A DICTIONARY OF KANIEN'KÉHA (MOHAWK) WITH CONNECTIONS TO THE PAST

Gunther Michelson, Karin Michelson, and Glenda Canadian Deer

This dictionary provides a record of the Kanien'kéha (Mohawk) language as spoken by fluent first- and second-language speakers at the Kahnawà:ke Mohawk territory outside of Montréal, Canada.

The Kanien'kéha language has been written since the 1600s, and these dictionary entries include citations from published, archival, and informal writings from the seventeenth century onwards. These citations are a legacy of the substantial documents of missionary scholars and several informal vocabulary lists written by Kanien'kéha speakers, among others. The introduction to the dictionary provides a description of the organization and orthography of the historical works so that they can be used in the future by those studying and learning the language.

A Dictionary of Kanien'kéha (Mohawk) with Connections to the Past allows scholars and students to learn the meaning, composition, and etymology of words in a language known for its particularly complex word structure. The organization of the entries, according to noun and verb roots, highlights the remarkable potential and adaptability of the language to express traditional concepts, as well as innovations that have resulted from contact with other customs and languages that have become part of the contemporary culture of the Kanien'kehá:ka.

GUNTHER MICHELSON (1920–2005) was a journalist with CBC Radio Canada and an independent scholar who immersed himself in the study of Haudenosaunee history, traditions, and language.

KARIN MICHELSON is a professor emeritus of linguistics at the University at Buffalo.

GLENDA CANADIAN DEER taught the Kanien'kéha (Mohawk) language at Kahnawà:ke, Québec, for twenty-four years.

GUNTHER MICHELSON

KARIN MICHELSON

GLENDA CANADIAN DEER

A Dictionary of Kanien'kéha (Mohawk) with Connections to the Past

UNIVERSITY OF TORONTO PRESS

Toronto Buffalo London

© University of Toronto Press 2024
Toronto Buffalo London
utorontopress.com

ISBN 978-1-4875-4843-8 (cloth)   ISBN 978-1-4875-4848-3 (EPUB)
ISBN 978-1-4875-4845-2 (paper)   ISBN 978-1-4875-4849-0 (PDF)

Library and Archives Canada Cataloguing in Publication

Title: A dictionary of Kanien'kéha (Mohawk) with connections to the past /
    Gunther Michelson, Karin Michelson, Glenda Canadian Deer.
Names: Michelson, Gunther, author. | Michelson, Karin, author. | Deer, Glenda, author.
Description: Includes bibliographical references.
Identifiers: Canadiana (print) 2024030862X | Canadiana (ebook) 20240308972 |
    ISBN 9781487548452 (softcover) | ISBN 9781487548438 (hardcover) |
    ISBN 9781487548483 (EPUB) | ISBN 9781487548490 (PDF)
Subjects: LCSH: Mohawk language—Dictionaries—English. | LCSH: English
    language—Dictionaries—Mohawk. | LCSH: Mohawk language—History. |
    LCGFT: Multilingual dictionaries.
Classification: LCC PM1883 .M53 2024 | DDC 497/.5542321—dc23

Cover design: John Beadle
Back cover illustration: Russell M. Deer

All royalties from the sale of this work are paid to the Iakwahwatsiratátie Language Nest
for further research and documentation of the Kanien'kéha (Mohawk) language.

We wish to acknowledge the land on which the University of Toronto Press operates.
This land is the traditional territory of the Wendat, the Anishnaabeg, the Haudenosaunee,
the Métis, and the Mississaugas of the Credit First Nation.

University of Toronto Press acknowledges the financial support of the Government of
Canada, the Canada Council for the Arts, and the Ontario Arts Council, an agency of the
Government of Ontario, for its publishing activities.

Canada Council Conseil des Arts
for the Arts du Canada

ONTARIO ARTS COUNCIL
CONSEIL DES ARTS DE L'ONTARIO
an Ontario government agency
un organisme du gouvernement de l'Ontario

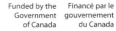
Funded by the Financé par le
Government gouvernement
of Canada du Canada

Canadä

Contents

PRELIMINARIES

Tables and Figures

Acknowledgements

For conversations, comments, questions, and encouragement, we would like to thank Clifford Abbott, whose work on dictionaries, grammars, and archival materials is exemplary and inspiring; Percy Abrams, whose careful and thoughtful reading of a draft of the introduction lead to a much improved version; Brian Carpenter of the American Philosophical Society, who in the midst of the pandemic scanned and sent a file we wanted right away; Ryan DeCaire, for sharing his innovative and exacting lexical and curriculum materials, and for saying just the right thing at the right time; Akwirente Bryan Deer, for help with names of trees and some difficult translations; Kenneth Deer, for urging us to work together on this project; Russell Deer, for proofreading, some editing, and most of all listening to all the ups and downs of completing a long project; Jean-Pierre Koenig, colleague, collaborator, and friend, for so often waiting on joint research while we were "just about finished" the dictionary; Megan Lukaniec, for discussions about the challenges of dictionaries, for both creators and users; and Akwiratékha' Martin, a special mention for reading the entire manuscript (and proofreading the final Kanien'kéha-English entries), attaching over 2000 notes, and following up, with Ryan DeCaire, with Zoom calls and texts.

Thanks to the University of Toronto Press and especially to Janice Evans and Brittney Sutherland of the Editorial and Production Division for editing and formatting recommendations.

Finally, we remember the friendship extended to Gunther Michelson by Mae Montour and family, Mike and Catherine Norton, Louis T. Curotte, Frank Natawe, and Jake Thomas as well as the knowledge and expertise they shared with Gunther.

Abbreviations

AMB   ambulative
ATTR   attributive
BEN   benefactive
CAUS   causative
CISL   cislocative
COIN   coincident
CONT   continuative
CONTR   contrastive
DISTR   distributive
DLC   duplicative (dualic)
FACIL   facilitative
HAB   habitual
INCH   inchoative
INSTR   instrumental
KIN   kinship term
LOC   locative
N   noun root
NEG   negative
PART   partitive
PNC   punctual

POSS   possessive
PROG   progressive
PURP   purposive
REFL   reflexive
REP   repetitive
REV   reversive
SRF   semi-reflexive
STV   stative
TRNL   translocative
V   verb root

At the head of an entry

/   between two forms: the two forms occur in different morphological contexts

[ ]   around vowels or consonants: the sounds are not present in all morphological contexts

(h)   before a consonant: the stem begins in the consonant that follows (h)

Guide to References Cited in Entries

The following is a list of the most frequently cited sources in the Kanien'kéha-English dictionary. A description of these works—when the work was written, background about the author, orthographic conventions, organization, and intended audience or function—is given in section 5 (Works Cited in Entries) under Preliminaries. The complete reference for each source as well as references for additional, less frequently cited sources can be found in the References section after the English-Kanien'kéha dictionary.

Anon
Vocabulary list, probably from the early 20th century; author unknown.

Beauvais
19th-century notes for plant-based recipes for medicines by Louis Kanonwatase Beauvais.

Biggar
Vocabulary of Laurentian Iroquois written down from prisoners taken back to France by Jacques Cartier.

Bruyas
17th-century Kanien'kéha-French dictionary by Jesuit missionary Jacques Bruyas.

Cory
Mid-20th-century vocabulary list by Presbyterian pastor Rev. David M. Cory.

Cuoq
19th-century Kanien'kéha-French dictionary by Sulpician missionary J.-A. Cuoq.

D'Ailleboust
Notebook, probably written by Annie D'Ailleboust, who owned a store in Kahnawà:ke with husband Teharerens.

Deering and Delisle
Teaching grammar of Kanien'kéha originally published in 1976.

Diabo
Mid-20th-century vocabulary list written by Louise Diabo of Kahnawà:ke.

Gabriel
English-Kanien'kéha (Kanehsatà:ke dialect) by Harvey Satewas Gabriel; page references are to the first edition (2014).

Galissonnière
17th-century French-Kanien'kéha dictionary; author uncertain.

Granger
1906 almanac by Jesuit priest L. S. Granger; includes ads in Kanien'kéha for products sold in Kahnawà:ke, Lachine, and Montréal.

Holm
Susquehannock vocabulary from the 1640s by Lutheran priest John Campanius Holm.

Horne
2003 "teaching textbook" by Josephine Horne of Kahnawà:ke, organized thematically.

Jamieson
Three short books 1958–1960 of Kanien'kéha vocabulary (Ohswé:ken dialect), created and compiled by Julia L. Jamieson.

Lafitau
Early 18th-century observations by Jesuit missionary Jean-Francois Lafitau.

Lazore
1985 vocabulary (2nd edition 1987, 3rd edition 2001) organized into 39 units, originally compiled by Hazel Lazore of the Kahnawà:ke Language Curriculum Center.

Ledger
Early 20th-century ledger from a store in Kahnawà:ke listing items in Kanien'kéha with amounts paid.

Letters
One from 1923 and four from 1945–1946. Orthography has been standardized.

Marcoux
Extensive 19th-century French-Kanien'kéha dictionary by Roman Catholic missionary Joseph Marcoux.

Megapolensis
A few words from 1644 by minister Johannes Megapolensis; page references are to Jameson (1909).

Old Kahnawake
Reminiscences by several authors, published in 1991 by the Kanien'kehaka Raotitiohkwa Cultural Center.

Onkweonwe
Only surviving issue, from 1900, of a news-paper developed and written by Charles A. Cooke of Wahta, Ontario.

Potier
18th-century Huron-Wendat dictionary by Jesuit missionary Pierre-Philippe Potier.

Pyrlaeus
18th-century German-Kanien'kéha dictionary by Moravian missionary John Christopher Pyrlaeus.

Rousseau
1945 publication (in French) by botanist Jacques Rousseau describing medicinal uses of plants growing in Kahnawà:ke.

Sagard
17th-century Huron-Wendat dictionary by Recollet missionary Gabriel (Théodat) Sagard.

Shea
17th-century French-Onondaga dictionary by an unidentified missionary.

Tewaterihwarenia'tha
Booklets produced by the Kanien'kehaka Raotitiohkwa Cultural Center, with pages of "Mohawk Vocabulary," "Old Words," "Tongue Twisters," and "Fun Words."

van den Bogaert
Vocabulary list appended to a journal from 1634–1635 by Harmen Meyndertsz van den Bogaert; page references are to G. Michelson's analysis (1988).

Wassenaer
Names of numbers and months from the 1600s by Nicolaes Janszoon van Wassenaer; page references are to Jameson (1909).

Waugh
Iroquois Foods and Food Preparation, published in 1916.

Preface

Kahnawà:ke is a Kanien'kehá:ka (Mohawk) territory located on the south shore of the St. Lawrence River across from Lachine and Montréal, Québec. Two large steel crosses, where Hwy 132 (Old Malone Highway) enters and exits the old village, commemorate the Québec Bridge collapse in August 1907, when 33 high-steel workers from Kahnawà:ke lost their lives. Land has been taken from the original territory; a vivid memory for many is the construction of the St. Lawrence Seaway from 1954–1959, for which the Canadian federal government appropriated over 1200 acres of the territory. The Kahnawa'kehrón:on (people of Kahnawà:ke) share a unique history, which has been written about in Devine (1922), Fenton and Tooker (1978), and Beauvais (1985). But many would agree that the best record of a people's traditions and history is through their language.

This dictionary began with the idea to review and edit Gunther Michelson's un-published manuscript *Notes to a Mohawk Dictionary*. Gunther had already published *A Thousand Words of Mohawk* in 1973, a dictionary of Kahnawà:ke Mohawk organized by verb and noun roots and intended as a resource to be used by those with or without technical linguistic knowledge. Over the next decades and until his passing in February 2005, he added new entries when there was an opportunity to consult with a speaker; he also added references to earlier attestations, and this was the reason for calling the continually evolving manuscript *Notes to a Mohawk Dictionary*.

Gunther read everything on Iroquoian, whatever the discipline: published books, unpublished manuscripts, peer-reviewed journal articles, obscure documents in institutional archives, pamphlets, bulletins, and ephemera. When he came across a term of historical, ethnological, or etymological relevance, he added it to the entries in his *Notes*. He made the manuscript available to anyone who requested a copy but, despite considerable urging and despite hearing how useful the 1973 dictionary was, he declined to submit the *Notes* for publication.

So what, one might ask, led to a decision that now was a good time to publish the dictionary? In part, the decision was based on a fruitful discussion in 2015 with Maggie Dittemore, head of the John Wesley Powell Library of Anthropology at the Smithsonian Institution, about manuscripts at the Smith-sonian written by scholars who died leaving their work unpublished. In large part, the decision was due to knowing that Gunther wanted what he had learned to be used by others who shared his curiosity about and enthusiasm for his interests. So, in May 2016, I asked Glenda Canadian Deer, retired from teaching Kanien'kéha in Kahnawà:ke, to work together to review and update the entries.

Initially, I thought a year or so might suffice, but because one word always leads to another, we have now been working on this project for seven years. From May 2016 until the end of 2019, we met two or three days a week every few months in Kahnawà:ke. Then during the pandemic, from March to December 2020, we switched to Zoom meetings for two hours Monday and Tuesday mornings almost every week, and from January 2021 until just recently, we worked together almost once a week. In the process of going over all the entries and subentries several times (*at least* half a dozen times through the entire manuscript), we added new entries, and then in the process of making sure we had those right we added many more. In the end there is probably as much new material as was in the original manuscript.

In August 2021, we began to share the complete draft of the Kanien'kéha-English entries with Ryan DeCaire and Akwiratékha' Martin, fluent second-language speakers from Wáhta and Kahnawà:ke, respectively, and they responded with valuable input. From August to December 2021, Akwiratékha' read every entry, corrected an embarrassing number of typos, recommended we add inflected forms and incorporations to some of the entries, provided some alternative English translations, and suggested some additional entries. These additions were reviewed with the third author and many, if not most, are included in the final version.

The organization is as Gunther conceived of it. Also from the original (though with some revisions) are the sections on orthography (section 1.2), dialects (section 2), organization (section 3), and overview of morphology (section 4). I added to the Introduction (section 1), and I wrote section 5 describing the works most often cited in the references and the final remarks in section 6.

Fluent speakers of Kanien'kéha are constantly making connections between words, between sentences, and between contexts. This is true whether they learned the language as a child before English or later as an adult. Somehow speakers have systematized these connections and have gotten to "know" the patterns of the language. What dictionaries (and grammars) attempt to accomplish is record and elucidate these patterns. But there are many ways of analyzing the structure of words, the components that make up words, and how words are related to other words. Some dictionaries list only words, some list "bases" and follow the base with words that have the base as a component, some organize words into thematic categories, and some— like this one—are organized according to roots. But it bears pointing out that whatever the analysis, those who write dictionaries and grammars are well aware that speakers do not say just a part of a word (whether root, stem, base, prefix, or suffix) in isolation, separated from the rest of a word. In fact, speakers often remark that even a whole word is only spoken and understood in a larger context.

Karin Michelson

PRELIMINARIES

1 Introduction

1.1 About dictionaries

Dictionaries have important functions when it comes to speaking, understanding, and writing a language. Bilingual dictionaries probably are used most often to look up a word in another language. Often dictionary users want to confirm the spelling of a word. Sometimes users want to know more about the meaning of a word, maybe its history or etymology. Beyond these obvious uses, dictionaries also provide a rich record of linguistic and cultural phenomena since they tell us what kinds of meanings are expressed by roots, the minimal lexical elements. The roots, together with the stems and words derived from the roots, are a reflection of how people approach the world, their customs and beliefs, and the concepts—intellectual and material—that have become ingrained in their language.

Dictionaries (and grammars) have to balance the regularities and irregularities of a language. Without regularities speakers could not express new thoughts, report events that have never happened before, talk about their emotions, or describe unfamiliar objects and ideas. But there are lots and lots of irregularities in language, "exceptions to the rule." The structure of words in Kanien'kéha and other Northern Iroquoian languages is elaborate, and only fluent speakers know, or have learned, which combinations of a root with another root or of a root with other components are actual words, and what meaning a word can have outside of the meaning that can be predicted from knowing the parts of words (i.e., outside of a literal meaning). Abrams (2006: 7) talks about the "word" in Onondaga like this: "A fluent Onondaga speaker will readily tell you if a particular string of sounds means something, whether it sounds like something meaningful but is not a word, or if it sounds like 'nothing' and has no meaning whatsoever."

A dictionary is a repository of both the regularities and irregularities of words, and as such, it provides evidence for the enduring yet evolving nature of language.

1.2 Orthography and pronunciation guide

The variety of Kanien'kéha described in this dictionary is spoken in the territory of Kahnawà:ke on the south shore of the St. Lawrence River across from Lachine, Québec, and the island of Montréal. The orthography is the standard one used today (see D. Lazore 1993). The English equivalents for the written sounds given in the list at the top of the next page are only approximations.

Sounds can be pronounced a little differently depending on where they occur in a word or sentence. This is especially so for vowels. The pronunciation of a vowel can vary depending on stress (whether the vowel is stressed or unstressed) and vowel length (whether a vowel is long or short), and certain consonant clusters can affect the pronunciation of a vowel as well.

Consonants

Kanien'kéha		*English equivalent*
k	(before consonants)	s<u>k</u>ate, ba<u>c</u>teria
k	(before vowels)	<u>g</u>ulley, a<u>gh</u>ast
kh		<u>k</u>ale, a<u>cc</u>ord
t	(before consonants)	s<u>t</u>ack, nu<u>t</u>meg
t	(before vowels)	<u>d</u>eck, a<u>d</u>orn
th		<u>t</u>ail, a<u>tt</u>ack
s	(before vowels or another consonant)	<u>s</u>oak, <u>st</u>ill
s	(between vowels)	ea<u>s</u>y
sh		"breathy" <u>S</u>orry!
hsi		<u>sh</u>ell
n		<u>n</u>ope
r		<u>r</u>ope (sort of)
w		<u>w</u>et
i		<u>y</u>es
h		<u>h</u>ello
'		uh <u></u>oh!

Vowels

Kanien'kéha	*English equivalent*
a	<u>a</u>rt, <u>au</u>to
i	k<u>ey</u>
e	t<u>a</u>ke, p<u>e</u>t
en	tr<u>u</u>nk, s<u>o</u>ng
o	g<u>oa</u>t
on	t<u>o</u>mb, s<u>oo</u>n

Diacritics

: after a vowel	long vowel
´ over a vowel	prominent vowel with a higher and level pitch
` over a vowel	prominent vowel with a mostly falling pitch

1.2.1 Writing h and glottal stop

For the most part writing Kanien'kéha is straightforward. However, it can be difficult to know with confidence when to write <h> in combination with other consonants. Writing the sound *h* when it occurs before or after another consonant is complicated, partly because there is greater variation—different speakers pronounce the *h* in a way that is more or less audible—and partly because in some cases the pronunciation has changed over time. The following description proceeds in the order *h* before and after *t*, *k*, *s*, *n*, *r*, and *w*. The convention < > around a letter will be used to draw attention to the written symbol rather than the sound and its pronunciation.

There are many roots that have *ht* and many that have *th*, and the difference between *ht* and *th* is relatively easy to hear, so roots with theses clusters are consistently written <ht> and <th>. An example with <ht> is *ohtè:ra'* 'root' and an example with <th> is *othè:sera'* 'flour'. There are also some roots that have an *h* sound both before and after *t*.

An example is the verb for 'look at', as in *katkáhthos* 'I look at (it)', or the verb for 'talk', as in *róhthare'* 'he is talking'. Quite often a root that ends in the causative suffix *-ht-* is followed by the habitual suffix *-ha'*, as in *katshokwaráhtha'* 'I make noise', derived from *-atsharokw-* 'be noisy'. Still, there is variation, and for a fair number of words some write <th> while others write <hth>. An example is the word for 'ball', written *athén:no* 'ball' in this dictionary but written *ahthén:no* by others. Although overall fewer in number, there are roots with *hk* and roots with *kh*. Words with *hkh* are frequent, but they all derive from stems that end in *-hkw-* (very often this is the instrumental suffix) plus the habitual suffix *-ha'*. This combination is pronounced *-hkhwa'* and is always written <hkhwa'>.

More challenging are roots that include *h* before or after *s*. In spoken Kanien'kéha of the mid-twentieth century, at least as is evident from the 1965 recordings of Mae

Montour made by G. Michelson, *hs* and *sh* are distinct. For example, *áhsire'* 'blanket' has a clear *hs* cluster, while *weshén:rate'* 'pink' has a clear *sh* cluster. In the 2003 work by Josephine Horne, there are <hs> words and <sh> words, suggesting that in her pronunciation *hs* and *sh* were distinct too (as supported by the recordings that accompany the work). There are words with *hsh* too, but these are mostly prefixes such as *hshako-*, the distributive ending *-hshon*, or the second person prefix *hs-* added to a stem that begins in *h* (Horne 2003: x). At some point, speakers began to pronounce the *sh* roots with an *h* before the *sh* (with "preaspiration"), and nowadays many write these roots with <hsh>.[1]

Because the consonants *s, t,* and *k* can combine with each other and with *h*, there are more possibilities. To add to the description so far, there are roots with *st* (*sa'nisténha* 'your mother') and roots with *hst* (*atháhsteren* 'pants, trousers'), roots with *sk* (*kaská:neks* 'I wish for') and *hsk* (*raóhskare'* 'his girlfriend'), roots with *ts* (*onà:tsa'* 'wheat'), *tsh* (*wa'ketshén:ri'* 'I found it'), and *hts* (*wa'kahtsóhare'* 'I washed my hands'). As might be expected, there is variation in writing these as well.

The situation with *n* and *r* is a bit more straightforward. In the 1965 recordings of Mae Montour, *hn* and *hr* are distinct from *nh* and *rh*. Sometimes the *nh* and *rh* are preceded by a breathiness that comes close to an *h* sound, so more like *hnh* or *hrh*.

More recently, most speakers pronounce roots with *nh* and *rh* with this preaspiration (although not necessarily each time the word is pronounced), and the *n* and *r* are voiceless. Mithun (1979) describes this phenomenon as spirantization. In this dictionary as in other contemporary works (including Horne 2003), roots with *hn* and *hr* are written <hnh> and <hrh>. It is important, though, to recognize that the first <h> is not a "true" *h* sound because a stressed vowel before it is not lengthened, which does happen with "true" *hn hr hw hi*. When writing roots at the head of an entry, the added *h* is written in parentheses to indicate that the *h* is not truly part of the root; for example, the root *-rho-* 'coat' is written *-(h)rho-* and the root is alphabetized with other r-stems. The clusters *hw* and *wh* are also distinct, and *wh* is pronounced like English *f* and written (with spirantization) <hwh>.

Glottal stop is a consonant sound, like *k t s h n r w* and *i* (when it is written for the sound *y*). But in the contemporary Kanien'kéha language glottal stop is usually not pronounced at the ends of words, so the question is whether to write the glottal in this position. In this dictionary, following Michelson's *Notes to a Mohawk Dictionary* as well as other recent work, the glottal stop is written in the following endings: the punctual aspect suffixes *-'*, *-e'*, and *-en'*, the habitual aspect suffix *-ha'*, the stative aspect suffixes *-'* and *-e'*, the (former) past suffix *-hkwe'*, and the noun suffixes *-a'* and *-e'*.

---

[1] It would require experimental study to determine how strongly the *sh* words are preaspirated. A good way to investigate this (and other aspects of the acoustics of Kanien'kéha sounds) would be with experimental instrumental studies using tools such as the software Praat.

2 Kanien'kéha Dialects

There are several other varieties of Kanien'-
kéha: Ohswé:ken (Six Nations of the Grand
River), Tyendinaga (The Mohawks of the Bay
of Quinte), Ahkwesáhsne, Kanehsatà:ke, and
Wáhta. In addition to lexical differences, there
are the regular differences laid out in Table 1
between the Eastern (Kahnawà:ke, Kanehsa-
tà:ke, Wáhta), Central (Ahkwesáhsne), and
Western (Tyendinaga, Ohswé:ken) dialects.
A purely orthographic difference is that the
Western dialect writes the palatal glide *y* as
<y> while the Eastern and Central dialects
use the vowel symbol <i>. But there are
also differences in the pronunciation of the
combinations written <ti>, <ki>, <ty>, <ky>,
<ts>, and <tsy> as shown in the first three
rows in Table 1.

The combination written <ti> in the
Eastern dialect is a palato-alveolar affricate
[dʒ], as in the first sound of the English word
*j*acket. The same words that have <ti> in the
Eastern dialect have <ki>, pronounced [gj] or
[kj], in the Central dialect. In the Western dialect some words have <ky> ('I go out' in row
1), pronounced [gj] or [kj], and others have
<ty> ('nine' in row 2), pronounced [dj] or [tj].
What happened historically is that the Eastern
and Central dialects merged *ty* and *ky*, but in
different ways: the Eastern dialect merged in
favour of *ty* (pronounced [dʒ] and written
<ti>); the Central dialect merged in favour of
ky (pronounced [gj]/[kj] and written <ki>).

The combinations <ts> and <tsy> are a
little less complicated. In the Eastern dialect
<ts> is an alveolar affricate [dz], as in some
pronunciations of *C*zar. In the Central and
Western dialects <ts>, when followed by the
vowel *i*, and <tsy> are pronounced [dʒ], as in
the first sound of *j*acket.

Another dialect difference is that in
Ahkwesáhsne the pronunciation of the *r*
sound is closer to *l*, even though <r> is
written. The last difference in Table 1 is a
grammatical one: the first person singular
possessive prefix *ak-* in Kanehsatà:ke and
Wáhta versus *akw-* elsewhere.

As a final word in this section, we would
like to remind those who are consulting this
dictionary that there is variation not only
between dialects but between speakers of the
same dialect. Speakers should not be surprised
if they pronounce some of the words in this
work differently from what is written. Sometimes a speaker will have an *h* where another
will have a glottal; for example, *ohswèn:ta'*
'coal'—from Michelson's manuscript and
pronounced that way by the third author—
is also pronounced *o'swèn:ta'*. Sometimes
speakers have a different vowel; for example,
ohsienhón:ta' 'stomach' is pronounced by
others as *ohsiahón:ta'*. Occasionally there
are multiple forms; for example, the word
for 'hip' in this dictionary is *oniahskwà:rha'*,
Michelson reported *ononskwárha'*, Horne
has *ohnhenskwà:rha'* (Horne 2003: 99; also
onn hens kwá ra from Mary Deer's 1965 class
notes), others have *oneskwà:rha* (Mithun
1977: 39, Lazore 1991: 58), and there is
ohnhoskwá:rha' (Deering and Delisle 1976:
397). Five different forms! A final example of
variation between speakers is the Kanien'kéha
word for 'it is lightning', with four forms:
tewanihne'kara'wánions (this dictionary) or
tewanine'karawánions (Deering and Delisle
1976: 134) or *wa'tewanine'kara'wánion* (*Old
Kahnawake* 1991: 20) or *tewani'nehkara'-
wánions* (Lazore 1991: 52, *The Eastern Door*
newspaper, Nov. 24, 2006). When Michelson
has one form, and the third author has a
slightly different form, both are given in this
dictionary; an example is *-hren-/-hre'n-* 'cut
into, make an incision'. Most of the time most

Table 1: Kanien'kéha dialects

Eastern		Central	Western		
	Kanehsatà:ke		Tyendinaga		
Kahnawà:ke	Wáhta	Ahkwesáhsne	Ohswé:ken		
tiá:ken's [dʒ]	tiá:ken's [dʒ]	kiá:ken's [gj]	kyá:ken's [gj]	'I go out'	
tióhton [dʒ]	tióhton [dʒ]	kióhton [gj]	tyóhton [dj]	'nine'	
otsì:tsa' [dz]	otsì:tsa [dz]	otsì:tsia [dʒ]	otsì:tsya [dʒ]	'flower'	
á:re'	á:re'	á:re'	á:re' [á:le']	'again'	
akwáhta	akáhta	akwáhta	akwáhta	'my shoe'	

people will have the same forms and the same pronunciation, but variation is a natural fact of language. The following quote from Horne (2003: vii) is apt: "Mohawk speakers may and do have distinct pronunciations and will sometimes have slightly different but equally correct ways of saying things and an assortment of terms for expressing concepts each with its own subtle flavors."

3 Organization of Entries

The head of most entries is a root, surrounded by dashes. For example, the entry for 'stick' begins with the root -nakar-. The root is identified as a noun root (N), verb root (V), or kinship term (KIN). The part-of-speech label N, V, or KIN is followed by an English gloss. If the entry is a noun root, the English gloss is followed by the Kanien'kéha noun word. This basic noun form is followed by one or more forms with a possessive (POSS) prefix, forms with a locative suffix (LOC), and forms with one of the attributive clitics (ATTR), when these are attested. If the noun root can be incorporated into verbs, examples of incorporation are also given.

If the entry is a verb root, the English gloss is followed by habitual, punctual, and stative aspect forms, and an imperative form. Note that some (even most) dictionaries always give a habitual aspect form, either a future or factual punctual aspect form, a stative aspect form, and an imperative, and always the same person, number, and gender form (for example, the first person singular or the masculine singular), in other words a stock set of "principal parts." But the Iroquoian languages have many, many inflected forms that could, theoretically, serve as principal parts. In addition, not every verb root attests all the aspect forms and the imperative. So no matter which three (or five or six) forms are chosen, the choice is somewhat arbitrary. Because of this wealth of inflected forms, the exact same set of forms is not given for every verb, although the set almost always includes a first person singular form and a masculine or feminine singular form (or both). Kinship stems are followed by a few examples of the kin relation. One advantage, incidentally, of giving different forms is that a greater number of phonological changes that result from combining a prefix with a stem are attested in the dictionary.

After these inflected forms are examples that show the derivational potential of the root: forms with non-modal prepronominal prefixes, the semi-reflexive or reflexive prefixes, derivational suffixes, and incorporated nouns. Some entries include an example sentence, preceded by a bullet (•), and sometimes there is a note that addresses some aspect of the structure or meaning of the entry or one of the subentries. Many entries end with references to earlier works, preceded by *Cf.* (for the Latin word *confer* 'compare').

In addition to roots, also listed as entries are locative endings (LOC) and attributive clitics (ATTR). Locative endings have a dash before them, and they are followed by the abbreviation LOC and an English gloss. Clitics have an equal sign, the abbreviation ATTR, and a gloss.

Entries without a label N, V, KIN, LOC, or ATTR are words that are not obviously analyzable into roots. Words that are not roots include particles, some place names, a few names of persons and nations, some animal and bird designations, onomatopoetic words (i.e., words that imitate a sound), and borrowings. (The terms *root* and *particle* are used here as they are generally understood by Iroquoianists: the *root* is the lexical unit that is not divisible into smaller components; a *particle* is a word, usually quite short, that is not inflected and often has a grammatical meaning or discourse function.)

Finally, it bears pointing out that translating a Kanien'kéha root or word from Kanien'kéha into English can be enormously challenging; sometimes no exact English word will do, so we use a phrase or sentence (and still may not be really satisfied).

4 Overview of Morphology

4.1 Minimal verb and noun forms

Every verb and almost every noun must have a pronominal prefix.[2] There are about 60 pronominal prefixes that reference participants ("arguments") of verbs, nouns, and kinship terms. The categories distinguished by the prefixes are person (first, second, third, and inclusive versus exclusive), number (singular, dual, plural), and gender (masculine, feminine-zoic, feminine-indefinite). Arguments that do not have a specific number or gender (the equivalent of 'one, someone, people') are referred to with the feminine-indefinite. The feminine-zoic is sometimes referred to as "neuter," especially when it occurs on words that refer to inanimate objects.

There are over 250 forms of the prefixes, and which form occurs depends on the first sound of the following stem (consonant, or the vowels *a e en i o on*). The forms of the prefixes are usually presented in tables or lists. Tables 2, 3, and 5 are based on similar tables in Martin (2016) and curriculum materials prepared by Ryan DeCaire for Onkwawenna Kentyohkwa at the Six Nations of the Grand River in Ontario, Canada. Table 4 gives possessive prefixes of nouns; these are similar in form to the objective/patient prefixes on verbs. In the tables, "M" is short for "male," "F" is short for "female." A capital "E" stands for an historically epenthetic vowel that occurs before some consonants and

---

[2] There is one regular "exception" to this. Noun roots that take the prefix *w-* when they are incorporated into a verb do not have any prefix when they occur as a stand-alone noun form.

consonant clusters; for example, the first person singular subjective/agent prefix *kE-* represents the form *ke-* (before sonorant consonants, glottal stop, and some consonant clusters) and *k-* (before all other consonants and before vowels). A vowel that is underlined "absorbs" (causes the deletion of) a following stem-initial vowel. Also, note that prefixes that begin in *h* do not have the *h* when the prefix occurs initially in a word, and masculine prefixes (for example, *ra-, ro-, ronwa-*) replace *r* with *h* (for example, *-ha-, -ho-, -honwa-*) when the prefix occurs after another prefix.

Most verbs and nouns also have an ending. Verbs (except the imperative) are inflected with an aspect ending—the habitual (imperfective), punctual (perfective), or stative. The aspect suffixes add a temporal perspective to the meaning of the verb. Section 4.6 describes the meaning of the aspect categories in more detail. Aspect endings are given in Table 6.

Nouns have a noun suffix, most often *-a'* or *-e'*, rather than an aspect suffix.

In addition to the aspect suffixes, there are three "modal" prefixes that also relate to the time or definiteness of an event: future, factual, and optative. The future and optative signal an event that has not begun, and the future and factual are used to signal that an event is definite or certain as opposed to hypothetical. The form of the future is always *en-*. The form of the optative is *a-*. The form of the factual when it is at the beginning of a word is *wa'-*. The form *wa-* occurs before a following pronominal prefix that begins in *h* since glottal stop does not occur before *h* in Kanien'kéha. The form *we-* occurs before second person and inclusive pronominal prefixes except the second person singular subjective/agent prefix; in the Kahnawà:ke dialect these prefixes all begin in *s* or *t* (for example, *seni-* second person dual, or *tia-/teni-* inclusive dual).

Table 2: Subjective (Agent) prefixes

	C-stem	i-stem	a-stem	e-stem	o-stem
I	kE-	k-	k-	k-	k-
We 2 incl	teni-	teni-	tia-	ten-	ten-
We 2 excl	iakeni-	iakeni-	iatia-	iaken-	iaken-
We 3 incl	tewa-	tewen-	tewa-	tew-	ti- (tew-)
We 3 excl	iakwa-	iakwen-	iakwa-	iakw-	iati- (iakw-)
You	hsE-	ts-/hs-	hs-	hs-	hs-
You 2	seni-	seni-	tsa-	sen-	sen-
You 3	sewa-	sewen-	sewa-	sew-	ts- (sew-)
He	ra-	ren-	ra-	hr-	hr-
She, It	ka-	ken-	wa-	w-	i-
She, s.o.	ie-	ie-	ion-	iak-	iak-
They M 2	hni-	hni-	hia-	hn-	hn-
They M 3	rati-	rati-	ron-	ronn-	ronn-
They F 2	keni-	keni-	tia-	ken-	ken-
They F 3	konti-	konti-	kon-	konn-	konn-

Table 3: Objective (Patient) prefixes

	C-stem	i-stem	a-stem	e-stem	o-stem
I	wakE-	wak-	wak-	wak-	wak-
We 2	ionkeni-	ionkeni-	iontia-	ionken-	ionken-
We 3	ionkwa-	ionkwen-	ionkwa-	ionkw-	ionti-
You	sa-	sen-	sa-	s-	s-
You 2	seni-	seni-	tsa-	sen-	sen-
You 3	sewa-	sewen-	sewa-	sew-	ts- (sew-)
He	ro-	ro-	ro-	raw-	ra-
She, It	io-	io-	io-	iaw-	ia-
She, s.o.	iako-	iako-	iako-	iakaw-	iaka-
They M 2, 3	roti-	roti-	rona-	ron-	ron-
They F 2, 3	ioti-	ioti-	iona-	ion-	ion-

Table 4: Possessive prefixes on nouns

	C-stem	i-stem	a-stem	e-stem	o-stem
my	akE-	ak-	akwa-	akw-	ak-
our 2	onkeni-	onkeni-	ontia-	onken-	onken-
our 3	onkwa-	onkwen-	onkwa-	onkw-	onti-
Your	sa-	sen-	sa-	s-	s-
Your 2	seni-	seni-	tsa-	sen-	sen-
Your 3	sewa-	sewen-	sewa-	sew-	ts-
His	rao-	rao-	rao-	raw-	ra-
Her, Its	ao-	ao-	ao-	aw-	a-
Her, Someone's	ako-	ako-	ako-	akaw-	aka-
Their (masc)	raoti-	raoti-	raon-	raon-	raon-
Their (fem)	aoti-	aoti-	aon-	aon-	aon-

Table 5: Transitive prefixes

	C-stem	i-stem	a-stem	e-stem	o-stem
I>You	kon-	kon-	koni-	koni-	koni-
I>You 2; we 2 excl>You (1,2)	keni-	keni-	tia-	ken-	ken-
I>You 3; we 3 excl>You (1,2,3)	kwa-	kwen-	kwa-	kw-	ti-
I>Him	ri-	ri-	rii-	rii-	rii-
I>Her, it	kE-	k-	k-	k-	k-
I>Her, them	khe-	khe-	khei-	khei-	khei-

We 2 incl >Him	tshiteni-	tshiteni-	tshitia-	tshiten-	tshiten-
We 3 incl> Him	tshitewa-	tshitewen-	tshitewa-	tshitew-	tshiti-
We 2 excl>Him	hshakeni-	hshakeni-	hshatia-	hshaken-	hshaken-
We 3 excl> Him	hshakwa-	hshakwen-	hshakwa-	hshakw-	hshati-
We 2 incl>Her, it	teni-	teni-	tia-	ten-	ten-
We 3 incl>Her, it	tewa-	tewen-	tewa-	tew-	ti- (tew-)
We 2 excl >Her, it	iakeni-	iakeni-	iatia-	iaken-	iaken-
We 3 excl>Her, it	iakwa-	iakwen-	iakwa-	iakw-	iati- (iakw-)
We 2,3 incl>Her, them	iethi-	iethi-	iethii-	iethii-	iethii-
We 2,3 excl>Her, them	iakhi-	iakhi-	iakhii-	iakhii-	iakhii-
You>Me	tak-/-hskE-	tak-	takwa-	takw-	tak-
You 2>Me; You (1,2)>Us 2	takeni-	takeni-	tatia-	taken-	taken-
You 3>Me; You (1,2,3)>Us 3	takwa-	takwen-	takwa-	takw-	tati-
You>Him	htshE-	htsh-	htsh-	htsh-	htsh-
You 2>Him	tshiseni-	tshiseni-	tshitsa-	tshisen-	tshisen-
You 3>Him	tshisewa-	tshisewen-	tshisewa-	tshisew-	tshits-
You>Her, it	hsE-	ts-/hs-	hs-	hs-	hs-
You 2>Her, it	seni-	seni-	tsa-	sen-	sen-
You 3>Her, it	sewa-	sewen-	sewa-	sew-	ts- (sew-)
You>Her, them	hshE-	hshe-	hshei-	hshei-	hshei-
You 2,3>Her, them	ietshi-	ietshi-	ietshii-	ietshii-	ietshii-
He>Me	rakE-	rak-	rakwa-	rakw-	rak-
He>Us 2	hshonkeni-	hshonkeni-	hshontia-	hshonken-	hshonken-
He>Us 3	hshonkwa-	hshonkwen-	hshonkwa-	hshonkw-	hshonti-
He>You	hia-	hien-	hia-	hi-	hi-
He>You 2	tshiseni-	tshiseni-	tshitsa-	tshisen-	tshisen-
He>You 3	tshisewa-	tshisewen-	tshisewa-	tshisew-	tshits-
He>Him	ro-	ro-	ro-	raw-	ra-
He>Her, it	ra-	ren-	ra-	hr-	hr-
He>Her, them	hshako-	hshako-	hshako-	hshakaw-	hshaka-
She, it>Me	wakE-	wak-	wak-	wak-	wak-
She, it >Us 2	ionkeni-	ionkeni-	iontia-	ionken-	ionken-
She, it >Us 3	ionkwa-	ionkwen-	ionkwa-	ionkw-	ionti-
She, it >You	sa-	sen-	sa-	s-	s-
She, it >You 2	seni-	seni-	tsa-	sen-	sen-
She, it >You 3	sewa-	sewen-	sewa-	sew-	ts-
She, it >Him	ro-	ro-	ro-	raw-	ra-
She, it >Her, it	io-	io-	io-	iaw-	ia-
She, it >Her, them	iako-	iako-	iako-	iakaw-	iaka-
She, They>Me	ionkE-	ionk-	ionkwa-	ionkw-	ionk-
She, They >Us 2,3	ionkhi-	ionkhi-	ionkhii-	ionkhii-	ionkhii-
She, They >You	iesa-/ionsa-	iesen-	iesa-	ies-	ies-
She, They >You 2,3	ietshi-	ietshi-	ietshii-	ietshii-	ietshii-
She, They >Him	ronwa-	ronwen-	ronwa-	ronw-	ronwai-
She, They >Her, it	konwa-	konwen-	konwa-	konw-	konwai-
She, They >Her, them	iontatE-	iontat-	iontat-	iontat-	iontat-
They M>Her, (them)	hshakoti-	hshakoti-	hshakona-	hshakon-	hshakon-
She, they>Them M	ronwati-	ronwati-	ronwan-	ronwan-	ronwan-
They F>Her, (them)	iakoti-	iakoti-	iakona-	iakon-	iakon-
She, they>Them F	konwati-	konwati-	konwan-	konwan-	konwan-

Table 6: Aspect suffixes

This table first groups together stative endings: *on, e', en, 'on, 'en,* and *ø.* Then within each stative category are grouped the habitual endings; for example, within the *on* stative there are the habitual endings *ha', s,* and *e's,* and within the *en* stative there are the habitual endings *ha, s,* and *as.* The distribution of the punctual endings looks helter-skelter, but in fact they are the most predictable: *ne'* occurs after stems that end in a glottal stop (though some stems that end in *a'* have no ending in the punctual, symbolized *ø*), *e'* occurs after stems that end in consonants other than a glottal stop, and *'* occurs after vowels. Table 6 is just one way of organizing the aspect endings; others might place the division between stem and suffix differently (for example, place the *n* of the punctual form *ne'* at the end of the stem instead) or group the habitual first and then the stative within the habitual groups. Finally, *this table does not include every distribution;* left out are stems that don't share a set of aspect endings with any other stem or with just one other stem. For the translations of the inflected forms, see the entry for the root.

Stem ends in	HAB	PNC	STV	Example verb
ht 't st kt	ha'	e'		-the't- pound: kethè:tha', waháthe'te', wakethè:ton
Vt Vk 'k o[k]³ hw				-arahtat- run: tekaráhtats, wa'tkaráhtate', tewakarahtá:ton
a' e' i'	s	ne'	on	-hri'- get broken: tekà:ri's, wa'tkà:ri'ne', teiohrì:'on
a'⁴		ø		-atsha'- burn: katia'tátsha's, wa'katia'tátsha', wakatia'tátshon'
ho⁵				-ahsentho- cry: tekahsénthos, wa'kahséntho', tewakahsénthon
Ci	e's	'		-ahtenti- go away: kahténtie's, wa'kahtén:ti', wakahténtion
ont ot 'kt r	ha'	en'	e'	-ate'skont- roast: kate'skóntha', wa'kate'skón:ten', wakatè:skonte'
hkw ek 'k	ha'	e'		-atek- burn, on fire: iotékha', wa'ó:teke', iotéken
a'[k]⁶				-nera'[k]- mistake: tekenéra'ks, wa'tkenéra'ke', tewakenéren'
en'	s	ne'		-a'sen'- fall: tewà:sen's, tòn:sen'ne', tio'sèn:'en
a'⁷		ø	en	-ta'- put inside: kéta's, wa'kéta', wakéten'
ha⁸				-owiha- split: tekohwíhas, wa'tkohwíha', tewakohwíhen
Vkw hkw 'kw skw ri	as	'		-atshokw- smoke: ratshókwas, wahatshó:ko', rotshókwen
et en ew 'w ok ii		e'		-attok- notice: kattó:kas, wa'káttoke', wakattó:ken
a on	s		'on	-ahton- disappear: wáhtons, ónhton', iohtòn:'on
a e	's	'		-ie- wake up: ítie's, wà:tie', watiè:'on
en	s	'	'en	-ahsithen- get numb: wakahsíthens, onkwahsíthen', wakahsithèn:'en
e en i on	s	'	ø	-atorishen- rest: : katoríshens, wa'katoríshen', wakatoríshen
[on]⁹ V[k]¹⁰ o'[k]		e'		-areser[on]- overflow: tewaréserons, tonré:sere', tioréseron -hwa'e[k]- strike: khwà:'eks, wa'khwà:'eke', wakhwà:'e

---

³ The stem-final *k* is absent in the stative aspect, and the vowel *o* is replaced by *on.*

⁴ The stem vowel *a* is replaced by the stative ending *on.*

⁵ The stem vowel *o* is replaced by the stative ending *on.*

⁶ The stem-final *k* is absent in the stative aspect, and the vowel *a* is replaced by *en.*

⁷ The stem vowel *a* is replaced by the stative ending *en.*

⁸ The stem vowel *a* is replaced by the stative ending *en.*

⁹ The stem vowel *on* is absent in the punctual aspect.

¹⁰ The stem-final consonant *k* is absent in the stative aspect.

4.2 Non-modal prepronominal prefixes

In addition to the three modal prefixes (future, factual, optative), there are eight non-modal prefixes that come before the pronominal prefixes. They are the repetitive, cislocative, translocative, partitive, duplicative, negative, coincident, and contrastive. They occur in structures that express repetition, locative and temporal concepts, manner, quantity, and negation.

Every prefix has at least two forms. In the tables below, the form of the prefix that occurs at the beginning of a word and directly before a pronominal prefix is given first, at the top left of the table and bolded. Below that is given the prefix in combination with the modal prefixes.[11] Modal prefixes can come before or after the non-modal prefixes. For example, the future *en-* precedes the repetitive *s-* (thus, *ens-* in Table 7), but the factual *a-* follows the repetitive (thus *sa-* in Table 7). The first column gives the basic form of the prefix in combination with the modal prefixes. The next column gives the forms of the prefixes before the "you" pronominal prefixes: the second person singular objective/patient, the second person dual and plural, and the inclusive (these prefixes begin in *s* or *t* in the Kahnawà:ke dialect). Finally, the non-modal prefixes can have a different form depending on what sounds follow, and these are given in the last, "phonology," column. A raised [c] indicates that the form occurs before certain consonant clusters. The raised [i] means that the form occurs before a following *y* sound (written <i> in Kahnawà:ke). A raised vowel [on] indicates a form that occurs before *on* when the *on* replaces the *wa* of the first person

singular objective/patient prefix *wak-*, or the third person singular feminine-zoic subjective/agent prefix *w-* and a following stem vowel *a*. Raised [h] indicates a form that occurs before prefixes that begin in *h*.

The repetitive (REP) indicates the repetition of an action or a return to a point of reference. The repetitive is found also with words that denote a specific category of being, and it is part of the structure that counts one object or being. The repetitive has the forms shown in Table 7.

The cislocative (CISL) indicates location close to, or movement towards, the speaker or another reference point (Table 8), and the translocative (TRNL) indicates location at a distance from, or movement away from, the speaker or another reference point (Table 9). The forms of the translocative can be especially complex in that disyllabic forms (for example, *iehé-, iahà:-*) occur when the prefix is stressed.

Table 7: Forms of the repetitive (REP)

	s-	"you" prefixes	phonology
		tsi-	se-[c], ts-[i]
Future	ens-	entsi-	ense-[c], ents-[i]
Factual	sa-	se-	se-[c], s-[on]
Optative	aonsa-	aonse-	aonse-[c], aons-[on]

Table 8: Forms of the cislocative (CISL)

	t-	"you" prefixes	phonology
		ti-	te-[c]
Future	ent-	enti-	ente-[c]
Factual	ta-	te-	te-[c], t-[on]
Optative	aonta-	aonte-	aonte-[c], aont-[on]

---

[11] The tables in this section are inspired by and based on the 2nd year curriculum prepared by Ryan DeCaire (*Tekeníhaton Iohserá:te Karihonnienníhtshera' 2022–2023*).

Table 9: Forms of the translocative (TRNL)

	ie-	"you" prefixes ie-	phonology iehé-
Future	ien-	ien-	ienhén-
Factual	ia'-	iahe-	iahà:-, ia-[h], iah-[on]
Optative	ia-	iaie-	

The partitive (PART) points to a location or time of an event or situation, and it occurs with verb roots that have to do with quantity (including counting) and manner (including intensity).

Table 10: Forms of the partitive (PART)

	ni-	"you" prefixes ni-	phonology
Future	nen-	nen-	
Factual	na'-	ne-	na-[h], n-[on]
Optative	na-	naie-	

The duplicative (DLC) most often conveys the involvement of two participants or a change from one state or location to another. The duplicative is also part of the various structures that are used to count two entities or beings.

Table 11: Forms of the duplicative (DLC)

	te-	"you" prefixes te-	phonology
Future	ten-	ten-	
Factual	wa't-	wa'ti-	wa'te-[c]
Optative	ta-	taie-	

The negative (NEG) negates an event or state. Negation requires both a prepronominal prefix and the negative particle *iah*, which comes before the verb. The negative prefix has only one form, *te-*. However, the negative prefix occurs only in the habitual and stative aspects and only before the repetitive and cislocative prefixes; otherwise, the contrastive (CONTR) is used to express negation. The contrastive (CONTR) most often occurs as a marker of negation (with the negative particle *iah*), but it also indicates an unusual or unexpected situation. The coincident (COIN) associates an event with a point in time. The contrastive and coincident have the basic forms *th-* and *sh-*, respectively. The forms of the contrastive and coincident are the same as the partitive with *th* and *sh* substituting for *n* in Table 10.

Several prepronominal prefixes can occur together. To give an idea of the complexity of the system, Table 12 gives the duplicative (DLC) with four other prefixes, including forms before the "you" prefixes and forms required by phonology (see Tables 7–10).

Some verb roots *must* occur with a nonmodal prefix; this is especially so with the duplicative. When a verb always occurs with a particular prefix, the English gloss of the verb root is followed by "with" and the abbreviation for the prefix; for example, "with DLC" means the verb always occurs with the duplicative, or "with CISL" means the verb is attested only with the cislocative.

Table 12: The duplicative (DLC) with other prepronominals

	DLC + REP	DLC + CISL	TRNL + DLC	PART + DLC
	tes-/tetsi-/tetse-/-tets-	tet-/teti-/tete-	ia'te-	na'te-
Future	tens-/tentsi-/tentse-/tents-	tent-/tenti-/tente-	ia'ten-	na'ten-
Factual	tonsa-/tonse-/tons-	tonta-/tonte-/tont-	ia't-/ia'ti-/ia'te-	na't-/na'ti-/na'te-
Optative	taonsa-/taonse-/taons-	taonta-/taonte-/taont-	ia'ta-/ia'taie-	na'ta-/na'taie-

4.3 Reflexive and semi-reflexive prefixes

These two prefixes occur after the pronominal prefixes and before the verb root. The reflexive (REFL) prefix identifies the agent of an event as the same participant that is affected by the event. With the duplicative prefix the verb indicates a reciprocal event. The reflexive has the form *atat-*, or *atate-* before glottal stop and certain consonant clusters. The semi-reflexive (SRF), sometimes called the "middle," adds the meaning that the main participant in the event has a greater involvement or interest in the situation or in the outcome of the situation. It commonly occurs with verbs that involve grooming or other body care. It can also add the meaning that someone or something is getting into a particular position or orientation. With some verbs it indicates that an event took place without it being brought about by an agent. Finally, with some verbs the semi-reflexive has the effect of changing the way that participants interact, for example, from buying to selling. Quite often the result of prefixing the semi-reflexive is unpredictable. The semi-reflexive has various forms: *at-, aten-, an-, ani-, ar-,* and *a-.*

4.4 Noun incorporation

Anyone who studies an Iroquoian language soon becomes aware how often nouns can be incorporated into verbs. The incorporated element can be a noun root, or a verb root plus nominalizer suffix. The nominalizer suffixes are - *'tsher-, -htsher-, -hser-, - 'ser-,* and *-enhser-.* An example of a word with a nominalizer suffix is *owistóhsera'* 'butter', derived from the verb root *-wisto-* 'be cold' with the nominalizer *-hser-*. (Sometimes a nominalizer occurs on a stem that is not obviously derived from a verb; in this case the form with the nominalizer is given at the head of the entry separated from the stem by a forward slash, for example, *-nonhkw-/-nonhkwa'tsher-* 'medicine'.) The causative and instrumental suffixes can function as nominalizers as well. Sometimes what is incorporated is a more complex structure; this is especially so in playful language (see the expression about carpenters in the entry *-ket-* 'scrape').

Often the combination of noun and verb results in a meaning that is (relatively) transparent, but just as often the outcome is unpredictable. In this dictionary, a verb with an incorporated noun is given as a subentry both in the entry for the noun root and in the entry for the verb root.

Frequently when a noun root is incorporated into a verb, the noun root has additional sounds. An example is the root *-shes[t]-* 'syrup'. The word for 'syrup' is *óshes,* without the *t* that is enclosed in square brackets. The incorporated form of the root ends in the *t,* as in *kashestákon* 'it is tasty syrup'.

Also frequently, a verb has two forms, one when there is no incorporated noun and the other with incorporated nouns. An example is the verb for 'wipe'. Without incorporation the form *-rakew-* occurs, as in *keraké:was* 'I wipe it', but with incorporation *-okew-* occurs, as in *katshatoké:was* 'I wipe away the steam' (*-atshat-* 'steam, mist'). The entry for this verb includes both forms, separated by a forward slash: *-rakew-/-okew-.* Sometimes the verb without incorporation has extra sounds at the beginning as compared with the incorporating form (in some works these additional sounds are analyzed as an "empty root," a root without any meaning). An example is the verb for 'be wet'. Without incorporation the form that occurs is -na'nawen-, as in ionà:nawen 'it is wet', but with incorporation -nawen-

occurs, as in ioientaná:wen 'it is damp, wet wood' (-ient- 'wood'). Again, the entry includes both forms: -na'nawen-/-nawen-.

4.5 Derivational suffixes

Derivational suffixes modify the meaning of the root. They occur after the verb root (the root plus derivational suffix is often referred to as the verb stem). The inchoative (INCH) is added to a verb that describes a state and derives a verb that describes progressing to that state. The causative (CAUS) derives a verb that requires an agent to bring about the event described by the verb. The instrumental (INSTR) derives a verb that denotes a characteristic function or behaviour related to the meaning of the verb. The reversive (REV) has the effect of reversing or undoing the situation described by the verb. The (DISTR) indicates that the action described by the verb occurs several times or in several places. The benefactive (BEN) modifies the meaning of a verb by adding a participant that benefits from or experiences a situation. The purposive (PURP) indicates that the event involves moving to a different locale. The facilitative (FACIL) suggests that an action occurs easily. The ambulative (AMB) expresses the idea of movement while an event is in progress. These are the most common meanings added by the derivational suffixes, but as is typical of derivational processes, a derivational suffix can also have less regular or less predictable effects on the meaning of a verb than those identified above.

The most common forms of the first seven of these suffixes are given in Table 13 with the aspect suffixes they select. (The facilitative and ambulative occur infrequently in this dictionary and so are omitted from the table.)

This dictionary has as its organizing principle the notion of a *root*—the part of

Table 13: Derivational suffixes

	HAB	PNC	STV
INCH -'-, -ha'-	-s	-ne'	-en, -on
CAUS -'t-, -ht-, -hst-, -st- -t-	-ha' -s	-e'	-on
INSTR -hkw-	-ha'	-e'	-en
REV -kw- -hsi-	-as -ons	-'	-en -on
DISTR -onnion-, -nion-, -on-, -hon-, -hshon-, -rion- -onkw-	-s -as	-'	ø -en
BEN -enni-/-en- -ni-/-en- -ni-/-hahs -ni-/-'s-	-s	-' -e'	ø
PURP -h-, -hn-, -'n-, -'nh-, -hr-, -hser-	-e's	-a'	-on

a word that cannot be broken down into a combination of other components and refers to an object, a being, a state, or an event. When a root occurs with a derivational suffix, inflected forms of the root plus derivational suffix are given as subentries of the root entry. As it turns out though, some roots always occur with a derivational suffix; an example is the verb root -hri-, which always occurs with the inchoative suffix in the stem -hri'- 'get broken into pieces, shatter' or with the causative suffix in the stem -hriht- 'break into pieces, smash'. Furthermore, some roots that occur only with derivational suffixes also incorporate nouns. In such cases, because the morphology is complex (verb root plus derivational suffix plus incorporations), the root plus derivational suffix is listed as its own entry rather than as a subentry under the root. Thus, the stems -*hri'*- 'get broken into pieces, shatter' and -*hriht*- 'break into pieces, smash' each have their own entry and the composition is described in a note at the end of the entries. For example, at the end of the entry for -*hriht*- there is the following note: "This stem is composed of a root -hri-, which occurs only with suffixes, and CAUS -ht-."

4.6 Aspects and aspect extensions

As described in section 4.1, a verb must have, minimally, a pronominal prefix and an aspect suffix. The basic aspects are habitual (HAB), punctual (PNC), and stative (STV). The habitual describes habitual activity, the punctual presents the event in its entirety, and the stative describes a state that results from an event (sometimes referred to as the stative-perfect) or an inherent state. The punctual aspect must occur with a modal prefix (future, factual, or optative).

A present ongoing event (translated into English with the present progressive) can be expressed with the habitual aspect for some verbs but with the stative aspect for others. Which verbs express ongoing action with the habitual versus the stative is challenging for learners; one idea is that verbs whose meaning implies a consequence (accomplishing something) use the habitual, while verbs whose meaning suggests an activity use the stative (Chafe 1980).

Verbs that have the Subjective (Agent) category of pronominal prefixes in the habitual and punctual aspects have the corresponding Objective (Patient) prefix in the stative aspect. This shift happens regardless of the meaning of the stative aspect—whether resultant state or ongoing activity.

Sometimes a verb inflected with the habitual or stative aspect is followed by another element that expresses additional temporal and aspectual meanings. The continuative (CONT) expresses the persistence of an action or state into the future. The past (PAST) conveys the idea that something used to be the case or was once the case. The progressive (PROG) occurs only after the stative aspect and conveys the idea that an event is progressing; often it is translated as doing something while going along. The progressive may also be classified as a derivational component because it can be inflected with the basic aspects. Table 14 summarizes the aspectual system, and Table 15 gives a verb inflected with each of the categories in Table 14.

Finally, verbs with the purposive (PURP) suffix and some verbs whose meaning includes motion (these verbs typically end in *e*) have an additional aspect form to the three basic ones. In this dictionary, this aspect form is labelled "present" following curriculum materials developed by Ryan DeCaire and Akwiratékha' Martin. It indicates that someone intends to ("is going to") do something. With the factual prefix it indicates that someone is on their way to carry out an action.

Table 14: The aspect system

Aspect	Prefix	Pronominal	Suffix
Habitual		Agent	Habitual
Habitual past		Agent	Past
Future	Future	Agent	Punctual
Factual	Factual	Agent	Punctual
Optative	Optative	Agent	Punctual
Stative (perfect)		Patient	Stative
Stative past		Patient	Past
Future past	Future	Patient	Stative
Optative past	Optative	Patient	Stative
Imperative		Agent	
Continuative			
Future habitual	Future	Agent	Habitual - Continuative - Punctual
Optative habitual	Optative	Agent	Habitual - Continuative - Punctual
Imperative		Agent	
Future perfect	Future	Patient	Stative - Continuative - Punctual
Optative perfect	Optative	Patient	Stative - Continuative - Punctual
Imperative		Agent	

Table 15: Aspect system for the verb 'search'[12]

Aspect	Prefix	Pronominal	Verb	Suffix	
Habitual		k	é:sak	s	I am searching
Habitual past		k	é:sak	skwe'	I used to search
Future	en	k	é:sak	e'	I will search
Factual	wa'	k	é:sak	e'	I searched
Optative	a	k	é:sak	e'	I would, should search
Stative (perfect)		wak	esá:k	on	I have searched
Stative past		wak	esak	ónhne'	I had searched
Future past	en	wak	esá:k	on	I will have searched
Optative past	a	onkw	esá:k	on	I would have searched
Imperative		s	é:sak		Search!
Continuative					
Future habitual	en	k	esák	sheke'	I will be searching
Optative habitual	a	k	esák	sheke'	I would, should be searching
Imperative		s	esák	shek	Keep searching!
Future perfect	en	wak	esak	ónhake'	I will have been searching
Optative perfect	a	onkw	esak	ónhake'	I would have been searching
Imperative		s	esak	ónhak	Be searching!

---

[12] This table is based on the pronunciation of Mike Norton; some speakers have *h* instead of the long vowel, as in *kéhsaks* 'I am searching' or *enkéhsake'* 'I will search'. The table is intended to show an inflectional paradigm of one verb, but it should be noted that not all speakers admit forms in every cell for every verb, especially when forms are spoken outside of a context.

4.7 Locative suffixes

The five locative suffixes (LOC) listed on the right can be added to noun roots in place of the noun suffix. Locative suffixes can be followed by the distributive (DISTR) ending -*hshon*.

-akta', near
-aktatie' or -aktontie', along, edge of
-kon, inside
-okon, under
-'ke, on, at

4.8 Attributive clitics

The attributive (ATTR) endings, technically clitics, can be added to nouns, verbs, or kinship terms. The entries for the clitics are preceded by an equal sign (=), the usual convention for clitics, and followed by an English translation. In the following list the labels in parentheses have been used in descriptions of other Iroquoian languages.

='a/=ha, diminutive (diminutive)
=haka/=aka, people of (characterizer)
=haton, forms ordinal numbers
=hne, at (locative)

=hronon, resident of (populative)
=hneha, way of (characterizer)
=keha, way of (characterizer)
=kenha, former, late (decessive)
=kha, characterized by (characterizer)
=kowa, great (augmentative)
=okon or =okon'a, pluralizer (plural, distributive)
=onwe, genuine (nativizer, authentic)
=shon'a, pluralizer (plural, distributive)
=tsi, intensifier (intensifier)
='ke, at (locative)

4.9 Representing variation

By "variation" is meant two quite different situations. One of them, which cannot be emphasized enough, is variation between speakers. This kind of variation was discussed in section 1.2.1 (about writing *h* and glottal stop) and at the end of section 2 (about dialects). Sometimes the different forms are given in the head of an entry separated by a forward slash. For example, the entry for 'cut into' is listed as -hren-/-hre'n-, and the different pronunciations are shown in the inflected forms, for example, *wà:khrene'* or *wà:khre'ne'* 'I cut it'.

The other kind of variation is when all speakers regularly use different forms depending on the morphology. When the variation is at the end of a root, the affected sounds are surrounded by square brackets. A sound may be present only when a (noun) root is incorporated. The example given in section 4.4 on noun incorporation was -*shes[t]*- 'syrup'. The final [t] is absent in the stand-alone noun *óshes* but present in the incorporation *kashestákon* 'it is tasty syrup'. Sometimes a sound is present in only some aspect forms. For example, the *k* at the end of -*hre[k]*- 'push' is present in the habitual form *iékhreks* 'I push it' but absent in the stative form *iewákhre* 'I have pushed it'. Sometimes it is a vowel that occurs in only some of the aspect forms, as is the case with the verb -*areser[on]*- 'overflow'. The stem-final vowel *on* is present in the habitual form *tewaréserons* 'it boils over, flows over' but absent in the punctual form *enteware:sere'* 'it will overflow'.

Variation at the beginning of a root often is conditioned by noun incorporation: one form occurs when there is no incorporated noun and the other with incorporated nouns. The verbs *-rakew-/-okew-* 'wipe' and *-na'nawen-/-nawen-* 'be wet' were discussed as examples of this in the section on noun incorporation (section 4.4). Both forms are listed at the head of the entry separated by a forward slash.

Another case of variation at the beginning of a root occurs when not all the pronominal prefixes point to the same root beginning. For example, the form *i:kate'* 'it stands' has the C-stem prefix *ka-*, but the form *rón:nete'* 'they are standing' has the e-stem prefix *ronn-*. Both C-stem and e-stem forms are listed in the entry, thus *-t-/-et-*.

Table 16 summarizes these kinds of variation and the conventions used to represent them. Note that some roots vary both at the beginning and the end!

Table 16: Types of variation

Variation at the end of a root	*Example*
Consonant(s) is present when the noun is incorporated	-shes[t]- syrup -ahta[hkw]- shoe -ahseriie['t]- string, rope, thread
Consonant is absent in one aspect (usually stative)	-ohro[k]- insert
Vowel is present in some aspect forms but not in others	-areser[on]- overflow -atstik[on]- vomit
Vowel is present in aspect forms but not before derivational suffixes	-atetsh[en]- dream -na'khw[en]- get angry -athont[e]- hear -atot[e]- be quiet, still
Variation at the beginning of a root	*Example*
Different forms occur with incorporated nouns	-rakew-/-okew- wipe -haratat-/-karatat- lift, raise up -hsa'-/-isa'- finish
Extra sounds (an "empty noun root") occur when there is no incorporated noun	-na'nawen-/-nawen- be wet -hio'thiie-/-o'thiie- be sharp -hren't-/-en't- hang
More than one stem class depending on the pronominal prefix	-t-/-et- stand -kehr-/-akehr- dish, plate, bowl
Different forms in different aspects	-awi-/-on- give
Variation both at the beginning and end of a root	*Example*
There is a different form with and without incorporated nouns, or pronominal prefixes point to different stems, *and* there is variation at the end	-astath[en]-/-ath[en]- dry -a'tarih[en]-/-tarih[en]- be hot -kwe'tar[on]-/-e'tar[on]- cut, slice -ihei[on]-/-enhei[on]- die
Variation depending on speaker	*Example*
Different speakers have slightly different pronunciations	-hre'n-/-hren- cut into

5 Works Cited in Entries

Since the sixteenth century, Kanien'kéha has been written down by travellers to Kanien'ke-há:ka territory. Some had an interest in recording the customs and language of the Kanien'ke-há:ka; a few (mainly missionaries) stayed among the Kanien'kehá:ka and became fluent in the language. More recent works, from the twentieth century, were compiled by those with a special interest or research focus. Just as important are documents written by Kanien'kehá:ka, such as letters, newspapers and journals, lists of vocabulary, and other records. These works—both historical and recent—each are impressive in their own way, reflecting different perspectives and unique relations to the Kanien'kéha language.

Cited words include names of nations and nationalities; general terms for kinds of persons (e.g., widow, priest); terms related to the supernatural; names of places and landmarks; words for times and seasons; names for illnesses; words for personal adornment; names for kinds of plants, animals, and tools; and expressions that relate to rites and traditions. Cognate words in early sources on other Iroquoian languages—Laurentian, Wendat, Onondaga, Susquehannock—are often included. The cited words are given at the end of an entry, in italics, preceded by *Cf.* and followed by the name of the author or other reference (see the Guide to References Cited in Entries) and the page number where the word can be found. If the word comes from a language other than Kanien'kéha, the name of the language precedes the cited word.

Sometimes it is interesting to see a term for a concept or object written or recorded throughout the centuries; sometimes earlier sources can suggest how the meaning of a word has evolved or provide an etymology. The following sections provide overviews of the most frequently cited works. The first section is about very early though sparse records of Kanien'kéha by Dutch travellers. The next two sections describe the dictionaries of Bruyas and Galissonnière from the seventeenth century and those of Marcoux and Cuoq from the nineteenth century. These dictionaries have similar orthographies—though they differ in interesting details, and each is based on different organizational principles. Next are sources from the eighteenth century, and the final section is about works written in the nineteenth and twentieth centuries. For those interested in reading more about how archival and historic resources are used for language reclamation, see Lukaniec (2022).

5.1 Early seventeenth-century vocabularies

Very early descriptions of the Haudenosaunee come from the Dutch during their presence in what was then known as New Netherland. There are three that include Kanien'kéha words and expressions; Jameson (1909) provides much detail about the original manuscripts, their translation and publication, and the circumstances that surrounded their writing. What follows is a short summary.

Reports of events that took place in 1623–1630 in New Netherland were compiled and published in Dutch by Nicolaes Janszoon van Wassenaer in semi-annual "news pamphlets" he called the *Historisch Verhael alder ghedenck-weerdichste Geschiedenissen die hier en daer in Europa,* etc., *voorgevallen syn* (Historical Account of all the most Remarkable Events which have happened in Europe, etc., Jameson 1909: 63). A translation into English from the original Dutch of pages concerning New Netherland was published in O'Callaghan (1850, Vol. III) and again, with revisions, in Jameson (1909). There are just a few Kanien'kéha words, including numbers 1–10 and names of months.

In 1895 in Amsterdam in the Netherlands, a manuscript was found by a General James Grant Wilson, which he translated and published in the *Annual Report of the American Historical Association* for 1895. Eventually, the author of the manuscript—a journal from a 1634–1635 journey to Iroquois territory—was identified as Harmen Meyndertsz van den Bogaert, a surgeon at Fort Orange (now Albany, the first permanent Dutch settlement in New York). Included is a "vocabulary" of almost 300 Kanien'kéha words. The manu-script was again translated and edited by Charles Gehring and William Starna (1988) with transcriptions and analyses of Kanien'-kéha words by Gunther Michelson, who also provided notes that give context to several of the Kanien'kéha terms. The words cited in the entries refer to the page numbers in the 1988 publication.

The minister Reverend Johannes Megapolensis wrote about the Kanien'kehá:ka in letters that were published in a pamphlet in 1644, which was reprinted or published in translation a number of times, the latest in Jameson (1909). Megapolensis's description includes the term for Kanien'kéha or Mohawk, *Kajingahaga* in his rendition, as well as the names of the three clans and a few other expressions.

5.2 Seventeenth-century dictionaries: Bruyas, Galissonnière

The earliest extensive and systematic record of the Kanien'kéha language is *Radices Verborum Iroquæorum*, or *Radical Words of the Mohawk Language, with their Derivatives*, by the Jesuit missionary Father Jacques Bruyas (1635–1712). Originally published in 1862, the work was written more than 150 years earlier, probably in the late 1600s. Until it was published as Volume X of Shea's Library of American Linguistics, it existed only in manuscript form, reportedly held at the St. Francis Xavier Mission Catholic Church in Kahnawà:ke. Bruyas arrived in Canada in 1666 and then worked continuously among the Iroquois, mainly at the Mohawk Mission of Sault St. Louis but also for several years, from 1667 to 1671, at Oneida and in 1673 with the Seneca. Devine (1922: 168) gives his Iroquois name as *Achiendasé*, or *Asennase* in Kanien'kéha ('a new name').

The book consists of two parts: a relatively short *Proemium* or grammatical description in Latin and the main part, the *Radices Verborum*, consisting of Kanien'kéha words translated into French. The grammatical introduction (pp. 5–19 in the 1970 AMS Press reprint) is couched largely in terms of Latin grammar. Verbs are analyzed as having four "principal parts" from which all the other aspect forms are derived. These principal parts have Latin labels, but from inspecting some of the examples it seems the first three correspond to what in contemporary descriptions are the stative, habitual, and punctual aspects, and the fourth is a negative (with either a stative or purposive ending). There are over 20 classes according to the stative ending. Some general formations are proposed for deriving, for example, progressive, causative, benefactive, and reflexive forms.

The very short section on nouns (less than a page) describes possession, terms for nationalities, and nouns derived with the nominalizer. Noun incorporation is described as compounding in the even shorter final section of the grammatical overview. More relevant for taking advantage of the wealth of information—not only lexical but also cultural particulars—is understanding the alphabetization and organization of the second part of the work (see also Michelson 1981).

The letters used by Bruyas are (in alphabetical order according to the Latin alphabet): <a e g h i k n o 8 r s t> and less frequently the Greek letters <θ χ> and a few diacritics. As in today's orthography, the digraphs <en> and <on> are used for nasal vowels. This convention is based on the spelling of French, which was the Jesuits' native language. Unlike the spelling of modern Kanien'kéha though, an oral vowel *a e i o* followed by the sound *n* is written with a double <nn> following the vowel; see, for example, the <enn> in the second syllable of the word for 'animal' in row (1) of Table 17. This spelling is also based on French; compare the masculine and feminine forms for the adjective 'good', *bon* and *bonne*, respectively. The <on> of the masculine form is a nasal vowel; the <onn> of the feminine form is an oral vowel plus the consonant *n*. This double function of <n> in French, both to mark nasal vowels and to indicate a consonant *n*, results in ambiguities in Kanien'kéha. This can be seen by comparing the words for 'animal', written with <enn>, and the word for 'potato', also written with <enn> (row (2) of Table 17). The first is an oral vowel plus *n*, the second is a nasal vowel plus *n*.

The symbol <8> is used for modern <w> and sometimes for the vowel <o>. Originally, this symbol stood for a digraph <ou> with <u> written right above the <o>, which resembles the number 8. Again, this spelling comes from French, where the sound *w* is written <ou> (for example, *oui* 'yes'). Examples of <8> for *w* and *o* are in the third and fourth rows of Table 17.

The letter <i> represents both *i* and *y* as in the orthography used today by Kahnawa'ke-hró:non, though occasionally Bruyas has <j> for *y* (row 5 in Table 17). One may once again compare French, where <i> represents a vowel sound *i* and, before another vowel, the glide *y* (for example, *bien* 'good').

Bruyas used both <k> and <g>, whereas today only <k> is written since the distribution of the sounds written <k> and <g> is predictable in Kanien'kéha. However, he used only <t> instead of both <t> and <d>; the letter <d> does occur, but it occurs as an element in the digraph <nd> in certain stems (an example is the word in row 6). In modern Kanien'kéha the <nd> corresponds to the consonant *n*; Bruyas probably adopted the convention of writing <nd> from the way Wendat was written. The Greek letter 'theta' <θ> is written quite often for <th> (row 7), and the Greek letter 'chi' <χ> occurs for <kh> (row 8) but relatively infrequently.

The sound written today as <h> is represented in a few ways, although often it is not represented at all. An <h> appears most consistently before or after the sonorant consonants, i.e., liquids and glides (written <r>, <n>, <8>, and <i>). Sometimes the diacritic symbol <'> is used for *h* before a consonant (row 9). One last convention is that a diaeresis (two dots) is written above the <n> of the nasal vowels, thus <eṅ> and <oṅ>, when these vowels are followed (at least in modern Kanien'kéha) by a glottal stop or glide (row 10). Otherwise, glottal stop is not recognized in the orthography used by Bruyas.

Table 17: Orthographic conventions in Bruyas

	Sound	Bruyas	French	page	Modern Kanien'kéha	English
1	e, ɛ	Gatsennen	animal domestique	205	katshé:nen	animal
2	ʌ̃	On'nennata	pomme de terre	71	ohnennà:ta'	potato
3	w	A8enha	fleur	24	awénha'	flower
4	o	Atker8θie	peigne	35	atkerothí:ha'	comb
5	j	Ojente	du bois	62	ó:iente'	wood
6	n	Garenda	prière, chanson	88	karén:na'	song, music
7	th	Oθesera	farine	103	othé:sera'	flour
8	kh	Gaχen	joindre	107	tekákhen	s.t. put tog.
9	h	On'nega	eau	69	ohné:ka'	liquid
10	ũw	Gahoñeja	canot	54	kahonwé:ia'	boat

The words of the dictionary, both verbs and nouns, are organized into conjugation classes. Stems that begin in the vowel *a* belong to the first conjugation, consonant stems to the second, stems beginning in *e* and *en* are assigned to the third, stems with initial *i* to the fourth, and stems that begin in *o* and *on* to the fifth. Between the fourth and fifth conjugations, Bruyas has a short section of forms that begin in *i*, mainly *i*-initial roots that typically occur only, or mostly, with incorporated nouns. Alphabetization of entries within the conjugations basically follows the Latin alphabet, but there are lapses and inconsistencies. Generally, <8> is alphabetized after <o> and before <r>, and <i> is alphabetized after <k>. Curious is the alphabetization of <8> (for *w*) relative to <n>. In the first conjugation (a-stems), entries that begin in <A8>) come after entries that begin <An> (where <A> is the initial stem vowel). But in the second conjugation (C-stems), entries in <Ga8> come before entries in <Gan> (where <Ga> is the pronominal prefix, and <8> and <n> are initial stem consonants).

The head entry for verb stems is given with the stative aspect ending, one of the four principal parts. Head entries of stems that begin in the vowels *a e en o on* are given without any pronominal prefix (i.e., they begin in the stem vowel). Consonant-stems and *i*-stems are given with the feminine-zoic subjective (agent) prefix, *ka-* and *ken-*, respectively (written by Bruyas <Ga> and <Gen>).[13] Verbs that occur only in the stative aspect and select the objective (patient) paradigm of prefixes usually have as the head of the entry the stative aspect form with the feminine-zoic prefix *io-*. The head entries of nouns are the basic or stand-alone noun forms. Usually the entries for verbs have several subentries with derivational suffixes or incorporated nouns, and entries for nouns include examples with the noun incorporated into different verbs.

Another valuable early work, likely from the seventeenth century (more on this below), is the *Petit Dictionnaire de la langue des Iroquois de la nation d'agnié*. An archivist at the Bibliotheque Royale in Paris, France, where the original manuscript is kept, wrote

---

[13] The stative aspect of verbs that occur in all three primary aspects is not attested often with a subjective (agent) prefix in our contemporary data. This means that many entries in Bruyas that have the feminine-zoic subjective prefix come across today as artificial or constructed. Certain entries suggest that Bruyas sometimes deliberately gave as a head of an entry a hypothetical form, a word that did not exist. For example, on p. 70 he gives the entry for 'kettle' or 'pail' (chaudière) as Kannatsia, *in comp.* Ontak *extra comp.*, meaning that the stem of Kannatsia occurs only as an incorporated noun in composition with a verb stem.

on the manuscript that it was written in the hand of M. le Marquis de la Galissonnière, who was governor of New France from 1747–1749. The manuscript consists of 84 leaves, each leaf comprising 2 pages. It is a very legible French-Kanien'kéha dictionary, with occasional comments in Latin. G. Michelson (2002) assesses some of the entries against the territory of the Kanien'kehá:ka during the early European presence and certain significant historical events. He concludes that the dictionary quite likely was not written by the Marquis de la Galissonnière and not in the eighteenth century but copied by him from an earlier manuscript. Michelson surmises that the author was a Jesuit father, Francois Boniface (1635–1674), and it was written much earlier, possibly in 1672 since that date is mentioned in the manuscript (59r) as an example of a higher number. Also according to Michelson, it was written in Kanien'kehá:ka territory, not at one of the Catholic missions in Québec. (A digital copy is available from Gallica.BnF.fr.)

Like Bruyas, the first verb form of an entry is a stative aspect form, and nouns are given in their basic, stand-alone form. Some of the entries include forms with incorporated nouns or other derivationally-related forms. Entries are also partially thematically organized in that certain entries include instances of a category; for example, the entry for *Animaux* includes names of species of animals, *fruit* gives all sorts of fruits, *crier* gives different cries. The organization into categories includes some that are more culturally relevant, such as kinds of songs and dances under *Chanter* and *Dancer*, respectively. Some entries include the parts of an object, like parts of a boat (*Canot*) or a gun *(Fusil)*.

The author uses the same orthographic conventions as Bruyas: the letters <a e g h i k

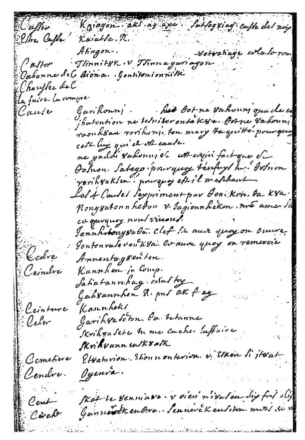

Figure 1: *Petit Dictionnaire*

n o 8 r s t> and less frequently Greek <θ χ>. One notable aspect of this dictionary is that more often than Bruyas's dictionary *h* is indicated with <'> above a previous vowel (in this work written to the right of the vowel since it is not possible to align the <'> diacritic above a vowel) and not infrequently he indicates stress with <'> above the stressed vowel. As in Bruyas, a diaeresis (two dots) is written above the <n> of the nasal vowels, thus <eñ> and <oñ>, when these vowels are followed (in modern Kanien'kéha) by a glottal stop or glide. Glottal stop generally is not represented, but where in modern Kanien'kéha it occurs between vowels the author sometimes has <h>.

Table 18: Orthographic conventions in *Petit Dictionnaire*

	Sound	Petit Dict.	French	page	Kanien'kéha	English
1	e, ɛ	gagarennion	transporter	81r	-karenie-	haul, take back and forth
2	ʌ̃	Aénna	Arc	8v	a'én:na'	bow
3	w	Aꝃenha	fleur	42r	awénha'	flower
4	o	Ogar'ꝃsta	Boyaux	14r	okahrósta'	intestine
5	j	jꝃhiꝃθie	Aigu	5r	iohio'thí:ie'	it is sharp
6	n	Joiandere	Bien	12v	ioiánere'	it is good
7	th	Oθesera	farine	40r	othé:sera'	flour
8	kh	χeiena	ma fille	41v	kheièn:'a	my daughter
9	h	o'téra	racine	71r	ohtè:ra'	root
10	ũw	garóñare	Aiguille	5r	karón:ware'	nail, wire
11	ʌ̃'	Gaiakeñon	Sortir	76v	-iakèn:'en	go out
12	ow	Tsinnöen	Rat	71v	otsinó:wen	mouse
13	ʔ	Aheren	Loin	52v	a'é:ren	over there, away

What is important for understanding the references to this work is that the manuscript is not *paginated*, i.e., it does not have numbers on each page. Instead, only the right page has numbers. This is called "foliation," and the numbers were added later, most likely by a manuscript curator. When a word occurs on the right-hand page of the manuscript, the reference to the page is the number written on the manuscript plus *r* (for *recto,* meaning right side); when a word occurs on the left-hand page, which is the back of the previous right-hand page, the reference to the page is the number of the previous page plus *v* (for *verso,* meaning the reverse or back of the previous page). If I were looking at the manuscript, the left side would be, for example, *8v* (for the back of page 8) and the right side would be *9r* (for the front of page 9). Then when I turn the page, the left side would be *9v* (for the back of page 9) and the right would be *10r* (for the front of page 10).

5.3 Nineteenth-century dictionaries: Marcoux, Cuoq

With the establishment of missionaries, initially from the Society of Jesus (Jesuits), among the Kanien'kéha and other Iroquois-speaking nations, systematically organized grammars and dictionaries of Kanien'kéha were written, copied, held in libraries or other archives, and sometimes published. Joseph Marcoux (1791–1855), given the Kanien'kéha name *Tharoniakanere* 'one who contemplates heaven', was a Roman Catholic priest who spent 36 years at the St. François-Xavier mission in Kahnawà:ke. He wrote several works, including the *Dictionnaire Francais-Iroquois* (1826). This is an extensive and rich source on Kanien'kéha. Its main, maybe only, shortcoming for second-language learners is that *h* and glottal stop are not written in all environments. The version of the dictionary cited in this work was shared by Marianne Mithun, who obtained a copy from a librarian working with Marcoux's materials in Saint-Jérôme, Québec. A microfilm copy of a Kanien'kéha-French dictionary, apparently from 1844, was deposited at the American Philosophical Society (APS) in 1952.

Figure 2: Marcoux's *Dictionnaire Francais-Iroquois*

Marcoux's orthographic conventions differ from the earlier works described here in three significant ways. First, he used only <k> and <t>; there are no words with <g> or <nd>. Second, for oral vowels plus *n* he wrote double <nn> only when the *n* was followed by *h*. An example is *kannhōha* 'door' (*kahnhóha'* in contemporary Kanien'kéha), with <annh>. This convention eliminates most of the ambiguities concerning oral versus nasal vowels followed by *n* in Bruyas and Galissonnière, but not all of them—it is still the case that in Marcoux <ennh> and <onnh> can represent either an oral or a nasal vowel followed by *nh*. An example of oral *e* followed by *nh* is *tekeri8akēnnhas* (nowadays *tekeri'wakéhnhas* 'I argue'); an example of

nasal *en* followed by *nh* is *Katēnnhas* (modern *katénhnha's* 'I am hiring help'). (See section 1.2.1 for today's spelling <hnh>.) Third, he put a macron over what today is the stressed vowel, as in *kannhōha* 'door'. Sometimes the stressed vowel is long in the contemporary language, as in *ohnēka* (*ohné:ka'* 'liquid, water'), and sometimes the stressed vowel is short, as in *iohnāsĕrote* (*iohnáwerote'* 'well'). We don't know whether Marcoux heard all stressed vowels as long and that is why he used the macron, or whether he simply preferred using a macron over any other symbol (say, an acute accent) to indicate stress. And as seen from the word *iohnāsĕrote* 'well', Marcoux wrote a breve over an unstressed and short vowel in a syllable after the stressed one. One final difference in Marcoux is that words with an intervocalic glottal stop are written with an *h* between the two vowels. An example is *atenhēnra (aten'èn:ra'* 'fence'). Otherwise, *h* occurs inconsistently. Thus, <Ke> at the beginning of a word represents either the first person singular prefix *ke-* or the transitive prefix *khe-* indicating a first person singular acting on a feminine-indefinite or third person nonsingular.

Jean André Cuoq (1821–1898), a member of the order of Saint-Sulpice, served in the last half of the nineteenth century at the Catholic missions at Kahnawà:ke and Lac des Deux-Montagnes. His Kanien'kéha name was *Orakwanentakon*, translated into French as 'l'étoile fixe'. He wrote several works about the Kanien'kéha language, including the work cited most here, the Kanien'kéha-French *Lexique de la Langue Iroquoise avec Notes et Appendices* (1866). It is organized into four parts.

The first part, Racine Iroquoises (pp. 1–59) with a Supplément aux Racine (pp. 61–73), lists Kanien'kéha verbs, nouns, particles, and some prefixes and endings in strict alphabetical order (*a e h i k n o r s t w*) with French translations (and it is not unusual to see several French words in the translation of a Kanien'kéha word). The words in the Supplément frequently are given with a suggested etymology, or origin if the Kanien'kéha word is borrowed from French or English. Sometimes words from other languages (for example, Algonquin, Hebrew) are cited for comparison. The second part, Dérivés et Composés (pp. 75–151), gives some of the same words that appear in the first part but with several forms to show the derivational potential of the stem. The third part, Notes Supplémentaires (pp. 153–82), gives details about 41 stems or words: their etymology or composition, words that are related structurally or semantically (for example, additional animal names in the entry for *Arosen* 'squirrel'), and notes about cultural traditions. The fourth part, Appendices (pp. 183–215), consists of 8 appendices. From a lexical perspective the most relevant are the second appendix on children's language, the third appendix on possible homonyms (some of which are not true homonyms and would be written distinctly today with consistent representation of glottal stop, *h*, and stress), and the eighth appendix, which gives the Kanien'kéha names of prominent persons. A few of the other appendices explain aspects of the grammar of Kanien'kéha, and as a demonstration of how words are composed in the fifth appendix, Cuoq gives the constructed example *Aonsonkaterennaientak-seraientaseronhatieseke* ("Ce qui forme un total de 19 syllabes et de 44 lettres," p. 202) and shows step-by-step how this word is derived.

Entries in the dictionary are headed by regularly inflected words written in an orthography that largely matches today's (see below). The head of verb entries is the first person singular habitual aspect form (for example, *Katkahthos* 'voir, regard', p. 14); if

the verb is one that occurs only in the stative aspect, then that form is given (for example, *Wakkate* 'être rich, avoir beaucoup', p. 55). Verbs that occur only with inanimate arguments are given with the feminine-zoic (neuter) singular prefix (for example, *Iokennores* 'pleuvoir', p. 7). And verbs that always occur with a prepronominal prefix are given with the prefix (for example, *Tekenaks* 'hercer, rateler', p. 45, with the duplicative prefix). Occasionally other inflected forms are given (for example, *Rawennio* 'le Seigneur, Dieu', p. 39, with the masculine singular). Nouns are given in their stand-alone form (for example, *Oniete* 'neige', p. 34).

The orthography is basically the modern one at Kahnawà:ke and Kanehsatà:ke except for glottal stop. Occasionally Cuoq did write *h* for an intervocalic glottal stop, but usually glottal stop is not written. He did not mark stress or vowel length, and he used <h> less frequently than it is used today. This does not cause a lot of confusion; it is perhaps most noticeable in that entries that begin in <Ke> correspond to verb forms beginning either in the first person singular subjective (agent) prefix *ke-* or in the transitive prefix *khe-* signaling a first person singular acting on a feminine-indefinite or third person nonsingular. Like Marcoux, he usually wrote double <nn> after oral vowels followed by *nh*.

It is apparent that Cuoq, who came after Marcoux, had made himself familiar with Marcoux's work, and he occasionally cites Marcoux for an observation. And as a final note to Marcoux, Clifford Abbott, Professor Emeritus at the University of Wisconsin, Green Bay, has been working on the letters and notes of Eleazer Williams (1788–1858), an Episcopalian missionary to the Oneida. Williams, in 1823, persuaded about 150 Oneidas to move to Wisconsin from New York, with 654 Oneidas relocating to Wisconsin by 1838. Williams spoke fluent

Kanien'kéha and lived at the same time as Marcoux (1791–1855). Abbott has concluded that Williams wrote in Kanien'kéha rather than Oneida. Moreover, Abbott's research has led him to believe that it is highly likely Williams's lexical and grammatical notes were influenced by, and sometimes perhaps even derived from, Marcoux's works.

5.4 Eighteenth-century sources

The Jesuit missionary Jean-Francois Lafitau (1681–1746) spent nearly six years from 1712 to 1717 at Saint-Louis du Sault, or Kahna-wà:ke, providing detailed observations about Haudenosaunee traditions and lifestyle. He is known for his "scientific" approach and is considered an early and innovative ethnologist and naturalist. The "discovery" of ginseng is attributed to him. His work was first published in 1724 in Paris as *Moeurs des Sauvages Amériquains, Comparées aux Moeurs des Premiers Temps*. The authoritative edition, in English, is Fenton and Moore's *Customs of the American Indians Compared with the Customs of Primitive Times*, published by the Champlain Society in 1974. This two-volume work includes a substantial introduction and extensive notes.

The next two eighteenth-century sources, Pyrlaeus and Claus, are cited less often than the dictionaries described in sections 5.2 and 5.3, partly because their orthographies and/or organizations are more challenging to penetrate, although that does not make them undeserving of future study. From the Moravian missionary John Christopher Pyrlaeus (Johann Christoph Pyrlaeus) (1713–1785) we have the 1742 German-Kanien'kéha manuscript entitled *Lexicon der Macquaischen Sprachen von Christopher Pyrlaeus, A Dictionary of the Mohawk Language by*

Incidentally, Cuoq makes no mention of Williams. Williams's dictionary notes have been archived at the University of Wisconsin, Green Bay, and a digital copy of the manuscripts with transcriptions and translations by Abbott are available at https://diglib.uwgb.edu/digital/collection/p17003coll3.

Christopher Pyrlaeus; a digital copy is available from the APS. The first 77 pages, some blank, are arranged into two columns, with German words alphabetically on the left and the page number where the Kanien'kéha can be found on the right. On these pages there are no page numbers, but at the top of each page is the letter that begins the German words on that page; for example, a page with German words beginning in the letter <g> has <g> written at the top of the page.

Following these pages is a page that has *Datum In nomine Jesu 1742* at the top. The remainder of the work gives the Kanien'kéha text first. The pages are numbered although not entirely consistently, at least so it appears from the digital copy. (See the description of Galissonnière above for the designations *r* and *v* for *recto* and *verso*, respectively.) A thorough and accurate description of the organization of the manuscript as well as systematic orthographic conventions requires more study. At least some expressions are thematically organized, for example, *Indianischer Nationen* ('Indian nations') on p. 43. Occasionally all words relating to a particular root or stem are listed together, for example, on p. 2 inflected forms of *Únque* (-*onkwe*- 'person') plus a few incorporations. The work also includes several religious texts with interlinear German translations.

Christian Daniel Claus (1727–1787) was born in the Federal Republic of Germany and came to this continent in 1749. He soon became acquainted with Johann Conrad Weiser, the Indian agent in Pennsylvania. After travelling with Weiser to the Hudson Valley in 1750, he became interested in the Iroquoian languages and is reported to have become fluent in Kanien'kéha. In 1755, he became deputy secretary of Indian affairs under Sir William Johnson, who was superintendent of northern Indians. From 1760–1774, he was deputy agent to Canadian Indians, and in 1778 he was appointed deputy agent for the Six Nations in Canada. For the rest of his life and career, he was involved with the Six Nations, especially in establishing lands for the Six Nations in Canada at Tyendinaga and Grand River. With Joseph Brant, he translated into Kanien'kéha *The Book of Common Prayer*, and he also produced *A Primer for the use of the Mohawk children*, first edition published in 1781 with a later edition printed in 1786.[14]

The 'Claus' papers, including extensive correspondence, have been digitized and are available at Canadiana Héritage (https://heritage.canadiana.ca/view/oocihm.lac_mikan _103767, accessed Oct. 6, 2020). References are identified by reel (for example, C-1478 is the first reel) followed by the image number that the cited word occurs in. For example, the word *aghgwesaghsne* occurs on image 388, which is the first page of a letter by John Deserontyon to Daniel Claus on March 9, 1779, at St. Regis (Ahkwesáhsne).

The orthography of these works is quite different from the works produced by the Catholic missionaries. To begin with, the missionaries wrote Kanien'kéha with a knowledge of French, whereas Claus spoke German and later English, and this difference in linguistic background is reflected in the orthography. The following is based primarily on the primer published in 1781. The consonant sounds are written with <c d g h k n r s t w y>. The oral stops *k* and *t* are written as they must have sounded to German and English ears, in other words for nowadays *k* are found <k> and <g>, and for nowadays *t* are found <t> and <d>. Occasionally <c> is also used for *k*. The sounds *s n r w y* do not need any comment except that occasionally one finds <ss>. Glottal stop is never written. The sound *h* is written both <h> and <gh>.

The vowels *a* and *e* are consistently written as we find them today. The vowel *i* is usually written <i> although at the end of a word it is sometimes written <y>, as in *Tayondàdy* 'Answer' on p. 21. The nasal vowel *en* is written <ea> most of the time, occasionally <en>, and occasionally <egh> in combination with a following *h* sound. The most varied conventions are for the vowels *o* and *on*. The oral vowel *o* is usually written <o>, but in combination with a following *h*, one finds <ough> (*Tyoughton* 'nine' on p. 18) and even once in a while <uh> (*yugh-nì-ron* 'it is hard' on p. 9).[15] The nasal vowel *on* is most often written <on> but occasionally <oe> and <oen>. With a following *h*, it is sometimes written <ough> (*A-gwé-gough* 'all' on p. 9) and <ogh> (*Kaghyadoghsera* 'book' on p. 1). Perhaps most confusing is that <ou> is sometimes (maybe most often) used where today we find the vowel *o* but also where we

---

[14] The editions differ only in that the later printing has one additional page after p. 18. The original then has 97 pages; the later one has 98 pages.

[15] The first 18 pages of the primer give lists of words that have from two to nine syllables. Just the Kanien'kéha words are given, so the translations of words from those pages are ours. The words in these lists indicate syllable divisions with a dash between syllables, but the rest of the work is not written in syllables.

find the vowel *on*. We don't know whether this is simply an inconsistency in the use of <ou> or whether Claus sometimes heard the vowel *on* as *o*. Stress, when it is written, is most often indicated with a grave accent over the vowel, although an acute accent occurs as well but infrequently.

A comparative vocabulary of 198 expressions in English, Macqua (Mohawk), Delaware, and Mahikan, compiled by the Moravian missionary David Zeisberger with a few additional terms contributed by John

Ettwein, also Moravian, dates from 1788 and is reproduced in Wheeler-Voegelin (1959).

Place names are recorded in Hough (1853) and Boyle (1898), often with a translation or tentative analysis.

Finally, there are occasional citations from two versions of the condolence: from 1782 by John Deserontyon, translated and edited by J.N.B. Hewitt, and Horatio Hale's edition, originally published in 1883, working from handwritten manuscript notebooks from the late eighteenth to mid-nineteenth centuries.

5.5 Other nineteenth- and twentieth-century sources

Documents from the late nineteenth and early-to-mid-twentieth century include ones written by Kanien'kehá:ka. Some are written just in Kanien'kéha and some are bilingual with English. They include notes and records, lists of uncommon as well as common terms and phrases, correspondence, and materials created for those learning Kanien'kéha. Vocabulary from these unique notebooks, periodicals, pamphlets, and letters is often cited (citations added by K. Michelson). The earliest Kahnawà:ke authors used the Jesuit missionary orthography with <en> and <on> for the nasal vowels and no representation of glottal stop or accent. However, most wrote spaces or dashes between syllables.

In 1972, Eddie Beauvais of Kahnawà:ke presented my father (I believe they knew each other well) with a photocopy of a handwritten book that contained recipes for medicines to treat various ailments. The book was written by Eddie's grandfather, Louis Kanonwatase Beauvais (1834–1902), and used by his father, Louis Kenwenteshon Beauvais (1864–1927), in his wild west shows. The photocopy has 27 (unnumbered) pages. It is described by Johnny Beauvais in *The Eastern Door* (Vol. 6, No. 28, August 15, 1997) and in Beauvais

(1985: 148), which also includes images from the book. According to Beauvais, the book was written in Kanien'kéha for security purposes. The work is referenced as "Beauvais," and it is cited when the name of a plant or product is reminiscent of a time when these were more often used.

Jacques Rousseau (1905–1970) was director of the Montreal Botanical Garden 1944–1956, and during a two-day visit to Kahnawà:ke in 1932, he explored the ethnobotany of Kahnawà:ke, specifically the medicinal qualities of local plants. Kate D'Ailleboust (Tekaherha), a monolingual Kanien'kéha speaker, provided the information; Harry Williams was the translator. Rousseau's 1945 publication *Le Folklore Botanique de Caughnawaga* is a meticulously organized work with the Latin labels for plants as well as the Kanien'kéha (and sometimes French and even English) terms.

The residents of Kahnawà:ke farmed, but they also made purchases in local stores as well as stores in Montréal and Lachine. A source related to commerce was discovered serendipitously. Several years ago when Kenneth and Russell Deer were clearing out the shed of their sister Mary Deer, Russell happened upon some old ledger sheets that came from the store founded by their grandfather Jean-Baptiste Teharerens at the turn of the twentieth century and later owned by his son Louis and Louis's wife Annie (née Paul) D'Ailleboust. The store is described in Beauvais (1985: 157–159), with a photo on p. 164. There is writing on about 30 sheets, some moderately to heavily damaged, with writing on front and back. We were able to make out most of the names of products, the quantities bought, and the amounts paid. It looks like the entries were made by two different persons with the handwriting of one much easier to read than the handwriting of the other.

Early twentieth-century records of everyday household products exist also in almanacs published by the St. Francis Xavier Mission Catholic Church in Kahnawà:ke. The almanacs, apparently published from 1899–1906 and then one in 1917, were written in Kanien'kéha by the Jesuit priest L. S. Granger (Kenwenteshon). Most include advertisements in Kanien'kéha for goods sold in Lachine and Montréal. Gunther had copies from 1901 and 1906 in his library; these are now available online from the Smithsonian Institution.

People often wrote letters in Kanien'kéha (or mostly in Kanien'kéha with some English phrases or sentences); five letters were found in Mary Deer's home. The earliest is from 1923, signed by Mary Armstrong and written to Annie D'Ailleboust (née Montour), the wife of Jean-Baptiste Teharerens, owner of the store from which the ledger sheets come. The other four letters are from 1945 and 1946, written by Annie D'Ailleboust (née Paul) to her mother-in-law Annie D'Ailleboust (née Montour); the envelopes of these four letters are addressed to John Canadian, Annie's third husband (Jean-Baptiste Teharerens was her first husband).

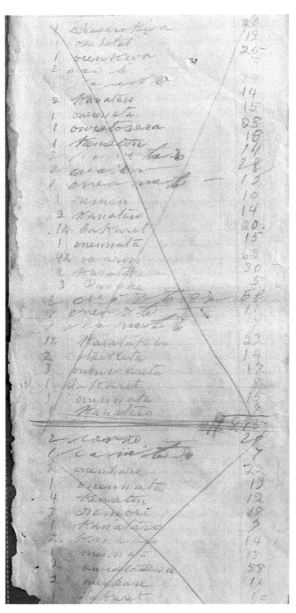

Figure 3: Ledger

Another discovery in Mary Deer's home was a notebook with 45 pages of English-Kanien'kéha vocabulary. A page in the middle of the notebook, also in Kanien'kéha and dated June 18, 1921, states that Onwari Kaentineson received $39, provided by Anen (Ka)Tsitsanien (Annie Montour D'Ailleboust). The author is alert to ambiguities in

English; for example, on p. 14 next to 'light' are given *ka a se ro te* ('lamp'), *te ios wa te* ('it is bright, light'), and *ia te iok ste* ('it is not heavy'); and next to 'can' are given *a ie kwe ni* ('be able') and *ka tse ka ris ta ken ra te* (literally, 'jar, tin'). The notebook is cited as D'Ailleboust.

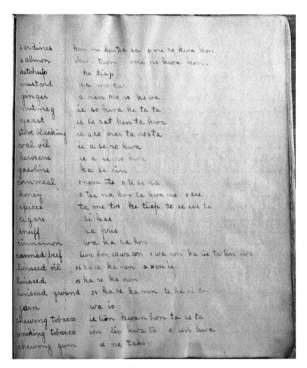

Figure 4: Annie D'Ailleboust's notebook

A relatively short English-Kanien'kéha dictionary was, or still is, held in the archives of the Kahnawake United Church. In 1967, Gunther was lent the handwritten exercise book, apparently from England, by Minister Montgomery. Gunther thought the work might date to the early twentieth century. The page numbers are from Gunther's typed version of the book, referenced as Anon (for anonymous author). The Kanien'kéha words are written in the standard orthography of the time with <en> and <on> representing the nasal vowels, <i> for both the vowel *i* and the glide *y*, only occasional use of <h>, no

representation of glottal stop, and oral vowels followed by *nh* written with a double <nn> (for example, *kann ho tokwa* 'key'). As seen from the example for 'key', the Kanien'kéha words are written with spaces between syllables. This notebook possibly may be the first part of a longer work written by Louise Diabo and described below.

In the Lounsbury collection at the American Philosophical Society is a composition-style notebook that has written on the front cover the name Mrs. Louise Diabo, Caughnawaga, Canada, P.Q. The back cover gives the production of the notebook as the U.S. The description by the APS gives the date of the notebook as 1951. There are 89 handwritten pages of an English-Kanien'kéha word list that begins with the word 'accident' on a page numbered 49 and ends with the word 'youthful'. After page 59 the pages are unnumbered. The page numbers given in the citations assume that the first page of the notebook is page 1 rather than 49.

There is no information about how this notebook ended up in Lounsbury's possession. From reading through the entries it is apparent that Diabo was asked to provide Kanien'kéha equivalents for English words since frequently a phrase or sentence is given, evidently to accommodate an English word that does not have a direct Kanien'kéha translation. For example, for 'hum' (p. 39) there is the sentence *ia kots kwe kon tsi ia ko te ren no te*, literally 'her mouth is closed as she is singing', and for 'chapter' (p. 8) Diabo provided *te ka ka shion kwen tsi ka ia ton nion*, literally 'it is separated, what is written'.

Intriguingly, the alphabetical list is almost identical to the list in the anonymous Kahnawake United Church manuscript (at least the portion of the manuscript typed by Gunther) though there are inconsistencies. Sometimes

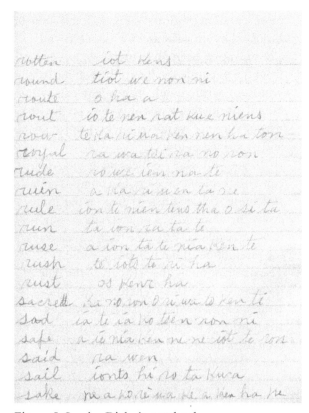

Figure 5: Louise Diabo's notebook

different words or phrases are given as the equivalent for an English item; for example, for 'acquainted' the anonymous (Anon) work has *te ion ta tien te ri* while Diabo has *te ia ko ta te renn ha on*, for 'belong' Anon has *ka ni ka ien a ko wenk* while Diabo has *onkak a ko wen*. The entries may have the same root but different pronominal prefixes; for example, for 'act' Anon has *a ion to ria ne ron* (feminine-indefinite) while Diabo has *a ha to ria ne ron* (masculine), for 'blind' Anon has *iah te ie ken* (feminine-indefinite) but Diabo has *iah te ha ken* (masculine), *ie wen na na ie* 'boast' in Anon (feminine-indefinite) but *ra wen na na ie* in Diabo (masculine). Or the aspect inflection may be different; for example, *ta ies ha ke te* 'bend' (punctual) in Anon versus *te iots hak ton* (stative) in Diabo. English words sometimes

are given in reverse order, for example, 'adopt' and 'adore', 'amount' and 'amuse', 'faint' and 'fair'. Occasionally an English-Kanien'kéha entry given in Anon is missing in Diabo ('angle' *tsi te ka io sa ien*, 'chip' *o ka ra*) or left blank in Diabo ('bark (noise)', 'detour'). Entries from 'control' to 'credit' in Anon are absent in Diabo's list. Occasionally there are slight differences in spelling; for example, *ka nen na wen* 'pipe' (Anon) versus *ka non na wen* (Diabo); *a then no* 'ball' (Anon) versus *at ten no* (Diabo); *kats he* 'vessel' (Anon) versus *ka tse* (Diabo); *as kwa* 'bridge' (Anon) versus *has kwa* (Diabo); *er har* 'cur' (Anon) versus *her har* (Diabo).

Also in the Lounsbury collection at the American Philosophical Society is a notebook from the mid-twentieth century by Reverend David M. Cory, a Presbyterian pastor who resided in Brooklyn, NY (he seems to have begun preaching about 1930 and he retired in 1990). There he met ironworkers from Kahnawà:ke and became interested in the Kanien'kéha language. He wrote words and phrases in a notebook that probably dates to around 1940. The small notebook is just over 100 unnumbered pages with more writing on the righthand page. It lists primarily nouns

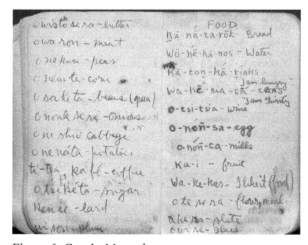

Figure 6: Cory's *Manual*

organized thematically under headings such as Animals and Birds, Food, Family, The Body, Colors, but there are also several pages of verbs. The page numbers in the citations assume that the title page is page 1.

Julia L. Jamieson is the compiler and editor of three short books (12–15 pages) of Kanien'kéha vocabulary, phrases, and short conversations from the Ohswé:ken dialect. On the first page of each book, she identifies herself as the "Founder, Organizer and Teacher of the Mohawk School at David Thomas Memorial Hall Six Nations Reserve near Brantford, Ontario." The vocabulary is organized into categories such as the usual Parts of the Human Body and Numbers, but also less usual such as Domestic Fowl and Parts of Harness. These charming and informative books include opening remarks and welcomes as well as translations of the Lord's Prayer, Psalm 23, and a passage from I Corinthians. Already in 1960 (Opening Remarks, Book 3), Jamieson states in English and Kanien'kéha how fast the language is being lost.

Onkweonwe is a newspaper developed and written by Charles A. Cooke of Wahta, Ontario, apparently produced every two weeks; the only surviving issue is from 1900.

The Kanien'kehaka Raotitiohkwa Cultural Center in Kahnawà:ke published a "journal," *Tewaterihwarenia'tha*, that includes puzzles, vocabulary lists, and a few stories in Kanien'-kéha. For example, the summer 1988 issue gives a page of Mohawk vocabulary, old words, and a tongue twister of 44 letters ('She is coming back from rabbit shopping'), as well as puzzles and a story. It is unclear how many issues of *Tewaterihwarenia'tha* were produced; the Cultural Center has issues from 1978–1980 and 1986–1990. Some of the issues (for example, Autumn 1989 with a description in Kainen'kéha for making corn-bread) do not mark stress but do indicate long

vowels with a colon, which is interesting for those intrigued by questions about how best to represent (and analyze) the accentual system of Kanien'kéha. The Kanien'kehaka Raotitiohkwa Cultural Center also published *Old Kahnawake (Oral History Project)* in 1991, a booklet of more than a dozen reminiscences in Kanien'kéha, English, and French.

A thematically-organized dictionary, *Kanien'kehá:ka Owenna'shón:'a* [Mohawk Words], compiled by Hazel Lazore, was published in 1987 by the Mohawk Language and Curriculum (Center). It was revised in 1991 (the edition cited here), and a third edition was published in 2001 as *Karonhianóhnha' Thematic Dictionary*. Vocabulary from this work as well as the next two works is cited when it attests a term that is otherwise not much cited or is considered "older" usage.

Two works included here are from the present century. Josephine S. Horne's 2003 *Kanien'kéha Iakorihonnién:nis* (teaching textbook) has a nice balance of vocabulary, verb paradigms, and conversational sentences, including questions and answers. The conversational and lexical material are organized into 26 sections, such as How to Address Relatives, Classroom Conversation, Talking to Children, Fruits & Vegetables, and Places, Towns & Cities, to name a few. The 113-page work comes with audio.

Harvey Satewas Gabriel's *Kanesata'ké:ha Tekawenna'thé:tha/Kanesatake Mohawk Dictionary* (2014) is a rich and thoughtful work reflecting the author's relation to the words of his language. There are occasional citations to words from Gabriel's dictionary for rather unusual phenomena that are not referenced elsewhere. (Gabriel has produced a second edition; the 2014 edition is the one cited here.) The dictionary is organized into three parts. The first, pp. 1–150, is an alphabetic list of English words—nouns, verbs, prepositions, adjectives including participles (for example, *conceited*)—followed by a Kanien'kéha inflected word that represents an equivalent of the English. When the equivalent is a complex Kanien'kéha word (which happens often), the Kanien'kéha word is followed by a literal English translation. For example, the entry for 'molasses' gives the Kanien'kéha word *kashestahòn:tsi*, which translates as 'black syrup'. Sometimes there is more than one Kanien'kéha equivalent, and sometimes the English entry cannot be expressed in a single word but requires one or more Kanien'kéha sentences. For example, the entry for 'firkin' is *oriwakahion'néha otára kát'tshe tó:ka áhsen nikaná'kwake ni'iotié:ni*, 'an old clay jar holds about three barrels'. The English entries include some place names (for example, Beauharnois, Chateauguay, Cornwall Island), biblical Christian terms (for example, 'apostle'), names for quite a few tools and musical instruments (for example, 'bugle', 'cymbals'), entries for spices (for example, 'cinnamon', 'cumin'), and the occasional traditional or community custom (for example, the entry for 'carry a basket' describes how parents would make marriage arrangements for their children). In some cases an entry that represents a more general category (for example, animals, birds, fish, flies) is followed by a list of species. Terms for tools are usually followed by an explanation in Kanien'kéha for their use. Occasionally older expressions are explained; for example, the entry for 'folly' includes an old expression *iáh tekaiá:ri* 'the bag is not full', literally, 'they don't have a full mind'.

The second section (25 pp) lists the Kanien'kéha word first and then the English translation. Gabriel states in the heading of this section that the older words were culled from three sources from 1836 to 1880. The final part, *Karahstáhnions* (13 pp), is an inventory of farm equipment, with drawings and both Kanien'kéha and English terms. The orthography is the standard for the variety spoken at Kanehsatà:ke, but with some inconsistences in the use of glottal stop and diacritics for stress and vowel length.

Finally, another work that deserves mention here, though no entries from it are cited, is David Kanatawakhon Maracle's 2002 Mohawk-English dictionary entitled *Yonte-weyenhstahkwa Kanyen'keha, A Mohawk Language Dictionary: A Root Dictionary to be Used as a Resource and Reference Text for any Mohawk Language Learning Situation*. He has produced a version for Kahnawà:ke using the Kahnawà:ke spelling conventions. For the past four decades Maracle has been providing clearly written works on the Kanien'kéha language based on his own speech and linguistic analysis of the language, which he learned as a young man from his grandfather and other elders at Tyendinaga. In 2017, he received an honorary doctorate from Brock University for his contributions. He passed away June 2023 in London, Ont.

According to the title Maracle's is a "root" dictionary. But in addition to giving noun and verb roots as heads of entries, the dictionary lists as heads of entries stems that include an incorporated noun or derivational ending, lexicalized whole words that are used to refer to specific objects, and particles. Stems with incorporated nouns are mostly given alphabetically after the noun root. For example, the entry for the noun root *ahonht* 'ear' (p. 12) gives the noun form ("in isolation") and as an example of incorporation ("in context") *ahonht* incorporated into *owanen* (*te-h-ahonht-owanen* 'he has big ears'). Following the entry for *ahonht* are several entries that have this root as an incorporated noun, for example, *ahonht-a-karewaht* 'hurting one's ear', *ahonht-a-nonhwak* 'one's ear being sore', *ahonht-a-ronhkwani* 'having an itchy ear'. Subentries are given in two representations: one that gives an analysis into morphemes (separated by dashes) and a representation in square brackets with stress and vowel length indicated and dashes between syllables. Note that glottal stop,

represented by an apostrophe as in other Kanien'kéha works, is alphabetized before the vowel *a*, that is, at the very beginning of the Kanien'kéha alphabet.

5.6 Sources on other languages

When the explorer Jacques Cartier voyaged up the St. Lawrence to the Gaspé in 1534, he encountered a group who was fishing in the area. He abducted and took two of the fishing party, the sons of Donnacona, the chief, back to France as concrete evidence of his visit to this continent and in the hope that the two could serve as guides during future trips. A list of fewer than 60 words was written down, in France, from the captives. When Cartier returned in 1535–1536 with the two young men, he was guided to Stadacona (Québec City today) and Hochelaga (Montréal). This time he took prisoner Donnacona, his two sons, and seven other men and brought them back to France. Additional vocabulary from these prisoners, about 160 words this time, was written down after the return to France. Cartier's first two voyages are described in manuscripts that were published in Paris (no original reports remain of the third voyage). The origin of the various manuscripts, their discovery, and their printing is a fascinating and quite complicated set of events summarized in Biggar (1924), who also provides a reproduction and translation of some of the manuscripts relating to the voyages. Barbeau (1949) also provides an overview. Consensus is that the language (or languages), now generally referred to as Laurentian, is Iroquoian (see Mithun 1984a).

Gabriel (baptized Théodat) Sagard, a Recollet missionary to the Wendat (Huron) 1623–1624, wrote about the history of Canada in *Le grand voyage du pays des Hurons*, pub-lished in 1632, and *L'histoire du Canada*, published in 1636. What is cited here are entries from his *Dictionnaire de la langue huronne*, published at the end of *Le grand voyage*. The pages are not numbered; instead they are each arranged into two columns, and at the top of each column are given the first two letters of the French words that occur in that column. When there are many words that begin in a particular sequence of two letters, both columns on the page will have the same letters at the head. For example, all the words that relate to *Manger* (English 'eat') are in a column headed *Ma*. There are enough French words that begin in the letters *ma* that there are 7 pages and 14 columns under *Ma*. References to Sagard include the letters and the column number that the Wendat word appears under; for example, the word for 'ear', *Ahontta*, occurs in the second *Me* column (for *Membres & parties du corps humain*), thus *Me2* in the citation to Sagard.

Missionaries of the Society of Jesus lived among the Wendat from 1632–1649. Their activities, observations, impressions, and (here and there) Wendat terms were recorded in annual bulletins published in Paris as the *Relations des Jésuites*. They were republished in 1959 by Reuben G. Thwaites in 73 volumes as the *Jesuit Relations and Allied documents*.

Pierre-Philippe Potier (1708–1781), of the Jesuit order, was born in present-day Belgium and came to New France to serve as a missionary to the Wendat (Huron) at several missions in Québec (Lorette) and

Ontario (Sandwich). He left some important manuscripts, three of which were published in Fraser (1920): *Elementa Grammaticae Huronicae* (1745), *Radices Huronicae* (1751), and *Extraits de l'évangele* (1747). The page numbers in the citations are from Fraser.

The Lutheran priest John Campanius Holm (1601–1683) was born in Sweden and came to New Sweden in what is today the state of Delaware, where he served as a missionary to the Lenape (Delaware). He produced a vocabulary of the Susquehannock language in the 1640s, *Vocabula Mahakuassica*. It was first published in 1696 by Holm's grandson, Thomas Campanius Holm, and then again in 1834 translated from the Swedish by Peter Stephen Du Ponceau. This last edition has been reprinted by Evolution Publishing and it is that edition which is cited here. Most of the words are also reproduced in Mithun (1981), which is a comparison of Susquehannock with other Northern Iroquoian languages. Susquehannock is no longer spoken.

The reference to Shea is a French-Onondaga dictionary from a seventeenth-century manuscript by an unidentified missionary. John Gilmary Shea produced and published the dictionary in 1860; it was reissued in 1970 by AMS Press. A digital copy of the original handwritten manuscript is available from BnF Gallica, the digital library of the *Bibliothèque nationale de France*.

6 Final Remarks on Words and Dictionaries

Working on, and hopefully using, a dictionary makes one aware of the phenomenal living record a dictionary is. Both traditional customs and everyday life are there in the roots and stems and words.

But a dictionary also offers a perspective on change—in the lives of speakers and in their language. In addition to talking about concepts established long ago, speakers of most languages very often find it necessary to refer to, or talk about, a new object or a new concept. Generally, languages accomplish this by either borrowing or using the existing resources of the language to create new words.

A feature of Kanien'kéha and other languages in the Iroquoian language family that stands out is how few borrowed words there are. There are some borrowings (especially personal names, terms for currency and measures, and words for kinds of food), but there aren't a great many. Most of them in the Kahnawà:ke dialect are from French, a reflection of where Kahnawà:ke territory is located and the history of the province of Québec. An example of a borrowed word is *arawén* 'oats' from French *avoinne*. This word is already attested in Marcoux's dictionary from 1826 (*raꞧēnn* 'Avoine'). Another example is the intriguing word *aremahnéha*, which refers to a kind of textile and apparently comes from *aremen* 'German' borrowed from French *allemand*. Often there is both a borrowing and a Kanien'kéha term, for example, for 'tea' the borrowing *tí:* and also *iekanerahtóhon* 'leaves are put in liquid'. Sometimes a borrowing is integrated into the morphology of Kanien'kéha; an example is the stem *-enhsion-* as in *rawénhsion* 'he is well dressed, elegant,' which as already noted by Cuoq (1866) is based on French *monsieur*.

Abbott (2016), writing about Oneida, and Bonvillain (1978), documenting borrowings in the Ahkwesáhsne dialect of Kanien'kéha, mention that one alternative to borrowing is a shift in the meaning of a root to a meaning that is needed to talk about new objects and concepts. Abbott gives as an example the root -*hwist*- 'metal', which in contemporary Oneida (Onʌyoteʔa·ká·) and Kanien'kéha means 'money'. The older meaning 'metal' is evident in few words, such as *ohwistanó:ron* 'gold' ('precious metal') and in the stem -*hwista'ek*-, literally 'strike metal'; this stem occurs in expressions for telling time and in the word *iehwista'ékstha'* 'bell'. The shifted meaning 'money' occurs often, for example, in *teiohwistahrì:'on* 'change' (more literally, 'the money is broken into pieces, shattered'), *wa'onkhwístani'* 'she or they lent me money', or *skahwísta* 'one dollar'. Interestingly, an alternative root for 'dollar' also shows a meaning shift, namely -*nake['t]*- 'birch bark (container), canoe', as in *tekanakè:take* 'two bills, two dollars'.

Sometimes the sources cited in the entries provide clues about subtle changes. For example, the translations in the older sources for -*aron'tat*- 'shoot' give *tirer du fusil* ('shoot a gun') but also *souffler* ('blow'). In fact, Marcoux (1826) is quite specific, stating *Souffler avec la bouche ou un soufflet* ('blow with the mouth or with bellows'). In some cases a root (or stem) is not used much anymore but is attested in all the older sources; an example is -*atontarikt*- 'laugh loudly or uncontrollably, guffaw'. Translations like *faire hüee* from Bruyas (1862), *Crier, plusieurs ensemble faire la hüee* from Galissonnière's seventeenth-century dictionary, and *hueé, faire des* from Marcoux (1826) suggest laughing in a particular manner, perhaps derisively with hooting. And sometimes an older root has pretty much been replaced by a different root. An example of this is *otsíkeri* 'cloud', which occurs in the seventeenth-century dictionaries of Bruyas (*Otsigre* 'nuée') and Galissonnière (*Iotsigere* 'Nuages'). Marcoux (1826) has *otsāta* 'Nuage', and indeed the root -*atshat*- 'steam, mist, fog, cloud' is used today when talking about clouds, as in *iotshatarónnion* 'there are fluffy clouds here and there'.

More than borrowings and semantic shifts, when it comes to establishing words for new objects and ideas the Kanien'kéha language makes use of existing structural patterns. Two examples are *tewahiakwí:rare* 'suit of clubs' (in a deck of cards, literally, 'it has a toe in it') and *iakonia'takahrónhstha'* 'cough drop' (literally, 'it widens the throat'). These words have the same structure as words that have presumably been part of the language a very long time, such as *teiakonia'tawèn:'eks* 'chokecherry' ('it wraps around the throat') or the older word for 'tea', *iekanerahtóhon* ('leaves are put in water').

A dictionary is so much more than a list of words. Consulting a dictionary, or even just reading around in one, can mean discovering the source of a word, thinking about a word's components and how exactly those components result in its meaning, realizing connections between words so that one word leads to another, learning how a word is used, and revisiting older words that are not used much anymore. Words evoke images, suggest contexts, and often recollect specific events. Translation of some words into another language can be challenging, even futile sometimes. And then, for dictionary writers, there are always more words.

KANIEN'KÉHA-ENGLISH DICTIONARY

A

-a- V be a size

With PART: **Tó: ní:wa'?** How big is it?
tsi ní:wa' the size of it, how big it is,
Tó: niiá:ka'? How big is she?
ken'k nì:ra' he is small, **tho nì:ra'** he is
that size.
With PART and TRNL: **kheh niehé:wa'**
(it is) a big piece.
With COIN and DLC: **sha'té:wa'** it is the
same size, **sha'tétena'** you and I are the
same size, **sha'tè:na'** the two are the
same size, **sha'tékena'** the two (females)
are the same size; it's worth it.
With N -kar- cost, value, and PART:
Tó: nikaká:ra'? What is the amount?
With N -nonhs- house, and PART:
tho nikanónhsa' the house is that size.
With V -'shatst[e]- be strong, NMZR
-enhser-, and PART:
tsi nike'shatsténhsera' all my might,
tsi niha'shatsténhsera' all his might.
• Kheh niehé:wa' onkwatá:tenre'. I have
a big piece left over (for example, a big
piece of fabric). • Sha'tékena' tóka'
iahsatáthreke'. It's worth it if you push
yourself.

-a- V take hold of someone

With N -hnia's- neck, collar: **wahihnià:sa'**
I put my arms around his neck,
wahakhnià:sa' he put his arms around
my neck.
With N -nentsh- arm: **wa'khenéntsha'**
I held her arm, I took her hand (to shake
it); and CISL: **tahinéntsha'** I took hold
of his arm, **tahakenéntsha'** he took hold
of my arm (maybe to dance).

-a- V touch, with TRNL, or TRNL and DLC

With N -hnenhs- shoulder: **iahihnénhsa'**
or **ia'thihnénhsa'** I touched his shoulder.

With N -hsnonhs- finger, hand:
iahihsnónhsa' or **ia'thihsnónhsa'**
I touched his hand.
With N -kwitsh- knee: **iahikwítsha'**
or **ia'thikwítsha'** I touched his knee.
With N -nentsh- arm: **iahinéntsha'**
or **ia'thinéntsha'** I touched his arm.

-ahetken- V be bad: **wahétken** it is bad.

With INCH -'-: **wahétken's** it is going
bad, **enwahétken'ne'** it will go bad,
onhétken'ne' it went bad, **iohetkèn:'en**
it has gone bad.
NOTE: This stem is related to -hetken-
be ugly.
• Onhétken'ne' ne teiotahià:kton. The
banana went bad.

-ahi- N fruit, berry: **káhi**

With **kátshe'** (-tshe['t]- bottle, jar):
kátshe' káhi pear.
With ATTR =shon'a, pluralizer:
kahihshòn:'a fruits.
With V -astath[en]-/-ath[en]- dry:
iohiáthen (it is) dried fruit.
With V -a[t]- be inside, and CISL:
tewà:ia pie.
With V -ate'skont- roast, bake:
wa'katahión:ten' I baked fruit.
With V -atskara- be bitter: **iohiatská:ra**
(it is) bitter fruit; grapefruit.
With -ek-/-ak- eat: **wa'kà:iake'** I ate fruit.
With V -es- be long, tall: **shà:iese'** or
shà:iase' thimbleberry.
With V -hio'tsis[t]- be salty, sour, and DLC:
teiohiahiò:tsis lemon.
With V -hon'tsi- be black, dark-coloured:
wahiahòn:tsi blackberry.
With V -hriht- break into pieces, smash,
and DLC: **wa'tkahià:rihte'** I crushed

berries, **tewahiahríhton** mashed berries or fruit.

With SRF -at-, V -hsa'kt[on]-/-a'kt[on]- bend, and DLC: **teiotahià:kton** banana.

With V -ke- amount to, and DLC: **tewà:iake** two fruits.

With V -kowan[en]-/-owan[en]- be big, and REP: **sewahió:wane'** apple; and ATTR =onwe, genuine: **sewahiowane'ón:we** crabapple.

With V -nohare-/-ohare- wash: **wa'kahióhare'** I washed fruit.

With V -o- be in water: **wà:io** jam.

With V -ohwiha- split in two, and DLC: **wa'tkahiohwíha'** I split the fruit.

With SRF -at- and V -onni- make: **iotahión:ni** (there are) a lot of fruit or berries.

With V -oren- split open, and DLC: **wa'tkahió:ren'** I split open the fruit.

With V -ri- cook, ripen: **wahiá:ris** cantaloupe, **onhiá:ri'** the fruit ripened, **iohiá:ri** the fruit is ripe; with V -ri- cook, ripen, and ATTR ='a/=ha, diminutive: **Ohiarí:ha** June; with V -ri- cook, ripen, and ATTR =kowa, great: **Ohiarihkó:wa** July.

NOTE: The root -ahi- is an a-stem, and it is the form that is incorporated into verbs, but the stand-alone noun form **káhi** has the prefix *ka-* indicating a C-stem. Note that **teiotahià:kton** is used for 'banana' nowadays, but the borrowing *ba na ne* is given in Horne (ca. 1970: 41), and *banane* appears in the Kahnawà:ke store ledger from the early 1900s.

Cf. Ohio in comp. *kahik* extra comp. fruit (Bruyas: 23); *Kahik ohia* in compo., fruit (Galissonnière: 43v); *kāhik* fruit (Marcoux: 182); *kahik* fruit (Cuoq: 9, 98); *waio* [jam] (Ledger: 55); *wa io* jam (Anon: 8); *ka-i* fruit (Cory: 15); *wá-io* jam (jelly) (Cory: 85); *wà:io* jam (Horne: 32); Wendat *Hahique* Tous menus fruicts (Sagard: Pl4); Wendat *ohia* fruit (Potier: 445)

-ahiakh- V go pick fruit or berries: **wa'kahiákhe'** I am going to pick berries, I am on my way to pick berries, **enionhiákha'** she will go and pick berries, **wahahiákha'** he went to pick berries.

With PAST -hne': **rohiakhónhne'** he went to pick berries, he has gone to pick berries.

-ahiakwir- N toe: **ohiakwí:ra'** POSS: **kahiakwirà:ke** (on) my toe, **rahiakwirà:ke** (on) his toe, **ionhiakwirà:ke** (on) her toe.

With V -kowan[en]-/-owan[en]- be big: **kahiakwirowá:nen** my big toe.

With V -r- put in, and DLC: **tewahiakwí:rare'** suit of clubs in cards.

With V -rakarere-/-karere- be noise travelling, and DLC: **tehahiakwirakaré:re'** his toes are making noise (talking about a dog).

-ahkar- N wood chips, shavings: **ohká:ra'** With V -eka'[w]-/-ka'[w]- find tasty, like the taste of: **wahkarákon'** cinnamon.

With V -ketskw- raise upright: **wa'kahkarakétsko'** I flipped the arm up to uncover the vent holes in the storm window; and SRF -at-: **watahkarakétskwas** storm window with vent holes.

With V -ohtshi- remove, pull out: **wahahkaróhtshi'** he is shaving it (a board or branch).

With V -tahkw- take out: **ionhkaratáhkwas** she is carving, **wahahkaratáhko'** he carved, **rohkaratáhkwen** he has carved, **sahkaratáhko** Carve! and CAUS -ht-: **ionhkaratahkwáhtha'** chisel.

-ahkararen- V ache, hurt: **wakahkará:rens**
I am aching, hurting, **rohkará:rens** he is
aching, hurting, **iakohkará:rens** she is
aching, hurting, **onkwahkará:ren'** I
ached, I hurt.

• Kahsi'tà:ke wakahkará:rens takò:ka'te'
anitskwà:ra. My foot is aching (because)
I bumped against the chair.

Cf. Akararen estre sensible à la douleur
(Bruyas: 23); *hokaráren* patient (Galissonnière: 64r); *ꝩakahkarārens* douleur,
sentir la (Marcoux: 130); *Wakahkararens*
être sensible à la douleur (Cuoq: 52);
iakokararens [(where) someone is hurting]
(Beauvais: 6); *ia ko ka ra rens* sore
(D'Ailleboust: 16)

-ahkatste- V endure pain: **wakahkátste'** I can
endure pain, **rohkátste'** he can endure
pain, **iakohkátste'** she can endure pain.
With NEG: **iah tehohkátste'** he can't
stand pain.

Cf. Atkatste estre patient à endurer
(Bruyas: 46); *hotkatste* patient (Galissonnière: 64r); *ꝩakakātste* endurer,
souffrir avec patience (Marcoux: 147);
Wakahkatste être fort, capable de résister,
dur au mal, à la douleur (Cuoq: 52);
Onondaga *hauiatagaste* Dur, Etre dur au
mal (Shea: 47)

-ahket- V go to a point and go or come back,
with REP: **sháhkets** he goes back and
forth, **saháhkete'** he went back,
saiónhkete' she went back.
With CISL: **tontaháhkete'** he came back.

-ahkwari['t]- N bear: **ohkwá:ri**
With V -a'a- be small, **ken'** particle, and
PART: **ken' niwahkwari'tà:'a** (it is) a
small bear.
With SRF -at-, V -her-/-hr- set on top of,
and PROG -atie-: **wakatahkwari'tahrátie'**
I have a bear (or bear skin) on my
shoulders.
With V -itie-/-tie-/-ontie- fly around, float
by: **wahkwari'tóntie'** a bear is running or
going along.
With V -kowan[en]-/-owan[en]- be big:
wahkwari'towá:nen (it is) a big bear.
With V -ra'ken- be white:
wahkwari'tarà:ken polar bear.

Cf. "The Mohawk Indians are divided
into three tribes, which are called *Ochkari,
Anaware, Oknaho*, that is the Bear, the
Turtle and the Wolf." (Megapolensis:
178); *ochquari* bear (van den Bogaert: 53);
Okꝩari, Okꝩarita in comp. ours (Bruyas:
23); *okꝩári* Ours (Galissonnière: 7v);
ochquaari Bär (Pyrlaeus: 12v); "*Ochquari*,
the Bear." (Ettwein in Wheeler-Voegelin:
49); *Ocquari* Bear (Zeisberger in Wheeler-
Voegelin: 61); *Okwari* [bear] (Onkweonwe: 3); *on-kwa-ri* bear (Cory: 12)

-ahkwas- V cover someone: **enhiiáhkwase'**
I will cover him, **wahakwáhkwase'** he
covered me, **wa'káhkwase'** I covered
(myself), **kheiahkwá:son** I have put a
cover on her.

-ahkwatase-/-tase- V go around: **rahkwatá:ses**
he keeps going around, **wa'kahkwatá:se'**
I went around, **rohkwatá:se** he has gone
around.
With DLC: **wa'tkahkwatá:se'** I went all
the way around, I made a round (I went
around the track, the block, a round at the
golf course), **tewakahkwatá:se** I have
gone around; and PROG -hatie-:
tewakahkwatasehátie' I am going round
and round.
With PART and DLC: **Tó: na'tehsahkwa-
tá:se'?** How many rounds did you make?
áhsen na'tkahkwatá:se' I went around
three times.

With CISL: **tahahkwatá:se'** he came around this way.

With TRNL: **ia'kahkwatá:se'** I went around that way, **ia'sahkwatá:se** Go around! and DLC: **ia'tkahkwatá:se'** I went all around that way.

With SRF -a-, N -nat- town, settlement, and DLC: **wa'tiakwanatatá:se'** we went all around town.

With SRF -a-, N -nonhs- house, and TRNL: **ia'kanonhsatá:se'** I went around the house.

With SRF -ate-, N -'sere[ht]- vehicle, car, and TRNL: **ia'kate'serehtatá:se'** I went around the car.

• Skenekwá:ti ia'sahkwatá:se. Go around to the left! Turn left!

-ahkwenni- N outfit, clothing

With SRF -at-: **atahkwénnia'** outfit, clothing; and POSS: **akwatahkwénnia'** my clothes; and **akohsá:tens** horse (-hsaten- carry a person on the back): **akohsá:tens aotahkwénnia'** harness.

With V -her-/-hr- set on top of: **wa'kahkwennià:ren' akohsá:tens** I put the harness on the horse, **wahiiahkwennià:ren'** I put the harness on him.

With SRF -at- and V -ien- put down, have: **wa'katahkwenniá:ien'** I stored it; and INSTR -hkw-: **iontahkwenniaientáhkhwa'** cupboard, storage shed, pantry, closet; with SRF -at-, V -ien- put down, have, and BEN -ni-/-hahs-: **koniatahkwenniaién:ni** I am leaving it in your care, **enkoniatahkwenniaién:hahse'** I will leave it in your care, **wa'kheiatahkwenniaién:hahse'** I left it in her care.

With SRF -at-, V -ieron- make fun of, play, DISTR -nion-, and DLC: **wa'thatahkwenniaierónnion'** he put on

a costume, **tehotahkwenniaierónnion** he has on a costume.

With V -onni- make: **rahkwennión:ni** tailor, **ionhkwennión:ni** seamstress.

With V -weienhon- be good at, capable at: **rahkwenniaweiénhon** he is a good tailor, he knows how to make clothes.

• Tewakatahkwenniaierónnion akwé:kon teiohstò:seronte'. I have on a costume that's all feathers.

-ahkwesen- N partridge: **ohkwé:sen**

With ATTR =ne, at: **Ahkwesáhsne** Mohawk Nation at Ahkwesáhsne.

With ATTR =hronon, resident of: **Ahkwesashró:non** Ahkwesáhsne Mohawks.

See also **ohkwesen'tarì:wase'** pheasant; **ohkwesen'tóia'** quail.

Cf. okꙋesen Perdrix (Galissonnière: 61v); *aghgwesaghsne* (Claus C-1478, 388); *Ak-wis-sas-ne* St. Regis River and Village, "where the partridge drums" (F. Marcoux in Hough: 180); *wakꙋēsas* Battres des ailes ... la perdrix (Marcoux: 37); *Akwesasne* à St. Regis, nom de lieu. Litt. Là où la perdrix bat des ailes (Cuoq: 2); Onondaga *ókꙋesseau* Perdrix (Shea: 78)

-ahkwihsron- V do intensely, try hard: **kahkwíhsrons** I try hard, I do it intensely, with effort, **enkahkwíhsron'** I will try hard, **wahahkwíhsron'** he tried hard, **rohkwíhsron** he is trying hard, **sahkwíhsron** Try hard!

With CISL: **tahahkwíhsron'** he did it intensely this direction.

With TRNL: **iahahkwíhsron'** he did it intensely that direction.

NOTE: The *hsr* of this stem sounds more like *shr*.

• Wakahkwíhsron akeweientéhta'ne' Onkwehonwehnéha akatá:ti'. I am trying

hard to learn to speak the Native language.
• Sahkwíhsron iahà:shrek. Push hard!
• Tasahkwíhsron satá:ti. Talk loud!

-ahnehkwan[on]- V swallow:
wahahnéhkwane' he swallowed it.
With TRNL: **iehahnehkwá:nons** he is
swallowing, **ienkahnéhkwane'** I will
swallow it, **ia'kahnéhkwane'** I
swallowed it, **iewakahnehkwá:non**
I have swallowed it.
With SRF -ate- and N -nekw- pea, pill:
wahatenekwahnéhkwane' or (with TRNL)
iahatenekwahnéhkwane' he took the
pill, **satenekwahnéhkwan** or (with TRNL)
ia'satenekwahnéhkwan Take the pill!

-ahnot- V tell about
With N -ia't- body: **riia'tahnótha'** I tell
about him, I tell on him,
wahshakoia'tahnó:ton' or
wahshakoia'tahnó:ten' he told on her, he
squealed on her, **wahatia'tahnó:ton'** or
wahatia'tahnó:ten' he squealed on me,
shakoia'tà:note' he is talking about her,
tóhsa sheia'tahnó:ten Don't tell on her!
With SRF -ate- and N -rihw- matter,
message: **raterihwahnótha'** he preaches,
lectures, **wahaterihwahnó:ton'** he
preached, **wakaterihwà:note'** I have
preached.
With N -wenn- voice, word:
kewennahnótha' I read,
enkewennahnó:ton' I will read,
wa'kewennahnó:ton' I read,
wakewennà:note' I am reading; and
BEN -ni-/-hahs-: **rakewennahnotá:ni** he
is reading to me, **enkhewennahnóthahse'**
I will read to her; with N -wenn- voice,
word, and INSTR -hkw-; and
kahiahtónhsera' (-hiatonhsera- book,
paper): **iewennahnotáhkhwa'**
kahiahtónhsera' books, stuff to read.

-ahonht- N ear: **ohónhta'**
POSS: **kahonhtà:ke** (on) my ear,
rahonhtà:ke (on) his ear, **ionhonhtà:ke**
(on) her ear.
With V -es- be long, and DLC:
tewahónhtes donkey, **tehahónhtes** he is
up to no good, he is doing something he is
not supposed to (for example, cheating on
his wife), **teionhónhtes** she is up to no
good. *This is an old expression.*
With V -kahront- make an opening, a hole,
and DLC: **tekahonhtakà:ronte'** I have
pierced ears.
With V -kwek- shut, close off, and DLC:
tehahónhtakweks his ear blocks up (like
when he has a cold),
wa'tkahónhtakweke' my ear blocked up,
tekahonhtakwé:kon I am hard of hearing, I am deaf, **tehahonhtakwé:kon** he is
deaf, **teionhonhtakwé:kon** she is deaf.
With V -nonhwak[t]- be sore, hurt:
wakahonhtanòn:waks I have an earache,
onkwahonhtanòn:wake' I got an earache.
With SRF -at-, V -ot- stand up, and DLC:
tekatahonhtótha' I am really trying to
listen (maybe I have my hand cupped to
my ear), **wa'tkatahonhtó:ten'** I tried
hard to listen; and PAST -hkwe':
tewakatahonhtó:tahkwe' I was trying
hard to listen.
With V -rakahr-/-kahr- make noise, and
DLC: **tekahonhtá:kahre'** I hear ringing
in my ears, **wa'tkahonhtá:kahre'** my
ears rang.
With V -ra'neken-/-neken- be side-by-side,
next to, and DLC: **taonhtané:ken** or
tehahonhtané:ken rabbit.
With V -ronhkwani-/-ronhkwen- itch:
wakahonhtarónhkwani my ear is itchy.

Cf. Ahonta oreille (Bruyas: 23); *ohonta*
oreille, *Tegahontagarente* Oreille perce
(Galissonnière: 23r); Laurentian

Ahontascon the ears (Biggar: 241);
Wendat *Ahontta* les oreilles (Sagard:
Me2); Wendat *ahonta* oreille (Potier: 445)

-ahranonhs- N temple, cheekbones
POSS: **kahranonhsà:ke** or
kehranonhsà:ke (on) my temples,
rahranonhsà:ke (on) his temples,
ionhranonhsà:ke or **iehranonhsà:ke**
(on) her temples.
With V -ia'[k]- hit, slap:
enkoniahranonhsáia'ke' I will smack
your face, **wahakwahranonhsáia'ke'**
he slapped me in the face.

Cf. Garanonsa temples (Galissonnière:
23r); *oranōnsa* Tempe (Marcoux: 384);
Oranonsa tempe, joue (Cuoq: 35)

-ahrho'ton- V show affection, cherish, with
DLC: **tekahrhò:tons** I show or give it (an
animal) affection, **tehakwahrhò:tons** he
shows me affection, **tenkheiahrhò:ton'**
I will show her affection,
wa'thiiahrhò:ton' I showed him affect-
tion.
With BEN -ni-: **tehiiahrho'tón:ni** I am
showing him affection,
tehakwahrho'tón:ni he is showing me
affection.
With REFL -atat-: **tekatatahrhò:tons** I
look after myself (for example, I don't
overdo it).

Cf. Garhotandi Consoler (Galissonnière:
22v); *tekeiarhotōnnis* caresser (Marcoux:
56); *Tekarhotonnis* flatter, caresser,
délicater, traiter avec douceur (Cuoq: 70);
taionhró:ton cherish (Gabriel: 22)

-ahri- N fishhook: **à:ria'**

Cf. aria hamecon (Galissonnière: 48r);
ārĭa Hameçon (Marcoux: 199); *Aria*
hameçon (Cuoq: 2)

-ahriohkawine- V fish: **rahriohkawí:ne's** he
is fishing, **wahahrióhkawine'** he fished.
With PURP -hser-:
wa'kahriohkwawinéhsere' I am going
fishing.

-ahrist- V urge, prevent: **enhsheià:riste'** you
will urge her, prevent her (from something), **wahiià:riste'** I urged, prevented
him.
• Wahiià:riste' tóhsa tho niahá:iere'. I
urged him not to do that.

-ahronk- V know a language: **kahrónkha'**
I speak, I understand a language,
enkà:ronke' I will learn the language,
wa'kà:ronke' I learned the language.
With INCH -ha'-: **wakahronkhà:'on**
I have learned, I know the language.
• Sahrónkha' ken Onkwehonwehnéha?
Do you understand the Indian language?

Cf. Arongen entendre, écouter, concevoir
(Bruyas: 26); *Arongen* Comprendre (Galis-
sonnière: 22r); *wachronia* understand
(Zeisberger in Wheeler-Voegelin: 64);
kahrōnkha Langue, entendre une langue
(Marcoux: 227); *Kahronkha* entendre,
comprendre, savoir une langue (Cuoq: 9);
Onondaga *garonka* Entend, j' (Shea: 52);
Susquehannock *Hije zœroncka* but I under-
stand (Holm: 6)

-ahronk- V hear about
With CAUS -t-: **iohrón:ka** it is audible, it
is loud.
With CAUS -'t- and BEN -enni-/-en-:
shakohronka'tén:ni he informs them,
lets them know, **wahiiahronkà:ten'** I
informed him, warned him,
wa'kheiahronkà:ten' I informed her,
warned her.
With N -rihw- matter, message:
wa'kerihwà:ronke' I heard the news,

sarihwahrón:ken you have heard the news.

With N -wenn- voice, word: **khewennahrónkha'** I hear her, her voice (for example, if she is lecturing, or on the radio), **wahiwennà:ronke'** I heard him, his voice, **riwennahrón:ken** I have heard him.

• Iohrón:ka nahò:ten' wahèn:ron'. It is audible (loud and clear) what he said.

• Wa'kerihwà:ronke' ónhka'k wa'íheie'. I heard someone died.

-ahsaht- N neck of a violin, guitar, fiddle: **ohsáhta'**

With V -ranie-/-karanie- rub, scrub: **wa'kahsahtakaránie'** I played the fiddle; and SRF -at- and CAUS -'t-: **iontahsahtakaraniè:tha'** fiddle.

-ahsahtahkar- N splinter

With SRF -at- and V -ion't-/-inion't- bring in, score: **onkwatahsahtahkarínion'te'** I got a splinter, **wakatahsahtahkariniòn:ton** I have a splinter.

With SRF -at-, V -ohar- attach at the end, and INCH -'-: **onkwatahsahtahkarohá:ra'ne'** I got a splinter.

With SRF -at-, V -okw- disperse, and DLC: **wa'tewatahsahtahkaró:ko'** it splintered.

-ahsarahkw- N shoe or moccasin cuff: **ohsaráhkwa'**

With V -es- be long, tall, and DLC: **teiohsaráhkwes** high top shoes or boots.

With V -her-/-hr- set on top of, and DLC: **wa'tionhsarahkwà:ren'** she put the cuff on, **tewahsarahkwáhere'** it (moccasin, shoe) has a cuff.

Cf. Asarak8a dessus de soulier (Bruyas: 27)

-ahsat- N dark, shadow

With LOC -kon, inside: **ahsá:takon** in the dark.

With SRF -at- and V -r- put in: **iotahsá:tare'** (it is) a shadow, **wakatahsá:tare'** I have a shadow, I am casting a shadow; and PROG -atie-: **rotahsatarátie'** he has a shadow as he is going along; with SRF -at-, V -r- put in, and BEN -hahs-: **onkwatahsatáhrhahse'** I saw a shadow.

Cf. Asatagon en secret (Bruyas: 27); Asatagon'son tenibres (Galissonnière: 78v); osāta ombre (Marcoux: 270); asātăkon Ténebres, dans les (Marcoux: 385); Asatakon dans les ténèbres (Cuoq: 2); o sa ta shadow (Anon: 41)

-ahsa'k- V cough: **kahsà:kha'** I cough, **wa'káhsa'ke'** I coughed, **rohsà:ken** he is coughing, **iakohsà:ken** she is coughing. With DISTR -nion-: **wahahsa'kánion'** he coughed (repeatedly).

-ahseht- V hide, kill: **ionhséhtha'** she hides it, **wa'káhsehte'** I hid it, **iakohséhton** she has hidden it, **shakohséhtha'** he kills them, **wahshakóhsehte'** he killed her, **shakohséhton** he has killed her, **tóhsa sheiáhseht** Don't kill her!

With BEN -enni-/-en-: **riiahsehtén:ni** I hide it on him or from him, **wa'koniahséhten'** I hid it on you or from you.

With SRF -at-: **katahséhtha'** I hide (myself), **enkatáhsehte'** I will hide, **wa'katáhsehte'** I hid, **wakatahséhton** I have hidden, I am hiding.

With N -ia't- body: **wa'kheia'táhsehte'** I hid her, **shakoia'tahséhton** he has hidden her.

With SRF -at-, N -kahr- eye, and DLC: **wa'thatkahráhsehte'** he covered his eyes, he hid his eyes, **tehotkahrahséhton** he has covered his eyes.

With SRF -at- and N -tsisto[hkw]- star: **rottsistohkwahséhton** he is a detective. *See also* -ri'wahseht- have a secret.

Cf. Ase'ton cacher, *Aseton* tuer en cachette (Bruyas: 28); *ase'ton* Cacher (Galissonnière: 15r); *ase'ton* tuer (Galissonnière: 81v); *keiaseta* Tuer, assasiner (Marcoux: 400); *Kasetha* cacher; assassiner, tuer en cachette (Cuoq: 12); *a hon wa se te* murder (Diabo: 48)

áhsen three, **áhsen iawén:re** thirteen, **áhsen niwáhsen** thirty, **áhsen tewen'niáwe** three hundred, **ahsénhaton** third, **áhsen nia'ká:ienhte'** three times.

Cf. Hasse [three] (Wassenaer: 73); *asen* trois (Bruyas: 27); *asen* 3 (Galissonnière: 59v); *áchso* 3 (Pyrlaeus: 11r); *āsen* Trois (Marcoux: 398); *Asen* trois (Cuoq: 2); Laurentian *Asche* Three (Biggar: 241); Wendat *Hachin* 3 (Sagard: No1); Onondaga *achen* Trois (Shea: 99); Susquehannock *Axe* three (Holm: 5)

-ahsen- V be tens

With DLC: **tewáhsen** twenty; and ATTR =haton, ordinal: **tewahsénhaton** twentieth.

With PART: **kaié:ri niwáhsen** forty. With NMZR -hser- and V -ot- stand: **iohsénhserote'** hundreds, thousands. • Iah thahskwé:ni' ahshní:non' né: tsi iohsénhserote'. You can't buy it because it's in the hundreds. • Tsi nikanó:ron iohsénhserote'. It's so expensive, it's in the hundreds.

Cf. Asenserøt dix par dessus (Bruyas: 27); *te-io-hen-ta-shen* Chelidonium majus (= vingt morceaux d'herbe) [greater

celandine] (Rousseau: 45); *iosén'tseronhte* percent (Gabriel: 94)

-ahsennen- V be half: **ahsén:nen**

With COIN and DLC: **wísk sha'tewahsén:nen** half past five, **skanà:tara sha'tewahsén:nen** a (loaf of) bread and a half. • Wísk tánon' ahsén:nen nikáksake. Five and a half cups. • Ahsén:nen iotatén:ron ne wà:io. There's half the jam left.

-ahsenni'tak- V get cold feet, with DLC: **tewakahsennì:taks** my feet are cold, **tehohsennì:taks** his feet are cold, **teiakohsennì:taks** her feet are cold, **wa'tewakahsennì:take'** I got cold feet.

-ahsenni'tontakw- V get frostbite, with DLC: **wa'tewakahsenni'tontá:ko'** I got frostbite, **wa'tiakohsenni'tontá:ko'** she got frostbite, **tehohsenni'tontákwen** he has frostbite.

-ahsentho- V cry, with DLC: **teionhsénthos** she is crying, **tenkahséntho'** I will cry, **wa'thahséntho'** he cried, **tewakahsénthon** I have cried.

-ahseriie['t]- N string, rope, thread: **ahserí:ie** With **iestatha'táhkhwa'** (-statha't-/ -atha't- dry): **iestatha'táhkhwa' ahserí:ie** clothesline. With **ie'nikhónhkhwa'** (-'nikhon- sew): **ie'nikhónhkhwa' ahserí:ie** sewing thread. With V -atiront- pull, stretch, and CISL: **tionhseriie'tatiróntha'** she is pulling string; with V -atiront- pull, stretch, and DLC: **tehonhseriie'tatiróntha'** they play tug-of-war, **tehonahseriie'tatí:ronte'** they are playing tug-of-war. With V -hren't-/-en't- hang down:

iohseriie'tèn:ton there is string hanging.
With V -hwatase/-tase- turn, twist:
kahseriie'tatá:ses I am winding thread
or string around something (like a spool),
wa'onhseriie'tatá:se' she wound the
string.
With V -ke- amount to, and PART:
Tó: niwahseriiè:take? How many
minutes?
With V -ohar- attach at the end:
wa'kahseriie'tohá:ren' I threaded the
needle.
With V -ohtshi- remove, pull out, and CISL:
takahseriie'tóhtshi' I pulled out the
thread.
With V -ont- attach, and DLC:
teiohseriiè:tonte' fringe.
With SRF -at-, variant -hseriie['t]-, and
V -o'kt- finish: **wa'katsheriie'tò:kten'**
I ran out of string or thread.
With V -r- put in, DISTR -on-, and DLC:
tekahseriiè:tarons I am embroidering it,
wa'tkahseriiè:taron' I embroidered it,
tewahseriiè:taron it is embroidered.

-ahset- V count: **kheiahsé:tas** I am counting
them, **wa'káhsete'** I counted it.
With CISL: **tkahsé:tas** I am counting,
tehshakohsé:tas he is counting them,
entkáhsete' I will count, **takáhsete'**
I counted, **tahshakóhsete'** he counted
them, **tewakahsé:ton** I have counted,
tasáhset Count! and DISTR -nion-:
tkahsetánions I am counting them all.
With N -enhni't- moon, month, and CAUS
-'t-: **iakenhni'tahsetà:tha'** calendar.
With N -ent- day, and CAUS -'t-:
iakentahsetà:tha' almanac.
With N -hstar- drop: **iehstarahsé:tas** she
is counting the drops, **wa'khstaráhsete'**
I counted the drops.
With N -ohser- winter, year:
iohserahsé:tas the count year, appears on

the front cover (as *ionhserahséta's)* of a
1979 calendar.
NOTE: Forms with the CISL are preferred.
• Wa'káhsete' tó: ní:kon enkakwé:ni'.
I counted how much it would equal.
• Tehshakohsé:tas tó: nihá:ti ken rón:ne's.
He is counting how many are here.

-ahsiharakw- V remove, yank out, with DLC:
wa'thahsihará:ko' he yanked it out.
NOTE: This stem is composed of a root
-ahsihar-, which occurs only with suffixes,
and REV -kw-.

-ahsihara'- V get wedged in, stuck, with DLC:
tewahsihá:ra's it gets wedged in, stuck,
tenwahsíhara'ne' it will get stuck,
wa'tewahsíhara'ne' it got stuck,
teiohsiharà:'on it has gotten stuck, it is
wedged in (for example, a rock under a
fence, something flushed down the toilet).
With N -ia't- body: **wa'tieia'tahsíhara'ne'**
she got stuck.
With N -neni- stone, rock:
teioneniahsiharà:'on there is a rock
stuck.
With N -(h)nhoh- door:
wa'tkahnhohahsíhara'ne' the door got
stuck, **teiohnhohahsiharà:'on** the door is
stuck.
NOTE: This stem is composed of a root
-ahsihar-, which occurs only with suffixes,
and INCH -'-.
• Akwé:kon teiohsiharà:'on, iah thé:nen
teionáktote'. It's all wedged in, piled
together, there's no space.

áhsikwe' or **ahsí:kware'** spear
Cf. assaghe rapier (van den Bogaert: 52);
Asegꙅe epée, halebarde (Bruyas: 27);
Aségꙅe Espee (Galissonnière: 37r); *āsĭkꙅe*
Hallebarde (Marcoux: 199); *Asikwe* dard,
lance, pique, hallebarde, baïonnette (Cuoq:

2); *a-si-kwe* spear (Cory: 34); *a si kwe* spare (Diabo: 76); Onondaga *gachégsa* Epée (Shea: 53)

-ahsio'tano- V get cold hands, with DLC: **tehohsiò:tanos** he has cold hands, **teiakohsiò:tanos** she has cold hands. With CAUS -hst-: **wa'tewakahsiò:tanohste'** my hands got cold.

-ahsir- N blanket, shawl: **áhsire'** POSS: **akwáhsire'** my blanket, **raóhsire'** his blanket, **akóhsire'** her blanket. With **tekenhnakhánion** (-ihn- skin, leather, -kha- attach, piece together): **tekenhnakhánion áhsire'** quilt. With V -her-/-hr- set on top of: **wahshakohsirà:ren'** he put the blanket or shawl on her; and REV -kw-: **wahshakohsirahrá:ko'** he took the shawl or blanket off her. With V -iio- be good, nice: **wakahsirí:io** I have a nice blanket, quilt, shawl. With V -i'tson-/-'tson- be dirty, and DLC: **teiohsirá'tson** it is a dirty blanket, shawl. With V -ke- amount to, and DLC: **tewahsí:rake** two blankets. With V -kste- be heavy: **iohsirákste'** (it is) a heavy blanket. With V -na'nawen-/-nawen- be wet: **iakohsiraná:wen** her shawl is wet; and CAUS -hst-: **wa'akohsiraná:wenhste'** her shawl got wet. With SRF -at- and V -nohare-/-ohare- wash: **wa'katahsiróhare'** I washed the blanket. With V -ot- stand: **wahsí:rote'** sailboat. With V -'nikhon- sew: **ionhsira'níkhons** she is sewing a blanket. With V -'sere-/-i'sere- drag: **ionhsirì:sere'** she is dragging the blanket.
• Karisé: ionnià:ton áhsire'. The blanket is made of wool.

Cf. "They call us [the Dutch] *Assirioni*, that is, cloth-makers, or *Charistooni*, that is, iron-workers, because our people first brought cloth and iron among them." (Megapolensis: 178); *Gasire* une couverte à grand poil, v. étoffe Iroquoise (Bruyas: 97); *Asire* Couverte (Galissonnière: 26r); *āsīre* Couverte (Marcoux: 93); *kasirahērha* hisser la voile [hoist the sail] (Marcoux: 201); *katsirōtha* mettre à la voile (Marcoux: 201); *Asire* couverture de lit (Cuoq: 2); *Katsirotha* hisser la voile (Cuoq: 80); *wa tshi rot ha* sailboat (Anon: 14); *ionts hi ro ta kwa* sail (Diabo: 67); *wattsirótha* sail boat (Lazore: 65)

ahsí:sa' or kasí:sa' pestle
NOTE: The translation of this word as 'corn' in Laurentian may have come about as a result of identifying the product of what is being pounded [corn] rather than the instrument used for pounding [pestle].
Cf. Asisat pilon (Bruyas: 28); *Gasisat* un pilon (Bruyas: 97); *Gasisat* pilon (Galissonnière: 66r); *asīsa* Pile pour piler (Marcoux: 291); *Asisa* pile, pilon (Cuoq: 2); *a'si'za'* Pestle (Waugh: 60); *ah shi sah* pestol (Jamieson 2: 5); Laurentian *Osizy* corn (Biggar: 242); Wendat *Achisa* Pilons à battre (Sagard: Me13)

-ahsithen- V become numb, fall asleep: **wakahsíthens** I get numb, **onkwahsíthen'** it fell asleep on me, I got numb, I got an (electric) shock, **wahohsíthen'** it fell asleep on him, he got numb, **wakahsithèn:'en** I am numb, it has fallen asleep on me.
• Kahsi'tà:ke onkwahsíthen'. My foot fell asleep.
Cf. Tsasiteñon avoir les pieds engourdis (Bruyas: 28); *Agachitenen* Engourdir (Galissonnière: 34v); *sakasītens* engordi,

être (Marcoux: 149); *Wakasithens* être engourdi (Cuoq: 52)

-ahsi't- N foot: **ohsì:ta'**

POSS: **kahsi'tà:ke** (on) my foot, **rahsi'tà:ke** (on) his foot, **ionhsi'tà:ke** (on) her foot.

With LOC -okon under: **kahsi'tó:kon** the bottom of my foot.

With V -akahron- be wide, and DLC: **tekahsi'takà:ron** I have wide feet.

With V -akera- stink, smell, and DLC: **tehahsi'tákeras** he has smelly feet.

With V -akwenhten- be flat, and DLC: **tekahsi'takwénhten** I have flat feet.

With V -atonris[t]- be damp, soggy, and DLC: **tewakahsi'tatón:ris** I have damp (sweaty) feet.

With SRF -ar-, V -enton[hw]- move back and forth, and DLC: **wa'tkarahsi'tén:tonhwe'** I moved my foot back and forth.

With V -es- be long, and DLC: **tekahsi'té:son's** I have long feet.

With SRF -ar-, V -her-/-hr- set on top of, and DLC: **è:neken wa'tkarahsi'tà:ren'** I elevated my feet.

With SRF -ar-, V -hwatase-/-tase- turn, twist, and DLC: **tehorahsi'tatá:se** he is pigeon-toed, **teiakorahsi'tatá:se** she is pigeon-toed.

With SRF -ar-, V -hwe'nonni-/-kwe'nonni- fold, and DLC: **tehorahsi'takwe'nón:ni** he is a widower. *This is an old expression.*

With V -ia'k- cut off, and CISL: **tonkwahsì:tia'ke'** I tripped, **tahohsì:tia'ke'** he tripped; and DISTR -hon-: **tewakahsi'tià:khons** I am always tripping all over.

With V -karewaht- injure, hurt: **onkwahsi'takaré:wahte'** I hurt my foot.

With V -nohare-/-ohare- wash: **wahiiahsi'tóhare'** I washed his feet; and

SRF -ar-: **wa'karahsi'tóhare'** I washed my feet.

With V -nonhwak[t]- be sore, hurt: **wakahsi'tanòn:waks** I have a sore foot.

With V -ohar- attach at the end, and INCH -'-: **wa'kahsi'tohá:ra'ne'** I got something stuck in my foot.

With SRF -ar- and V -ohro[k]- insert: **waharahsi'tò:roke'** he slipped on his shoes or slippers; and CAUS -st-: **ionrahsi'tohrókstha'** slippers, slip-on (backless) shoes.

With SRF -ar- and V -ohtshi- remove, pull out: **wa'karahsi'tóhtshi'** I took my foot out of it; and BEN -en-: **onkwarahsi'tóhtshien'** my foot came out of it (for example, a shoe).

With SRF -ar- and V -ohw- swell: **rarahsì:tos** his foot swells, **waharahsì:to'** his foot swelled, **wakarahsì:to** my feet are swollen.

With V -ok- chafe, get a blister: **onkwahsì:toke'** I got a blister on my foot.

With SRF -ar-, V -ontawe't- shake, pump, vibrate, and INSTR -hkw-: **ionrahsi'tontawe'táhkhwa'** pedal (for example, of an old sewing machine).

With SRF -ar-, V -ot- stand, and DLC: **wa'tkarahsi'tó:ten'** I put my foot up.

With V -o'ka't- run into, bump against, and CISL: **tahakwahsi'tò:ka'te'** he (accidently) hit my foot.

With V -rakarere-/-karere- be noise travelling, and DLC: **tekahsi'takaré:re'** my feet are making noise.

With SRF -ar-, V -rakew-/-okew- wipe, and CAUS -ht-: **ionrahsi'tokewáhtha'** foot mat.

With V -ronhkwani-/-ronhkwen- itch: **wakahsi'tarónhkwani** my foot is itchy.

With V -[t]- be one, and REP: **sewahsì:ta** one foot (measure).

With SRF -ar -, V -tenihon- shake, and DLC:

wa'tkarahsi'tateníhon' I shook my foot (back and forth, in a circle).

With SRF -ar-, V -'sere-/-i'sere- drag, and DLC: **teionrahsi'tì:sere's** she is dragging her feet, **wa'tkarahsi'tì:sere'** I dragged my feet.

Cf. Asi pied, *Raosige* à son pied, *Hondasitagon* Recollectos, ils ont les pieds nuds (Bruyas: 22); *ronasītăkon* les récollets, i.e. les va nus pieds (Marcoux: 264); *Ronasitakon* les Récollets (Cuoq: 2-3); *ro si ta kon* brother (Anon: 10); Laurentian *Ouchidascon* the feet (Biggar: 242); Wendat *Achita* Pieds (Sagard: An5)

-ahskats[t]- V be beautiful: **ióhskats** it is beautiful.

With PAST -'ne': **iohskatstòn:ne'** it was beautiful.

With N -ia't- body: **roia'táhskats** he is handsome, **iakoia'táhskats** she is beautiful, glamorous.

With N -renn- song, music: **iorennáhskats** it is a beautiful song, beautiful music.

• Ióhskats wa'tietsi'nehtará:ron' ako'wháhsa'. It's beautiful, the skirt she beaded.

-ahskontar- N back of the heel: **ohskón:tara'**

POSS: **kahskontarà:ke** (on) my heel, **rahskontarà:ke** (on) his heel, **ionhskontarà:ke** (on) her heel.

-ahskw- N bridge: **áhskwa'**

With V -her-/-hr- set on top of: **wahahskwà:ren'** he put up a bridge, **wahskwáhere'** (there is) a bridge; and **karístatsi** stove, iron, and **rotiió'te'** (-io'te-/-io'ten- work): **karístatsi rotiió'te' ronhskwahéhrha'** ironworkers.

With V -iahia'k-/-iia'k- cross over, and DLC: **wa'tkahskwí:ia'ke'** I crossed the bridge.

With V -ihen- be in the middle of, and COIN and DLC: **sha'tewahskwí:hen** middle of the bridge.

With V -o- be in water: **wahskóhon** bridge over water.

With V -ohar- attach at the end: **iohskóhare'** suspension bridge.

With SRF -at-, V -ohw- put in liquid, and TRNL: **iahatáhskohwe'** he put in a dock.

• Wentó:re' takahskwí:ia'ke' né: tsi iote'serehtakà:te'. It's hard for me to get across the bridge because there are a lot of cars.

Cf. Ask8a eschaffaut (Bruyas: 28); *8ask8ahere* Avant de la cabanne (Galissonnière: 15r); *8askōhon* Pont (Marcoux: 297); *Waskohon* pont (Cuoq: 58); *Quebec Tewaskohon* [Quebec Bridge] (Onkwehonwe: 3); *waskohon* bridge holding one side to other (Mary Deer's class notes, Feb. 1966); *as kwa* bridge (Anon: 26); *has kwa* bridge (Diabo: 6)

-ahskwen'n- N porch: **ahskwèn:na'**

With LOC -aktontie', along, edge of: **ahskwen'naktóntie'** along the porch.

With LOC -kon, inside: **ahskwèn:nakon** enclosed porch, usually at the entrance to a house.

With LOC -okon, under: **ahskwen'nó:kon** under the porch.

With V -akarenhr[e]- lean to one side, slant: **wahskwen'nakarèn:re'** the porch is leaning, crooked; and CAUS -t-: **wahskwen'nakarenhrá:ton** a shed or lean to-type structure attached to a building.

With V -hnhonter- attach end-to-end, add on: **wahahskwen'nahnhónteren'** he added on a porch, **wahskwen'nahnhón:tere'** (it is) an attached, enclosed porch.

With V -hseronni- dress, prepare:

rahskwen'nahserón:ni he is fixing the porch.

With V -ont- attach: **iohskwèn:nonte'** there's a porch.

Cf. Askꝟannonte l'avant d'une cabane (Bruyas: 29); *aksēnna* Appentis (Marcoux: 18); *Askwenna* appentis, vestibule (Cuoq: 2); *as kwen na* porch (Anon: 20)

-ahsohkw- N colour: **ohsóhkwa'** colour, **ionhsóhkhwa'** crayons

With ATTR =shon'a, pluralizer: **ohsohkwa'shòn:'a** (different) colours.

With SRF -at- and V -atak- be brightly-coloured, vivid: **iotahsohkwatá:kon** it is brightly-coloured.

With V -ke- amount to, and CONTR, TRNL and DLC: **thia'tewahsóhkwake** all different colours.

With V -o'ten- be a kind of, and PART: **Oh niwahsohkò:ten?** What colour is it?

With V -(h)rho- coat: **ionhsohkwáhrhos** she is colouring it; and CAUS -hst- and INSTR -hkw-: **ionhsohkwahrhohstáhkhwa'** crayons.

With V -[t]- be one, and COIN: **né: shonhsóhkwa** it's the same colour.

With SRF -at-, V -tiha- be different, and DLC: **tetiatahsohkwatíhen** they are different colours.

NOTE: This stem is composed of -ahso[hw]- dye, colour, and INSTR -hkw-.

-ahso[hw]- V dye, colour: **wa'káhsohwe'** I coloured it, dyed it, **wakahsóhon** I have coloured it, dyed it, **wahsóhon** it is dyed, coloured.

With SRF -at- and REV -kw-: **watahsókwas** the colour fades, runs, **ontahsó:ko'** the colour faded, ran, **iotahsókwen** the colour has faded.

With INSTR -hkw-, *see* -ahsohkw- colour.

-ahsonht- N wall: **ahsónhta'**

With LOC -'ke, on, at: **ahsonhtà:ke** on the wall.

With V -ot- stand, and DLC: **tewahsónhtote'** partition, **wa'thahsonhtó:ten'** he put up a wall; and REV -kw-: **wa'thahsonhtotá:ko'** he took down a wall; with V -ot- stand, and PART and DLC: **wísk na'tewahsónhtote'** it is divided into five, it has five divisions, five rooms; with V -ot- stand, DISTR -on-, and DLC: **tewahsonhtó:ton** there are partitions, rooms.

With V -o'ka't- run into, bump against, and CISL: **takahsonhtò:ka'te'** I ran into the wall.

With V -rakahr-/-kahr- make noise, and DLC: **tewahsonhtá:kahre'** the walls are making noise.

With unclear V, and DLC: **tehonahsónhta** they live in attached buildings (a duplex or townhouses).

• Átste' tsi niiothó:re' tewahsonhtá:kahre'. It is so cold out that the walls are making noise (cracking).

-ahsont- N night

With V -es- be long, tall, and PART: **tsi niwahsón:tes** during the night.

With V -a'tarih[en]-/-tarih[en]- be hot, warm: **iohsontataríhen** it is a hot night.

With V -kwek- be the whole of: **ahsontakwé:kon** all night.

With V -no- be cold: **iohsón:tano** it is a cold night; and CAUS -hst-: **enwahsón:tanohste'** the night will cool off.

With V -[t]- be one, and REP: **sewahsón:ta** one night.

With unclear beginning: **kwa'ahsón:te'** or **kwa'shón:te'** last night; and ATTR ='ke, at: **kwa'ahsontè:ke** or **kwa'shontè:ke** nighttime.

-ahsonter- V join, connect
   With DLC: **tekahsontéhrha'** I am joining it, connecting it, **tenkahsónteren'** I will join it, connect it, **wa'thahsónteren'** he connected it, **tewakahsón:tere'** I have connected it, **tewahsón:tere'** it is connected; and DISTR -onnion-: **tewahsonterónnion** they are connected.
   With REV -kw- and DLC: **wa'thahsonterá:ko'** he disconnected it.
   With SRF -at- and TRNL: **ia'katahsónteren'** I am continuing (with what I am doing).
   With N -wenn- voice, word, DISTR -onnion-, and DLC: **tekawennahsonterónnion** morphology, *title of Martin (2016)*.
   See also -hnhonter- attach end-to-end, add on, which has a similar meaning but occurs only with incorporated nouns.

-ahsonthen- N midnight: **ahsónthen**
   With ATTR =hne, at; and **nikahá:wi'** (-hawi-/-enhawi- carry): **ahsonthèn:ne nikahá:wi'** nighttime.
   With ATTR =kha, characterized by; and **karáhkwa'** (-rahkw- sun): **ahsonthénhkha karáhkwa'** moon.
   Cf. Asonθen minuit (Bruyas: 29); *ȣasonten* minuit (Galissonnière: 60r); *Achsóndha* Mitternacht (Pyrlaeus: 2v); *asōnthen* Minuit (Marcoux: 250); *Asonthen* au milieu de la nuit, à minuit (Cuoq: 80); *a shon then* midnight, *ka ra kwa a son then kha* moon (Anon: 6)

-ahstesk- V go dry, evaporate: **ónhsteske'** it evaporated, it went dry.
   With TRNL: **ienwáhsteske'** it will boil right down, go dry, **iahónhsteske'** it totally boiled away, evaporated, **ieiohstéskon** it has evaporated.

Cf. asennen nienwasteske 10 karen iateniotatenre [it will boil down to half, 10 gallons will get left over] (Beauvais: 10)

-ahstoht- V reduce, shrink, take in: **kahstóhtha'** I reduce it, make it smaller, take it in, **wa'ónhstohte'** she shrunk it, made it smaller.
   With N -atia'tawi- dress, shirt, jacket, and NMZR -'tsher-: **wa'katia'tawi'tsheráhstohte'** I took in the dress, etc.
   With N -rihw- matter, message: **wa'kerihwáhstohte'** I consider the matter unimportant, insignificant; and BEN -en-: **wahirihwahstóhten'** I didn't think very highly of him, I didn't think much of him, **wa'kherihwahstóhten'** I didn't think highly of her.
   NOTE: This stem is composed of a root -ahsto-, which occurs only with suffixes, and CAUS -ht-.
   • Ako'wháhsa' wa'ónhstohte' wa'ón:tiwe'. She took in her skirt [because] she got skinny (i.e., lost weight).

-ahsto'- V shrink, get small: **wa'ónhsto'ne'** she got small, she shrunk, **ónhsto'ne'** it shrunk, it got small.
   With PROG -hatie-: **wakahsto'onhátie'** I am shrinking.
   NOTE: This stem is composed of a root -ahsto-, which occurs only with suffixes, and INCH -'-.

-ahsto's- V think small of
   With N -rihw- matter, message: **kherihwahstò:se'** I find her issue, whatever she brought up, is small, I don't think much of it, **wa'kherihwáhsto'se'** I found her issue insignificant.
   NOTE: This stem is composed of a root -ahsto-, which occurs only with suffixes, and BEN -'s-.

-ahswahser- N fine wood shavings, sawdust: **ohswáhseri**

With V -ta'-/-eta'- put inside, and CISL: **taionhswahseráta'** or (with a variant -ahsewahser-) **taionhsewahseráta'** she put sawdust inside it (for example, when doing beadwork).

Cf. oseßāsĕri Sciure de bois (Marcoux: 359); *ohse'wáhseri* chaff, the outer husk of the grain/sawdust (Gabriel: 21)

-ahswen't-/-a'swen't- N coal: **ohswèn:ta'** or **o'swèn:ta'**

With V -ha[w]-/-enha[w]- hold, bring, take, and TRNL: **iahahswen'ténhawe'** he took coal.

With V -hninon- buy: **wa'kahswen'tahní:non'** I bought coal.

With SRF -at- and V -ien- put down, have: **katahswèn:taiens** I am saving coal; with V -ien- put down, have, PURP -hn-, and REP: **sahahswen'taiénhne'** he is going to return, bring back some coal.

With V -ontho- burn, put in the fire: **kahswen'tónthos** I am putting coals in to burn (into a stove or coal oven), **wahahswen'tóntho'** he put coals in to burn, **sahswen'tóntho** Put the coals in!

With SRF -at- and V -o'kt- finish: **wa'katahswen'tò:kten'** I ran out of coal.

Cf. Osßen charbon (Bruyas: 29); *Osßenta* noir (Bruyas: 101); *Osßenθa* Charbon (Galissonnière: 17v); *osßēnta* Charbon (Marcoux: 61); *Oswenta* charbon éteint (Cuoq: 139); *os wen ta* coal (Anon: 14)

-ahta[hkw]- N shoe: **áhta**

POSS: **akwáhta** my shoe(s), **raóhta** his shoe(s), **akóhta** her shoe(s).

With **teiohnatiróntha'** (-ihn- skin, leather, -atiront- pull, stretch): **teiohnatiróntha' áhta** rubber boots.

With **teionrerenhstáhkhwa'** (-areren-

race): **teionrerenhstáhkhwa' áhta** running shoes.

With ATTR =onwe, genuine: **ahtahkwa'ón:we** moccasin.

With INCH -'-: **wa'kheiáhta'** I put shoes on her; and SRF -ar-: **karáhta's** or (with DLC) **tekaráhta's** I am putting on shoes, **wa'karáhta'** or **wa'tkaráhta'** I put on shoes, **roráhten** or **tehoráhten** he has on shoes.

With REV -hsi-: **wa'kheiahtáhsi'** I took the shoes off her.

With V -akaion-/-kaion- be old: **ahtahkwaká:ion** a large red fall raspberry.

With V -ati-/-onti- lose, throw: **onkwahtahkón:ti'** I lost my shoe(s); and TRNL: **iahonkwahtahkón:ti'** I threw the shoe.

With SRF -ar-, V -hna'neta'-/-neta'- line, double, and DLC: **wa'tkarahtahkwanéta'** I put on galoshes (over my shoes), boots, **tesarahtahkwanéta** Put on boots! and CAUS -hst- and INSTR -hkw-: **teionrahtahkwaneta'ahstáhkhwa'** overshoes, galoshes, boots.

With V -i'tson-/-'tson- be dirty: **teiakohtahkwá'tson** her shoes are dirty; and INCH -'-: **wa'thohtahkwá'tson'ne'** his shoes got dirty.

With V -kareni- take back and forth, and DLC: **teiakohtahkwakaré:ni** she is running around (with different men). This word has also been attested with a falling tone, **teiakohtahkwakarè:ni**, *see* -rakare'ni-/-kare'ni- be loud.

With otherwise unattested V -na'kor-: **kahtahkwanà:kore'** I wear out my shoes fast, **ionhtahkwanà:kore'** she wears out her shoes fast.

Cf. achta shoes (van den Bogaert: 53); *Ata* soulier, extra comp., *Atakßa* in comp. (Bruyas: 31); *ata'kßagaion* framboises

(Galissonnière: 43v); *a-ta-wka-ka-ion*
Rubus odoratus (Rousseau: 48, who points
out that the coureurs des bois used to line
their shoes with this plant); *ahtahkwa-
ká:ion* These were pink berries. (Old
Kahnawake: 10); *ahtakwakén:ion*
old shoes (also a name for a wild purple
berry) (Gabriel: 119); *tsiotakwa'ka'ré:ni*
harlot, loud shoes (Gabriel: 64);
teiohtahkwakarè:ni Woman of loose
morals (Horne: 92); Laurentian *Atha* Shoes
(Biggar: 242); Wendat *'ak8a (atak8a)*
souliers (Potier: 445); Onondaga *attak8a*
Soulier (Shea: 95); Susquehannock
Atackqua shoes (Holm: 5)

-ahtahkwitahkwen- V get overtired, with DLC:
wa'tewakahtahkwitáhkwen' I got overtired, **wa'thohtahkwitáhkwen'** he got
overtired, **wa'tiakohtahkwitáhkwen'** she
got overtired.

-ahtakw- V attempt but fail, with DLC and
CISL: **tetewakahtákwas** I try but fail,
tethohtákwas he tries again,
tontaiakohtá:ko' she tried again.

-ahtarion- V have on shoes, with DLC:
tewakahtárion I have on shoes,
tehohtárion he has on shoes,
teiakohtárion she has on shoes.

-ahta'- V become full: **wakáhta's** I get full,
onkwáhta'ne' I got full, **wakahtà:'on** I
am done eating.
• Onkwáhta'ne' ia'tewatié:rihse' tsi
ní:kon wà:keke'. I'm finished eating,
I had enough of what I ate.

-ahta'nawen- V be dressed warmly:
iohtà:nawen it is warm (what I have on),
wakahtà:nawen I am dressed warmly.
With SRF -at- and CAUS -hst-:

ratahta'nawénhstha' he dresses warmly,
wa'katahtà:nawenhste' I got dressed
warmly, **rotahta'nawénhston** he has
dressed warmly.
• Iohtà:nawen ne akwáhta. My shoes are
warm.

-ahtenti- V go away, leave, walk: **kahténtie's**
I go away, I walk, **enkahtén:ti'** I will go
away, **wa'kahtén:ti'** I went away, I
walked, **wakahténtion** I have gone away.
With TRNL: **ia'kahtén:ti'** I walked that
way, I took a couple of steps.
With REP: **sakahtén:ti'** I went away
again, I went home; and PURP -h-:
shahtentiónhe' he is going to go home,
sahahtentiónhe' he is on his way home.
With DLC and CISL: **tontakahtén:ti'**
I came back home.
With CAUS -ht-; and **kahnà:ta'**
(-hna't-/-hna'tahtsher- purse):
ionhtentiéhtha' kahnà:ta' suitcase.
With CAUS -'t-: **rahtentià:tha'** he starts
it, he runs it (the train or bus), (he is) an
engineer, **wa'kahténtia'te'** I started it,
rohtentià:ton he is running it.
With SRF -ate-, N -rihw- matter, message,
and CAUS -'t-: **wa'katerihwahténtia'te'**
I started, prepared to do something.
• Ionteienahninòn:tha' rohtentià:ton.
He runs a gas station. • Iah ki' thé:nen
tewà:tons nahò:ten' aionterihwahténtia'te'
ne kahéhtakon tsi niionà:nawen. You
couldn't get anything started in the garden
(with) how wet it is. (Letter 1945, June)
Cf. "They call the polar star, *Ia te
Ouattenties*, 'The One Which Does Not
Walk', because it has a movement imper-
ceptible to the eye and appears always
fixed at the same point." (Lafitau II: 137);
Attention partir (Bruyas: 34); *Atention*
partir (Galissonnière: 63v); Wendat
Atontarégue satandi Mene-la à Kebec

(Sagard: Me1); Onondaga *chattendia* tu pars (Shea: 77); Susquehannock *Hoona sattaande* now I am going away (Holm: 6)

-ahton- V disappear: **wáhtons** it disappears, **enwáhton'** it will disappear, **ónhton'** it disappeared, **iohtòn:'on** it has disappeared.
With PROG -hatie-: **ionahtonhátie'** they are disappearing.
With BEN -ni-/-'s-: **onkwáhton'se'** I lost it, misplaced it, **wahóhton'se'** he lost it, misplaced it, **wakahtón:ni** I have lost it, misplaced it.
With SRF -at- and N -hah- road: **onthaháhton'** the road disappeared.
With SRF -at- and N -hwist- metal, money: **onthwistáhton'** the money got lost; and BEN -'s-: **onkwathwistáhton'se'** I lost or misplaced the money.
With SRF -at- and N -ia't- body: **wahatia'táhton'** he got lost, **iakotia'tahtòn:'on** she is lost.
With N -nonhwar- brain: **rononhwarahtòn:'on** he is drunk; and CAUS -'t- and NEG: **iah teiakononhwarahtòn:tha'** it doesn't make one drunk.
With SRF -ate- and N -rahkw- sun: **onterahkwáhton'** eclipse.
With N -rihw- matter, message, and CAUS -'t-: **waharihwáhton'te'** he put an end to the matter.
With SRF -ate- and N -wenn- voice, word: **wahatewennáhton'** he lost his voice.
With N -'nikonhr- mind: **onke'nikonhráhton'** I fainted, **waho'nikonhráhton'** he fainted.
• Onkwáhton'se' akhnà:ta'. My purse disappeared, I misplaced my purse.
• Iah teionkwaterièn:tare' oh nontié:ren ionahtonhátie'. We don't really know why they (for example, butterflies) are disappearing.

-ahts- N hand
With V -hwe'nonni-/-kwe'nonni- fold: **wa'kahtsakwe'nón:ni'** I made a fist, **rohtsakwe'nón:ni** he is making a fist, **sahtsakwe'nón:ni** Make a fist!
With V -nohare-/-ohare- wash: **enhahtsóhare'** he will wash his hands, **wa'kahtsóhare'** I washed my hands, **iakohtsóhare** she has washed her hands.

-ahtsat[at]- V put out, extend the hand, with DLC, and CISL or TRNL: **tontaháhtsatate'** he put out his hand, **ia'tenkáhtsatate'** I will hold out my hand, **ia'tewakáhtsate'** I have put out my hand, my hand is held out.

-ahtsaton- V point, with TRNL: **iehahtsá:tons** he points to it, **ia'kahtsá:ton'** I pointed to it, **iahiiahtsá:ton'** I pointed to him, **ia'kheiahtsá:ton'** I pointed to her, **iewakahtsá:ton** I am pointing, I have pointed to it.

-ahtsa'n- N palm of the hand, handful: **ohtsà:na'**
POSS: **kahtsa'nà:ke** (on) my palm.
With LOC -okon, under: **kahtsa'nó:kon** underneath my hand, the underpart of my hand, **rahtsa'nó:kon** underneath his hand, **ionhtsa'nó:kon** underneath her hand.
With V -ia'[k]- hit, slap: **enkoniahtsa'náia'ke'** I will slap your hand, **wa'onkwahtsa'náia'ke'** she slapped my hand.
With V -ke- amount to, and DLC: **tewahtsà:nake** two handfuls; or PART: **áhsen niwahtsà:nake** three handfuls.
With V -ronhkwani-/-ronhkwen- itch: **wakahtsa'narónhkwani** the palm of my hand is itchy.
With V -[t]- be one, and REP: **sewahtsà:na** one handful.

Cf. Atsia extra comp. *Atsianna* in comp.
le dedans de la main. *Te ꝑatsiannage* 2
jointées (Bruyas: 42); *ꝑatsanna* poignee
(Galissonnière: 67r); *tsiotsiāna* Poigné
(Marcoux: 295); *Otsiana* poigné (Cuoq:
37)

-ahtsohkw- N morsel, portion
    With V -a'a- be small, **ken'** particle, and
    PART: **ken' niwahtsohkwà:'a** (it is) a
    small morsel, a small portion.
    With V -kowan[en]-/-owan[en]- be big:
    wahtsohkowá:nen (it is) a big morsel,
    a large portion.
    Cf. Otsiokꝑa portion, morceau de chair
    (Bruyas: 107); *otsiōkꝑa* Morceau (Mar-
    coux: 256); *Otsiokwa* morceau (Cuoq: 38)

aiá:wens hopefully, I hope so
    • Aiá:wens tho naiá:wen'. I hope it
    happens.

aió:ha' mink
    Cf. eyo mink (van den Bogaert: 53); *Aioha*
    vison (Cuoq: 1); *Aioah* [mink] (Onkwe-
    onwe: 3); *ah yo hah* mink (Jamieson 1: 5);
    Aió:ha Mink (Horne: 110); Wendat
    Hahyuha Renard noir (Sagard: An2)

Aionhwá'tha' Mohawk title name 2

-ak- eat. *See* -ek-/-ak-

=aka ATTR people of. *See* =haka/=aka

-akahron- V be wide, with DLC
    With SRF -at-: **tewatakà:ron** it is wide.
    With N -ahsi't- foot: **tekahsi'takà:ron**
    I have wide feet.
    With N -(h)nhoh- door:
    tekahnhohakà:ron (it is) a wide door.
    With N -nia't- throat, and CAUS -hst-:
    iakonia'takahrónhstha' cough drop,

mints (this word lacks the DLC prefix).
    With N -'khah- step: **teha'khahakà:ron**
    he has wide, long strides.

-akaion-/-kaion- V be old: **aká:ion** it is old.
    With DISTR -hshon-: **okaiónhshon** old
    things, antiques; **rotikaiónhshon** ances-
    tors, term used in Ohkiwe ceremony.
    With INCH -'-: **onká:ion'ne'** or
    wa'oká:ion'ne' it got old, **iokaiòn:'on**
    it has gotten old, it is old.
    With SRF -at-, variant -kaion-, and CAUS
    -hst-: **katkaiónhstha'** I waste it.
    With N -ahta[hkw]- shoe:
    ahtahkwaká:ion a large red fall rasp-
    berry.
    With SRF -at-, N -enhniser- day, and
    CAUS -hst-: **katenhniserakaiónhstha'**
    I waste the day (daydreaming, dilly-
    dallying), **wa'ontenhniseraká:ionhste'**
    she frittered away the time.
    With N -hstien['t]- bone, and INCH -'-:
    wakhstien'takaiòn:'on I have old bones,
    iakohstien'takaiòn:'on she has old
    bones.
    With N -ia't- body, V -ase- be fresh, new,
    NMZR -'tsher-, and INCH -'-:
    iakoia'tase'tsherakaiòn:'on unmarried
    woman, spinster.
    With SRF -at-, N -kar- cost, value, and
    CAUS -hst-: **enkatkaraká:ionhste'** I
    will neglect to pay my bill, what I owe,
    wahatkaraká:ionhste' he left unpaid
    what he owed.
    With N -na'tar[o][k]- bread, and INCH -'-:
    iona'tarakaiòn:'on (it is) stale, old bread.
    With V -nekenhteron- handsome man,
    NMZR -'tsher-, and INCH -'-:
    ronekenhteron'tsherakaiòn:'on
    bachelor.
    With N -nenh- seed, and INCH -'-:
    ionenhakaiòn:'on heirloom seed(s).
    With N -(h)nhr- sickness, disease, and

BEN -'s-: **wakehnhrakaiòn:se'** I have tuberculosis, **wahohnhraká:ion'se'** he got tuberculosis.
With N -nonhs- house, and INCH -'-: **wa'kanonhsaká:ion'ne'** the house got old, **iononhsakaiòn:'on** (it is) an old house.
With N -rihw- matter, message, and ATTR =hneha, way of: **orihwakaionhnéha** old-fashioned; with N -rihw- matter, message, V -nera'[k]- mistake, and NMZR -hser-: **iorihwanera'akhseraká:ion** original sin.
With N -wenn- voice, word: **owennaká:ion** or (with INCH -'-) **iowennakaiòn:'on** (it is) an old word.
With N -'sere[ht]- vehicle, car, and INCH -'-: **wa'ka'serehtaká:ion'ne'** the car got old, **io'serehtakaiòn:'on** (it is) an old car.
• Raon'éskwani ahatenhniseraká:ionhste'. He likes to take breaks, waste time.

aká:ratsi American elm, rock elm

Cf. akārătsi orme (Marcoux: 272); *Akaratsi* orme blanc (Cuoq: 61); *a-ga-ra-ti* Ulmus americana [American elm] (Rousseau: 40); *A ga rah tsi* Elm (Jamieson 2: 3); *Aká:ratsi* Elm (Horne: 112)

-akarenhr[e]- V lean to one side, slant: **wakarèn:re'** it is leaning, crooked, on a slant.
With INCH -'-: **onkarèn:re'ne'** it leaned; and REP: **ísi' nonkwá:ti sonkarèn:re'ne'** it leaned toward the other side.
With N -ahskwen'n- porch: **wahskwen'nakarèn:re'** the porch is leaning, crooked; and CAUS -t-: **wahskwen'nakarenhrá:ton** a shed or lean to-type structure attached to a building.
With N -ia't- body: **raia'takarèn:re'** he is crooked, lopsided, **ieia'takarèn:re'** she is crooked, lopsided.

With N -nonhs- house: **kanonhsakarèn:re'** the house is leaning.
With N -ronhkwe'n- spine, back: **karonhkwe'nakarèn:re'** the roof is slanted.
NOTE: The older sources also give the meaning 'afternoon, end of the day', suggesting that the sun is going the other direction.

Cf. Gagarenron pancher du'un costé, *Onne jogarenre* il est après midi (Bruyas: 45); *iokarēnre* après midi (Marcoux: 249); *Iokarenre* le déclin du jour, l'après-midi (Cuoq: 6)

akarè:t cake. A borrowing from French *galette*. A nominalized form occurs incorporated in *teiokare'tsheratsikhè:tare* cookies (-tsikhe't- sweet) (Lazore: 15). Note that today **teiona'taratsikhè:tare'** (-na'tar[o][k]- bread, -tsikhe't- sweet) is mostly used.

Cf. a ka ret cake (Anon: 7); *hakaret* [cake] (Ledger: 47); *a ka ret* cakes (D'Ailleboust: 23)

-akatste- V last long, endure: **wakátste'** it lasts long, it endures.
With NEG: **iah tewakátste'** it doesn't last long.
• Wakátste' ne iekhonnià:tha' karístatsi. The iron stove lasts a long time. • Iah tewakátste' otsì:tsa'. The flower doesn't last long.

Cf. Gagatste fort, dur (Bruyas: 46); *Gagatste* Dur (Galissonnière: 32v); *ȣakātste* durable (Marcoux: 132); *Wakatste* être ferme, solide, durable (Cuoq: 53); *wa kats te* durable (Anon: 34); *wa kats te* durable (Diabo: 21)

Á:ke! Gee!

-akehr-/-kehr- N dish, plate, bowl: **akè:ra'**
With **teionthnekontáhkhwa'** (-hnek-
liquid, -ont- attach):
teionthnekontáhkhwa' akè:ra' teacup.
With ATTR =shon'a, pluralizer:
akehra'shòn:'a different kinds of dishes.
POSS: **akkè:ra'** my dish, **raokè:ra'** his
dish, **akokè:ra'** her dish.
With V -[t]- be one, NMZR -'tsher-, and
REP: **skakehrà:tshera** one dish.

akéhton tumpline
NOTE: This word is probably related
to -keht[e]- carry on the back. Burden
straps or tumplines are described in
Orchard (1929).

Cf. Gage'ton collier à porter (Bruyas: 49);
Age'ton Collier a porter (Galissonnière:
21r); *akēhton* Collier de charge (Marcoux:
71); *Akehton* Collier de charge (Cuoq: 1);
ah geh donh tumpline (Jamieson 2: 6)

-akenhiat- V at the end or peak
With SRF -at- and N -kwir- tree, sapling:
tsi iotkwirakèn:iate' at the top of the
tree.
With N -nat- town, settlement:
kanatakèn:iate' on the edge of town.
With SRF -ate- and N -nont- mountain, hill:
tsi iotenontakèn:iate' at the top of the
mountain or hill.
• À:kweks ká:rate' tsi iotkwirakèn:iate'.
The eagle is standing at the top of the tree.

Cf. Gagenhiat extremité de quelque chose
(Bruyas: 47); *Agenhiat* haut le faiste
(Galissonnière: 48r); *–Akenhiate* le haut, le
faîte, le sommet (Cuoq: 62); *Wakenhiate* le
haut, le faîte, le bout (Cuoq: 54)

-akenhnh- N summer
With LOC -'ke, on, at: **akenhnhà:ke**
in the summer.

With V -ihen- be in the middle of, and
COIN and DLC: **sha'tewakenhnhí:hen**
middle of the summer.
With SRF -at-, variant -kenhnh-, and
V -o'kt- finish: **ontkenhnhò:kten'**
summer ended, summer is over.
With unclear V, and DLC:
teniokenhnhón:ti' it will become summer, **teiokenhnhóntion** it has become
summer.

Cf. Gagennha esté, *Gagennhagé* pendant
l'eté (Bruyas: 47); *Gagennhe* Esté (Galissonnière: 37v); *Agénha* Somer (Pyrlaeus:
183); *akennhake* été (Marcoux: 159);
Akennhake été, en été (Cuoq: 1);
Teiokennhonties l'eté s'ouvrir, c.-à-d.
être au printemps (Cuoq: 77); *Akennhake*
[summer] (Granger: 4); *a kenn ha ke*
summer (Anon: 6); *A-ken-há-ke* summer
(Cory: 73); *Ah gen hah ge neh* Summer
(Jamieson 1: 8)

-akera- V stink, smell: **wákeras** it stinks,
it smells.
With INCH -'-: **enwákera'ne'** it will
smell, **ónkera'ne'** it started to smell.
With N -ahsi't- foot, and DLC:
tehahsi'tákeras he has smelly feet.
With N -enser- smell, scent: **wenserákeras**
it smells bad.
With N -hakenht- soot: **kahakenhtákeras**
it smells of soot.
With N -hneht- pine: **kahnehtákeras**
turpentine.
With N -hont- green, and ATTR =kowa,
great: **kahontakeraskó:wa** goldenrod.
With N -ia't- body: **raia'tákeras**
he smells, **ieia'tákeras** she smells,
kaia'tákeras goat.
With N -ien'kwar- smoke:
raien'kwarákeras he smells of smoke,
kaien'kwarákeras it smells of smoke.

With N -ihwhar- fur: **tsihwharákeras** your fur smells (talking to a dog), **renhwharákeras** his fur smells.
With N -iie-/-ien- oil, grease (variant -enien-): **wenienákeras** it smells like oil or gasoline.
With N -karien't- carcass: **kakarien'tákeras** (it is) a smelly carcass.
With N -nehohs- urine: **ranehohsákeras** he smells pissy; and INCH -'-: **wahanehohsákera'ne'** he got to smell pissy.
With N -nehsio- cabbage, and CAUS -'t-: **kanehsio'tákeras** (it is) a smelly cabbage.
With N -ris[er]- socks, and INCH -'-: **wahariserákera'ne'** his socks got smelly.
With N -tsi'nonw- insect, bug: **katsi'nonwákeras** bedbug.
With N -tsi'ts- flower: **katsi'tsákeras** (it is) a smelly plant.
With N -wero'kw- jug, bulb, lamp chimney, carcass: **kawero'kwákeras** (it is) a smelly carcass.
With V -'khar- have on a slip, and DLC: **teie'kharákeras** her slip or skirt smells (talking about someone who doesn't wash).

Akí:! Ouch!

akonhonwà:tha' broom

akò:ren somebody else, another one
With ATTR =shon'a, pluralizer: **akohren'shòn:'a** other people, the others.

-aksen- V be bad
With N -atera'sw- luck: **rotera'swáksen** he has bad luck.
With V -atkon- be the devil, demon, and NMZR -'ser-: **otkon'seráksen thí:** The devil is with you! *An expression used when someone is misbehaving.*

With N -i't- excrement: **io'táksen** it is spoiled, it is bad; and INCH -'-: **io'táksen's** it is going bad, **enio'táksen'ne'** it will go bad, **wa'o'táksen'ne'** it went bad, **io'taksèn:'en** it has gone bad; and PROG -hatie-: **io'taksen'enhátie'** it is going bad; with INCH -'- and DLC: **teionkeni'táksen's** we two get mad at each other, **wa'tionkeni'táksen'ne'** we two got mad at each other, **teioti'taksèn:'en** they (females) have gotten mad at each other.
With N -kahr- eye, and REP: **skakahráksen** walleye, pickerel, yellow pike.
With N -onhnh- life: **konhnháksen** I don't feel good, I feel sick, **ronhnháksen** he doesn't feel good, **iakonhnháksen** she doesn't feel good; with N -onhnh- life, and INCH -'-: **wa'konhnháksen'ne'** I got sick; with N -onhnh- life, and CAUS -'t-: **onkonhnháksa'te'** it made me feel sick.
With N -rihw- matter, message: **karihwáksen** (it is) a bad matter.
With N -serenht- sleep, and INCH -'-: **roserenhtáksen's** he gets bad dreams, **onkeserenhtáksen'ne'** I had a bad dream, **wa'akoserenhtáksen'ne'** she had a bad dream.
With N -'khah- step: **ke'khaháksen** my walk or gait is wrong (I'm limping or off-balance).
With N -'nikonhr- mind: **ra'nikonhráksen** he is a negative person, **ie'nikonhráksen** she is negative; with N -'nikonhr- mind, and INCH -'-: **wake'nikonhráksen's** I feel bad, I am sad, **onke'nikonhráksen'** or **onke'nikonhráksen'ne'** I got sad; with N -'nikonhr- mind, and CAUS -'t-: **rake'nikonhraksà:tha'** he hurts my feelings, **wahi'nikonhráksa'te'** I hurt his feelings, **rake'nikonhraksà:ton** he has hurt my feelings.
With N -'shenn- aim: **ra'shennáksen** he has a bad aim.

Cf. sariwacksi a blasphemer (van den Bogaert: 60); *Satkon'seráksen* You bad devil *Only swear word in Mohawk* (Horne: 92); Susquehannock *Serωquacksi* you are bad (Holm: 8)

-akta' LOC near. For example: **kanonhsákta'** near the house; **Tiohtià:ke ákta'** near Montreal.
NOTE: This is both a suffix and a particle **ákta'**.

ákte' elsewhere

-aktontie' LOC along, edge of

akwáh or **kwah** very, quite, just, really

akwé:kon all, whole. For example: **akwé:kon ne Kanien'kehá:ka** all the Mohawks; **akwé:kon wa'kahióhare'** I washed all the fruit.
NOTE: For the related V, *see* -kwek- be the whole of.

à:kweks eagle
Cf. ākweks Aigle (Marcoux: 11); *Akweks* aigle (Cuoq: 2); *a kweks* eagle (Anon: 17); *á-kweks* eagle (Cory: 89, 101); *Á:kweks* Eagle (Horne: 113)

-akwenhten- V be flat
With SRF -at- and DLC: **tewatakwénhten** it is flat; and INCH -'-: **tenwatakwénhten'ne'** it will get flat, **wa'tewatakwénhten'ne'** it got flat.
With CAUS -hst-, variant -takwenhten-, and DLC: **wa'tektakwénhtenhste'** I flattened it.
With N -ahsi't- foot, and DLC: **tekahsi'takwénhten** I have flat feet.
With N -nenhst- corn:

tsikenenhstakwénhten a berry that looks almost like a cranberry, smells foul (like smelly feet) but is delicious when cooked, 'moose cherry' in GM, *djigιnǫstagwą́ʰdą* Tree cranberry (Waugh: 128).
With N -nen't- evergreen, and NMZR -'tsher-: **onen'takwenhtèn:tshera'** cedar.
With N -she'rh- dough, gravy, CAUS -hst- and DLC: **wa'tkeshe'rhakwénhtenhste'** I rolled out the dough.
• Wa'tewatakwénhten'ne' ne okahkwèn:ta'. The tire went flat.

amónia pneumonia
• Amónia iakoié:na. She got pneumonia.

-anihne'kara'wanion- V lightning, with DLC: **tewanihne'kara'wánions** it is lightning, **wa'tewanihne'kara'wánion'** it did lightning.

-anihtia[k]- V put around one's neck: **kaníhtiaks** I put it around my neck, **wa'kaníhtiake'** I put it around my neck, **wakaníhtien** I have it around my neck.
With CAUS -st-: **ionnihtiákstha'** necklace, yoke (of a shirt or dress).
• Ohstarò:kwa' wa'kaníhtiake'. I put pearls around my neck.

-anistiake- V urinate: **enkanistiá:ke'** I will urinate, **wahanistiá:ke'** he urinated, **wakanistiá:ke** I am urinating.

-anitsheho- V eat like a glutton: **ranítsheho** he likes to eat, he is a glutton, **ionnítsheho** she is a glutton, **wahanitshého'** he ate gluttonously; **anítsheho** glutton (talking about a dog who loves its treats).
Cf. Ennitsehwa pance, *Ennitseho* le ventre enflé (Bruyas: 110); *Wa ha nihts hehr hoh* overate (Jamieson 2: 9)

-anitshehwen't- N milkweed:
anitshehwèn:ta'
NOTE: Possibly related to
tsikenitshehwèn:ta' pollywog.
Cf. utshe'wa'nda Milkweed (Waugh: 117);
o-tse-wen-da Asclepias syriaca [milkweed]
(Rousseau: 59)

-ani'teni- V fart: **wahani'té:ni'** he farted,
roni'ténion he has farted.
With DISTR -onkw-: **rani'teniónkwas**
he is farting, **wahani'tenión:ko'** he farted
(repeatedly).

-ani'tia'khon- V be wrinkled, with DLC:
teioni'tià:khon it is all wrinkled.
NOTE: Possibly composed of SRF -an-,
-i't- exrement, -ia'k- cut, sever, and DISTR
-hon-. A stem -ani'tia'k- occurs also in the
word **tekonní'tia'ks** little black insects.

-anonhton- V think
With DISTR -nion-: **kanonhtónnions** I
think, **enkanonhtónnion'** or (with unclear
ending -hw-) **enkanonhtónnionhwe'** I
will think, **wahanonhtónnion'** or
wahanonhtónnionhwe' he thought about
it; and CONT -hak- or -hek-:
skén:nen sanonhtonniónhak or **skén:nen
sanonhtonniónhek** Have peace as you are
thinking (used for English 'Excuse me!').
With DISTR -nionkw-:
ranonhtonniónkwas he is thinking it
over, considering it,
wahanonhtonnión:ko' he was thinking it
over, he considered it.
With CISL: **thanónhtons** he gets his way,
he likes to control things, **tionnónhtons**
she gets her way, **entkanónhton'** I will
get my way, **tahanónhton'** he got his
way, **thonónhton** he has had his way;
and CONTR: **iah í:se' thaontahsanónhton'**
you won't get your way; with CISL and

BEN -'s-: **entehshakonónhton'se'** he will
force himself on her, **tahakwanónhton'se'**
he forced me to have sex against my will,
without my consent, **tahianónhton'se'** he
forced you to have sex,
aontaiontatenónhton'se' someone would
force her to have sex.
• Skén:nen sanonhtonniónhak tsi sahén:ton
wa'katóhetste'! Have peace thinking as I
passed in front of you! (Excuse me for
passing in front of you!) • Wahanonhtónnionhwe' tóka' tho ièn:re'. He's thinking
about whether to go there. • Ó:nen'k tsi
akwé:kon akáonha entionnóhton'. She has
to control everything.

anonhwaráweron or **anon'waráweron**
woodchuck

-anonhwet- V sleep over: **kanòn:wets** I sleep
over, **enkanòn:wete'** I will sleep over,
wahanòn:wete' he slept over,
wakanonhwé:ton I have slept over.
With TRNL: **ienhanòn:wete'** he will sleep
over there, **iahanòn:wete'** he slept over
there, **iewakanonhwé:ton** I have slept
over there.
With PURP -h-: **ranonhwéthe'** he is coming to sleep over, **wahanonhwéthe'** he is
going to sleep over there,
wa'kanonhwétha' I went to sleep over.
With CAUS -st-: **tsi ionnonhwétstha'**
bedroom.
• Ontiátshi tsi tiè:teron wa'kanonhwéthe'.
I am going to sleep over at my friend's
house. • Iah nòn:wa sahsothnéha thahsa-
nonhwéthe'. You won't go over to your
grandmother's to sleep over.

-anonhwetshaweron- V tumble over, get
upside down, with DLC:
wa'tkanonhwetsháweron' I tumbled
over, I got upside down,

wa'thanonhwetsháweron' he got upside down.
With TRNL: **ia'tkanonhwetsháweron'**
I tumbled over that way.
NOTE: This stem may be composed of a
variant of -anonhwet- sleep over, and
-aweron- spill out of.

anò:tien muskrat
Cf. Tiotennŝton v. *annŝgien* rat-musque
(Galissonnière: 7v); *annógien* muskrat
(Pyrlaeus: 201); *Anokien* rat musqué
(Cuoq: 2); *a no tien* muskrat (Anon: 16);
Anotien [muskrat] (Onkweonwe: 3);
a-nó-tien muskrat (Cory: 89); *ah no kyenh*
muskrat (Jamieson 1: 5); *Anò:tien* Muskrat
(Horne: 109)

-ano'serikhon- V clench teeth, grit teeth, with
DLC: **tekano'seríkhons** I am clenching,
gritting my teeth, **tehano'seríkhons** he is
clenching his teeth, **wa'tionno'seríkhon'**
she clenched her teeth.
With CONTR, TRNL, and DLC:
thia'tehono'seríkhon he is gritting his
teeth, he is grimacing.
Cf. tia te ho no se ri kon tsi ro ies hon grin,
literally, he is gritting his teeth or grimacing [as] he is laughing (-ieshon- laugh)
(Diabo: 35)

aonhà:'a most. For example: **aonhà:'a
tkowá:nen** the biggest.

-arahsar[on]- V brace with the foot, with DLC:
tekaráhsarons I brace it with my foot,
wa'tharáhsaren' he braced it.

-arahsentho- V kick: **karahsénthos** I kick it,
wa'karahséntho' I kicked it,
wahiiarahséntho' I kicked him,
wa'onkwarahséntho' she kicked me,
rorahsénthon he has kicked it or him.

-arahsoharen- V put on shoes without socks,
with DLC: **tekarahsohá:rens** I am putting
on shoes without socks (maybe when I'm
running out to start the car),
wa'tkarahsohá:ren' I put on shoes without socks.
Cf. Wendat *Arassiou* Souliers (Sagard:
Ha2)

-arahtat- V run, with DLC: **tekaráhtats** I run,
tenkaráhtate' I will run, **wa'tharáhtate'**
he ran, **tewakarahtá:ton** I have run,
tóhsa tesaráhtat Don't run!
Cf. Tŝara'taton courir (Bruyas: 25);
Tŝara'taton Courir (Galissonnière: 25v);
tekarātats courir, aller vite (Marcoux: 91);
Tekaratats courir (Cuoq: 44); Laurentian
Thodoathady Run (Biggar: 245); Wendat
Saratate cour (Sagard: Co5)

-arat- V lie down: **ká:rats** I am lying down,
wa'ón:rate' she lay down.
With TRNL: **ia'ká:rate'** I went to lie
down, **ia'ón:rate'** she went to lie down,
ieiakorá:ton she has gone to lie down.

arawén oats
With **othè:sera'** (-the'ser- flour):
arawén othè:sera' porridge.
NOTE: The final syllable of this word is
pronounced like English *when*. It is a borrowing from French *l'avoine*, as pointed
out by Cuoq.
Cf. raŝēnn Avoine (Marcoux: 28); *Rawenn*
corr. du fr.: l'avoine (Cuoq: 39); *harawen*
[oats], *arawen otesera* [porridge] (Ledger:
66); *Rawe'n* oats (Onkweonwe: 4);
a ra wen o te se ra oatmeal (D'Ailleboust:
23)

-ara'se- V be attractive, appealing: **iorà:se'**
it is appealing.
With CAUS -hst-: **rara'séhstha'** he is

proud (he has his nose in the air), he admires himself, he is a show-off, **ionra'séhstha'** she is proud, a show-off, **wahará:sehste'** he admired himself; and PROG -hatie-: **rora'sehstonhátie'** he is going along proud, showing off.

With CAUS -hst- and BEN -enni-/-en-: **shakora'sehstén:ni** he is flirting with her, **ronwara'sehstén:ni** she is flirting with him, **wahakwara'séhsten'** he flirted with me.

With N -ia't- body: **roia'tarà:se'** he is attractive, **iakoia'tarà:se'** she is attractive; and DLC: **tehotiia'tarà:se'** they are a very nice couple, they are compatible.

Cf. Shakora'sestén:ni He is flirting with her (Tewaterihwarenia'tha, Summer 1988: 24, listed under "Old Words")

-ara'se- KIN cousin, with ATTR ='a/=ha, diminutive: **ontiara'sè:'a** my cousin, **onkwara'sè:'a** our cousin, **ronara'sè:'a** his cousin, **ionara'sè:'a** her cousin.

aremahnéha a type of textile. Possibly from French *allemand* 'German', with ATTR =hneha, way of.

Cf. Aramanhneha (Granger: 36); *a re men* German (Anon: 19)

-areni- V spread around, disperse, with DLC: **tewarénie's** it goes all over, **wa'tewaré:ni'** it went all over, it fell apart.

With REP: **tentsitewaré:ni'** we will disperse, **tonsahonré:ni'** they dispersed.

With CAUS -'t-: **tekarenià:tha'** I spread it around, I deliver things, **wa'tkarénia'te'** I spread it around, **tewakarenià:ton** I have spread it around, **tesarénia't** Spread it around!

With SRF -at-, N -a'kenhr- ashes, dirt, and CAUS -'t-: **tekata'kenhrarenià:tha'** I

spread dirt.

With SRF -at-, N -hiatonhser- book, paper, and CAUS -'t-: **tehathiatonhserarenià:tha'** mailman.

With SRF -ate-, N -nenh- seed, and CAUS -'t-: **tekontenenharenià:tha'** they are spreading seeds, **wa'tkatenenharénia'te'** I spread the seeds.

With SRF -ate-, N -rihw- matter, message, and CAUS -'t-: **tewaterihwarenià:tha'** newspaper.

With SRF -ate-, N -'nehsaronhkw- sand, and CAUS -'t-: **wa'thonte'nehsaronhkwarénia'te'** they spread sand.

With SRF -ate-, N -'nehtar- gravel, and CAUS -'t-: **tekate'nehtararenià:tha'** I spread gravel.

• Iononhsakaiòn:'on wa'tewaré:ni'. The old house fell apart. • Tonsaiakwaré:ni' tsik nón: thionsaiákwe'. We dispersed, we went in all different directions.

• Otsi'tèn:'a tekontenenharenià:tha'. The birds are spreading the seeds.

-areren- V race, with DLC: **tekaré:rens** I race, **tenkaré:ren'** I will race, **wa'tharé:ren'** he raced, **tewakaré:ren** I have raced

With PURP -hser-: **wa'tkarerénhsere'** I am going to race.

With CAUS -hst- and INSTR -hkw-; and **áhta** (-ahta[hkw]- shoe): **teionrerenhstáhkhwa' áhta** running shoes.

-areser[on]- V overflow, with CISL: **tewaréserons** it boils over, flows over (for example, a cake as it is baking flows over over the sides of the pan), **entewaré:sere'** it will flow over, **tonré:sere'** it flowed over, **tioréseron** it has overflowed.

á:re' again, repeatedly

áre'kho not yet

> *Cf. Areko* pas encore (Bruyas: 26); *areχo* pas encore (Galissonnière: 34r); *ārĕko* pas encore (Marcoux: 146); *Arekho* pas encore (Cuoq: 2); *a-rē-kho* not yet (Cory: 45)

-are'sen- V get fat: **wakáre'sen** I am fat, **róre'sen** he is fat, **iakóre'sen** she is fat, **wa'ónre'sen'** she got fat, **rore'sèn:'en** he has gotten fat.
> With CAUS -hst-: **wahiiáre'senhste'** I fattened him up.
> With N -onhwents-/-onhonts- earth, world, and CAUS -hst-: **wa'konhontsáre'senhste'** I fertilized.

-ariha- KIN sisters-in-law between females: **ontiaríha** my sister-in-law, **onaríha** her sister-in-law, **tiári** Sister-in-law!
> With ATTR =okon, pluralizer: **onkwarihó:kon** my sisters-in-law

arohátien never mind

> • Arohátien iokennó:ron sha'té:ioht tsi tho wà:ke'. Never mind it's raining, I'm still going to go (i.e., I'm going to go even if it's raining.)

-aron'tat- V shoot: **karòn:tats** I shoot, **enkaròn:tate'** I will shoot, **waharòn:tate'** he shot it (*oskenón:ton* a deer, *ne káhonre'* the gun), **wahakwaròn:tate'** he shot at me, **wakaron'tá:ton** I have shot.
> With DISTR -hon-: **raron'táthons** he is shooting (several times)
>
> *Cf. Alle sarondade* shoot! (van den Bogaert: 20); *Arontaton* souffler, tirer le fusil et arroser d'eau medicinale (Bruyas: 26); *arontaton* Souffler (Galissonnière: 76v); *karōntats* Souffler avec la bouche ou un soufflet (Marcoux: 369); tirer du fusil (Marcoux: 183); *a ion ron ta te* shoot

(Diabo: 72); *yen ron dahts thah* blow-gun (Jamieson 2: 6); Wendat *Sarontat* Souffle le feu (Sagard: Fe6); Onondaga *warõntat* to blow (Zeisberger: 25); Susquehannock *Kahʒroonta* a gun (Holm: 6)

aró:sen red squirrel

> *Cf. Arosen* escureuil (Bruyas: 26); *Arosen* Escurieux (Galissonnière: 7v); *arōsen* ecureuil (Marcoux: 139); *Arosen* écureuil (Cuoq: 2); *a ro sen* squirrel (Anon: 16); *Arosen* [squirrel] (Onkweonwe: 3); *a-ró-sen* squirrel (Cory: 12); *a ro senh* squirrel (Jamieson 1: 5); *Aró:sen* Squirrel (Horne: 110); Wendat *Arousen* Escureux communs (Sagard: An2)

-ase- V be fresh, new: **á:se'** it is fresh.
> With ATTR =shon'a, pluralizer: **ase'shòn:'a** vegetables.
> With N -ia't- body: **ieià:tase'** elegant, attractive young woman; and NMZR -'tsher-, V -akaion-/-kaion- be old, and INCH -'-: **iakoia'tase'tsherakaiòn:'on** unmarried woman, spinster; with NMZR -'tsher- and V -nonhwe'- like: **raia'tase'tsheranòn:we's** he likes women (he is a playboy).
> With N -neraht- leaf, ATTR =kowa, great, and CISL: **tionerahtase'kó:wa** white pine.
> With N -rihw- matter, message: **orì:wase'** news, **Oh nahò:ten' orì:wase'?** What's new?
> With N -wir- offspring: **owí:rase'** a new baby.

ase'kén because

asé'tsi it is new
> With N -nonhs- house: **kanonhsasé'tsi** a new house.
> NOTE: **asé'tsi** can occur by itself as a word or with an incorporated noun.

• Asé'tsi ke'serehtahninòn:re'. I am going to buy a brand new car.

-ashar- N strap, leash: **ashá:ra'**
With V -ine- lead: **rasharí:ne'** he is leading it on a leash.
With V -ont- attach: **wa'kasharón:ten'** I put it on a leash.

Cf. Asara corde à lier, collier (Bruyas: 26); *Asara* le collier qui se met au front (Bruyas: 49); *8asārōnte* enchainé à la chaine (Marcoux: 145); *Ashara* anse, corde (Cuoq: 2, who points out that this word refers to anything that is attached to an object and functions to carry or drag it); Onondaga *gachaâ* collier a porter (Shea: 33)

-asharanie- V wash by hand, with DLC:
teionsharánies she is washing (something dainty, like underwear or a baby's dress), **wa'tkasharánie'** I washed it.

-ashew- V separate chaff, winnow: **rashé:was** he is separating the chaff, **wa'káshewe'** I separated the chaff, **roshé:wen** he has separated the chaff; **oshé:wa'** bud, chaff, shavings (from a tree, or root).

Cf. Ase8an Cribler (Galissonnière: 26v); *kasē8as* Cribler (Marcoux: 95); *ionshe8āta* Van (Marcoux: 409); *Kasewas* Cribler, *iosewasĕri* criblure, vannure (Cuoq: 12); *onentakwententshera osewa* [cedar shavings] (Beauvais: 16); *ohse'wáhseri* chaff, the outer husk of the grain (Gabriel: 21)

-askanek- V wish for, hope for: **kaská:neks** I wish for something, **enkaská:neke'** I will wish for it, **wa'kaská:neke'** I wished for it, **wakaskanékon** I have wished for it.
• Kaská:neks ó:ia' aonsonke'serehtaién:ta'ne'. I would really like to get another car.

-askawe't- N barefoot
With V -ot- stand, and DLC:
tehaskawè:tote' he is barefoot, **teionskawè:tote'** she is barefoot; and PROG -atie-: **tehaskawe'totátie'** he is going barefoot, **teionskawe'totátie'** she is going barefoot.
With SRF -at-, V -ot- stand, and DLC: **wa'thataskawe'tó:ten'** he got barefoot, **wa'tiontaskawe'tó:ten'** she got barefoot.

-askwa'ser- V trample, with DLC
With DISTR -onkw- and CAUS -ht-:
wa'thiiaskwa'serónkwahte' I trampled him, **wa'tehsheiaskwa'serónkwahte'** you trampled her, **teioskwa'seronkwáhton** it got trampled, crushed underfoot; and SRF -at-: **wa'tewataskwa'serónkwahte'** it nicked itself (for example, a horse galloping, its hooves nicking its legs).
With SRF -at- and DISTR -onnion-:
tewataskwa'serónnions it is running hard with the hooves clicking together, hitting against each other (talking about a horse), **wa'tewataskwa'serónnion'** it ran with hooves hitting against each other.

-astath[en]-/-ath[en]- V dry: **iostáthen** it is dry, **enwastáthen'** it will dry, **onstáthen'** it dried.
With INCH -'-: **iostathèn:'en** it has dried.
With N -ahi- fruit, berry: **iohiáthen** (it is) dried fruit.
With N -haranawen't- sap:
wa'kaharanawen'táthen' the sap dried up.
With N -hnenna't- potato:
iohnenna'táthen potato chips.
With N -ient- wood: **ioientáthen** (it is) dry wood.
With N -na'tar[o][k]- bread: **iona'taráthen** (it is) dry bread.

With N -nia't- throat: **wakenia'táthens** I am thirsty, **onkenia'táthen'** I got thirsty.
With N -nor- husk, braided corn: **enkanoráthen'** the husks will dry, **wa'kanoráthen'** the husks dried, **ionoráthen** the corn is dry.
With CAUS -'t-, *see* -statha't-/-atha't- dry.

-astoron- V walk fast: **kastó:rons** I walk fast, **enkastó:ron'** I will walk fast, **wahastó:ron'** he walked fast.
With PROG -tie-: **iakostoróntie'** she is walking fast as she is going.
Cf. sastorum hurry up (van den Bogaert: 57); *Astoron viste* (Bruyas: 30); *Gastoron dépêche, fais viste* (Bruyas: 101); *Astoron se haster* (Galissonnière: 48r); *8akastorōntie se dépecher en marchant* (Marcoux: 114); *Kastorons aller vite, se hâter en marchant* (Cuoq: 12)

-a[t]- V be inside: **í:wa** it is inside it.
(In contemporary Kanien'kéha as spoken at Kahnawà:ke, *t* is not pronounced when it is at the end of a word, which means that unless a suffix follows, forms of this verb end in *-a* instead of *-at*.)
With N -ahi- fruit, berry, and CISL: **tewà:ia** pie.
With N -hnek- liquid: **rohné:ka** he drank too much, he is drunk; and DISTR -rion-: **enkahnekatárion'** it will fill up with water.
With N -hsto'ser- small feathers, and CISL: **tkahstò:sera** it has feathers in it, a down-filled jacket, duvet, pillow.
With N -nen'- pit, pellet, and CISL: **tkanèn:'a** there is a pit in it.
With N -nor- husk, braided corn, and CISL: **tkanó:ra** corn husk mattress.
With N -tsir- spark, fire, embers: **rotsí:ra** he is quick-tempered, ready to get into it, **iakotsí:ra** she is quick-tempered.

With N -'nehtar- gravel: **iako'néhtara** she has kidney stones, gall stones.
With N -'wahr- meat, and CISL: **tka'wà:ra** meat pie(s).
With INCH -'-, *see* -ta'-/-eta'- put inside.
With REV -hkw-, *see* -tahkw- take out.
• Akhna'tahtsherá:kon í:wa teiohwista-hrì:'on. I have change in my pocket.

-ata- N twig, stick, fabric: **á:ta'** fabric, material.
With NMZR -htsher-, *see* -atahtsher- twig, yard (measure).
• Á:ta' wa'khninòn:re'. I am going to buy material.
Cf. Ata, Atatsera cheville, petit baton (Bruyas: 31) or possibly *Ata, Atasera petit escorce ou bois sec pour servir de flambeaux à la chasse des tourtes pendant la nuit* [little bark or dry wood to be used as torches when hunting doves/pigeons during the night] (Bruyas: 32); *Atak petit baston avec quoy on remüe les cendres* [little stick with which one stirs ashes] (Galissonnière: 12r); *ātak Baguette* (Marcoux: 33); *Atak baguette, petit canne, règle, mesure, aune, corde de bois à brûler* (Cuoq: 2); *a ta* yard (Anon: 21); *a ta* yards (D'Ailleboust: 28)

-atahkont- V get annoyed, fed up, with BEN -enni-/-hahs-: **onkwatahkónthahse'** I got annoyed, **wahotahkónthahse'** he got annoyed, **rotahkontén:ni** he gets annoyed.

-atahkwahswen- V dislike, hate: **koniatahkwáhswens** I dislike you, hate you, **kheiatahkwáhswens** I dislike her, **wahiiatahkwáhswen'** I disliked him.
NOTE: This stem probably includes -hsw[en]- dislike.

-atahonhsanera'[k]- V mishear, and DLC:
tekatahonhsanéra'ks I mishear things,
wa'tkatahonhsanéra'ke' I misheard it,
I didn't hear it right (I thought they said
something else), **tehotahonhsanéren'**
he has misheard it.
NOTE: This stem is composed of a root
-ahonhs-, having to do with hearing, and
-nera'[k]- mistake.

-atahonhsat- V listen: **wakatahónhsate'** I am
listening, **riiatahónhsate'** I am listening
to him, **rakwatahónhsate'** he is listening
to me.
With CAUS -t-: **katahónhsatats** I listen,
enkatahónhsatate' I will listen,
wahiiatahónhsatate' I listened to him,
satahónhsatat Listen!
With SRF -ate- and N -renn- song, music:
wakaterennatahónhsate' I am listening
to music; and CAUS -t-:
katerennatahónhsatats I listen to music.

-atahrate'kw- V turn away, dodge:
iontahratè:kwas she is turning her head
away (maybe someone is coming to kiss
her cheek and she turns away to avoid it),
wa'katahratè:ko' I turned my head
away, I dodged it, **rotahratè:kwen** he has
turned his head away.

-atahronti- V look away: **katahróntie's** I look
the other way, **wa'katahrón:ti'** I looked
the other way, **wa'kheiatahrón:ti'** I
looked away from her, I didn't look at her,
I didn't make eye contact, **rotahróntion**
he is looking the other way.

-atahsaw- V start, begin, with CISL:
tkatahsáhwhas I start, **entkatáhsawen'**
I will start, **tahatáhsawen'** he is starting,
he started, **tontáhsawen'** it started,
tewakatáhsawe' I have begun,
tiotáhsawe' at the beginning.

-atahtsher- N twig, yard (measure):
atáhtshera' yardstick.
With V -ke- amount to, and DLC:
tewatahtsherá:ke two yards, two metres;
or PART: **Tó: niwatahtsherá:ke?** How
many yards or metres?
With V -o'ten- be a kind of, and PART:
niwatahtsherò:ten the kind of twig it is;
and **onekwénhtara'** (-nekwenhtar- red):
onekwénhtara' niwatahtsherò:ten red
willow.
With V -[t]- be one, and REP:
sewatáhtshera one yard, one metre.
NOTE: This stem is composed of -ata- twig,
stick, fabric, and NMZR -htsher-.

Cf. seꝛatātsĕra corde, mesure de bois
(Marcoux: 86); *Sewatatserat* 1 aune, 1
verge, 1 corde de bois (Cuoq: 81);
o-ne-wen-ta-ra ni-wa-ta-tse-ro-ten Cornus
obliqua [(red) dogwood] (Rousseau: 54)
se wa dah tse rah yard (Jamieson 2: 11)

-atak- V be brightly-coloured, vivid: **iotá:kon**
it is brightly-coloured.
With SRF -at- and N -ahsohkw- colour:
iotahsohkwatá:kon it is brightly-
coloured.

-atatenr- V have leftovers, a surplus:
wa'otá:tenre' it got left over,
onkwatá:tenre' I was left with leftovers,
a surplus (for example, food, or splints
from making a basket), **wakatatén:ron**
I have leftovers, **iotatén:ron** it is left over.
With CISL: **tiotatén:ron** there is something left.
With TRNL and REP: **ientsotá:tenre'** it
will be left; and DLC: **ia'tonsaiotá:tenre'**
it got left over, **ia'tetsotatén:ron** it is left.
With SRF -ate- and N -khw- food:
wakatekhwatatén:ron I have food left
over, **iotekhwatatén:ron** there is food
left over.

• Áhsen ní:kon sewahió:wane' sá:ien'.
Tékeni tontaserá:ko, énska iotatén:ron.
You have three apples. Take away (or
remove) two, there is one left. • Ohà:ta'
khok ia'tetsotatén:ron. Just the (apple)
core is left over. • Saka'tariha'tánion' ne
wakatekhwatatén:ron. I heated up the
leftovers.

Cf. *waotatenre* [it's left to pay, i.e., it's
the amount still owed] (Ledger: 65);
wa-o-ta-ten-re leftover (Cory: 84, 97)

-atateri'wahst- V be sorry, regret, with BEN
-ni-/-en- and REP: **shatateri'wáhstani** he
is (always) sorry, **ensehsatateri'wáhsten'**
you will be sorry, you will regret it,
sakatateri'wáhsten' I was sorry, I
regretted it.

-atathar- V be a busybody: **ratáthare'** he is
a busybody, into everything, **iontáthare'**
she is a busybody; **atáthare'** busybody
(name of a dog).

-atati- V speak: **iontá:tis** she speaks,
enkatá:ti' I will speak, **wa'katá:ti'**
I spoke, **satá:ti** Speak! **atá:tis** whistle.
With CISL: **taiontá:ti'** she spoke up; and
NEG: **iah thé:nen tetiakotá:ti** she didn't
say anything, didn't answer with anything.
With TRNL: **ia'ontá:ti'** she spoke up, she
spoke for it (she treated someone to it).

Cf. "There are still, in Virginia, some
miserable remains of a people whom the
Iroquois call *atati-onoué*, that is to say,
'those who speak a common language
with them'." (Lafitau II: 262); "The
Ontationoué, that is those who speak the
language of men; so called by the Iroquois
because they understand each other" (M.
de Joncaire in O'Callaghan I: 24); *a ta tis*
whistle (Anon: 43); *a ta tis* whistle (Diabo:
86); Laurentian *Asigny quadadya* come

and speak to me (Biggar: 243); Wendat
Tesatakia Tu ne parles point (Sagard: Pa7)

-atatie' LOC along, edge of

-atawe- N flea: **otá:we**
With NMZR -hser- and V -r- put in:
wakatawéhserare' I have fleas on me,
rotawéhserare' he has fleas on him,
iakotawéhserare' she has fleas on her.

Cf. *Tásek* pulce (Galissonnière: 70r);
atāwek puce (Marcoux: 311); *da weh* flea
(Jamieson 3: 8); *Otá:we* Flea (Horne: 113)

-ataweia't- V enter
With CISL: **thataweià:tha'** he comes in,
enthatáweia'te' he will come in,
tahatáweia'te' he came in, **thotaweià:ton**
he has come in, **tasatáweia't** Come in!
tatsatáweia't You two come in!
tasewatáweia't You all come in! and
PROG -hatie-: **tahotaweia'tonhátie'** he is
coming in.
With TRNL: **iehataweià:tha'** he goes in,
iahatáweia'te' he went in,
iehotaweià:ton he has gone in,
ia'satáweia't Go in!
With INSTR -hkw- and TRNL:
tsi iontaweia'táhkhwa' inn, hotel.

-ata'tihon- V be stiff: **iota'tíhon** it is stiff.
With INSTR -hkw-: **enhsata'tíhonhkwe'**
you will stiffen it (like when you starch a
shirt), **wa'kata'tíhonhkwe'** I stiffened it.

-ateh[en]- V become embarrassed, ashamed:
katéhens I get embarrassed, ashamed,
iontéhens she gets embarrassed, ashamed,
wa'katéhen' I got embarrassed, ashamed,
wakatehèn:'en I am embarrassed,
ashamed; **iotéha** it is shameful.
With CAUS -'t-: **rakwatehà:tha'** he
embarrasses me, **wa'kheiatéha'te'** I

embarrassed her, **wa'onkwatéha'te'**
she embarrassed me.

With BEN -'s-: **riiatehà:se'** I am embarrassed for him, **wahakwatéha'se'** he was embarrassed for me.

With NMZR -hser-: **atehénhsera'** embarrassing situation; and V -ien- put down, have, and NEG: **iah teiakotehenhserá:ien'** she has no shame (she will do anything, like lie and not be bothered by it).

Cf. Ateheñon avoir honte, *Atenhensera* honte (Bruyas: 32); *Ateheñon* honte, avoir, *Atehensera* honte (Galissonnière: 49r); *katēhens* avoir honte, *atehēnsĕra* Honte (Marcoux: 202); *Katehens* avoir honte, *Atehensera* honte (Cuoq: 63, 107); *wa'katéhen'* I was embarrassed (Horne: 91)

-atehontsoni- want, need. *See* -atonhwentsoni-/-atonhontsoni-/ -atehontsoni-

-atek- V burn, on fire: **iotékha'** it is burning, **enió:teke'** it will burn, **wa'ó:teke'** it burned, **iotéken** it has burned, it is burnt. With CAUS -'t-: **katekà:tha'** I start a fire, **enkaté:ka'te'** I will start a fire, **wa'katé:ka'te'** I started a fire, **wakatekà:ton** I have started a fire; and INSTR -hkw-: **ionteka'táhkhwa'** matches, lighter, **tsi ionteka'táhkhwa'** fireplace, stove; and **ò:wahste'** (-'wahst- little stick, peg): **ionteka'táhkhwa' ò:wahste'** matchsticks.

With N -(h)rh- woods: **iohrhatékha'** (there is) a forest fire.

With N -'nionhr- inside of a chimney: **io'nionhratékha'** the inside of the chimney is in flames, **wa'o'niòn:rateke'** the inside of the chimney burned, **onke'niòn:rateke'** I had a fire in my chimney.

With N -'sere[ht]- vehicle, car: **io'serehtatékha'** the car is burning; and SRF -ate- and CAUS -'t-: **ronte'serehtatekà:tha'** they set fire to the cars.

See also -non'kwatek- house fire.

Cf. Isteχa il y a du feu (Bruyas: 32); *Ategen* Feu, j'en avoir (Galissonnière: 41r); *iōteks* Bruler neut. consumer (Marcoux: 48); *Iotekha* y avoir du feu, être en feu, brûler (Cuoq: 7); *ion te ka ta kwa* matches (Anon: 8); *io tek ha* fire (Diabo: 29); Wendat *Outeca* Y a-il du feu? (Sagard: Fe5); Onondaga *outéka* il y a du feu (Shea: 56);

-atekhwahra- N table: **atekhwà:ra**
With ATTR =ne, at: **atekhwaráhne** on the table.

With NMZR -'tsher-, and V -hnir- be hard, solid: **iotekhwahra'tsherahní:ron** (it is) a hard or solid table.

With NMZR -'tsher-, V -ihen- be in the middle of, and COIN and DLC: **sha'tewatekhwahra'tsherí:hen** (it is) in the middle of the table.

With NMZR -'tsher-, and V -kowan[en]-/ -owan[en]- be big: **watekhwahra'tsherowá:nen** (it is) a big table.

With NMZR -'tsher-, V -'rhoro[k]-/-oro[k]- cover, and CAUS -st-: **iontekhwahra'tsherorókstha'** tablecloth.

NOTE: This stem is composed of SRF -ate-, -khw- food, and -her-/-hr- set on top of.

atená:ti caribou

Cf. Atindati Caribou (Galissonnière: 7r); *atināti* Caribou (Marcoux: 56); *Atinati* renne, caribou (Cuoq: 3); *Atenati* [elk] (Onkeonwe: 3); *A-ti-na-ti* elk (Cory: 13); *Atená:ti* Elk (Horne: 109)

-atena'tar- N sunfish: **atenà:tara'**
With V -ien-/-ient- put down, have:
iotena'tará:ien' a snake that's coiled.
NOTE: The word for 'sunfish' evoked the
expression for a coiled snake even though
there would appear to be no semantic
connection between a kind of fish and a
snake.

Cf. atenà:tara sunfish, literal bread
(Gabriel: 54)

-atena'tkar- V spin, with BEN -ni-/-en-:
wa'otenà:tkaren' it is spinning (talking
about *okahkwèn:ta'* the wheels on a car),
onkwatenà:tkaren' my wheels or tires
spun, **wahotenà:tkaren'** his wheels or
tires spun, **rotena'tkará:ni** his wheels or
tires are spinning.
NOTE: This stem looks like it is composed
of SRF -ate- and a root -na'tkar- side of a
hill, slope.
• Wahanawa'tstotáhrhe'ne' kwah nek ne
rotena'tkará:ni. He got stuck in the mud
[and] his tires are just spinning.

atenénha' Mike Norton described this as a
black bug that sits on top of water and gets
inside of an animal as it drinks, and then it
tears up the animal's insides.

Cf. Atenenha Noyau (Galissonnière: 60r);
Atenénha Peach game (Tewaterihwarenia'tha, Summer 1988: 24); *atenénha*
peach stone game (Deering and Delisle:
287)

-atene'rhohar- V sting, with DLC:
wa'thakwatene'rhohá:ren' it (an insect)
stung me, **wa'thotene'rhohá:ren'** it stung
him.
NOTE: This stem is composed of the SRF
-ate-, a root -ne'rh- (not attested elsewhere), and -ohar- attach at the end.

• Ra'nionkwaristà:ke wa'thotene'rho-
há:ren' otsina'kontahkwà:ne'. The bee
stung him on the snout.

-atenhre'ons[k]- V be widowed:
wakatenhrè:'ons I am a widow(er),
rotenhrè:'ons he is a widower,
iakotenhrè:'ons she is a widow,
wahotenhrè:'onske' he became a
widower, **wa'akotenhrè:'onske'** she
became a widow.

Cf. hohreons Veuf (Galissonnière: 82r);
ꝸakaterēhons Veuf (Marcoux: 414);
Wakaterehons être, devenir veuf ou veuve
(Cuoq: 53); *ia ko te re ons* widow (Anon:
2)

-atenhrion- V warm oneself: **wa'katèn:ion'** or
wa'katèn:rion' I warmed myself (maybe
by the fire), **wahatèn:ion'** he warmed
himself, **wa'ontèn:ion'** she warmed herself.
NOTE: Most of the time the *r* in the stem is
not pronounced.

-ateniawak- V flail, paddle the arms, with
DLC: **tenhateniá:wake'** he will flail,
paddle his arms (maybe he fell in the water
and can't swim), **wa'thateniá:wake'** he
flailed, paddled his arms.

-ateniha't- V take turns, with DLC:
tehontenihà:tha' they are taking turns,
tentewateníha'te' we (you all and I) will
take turns, **wa'ttiateníha'te'** you and I
took turns, **wa'tiatiateníha'te'** we two
took turns, **wa'thiateníha'te'** the two
took turns, **wa'ttiateníha'te'** the two
(females) took turns, **teiontiatenihà:ton**
we two have taken turns.
• Tentewateníha'te' ienionkwá:ti'
athén:no. We will take turns throwing
the ball.

-atenna't- V take along a lunch or meal,
with TRNL: **iekatennà:tha'** I take along
a lunch, **ia'katén:na'te'** I took along a
lunch or meal.
With PROG -hatie-: **rotenna'tonhátie'**
he is bringing his meal.
With NMZR -hser-, *see* -atenna'tsher-
groceries.

-atenna'tsher- N groceries: **atennà:tshera'**
With ATTR =shon'a, pluralizer:
atenna'tshera'shòn:'a groceries.
With V -hninon- buy, and PURP -hr-:
wa'katenna'tsherahninòn:re' I am
going to buy groceries.
With V -noron- be expensive, precious:
watenna'tsheranó:ron they are expensive groceries.
*Cf. Strong & Strong Hiatenhninons
Tsi natennatsera sonha, Kahik sonha.
Onnhonsa sonha.* [S & S they sell all kinds
of groceries, fruits, eggs] (Granger: inside
front cover); *a ten na tse ra* provisions
(D'Ailleboust: 29)

-ateno'sen- V be family: **rontenò:sen** they
are family, **kontenò:sen** they (female)
are family.
NOTE: GM gave the additional forms
tewatenò:sen Sisters! Women! and with
ATTR ='a/=ha, diminutive: **ronteno'sénha**
brothers, brothers and sisters.
Cf. AtennꟅsen être frère et sœur (Bruyas:
33); *tegiatendꟅsenha* Sœur (Galissonnière:
62v); *ontennosēnha* frere et sour
(Marcoux: 180); *-atennosenha* Frère
à sœur, sœur à fr. (Cuoq 1866: 147);
en dya den noh senh hah My sister
(Jamieson 2: 4); *Te wah dah no senh*
Sisters (Jamieson 1: 2)

-atenro- KIN friends: **ontiatén:ro'** we two
(are) friends, my friend, **onkwatén:ro'**

my friends, **tsatén:ro'** your friend,
ronatén:ro' his friend, **tiatén:ro'** Friend!
With ATTR =shon'a, pluralizer:
onkwatenro'shòn:'a we are all friends,
ronatenro'shòn:'a all his friends.
With DLC: **tehiatén:ro'** the two match, go
together, **tetiatén:ro'** the two (females)
match, **tehontén:ro'** they match,
tekontén:ro' they (females) match.
With INCH - '-: **wa'ontiatén:ro'ne'** he
and I became friends, **wahonatén:ro'ne'**
they became friends; and DLC:
wa'thiatén:ro'ne' the two got along,
wa'thontén:ro'ne' they got along,
wa'tkontén:ro'ne' they (females) got
along; with CONTR and DLC:
iah tha'teiontiatenrò:'on it didn't agree
with me (for example, *nahò:ten' wà:keke'*
what I ate), **iah tha'tehonatenrò:'on** it
didn't agree with him.
With CAUS -hw- and CISL:
taiatiatén:rohwe' we worked together,
tahontén:rohwe' they worked together.
NOTE: GM translated this stem as 'friends
between males, unrelated husbands of
two sisters'.
Cf. Atenro estre camarade (Bruyas: 35);
Giatenro Camarade (Galissonnière: 15v);
ontenro, onkiatēnro Ami (Marcoux: 14);
Tkatenros se mettre avec qlq. en opposi-
tion à d'autres, se liguer (Cuoq: 50);
on ten ro friend (Anon: 38); *(on)-tia-tén-ro*
friend (Cory: 16); *ontiatén:ro'* my friend
(m) (Deering and Delisle: 40);
Ontiatén:ro' My man friend (man speaking) (Horne: 6); Wendat *Yathoro* mon
camarade (Sagard: Pa18); Susquehannock
Agændeero we are good friends (Holm:
5)

-aten'enhr- N fence: **aten'èn:ra'**
With LOC -kon, inside: **aten'èn:rakon**
in the yard.

With LOC -okon, underneath:
aten'enhró:kon under the fence.
With LOC -'ke, on, at: **aten'enhrà:ke**
on the fence.
With V -kahront- make an opening, a
hole: **ioten'enhrakà:ronte'** gate.
With V -kwek- be the whole of:
aten'enhrakwé:kon the whole yard.
With V -rihsi- take apart, take off:
wahaten'enhraríhsi' he took apart
(destroyed) the fence.
With V -te- be present, exist:
tsi ioten'èn:rate' at the end of the yard.
• O'khóhkwa' wa'katkáhtho' tsi ioten'èn:-
rate'. I saw a ghost at the end of the yard.
Cf. *Aten'ra* palissade (Bruyas: 33); *Atenra*
Palissade (Galissonnière: 61v); *atenhēnra*
Palissade (Marcoux: 278); *Atenhenra*
enclos, parc (Cuoq: 3); *a ten hen ra* fence
(Diabo: 28)

-aten'kehwha- V get jealous: **raten'kéhwhas**
he gets jealous, **enhaten'kéhwha'** he will
get jealous, **wahaten'kéhwha'** he got
jealous, **wahakwaten'kéhwha'** he got
jealous of me, **roten'kéhwhen** he is
jealous.

-aten'nahkara'w- V stick out one's tongue,
with DLC: **wa'tkaten'náhkara'we'** I
stuck out my tongue,
wa'tionten'náhkara'we' she stuck out
her tongue.
With DISTR -nion-:
tehaten'nahkara'wánions he keeps
sticking out his tongue,
wa'tkate'nahkara'wánion' I stuck my
tongue (in and) out.
With BEN -enni-/-en-:
tekheiaten'nahkara'wén:nis I stick out
my tongue at her,
wa'tekheiaten'nahkarà:wen' I stuck out
my tongue at her.

-aten'niot- V have a wedding, a feast:
wa'katen'nió:ten' I had a wedding,
watèn:niote' there's a wedding, a feast.
With PURP -'n-: **katen'niotà:ne'** I am
going to have a wedding,
wa'katen'niotà:ne' I am going to a
wedding, **wa'katen'niotà:na'** I went to
a wedding; and PAST -hne':
wakaten'niota'nónhne' I had gone, I
went to a wedding.

-aten'nits-/-aten'nitsher- N cane: **atèn:nits**
With V -hawi-/-enhawi- carry:
raten'nitsherenhá:wi' he is carrying a
cane.
With V -ohro[k]- insert:
roten'nitsherò:ron he has crutches
(under his arms), **iakoten'nitsherò:ron**
she has crutches (under her arms).
With V -ot- stand: **wakaten'nítsherote'**
I am using a cane, **wahaten'nitsheró:ten'**
he used a cane; and PROG -atie-:
roten'nitsherotátie' he is using a cane
going along.
NOTE: The incorporating variant is composed of a truncated form of -aten'nits-
and NMZR -tsher-.
Cf. *Atennise* baston sur lequel s'appuye
(Bruyas: 33); *Ennhise* Baston sur lequel
s'appuye (Galissonnière: 12r); *atēnnits*
Baton (Marcoux: 36); *Atennits* bâton,
canne, béquille, cross d'évêque (Cuoq: 3);
a ten nits cane (D'Ailleboust: 5)

ateráhki or **ateráhkwi** felt inside of a boot
(for example, a skidoo boot), any old rag
or cloth used to line the inside of a shoe
Cf. *a de rah dih* stocking (Jamieson 2: 10)

-ateratst- V do over, with CISL: **entkáteratste'**
I will do it over, **entitewáteratste'** we
will do it over, **takáteratste'** I did it over.

• Tó: nienká:ienhte' entehsáteratste'? How many times will you do it over? • Ó:nen tóhka nia'ká:ienhte' takáteratste'. I did it over a few times.

aterawénhta' snowsnake

-atera'sw- N luck: **aterà:swa'**
With V -iio- be good, nice: **watera'swí:io** it is good luck, **rotera'swí:io** he has good luck; and CAUS -hst-: **enwakatera'swí:iohste'** I will get lucky, **onkwatera'swí:iohste'** I got lucky.

-atere- KIN grandchild: **Átskwi kwátere'** Well, grandchild! So, child! (can be used by an older person to address any young person)
With ATTR ='a/=ha, diminutive: **riiaterè:'a** my grandson, **kheiaterè:'a** my granddaughter.
With ATTR =okon'a, pluralizer: **kheiatere'okòn:'a** my grandchildren.
With NMZR -'ser-: **aterè:sera'** grandchildren.
With NMZR -'ser-, V -hna'ne[t]-/-ne[t]- be lined, doubled, and DLC: **teiotere'será:ne** great-grandchild.
With NMZR -'ser- and V -ka'te- have many: **wakatere'serakà:te'** I have a lot of grandchildren.
With V -shen- have as kin: **wakaterè:shen** I have a grandchild; and DLC: **tékeni tewakaterè:shen** I have two grandchildren; or PART: **áhsen niwakaterè:shen** I have three grandchildren.

-ateriahtiht- V leave a situation: **kateriahtíhtha'** I leave (abruptly), **wa'kateriáhtihte'** I went away, removed myself from a situation (maybe I arrived at a meeting and just turned around and left), **wahateriáhtihte'** he went away, he left.

-ateriahtikhon- V express frustration or anger, mistreat, with DLC: **tehateriahtíkhons** he slams things around, throws things in frustration, he takes it out on something, **wa'thateriahtíkhon'** he slammed around, **wa'thiiateriahtíkhon'** I mistreated him, took it out on him.

-ateronhia'tahkw- V resist, be uncooperative: **rateronhia'táhkhwa'** he resists, **wa'kateronhià:tahkwe'** I resisted (I didn't want to do what I was told).
With BEN -enni-/-en-: **shakoteronhia'tahkwén:ni** he is resisting her, **wahakwateronhia'táhkwen'** he resisted me.

-ateronhienht- V become scared, frightened, with BEN -enni-/-en-: **wakateronhienhtén:ni** I am scared, **enwakateronhiénhten'** I will be scared, **onkwateronhiénhten'** I got scared, **tóhsa othé:nen sateronhiénhten** Don't be scared of anything!

-atero'ser- N friendship: **aterò:sera'**
With V -awi-/-on- give, and DLC: **tenkoniaterò:seron'** I will introduce you, **tenhonwanaterò:seron'** she will introduce them to each other, **wa'tekheiaterò:seron'** I introduced them to each other.
With V -ka'te- have many: **wakatero'serakà:te'** I have a lot of friends.
Cf. Atenrotsera Camaradise (Bruyas: 35); "The *Athenrosera*, or particular friendship between young people" (Lafitau I: 361); *a te ro se ra* friend (D'Ailleboust: 5)

-atesen-/-atosen- dozen
With NMZR -'tsher-, V -[t]- be one, and REP: **sewatesèn:tshera** one dozen.

With NMZR -'tsher -, V -ke- amount to, and DLC: **tewatesen'tsherá:ke** two dozen.

Cf. Sewatesenjera [one dozen] (Onkwe-onwe: 4); *ra to sen* dozen (D'Ailleboust: 28); *sewatosénthsera* a dozen eggs (Gabriel: 44)

-ateshwe'nont- V make a pouch: **wa'kateshwe'nón:ten'** I made a little pouch (out of the front of my apron or shirt, to carry things), **sateshwe'nón:ten** Make a little pouch!
NOTE: This stem may include a component related to Oneida -ashe'nut- 'basket' (Kahrhó:wane McComber, p.c., October 2022)

-atetsh[en]- V dream: **wakatétshens** I dream, **enwakatétshen'** I will dream, **onkwatétshen'** I dreamed, **iakotetshèn:'en** she is dreaming.
With CAUS -'t- and BEN -enni-/-en-: **rakwatetsha'tén:ni** I am dreaming of him, **wahakwatetshà:ten'** I dreamed of him, **wa'onkwatetshà:ten'** I had a dream about her.
With NMZR -hser-: **atetshénhsera'** dream.
With NMZR -hser- and V -kowan[en]-/ -owan[en]- be big: **wakatetshenhser-owá:nen** I have made a big issue of it, bigger than it really is.
• Iah tekè:iahre' nahò:ten' onkwatétshen'. I don't remember what I dreamed.

Cf. Ongꙅatetsen j'ai eu un mauvais songe (Bruyas: 35); *onkꙅatetsens* j'ay songe (Galissonnière: 76r); *katētsens* Rêver (Marcoux: 345); *Katetsens* rêver, avoir un songe (Cuoq: 13); *a ia ko tets hen* dream (Anon: 34); *a ia ko te tsen* dream (D'Aille-boust: 10); *a ia ko tets hen* dream (Diabo: 20)

-atetshen- V be greedy: **wakatétshen** I want everything, I am greedy, **rotétshen** he is greedy, **iakotétshen** she is greedy.

Cf. wakatētshen Friand (Marcoux: 181), intemperant (Marcoux: 214); *Wakatetsen* être gourmand, sensuel (Cuoq: 53)

-atewe- V gurgle, smile, look happy: **rótewe'** he is gurgling, smiling (talking about a baby), **iakótewe'** she is gurgling.

-ateweien'ton- V put away, conserve, save: **kateweièn:tons** I put it away, I conserve it, save it, **enkateweièn:ton'** I will put it away, put it aside, **wa'kateweièn:ton'** I put it away, put it aside, **roteweièn:ton** he has saved it.
With PROG -hatie-: **roteweien'tonhátie'** he is putting things away as he goes along.
With DISTR -nion-: **kateweien'tónnions** I put stuff away, **enkateweien'tónnion'** I will put it away, **wahateweien'tónnion'** he put things away.
With CISL: **thateweièn:tons** he does a good job, **taiatiateweièn:ton'** we two did a good job, **tewakateweièn:ton** I have done a good job, **tasateweièn:ton** Do a good job!

Cf. Ateꙅejenton garder, faire bien (Bruyas: 34); *Ateꙅeienton* Estre sur ses gardes (Galissonnière: 45r); *kateꙅeiēntons* garder, conserver (Marcoux: 166); *Kateweientons* fair bien, se donner de la peine, s'appli-quer, se bien conduire, garder, conserver qq. ch. (Cuoq: 14)

-atewennaientonhw- V scold: **wahshakotewennaién:tonhwe'** he scolded her or them, **wahiiatewennaién:tonhwe'** I scolded him.

NOTE: This stem includes the SRF -ate-
and -wenn- voice, word; the remainder
is unclear.

-atewennatkon- V talk back, have a sassy
mouth: **rotewennátkon** he talks back,
he has a sassy mouth, **iakotewennátkon**
she talks back, she has a sassy mouth.
NOTE: This stem includes the SRF -ate-
and -wenn- voice, word; the remainder
is unclear.

-atewenteht- V abandon: **wahiiatewén:tehte'**
I left him (my spouse), **shakotewentéhton**
he has abandoned them (for example, his
family).
With BEN -'s-: **enkoniatewentéhta'se'**
I will let you have some,
wa'onkwatewentéhta'se' she let me have
some.
• Énska enkoniatewentéhta'se' tiohnhónskwaron owí:ra'. I will let you have one
of the calves.

-atewe't- V give birth (usually an animal):
ontéwe'ton' it gave birth.

Cf. Atéʃeton Accoucher (Galissonnière:
3v); *katēʃĕtons* enfanter (Marcoux: 148)

-ate'kw- V run away: **ratè:kwas** he runs
away, **entiatè:ko'** you and I will run
away, **wa'katè:ko'** I ran away, **rotè:kwen**
he has run away, **satè:ko** Go away!
With PROG -hatie-: **wakate'kwenhátie'**
I am running away.
With BEN -ni-/-hs-: **shakote'kwá:ni** he is
running away from her,
wahakwatè:kwahse' he ran away from
me.
With SRF -ate- and N -rihw- matter, message: **wa'katerihwatè:ko'** I avoided the
matter.

-ate'nienten- V try, try on, measure:
kate'nién:tens I measure it, or (with a
different habitual ending) **kate'niéntha'**
I am trying, **enkate'nién:ten'** I will try
it on, I will measure it, **wa'kate'nién:ten'**
I tried it on, I measured it.
With NEG: **iah tewakate'nién:ten** I didn't
try it on.
With DISTR -nion-: **kate'nienténnions**
I am measuring things.
With CAUS -hst-: **kate'nienténhstha'**
I am measuring it, **enkate'nién:tenhste'**
I will measure it, **wa'kate'nién:tenhste'**
I measured it, **wate'nienténhston** it is
measured; and INSTR -hkw-:
ionte'nientenhstáhkhwa' ruler, tape
measure.
With CAUS -hst- and CISL:
thate'nienténhstha' he is tracing it, copying it, **entkate'nién:tenhste'** I will trace
it, copy it, **takate'nién:tenhste'** I traced
it, copied it, **tiakote'nienténhston** she has
traced it, copied it.
• Kate'niéntha' tho nátiere' nahò:ten'
wahseri'wanón:ton'. I am trying to do
what you asked. • Wa'kate'nién:ten' tóka'
ia'ttié:ri'ne'. I tried it on to see if I fit it.
• Kate'nienténnions tó: niwatahtsherá:ke
én:katste'. I am measuring how many
yards I will use.

-ate'serontie- V lightning strike, thunderclap:
wa'ote'serón:ti' a lightning bolt struck,
there was a thunderclap, **iote'seróntie'**
lightning is striking.

Cf. ʃateserōnties Tonnerre, le tonnerre tombe (Marcoux: 390);
te-se-ron-tion thunderclap (Cory: 75);
Wah o deh se ron dih A lightning
struck (Jamieson 2: 6)

-ate'skont- V roast, bake: **kate'skóntha'** I
roast it, **enkate'skón:ten'** I will roast it,
wa'kate'skón:ten' I roasted it,
wakatè:skonte' I have roasted it,
watè:skonte' a roast.
With N -ahi- fruit, berry:
wa'katahión:ten' I baked fruit.
With N -hnenna't- potato:
wa'kathnenna'tón:ten' I baked potatoes.
With N -na'tar[o][k]- bread:
wa'katena'tarón:ten' I baked bread,
watenà:taronte' bread baked in the oven.
With N -sahe't- bean: **watshahè:tonte'**
baked beans.
NOTE: This stem is composed of the SRF
-ate-, an incorporated noun -'sk-, and a
verb root -ont- (*see* -ontho- burn, put in
the fire); the root -'sk- is probably a variant of -'skonw- roasted meat.

Cf. Ont mettre au feu, *Gannataront* mettre
du pain au four, au feu (Bruyas: 122);
Gaskontoon rostir v. cuire (Galissonnière:
73v); *keskōntha* rotir, faire (Marcoux:
348); *Keskontha* griller, rôtir (Cuoq: 21)

-ate'wahshar- V put on earrings:
ate'wáhshare' earring.
With DLC: **wa'tionte'wahshá:ren'** she
put on earrings, **tewakate'wáhshare'** I
have on earrings.

Cf. Ateꝸasaron pendant d'oreilles (Bruyas:
33); *Tionteꝸasaronkꝸa* pendant d'oreille
(Galissonnière: 64v); *ateꝸāsăre* Boucle
d'oreille (Marcoux: 44); *Atewasare*
pendant d'oreilles (Cuoq: 3); *ah deh wah
sa ronh* ear-ring (Jamieson 2: 5)

-ate'waht- V miss a target, with REP:
skate'wáhtha' I miss it (what I aim for),
saháte'wahte' he missed it,
sahiiáte'wahte' I missed him,
shote'wáhton he has missed it.
With DISTR -nion-: **skate'wahtánions**
I miss them.
With SRF -ate- and N -rihw- matter,
message: **sakaterihwáte'wahte'** I did
something wrong.

-athahioni- V belong to the Wolf clan:
wakathahión:ni I am Wolf clan.

-athahsteren[k]- V put on pants, trousers
atháhsteren pants, trousers, **tekahsí:nes
atháhsteren** long pants (-hsin- leg, -es- be
long); **ken' na'tekahsinésha atháhsteren**
shorts (-hsin- leg, -esha- be short);
**iontia'tahseronnia'táhkhwa'
atháhsteren** dress pants (-ia't- body,
-hseronni- dress, prepare);
iakoio'ténhstha' atháhsteren work pants
(-io'te-/-io'ten- work); **oronhia'kó:wa
atháhsteren** jeans (-ronhi- sky, heaven),
and **iawentskwè:nonte'** (-entskwe'n-
chest, -ont- attach): **oronhia'kó:wa
atháhsteren iawentskwè:nonte'** overalls.
POSS: **akwatháhsteren** my pants.
With DLC: **tehotháhsteren** he has trousers
on, **wa'tkatháhsterenke'** I put pants on;
and REV -hsi-: **wa'thathahsterénhsi'** he
took off his pants.
With NMZR -'tsher- and V -i'tson-/-'tson-
be dirty: **tehothahsteren'tsherá'tson** his
pants are dirty.
With NMZR -'tsher- and V -kowan[en]-/
-owan[en]- be big: **wathahsteren'tsher-
owá:nen** (they are) big trousers.
With NMZR -'tsher- and V -noron- be
expensive, precious: **wathahsteren'-
tsheranó:ron** they are expensive pants.
NOTE: The beginning of this stem is the
SRF -at-. A form without the SRF is
wa'tekheháhsterenke' I put pants on her.

-atha't- dry. *See* -statha't-/-atha't-

-ath[en]- dry. *See* -astath[en]-/-ath[en]-

-athenno-/-athenno'tsher- N ball: **athén:no**
With **iehwa'ékstha'** (-hwa'e[k]-/-a'e[k]-
hit, strike): **athén:no iehwa'ékstha'** bat.
With LOC -'ke, on at: **athenno'tsherà:ke**
on the ball.
With V -ati-/-onti- lose, throw, and TRNL:
iahonkwathenno'tsherón:ti' I threw the
ball.
With V -a'sen's-/-en's- drop unintentionally: **onkwathennò:tsheren'se'** I dropped
the ball.
With V -es- be long: **wathennò:tsheres**
(it is) a long ball, a football.
With V -hkhwa- take away from:
wahiiathenno'tsheráhkhwa' I took the
ball away from him.
With V -ke- amount to, and DLC:
tewathenno'tsherá:ke two balls.
With V -kowan[en]-/-owan[en]- be big:
wathenno'tsherowá:nen (it is) a big ball.
With V -o'[k]- slap, flutter, flap, and DLC:
tekathénno'ks I play ball,
tenhonthénno'ke' they will play ball; and
CAUS -st-: **teionthenno'ókstha'** playing
field.
NOTE: The incorporating form has the
NMZR -'tsher-.

-athonro- V dive: **rathón:ros** he is diving,
wahathón:ro' he dove.
With TRNL: **iahathón:ro'** he dove that
way.
With PROG -hatie-: **rothonrohátie'** he is
diving.

-athont[e]- V hear: **wakathón:te'** I hear it.
With INCH -'-: **enwakathón:te'ne'** I will
hear it, **onkwathón:te'ne'** I heard it,
rothontè:'on he has heard it.
With CAUS -t-: **kathón:tats** I consent, I
agree, **enkathón:tate'** I will consent,
agree, **wahathón:tate'** he consented,
wakathontá:ton I have consented.

-athonwisen- V be a female, with CISL:
tewakathonwí:sen I am a female,
tiakothonwí:sen she is a female,
tionathonwí:sen they are females.

Cf. Tejontonꬸꙅas Danse des femmes ou
l'une chante et les autres respondent
(Galissonnière: 27v); *tsiakokonꙅꙇsen*
Femme (Marcoux: 171); *Sewathonwisen*
être du sexe féminin (Cuoq: 41);
tsia kot hon wi sen female (Anon: 2);
tsio-ton-wi-sen women, *tsio-na-ton-wi-sen*
(pl.) (Cory: 33); Onondaga *hotonhissen*
Madame (Shea: 68)

-athor[e]- V be cold: **iothó:re'** it is cold.
With ATTR =kowa, great, and REP:
Tsothohrhkó:wa January.
With ATTR ='a/=ha, diminutive, and
REP: **Tsothóhrha** December.
With ATTR ='ke, at:
othorè:ke (nonkwá:ti) north.
With CAUS -t-: **wathó:rats** it gets cold,
enwathó:rate' it will get cold,
onthó:rate' it got cold.
With NMZR -hser-: **athoráhsera'** rheu-
matism, arthritis.

Cf. Joθore il fait froid (Bruyas: 41); *jꙅθore*
il fait froid (Galissonnière: 43v); *Tsiꙅθore*
Decembre (Galissonnière: 53v); *iotōre*
Froit, il fait froid (Marcoux: 181);
tsiotorha dec. (Marcoux: 258); *Tsiotorkoꙅa*
janvier (Marcoux: 257); *Atho* le Dieu de
l'hiver, *Othoreke* le nord, au nord (Cuoq:
3, 37); *athorasera ononkwa* [rheumatism
medicine] (Beauvais: 27); *Tsiotorha*
December (Granger: 16); *Tsiotorkowa*
January (Granger: 5); *Tsiotorha* [January],
Tsiotorhkó:wa [December] (Calendar
1979); Laurentian *Athau* Cold (Biggar:
244); Wendat *Ottoret* Froid (Sagard: As2);
Onondaga *hôtôré* il fait froid (Shea: 58)

-athoriahseron's- V catch a cold:
wakathoriahseròn:se' I have a cold,
onkwathoriáhseron's' I caught a cold,
wahothoriáhseron's' he caught a cold.

-ati-/-onti- V lose, throw: **wakátie's** I lose it,
enwaká:ti' I will lose it, **onkwá:ti'** I lost
it, **wakátion** I have lost it.
With CISL: **tahó:ti'** he threw it this way.
With TRNL: **iewakátie's** I throw it away,
iahonkwá:ti' I threw it that way, **ia'sá:ti**
Throw it there, that way!
With TRNL and REP: **ionsaiakó:ti'** she
threw it back or over, she postponed it,
ionsonkwá:ti' I postponed it, I put it off,
ionsahoná:ti' they postponed it.
With N -ahta[hkw]- shoe:
onkwahtahkón:ti' I lost my shoe(s);
and TRNL: **iahonkwahtahkón:ti'** I threw
the shoe.
With N -athenno-/-athenno'tsher- ball,
and TRNL: **iahonkwathenno'tsherón:ti'**
I threw the ball.
With N -ent- day, and CAUS -ht-:
onkwentóntiehte' I fasted, I went without, **rawentontiéhton** he has fasted; and
PART: **Tsi niiakawentontiéhtha'** Lent.
With N -hneht- pine: **kahnehtóntion** it
is paved.
With N -hnek- liquid: **onkhnekón:ti'** I
threw water on it (maybe with the hose);
and DLC: **teiohnekóntie's** the water is
boiling; and CAUS -ht-: **tekhnekontiéhtha'**
I am boiling it, **wa'tekhnekóntiehte'** I
boiled it, **tekahnekontiéhton** it is boiled,
teshnekóntieht Boil it! and N -hnenna't-
potato: **wa'tekhnenna'tahnekóntiehte'**
I boiled potatoes; and N -sahe't- beans:
wa'teksahe'tahnekóntiehte' I boiled
beans.
With SRF -at- and N -honkar- invitation:
wakathonkaróntie's I extend an invitation (to an event), **enwakathonkarón:ti'**
I will extend an invitation,

wahothonkarón:ti' he extended an
invitation, **iakothonkaróntion** she has
extended an invitation.
With N -hstar- drop: **onkhstarón:ti'** I
sprinkled drops (maybe on clothes before
ironing them), **wa'ohstarón:ti'** it started
to rain lightly, **iohstaróntion** it is raining
lightly.
With N -ia't- body: **watia'tóntie's** I miss
it (the bus, train, airplane), **ontia'tón:ti'**
I missed it; with N -ia't- body, and TRNL
and DLC: **átste' ia'tshia'tón:ti** Let him
out, throw him out! (talking about a dog);
with SRF -at-, N -ia't- body, and CISL or
TRNL: **tionkwatia'tóntie's** she keeps
jumping me, attacking me,
iahiiatia'tón:ti' I jumped him.
With N -ien'kwar- smoke, and TRNL:
ieniakoien'kwarón:ti' she will drop
(blow) the smoke there.
With SRF -an- and N -itsker- spit, saliva:
ronitskeróntie's he is spitting,
onkwanitskerón:ti' I spit,
ronitskeróntion he has spit,
sanitskerón:ti Spit it out!
With N -nahkw- marriage: **ronahkóntie's**
he walks out on his spouse(s).
With N -na'kar- horn, antler, dice, and
TRNL: **iahonkena'karón:ti'** I threw the
dice.
With N -nenh- seed: **onkenenhón:ti'** I
dropped seeds (in the ground).
With N -nennawen['t]- tobacco pipe:
wahonennawen'tón:ti' he lost his pipe.
With N -nennio'kw- snowball, and TRNL:
iahonennio'kón:ti' he threw a snowball.
With N -nen'- pit, pellet: **enionen'ón:ti'**
it will snow ice pellets, **wa'onen'ón:ti'**
it snowed ice pellets, **ionen'óntion** it is
snowing ice pellets.
With N -nonhs- house: **wahotinonhsón:ti'**
they just left their houses (abandoning
them); and CAUS -ht-:
rotinonhsontiéhtha' they leave, close up

the houses, **wahotinonhsóntiehte'** they abandoned their houses.

With SRF -ate-, N -nont- mountain, hill, and DLC and CISL: **tetiotenontóntie's** a big wave comes back in (for example, after a tide has gone out), **tentiotenontón:ti'** a big wave will come back in, **tontaiotenontón:ti'** a big wave came back in.

With N -wenn- voice, word: **shakowennóntie's** he disobeys her, **wahiwennón:ti'** I disobeyed him, **wahakewennón:ti'** he disobeyed me.

With N -wis- ice, glass: **eniowisón:ti'** it will hail, **iowisóntion** it is hailing.

With N -'khah- step, and TRNL: **iewake'khahóntie's** I am taking steps, **iahonke'khahón:ti'** I took a step.

With N -'nehsaronhkw- sand: **wahoti'nehsaronhkón:ti'** they threw sand on it.

With N -'nehtar- gravel: **wahoti'nehtarón:ti'** they threw gravel on it, **ka'nehtaróntion** it is gravelled.

With SRF -ate-, N -'nikonhr- mind, and TRNL: **ia'kate'nikonhrón:ti'** I expressed myself.

• Onkwá:ti' teiehtharáhkhwa'. I lost my phone. • Tsiahià:khsera niió:re' ionsonkwá:ti'. I put it off for a week.

-atianeron- V get scared, haunted

With INCH -'-: **wakatiáneron's** I get scared, I feel spooky, **enwakatiáneron'ne'** I will get scared, **onkwatiáneron'ne'** I got spooked.

With CAUS -hst-: **iakotianerónhstha'** (it is) a scary thing or place, it is haunted, a ghost.

Cf. Atianneron avoir des visions, estre effrayé (Bruyas: 36); *ᴤakatiānĕrons* fair peur par quelque vision (Marcoux: 313);

Wakatianerons voir un fantôme, un spectre, avoir une vision (Cuoq: 53)

-atiaren't- N orange colour: **atiarèn:ta'** With ATTR ='a/=ha, diminutive: **atiaren'tà:'a** canary. With ATTR =kowa, great: **atiaren'ta'kó:wa** oriole.

Cf. otiarenta fleur de citrouille (Bruyas: 36); *otiarēnta* fleur de Citrouille (Marcoux: 69); *Otiarenta* fleur de citrouille (Cuoq: 37)

-atia'k- N some: **ótia'ke'** some, **ronátia'ke'** the rest of them, **onátia'ke'** the rest of them (females). With DISTR -shon: **ronatia'kè:shon** all the rest of them, the different people.

-atia'karetst- V stretch to reach, reach over, with TRNL and DLC: **ia'tekatia'karétstha'** I reach over, I stretch over to reach something, **ia'thatià:karetste'** he reached over, **ia'tewakatia'karétston** I am reaching over for it.

-atia'karonti- V gallop: **watia'karóntie's** it is galloping, **ontia'karón:ti'** it started galloping, **wahatia'karón:ti'** he galloped. With PROG -hatie-: **iotia'karontionhátie'** it is going along galloping.

-atia'takwenhtahrho- V lie down on top of, with TRNL: **ia'katia'takwenhtáhrho'** I lay down on top of it, **iahatia'takwenhtáhrho'** he lay down on top of it, **ia'ontia'takwenhtáhrho'** she lay down on top of it.

-atia'tawi- N dress, shirt, jacket, coat: **atià:tawi** With **io'nhehsen'tónnion** (-'nhehs- silk,

satin, -hren't-/-en't- hang down):
io'nhehsen'tónnion atià:tawi ribbon shirt.
POSS: **akwatià:tawi** my dress, coat, shirt, **raotià:tawi** his shirt.
With CAUS -'t-: **wa'katià:tawi'te'** I put on a dress, shirt; with CAUS -'t- and DISTR -nion-: **ionkwaia'tawi'tánion** we have on coats, etc.; with CAUS -'t- and REV -hsi-: **wa'katia'tawi'táhsi'** I took off my dress, shirt.
With NMZR -'tsher-, and V -ahstoht- reduce, shrink, take in: **wa'katia'tawi'tsheráhstohte'** I took in the dress, etc.
With NMZR -'tsher-, V -i'tson-/-'tson- be dirty, and DLC: **tewakatia'tawi'tsherá'tson** my dress or shirt is dirty.
With NMZR -'tsher-, and V -na'nawen-/ -nawen- be wet: **iakotia'tawi'tsheraná:wen** her dress, shirt is wet; and CAUS -hst-: **onkwatia'tawi'tsheraná:wenhste'** my dress, shirt got wet.
With NMZR -'tsher-, and V -onni- make: **enkatia'tawi'tsherón:ni'** I will make a dress, a shirt; and BEN -enni-/-en-: **riiatia'tawi'tsheronnién:ni** I am making a shirt for him, **wahiiatia'tawi'tsherónnien'** I made a shirt for him.
NOTE: This stem is composed of SRF -at-, -ia't- body, and -awi- wrap around, encircle. A form without the SRF is **wa'kheià:tawi'te'** I put a dress on her.
• Kwah iah thé:nen ne coat teionkwatia't-awi'tánion. We didn't wear any coats. (Letter 1945, June)

atiehwà:ta' butternut (tree)
Cf. a tie wa ta walnut (Anon: 18); *tie-wa-ta* Juglans cinerea [butternut or white walnut] (Rousseau: 39); *Ate'wáhta'* Butternut (Horne: 112)

-atierenht- V be first, with CISL: **tiotierénhton** first, **í: takatié:renhte'** I went first.
• Takatié:renhte' ia'katiá:nenhte'. I went first sledding (down the hill).

-atierenk- V be surprised by, suddenly take notice, with CONTR: **tha'katié:renk** I was suddenly surprised.
• Tha'katié:renk tho wahokè:tohte'. I was surprised that he appeared.

-atieskwani- V ridicule, with CONTR: **thikatiéskwani** I ridicule (someone), **thenkatiéskwani'** I will ridicule, **thiwakatiéskwani** I have ridiculed.
NOTE: Mike Norton said this is an old word.

-atie'ni- V be plenty, hold a lot, accumulate: **iotiè:ni** there is plenty of it, it is accumu-lated, there's enough, it holds a lot.
With CAUS -ht-: **ontiè:nihte'** there got to be enough, it got full, **wa'katiè:nihte'** I got plenty of it, I filled it (e.g., a basket), **rotie'níhton** he has filled it.
With SRF -ate- and N -rihw- matter, message: **wakaterihwatiè:ni** I talk a lot, I'm a blabbermouth, **roterihwatiè:ni** he talks a lot, **iakoterihwatiè:ni** she talks a lot.
Cf. Sok ki' ní:'i enkatkátston tó:'k nikaná:tsa né:ne iotié:ni ... So then I know to make a large pot of soup ... [So then *I* will make soup, a pot that holds a lot] (Old Kahnawake: 8)

-atihentho- V pull, with CISL: **tkatihénthos** I pull it, **entkatihéntho'** I will pull it, **takatihéntho'** I pulled it, **tewakatihénthon** I have pulled it.
With N -atonriser- breath: **takatonriseratihéntho'** I inhaled.

With N -hnek- liquid: **tkahnekatihénthos** waves go out, **entkahnekatihéntho'** the water will go out (as in the tide).
With N -hnenhs- shoulder: **tahihnenhsatihéntho'** I pulled at, touched his shoulder.
With N -rihw- matter, message: **tkerihwatihénthos** I pull or draw out the matter, **taharihwatihéntho'** he pulled or drew out the matter.
• Takatihéntho' akoratskèn:ta'. I pulled, tugged her braid.

-atihentonhw- V lightly shake someone: **wahiiatihén:tonhwe'** I lightly shook him, **wa'onkwatihén:tonhwe'** she lightly shook me.

-atioha KIN brothers-in-law between males: **ontiatióha** my brother-in-law, **ronatióha** his brother-in-law, **tiátio** Brother-in-law!

atí:ron raccoon

Cf. adiron cats (van den Bogaert: 53); *Atiron* Chat-Sauvage (Galissonnière: 7r); *atiron* chat-sauvage (Cuoq: 156); *Atiron* [raccoon] (Onkweonwe: 3); *a di ronh* raccoon (Jamieson 1: 5); *Atí:ron* Raccoon (Horne: 110); Wendat *Tiron* Chat sauuage (Sagard: An3)

-atiront- V pull, stretch
With CISL: **thatiróntha'** he pulls it, **enthatirón:ten'** he will pull it, **tahatirón:ten'** he pulled it, **thotí:ronte'** he is pulling it; and PROG -atie-: **tonkwatirontátie'** I am pulling it.
With DLC: **tekatiróntha'** I stretch it, **tenkatirón:ten'** I will stretch it, **tewakatí:ronte'** I have stretched it.
With N -ahseriie['t]- string, rope, thread, and CISL: **tionhseriie'tatiróntha'** she is pulling string; with N -ahseriie['t]- string,

rope thread, and DLC: **tehonhseriie'tatiróntha'** they play tug-of-war, **tehonahseriie'tatí:ronte'** they are playing tug-of-war.
With N -ihn- skin, rubber, and DLC: **teiohnatiróntha'** it is elastic, an elastic band; and **áhta** (-ahta[hkw]- shoe): **teiohnatiróntha' áhta** rubber boots.
With N -nentsh- arm: **kanentshatiróntha'** notched stick, invitation wampum; and INSTR -hkw- and CISL: **tiakonentshatirontáhkhwa'** they present wampum as an invitation.
With N -'nerohkw- box, and DLC: **teie'nerohkwatiróntha'** accordion.
With N -'nikonhr- mind, and CISL: **tho'nikonhratí:ronte'** he is attracted to it.
• Akohsá:tens tahotirontátie' ienekera-ráhkhwa'. The horse is pulling the hay wagon.

-atiw- V be skinny: **wakatí:wen** I am skinny, **rotí:wen** he is skinny, **iakotí:wen** she is skinny, **enká:tiwe'** I will be skinny.
With REFL -atat- and CAUS -ht-: **katatiwáhtha'** I am dieting, **enkatatí:wahte'** I will put myself on a diet, **wa'ontatí:wahte'** she put herself on a diet.
With SRF -ate- and N -nakar- stick: **iotenakaratí:wen** blue beech, American hornbeam.

-atkahkwarihsi- V open one's eyes, with DLC: **tekatkahkwaríhsions** I open my eyes, **wa'tiontkahkwaríhsi'** she opened her eyes, **tewakatkahkwaríhsion** I have opened my eyes, my eyes are open.

-atkahrhar- V snare: **enhatkahrhá:ren'** he will snare it (a rabbit), **wahatkahrhá:ren'** he snared it.

With PURP -'n-: **enhatkahrharà:na'** he will go snaring.

-atkahri- V play
With CAUS -'t-: **katkahrì:tha'** I play with it, **enkatkà:ri'te'** I will play with it, **wahatkà:ri'te'** he played with it, **wakatkahrì:ton** I am playing with it; and INSTR -hkw-: **iontkahri'táhkhwa'** toy. With NMZR -'tsher- and V -onni- make: **wakatkahri'tsherón:ni** I am playing, **rotkahri'tsherón:ni** he is playing.

-atkahtho- V look at: **katkáhthos** I look at it, **enkatkáhtho'** I will look at it, **wa'katkáhtho'** I looked at it, **wahiiatkáhtho'** I looked at him, **rotkáhthon** he has looked at it. With TRNL: **iahiiatkáhtho'** I looked his way. With CISL: **tahakwatkáhtho'** he looked my way; **tiakotkáhthon ken** Imagine that, can you believe it?! With DISTR -onnion-: **tekatkahthónnions** I am looking around, and CONT -hek-, and CONTR, DLC, and REP: **tha'tensehsatkahthonniónheke'** you will just keep looking from side to side.
Cf. *thadenseghsatkaghthonnyonhheke* you may look about you (Hale: 120); Laurentian *Quatgathoma* Look at me (Biggar: 243)

-atkanonni- V be tiny: **rotkanón:ni** he is tiny, **iakotkanón:ni** she is tiny.

-atkarohkw- N rag: **otkaróhkwa'**
With V -ien- put down, have, and TRNL: **ia'satkaróhkwaien** An older, playful expression, like 'you silly goose!'

-atkatston- V make soup: **katkátstons** I make soup, **enkatkátston'** I will make soup,

wahatkátston' he made soup, **rotkátston** he is making soup.

-atka'w- V let go: **katkà:was** I let it go, **wa'kátka'we'** I let it go, **wa'kheiátka'we'** I let her or them go, **riiatkà:wen** I have let him go. With TRNL: **ia'kheiátka'we'** I let her or them go that way or over there. With CISL: **tahátka'we'** I provided it, turned it over.
• *nene akononsa tsi shakoniakwe tsi kakariakon ii takatkawe.* [it's her house that he or someone was lending her [renting from her], it [rent] is paid, which *I* provided] (Receipt in D'Ailleboust's notebook)

-atken- V rot, spoil: **iótkens** it is rotten, **eniótken'** it will rot, **wa'ótken'** it rotted, **iotkèn:'en** it has rotted. With N -hnenna't- potato: **iohnenna'tátkens** the potatoes are rotten, **wa'ohnenna'tátken'** the potatoes rotted. With N -non't- milk: **ionon'tátkens** the milk is rotten, curdled, **enionon'tátken'** the milk will rot, **ionon'tatkèn:'en** the milk has become rotten. With N -wero'kw- jug: **iowero'kwátkens** it is bloated (ready to burst), decaying (for example, an animal in the bush or a drowned person), **wa'owero'kwátken'** it rotted, **iowero'kwatkèn:'en** it has rotted; and PROG -hatie-: **iowero'kwatken'enhátie'** it is rotting. With N -'nhonhs- egg: **io'nhonhsátkens** the eggs are rotten.

-atkennisa'- V meet, assemble: **katkennísa's** I have meetings, **wahontkennísa'** they met, they had a meeting, **ionkwatkenníson'** we are meeting, **watkenníson'** meeting.

With PAST -'ne': **ronatkennison'òn:ne'** they had met.

With PURP -'nh-: **rontkennisa'à:nhe'** they are going to have a meeting, **wa'katkennisa'à:nhe'** I am going, I am on my way to a meeting, **katkennisa'à:nhe's** I go to meetings, **enkatkennisa'à:nha'** I will go to a meeting, **wa'katkennisa'à:nha'** I went to a meeting; and PAST -hne': **rotkennisa'ahnhónhne'** he went, he had gone to a meeting.

NOTE: The short accented vowel in the first four words suggests that this stem goes back to an earlier form *-atkennis'a-.

-atken'serahkw- V put off:
wa'katkèn:serahkwe' I put it off, I will deal with it later.

With SRF -ate- and N -rihw- matter, message: **raterihwatken'seráhkhwa'** he makes excuses, **wa'katerihwatkèn:serahkwe'** I made an excuse, **roterihwatken'seráhkwen** he is making excuses.

• Wa'katerihwatkèn:serahkwe' iah tho thá:ke'. I made an excuse, I'm not going.

-atken'tsohkaw- V become confirmed (religious): **wahatken'tsóhkawe'** he was confirmed (into the religion).

-atkon- V be the devil, demon: **ótkon**
With **ia'saia'ténha** (-ia't- body, -ha[w]-/ -enha[w]- bring, take):
Ótkon ia'saia'ténha! May the devil take you! Go to the devil!

With CAUS -hst-: **iontkónhstha'** she practices, dabbles in witchcraft, she makes spells, **enkátkonhste'** I will make a spell, **iakotkónhston** she is dabbling in witchcraft.

With NMZR -'ser- and V -aksen- be bad: **otkon'seráksen thí:** The devil is with you!

An expression used when someone is misbehaving.

With NMZR -'ser- and V -attokha- be stingy: **rotkon'serattókha'** he is really stingy, cheap.

With NMZR -'ser- and V -henreht- yell, holler, and DLC: **tehotkon'serahenréhtha'** he is making a heck of a noise, yelling.

With SRF -at- and N -ia't- body: **rotia'tátkon** he is a mystic, he has power.

With NMZR -'ser- and V -ien-/-ient- put down, have, and TRNL: **ia'satkon'será:ien** Go to the devil!

Cf. "They have also naturally a very high opinion of themselves; they say *Ihy Ithkon*, ('I am the Devil') by which they mean that they are superior folks. In order to praise themselves and their people, whenever we tell them that they are very expert at catching deer, or doing this and that, they say, *Tkoschs ko, aguweechon Kajingahaga kouaane Jountuckcha Othkon*; that is 'Really all the Mohawks are very cunning devils'." [GM: word-by-word, but deemed not good Kanien'kéha: tó:ske' akwé:kon Kanien'kehá:ka kowá:nen ionttókha' ótkon] (Megapolensis: 176); *Atkon* demon. Il se dit aussi d'un homme hardy, &tc. à qui rien n'est difficile (Bruyas: 36); "*Otkon*, Okki, Manitou, that is to say the Spirit" (Lafitau I: 236); *hotkon* Demon (Galissonnière: 29r); *8akātkon* Sorcier (Marcoux: 368); *Otkon* génie, esprit, être mystérieux et puissant (Cuoq: 37); *ro tia tat kon* magic (Diabo: 46); *N'ot-kon* Devil (Cory: 19); *rótkon* a seer, he has spiritual power (Deering and Delisle: 289); Iroquois "The Iroquois ... called us '*Otkon*', that is in their language, 'most penetrating wits'." (Hennepin in Ketchum I: 61); Wendat *Oki* diable (Sagard: Yo2); Onondaga *ótcon* Ghost (Zeisberger: 83)

-atkonhen- V put one's head down on something: **iontkón:hens** she puts her head
down, **enkatkón:hen'** I will put my head
down, **wa'katkón:hen'** I put my head
down, **iakotkón:hen** she has put her head
down.
With TRNL: **ia'katkón:hen'** I put my head
down there.

-atkon'ser- V use as a pillow or cushion:
wahatkòn:seren' he used a pillow;
atkòn:sera' pillow.
With NMZR -htsher- and LOC -'ke, on, at:
atkon'serahtsherà:ke on the pillow.
With NMZR -htsher-, V -'rhoro[k]-/-oro[k]-
cover, and CAUS -st-: **iontkon'serahtsherorókstha'** pillow case.

ató:ken' axe
POSS: **akwató:ken'** my axe.

Cf. atoga axes (van den Bogaert: 52);
Atogen hache (Galissonnière: 47v); *Atoken*
hache, cognée (Cuoq: 3); *a to ken* axe
(Anon: 12); *ah do genh* axe (Jamieson
2: 5); Laurentian *Addogué* A hatchet
(Biggar: 243); Wendat *Atouhoin* Hache
(Sagard: Me13); Susquehannock *Adωgen*,
hadoogan An axe (Holm: 5, 6)

-atokw-/-atokwahtsher- N spoon: **atókwa**
With V -awenht[e]- be extra:
iotokwahtsherawénhte' an extra spoon.
With V -ke- amount to, and PART: **áhsen
niwatokwahtsherá:ke** three spoons.
With V -kowan[en]-/-owan[en]- be big:
watokwahtsherowá:nen (it is) a big
spoon.
With V -nohare-/-ohare- wash:
wa'katokwahtsheróhare' I washed the
spoon.
NOTE: The incorporating form has the
NMZR -htsher-.

-aton- V become, be possible: **wá:tons** it is
possible, **enwá:ton'** it will be possible,
it can be, **ón:ton'** it became, it could be,
aón:ton' it would be possible, **iotòn:'on**
it has become possible, **rotòn:'on** he has
become, he has turned into.
With NEG: **iah tewá:tons** it is not possible.
With CONTR: **iah thaón:ton'** it won't be
possible, it can't be.
• Enwá:ton' ken entkatáweia'te'? Can I
come in? • Onekwá:ra' ón:ton' raonekwénhsa'. His blood turned into a clot, he
got a blood clot. • Kwah iah thaón:ton' né:
iah thaiotékhake'. You have to keep a fire
going (because the days are so cold).
(Letter 1945, Apr)

-aton- V get underneath
With **nà:kon** down, and CISL:
nà:kon taká:ton' I got to be underneath
(maybe when playing with other kids),
I got short-changed or I overpaid (maybe
I gave someone something nice and got
nothing in return), **nà:kon tahá:ton'** he
got to be underneath, he got short-changed,
nà:kon taión:ton' she got to be underneath, she got short-changed.
With **ó:kont** (meaning unclear):
ó:kont wa'ká:ton' I came for nothing,
ó:kont wahá:ton' he came for nothing.

-aton-/-ihron-/-en- V say: **ión:tons** she is
saying, **enkì:ron'** I will say, **wahèn:ron'**
he said, **iaká:wen** she has said.
With DISTR -nion-: **enkonnihrónnion'**
they will talk about things.

-atonhkaria'k- V get hungry: **katonhkária'ks**
I am hungry, **enkatonhkária'ke'** I will
get hungry, **wahatonhkária'ke'** he got
hungry, **wakatonhkarià:kon** I was
hungry.

atónhnhets soul, spirit

NOTE: This word is composed of the SRF -at- and -onhnhe[t]- be alive, but it is unclear what the final *s* is.

Cf. Naie tionnhe'kon nong8atonnheston notre ame nous fait vivre (Bruyas: 16); *Atonnheson* Ame (Galissonnière: 6v); *atōnnhets, atonnhētston* Ame (Marcoux: 14); *A-gwa-doen-hets* My soul (Newhouse: 289); *a-tonn-hests* soul (Cory: 18); *a tonn hets* soul (Diabo: 76); *Sa ha kehts koh ne wa ga don hehts* He restoreth my soul (Jamieson 3: 11)

-atonhnhii- V deny: **ratonhnhí:ias** he denies it, **wahatónhnhiie'** he denied it, **rotonhnhí:hen** he is denying it.
With REP: **sakatónhnhiie'** I denied it.
With NEG: **iah tehotonhnhí:hen** he didn't deny it.
With FACIL -'tskon, easily: **rotonhnhiià:tskon** he (always) denies it.

-atonhwentsoni-/-atonhontsoni-/-atehontsoni- V want, need, with DLC:
tewakatonhwentsó:ni or **tewakatonhontsó:ni** or **tewakatehontsó:ni** I want or need it, **Nahò:ten' tesatehontsó:ni?** What do you want?

-atonni- N paternal family, godfather
POSS: **akatón:ni** my paternal family, my godfather.

Cf. Atonni Originaire de ql lieu du costé du pere (Galissonnière: 63r); "The *Athonni* or father's household is foreign," (Lafitau I: 339); *akatónni* godparents (Mary Deer's class notes, Feb. 1966); Wendat *Houatondi* C'est vn de nos gens, c'est vn des nostres (Sagard: Pa18)

-atonrie- V breathe: **katón:rie'** I am breathing, **ratón:rie'** he is breathing, **iontón:rie'** she is breathing, **eniontón:rie'** she will breathe, **wahatón:rie'** he breathed, **iakotón:rie'** she is breathing, she is taking a breath.
See also -onri- breath.

Cf. Atonrion respirer (Bruyas: 40); *Atonrion* respirer (Galissonnière: 72v)

-atonriser- N breath
With V -atihentho- pull, and CISL: **takatonriseratihéntho'** I inhaled.
With V -a'senht-/-enht- drop, and TRNL: **iahatonríserenhte'** he breathed into it.
With V -hre[k]- push, and TRNL: **ia'katonriserà:reke'** I exhaled.
With V -o'kt- finish: **wahatonriserò:kten'** he took his last breath (and died).
See also -onri- breath.

-atonris[t]- V be damp, soggy: **iotón:ris** it is damp.
With INCH -'-: **wa'otonrísta'ne'** it got damp.
With N -ahsi't- foot, and DLC: **tewakahsi'tatón:ris** I have damp (sweaty) feet.
With SRF -ate- and N -na'tar[o][k]- bread: **iotena'taratón:ris** (it is) damp, soggy bread.
With SRF -ate- and N -nonhs- house: **iotenonhsatón:ris** (it is) a damp house.

-atonron- V be adept, useful, helpful: **katón:ron** I am useful, helpful, **ratón:ron** he is useful, helpful, **iontón:ron** she is useful, helpful.
With NEG: **iah thé:nen tehatón:ron** he is worthless, good-for-nothing, a lazybones.
• **Nahò:ten' akwáh ratón:ron?** What is he good at?

-atont- V eat a meal together, with DLC:
skáthne tentewá:tonte' we (you all and
I) will eat together, **wa'titewá:tonte'** we
ate together, **wa'tiakwá:tonte'** we (they
all and I) ate together, **teionkwatón:ton**
we are eating together.

Cf. Tꜱatonton se mettre deux au même plat
ou à faire même chose (Bruyas: 38);
Tꜱaton se joindre pour manger dans un
meme plat (Galissonnière: 50v); *teiōntonts*
Campagnie, Manger en (Marcoux: 74);
Tekatonts se mettre deux ou plusieurs pour
fair une chose; manger ensemble (Cuoq:
45)

-atontarikt- V laugh loudly or uncontrollably,
guffaw, with DLC: **tekatontaríktha'** I
laugh loudly, **tenkatón:tarikte'** I will
laugh loudly, **wa'thatón:tarikte'** he
laughed loudly, **teiakotontaríkton** she
is laughing uncontrollably.

Cf. Tꜱatonarikton faire hüee (Bruyas: 40);
Tꜱatonarikton Crier, plusieurs ensemble
faire la hüee (Galissonnière: 26v);
tekatontarīkta Crier en riant (Marcoux:
95); *Tekatontariktha* rire aux éclats, à
gorge déployé (Cuoq: 45);
Wa'thiatón:tarikte They roared with
laughter (Tewaterihwarenia'tha, Summer
1988: 24, listed under "Old Words")

Atón:wa' Personal Chant, one of four sacred
ceremonies

Cf. Atonront chanter un air auquel on
repond par des hen hen (Bruyas: 40);
"After the meal, the master of the feast
begins the *athonront* or pyrrhic, a dance
exclusively for the men." (Lafitau I: 319),
"The chief then 'lifts up the song' and
begins the dance of the *athonront*, striking
on one of the posts of the house with his
ball-headed war club and all answer him
with their *he! he!* while he dances." (Lafi-

tau II: 112); *Atonronten* chanter au hen hen
(Galissonnière: 17v); *Katonrontha* chanter
la chanson de guerre (Cuoq: 15); Wendat
atonront chanter en guerrier une chanson
laquelle s'assemblée repond par de hen,
hen, reiterer, et qui l'accordent en cadence
(Potier: 200)

-aton'ne[k]- V get startled, scared, anxious,
with CISL: **tkatón'neks** I get startled, I get
a scare, **taiontón'neke'** she got startled,
she got a scare, **tewakatón'ne** I am anxious, **thotón'ne** he is anxious,
tiakotón'ne she is anxious.
With NEG: **iah tethoton'nékon** he didn't
get startled.
With CAUS -t- and BEN -en-:
tahakwaton'nékten' he startled me,
takheiaton'nékten' I startled her.
With FACIL -htskon, easily:
tewakaton'néhtskon I am easy to startle.
• Tisatón'ne thé:nen neniá:wen'. You are
anxious something will happen.

-atorat- V hunt: **kató:rats** I hunt,
enkató:rate' I will hunt, **wa'kató:rate'**
I hunted, **wakatorá:ton** I have hunted.
With PAST -kwe': **kató:ratskwe'** I used
to hunt.
With PAST -'ne': **wakatoratòn:ne'** I
hunted (at one time).
With PURP -h-: **wa'katoráthe'** I am going
hunting, **enkatorátha'** I will go hunting,
wa'katorátha' I went hunting,
wakatoráthon I have gone to hunt.
With CAUS -st- and INSTR -hkw-:
Tsi iontoratstáhkhwa' Vermont.
With SRF -an- and N -its- fish:
kanitsató:rats I am fishing; and PURP -h-:
wa'kanitsatoráthe' I am going fishing.

-atorishen- V rest, take a break: **katoríshens**
I rest, **enkatoríshen'** I will rest,

wahatoríshen' he rested, he took a break, he quit, **wakatoríshen** I am resting.
• Iah nòn:wa thatiá:ken'ne' enkatoríshen'. I am not going out today, I am going to rest.

-atot[e]- V be quiet, still, with DLC: **teiotó:te'** it is quiet, it is still.
With CONTR: **tha'tewakató:te'** I am quiet, still, **tha'tehotó:te'** he is quiet, **tha'teiakotó:te'** she is quiet, **tha'teiotó:te'** it is quiet; and CAUS -t-: **tha'tható:tate'** he got quiet, still, **tha'tewató:tate'** it got quiet, still, **tha'tesató:tat** Be quiet!
With CONT -k-: **tó:tek** Quiet!

-ato'tsine- V slide, skate: **ato'tsí:ne** skates.
With CAUS -ht- and DLC: **tekato'tsinéhtha'** I slide, **wa'tkato'tsí:nehte'** I slid; and TRNL: **ia'tehato'tsinéhtha'** he slides across that way, **ia'thato'tsí:nehte'** he slid that way, **ia'tewakato'tsinéhton** I have slid that way.
With NMZR -htsher-, V -ont- attach, and DLC: **tekato'tsinehtsheróntha'** I am putting on skates, I am skating, **wa'tkato'tsinehtsherón:ten'** I put on skates; and PURP -'n-: **wa'tiakwato'tsinehtsherontà:ne'** we all are going skating.

-ato'wi- N falseface: **atò:wi** or **atòn:wi**
With NMZR -htsher-: **ato'wíhtshera'** Falseface Society.
NOTE: Today the more common term for falseface is **ratórie's** (-ori- drive, drive away) i.e., he drives away (the sickness).

atsà:kta' at the river, by the riverside
With LOC -aktontie', along, edge of: **atsa'któntie'** along the riverbank.

-atshakan- V speak a foreign language: **ronatshá:kanen** Eastern Seaboard Indians, Abenakis.
Cf. anesagghena Mahicanders (van den Bogaert: 62); "the Mahakans, otherwise called *Agotzagena.*" (Megapolensis: 172); "The wolves, whom the Iroquois call *Agotsaganens*, are the nearest to the settlement of Renselaerswick and to Fort Orange." (Jogues in Jameson: 262); *ne ratsagannha* le Mahingan (Bruyas: 28); Sagotinnéon *agotsagannha* il a defait les Loups (Bruyas: 70); *Atsagannha* Estranger ... qui parle ... un autre langue (Galissonnière: 38r); *Agozhágane* Mahikander, Delawares (Pyrlaeus: 43); *Aktsakann* je suis abénaquis (Cuoq: 155); *ronatshá:kanen* Abenaki, Hurons (Deering and Delisle: 285); Iroquois "The five Nations call the Mahikans, Delawares and all New England Savages: *Agozhagánta.*" (Zeisberger in Wheeler-Voegelin: 45); Iroquois: "The Delawares [are called] by the five Nations, *Akotshakaw.*" (John Norton in Klinck and Talman: 198); Wendat *Anasaquanan* Canadiens (Sagard: N̥a1); Wendat *aǫsaannen* abnaquis (Potier: 154); *asaǫnnen* parler une langue étrangère que ceux a qui on parle n'entendent pas, (Potier: 174); *hondasaǫnnen* Les Loups (Nation) (Potier: 174)

-atsharit[e]- V solicit, with DLC: **tehontsharí:tes** they are soliciting, asking or begging for something (for a donation to a cause, for candy at Hallowe'en, someone begging for a sandwich), **wa'thatshá:rite'** he solicited, **wa'tiontshá:rite'** she solicited, **tehonatsharí:ton** they have solicited.

-atsharokw- V be noisy: **iotsharókwen**
there's a lot of noise (for example, a lot
of people are all talking at once, kids are
playing in the pool).
With CAUS -ht-: **katsharokwáhtha'** I
make noise (listen to the radio, noisily
flip pages of a book), **wahatsharókwahte'**
he made a lot of noise,
wakatsharokwáhton I am making noise.
Cf. Atsarog8an bruit de plurieurs qui
parlent (Bruyas: 42); *iotsarōk8en* Bruit, il
y a du (Marcoux 48); *Katsarokwas* faire
courir des bruits, répandre des nouvelles
vraies ou fausses, parler en l'air sans être
sûr de ce que l'on dit (Cuoq: 15)

-atshat- N steam, mist, fog, cloud: **otshá:ta'**
With V -ien-/-ient- put down, have, and
DLC: **teiotshá:taien'** it is misty, foggy.
With V -ineken'- emerge:
enwatshatíneken'ne' the steam will
come out or emerge.
With V -kwente- be an opening, clearing,
and DLC: **teiotshatakwén:te'** there are
scattered clouds (there's space between
the clouds).
With V -okw- disperse: **iotshatókwen**
the fog or mist has lifted; and REP:
sontsható:ko' the fog or mist lifted,
went away again.
With V -ot- stand: **iotshá:tote'** it (the
ground) is steaming, there is a mist,
enwatsható:ten' it will steam or mist,
ontsható:ten' it steamed or became mist.
With V -r- put in, and DISTR -onnion-:
iotshatarónnion there are fluffy clouds
here and there.
With V -rakew-/-okew- wipe:
katshatoké:was I wipe away the steam,
wa'katsható:kewe' I wiped away the
steam, **iotshatoké:wen** it is clear (the
sky is clear, the windows are unfoggy).

-atsha'- V burn: **wátsha's** it burns, **enwátsha'**
it will burn, **óntsha'** it burned.
With CAUS -ht-: **katsha'áhtha'** I burn it,
enkátsha'ahte' I will burn it,
wa'kátsha'ahte' I burned it,
wakatsha'áhton I have burned it,
watsha'áhton it is burnt.
With SRF -at- and N -ia't- body:
kwah katia'tátsha's I am burning (with
discomfort or irritation), **wa'ontia'tátsha'**
she got burned, **rotia'tátshon'** he has
gotten burned; and CAUS -ht-:
wahakwatia'tátsha'ahte' he burned me.
With SRF -at- and N -ient- wood:
wakatientátshon' I have a Native mother
and a White father, **rotientátshon'** he has
a Native mother and a White father.
With SRF -ate- and N -iie-/-ien- oil, grease:
wateienátsha's or (with variant -weien-)
wateweienátsha's the (cooking) oil is
burning, **onteweienátsha'** the oil burned.
With SRF -ate-, N -na'tar[o][k]- bread, and
and CAUS -ht-: **wa'katena'tarátsha'ahte'**
I made toast, **rotena'taratsha'áhton** he
is making toast, **watena'taratsha'áhton**
toast.
With SRF -ate-, N -'nonhkw- bottom of
something, and CAUS -ht-:
wa'kate'nonhkwátsha'ahte' I burned
the bottom of it.
• Katia'tátsha's skáthne aiakenè:sheke'.
It burns me to be together with her (she
is irritating to me).

-atsha'rhon-/-atsha'nhon- V drip:
watshà:rhons or **watshà:nhons** it is
dripping, leaking (a faucet or the roof),
ontshà:rhon' or **ontshà:nhon'** it dripped.

-atsheiaron- V be shy: **wakatshé:iaron**
I am shy, **rotshé:iaron** he is shy,
iakotshé:iaron she is shy.

-atshen- V be or act timid: **wakátshen** I am timid, I shy away from fights, **rótshen** he is timid.
With CAUS -ht-: **wahátshenhte'** he backed away, he stood down (from an argument or a fight), **rotshénhton** he is backing down.

-atshennonni- V become happy, glad: **katshennón:nis** I become happy, **enkatshennón:ni'** I will become happy, **wahatshennón:ni'** he became happy, **wakatshennón:ni** I am happy.
With CAUS -'t-: **iotshennónnia't** it is a happy thing, a happy event; and REP: **entsitewatshennónnia'te'** we will rejoice at it again.
With FACIL -'tskon: **wakatshennonnià:tskon** I become happy easily.

-atshentho- V for the sun to set, with TRNL and DLC: **ia'tewatshénthos** the sun is going down, **ia'tewatshéntho'** the sun went down, the sun set.
Cf. Te ꙩatseθo nongati du coste du soleil couchant (Bruyas: 43); *iateꙩatsōthos* soleil se couche (Marcoux: 367); *Iatewatshothos* l'occident, le couchant (Cuoq: 62)

-atshi- KIN friends, usually between females: **ontiátshi** we two (are) friends, my friend, **tsátshi** your friend.
With INCH - '-: **wa'ontiátshi'ne'** we two became friends, **wa'onátshi'ne'** the two females became friends.
NOTE: GM translated this term also as 'wives between two brothers'.
Cf. Atsi camarade (Bruyas: 43); *Giatsi* Camarade (Galissonnière: 15v); *onkiātsi* Ami (Marcoux: 14); Laurentian *Aguiase* My friend (Biggar: 245); Wendat *Eadsé* ma compagne (Sagard: Pa18)

atshinénha' leggings

atshohkwáhtshera' treasures, riches, material goods

atshò:kten hoe
Cf. atsochta adzes (van den Bogaert: 52); *otsokton* houe de fer (Galissonnière: 49r); *atsōkton* pioche (Marcoux: 291); *Atsokton* pioche, bêche (Cuoq: 3); *ats hok ten* hoe (Anon: 12); *a tsok ten* hoe (D'Ailleboust: 26); *ahts hok denh* hoe (Jamieson 2: 5); Laurentian *Asogné* a hatchet (Biggar: 80)

-atshokw- V smoke: **katshókwas** I smoke, **enkatshó:ko'** I will smoke, **wahatshó:ko'** he smoked, **rotshókwen** he is smoking.

-atshon'nionhkw- V mourn: **wakatshon'niónhkwen** I am mourning, **rotshon'niónhkwen** he is mourning, **iakotshon'niónhkwen** she is mourning.
• Kahon'tsistóskon iakótston iakotshon'niónhkwen. She is wearing all black, she's mourning.

-atshori- V slurp, eat soup: **katshó:ris** I have soup, I slurp soup, **enkatshó:ri'** I will have soup, **wahatshó:ri'** he ate soup, **iakotshó:ri** she is having soup.
Cf. Atsori manger de la sagamité (Bruyas: 43); *katsōris* Soupe, manger la (Marcoux: 370); *Katsoris* manger avec la cuiller, avec la micoine (Cuoq: 15)

-atskara- V be bitter: **iotská:ra** it is bitter tasting.
With N -ahi- fruit, berry: **iohiatská:ra** (it is) bitter fruit, grapefruit.
With N -hnek- liquid: **iohnekatská:ra** (it is) a bitter liquid.
With N -htehr- root: **iohtehratská:ra** (it is) a bitter root.

Cf. iotskarat l'eau de vie (Bruyas: 49);
jotskarat Amer [bitter] (Galissonnière: 6v);
on'nega ꭶitskarat Eau de vie (Galissonnière: 33r); *iotskārat* Amer (Marcoux: 14);
ots ka ra o ne ka whisky, *literally,* bitter
liquid (-hnek- liquid) (Diabo: 86);
yohts gah rah bitter (Jamieson 1: 4)

-atska'hon- V eat, have a meal, with DLC:
teiontskà:hons she eats, **tenkatskà:hon'**
I will eat, **wa'thatskà:hon'** he ate,
tewakatskà:hon I have eaten, I am eating, **teiontiatskà:hon** we two are eating.
With INSTR -hkw-: **teiontska'hónhkhwa'**
restaurant.

-atskennenont- V become pale, with DLC:
wa'thatskennenón:ten' he got pale,
wa'tiontskennenón:ten' she got pale,
tehotskenné:nonte' he is pale,
teiakotskenné:nonte' she is pale.

Átskwi or **Hátskwi** So, well! **Átskwi órie'!**
or **Átskwi kwátere!** Well there! (to a
young person)

-atsnenht- V go down, descend
With CISL: **tkatsnénhtha'** I come
down, **tahátsnenhte'** he came down,
tewakatsnénhton I have come down,
tasátsnenht Come down! with CISL and
PROG -hatie-: **tonkwatsnenhtonhátie'** I
am on my way down; with CISL and DLC:
tontakátshnenhte' I came back down.
With TRNL: **iekatsnénhtha'** I go down,
iahátsnenhte' he went down,
iewakatsnénhton I have gone down,
ia'sátsnenht Go down!
With SRF -a-, N -nont- mountain, hill, and
TRNL: **iekanontatsnénhtha'** I go downhill, **iahanontátsnenhte'** he went downhill, **iewakanontatsnénhton** I have gone
downhill; and PROG -hatie-:

iewakanontatsnenhtonhátie' I am going
downhill.
With SRF -ate-, N -wer- wind, air, and
TRNL: **ia'katewerátsnenhte'** I went
downwind.

átsta's sassafras
Cf. a-tsa Dentaria diphylla [toothwort]
(Rousseau: 45)

-atsterist- V bother: **katsterístha'** I bother
with it, I fuss with it, **kheiatsterístha'**
I am bothering her, bugging her,
rakwatsterístha' he is bothering, bugging
me, **wa'katsté:riste'** I bothered, fussed
with it, **wahshakotsté:riste'** he bothered,
bugged her, **iakotsteríston** she has
bothered, fussed with it.
With SRF -ate- and N -rihw- matter, message: **wa'katerihwatsté:riste'** I bothered
with the matter.
• Akenónhkwis katsterístha'. I am bothering with my hair, touching, fussing with it.

átste' outside

-atste'niaron- V be diligent, persist, urge,
encourage: **kheiatste'niá:ron** I am urging
her, encouraging her to apply herself,
wahiiatste'niá:ron' I encouraged him,
wakatste'niá:ron' I keep at it, put in a
good effort, I am diligent, persistent,
rotste'niá:ron' he is diligent, persistent,
iakotste'niá:ron' she is diligent,
persistent.
• Wahiiatste'niá:ron' ahahkwíhsron'
ahoió'ten'. I am urging him to try hard
at working.

-atstiehser- N kidney: **otstiéhseri**
POSS: **akwatstiéhseri** my kidney.
With V -awi-/-on- give:
wa'onkwatstiéhseron' they gave me

a kidney (as in transplant).

• Ó:ia' wa'onkwatstiéhseron' né: tsi iotsi-ió:ha ne akwá:wen. They gave me another kidney because mine was weak, sickly.

-atstikahwha- V travel, with DLC: **teiontstikáhwhas** she is a a traveller, she goes all over, **wa'thatstikáhwha'** he travelled all over, **tewakatstikáhwhen** I have travelled.
With PROG -hatie-: **tewakatstikahwhen-hátie'** I am travelling from place to place.

-atstik[on]- V vomit, with CISL: **thatstí:kons** he is vomiting, **entkátstike'** I will vomit, **tahátstike'** he vomitted, **thotstí:kon** he has vomitted.

-attakara'w- V stick up or out: **iottakarà:wen** it is sticking up or out (for example, nails on a porch, roots on a path), **onttá:kara'we'** it stuck up or out.
With DISTR -nion-: **iottakara'wánion** things are sticking up here and there.

• Ohson'karà:ke kahnehtáhrhon iottaka-rà:wen. The linoleum is sticking up on the floor.

-attatakw- V explode, pop: **onttatá:ko'** it exploded.
With CAUS -ht-: **wa'kattatákwahte'** I exploded it.
With N -hnek- liquid: **wathnekatákwas** soda, fizzy drink.
With N -nenhst- corn, and CAUS -ht-: **watenenhstatakwáhton** popcorn.
NOTE: This stem is composed of the SRF -at- and a root -tatakw-. After incorporated nouns, the form of the root is -takw-.

-atteht- V rebuke, with BEN -enni-/-en-: **riiattehtén:ni** I am rebuking him, warning him not to do it again,

wahakwattéhten' he rebuked me, **wahiiattéhten'** I rebuked him.

-atten'kw- V expand, rise: **wattèn:kwas** it expands, it rises, **enwattèn:ko'** it will expand, rise, **onttèn:ko'** it expanded.
With NEG: **iah teiottèn:kwen** it didn't expand, rise.
With CAUS -ht-: **iontten'kwáhtha'** or **iethen'kwáhtha'** baking powder, **wa'onttèn:kwahte'** she made it expand.

-attok- V notice, perceive: **kattó:kas** I notice it, sense it, perceive it, **enkáttoke'** I will notice, **waháttoke'** he noticed, **wakattó:ken** I have noticed.

-attokha- V be smart, knowledgeable: **kattókha'** I am smart, knowledgeable, **rattókha'** he is smart, knowledgeable, **ionttókha'** she is smart, knowledgeable.
With CONT -k-: **enhattókhake'** he will be smart.
With NMZR -htsher-: **attokháhtshera'** wisdom, knowledge.
With SRF -ate- and N -'nikonhr- mind: **rate'nikonhrattókha'** he has a bright, a wise mind.

-attokha- V be stingy: **rattókha'** he is stingy, cheap, **ionttókha'** she is stingy.
With V -atkon- be the devil, demon, and NMZR -'ser-: **rotkon'serattókha'** he is really stingy, cheap.

-attokha- V have loose morals, with NEG: **iah tehattókha'** he has loose morals, he has all kinds of women, **iah tewattókha'** she has loose morals, she runs around.

-attokw- V disperse, with DLC: **tewattókwas** it goes all over, **tenwattó:ko'** it will go all over, **wa'tewattó:ko'** it went all over,

it dispersed, **teiottókwen** it has gone all over.
With CAUS -ht-: **tekattokwáhtha'** I go digging around, **wa'tkattókwahte'** I dug around, I rummaged, **tehottokwáhton** he has rummaged.

-attsikenhro'k- V blink, with DLC:
tekattsikèn:ro'ks I am blinking,
tehattsikèn:ro'ks he is blinking,
teionttsikèn:ro'ks she is blinking,
wa'tionttsikèn:ro'ke' she blinked.
NOTE: This stem may include the SRF -at- and -o'[k]- slap, flutter, flap.

-awak- V shake: **ká:waks** I am shaking it out (for example, sheets or a blanket),
enká:wake' I will shake it, **wa'ká:wake'** I shook it, **wakawá:kon** I have shaken it.
With N -a'kenhr- ashes, dirt:
ka'kenhrá:waks I am sifting dirt or ashes, **wa'ka'kenhrá:wake'** I sifted the dirt.
With N -hakenht- soot: **rahakenhtá:waks** chimney sweep, **enkhakenhtá:wake'** I will knock or shake the soot off of it,
wahahakenhtá:wake' he shook the soot off.
With N -iar- bag: **kaiarawá:kon** last born child.
With SRF -at- and N -ia't- body:
enhatia'tá:wake' he will shake himself off (talking about a dog), he will shake it off, **wahatia'tá:wake'** he shook himself off, **rotia'tawá:kon** he is shaking himself off.
With SRF -an- and N -itahs- tail:
ranitahsá:waks he wags his tail,
wahanitahsá:wake' he wagged his tail, **ronitahsawá:kon** he is wagging his tail.
With N -the'ser- flour: **kethe'será:waks** I am sifting flour, **wa'kethe'será:wake'** I sifted the flour, **wakethe'serawá:kon** I have sifted the flour.

With N -wei- wing: **wa'kheweiá:wake'** I fanned her; and SRF -ate-:
kateweiá:waks I am fanning myself,
wa'kateweiá:wake' I fanned myself,
wakateweiawá:kon I have fanned myself; and CAUS -st-: **ionteweiawákstha'** fan.

-awehrho- V cover, close off
With N -rahkw- sun, and CAUS -hst-:
iorahkwawehrhóhston it is in the shade; and SRF -ate-: **ionterahkwawehrhóhstha'** umbrella, **enhsaterahkwawéhrhohste'** you will get in the shade,
wa'katerahkwawéhrhohste' I got in the shade, **wakaterahkwawehrhóhston** I am in the shade.
With N -'nionhr- inside of a chimney:
wa'ke'nionhrawéhrhon' I closed the damper to the chimney,
waha'nionhrawéhrhon' he closed the chimney damper.
With SRF -at- and unclear N:
wa'katahonhtawéhrhon' I insulated the house (outside, around the foundation).

-awen- N water
With LOC -'ke, on, at: **awèn:ke** in the water; and DISTR -hshon: **awen'kéhshon** all over in the water.
With SRF -at-: **katá:wens** I swim, I am swimming, I am taking a bath,
enkatá:wen' I will swim, take a bath,
wahatá:wen' he swam, took a bath,
rotá:wen he has swum, taken a bath; and PURP -h-: **katawénhe'** I am going to swim, take a bath, **wahatawénhe'** he is going swimming, going to take a bath,
enkatawénha' I will go to swim,
wahatawénha' he went swimming; and PAST -hne': **rotawenhónhne'** he went swimming, he has gone swimming.
With SRF -at- and REV -hsi-:
wa'katawénhsi' I finished my bath.

With SRF -at-, CAUS -hst-, and INSTR
-hkw-: **iontawenhstáhkhwa'** bathtub.
• Katawénhe' iotohétston néntie. I am
going to swim this afternoon.

Cf. A8en eau, *A8enge* dans l'eau (Bruyas:
24); *asēnke* dans l'eau (Marcoux: 135);
Awenke dans l'eau (Cuoq: 83); *Awèn:ke*
In the water (Horne: 58); Laurentian *Ame*
Water (Biggar: 242); Wendat *Aoüen* Eau
(Sagard: Ea1)

-awen- N belonging: **akwá:wen** mine,
ì:'i akwá:wen it is mine, **í:se' sá:wen**
it is yours, **raónha raó:wen** it is his,
akaónha akó:wen it is hers,
ì:'i ontiá:wen it is ours (dual),
ì:'i onkwá:wen it is ours (plural),
ronónha raoná:wen it is theirs
(belonging to males, or males and
females), **onónha aoná:wen** it is theirs
(belonging to females).
With ATTR =kenha, former, late:
akwawenhkénha is used to be mine.
With ATTR =shon'a, pluralizer:
raowenhshòn:'a his things.
With NEG: **iah í: tewaká:wen** it is not
mine.

awénha' flower. *This is an old word.*
Cf. A8enha fleur (Bruyas: 24); *A8enha*
fleur (Galissonnière: 42r)

-awenhrat- V overflow: **kawèn:rats** I overflow it, **enkawèn:rate'** I will overflow it,
wahawèn:rate' he overflowed it,
wakawenhrá:ton I have overflowed it.
With TRNL: **iehawèn:rats** he is putting it
over, passing it over, **iahawèn:rate'** or
(with DLC) **ia'thawèn:rate'** he put it,
passed it over, **ieiakowenhrá:ton** she has
passed it over.
With SRF -at-: **ontawèn:rate'** it overflowed; and TRNL and DLC:

ia'tenkatawèn:rate' I will go over it
(for example, the fence or a log),
ia'thatawèn:rate' he went over it,
ia'teiakotawenhrá:ton she has gone
over it.
With N -kahser- tears, and DISTR -hon-:
iekahserawenhráthons she is in tears,
wa'kkahserawenhráthon' I shed tears.

Cf. desawennawenrate your voice coming
through (Hale: 116–7)

-awenht[e]- V be extra: **iowénhte'** it is left
over, there is an extra amount;
énska iowénhte' one more;
skáksa iowénhte' an extra cup (-ks- dish,
plate).
With CAUS -t-: **kawénhtats** I add the difference, **enkawénhtate'** I will add the
difference, **wa'kawénhtate'** I added more
to it, **wakawenhtá:ton** I have added more
to it.
With N -atokw-/-atokwahtsher- spoon:
iotokwahtsherawénhte' an extra spoon.

Cf. A8ente joindre quelque chose; estre
avec ou au dessus du principal, *A8entaton*
accroitre à quelqu'un (Bruyas: 25);
io8ēnhte Surplus, au surplus (Marcoux:
375); *Kawentats* mettre par dessus, faire
un supplément, mettre du surplus (Cuoq:
18)

-awenren- V outgrow, with DLC:
wa'tewakawén:ren' I outgrew it,
teiakowenrèn:'en she has outgrown it,
she doesn't fit it.
With N -'whahs- skirt:
wa'tewake'whahsawén:ren' I outgrew
the skirt.

-awenrie- V stir, with DLC: **tekawénrie's**
I stir it, **tenkawénrie'** I will stir it,
wa'tkawénrie' I stirred it,

tewakawénrie' I have stirred it, I am stirring it.

With SRF -at-: **tekatawénrie's** I wander, I stroll (maybe I'm moving through a crowd), **wa'thatawénrie'** he wandered, he strolled.

With N -a'kenhr- ashes, dirt: **Tewa'kenhrawénrie'** Stirring of the Ashes (rite).

With N -a'ser- blade, axe: **a'serawénrie'** stirring paddle (for taking cornbread out of the water).

With SRF -at- and N -erien't- disposition: **tekaterien'tawénrie's** I make mistakes, **wa'tkaterien'tawénrie'** I made a mistake, **teiakorien'tawenriè:'on** she has made a mistake.

With N -hsienhont-/-hsiahont- stomach: **tewakhsienhontawénrie'** my stomach is rumbling, **tehohsienhontawénrie'** his stomach is rumbling.

With SRF -a- and N -nonhwar- brain: **tekanonhwarawénrie'** I am crazy, **tenkanonhwarawénrie'** I will get crazy, **wa'tkanonhwarawénrie'** I went crazy; and CAUS -'t-: **teiakononhwarawenriè:tha'** it makes her or someone crazy (maybe from taking drugs or drinking too much alcohol), **wa'thononhwarawénrie'te'** it made him crazy.

With N -she'rh- dough, gravy: **wa'thashe'rhawénrie'** he stirred the dough, the gravy.

With N -tsir- spark, fire, embers: **wa'tektsirawénrie'** I stirred the embers, **testsirawénrie** Stir the embers!

Cf. te-ion-non-wa-ra-wen-rhe-ta Datura Stramonium (= l'herbe qui rend fou) [jimsonweed] (Rousseau: 56)

-awen'e[k]- wrap. *See* -hwawen'e[k]-/ -awen'e[k]-

-aweron- V spill out of: **káwerons** I spill it, **enkáweron'** I will spill it, **wa'káweron'** I spilled it, **iakóweron** she has spilled it.

With CISL: **tkáwerons** I pour it, **takáweron'** I poured it, **tasáweron** Pour it!

With TRNL: **ieniónweron'** she will spill it, pour it out, **iaháweron'** he spilled it, poured it out, **ia'sáweron** Pour it, add it!

With SRF -at-: **ontáweron'** it spilled out.

With N -hnek- liquid, and CISL or TRNL: **takhnekáweron'** I poured the water (this way), **ia'khnekáweron'** I poured the water out, I added liquid to it.

With SRF -at- and N -hon'kw- throat: **wa'kathon'kwáweron'** I looked up with my head back, **sathon'kwáweron** Look up, put your head back!

With N -iie-/-ien- oil, grease, and TRNL: **ia'keienáweron'** I put oil or gas in it.

With N -na'ts- pail: **rana'tsáwerons** he keeps spilling it out of the pail, **wahana'tsáweron'** he spilled the pail.

With N -nontar- soup: **wa'kenontaráweron'** I spilled the soup.

With N -non't- milk: **wahanon'táweron'** he spilled the milk; and CISL: **tahanon'táweron'** he poured the milk; with N -non't- milk, variant -aweront-, and INSTR -hkw-: **ienon'tawerontáhkhwa'** milk pitcher.

With SRF -ate-, N -tshe['t]- bottle, jar, and TRNL and DLC: **ia'tkatetshe'táweron'** I gulped or chugged it down.

See also -anonhwetshaweron- tumble over.

• Takenon'táweron' ne arawén othè:sera'. I poured milk on the porridge.

-awe'ehst- V pierce, with DLC: **tekawe'éhstha'** I pierce it, **tenkáwe'ehste'** I will pierce it, **wa'tháwe'ehste'** he pierced it, **wa'tionkwáwe'ehste'** they gave me a

needle (for example, a flu shot),
tewakawe'éhston I have pierced it.
With SRF -at-, N -hskaw- bush, and TRNL:
ia'tkatskawáwe'ehste' I went into the
bush.
With N -nenhst- arm:
wa'tionkenentsháwe'ehste' they gave
me a needle in the arm.
With SRF -ate-, N -(h)rh- woods, and TRNL:
ia'tkatehrháwe'ehste' I went into the
woods.
With N -rihw- matter, message:
tenkerihwáwe'ehste' I will put the
subject forth, look into it.
With N -'wahr- meat, and INSTR -hkw-:
teie'wahrawe'ehstáhkhwa' meat fork.

Cf. Ti agotkonniaeston Nez Percés
(Bruyas: 78)

-awi- V wrap around, encircle
With SRF -ani- and N -hsnonhs- finger,
hand: **anihsnónhsawi** ring,
akwanihsnónhsawi my ring; and CAUS
-'t-: **kanihsnonhsawì:tha'** I am putting
on a ring(s), **enkanihsnónhsawi'te'** I will
put on a ring(s), **wa'kanihsnónhsawi'te'**
I put on a ring(s), **wakanihsnonhsawì:ton**
I have a ring(s) on.
With SRF -at- and N -ia't- body: **atià:tawi**
dress, shirt (*see* -atia'tawi- for more
forms).
With N -nentsh- arm, and CAUS -'t-:
onentshawì:ta' wrist, cuffs (of a shirt)
(*see* -nentshawi't- for more forms).

-awi-/-on- V give: **koniá:wis** I give it to you,
kheiá:wis I give it to her, **enkón:ion'** I
will give it to you, **enhá:kon'** he will give
it to me, **wa'ón:kon'** she gave it to me,
rakwá:wi he has given it to me, **tá:kon**
Give it to me!
With CISL: **tionkwá:wis** she gives it to
me, hands it to me, **tahá:kon'** he gave,

handed it to me, **tkoniá:wi** I have given,
handed it to you.
With REFL -atat- and DLC: **teiontiatatá:wi**
you and I are trading, **tentiatá:ton'** I will
trade with you, **wa'tiatiatá:ton'** we two
traded, **tetsatá:ton** You two trade it!
With N -atero'ser- friendship, and DLC:
tenhonwanaterò:seron' she will introduce them to each other, **wa'tekheiate-
rò:seron'** I introduced them to each other.
With N -atstiehser- kidney:
wa'onkwatstiéhseron' they gave me a
kidney (as in transplant).
With N -hah- road: **shakohahá:wis** traffic
cop, school crossing guard.
With N -honkar- invitation:
kwahonkará:wis I or we are giving you
an invitation, **enkhehón:karon'** I will
give her an invitation, **wa'konhón:karon'**
I gave you an invitation; and NEG:
iah tekhehonkará:wi I didn't invite her;
with N -honkar- invitation, and DISTR
-hon-: **wa'khehonkarawíhon'** I gave
them invitations; with SRF -ate-, N
-honkar- invitation, and PURP -hr-:
wa'kathonkarawì:re' I am going around
giving out invitations.
With N -hsenn- name: **khehsenná:wi** I
give her a name, **ionkhsenná:wi** she gives
me a name, **wahohsén:non'** he gave him
a name.
With N -hwist- metal, money:
khehwistá:wis I give her money,
wa'khehwíston' I gave her money; and
REFL -atat- and DLC: **tehatathwistá:wis**
he makes change.
With N -nennotsher- package, parcel:
wahakenennótsheron' he gave me a
package.
With N -rihw- matter, message:
rakerihwá:wis he allows me, gives me
permission, **wahiríhon'** I let him,
wa'onkeríhon' she or they allowed me.

With N -tsi'ts- flower: **wahaktsì:tson'** he gave me flowers.
• Ká:nen tentiatá:ton'. I will trade seeds with you. • Wa'onkeríhon' takhewén:-nahkwe'. They let me talk for them.

-awiskwaht- V sideswipe, miss a target, with DLC: **tehawiskwáhtha'** he misses the target, **wa'thawískwahte'** he missed the target, **wa'thakwawískwahte'** he side-swiped me, he brushed by me (without touching me).
• Wahakwaròn:tate' nek tsi wa'thakwawís-kwahte'. He shot at me but he missed me.

-a'a- V be small, with **ken'** particle and PART:
ken' niwà:'a it is small, **ken' niwà:sa'** they are small.
With N -ahkwari['t]- bear:
ken' niwahkwari'tà:'a (it is) a small bear.
With N -ahtsohkw- morsel, portion:
ken' niwahtsohkwà:'a (it is) a small morsel, a small portion.
With N -hnek- liquid: **Ken' nikahnekà:'a** Little Water Medicine.
With N -htehr- root: **ken' niiohtehrà:sa'** (they are) small roots.
With N -itiohkw- group:
ken' nikentiohkwà:'a (it is) a small group.
With N -nat- town, settlement:
ken' nikanatà:'a (it is) a small town.
With N -nenhr- crowd:
ken' nikanenhrà:'a (it is) a small crowd.
With N -nennotsher- package, parcel:
ken' nikanennotsherà:'a (it is) a little package.
With N -rihw- matter, message, and ATTR =shon'a pluralizer:
ken' niiorihwasa'shòn:'a miscellaneous matters.

-a'ar- N net, curtain, veil: **à:'are'**
With SRF -at- and V -her-/-hr- set on top of: **iakota'aráhere'** she has on a veil.
With V -hwawen'e[k]-/-awen'e[k]- wrap, and DLC; and **awenhétsha'** (-enhetsh-sausage): **tewa'arawèn:'e awenhétsha'** farmer's sausage.
With V -kha- attach, piece together, REV -hsi-, and DLC: **wa'tka'arakháhsi'** I parted the curtains or drapes, I put them to the side, **tesa'arakháhsi** Put the curtains to the side!
With SRF -at- and V -nohare-/-ohare- wash: **wa'kata'aróhare'** I washed the curtains; and DISTR -nion-: **wa'kata'aroharénion'** I washed the curtains.
With V -rik- put together, and DLC: **wa'tka'á:rarike'** I put together the curtains, **tesa'á:rarik** Put the curtains together!
With SRF -at- and V -ta'-/-eta'- put inside: **wata'aráta's** screen, **wahata'aráta'** he put in a screen.
With unclear V, and DLC **tewa'á:raton tehonttsihkwà:'eks** lacrosse game (-tsihkw- fist, button, -hwa'e[k]-/-a'e[k]- hit, strike); with SRF -at-, unclear V, and DLC: **teiota'á:raton** there are cobwebs; and **takwa'áhson** spider: **takwa'áhson teiota'á:raton** spider web; and REV -kw-: **tekata'arátónkwas** I am removing the cobwebs, **wa'tkata'aratón:ko'** I removed the cobwebs, **tewakata'aratónkwen** I have removed the cobwebs.

-a'as- V stab: **kà:'as** I stab it, **enkà:'ase'** I will stab it, **wa'kà:'ase'** I stabbed it, **wahshakò:'ase'** he stabbed her.

-a'awi-/-en'awi- V float, drift: **io'á:wi** it is floating, drifting.

With CAUS -ht-: **wahata'á:wihte'** he removed himself, he (discreetly) made his way out, **wakata'awíhton** I am on my way (without drawing attention to my leaving); and PROG -hatie-: **rota'awihtonhátie'** he is removing himself.

With N -neraht- leaf: **ionerahten'á:wi** the leaves are floating.

With N -wis- ice, glass: **iowisen'á:wi** the ice is floating, (it is) an ice flow.

See also -ri'wen'awiht- gossip.

-a'eht- N claw: **o'éhta'**

POSS: **rao'éhta'** his claws.

With V -ot- stand, and DLC: **teka'éhtote'** I am on my toes; and PROG -atie-: **teka'ehtotátie'** I am on my tiptoes, going along.

With SRF -at-, V -ot- stand, and DLC: **wa'tkata'ehtó:ten'** I stood up on my toes, **tesata'ehtó:ten** Stand on your toes!

-a'e[k]- hit, strike. *See* -hwa'e[k]-/-a'e[k]-

-a'enn- N bow: **a'én:na'**

POSS: **akwa'én:na'** my bow, **rao'én:na'** his bow, **ako'én:na'** her bow.

With SRF -at-, V -hsa'kt[on]-/-a'kt[on]- bend, and DLC: **teiota'ennà:kton** (it is) a bow that is bent.

With SRF -at- and V -(h)rho- coat: **shakota'ennáhrhos** he witches her, **wa'kheiata'ennáhrho'** I witched her.

With SRF -at- and unclear V: **rata'én:naras** he is a witch, **wata'én:naras** she is a witch, **ionta'én:naras** she is a witch; and NMZR -htsher-: **ata'ennaráhtshera'** witchcraft.

Cf. aénna Arc (Galissonnière: 8v); *Gaterennonnianni* Ensorceler (Galissonnière: 76v); *katenhēnnăras* Sorcier (Marcoux: 368); *Ahenna* arc, archet (Cuoq: 1); *Kahennarhos* ensorceler, *Katahennaras* être sorcier, sorcière (Cuoq: 75); *wa ta en na ras* witch (Diabo: 87); *raén:naras* he is a witch, *ata'ennaráhtshera'* witchcraft (Deering and Delisle: 289); *taiontaten'ennáhro* charm, to cast a spell to each other (Gabriel: 21); Laurentian *Ahena* A bow (Biggar: 243); Wendat *Anda* Arc (Sagard: Ar2); Onondaga *ahêna* Arc (Shea: 22)

a'é:ren over there
• A'é:ren wa'kátie' ne otsi'tèn:'a. The bird is flying over there.

-a'kara[hw]- V become dark

With DLC and CISL: **tetiò:karas** it is dark, **tentiò:karahwe'** it will get dark, **tontaiò:karahwe'** it got dark, **tetio'karà:'on** it has gotten dark.

With PROG -hatie- and CISL: **taio'kara'onhátie'** it is getting to be evening.

With ATTR =hneha, way of: **o'karahsnéha** evening.

-a'karit[e]- V be healthy, thrive: **io'karí:te'** it is thriving.

With SRF -at-: **wakata'karí:te'** I am healthy, **rota'karí:te'** he is well, **iakota'karí:te'** she is well; and NEG: **iah tehota'karí:te'** he is not well.

With SRF -at- and CONT -k-: **enwakata'karí:teke'** I will be in good health.

With SRF -at-, CAUS -t- and REP: **saionta'karí:tate'** she got well again.

-a'kenhr- N ashes, dirt: **o'kèn:ra'**

With LOC -okon, under: **o'kenhró:kon** underground, under the dirt.

With SRF -at-, V -areni- spread around, disperse, CAUS -'t-, and DLC:

tekata'kenhrarenià:tha' I spread dirt.
With V -awak- shake out, off:
ka'kenhrá:waks I am sifting dirt or
ashes.
With V -awenrie- stir, and DLC:
Tewa'kenhrawénrie' Stirring of the
Ashes (rite).
With V -hon'tsi- be black, dark-coloured:
wa'kenhrahòn:tsi (it is) black soil, dirt.
With SRF -at- and V -hseronni- dress,
prepare: **wa'kata'kenhrahserón:ni'**
I prepared the soil.
With V -kareni- take back and forth:
ra'kenhrakarénie's he is carrying dirt
back and forth.
With V -keri- be broth: **o'kenhrákeri'** lye.
With SRF -at-, V -o- be in water, and
INSTR -hkw-: **ata'kenhróhkwa'** grey;
and V -hon'tsi- be black, dark-coloured:
ata'kenhrohkwahòn:tsi dark grey.
With V -ohro[k]- insert, and REV -hsi-:
enhon'kenhrohrókhsi' they will do a
reading of the Handsome Lake Code.
With V -ohtshi- remove, pull out:
sa'kenhróhtshi Take the ashes out (of
the stove)!
With SRF -at-, V -okw- take out of liquid,
and BEN -hs-:
í:wehre' aonkwata'kenhrókwahse'
I feel faint from hunger, **í:wehre'**
ahota'kenhrókwahse' he feels faint
from hunger.
With SRF -at- and V -otka'w- go through,
channel, and DLC:
tenkonta'kenhrótka'we' they (plants)
will come, poke through the soil.
With V -o'kwat- dig: **ka'kenhró'kwats** I
am digging up dirt, **wa'ka'kenhró'kwate'**
I dug in the dirt.
With V -rakew-/-okew- wipe:
ka'kenhroké:was I am dusting,
waha'kenhró:kewe' he wiped the dust
off.

-a'ker- N snowflake: **ò:kera'**
With V -a'sen'-/-en'- fall down:
enwà:keren'ne' it will snow,
òn:keren'ne' it snowed, **io'kerèn:'en**
it is snowing.
With V -onni- make: **wa'kerón:ni'** it is
making snow, changing to snow.
With SRF -at- and V -teni[on]- disperse,
flurry: **iota'keraténion** it is starting to
snow, there's a flake here and a flake
there.

-a'ker- V float, be in water: **io'kéhrha'** it is in
the water.
With AMB -hne-: **io'kerà:ne'** it is going
floating.
With DISTR -onnion-: **io'kerónnion** it is in
there floating (for example, beans, corn).
With SRF -at- and INSTR -hkw-:
wa'katà:kerahkwe' I floated; and BEN
-en-: **onkwata'keráhkwen'** I got the
measles or chicken pox,
wahota'keráhkwen' he got the measles,
wa'akota'keráhkwen' she got the
measles.
With N -honw[ei]- boat, and AMB -hne-:
iohonwa'kerà:ne' the boat is floating.
With N -nonskwar-/-nenskwar- green fruit,
smallpox, and possibly BEN -en- and INCH
-'-: **iakonenskwarà:keren's** smallpox.
Cf. *ia ko ta ke ra kwen ni* measles (Anon:
21); *ia ko nens kwa ra ke rens* smallpox
(Anon: 21)

-a'kotar- N Achilles tendon: **o'kó:tara'**
POSS: **ka'kotarà:ke** my Achilles tendon,
ra'kotarà:ke his Achilles tendon,
ion'kotarà:ke her Achilles tendon.
With V -es- be long, tall, and DLC:
teha'kó:tares he has long feet.

-a'kt[on]- bend. *See* -hsa'kt[on]-/-a'kt[on]-

-a'nianawen[k]- V put on mittens, gloves:
a'niá:nawen mitten, glove.
POSS: **akwa'niá:nawen** my mitten(s).
With DLC: **tewaka'niá:nawen** I have
gloves, mitts on, **wa'tka'niá:nawenke'**
I put gloves, mitts on,
wa'thiia'niá:nawenke' I put gloves, mitts
on him.

-a'senht-/-enht- V drop
With CISL: **tka'sénhtha'** I drop it, pull it
down, **tewa'sénhtha'** waterfall,
entkà:senhte' I will bring it down,
takà:senhte' I brought it down,
tho'sénhton he has knocked, pulled it
down, **tasà:senht** Knock it down!
With TRNL: **ieka'sénhtha'** I drop it down
or in, **ienkà:senhte'** I will drop it,
ia'kà:senhte' I dropped it,
iewaka'sénhton I have dropped it.
With SRF -at-: **ontà:senhte'** it landed (on
the ground).
With N -atonriser- breath, and TRNL:
iahatonríserenhte' he breathed into it.
With N -hakenht- soot:
wahahakénhtenhte' he knocked the soot
out or off of it.
With N -hnaw- rapid, strong current, and
REP: **ó:nen ensekhná:wenhte'** I will
leave, go home, go downstream, look for
work (*this is an old expression*); and PROG
-hatie-: **sewakhnawenhtonhátie'** I am
leaving.
With SRF -at-, N -honw[ei]- boat, INSTR
-hkw-, and DLC: **teionthonwenhtáhkhwa'**
toboggan.
With N -hs- lip and BEN -enni-/-en-:
rakhsenhtén:ni he criticizes me, he
insults me, **shakohsenhtén:ni**
he criticizes, insults her or them,
wa'khehsénhten' I criticized her, I
insulted her.
With N -hson'kar-/-hswen'kar- board:
wahonwahsòn:karenhte' they raided

him, his place, **wa'esahsòn:karenhte'**
they raided you.
With N -hstar- drop, and TRNL:
ia'khstá:renhte' I put a drop in it.
With N -hsto'ser- small feathers:
wa'khstò:serenhte' ne kítkit I pulled
the chicken feathers.
With SRF -at-, N -ian- footprint, track, and
CISL: **tkatianénhtha'** I am sledding, ski-
ing, **takatiá:nenhte'** I sledded, I skied;
with SRF -at-, N -ian- footprint, track, and
INSTR -hkw-: **iontianenhtáhkhwa'** sled.
With N -ia't- body: **wa'kheià:tenhte'** I
dropped her, **wa'tià:tenhte'** I dropped it
(the animal).
With N -ihwhar- fur: **kihwharénhtha'**
I take the fur off, **wa'kihwhá:renhte'**
I took the fur off.
With N -itst- fish scale, scab:
wahéntstenhte' he scaled the fish.
With SRF -an-, N -i't- excrement, and
INSTR -hkw-: **ionni'tenhtáhkhwa'** outhouse, bathroom (an older, alternative
expression for **átste' ieienhtáhkhwa'**,
átste' outside, -eht- V go somewhere).
With N -nahstonhkw- window, windowsill, and CISL: **tahanahstónhkwenhte'**
he lowered the window, he closed the
window, **tasenahstónhkwenht** Lower
the window!
With N -na'watsist- bark:
wahana'watsístenhte' he took off the
bark.
With N -niar- neck: **wahskwaniá:renhte'**
you finished all our food; and SRF -ate-:
kateniarénhtha' I am dropping my head
or neck (because I am moping or feeling
dejected), **enkateniá:renhte'** I will drop
my neck, **wakateniarénhton** I have
dropped my neck; and CISL:
tkateniarénhtha' I put down my neck
(so my chin is on my chest, maybe while
exercising), **entkateniá:renhte'** I will put
down my neck, **tahateniá:renhte'** he put

down his neck, **tasateniá:renht** Put down
your neck!
With N -nieht- snow, and TRNL:
iahaniéhtenhte' he moved, threw the
snow off it.
With N -nien'ser- trigger, and CISL:
tahanièn:serenhte' he pulled the trigger.
With N -rihw- matter, message:
shakorihwénhtha' he sentences them,
he is a judge, **enhiarì:wenhte'** he will
sentence you, **wahirì:wenhte'** I sentenced
him.
With N -rist- iron, steel: **wa'kerístenhte'**
I pleated it, **karisténhton** it is pleated, it
has pleats.
With N -tsihenhst- crispiness, char:
wa'ktsihénhstenhte' I singed the hair off
it, **wahatsihénhstenhte'** he singed the
hair off.
With N -wer- wind, air: **wa'káwerenhte'**
the air pressure dropped, **iowerénhton** the
air is heavy.
With N -'nenhr- cluster of branches, and
DLC: **wa'tke'nèn:renhte'** I pruned the
branches.
With N -'watsist- rough, outer bark:
wa'ke'watsístenhte' I took the bark off.
NOTE: This stem is composed of a root
-a'sen-/-en-, which occurs only with suffixes, and CAUS -ht-.
• Tewenhnì:take ahsatehnhó:ton' enhiarì:-
wenhte'. He will sentence you to two
months in jail.

-a'sen'-/-en'- V fall down
With CISL: **tewà:sen's** it falls down,
entewà:sen'ne' it will fall down,
tòn:sen'ne' it fell down, **tio'sèn:'en**
it has fallen down; and PROG -hatie-:
taio'sen'enhátie' it is falling.
With TRNL: **iahòn:sen'ne'** it fell down
(that way).
With N -a'ker- snowflake:
enwà:keren'ne' it will snow,

òn:keren'ne' it snowed, **io'kerèn:'en**
it is snowing.
With N -hnek- liquid, and CISL:
tiohnekèn:'en there is a (small) waterfall.
With N -ia't- body, and TRNL:
ia'tià:ten'ne' I fell down or off,
iehoia'tèn:'en he has fallen down or off.
With N -itsker- spit, saliva: **iakótskeren's**
she is drooling, **wahótskeren'ne'** he
drooled.
With N -kahser- tears, and CISL:
takakáhseren'ne' the tears are falling
(maybe I hit something and tears form).
With N -nen't- evergreen: **kanèn:ten's**
tamarack, jack pine.
With N -nonhwe'rh- body hair, fuzz:
rononhwè:rhen's his hair is falling out,
he is shedding hair,
wahononhwè:rhen'ne' he shed hair.
With N -rahkw- sun, and TRNL:
ia'karáhkwen'ne' the sun went down;
and PROG -hatie-:
ó:nen wa'orahkwen'enhátie' the sun
is going down.
With N -wis- ice, glass, and CISL:
takawí:sen'ne' the glass fell.
NOTE: This stem is composed of a root
-a'sen-/-en-, which occurs only with suffixes, and INCH -'-.

-a'sen's-/-en's- V drop unintentionally:
waka'sèn:se' I drop it, **onkwà:sen'se'**
I dropped it, **wahò:sen'se'** he dropped it.
With N -athenno-/-athenno'tsher- ball:
onkwathennò:tsheren'se' I dropped
the ball.
With N -hstar- drop: **onkhstá:ren'se'**
I dropped a drop (for example, when I
was cooking a drop fell on the floor).
With N -neni- stone, rock:
onkenén:ien'se' I dropped the stone.
With N -'nonhkw- bottom of something,
and DLC: **wa'tewake'nónhkwen'se'**
my pants fell down.

With N -wis- ice, glass: **onkewí:sen's̉e'**
I dropped the glass.
NOTE: This stem is composed of a root
-a'sen-/-en-, which occurs only with suffixes, and BEN -'s-.

-a'ser- N blade, axe
With V -awenrie- stir: **a'serawénrie'**
stirring paddle (for taking cornbread
out of the water).
With V -onni- make: **O'serón:ni** French;
and ATTR =keha, way of: **O'seroni'kéha**
French language.

Cf. Kristoni asseroni Dutch (van den
Bogaert: 62); *Asera* hache, in comp.
(Bruyas: 28); *Aseronnige* des Europeans
(Bruyas: 72); *onseronni* les Français
(Bruyas: 80); *Aseronni* francais (Galissonnière: 43r); *Asseróni* Europaer (Pyrlaeus:
2v); *õnseronni* Francais (Marcoux: 179);
Onseronni francais ou descendant de
francais, litt., faisseur de haches (Cuoq:
69); *o se ron ni* french (Anon: 19);
O-se-ron-ni ne-ha French [language]
(Cory: 57); *aserawą'lyı'* Paddle (Waugh:
70); *ah seh ra wen ryeh* paddle (for stirring
soup) (Jamieson 2: 5); Onondaga *asseróni*
white[s] (Zeisberger: 229)

-a'shar- N knife: **à:share'**
With **iontkonhston'rhià:kstha'**
(-konhston'rh- beard, whiskers, -ia'k- cut):
iontkonhston'rhià:kstha' à:share' razor
blade.
With ATTR =kowa, great: **a'share'kó:wa**
sword, war chief.
With V -hio'thiie-/-o'thiie- be sharp,
pointy: **io'sharo'thí:ie'** (it is) a sharp
knife.
With V -ke- amount to, and DLC:
tewa'shá:rake two knives.
With V -ot- stand, and DISTR -onkw-:
wahiia'sharotón:ko' I stabbed him

(put the blade in and out several times).
With unclear V, and DLC: **teka'sharí:sas**
I am using scissors, **wa'tion'shá:rise'**
she used scissors; and SRF -at-:
tewata'sharí:sas scissors.

-a'sharo'[k]- V clap hands, with DLC:
teka'sháro'ks I clap my hands,
wa'tha'sháro'ke' he clapped,
wa'tion'sháro'ke' she clapped,
tewaka'sháro' I am clapping.
NOTE: This stem probably includes
-o'[k]- slap, flutter, flap.

-a'swaht- V extinguish a fire: **ka'swáhtha'**
I extinguish a fire, turn off the light,
ron'swáhtha' they extinguish, firemen,
enkà:swahte' I will turn off the light,
wa'kà:swahte' I turned off the light,
waka'swáhton I have turned off the light.
With ATTR ='ke, at: **ron'swahthà:ke** fire
station.

-a'swen't- coal. *See* -ahswen't-/-a'swen't-

-a'taniharon- V string: **ra'taníharons** he is
stringing them (for example, beads or popcorn), **wa'ka'taníharon'** I strung them.

-a'tarih[en]-/-tarih[en]- V be hot, warm:
io'taríhen it is hot, **waka'taríhens** I
get hot, **onkwa'taríhen'** I got hot,
waka'tarihèn:'en I am hot.
With CAUS -'t-: **ka'tarihà:tha'** I heat it,
enka'taríha'te' I will heat it,
enwa'taríha'te' it will get hot,
on'taríha'te' it got hot, **waka'tarihà:ton**
I have heated it; and DISTR -nion- and REP:
enska'tariha'tánion' I will reheat them
(for example, leftovers),
saka'tariha'tánion' I reheated them.
With CAUS -'t- and INSTR -hkw-:
ion'tariha'táhkhwa' forge.

With N -ahsont- night: **iohsontataríhen** it is a hot night.

With N -enhniser- day: **iawenhniserataríhen** it is a hot day.

With N -honro't- pipe, tube: **iohonro'tataríhen** the stove pipe is hot.

With N -ken'tstar- top part of the forehead: **wakken'tstarataríhen** my forehead is hot, **roken'tstarataríhen** his forehead is hot, **iakoken'tstarataríhen** her forehead is hot.

With NMZR -hser-, V -no- be cold, and CAUS -hst-: **wa'ka'tarihenhserá:nohste'** I got a cold, **waka'tarihenhseranóhston** I have a cold.

With N -nontar- soup, and CAUS -'t-: **wa'kenontarataríha'te'** I heated up the soup.

With N -nonw- bottom water, dregs: **iononwataríhen** (it is) warm water.

With NMZR -hser-, V -onko- penetrate, CAUS -ht-, and DLC: **teka'tarihenhseronkóhtha'** I am sweating, **wa'tha'tarihenhserón:kohte'** he got sweaty, **teiako'tarihenhseronkóhton** she has sweated.

With N -rist- iron, steel: **ioristataríhen** the stove or iron is hot.

With N -tsenh- fire: **iotsenhataríhen** it is a hot fire.

With N -wer- wind, air: **iowerataríhen** it is a warm wind.

-a'ther- N basket: **à:there'**

With **iontkéhtats** (-keht[e]- carry): **iontkéhtats à:there'** burden basket.

POSS: **akwà:there'** my basket.

With LOC -kon, inside: **a'thé:rakon** inside the basket.

With SRF -at- and V -hsa'-/-isa'- finish, complete: **wa'onta'therísa'** she finished (making) a basket.

With SRF -at-, V -hwe'nonni-/-kwe'nonni-fold, and DLC: **teiota'therakwe'nón:ni** (it is) a round basket.

With V -iio- be good, nice: **iako'therí:io** she has a nice basket, her basket is beautiful.

With V -ke- amount to, and DLC: **tewa'thé:rake** two baskets.

With V -kste- be heavy: **io'therákste'** (it is) a heavy basket.

With V -onni- make: **ion'therón:ni** she is making a basket; and SRF -at- and CAUS -'t-: **enhata'therónnia'te'** he will make a basket with it.

With V -[t]- be one, and REP: **sewa'thé:ra** one basket.

-a'tohser- N tent, cage: **a'tóhsera'**

With LOC -kon, inside: **a'tohserá:kon** in the tent, in the cage.

With SRF -at- and V -ot- stand: **ronta'tohserótha'** they are putting up a tent, **wa'kata'tohseró:ten'** I put up a tent.

B

barakén: corduroy

bararón: bullfrog

With **raotsì:tsa'** (-tsi'ts- flower): **bararón: raotsì:tsa'** pond lily.

Cf. wa-wa-ron ra-o-tsi-tsa Nuphar variegatum (=la fleur du ouaouaron) (Rousseau: 43)

E

-e- V walk, come, go: **í:ke'** I am walking, **ì:re'** he is walking, **í:ien'** she is walking, **tho nonkwá:ti wà:ke'** I am going over there, **tho nonkwá:ti wà:re'** he is going over there, **tho nonkwá:ti wà:'en'** she is going over there, **ì:re's** he is walking around, **wà:s** Go! Get going!
With NEG: **iah ken tè:re's** he isn't present, **iah ken té:ien's** she isn't present.
With PART: **Ka' nón: nì:re's?** Where is he?
With PART and PAST -kwe': **Ka' nón: nì:re'skwe'?** Where was he?
With CISL: **a'é:ren íthre's** he is over there, **éntke'** I will come, **tá:ke'** I am coming, I came, **tà:re'** he is coming, he came, **takón:ne'** they (female) are coming, **ká:ts** Come! **kásene** or **tásene** Come (du)! **kásewe** or **tásewe** Come (pl)!
With CISL and PAST -hne': **thawenónhne'** he has come over.
With CISL and PROG -hatie-: **ken nonkwá:ti tahawenonhátie'** he is coming this way, **ákta' taiawenonhátie'** it's coming closer.
With CISL and NEG: **iah ónhka tho tétien's** there's nobody there, **iah tho téthre's** he isn't there.
With CISL and DLC: **téntke'** I will come back, **tontahón:ne'** they are coming back.
With CISL and PART: **tho nontá:ke'** I came from there, **ka' nitiakawé:non** where she is (coming) from, **ken nonkwá: nontá:se** Come this way!
With TRNL: **tho nonkwá:ti ié:ke's** I am over there, **tho nonkwá:ti ién:ke'** I will go over there, **tho nonkwá:ti iehawé:non** he went that way, he has gone that way, **tho iahà:se** Go over there!
With TRNL and PAST -hne': **tho nonkwá:ti iewakenónhne'** I have gone that way.

With TRNL and PART: **tho niahà:ke'** I went that way.
With TRNL, PART and DLC: **Tó: nia'ténkene'?** How much will it go (sell) for? **Tó: niahà:tkene'?** How much did it go for?
• Kanonhsoharà:ke wà:ke'. I am going upstairs. • Onhontsó:kon (*or* Onhwentsó:kon) nontá:ke'. I came from the basement.
• Onhontsó:kon niahà:ke'. I went down to the basement. • Notsì:tsa' tsi nón: takón:ne' ne thí:ken ahskwen'naktóntie' kaiénthon. Flowers are coming up where they are planted all along the porch. (Letter 1945, Apr)

Cf. Enskat te8ennia8e kont (ou nikakontserāke iateionēnon [is going for] ne ken kanōnsŏte. Cette maison sa coute £100. (Marcoux 1828: 99) • *25 niwatokwatserake Ne iatenkene 25 cents* [25 spoons, it will go for 25 cents] (Granger: 2); Susquehannock *Kaatzie* come here (Holm: 6); Laurentian *Canada undagneny* whence come you? (Biggar: 245)

eh tho there, thus. *See* **e'thó:**

eh tho ní:ioht it is thus, it is so

eh tho nón:we there

-eharar- V have dandruff: **rawéharare'** he has dandruff, **iakawéharare'** she has dandruff.

-ehiahr- V remember: **kè:iahre'** I remember.
With NEG: **iah tekè:iahre'** I don't remember.
With INCH -'-: **kehià:ra's** I remember, **rehià:ra's** he remembers, **enkehià:ra'ne'** I will remember, **wa'kehià:ra'ne'** I

remembered, **wa'kheiehià:ra'ne'** I remembered her, **rawehiahrà:'on** he has remembered; and PAST -'ne': **wakehiahra'òn:ne'** I had remembered; and REP and NEG: **iah teskehià:ra's** I don't remember anymore.
With INSTR -hkw-, BEN -enni-/-en-, and REP: **tió:konte' shiiehiahrahkwén:ni** I am always reminding him, **enskoniehiahráhkwen'** I will remind you, **sakoniehiahráhkwen'** I reminded you, **sahakwehiahráhkwen'** he reminded me.
With REFL -atat- and INSTR -hkw-: **iontatehiahráhkhwa'** memorial.

-ehiahron- V raise a child: **enkheiehià:ron'** I will raise her, **wahakehià:ron'** he raised me.
With PROG -tie-: **riiehiahróntie'** I am raising him, **kheiehiahróntie'** I am raising her.
With SRF -at-: **enkatehià:ron'** I will grow up, **wahatehià:ron'** he grew up, **rotehià:ron** he has grown up; and PROG -tie-: **rotehiahróntie'** he is growing up, **iakotehiahróntie'** she is growing up, **iotehiahróntie'** it is growing, **ionatehiahróntie'** they are growing.
With SRF -ate-, N -'nikonhr- mind, and SRF -at-: **wahate'nikonhratehià:ron'** his mind expanded, he matured.
• Ionatehiahróntie' ne kaienthóhsera'. The plants (vegetables) are growing.

-ehnhonsa' KIN in-law, different generations: **rakwehnhónsa'** my father-in-law, **ionkwehnhónsa'** my mother-in-law, **riiehnhónsa'** my son-in-law,
With REFL -atat-: **rontatehnhónsa'** they are in-laws.
NOTE: This term is used when the younger member in the in-law relation is male; for example: **ionkwehnhónsa'** my mother-

in-law (man speaking), **riiehnhónsa'** my son-in-law (woman speaking). See Deering and Delisle: 31–35, Horne: 4–9.

-ehr- V think, want: **í:kehre'** I think so, I want to, **íhsehre'** you think so, you want to, **ì:rehre'** he think so, he wants to, **í:ienhre'** she thinks so, she wants to, **ítenehre'** you and I want to, **rón:nehre'** they want to, **wà:kehre'** I thought.
With NEG: **iah té:kehre'** I do not want to.
With SRF -at- (and possibly short form of **ok** just?): **wahá:tehrek** he took advantage of the moment.
• Tió:konte' ì:rehre' enthanónhton'. He always wants to get his way. • Wahá:tehrek ahatè:ko'. First chance he got he ran away.

-ehrhit- V be a tree: **kéhrhite'** there is a tree. (See Lounsbury (1960: 50) for the exceptional *k-* prefix.)
With DISTR -on-: **kehrhí:ton** there are trees.
Cf. Gerhit arbre de bout (Bruyas: 89); *kērhĭte* Arbre, debout (Marcoux: 20); *Kerhite* pl. *kerhiton* arbre fruitier (Cuoq: 20); Wendat *Yharhy* arbre (Sagard: Pll); Wyandot *ká:rhi* tree (Barbeau 1960: 146)

-ehsak-/-ihsak-/-esak-/-isak- V look for: **kéhsaks** or **ké:saks** I am looking for it, **réhsaks** he is looking for it, **iakéhsaks** she is looking for it, **enkéhsake'** or **enké:sake'** I will look for it, **wa'kéhsake'** or **wa'ké:sake'** I looked for it, **wakehsá:kon** or **wakesá:kon** I have looked for it.
With PURP -h-: **wa'kesákhe'** I am going looking for it.
With N -ia't- body: **kheia'tíhsaks** or **kheia'tí:saks** I am looking for her, I miss her, **wahiia'tíhsake'** or **wahiia'tí:sake'** I

looked for him, I missed him,
riia'tihsá:kon or **riia'tisá:kon** I have
looked for him, I have missed him.
With N -karien't- carcass:
wa'kkarien'tíhsake' I looked for the
carcass.
With SRF -ate-, N -nakt- bed, place, and
PURP -h-: **wahatenaktisákha'** he went
looking for a place or spot.
With SRF -at-, N -onhnh- life, and PURP
-h-: **wa'katonhnhisákhe'** I am going
looking for work, **wa'katonhnhisákha'**
I went to look for work; and PAST -hne':
rotonhnhisakhónhne' he has gone looking for work.
With N -rihw- matter, message:
wa'kerihwí:sake' I searched for information.
NOTE: The first and third variants, -ehsak-
and -esak-, occur in the basic aspect forms
with some speakers having -ehsak- and
some -esak-. With incorporated nouns,
some speakers use -ihsak- and some use
-isak-. The forms -esak- and -isak- occur
before the PURP -h-.

éhsa' black ash

-eht- V go somewhere: **é:ren kéhtha'** I go
away from here, **é:ren én:kehte'** I will
go away, **é:ren wà:rehte'** he went away,
é:ren í:seht Go away, get away!
With CISL: **ohén:ton tà:rehte'** he came
forward, **ohén:ton tá:ienhte'** she came
forward.
With PART and CISL: **ken nonkwá:
nontà:rehte'** he came this way,
ken nonkwá: nontá:ienhte' she came
this way.
With REP: **ohnà:ken sà:rehte'** he went
backward.
With INSTR -hkw- and TRNL; and **átste'**
outside: **átste' ieienhtáhkhwa'** outhouse,
bathroom.

NOTE: This stem is probably composed
of -e- walk, go, and a suffix -ht- which
looks like the CAUS.

-ehtahkw- V believe, with CISL:
tkehtáhkhwa' I believe it,
tkoniehtáhkhwa' I believe you,
enthiiéhtahkwe' I will believe him,
tahréhtahkwe' he believed it,
thawehtáhkwen he has believed it.
With PAST -'ne': **thiiehtahkwèn:ne'**
I did believe him (but no longer).

ehta'kéhshon on foot

-ek-/-ak- V eat: **í:keks** I eat it, **íhseks** you
(sg) eat it, **ì:raks** he eats it, **í:ienks** she
or someone eats it, **í:waks** she or it eats it,
énteneke' you and I will eat it, **wà:keke'**
I ate it, **ón:wake'** she or it ate it,
waké:kon I have eaten it.
With **takwa'áhson** spider:
takwa'áhson í:waks cancer.
With N -ahi- berry, fruit: **wa'kà:iake'**
I ate fruit.
With N -hneht- pine: **rohnehtá:kon** he is
chewing, **iakohnehtá:kon** she is chewing,
shnéhtak Be quiet! *Used when someone
is saying something silly or stupid.*
With N -nenhst- corn: **kenénhstaks** I eat
corn, **wakenenhstá:kon** I am eating corn.
With SRF -a- and N -nen't- evergreen:
anèn:taks porcupine.
With N -ront- log, beam: **Atirón:taks**
Ojibwe.
With N -tsi'non[ht]- louse, lice:
katsi'nónhtaks monkey; and ATTR
=kowa, great: **katsi'nonhtakskó:wa**
gorilla.

-eka'[w]-/-ka'[w]- V find tasty, like the taste
of: **waké:ka's** I find it tasty, I like the
taste of it, **enwaké:ka'we'** I will find it
tasty, **onké:ka'we'** I found it tasty,

wakekà:'on I have found it tasty,
iawékon' it is delicious, yummy.
With PAST -kwe': **waké:ka'skwe'** I used
to like it.
With PAST -'ne': **iawekon'òn:ne'** it was
delicious.
With N -ahkar- wood chips, shavings:
wahkarákon' cinnamon.
With N -enser- smell, scent: **wenserákon'**
it smells good.
With N -hont- green: **kahontákon'** sweetgrass.
With N -hwa'tst- foam, and REP:
tsohwà:tstaka'we' seagull.
With SRF -at-, N -ia't- body, and CAUS
-hst-: **wakatia'takon'ónhston** I have
on perfume; and INSTR -hkw-:
iontia'takon'onhstáhkhwa' perfume.
With N -iie-/-ien- oil, grease (variant
-enien-) and CAUS -st-: **wenienakà:stha'**
it (a car) takes a lot of gas.
With N -nontar- soup: **kanontarákon'**
it is delicious soup.
With N -shes[t]- syrup: **kashestákon'**
it is tasty syrup.
• **Waké:ka's ne kahrhata'kéha á:keke'.**
I like to eat blueberries.

-en- say. *See* -aton-/-ihron-/-en-

-en- V happen, with PART: **tsi niiá:wens** the
way it happens, **tsi neniá:wen'** how it will
happen, **tsi na'á:wen'** what happened,
tsi niiawèn:'en the way it has happened,
e'thó: naiá:wen' or **eh tho naiá:wen'** As
it is! Amen!
With ATTR =tsi, intensifier, and CONTR and
CISL: **thontaiawénhstsi** all of a sudden.
With N -ia't- body: **tsi niwatià:tawens**
what is happening to me, what is wrong
with me.

è:neken up, above, **è:neken nonkwá:ti**
west, **è:neken tiótte'** it is high

-enhahs- V call (bad) names, call down:
wahawénhahse' he called him names, put
him down, **wa'onkwénhahse'** she called
me names, put me down.

-enha[w]- hold, bring, take. *See* -ha[w]-/
-enha[w]-

-enhawi- carry. *See* -hawi-/-enhawi-

-enhei[on]- die. *See* -ihei[on]-/-enhei[on]-

-enhetsh- N sausage: **awenhétsha'** sausage.
With **tewa'arawèn:'e** (-a'ar- net,
-hwawen'e[k]-/-awen'e[k]- wrap):
tewa'arawèn:'e awenhétsha' farmer's
sausage.
With **onekwénhsa'** (-nekwenhs- blood):
onekwénhsa' awenhétsha' blood sausage.

-enhniser- N day: **awenhnísera'**
With SRF -at-, V -akaion-/-kaion- be old,
and CAUS -hst-: **katenhniserakaiónhstha'**
I waste the day (daydreaming, dilly-
dallying), **wa'ontenhniseraká:ionhste'**
she frittered away the time.
With V -a'tarih[en]-/-tarih[en]- be hot,
warm: **iawenhniserataríhen** it is a hot
day.
With V -es- be long, tall, and PART:
tsi niwenhníseres during the day.
With V -iio- be good, nice: **wenhniserí:io**
(it is) a nice day.
With V -ke- amount to, and PART, TRNL,
and DLC, or CONTR, TRNL, and DLC:
nia'tewenhniserá:ke or
thia'tewenhniserá:ke every day.
With V -kwek- be the whole of:
enhniserakwé:kon all day.
With V -no- be cold: **iawenhniserá:no**
it is a cold day; and PART:
tsi niiawenhniserá:no it is a really cold
day; with V -no- be cold, and CAUS -hst-:

enwenhniserá:nohste' the day will cool off.

With V -nonhiani- be extreme, menacing, drastic, and DLC: **teiawenhniseranòn:iani** it is really drastic weather (raining, snowing, windy).

With SRF -at-, V -o'kt- finish, BEN -hahs-, and CISL: **tonkwatenhniserò:kthahse'** the day was not long enough for me.

With V -te- be present, exist: **òn:wa wenhniserá:te'** today; and DISTR -nion-: **wenhniseraténion** daily, every day.

-enhni't- N moon, month: **awenhnì:ta'** month.

With **akhsótha** (-hsot- grandparent): **akhsótha awenhnì:ta'** moon, but note that **ahsonthénhkha karáhkwa'** (-ahsonthen- midnight, -rahkw- sun) is heard more often.

POSS: **akawenhnì:ta'** her moon time, her monthly (period).

With V -ahset- count, and CAUS -'t-: **iakenhni'tahsetà:tha'** calendar.

With V -ihen- be in the middle of, and COIN and DLC: **sha'tewenhni'tí:hen** middle of the month.

With V -ke- amount to, and DLC: **tewenhnì:take** two months.

With SRF -at- and V -o'kt- finish: **ontenhni'tò:kten'** the month ended, the end of the month.

With V -[t]- be one, DISTR -hshon-, and REP: **sewenhni'tátshon** each month, monthly.

-enhsion- V look well-dressed, elegant, well-to-do: **rawénhsion** he is well-dressed, elegant, **iakawénhsion** she is well-dressed, elegant. Based on French *monsieur*.

With SRF -at- and CAUS -hst-: **wakatenhsiónhston** I am trying to be elegant (like I come from the right side of the tracks).

Cf. Rawension vel *Rawensie* monsieur, un monsieur, un bourgeois. Mot tiré du francais. (Cuoq: 39); *sién:shion, rawén:shie* sir (Gabriel: 121)

-enht- drop. *See* -a'senht-/-enht-

-enien- oil, grease. *See* -iie-/-ien-

enká:r one quarter. A borrowing from French *un quart.*
 • Enká:r shé:kon í:wa wà:io ne katshè:ta-kon. A quarter (amount) of jam is still in the jar.

-ennakahr-/-ennakarere- V whistle: **kenná:kahre'** I whistle, **renná:kahre'** he is whistling, **iakenná:kahre'** she is whistling, **wenná:kahre'** it whistles, **wahrenná:kahre'** he whistled, **kennakaré:re's** I am going about, whistling.
 • Wenná:kahre' ne ówera'. The wind is whistling.

-enneker- hay. *See* -neker-/-enneker-

énnekoks or **ánekoks** buckwheat. Probably from English *pancakes.*

Cf. on noh gohk buckwheat (Jamieson 1: 6); compare *Otskenrah* buckwheat (Onkweonwe: 4)

-enniser- N shelf

With V -her-/-hr- set on top of: **wenniseráhere'** (there is) a shelf, a mantel; and DISTR -onnion-: **wenniserahrónnion** there are shelves here and there.

Cf. Ennisera échaffaut, *Enniserare* il y a un échaffaut (Bruyas: 109); *Enniserare*

Eschaffaut (Galissonnière: 35v);
ꝸenniserāhĕre echafaud (Marcoux: 136);
Ennisera échafaud (Cuoq: 4)

-enniseren'- V sigh, with CISL:
tahawenníseren'ne' he sighed,
taiakawenníseren'ne' she sighed.

Enníska February
With ATTR =kowa, great: **Enniskó:wa**
March.
Cf. En^cniska Janvier, *En^cniksò* febvrir
(Galissonnière: 53r); *enniska* février,
enniskoꝸa mars (Marcoux: 257); *Enniska*
February (Granger: 6); *Enniskowa* March
(Granger: 7); *Enníska* [February],
Enniskó:wa [March] (Calendar 1979)

-enser- N smell, scent: **awénsera'**
With V -akera- stink, smell: **wenserákeras**
it smells bad.
With V -eka'[w]-/-ka'[w]- find tasty, like
the taste of: **wenserákon'** it smells good.
With V -ien- put down, have:
iawenserá:ien' it has a smell to it.
With V -iio- be good, nice: **wenserí:io**
it smells good.

énska one, **énska iawén:re** eleven,
tewáhsen énska twenty-one,
énska tewen'niáwe one hundred,
énska'k only one.
Cf. Skat un (Bruyas: 27); *Skat* 1 (Galissonnière: 59v); *ēnskat* Un (Marcoux: 405);
Enskat un (Cuoq: 85); Laurentian *Segada*
One (Biggar: 241); Wendat *Escate* 1
(Sagard: No1); Susquehannock *Onskat*
one (Holm: 7)

-ent- N day
With LOC -akta', near: **Entákta'** Saturday.
With V -ahset- count, and CAUS -'t-:
iakentahsetà:tha' almanac.

With V -ati-/-onti- lose, throw, and CAUS
-ht-: **onkwentóntiehte'** I fasted, I went
without, **rawentontiéhton** he has fasted;
and PART: **Tsi niiakawentontiéhtha'**
Lent.
With V -ent- wear out, end, INCH -'-, and
ATTR ='ke, at: **Awententa'ón'ke**
Monday.
With V -hawi-/-enhawi- carry, CAUS -ht-,
and CISL: **Thentenhawíhtha'** Venus.
With V -hroh[o]- block, put across (as a
barrier) and DLC and CISL:
tontawentahróho' (it is) early dawn (the
sun is just below the horizon).
With V -iio- be good, nice: **wentí:io** (it is)
a nice day.
With V -na'nawen-/-nawen- be wet:
iawentaná:wen it is a mild day.
With V -tokenhti- be holy, and ATTR ='ke,
at: **Awentatokenhtì:ke** Sunday.
NOTE: An obscure form of this root occurs,
with the PART, in **nón:ta** so many nights or
days, for example, Tó: nón:ta rohténtion?
How many nights or days was he gone? or
Tó: nón:ta tsi náhe'? How long ago?
Cf. entākta Samedi (Marcoux: 355);
Entakta [Saturday] (Granger: 4); *en tak ta*
saturday (Anon: 6); *en-tak-ta* Saturday
(Cory: 71); *kaieri niꝸasontasen iakaꝸen-
tontiēta* careme [Lent] (Marcoux: 56);
Tsi iakowentontiéhtha' Lent (Horne: 52)

-ent- V wear out, end
With N -ent- day, INCH -'-, and ATTR ='ke,
at: **Awententa'ón'ke** Monday.
With N -hwist- metal, money, and INCH -'-:
wa'kahwistén:ta'ne' it (the telephone,
bells) stopped ringing.
With N -khw- food, and INCH -'-:
kekhwén:ta's I finish eating,
eniekhwén:ta'ne' she will finish eating,
wa'kekhwén:ta'ne' I finished eating,
rokhwentà:'on he has finished eating.

With N -rihw- matter, message, and
INCH -'-: **karihwén:ta's** it wears out,
enkarihwén:ta'ne' it will wear out,
wa'karihwén:ta'ne' it wore out,
iorihwentà:'on it has worn out; with
N -rihw- matter, message, and CAUS
-ho-: **wa'kerihwéntho'** I wore it out.
With SRF -ate-, V -rio-/-riio- beat up, kill,
NMZR -hser-, and INCH -'-:
onteriiohserén:ta'ne' the war ended.
With N -tsenh- fire, and INCH -'-:
wa'katsenhén:ta'ne' the fire is out, the
meeting is over.
With N -weienn- manner, and INCH -'-:
wa'keweiennén:ta'ne' I got it ready, I
finished doing it, **wa'eweiennén:ta'ne'**
she got it ready, **roweiennentà:'on** he is
getting it ready, **kaweiennentà:'on** it is
ready, it is done; and SRF -ate-:
enwateweiennén:ta'ne' it will get
finished, it will be over,
onteweiennén:ta'ne' it got finished; and
REFL -atate-: **ratateweiennén:ta's** he gets
ready, **wa'katateweiennén:ta'ne'** I got
ready.
• Aiá:wens ki' iohsnó:re' ne aonteriiohse-
rén:ta'ne' ne Japan. Hopefully war with
Japan will end soon. (Letter 1945, June)

Cf. aꞵententahōnke Lundi (Marcoux: 233);
Awententaonke [Monday] (Granger: 4);
a wen ta ta on ke monday (Anon: 6);
a-wen-ta-ta-on-ke Monday (Cory: 71)

-ente- V be daylight: **wén:te'** it is daylight.
With INCH -'-: **enwén:te'ne'** it is beginning to be daylight; and PROG -hatie-:
iawente'onhátie' or (with CISL)
taiawente'onhátie' the sun is coming
up, it is becoming daylight.

éntie nikahá:wi' it is 12 o'clock,
éntie ní:kare' (it is) noon time, lunch,
12 o'clock, **éntie nonkwá:ti** south.

Cf. Kafee, tii. Entie Nonkwati Nitionenon.
[Coffee, Tea. Having come from the
south.] (Granger: 2)

-enton[hw]- V move back and forth, with DLC
With SRF -ar- and N -ahsi't- foot:
wa'tkarahsi'tén:tonhwe' I moved my
foot back and forth.
With SRF -at- and N -ho'kw- buttocks:
teiontho'kwén:tons she is wiggling her
bum, **wa'tiontho'kwén:tonhwe'** she
wiggled her bum.
With N -ien'kwar- smoke:
wa'thaien'kwarén:tonhwe' he (the
priest) moved the thurible (incense burner)
back and forth.
With SRF -an- and N -itahs- tail:
tehanitahsén:tons he is moving his tail
back and forth, he is waving or wagging
his tail, **wa'thanitahsén:tonhwe'** he
waved or wagged his tail.
With SRF -a- and N -nentsh- arm:
wa'tionnentshén:tonhwe' she moved
her arm back and forth.

-entonni- V be lonesome, lonely: **kentón:nis**
I am lonesome, **rentón:nis** he is lonesome, **iakentón:nis** she is lonesome,
wa'kentón:ni' I got lonesome,
wahrentón:ni' he got lonesome,
wa'akentón:ni' she got lonesome.
With CAUS -t-: **iawentónnia** it is lonesome.
• Iawentónnia nòn:wa ne átste' ioron-
hió:ron. It's lonesome, now it's gloomy
(cloudy, overcast) outside. • Iawentónnia
ne kèn:tho nòn:wa tsi niiawenhniserá:no.
It's lonesome here when the days are cold.
(Letter 1945, Apr)

Cf. Entonni s'ennuyer, *Jaꞵenthônniat*
O qu'il ennuye bien ici! (Bruyas: 112);
Entonni Sennuyer (Galissonnière: 34v);
kentōnnis S'ennuyer (Marcoux: 149);

Kentonnis s'ennuyer, trouver le temps
long (Cuoq: 19)

-entor- V be lazy: **kentóhrha'** I am lazy,
rentóhrha' he is lazy, **iakentóhrha'**
she is lazy, **enkentó:ren'** I will be lazy,
wahrentó:ren' he got lazy.
With INCH -'-: **wakentorà:'on** I have
become lazy.

-entor[e]- V be difficult: **wentó:re'** it is
difficult or hard.
With NEG: **iah tewentó:re'** it is not
difficult.
With CONT -k-: **enwentó:reke'** it will
be difficult.
With INCH -en'-: **enwentó:ren'ne'** it will
become difficult, **ontó:ren'ne'** it became
difficult.
With CAUS -hst-: **wahrentó:rahste'** he
became difficult, **wa'akentó:rahste'**
she became difficult.
With CAUS -hst- and INCH -'-:
ontoráhsta'ne' it was made difficult,
it got difficult.
With BEN -'s-: **wakentorà:se'** I am
having a hard time.
• Wentó:re' tsi nikaio'tenhserò:ten.
It's hard the kind of work it is.

-entshot- V kneel, with DLC: **tekéntshote'**
I am kneeling, **tehréntshote'** he is kneeling, **teiakéntshote'** she is kneeling.
With SRF -at-: **tekatentshótha'** I go on
my knees, **tenkatentshó:ten'** I will kneel
down, **wa'tiontentshó:ten'** she knelt
down; and INSTR -hkw-:
teiontentshotáhkhwa' kneeler, prayer
bench (in front of the coffin at a wake,
or before an altar or pew).
With INCH -'- and TRNL:
ia'tkentshó:ta'ne' I fell onto my knees;
and DISTR -seron-: **ia'tkentshotà:seron'**
I went or fell down on (both) my knees.

NOTE: This stem is composed of -ot- stand,
and an incorporated noun -entsh- knee. A
similar root (-ontsh-) is attested in Galissonnière (*Ontsa* Genou, 45v) and Cuoq
(*Ontsa* genou, fémur, 35) and in Oneida
(-utsh- knee). *See* -kwitsh- for the root
used today.

-entskwe'n- N chest: **otskwè:na'**
POSS: **kentskwe'nà:ke** (on) my chest,
rentskwe'nà:ke (on) his chest,
iakentskwe'nà:ke (on) her chest.
With V -nonhwak[t]- be sore, hurt:
wakentskwe'nanòn:waks my chest hurts,
iakotskwe'nanòn:waks or
iakawentskwe'nanòn:waks her chest
hurts.
With V -ont- attach; and **oronhia'kó:wa
atháhsteren** jeans (-ronhi- sky, blue,
-athahsteren- put on pants, trousers):
**oronhia'kó:wa atháhsteren
iawentskwè:nonte'** overalls.

-en'- fall down. *See* -a'sen'-/-en'-

-en'awi- float, drift. *See* -a'awi-/-en'awi-

-en'nahs- N tongue: **awen'náhson**
POSS: **akwen'náhson** my tongue,
ken'nahsà:ke (on) my tongue,
rawen'náhson his tongue,
akawen'náhson her tongue.
With V -es- be long: **sen'náhses** you have
a long tongue.
With SRF -at-, V -ke'tot- protrude, and
CISL: **tkaten'nahsake'tótha'** I stick out,
show my tongue, **takaten'nahsake'tó:ten'**
I stuck out my tongue,
thoten'nahsakè:tote' he has his tongue
sticking out.
With SRF -at- and V -otshi- burn oneself:
wa'katen'nahsótshi' I burned my tongue.
Cf. Ennasa langue (Bruyas: 108);

Ga8ennasa langue (Galissonnière: 23r);
ennāsa, a8ennāsa Langue (Marcoux: 227);
Ennasa langue (Cuoq: 3, 83);
a wen nha son tongue (Anon: 3);
enh nah sah tongue (Jamieson 3: 3); Laurentian *Esnache* the tongue (Biggar: 241);
Wendat *Dachia* la langue (Sagard: Me3);
Onondaga *hônacha* Langue (Shea: 66)

-en'niawe- V hundred, with DLC:
tewen'niáwe hundred,
énska tewen'niáwe one hundred,
oié:ri tewen'niáwe one thousand.
With an ending -k-, and DISTR -hon-:
tewen'niawe'ékhon hundreds.
With SRF -at-: **tehoten'niáwe** he is 100,
teiakoten'niáwe she is 100.

Cf. Ennia8e cent (Bruyas: 109); *skat te8ennia8e* Cent (Galissonnière: 16v);
Hoskat t'owánnìauwe 100 (Pyrlaeus: 11r);
Huskat-Tunihyowy 100 (Weiser: 386);
Uskat Towaniyawe C. (Primer: 95);
Ounskut Towwaunowwau 100 (Hawley: 137); *enskat te8ennia8e* cent (Marcoux: 59); *te8ennia8e ou enskat te8ennia8e* 100 (Cuoq 1866: 133); *En-ska-de-wen-nya-weh* 100 (Oronhyatekha: 6); *enska te wen nia we* 100 (D'Ailleboust: 18); *én-skā te-wen-nia-we* 100 (Cory: 39); *enhs gah deh wenh nya wehr* 100 (Jamieson 1: 3); *tewen'niawe'ékhon* hundreds (many) (Lazore: 6); *Énska tewen'niáwe ...* One hundred (100) ... (Horne: 107)

-en's- drop unintentionally. *See -a'sen's-/-en's-*

-en't- hang down. *See -hren't-/-en't-*

-erahs- N moss: **aweráhsa'**
With V -r- put in: **iaweráhsare'** it has moss on it.

Cf. A8enra Mousse (Galissonnière: 58r);
a8enrāsa Mousse (Marcoux: 255);
Awenrasa mousse (Cuoq: 3); *a-we-ra-sa* Myriophyllum exalbescens [northern watermilfoil] (Rousseau: 51); Wendat *Einra* Mousse (Sagard: Pl2); *enra dic a8enra* mousse sur les arbres (Potier: 454)

é:ren away, **é:ren nón:we** elsewhere. For example: **é:ren í:seht** Go away, get away!

è:rhar dog

é:ri cherry
Cf. Eri Cerise (Galissonnière: 8v, 43v);
hēri Mérisier (Marcoux: 246); *Eri* cérise de France (Cuoq: 4); *e ri* cherry (Anon: 7); *eri* Prunus serotina (Rousseau: 46); *erih go wah* cherry (Jamieson 1: 6)

-eri[ahs]- N heart: **awé:ri** heart; also suit of hearts in cards.
POSS: **akwé:ri** or **akwerià:ne** my heart,
rawé:ri or **rawerià:ne** his heart,
akawé:ri or **akawerià:ne** her heart.
With V -hnir- be hard, solid, firm:
raweriahsahní:ron he is hard-hearted, cruel.
With V -hri'- get broken into pieces, shatter, and DLC: **teiakaweriahsahrì:'on** she has a broken heart.
With V -ishonhkw- quake, tremble, and DLC: **tewakeriahsishónhkhwa'** my heart is racing, beating fast,
tehaweriahsishónhkhwa' his heart is racing, **wa'tewakeriahsíshonhkwe'** I had a heart attack, **wa'tiakaweriahsíshonhkwe'** she got a heart attack.
With V -o'ka't- run into, bump against, and CISL: **tonkweriahsò:ka'te'** it touched me, it went right to my heart.

-erien't- N disposition

With SRF -at-, V -awenrie- stir, and DLC:
tekaterien'tawénrie's I make mistakes,
wa'tkaterien'tawénrie' I made a mistake, **teiakorien'tawenriè:'on** she has
made a mistake.

With V -iio- be good, nice: **wakerien'tí:ios**
I am satisfied, **onkwerien'tí:io'** I became
satsified, **wahawerien'tí:io'** he became
satsified.

With SRF -at-, V -kari- bite, and DLC:
tekaterien'takárias I get irritated,
annoyed, it gets on my nerves,
wa'tkaterien'taká:ri' I got irritated,
annoyed, **tewakaterien'takária** I am
noisy, **teiakoterien'takária** she is noisy,
teioterien'takária it is noisy (for example, cars going by at night); and CAUS -ht-:
wa'thaterien'takáriahte' he made noise,
tehoterien'takariáhton he is making
noise.

With SRF -at- and V -r- put in:
wakaterièn:tare' I know, **roterièn:tare'**
he knows, **iakoterièn:tare'** she knows;
and NEG: **iah tewakaterièn:tare'** I don't
know; with SRF -at-, V -r- put in, and INCH
-'-: **enwakaterièn:tara'ne'** I will know,
onkwaterièn:tara'ne' I found out, I
discovered, **wakaterien'tarà:'on** I have
found out.

With SRF -at- and V -tshenri- find:
wa'katerien'tatshén:ri' I got an idea;
and FACIL -'tskon, easily:
wakaterien'tatshenriè:tskon I am
creative.

• Onkwerien'tí:io' nahò:ten' wa'kateriserihá:ren'. I am satisifed with what I
got for Christmas. • Onkwaterièn:tara'ne'
nahò:ten' rotiri'wahséhton. I found out
what their secret is.

-es- V be long, tall, high, deep: **í:iens**
it is long.
With PART and TRNL: **kheh nié:iens**
(it is) a long piece.

With N -ahi- fruit, berry: **shà:iese'** or
shà:iase' thimbleberry.
With N -ahonht- ear, and DLC:
tewahónhtes donkey, **tehahónhtes**
he is up to no good, he is doing something
he is not supposed to (for example, cheating on his wife), **teionhónhtes** she is up
to no good. *This is an old expression.*
With N -ahsarahkw- cuff of a shoe or
mocassin, and DLC: **teiohsaráhkwes**
high top shoes or boots.
With N -ahsi't- foot, and DLC:
tekahsi'té:son's I have long feet.
With N -ahsont- night, and PART:
tsi niwahsón:tes during the night.
With N -athenno-/-athenno'tsher- ball:
wathennò:tsheres (it is) a long ball,
a football.
With N -a'kotar- Achilles tendon, and
DLC: **teha'kó:tares** he has long feet.
With N -enhniser- day, and PART:
tsi niwenhníseres during the day.
With N -en'nahs- tongue: **sen'náhses**
you have a long tongue.
With N -hahser- light, lamp: **kaháhseres**
(it is) a long mass.
With N -hneni- applied to animates:
khnén:ies I am tall, **rahnén:ies** he is tall,
iehnén:ies she is tall.
With N -hnia's- neck, collar, and ATTR
=kowa, great: **kahnia'seskó:wa** giraffe;
with SRF -at-, N -hnia's- neck, collar, and
CAUS -t-: **wahathnià:seste'** he stretched
his neck, **wakathnia'séston** I am stretching my neck.
With N -hnot- indicating depth: **iohnó:tes**
it is deep; and N -nieht- snow:
ioniehtahnó:tes it is deep snow; and N
-rat- heel, and DLC: **teioratahnó:tes** high-
heeled shoes.
With N -hs- indicating high sides, and DLC:
teióhses it is high (anything with high
sides, such as boots or cans).
With N -hsin- leg, and DLC: **tekhsiné:son's**

I have long legs; and **atháhsteren** (-athahsteren- put on pants, trousers): **tekahsí:nes atháhsteren** long pants.

With N -htehr- root, and REP: **tsohtè:rese'** sarsaparilla.

With N -iahia'khser- week, and PART: **tsi niiahià:khseres** during the week.

With N -ia'kar-/-ia'kwar- midriff, and DLC: **tetià:kares** I am long-waisted, **teieià:kares** she is long-waisted; and PART: **Tó: na'tehsià:kares?** How long is it to your waist (from your shoulder)?

With N -ihwhar- fur: **iohwhá:res** (it is) long-haired fur, **rohwhá:res** he has long fur.

With N -itahs- tail: **rentáhses** he has a long tail.

With N -i'tsonhkw- jump, stride, and DLC: **teki'tsónhkwes** I jump far, **tehen'tsónhkwes** he jumps far, **teie'tsónhkwes** she jumps far.

With N -kahreht- eyelash, and DLC: **tehokahrehté:son's** he has long eye-lashes, **teiakokahrehté:son's** she has long eyelashes.

With N -konhs- face, and REP: **tsikónhses** pike.

With N -konhston'rh- beard, whiskers, and DLC: **tehokonhstòn:rhes** he has a long beard, **teiotikonhstòn:rhes** barley.

With N -konwar- falseface, face, and PART: **nikakón:wares** it has a long face (talking about an animal, maybe a horse or moose).

With N -nakar- stick: **kanaká:res** (it is) a long stick.

With N -na'kar- horn, antler, and DLC: **teiotinà:kares** oxen.

With N -na'tkar- bluff, slope, and DLC: **tekanà:tkares** (it is) a steep slope or hill.

With N -nenhr- crowd, and DLC: **tekanèn:res** square dance.

With N -nennawen['t]- tobacco pipe: **kanennawèn:tes** (it is) a long pipe.

With N -nonhkwis[er]- head hair: **rotinonhkwíseres** "the long-haired ones," a conservative group in Kanehsatà:ke; and SRF -ate- and CAUS -t-: **wa'katenonhkwísereste'** I let my hair grow.

With N -nonhs- house: **kanónhses** long-house.

With N -nont- hill, mountain: **ionón:tes** (it is) a high mountain.

With N -non'onser- squash: **kanon'ónseres** cucumber, zucchini.

With N -ohser- winter, year, and PART: **tsi niióhseres** during the winter.

With N -ratsken't- braid: **roratskèn:tes** he has a long braid, **iakoratsken'té:son's** she has long braids.

With N -rihw- matter, message: **rorì:wes** he is taking a long time, **iakorì:wes** she is taking a long time; with N -rihw- matter, message, and NEG: **iah tekarì:wes** not long (after), it won't be long; with N -rihw- matter, message, and PART: **tsi nikarì:wes** while.

With N -sto'kw- beak: **rastò:kwes** his beak is long, **kastò:kwes** stork.

With N -tsi'er- fingernail, and DLC: **tektsi'eré:son's** I have long nails; and ATTR =kowa, great: **tekatsi'ereskó:wa** eagle.

With N -wenn- voice, word: **kawén:nes** (it is) a long word.

With N -'khah- step, and DLC: **teha'khahé:son's** he has long strides.

With N -'kohs- tail of a bird: **ro'kóhses** he is wearing a long coat, a trench coat; **iako'kóhses** she is wearing a long coat.

With N -'nionkwarist- snout: **ra'nionkwarístes** he has a long snout.

With N -'whar- tunnel, hollow: **ka'whá:res** (it is) a long hall.

With ATTR ='a/=ha, diminutive, *see* -esha- be short.

-esak- look for. *See* -ehsak-/-ihsak-/-esak-/
-isak-

-esha- V be short, with particle **ken'** and
PART: **ken' niiénsha** it is short.
With N -hnot- indicating depth:
ken' niiohnotésha it is shallow.
With N -honr- gun: **ken' nikahonrésha**
handgun, pistol.
With N -hont- green: **ken' niiohontésha**
strawberry; and **teiontenonhwerá:tons**
(-nonhweraton- greet, give thanks):
**Teiontenonhwerá:tons ken' niio-
hontésha** Strawberry Festival; and ATTR
=kowa, great: **ken' niiohontesha'kó:wa**
pineapple.
With N -hs- indicating high sides, and
DLC: **ken' na'teiohsésha** it is low-sided,
(for example, talking about loafers or low-
topped shoes).
With N -hsin- leg; and **atháhsteren**
(-athahsteren- put on pants, trousers):
ken' na'tekahsinésha atháhsteren
shorts.
With N -ia'kar-/-ia'kwar- midriff, and DLC:
ken' na'tetia'karésha I am short-waisted.
With N -itahs- tail: **ken' nihentahsésha** he
has a short tail.
With N -nentsh- arm, and DLC; and
atià:tawi (-atia'tawi- dress, shirt):
ken' na'tekanentshésha atià:tawi short-
sleeved shirt.
NOTE: This stem is composed of -es- be
long, tall, high, deep, and ATTR ='a/=ha,
diminutive.

-eshenrat- V be pink: **weshén:rate'** (it is)
pink.

é:so many, much, lots, **é:so'tsi** much, very.
• É:so enhsatkáhtho' ne okarièn:ta' ohahaktóntie'. You see a lot of carcasses at the
side of the road.

-et- stand. *See* -t-/-et-

-etahkw- take out. *See* -tahkw-/-etahkw-

-eta'- put inside. *See* -ta'-/-eta'-

Étien Indian agent
With ATTR =hne, at: **Etiénhne** at the
Indian agent's.
Cf. etiénhne (at) the agent's (Old Kahna-
wake: 14)

-e'ne- V be evident: **wè:ne'** it seems.
With CAUS -hst-: **wa'kè:nehste'** I made it
evident (so that people are aware of it).

-e'tar[on]- cut, slice off a piece or chunk.
See -kwe'tar[on]-/-e'tar[on]-

e'thó: or **eh tho** or **tho** there, thus,

e'thó: naiá:wen' or **eh tho naiá:wen'**
As it is! May it thus happen! Amen!

e'thó:ne' or **eh thó:ne'** and then

H

=ha ATTR diminutive. *See* ='a/=ha

-hah- N road: **oháha'**

With LOC -aktontie', along, edge of: **ohahaktóntie'** on the side of the road.

With LOC -'ke, on, at: **ohahà:ke** on the road.

With SRF -at- and V -ahton- disappear: **onthaháhton'** the road disappeared.

With V -awi-/-on- give: **shakohahá:wis** traffic cop, school crossing guard.

With SRF -at-, V -hsa'kt[on]-/-a'kt[on]- bend, and DLC: **teiothahà:kton** the road has a bend in it.

With SRF -at- and V -hwatase-/-tase- turn, twist: **wahathahatá:se'** he took a winding road; and DLC: **teiothahatá:se** the road has a curve in it.

With V -iahia'k-/-iia'k- cross over, and DLC: **wa'thahahí:ia'ke'** he crossed the road.

With SRF -at-, V -ia'ser-/-'ser- stack, and DLC: **teiothahà:sere'** crossroads.

With V -iehwa-/-ioha- look for in vain: **wakhahaiè:was** I am looking for the road and can't find it.

With V -ieronni- be a mark: **kahahaierón:ni** there is a mark on the road (for example, white or yellow road markings).

With SRF -at- and V -ine- lead: **rathahí:ne's** he is a wanderer, a tramp.

With V -ke- amount to, and DLC: **teioháhake** two roads or lanes (for example, two lanes of traffic, or two lanes, one in each direction).

With SRF -at-, V -kwat- curve, and DLC: **teiothahakwá:ton** it is a winding, curvy road.

With V -(h)nhoton- close: **kahahahnhó:ton** the road is closed.

With V -r- put in, and INCH -'-: **wahaháhara'ne'** he got onto the road.

With V -te- be present, exist (and variant -ha- of -hah-), and CISL: **ísi' nonkwá: tiohá:te'** there's a road over there; with V -te- be present, exist, and PROG -tie-: **iohatátie'** there is a road; with **tékeni** two, and V -te- be present, exist, and DLC: **tékeni teiohá:te'** Two Row wampum belt; with V -te- be present, exist, and DISTR -nion-: **iotihaténion** it has stripes, straight lines or rows, **kahòn:tsi tánon' karà:ken iotihaténion** black and white stripes.

With V -tshenri- find: **wa'khahatshén:ri'** I found the road.

With unclear V, and DLC: **teionkeniháha** we're across the road from each other.

• Tóhsa ohahaktóntie' enhsanistiá:ke'. Don't pee on the side of the road! (or you will get a sty, *an old saying*) • Iowisáhrhon ne ohahà:ke. The road is icy.

Cf. Johati a path or road (van den Bogaert: 58); *Aha* v. *Ahaha* chemin (Bruyas: 22); *teiohāhake* Collier de porcelaine à 2 rangs, *asen niiohāhǎke* à 3 (Marcoux: 71); Laurentian *Addé* a trail (Biggar: 244); Wendat *Hahattey* Chemin (Sagard: Te5); Onondaga *ꞩhate* vel *ꞩhaha* chemin (Shea: 32)

-hahs- N hip: **oháhsa'**

POSS: **khahsà:ke** (on) my hip

Cf. ohāsa jointure de la hanche (Marcoux: 199); *Ohasa* jointure de la hanche (Cuoq: 30)

-hahsen[t]- V hold mass, say mass: **roháhsen** he says mass.

With INSTR -hkw-: **tsi iehahsentáhkhwa'** altar.

Cf. Gahasen tenir conseil, être assemblé (Bruyas: 53); *Gahasen* S'assembler pour tenir conseil (Galissonnière: 9v); *rohāsen* dire Masse (Marcoux: 248); *Wakhasen* dire la messe (Cuoq: 114); *tsi ro ha shen mass* (Anon: 10)

-hahser- N light, lamp: **oháhsera'**
With V -es- be long: **kaháhseres** (it is) a long mass.
With V -ha[w]-/-enha[w]- hold, bring, take, and TRNL: **iehahserénhas** lantern.
With V -ienawa's-/-wa's- help someone: **rohahserawà:se'** altar boy.
With V -o- be in water, and INSTR -hkw-; and **kén:ie'** (-iie-/-ien- oil, grease): **iehahseróhkhwa' kén:ie'** oil for a kerosene lamp, coal oil.
With V -ot- stand: **wa'khahseró:ten'** I turned on the light, **kaháhserote'** the light is on.
With V -tokenhti- be holy: **ohahseratokénhti** (church) candle.

Cf. Gahahsera Conseil (Galissonnière: 22r); *Ohaseratogeᶜti* Messe (Galissonnière: 56r); *ohaseratokēnti* Messe (Marcoux: 248); *Ohasera* chandelle, cierge (Cuoq: 30, 167); *iehaserokwa* [coal oil] (Ledger: 48); *iont ha se ro kwa* coal oil (Anon: 14); *ie a se ren as* lantern, *ie a se ro kwa* coal oil, kerosene (D'Ailleboust: 24, 25); *o ha se ra* lamp, *o ha se ra to ken ti* candle (D'Ailleboust: 35); *o-há-se-ra* lamp (Cory: 34); *o ha se ra on we* candle (Diabo: 7); *ie ha se ren has* lantern (Diabo: 43); *oh hah she rah* lamp (Jamieson 2: 9) *Ohahsera* Lamp (Tewaterihwarenia'tha, Autumn 1989: 27)

=haka/=aka ATTR people of
With N -neni- stone, rock, and V -ot- stand: **Oneniote'á:ka** Oneida.
With N -nien'- flint, and LOC -'ke, on, at: **Kanien'kehá:ka** People of the Flint.
With N -nont- mountain, hill, and LOC -'ke, on, at: **Ononta'kehá:ka** Onondaga; with N -nont- mountain, hill, V -kowan[en]-/-owan[en]- be big, and REP: **Shotinontowane'á:ka** Seneca.
With V -(h)rhen'- become day, and CISL: **Tiohrhen'shá:ka** English.
With unrecognized root: **Kaiokonhá:ka** Cayuga.

-hakenht- N soot: **ohá:kenhte'**
With V -akera- stink, smell: **kahakenhtákeras** it smells of soot.
With V -awak- shake: **rahakenhtá:waks** chimney sweep, **enkhakenhtá:wake'** I will knock or shake the soot off of it, **wahahakenhtá:wake'** he shook the soot off.
With V -a'senht-/-enht- drop: **wahahakénhtenhte'** he knocked the soot out or off of it.
With V -r- put in: **iohakénhtare'** it is full of soot.
With unclear V, and CAUS -ht-: **kahakenhtaríkhton** bacon, ham. *This is an older word.*

Cf. Ohagenta suye de la cheminé (Bruyas: 53); *ohagenta* Suie (Galissonnière: 77v); *ohākĕnte* Suie (Marcoux: 373); *Ohakenta* mâchefer, suie (Cuoq: 29); *kaakentariton* [bacon] (Ledger: 74); *ka ha ken ta rik ton* bacon (Anon: 7)

-hakwaien- V be bow-legged, with DLC: **tehahá:kwaien'** he is bow-legged, **teiehá:kwaien'** she is bow-legged.

Hánio! or **Hánion!** Come on!

-har-/-ihar- V hang up **kháhrha'** I hang it up, **enkhá:ren'** I will hang it up, **wa'ehá:ren'**

she hung it up.

With NEG: **iah teiakóhare'** she didn't hang it up.

With DISTR -onnion-: **wa'kharónnion'** I hung them up.

With REV -kw-: **wahahará:ko'** he took it off, he unhung it.

With BEN -'s-: **wa'konhá:ra'se'** I caught you at it, I found out what you were up to, **wahihá:ra'se'** I caught him at it, **wahonwatihá:ra'se'** they found out what they were up to, **rihará:se'** I am catching him at it.

With SRF -at- and N -honw[ei]- boat: **kathonwiháhrha'** I swing, **wahathonwihá:ren'** he swung, **wakathonwíhare'** I am swinging; and INSTR -hkw-: **ionthonwiharáhkhwa'** swing.

With N -itahs- tail: **kentahsíhare'** kite.

With N -kon'tsher- pound: **wahakon'tsherihá:ren'** he weighed it; and REFL -atat-: **wahatatkon'tsherihá:ren'** he weighed himself.

With SRF -ate- and N -ris[er]- socks: **wa'kateriserihá:ren'** I hung up my socks, I got a present for Christmas; with N -ris[er]- socks, and BEN -hahs-: **wahiriseriháhrhahse'** I gave him a Christmas present.

• Rihará:se' tsi ronó:wen. I catch him at lying. • Rihará:se' rate'niéntha' aonhatáweia'te'. I catch him at trying to come in.

-haranawen't- N sap: **oharanawèn:ta'**

With V -astath[en]-/-ath[en]- dry: **wa'kaharanawen'táthen'** sap dried up.

With V -na'nawen-/-nawen- be wet: **enkaharanawen'taná:wen'** it will start running sap, **ó:nen wa'kaharanawen'taná:wen'** now the sap is melted and running, **ioharanawen'taná:wen** it is running sap.

-haratat-/-karatat- V lift, raise up: **khará:tats** I lift it, raise it up, **enkhará:tate'** I will lift it, **wahahará:tate'** he raised it up, **wakharatá:ton** I have raised it up, **shará:tat** Raise it!

With PROG -hatie-: **wakharatatonhátie'** I am lifting it, raising it up.

With N -hnek- liquid: **iohnekakaratá:ton** the water (level) is high.

With N -hsenn- name: **Enhonwatihsennakará:tate'** Naming Ceremony.

With SRF -at- and N -hsin- leg: **enhsatshinakará:tate'** you will lift up your leg (so you stand on one leg), **wa'katshinakará:tate'** I lifted up my leg.

With N -ia't- body: **iakoia'takará:tats** elevator.

With N -nahstonhkw- window, windowsill: **wahanahstonhkwakará:tate'** he raised the window, he opened the window, **senahstonhkwakará:tat** Raise the window!

With N -neni- stone, rock: **wa'keneniakará:tate'** I wound it (the clock or watch).

With SRF -a- and N -nentsh- arm: **wa'kanentshakará:tate'** I raised my arms.

With N -nonhs- house: **wahatinonhsakará:tate'** they raised the house.

With N -rihw- matter, message: **waharihwakará:tate'** he started or led the proceedings.

With N -'sere[ht]- vehicle, car: **ro'serehtakaratá:ton** he has raised up the car.

• Father Hauser waharihwakará:tate'. Father Hauser led the service. (Letter 1946)

Cf. *Garihsagaraton* dire des mots du festin (Galissonnière: 31v)

-harennaht- N lead, purple, bruise:
oharennáhta'
With V -ohar- attach at the end:
kaharennahtóhare' lead, lead pencil.
This is an older word for pencil.
With SRF -at- and V -r- put in:
wakatharennáhtare' I have a bruise;
and INCH -'-: **onkwatharennáhtara'ne'**
I got a bruise.
With V -(h)rho- coat, and INSTR -hst-:
ieharennahtahrhóhstha' stove polish.
• Watié:sen aonkwatharennáhtara'ne'.
It's easy for me to bruise.

=haton ATTR forms ordinal numbers.
For example: **ahsénhaton** third,
tékeni iawenréhaton twelfth,
tewahsénhaton twentieth.

-ha[w]-/-enha[w]- V hold, bring, take:
íkhawe' I am holding it, I have it,
íhshawe' you are holding it, **ráhawe'**
he is holding it, **iéhawe'** she is holding it.
With CONT -k-: **enkhá:wake'** I will hold
it.
With PAST -hkwe': **khá:wahkwe'** I was
holding it.
With CISL: **tékhas** I bring it, **tháhas** he
brings it, **tiéhas** she brings it, **entékhawe'**
I will bring it, **entháhawe'** he will bring
it, **tákhawe'** I brought it, **thóha** he has
brought it, **tásha** Bring it! **tasewáha**
Bring it! (pl).
With TRNL: **iékhas** I take it, **iénkhawe'**
I will take it, **iahà:khawe'** I took it,
iaháhawe' he took it, **iahà:sha** Take it!
ia'sewáha Take it! (pl)
With N -ahswen't-/-a'swen't- coal, and
TRNL: **iahahswen'ténhawe'** he took coal.
With N -hahser- light, lamp, and TRNL:
iehahserénhas lantern.
With N -hwist- metal, money:
khwisténhawe' I have money in my hand.
With N -ian- footprint, track:

wa'tianénhawe' I followed the tracks,
wa'kheianénhawe' I followed her tracks.
With N -iar- bag: **tiarénhawe'** I am holding the bag; and TRNL: **iehaiarénhas** he
is carrying, taking the (golf) bag,
ientiarénhawe' I will take the bag.
With N -ia't- body, and CISL or TRNL:
entekheia'ténhawe' I will bring her,
ia'kheia'ténhawe' I took her there.
With N -ron'onhkw- pompom:
raron'onhkwénhawe' he is the
champion.
With N -'nikonhr- mind, and TRNL:
iahi'nikonhrénhawe' I swayed,
persuaded him.
• Tásha akehra'shòn:'a! Bring the dishes!
• Iahà:sha, satatié:nawa's! Take it, help
yourself! (to the leftovers, for example)

-hawi-/-enhawi- V carry: **khá:wi'** I am
carrying it, **khá:wi's** I carry it around.
With CISL: **takhá:wi'** I am bringing it.
With PART: **nikahá:wi'** it's at this time.
With CAUS -ht-: **é:ren wa'khá:wihte'**
I carried or took it away, I moved it aside.
With N -aten'nits-/-aten'nitsher- cane:
raten'nitsherenhá:wi' he is carrying a
cane.
With N -ent- day, CAUS -ht-, and CISL:
Thentenhawíhtha' Venus.
With N -hwist- metal, money:
khwistenhá:wi' I am carrying money.
With N -ian- footprint, track:
riianenhá:wi' I am following his tracks.
With N -iar- bag: **tiarenhá:wi'** I am carry-
ing the bag.
With N -ia't- body: **kheia'tenhá:wi'** I am
carrying her.
With N -nahkw- marriage:
ranahkwenhá:wi's he is living together
(with someone) without being married,
ienahkwenhá:wi's she is living together
without being married.

Cf. θentenhaꙅiθa il apporte le jour (Bruyas: 111); "They call Venus, or the morning star, *Te Ouentenhaouitha*, 'It brings the day'," (Lafitau II: 135); *ninakꙅenhāꙅis* cohabiter, si d'une union illegit (Marcoux: 70)

-ha't- N (apple) core, Adam's apple: **ohà:ta'**
With V -iio- be good, nice: **roha'tí:io** he has a nice (singing) voice, **iakoha'tí:io** she has a nice voice.

-hehs- N decayed, rotted wood: **ohéhsa'**
With SRF -at-: **athéhsa'** brown; and V -hon'tsi- be black, dark-coloured: **athehsahòn:tsi** dark brown; and V -ra'ken- be white, light-coloured: **athehsarà:ken** light brown, beige.
Cf. ohésa Bois pourry (Galissonnière: 13r); *ohēsa* Arbre, vieux (Marcoux: 20); *Ohesa* vieil arbre couvert de mousse et déjà pourri (Cuoq: 30)

-heht- N field, meadow, garden
With LOC -kon, inside: **kahéhtakon** in the garden.
With LOC -'ke, on at: **kahehtà:ke** (on) the farm.
With V -ien- put down, have: **kahéhtaien'** there is a field or garden.
With SRF -at- and V -ori- drive, drive away: **athehtó:ri** scarecrow.

hén: or **én:** yes

-henreht- V yell, holler, with DLC:
tewakhenréhtha' I am yelling,
wa'thohén:rehte' he yelled,
wa'tiohén:rehte' it made a loud noise,
tehohenréhton he has yelled.
With TRNL: **ia'tewakhén:rehte'** I yelled out.
With DISTR -nion-: **wa'thahenrehtánion'**

he honked the horn.
With INSTR -hkw-:
teiakohenrehtáhkhwa' bullhorn.
With V -atkon- be the devil, demon, and NMZR -'ser-: **tehotkon'serahenréhtha'** he is making a heck of a noise, yelling.
NOTE: The word **teiakohenrehtáhkhwa'** has an interesting history. Long ago there was a platform in front of the Catholic Church that someone could stand on to make announcements; people referred to this platform as *tsi teiakohenrehtáhkhwa'*. • Kwah òn:wa'k wa'tiohén:rehte' ne kahonweia'kó:wa. The ship made a noise just a while ago. • Ohkwá:ri ro'nhí:ien, tehotkon'serahenréhtha'. Ohkwá:ri is barking, he is making a heck of a noise.
Cf. Kahenreton faire un cry de nouvelle (Bruyas: 53); *Kahenreᶜton* Crier, faire ... pour dire la nouvelle (Galissonnière: 26v); *teꙅakhenrātha* Beugler (Marcoux: 39); *Tewakhenretha* crier fort (Cuoq: 48); *ta ia ko hen re te* shout (Diabo: 72)

-hent- N grass: **óhente'** grass, **kahén:ta'** meadow, big field, prairie.
With LOC -'ke, on, at: **kahentà:ke** on the meadow, field, lawn, in the grass.
With V -ia'k- cut, sever: **rahéntia'ks** he cuts the grass.
With V -ien- put down, have: **kahén:taien'** there is a field.
With V -r- put in, and CAUS -hst-: **iakohentaráhstha'** poison ivy.
Cf. Gahenta prairie (Bruyas: 53); *ka hen ta ke* meadow (Anon: 19); *tiot kon ho hen te ni iot* evergreen, *literally,* always green is how it is (Diabo: 24); *ka hen ta ke* field (Diabo: 28)

-hente- V go ahead, advance: **khén:te'** I am ahead, I am in front, **rahén:te'** he is going ahead, **kahén:te'** it goes on, **énkhente'** I

will go ahead, **waháhente'** he went ahead, **wakhén:ton** I have gone ahead.
With CAUS -ht-: **rahentéhtha'** he puts it in front, ahead, **wa'khén:tehte'** I put it ahead, I advanced it, pushed it forward (maybe I want mine to be first, or I didn't wait my turn).
• Ka'nosháhtshera' kahén:te' nòn:wa. Jealousy is going around now.
• Wahahén:tehte' ne raoio'ténhsera'. He pushed forward, advanced his own work.

-henton- N front, in front: **ohén:ton**
POSS: **akhén:ton** in front of me, **sahén:ton** in front of you, **raohén:ton** in front of him, **akohén:ton** in front of her.
With **karihwatéhkwen** (-rihw- matter, message): **Ohén:ton Karihwatéhkwen** Preface, Thanksgiving Address.
• Satè:ko akhén:ton. Get away from me!
• Akohén:ton wahatóhetste'. He passed in front of her. • tánon' akwé:kon ne ronatia'-kè:shon né: ki' sénha ohén:ton ne Maggie. (I send regards to) all of the rest of them, but most of all to Maggie. (Letter 1923)
Cf. Oghentonh karighwateghkwenh The preliminary ceremony (Hale: 116–7)

-her- N corn stalk: **óhere'**

-her-/-hr- V set on top of: **khéhrha'** I put it on the top or surface of something, **énkhren'** I will set it down, **wà:khren'** I set down, **wahà:ren'** he set it down, **wa'è:ren'** she set it down, **káhere'** it is set on top, **tho íshren** Put it on there! With TRNL: **è:neken iahà:khren'** I put it up there.
With DLC and CISL: **tetkáhere'** it is full; and CONTR: **iah tha'tetkáhere'** it is not full.
With REP: **skáhere'** it's over (an amount).
With REV -kw-: **rahrákwas** he takes it off

of it, **wahahrá:ko'** he took it off of it.
With SRF -at-, N -ahkwari['t]- bear, and PROG -atie-: **wakatahkwari'tahrátie'** I have a bear (or bear skin) on my shoulders.
With N -ahkwenni- outfit, clothing; and **akohsá:tens** horse: **wa'kahkwennià:ren'** **akohsá:tens** I put the harness on the horse.
With N -ahsarahkw- cuff of a shoe or moccasin, and DLC: **wa'tionhsarahkwà:ren'** she put the cuff on, **tewahsarahkwáhere'** it (moccasin, shoe) has a cuff.
With N -ahsir- blanket, shawl: **wahshakohsirà:ren'** he put the blanket or shawl on her; and REV -kw-: **wahshakohsirahrá:ko'** he took the shawl or blanket off her.
With SRF -ar-, N -ahsi't- foot, and DLC: **è:neken wa'tkarahsi'tà:ren'** I elevated my feet.
With N -ahskw- bridge: **wahahskwà:ren'** he put up a bridge, **wahskwáhere'** (there is) a bridge.
With SRF -at- and N -a'ar- net, curtain, veil: **iakota'aráhere'** she has on a veil.
With N -enniser- shelf: **wenniseráhere'** (there is) a shelf, a mantel; and DISTR -onnion-: **wenniserahrónnion** there are shelves here and there.
With N -hnaw- rapid, strong current: **kahnawáhere'** (there is) a rapid.
With N -hnia's- neck, collar, and DLC: **tekahnia'sáhere'** it has a collar.
With SRF -at- and N -hwa'tst- foam: **iothwa'tstáhere'** there is foam on top of it.
With N -hwist- metal, money, and DLC: **tekahwistáhere'** a general.
With N -ia't- body: **ieia'táhere'** she is laid out (at a wake), **wahonwaia'tà:ren'** they laid him out; and INSTR -hkw-: **iontatia'tahráhkhwa'** funeral parlour.

With SRF -ate- and N -iie-/-ien- oil, grease: **ioteienáhere'** there is oil or grease on it.
With N -itskw- haunches: **kentskwáhere'** foundation; and SRF -an-: **wa'kanitskwà:ren'** I sat or perched on it; **anitskwà:ra** chair, seat.
With N -i't- excrement, and ATTR ='ke, at: **Ken'taherè:ke** Scotland.
With N -kahr- eye, and DLC: **tekkahráhere'** I have my eye on it, I am watching it.
With SRF -ate- and N -khw- food: **atekhwà:ra** table (see -atekhwahra-).
With N -ko'ts- crest, comb: **roko'tsáhere'** he (a rooster) has a comb.
With N -ks- dish, plate, and DISTR -onnion-: **wa'keksahrónnion** I set the table.
With N -nahst- rafters: **wahanahstà:ren'** he put up the rafters, **kanahstáhere'** (there are) rafters.
With N -na'kar- horn, antler, and DLC: **tenhonwana'karà:ren'** they will install him as chief.
With N -na'skw- body, curled-up, and TRNL: **ieiena'skwáhere'** she is lying down; and SRF -ate-: **ia'katena'skwà:ren'** I went to lie down.
With N -na'ts- pail: **kana'tsáhere'** the pot, dinner is on (the stove), it's cooking; and INSTR -hkw-: **iena'tsahráhkhwa'** frying pan.
With N -nerahontsh- wing, shoulder blade, and DLC: **tekanerahontsháhere'** it has a fender.
With N -niar- neck, and possessive form of shoulder (-hnenhs- shoulder): **iehnenhsà:ke ieniaráhere'** her head is nodding, she is putting her neck towards her shoulder.
With N -niatar- river, lake: **kaniataráhere'** there is a river, a lake.
With N -nia'kw- throat: **onia'kwáhehr** camel.

With N -nont- mountain, hill: **ionontáhere'** there's a hill; and DISTR -onnion-: **ionontahrónnion** there are mountains; with N -nont- mountain, hill, and INCH -'-: **wa'enontà:ra'ne'** she went uphill.
With N -nontsi[st]- head: **kanontsistáhere'** it has an engine (a train, tractor, lawn-mower).
With SRF -at- and N -onhnh- life: **wakatonhnháhere'** I am happy, joyful, **wa'katonhnhà:ren'** I became happy; and BEN -hahs-: **wahiiatonhnhahéhrhahse'** I celebrated him (his birthday); with N -onhnh- life, and NMZR -htsher-: **atonhnhahráhtshera'** happiness.
With SRF -ate-, N -rahkw- sun, and CISL: **tioterahkwáhere'** it is a full moon.
With SRF -ate- and N -rawa't- muck, sludge: **ioterawa'táhere'** there is muck.
With SRF -ate- and N -renn- song, music: **waterennahéhrha'** record player.
With N -(h)rh- woods: **kahrháhere'** there are woods.
With N -rihw- matter, message: **wa'erihwà:ren'** she brought the matter forth, **karihwáhere'** issue, agenda.
With N -ronwar-/-nonwar- wire, nail, needle: **karonwaráhere'** there is a wire; and DISTR -onnion-: **karonwarahrónnion** there are wires up.
With N -ron'onhkw- pompom: **karon'onhkwáhere'** there is a pompom; and REV -kw-: **wahatiron'onhkwahrá:ko'** they won the championship.
With N -tshe['t]- bottle, jar: **wa'ketshe'tà:ren'** I set down a bottle.
With SRF -ate- and N -wei- wing: **ateweià:ra'** cape, shawl; and DLC: **tewakateweiáhere'** I have a cape on, I am wearing a shawl.
With N -wis- ice, glass: **wa'ewisà:ren'** she set down the glass.
With N -'nerohkw- box:

ka'nerohkwáhere' there is a box set
on it.
With N -'nhehs- snow crust:
io'nhehsáhere' there is an icy crust on
the snow.
With N -'nikonhr- mind, INCH -'-, and
DLC: **tehi'nikonhrà:ra's** I get suspicious
of him, **wa'thi'nikonhrà:ra'ne'** I got
suspicious of him, **tehi'nikonhrahrà:'on**
I have gotten suspicious of him, I am suspicious of him.
With N -'notst- nakedness: **ra'notstáhere'**
he is sitting there bare.
NOTE: This root occurs with many incorporated nouns, and not all the inflected forms
of some of the N plus V combinations are
given here; for the additional forms, see
the N entry.
• Raotsinà:kwa' akwé:kon tetkáhere'
ohrhónria'. His lungs are full of mucus.
• Skahawísta skáhere'. It's over one
dollar.

-hetken- V be ugly: **kahétken** she or it is
ugly, **rahétken** he is ugly, **iehétken**
she is ugly.
With CAUS -ht- and CONTR:
iah thahshétkenhte' you can't ruin it,
you can't make it ugly.
NOTE: This stem is used most often to talk
about an animal; it is related to -ahetken-
be bad.

-hetkw- N rectum: **ohétkwa'**

-he[w]- V arrive
With TRNL: **ia'káhewe'** it is time;
iénkhewe' I will get it, I will understand,
iahà:khewe' I got it, I understood, I
remembered, and NEG: **iah thiehékhes**
I don't get it, I don't know, I can't
remember, **iah thiewákhe'** I didn't get
it, I didn't understand.

With REFL -atat- and N -ia't- body:
wa'katatià:thewe' I arrived, I brought
my body here, **wahatatià:thewe'** he
arrived, **wa'ontatià:thewe'** she arrived.
• Ia'káhewe' ake'rhotsherá:ko'. It's time
for me to pick beans.

-hiaton- V write: **khiá:tons** I am writing,
kahiá:tons it writes (for example, a
computer or typewriter), **enkhiá:ton'**
I will write, **wahahiá:ton'** he wrote,
wakhiá:ton I have written.
With INSTR -hkw-: **iehiatónhkhwa'**
pencil; **ohiatónhkwa'** letter, number,
written character; and ATTR =shon'a,
pluralizer: **ohiatonhkwa'shòn:'a** letters,
characters.
With BEN -ni-/-'s-, and CISL:
tiesahiatón:ni she writes to you,
tahakhiá:ton'se' he wrote to me.
With NMZR -hser-, see -hiatonhser- book,
paper.

-hiatonhser- N book, paper: **kahiatónhsera'**
With **iewennahnotáhkhwa'** (-wenn-
voice, word, -ahnot- tell about):
iewennahnotáhkhwa' kahiatónhsera'
books, stuff to read.
With SRF -at-, V -areni- spread around,
disperse, CAUS -'t-, and DLC:
tehathiatonhserarenià:tha' mailman.
With SRF -at- and V -hninon- buy:
rathiatonhserahní:nons he sells paper,
books, newspapers.
With V -ien- put down, have, and DLC:
tehatihiatonhserá:iens they are playing
cards; and INSTR -hkw-:
teiehiatonhseraientáhkhwa' cards.
With V -na'nawen-/-nawen- be wet:
iohiatonhseraná:wen the book or paper
is wet.
With V -nenhskw- steal:
wahakhiatonhseranénhsko' he stole the
book from me.

With V -ota's- receive:
rohiatonhserotà:se' he gets mail,
enhohiatonhseró:ta'se' he will get mail,
onkhiatonhseró:ta'se' I received a book,
I got mail.
With V -ra'nentakt-/-nentakt- stick something to: **wa'ehiatonhseranén:takte'**
she put up wallpaper; and INSTR -hkw-:
iehiatonhseranentaktáhkhwa' wall-
paper.
With V -tahkw- take out, and CAUS -ht-:
tsi iehiatonhseratahkwáhtha' post
office.
With V -tens- be thick paper:
kahiatonhserá:tens it is thick paper,
cardboard.
With V -tokenhti- be holy:
kahiatonhseratokénhti gospel, Bible.
NOTE: This stem is composed of -hiaton-
write, and NMZR -hser-.

-hiohs- N elbow: **ohióhsa'**
POSS: **khiohsà:ke** (on) my elbow,
rahiohsà:ke (on) his elbow, **iehiohsà:ke**
(on) her elbow.
With LOC -'ke, on, at: **ohiohsà:ke** corner.
With V -ia'k- hit, bang, and TRNL:
iahonkhióhsia'ke' I banged my elbow.
With V -ien- put down, have, and DLC:
tsi tekahióhsaien' at the corner.
With V -ienht- hit against, and TRNL:
iahonkhióhsaienhte' I banged my elbow
against it, **iahohióhsaienhte'** he hit his
elbow against it; with SRF -at- and V
-ienht- hit against: **wahiiathióhsaienhte'**
I elbowed him, I hit him with my elbow,
wahakwathióhsaienhte' he elbowed me.
With V -i'tson-/-'tson- be dirty, and DLC:
tewakhiohsá'tson I have a dirty elbow.
With V -ot- stand, and DLC: **tekhióhsote'**
I have my elbow on something (like a
table); and DISTR -on-: **tekhiohsó:ton**
I have my elbows on something; with

SRF -at-, V -ot- stand, and DLC:
tekathiohsótha' I am putting my elbow(s)
on it, **wa'tkathiohsó:ten'** I put my elbows
on it, **wa'thiiathiohsó:ten'** I nudged him
with my elbow.
With SRF -at- and V -te- be present, exist:
tsi iothióhsate' (at) the corner; and DISTR
-onnion-: **tsi iothiohsatónnion** (at) the
corners.
With V -'rhenien'-/-ienen'- fall down, and
DLC: **wa'tekhiohsié:nen'ne'** I am so
tired, just worn out, worn down,
wa'thahiohsié:nen'ne' he is worn out,
wa'tiehiohsié:nen'ne' she is worn out.

-hionh- N creek: **kahiónha'**
With LOC -atatie', along, edge of:
kahionhatátie' there's a creek going
along.
With V -ti- be on the other side, and PART:
ísi' na'kahiónhati the other side of the
creek.
• Isi' na'kahiónhati tiohá:te'. The road is
on the other side of the creek.
Cf. Gaihonha rivière (Bruyas: 63);
Gaihona riviere (Galissonnière: 73v);
Kahiōnha, Kahiōnhăte, Kahionhatāties
Riviere (Marcoux: 346); *Kahionha* rivière,
fleuve (Cuoq: 9); *Geihate* River (Zeisberger in Wheeler-Voegelin 57);
ka ion ha ta tie brook (Anon:19);
kahionhatátie creek, stream (Lazore: 32)

-hio'kt-/-hio'ket- V dull, with DLC:
wa'tekhiò:kete' I made it dull.
With SRF -at-: **wa'tewathiò:kete'**
it got dull, **teiothiò:kton** it is dull.

-hio'thiie-/-o'thiie- V be sharp, pointy:
iohio'thí:ie' it is sharp or pointy.
With N -a'shar- knife: **io'sharo'thí:ie'**
(it is) a sharp knife.
With N -tsi'er- fingernail: **rotsi'ero'thí:ie'**

he has sharp claws, sharp nails,
iotsi'ero'thí:ie' it has sharp claws, nails.

-hio'thiion- V sharpen: **khio'thí:ions** I am
sharpening it, **wa'khio'thí:ion'** I sharpened it, **rohio'thí:ion** he has sharpened it.

-hio'tsis[t]- V be salty, sour
    With CISL: **tiohiò:tsis** salt.
    With DLC: **teiohiò:tsis** it is salty, sour;
    and INCH -'-: **teniohio'tsísta'ne'** it will
    turn sour, salty, **wa'tiohio'tsísta'ne'** it
    got sour, salty; and CONTR:
    iah tha'teiohio'tsistà:'on it didn't get
    sour, salty.
    With N -ahi- fruit, berry, and DLC:
    teiohiahiò:tsis lemon.
    With N -hnek- liquid, ATTR =hne, at,
    and DLC: **teiohnekahio'tsíshne** ocean.
    With N -hont- green; and **ostawí:na'**
    (-stawin- stalk, celery): **teiaontahiò:tsis
    ostawí:na'** or **tiohontahiò:tsis ostawí:na'**
    rhubarb.
    With V -kowan[en]-/-owan[en]- be big:
    kahio'tsistowá:nen's coarse salt, rock
    salt.
    With N -non'onser- squash, and DLC:
    teionon'onserahiò:tsis pickles.
    With V -(h)rho- coat, and DLC:
    wa'tekhio'tsistáhrho' I salted it,
    tekahio'tsistáhrhon it is covered in salt.
    With N -'wahr- meat, and DLC:
    teio'wahrahiò:tsis salt pork.
    Cf. Tiohiotsist chose salée (Bruyas: 54);
    te ohiotsis sal (Galissonnière: 74r);
    teiohiōtsis Sel (Marcoux: 361); *Teiohiotsis*
    sel (Cuoq: 43); *tioiotsis* [salt] (Ledger: 53);
    tio io tsis salt (D'Ailleboust: 22); *tioiótsis*
    salt (Cory: 85); *de hyo hyo jihs* salt (Jamie-
    son 1: 4); *tiohiò:tsis* salt (Horne: 29);
    Onondaga *deyoyodzieh* Aigre (Shea: 16)

-hi'kar- N gear: **ohì:kara'**

With V -ke- amount to, and PART:
Tó: nikahi'kará:ke? How many gears?
With V -otahrho[k]- hook:
enkhi'karotáhrhoke' I will put it in gear.
Cf. Ohikara pointe, dent d'un instrument
(Cuoq: 30)

-hi'kt- N thorn: **ohì:kta'**
    With V -ont- attach, and DISTR -on-:
    iohi'któn:ton it is thorny.
    Cf. Ohᵴikta Espine (Galissonnière: 37v);
    ohīkta épine (Marcoux: 155); *Ohikta*
    épine (Cuoq: 30); *o hik tha* thorn (Anon:
    18); *o-hik-ta* Crataegus sp. [hawthorn]
    (Rousseau: 45); *Ohì:kta'* Thorn bush
    (Horne: 112)

-hkhwa- V take away from: **khéhkhwas**
    I take it away from her, **enkónhkhwa'**
    I will take it away from you, **wahíhkhwa'**
    I took it away from him.
    With SRF -at-: **katéhkhwas** I take things
    away, **rotéhkhwen** he has taken things
    away.
    With N -athenno-/-athenno'tsher- ball:
    wahiiathenno'tsheráhkhwa' I took the
    ball away from him.
    With SRF -at- and N -onhwents-/-onhonts-
    earth, world: **rontonhwentsáhkhwas** they
    take the land away.
    With N -wir- offspring:
    wahshakowiráhkhwa' he took her child
    away from her.
    • Rontonhwentsáhkhwas ne Kó:ra. The
    government takes the land away.

-hkw- V pick up, with DLC **tekéhkhwa'** I
    pick it up, **teháhkhwa'** he picks it up,
    teiéhkhwa' she picks it up, **tén:kehkwe'**
    I will pick it up, **wà:tkehkwe'** I picked it
    up, **wà:thrahkwe'** he picked it up,
    wà:tionhkwe' she picked it up,
    tewakéhkwen I have picked it up,

té:sehkw Pick it up!
With TRNL: **iahà:tkehkwe'** I picked it
up, **iahà:thrahkwe'** he picked it up,
iahà:tionhkwe' she picked it up.
With CAUS -'t-: **wa'tewákhkwa'te'**
something hit me, attacked me,
wa'thóhkwa'te' it hit him,
teiakohkwà:ton it has attacked her.
With BEN -enni-/-en-: **tekhehkwén:ni**
I take it, I swipe it from her,
wa'thíhkwen' I swiped it from him,
wa'tekhéhkwen' I swiped it from her.
With N -hwist- metal, money, and BEN
-enni-/-en-: **wa'thihwistáhkwen'** I took,
swiped money from him.
With N -ia't- body: **wa'tekheià:tahkwe'**
I picked her up, **teiakoia'táhkhwa'** hawk.
With SRF -an- and N -i'tsonhkw- jump,
stride: **tekani'tsonhkwáhkhwa'** I am
jumping, **wa'tionni'tsónhkwahkwe'**
she jumped; and DISTR -nion-:
teionni'tsonhkwahkwánions she is
jumping up and down,
wa'tionni'tsonhkwahkwánion' she
jumped up and down; with SRF -an-,
N -i'tsonhkw- jump, stride, and PROG
-hatie-: **teiakoni'tsonhkwahkwenhátie'**
she is jumping along, she is skipping.
With N -konhretsh- block of wood:
wa'thakonhrétshahkwe' he picked up
the block of wood.
With SRF -a- and N -nat- town, settlement:
wa'tkaná:tahkwe' I moved (from one
place to another), **teiakonatáhkwen** she
has moved; and CAUS -'t-:
teionnatahkwà:tha' she is moving it
(to another place), **wa'thanatáhkwa'te'**
he moved it, **tewakanatahkwà:ton** I have
moved it.
With N -nieht- snow: **wa'tkaniéhtahkwe'**
the snow left.
With N -nonhwenhsker- dust:
wa'tkenonhwénhskerahkwe' I picked up

the dust, **teienonhwenhskeráhkhwa'**
dustpan.
With N -nonni- dance: **tekenonniáhkhwa'**
I dance, **tenkenónniahkwe'** I will dance,
wa'tkenónniahkwe' I danced,
tewakenonniáhkwen I am dancing.
With N -nonw- water at the bottom, dregs:
tenkanón:wahkwe' it will get murky,
wa'tkanón:wahkwe' it got murky.
With N -rihw- matter, issue:
teierihwáhkhwa' she sings (hymns, in a
choir), **tekarihwáhkhwa'** organ,
wa'tierì:wahkwe' she sang,
tehorihwáhkwen he is singing; and CAUS
-'t-: **teierihwahkwà:tha'** hymnal, hymn
book.
With N -wenn- voice, word:
tehakewennáhkhwa' he talks for me, he
speaks on my behalf, **wa'thiwén:nahkwe'**
I spoke for him.
With N -wer- wind, air: **tekaweráhkhwa'**
the wind picks up, it gets windy,
wa'tkáwerahkwe' it got windy.
With SRF -ate- and N -'khah- step:
tenkate'kháhahkwe' I will take a step,
wa'thate'kháhahkwe' he took a step.

-hkwi't- V move over
With SRF -at-: **é:ren enkáthkwi'te'** I will
move over, **waháthkwi'te'** he moved
over; and TRNL: **ienkáthkwi'te'** I will
move over that way.
With DLC: **Tekahkwì:tha'** Lily of the
Kanien'kehá:ka (Mohawks).

-hnakenhs- N hide: **ohnakénhsa'**
With V -ke- amount to, and DLC:
tekahnakénhsake two hides.

-hnaw- N rapid, strong current, swift water
With LOC -atatie', along, edge of:
kahnawatátie' (it is) a stream.
With LOC -'ke, on, at: **Kahnawà:ke** at the

rapids, Kahnawà:ke Mohawk territory; and ATTR =hronon, resident of: **Kahnawa'ke-hró:non** Kahnawà:ke residents.

With V -a'senht-/-enht- drop, and REP: **ó:nen ensekhná:wenhte'** I will leave, go home, go downstream, look for work (*this is an old expression*); and PROG -hatie-: **sewakhnawenhtonhátie'** I am leaving, I am going down the rapids or the stream.

With V -her-/-hr- set on top of: **kahnawáhere'** (there is) a rapid.

With V -ot- stand: **iohná:ote'** it is pouring out.

With V -te- be present, exist: **iohná:wate'** (it is) swift water, a rapid.

Cf. 8atkennisat ganna8age si 8agennon Je suis allé et venu de Ganna8age en un jour (Bruyas: 109); *Cahnuaga, or Cocknawaga* (Long: 5); *Kahna8āke* Sault St. Louis (Marcoux: 357); *Ohna8a* courant, cours d'eau rapide, saut, cascade, chûte d'eau (Cuoq: 32); *Kahnawake* Sault St. Louis, nom de lieu dont l'orthographe anglaise a fait *Caughnawaga* (Cuoq: 9); *Kanawáke* Caughnawaga (Cory: 83); Wendat *anda8a,e* au Sault, *ganna8age* (Potier: 154)

-hnawer- N well: **ohnáwera'**
With LOC -kon, inside: **ohnawerá:kon** in the well.

With V -ot- stand: **iohnáwerote'** (there is) a well; and CISL: **ísi' tiohnáwerote'** there is a well over there; with V -ot- stand, and ATTR =onwe, genuine: **iohnawerote'ón:we** a (natural) spring.

With SRF -at- and V -ot- stand: **Ronathnáwerote'** Mohawks and Senecas, as referred to in council (possibly also refers to Turtle clan 'keepers of the well').

-hna'ne[t]-/-ne[t]- V be lined, doubled, with DLC: **tekahnà:ne** or **teiohnà:ne** it is lined, doubled.

With DISTR -rion-: **tekahna'netárion** or **teiohna'netárion** they are doubled, **wa'tekhna'netárion'** I doubled things.

With KIN -atere- grandchild, and NMZR -'ser-: **teiotere'será:ne** great-grandchild.

With N -hson-/-hsw- back: **tekahswá:ne** pie.

With KIN -hsot- grandparent, and NMZR -hser-: **teiohsotsherá:ne** great-grand-parent(s).

With SRF -ate-, N -ronto-/-ronto'tsher- wooden box, and INSTR -hkw-: **tewateronto'tsheranetáhkhwa'** cover for a vault that holds a coffin.

With REV -hkw-, *see* -hna'netahkw-/ -netahkw- remove a lining, make a copy.

With INCH -'-, *see* -hna'neta'-/-neta'- line, double.

• Óhwhare' tekahnà:ne akwa'nià:nawen. It has fur inside my mittens. • Teiohnà:ne tsi ní:kon wa'kária'ke'. I paid double the price.

-hna'netahkw-/-netahkw- V remove a lining, make a copy, with DLC:
tekhna'netáhkwas I am making a copy, taking out the lining, **tenkhna'netáhko'** I will make a copy, take out the lining, **wa'tiehna'netáhko'** she made a copy, took out the lining, **tehohna'netáhkwen** he has made a copy, taken out the lining.

With N -wenn- voice, word: **tehawennanetáhkwas** he is translating.

NOTE: This stem is composed of -hna'ne[t]-/-ne[t]- be lined, doubled, and REV -hkw-.

• Wa'tekhna'netáhko' kahiatónhsera'. I made a copy of the (piece of) paper.

Cf. ... tsi nió:re enwá:ton teniehna'netáhko tsi wathtsiseró:roks ne iekahrá:ke. ... until she was able to peel [remove] the cataracts. (Old Kahnawake: 2)

-hna'neta'-/-neta'- V line, double, with DLC:
tenkhna'néta' I will line it, double it,
wa'tekhna'néta' I lined it, doubled it.
With SRF -at- and CISL: **tentionthna'néta'**
she will repeat (a process).
With SRF -ar- and N -ahta[hkw]- shoe:
wa'tkarahtahkwanéta' I put galoshes
on (over my shoes), I put on boots,
tesarahtahkwanéta Put on your boots!
and CAUS -hst- and INSTR -hkw-:
teionrahtahkwaneta'ahstáhkhwa'
overshoes, galoshes, boots.
With N -hson-/-hsw- back, and CISL:
entkonhswanéta' I will back you up,
take your part, **tahakhswanéta'** he took
my part.
With SRF -ate- and N -nahstonhkw-
window, windowsill:
tewatenahstonhkwanéta's double
window, storm window.
With SRF -ate- and N -(h)nhoh- door:
tewatehnhohanéta's storm door.
NOTE: This stem is composed of
-hna'ne[t]-/-ne[t]- be lined, doubled,
and INCH -'-.
• Okénha' ionnià:ton tenkhna'néta'
akwáhta. It is made of felt (and) I'm
going to line my shoe with it.

-hna't-/-hna'tahtsher- N purse: **kahnà:ta'**
With **ionhtentiéhtha'** (-ahtenti- go away,
leave): **ionhtentiéhtha' kahnà:ta'** suitcase.
POSS: **akhnà:ta'** my purse, **akohnà:ta'**
her purse; and NEG: **iah í: tewakhnà:ta'**
it is not my purse.
With LOC -kon, inside:
akhna'tahtsherá:kon in my purse, in
my pocket.
With V -iio- be good, nice:
kahna'tahtsherí:io (it is) a nice purse.
With V -ke- amount to, and DLC:
tekahna'tahtsherá:ke two purses.

With V -ont- attach: **iohna'táhtsheronte'**
pocket.
NOTE: The incorporating form has the
NMZR -htsher-.
*Cf. Gan^cnata sac à petun ou autre petit sac,
pochette (Bruyas: 69); Gan^cnátak Sac a
petun (Galissonnière: 74r)*

-hna'tsh- N buttocks: **ohnà:tsha'**
POSS: **khna'tshà:ke** (on) my buttocks.
With SRF -ani-, V -ketskw- raise upright,
and CISL: **tewanihna'tshakétskwas** it is
bucking (a horse or a cow).
With SRF -at- and V -nohare-/-ohare- wash:
Wà:s sathna'tshóhare! Go, wash your
butt!

=hne ATTR at. For example: **kanonhséshne**
at the longhouse; **Ahkwesáhsne**
Ahkwesáhsne Mohawk Nation territory.

=hneha ATTR way of. For example:
Onkwehonwehnéha the Native way;
arihwawa'konhnéha purple,
o'karahsnéha in the evening.

-hneht- N pine, (chewing) gum: **ohnéhta'**
With V -akera- stink, smell:
kahnehtákeras turpentine.
With V -ati-/-onti- lose, throw:
kahnehtóntion it is paved.
With V -ek-/-ak- eat: **rohnehtá:kon** he is
chewing, **iakohnehtá:kon** she is chewing,
shnéhtak Be quiet! *An expression used
when someone is saying something silly or
stupid.*
With V -hon'tsi- be black, dark-coloured:
kahnehtahòn:tsi tar.
With V -(h)nhont- have in one's mouth:
wakhnehtáhnhonte' I have gum in my
mouth.
With V -r- put in: **iohnéhtare'** it has pitch
or gum on it.

With V -(h)rho- coat: **kahnehtáhrhon**
linoleum, tablecloth: **kahnehtáhrhon
atià:tawi** raincoat (-atia'tawi- dress, etc.).
With V -ti- be on the other side, and REP:
Skahnéhtati Albany, NY (nowadays,
Schenectady).

Cf. Onne^cta gomme, bray, pin (Bruyas:
73); *Onne^cta* Pin (Galissonnière: 8v);
Ochnéchta Weiss Pine (Pyrlaeus: 207);
ohnētta Pin (Marcoux: 291); *Ohneta* pin
(Cuoq: 30); *S'kanedadih* Albany, Beside
the pines (Brant-Sero and Hill in Boyle:
172); *Skanektati* Albany NY (Gabriel: 5);
*onentasonha howatsiste tsi non niionetar-
onnion* [bark of an evergreen where there
is pitch] (Beauvais: 27); *Oh neh da* Pitch
(Jamieson 2: 3); *ohnéhta* pine tree (Lazore:
61); Laurentian *Haneda* Green tree
(Biggar: 81), According to them this tree
cured every kind of disease. They call it
in their language *Annedda* (Biggar: 213);
Wendat *andeta* pin arbre (Potier: 449);
Onondaga *ôhnêtta* pin blanc (Shea: 79)

-hnek- N liquid: **ohné:ka'**
With LOC -okon, under: **ohnekó:kon**
under the water.
With V -a[t]- be inside: **rohné:ka** he
drank too much, he is drunk; and DISTR
-rion-: **enkahnekatárion'** it will fill up
with water.
With V -ati-/-onti- lose, throw:
onkhnekón:ti' I threw water on it; and
DLC: **teiohnekóntie's** the water is boiling;
and CAUS -ht-: **wa'tekhnekóntiehte'**
I boiled it, **tekahnekontiéhton** it is
boiled.
With V -atihentho- pull, and CISL:
tkahnekatihénthos waves go out,
entkahnekatihéntho' the water will go
out (as in the tide).
With V -atskara- be bitter: **iohnekatská:ra**
(it is) a bitter liquid.

With V -attatakw- explode, pop:
wathnekatákwas soda.
With V -aweron- spill out of, and CISL or
TRNL: **takhnekáweron'** I poured the
water, **ia'khnekáweron'** I poured the
water out, I added liquid to it.
With V -a'a- be small, **ken'** particle, and
PART: **Ken' nikahnekà:'a** Little Water
Medicine.
With V -a'sen'-/-en'- fall down, and CISL:
tiohnekèn:'en there is a (small) waterfall.
With V -haratat-/-karatat- lift, raise up:
iohnekakaratá:ton the water (level) is
high.
With V -hio'tsis[t]- be salty, sour, ATTR
=hne, at, and DLC: **teiohnekahio'tsíshne**
ocean.
With SRF -at-, V -hwe'nonni-/-kwe'nonni-
fold, and BEN -en-:
onkwathnekakwe'nónnien' something
is going around and around in my throat
(instead of going down).
With V -inekenht- make come out:
wa'khnekínekenhte' I squeezed the
liquid out of it, **kahnekinekénhton** juice.
With V -kentst- be leftover scraps, refuse:
wa'khné:kentste' I drained it.
With V -keri- be broth: **ohnekákeri'**
broth, **kítkit ohnekákeri'** chicken broth.
With V -no- be cold: **ohné:kanos** fresh,
cold water, **iohné:kano** it is cold water.
With V -nont[en]- feed someone:
wa'khehné:kanonte' I gave her or them
water (to drink).
With V -o- be in water: **kahné:ko** there's
water (in the basement, in the creek).
With V -ont- attach: **wakhné:konte'** I am
perspiring; with SRF -at-, V -ont- attach,
INSTR -hkw-, and DLC; and **akè:ra'**
(-akehr-/-kehr- dish, plate, bowl):
teionthnekontáhkhwa' akè:ra' teacup.
With V -ot- stand, and CISL: **tiohné:kote'**
fountain.

With V -otsenh- go scoop out of:
wa'khnekotsénhe' I am going to get
water.
With V -otsenht- scoop out of:
wahahnekótsenhte' he scooped out
water.
With V -o'ten- be a kind of, DISTR -shon-,
and PART: **tsi nikahneko'tèn:shon** all
kinds of drinks.
With V -r- put in: **kahné:kare'** there is
liquid in it, level (tool).
With SRF -at-, V -rakew-/-okew- wipe,
and REP: **shothnekoké:wen** he is sober.
With SRF -at-, V -(h)rho- coat, and CAUS
-hst-: **ionthnekahrhóhstha'** untranslated
(Beauvais: 2), but probably rubbing alcohol.
With V -rihsi- take apart, take off:
wa'khnekaríhsi' I diluted it.
With V -sera[hw]-/-osera[hw]- gush, spew:
wahakhnekóserahwe' he squirted water
at me.
With V -tahkw- take out, and CAUS -ht-:
iehnekatahkwáhtha' pump.
With V -ta'-/-eta'- put inside:
wa'khnekáta' I put water in it.
With V -teni- change, and DLC:
wa'tekhnekaté:ni' I changed the water.
With N -tsikhe't- sweet, V -r- put in, and
DLC: **teiohnekatsikhè:tare'** soda.
NOTE: This root occurs incorporated into
many verbs, and not all the derived and
inflected forms of some of the N plus V
combinations are given here; for the additional forms, see the V entry.
Cf. Onᶜnega eau (Bruyas: 69); Onᶜnéga
Eau, Onᶜneganos Eau froide (Galissonnière: 33r); *ohnēka* Eau (Marcoux: 135);
teiohnekōnties bouillir (Marcoux: 45);
Ohneka eau, liqueur, liquide en général
(Cuoq: 30, 124); *ne hakwekon skatne
tekanekontieton* [everything is boiled
together] (Beauvais: 6); *ta io ne kon ti*

boil (Anon: 26); *te-io-ne-kon-ties* boiling
(water) (Cory: 64); *ta io ne kon ti* boil
(Diabo: 5); *Teiohnekóntie's* Boiling water
(Horne: 85); Susquehannock *Caneega*
water (Holm: 5), *Oneegha* water (Holm: 7)

-hnekir-/-hnekihra- V drink: **khnekíhrha'**
  I drink, **enkhnekì:ra'** I will drink,
  wahahnekì:ra' he drank, **wakhnekì:ren**
  I am drinking, I have drunk.

-hnenhs- N shoulder: **ohnénhsa'**
  POSS: **khnenhsà:ke** (on) my shoulder,
  rahnenhsà:ke (on) his shoulder,
  iehnenhsà:ke (on) her shoulder.
  With V -a- touch, and TRNL, or TRNL and
  DLC: **iahihnénhsa'** or **ia'thihnénhsa'** I
  touched his shoulder.
  With V -atihentho- pull, and CISL:
  tahihnenhsatihéntho' I pulled at, touched
  his shoulder.
  With SRF -at- and V -ot- stand:
  wa'kathnenhsó:ten' I put my shoulder
  up against it (in order to hold it up),
  wahathnenhsó:ten' he put his shoulder
  up against it, he leaned into it with his
  shoulder.
  With SRF -at-, V -otahrho[k]- hook, and
  DISTR -hon-: **athnenhsotáhrhon** suspenders.

  Cf. a tnon so tar hon suspenders (Anon: 5)

-hnenies- be tall. *See* -es-

-hnenna't- N potato: **ohnennà:ta'**
  With V -ate'skont- roast, bake:
  wa'kathnenna'tón:ten' I baked potatoes.
  With V -atken- rot, spoil:
  iohnenna'tátkens the potatoes are rotten,
  wa'ohnenna'tátken' the potatoes rotted.
  With V -astath[en]-/-ath[en]- dry:
  iohnenna'táthen potato chips.

With N -hnek- liquid, V -ati-/-onti- lose, throw, CAUS -ht-, and DLC: **wa'tekhnenna'tahnekóntiehte'** I boiled potatoes.

With V -hriht- break into pieces, smash, and DLC: **wa'tekhnenna'tà:rihte'** I mashed potatoes.

With V -ientho- plant: **wa'khnenna'taiéntho'** I planted potatoes.

With V -kenser[on]- plane, slice, and DLC: **wa'thahnenna'takén:sere'** he sliced potatoes.

With V -o- be in water: **wa'khnennà:to'** I boiled potatoes; and INSTR -hkw-: **iehnenna'tóhkhwa'** pot for cooking potatoes.

With SRF -at-, V -ont- attach, and DLC: **tesathnennà:tonte'** you are so cakey (a Kahnawà:ke expression), you are not all there (the lights are on but nobody's home), **tehothnennà:tonte'** he is so cakey.

With V -ri- cook, ripen, and CAUS -ht-: **wa'khnennà:tarihte'** I cooked potatoes.

With V -takeri'ta['w]-/-keri'ta['w]- fry: **khnenna'takerì:ta's** I fry potatoes, **wa'ehnenna'takerì:ta'we'** she fried potatoes, **iakohnenna'takerì:ta** she is frying potatoes.

Cf. On^cnennata pommes de terre (Bruyas: 71); *onennata* [potato] Ledger: 47, Laurentian *Canonotha* clover (Biggar: 246)

-hneren[k]- V tie, fasten: **íkhnerenks** I tie it, **énkhnerenke'** I will tie it, **wahà:nerenke'** he tied it, **wákhneren** I have tied it, **tekà:neren** it is tied (together).

With DLC: **wa'tékhnerenke'** I fastened it, I did it up (for example, my jacket), **téshnerenk** Do it up! and REV -hsi-: **wa'tekhnerénhsi'** I untied it.

-hnha[k]- wrap, tie around. *See* -hwahnha[k]-/ -hnha[k]-

-hnhonter- V attach end-to-end, add on

With INCH -'-: **wa'khehnhóntera'ne'** I caught up to her, **wa'onkhnhóntera'ne'** she caught up to me, **wahihnhóntera'ne'** or (with REP) **sahihnhóntera'ne'** I caught up to him, **rihnhonterà:'on** I have caught up to him.

With N -ahskwen'n- porch: **wahahskwen'nahnhónteren'** he added on a porch, **wahskwen'nahnhón:tere'** (it is) an attached, enclosed porch.

With N -hson'kar-/-hswen'kar- board, and DLC: **wa'thahson'karahnhónteren'** he added on to the board by attaching another.

With N -nonhs- house: **wahanonhsahnhónteren'** or (with SRF -ate-) **wahatenonhsahnhónteren'** he added on a room to the house.

With N -ronwar-/-nonwar- wire, nail, pin, and DLC: **teharonwarahnhontéhrha'** he attaches wires, (he is) an electrician, **wa'tharonwarahnhónteren'** he connected the wires.

With N -'sere[ht]- vehicle, car, and DLC: **teka'serehtahnhón:tere'** the cars are hooked together; and SRF -ate-: **tewate'serehtahnhontéhrha'** double-runner sleigh with front and back hooked together, a trailer.

See also -ahsonter- join, connect, which has a similar meaning but occurs (mostly) without incorporated nouns.

• Sahakhnhóntera'ne' sahakwatohétsten'. He caught up to me [and] he passed me.

-hniahskari[k]- V buckle: **ohniáhskari**

With DLC: **wa'tekhniáhskarike'** I buckled it up (my shoes, my jacket), **wa'tiehniáhskarike'** she buckled it up, **teshniáhskarik** Buckle it up!

-hniar- N snake: **ò:niare'**
With ATTR =kowa, great: **ohniare'kó:wa** serpent.
With V -r- put in, and INCH -'-: **rohniá:rara's** he sees things (that are not real), he is having hallucinations, **wahohniá:rara'ne'** he saw things, he hallucinated.
• Akwé:kon ne ò:niare' ionathwe'nón:ni. The snakes are all in a ball (typically seen in the spring).

-hnia's- N neck, collar: **ohnià:sa'**
POSS: **khnia'sà:ke** (on) my neck, **rahnia'sà:ke** (on) his neck, **iehnia'sà:ke** (on) her neck.
With LOC -kon, inside; and **ononhsato-kenhtì:ke** (-nonhs- house, -tokenhti- be holy): **ononhsatokenhtì:ke kahnià:sakon** part of a church that goes up to the bell tower.
With V -a- take hold of someone: **wahihnià:sa'** I put my arms around his neck, **wahakhnià:sa'** he put his arms around my neck.
With V -es- be long, tall, and ATTR =kowa, great: **kahnia'seskó:wa** giraffe; with SRF -at-, V -es- be long, tall, and CAUS -t-: **wahathnià:seste'** he stretched his neck, **wakathnia'séston** I am stretching my neck.
With V -her-/-hr- set on top of, and DLC: **tekahnia'sáhere'** it has a collar.
With V -ienawa'k-/-wa'k- hold, support: **khehnia'sawà:kon** I have my arms around her neck, **rihnia'sawà:kon** I have my arms around his neck.
With V -i'tson-/-'tson- be dirty, and DLC: **tehohnia'sá'tson** he has a dirty neck, a dirty collar, **teiohnia'sá'tson** it has a dirty collar.
With V -kwaront- bulge, lump: **iakohnia'sakwá:ronte'** goiter.

With SRF -at- and V -nohare-/-ohare- wash: **rathnia'sóhares** he is gargling, **wa'kathnia'sóhare'** I gargled.
With V -nonhwak[t]- be sore, hurt: **wakhnia'sanòn:waks** my neck hurts.
With SRF -at- and V -ohw- swell: **wakathnià:so** my neck is swollen.
With V -ot- stand, and DLC: **wa'tekhnia'só:ten'** I got all dressed up, all done up, **wa'thahnia'só:ten'** he got all dressed up, **wa'tiehnia'só:ten'** she got all dressed up; with SRF -at- and V -ot- stand: **kathnia'sótha'** I immerse myself (in water) up to my neck, **wa'kathnia'só:ten'** I immersed myself; with SRF -at-, V -ot- stand, and INSTR -hkw-: **ionthnia'sotáhkhwa'** velvet.
With SRF -at- and V -otshi- burn oneself: **kathnia'sótshions** my throat is burning, **wa'kathnia'sótshi'** I burned my throat.
Cf. teiontniasotakwa (velvet) (Onkwe-onwe: 4)

-hnien'tskwir- N shrub, small tree having new buds: **ohnièn:tskwire'**
With V -ra'nekar[on]-/-nekar[on]- burst open, and DLC: **wa'tkahnien'tskwirané:kare'** the twigs are bursting (with buds or leaves).

-hnih-/-hnii- V bark: **rahní:has** he barks, **wahà:niie'** he barked, **rohní:hen** he is barking.
NOTE: There are two pronunciations of this root; for the alternative forms, *see* -'nhii-.

-hnihshen- V be guilty: **wakhníhshen** I am guilty, **rohníhshen** he is guilty, **iakohníhshen** she is guilty.

-hnihsheron- V be on edge, feel edgy, jittery: **tewakhníhsherons** I feel edgy, jittery, **tesahníhsherons** you are on edge, jittery.

-hninon- V buy: **khní:nons** I buy,
enkhní:non' I will buy it, **wahahní:non'**
he bought it, **wahihní:non'** I bought it
from him, **wakhní:non** I have bought it.
With PURP -hr-: **wa'khninòn:re'** I am
going to buy it.
With SRF -aten-: **katenhní:nons** I am
selling something, **wa'katenhní:non'**
I sold it, **rotenhní:non** he has sold it,
wa'kheiatenhní:non' I squealed or tattled
on her, **wahakwatenhní:non'** he squealed
on me; with SRF -aten- and CAUS -'t-:
iontenhninòn:tha' store; with SRF -aten-
and BEN -'s-: **shakotenhninòn:se'** he sells
it to them, for them,
enkheiatenhní:non'se' I will sell it to
her, for her, **wahiiatenhní:non'se'** I sold
it to him, for him.
With N -ahswen't-/-a'swen't- coal:
wa'kahswen'tahní:non' I bought coal.
With N -atenna'tsher- groceries:
wa'katenna'tsherahní:non' I bought
groceries; and PURP -hr-:
wa'katenna'tsherahninòn:re' I am
going to buy groceries.
With SRF -at- and N -hiatonhser- book,
paper: **rathiatonhserahní:nons** he sells
paper, books, newspapers.
With N -honr- gun: **wahahonrahní:non'**
he bought a gun.
With SRF -at- and N -hwist- metal, money:
wahathwistahní:non' he spent his
money.
With N -iie-/-ien- oil, grease:
wa'keienahní:non' I bought gas; and
SRF -ate-: **ronteienahní:nons** they sell
gas; and CAUS -'t-: **ionteienahninòn:tha'**
gas station.
With N -kahkwen't- wheel, tire:
wa'kkahkwen'tahní:non' I bought a tire;
and PURP -hr-: **wahakahkwen'ta-
hninòn:re'** he is going to buy a tire.
With SRF -ate- and N -nonhkw-/

-nonhkwa'tsher- medicine:
ratenonhkwa'tsherahní:nons he sells
medicine; and CAUS -'t-:
tsi iontenonhkwa'tsherahninòn:tha'
drugstore, pharmacy.
With SRF -ate- and N -rist- iron, steel:
rateristahní:nons he is selling something
made of iron or steel (maybe a stove).
With N -wir- offspring: **wa'ewirahní:non'**
she had a baby; and PURP -hr-:
iewirahninòn:re' she is going to have a
baby.
With SRF -ate- and N -'nhonhs- egg:
kate'nhonhsahní:nons I sell eggs.
With N -'sere[ht]- vehicle, car, and PURP
-hr-: **ke'serehtahninòn:re'** I am going
to buy a car.
Cf. Atenninnon traitter (Bruyas: 77);
Aten'ninnon (Acheter) (Galissonnière: 3v);
Susquehannock *Skaddanijnu* will you sell
or barter something? (Holm: 8)

-hnio- V grow (vegetation): **wa'kà:nio'** it
grew.
With NEG: **iah thé:nen teiohniò:'on**
nothing grew.
With PROG -tie- and CISL: **taiohniótie'**
it is growing.
With INSTR -hkw-: **ohnióhkwa'** sprout;
and V -ont- attach: **wa'kahniohkón:ten'**
it sprouted.
• Taiohniótie' ne ohnennà:ta'. The potatoes are growing.

-hnionwar- N thistle, picker, bramble:
ohnión:wara'
With LOC -akta, near, and DLC:
Teiohnionwarákta' At the Wood's Edge
rite.
With V -ont- attach, DISTR -on-, and DLC:
teiohnionwarón:ton it has pickers; and
ATTR ='a/=ha, diminutive:
teiohnionwarontòn:'a gooseberry.

With V -ont- attach, DISTR -onnion-, and DLC: **tewakhnionwarontónnion** I have a pins-and-needles sensation, **wa'tewakhnionwarontónnion'** I got a pins-and-needles sensation.

Cf. Deyughnyonkwarakta At the woods edge (Hale: 116–7); *Onniongꞔar* épine, ronce (Bruyas: 78); *Ohiongꞔare* Espine (Galissonnière: 37v)

-hniot-/-ot- V stand something up: **khniótha'** I stand it up, **enkhnió:ten'** I will stand it up, **wa'khnió:ten'** I stood it up, **kà:niote'** it is standing up.
With SRF -at-: **wa'kathnió:ten'** I put on a brooch, **iakóthniote'** she has on a brooch; **athnió:ta'** brooch, badge.
NOTE: For examples with incorporated nouns, *see* -ot-.

-hnio'kw- N hook: **kahnió:kwa'**

Cf. Kanniogꞔa cramaillere (Bruyas: 78); *Kaniogꞔa* cremaillere (Galissonnière: 26v); *Kaniōkꞔa* Crémaillere (Marcoux: 94); *Kaniokwa* crochet, gaffe, crémaillère (Cuoq: 10); *ka nio kwa* hook (Diabo: 38)

-hnio'tskahr- V hiccup: **wakhnió:tskahre'** I have hiccups, **rohnió:tskahre'** he has hiccups, **iakohnió:tskahre'** she has hiccups, **onkhnió:tskahre'** I got hiccups.

-hnir- V be hard, solid, firm: **iohní:ron** it is hard.
With INCH -ha-: **iohníhrhas** it gets hard, **eniohníhrha'** it will get hard, **wa'ohníhrha'** it got hard, **iohnihrhà:'on** it has gotten hard, it is hard.
With N -atekhwahra- table, and NMZR -'tsher-: **iotekhwahra'tsherahní:ron** (it is) a hard or solid table.
With N -eri[ahs]- heart:

raweriahsahní:ron he is hard-hearted, cruel.
With N -hsi- palm of the hand: **rohsiahní:ron** his grip is strong.
With N -ia't- body, and CAUS -t-: **iakoia'tahní:rats** it makes the body strong.
With N -konhs- face: **rokonhsahní:ron** he has a hard face, he is pushy, he will stick to it (for example, to a lie), **iakokonhsahní:ron** she has a hard face.
With N -niar- neck: **wakeniarahní:ron** I have a strong neck.
With N -rihw- matter, message, and CAUS -t-: **kerihwahní:rats** I confirm it, **enkerihwahní:rate'** I will confirm it, **waharihwahní:rate'** he confirmed it, **wakerihwahnirá:ton** I have confirmed it.
With N -'nikonhr- mind: **wake'nikonhrahní:ron** I am strong-willed; and CAUS -t-: **wa'khe'nikonhrahní:rate'** I comforted her.
With N -'nonhkw- bottom of something; and **anòn:warore'** (-nonhwar- brain, -'rhoro[k]-/-oro[k]- cover): **io'nonhkwahní:ron anòn:warore'** top hat.
With unclear N, CAUS -t-, and DLC: **tehrontahní:rats** he is compressing it, packing it down, **wa'throntahní:rate'** he compressed it, **tewakontahnirá:ton** I have compressed it, **teiontahní:rats** steamroller.

-hnitsh- N thigh: **ohnítsha'**
POSS: **khnitshà:ke** (on) my thigh.
With V -nonhwak[t]- be sore, hurt: **wakhnitshanòn:waks** my thigh hurts.

-hnonhwahsen- V stay with one's in-laws: **kehnonhwáhsen** I am living with my in-laws, **rahnonhwáhsen** he is living with his in-laws, **iehnonhwáhsen** she is living with her in-laws.

-hnotes- be deep. *See -es-*

-hon- V mid
>With N -ohser- winter, year: **Ohséhrhon** Midwinter; and COIN and DLC: **Sha'tekohséhrhon** January, Midwinter.

-honkar- N invitation
>With SRF -at- and V -ati-/-onti- lose, throw: **wakathonkaróntie's** I extend an invitation (to an event), **enwakathonkarón:ti'** I will extend an invitation, **wahothonkarón:ti'** he extended an invitation, **iakothonkaróntion** she has extended an invitation.
>
>With V -awi-/-on- give: **kwahonkará:wis** I or we are giving you an invitation, **enkhehón:karon'** I will give her an invitation, **wa'konhón:karon'** I gave you an invitation; and NEG: **iah tekhehonkará:wi** I didn't invite her; with V -awi-/-on- give, and DISTR -hon-: **wa'khehonkarawíhon'** I gave them invitations; with SRF -at-, V -awi-/-on- give, and PURP -hr-: **wa'kathonkarawì:re'** I am going around giving out invitations.
>
>With V -ia'k- cut, sever: **wa'khehonkária'ke'** I asked her to take on a task (maybe taking notes for a meeting), I volunteered her.
>
>• Akwé:kon wa'khehón:karon' ne ronatenro'shòn:'a. I invited all his friends.
>• Wa'kathonkarawì:re' katen'niotà:ne'. I am going around inviting (people) (because) I'm going to have a wedding.
>
>*Cf. Gahꙅengare* buchette, soit pour festin soit pour autre entreprise, *Gahꙅengaron* donner cette buchette, ce billet (Bruyas: 56); *Kehonkarāꙅis* inviter, convier (Marcoux: 215)

-honr- N gun: **káhonre'**
>With V -esha- be short, **ken'** particle, and PART: **ken' nikahonrésha** handgun, pistol.
>With V -hninon- buy: **wahahonrahní:non'** he bought a gun.
>With V -ot- stand: **iohón:rote'** kettle with a spout.

-honrawatst- V brass instrument: **iehonrawátstha'**
>*Cf. Johonraꙅatsta* joüer de la trompette (Galissonnière: 81r); *iehonraꙅatsta* Trompette (Marcoux: 398);
>*ie hon ra wats tha* cornet (Anon: 22); *iehonrawátsha* horns (Lazore: 73); *iehonrawáhstha* bugle (Gabriel: 17)

-honria'k- V choke, with DLC: **wa'tewakhónria'ke'** I choked, **wa'tiakohónria'ke'** she choked, **wa'tehshakohónria'ke'** he choked her, he strangled her.

-honro't- N pipe, tube: **ohonrò:ta'**
>With LOC -kon, inside: **ohonrò:takon** inside of the pipe.
>With V -a'tarih[en]-/-tarih[en]- be hot, warm: **iohonro'tataríhen** the (stove) pipe is hot.
>With V -hroh[o]- block, put across (as a barrier), and DLC: **teiehonro'tahróhos** flute.
>With V -ke'tot- protrude: **iohonro'takè:tote'** the pipe is sticking out (out of a wall, out of the roof); and CONTR and TRNL: **thiehohonro'takè:tote'** someone with a Native father and White mother.
>With SRF -at-, V -kha- attach, piece together, REV -hsi-, and DLC: **wa'tewathonro'takháhsi'** the pipe separated.

With V -ohw- put into liquid, and TRNL: **ia'akwahonrò:tohwe'** we put the tube, the hose in the water.

With V -okha- leak, drip: **iohonro'tókhas** the pipe is leaking.

With V -onni- make: **wa'khonro'tón:ni'** I made it into a tube.

With V -ot- stand, and DISTR -on-: **kahonro'tó:ton** organ; dandelion.

With SRF -at-, V -ra'nekar[on]-/-nekar[on]- burst open, and DLC: **wa'tewathonro'tané:kare'** the pipe burst.

-hont- N green: **óhonte'**

With V -akera- stink, smell, and ATTR =kowa, great: **kahontakeraskó:wa** goldenrod.

With V -eka'[w]-/-ka'[w]- find tasty, like the taste of: **kahontákon'** sweetgrass.

With V -esha- be short, **ken'** particle, and PART: **ken' niiohontésha** strawberry; and **teiontenonhwerá:tons** (-nonhweraton- greet, give thanks): **Teiontenonhwerá:tons ken' niiohontésha** Strawberry Festival; and ATTR =kowa, great: **ken' niiohontesha'kó:wa** pineapple.

With V -hio'tsis[t]- be salty, sour, and DLC; and **ostawí:na'** (-stawin- stalk, celery): **teiaontahiò:tsis ostawí:na'** or **tiohontahiò:tsis ostawí:na'** rhubarb

Cf. Kanniohontesha fraises (Galisson-nière: 43v); *ka-hon ta-kon* Hierochloe odorata [sweetgrass] (Rousseau: 67); *te-io-hon-ta-ri-on* Euporbia Helioscopie (= herbe cassée en miettes) [sun spurge] (Rousseau: 41)

-honw[ei]- N boat: **kahonwé:ia'**

POSS: **akhonwé:ia'** my boat.

With ATTR =kowa, great: **kahonweia'kó:wa** ship.

With SRF -at- and CAUS -'t-: **kathonweià:tha'** I go boating; and PROG -hatie-: **ronathonweia'tonhátie'** they are boating; with SRF -at-, CAUS -'t-, and PURP -'n-: **wa'kathonweia'tà:ne'** I am going boating, for a boat ride.

With V -a'ker- float, be in water, and AMB -hne-: **iohonwa'kerà:ne'** the boat is floating.

With SRF -at-, V -a'senht-/-enht- drop, INSTR -hkw-, and DLC: **teionthonwenhtáhkhwa'** toboggan.

With SRF -at- and V -har-/-ihar- hang up: **kathonwiháhrha'** I swing, **wahathonwihá:ren'** he swung, **wakathonwíhare'** I am swinging; and INSTR -hkw-: **ionthonwiharáhkhwa'** swing.

With SRF -at- and V -hre[k]- push: **kathonwà:reks** I go boating, **enkathonwà:reke'** I will go boating; and PROG -hatie-: **wakathonwahrehátie'** I am boating.

With V -itie-/-tie-/-ontie- fly around, float by: **kahonweióntie'** the boat floats by, goes by.

With V -ohw- put into liquid, and TRNL: **iahahón:io'** he put the boat into the water.

With V -'sere-/-i'sere- drag, and DISTR -hshon-: **onkhonwi'seréhshon'** I am riding around (in a car); with SRF -at-, V -'sere-/-i'sere- drag, CAUS -ht-, and PURP -'n-: **wa'kathonwi'serehtà:ne'** I am going for a car ride.

• Kana'tsherá:kon kahonweia'kó:wa kahonweióntie'. The ship is going by in the seaway.

-hon'kw- N throat: **ohòn:kwa'**

With SRF -at- and V -aweron- spill out of: **wa'kathon'kwáweron'** I looked up with my head back, **sathon'kwáweron** Look up, put your head back!

With V -ia'[k]- hit, slap:
wahakhon'kwáia'ke' he hit me in the
throat.
With variant -hon'k-, V -ia'k- break, cut in
two, and DLC: **wa'thihòn:tia'ke'** I cut his
throat, **wa'thohòn:tia'ke** he cut his throat.

-hon'tsi- V be black, dark-coloured: **kahòn:tsi**
it is black, **rahòn:tsi** he is a Black person.
With **ata'kenhróhkwa'** grey (-a'kenhr-
ashes, dirt): **ata'kenhrohkwahòn:tsi** dark
grey.
With N -ahi- fruit, berry: **wahiahòn:tsi**
blackberry.
With N -a'kenhr- ashes, dirt:
wa'kenhrahòn:tsi (it is) black soil, dirt.
With SRF -at- and N -hehs- decayed, rotted
wood: **athehsahòn:tsi** dark brown.
With N -hneht- pine: **kahnehtahòn:tsi** tar.
With N -htehr- root: **kahtehrahòn:tsi**
fern.
With N -nonhkwis[er]- head hair:
rononhkwiserahòn:tsi he has black hair.
With ending -st- and V -oskon- be all,
pure: **kahon'tsistóskon** it is all black.

-hoser- N basswood: **ohósera'**

Cf. ohoᶜsera bois blanc (Galissonnière:
8v); *ohōsĕra* Tilleul (Marcoux: 388);
Ohosera tilleul, bois-blanc du Canada
(Cuoq: 30); *oosera otera* [basswood root]
(Beauvais: 3); *o-ho-se-ra* Tilia americana
[basswood] (Rousseau: 51); *O hoh seh rah*
Basswood (Jamieson 2: 3); *Ohósera'* Bass-
wood (Horne: 112)

-ho'kser- N slippery elm: **ohò:ksera'** or
ohò:kseri

-ho'kw- N buttocks: **ohò:kwa'**
POSS: **kho'kwà:ke** (on) my buttocks,
raho'kwà:ke (on) his buttocks,
ieho'kwà:ke (on) her buttocks.

With SRF -at-, V -enton[hw]- move back
and forth, and DLC: **teiontho'kwén:tons**
she is wiggling her bum,
wa'tiontho'kwén:tonhwe' she wiggled
her bum.

-hr- set on top of. *See* -her-/-hr-

-hrahrho- V go ashore: **khráhrhos** I go to
shore, **enkhráhrho'** I will go ashore,
wahahráhrho' he got to shore,
rohráhrhon he has gotten to shore.
With TRNL: **ia'khráhrho'** I went to shore,
I landed.
With CAUS -hst-: **tsi iehrahrhóhstha'**
wharf.

-hraht- N corn ear: **ohráhta'**

Cf. oh rah deh Corn cob (Jamieson 2: 3);
ieniakwahrahtenhte [we would remove the
cobs] (incorporated into -a'senht-/-enht-
drop) (Tewaterihwarenia'tha, Autumn
1989: 6)

-hrarak- V bore a hole: **rahrá:raks** he bores
a hole, **enkhrá:rake'** I will bore a hole,
wahahrá:rake' he bored a hole.
With N -ront- log, beam: **kerontahrá:raks**
I am boring into wood,
wa'kerontahrá:rake' I bored into wood.

-hra'kwenhtar- V be on one's stomach, with
DLC: **tekhra'kwénhtare'** I am on my
stomach, **tehahra'kwénhtare'** he is on
his stomach, **teiehra'kwénhtare'** she is
on her stomach.
With INCH -'- and TRNL:
ia'thahra'kwénhtara'ne' he fell down,
landing on his stomach, on his belly,
ia'tiehra'kwénhtara'ne' she fell on her
stomach.
With SRF -at-, CAUS -ho-, and TRNL:
ia'tkathra'kwenhtáhrho' I lay on my

stomach, **ia'thathra'kwenhtáhrho'** he lay on his stomach.

-hre[k]- V push

With TRNL: **iékhreks** I push it, **ieiónkhreks** she is pushing me, **iénkhreke'** I will push it, **iahà:khreke'** I pushed it, **ia'khè:reke'** I pushed her, **iewákhre** I have pushed it, **iahà:shrek** Push it!

With DISTR -hseron-, and TRNL: **iekhréhserons** I push it around.

With N -atonriser- breath, and TRNL: **ia'katonriserà:reke'** I exhaled.

With SRF -at- and N -honw[ei]- boat: **kathonwà:reks** I go boating, **enkathonwà:reke'** I will go boating; and PROG -hatie-: **wakathonwahrehátie'** I am boating.

With N -tsenh- fire, and DISTR -hseron-: **ktsenhahréhserons** I poke around in the fire, **wahatsenhahréhseron'** he poked the fire.

With N -wer- wind, air, and TRNL: **iekewerà:reks** I am blowing out air, **iahawerà:reke'** he blew out air.

-hren-/-hre'n- V cut into, make an incision:
khrè:nas or **khré:nas** I cut into it, I make an incision, **énkhre'ne'** or **énkhrene'** I will cut into it, **wà:khre'ne'** or **wà:khrene'** I cut it, **wahà:re'ne'** or **wahà:rene'** he cut it, **wahì:re'ne'** or **wahì:rene'** I cut him, **wakhrè:nen** or **wakhré:nen** I have made a cut.

With REFL -atat-: **wa'katáthre'ne'** or **wa'katáthrene'** I cut myself.

Cf. Gahren le coup tomber sur quelqu'un (Bruyas: 87); *Garennhon* decouper (Galissonnière: 25r); *kerēnas* Couper (Marcoux: 91); *Kerenas* inciser, couper (Cuoq: 20); Wendat *Aixrein* Couper le bord de la robe (Sagard: Co4);

Susquehannock *Kareenach* a knife (Holm: 6)

-hren't-/-en't- V hang down: **iohrèn:ton** it is hanging.

With DISTR -onnion-: **iohren'tónnion** they are hanging.

With CISL: **tiohrèn:ton** it is hanging there.

With N -ahseriie['t]- string, rope, thread: **iohseriie'tèn:ton** there is string hanging.

With N -hson'kar-/-hswen'kar- board: **iohson'karèn:ton** tavern, bar, boarding house (referring to the sign that hangs outside).

With N -ia't- body, AMB -hne-, and CISL: **ohnà:ken tahoia'ten'tòn:ne'** he is coming in the back, behind.

With N -itahs- tail: **iotahsèn:ton** there is a tail hanging (for example, from a hat).

With N -kahser- tears, DISTR -onnion-, and DLC: **teiakokahseren'tónnion** she has teardrops hanging (from her eyes); and AMB -hne-: **tesakahseren'tonniòn:ne'** you (sg) are going along with tears.

With N -na'kwarohs- loose, flabby skin, **iona'kwarohsèn:ton** the skin is hanging loose (like when someone has a turkey neck, or the turkey's wattle).

With N -niar- neck: **wakeniarèn:ton** I have my head or neck hanging (to my chest); and AMB -hne-: **roniaren'tòn:ne'** he has his head down walking, **iakoniaren'tòn:ne'** she has her head down walking.

With N -niatar- river, lake: **ioniatarèn:ton** loon.

With N -wis- ice, glass, and DISTR -onnion-: **iowisen'tónnion** icicles.

With N -'nhehs- silk, satin, and DISTR -onnion-: **io'nhehsen'tónnion atià:tawi** ribbon shirt (-atia'tawi- dress, shirt).

With N -'nikonhr- mind: **wake'nikonhrèn:ton** I am depressed.

With N -'now- hump, padlock:
io'nowèn:ton there is a lock hanging.
• Ohiohsà:ke káhrhon tiohrèn:ton. The
cradleboard is hanging in the corner.

Cf. desakaghserentonionne you are weeping on your way (Hale: 116–7)

-hretsaron- V encourage: **wa'khehretsá:ron'**
I encouraged her or them, **rihretsá:ron**
I am encouraging him.
• Wa'khehretsá:ron' aontaionteweièn:ton'
tsi taietsi'nehtará:ron'. I encouraged her
to do a good job with her beadwork.

-hrewaht- V punish: **khehrewáhtha'** I punish
her or them, **enkhehré:wahte'** I will
punish them, **wa'onkhré:wahte'** she or
someone punished me, **khehrewáhton** I
have punished her.
With REFL -atat- and REP:
sakatathré:wahte' I repented,
shotathrewáhton he has repented.

-hre'n- cut into, make an incision. *See*
-hren-/-hre'n-

-hrie'n- N pack, load
With SRF -at- and V -onni- make:
rathrie'nón:ni he packs it,
wa'kathrie'nón:ni' I made a pack.
With V -[t]- be one, and REP: **skahriè:na**
one pack, one load.
• Roientakohónhne' skahriè:na shahá:wi'.
He went to get wood, he brought back
one load.

Cf. Ohriè:na A burden (Tewaterihwarenia'tha, Summer 1988: 24, listed under
"Old Words")

-hriht- V break into pieces, smash, with DLC:
tekhríhtha' I break it, smash it, crush it,
ténkhrihte' I will break it, **wa'tékhrihte'**
I broke it, **tewakhríhton** I have broken it.

With DISTR -nion-: **tekhrihtánions** I am
cutting or chopping them up (for example,
vegetables), **wa'tiehrihtánion'** she broke
them, she smashed them.
With N -ahi- fruit, berry: **wa'tkahià:rihte'**
I crushed berries, **tewahiahríhton** mashed
berries or fruit.
With N -hnenna't- potato:
wa'tekhnenna'tà:rihte' I mashed potatoes.
With N -ks- dish, plate: **wa'tieksà:rihte'**
she broke the dish.
With N -neni- stone, rock:
tekeneniahríhtha' I break up stones,
tekaneniahríhtha' stone crusher,
wa'thanenià:rihte' he smashed, broke up
stones, **tekaneniahríhton** crushed stone.
With SRF -at- and N -onhwents-/-onhonts-
earth, world: **tehatonhontsahríhtha'** he is
breaking up the earth,
wa'thatonhontsà:rihte' he broke up the
earth.
With N -wis- ice, glass: **tehawisahríhtha'**
he is breaking up ice, **wa'thawisà:rihte'**
he broke the glass.
With N -'nionkser- onion:
wa'tha'nionkserà:rihte' he cut up
onions.
With N -'now- hump, padlock:
wa'tke'nowà:rihte' I broke, smashed the
padlock.
With N -'wahr- meat: **teka'wahrahríhton**
hash meat.
NOTE: This stem is composed of a root
-hri-, which occurs only with suffixes, and
CAUS -ht-.

-hri'- V get broken into pieces, shatter, with
DLC: **tekà:ri's** it breaks, **tenkà:ri'ne'**
it will break, **wa'tkà:ri'ne'** it broke,
teiohrì:'on it is broken.
With N -eri[ahs]- heart:
teiakaweriahsahrì:'on she has a broken
heart.

With N -hwist- metal, money:
teiohwistahrì:'on change.
With N -ks- dish, plate: **wa'tkaksà:ri'ne'** the dish broke.
With N -wis- ice, glass: **wa'tkawisà:ri'ne'** the glass broke.
NOTE: This stem is composed of a root -hri-, which occurs only with suffixes, and INCH -'-.

-hroh[o]- V block, put across (as a barrier)
With DLC: **wa'tekhróho'** I put something across, I put up a barrier, **tekahróho** it is put across, in the way (for example, a chain across a road or yellow tape); and DISTR -nion-: **tekahrohánion** there are obstacles in the way.
With SRF -at- and CAUS -hst-:
enkathróhohste' I will shield myself, **wahathróhohste'** he shielded himself, **iakothrohóhston** she is turned away, shielding herself (as if she doesn't want to be recognized); and INSTR -hkw-:
ionthrohohstáhkhwa' shield.
With N -ent- day, and DLC and CISL:
tontawentahróho' (it is) early dawn (the sun is just below the horizon).
With N -honro't- pipe, tube, and DLC:
teiehonro'tahróhos flute.
With N -ronkwahs- chain, and DLC:
tekaronkwahsahróho (there is) a chain going across.
With N -ront- log, beam, and DLC:
tekarontahróho (there is) a beam extended across (for example, at the end of a road, across an entrance or waterway); and DISTR -nion-: **tekarontahrohánion** there are beams extended across; with SRF -ate-, N -ront- log, beam, CAUS -hst-, and DLC:
tewaterontahrohóhstha' axle.
With N -wer- wind, air, and CAUS -hst-:
iowerahrohóhston it is sheltered from the wind; and SRF -ate-:
wakatewerahrohóhston I am shielding

or sheltering myself from the wind; and PROG -hatie-: **wakatewerahrohohston-hátie'** I am going along sheltering from the wind.
Cf. Onondaga *deyosseraronhꙅa* Digue [dam] (Shea: 45)

-hronhw- V go across, angle across, with DLC:
tekà:ronhwe' it is put, angled across (for example, a chain or barrier).
With DISTR -nion-: **tekahronhwánion** they are put across.
With N -nat- town, settlement, and DLC:
Tekanatà:ronhwe' Malone, NY.
With N -ront- log, beam:
tekarontà:ronhwe' (there are) beams across.
• Ohéhsa' ón:ton' tekarontà:ronhwe'. The beams (of the house) became rotted, decayed.

=hronon ATTR resident of. For example:
Kahnawa'kehró:non Kahnawà:ke residents, **Ahkwesashró:non** Akwesáhsne residents, **Wastonhró:non** American(s), **Sita'ehró:non** Jewish, **ieronhia'kehró:non** angel(s).
Cf. "The Indians, called in Canada, *gens des terres, Garhagonronnon,* ... are called also *Têtes de Boule.*" (Lafitau I: 358); *ganniegeronnon* Agniers (Bruyas: 36); *si ta e ro non* jewish, *was ton ro non* american (Anon: 19); Wendat *Chauhaguéronon* Montagnets, *Quieunontatéronons* Les Petuneux, (Sagard: Na2) *Sontouhoironon, Aguierhonon, Onontagueronon* Les Yroquois (Sagard: Na1); Wendat *annieneeronnon* Aniers (Potier: 154)

-hronw- N crevice, ditch
With LOC -kon, inside: **Ohrón:wakon** Hamilton, ON.

With V -onni- make, and DLC: **tekahronión:ni** (there is) a ditch; and PROG -hatie-: **tekahronionnihátie'** (there is) a ditch going along.

-hrori- V tell: **khehró:ris** I tell her, **enkonhró:ri** I will tell you, **wa'khehró:ri'** I told her, **rihró:ri** I have told him, **takhró:ri** Tell me! With DISTR -nion-: **wa'khehroriánion'** I told them all; and TRNL and REP: **iensehshehroriánion'** you will tell all of them over there (back home). With SRF -at-: **kathró:ris** I tell about it, **enionthró:ri'** she will tell about it, **wa'kathró:ri'** I told about it, **rothró:ri** he has told, he is telling about it; and **ákte'** elsewhere, and PART: **ákte' nihathró:ris** he tells something else, he lies. With SRF -at- and CAUS -'t-: **kathrorià:tha'** I talk about it, **wa'kathrória'te'** I talked about it, **wa'kheiathrória'te'** I talked about her.

-hs- N lip: **óhsa'** POSS: **khsá:kon** inside my mouth, **rahsá:kon** inside his mouth, **iehsá:kon** inside her mouth. With V -a'senht-/-enht- drop, and BEN -enni-/-en-: **rakhsenhtén:ni** he criticizes me, he insults me, **shakohsenhtén:ni** he criticizes, insults her or them, **wa'khehsénhten'** I criticized her, I insulted her. With V -kahront- make an opening, a hole: **tsi khsakà:ronte'** my mouth, **tsi rahsakà:ronte'** his mouth, **tsi iehsakà:ronte'** her mouth. With SRF -at-, V -kara'w- be open, and DLC: **wa'tkátskara'we'** I opened my mouth, , **tehotskarà:wen** his mouth his open, **teiakotskarà:wen** her mouth is open; with V -kara'w- be open, CAUS -ht-,

and DLC: **wa'tewakhskarà:wahte'** I yawned, **wa'thohskarà:wahte'** he yawned, **wa'tiakohskarà:wahte'** she yawned; and DISTR -nion-: **tewakhskara'wahtánions** I am yawning, **tehohskara'wahtánions** he is yawning, **teiakohskara'wahtánions** she is yawning. With SRF -at- and V -kwek- shut, close off: **kátskweks** I shut my mouth, **enkátskweke'** I will close my mouth, **wahátskweke'** he closed his mouth, **iakotskwé:kon** she has closed her mouth, her mouth is closed, **sátskwek** Close your mouth, be quiet! With V -nonhwak[t]- be sore, hurt: **wakhsanòn:waks** my lips are sore. With SRF -at- and V -oken- merge, fork: **ratshó:ken** he is a liar, **iontshó:ken** she is a liar.
• Tsi ní:kon enhí:ken' tió:konte' rakhsenhtén:ni. Whenever I see him he is always criticizing me.

-hsakaionhtanion- V yell, hoop and holler: **rahsakaionhtánions** he yells (a warning), **wahahsakaionhtánion'** he yelled, hooped and hollered.

Cf. Gasagaionton faire le cry de victorieux (Bruyas: 95); *Gasagaionton* Cris de victorieux le faire (Galissonnière: 26v); *ksakaiōntha* Cri de victoire, la faire (Marcoux: 99); *Ksakaionts* pousser le cri de victoire, d'alarme (Cuoq: 136); *a ion sa ka ien te* yell (Diabo: 89)

-hsakawente- V have a high-pitched, loud voice: **wakhsakawén:te'** I have a high-pitched, loud voice, **rohsakawén:te'** he has a high-pitched, loud voice, **iakohsakawén:te'** she has a high-pitched, loud voice.

-hsat- V be leaning back, with TRNL:
iékhsate' I am leaning back.
With INCH -'-: **iahahsá:ta'ne'** he fell
backwards, **iehohsatà:'on** he has fallen
backwards.
With SRF -at- and CAUS -ho-:
ia'katshátho' I leaned back.

-hsaten- V carry a person on the back:
wakhsá:tens I go on horseback,
khehsá:tens I am carrying her on my
back, giving her or someone a ride on my
back (I am on all fours, playing with a
child), **enkhehsá:ten'** I will give her a
ride on my back, **wa'khehsá:ten'** I gave
her a ride on my back; **akohsá:tens** horse;
and ATTR =hne, at: **akohsaténhsne** barn.
With PROG -hatie-: **rohsatenhátie'** he is
riding, **khehsatenhátie'** I am riding her
on my back.

-hsa'-/-isa'- V finish, complete: **íkhsa's**
I finish it, **íhthsa's** you (sg) finish it,
ráhsa's he finishes it, **énkhsa'** I will
finish it, **wà:khsa'** I finished it, **waháhsa'**
he finished it, **róhson'** he has finished it.
With CAUS -ht- and TRNL: **ieiehsa'áhtha'**
she uses it up, **iahà:khsa'ahte'** or
iahà:khsahte' I used it up, **iaháhsa'ahte'**
or **iaháhsahte'** he used it up,
iewakhsa'áhton I have used it up.
With SRF -at- and N -a'ther- basket:
wa'onta'therísa' she finished (making)
a basket.
With N -ia't- body: **Shonkwaia'tíson'**
Our Creator.
With SRF -ate- and N -khw- food:
ratekhwísa's he eats it all,
wa'katekhwísa' I ate it up, I finished it,
rotekhwíson' he has finished eating it.
With N -rihw- matter, message:
kerihwísa's I make a commitment, I
promise, **wa'kerihwísa'** I made a commitment, I promised, **rorihwíson'** he has

promised; and SRF -ate- and DLC:
tehiaterihwísa'as the two are going out
together, they are dating, they are engaged.
With SRF -ate- and N -'nikonhr- mind:
wa'kate'nikonhrísa' I made up my mind,
rote'nikonhríson' he has made up his
mind, he has matured; with N -'nikonhr-
mind, CAUS -ht-, and CISL:
tonke'nikonhráhsa'ahte' I am focusing
on it, giving it my full attention,
tewake'nikonhrahsa'áhton I have given
it my full attention.
NOTE: The short accented vowel in forms
with incorporated nouns suggests that this
root goes back to earlier *-hs'a-/-is'a-.
• Akwé:kon iaháhsa'ahte' ne kén:ie'
kà:sere onontsístakon iaháweron'. He
finished or used up all the oil, he poured it
into the engine. • Tonke'nikonhráhsa'ahte'
tsi wahiiatahónhsatate'. I paid attention
when I listened to him.

-hsa'kenser- N frost: **ohsa'kénsera'**
With V -ien- put down, have:
enkahsa'kenserá:ien' it will get frost on
the ground, **wa'kahsa'kenserá:ien'** frost
got on the ground, **iohsa'kenserá:ien'**
there is frost on the ground.
With V -r- put in: **iohsa'kénserare'** there
is frost on it (for example, on a window);
and INCH -'-: **eniohsa'kénserara'ne'** it
will get frost on it,
wa'ohsa'kénserara'ne' it got frost on it.
With V -(h)rho- coat:
wa'kahsa'kenseráhrho' it got covered in
frost.

-hsa'kt[on]-/-a'kt[on]- V bend, with DLC:
tekhsà:ktons I bend it, I fold it,
wa'tekhsà:kete' I bent it, **tehohsà:kton**
he has bent it.
With DISTR -nihon-: **tehahsa'ktaníhons**
he is bending it this way and that way,
wa'thahsa'ktaníhon' he bent it this way

and that way.

With SRF -at-: **tekatshà:ktons** I bend over, **wa'tkatshà:kete'** I bent over, **tewakatshà:kton** I am bent over, **teiotshà:kton** it is bent or crooked.

With SRF -at- and N -ahi- fruit, berry: **teiotahià:kton** banana.

With SRF -at- and N -a'enn- bow: **teiota'ennà:kton** (it is) a bow that is bent.

With SRF -at- and N -hah- road: **teiothahà:kton** the road has a bend in it.

With SRF -at- and N -kwir- tree, sapling: **teiotkwirà:kton** the tree is bent or crooked.

With SRF -ate- and N -nekot- steps, ladder, stairs: **teiotenekotà:kton** the stairs have a bend or curve in them.

With SRF -ate- and N -nentsh- arm: **wa'tkatenentshà:kete'** I bent my arm.

NOTE: The punctual forms have a variant of the stem -hsa'ket-, with an epenthetic *e*.

-hsenn- N name: **kahsén:na'**

With ATTR =shon'a, pluralizer: **kahsenna'shòn:'a** names.

With V -awi-/-on- give: **khehsenná:wi** I give her a name, **ionkhsenná:wi** she gives me a name, **wahohsén:non'** he gave him a name.

With V -haratat-/-karatat- lift, raise up: **Enhonwatihsennakará:tate'** Naming Ceremony.

With V -ien- put down, have: **ronwahsén:naien'** they praise him (in a religious sense), they worship him.

With V -ieron- make fun of, play, and CONTR: **thihonwahsennaié:ron** they are making fun of his name.

With V -keht[e]- carry on the back: **rohsennakéhte'** he doesn't have a clan, so they give him a name, **iakohsennakéhte'** she doesn't have a clan, so they give her a name.

With V -kowan[en]-/-owan[en]- be big:

rahsennowá:nen he has a big name, a big reputation, he is famous, (he is) a chief; and INCH -ha'-: **wahahsennowáhnha'** he got a big name, a reputation.

With REFL -atat- and V -r- put in: **wa'katatshén:naren'** I signed it.

With V -rohro[k]- gather, collect: **rahsennarò:roks** he is collecting names, (he is) a census taker.

Cf. Gasendꝸannen être considérable, grand guerrier (Bruyas: 95); "The first [social class] is (that of) the *Iesendouans*, that is the noble families;" (Lafitau I: 341); *ra'sĕññowā'nĕⁿ'* 'he a chief (is) (Deserontyon: 100)

-hsere- V follow, chase: **khéhsere'** I am following her, **íkhsere's** I chase it, **khéhsere's** I am chasing her around, here and there, **enkhéhsere'** I will follow her, **wa'khéhsere'** I followed her, **ítsher** Chase it!

With DISTR -hshon-: **enkhehseréhshon'** I will chase her from place to place.

-hseriie['t]- string, rope, thread. *See* -ahseriie['t]-

-hserohen- V be quick-tempered: **khseró:hen** I am quick-tempered, **rahseró:hen** he is quick-tempered, **iehseró:hen** she is quick-tempered.

With INCH -'-: **enkhseró:hen'ne'** I will become angry, **wahahseró:hen'ne'** he got fierce, **wa'kahseró:hen'ne'** it got fierce (for example, a dog baring its teeth).

Cf. Gaserohen être méchant homme (Bruyas: 96); *Kserōhen* Barbare (Marcoux: 35); *Kserohen* être méchant (Cuoq: 26); *ka se ro hen* fierce (Diabo: 28)

-hseronni- V dress, prepare

With SRF -at-: **katsherón:nis** I get

dressed, **wa'ontsherón:ni'** she got dressed; **atsherónnia'** clothing.
With SRF -at- and DISTR -nion-: **katsheronniánions** I am putting on clothes, I am getting dressed, **wa'ontsheronniánion'** she put on clothes, she got dressed, **satsheronniánion** Put on your clothes!
With SRF -at- and CAUS -'t-: **né: katsheronnià:tha'** that's what I wear, **enkatsherónnia'te'** I will wear that.
With N -ahskwen'n- porch: **rahskwen'nahserón:ni** he is fixing the porch.
With SRF -at- and N -a'kenhr- ashes, dirt: **wa'kata'kenhrahserón:ni'** I prepared the soil.
With SRF -at- and N -ia't- body: **katia'tahserón:nis** I am dressing up, **wa'katia'tahserón:ni'** I dressed up; and CAUS -'t- and INSTR -hkw-: **iontia'tahseronnia'táhkhwa'** dressy clothing.
With V -ihei[on]-/-enhei[on]- die, and CAUS -'t-: **renheion'tahserón:ni** he is an undertaker.
With SRF -at- and N -kwir- tree, sapling: **wahatkwirahserón:ni'** he trimmed the tree.
With N -nat- town, settlement: **wahatinatahserón:ni'** they fixed up (decorated) the town.
With N -nehw- animal skin, hide: **wa'kenehwahserón:ni'** I prepared the skin or hide.
With N -nenhr- crowd: **rotinenhrahserón:ni** they lined up, **sewanenhrahserón:ni** Form a line! (pl).
With N -onhnh- life: **konionhnhahserón:ni** I make you feel better, healthier, **wa'kheionhnhahserón:ni'** I made her feel better.
With SRF -ate- and N -rihw- matter, message: **wa'atiaterihwahserón:ni'** we two

arranged it, **wahonterihwahserón:ni'** they made arrangements.
With N -ront- log, beam: **kerontahserón:ni** I square a log or beam, **waharontahserón:ni'** he squared the log.
With N -tsinaren't-/-tsiniaren't- hoof: **wa'ktsiniaren'tahserón:ni'** (ne akohsá:-tens) I worked on the hoofs (of the horse).
With N -'sere[ht]- vehicle, car: **ra'serehtahserón:ni** mechanic; and CAUS -'t-: **ie'serehtahseronnià:tha'** garage (for repairing cars).

-hseronni[k]- V put on stockings, socks: **wa'khehserón:nike'** I put stockings, socks, footies on her.
With SRF -at-: **wa'katsherón:nike'** I put on stockings, socks, footies, **iakotsherón:ni** she has on stockings; and REV -hsi-: **wa'katsheronniáhsi** I took off my stockings.

-hshon distributive ending added to locative suffixes.

-hsi- N palm of the hand: **óhsia'**
With LOC -okon, under, and POSS: **khsió:kon** (on) my palm(s), **rahsió:kon** (on) his palm(s), **iehsió:kon** (on) her palm(s).
With V -hnir- be hard, solid: **rohsiahní:ron** his grip is strong.
With V -ok- chafe, get a blister: **wakhsió:kas** I have a blister on my hand.
With V -otarihsi- unhook, and BEN -en-: **onkhsiotaríhsien'** it came out of my hand, I lost my grip, **wahohsiotaríhsien'** he lost his grip.

-hsiara'- V have seizures, be epileptic: **wakhsiá:ra's** I am epileptic, **rohsiá:ra's** he is epileptic, **iakohsiá:ra's** she is epileptic, **wahohsiá:ra'ne'** he had a seizure.

Cf. ꝸaksiāras epilepsie, etre attaqué d'
(Marcoux: 155); *Wakiaras* être épileptique
(Cuoq: 57); *iakosiaras ononkwa* [epilepsy
medicine] (Beauvais: 17)

-hsienhont-/-hsiahont- N stomach:
ohsienhón:ta' or **ohsiahón:ta'**
POSS: **akhsienhón:ta'** my stomach.
With V -awenrie- stir, and DLC:
tewakhsienhontawénrie' my stomach is
rumbling, **tehohsienhontawénrie'** his
stomach is rumbling.
With V -nonhwak[t]- be sore, hurt:
wakhsienhontanòn:waks I have a stomach ache, **onkhsienhontanòn:wake'** I got
a stomach ache.

Cf. osiahōnta ventre (Marcoux: 411);
Osienhonta bas ventre, abdomen (Cuoq:
36); Laurentian *Eschehenda* the belly
(Biggar: 242)

-hsin- N leg: **ohsí:na'**
POSS: **khsinà:ke** (on) my leg, **rahsinà:ke**
(on) his leg, **iehsinà:ke** (on) her leg.
With SRF -at- and ATTR =ʼa/=ha,
diminutive: **atshíhnha** garter.
With V -es- be long, and DLC:
tekhsiné:son's I have long legs; and
atháhsteren (-athahsteren- put on pants,
trousers): **tekahsí:nes atháhsteren** long
pants.
With V -esha- be short, **ken'** particle, and
PART and DLC; and **atháhsteren**
(-athahsteren- put on pants, trousers):
ken' na'tekahsinésha atháhsteren
shorts.
With SRF -at- and V -haratat-/-karatat- lift,
raise up: **enhsatshinakará:tate'** you will
lift up your leg (so you stand on one leg),
wa'katshinakará:tate' I lifted up my leg.
With V -ia'ser-/-'ser- stack, and DLC:
tekhsinà:sere' my legs are crossed; and
SRF -at-: **tenhsatshinà:seren'** you will

cross your legs, **wa'tkatshinà:seren'** I
crossed my legs.
With V -kwatho- hem, and DLC:
wa'tekhsinakwátho' I hemmed it.
With SRF -at- and V -ohro[k]- insert:
katshinò:roks I am putting on leggings,
wa'katshinò:roke' I put on leggings,
wakatshinò:ron I have put on leggings;
atshinò:ron leggings.
With SRF -at- and V -ohw- swell:
wahatshí:no' his leg swelled, **rotshí:no**
his leg is swollen.
With V -ok- chafe, get a blister:
onkhsí:noke' it chafed my leg.
With SRF -at-, V -otahrho[k]- hook, and
DLC: **wa'thakwatshinotáhrhoke'** he
tripped me.
With SRF -at-, V -o'[k]- slap, flutter, flap,
and CAUS -ht-: **katshino'káhtha'** I am
limping, **wahatshinò:kahte'** he limped;
and PROG -hatie-: **rotshino'kahtonhátie'**
he is going along limping.

Cf. Atsinnha jartière (Bruyas: 43);
Gatsinnha Jartiere (Galissonnière: 49v);
atsīnnha Jarretiere (Marcoux: 219);
Atsinnha jarretière (Cuoq: 3); *a tshinn ha*
garters (Anon: 5)

-hsineko't- N ankle: **ohsinekò:ta'**
POSS: **khsineko'tà:ke** (on) my ankle,
rahsineko'tà:ke (on) his ankle,
iehsineko'tà:ke (on) her ankle.
With SRF -at- and V -tahkw- take out:
wa'katshineko'tatáhko' I sprained
my ankle.

Cf. Osinnigota cheville du pied (Bruyas:
97); *osenigꝸta* cheville du pied (Galissonière: 24r); *ochsinnagōta* Knöchel
(Pyrlaeus: 199); *osinekōta* Cheville du
pied (Marcoux: 67); *Osinekota* cheville du
pied (Cuoq: 36); *o si ne ko ta* ankle (Anon:
3); Laurentian *Agochinegodascon* the

knees (Biggar: 242); Wendat *Ochingoda*
Les genoüils (Sagard: Me5)

-hskar- N friend of the opposite sex:
ákhskare' my boyfriend, girlfriend,
sáhskare' your boyfriend, girlfriend,
raóhskare' his girlfriend, **akóhskare'**
her boyfriend.

-hskar- N flax: **óhskare'**
Cf. Oskaro du chanvre (Bruyas: 97);
Oskare Chanvre (Galissonnière: 17v);
ōskăre Lin (Marcoux: 231); *Oskare*
lin, chanvre (Cuoq: 36); *os ka re
ka nen ken ie* linseed oil (Anon: 14);
os ka re ka nen linseed, *os ka re
ka nen a wen ie* linseed oil (D'Ailleboust: 25)

-hskaw- N bush
With LOC **-aktontie'**, along, edge of:
ohskawaktóntie' near the bush.
With LOC **-kon**, inside: **ohská:wakon**
in the bush.
With SRF **-at-**, V **-awe'ehst-** pierce, and
TRNL and DLC: **ia'tkatskawáwe'ehste'**
I went into the bush.
With V **-ot-** stand: **kahská:ote'** (there is)
a bunch of trees.

-hsken'rakehte- V be a male:
rohsken'rakéhte' male person, warrior,
rotihsken'rakéhte' warriors.
NOTE: According to Mike Norton, this
stem describes a boy whose voice has
changed. The stem probably includes
-keht[e]- carry on the back.
Cf. Gaskenra la guerre, *Hoskenragetete*
Soldat (Bruyas: 98); *Hoskenrᶜcheᶜte*
Guerrier (Galissonnière: 47r);
roskenrakēhte guerrier (Marcoux: 194);
Roskenrakehte homme de guerre (Cuoq:

36); *ros ken ra khe te* male (Anon: 2);
Wendat *oskenraę^te* La guerre (Potier:
453); Onondaga *haguechkenraguettat*
je suis Soldat (Shea: 94)

-hskerewak- V belong to the Bear clan:
wakhskeré:wake' I am Bear clan,
rohskeré:wake' he is Bear clan.
Cf. oskerɛage Ours (Galissonnière: 7v);
"*Hoskereouak*, ... the [Great] Bear," (Lafitau I: 291); *Rosgeréwage* er ist aus dem
Geschlecht des Baeren (Pyrlaeus: 481);
roghskerewake Bear clan (Hale: 120–1)

-hskwen't- N lips: **ohskwèn:ta'**
POSS: **khskwen'tà:ke** (on) my lip,
rahskwen'tà:ke (on) his lip,
iehskwen'tà:ke (on) her lip.
With V **-ia'[k]-** hit, slap:
enkonhskwen'táia'ke' I will smack
you in the lips.

-hsnie- V take care of someone, with DLC:
tekhéhsnie' I take care of her.
With INCH **-'-**: **tenhákhsnie'ne'** he will
take care of me, **tenhíhsnie'ne'** I will take
care of him, **wa'tekhéhsnie'ne'** I took
care of her, **tehshakohsniè:'on** he has
taken care of her.

-hsnienen- V help someone: **khehsnié:nens**
I help her or someone (do something),
enkonhsnié:nen' I will help you,
enhsekhsnié:nen' you will help me,
wahshakohsnié:nen' he helped her,
khehsnié:nen I am helping her.
With unusual SRF **-ata-**:
wa'katahsnié:nen' I helped out,
wahontahsnié:nen' they helped out.
• Enwá:ton' ken enhsekhsnié:nen'?
Can you help me? • Khehsnié:nen
taionná:tahkwe'. I'm helping her move.

-hsnonhs- N finger, hand: **ohsnónhsa'** or **oshónhsa'** finger, hand, donut.
POSS: **kehsnonhsà:ke** (on) my hand(s) or finger(s), **rahsnonhsà:ke** (on) his hand(s), **iehsnonhsà:ke** (on) her hand(s).
With V -a- touch, and TRNL, or TRNL and DLC: **iahihsnónhsa'** or **ia'thihsnónhsa'** I touched his hand.
With SRF -ani- and V -awi- wrap around, encircle: **anihsnónhsawi** ring, **akwanihsnónhsawi** my ring; and CAUS -'t-: **kanihsnonhsawì:tha'** I am putting on a ring(s), **enkanihsnónhsawi'te'** I will put on a ring(s), **wa'kanihsnónhsawi'te'** I put on a ring(s), **wakanihsnonhsawì:ton** I have a ring(s) on.
With V -htohrarak-/-ohrarak- squeeze, press down, and DLC: **wa'tkonhsnonhsò:rarake'** I squeezed your hands or fingers.
With V -ienawa'k-/-wa'k- hold, support: **khehsnonhsawà:kon** I am holding her hand.
With V -ishonhkw- quake, tremble, and DLC: **tewakehsnonhsishónhkhwa'** my hands are trembling, shaking.
With V -karewaht- injure, hurt: **onkehsnonhsakaré:wahte'** I hurt my finger or hand.
With V -kowan[en]-/-owan[en]- be big, and DLC: **tekehsnonhsowá:nen's** I have big fingers, big hands.
With SRF -ani- and V -ohro[k]- insert: **anihsnonhsò:ron** or (with CAUS -st-) **ionnihsnonhsohrókstha'** thimble.
With SRF -ani- and V -ohw- swell: **kanihsnónhsos** my hand swells, **wa'kanihsnónhso'** my hand swelled, **wakanihsnónhso** my hand is swollen.
With V -onkw- bump, hit, and TRNL and DLC: **ia'tewakehsnonhsón:ko'** I hit my finger, my hand.
With V -onni- make: **wa'kehsnonhsón:ni'** I made donuts.

With V -ont- attach, DISTR -on-, and DLC: **teiohsnonhsón:ton** it has fingers (for example, *akwa'niá:nawen* my gloves).
With SRF -ate- and V -rakarehrahst-/-karehrahst- make noise: **katehsnonhsakarehráhstha'** I am making noise with my hand (for example, snapping my fingers, tapping on the table).
With SRF -ani-, V -ra'neken-/-neken- be side-by-side, next to, and DLC: **tenhsanihsnonhsané:ken'** you will put your fingers together (and make a piercing whistle), **wa'tkanihsnonhsané:ken'** I put my fingers together.
With V -ronhkwani-/-ronhkwen- itch: **wakehsnonhsarónhkwani** my hands are itchy.
With SRF -ani-, V -tenihon- shake, and DLC: **tekanihsnonhsateníhon** I am waving my hand.
NOTE: The *hsn* of this root sounds more like *shn*; also, some speakers do not pronounce the *n*.

-hsnor[e]- V be fast: **iohsnó:re'** it is fast.
With PROG -atie-: **iohsnorátie'** it is going by fast.
With SRF -at- and CAUS -t-: **kathsnó:rats** I am hurrying up, **wa'kathsnó:rate'** I hurried up, I went fast, **rothsnorá:ton** he has hurried up, **sathsnó:rat** Hurry up!
With INSTR -hkw- and REP: **enshihsnó:rahkwe'** I will confront him, go back and tell him (what he said) is not so, I will tell him off, **sakhehsnó:rahkwe'** I confronted her, I told her or someone off.
With N -ia't- body: **raia'tahsnó:re'** he is fast, he does things fast; and NEG: **iah tetia'tahsnó:re'** I am not fast.
With N -kahr- eye: **kkahrahsnó:re'** I am giving it a glance, a quick look (without really looking), **rakahrahsnó:re'** he gives it a glance, **iekahrahsnó:re'** she gives it a glance.

With N -na'kw- anger: **rana'kwahsnó:re'** he gets angry easily, **iena'kwahsnó:re'** she gets angry easily.

NOTE: The *hsn* of this root sounds more like *shn* and could be written without the *h*.

Cf. Josnoron aller faire viste q. chose, *Gasnoraton* dépêcher q. chose, haster (Bruyas: 99); *Iosnore* vite (Cuoq: 7); *ios no re* quick (Diabo: 60); Susquehannock *Zatznⱳri* Be quick (Holm: 9)

-hsohi't-/-hsohiht- N hazelnut: **ohsóhi'te'** or **ohsóhihte'**

Cf. osōhĭte Noisettier (Marcoux: 262); *Osohite* noisette (Cuoq: 36); *osoite* [nut] (Beauvais: 3); *o-so-hi-te* Corylus cornuta [beaked hazelnut] (Rousseau: 38)

-hsohkw- N spout

With V -ont- attach: **iohsóhkonte'** (there is) a spout.

• Kawistohserókwen takáweron' iohsóhkonte' kátshe'. I poured cream out of the container with the spout.

-hson-/-hsw- N back

POSS: **khsòn:ne** my back, behind me, **rahsòn:ne** his back, behind him, **iehsòn:ne** her back, behind her.

With V -hna'ne[t]-/-ne[t]- be lined, doubled, and DLC: **tekahswá:ne** pie.

With V -hna'neta'-/-neta'- line, double, and CISL: **entkonhswanéta'** I will back you up, take your part, **tahakhswanéta'** he took my part.

With V -ket- scrape: **rakhswaké:tas** he is scratching my back, **wahíhswakete'** I scratched his back, **tákhswaket** Scratch my back!

With SRF -at-, V -ra'kar- be leaning against, and TRNL: **ia'katshwarà:karen'** I leaned my back up against something.

• Khsòn:ne ne tká:ien'. It's (lying) behind me.

Cf. Gasonne le dos (Bruyas: 100); *Gesonne* mon dos (Galissonnière: 32r); *esōnne* dos (Marcoux: 129); *ieshonne ken niwaa* [on the small of the back] (Beauvais: 6); *ohs wah* back (Jamieson 3: 3)

-hsonw- V be a hole: **iohsón:we'** (there is) a hole.

With SRF -ani- and V -hwatase-/-tase- turn, twist: **anihsonwatá:se** borer; with V -hwatase-/-tase- turn, twist, CAUS -'t-, and INSTR -hkw-: **iehsonwatase'táhkhwa'** hand drill.

With V -kahront- make an opening, a hole: **iohsonwakà:ronte'** there is a hole in it.

With V -kowan[en]-/-owan[en]- be big: **iohsoniowá:nen** (it is) a big hole.

With V -onni- make: **wahahsonión:ni'** he made a hole, **wakhsonión:ni** I have made a hole.

-hson'kar-/-hswen'kar- N board: **ohsòn:kare'** or **ohswèn:kare'**

With LOC -'ke: **ohson'karà:ke** or **ohswen'karà:ke** on the floor.

With V -a'senht-/-enht- drop: **wahonwahsòn:karenhte'** they raided him, his place, **wa'esahsòn:karenhte'** they raided you.

With V -hnhonter- attach end-to-end, add on, and DLC: **wa'thahson'karahnhónteren'** he added on to the board by attaching another one.

With V -hren't-/-en't- hang down: **iohson'karèn:ton** tavern, bar, boarding house (referring to the sign that hangs outside).

With V -ia'k- break, cut in two, INSTR -st-, and DLC: **teiehson'karià:kstha'** saw.

With V -ientot- stack in a pile, and DLC: **wa'thahson'karaientó:ten'** he stacked the boards.

With V -ket- scrape: **rahson'karaké:tas** (he is) a carpenter; and NMZR -'sher-, V -nekenhteron- handsome man, and DLC: **tehnihson'karaketa'sheranekénhteron** two young carpenters (*a playful expression from Mike Norton*).

With V -oia'[k]- throw straight at, CAUS -ht-, and DLC: **wa'tekhson'karó:ienhte'** I threw it on the floor, **wa'thihson'karó:ienhte'** I threw him on the floor (as we were wrestling); and REFL -atat- and DISTR -nion-: **tehontatshon'karoienhtánions** they throw each other on the floor.

With V -oren- split open, and DLC: **Tekahson'karó:rens** Hogansburg, NY.

Cf. iossenkarēnton Auberge (Marcoux: 27); *ra shon ka ra ke tas* carpenter (Anon: 11); *tekasūkaró:rᾶs* Hogansburg ('saw mill') (Floyd Lounsbury, notes archived at the American Philosphical Society); *Tekahshon'karó:renhs* Hogansburg (Horne: 60)

-hson'nion- V be an omen, a premonition: **kahsòn:nions** it is an omen.

With BEN -'s-: **wakhson'niòn:se'** I have a premonition, **rohson'niòn:se'** he has a premonition, **onkhsòn:nion'se'** I got a premonition, **wa'akohsòn:nion'se'** she got a premonition.

-hsot- KIN grandparent

With ATTR ='a/=ha, diminutive: **rakhsótha** my grandfather, **akhsótha** my grandmother, **iahsótha** your grandfather, **sahsótha** your grandmother, **rohsótha** his or her grandfather, **ronwahsótha** her grandfather, **rákhso** Grandfather! **ákhso** Grandmother!

With **iakonatahrén:nen** (-natahr[e]- visit): **akhsótha iakonatahré:nen** it is (my, her)

moon time, monthly (period), my grandmother (moon) is visiting.

With ATTR =kenha, former, late: **rakhsothkénha** my late grandfather.

With ATTR =okon, pluralizer, and ATTR =kenha, former, late: **ionkhihsothokon'kénha** our ancestors.

With NMZR -hser-: **kahsótshera'** grandparents, grandparents plus great-grandparents.

With NMZR -hser-, and ATTR =kenha, former, late: **onkwahsotshera'kénha** our ancestors.

With NMZR -hser-, V -hna'ne[t]-/-ne[t]- be lined, doubled, and DLC: **teiohsotsherá:ne** great-grandparent(s).

With V -shen- have as kin: **rohsótshen** he has grandparents, **iakohsótshen** she has grandparents, **rotihsótshen** they have grandparents.

• Kahsótshera' tahiatáweia'te' ionsahni-iá:ken'ne'. The two grandparents came in [and] went out again. • Kahsótshera' tahontáweia'te'. All the grandparents (or grandparents, great-grandparents) came in.

-hso'kw- N nut: **ohsò:kwa'**

With **akohsá:tens** horse (-hsaten- carry a person on the back): **akohsá:tens ohsò:kwa'** chestnut.

With ATTR =shon'a, pluralizer: **ohso'kwa'shòn:'a** all kinds of nuts.

With V -ia'[k]- hit, slap: **wahihso'kwáia'ke'** I smacked him on the head.

With V -keri- be broth: **ohso'kwákeri'** coffee.

With V -ket- scrape, and CAUS -'t-: **iehso'kwaketà:tha'** nutmeg.

-hst- V use: **íkhsta** I am useful, **ráhsta** he is useful, **káhsta** it is useful.

With NEG: **iah thé:nen tékahsta** it's not useful.

With NEG and REP: **iah thé:nen tesékhsta** I am not strong, of no use anymore.
With SRF -at-: **kátstha'** I am using it, **rátstha'** he uses it, **ióntstha'** she uses it, **róntstha'** they are using it, **én:katste'** I will use it, **wà:katste'** I used it, **wà:ratste'** he used it, **wakátston** I have used it, I am wearing it, **iakótston** she has used it, she is wearing it.
With SRF -at- and REV -hsi-: **ó:nen wa'katstáhsi'** I have no use for it now.
With N -rihw- matter, message: **karihwáhsta** it is useful (a useful matter).
• Kátstha' ne iohón:rote' takhnekóntiehte' ohné:kanos. I use the kettle to boil water.
• Wakátston ohstarò:kwa'. I am wearing a necklace. • Iah thé:nen teháhsta rentóhrha'. He's of no use, he's lazy.

-hstar- V weep, cry, with SRF -at-:
katstáhrha' I weep, **enkatstá:ren'** I will cry, **wakátstare'** I am weeping.
NOTE: Frank Natawe said this stem was "oratorial."

Cf. onstara cry (van den Bogaert: 58); *Gastaren* pleurer (Galissonnière: 66v); *Katstārha* Pleurer (Marcoux: 294); *Katstarha* pleurer, verser des larmes (Cuoq: 16); *a ionts ta ren* weep (D'Ailleboust: 12)

-hstar- N drop: **ohstá:ra'**
With V -ahset- count: **iehstarahsé:tas** she is counting the drops, **wa'khstaráhsete'** I counted the drops.
With V -ati-/-onti- lose, throw: **onkhstarón:ti'** I sprinkled drops (maybe on clothes before ironing them), **wa'ohstarón:ti'** it started to rain lightly, **iohstaróntion** it is raining lightly.
With V -a'senht-/-enht- drop, and TRNL: **ia'khstá:renhte'** I put a drop in it.

With V -a'sen's-/-en's- drop unintentionally: **onkhstá:ren'se'** I dropped a drop (for example, when I was cooking a drop fell on the floor).
With V -ke- amount to, and DLC: **tekahstá:rake** two drops.
With V -ohw- put into liquid, and TRNL: **iekhstá:rohs** I am putting a drop into something that's liquid (maybe a drop of food colouring), **ienkhstá:rohwe'** or **ienkhstá:ro'** I will put in a drop, **ia'khstá:rohwe'** or **ia'khstá:ro'** I put in a drop, **ieiakohstaróhon** she has put in a drop.
With SRF -at-, V -okw- disperse, CAUS -ht-, and DLC: **wa'tekheiatstarókwahte'** I splashed her, **wa'thakwatstarókwahte'** he splashed me.
With V -ont- attach: **khehstaróntha'** I am nursing her, **wa'khehstarón:ten'** I nursed her.
With V -[t]- be one, and REP: **skahstá:ra** one drop.
With SRF -at- and V -teni[on]- disperse, flurry: **ontstaraté:ni'** it started to rain lightly, drizzle, **iotstaraténion** it is raining lightly.

-hstarathe- V be shiny, with DLC:
teiohstaráthe' it is shiny.
With INCH -'-: **wa'tiohstaráthe'ne'** it got shiny.
With CAUS -'t-: **teiehstarathè:tha'** she is polishing it, **wa'tekhstaráthe'te'** I polished it, **tewakhstarathè:ton** I have polished it; and INSTR -hkw-: **teiehstarathe'táhkhwa'** polish.
With N -neraht- leaf: **teionerahtahstaráthe'** plantain.
NOTE: This stem probably includes -hstar- drop, and -the- be shiny, bright, which is also present in -rihwathe't- make clear, explain.

-hstaro'kw- N necklace made of big beads, chain: **ohstarò:kwa'**
With V -nia[k]- wrap around the neck: **wa'khehstaro'kwániake'** I put a necklace on her; and SRF -at-: **wa'katstaro'kwániake'** I put on a necklace, **iakotstaro'kwánien** she has on a necklace.

-hstawen- N rattle: **ohstá:wen**
With ATTR =kowa, great: **ohstawa'kó:wa** turtle rattle.
With NMZR -hser- and V -a'senht-/-enht- drop: **Hahstawenhserénhtha'** Mohawk title name 8.

Cf. Astaᴤen tortue que le jongleur tient en main en chantant (Bruyas: 30); *Ostaᴤen* tortue que l'on bat en chantant (Galissonnière: 17v); *oh steh wen dah* rattle (Jamieson 2: 5); *ohstá:wen* rattle (Deering and Delisle: 286); Wendat *ᴧstaᴤencha* tortue ... serpent à sonnettes ... chichikoi (Potier: 453); Onondaga *gastahᴤenchera Chichicoi ...* une gourde ... avec laquelle ils battent la mesure dans leur chansons (Shea: 32)

-hstien['t]- N/V bone: **óhstien** bone, **ónkhstien'** I got a bone (stuck in my throat), **wahóhstien'** he got a bone stuck, **wa'akóhstien'** she got a bone stuck. POSS: **ákhstien** my bones, **raóhstien** his bones, **akóhstien** her bones; and ATTR =shon'a, pluralizer: **akhstien'shòn:'a** my bones.
With LOC -kon, inside, and ATTR ='a/=ha, diminutive: **ohstien'takón:ha** bone marrow.
With V -akaion-/-kaion- be old, and INCH -'-: **wakhstien'takaiòn:'on** I have old bones, **iakohstien'takaiòn:'on** she has old bones.
With V -ke- amount to, and DLC:

tekahstièn:take two bones.
With V -kwe'niio- be in charge of: **kahstien'takwe'ní:io** spine.
With V -r- put in, and DLC: **tekahstièn:tare'** crossbones (indicating poison).
With V -rakahr-/-kahr- make noise: **iohstien'tá:kahre'** (my) bones are cracking.
• Iohstien'tá:kahre' khsineko'tà:ke. My ankles are cracking.

-hstio'kanont-/-hstio'kan- V gnaw at a bone: **rahstio'ká:nonts** he is gnawing at a bone, **wahahstiò:kane'** he gnawed the bone.

-hstonter- N joint: **ohstónteri**
With DISTR -onnion- and DLC: **tewakhstonterónnion** my joints, **tehohstonterónnion** his joints, **teiakohstonterónnion** her joints.
With NMZR -'tsher-: **ohstonterì:tshera'** a root that looks like it has joints.

-hsto'ser- N small feathers, little soft down or plumes, fluff: **ohstò:seri**
With V -a[t]- be inside, and CISL: **tkahstò:sera** it has feathers in it, a down-filled jacket, duvet, pillow.
With V -a'senht-/-enht- drop: **wa'khstò:serenhte' ne kítkit** I pulled the chicken feathers.
With V -ke- amount to, and DLC: **tekahsto'será:ke** two feathers.
With V -ont- attach: **iohstò:seronte'** it has feathers.
• Tkahstò:sera ká:iare' tia'tò:ron. I am inside a down sleeping bag.

-hsw- V smell something: **wakéhswas** I smell something, **róhswas** he smells something, **iakóhswas** she smells something, **enwakésho'** I will smell it, **onkésho'** I smelled it.

NOTE: The *hsw* of this root sounds more like *shw*.
• Onkésho' kawero'kwákeras. I smelled the rotting, smelly carcass.

-hsw- V be playful, kid, tease: **wákhswa** I like to tease, **róhswa** he likes to tease, **iakóhswa** she likes to tease.
   With SRF -at- and CAUS -'t-: **katswà:tha'** I am playing (a game), I am fooling around, kidding, **enkátswa'te'** I will play, I will fool around, **wahátswa'te'** he played, he fooled around, **wakatswà:ton** I am fooling around, **ronatswà:ton** they are playing (a game); and PROG -hatie-: **wakatswa'tonhátie'** I am fooling around.
   With CAUS -'t- and V -onni- make: **wahihswa'tón:ni'** I teased him, joked with him, **wahakhswa'tón:ni'** he teased me, joked with me.

-hsw- back. *See* -hson-/-hsw-

-hswathe- V be bright, and DLC: **teiohswáthe'** it is bright.
   With INCH -'-: **teniohswáthe'ne'** it will get bright, **wa'tiohswáthe'ne'** it got bright, **wa'tewakhswáthe'ne'** it dawned on me, I got enlightened.
   With CAUS -'t- and BEN -en-: **wa'thihswathè:ten'** I enlightened him, **wa'tionkhswathè:ten'** she enlightened me.

-hsw[en]- V dislike: **íkhswens** I dislike it, **ríhswens** I dislike him, **shéhswens** you dislike them, your enemies, **énkhswen'** I will dislike it, **wà:khswen'** I disliked it.
   With CAUS -'t- and BEN -ni-/-en-: **wakhswà:tani** I get annoyed, it gets to me and it bothers me, **enhohswà:ten'** he will get annoyed, **onkhswà:ten'** I got annoyed, it got to me.

With REFL -atat- and NMZR -hser-: **atathswénhsera'** dislike.
See also -atahkwahswen- dislike, hate.
• Íkhswens tsi niwahsohkò:ten' ne atià:tawi. I dislike the colour of the dress.

-hswen'kar- N upper lip: **ohswèn:kara'** POSS: **khswen'karà:ke** (on) my lip, **rahswen'karà:ke** (on) his lip, **iehswen'karà:ke** (on) her lip.

-hswen'kar- board. *See* -hson'kar-/ -hswen'kar-

-htehr- N root: **ohtè:ra'**
   With ATTR =shon'a, pluralizer: **ohtehra'shòn:'a** all kinds of roots.
   With V -atskara- be bitter: **iohtehratská:ra** (it is) a bitter root.
   With V -a'a- be small, **ken'** particle, and PART: **ken' niiohtehrà:sa'** (they are) small roots.
   With V -es- be long, and REP: **tsohtè:rese'** sarsaparilla.
   With V -hon'tsi- be black, dark-coloured: **kahtehrahòn:tsi** fern.
   With V -o- be in water: **enkhtè:ro'** I will put the root in water, I will boil the root.
   With V -o'ten- be a kind of, and PART; and **otsì:nekwar** (-tsi'nekwar- yellow): **otsì:nekwar nikahtehrò:ten** goldthread.
   With unclear V: **ohtehrò:tsi** skinny stick (plant), American hornbeam.

Cf. Gaᶜteᶜra racine à coudre canot (Bruyas: 103); *Oᶜtéra* racine (Galissonnière: 71r); *ochtéra* Wurzel (Pyrlaeus: 2r); *ohtēra* Racine (Marcoux: 321); *Ohtera* racine, *tsiohteresekowa* salsepareille (Cuoq: 31); *te-io-te-ren-hak-ton* Solidago canadensis [goldenrod] (Rousseau: 65); *tsioteresekowa* [sarsaparilla] (Beauvais: 14); Onondaga *ouktera* Racinne (Shea: 85)

-hteron- V be scared, afraid

With BEN -ni-: **wakhterón:ni** I am scared, afraid, **rohterón:ni** he is scared, afraid, **iakohterón:ni** she is scared, afraid.

With INCH -'-: **wákhteron's** I get scared, **róhteron's** he gets scared, **enwákhteron'ne'** I will get scared, **ónkhteron'ne'** I got scared, **wahóhteron'ne'** he got scared.

With INSTR -hkw- and BEN -enni-/-en-: **ionkhteronhkwén:ni** she scares me, **wahakhterónhkwen'** he scared me, **wahihterónhkwen'** I scared him; and REFL -atat-: **katathteronhkwén:ni** I scare myself, **wa'katathterónhkwen'** I scared myself; and DLC: **wa'tiatiatathterónhkwen'** the two of us scared ourselves, **wa'ttiatathterónhkwen'** the two (females) scared themselves, **wa'thontathterónhkwen'** they scared themselves.

With SRF -at-: **ióthteron** it is dangerous, scary.

With SRF -at-, N -ia't- body, and SRF -at-: **rotia'táthteron** he is a scary person, he is off-putting, **iakotia'táthteron** she is a scary person.

With SRF -at-, N -onkwe['t]- person, human being, and SRF -at-: **rotonkwe'táthteron** he is a frightening person, he makes one feel uncomfortable. • Iakohterón:ni aontaió:karahwe'. She is scared of the dark. • Átste' tiorá:kahre' ónkhteron'ne'. There's a noise outside [and] I got afraid.

-hthar- V talk, converse: **wákhthare'** I am talking, **róhthare'** he is talking, **iakóhthare'** she is talking.

With CONT -k-: **enwakhthá:rake'** I will be talking.

With DLC: **teiakenihtháhrha'** we two talk (all the time), **tentenihthá:ren'** you and I will talk, **wa'tiakenihthá:ren'** we two

talked, **teionkeníhthare'** we two are talking.

With BEN -ni-/-hahs-: **rakhthará:ni** he is talking to me, **wahakhtháhrhahse'** he talked to me, **takhtháhrhahs** Talk to me!

With INSTR -hkw-: **wa'akwahthá:rahkwe'** we talked about it, **ionkwahtharáhkwen** we are talking about it, **rotihtharáhkwen** they are talking about it; and DLC: **teiehtharáhkhwa'** telephone.

-htohrarak-/-ohrarak- V squeeze, press down, with DLC: **tekhtò:raraks** I squeeze it, press down on it, **tekahtò:raraks** pliers, **tenhahtò:rarake'** he will squeeze it, **wa'tekhtò:rarake'** I squeezed it, **tewakhtohrará:kon** I have squeezed it, **teshtò:rarak** Squeeze it!

With N -hsnonhs- finger, hand: **wa'tkonhsnonhsò:rarake'** I squeezed your hands or fingers.

With N -ia't- body (and without DLC): **wa'ontia'tò:rarake'** she held me down, **wahoia'tò:rarake'** he held him down, he pinned him (as in wrestling), **wahonwaia'tò:rarake'** they squashed him, he got squashed (in an elevator, run over by a car).

With N -ihn- skin, leather: **wa'thihnò:rarake'** I pinched him, **wa'thakihnò:rarake'** he pinched me.

With N -onri- breath: **teiakaonriò:raraks** she is wheezing, gasping for breath, **wa'thaonriò:rarake'** he wheezed.

With N -rist- iron, steel: **tekaristò:raraks** printing machine, **tewakeristohrará:kon** I have printed, typed; and CAUS -st-: **teieristohrarákstha'** typewriter.

-htsi- KIN older sibling, with ATTR ='a/=ha, diminutive: **rakhtsì:'a** my older brother, **akhtsì:'a** my older sister, **iahtsì:'a** your older brother, **sahtsì:'a** your older sister.

With ATTR =kenha, former, late:
rakhtsi'kénha my late brother.

-htskon or -hskon FACIL, easily

-hwahnha[k]-/-hnha[k]- V wrap, tie around
With DLC: **tekhwáhnhaks** I wrap something around something, **tenkhwáhnhake'** I will wrap it around it, **wa'tekhwáhnhake'** I wrapped it around it, **wa'thahwáhnhake'** he wrapped it around it, **tewakhwáhnhen** I have wrapped it around it, **tekahwáhnhen** it is wrapped around.
With N -ia'kar-/-ia'kwar- midriff, and DLC: **wa'ttia'kwaráhnhake'** I put the bellyband on (a horse), **tetsa'kwaráhnhak** Put the bellyband on! and INSTR -st-: **tekonwaia'kwarahnákstha'** bellyband.
With SRF -at- and N -ia't- body: **wahatia'táhnhake'** he put on a belt; **atia'táhnha'** belt.
With SRF -at- and N -kahr- eye: **atkahráhnha'** eyeglasses.
With SRF -at-, N -konhs- face, and DLC: **teiontkonhsáhnhaks** she is putting on a (Covid) mask, **tenhsatkonhsáhnhake'** you will put on a mask, **tewakatkonhsáhnhen** I have on a mask.
With SRF -ate- and N -nentsh- arm: **atenentsháhnha'** bracelet, wristwatch.
With SRF -ate- and N -nentshawi't- wrist: **atenentshawi'táhnha'** anything tied around the wrist (beads, leather).
With N -sha'kent- bulrush, and DLC: **teiosha'kentáhnhen** (it is) surrounded by bulrushes.
• Kà:nhes wa'tekhwáhnhake'. I wrapped ribbon around it.

-hwaneren[k]-/-neren[k]- V tie up:
khwánerenks I tie it up,
enkhwánerenke' I will tie it up,
wa'khwánerenke' I tied it up,

wakhwáneren I have tied it up.
With CAUS -st-: **iehwanerénkstha'** string, twine.
With N -ithohkw- bundle: **wa'kithohkwánerenke'** I tied up the bundle, **kenthohkwáneren** (it is) a bundle, tied up.
With N -itstohkw- pack, pile: **wa'kitstohkwánerenke'** I tied the pack, **kentstohkwáneren** (it is) a pack, tied up.
With N -kahrohst- intestines: **tenikahrohstáneren** we are inseparable friends, **tehnikahrohstáneren** the two are inseparable friends.
With N -nennotsher- package, parcel: **wa'kenennotsheránerenke'** I tied the package; and CAUS -st- and INSTR -hkw-: **ienennotsheranerenkstáhkhwa' ahserí:ie** string or cord used to wrap a package (-ahseriie['t]- string, rope).
With N -nohkw- bundle: **kenohkwánerenks** I am tying up the bundle, **wa'kenohkwánerenke'** I tied up the bundle, **kanohkwáneren** (it is) a bundle, tied up, **senohkwánerenk** Tie up the bundle!
With N -nonhkwen'- corn cob, and DLC: **tekanonhkwen'áneren** corn cob game.
• Iehwanerénkstha' wà:katste' wa'khwánerenke'. I used string or twine to tie it up.

-hwaseron- V take the bark off: **khwáserons** I take the bark off, **enkhwáseron'** I will take the bark off, **wahahwáseron'** he took the bark off, **wakhwáseron** I have removed the bark.

-hwaserotatie- V go out (dressed) just as one is: **khwaserotátie'** I am going out just the way I am (it might be cold out but I go out dressed as I am), **rahwaserotátie'** he is going out just the way he is, **iehwaserotátie'** she is going out just the way she is.

-hwatase-/-tase- V turn, twist: **khwatá:ses**
I am turning, twisting it (for example,
tightening the lid on a jar), **wa'khwatá:se'**
I twisted it.
With DLC: **tekhwatá:ses** I put or twisted
it around something (for example, I'm
making a ball from yarn), **tenkhwatá:se'**
I will put it around, **wa'tekhwatá:se'** I
put it around.
With REV -hsi-: **wa'khwatas̈hsi'** I
opened, untwisted it.
With CAUS -'t-: **iehwatasè:tha'** or (with
N -ronwar-/-nonwar- wire, nail, needle,
pin): **ieronwaratasè:tha'** screwdriver.
With N -ahseriie['t]- string, rope, thread:
kahseriie'tatá:ses I am winding thread or
string around something (like a spool),
wa'onhseriie'tatá:se' she wound the
string.
With SRF -ar-, N -ahsi't- foot, and DLC:
tehorahsi'tatá:se he is pigeon-toed,
teiakorahsi'tatá:se she is pigeon-toed.
With SRF -at- and N -hah- road:
wahathahatá:se' he took a winding road;
and DLC: **teiothahatá:se** the road has a
curve in it.
With SRF -ani- and V -hsonw- be a hole:
anihsonwatá:se borer; with V -hsonw-
be a hole, CAUS -'t-, and INSTR -hkw-:
iehsonwatase'táhkhwa' hand drill.
With N -ihn- skin, leather: **wahihnatá:se'**
I twisted his skin, I pinched him,
wahakihnatá:se' he pinched me.
With N -nennio'kw- snowball, and DLC:
teionennio'kwatá:se or **teionien'kwa-
tá:se'** (it is) a snowstorm.
With N -niar- neck:
Wà:s enkonniaratá:se' Go on, I will
wring your neck (talking to a dog).
With N -tsi'nehtar- small bead(s), and DLC:
teietsi'nehtaratá:ses she does beadwork,
wa'tektsi'nehtaratá:se' I did beadwork.
With N -wer- wind, and DLC:

teioweratá:se it is very windy,
wa'tkaweratá:se' it got very windy.
With N -'nenhar- grape, raisin, CAUS -'t-,
and DISTR -on-: **o'nenharatasè:ton**
sprouts from vines that curl around something (a wall or fence); with N -'nenhar-
grape, raisin, NMZR -'tsher-, and V
-kehron[t]- put down here and there:
o'nenharatase'tsherakè:ron shoots or
vines that are lying on the ground.

-hwatsir- N family: **kahwá:tsire'** family,
ohwá:tsire' maternal family
POSS: **akhwá:tsire'** my family.
With V -ien- put down, have:
iakwahwatsí:raien' we have a family.
With V -kowan[en]-/-owan[en]- be big:
khwatsirowá:nen I have a big family.

Cf. awátsire maternal family, *kawatsire*
household (Mary Deer's class notes, Feb.
1966)

-hwawen'e[k]-/-awen'e[k]- V wrap, with DLC:
tekhwawèn:'eks I wrap it,
tenkhwawèn:'eke' I will wrap it,
wa'tekhwawèn:'eke' I wrapped it,
tewakhwawèn:'e I have wrapped it.
With SRF -at- and CAUS -t-:
athwawen'éktha' or (with CAUS -st- and
INSTR -hkw-) **teionthwawen'ekstáhkhwa'**
diaper.
With N -a'ar- net, curtain; and
awenhétsha' (-enhetsh- sausage):
tewa'arawèn:'e awenhétsha' farmer's
sausage.
With N -nia't- throat:
teiakonia'tawèn:'eks chokecherry.
With SRF -ate- and N -nor- husk:
teiotenorawèn:'en ground tomato.

-hwa'ehst- V end up, show up somewhere,
land, with TRNL: **tho iahonkhwà:'ehste'**
I ended up there, I showed up there,

tho iahohwà:'ehste' he landed there, ended up there, washed up (ashore).

-hwa'e[k]-/-a'e[k]- V hit, strike: **khwà:'eks** I hit it, strike it, **enkhwà:'eke'** I will strike it, **wahahwà:'eke'** he struck it, **wakhwà:'e** I have struck it, **kahwà:'e** straw.
  With CAUS -st-; and **athén:no** (-athenno-/-athenno'tsher- ball): **athén:no iehwa'ékstha'** bat.
  With N -hwist- metal, money: **enhahwistà:'eke'** he will ring the bells, **énska enkahwistà:'eke'** one hour; and DLC: **tékeni tenkahwistà:'eke'** two hours; or PART: **Tó: niiohwistà:'e?** What time is it? with N -hwist- metal, money, and CAUS -st-: **iehwista'ékstha'** bell.
  With N -tsihkw- fist, button, knot (of a tree), puck, and DLC: **tehattsihkwà:'eks** he plays hockey or lacrosse; **tewa'á:raton tehonttsihkwà:'eks** lacrosse game (-a'ar-net, curtain), **wa'thattsihkwà:'eke' ohahà:ke** he played road hockey (-hah-road), **tehottsihkwà:e'** he has played hockey, lacrosse; and PURP -h-: **wa'thonttsihkwa'ékhe' owisà:ke** they are going to play hockey (-wis- ice, glass).

-hwa'tst- N foam: **ohwà:tsta'**
  With V -eka'[w]-/-ka'[w]- find tasty, and REP: **tsohwà:tstaka'we'** seagull.
  With SRF -at- and V -her-/-hr- set on top of: **iothwa'tstáhere'** there is foam on top of it.
  With V -ot- stand: **iohwà:tstote'** (there is) foam, **wa'kahwa'tstó:ten'** it got to be foam.

-hwen'kar- N snowshoe: **kahwèn:kare'**
  With SRF -at-, V -ont- attach, and DLC: **wa'thathwen'karón:ten'** he put on snowshoes, **tehothwèn:karonte'** he has on snowshoes.
  Cf. Gahꜱengare raquettes (Bruyas: 55); *Gahꜱengare* raquette (Galissonnière: 71r); *Kaꜱēnkăre* Raquette (Marcoux: 324); *Kawenkare* raquette (Cuoq: 16)

-hwesen- N wood shavings: **kahwé:sen**
  Cf. Gahꜱesen polir, doler, gratter escorce (Bruyas: 56); *Gahꜱesen* gratter escorce (Galissonnière: 46v)

-hwe'nonni-/-kwe'nonni- V fold: **khwe'nón:nis** I fold it, **enkhwe'nón:ni'** I will fold it, **wahahwe'nón:ni'** he folded it, **rohwe'nón:ni** he has folded it, **shwe'nón:ni** Fold it!
  With SRF -at- and DLC: **teiothwe'nón:ni** it is round, a circle; and **í:iens** (-es- be long): **í:iens tsi teiothwe'nón:ni** oval.
  With SRF -ar-, N -ahsi't- foot, and DLC: **tehorahsi'takwe'nón:ni** he is a widower. *This is an old expression.*
  With N -ahts- hand: **wa'kahtsakwe'nón:ni'** I made a fist, **rohtsakwe'nón:ni** he is making a fist, **sahtsakwe'nón:ni** Make a fist!
  With SRF -at-, N -a'ther- basket, and DLC: **teiota'therakwe'nón:ni** (it is) a round basket.
  With SRF -at-, N -hnek- liquid, and BEN -en-: **onkwathnekakwe'nónnien'** something is going around and around in my throat (instead of going down).
  With SRF -ate-, N -ks- dish, plate, and DLC: **teioteksakwe'nón:ni** (it is) a round dish.
  • **Wa'khwe'nón:ni' akhsí:na'.** I folded up my legs (doing yoga).

-hwish- N burden, effort
  With ending -en-: **onkhwíshen'** it got burdensome or heavy for me, a struggle,

wahohwíshen' it got heavy, a struggle for him.
With V -ihei[on]-/-enhei[on]- die, and DLC: **tekhwishenhé:ions** I get tired, **wa'tekhwishénheie'** I got tired, **tewakhwishenhé:ion** I am tired; and N -'nikonhr- mind: **wa'tke'nikonhrahwishénheie'** my mind got tired, **tewake'nikonhrahwishenhé:ion** my mind is tired.
With V -r- put in, and REV -kw-: **onkhwishará:ko'** the burden or weight got lifted off me (off my shoulders).

-hwist- N metal, money: **ohwísta'**
With SRF -at- and V -ahton- disappear: **onthwistáhton'** the money disappeared; and BEN -'s-: **onkwathwistáhton'se'** I lost or misplaced the money.
With V -awi-/-on- give: **khehwistá:wis** I give her money, **wa'khehwíston'** I gave her money; and REFL -atat- and DLC: **tehatathwistá:wis** he makes change.
With V -ent- wear out, end, and INCH -'-: **wa'kahwistén:ta'ne'** it (the telephone, bells) stopped ringing.
With V -ha[w]-/-enha[w]- V hold, bring, take: **khwisténhawe'** I have money in my hand.
With V -hawi-/-enhawi- carry: **khwistenhá:wi'** I am carrying money.
With V -her-/-hr- set on top of, and DLC: **tekahwistáhere'** a general.
With V -hkw- pick up, BEN -en-, and DLC: **wa'thihwistáhkwen'** I took, swiped money from him.
With SRF -at- and V -hninon- buy: **wahathwistahní:non'** he spent his money.
With V -hri'- get broken into pieces, shatter, and DLC: **teiohwistahrì:'on** change.
With V -hwa'e[k]-/-a'e[k]- hit, strike: **enhahwistà:'eke'** he will ring the bells,

énska enkahwistà:'eke' one hour; and DLC: **tékeni tenkahwistà:'eke'** two hours; or PART: **Tó: niiohwistà:'e?** What time is it? with V -hwa'e[k]-/-a'e[k]- hit, strike, and CAUS -st-: **iehwista'ékstha'** bell.
With V -ien- put down, have: **wakhwístaien'** I have money, **kahwístaien'** there is money; and NEG: **iah tekahwístaien'** there is no money; with V -ien- put down, have, and PROG -atie-: **wakhwistaientátie'** I have money with me; with SRF -at- and V -ien-/-ient- put, have: **kathwístaiens** I save money, **wahathwístaien'** he saved money; with V -ien-/-ient- put, have, and INSTR -hkw-: **tsi iehwistaientáhkhwa'** bank.
With SRF -at-, and SRF -at-, V -ies[en]- be easy, available, and CAUS -ht-: **rathwistatiesáhtha'** he spends money easily, easy come-easy go, he's a sport.
With V -naker[e]- reside, be plenty: **kahwistanákere'** there is plenty of money; and NEG: **iah tekahwistanákere'** there isn't a lot of money.
With V -ni[h]- lend: **wa'onkhwístani'** she or they lent me money.
With V -noron- be expensive, precious: **kahwistanó:ron** money is scarce, hard to come by; **ohwistanó:ron** gold.
With V -o- be in water: **tsi kahwísto** a mine.
With V -onni- make: **rahwistón:ni** blacksmith.
With V -otahrho[k]- hook, and DLC: **wa'tionkhwistotáhrhoke'** they put handcuffs on me, **wa'thihwistotáhrhoke'** I put handcuffs on him.
With V -rakahr-/-kahr- make noise: **iohwistá:kahre'** a bell is ringing, money is jangling, **wa'ohwistá:kahre'** it rang (for example, church bells).
With V -ra'ken- be white: **kahwistarà:ken** silver.

With V -rohro[k]- gather, collect: **khwistarò:roks** I am collecting money, **kahwistarò:roks** collection (at church), **enhatihwistarò:roke'** they will collect money.

With V -[t]- be one, and REP: **skahwísta** one dollar.

With V -tahkw- take out: **wa'khwistatáhko'** I got paid (for doing my job), **wa'ts enhshwistatáhko'** later you will get paid for it, get punished; and TRNL: **ia'khwistatáhko'** I took money out (from) there.

With SRF -at- and unclear V (possibly related to the root in the last subentry under -kahser- tear): **rothwistahríhrhon** he lets his money go, he keeps spending money, **iakothwistahríhrhon** she keeps spending money.

• Kahwístaien' ahshní:non' kákhwa'. There is money to buy food. • Wakhwísta-ien' akkária'ke' takatskà:hon'. I have money to pay to eat. • Ia'khwistatáhko' tsi iehwistaientáhkhwa'. I took money out of the bank.

I

-i- V be the total of
  With PART: **nihá:ti** (there are) so many, that many, **nikón:ti** (there are) so many (females, animals).
  With N -ia't- body, CAUS -st-, and TRNL and DLC: **ia'tenhoià:tiste'** he will be all alone, **ia'tewatià:tiste'** I was left all alone, **ia'tewatia'tíston** I am all alone; and REP: **ia'tesewatia'tíston** I am all alone again, **ia'teshoia'tíston** he is all alone again.
  NOTE: This may be the root -i[k]- fill up.
  • É:so nikón:ti è:rhar. There are a lot of dogs.

iah or **iáhten** negative particle, not

iah thé:nen nothing

-iahe't- N perch: **oiahè:ta'**
  Cf. o ia he ta perch (Anon: 17); *oiahè:ta* perch (Lazore: 41)

-iahia'k-/-iia'k- V cross over, with DLC:
  tetià:ia'ks I cross over, **tenhaià:ia'ke'** he will cross over, **wa'thaià:ia'ke'** he crossed over, **tewatiahià:kon** I have crossed over.
  With CISL: **tenthaià:ia'ke'** he will cross over coming this way.
  With TRNL: **ia'tenhaià:ia'ke'** he will cross over going that way, **ia'ttià:ia'ke'** I crossed over that way.
  With N -ahskw- bridge: **wa'tkahskwí:ia'ke'** I crossed the bridge.
  With N -hah- road: **wa'thahahí:ia'ke'** he crossed the road.
  With N -ohser- winter, year, and PART: **Tó: na'tesohseriià:kon?** How old are you?
  With N -rist- iron, steel, and TRNL: **ia'teharistí:ia'ks** he goes across the

(U.S.-Can.) border, **ia'tenteniristí:ia'ke'** you and I will go across the border, **ia'tewakeristiià:kon** I have gone across the border.
  With N -tsenh- fire: **tenhatitsenhí:ia'ke'** they will cross the fire, they will debate.
  With N -'now- hump, padlock: **tewake'nowiià:kon** I am a hunchback, **teho'nowiià:kon** he is a hunchback, **teiako'nowiià:kon** she is a hunchback.
  With NMZR -hser-, see -iahia'khser- week.

-iahia'khser- N week
  With V -es- be long, tall, and PART: **tsi niiahià:khseres** during the week.
  With V -ihen- be in the middle of, and COIN and DLC: **sha'teiahia'khserí:hen** middle of the week.
  With V -ke- amount to, and DLC: **teiahia'khserá:ke** two weeks.
  With SRF -at- and V -o'kt- finish: **ontiahia'ksherò:kten'** the week ended, the end of the week.
  With V -[t]- be one, and REP: **tsiahià:khsera** one week, **tsiahià:khsera tsi náhe'** last week, a week ago.
  • Wa'khwistatáhko' ontiahia'khserò:kten'. I got paid at the end of the week.
  Cf. tsioiaiāksĕra Semaine (Marcoux: 361); *Iaiaksera* espace de six jours (Cuoq: 86); *o ia iak se ra* week (Anon: 6); *o ia iak se ra* week (D'Ailleboust: 33); *oia-iak-se-ra* week (Cory: 71)

-iahs- N cross: **kaiáhsa'**
  With V -ont- attach, and DLC: **tehaiahsóntha'** he makes the sign of the cross, he is a Catholic, **teieiahsóntha'** she makes the sign of the cross, she is a Catholic.

-iahse- V be together, be two, with DLC:
tehniiáhse two males, a male and a
female, **tekeniiáhse** two females,
teiakeniiáhse we two are together,
teiakwaiáhse we all are together.
With SRF -at- and CAUS -t-:
wa'thiatiáhsete' the two came to be
together, **wa'tiakwatiáhsete'** we all
came to be together.

iáhten no, not

ià:ia'k six, **ià:ia'k iawén:re** sixteen,
ià:ia'k niwáhsen sixty, **iahià:khaton**
sixth, **ià:ia'k nia'ká:ienhte'** six times,
Ià:ia'k nihononhwentsá:ke Six Nations.
Cf. Iajack [six] (Wassenaer: 73); *yáyak* 6
(Pyrlaeus: 11r); *Yayack* six (Weiser: 386);
Yàyak VI. (Primer: 94); *achiak* six
(Zeisberger in Wheeler-Voegelin: 64);
Laurentian *Aiaga* Seven (Biggar: 241);
Wendat *ꜱahia* 6 (Potier: 106); *Houhahéa* 6
(Sagard: No2); Susquehannock *Jaiack* 6
(Holm: 6)

iá:ken it is said

-iakenhw- V take out, put out, with TRNL or
CISL: **ia'tiá:kenhwe'** I took it outside,
iahaiá:kenhwe' he took it outside,
tahaiá:kenhwe' he brought it outside,
iehoiakénhen he has taken it outside.
NOTE: This stem is composed of a root
-iaken-, which occurs only with suffixes,
and CAUS -hw-.

-iaken'- V go out: **tiá:ken's** I go out,
entiá:ken'ne' I will go out,
wahaiá:ken'ne' he went out,
watiakèn:'en I have gone out.
With PAST -'ne': **watiaken'èn:ne'** I had
gone out.
With PURP -ser-: **wa'tiakèn:sere'** I am

going to go out.
With CISL: **tahaiá:ken'ne'** he came out.
With TRNL: **iahaiá:ken'ne'** he went out.
NOTE: This stem is composed of a root
-iaken-, which occurs only with suffixes,
and INCH -'-.
• Tahaiá:ken'ne' wa'tiakenihthá:ren'. He
came out [and] we talked. • Iahaiá:ken'ne'
ahatshó:ko'. He went out to smoke.

-ian- N footprint, track: **oiá:na'**
With SRF -at-, V -a'senht-/-enht- drop, and
CISL: **tkatianénhtha'** I am sledding, skiing, **takatiá:nenhte'** I sledded, I skied;
with SRF -at-, V -a'senht-/-enht- drop, and
INSTR -hkw-: **iontianenhtáhkhwa'** sled.
With V -ha[w]-/-enha[w]- bring, take:
wa'tianénhawe' I followed the tracks.
With V -hawi-/-enhawi- carry:
riianenhá:wi' I am following his tracks,
kheianenhá:wi' I am following her
tracks.
With V -kahrhate- be turned out, and DLC:
tehaianakáhrhate' his feet are turned
out, **teieianakáhrhate'** her feet are turned
out, **tekaianakáhrhate'** its feet are turned
out (talking about a dog).
With V -kste- be heavy: **roianákste'** he
walks heavy, he lumbers (as if he is making an effort at walking).
With V -onni- make, and DLC:
tehatiianón:ni they leave their footprints,
their tracks, **tekaianón:ni** there is a path;
and PROG -hatie-: **tehatiianonnihátie'**
they are leaving their footprints or tracks,
tekaianonnihátie' there is a path going
along.
With V -[t]- be one, and REP: **tsoiá:na** one
pair; and DISTR -hshon-: **tsoianátshon** one
step at a time.
With V -te[ht]- be strong-tasting, energetic:
roiá:nate' he has a heavy step or tred,
iakoiá:nate' she has a heavy step or tred.

-iane[r]- V be titled, a chief: **roiá:ner** he is a chief, **iotiiá:ner** clan mothers.

With DISTR -hshon-: **rotiianéhshon** they have titles, they are the ones with titles, chiefs, **iotiianéhshon** they (females) are titleholders; and **ka'nisténhsera'** (-'nisten- mother): **iotiianéhshon ka'nisténhsera'** clan mothers.

Cf. aquayanderen a chief (van den Bogaert: 60); *Gaiander* homme ou femme considérable, *Gaianderesera* noblesse (Bruyas: 58); "... deputies [to the chiefs] who share with them the soveignty of the territory and are called also the *Agoïanders*." (Lafitau I: 293); "The *Agayandres* or Sachems of the Five Nations" (Colden: 163); "Chaque village se partage en plusieurs bandes dont chacune a son chef, son *roianer*." (Cuoq: 154); *Ro-iá-ner* "Lord" (Cory: 19); *roianerh* principal chief (Mary Deer's class notes, Feb. 1966); *ro ia ner* chief (Diabo: 9); *roiá:ner* the chiefs (Old Kahnawake: 4); Oneida "... the nobles of the country. They are called *Agoïandères*," (Millet in Thwaites 58: 185); Onondaga *hᴈyané* Ancien, chef de conseil (Shea: 20); Onondaga *ne aquàs hojáner* Chief, Vornehmste (Zeisberger: 36); *hotijaner* magistrate (Zeisberger: 118)

-ianer[e]- V be good: **ioiánere'** it is good.

With ATTR =kowa, great: **Kaianere'kó:wa** the Great Law.

With CONT -k-: **aioiánereke'** it would be good.

With PAST -hkwe': **ioiánerehkwe'** it was good, nice.

With PROG -atie-: **ioianerátie'** it is going well.

With INCH -en'-: **enioiáneren'ne'** it will become good.

With NMZR -enhser-: **kaianerénhsera'**

law; and ATTR =kowa, great: **Kaianerenhsera'kó:wa** alternative term for the Great Law.

With NMZR -enhser-, V -o'ten- be a kind of, and PART: **niionkwaianerenhserò:ten** our laws, our traditions.

• Ioiánerehkwe' shiwasé'tsi. It was nice when it was new.

Cf. ongwayanereghseragh [our law] (Little Abraham in Claus C-1478, 472, line 12)

-iar- N bag: **ká:iare'**

With LOC -kon, inside: **kaiá:rakon** inside the bag.

With V -awak- shake: **kaiarawá:kon** last born child.

With V -ha[w]-/-enha[w]- V hold, bring, take: **tiarénhawe'** I am holding the bag; and TRNL: **iehaiarénhas** he is carrying, taking the (golf) bag, **ientiarénhawe'** I will take the bag.

With V -hawi-/-enhawi- carry: **tiarenhá:wi'** I am carrying the bag.

With SRF -at- and V -i[k]- fill up: **wa'ontiá:rike'** she filled the bag; with V -i[k]- fill up, and CONTR and TRNL: **iah thiekaiá:ri** he or she is not all there.

With V -ke- amount to, and DLC: **tekaiá:rake** two bags.

With V -kste- be heavy: **ioiarákste'** (it is) a heavy bag.

With V -[t]- be one, and REP: **skaiá:ra** one bag.

Cf. Gaiare sac, *Tiarenhaᴈi* porter le sac, faire des presents (Bruyas: 58); *Gaiare* Sac (Galissonnière: 14r); *Kāiăre* sac, poche (Marcoux: 353); *Kaiare* sac, poche (Cuoq: 9); *Kiarenhawis* être porteur du sac (terme de diplomatie); citing Marcoux: "Ratiiarenhawis, les Ambassadeurs, les Députés, ceux qui portent le sac tout malpropre qui contient les colliers de porcelaine sur lesquels est figuré en hiéroglyphes, ou plutôt en imagination, le suject de l'Ambassade." (Cuoq: 100); *ka ia re* bag (Anon: 25); *ka ia re* bag (Diabo: 4)

-iaron- N amulet: **oiá:ron**

Cf. "... his *Oiaron* and his Manitou which may be regarded as his talismans in which all his virtue resides." (Lafitau II: 210); *oiaron* objet de prédilection (Cuoq: 67)

-iat- V call by a name: **ióntiats** my name is, **ronwá:iats** his name is, **iontátiats** her name is.
• Oh nahò:ten' ní:se' iesá:iats? What is your name?

iá:we it is as if it were, instead of
• Né:ne iá:we aiesaió'ten' ó:ia'k sén:ta's. Instead of working you are just sleeping.
• Kaná:takon wà:ke' né:ne iá:we akenatà:ra'. I am going to town instead of going visiting. • Owistóhsera' wahahní:non' né:ne iá:we onòn:ta'. He bought butter instead of milk.

iawén:re Added to number words to form numbers in the teens. For example: **wísk iawén:re** fifteen.

-ia'k- V cut, sever: **ítia'ks** I cut it, I am cutting it, **ítsa'ks** you (sg) cut it, **rá:ia'ks** he cuts it, **éntia'ke'** I will cut it, **wà:tia'ke'** I cut it, **wáhsia'ke'** you cut it, **watià:kon** I have cut it.
With N -hent- grass: **rahéntia'ks** he cuts the grass.
With N -honkar- invitation: **wa'khehonkária'ke'** I asked her to take on a task (like, taking notes for a meeting), I volunteered her.
With SRF -an- and N -itstenhr- rock, boulder: **ionitstenhrià:kon** cliff.

With N -kahreht- eyelash: **enhskahréhtia'ke'** you will take or cut off the (strawberry) stems, tops.
With N -kar- cost, value: **rakária'ks** he is paying, **enhatikária'ke'** they will pay, **wahakária'ke'** he paid, **rokarià:kon** he has paid; and BEN -i-/-hs-: **eniethikária'khse'** we will pay her, **wahikária'khse'** I paid him, **wahakkária'khse'** he paid me, **khekarià:ki** I have paid her, **iethikarià:ki** we have paid her.
With SRF -at- and N -konhston'rh- beard, whiskers: **katkonhstòn:rhia'ks** I am shaving, **enhatkonhstòn:rhia'ke'** he will shave, **wahatkonhstòn:rhia'ke'** he shaved, **rotkonhston'rhià:kon** he has shaved; and CAUS -st-: **iontkonhston'rhià:kstha'** razor.
With SRF -at- and N -kwir- tree, sapling: **ratkwíria'ks** he is cutting down a tree, **wahatkwíria'ke'** he cut down a tree.
With N -nats- wheat: **wa'kenatsí:ia'ke'** I cut wheat; and CAUS -st- or -t-: **ienatsiià:kstha'** or **ienatsiià:ktha'** sickle.
With N -neker-/-enneker- hay: **ranekerí:ia'ks** he is cutting hay, **wahanekerí:ia'ke'** or (with SRF -ate-) **wahatenekerí:ia'ke'** he cut hay; and CAUS -st-: **iakennekeriià:kstha'** scythe.
With N -nekwenhs- blood: **kanekwénhsia'ks** it stops the blood, the bleeding.
With SRF -ate-, N -nen't- evergreen, and DISTR -hon-: **ontenen'tià:khon'** the evergreen (branches) are broken (maybe after a heavy snowstorm).
With SRF -at- and N -onhwents-/-onhonts- earth, world: **watonhóntia'ks** landslide, **ontonhóntia'ke'** a landslide happened, **iotonhontià:kon** there was a landslide.
With SRF -at-, N -tsikhe't- sweet, and BEN -hs-: **ó:nen wesattsikhè:tia'khse'**

A saying, something like 'Enough already! That's it! You're done!'
With N -tsi'er- fingernail: **wa'khetsi'éria'ke'** I cut her nails; and SRF -at-: **wa'kattsi'éria'ke'** I cut my nails.
With N -tsi'ts- flower, outside of the lips: **wahatsì:tsia'ke'** he cut the flowers.
With SRF -ate- and N -wenn- voice, word: **atewénnia'ke'** goose (domesticated).
With N -'nhaht- branch: **enke'nháhtia'ke'** I will cut the branch, **waha'nháhtia'ke'** he cut the branch, **wake'nhahtià:kon** I have cut the branch, **se'nháhtia'k** Cut the branch! and DISTR -hon-: **waha'nhahtià:khon'** he cut the branches.
With SRF -a- and N -'nikonhr- mind: **ion'nikòn:ria'ks** she is giving up, she quits, **enha'nikòn:ria'ke'** he will give up, **wa'on'nikòn:ria'ke'** she gave up, **iako'nikonhrià:kon** she has given up.
With N -'nist- stem: **wa'ke'nístia'ke'** I cut the stem.
NOTE: This root occurs productively with the DLC and CISL; see the next two entries. It may also be present in -honria'k- choke.

-ia'k- V break, cut in two, with DLC: **tétia'ks** I break it, I am breaking it, **tehá:ia'ks** he breaks it, **téntia'ke'** I will break it, **wà:ttia'ke'** I broke it, **teiakoià:kon** she has broken it.
With DISTR -hon-: **tekaià:khon** it is separated into portions.
With SRF -at-: **tewátia'ks** it breaks, **wa'tewátia'ke'** it broke, **teiotià:kon** it is broken, **tewakatià:kon** I am broke (have no money).
With N -hon'kw- throat (variant -hon'k-): **wa'thihòn:tia'ke'** I cut his throat, **wa'thohòn:tia'ke** he cut his throat.
With N -hson'kar-/-hswen'kar- board, and INSTR -st-: **teiehson'karià:kstha'** saw.
With N -ient- wood: **tehaiéntia'ks** he is

chopping wood.
With SRF -an- and N -itahs- tail: **wa'tkanitáhsia'ke'** I broke my tailbone.
With N -nakar- stick: **wa'tkenakária'ke'** I broke the stick.
With SRF -ate- and N -na'aht- rib: **wa'tkatena'áhtia'ke'** I broke my rib.
With N -na'kar- horn, antler: **tenhina'kária'ke'** I am going to cut off his horns. *This is an old expression used by a woman who is fed up with her husband.*
With SRF -ate- and N -nekwenhs- blood: **tewatenekwénhsia'ks** a kind of plant.
With SRF -ate- and N -nentsh- arm: **wa'tkatenéntshia'ke'** I broke my arm.
With SRF -a- and N -nont- mountain, hill: **wa'thonnóntia'ke** they dug or made a ditch.
With SRF -ate- and N -ronhkwe'n- spine, back: **wa'thateronhkwè:nia'ke'** he broke his back.
With N -ronwar-/-nonwar- wire, nail, pin: **wa'tkeronwária'ke'** I cut the wire.
With N -wer- wind, air: **wa'tkawerí:ia'ke'** the wind died down, it got calm, **teioweriià:kon** the wind has died down, it is calm.
With N -'nhonhs- egg: **teka'nhónhsia'ks** it hatches, incubator, **wa'tka'nhónhsia'ke'** it hatched.

-ia'k- V cut off, with CISL: **thá:ia'ks** he is cutting off a piece (shortening it), **tátia'ke'** I cut some off, **tahá:ia'ke'** he cut it off, **thoià:kon** he has cut it off.
With N -ahsi't- foot: **tonkwahsì:tia'ke'** I tripped, **tahohsì:tia'ke'** he tripped; and DISTR -hon-: **tewakahsi'tià:khons** I am always tripping all over.

-ia'k- V hit, bang, with TRNL
With N -hiohs- elbow, and TRNL: **iahonkhióhsia'ke'** I banged my elbow.

With N -kwitsh- knee: **iahonkkwítshia'ke'** I banged my knee.

With N -nentsh- arm: **iahonkenéntshia'ke'** I banged my arm.

With N -nient- shin: **iahonkeniéntia'ke'** I banged my shin.

• Ohiohsà:ke iahonkkwítshia'ke'. I banged or hit the corner (of a piece of furniture) with my knee.

-ia'[k]- V hit, slap

With N -ahranonhs- temple, cheekbones: **enkoniahranonhsáia'ke'** I will smack your face, **wahakwahranonhsáia'ke'** he slapped me in the face.

With N -ahtsa'n- palm of the hand: **enkoniahtsa'náia'ke'** I will slap your hand, **wa'onkwahtsa'náia'ke'** she slapped my hand.

With N -hon'kw- throat: **wahakhon'kwáia'ke'** he hit me in the throat.

With N -hskwen't- lips: **enkonhskwen'táia'ke'** I will smack you in the lips.

With N -hso'kw- nut: **wahshakohso'kwáia'ke'** he smacked her on the head.

With N -kahr- eye: **wahikahráia'ke'** I gave him a black eye; and SRF -at-: **rotkahráien'** he has a black eye.

With N -ken'tstar- top part of the forehead: **enkonken'tstaráia'ke'** I will smack your forehead.

With N -kwitsh- knee: **wahakkwitsháia'ke'** he hit me in the knee.

With N -na'kar- horn, antler: **iena'karáia'ks** piano.

With N -nekwen't- belly: **wahonwanekwen'táia'ke'** she hit him in the belly.

With N -nenhr- crowd, and CISL: **taienenhráia'ke'** she treated everyone,

she paid for everyone.

With N -(h)nhoh- door: **wa'kehnhoháia'ke'** I knocked on the door; and DISTR -hon-: **kehnhohaia'ákhons** I am knocking on the door, **wa'kehnhohaia'ákhon'** I knocked (gave several knocks) on the door.

With N -nient- shin: **wahakenientáia'ke'** he hit me in the shin.

With N -ronwar-/-nonwar- wire, nail, needle, pin: **karonwaráia'ks** piano, telegram; and TRNL: **ia'kenonwaráia'ke'** I sent a telegram.

With N -tsi'ts- flower, outide of the lips, and DLC: **wa'thaktsi'tsáia'ke'** he smacked me in the mouth.

With N -'rhiotsh- chin: **wahake'rhiotsháia'ke'** he hit me in the chin.

NOTE: Forms with a short accented vowel suggest that this root goes back to an earlier form *-i'ak-.

• Taienenhráia'ke' wa'ehní:non' ne otskihè:ta'. She bought candy for everyone.

-ia'kar-/-ia'kwar- N midriff, vest, blouse: **oià:kara'**

With V -es- be long, tall, and DLC: **tetià:kares** I am long-waisted, **teieià:kares** she is long-waisted; and PART: **Tó: na'tehsià:kares?** How long is it to your waist (from your shoulder)?

With V -esha- be short, **ken'** particle, and PART and DLC: **ken' na'tetia'karésha** I am short-waisted.

With V -hwahnha[k]-/-hnha[k]- wrap, tie around, and DLC: **wa'ttia'kwaráhnhake'** I put the bellyband on (a horse), **tetsa'kwaráhnhak** Put the bellyband on! and INSTR -st-: **tekonwaia'kwarahnhákstha'** bellyband.

With V -otahrho[k]- hook, and DLC:

wa'ttia'karotáhrhoke' I draped it over something (for example, a towel or a belt over a chair), **wa'tieia'karotáhrhoke'** she draped it over.

-ia'kwahrhie'na- V hug, put one's arms around, with DLC: **tenhiaia'kwahrhiè:na'** he will put his arms around you, **wa'thiia'kwahrhiè:na'** I put my arms around him, I hugged him, **wa'tehshakoia'kwahrhiè:na'** he put his arms around her, he hugged her.

-ia'kwatahkw- V arch of the foot, with DLC: **tekaia'kwatáhkwen** arch of the foot.

-ia'ser-/-'ser- V stack, with DLC: **tetia'séhrha'** I stack it, put one thing on top of another, **tentià:seren'** I will stack it, **wa'ttià:seren'** I stacked it, **tewatià:sere'** I have stacked it, **tekaià:sere'** it is stacked.
With DISTR -onnion-: **tetia'serónnions** I stack things, **wa'ttia'serónnion'** I stacked things, **tetsa'serónnion** Stack them!
With SRF -at- and -hah- road: **teiothahà:sere'** crossroads.
With N -hsin- leg: **tekhsinà:sere'** my legs are crossed; and SRF -at-: **tenhsatshinà:seren'** you will cross your legs, **wa'tkatshinà:seren'** I crossed my legs.
With N -na'tar[o][k]- bread: **tekana'tarà:sere'** sandwich.
With N -nentsh- arm: **tekenentshà:sere'** I have my arms crossed; and SRF -ate-: **wa'tkatenentshà:seren'** I crossed my arms.
With SRF -ate- and N -rahkw- sun: **wa'tewaterahkwà:seren'** eclipse.
With SRF -ate- and N -renhs- lower leg: **wa'tkaterenhsà:seren'** I crossed my legs (maybe doing yoga).
With N -ront- log, beam, and DISTR

-onnion-: **wa'tharonta'serónnion'** he stacked logs, **tekaronta'serónnion** there are stacked logs or beams.
With N -'nerohkw- box: **wa'tha'nerohkwà:seren'** he stacked the box on top of the other, **teka'nerohkwà:sere'** the boxes are stacked on top of one another; and DISTR -onnion-: **teka'nerohkwa'serónnion** the boxes are all on top of one another.

-ia't- N body: **oià:ta'**
POSS: **tia'tà:ke** (on) my body, **raia'tà:ke** (on) his body, **ieia'tà:ke** (on) her body.
With LOC -kon, inside: **tià:takon** it is inside my body, **kaià:takon** it is inside its body; and **tiakéta's** (-ta'-/-eta'- put inside): **kaià:takon tiakéta's** dressing (chicken, turkey).
With V -ahnot- tell about: **riia'tahnótha'** I tell about him, I tell on him.
With V -ahseht- hide, kill: **wa'kheia'táhsehte'** I hid her.
With V -ahsihara'- get wedged in, stuck, and DLC: **wa'tieia'tahsíhara'ne'** she got stuck.
With V -ahskats[t]- be beautiful: **roia'táhskats** he is handsome.
With SRF -at- and V -ahton- disappear: **wahatia'táhton'** he got lost.
With V -akarenhr[e]- lean to one side, slant: **raia'takarèn:re'** he is crooked, lopsided.
With V -akera- stink, smell: **raia'tákeras** he smells, **kaia'tákeras** goat.
With V -ara'se- be attractive, appealing: **iakoia'tarà:se'** she is attractive.
With V -ase- be fresh, new: **ieià:tase'** elegant, attractive, well-dressed, young woman; and NMZR -'tsher-, V -akaion-/ -kaion- be old, and INCH -'-: **iakoia'tase'tsherakaiòn:'on** unmarried woman, spinster.
With V -ati-/-onti- lose, throw:

ontia'tón:ti' I missed it (the bus, train, airplane); and SRF -at- and CISL or TRNL: **iahiiatia'tón:ti'** I jumped him, attacked him.

With SRF -at- and V -atkon- be the devil, demon: **rotia'tátkon** he is a mystic, he has power.

With SRF -at- and V -atsha'- burn: **wahatia'tátsha'** he got burnt.

With SRF -at- and V -awak- shake: **wahatia'tá:wake'** he shook himself off.

With SRF at- and V -awi- wrap around, encircle: **atià:tawi** dress, shirt, jacket, coat (*see* -atia'tawi- for more forms).

With V -a'senht-/-enht- drop: **wa'kheià:tenhte'** I dropped her.

With V -a'sen'-/-en'- fall down, and TRNL: **ia'tià:ten'ne'** I fell down or off.

With V -ehsak-/-ihsak-/-esak-/-isak- look for: **kheia'tíhsaks** or **kheia'tí:saks** I am looking for her, I miss her.

With SRF -at-, V -eka'[w]-/-ka'[w]- find tasty, and CAUS -hst-: **wakatia'takon'ónhston** I have on perfume.

With V -en- happen, and PART: **tsi niwatià:tawens** what is happening to me, what is wrong with me.

With V -haratat-/-karatat- lift, raise up: **iakoia'takará:tats** elevator.

With V -ha[w]-/-enha[w]- hold, bring, take, and CISL: **entekheia'ténhawe'** I will bring her.

With V -hawi-/-enhawi- carry: **kheia'tenhá:wi'** I am carrying her.

With V -her-/-hr- set on top of: **ieia'táhere'** she is laid out (at a wake), **wahonwaia'tà:ren'** they laid him out; and INSTR -hkw-: **iontatia'tahráhkhwa'** funeral parlour.

With REFL -atat- and V -hew- arrive: **wa'katatià:thewe'** I arrived.

With V -hkw- pick up, and DLC: **wa'tekheià:tahkwe'** I picked her up,

teiakoia'táhkhwa' hawk.

With V -hnir- be hard, solid, firm, and CAUS -t-: **iakoia'tahní:rats** it makes the body strong.

With V -hren't-/-en't- hang down, AMB -hne-, and CISL: **ohnà:ken tahoia'ten'tòn:ne'** he is coming in the back, behind.

With V -hsa'-/-isa'- finish, complete: **Shonkwaia'tíson'** Our Creator.

With SRF -at- and V -hseronni- dress, prepare: **wa'katia'tahserón:ni'** I dressed up.

With V -hsnor[e]- be fast: **raia'tahsnó:re'** he is fast, he does things fast.

With SRF -at-, and SRF -at- and V -hteron- be scared, afraid: **rotia'táthteron** he is a frightening person, he is off-putting.

With V -htohrarak-/-ohrarak- squeeze, press down: **wahoia'tò:rarake'** he held him down, he pinned him (wrestling).

With SRF -at- and V -hwahnha[k]-/-hnha[k]- wrap, tie around: **wahatia'táhnhake'** he put on a belt; **atia'táhnha'** belt.

With V -i- be the total of, CAUS -st-, and TRNL and DLC: **ia'tewatià:tiste'** I was left all alone.

With SRF -at- and V -ienht- hit against: **wahakwatià:taienhte'** he bumped into me.

With V -ihei[on]-/-enhei[on]- die: **wa'eia'takénheie'** she became paralyzed, **watia'takenhé:ion** I do things slowly, I take my time.

With V -inekenhw- let out, and TRNL: **ietia'tínekenhs** I let it out (an animal).

With V -ionni- be lying, be extended: **tia'tión:ni** I am lying down.

With V -ion't-/-inion't- bring in, and CISL: **takheia'tínion'te'** I brought her in.

With V -ishonhkw- quake, tremble: **ontia'tíshonhkwe'** I trembled.

With V -i[t]- be inside: **tià:ti** I am in it.

With V -itahkhe- be in something moving: **tia'titáhkhe'** I am in something moving.

With V -ita'- put into (a vehicle): **wahiia'títa'** I gave him a ride.

With V -kareni- take back and forth: **iakoia'takarénie's** bus.

With V -kehron[t]- put down here and there: **ieia'takè:ron** there are people lying down.

With V -ken- see: **roià:taken** he stands out, he is conspicuous.

With V -keront-/-okeront- square: **tia'tokerón:te'** I am lying on my side.

With V -kste- be heavy: **roia'tákste'** he is heavy.

With V -kwe'niio- be in charge of: **ieia'takwe'ní:io** she is in charge.

With V -na'nawen-/-nawen- be wet: **watia'taná:wen** I am wet.

With V -nekheren- find something strange, unusual: **wahiia'tanekhé:ren'** I find him strange.

With V -nera'[k]- mistake, and DLC: **wa'tkonia'tanéra'ke'** I mistook you for someone.

With V -nonhn- mind, guard: **wahoia'tanòn:na'** he guarded him.

With V -nonhst[e]- treasure, protect, aid: **riia'tanónhstha'** I protect him.

With V -nonhwak[t]- be sore, hurt, ache, and DISTR -hon-: **watia'tanonhwákhons** my body aches.

With REFL -atat-, V -noron- be expensive, precious, and CAUS -hst-: **katatia'tanorónhstha'** I take care of myself.

With V -ohro[k]- insert: **tia'tò:ron** I am inside of it, underneath it.

With V -ohseronkw- caress, pat: **kheia'tohserónkwas** I am caressing her, patting her.

With V -ohtahrho- tidy: **wahonwaia'tohtáhrho'** he got a penalty.

With SRF -at- and V -ohw- swell:

iakotià:to her stomach is swollen.

With V -ohwiha- split in two, and DLC: **wa'ttia'tohwíha'** I split it in two.

With SRF -at-, V -onko- penetrate, CAUS -ht-, and DLC: **tewakatia'tonkóhtha'** I have diarrhea.

With V -onkw- bump, hit, TRNL and DLC: **ia'thatia'tón:ko'** he bumped into me.

With V -onni- make: **kaia'tón:ni** doll.

With V -ont- attach, REV -kw-, and CAUS -ht-: **wa'kheia'tontákwahte'** I excluded her; with SRF -at-, V -ont- attach, and INSTR -hkw-: **wahatia'tón:tahkwe'** he faked it, **wakatia'tontáhkwen** I am pretending, faking it.

With V -oreht- judge, and DLC: **tehaia'toréhtha'** he is a judge.

With V -otahrhe'- get hooked on something: **wa'tia'totáhrhe'ne'** I got hooked or snagged on it.

With V -o'ten- be a kind of, and PART: **tsi nihaia'tò:ten** the way he is.

With V -r- put in: **kaià:tare'** picture; and SRF -at- and INSTR -hkw-: **ohnà:ken eniakoià:tarahkwe'** she will be late.

With SRF -at-, V -rakew-/-okew- wipe, and CAUS -ht-: **iontia'tokewáhtha'** towel(s).

With V -ra'kar- be leaning against: **tia'tarà:kare'** I am leaning up against it.

With SRF -at-, V -ra'nekar[on]-/-nekar[on]- burst open, and DLC: **tehotia'taneká:ron** he has a hernia.

With V -ra'nentakt-/-nentakt- stick to, and ATTR =hne, at: **Ronwaia'tanentaktónhne** Friday.

With V -rio-/-riio- beat up, kill: **watia'tários** I feel there's a heaviness on me, I am feeling out of sorts.

With V -skenni- rush, and DLC: **wa'thatia'taskén:ni'** he beat me to it, he got there before I did.

With V -steri- be funny, jolly: **iakoia'tasté:ris** she is funny, jolly.

With V -[t]- be one, and REP: **shaià:ta** one

male, **tseià:ta** one female.
With V -ta'-/-eta- put inside:
wahonwaia'táta' they buried him; and
CAUS -hst- and INSTR -hkw-:
iontatia'tata'ahstáhkhwa' grave, cemetery.
With V -te[ht]- be strong-tasting,
energetic: **roià:tate'** he is hyperactive,
always moving, never sits still.
With V -tokenhti- be holy:
iakoia'tatokénhti nun.
With V -tshahni[ht]- be industrious,
energetic, active: **roia'tatshà:ni** he is
energetic, active.
With V -weienst- learn, study, practice:
roia'taweiénston it looks good on him.
With V -'nikonhrhen- forget, and REP:
sahiia'ta'nikónhrhen' I forgot him.
With V -'rhenienht-/-ienenht- knock down:
wahatia'tié:nenhte' he knocked me
down.
With V -'rhenien'-/-ienen'- fall down:
wa'tia'tié:nen'ne' I fell down or over.
With SRF -at-, V -'rhoro[k]-/-oro[k]- cover,
and CAUS -st-: **watia'torókstha'** envelope.
NOTE: This root occurs incorporated into
many verbs, and not all the derived and
inflected forms of some of the N plus V
combinations are given here; for the additional forms, see the V entry.

-ia'tahkariio- V be flexible, agile:
roia'tahkarí:io he is flexible,
iakoia'tahkarí:io she is flexible,
ioia'tahkarí:io it is flexible (an animal).
With SRF -at- and CAUS -hst-:
wa'katia'tahkarí:iohste' I exercised,
iakotia'tahkariióhston she is exercising;
and DISTR -nion-:
katia'tahkariiohstánions I exercise.

-ia'takehnha- V help, support:
ratia'takéhnhas he helps me out with it,

he supports me, **enkheia'takéhnha'** I will
help her, support her, **wahatia'takéhnha'**
he helped me, **ratia'takéhnhen** he is
helping me.
With REFL -atat-: **eniontatia'takéhnha'**
she will help herself,
wa'katatia'takéhnha' I helped myself.

-ia'taterist- V bless: **wahshakoia'taté:riste'**
he blessed them, **sheia'taté:rist** Bless
them!

-ia'tohka'w- V give last rites:
enhshakoia'tóhka'we' he will give her
the last rites, **wahoia'tóhka'we'** he gave
him the last rites.

-ia'tont[a]- V be in someone's way, underfoot:
roia'tón:ta he is just in the way,
iakoia'tón:ta she is just in the way.
With SRF -at- and BEN -hahs-:
onkwatia'tónthahse' someone got in the
way, annoying me or making me feel
discomfitted, **wahotia'tónthahse'** it made
him feel discomfitted.
• Onkwatia'tónthahse' tsi nihaia'tò:ten.
It was annoying how he was (underfoot,
a pest).

-ie- V wake up: **ítie's** I wake up, **rá:ie's** he
wakes up, **wà:tie'** I woke up, **wahá:ie'** he
woke up, **wa'é:ie'** she woke up, **watiè:'on**
I am awake, **roiè:'on** he is awake,
iakoiè:'on she is awake.
With CAUS -ht-: **wahí:iehte'** I woke him
up.

-iehwa-/-ioha- V look for in vain: **watiè:was**
I can't find it, **enwatióha'** I won't find it,
ontióha' I couldn't find it, **wahoióha'** he
couldn't find it, **watiohà:'on** I couldn't
find it.
With N -hah- road: **wakhahaiè:was** I am
looking for the road and can't find it.

With SRF -ate-, N -rihw- matter, message, and CAUS -ht-: **katerihwaiehwáhtha'** I deny it, **wa'katerihwaiè:wahte'** I pretended to not know, I denied it, **wakaterihwaiehwáhton** I am pretending to not know.

• Watiè:was akehnhotónkwa'. I can't find my keys.

-iehwahtahkw- V wake up suddenly, with TRNL: **ia'tiehwáhtahkwe'** I woke up suddenly, **iahaiehwáhtahkwe'** he woke up suddenly.

-iehwat[on]- V wake up early: **tiè:wate'** I wake up early, **raiè:wate'** he wakes up early, **ieiè:wate'** she wakes up early. With NEG: **iah tehaiè:wate'** he doesn't wake up early. With SRF -at-: **wa'katiehwá:ton'** I stayed up all night, I woke myself up early (maybe by setting the alarm), **wahatiehwá:ton'** he stayed up all night, **wa'ontiehwá:ton'** she stayed up all night.

-ien- KIN child, young age, with ATTR ='a/=ha, diminutive: **riièn:'a** my son, **kheièn:'a** my daughter. With ATTR =okon'a, pluralizer: **kheien'okòn:'a** my children.

-ien- oil, grease. *See* -iie-/-ien-

-ien- V put down, have: **ítiens** I put it down, **ítsens** you (sg) put it down, **rá:iens** he puts it down, **éntien'** I will put it down, **énhsien'** you will put it down, **wà:tien'** I put it down, **wahá:ien'** he put it down, **wátien'** I have it, **kèn:tho ítsen** Put it down here! **kèn:tho ká:ien'** it is here, **ó:ia' shé:kon ká:ien'** there is another one. With DISTR -on-, and PART: **tsik nón: nikaién:ton** it is scattered here and there.

With PURP -hn-, and REP: **sahaiénhne'** he is going to return it, **sahaiénhna'** he returned it. With CISL: **tho tká:ien'** it is there; and DLC: **tontahá:ien'** he brought it back. With CISL: **ó:nen tewátien'** I am older now, **ó:nen thó:ien'** he is older now, **ó:nen tiakó:ien'** she is older now; and PART: **Tó: nithó:ien'?** How old is he? **nitió:ien'** it is that old, a certain age. With INCH -'- and CISL: **tahoién:ta'ne'** he got old. With PART and CISL, and **ken'** particle: **ken' nithoièn:'a** he is young, **ken' nitiakoièn:'a** she is young, **ken' nithotiièn:'a** they are young, **ken' nithotiièn:sa'** young people, **ken' nitiotiièn:sa'** young women. With TRNL: **iahá:ien'** he left it there; and REP: **ionsahá:ien'** he took it back. With DLC: **tehá:iens** he is playing (cards, Bingo), he is gambling, **tentení:ien'** you and I will play. With SRF -at-: **kátiens** I sit down, **wa'kátien'** I sat down, **sátien** Sit! and BEN -ni-/-hahs-: **wa'kheiatién:hahse'** I stayed with them, **wa'onkwatién:hahse'** she or they stayed with me. With REFL -atat- and BEN -ni-/-hahs-: **katatién:ni** I am saving it, **ratatién:ni** he is saving it, **iontatién:ni** she is saving it, **wa'katatién:hahse'** I saved it. With SRF -at- and N -ahkwenni- outfit, clothing: **wa'katahkwenniá:ien'** I stored it; and INSTR -hkw-: **iontahkwenniaientáhkhwa'** cupboard, storage shed, pantry; with SRF -at-, N -ahkwenni- outfit, clothing, and BEN -ni-/-hahs-: **enkoniatahkwenniaién:hahse'** I will leave it in your care, **wa'kheiatahkwenniaién:hahse'** I left it in her care. With SRF -at- and N -ahswen't-/-a'swen't- coal: **katahswèn:taiens** I am saving coal.

With N -ateh[en]- become embarrassed, ashamed, NMZR -hser-, and NEG: **iah teiakotehenhserá:ien'** she has no shame (she'll do anything).

With N -atena'tar- sunfish: **iotena'tará:ien'** a snake that's coiled.

With N -atkarohkw- rag, and TRNL: **ia'satkaróhkwaien** an older, playful expression, like 'you silly goose!'

With V -atkon- be the devil, demon, NMZR -'ser-, and TRNL: **ia'satkon'será:ien** Go to the devil!

With N -atshat- steam, mist, fog, and DLC: **teiotshá:taien'** it is misty, foggy.

With N -enser- smell, scent: **iawenserá:ien'** it has a smell to it.

With N -heht- field, meadow, garden: **kahéhtaien'** there is a field or garden.

With N -hent- meadow, big field, prairie: **kahén:taien'** there is a field.

With N -hiatonhser- book, paper, and DLC: **tehatihiatonhserá:iens** they are playing cards; and INSTR -hkw-: **teiehiatonhseraientáhkhwa'** cards.

With N -hiohs- elbow, and DLC: **tsi tekahióhsaien'** at the corner.

With N -hsa'kenser- frost: **iohsa'kenserá:ien'** there is frost.

With N -hsenn- name: **ronwahsén:naien'** they praise him, worship him.

With N -hwatsir- family: **iakwahwatsí:raien'** we have a family.

With N -hwist- metal, money: **wakhwístaien'** I have money; and SRF -at-: **wahathwístaien'** he saved money.

With N -ient- wood, and INSTR -hkw-: **ieientaientáhkhwa'** wood shed.

With V -ihei[on]-/-enhei[on]- die, CAUS -'t-, INSTR -hkw-, and CISL: **tsi tiakenheion'taientáhkhwa'** morgue, hospital.

With N -i't- excrement: **wahaní'taien'** he defecated.

With N -i'tar- chimney, clan:

waki'tá:raien' I have a clan.

With N -karien't- carcass: **kakarièn:taien'** there is a carcass.

With N -ks- dish, plate, and CISL; and **nà:kon** down: **nà:kon tiéksaiens** saucer.

With N -nahskw- pet, domestic animal: **wakenáhskwaien'** I have a pet.

With N -nat- town, settlement, and CISL: **tkaná:taien'** there's a town there; with SRF -ate- and N -nat- town, settlement: **wa'katená:taien'** I made myself at home.

With N -naw- swamp, and CISL: **tkaná:waien'** there's a swamp there.

With N -na'kar- horn, antler, dice, and DLC: **tekena'kará:iens** I am playing dice.

With N -na'skw- body, curled-up, INCH -'-, and TRNL: **ia'kena'skwaién:ta'ne'** I fell down, I tumbled down.

With N -nekw- pea, pill, and TRNL: **ia'senékwaien** Take a pill! That's enough!

With N -neni- stone, rock, INSTR -hkw-, and DLC: **teieneniaientáhkhwa'** marbles.

With N -nerokw- vest, top: **kaneró:kwaien'** it (an animal) is lying down.

With N -nieht- snow: **kaniéhtaien'** there is snow (on the ground).

With N -nons- crouch, squat, and DLC: **tekenón:saien'** I am crouching.

With SRF -ate- and N -nonw- bottom water, dregs: **katenón:waiens** I sink, go underwater.

With N -nonwe[ht]- object for witchcraft: **iononwéhtaien'** she has an object that she uses for witchcraft.

With N -onhar- frozen ground: **iaonhará:ien'** the ground is frozen.

With SRF -at- and N -onri- breath: **rotonriá:ien'** he is whining.

With SRF -ate- and N -renn- song, music: **roterén:naien'** he is praying; and INSTR -hkw-: **ionterennaientáhkhwa'** church.

With N -rihton- black oak, and NMZR

-'tsher-: **ionkwarihton'tsherá:ien'** we have police.

With SRF -ate-, N -rist- iron, steel, and INSTR -hkw-: **ionteristaientáhkhwa'** steel trap.

With N -tsenh- fire: **ratitsénhaiens** they council; and INSTR -hkw-: **ietsenhaientáhkhwa'** town or council hall.

With N -tsihkw- fist, button, and DLC: **tektsíhkwaiens** I am playing billiards, checkers (a game with pieces).

With SRF -at- and N -tsist- fire: **Ronattsístaien'** Firekeepers, Onondagas as referred to in council.

With N -tsi'ts- flower, and PURP -hn-: **wa'etsi'tsaiénhne'** bridesmaid.

With N -wir- offspring: **wakewí:raien'** I have a child.

With N -'nonhkw- bottom of something, and CISL: **tka'nónhkwaien'** it has a bottom (for example, a basket or a pie).

With N -'now- hump, padlock: **ke'nó:waien'** I am crouched down.

With N -'onwar- seedling: **wa'ke'onwará:ien'** I started the seedling.

With SRF -ate- and N -'sere[ht]- vehicle, car: **wa'kate'seréhtaien'** I parked the car.

With V -'shatst[e]- be strong, and NMZR -enhser-: **wake'shatstenhserá:ien'** I have strength or energy.

With INCH -'-, *see* -ienta'- get, obtain.

NOTE: This root has the variant -ient- before some suffixes. The root occurs with many incorporated nouns, and not all the inflected and derived forms of some of the N plus V combinations are given here; for the additional forms, see the N entry.

• Wahiiatahkwenniaién:hahse' akè:sere kahnhotónkwa'. I left the keys to my car in his care.

Cf. Gaien y avoir (Bruyas: 59); *θonn'etisaien* quel aage as tu? (Galissonnière: 2r); Wendat *Sakieiu* Assieds-toy (Sagard: Sa1); Susquehannock *Tzátzie* sit and stay (Holm: 9)

-iena- V hold, catch, touch: **tié:nas** I grab hold of it, **entié:na'** I will hold it, **enhsié:na'** you will hold it, **wahaié:na'** he held it, he caught her or it, **wahoié:na'** he caught him, **wahiié:na'** I caught him, **watienà:'on** I have gotten hold of it.

With CISL: **ttié:nas** I catch it, **thaié:nas** he catches it, **tieié:nas** she catches it, **enttié:na'** I will catch it, **tatié:na'** I caught it, I grabbed it, **tahiié:na'** I caught him (as he passed by).

With TRNL: **ia'tié:na'** I touched it, **iahiié:na'** I touched him, **tóhsa ia'tsé:na** Don't touch it!

With DLC: **teiakeniié:nas** we two work together (as a team), **wa'tiakeniié:na'** we two worked together.

With REFL -atat- and DLC: **tehontatié:nas** they are wrestling, **tenkontatié:na'** they (females, plants) will hold on to one another.

With N -rihw- matter, message: **Ratirihwaié:nas** they receive the message; Oneidas and Cayugas as referred to in council, **wa'erihwaié:na'** she agreed to the issue; and CONTR: **iah thakerihwaié:na'** I won't take hold of, agree to the matter.

• Tóhsa ia'tsé:na io'taríhen enhsatia'tátsha'. Don't touch it, it's hot [and] you'll burn yourself.

-ienawa'ahst- V take someone in, shelter someone, with SRF -at-: **wahiiatiénawa'ahste'** I took him in, took care of him, **kheiatienawa'áhston** I am sheltering her.

-ienawa'k-/-wa'k- V hold, support: **watienawà:kon** I am holding it,

kheienawà:kon I am holding her; and PROG -hatie-: **roienawa'konhátie'** he is holding him as they are going along. With DLC: **teionkeniienawà:kon** we two are working together.

With N -hnia's- neck, collar: **khehnia'sawà:kon** I have my arms around her neck, **rihnia'sawà:kon** I have my arms around his neck.

With N -hsnonhs- finger, hand: **khehsnonhsawà:kon** I am holding her hand.

With REFL -atate-, N -nentsh- arm, and DLC: **teionkwatatenentshawà:kon** we are locking our arms, **tehonatatenentshawà:kon** they are locking their arms, Chain Belt, Covenant Belt. With N -rihw- matter, message: **arihwawà:kon** Bishop; and ATTR =kowa, great: **arihwawa'konhkó:wa** the Pope; with N -rihw- matter, message, and ATTR =hneha, way of: **arihwawa'konhnéha** purple (the colour of garments worn by Bishops); and NMZR -'tsher- and V -ra'ken- be white: **arihwawa'kon-hne'tsherarà:ken** lavender; with N -rihw- matter, message, and DLC: **tehotirihwaienawà:kon** they are a couple, **teionkenirihwaienawà:kon** he/she and I are a couple, my spouse. With N -ronhi- sky, heaven, and CISL: **Tharonhiawà:kon** Holder of the heavens. NOTE: GM reported that **Tharonhiawà:kon** also referred to a giant, appearing to some people out of nowhere and seen standing at the Catholic church or some other tall building, resting his elbow on the church steeple or roof. The third author remembers her father talking about this benevolent giant, but her father did not use this term to refer to him.

-ienawa's-/-wa's- V help someone: **ratienawà:se'** he helps me (to do some-thing), **wahatié:nawa'se'** he helped me, **wa'kheié:nawa'se'** I helped her, **ahstié:nawa'se'** you should help me. With REFL -atat-: **wa'katatié:nawa'se'** I helped myself (to something), **satatié:nawa's** Help yourself! (for example, help yourself to some coffee). With N -hahser- light, lamp: **rohahserawà:se'** altar boy. With N -rihw- matter, message: **wa'kherì:wawa'se'** I helped her look for it, find out information; and REFL -atate-: **wa'katateri:wawa'se'** I found information for myself.

-ienenht- knock over, knock down. *See* -'rhenienht-/-ienenht-

-ienen'- fall down. *See* -'rhenien'-/-ienen'-

-ienht- V hit against with something: **wà:tienhte'** I hit it with something, **wahá:ienhte'** he hit it, **wa'khé:ienhte'** I hit her, **wa'óntienhte'** she hit me, **óntienhte'** it hit me, **wa'otí:ienhte'** they (plants) got frost, were affected by frost, **watiénhton** I have hit it. With DISTR -nion-: **tienhtánions** I am hitting it against it repeatedly, **wa'tienhtánion'** I hit it repeatedly. With TRNL and DLC: **tékeni ia'tká:ienhte'** two times; or PART: **nienká:ienhte'** it will be so many times, **áhsen nia'ká:ienhte'** three times.

With REFL -atat- and DLC: **wa'tkatátienhte'** I struggled, I had a hard time, **wa'tiontátienhte'** she struggled, **tehotatiénhton** he is struggling, finding it hard to get by.

With N -hiohs- elbow, and TRNL: **iahonkhióhsaienhte'** I banged my elbow against it, **iahohióhsaienhte'** he hit his elbow against it; with SRF -at- and N -hiohs- elbow: **wahiiathióhsaienhte'** I

elbowed him, I hit him with my elbow, **wahakwathióhsaienhte'** he elbowed me.
With SRF -at- and N -ia't- body: **wahakwatià:taienhte'** he bumped into me, **wa'kheiatià:taienhte'** I bumped into her.
With N -(h)nhoh- door: **wahahnhóhaienhte'** he slammed the door.
With N -nontsi[st]- head, and TRNL: **iahonkenontsístaienhte'** I banged my head.
With N -'rhiotsh- chin, and TRNL: **iahonke'rhiótshaienhte'** I banged my chin.
• Kanekotà:ke **wahá:ienhte'** iene'konhréksta'. He hit the steps with a hammer.
• Karontà:ke **wa'tienhtánion'**. I hit it (a rug, rake, stick) against the beam or pole.
• **Wa'tiontátienhte'** wahonwanehià:ron' ne ronwatiien'okòn:'a. She had a hard time to bring up her children.

-ienht- N gums: **oiénhta'**
POSS: **atiénhta'** my gums, **tienhtà:ke** on my gums, **raoiénhta'** his gums, **akoiénhta'** her gums.
With V -nonhwak[t]- be sore, hurt: **iakoienhtanòn:waks** she has sore gums.
With SRF -at- and V -ohw- swell: **iakotiénhto** her gums are swollen.

-ienkwir- N -arrow: **kaién:kwire'**

-ienser[on]- V skin an animal: **raiénserons** he skins it, **entién:sere'** I will skin it, **wa'tién:sere'** I skinned it, **roiénseron** he has skinned it.

-ient- N wood: **ó:iente'**
With V -astath[en]-/-ath[en]- dry: **ioientáthen** (it is) dry wood.
With SRF -at- and V -atsha'- burn: **wakatientátshon'** I have a Native mother

and a White father, **rotientátshon'** he has a Native mother and a White father.
With V -ia'k- break, and DLC: **tehaiéntia'ks** he is chopping wood.
With V -ien- put down, have, and INSTR -hkw-: **ieientaientáhkhwa'** wood shed.
With V -ion't-/-inion't- bring in, and CISL: **tahaientínion'te'** he brought in wood.
With SRF -at-, V -kahrhatho- turn over, and BEN -'s-: **onkwatientakahrhátho'se'** it didn't go well for me, not as planned, **wahotientakahrhátho'se'** it didn't go well for him.
With V -koh- go get something: **wahaientakóhe'** he is going to get wood.
With V -kowan[en]-/-owan[en]- be big: **Kaientowá:nen** Peach Pit (Great Bowl) game.
With V -kw- pick, and CAUS -ht-: **ieientakwáhtha'** vehicle for transporting wood.
With V -na'nawen-/-nawen- be wet: **ioientaná:wen** (it is) damp or wet wood.
With V -ohwiha- split in two, and DLC: **tehaientohwíhas** he is splitting wood, **wa'ttientohwíha'** I split wood.
With V -ontho- burn, put in the fire: **tientónthos** I put wood in the fire, **entientóntho'** I will put wood in the fire, **wa'tientóntho'** I put wood in to burn, **roientónthon** he has put wood in to burn; and REP: **sahaientóntho'** he is putting more wood in to burn.
With V -ot- stand, and DLC: **tehaientótha'** he is stacking wood, **tentientó:ten'** I will stack wood, **wa'thaientó:ten'** he stacked wood.
With V -ra'neken-/-neken- be side-by-side, next to, and DLC: **Thaientané:ken** two pieces of wood side-by-side (tied together); name of Mohawk chief Joseph Brant.
With SRF -at- and V -statha't-/-atha't- dry: **wa'katientátha'te'** I dried wood.
See also -ientot- stack in a pile.

Cf. Oienta Jeu de Paille (Galissonnière: 50v); *iotientātson* Métis (Marcoux: 248); *Oiente* bois de chauffage (Cuoq: 31); *wakatientatson* être bois-brûlé, métis des Pays-Hauts (Cuoq: 129)

-ienta'- V get, obtain: **watién:ta's** I obtain it, **enwatién:ta'ne'** I will obtain it, **ontién:ta'ne'** I got it, **watientà:'on** I have gotten it.
With REP: **sontién:ta'ne'** I got it again, I got another one.
With N -kahr- eye, and TRNL and DLC: **ia'tekkahraién:ta'ne'** my eye focused on it, I understand it better now, it's clearer.
With N -tsihenhst- crispiness, char, and REP: **ó:ia enshotitsihenhstaién:ta'ne'** they will get another priest [Father Granger would be replaced] (Old Kahnawake: 4)
With N -'nikonhr- mind: **wake'nikonhraién:ta's** I understand, **onke'nikonhraién:ta'ne'** I understood it.
With: N -'sere[ht]- vehicle, car, and REP: **ó:ia' sonke'serehtaién:ta'ne'** I got a car again, I got another car.
NOTE: This stem is composed of the variant -ient- of -ien- put down, have, and INCH -'-.

-ientehrha'- V make somebody's acquaintance, get to know: **enkheientéhrha'ne'** I will get to know her, **wa'konientéhrha'ne'** I made your acquaintance, I got to know you.
With REFL -atat- and DLC: **tentiatatientéhrha'ne'** you and I will get to know each other, the two (females) will get to know each other, **wa'thontatientéhrha'ne'** they got to know each other, **wa'tkontatientéhrha'ne'** they (females) got to know each other.

-ientere'- V recognize: **tién:tere's** I recognize it, **kheién:tere's** I recognize her, **entién:tere'ne'** I will recognize it, **wahaién:tere'ne'** he recognized it, **kheienterè:'on** I have recognized her.
With NEG: **iah tehiién:tere's** I don't recognize him.

-ienteri- V know someone: **konienté:ri** I know you, **kheienté:ri** I know her.

-ientho- V plant: **tiénthos** I plant, **tsénthos** you (sg) plant, **raiénthos** he plants, he is a farmer, **entiéntho'** I will plant, **wahaiéntho'** he planted, **watiénthon** I have planted.
With NMZR -hser-: **kaienthóhsera'** plants.
With REV -kw-: **tienthókwas** I harvest, **wa'tienthó:ko'** I harvested, **roienthókwen** he has harvested, **Kaienthókwen** Harvest ceremony.
With N -hnenna't- potato: **wa'khnenna'taiéntho'** I planted potatoes.

-ientot- V stack in a pile, with DLC: **tetientótha'** I stack them, pile them up, **entientó:ten'** I will stack, pile them, **wa'tientó:ten'** I stacked, piled them, **tewatién:tote'** I have stacked, piled them, **tekaién:tote'** it is a stack, a pile.
With N -hson'kar-/-hswen'kar- board: **wa'thahson'karaientó:ten'** he stacked the boards.
With N -ks- dish, plate: **tehaksaientótha'** he is stacking dishes, **wa'thaksaientó:ten'** he stacked dishes.
With N -'nerohkw- box: **wa'tha'nerohkwaientó:ten'** he stacked boxes.
NOTE: This stem is composed of -ient- wood, and -ot- stand.

-ien'kw- N tobacco: **oièn:kwa'**

With ATTR =onwe, genuine:
oien'kwa'ón:we Native tobacco.
With V -(h)nhont- have in one's mouth:
roien'kwáhnhonte' he has tobacco in his mouth.
With SRF -at- and V -(h)nhonta'- put in one's mouth: **ratien'kwahnhónta's** he puts tobacco in his mouth,
wahatien'kwahnhónta' he put tobacco in his mouth.
With V -ontho- burn, put in the fire:
enhsien'kóntho' you will put tobacco in the fire, **wa'tien'kóntho'** I burned tobacco.

Cf. Ojeng𝑠a petun (Bruyas: 61); *Oieng𝑠a* Petun (Galissonnière: 65v); *oiēnk𝑠a* Tabac (Marcoux: 380); *Oienkwa* tabac (Cuoq: 31); *Oyenkondonh* warriors (Hale: 122–3); *ot-kon ra-io-ien-kwa* Verbascum Thapsus [devil's tobacco, mullein] (Rousseau: 57); Onondaga *oyeng𝑠a* tabac (Shea: 96); Susquehannock *Ojeengqua* tobacco (Holm: 7)

-ien'kwar- N smoke: **oièn:kwara'**
With V -akera- stink, smell:
raien'kwarákeras he smells of smoke,
kaien'kwarákeras it smells of smoke.
With V -ati-/-onti- lose, throw, and TRNL:
ieniakoien'kwarón:ti' she will drop (blow) the smoke there.
With V -enton[hw]- move back and forth, and DLC: **wa'thaien'kwarén:tonhwe'** he (the priest) moved the thurible (incense burner) back and forth.
With V -o- be in water, BEN -'s-, and DLC:
wa'tewatièn:kwaro'se' I got smoke in my eyes, **wa'thoièn:kwaro'se'** he got smoke in his eyes.
With SRF -at-, V -okw- disperse, and DLC:
tewatien'kwarókwas puffball.
With SRF -at- and V -onni- make:
iotien'kwarón:ni it is smoky.

With V -ot- stand: **ioièn:kwarote'** the smoke is rising.

Cf. te-wa-tien-wha-ro-kwas Lycoperdon sp [puffball] (Rousseau: 32); compare *o'tgu̧ raona'daro* Puffball ("devil's bread") (Waugh: 121); *tho thí:ken ieniakoien'-kwarón:ti* … she blew the smoke (into a glass milk bottle) (Old Kahnawake: 2)

-ier- V do
With PART: **tsi nitiéhrha'** how I do it, what I do, **tho nitiéhrha'** that's how I do it, **tsi néntiere'** how I will do it,
tsi nà:tiere' how I did it, **tsi niwatié:ren** how I have done it; and PROG -hatie-:
tsi niwatierenhátie' what I am doing as I am going along.
With SRF -at- and PART: **tsi nikatiéhrha'** what I am doing, **Oh nihsatiéhrha'?** What are you doing? **Oh nontié:ren?** or **Oh niiotié:ren?** Why? What's the matter?
iah othé:nen teiotié:ren it doesn't matter.
With SRF -at- and REP: **sewatié:rens** sometimes.
With **ken'** particle, and PART:
ken' nà:tiere' I touched something,
ken' na'é:iere' she touched it,
tóhsa ken' nà:tser or **tóhsa ken' nà:tse** Don't touch it!
With **ken'** particle, and CONTR and TRNL:
iah thé:nen nahò:ten' ken' thiewatié:ren I didn't do anything at all, **iah thé:nen nahò:ten' ken' thieiakoié:ren** she didn't do anything at all.
With CAUS -'t-, and PART and TRNL:
ísi' nonkwá:ti niahaié:ra'te' he went the other way.
With SRF -at-, CAUS -'t-, and PART:
tho nonkwá:ti nenkatié:ra'te' I will face that way, **ákte' na'katié:ra'te'** I looked the other way.
With SRF -at-, BEN -'s-, and CISL:
thotierà:se' he gets offended,

enthotié:ra'se' he will get offended, **tonkwatié:ra'se'** I got offended, **tóhsa tasatié:ra's** Don't get offended! With COIN: **sha'oié:ra** it is natural.

Cf. Wendat *Danstan téaquierha* Je ne fais rien (Sagard: Fa2)

-ieren- V resemble, look like, with REP: **shiié:ren** I am like him (in manner or features).

With SRF -at- and DLC: **tetsitiatié:ren** you and I resemble each other, you and I look like one another, **tetsatiatié:ren** we two resemble, look like one another, **tetsitsatié:ren** you two look alike, you look like her or him, **teshiatié:ren** the two look alike, **testiatié:ren** the two (females) look alike.

• Teshiatié:ren ro'níha. He looks like his father.

-ieri- V be right

With CISL: **tkaié:ri** it is right; and NEG: **iah tetkaié:ri** it is not right.

With CISL and CONT -k-: **aontakaié:rike'** it would be right.

With TRNL and DLC: **tho ia'tekaié:ri** that's enough, **ia'tetié:ri** it fits me, **shé:kon ia'teieié:ris** it still fits her; and CONTR and REP: **iah thia'testié:ris** it doesn't fit me anymore.

With INCH -'-, and TRNL and DLC: **ia'ttié:ri'ne'** it fit me.

With BEN -hs-, and TRNL and DLC: **ia'tewatié:rihse'** I had enough, **ia'thoié:rihse'** he had enough; and NEG: **iah tha'tewatieríhse'** I didn't have enough.

With N -rahkw- sun, and TRNL: **iekarahkwaié:ri** it is a full moon, a moonlit night.

With N -rihw- matter, message, and CISL: **tewakerihwaié:ri** I have good intentions,

good morals, I am kind, **thorihwaié:ri** he has good intentions, he is kind, **tiakorihwaié:ri** she has good intentions, she is kind, **tkarihwaié:ri** the issue is right; and NEG: **iah tetkarihwaié:ri** the matter is not right, **iah tethorihwaié:ri** he is not a good person; and ATTR =kowa, great: **Thorihwaieri'kó:wa** he is most righteous, begging song they sing on New Year's Eve.

• Ka' niká:ien' tkaié:ri? Which one is right? • Shé:kon ia'tetié:ris ne oronhia'-kó:wa akwatháhsteren. My jeans still fit me. • Ia'tewatié:rihse' tekato'tsinehtsher-óntha'. I had enough of skating. • Iah tetkarihwaié:ri tsi nihontiéhrha'. It's not right what they are doing.

-ierit- V complete, celebrate (another year): **entié:rite'** I will be a certain age, I will have a birthday, **wísk wa'tié:rite'** I celebrated my fifth birthday, I am 5 years old.

With REP: **ensehsié:rite'** you will have another year, another birthday, **tsakoierí:ton** it is her birthday.

With N -rihw- matter, message: **wa'kerihwaié:rite'** I completed the task (to the point of exhaustion), **wakerihwaierí:ton** I am done doing it (I am done in, worn out); and CISL: **tierihwaié:rits** she does good deeds, **tahaierihwaié:rite'** he did good deeds, **thorihwaierí:ton** he has done a good deed.

-ieron- V make fun of, play: **aié:ron** clown.

With CONTR: **thiiontié:ron** she or they are making fun of me, **thihiaié:ron** he is making fun of you, **thenkonié:ron'** I will make fun of you, **thahatié:ron'** he made fun of me.

With SRF -at- and CAUS -hst-: **rotierónhston** he is clowning around.

With SRF -at-, DISTR -nion-, and DLC: **tekatierónnions** I am playing a part (in a play), I am performing, **wa'thatierónnion'** he acted in a play, he performed.

With SRF -at-, DISTR -nion-, BEN -'s-, and DLC: **wa'tewakatierónnion'se'** something unexpected happened to me (for example, a tire on my car blew out, I thought I saw something like a ghost), **wa'thotierónnion'se'** something unexpected happened to him.

With SRF -at-, N -ahkwenni- outfit, clothing, DISTR -nion-, and DLC: **wa'thatahkwenniaierónnion'** he put on a costume, **tehotahkwenniaierónnion** he has on a costume.

With N -hsenn- name, and CONTR: **thihonwahsennaié:ron** they are making fun of his name.

With SRF -at-, N -nonhs- house, DISTR -nion-, and DLC: **tekatenonhsaierónnions** I decorate my house, **wa'tkatenonhsaierónnion'** I decorated my house.

With N -rihw- matter, message, DISTR -nion-, and DLC: **tehakerihwaierónnions** he tricks me, deceives me, **wa'thakerihwaierónnion'** he tricked me, **wa'tekherihwaierónnion'** I tricked her.

• Wa'thatierónnion' athenno'tsherà:ke rá:rate'. He performed, standing (balancing) on the ball. • Raon'éskwani tahshakorihwaierónnion'. He likes to play tricks on people.

Cf. É:so senhs thiionkhiié:ron ne Skaniatará:ti thati'terón:ton. The people of Lachine used to make fun of us. (Old Kahnawake: 32)

-ieronni- V be a mark: **kaierón:ni** it is marked, there is a mark.

With CAUS -tst-: **tieronnítstha'** I mark it, I make identification marks (for instance, pile up stones), **wahaierón:nitste'** he

marked it, **roieronnítston** he has marked it, **kaieronnítston** it has a mark on it.

With N -hah- road: **kahahaierón:ni** there is a mark on the road (for example, white or yellow road markings).

-ieron['t]- N body, shape: **oieròn:ta'** POSS: **tieron'tà:ke** or **tieròn:ke** (on) my body, **raieron'tà:ke** (on) his body, **kaieron'tà:ke** on its body (an animal's).

With V -o'ten- be a kind of, and PART: **tho nikaieron'tò:ten** that is the shape; or COIN: **né: sha'kaieron'tò:ten'** it is the same shape.

Cf. tho nikaierontó:ten tsi ní:iot ne tsí:'s ieráhkhwa o'neróhkwa … it [our first ambulance] was shaped like a cheesebox [cheese container box] … (Old Kahnawake: 14)

-ies[en]- V be easy, available

With SRF -at-: **watié:sen** it is easy; and INCH -'-: **enwatié:sen'ne'** it will become easy, **ontié:sen'ne'** it became easy, **iotiesèn:'en** it has become easy.

With CAUS -ht-: **shakoiesáhtha'** he mistreats her or them, he puts her down, **wahonwaié:sahte'** she mistreated him.

With SRF -at- and CAUS -ht-: **iontiesáhtha'** she wastes things, she is wasteful, **wahatié:sahte'** he wasted it, **wakatiesáhton** I am wasting it, I have wasted it.

With INCH -ha'-, and NEG: **iah thé:nen tekaiésha's** nothing is wasted, **iah thé:nen thakaiésha'** nothing will go to waste.

With SRF -at- and CAUS -hst-: **wakatiesénhston** I have it for sale, **ronatiesénhston** they have things for sale, **watiesénhston** it is on sale.

With SRF -at-, N -hwist- metal, money, and SRF -at- and CAUS -ht-:

rathwistatiesáhtha' he spends money easily, easy come-easy go, he's a sport.
• Tékeni teiokahkwèn:tonte' wakatiesénhston. I have a bicycle for sale.

-ieshon- V laugh: **iakoiéshon** she is laughing, **ontiéshon'** I laughed, **wahoiéshon'** he laughed.

-iest- V mix
  With DLC: **tetiéstha'** I am mixing it together, **téntieste'** I will mix it, **wà:ttieste'** I mixed it, **tewatiéston** I have mixed it; and DISTR -nion-: **tetiestánions** I am mixing them all together, **wa'tieiestánion'** she mixed them; and TRNL: **ia'tentiestánion'** I will add them in, mix them all together.
  With CISL: **tahá:ieste'** he added, contributed it, **thoiéston** he has contributed it.
  With SRF -at- and DLC: **tentiátieste'** you and I will share it, chip in on it, **wa'tiatiátieste'** we two shared.
  With REV -hsi- and DLC: **tetiestáhsions** I sort it, **tenhaiestáhsi'** he will sort it, **wa'thaiestáhsi'** he sorted it, **tehoiestáhsion** he has sorted it.
  With N -sahe't- bean, and TRNL: **ia'ksahè:taieste'** I added, mixed in beans.
  With N -the'ser- flour, and TRNL: **ia'ethe'será:ieste'** she added, mixed in flour.
  With N -'nhonhs- egg, and TRNL: **ia'ke'nhónhsaieste'** I added, mixed in eggs.
  • Tahá:ieste' tó: ní:kon tiakoto'ktá:ni ohwísta'. He added how much money she was short of.

-ie'wenta'- V recover, with REP:
  satie'wén:ta'ne' I got better, I recovered, **sahaie'wén:ta'ne'** he got better, **tsakoie'wentà:'on** she has recovered.

With PROG -hatie-:
  tsakoie'wenta'onhátie' she is recovering.

-ihar- hang up. *See* -har-/-ihar-

-ihei[on]-/-enhei[on]- V die: **renhé:ions** he is dying, **wa'kíheie'** I died, **wahrénheie'** he died, **wa'íheie'** she died, **rawenhé:ion** he is dead, **iakawenhé:ion** she is dead, **iawenhé:ion** it is dead (an animal), **kenhé:ion** death.
  With CAUS -'t-: **awenheiòn:ta'** dead body, cadaver; and SRF -an- or -enn-: **wahanihé:ia'te'** he pretended to be dead, he made up he was dead, **wenniheià:tha'** opossum.
  With CAUS -'t- and V -hseronni- dress, prepare: **renheion'tahserón:ni** he is an undertaker.
  With N -hwish- burden, effort, and DLC: **tekhwishenhé:ions** I get tired, **wa'tekhwishénheie'** I got tired, **tewakhwishenhé:ion** I am tired; and N -'nikonhr- mind: **wa'tke'nikonhrahwishénheie'** my mind got tired, **tewake'nikonhrahwishenhé:ion** my mind is tired.
  With N -ia't- body (and variant -kenhei[on]-): **wahaia'takénheie'** he became paralyzed, **wa'eia'takénheie'** she became paralyzed, **watia'takenhé:ion** I do things slowly, I take my time, I am a slowpoke.
  With CAUS -'t-, V -ien- put down, have, INSTR -hkw-, and CISL: **tsi tiakenheion'taientáhkhwa'** morgue, (in older usage) hospital.
  With CAUS -'t- and V -kareni- take back and forth: **wenheion'takarénie's** hearse.
  With CAUS -'t-, V -r- put in, and INSTR -hkw-: **iakenheion'taráhkhwa'** coffin.
  With N -rihw- matter, message, V -nera'[k]- mistake, NMZR -hser-, V

-akaion-/-kaion- be old, and NMZR -hser-: **wa'karihwanera'akhserakaionhserén-heie'** the woman of ill repute died *(a playful expression from Mike Norton)*.

Cf. Genheion mourir, *Genhejonta* moribond, *Gaiatagenheion* être flasque (Bruyas: 113); *Genheionta* Cadavre (Galissonnière: 15v); *Kenheion* la mort (Cuoq: 115); Laurentian *Quenheya* the heavens [probably *kenhé:ion* death] (Biggar: 244f); Wendat "where those called *Aiheonde*, who take care of the graves," (Brebeuf in Thwaites 10: 281); Wendat "where the undertakers and embalmers of each family whom they call *A,iheionné*," (Lafitau II: 247)

-ihen- V be in the middle of, with COIN and DLC

With N -ahskw- bridge: **sha'tewahskwí:hen** middle of the bridge.
With N -akenhnh- summer: **sha'tewakenhnhí:hen** middle of the summer.
With N -atekhwahra- table, and NMZR -'tsher-: **sha'tewatekhwahra'tsherí:hen** (it is) in the middle of the table.
With N -enhni't- moon, month: **sha'tewenhni'tí:hen** middle of the month.
With N -iahia'khser- week: **sha'teiahia'khserí:hen** middle of the week.
With N -nat- town, settlement: **sha'tekanatí:hen** centre of the town, of the village.
With N -ohser- winter, year: **sha'teiohserí:hen** middle of the winter.
With N -tshe['t]- bottle, jar: **sha'tekatshe'tí:hen** half a bottle or jar.

-ihn- N skin, leather: **óhna'**
With V -atiront- pull, stretch, and DLC:

teiohnatiróntha' it is elastic, an elastic band; and **áhta** (-ahta[hkw]- shoe): **teiohnatiróntha' áhta** rubber boots.
With V -htohrarak-/-ohrarak- squeeze, press down, and DLC: **wa'thihnò:rarake'** I pinched him, **wa'thakihnò:rarake'** he pinched me.
With V -hwatase-/-tase- turn, twist: **wahihnatá:se'** I twisted his skin, I pinched him, **wahakihnatá:se'** he pinched me.
With V -kenra- be pale: **renhnakén:ra** he is light-skinned, **iehnakén:ra** she is light-skinned.
With V -kha- attach, piece together, DISTR -nion-, and DLC: **tekihnakhánions** I am piecing cloth together; and **áhsire'** (-ahsir- blanket): **tekenhnakhánion áhsire'** quilt.
With V -ner- make pregnant, and CAUS -'t-: **ohnanerì:ta'** vagina; POSS: **iehnaneri'tà:ke** her vagina.
With SRF -an- and V -ont- attach: **wakaníhnonte'** I have a skin tag; **ioníhnonte'** (there is) a skin tag, a little bump on the skin; and DISTR -on-: **ionihnón:ton** (there are) several tags or bumps.
With V -ra'ken- be white, light-coloured: **kihnarà:ken** I am a light-skinned person, a White person, **renhnarà:ken** he is light-skinned, **iehnarà:ken** she is light-skinned.
With V -ra'nentakt-/-nentakt- stick something to: **wa'kihnanén:takte'** I patched it.
With SRF -an-, V -tokeri[k]-/-okeri[k]- gather, shirr, and DISTR -hon-: **wakanihnokeríkhon** I am wrinkled, **iakonihnokeríkhon** she is wrinkled.
With V -'rhoro[k]-/-oro[k]- cover: **ohnó:ron** penis.

-ihnhe't[ar]- N quill: **ohnhè:ta'**
With SRF -an-: **anihnhè:ta'** wart; a miser.
With SRF -an- and V -ont- attach:

wakanihnhè:taronte' I have a wart; and DISTR -on-: **ronihnhe'tarón:ton** he has warts.

• Anèn:taks raronkwe'nakwé:kon ohnhè:ta' kà:niote'. The porcupine has quills all on his back.

Cf. *Onnheta* porcépi (Bruyas: 74); *Onnhe^cta* porc-épyc (Galissonnière: 7r); *Jagonninne^cteront* Verrüe (Galissonnière: 82v); *oninnhēta* Verrue, *8akenninnhētĕron* on avoir (Marcoux: 413); *Onnheta* poil, piquants de porc-épic (Cuoq: 34)

-ihnonk- V call to someone, pass by for someone

With CISL: **thakì:nonks** he is calling me, **tahakì:nonke'** he called me.

With TRNL: **iekhè:nonks** I am calling her, **ienhonwèn:nonke'** she or they will call him, **iahì:nonke'** I called him.

With PURP -hs-: **rakihnónkhse'** he is coming for me, **wa'konhnónkhse'** I am going to get you, **wa'khehnónkhsa'** I went to get her.

With PURP -hs- and REP: **sekhehnónkhse'** I come for her, **sakhehnónkhse'** I am going to get her, **sakhehnónkhsa'** I went to get her.

With PURP -hs- and CISL: **tahakihnónkhsa'** he came to get me; and DLC: **tontahakihnónkhsa'** he came to pick me up.

• Iahì:nonke' tahatskà:hon'. I called him to eat.

-ihron- say. *See* -aton-/-ihron-/-en-

-ihsak- look for. *See* -ehsak-/-ihsak-/-esak-/-isak-

-iht- N prairie, meadow, with LOC -'ke, at, on: **Kenhtà:ke** Laprairie, Québec

Cf. *Kēntake* la Prairie de la magdeleine (Marcoux: 302); *Kenta* abbrév. de *kahenta*. De là le nom de *Kentake* Laprairie, paroissse limitrophe de Caughnawaga (Cuoq: 19); *Kenhtà:ke* Laprairie (Horne: 61)

-ihwhar- N fur: **óhwhare'**

With (possibly) AMB -hne-: **ohwharà:ne'** caterpillar.

With V -akera- stink, smell: **tsihwharákeras** your fur smells (talking to a dog), **renhwharákeras** his fur smells.

With V -a'senht-/-enht- drop: **kihwharénhtha'** I take the fur off, **wa'kihwhá:renhte'** I took the fur off.

With V -es- be long: **iohwhá:res** (it is) long-haired fur, **rohwhá:res** he has long fur.

With V -ont- attach: **rohwhá:ronte'** he has fur.

With V -r- put in: **iohwhá:rare'** fungus.

With V -rohro[k]- gather, collect: **renhwhararò:roks** he collects furs.

• Wa'kihwhá:renhte' ne kanéhon. I took the fur off the hide or skin.

-iia'k- cross over. *See* -iahia'k-/-iia'k-

-iie-/-ien- N oil, grease: **kén:ie'**

With **iekhonnià:tha'** (-khw- food, -onni- make): **iekhonnià:tha' kén:ie'** cooking oil.

With LOC -'ke, on: **keniè:ke** in the oil.

With V -akera- stink, smell (and variant -enien-): **wenienákeras** it smells like oil or gasoline.

With SRF -ate-, V -atsha'- burn: **wateienátsha's** or (with variant -weien-) **wateweienátsha's** the (cooking) oil is burning, **onteweienátsha'** the oil burned.

With V -aweron- spill out of, and TRNL: **ia'keienáweron'** I put oil or gas in it.

With V -eka'[w]-/-ka'[w]- find tasty, like the taste of, and CAUS -st- (and variant -enien-): **wenienakà:stha'** it (a car) takes a lot of gas.

With SRF -ate-, V -her-/-hr- set on top of: **ioteienáhere'** there is oil or grease on the surface of it, **onteienà:ren'** oil (droplets) came up (maybe while cooking).

With V -hninon- buy: **wa'keienahní:non'** I bought gas; and SRF -ate-: **ronteienahní:nons** they sell gas; and CAUS -'t-: **ionteienahninòn:tha'** gas station.

With SRF -ate- and V -o- be in water: **ioteié:no** there is grease or oil drippings (drippings to make gravy or oily spots floating on water).

With SRF -ate- and V -o'kt- finish: **wa'kateienò:kten'** I ran out of oil or gas.

With V -rakew-/-okew- wipe: **wa'keienó:kewe'** I wiped off the oil or grease.

With V -(h)rho- coat: **keienáhrhos** or (with SRF -ate-) **kateienáhrhos** I coat it with oil or grease; and CAUS -hst- (with variant -enien-): **iakenienahrhóhstha'** shellac.

With V -ta'-/-eta'- put inside: **enkeienáta'** I will put oil or gas in it, **wa'keienáta'** I put oil or gas in it.

NOTE: The variant -iie- occurs in the stand-alone noun form. The variant -ien- is the most frequent incorporating form but -enien- and -weien- also occur.

-iio- V be good, nice

With ATTR =hne, at: **Niióhne** Sunday.

With N -ahsir- blanket, shawl: **wakahsirí:io** I have a nice blanket, quilt, shawl.

With N -atera'sw- luck: **watera'swí:io** it is good luck, **rotera'swí:io** he has good luck; and NEG: **iah tehotera'swí:io** he is not lucky; with N -atera'sw- luck, and

CAUS -hst-: **enwakatera'swí:iohste'** I will get lucky, **onkwatera'swí:iohste'** I got lucky.

With N -a'ther- basket: **iako'therí:io** she has a nice basket, her basket is beautiful.

With N -enhniser- day: **wenhniserí:io** (it is) a nice day.

With N -enser- smell, scent: **wenserí:io** it smells good.

With N -ent- day: **wentí:io** (it is) a nice day.

With N -erien't- disposition: **wakerien'tí:ios** I am satisfied, **onkwerien'tí:io'** I became satsified, **wahawerien'tí:io'** he became satsified.

With N -ha't- (apple) core, Adam's apple: **roha'tí:io** he has a nice (singing) voice.

With N -hna't-/-hna'tahtsher- purse: **kahna'tahtsherí:io** (it is) a nice purse.

With N -io'tenhser- work: **raio'tenhserí:io** he does good work.

With N -khw- food: **kakhwí:io** (it is) good food.

With N -ksa['t]- child: **raksa'tí:io** he is a nice boy, a good boy.

With N -nahkw- marriage, and DLC: **teiakeninahkwí:io** we two have a good marriage, **tehninahkwí:io** they have a good marriage.

With N -nakt- bed, place: **ronaktí:io** he has a good spot; and INCH -'-: **wahonaktí:io'ne'** he got a nice spot, he got comfortable.

With N -nenhst- corn: **kanenhstí:io** (it is) good corn.

With N -niatar- river, lake: **Kaniatarí:io** Lake Ontario; and REP: **Skaniatarí:io** name of the Seneca prophet Handsome Lake and Seneca title name.

With N -nonhs- house: **kanonhsí:io** (it is) a nice house, **tsi kanonhsí:io** parlour.

With N -nont- mountain, hill: **Ronontí:io** King, the king in a deck of cards, **Ionontí:io** Queen.

With N -onkwe['t]- person, human being: **ronkwe'tí:io** he is handsome, a good-looking person, **iakonkwe'tí:io** she is pretty, beautiful; with NMZR -hser-: **ronkwehserí:io** he is a kind fellow.
With N -rihw- matter, message: **orihwí:io** really; and ATTR =onwe, genuine: **orihwiio'ón:we** it is really, unquestionably true; with N -rihw- matter, message: **Karihwí:io** the Good Message; and CAUS -hst-: **Karihwiióhston** Christian religion.
With N -ronto-/-ronto'tsher- wooden box: **iakoronto'tsherí:io** she has a nice casket or coffin, she has nice cupboards.
With N -serenht- sleep, and INCH -'-: **onkeserenhtí:io'ne'** I had a nice dream.
With N -wenn- voice, word: **Rawenní:io** God; with REFL -atate- and N -wenn- voice, word: **katatewenní:io** I am free, **iontatewenní:io** she is free; and INCH -'-: **enkatatewenní:io'ne'** I will become free; with N -wenn- voice, word, and CAUS -hst-: **konwenniióhstha'** I give you a free hand, I allow you, **enkonwenní:iohste'** I will allow you; and REFL -atate-: **iontatewenniióhstha'** she takes something freely (without asking), she takes advantage, **wahatatewenní:iohste'** he helped himself to it; with N -wenn- voice, word, and CONTR: **thikawenní:io** it's alright, **thikawenní:io kátke** anytime, **thikawenní:io ka' nón:** anywhere, anyplace.
With SRF -ate-, N -'nikonhr- mind, and CAUS -hst-: **wakate'nikonhriióhston** I am patient.
With N -'shenn- aim: **ra'shenní:io** he has a good aim.

Cf. Ni-io-ne Sunday (Colloq.) (Cory: 70); *Niiohne* [Sunday] (handwritten R.C. religious journal found in home of Mary Deer, daily entries from 1915–1922)

-i[k]- V fill up
With SRF -at- and N -iar- bag: **wa'ontiá:rike'** she filled the bag; with N -iar- bag, and CONTR and TRNL: **iah thiekaiá:ri** he or she is not all there.
With SRF -ate- and N -'nerohkw- box: **wahate'neróhkwike'** he filled the box. *See* -i- be the total of.
• Wahatiá:rike' ónerahte' waháta'. He filled the bag, he put in leaves.

íksa term used when speaking to a child: **Átskwi íksa!** Well, child! **Óksa íksa!** Hurry up child!
NOTE: GM described the use of this term as follows: "formal term used when addressing a female person of any age or standing, irrespective of one's own sex." And from Mary Deer's Mohawk class notes, Nov. 1965: "*ik-sa* addressing a friend (fem)." Nowadays the term is not restricted to female persons.

Cf. Iksa voc. irreg. de *ontsi*, amie, camarade entre femmes (Cuoq: 63); Laurentian *Ysaa* My wife (Biggar: 246)

-ine- V lead
With N -ashar- strap, leash: **rasharí:ne'** he is leading it on a leash.
With SRF -at- and N -hah- road: **rathahí:ne's** he is a wanderer, a tramp.
With N -na'kar- horn, antler, and DLC: **Tehana'karí:ne'** He is leading it by the horns (Mohawk title name 7).
With N -nentsh- arm: **shakonentshí:ne'** he is going along holding her arm; and REFL -atate- and DLC: **tetiatatenentshí:ne'** you and I are holding arms as we walk.
With N -(h)nhr- sickness, disease (and possibly a variant -tarine- of -ine-): **kahnhratarí:ne's** the disease is going around, an epidemic, **wa'kahnhrá:tarine'** the disease went around.

Cf. Ethononweh yenyontatenonshine
Thither shall they be led by the hand
(Hale: 118–9)

-inekenht- V make come out
  With N -hnek- liquid:
  wa'khnekínekenhte' I squeezed the
  liquid out of it, **kahnekinekénhton** juice.
  NOTE: This stem is composed of a root
  -ineken-, which occurs only with suffixes,
  and CAUS -ht-.
  • Wa'khnekínekenhte' otsì:nekwar
  niwahiò:ten. I squeezed the juice out
  of the orange.

-inekenhw- V let out
  With N -ia't- body, and TRNL:
  ietia'tínekenhs I let it out (an animal),
  ia'kheiia'tínekenhwe' I let her out,
  iehiia'tinekénhen I have let him out.
  NOTE: This stem is composed of a root
  -ineken-, which occurs only with suffixes,
  and CAUS -hw-.

-ineken'- V emerge
  With N -atshat- steam, mist:
  enwatshatíneken'ne' the steam will
  come out or emerge.
  With N -kahr- eye, and DLC:
  tekkahríneken's I open my eyes big or
  wide, **wa'tiekahríneken'ne'** she opened
  her eyes wide, **tewakkahrinekèn:'en** my
  eyes are opened wide.
  With N -nenhr- crowd, and PROG -hatie-:
  rotinenhrineken'enhátie' they are in a
  parade.
  With N -rahkw- sun, and CISL:
  tkarahkwíneken's the sun is rising,
  entkarahkwíneken'ne' the sun will come
  up, **takarahkwíneken'ne'** the sun came
  up, **tiorahkwinekèn:'en** the sun has come
  up.
  With N -wenn- voice, word, and CISL:

thawenníneken's he speaks up,
takewenníneken'ne' I spoke up.
  NOTE: This stem is composed of a root
  -ineken-, which occurs only with suffixes,
  and INCH -'-.

-inion't- bring in, score. *See* -ion't-/-inion't-

í:non far
  With ATTR ='a/=ha, diminutive: **inónha**
  further along.

Io expression of approbation
  Cf. Io (il faut trainer un peu sur l'o) oui
  (Cuoq: 6)

-ioha- look for in vain. *See* -iehwa-/-ioha-

iohnhonwá:taien' pond

iokháhon garlic

-ionni- V be lying, be extended
  With N -ia't- body: **tia'tión:ni** I am lying
  down (stretched out), **raia'tión:ni** he is
  lying down, **ieia'tión:ni** she is lying
  down.
  With N -nen't- evergreen: **onen'tión:ni**
  low-growing evergreen, yew.
  With N -nonhs- house: **Rotinonhsión:ni**
  they of the extended house, the Haudenosaunee.
  Cf. hotinnonsionni les faiseurs de cabane
  (Bruyas: 51); "*Honontonchionni* I think
  do's signify as much as *Konossioni*, which
  is the whole howse, or all the Indians
  together;" (Dellius in Brodhead IV: 78);
  " ... *Agonnonsionni* or the Builders of
  Lodges," (Lafitau I: 86); *Aquanoschióni*
  [Iroquois] (Pyrlaeus: 235); *Ongwanongh-
  syonigh* [we of the league] (Claus C-1478:
  472, line 5); "and since that Time they are
  called the Six Nations, *Aquanosshioni-*

hága." (Ettwein in Wheeler-Voegelin: 47);
"*Rodinonghjónigh*, the people of the Long-
house" (Joseph Brant in Boyce: 291); "The
Confederate Nations call themselves
Rodinonghjonigh, which means House-
makers," (John Norton in Boyce: 293);
"*Kanonsionni* is a compound word, formed
of kanonsa, house, and ionni, extended, or
drawn out." (Hale: 75); "*Rononsionni* ou
faiseur de cabanes, comme s'appelait
l'Iroquois." (Forbes: 301); *Kiatonni* être
couché, alité, étendu sur un lit ou terre,
etre gisant (Cuoq: 22); Wendat "In fact,
from the earliest times, these five Iroquois
Nations have been called in their language,
which is Huron, *Hotinnonchiendi*, — that
is, 'the completed Cabin', as if to express
that they constituted but one family."
(Le Mercier in Thwaites 41: 87); Wendat
hotinnonchiondi Iroquois (Potier: 154)

ionton'wesà:tha' drawknife
NOTE: A slightly different word is
iehwesà:tha (Lazore: 71); cf. *Iehwasáhtha*
(Gabriel: Part II, 7)

-ion't-/-inion't- V bring in, score: **raiòn:tha'**
he scores, **wà:tion'te'** I scored,
wa'é:ion'te' she scored,
seréka ahoiòn:ton he almost scored.
With NEG: **iah tehoiòn:ton** he didn't
score.
With CISL: **tátion'te'** I brought it in,
tewatiòn:ton I have brought it in.
With TRNL: **iahà:tion'te'** I brought it in
(that way).
With SRF -at- and N -ahsahtahkar- splinter:
onkwatahsahtahkarínion'te' I got a
splinter, **wakatahsahtahkariniòn:ton**
I have a splinter.
With: N -ia't- body, and CISL or TRNL:
takheia'tínion'te' I brought her in,
iahiia'tínion'te' I brought him in.
With N -ient- wood, and CISL:

tahaientínion'te' he brought in wood.
With SRF -at-, N -tsi'er- fingernail, and
BEN -en-: **onkwattsi'eriniòn:ten'** I got
an ingrown nail, **wahottsi'eriniòn:ten'**
he got an ingrown nail.
• Akwé:kon tahá:ion'te' nahò:ten'
wahatenna'tsherahní:non'. He brought
in all the groceries he bought.

iotká:non it is worn (after being used a lot)

-io'tat- V obstruct, hinder: **raió'tats** he gets
in the way of it, obstructs it, presents an
obstacle, **ieió'tats** she gets in the way,
entió'tate' I will get in the way,
wahaió'tate' he got in the way.
With BEN -i-: **tatio'tá:ti** you are wasting
my time, you are in my way, hindering me,
ratio'tá:ti he is wasting my time,
iontio'tá:ti she is wasting my time.

-io'te-/-io'ten- V work: **watió'te'** I am
working, **enwatió'ten'** I will work,
wahoió'ten' he worked, **watio'tèn:'en**
I have worked, **saió'ten** Work!
With **karistà:ke** (-rist- iron, steel):
karistà:ke rotiió'tens they work on
steel, ironworkers; or **karístatsi rotiió'te'**
ronhskwahéhrha' ironworkers (-ahskw-
bridge, -her-/-hr- set on top of).
With PURP -hser-: **watio'ténhsere'** I
am going to work; and CONTR:
iah thahoio'ténhsere' he is not going
to work.
With PURP -hser- and REP:
sahoio'ténhsere' he is going back to
work.
With BEN -hs-: **kheio'ténhse'** I am working for her or them, **wahiió'tenhse'** I
worked for him.
With CAUS -hst-: **iakoio'ténhstha'**
anything used for working (for example,
iakoio'ténhstha' tehohtárion he has on
work boots, **iakoio'ténhstha' atháhsteren**

work pants).

With NMZR -hser-, *see* -io'tenhser- work.

• Tetsá:ron ken seniio'ténhsere' enióhr-hen'ne'? Are you both going to work tomorrow?

-io'tenhser- N work: **kaio'ténhsera'**
POSS: **raoio'ténhsera'** his work, **akoio'ténhsera'** her work.
With V -iio- be good, nice: **raio'tenherí:io** he does good work.
With V -ka'te- have many: **watio'tenherakà:te'** I have plenty of work.
With V -noron- be expensive, precious: **kaio'tenheranó:ron** jobs are scarce, hard to find.
With V -o'ten- be a kind of, and PART: **tsi nikaio'tenherò:ten** what kind of work it is.
NOTE: This stem is composed of -io'te-/ -io'ten- work, and NMZR -hser-.
• Kwah tekèn:'en tsi raio'tenherí:io. He really does good work, he is a great worker.

-isak- look for. *See* -ehsak-/-ihsak-/-esak-/ -isak-

-isa'- finish, complete. *See* -hsa'-/-isa'-

í:se' you (singular, dual, plural)

-ishonhkw- V quake, tremble, shiver, shake
With N -eri[ahs]- heart, and DLC: **tewakeriahsishónhkhwa'** my heart is racing, beating fast, **tehaweriahsishónhkhwa'** his heart is racing, **wa'tewakeriahsíshonhkwe'** I had a heart attack, **wa'tiakaweriahsíshonhkwe'** she got a heart attack.
With N -hsnonhs- finger, hand, and DLC: **tewakehsnonhsishónhkhwa'** my hands

are trembling, shaking.
With N -ia't- body: **watia'tishónhkhwa'** I am quaking, trembling, shivering, **ontia'tíshonhkwe'** I trembled, I shivered, **wahoia'tíshonhkwe'** he trembled, he shivered.

ísi' over there

-i[t]- V be inside (a vehicle) (In contemporary Kanien'kéha as spoken at Kahnawà:ke, *t* is not pronounced when it is at the end of a word, which means that unless a suffix follows, forms of this verb end in -*i* instead of -*it*.)
With N -ia't- body: **tià:ti** I am in it, **raià:ti** he is in it, **kaià:ti** it is in it; and CONT -k-: **entia'tí:take'** I will stay in it.
With REV -hkw-, *see* -itahkw- get out or off (a vehicle).
Wth INCH -'-, *see* -ita'- put into (a vehicle).
• A'thé:rakon kaià:ti. It (a dog or cat) is in the basket.

-itahkhe- V be in something moving
With N -iat't- body: **tia'titáhkhe'** I am in something moving, **raia'titáhkhe'** he is in something moving, **ieia'titáhkhe'** she is in something moving.

-itahkw- V get out or off (a vehicle), with SRF -at-: **katitáhkwas** I get off, I get out, **enkatitáhko'** I will get off, get out, **wa'katitáhko'** I got off, got out, **rotitáhkwen** he has gotten off, out.
NOTE: This stem is composed of -i[t]- be inside (a vehicle), and REV -hkw-.

-itahs- N tail: **otáhson**
POSS: **raotáhson** his tail, **rentahsà:ke** on his tail.
With SRF -an- and V -awak- shake: **ranitahsá:waks** he wags his tail, **wahanitahsá:wake'** he wagged his tail,

ronitahsawá:kon he is wagging his tail.
With SRF -an- and V -enton[hw]- move back and forth, and DLC: **tehanitahsén:tons** he is moving his tail back and forth, he is waving or wagging his tail, **wa'thanitahsén:tonhwe'** he waved or wagged his tail.
With V -es- be long: **rentáhses** he has a long tail.
With V -esha- be short, **ken'** particle, and PART: **ken' nihentahsésha** he has a short tail.
With V -har-/-ihar- hang up: **kentahsíhare'** kite.
With V -hren't-/-en't- hang down: **iotahsèn:ton** there is a tail hanging (for example, from a hat).
With SRF -an-, V -ia'k- break, cut in two, and DLC: **wa'tkanitáhsia'ke'** I broke my tailbone.
With SRF -an-, V -karenhr[on]- rock, and DLC: **tehanitahsakarèn:ron** he is wagging his tail (for example, a dog is sleeping and in his sleep he's moving his tail).
With V -ont- attach: **rentáhsonte'** he has a tail, **kentáhsonte'** it has a tail; and **otsísto** (-tsisto[hkw]- star): **otsísto kentáhsonte'** comet.
With SRF -an-, V -tenihon- shake, and DLC: **tehanitahsateníhon** he is wagging his tail, **wa'thanitahsateníhon** he wagged his tail.

Cf. a-ro-son ra-o-te-son Achillea Millefolium [yarrow, 'squirrel's tail'] (Rousseau: 64); *arosen otasa* [yarrow] (Beauvais: 13)

-ita'- V put into (a vehicle)
With SRF -at-: **katíta's** I get on it, in it, **enkatíta'** I will get on it, in it, **wahatíta'** he got on it, in it, **rotíten'** he has gotten on it, in it, **satíta** Get on, get in! and TRNL: **ia'satíta** Go in!

With N -ia't- body: **wahiia'títa'** I gave him a ride.
NOTE: This stem is composed of -i[t]- be inside (a vehicle), and INCH -'-.
• A'tohserá:kon ia'satíta! Go in the tent, get into the cage!

-ita'[w]- V sleep, fall asleep: **wakí:ta's** I am sleeping, **ró:ta's** he is sleeping, **enwakí:ta'we'** I will sleep, **onkí:ta'we'** I dropped off to sleep, I fell asleep.
With PURP -h-: **enwakità:wha'** I will go to sleep, **onkità:wha'** I went to sleep, I went to bed, **wà:s sentà:wha** Go, go sleep!
With CAUS -st-: **iakotà:stha'** pyjamas.
With SRF -an- and CAUS -st-: **ranità:stha'** he pretends to be sleeping, **wa'kaní:ta'ste'** I pretended to be sleeping, **wakanità:ston** I am pretending to sleep.
With CAUS -st- and BEN -enni-/-en-: **iontatita'stén:ni** she puts her to sleep, **enhshetà:sten'** you will put her to sleep, **wa'ontatità:sten'** she put her to sleep.

Cf. Laurentian *agnydahoa* let us go to bed (Biggar: 243)

-iten[ht]- V be poor: **wakí:ten** I am poor, **ró:ten** he is poor, **iakó:ten** she is poor, **rotí:ten** they are poor.
With ATTR ='a/=ha, diminutive: **Kenténha** October.
With ATTR =kowa, great: **Kentenhkó:wa** November.
With PAST -'ne': **wakitenhtòn:ne'** I was poor.
With CAUS -ht- and INCH -'-: **eniakoténhta'ne'** she will become poor, **wahoténhta'ne'** he became poor.
With SRF -an- and CAUS -ht-: **wa'kaní:tenhte'** I humbled myself, **wahaní:tenhte'** he humbled himself, **wa'onní:tenhte'** she humbled herself,

roniténhton he is humble, **iakoniténhton** she is humble; and PROG -hatie-: **iakonitenhtonhátie'** she is (always) humbling herself.

Cf. Gannitenton battre sur les écorces le soir qu'on a brulé ou tué quelque prisonnier, pour chasser lâme du défunct (Bruyas: 79); *kentenha* oct., *kentenkoꙅa* nov. (Marcoux: 258); *Kentenha* October (Granger: 14); *Kentenkowa* November (Granger: 15); *Kenténha* [October], *Kentenhkó:wa* [November] (Calendar 1979)

-itenr- V pity, feel sorry for: **ritén:ras** I take pity on him, **enkhé:tenre'** I will feel sorry for her, **wa'khé:tenre'** I felt sorry for her, I took pity on her, **ritén:ron** I have pitied him, **khetén:ron** I have pitied her, **takí:tenr** Take pity on me!
With NEG: **iah tekhetén:ras** I don't pity her or them.
With REFL -atat-: **atatitén:ron** pity, charity, **iotatitén:ra** it is sad, pitiful; and PART: **ó: tsi niiotatitén:ra** it's so sad!
With REFL -atat- and DLC: **tetiatatí:tenre'** the two (females) take pity on each other, **tentiatatí:tenre'** the two will pity each other, **wa'tiatiatatí:tenre'** we two pitied each other.
With REFL -atenn- and NMZR -htsher-: **atennitenráhtshera'** pity.
With REFL -atenn- and FACIL -htskon, easily: **wakatennitenráhtskon** I feel bad (for them), I feel compassion.
• Wa'khé:tenre' ne átste' ratì:teron (*or* átste' ronnòn:wets). I pity the homeless people, those who live outside (*or* sleep outside).

Cf. eghtenyontatitenranyon they are to condole with each other (Hale: 118–9); *a-ta-ni-ten-ron* grace (Cory: 18); *a ta ti ten ron* charity (Diabo: 8)

-ithohkw- N bundle (hay, straw, wool): **kenthóhkwa'**
With V -hwaneren[k]-/-neren[k]- tie up: **wa'kithohkwánerenke'** I tied up the bundle, **kenthohkwáneren** (it is) a bundle, tied up.
With V -ke- amount to, and DLC: **tekenthóhkwake** two bundles (for example, two bales of hay, two skeins of wool).
With V -onni- make: **wa'kithohkón:ni'** I made a bundle, **wahenthohkón:ni'** he made a bundle, **wa'ethohkón:ni'** she made a bundle; and DISTR -nion-: **wahenthohkonniánion'** he made bundles.
With V -ot- stand: **wa'kithohkó:ten'** I made a bundle.
With V -rihsi- take apart, take off: **kithohkwaríhsions** I am taking the bundle apart, **wahenthohkwaríhsi'** he took the bundle apart.
With V -[t]- be one, and REP: **skenthóhkwa** one bundle, one bunch.
NOTE: This root can have the variant -thohkw-, a C-stem.

-itie-/-tie-/-ontie- V fly around, float by: **kátie'** it is flying, **kítie's** I am flying around, **tsítie's** you (sg) fly around, **rátie's** he flies around, **iétie's** she flies around, **kátie's** it is flying around, **ratíties's** they are flying around, **kontítie's** they (females) are flying around.
With DISTR -hshon-: **enkitiéhshon'** I will fly all around (because I am in a rush).
With N -ahkwari['t]- bear: **wahkwari'tóntie'** a bear is running or going along.
With N -honw[ei]- boat: **kahonweióntie'** the boat floats by, goes by.
With N -neraht- leaf: **kanerahtóntie'** there are leaves flying around.
With N -tsisto[hkw]- star: **katsistohkóntie'** meteor.

ítiete' dock (a plant)

Cf. itiete [dock] (Beauvais: 4), *i´diedę*
Yellow dock (Waugh: 117); *i-tie-te*
Rumex sp [curly dock] (Rousseau: 41)

-itiohkw- N group (of people): **otióhkwa'**
With V -a'a- be small, **ken'** particle, and
PART: **ken' nikentiohkwà:'a** (it is) a
small group.
With SRF -an-, V -kenni- compete, and
DLC: **tehonnitiohkwakénnie's** they vote,
councilors, **wa'tkanitiohkwakén:ni'** I
voted.
With V -kowan[en]-/-owan[en]- be big:
kentiohkowá:nen (it is) a big group,
ionkwentiohkowá:nen we are a big
group.

-iton- V mean: **né: tsí:ton** you mean it,
né: rén:ton he means it, **né: ié:ton**
she means it, **kén:ton** it means.
• Nahò:ten' kén:ton? What does it mean?

-its- N fish: **kéntson'**
With ATTR =shon'a, pluralizer:
kentson'shòn:'a fish.
With ATTR =kowa, great, and ATTR =hne,
at: **Kentsa'kowáhne** Fort Covington, NY.
With SRF -an- and V -atorat- hunt:
kanitsató:rats I am fishing; and PURP -h-:
wa'kanitsatoráthe' I am going fishing.
With V -okw- take out of liquid:
kentsókwas pelican, (GM) heron (cf.
ken-tso-kwas heron, from Mary Deer's
class notes, Nov. 1965).
With V -takeri'ta['w]-/-keri'ta['w]- fry:
wa'kitsakerì:ta'we' I fried fish.

Cf. cinsie fish (van den Bogaert: 56);
Gentsion poisson (Bruyas: 115); *Gentsion*
poisson (Galissonnière: 67r); *Guntshian*
Fish (Zeisberger in Wheeler-Voegelin:
61); *kén-tsion* Fish (Cory: 13);
kx̃tsa'kowáh·neh Ft. Covington (Floyd

Lounsbury, notes archived at the American
Philosphical Society); *Kentsa'kowáhne*
Fort Covington (Horne: 61); Laurentian
Quejon Fish (Biggar: 242); Wendat *ęntson*
poisson (Potier: 455)

-itshenen- pet, domestic animal. *See*
-tshenen-/-itshenen-

-itskar[on]- V shoe sole, cover, rug:
kítskarons I put a cover on the floor
(for example, a rug, linoleum),
enkítskaron' I will put down a cover, a
rug, **wa'kítskaron'** I put down a cover,
wakítskaron I have put down a cover,
kéntskare' cover, linoleum, carpeting.
With INSTR -hkw-: **ietskarónhkhwa'** rug,
runner, carpet; and ATTR =kowa, great:
ietskaronhkhwa'kó:wa a type of fern.
With SRF -an- and INSTR -hkw-:
ionnitskaráhkhwa' sheet(s).
With V -kehron[t]- put down here and
there: **kentskarakè:ron** there are rugs
here and there.
With SRF -an-, V -ra'nentahsi-/-nentahsi-
get unstuck: **onnitskaranentáhsi'** the sole
(of a shoe) came off; and BEN -en-:
onkwanitskaranentáhsien' the sole of
my shoe came off on me.
With V -tens- be thick: **kentská:ratens**
it is a thick sole or rug.
• Onnitskara'nentáhsi' ne akwáhta. The
soles came off my shoes.

*Cf. onontsi ienatonkhwa ietskaronkhwa-
kowa kateraontsi* [head is what they call
it, a big carpet fern = fiddlehead fern?]
(Beauvais: 13)

-itsker- N spit, saliva: **ótskeri**
POSS: **akítskeri** my saliva, **raótskeri**
his saliva, **akótskeri** her saliva.
With SRF -an- and V -ati-/-onti- lose,
throw: **ronitskeróntie's** he is spitting,

onkwanitskerón:ti' I spit,
ronitskeróntion he has spit,
sanitskerón:ti Spit it out!
With V -a'sen'-/-en'- fall down:
iakótskeren's she is drooling,
wahótskeren'ne' he drooled.
With SRF -an-, V -r- put in, and INSTR
-hkw-: **ionnitskeraráhkhwa'** spittoon.
With SRF -an- and V -sera[hw]-/
-osera[hw]- gush, spew:
enhianitskeróserahwe' he will spit at
you, **wahakwanitskeróserahwe'** he spit
at me.

-itskw- N haunches: **ótskwa'**
With V -her-/-hr- set on top of:
kentskwáhere' foundation; and SRF -an-:
wa'kanitskwà:ren' I sat or perched on it,
sanitskwà:ren Sit down! **anitskwà:ra**
chair, seat; POSS: **raonitskwà:ra** his chair;
and NMZR -'tsher-, V -o'ka't- run into,
bump against, and CISL:
takanitskwahra'tsherò:ka'te' I banged
into the chair.
With V -ot- stand: **kítskote'** I am sitting,
iétskote' she is sitting, **réntskote'** he is
sitting; crusty bread, **wa'khetskó:ten'** I
sat her down; and DISTR -on-:
kontitskó:ton they are sitting; with
SRF -an- and V -ot- stand: **enkanitskó:ten'**
I will sit down, **wa'kanitskó:ten'** I sat
down; and REV -kw-: **wa'kanitskotá:ko'**
I got up (from the seat); and CAUS -ht- and
CISL: **takanitskotákwahte'** I got up fast
(from the seat).
With SRF -an-, V -ra'neken-/-neken- be
side-by-side, next to, and DLC:
tetianitskwané:ken you and I are sitting
next to each other.
• Karonwarà:ke kontitskó:ton otsi'tèn:'a.
The birds are sitting on the wires. • Ká:ts
ken nonkwá:ti sanitskó:ten! Come sit over
here, on this side!

Cf. Enniskotáon se mettre devant
quelqu'un sur son derrière pour conférer
avec luy, ou lui faire le rapport (Bruyas:
109); *réntskote* crusty bread (Old Kahnawake: 8)

-itskwahrhe- N frog: **otskwà:rhe'**

-itst- N fish scale, scab: **ótsta'**
With V -a'senht-/-enht- drop:
wahéntstenhte' he scaled the fish.
With V -r- put in: **wakítstare'** I have
scabs, **iótstare'** it is scabby; and DISTR
-onnion-: **wakitstarónnion** I have scabs
all over, here and there; with V -r- put in,
and INCH -'-: **wahótstara'ne'** he got
scabs.
With V -(h)rho- coat, and CAUS -hst-:
ietstahrhóhstha' shingle.
With V -ronkw- remove, scrape off:
wa'kitstarón:ko' I took the scab off,
wahentstarón:ko' he took the scab off,

-itstenhr- N rock, boulder: **otstèn:ra'**
With LOC -'ke, on, at: **otstenhrà:ke**
on the rock.
With SRF -an- and V -ia'k- cut, sever:
ionitstenhrià:kon cliff.
With V -kahront- make an opening, a hole:
iotstenhrakà:ronte' cave.
With V -kowan[en]-/-owan[en]- be big:
kentstenhrowá:nen (it is) a big rock.
With V -ot- stand, and DLC:
tenhentstenhró:ten' he will stack rocks,
make a foundation, **wa'thentstenhró:ten'**
he stacked rocks.
See also **skentstèn:ri** buffalo carp.
• Otstenhrà:ke kítskote'. I'm sitting on
the rock.

-itstohkw- N pack, pile (laundry, clothes, coal,
wood): **otstóhkwa'**
With V -hwaneren[k]-/-neren[k]- tie up:

wa'kitstohkwánerenke' I tied the pack, **kentstohkwáneren** (it is) a pack, tied up. With V -ke- amount to, and DLC: **tekentstóhkwake** two packs, piles. With V -ot- stand: **iotstóhkote'** it is piled; and DISTR -on-: **iotstohkó:ton** there are piles here and there.

ì:'i; í:, nì:'i I, me, we, us

-i'sere- drag. *See* -'sere-/-i'sere-

-i't- N excrement: **ó'ta'**
With SRF -an-: **anì:tas** skunk.
With V -aksen- be bad: **io'táksen** it is spoiled, it is bad; and INCH -'-: **io'táksen's** it is going bad, **enio'táksen'ne'** it will go bad, **wa'o'táksen'ne'** it went bad, **io'taksèn:'en** it has gone bad; and PROG -hatie-: **io'taksen'enhátie'** it is going bad; with V -aksen- be bad, INCH -'-, and DLC: **teionkeni'táksen's** we two get mad at each other, **wa'tionkeni'táksen'ne'** we two got mad at each other, **teioti'taksèn:'en** they (females) have gotten mad at each other.
With SRF -an-, V -a'senht-/-enht- drop, and INSTR -hkw-: **ionni'tenhtáhkhwa'** outhouse, bathroom (an older and alternative expression to **átste' ieienhtáhkhwa'**).
With V -her-/-hr- set on top of, and ATTR ='ke, at: **Ken'taherè:ke** Scotland.
With V -ien- put down, have: **raní'taiens** he is defecating, he is pooping, **wahaní'taien'** he defecated, **iakoní'taien'** she has defecated.
With V -ke'tot- protrude, and CISL: **tio'takè:tote'** squash.
With SRF -an-, V -onni- make, and DLC: **teioni'tón:ni** it is tangled, complicated, a mess, **tewakani'tón:ni** it is tangled on me (for example, talking about my hair); and CAUS -'t-: **tehani'tonnià:tha'** he messes it up, he complicates things,

wa'thani'tónnia'te' he messed it up, **teiakoni'tonnià:ton** she has messed it up.
With SRF -an- and V -rakew-/-okew- wipe: **wahani'tó:kewe'** he wiped his bum, **wà:s sani'tó:kew** Go wipe yourself! and CAUS -ht-: **ionni'tokewáhtha'** toilet paper.
With V -ra'nentak-/-nentak- stick to: **ro'tanén:taks** he is constipated, **iako'tanén:taks** she is constipated.
• Wà:s tsi ionni'tenhtáhkhwa' iahà:se. Go to the bathroom! • Teioni'tón:ni nahò:ten' í:we' kaná:takon. It's a mess what's going on in town. • Akwé:kon teioni'tón:ni akenónhkwis. My hair is all tangled.

-i'tar- N chimney, clan, clay: **o'tá:ra'**
With LOC -kon, inside, and ATTR =haka/ =aka, people of: **ken'tarakonhá:ka** swallow.
With V -ien- put down, have: **waki'tá:raien'** I have a clan.
With V -kahrhatho- turn over: **ki'tarakahrháthos** I am ploughing, **wahen'tarakahrhátho'** he ploughed, **ken'tarakahrháthon** it is ploughed; and CAUS -hst-: **ie'tarakahrhathóhstha'** plough.
With V -ont- attach, PROG -atie-, and DLC: **tsi teken'tarontátie'** along the edge of the roof.
With V -ot- stand: **ken'tá:rote'** there is a chimney.
With V -o'ten- be a kind of, and PART: **Oh nisen'tarò:ten?** What clan are you?
With V -takeri'ta['w]-/-keri'ta['w]- fry: **ken'tarakerì:ta** lime.
• Tsi teken'tarontátie' tho konttsi'nahkón:ni. They build their nests along the edge of the roof.

Cf. Asen n'iongsatarage nous sommes 3 familles (Galissonnière: 40r); *katarakenrītha* Chaux (Marcoux: 65); *Katarakarita* chaux; *Tkataroton* les

Eboulis (nom de lieu), St. Placide (Cuoq: 139); *ka ta ra ke ri ta* lime (Anon: 14); *ka ta ra kon ha a* sparrow (Anon: 17); *ka ta ra ke ri ta* lime (D'Ailleboust: 6); *ken'tarakerí:ta* lime (Lazore: 27); and possibly *Gentare* poil rouge que l'on met autour de la teste ou au col (Bruyas: 114)

-i'teron- V put someone down: **khé'terons** I put her down (a baby on the floor), **enkhé'teron'** I will put her down, **wahí'teron'** I put him down, **khé'teron** I have put her down.
With TRNL: **ia'ontatí'teron'** they put or left her there.
With PURP -hn-: **waho'terónhne'** best man (he's going to bring him), **wa'ontati'terónhne'** maid of honour (she's going to bring her).
• Kanonhsowanèn:ke ia'ontatí'teron'. They put her in the hospital (maybe to leave her there since she won't get better).

-i'teron[t]- V reside: **kì:teron** I live, reside, **ratì:teron** they reside, **skáthne nì:teron** they two live together, **skáthne iakwèn:teron** we are living together, they are staying with me.
With CISL: **tkì:teron** I reside there, I am home, **thèn:teron** he is home, **tiè:teron** she is home, **tiakenì:teron** my husband, my wife; and CONT -k-: **entki'terón:take'** I will be home; and PAST -hkwe': **tki'terón:tahkwe'** I was home; and NEG: **iah ónhka tetiè:teron** there is nobody home.

-i'tonhkw- N flame, fever, omen: **o'tónhkwa'** (can refer to a flame that if seen at night is an omen that means someone is going to pass)
With V -no- be cold, CAUS -hst-, INSTR -hkw-, and DLC: **teie'tonhkwanohstáhkhwa'** mint (herb)

(from Rousseau: 58, who says an infusion of this herb reduces fever in children).
With V -ra'ken- be white, light-coloured: **ken'tonhkwarà:ken** lantern that has a bag inside with naphtha, and the flame is more white than yellow.
With V -(h)rho- coat: **waki'tonhkwáhrhos** I have a fever, **iako'tonhkwáhrhos** she has a fever, **io'tonhkwáhrhos** it is feverish, inflamed, **waho'tonhkwáhrho'** he got a fever; and ATTR =kowa, great: **iako'tonhkwahrhoskó:wa** typhoid fever.
With SRF -an-, V -rik- put together, DISTR -hon-, and DLC: **tewani'tonhkwaríkhons** the flame is flickering, **wa'tewani'tonhkwaríkhon'** the flame flickered.

-i'tonser- N fat: **o'tónsera'**
Cf. odossera bacon (van den Bogaert: 59); *Oθonsera* Graisse (Galissonnière: 46v); *othōnsĕra* Lard (Marcoux: 228); *Othonsera* lard (Cuoq: 37); *Otochsera* Bacon (Zeisberger in Wheeler-Voegelin: 61)

-i'tonw- N pile, heap: **o'tón:wa'**
With V -ke- amount to, and DLC: **teken'tón:wake** two piles.
With V -kowan[en]-/-owan[en]- be big: **io'toniowá:nen** (it is) a big pile, a big heap.
With V -ot- stand: **wa'ki'tonió:ten'** I made a pile, **wahen'tonió:ten'** he made a pile, **wahati'tonió:ten'** they made a pile, **io'tón:iote'** there's a pile of something; and PROG -atie-: **io'toniotátie'** it is piled all over.
• Iontia'tokewáhtha' wa'ki'tonió:ten'. I made a pile of towels, I piled the towels.

-i'tson-/-'tson- V be dirty, with DLC: **teió'tson** it is dirty.

With SRF -at- and INCH -'-:
wa'tió'tson'ne' it got dirty.
With CAUS -hst-: **tehen'tsónhstha'** he
dirties it (and leaves it for someone else to
clean up), **teie'tsónhstha'** she just leaves
it there dirty, **wa'tkí'tsonhste'** I dirtied it
(and just left it).
With N -ahsir- blanket, shawl:
teiohsirá'tson it is a dirty blanket or
shawl.
With N -ahta[hkw]- shoe:
teiakohtahkwá'tson her shoes are dirty;
and INCH -'-: **wa'thohtahkwá'tson'ne'**
his shoes got dirty.
With V -athahsteren[k]- put on pants,
trousers, and NMZR -'tsher-:
tehothahsteren'tsherá'tson his pants are
dirty.
With N -atia'tawi- dress, shirt, and NMZR
-'tsher-: **tewakatia'tawi'tsherá'tson** my
dress or shirt is dirty.
With N -hiohs- elbow: **tewakhiohsá'tson**
I have a dirty elbow.
With N -hnia's- neck, collar:
tehohnia'sá'tson he has a dirty neck, a
dirty collar, **teiohnia'sá'tson** it has a dirty
collar.
With N -ihwhar- fur: **tehohwhará'tson** he
has dirty fur.
With N -nonhs- house:

tewakenonhsá'tson I have a dirty house.
With N -wenn- voice, word:
teiakowenná'tson she has a dirty mouth
(uses foul language).
• Teiohnia'sá'tson ne raotià:tawi. His shirt
has a dirty collar.

-i'tsonhkw- N jump, stride
With V -es- be long, and DLC:
teki'tsónhkwes I jump far,
tehen'tsónhkwes he jumps far,
teie'tsónhkwes she jumps far.
With SRF -an-, V -hkw- pick up, and DLC:
tekani'tsonhkwáhkhwa' I jump,
wa'tionni'tsónhkwahkwe' she jumped,
tehoni'tsonhkwáhkwen he is jumping;
and DISTR -nion-:
teionni'tsonhkwahkwánions she is
jumping up and down,
wa'tionni'tsonhkwahkwánion' she
jumped up and down; with SRF -an-,
V -hkw- pick up, PROG -hatie-, and DLC:
teiakoni'tsonhkwahkwenhátie' she is
jumping along, she is skipping.

-i'tson'k- V sneeze, with DLC:
wa'tewakí'tson'ke' I sneezed (once).
With DISTR -nion-: **teiako'tson'kánions**
she is sneezing, **wa'tho'tson'kánion'** he
sneezed.

K

=k only. Short form for the particle **ok**

káhi fruit, berry. *See* -ahi-

kahionwa'takè:ron puddles
NOTE: This word may be composed of a variant -hionwa't- of -hionh- creek, and -kehron[t]- put down here and there.

-kahkarenhre- V be cross-eyed:
rakahkarèn:re' he is cross-eyed,
iekahkarèn:re' she is cross-eyed.

-kahkwen't- N wheel, tire: **okahkwèn:ta'**
With V -hninon- buy:
wa'kkahkwen'tahní:non' I bought a tire;
and PURP -hr-: **wahakahkwen'ta-hninòn:re'** he is going to buy a tire.
With V -ke- amount to, and DLC:
tekakahkwèn:take two wheels, two tires.
With V -ohro[k]- insert, and REP:
sakkahkwen'tò:roke' I changed the tire.
With V -ohtshi- remove, pull out:
rokahkwen'tóhtshion he has taken off the tire(s).
With V -ont- attach, and **énska** one:
énska iokahkwèn:tonte' wheelbarrow;
with V -ont- attach, and DLC, and **tékeni** two: **tékeni teiokahkwèn:tonte'** bicycle.
With V -r- put in, and DLC:
tenkkahkwèn:taren' I will put a circle around it.

-kahner- V look at, with DLC: **tekkà:nere'**
I look at it, **tekhekà:nere'** I am looking at her, **tehakkà:nere'** he is looking at me.
With CONT -k-: **tenkkà:nerake** I will look at it, **teskà:nerak** Watch it!
With PAST -hkwe': **tekkà:nerahkwe'**
I was looking at it.
With TRNL: **ia'tekkà:nere'** I look over there.
With SRF -at- and BEN -en-:
wa'thatkà:neren' he stared at it,
wa'thakwatkà:neren' he stared at me,
wa'thiiatkà:neren' I stared at him.
• ... kwah ion'wé:sen tsi ia'tekkà:nere' tsi niió:re' tsi iotkónniens. ... it so nice when I look over there, how neat it (the yard) is. (Letter 1945, April) • Iotsistohkwarónnion wa'tkatkà:neren' tsi tkaronhiá:te'. I stared at the stars in the sky.

káhonk wild goose
Cf. kahanckt geese (van den Bogaert: 54); *Gahonk* Outarde (Galissonnière: 61v); *Gahunc* Wilde Ganss (Pyrlaeus: 203); *Gahuchk* Goose (Zeisberger in Wheeler-Voegelin: 61); *kāhonk* outarde (Marcoux: 273); *Kahon* outarde (Cuoq: 9); Wendat *Ahonque* Outarde (Sagard: An1); Onondaga *kahonk* Outarde (Shea: 76); Onondaga *gàhuchk* Goose (Zeisberger: 85)

-kahr- N eye: **okà:ra'**
POSS: **kkahrà:ke** (on) my eye,
rakahrà:ke (on) his eye, **iekahrà:ke** (on) her eye.
With **iottsiseró:ron** (-tsiser- pane of glass, -'rhoro[k]-/-oro[k]- cover), and POSS: **iottsiseró:ron rakahrà:ke** he has cataracts.
With LOC -kon, inside, and POSS:
kkà:rakon in my eye.
With SRF -at-, V -ahseht- hide, kill, and DLC: **wa'thatkahráhsehte'** he covered, hid his eyes, **tehotkahrahséhton** he has covered his eyes.
With V -aksen- be bad, and REP:
skakahráksen walleye, pickerel.
With V -her-/-hr- set on top of, and DLC:
tekkahráhere' I have my eye on it, I am

watching it, **tehakahráhere'** he has his eye on it, **teiekahráhere'** she has her eye on it.

With V -hsnor[e]- be fast: **kkahrahsnó:re'** I am giving it a glance, a quick look (without really looking), **rakahrahsnó:re'** he gives it a glance, **iekahrahsnó:re'** she gives it a glance.

With SRF -at- and V -hwahnha[k]-/-hnha[k]- wrap, tie around: **atkahráhnha'** eyeglasses.

With V -ia'[k]- hit, slap: **wahikahráia'ke'** I gave him a black eye; and SRF -at-: **rotkahráien'** he has a black eye.

With V -ienta'- get, obtain, and TRNL and DLC: **ia'tekkahraién:ta'ne'** my eye focused on it, I understand it better now, it's clearer.

With V -ineken'- emerge, and DLC: **tekkahríneken's** I open my eyes big or wide, **wa'tiekahríneken'ne'** she opened her eyes wide, **tewakkahrinekèn:'en** my eyes are opened wide.

With V -nenhskw- steal, and DLC: **tehikahranénhskwas** I am snooping on him, spying on him, **wa'thikahranénhsko'** I spied on him.

With V -ni'keronkw- twitch: **wakkahrani'kerónkwas** my eye is twitching, **onkkahrani'kerón:ko'** my eye twitched.

With V -otahrhe'- get hooked on something: **wa'kkahrotáhrhe'ne'** I cast my eye on it, I fixated on it, **wahakahrotáhrhe'ne'** he fixed his eye on it.

With V -o'ka't- run into, bump against, and TRNL: **iahokahrò:ka'te'** it went into his eye (for example, an insect), **iahikahrò:ka'te'** I (accidentally) hit or touched his eye; and REFL -atat-: **ia'katatkahrò:ka'te'** I poked myself in the eye.

With V -ronhkwani-/-ronhkwen- itch: **wakkahrarónhkwani** I have an itchy eye.

With SRF -at- and V -sera[hw]-/-osera[hw]- gush, spew: **wa'katkahróserahwe'** I rinsed my eyes with water.

With SRF -at- and V -ta'-/-eta'- put inside: **wa'katkahráta'** I looked at it through a telescope, binoculars; and CAUS -hst- and INSTR -hkw-: **iontkahrata'ahstáhkhwa'** telescope, binoculars.

With SRF -at-, V -tiha- be different, and DLC: **tetiatkahratíhas** you and I see things differently (for example, a colour as red versus yellow), **wa'titiatkahratíha'** we saw it differently, **wa'thiatkahratíha'** the two saw it differently.

-kahr- make noise. *See* -rakahr-/-kahr-

-kahreht- N eyelash: **okahréhta'**
POSS: **akkahréhta'** my eyelash.
With V -es- be long, and DLC: **tehokahrehté:son's** he has long eyelashes, **teiakokahrehté:son's** she has long eyelashes.
With V -ia'k- cut, sever: **enhskahréhtia'ke'** you will take or cut off the (strawberry) stems, tops.
With V -ohtshi- remove, pull out: **wa'kkahrehtóhtshi' ken' niiohontésha** I took off the top of the strawberry.

kahrhata'kéha blueberry
NOTE: May be composed of -(h)rhat- hedge, and ATTR =keha, way of.

Cf. Garhatageha des bluets (Bruyas: 89); Karhatakēha Bluet, fruit (Marcoux: 41); Karhatakeha petits fruits des bois (Cuoq: 106); karatakeha [blueberries] (Ledger: 47); ka ra ta ke ha blueberries (D'Aille-boust: 22); gar ha dah ge hah blueberry (Jamieson 1: 6)

-kahrhate- V be turned out (to the side)
With N -ian- footprint, track, and DLC:
tehaianakáhrhate' his feet are turned
out, **teieianakáhrhate'** her feet are turned
out, **tekaianakáhrhate'** its feet are turned
out (talking about a dog).

-kahrhateni- V turn around, empty:
rakahrhaténie's he is emptying it,
wahakahrhaté:ni' he emptied it,
rokahrhaténion he has emptied it.
With DLC: **tehakahrhaténie's** he is
turning it around, **wa'tekkahrhaté:ni'**
I turned it around, **wa'thikahrhaté:ni'**
I turned him around, **tehokahrhaténion**
he has turned it around; and DISTR -hon-:
tekkahrhateníhon I am turning things
around, **wa'thakahrhateníhon'** he
turned things around.
With SRF -at- and DLC:
tekatkahrhaténie's I turn around,
tenkatkahrhaté:ni' I will turn around,
wa'tkatkahrhaté:ni' I turned around,
tewakatkahrhaténion I have turned
around; and PROG -hatie-:
tewakatkahrhatenionhátie' I am turning around.
With CAUS -'t-: **enkkahrhaténia'te'** I
will roll it, **wahakahrhaténia'te'** he
rolled it, **rokahrhatenià:ton** he has
rolled it; and PROG -hatie-:
wakkahrhatenia'tonhátie' I am rolling
it; with SRF -at- and CAUS -'t-:
wa'katkahrhaténia'te' I rolled (for
example, down the hill).
With SRF -ate-, N -neni- stone, rock,
DISTR -hon-, and DLC:
tewateneniakahrhateníhon grindstone.
With SRF -at-, N -onhwents-/-onhonts-
earth, world, BEN -en-, and DLC:
wa'tewakatonhontsakahrhaténien'
I got disoriented.
With SRF -at-, N -tsisto[hkw]- star, CAUS
-'t-, PROG -hatie-, and CISL:

taiottsistohkwakahrhatenia'tonhátie'
stars come rolling out (*a playful expression
from Mike Norton*).

-kahrhatho- V turn over: **rakahrháthos** he
turns it over, **enkkahrhátho'** I will turn it
over, **wahakahrhátho'** he turned it over,
wakkahrháthon I have turned it over.
With SRF -at-: **wa'katkahrhátho'** I turned
over, I rolled over.
With SRF -at-, N -ient- wood, and BEN -'s-:
onkwatientakahrhátho'se' it didn't go
well for me, not as planned,
wahotientakahrhátho'se' it didn't go
well for him.
With N -i'tar- chimney, clan, clay:
ki'tarakahrháthos I am ploughing,
wahen'tarakahrhátho' he ploughed,
ken'tarakahrháthon it is ploughed;
and CAUS -hst-: **ie'tarakahrhathóhstha'**
plough.
With N -ra'wist- peel, pancake:
wa'kera'wistakahrhátho' I flipped the
pancake, **sera'wistakahrhátho** Flip the
pancake!
With SRF -ate- and N -'sere[ht]- vehicle,
car: **onkwate'serehtakahrhátho'** I
flipped over in or on my vehicle (in my
car, on my bike).
*Cf. Gandigonragarhaθon renverser l'esprit
à quelqu'un* (Bruyas: 45)

-kahri's- V get something into one's eye:
onkkà:ri'se' something went into my eye,
I got something in my eye, **wahokà:ri'se'**
he got something in his eye,
wa'akokà:ri'se' she got something in her
eye, **wakkahrì:sen** I have something in
my eye.

-kahrohst- N intestine: **okahróhsta'**
POSS: **akkahróhsta'** my intestines.
With V -hwaneren[k]-/-neren[k]- tie up,

and DLC: **tenikahrohstáneren** we are inseparable friends, **tehnikahrohstáneren** the two are inseparable friends. *This is an old expression.*

With V -tahkw- take out: **wa'kkahrohstatáhko'** I took out the intestines.

Cf. Ogar8sta Boyaux (Bruyas: 46): *Ogar^c8sta* Boyaux (Galissonnière: 14r); *ogarōsta* Boyeau (Marcoux: 46); *Okahrosta* tripes, boyaux, intestins (Cuoq: 67); *o ka rohs tha* intestine (Jamieson 3: 3)

-kahront- V make an opening, a hole: **wa'kkahrón:ten'** I made a hole in it, **iokà:ronte'** there is an opening or hole.
With DISTR -on-: **iokahrón:ton** there are openings or holes.
With N -ahonht- ear, and DLC: **tekahonhtakà:ronte'** I have pierced ears.
With N -aten'enhr- fence: **ioten'enhrakà:ronte'** gate.
With N -hs- lip: **tsi khsakà:ronte'** my mouth, **tsi rahsakà:ronte'** his mouth, **tsi iehsakà:ronte'** her mouth.
With V -hsonw- be a hole: **iohsonwakà:ronte'** there is a hole in it.
With N -itstenhr- rock, boulder: **iotstenhrakà:ronte'** cave.
With N -na'ts- pail: **iona'tsakà:ronte'** there is a hole in the pail.
With N -(h)nhoh- door: **kehnhohakahróntha'** I am making a hole in the door, **wa'kehnhohakahrón:ten'** I made a hole in the door.
With N -(h)nho'kw- cheek: **iakohnho'kwakà:ronte'** she has a dimple; and DISTR -on-: **iakohnho'kwakahrón:ton** she has dimples (on both sides of her face).
With N -'nionhr- inside of a chimney: **io'nionhrakà:ronte'** there is a hole in the chimney.

With N -'rhiotsh- chin: **ro'rhiotshakà:ronte'** he has a dimple in his chin.
With N -'whar- tunnel, hollow: **tsi io'wharakà:ronte'** at the tunnel (in Kahnawà:ke).
• Iokahrón:ton ne ienonwakentstáhkhwa'. A colander has holes in it. • Wa'kehnhoha-kahrón:ten' ake'nowáta'. I made a hole in the door to put in a lock.

-kahro'kw- N eyeball: **okahrò:kwa'**

-kahser- N tears: **okáhseri**
With V -awenhrat- overflow, and DISTR -hon-: **iekahserawenhráthons** she is in tears, **wa'kkahserawenhráthon'** I shed tears.
With V -a'sen'-/-en'- fall down, and CISL: **takakáhseren'ne'** the tears are falling (maybe I hit something and tears form).
With V -hren't-/-en't- hang down, DISTR -onnion-, and DLC: **teiakokahseren'tónnion** she has tear-drops hanging (from her eyes); and AMB -hne-: **tesakahseren'tonniòn:ne'** you (sg) are going along with tears.
With unclear V (possibly related to the root in the last subentry under -hwist- metal, money): **wakkahserahrì:'on** I have shed tears, my tears are falling, **iakokahserahrì:'on** she has shed tears.

Cf. te8akkaserentōnnions avoir les larmes aux yeux (Marcoux: 228); *desakaghserentonionne* you are weeping on your way (Hale:116–7)

-kahserot- N Green Corn festival: **okahseró:ta'**

Cf. Okaserota le blé d'inde en lait, *litt.* En larmes=okaseri (Cuoq: 31); *o gah se ro dah* Green corn bread (Jamieson 2: 3); *okahseró:ta'* Green

Corn [festival] (Deering and Delisle: 288); *Okahseró:ta* [Green Corn festival] (Lazore: 50)

kahstó:wa' traditional head piece
With ATTR =kowa, great: **Ohstowa'kó:wa** Great Feather Dance; one of the four sacred ceremonies of the Haudenosaunee.

kahswénhtha' wampum belt
Cf. "The Onkwehón:we called the [Two Row] Wampum Belt, *Kaswén:ta.*" (Thomas: 2)

-kahte- V be raw: **iokáhte'** it is raw.
With N -neraht- leaf: **onerahtakáhte'** lettuce.
With N -non'onser- squash: **onon'onserakáhte'** watermelon.
With N -tsihkw- fist, button: **otsihkwakáhte'** radish.

-kahtso't- N dry crusty sleep in the eyes: **okahtsò:ta'**
With V -ont- attach, and DLC: **tesakahtsò:tonte'** your eyes are crusty with sleep, **tehokahtsò:tonte'** his eyes are crusty with sleep, **teiakokahtsò:tonte'** her eyes are crusty with sleep.

káhwhe coffee
Cf. ka fe coffee (D'Ailleboust: 24); *kafé* coffee (Cory: 14); *Káhwhe* Coffee (Horne: 30)

kaié:ri four, **kaié:ri iawén:re** fourteen, **kaié:ri niwáhsen** forty, **kaieríhaton** fourth, **kaié:ri nia'ká:ienhte'** four times.

-kaiet- N yogurt: **okaié:ta'**
Cf. okaiétha yogurt (Gabriel: 150)

Kaiokonhá:ka Cayuga

Cf. "*Goyogouens* [Cayuga]" (Lafitau I: 87); *Gajuguhãga Gajuquer* (Pyrlaeus: 215); *Cayokwen* [Cayuga] (Joseph Brant in Penrose: 106); "*Cayugwa* is a name the meaning of which is obsolete" (Joseph Brant in Boyce: 291); *Koi-ok-wen* Cayuga, "from the water to the shore," as the landing of prisoners (De Lorimier in Hough: 181); *Koiokwenronons* Cayugas (Cuoq: 164); Wendat *goiogoinronnon goiogoin* (Potier: 154)

-kaion- be old. *See* -akaion-/-kaion-

kaión:ni wampum belt
NOTE: GM notes that the names *Tekahionwake* Pauline Johnson, *Ahyouwaighs* John Brant, and *Skahionwí:io* include this root.
Cf. Gaionni collier de porcelaine (Bruyas: 63); *Gaionni* collier de porcelaine (Galissonière: 21r); "*Gaïonni*, meaning belts of this sort," (Lafitau I: 311); *Gajojõni* Ein Belt of Wampum (Pyrlaeus: 210); *kayõn'ni'* a wampum belt (Deserontyon: 103); *kaiõnni* Porcelaine, Collier de (Marcoux: 297); *Kaionni* collier diplomatique, collier de porcelaine, de wampum (Cuoq: 9); *kaionni* wampum (Mary Deer's class notes, Feb. 1966); *kaión:ni* Wampum belt (Deering and Delisle: 286); *kaión:ni* wampum (Old Kahnawake: 4)

kakwín Queen (in cards)
NOTE: The *í* is pronounced like the *i* in the English word *twin*.
Cf. Ka kwin Queen (Anon: 9)

Kananóhkhwi Gananoque

kanáthen front, downtown
With DISTR -hshon: **kanathénhshon** in the village.

• Wà:s kanáthen nonkwá:ti niahà:se.
Go to the front! (talking to the dog)

Kanatién French person

kana'tsówi (water) drum

Kanehsatà:ke Mohawk territory at Oka,
Québec
Cf. " ... Onondagas ... built a village on
the Island of Montreal a few miles from
that city on the side of a Hill from which
it took the name of *Kaneghsadáge*, it has
since been removed to the lake of two
Mountains" (John Norton in Boyce: 292);
Kanesatakehrōnon la nat. du Lac des deux
mont. (Marcoux: 259); *Kanesatake* Litt.
au bas de la cote. Le village du Lac des
deux Montagnes est en effet situé au pied
d'une colline (Cuoq: 10); *Ka ne sá ta ke*
Oka (Cory: 83); *Kaneghsadakeh* On the
hill side (Hale: 118–9); Iroquois
Ca-nes-se-da-ge "It is usually rendered
side hill, but is capable of other defini-
tions." (Beauchamp 1907: 264)

káneka anywhere
• Káneka ken wáhse'? Are you going
anywhere? • Iah káneka thá:ke' nòn:wa.
I'm not going anywhere today.

kanekhé:re certainly, no wonder

kanenna'kè:ne in the autumn
Cf. Kannennage l'automne (Bruyas: 71);
Gannonáger Herbst (Pyrlaeus: 183);
kanennāke Automne, *kanennnakēhne* dans
l' (Marcoux: 30); *Kanennakehne* [autumn]
(Granger: 4); *ka nen na ke ne* autumn
(Anon: 6); *Ka-ne-ná-ké-ne* fall (Cory: 73);
Ga nen nah ge neh Autumn (Jamieson 1:
8)

káneron white ash

Kanón:no Manhattan, New York City
Cf. Kanonnewage [kanón:no wà:ke'] the
Manhatas (van den Bogaert: 62); *Ganuhnu*
(or *Ganuhno*) New York (Pyrlaeus: 63);
Ka no-no New York, signification not
known (F. Marcoux in Hough: 181);
Kanonno New York, jonc dans l'eau,
pays de joncs (Cuoq: 11); "*Ka-noo'-no*
is fresh water basin, according to Brant-
Sero, who called it the name of New York
harbor in Mohawk, thence applied to the
city and the State." (Beauchamp 1907:
259); *Ka non no* New York (Anon: 17);
Kanónno New York (Cory: 83); *Kanón:no*
Brooklyn, New York (Horne: 61); Wendat
annond8 La menade (Potier: 154)

-kanont- V lick: **wahaká:nonte'** he licked it.
With DISTR: -hon-: **iekanónthons** she is
licking it, **wakkanónthons** it (an animal)
is licking me, **shakokanónthons** he is
licking her; **rokanónthon** he has licked it.

-kar- N cost, value
With SRF -at-, V -akaion-/-kaion- be old,
and CAUS -hst-: **enkatkaraká:ionhste'**
I will neglect to pay my bill, what I owe,
wahatkaraká:ionhste' he left unpaid
what he owed.
With V -ia'k- cut, sever: **rakária'ks** he
is paying, **enhatikária'ke'** they will pay,
wahakária'ke' he paid, **rokarià:kon** he
has paid; and BEN -i-/-hs-:
eniethikária'khse' we will pay her,
wahikária'khse' I paid him,
wahakkária'khse' he paid me,
khekarià:ki I have paid her, **iethikarià:ki**
we have paid her.
With V -onni- make: **wakkarón:nis** I suffer for it, I pay for it, **rokarón:nis** he pays
for it, **iakokarón:nis** she pays for it,

onkkarón:ni' I suffered for it (I went out to eat and now I'm paying!); and CAUS -'t-: **wakkaronnià:tha'** it harms me, **wahokarónnia'te'** it harmed him; with SRF -at- and V -onni- make: **wahatkarón:ni'** he had an expense. With SRF -at- and V -ot- stand: **wakatká:rote'** I have a bill, I owe money, **rotká:rote'** he has bills, he owes money, **iakotká:rote'** she has bills, she owes money; with V -ot- stand, and BEN -ni-/ -hahs-: **khekarotá:ni** I give her credit, **wahikaróthahse'** I gave him credit; with V -ot- stand, and REV -hsi-: **rakarotáhsions** he collects money, conductor, cashier, **iekarotáhsions** she collects money; and BEN -enni-/-en-: **rakkarotahsién:nis** he is asking me for his money, he is collecting from me, **ronwakarotahsién:nis** they are asking him for their money, **wahikarotáhsien'** I collected money off him. With V -o'kt- finish: **wahakarò:kten'** he paid off, ended his debt. • Sewenhni'tátshon shakokarià:ki. He pays her by the month. • Wakkarón:nis ne onékwa' iah tha'teiontiatenrò:'on. I'm suffering for it, the pill didn't agree with me.

Cf. Gagariagon payer ses dettes, *Gagaʀst* Avoir, faire ses dettes, *Gagarokte* achever de tout payer (Bruyas: 45); *Gagaronnion* faire tort à quelqu'un, lui causer quelque perte (Bruyas: 46); *ꝸahoňatkaronni* fair perte, on luy a (Galissonnière: 80); *ꝸakatkãrŏte* avoir des dettes, *kkarotāsions* demander ses dette (Marcoux: 122); *Wakkarŏte* av. une dette, des dettes, *Kkaroktha* payer ses dettes (Cuoq: 130); *o ka ra* debt (Anon: 31); *a ka ra* debt (Diabo: 15); *ia ko ka ro te* owe (Diabo: 51)

-kar- N story, tale: **oká:ra'**
With NEG: **iah í: tewakká:ra'** it is not my story.
With V -ka'te- have many: **wakkarakà:te'** I have a lot of stories, **rokarakà:te'** he has a lot of stories.

-kar- N inner bark: **ó:kare'**
Cf. nene tosa aiakaonhaksate aseron okara sewaiowane okwire [so it doesn't make them feel bad you should put in some bark from an apple tree] (Beauvais: 5)

-karanie- rub, scrub. *See* -ranie-/-karanie-

-karatat- lift, raise up. *See* -haratat-/-karatat-

-karaton- V tell stories: **kká:ratons** I tell stories, **enhaká:raton'** he will tell a story, **wahaká:raton'** he told a story, **roká:raton** he is telling a story, he has told a story.
With DISTR -onnion-: **rakaratónnions** he is telling stories.
With BEN -ni-/-hahs-: **khekaratón:ni** I am telling her a story, **wa'onkkaratón:hahse'** she told me a story, **takkaratón:hahs** Tell me a story!
With INSTR -hkw-: **iekaratónhkhwa'** legend.

-kara'w- V be open
With SRF -at-, N -hs- lip, and DLC: **wa'tkátskara'we'** I opened my mouth, **tehotskarà:wen** his mouth is open, **teiakotskarà:wen** her mouth is open.
With N -hs- lip, CAUS -ht-, and DLC: **wa'tewakhskarà:wahte'** I yawned, **wa'thohskarà:wahte'** he yawned, **wa'tiakohskarà:wahte'** she yawned; and DISTR -nion-: **tewakhskara'wahtánions** I am yawning, **tehohskara'wahtánions**

he is yawning, **teiakohskara'wahtánions** she is yawning.

-karehrahst- make noise. *See* -rakarehrahst-/ -karehrahst-

-karenhr[on]- V rock
 With DLC: **tekkarèn:ron** I am rocking it, **wa'tekkarèn:ron'** I rocked it, **wa'tekhekarèn:ron'** I rocked her; and SRF -at-: **tewatkarèn:ron** it is rocking.
 With REFL -atat- and INSTR -hkw-: **iontatkarenhrónhkhwa' anitskwà:ra** rocking chair.
 With REV -kw-: **kkarenhrákwas** I turn (in a direction), **wa'kkarenhrá:ko'** I turned, **rokarenhrákwen** he has turned; and CAUS -ht-: **iekarenhrakwáhtha'** reins.
 With SRF -an-, N -itahs- tail, and DLC: **tehanitahsakarèn:ron** he is wagging his tail (for example, a dog is sleeping and in his sleep he's moving his tail).
 • Skeweientehtáhkwen nonkwá:ti wa'kkarenhrá:ko'. I turned right.

-kareni- V take back and forth: **kkarénie's** I am taking it back and forth, **wahakaré:ni'** he took it back and forth, **iakokarénion** she has taken it back and forth.
 With CAUS -'t-: **iekarenià:tha'** shovel.
 With N -ahta[hkw]- shoe, and DLC: **teiakohtahkwakaré:ni** she is running around (with different men). This word has also been attested with a falling tone, **teiakohtahkwakarè:ni**, *see* -rakare'ni-/ -kare'ni- be loud.
 With N -a'kenhr- ashes, dirt: **ra'kenhrakarénie's** he is carrying dirt back and forth.
 With N -ia't- body: **iakoia'takarénie's** bus.
 With V -ihei[on]-/-enhei[on]- die, and

CAUS -'t-: **wenheion'takarénie's** hearse.
 With N -neni- stone, rock: **keneniakarénie's** I am carrying stones back and forth.
 With N -(h)nhoh- door: **rahnhohakarénie's** he goes in and out, **wahahnhohakaré:ni'** he went in and out, **rohnhohakarénion** he is going in and out.
 With SRF -at- and N -onkwe['t]- person, human being: **watonkwe'takarénie's** bus.
 With N -'nehtar- gravel: **ra'nehtarakarénie's** he is carrying gravel back and forth.
 • Tió:konte' rohnhohakarénion ne Ohkwá:ri. Ohkwá:ri (a dog) is always going in and out.

-karere- be noise travelling. *See* -rakarere-/ -karere-

-karewaht- V injure, hurt: **shakokarewáhtha'** he injures her or them, **wahakkaré:wahte'** he injured me, **onkkaré:wahte'** I got hurt, I hurt myself, **wahokaré:wahte'** he got hurt, **shakokarehwáhton** he has hurt her.
 With N -ahsi't- foot: **onkwahsi'takaré:wahte'** I hurt my foot.
 With N -hsnonhs- finger, hand: **onkehsnonhsakaré:wahte'** I hurt my finger or hand.

-kare'ni- be loud. *See* -rakare'ni-/-kare'ni-

-kari- V bite: **khekárias** I bite her, **wa'kheká:ri'** I bit her, **wa'onkká:ri'** she bit me, **ionkkárien** she has bitten me, **iokária** there's a lot of mosquitoes.
 With REFL -atat-: **wa'katatká:ri'** I bit myself.
 With CAUS -ht- and AMB -hne-: **okariahtà:ne'** mosquito.
 With SRF -at-, N -erien't- disposition, and

DLC: **tekaterien'takárias** I get irritated, annoyed, it gets on my nerves, **wa'tkaterien'taká:ri'** I got irritated, annoyed, **tewakaterien'takária** I am noisy, **teiakoterien'takária** she is noisy; and CAUS -ht-: **wa'thaterien'takáriahte'** he made noise, **tehoterien'takariáhton** he is making noise.

With N -nat- town, settlement: **Ranatakárias** President of the United States (i.e., he destroys the town); and ATTR =hne, at: **Ranatakariáhsne** Washington, D.C.; with N -nat- town, settlement, and CISL: **takenataká:ri'** I made a fuss in town, I raised Cain.

With SRF -at-, N -onhnh- life, and DLC: **wa'thatonhnhaká:ri'** he was orphaned, **wa'tiontonhnhaká:ri'** she became an orphan, **teiakotonhnhakarì:'on** she is an orphan.

Cf. Jogariat O qu'il mange ici à cause des puce, *Jogaratianne* maringouins, *Tsatonnhakarien* souffrir beaucoup (Bruyas: 45); *Garigon* Mordre (Galissonnière: 57v); *Jogarias* vermine (Galissonnière: 82v); *okariatāne* Maringouin, *iokāriat* il y a des (Marcoux: 243); *Okariatane* maringouin, *Iokariat* il y a des maringouins, litt. ça mord, ça pique (Cuoq: 116)

-karien't- N carcass: **okarièn:ta'**
With V -akera- stink, smell: **kakarien'tákeras** (it is) a smelly carcass.
With V -ehsak-/-ihsak-/-esak-/-isak- look for: **wa'kkarien'tíhsake'** I looked for the carcass.
With V -ien- put down, have: **kakarièn:taien'** there is a carcass.
With V -rohro[k]- gather, collect: **rakarien'tarò:roks** he collects carcasses, **wahakarien'tarò:roke'** he collected carcasses.

With V -tshenri- find: **wa'kkarien'tatshén:ri'** I found a carcass.
• É:so enhsatkáhtho' ne okarièn:ta' ohahaktóntie'. You see a lot of carcasses on the side of the road.

Cf. Okariēntha Carcasse (Marcoux: 56); *Okarienta* carcasse (Cuoq: 31); *okarié'ta* an animal that is weak and skinny (Gabriel: 12)

karisé: wool. Possibly a borrowing from English *kersey*, a coarse woolen cloth.

karístatsi stove, piece of iron or steel
POSS: **raorístatsi** his stove; and **ronontí:io** (-nont- mountain, hill, -iio- be good, nice): **ronontí:io raorístatsi** large, black metal stove (*literally,* king's stove).
With ATTR =kowa, great: **karistatsi'kó:wa** crowbar.
NOTE: These words all include a root -rist- iron, steel.

Cf. Garistatsi fer, métail (Bruyas: 93); *Kalistasi* fer (Galissonnière: 40v); *Karistatsi* Fer (Marcoux: 171); *Karistatsi* métal noir, fer (Cuoq: 11)

-kar[on]- V peel off bark: **raká:rons** he is peeling off bark, **énkkare'** I will peel off the bark, **wakká:ron** I have peeled off the bark, **ískar** Peel off the bark!

Cf. Gagaron escorce dont on se sert pour lier, en lever (Bruyas: 45); *Kkarons* écorcer, ôter l'écorce (Cuoq: 24); *enié:kare* [she will peel off the bark] (Old Kahnawake: 2)

kà:ron less than. For example, **kà:ron ní:iens** it is not as long, it does not equal.

kasí:sa' or **ahsí:sa'** pestle

katerón: weight measure, perhaps a quarter pound.

Cf. Katerōn Quarteron (Marcoux: 316); *toka iostathen akwekon noterasona, onenontste 3 kateron, onontsi 3 kateron, kateraontsi 7 aonts* [maybe all the roots are dried, 3 katerón: mandrake, 3 katerón: heads, 7 ounces fern] (Beauvais: 9)

katiéhson husk face
NOTE : Frank Natawe suggested the literal meaning 'it flies about'.
Cf. gah jih sah false face (corn-husk) (Jamieson 2: 5); Onondaga "*Kah-je-sah*, a name for a mat, is applied to the corn-husk masks, worn by doorkeepers at public feasts." (Beauchamp 1922: 37)

káti' then, well, therefore, consequently
Né: kati' ken nè:'e. So what! Uh-huh.

kátke when? **katkehshòn:'a** sometime (in the future, we don't know when)

káton' or; let's
• **È:rhar káton' takò:s sanáhskwaien'?** Do you have a dog or a cat?
Cf. Káton' entiatawénha'. Let's go swimming. (Horne: 14)

káton' ken? can you? would you?
• **Káton' ken aontahsóhetste'?** How about you pass it this way?

-kawe- V paddle: **raká:wes** he paddles, **enkká:we'** I will paddle, **wahaká:we'** he paddled; **aká:we'** paddle, oar.
With PROG -hatie-: **wakkawehátie'** I am paddling, pedalling, **rokawehátie'** he is paddling, pedalling.
With CAUS -'t- and INSTR -hkw-: **iekawe'táhkhwa'** (bike) pedal.
With NMZR -'tsher-, V -ke- amount to, and

DLC: **tekakawe'tsherá:ke** two paddles.
• **Rokawehátie' tékeni teiokahkwèn:tonte'.** He is pedalling the bicycle.

ka' nonkwá:ti which way?

ka' nón:we where? **ka'k nón:we** somewhere, **tiok nón:we** everywhere

-ka'enion- V look closely, scrutinize: **kka'én:ions** I am looking at it closely, carefully, **enhakka'én:ion'** he will look closely at me, **wahaka'én:ion'** he looked closely at it, **roka'én:ion** he has looked closely at it.
With BEN -'s: **wahakka'én:ion'se'** he looked at it for me, **wa'onkka'én:ion'se'** she looked at it for me.
With N -rahkw- sun, and CAUS -'t-: **karahkwaka'eniòn:tha'** clock, sundial.
• **Kwah tekèn:'en enhska'én:ion'.** Look at it! Really look at it! (for example, when you are cutting out a pattern).
• **Wahakka'én:ion'se' ka'serehtí:io ken.** He looked at it for me [whether] it was a good car.
Cf. Gagaieñon desirer de voir son pays (Bruyas: 44); *Kagakennion* Voir sans estre veu (Galissonnière: 83v); *Kkahēnhiŏns* examiner (Marcoux: 81); *Kkahenhions* examiner, considérer, regarder attentivement (Cuoq: 23)

ka'ní:ka mortar (as in mortar and pestle)

Ka'taróhkwen or **Ken'taróhkwen** Kingston, Ontario
Cf. Gataróchco Fort Frontenac (Pyrlaeus: 63); "As soon as they arrived at *Cadarackui*," (Colden: 79); *Cadaroghkon* [Bay of Quinte] (Deserontyon in Torok: 75); *Cataroqui* Ancient name of Kingston, "a bank of clay rising out of the waters."

(De Lorimier in Hough: 181); *Kaghdarongwenh* Kingston, Built a fort (Brant-Sero and Hill in Boyle: 172); *Katarokwen* ancien nom de la ville de Kingston (Cuoq: 13); *takataró:kwen* Kingston Ontario, where the cement is on it because of the walls made of cement (Gabriel: 76); *Ka'taróhkwen* Kingston (Horne: 61); Iroquois "Fort Frontenac or *Catarokouy*" (Hennepin in Ketchum I: 54); Iroquois *Catarocoui* ou Fort Frontenac (Jaillot map 1685); Wendat *ɑtarokʒi, catarakʒi* (Potier: 154); Onondaga *Cat-a-ra-qui* Fort in the water (Beauchamp 1893: 64)

-ka'te- V have many: **wakkà:te'** I have many.
With CONT -k-: **enwakkà:teke'** I will have many.
With PAST -hkwe': **wakkà:tehkwe'** I used to have many.
With SRF -at-: **iotkà:te'** often.
With KIN -atere- grandchild, and NMZR -'ser-: **wakatere'serakà:te'** I have a lot of grandchildren.
With N -atero'ser- friendship: **wakatero'serakà:te'** I have a lot of friends.
With N -io'tenhser- work: **watio'tenhserakà:te'** I have plenty of work.
With N -kar- story, tale: **rokarakà:te'** he has a lot of stories.
With N -nentstakwar- dirty laundry: **wakenentstakwarakà:te'** I have lots of dirty laundry.
With N -rihw- matter, message: **iakorihwakà:te'** she has a lot to say (like she never shuts up).
With N -wir- offspring: **iakowirakà:te'** she has a lot of children.
With N -'sereht- vehicle, car: **ro'serehtakà:te** he has a lot of cars; and SRF -ate-: **iote'serehtakà:te'** there are a lot of cars.

-ka'[w]- find tasty, like the taste of. *See* -eka'[w]-/-ka'[w]-

-ke- V amount to. For example, with N -nonhs- house, and DLC: **tekanónhsake** two houses; or PART: **kaié:ri nikanónhsake** four houses.

=keha ATTR way of. For example: **Kanien'kéha** language of the Kanien'kehá:ka (People of the Flint); **kahrhata'kéha** blueberry.

-kehon- V cut corn stalks, harvest corn: **wakkéhon** I am harvesting corn, cutting the corn stalks, **rokéhon** he is cutting the corn stalk, **iakokéhon** she is cutting the corn stalk. *These are old words.*

-kehr- dish, plate, bowl: *See* -akehr-/-kehr-

-kehron[t]- V put down here and there: **kkè:rons** I put it down here and there, I am laying it out, **wahakè:ron'** he put them down, **rokè:ron** he has put them down, **é:so kakè:ron** lots of things are here and there, all over (on the ground).
With SRF -at-: **ratkè:rons** he peddles, sells things, **enkatkè:ron'** I will peddle, sell it, **wahatkè:ron'** he peddled it, sold it, **iakotkè:ron** she is selling, **ionatkè:ron** they (females) are selling, **watkè:ron** it is for sale.
With SRF -at- and PURP -hnh-: **wa'katkehrónhnhe'** I am going to sell (things), **enkatkehrónhnha'** I will go to sell, **wa'katkehrónhnha'** I went to sell.
With SRF -at- and PROG -atie-: **rotkehrontátie'** he is selling things.
With SRF -at- and REV -kw-: **katkehrontákwas** I am shopping, **wahatkehrontá:ko'** he shopped, **iakotkehrontákwen** she has shopped;

and PURP -h-: **wahatkehrontakóha'** he
went shopping.
With N -ia't- body: **ieia'takè:ron** there
are people lying down.
With V -itskar[on]- shoe sole, cover, rug:
kentskarakè:ron there are rugs here and
there.
With N -na'ts- pail, and TRNL:
iahana'tsakè:ron' he put pails all around
there.
With N -neraht- leaf: **kanerahtakè:ron**
here and there there are leaves on the
ground.
With N -nieht- snow: **kaniehtakè:ron**
there are patches of snow here and there.
• Rotkehrontátie' ase'shòn:'a. He is selling vegetables. • Wahatkehrontakóha'
atennà:tshera'. He went shopping for
groceries.

Cf. tyeyadakeron Yonder are lying bodies
(Hale: 118–9); *Tontaiakotahonhtaneken'-
tsheratkehrontakohátie* She is coming back
from rabbit shopping. ("Tongue Twister,"
44 letters, Tewaterihwarenia'tha, Summer
1988: 24)

-keht[e]- V carry on the back: **wakkéhte'**
I am carrying it, I have it on my back,
rokéhte' he has it on his back, **iakokéhte'**
she has it on her back.
With SRF -at- and CAUS -t-: **ratkéhtats**
he puts it on his back, **wahatkéhtate'**
he carried it on his back; and **à:there'**
(-a'ther- basket): **iontkéhtats à:there'**
burden basket.
With N -hsenn- name: **rohsennakéhte'**
he doesn't have a clan, so they give him a
name, **iakohsennakéhte'** she doesn't have
a clan, so they give her a name.
With N -nohkw- bundle: **ronohkwakéhte'**
he is carrying a bundle on his back; and
SRF -ate- and CAUS -t-:
ratenohkwakéhtats hobo, peddler.

See also -hsken'rakehte- be a male, and
akéhton tumpline.

-kehwhen't- N (corn) chaff: **okehwhèn:ta'**

-ken- V see: **íkkens** I see, **rá:kens** he sees,
ié:kens she sees, **enié:ken'** she will see,
wà:kken' I saw her or it (an animal),
wahonwatí:ken' she saw them, **iakó:ken**
she or it has seen her or someone, **ió:ken**
it is seen, it is visible.
With NEG: **iah tehá:ken** he is blind,
iah teié:ken she is blind.
With REP: **enséhsken'** you (sg) will see
her or it again, **enséhsekken'** you (sg)
will see me again, **enskón:ken'** I will see
you again, **sahí:ken'** I saw him again.
With TRNL: **ohén:ton iehá:kens** he sees
ahead, into the future.
With CONTR, TRNL, and REP:
iah thietsó:ken it is no longer visible
(you can't see it).
With REFL -atat-: **atátken** mirror; and
NMZR -'tsher- and V -ohar- attach at the
end: **watatken'tsheróhare'** dresser.
With REFL -atat- and DLC: **tetiatátkens**
you and I see each other, we meet; and
PAST -hne': **teiontiatatkénhne'** we two
had seen each other; with REFL -atat-,
and DLC and REP: **taonsetewatátken'**
we (you all and I) should meet again.
With SRF -at- and BEN -'s-: **katkèn:se'**
I look into it, examine it, **enkátken'se'** I
will look into it, **wa'onkwátken'se'** she
examined me, **wakatkèn:se'** I have
looked into it.
With N -ia't- body: **roià:taken** he stands
out, he is conspicuous, **iakoià:taken** she
is conspicuous.
• Wahonwatí:ken' tehotíhthare'. She saw
them talking. • Akwé:kon ió:ken tsi
katsinonhiahtatátie'. You can see all the
veins, all my veins are visible. • Wa'kát-
ken'se' tóka' teiotsikhè:tare'. I checked to

see if it's sweet. • July kati' nòn:wa enionkwahrhá:rake' ne taonsetewatátken'. We will be waiting to meet again in July. (Letter 1945, Apr)

ken marks a yes-no question

ken: or **kenh** or **kèn:tho** right here, right there

-**kenh**- N felt (the fabric): **okénha'** With V -nohare-/-ohare- wash: **kakenhóhare** mop.

Cf. Ogenha couverte (Bruyas: 47); *ogenha* Couverte (Galissonnière: 26r); Etoffe (Galissonnière: 38r); *okēnha* etoffe, drap (Marcoux: 159); *Okenha* drap, étoffe (Cuoq: 31)

=**kenha** ATTR former, late. For example: **rakhsothkénha** my late grandfather; **onkwahsotshera'kénha** our ancestors; **rone'kénha** her late husband, his late wife; **akenonhsa'kénha** my former house.

-**kenhr[on]**- V shun: **khekèn:rons** I shun her, I don't want anything to do with her (for example, talking about a homeless person), **wahakkèn:ron'** he shunned me.
With BEN -ni-: **khekenhrón:nis** I am intolerant of her, **rakkenhrón:nis** he is intolerant of me.
With CAUS -'t-: **iokenhrà:ton** it is unappealing, not likeable, and BEN -en-: **onkkenhrà:ten'** I disliked it right away, I rejected it, **wahokenhrà:ten'** he rejected it.
With NMZR -'ser- and V -onni- make: **wahikenhra'serón:ni'** I insulted him, I belittled him, **wa'khekenhra'serón:ni'** I insulted her, I put her down.

kenkwitè:ne in the spring

Cf. Geng8ite (Bruyas 113); *Geng8ite* printems (Galissonnière: 69v); *Gaquĩtek* Frueling (Pyrlaeus: 183); *kenk8ĩte, kenk8itēhne* Printems (Marcoux: 306); *Kenkwite* printemps (Cuoq: 18); *Kenkwitehne* [spring] (Granger: 4); *ken kwi te ne* spring (Anon: 6); *Ko-kwí-té-ne* spring (Cory: 73); *Gen gwi de neh* Spring (Jamieson 1: 8)

-**kenni**- V compete, with DLC
With SRF -at-: **tehontkénnie's** they are competing, **wa'thontkén:ni'** they competed, **teiakotkénnion** she has competed.
With SRF -an- and N -itiohkw- group: **tehonnitiohkwakénnie's** they vote, councilors, **wa'tkanitiohkwakén:ni'** I voted.
With SRF -ate- and N -nonni- dance: **tekatenonniakénnie's** I jig, **wa'thatenonniakén:ni'** he jigged, **teiakotenonniakénnion** she is jigging.
With N -'nikonhr- mind: **wa'thi'nikonhrakén:ni'** I convinced him, I won him over, **wa'thake'nikonhrakén:ni'** he won me over.
With SRF -ate-, N -'shenn- aim, and TRNL: **ia'thate'shennakén:ni'** he aimed for it.

-**kennor**- V rain: **iokennó:re's** it rains, **eniokén:nore'** it will rain, **wa'okén:nore'** it rained, **iokennó:ron** it is raining.
With PROG -hatie-: **iokennoronhátie's** it is raining off and on; and CISL: **taiokennoronhátie'** rain is on the way.

-**kenra**- V be pale: **iokén:ra** it is pale, light-coloured.
With N -ihn- skin, leather: **renhnakén:ra** he is light-skinned, **iehnakén:ra** she is light-skinned.

With N -nats- wheat: **onatsakén:ra** rice.
With N -nenh- seed: **onenhakén:ra** Indian white corn.
With N -rist- iron, steel: **karistakén:ra** tin.
With N -ronhi- sky, heaven, blue: **oronhiakén:ra** light blue.
With N -tsi'ts- flower: **iotsi'tsakén:ra** (it is) a light-coloured flower.
With N -'nahs- feather, plume: **o'nahsakén:ra** swan.

kèn:reks lion

Cf. Genreks Lyon (Galissonnière: 7r); *kēnreks* Lion (Marcoux: 231); *Kenreks* lion, tigre (Cuoq: 19); *ken reks* lion (Anon: 16); *kén-reks* lion (Cory: 89); *gen rehks* lion (Jamieson 2: 11); Wyandot *yę'ric* lion (Barbeau 1960: 104)

-kenser[on]- V plane, slice, scrape, with DLC:
tehakénserons he is planing it,
tenhakén:sere' he will plane it,
wa'tekkén:sere' I planed it, I scraped it, I sliced it, **tehokénseron** he has planed it.
With DISTR -onkw-: **wa'tekkenserón:ko'** I sliced it all.
With N -hnenna't- potato: **wa'thahnenna'takén:sere'** he sliced potatoes.
With N -'nionkser- onion: **wa'tha'nionkserakén:sere'** he sliced onions.
With N -'wahr- meat: **wa'tha'wahrakén:sere'** he sliced meat.

-kentst- V be leftover scraps, refuse
With SRF -at-: **watkéntston** (there are) scraps left.
With N -hnek- liquid: **wa'khné:kentste'** I drained it (for example, beans or potatoes), **iakohnekéntston** she has drained it.
With SRF -ate- and N -khw- food: **watekhwakéntston** there are food scraps left.
With N -nonw- bottom water, dregs: **kenonwakéntstha'** I am draining it, straining it, **enienón:wakentste'** she will drain it, **wa'kenón:wakentste'** I drained it, **iakononwakéntston** she has drained it; and INSTR -hkw-: **ienonwakentstáhkhwa'** colander.

Cf. watkénhston it has been put to waste (Gabriel: 26)

ken' náhe' some time after, a while ago

-ken'ker- N eyebrow: **okèn:kera'**
POSS: **kken'kerà:ke** (on) my eyebrow, **raken'kerà:ke** (on) his eyebrow, **ieken'kerà:ke** (on) her eyebrow

-ken'kwar- N forehead: **okèn:kwara'**
POSS: **kken'kwarà:ke** (on) my forehead, **raken'kwarà:ke** (on) his forehead, **ieken'kwarà:ke** (on) her forehead.

ken'takén:ra soft maple

-ken'tok-/-ken'to'k- V knock, flick with the finger.
With DLC: **wa'tionkkèn:toke'** she flicked her finger against my forehead, **wa'thikèn:toke'** I flicked my finger against his forehead.
With DISTR -hon- and CISL: **thaken'to'ókhons** he is knocking, **takken'to'ókhon'** I knocked.

-ken'tor[en]- V bandage: **wa'kheken'tó:ren'** I put a bandage on her.
With SRF -at-: **ratken'tó:rens** he is putting a bandage on (himself), **eniontken'tó:ren'** she will put a bandage on, **wahatken'tó:ren'** he put a bandage on, **iakotkèn:tore'** she has a bandage on.

With SRF -at- and REV -kw-:
wa'katken'torá:ko' I took off the bandage.

With SRF -at- and INSTR -hkw-:
iontken'toráhkhwa' bandage.

-ken'tstar- N top part of the forehead, where the hairline begins: **okèn:tstara'** POSS: **kken'tstarà:ke** (on) my forehead, **raken'tstarà:ke** (on) his forehead, **ieken'tstarà:ke** (on) her forehead.

With V -a'tarih[en]-/-tarih[en]- be hot, warm: **wakken'tstarataríhen** my forehead is hot, **roken'tstarataríhen** his forehead is hot, **iakoken'tstarataríhen** her forehead is hot.

With V -ia'[k]- hit, slap: **enkonken'tstaráia'ke'** I will smack your forehead.

• Okèn:tstara' wahá:ton'. He became bald.

-ker- N corn tassle, silk: **ókera'**

-keri- V be broth
With N -a'kenhr- ashes, dirt: **o'kenhrákeri'** lye.
With N -hnek- liquid: **ohnekákeri'** broth; and **kítkit** chicken: **kítkit ohnekákeri'** chicken broth.
With N -hso'kw- nut: **ohso'kwákeri'** coffee.
With N -nen't- evergreen: **onon'tákeri'** or **onen'tákeri'** beer.
With N -ront- log, beam: **orontákeri'** (maple) sap.

-keri'ta['w]- fry. *See* -takeri'ta['w]-/ -keri'ta['w]-

-keront-/-okeront- V square
With SRF -ate- and DLC: **teiotekerón:te'** it is square; the suit of diamonds in cards.
With N -ia't- body: **tia'tokerón:te'** I am

lying on my side; and SRF -at- and CAUS -t-: **wa'katia'tokerón:tate'** I got on my side.

With N -nontsi[st]- head, and DLC: **Tehotinontsistokerón:te'** (they are) Germans.

With N -ronhkwe'n- spine, back: **ioronhkwe'nakerón:te'** the roof is squared, pitched.

Cf. Atageronte quarré (Bruyas: 31); *Gannnsogeronte* maison, cabane dont le toit est en talus (Bruyas: 82); *tio te ke ron te* square (Anon: 21); *í:iens teiotekerón:te'* rectangle (-es- be long, tall) (Lazore: 89)

-kerothiha-/-kerothiw- V comb: **rikerothí:ha** I am combing, brushing his hair.
With SRF -at-: **katkerothí:ha** I am combing, brushing (myself), **wa'katkeróthiwe'** I combed, brushed my hair; **atkerothí:ha** comb.

-ket- V scrape: **raké:tas** he scrapes it, **énkkete'** I will scrape it, **wahá:kete'** he scraped it, **wa'kón:kete'** I scratched you (on the surface, or moving back and forth), **wahákkete'** he scratched me, **wakké:ten** I have scraped it.
With SRF -at-: **katké:tas** I am scratching myself.
With N -hson-/-hsw- back: **rakhswaké:tas** he is scratching my back, **wahíhswakete'** I scratched his back, **tákhswaket** Scratch my back!
With N -hson'kar-/-hswen'kar- board: **rahson'karaké:tas** (he is) a carpenter; and NMZR -'sher-, V -nekenhter- handsome man, and DLC: **tehnihson'karaketa'-sheranekénhteron** two young carpenters (*a playful expression from Mike Norton*).
With N -hso'kw- nut, and CAUS -'t-: **iehso'kwaketà:tha'** nutmeg.

• Enwá:ton ken enhsékhswakete'. Can you scratch my back?

-ketskw- V raise upright: **rakétskwas** he raises it upright (from horizontal to vertical position), **khekétskwas** I get her up, **enkkétsko'** I will raise it, **wahakétsko'** he raised it, **wakkétskwen** I have raised it.
With SRF -at-: **katkétskwas** I get up, **wa'katkétsko'** I got up, **wakatkétskwen** I have gotten up.
With N -ahkar- wood chips, shavings: **wa'kahkarakétsko'** I flipped the arm up to uncover the vent holes in a storm window; and SRF -at-: **watahkarakétskwas** storm window with vent holes.
With SRF -ani-, N -hna'tsh- buttocks, and CISL: **tewanihna'tshakétskwas** it is bucking (a horse or a cow).
With N -(h)nhoh- door: **wa'kehnhohakétsko'** I lifted up the (trap) door.
With N -ra'wist- peel, and CISL: **thara'wistakétskwas** he is turning the page, **takera'wistakétsko'** I turned the page, **tewakera'wistakétskwen** I have turned the page, **tasera'wistakétsko** Turn the page!
With N -ront- log, beam: **kerontakétskwas** I raise a log.
With SRF -ate-, N -'nerohkw- box, and DLC: **tewate'nerohkwakétskwas** cart (with two wheels, pulled by a horse).
With N -'nikonhr- mind: **Ka'nikonhrakétskwen** Condolence; and REP: **saionke'nikonhrakétsko'** she lifted my spirits.
Cf. Garontagetsk8an gaianderesera lever l'arbre de paix (Bruyas: 49); *Kerontaketskwas* lever l'arbre, c.-à.-d. élire un chef (Cuoq: 107)

-ke'rh- N unkempt, messy hair
With V -r- put in, and DLC: **tekkè:rhare'** my hair is every which way (like after I've gotten up in the morning), **tehakè:rhare'** his hair is messy, **teiekè:rhare'** her hair is messy.
• Tekkè:rhare' né: tsi iaò:te átste'. My hair is messy because it's windy out.

-ke'toht- V appear, emerge: **roke'tóhtha'** he emerges, he appears, **enwakkè:tohte'** I will appear, **wahokè:tohte'** he appeared, **wakke'tóhton** I have appeared.
With REP: **sahokè:tohte'** again he appeared (he is back again).

-ke'tot- V protrude: **iokè:tote'** it is protruding, sticking out.
With SRF -at-: **ratke'tótha'** he shows himself, he peeks (in), **wahatke'tó:ten'** he showed himself.
With SRF -at- and CISL: **tewatke'tótha'** it keeps looking in or this way (an animal), **tahatke'tó:ten'** he looked in, **tontke'tó:ten'** it looked in (an animal), **thotkè:tote'** he is looking in, **tiotkè:tote'** it is showing over here.
With SRF -at- and TRNL: **iahatke'tó:ten'** he looked out or that way, **iahontke'tó:ten'** it looked out or that way (an animal), **átste' ieiotkè:tote'** it is showing outside.
With SRF -at-, N -en'nahs- tongue, and CISL: **tkaten'nahsake'tótha'** I stick out, show my tongue, **takaten'nahsake'tó:ten'** I stuck out my tongue, **thoten'nahsakè:tote'** he has his tongue sticking out.
With N -honro't- pipe, tube: **iohonro'takè:tote'** the pipe is sticking out (out of a wall, out of the roof); and CONTR and TRNL: **thiehohonro'takè:tote'**

someone with a Native father and White mother.

With N -i'ta- excrement, or N -neri'tst-bellybutton, navel, and CISL: **tio'takè:tote'** or **tioneri'tstakè:tote'** squash.

-kha- V attach, piece together, with DLC: **tekékhas** I attach things, piece them together (for example, pieces of a puzzle), **wa'tiékha'** she pieced it together, **teiakókhen** she has pieced it together, **tekákhen** it is joined, put together, **tehníkhen** they are twins, **tekeníkhen** they are female twins.

With DISTR -nion-: **tekekhánions** I am joining them together, **wa'tiekhánion'** she put it together.

With REV -hsi-: **tekekháhsions** I am separating it, **wa'tkekháhsi'** I separated it, **tewakekháhsion** I have separated it; and SRF -ate-: **wa'tiatiatekháhsi'** we two separated (either formally, i.e., divorce, or as we are walking along).

With N -a'ar- net, curtain, and REV -hsi-: **wa'tka'arakháhsi'** I parted the curtains or drapes, I put them to the side, **tesa'arakháhsi** Put the curtains to the side!

With SRF -at-, N -honro't- pipe, tube, and REV -hsi-: **wa'tewathonro'takháhsi'** the pipe separated.

With N -ihn- skin, leather, and DISTR -nion-: **tekihnakhánions** I am piecing cloth together; and **áhsire'** (-ahsir- blanket, shawl): **tekenhnakhánion áhsire'** quilt.

With N -nat- town, settlement, variant -okha- of the root, DISTR -nion-, and DLC: **tsi tekanatokhánion** at the streets.

With N -rihw- matter, message: **tekarihwákhen** a word or message that is put together, a sentence that is put together.

With N -'now- hump, padlock, and

kanà:taro (-na'tar[o][k]- bread): **teio'nowákhen kanà:taro** crusty bread.

=kha ATTR characterized by

khá:re' ó:nen finally

khé:re instead, **khé:re káti' ken** I suppose so, I guess so

-khw- N food: **kákhwa'** POSS: **raókhwa'** his food; and **ráskan** (-skan- skeleton): **ráskan raókhwa'** mushroom.

With SRF -ate- and possibly DISTR -nionkw-: **wa'katekhwanión:ko'** I took bites out of it (like when I'm eating a whole apple).

With SRF -ate- and V -atatenr- have left-overs, a surplus: **wakatekhwatatén:ron** I have food left over, **iotekhwatatén:ron** there is food left over.

With V -ent- wear out, end, and INCH -'-: **kekhwén:ta's** I finish eating, **eniekhwén:ta'ne'** she will finish eating, **wa'kekhwén:ta'ne'** I finished eating, **rokhwentà:'on** he has finished eating.

With SRF -ate- and V -her-/-hr- set on top of: **atekhwà:ra** table (*see* -atekhwahra- for more forms).

With SRF -ate- and V -hsa'-/-isa'- finish, complete: **ratekhwísa's** he eats it all, **wa'katekhwísa'** I ate it up, I finished it, **rotekhwíson'** he has finished eating it.

With V -iio- be good, nice: **kakhwí:io** (it is) good food.

With SRF -ate- and V -kentst- be leftover scraps, refuse: **watekhwakéntston** there are food scraps left.

With SRF -ate- and V -kw- pick: **katekhwákwas** I take a bite of food, I bite into it, **wa'katekhwá:ko'** I took a bite of food, **wakatekhwákwen** I have taken a bite.

With V -onni- make: **kekhón:nis** I cook,
prepare a meal, **wa'kekhón:ni'** I cooked,
rokhón:ni he is cooking; and CAUS -'t-:
iekhonnià:tha' one cooks with it,
tsi iekhonnià:tha' kitchen; with SRF -ate-
and V -onni- make: **katekhón:nis** I eat,
wa'katekhón:ni' I ate, **ionkwatekhón:ni**
we ate, we had a meal.
With REFL -atate- and V -tokeri[k]-/
-okeri[k]- gather, shirr:
wa'katatekhókerike' I cut down on
eating.
With V -weienhon- be good at, capable at:
kekhwaweiénhon I know how to cook.

kí:ken or **kí:** this, these

kítkit chicken; **kítkit rá:tsin** rooster (-tsin-
be a male animal)

ki' in fact, actually, indeed

ki' nà:'a Oh sure! Like heck! Nonsense!
NOTE: GM translated this as 'probably' and
Horne (2003: 94) as 'Oh well!'. It is often
used by non-speakers in, for example,
"Your SISTER, ki' nà:'a!" ("You are so full
of s**t!")

Kóh Here! (presenting something)

-koh- V go get something: **rakóhe'** he is here
to get it, **wa'kkóhe'** I am going to get it,
iekóhe's she goes to get it, **enkkóha'** I
will go get it, **wa'kkóha'** I went to get it,
skóha Get it!
With PAST -hne': **wakkohónhne'** I have
gone to get it.
With CISL: **tahatikóhe'** they are coming
to get it; and PAST -hne': **thotikohónhne'**
they have come to get it.
With N -ient- wood: **wahaientakóhe'**
he is going to get wood.

-koh- N blockage, clog
With V -ohro[k]- insert:
wahatikohò:roke' they blocked it,
rotikohò:ron they have blocked it; and
DISTR -hon-: **rotikohohrókhon** they
filled them in, they blocked it; with SRF
-at- and V -ohro[k]- insert: **iotkohò:ron**
it is blocked or clogged.
With V -ohtshi- remove, pull out:
wa'kkohóhtshi' I unblocked it, unclogged it.
• Oneráhsa' rotikohohrókhon. They
corked (the bottles).

-koharohs- N something soaking wet:
okoharóhsa' or **akoharóhsa'**
• Akwé:kon okoharóhsa' ón:ton'
akwatahkwénnia' ontia'taná:wenhste'.
My clothes got all soaking wet [when]
I got wet.

-kon LOC inside

-konhkwar- N nipple: **okónhkwara'**
With **owirà:'a** (-wir- offspring), and
POSS: **owirà:'a akokónhkwara'** nipple
for a baby bottle, pacifier.
Cf. okonkwara [nipple for a bottle]
(Ledger: 85)

-konhre[k]- V hit, punch: **kkòn:reks** I hit it,
enkkòn:reke' I will hit it,
wahakkòn:reke' he hit me, he punched
me, **wahonwakòn:reke'** she hit him, she
punched him, **wakkonhré:kon** or
wakkòn:re I have hit it, **skòn:rek** Hit it!
With N -'nahkw- drum, barrel, and CAUS
-st-: **ie'nahkwakonhrékstha'** drumstick.

-konhretsh- N block of wood: **okonhrétsha'**
With LOC -'ke, on, at: **okonhretshà:ke**
on the block of wood.
With V -hkw- pick up, and DLC:

wa'thakonhrétshahkwe' he picked up the block of wood.
With V -ke- amount to, and DLC:
tekakonhrétshake two blocks of wood.
With V -kste- be heavy:
iokonhretshákste' (it is) a heavy block of wood.

-konhs- N face: **okónhsa'** face
POSS: **kkonhsà:ke** (on) my face, **rakonhsà:ke** (on) his face, **iekonhsà:ke** (on) her face.
With V -es- be long, and REP: **tsikónhses** pike.
With V -hnir- be hard, solid:
rokonhsahní:ron he has a hard face, he is pushy, he will stick to it (maybe to a lie), **iakokonhsahní:ron** she has a hard face.
With SRF -at-, V -hwahnha[k]-/-hnha[k]- wrap, tie around, and DLC:
teiontkonhsáhnhaks she is putting on a (Covid) mask, **tenhsatkonhsáhnhake'** you will put on a mask, **tewakatkonhsáhnhen** I have on a mask.
With SRF -at- and V -nohare-/-ohare- wash:
wa'katkonhsóhare' I washed my face, **satkonhsóhare** Wash your face!
With V -ot- stand, INCH -'-, and CONTR and TRNL: **thiahakonhsó:ta'ne'** he landed on his face, face first.
With V -ra'nentakt-/-nentakt- stick something to: **enkkonhsanén:takte'** I will paste a stamp on it, **wahakonhsanén:takte'** he stuck a stamp on it.

Cf. Laurentian *Hegouscon* the face (Biggar: 241y); Wendat *Aonchia* visage (Sagard: Me2)

-konhston'rh- N beard, whiskers, mustache: **okonhstòn:rha'**
With V -es- be long, and DLC:
tehokonhstòn:rhes he has a long beard, **teiotikonhstòn:rhes** barley.
With SRF -at- and V -ia'k- cut, sever:
katkonhstòn:rhia'ks I am shaving, **enhatkonhstòn:rhia'ke'** he will shave, **wahatkonhstòn:rhia'ke'** he shaved, **rotkonhston'rhià:kon** he has shaved; and CAUS -st-: **iontkonhston'rhià:kstha'** razor; and **à:share'** (-a'shar- knife): **iontkonhston'rhià:kstha' à:share'** razor blade.
With V -ont- attach, and DLC:
tehokonhstòn:rhonte' he has a beard or mustache.
With V -[t]- be one, and REP:
shakonhstòn:rha Santa Claus.

Cf. teiotikonstonrhes Bled barbe (Marcoux: 41); *tio ti kons ton rhes* rye (Anon: 7); *tio ti kon ston res* barley (D'Ailleboust: 26); *de yo dih genhs tenr hoh de* barley (Jamieson 1: 6); *teioti'konh'stón:re's* barley, long whiskers (Gabriel: 11); *teiotikonhstòn:rhes* (or *onatsa'kó:wa*) barley (Lazore: 12)

-konniens- be very clean, neat. *See* -kwenniens-/-konniens-

-kon[t]- V persist, persevere
With CISL: **tió:konte'** or (with SRF -at-) **tiótkon** always, all the time.
With CONTR, TRNL, and DLC:
thia'teká:konte' again and again, always.
With INSTR -hkw- and TRNL or CISL:
ienkkón:tahkwe' I will keep doing it, I will continue, **iahakón:tahkwe'** he kept doing it, he continued, **takakón:tahkwe'** it continued, persisted.
With SRF -at-: **ronwatkóntha'** they bully him, they pick on him, **wahiiatkón:ten'** I got after him, I got on his case, **wa'kheiatkón:ten'** I got on her case, **shakótkonte'** he is bullying her.
With N -'nikonhr- mind, and CISL:

tewake'nikòn:rakonte' I keep at it, I persevere, **tio'nikòn:rakonte'** it is continuous; and INSTR -hkw-: **tewake'nikonhrakontáhkwen** I have my mind set on it, I am focused on it, **tho'nikonhrakontáhkwen** he is focused on it, **tiako'nikonhrakontáhkwen** she is focused on it.

• Tóka' 5 weeks takakón:tahkwe' tsi wa'okén:nore'. Maybe it has been 5 weeks of straight rain. (Letter 1945, June)

-kont- N bridge of the nose: **okón:ta'**
With V -ot- stand: **rokón:tote'** he has a bump on his nose.

Cf. ionterho tsi teiekontiakon iekenkwarake [have them smear it on the bridge of the nose, on the forehead] (Beauvais: 2); Cayuga *ogǫ́da'* bridge of one's nose (Dyck et al.: 46); Seneca *ogö:do'* nose (Chafe, English-Seneca Dictionary: 113)

-konte'n- N lamprey: **okontè:na'**

Cf. okontēna Anguille (Marcoux: 16); *Okontena* anguille (Cuoq: 32)

-kontsher- N paint: **okóntshera'**
With ATTR =shon'a, pluralizer: **okontshera'shòn:'a** paints.
With SRF -at-, variant -kont- of -kontsher-, obscure V -e'ek- and DISTR -hon-: **katkonte'ékhons** I am putting on rouge (makeup) on my cheeks, cheekbones, **wa'katkonte'ékhon'** I put on rouge, **iakotkonte'ékhon** she has on rouge; with SRF -at- and CAUS -t-: **iontkonte'éktha'** rouge. (This is a tentative analysis suggested by Akwiratékha' Martin.)
With V -(h)rho- coat: **kkontsheráhrhos** I am painting it, **wahakontsheráhrho'** he painted it, **rokontsheráhrhon** he has painted it.

-konwar- N falseface, face: **okón:wara'** *An older word, not used much nowadays.*
With V -es- be long, and PART: **nikakón:wares** it has a long face (talking about an animal, maybe a horse or moose).
With V -otahrho[k]- hook: **wa'kkonwarotáhrhoke'** I put the bridle on (a horse), **skonwarotáhrhok** Put the bridle on! and SRF -at- and INSTR -st-: **atkonwarotahrhókstha'** bridle.
With SRF -at- and V -'rhoro[k]-/-oro[k]- cover: **iakotkonwaró:ron** she has on a mask; and CAUS -st-: **iontkonwaróokstha'** Hallowe'en mask.

Cf. Gagonhara le milieu ou le gros os du nez, inde: *Nigagonhres* dit on d'un long visage (Bruyas: 49); *akōnwara* Masque (Marcoux: 244); *Akonwara* visage, masque (Cuoq: 1); *Akónwara'* mask (Hewitt: 335); *ia kot kon wa ro ron* mask (Anon: 39); *a gon wah rah* mask (Jamieson 2: 5); *aht kon wa ro dahr hohs* halter (Jamieson 3: 5)

kon'tátie' all day
With DISTR -hshon: **kon'tatiè:shon** all day long.
• Kon'tátie' watió'te' katenónhnha'. I work all day minding (them).
• Louie kon'tátie' tsi sewanónhsote' iè:re's. Louie is over at your (plural) house all day. (Lettter 1945, Jan)

-kon'tsher- N pound
With V -har-/-ihar- hang up: **wahakon'tsherihá:ren'** he weighed it; and REFL -atat-: **wahatatkon'tsherihá:ren'** he weighed himself.
With V -[t]- be one, and REP: **skakòn:tshera** one pound.

kó:ra government, governor: **kó:ra** government, **rakó:ra** governor, president, he works for the government, **iekó:ra** she works for the government.

With ATTR =hne, at: **Koráhne** Canada.

Cf. "the king of England called by us *Corachkoo*" (Brodhead IV: 909); *kolahkowah* King (Gallatin: 383); *Kora koʁa* le grand gouverneur, le roi d'Angleterre, la Reine (Cuoq 1866: 90); "KORA. M. l'abbé Ferland assigne la véritable origine de ce mot, en le faisant venir du nom du célèbre Arendt Van Corlaer." (Cuoq: 167); *Kő-rā* "King" (Dutch governor) (Cory: 51); *go rah* queen (Jamieson 2: 11); *rakóhra* governor (Gabriel: 62); Wyandot *kurà'kuwá* man of authority, important person, man of wealth (Barbeau: 261, 262, 271)

=kowa ATTR great. For example:
Kaianere'kó:wa the Great Law;
kaniatara'kehkó:wa ocean;
ohniare'kó:wa serpent;
onon'onsera'kó:wa pumpkin;
otsinowen'kó:wa rat; **skanaie'kó:wa** peacock; **tako'skó:wa** wildcat, tiger;
Tsi kanataien'kó:wa Philadelphia, PA.

-kowan[en]-/-owan[en]- V be big: **kkowá:nen** I am big, **rakowá:nen** he is big, **iekowá:nen** she is big, **kakowá:nen** it (an animal) is big, **kowá:nen** it is big.
With CISL: **kwah né: tkowá:nen** this is the greatest.
With CAUS -ht-: **kkowanáhtha'** I am making it bigger, enlarging it, **wa'ekó:wanahte'** she enlarged it.
With N -ahi- fruit, berry, and REP: **sewahió:wane'** apple; and ATTR =onwe, genuine: **sewahiowane'ón:we** crabapple.
With N -ahiakwir- toe: **kahiakwirowá:nen** my big toe.

With N -ahkwari['t]- bear: **wahkwari'towá:nen** (it is) a big bear.
With N -ahtsohkw- morsel, portion: **wahtsohkowá:nen** (it is) a big morsel, a big portion.
With N -atekhwahra- table, and NMZR -'tsher-: **watekhwahra'tsherowá:nen** (it is) a big table.
With V -atetsh[en]- dream, and NMZR -hser-: **wakatetshenhserowá:nen** I have made a big issue of it, bigger than it really is.
With V -athahsteren- put on pants, trousers, and NMZR -'tsher-: **wathahsteren'tsherowá:nen** (they are) big trousers.
With N -athenno-/-athenno'tsher- ball: **wathenno'tsherowá:nen** (it is) a big ball.
With N -atokw-/-atokwahtsher- spoon: **watokwahtsherowá:nen** (it is) a big spoon.
With empty N -e't-: **iawe'towá:nen** it is a large amount.
With V -hio'tsis[t]- be salty, sour: **kahio'tsistowá:nen's** coarse salt, rock salt.
With N -hsenn- name: **rahsennowá:nen** he has a big name, big reputation, he is famous, (he is) a chief; and INCH -ha'-: **wahahsennowáhnha'** he got a big name, a reputation.
With N -hsnonhs- finger, hand, and DLC: **tekehsnonhsowá:nen's** I have big fingers, big hands.
With V -hsonw- be a hole: **iohsoniowá:nen** (it is) a big hole.
With N -hwatsir- family: **khwatsirowá:nen** I have a big family.
With N -ient- wood: **Kaientowá:nen** Peach Pit game.
With N -itiohkw- group: **kentiohkowá:nen** (it is) a big group, **ionkwentiohkowá:nen** we are a big group.

With N -itstenhr- rock, boulder: **kentstenhrowá:nen** (it is) a big rock.
With N -i'tonw- pile, heap: **io'toniowá:nen** (it is) a big heap.
With N -nehson- hell, ATTR =hronon, resident of, and NMZR -'tsher-: **ranehsonhronon'tsherowá:nen** (he is) a big devil.
With N -nenhr- crowd: **kanenhrowá:nen** (it is) a big crowd.
With N -neni- stone, rock: **onenió:wane'** bullet.
With N -nennawen['t]- tobacco pipe, and REP: **Shotinennawen'tó:wane'** Cayugas, as referred to in council.
With N -neri'tst- bellybutton: **saneri'tstowá:nen** you have a big bellybutton.
With N -(h)nhoskw- cheeks, jowl, and DLC: **teiehnhoskowá:nen's** she has big cheeks.
With N -nonhkware't- hair: **iakononhkware'towá:nen** she has big hair.
With N -nonhs- house: **kanonhsowá:nen** (it is) a big house; and ATTR ='ke, at: **kanonhsowanèn:ke** at the hospital; with SRF -ate-, N -nonhs- house, and CAUS -ht-: **wa'katenonhsó:wanahte'** I made the house bigger.
With N -nont- mountain, hill: **ionontowá:nen's** (there are) big mountains (for example, the Rockies or Adirondacks); and ATTR =haka/=aka, people of, and REP: **Shotinontowane'á:ka** Seneca.
With N -onhnh- life, and CISL: **tsonhnhó:wane'** whale.
With N -renh- vine, (tree) limbs, and REP: **Sharenhó:wane'** Mohawk title name 4.
With N -rihw- matter, message, and CAUS -ht-: **waharihó:wanahte'** he announced it.
With N -tsenh- fire: **Katsenhowá:nen** Grand Council.

With N -wer- wind, air, and REP: **skawiró:wane'** or **skaweró:wane'** turkey.

Cf. Sagok8annatanni Onnontio Onnontio a enlevé, s'est fait maitre de (Bruyas: 51); *Ragoáno* Chief (Pyrlaeus: 234); *ratigowaneaghse* [chiefs] (Little Abraham in Claus C-1478, 476, line 18); *rakowanas* leading chiefs of each of the five cantons (Schoolcraft: 122); "Takaweanadennyoh Kanyenkehàga *Rakowànea* Thayendanegea, Roewayats" Translated into the Mohawk Language by Captn Joseph Brant (Pilling: 15); *Rakowanenh* High Chief (Hale: 136); Laurentian *Agouhanna* Seigneur (Biggar: 245); Wendat *hati8annens* les anciens, les viellards, les gens de conseil qui deliberent des affaires, qui les decident et qui les reglent (Potier: 254); Onondaga *hachennoanen* Chef (Shea: 32); Onondaga *ne hagoáno* Chief (Zeisberger: 36)

-ko'ts- N crest (of a bird), comb (of a rooster): **okò:tsa'**
With V -her-/-hr- set on top of: **roko'tsáhere'** he (a rooster) has a comb.
With SRF -at- and V -onni- make: **wa'katko'tsón:ni'** I fixed my hair, **iakotko'tsón:ni** she has fixed her hair; with V -onni- make, and PURP -'n-: **wa'onkko'tsonnià:ne'** I'm going to get my hair done.
With V -o'ten- be a kind of, and PART: **nikko'tsò:ten** my hair style, **niieko'tsò:ten** her hair style.

Cf. Okotsia huppe, touffe de plummes que portent certains oiseaux (Cuoq: 32); De là: *Iokotsiote* nom d'un oiseau du Canada ... On l'appelle ici, *récollet*, à cause d'une certain resemblance entre sa huppe et le capuchon des Religieux de St. François (Cuoq: 173–4)

-ks- N dish, plate: **káksa'**
    With LOC -kon, inside: **káksakon** in the dish.
    With V -her-/-hr- set on top of, and DISTR -onnion-: **keksahrónnions** I am setting the table, **wa'keksahrónnion'** I set the table, **seksahrónnion** Set the table!
    With V -hriht- break into pieces, smash, and DLC: **wa'tieksà:rihte'** she broke the dish.
    With V -hri'- get broken into pieces, shatter, and DLC: **wa'tkaksà:ri'ne'** the dish broke.
    With SRF -ate-, V -hwe'nonni-/-kwe'nonni- fold, and DLC: **teioteksakwe'nón:ni** (it is) a round dish.
    With V -ien- put down, have, and CISL; and **nà:kon** down: **nà:kon tiéksaiens** saucer.
    With V -ientot- stack in a pile, and DLC: **tehaksaientótha'** he is stacking dishes, **wa'thaksaientó:ten'** he stacked dishes.
    With V -ke- amount to, and DLC: **tekáksake** two dishes, cups, pecks; or PART: **wísk nikáksake** five dishes, cups.
    With V -nohare-/-ohare- wash: **keksóhares** I am washing dishes, **wa'keksóhare'** I washed dishes, **wakeksóhare** I have washed dishes; and DISTR -nion-: **wa'keksoharénion'** I washed dishes.
    With V -rakew-/-okew- wipe, and DISTR -nion-: **wa'keksokewánion'** I wiped (dried) the dishes.
    With V -[t]- be one, and REP: **skáksa** one dish.

-ksa['t]- N child
    With ATTR ='a/=ha, diminutive: **raksà:'a** boy, **eksà:'a** girl, **íksa** Child!
    With ATTR =okon'a, pluralizer: **ratiksa'okòn:'a** children, **kontiksa'okòn:'a** girls.
    With DLC: **tehniksà:'a** two boys, two children, **tekeniksà:'a** two girls.

With COIN shi-: **shikeksà:'a** when I was a child.
    With V -iio- be good, nice: **raksa'tí:io** he is a nice boy, a good boy.

-kste- V be heavy: **iókste'** it is heavy.
    With NEG: **iah teiókste'** it is not heavy.
    With BEN -'s-: **wakekstè:se'** I find it heavy, **rokstè:se'** he finds it heavy, **iakokstè:se'** she finds it heavy.
    With N -ahsir- blanket, shawl: **iohsirákste'** (it is) a heavy blanket.
    With N -a'ther- basket: **io'therákste'** (it is) a heavy basket.
    With N -ian- footprint, track: **roianákste'** he walks heavy, he lumbers (as if he is making an effort at walking).
    With N -iar- bag: **ioiarákste'** (it is) a heavy bag.
    With N -ia't- body: **roia'tákste'** he is heavy.
    With N -konhretsh- block of wood: **iokonhretshákste'** (it is) a heavy block of wood.
    With N -nennotsher- package, parcel: **ionennotsherákste'** (it is) a heavy package.
    With N -nieht- snow: **ioniehtákste'** (it is) heavy snow.
    With N -wer- wind, air: **iowerákste'** the air is heavy.
    With N -'nerohkw- box: **io'nerohkwákste'** (it is) a heavy box, and BEN -'s-: **wake'nerohkwakstè:se'** I find the box heavy.
    With N -'sere[ht]- vehicle, car: **io'serehtákste'** freight train.
    • Iókste' tsi ní:tsi sanonhtónnion. It's heavy how you're thinking (maybe you heard someone died or other bad news).

-ksten- V be old (animate), with ATTR ='a/=ha, diminutive: **rokstén:ha** he is old,

(he is) an old man, **iakokstén:ha** she is old, **akokstén:ha** or **okstén:ha** (she is) an old woman, **rotikstén:ha** old people.
With ATTR =okon'a, pluralizer: **rotikstenhokòn:'a** old people.
With INCH -ha'-: **wahokstén:ha'ne'** he got old; and PROG -hatie-: **rokstenha'onhátie'** he is getting old, **iakokstenha'onhátie'** she is getting old.
With N -'nikonhr- mind: **ro'nikonhrakstén:ha** he has an old soul or spirit (can be said of younger persons who are ahead of their years).

Cf. ochtaha an old man (van den Bogaert: 54); "After the Agoïanders comes the senate, composed of the Old Men or Old People, called in their language, *Agokstennha.*" (Lafitau I: 294); *Rockstáha* ein alter Mann, *agokstáha* eine alte Frau (Pyrlaeus: 2l); *ne rokstēnha* Doyen (Marcoux: 131); *roks ten ha* old (Diabo: 51); *rikstenha* my husband, *kekstenha* my wife (Mary Deer's class notes, Oct. 12, 1971)

-kw- V pick: **íkkwas** I am picking it, **rákwas** he picks, **iékwas** she picks, **wà:kko'** I picked it, **wahá:ko'** he picked it, **wákkwen** I have picked it.
With TRNL: **iahákko'** I got it, **iahá:ko'** he got it, **iewákkwen** I have gotten it.
With PART and TRNL: **Tó: nia'ká:ko'?** How much did it go (sell) for?
With N -ient- wood, and CAUS -ht-: **ieientakwáhtha'** vehicle for transporting wood.
With SRF -ate- and N -khw- food: **katekhwákwas** I take a bite of food, I bite into it, **wa'katekhwá:ko'** I took a bite of food, **wakatekhwákwen** I have taken a bite.
With N -nenhst- corn: **kenenhstákwas** I harvest corn.

With N -'rhotsher- string bean: **ke'rhotsherákwas** I am picking beans, **wa'ke'rhotsherá:ko'** I picked beans.
With N -tsi'ts- flower: **ktsi'tsákwas** I am picking flowers, **wahatsì:tsako'** he picked flowers.

kwah or **akwáh** very, just

kwah tekèn:'en or **kwah tokèn:'en** really

-kwaho- N wolf, belong to the Wolf clan: **okwáho** wolf, **wakkwáho** I am Wolf clan.

Cf. "The Mohawk Indians are divided into three tribes, which are called *Ochkari, Anaware, Oknaho*, that is the Bear, the Turtle and the Wolf." (Megapolensis: 178); *ochquoha* wolf (van den Bogaert: 53); *Hotigsaho* ceux qui sont de la famille du Loup (Galissonnière: 7v); "... *Hoghouaho* ... the [great] wolf" (Lafitau I: 29l); *Oquácho* aus dem Geschlecht des Wolfes (Pyrlaeus: 481); "*Oquacho*, the Wolf, the lowest Class." (Ettwein in Wheeler-Voegelin: 49); *rotiksāho* la bande du loup (Marcoux: 234); *rokwaho* être de la bande du loup (Cuoq: 32); *Okwaho* [wolf] (Onkweonwe: 3); *o kwa ho* wolf (Anon: 16); *okwáho* wolf (Cory: 12); *oh gwah hoh* wolf (Jamieson 1: 5); *Okwáho* Wolf (Horne: 110)

-kwahro't- N boil: **okwahrò:ta'** boil; a kind of medicine.
With SRF -at- and V -kwaront- bulge, lump: **onkwatkwahro'takwarón:ten'** I got a boil, **wakatkwahro'takwá:ronte'** I have a boil.

-kwaht- V bump, hit: **wahíkwahte'** I bumped him, I hit him (maybe with my car),

wahákkwahte' he bumped me, **wahshakókwahte'** he bumped her.

-kwaras- bruise, dent. *See* -takwaras-/-kwaras-

-kwarihsi- straighten. *See* -takwarihsi-/ -kwarihsi-

-kwariht- spread, open out. *See* -takwariht-/ -kwariht-

-kwaront- V bulge, lump: **iokwá:ronte'** it has a bulge, a lump.
With DISTR -on-: **iokwarón:ton** it has bulges in it.
With INCH -'-: **wa'okwarón:ta'ne** a bulge or lump came up, it got a bulge or lump in it.
With N -hnia's- neck, collar: **iakohnia'sakwá:ronte'** goiter.
With SRF -at- and N -kwahro't- boil: **onkwatkwahro'takwarón:ten'** I got a boil, **wakatkwahro'takwá:ronte'** I have a boil.
With N -niatar- river, lake: **Ioniatarakwá:ronte'** Chambly, Québec.
With N -nont- mountain, hill, and PROG -ontie-: **tsi ionontakwarontóntie's** on the waves.
With N -'now- hump, padlock: **io'nowakwá:ronte'** camel.

kwaroró:ha barn owl

-kwat- V curve, with SRF and DLC: **teiotkwá:ton** there is a curve.
With N -hah- road: **teiothahakwá:ton** it is a winding, curvy road.
With N -'nhaht- branch: **teiote'nhahtakwá:ton** it is a crooked branch, there is a curve in the branch.
With CAUS -ho-, *see* -kwatho- hem.

-kwatakw- V fix: **rakwatákwas** he is fixing it, **enkhekwatá:ko'** I will dress her, get her ready, **wahakwatá:ko'** he fixed it, **rokwatákwen** he has fixed it.
With REP: **sakkwatá:ko'** I fixed it again.
With SRF -at-: **ratkwatákwas** he is getting ready, getting dressed, **wahatkwatá:ko'** he got ready, he dressed, **rotkwatákwen** he is ready, he is dressed.
With SRF -at- and REP: **sahatkwatá:ko'** he got better (after being sick); and NEG: **iah tetsakotkwatákwen** she didn't get better.

-kwatho- V visit, pass by: **kkwáthos** I visit (once in a while), **enkkwátho'** I will visit, stop by, **wahakwátho'** he dropped in, **rokwáthon** he has visited.
With CISL: **tahakwátho'** he came by.
With TRNL: **iehakwáthos** he goes over there, passes by there, **ienkkwátho'** I will visit, pass by, **iahakwátho'** he passed by.
With PURP -hser-: **rakwathóhsere'** he is going to come by.
• Enwá:ton' ken iontenhninòn:tha' ienhskwátho'? Can you go to the store?

-kwatho- V hem, with DLC: **tekkwáthos** I am hemming it, **wa'tiekwátho'** she hemmed it, **teiakokwáthon** she has hemmed it.
With N -hsin- leg: **wa'tekhsinakwátho'** I hemmed it.
With N -nentsh- arm: **raotià:tawi wa'thanentshakwátho'** he rolled up the sleeves of his shirt, coat.
With N -'nist- stem: **tehati'nistakwáthos** they are riveting, putting in rivets, **tenhati'nistakwátho'** they will put in rivets.
NOTE: This stem is composed of V -kwat- curve, and CAUS -ho-.
• Akwatháhsteren wa'tekhsinakwátho'. I hemmed my trousers.

Cf. tekkꝹathos ourler (Marcoux: 273);
Tekwathons plier et replier (Cuoq: 47)

-kwatshe- V be well-off, rich: **wakkwátshe'**
I am well-off, **rokwátshe'** he is well-off,
iakokwátshe' she is well-off.
With INCH -'-: **wahokwátshe'ne'** he got
rich.

kwa'kóhrien whippoorwill

Cf. kwa-ko-ri-en ra-o-ta Cypripedium
Calceolus [lady slipper] (Rousseau: 69);
gwah go rih whip-poor-will (Jamieson 1:
7); *wa'kória* whip-o-will (Lazore: 77)

Kwé: or **Kwé** Hello!

Cf. "... the envoy, in place of a death cry,
utters rather a cry of triumph, shouting
kôhé" (Lafitau II: 150); *Kwe* mot de salut
en s'abordant (Cuoq: 27); Wendat "... for
ordinary salutation, they content themselves with a 'good day', which in their
language is expressed by saying *Quoe*"
(Bressani in Thwaites 38: 249)

-kwek- V be the whole of
With N -ahsont- night: **ahsontakwé:kon**
all night.
With N -aten'enhr- fence:
aten'enhrakwé:kon the whole yard.
With N -enhniser- day: **enhniserakwé:kon**
all day.
With N -onhwents-/-onhonts- earth, world:
onhontsakwé:kon the whole world.
With **karonhia'kehró:non** angels (-ronhi-
sky, heaven) and NMZR -'tsher-:
karonhia'kehronon'tsherakwé:kon all
the angels, kingdom of angels *(a playful
expression from Mike Norton)*.

-kwek- V shut, close off: **íkkweks** I shut it
off, **énkkweke'** I will close it off,
wakkwé:kon I have shut it off.

With N -ahonht- ear, and DLC:
tehahónhtakweks his ear blocks up (like
when he has a cold), **tekahonhtakwé:kon**
I am hard of hearing, I am deaf,
tehahonhtakwé:kon he is deaf,
teionhonhtakwé:kon she is deaf.
With SRF -at- and N -hs- lip: **kátskweks** I
shut my mouth, **enkátskweke'** I will close
my mouth, **wahátskweke'** he closed his
mouth, **iakotskwé:kon** she has closed her
mouth, her mouth is closed, **sátskwek**
Close your mouth, be quiet!
See also -'nionkwek- blocked nose.

kwé:nati penguin

-kwenhrar- V occur together, as in a patch:
iokwèn:rare' a patch, a bunch of things
that are together (for example, a bunch of
fish swimming together); and DISTR -on-:
iokwenhrá:ron patches here and there.
• Wa'ketshén:ri' ken' niiohontésha tsi
nón:we iokwèn:rare'. I found where there
is a strawberry patch.

Cf. GagꝹenraronQ être par ci par là en
divers endroits, *Asen niagogꝹenrare
ganniege* les 3 terres d'agnie (Bruyas: 52);
Iokwenrare, pl. *Iokwenraron* temps, lieux
séparés par des distance; intervalles de
temps, de lieux (Cuoq: 6)

-kweni- V be able to do: **kkwénie's** I am able,
enkkwé:ni' I will be able to, I can do it,
enkakwé:ni' it can (be), **wa'kkwé:ni'** I
was able, **wakkwénion** I am able, I can.
With NEG: **iah thahskwé:ni'** you can't.
With COIN and DLC: **sha'tekenikwé:ni'**
they are equally able to do it.
With SRF -at-: **wahontkwé:ni'** they won,
rotkwénion he has won; and PROG
-hatie-: **rotkwenionhátie'** he is winning.
• Enkakwé:ni' ken eh naiá:wen'? Do you
agree it will happen? • Wahakwé:ni'

ahakhró:ri'. He was able to tell me.
• Sha'tekenikwé:ni' akenirahstánion'.
The two can both draw, do art.

-kwennien-/-konnien- V be very clean, neat:
rokwénniens or **rokónniens** he is very
clean, very neat.
With SRF -at-: **rotkwénniens** or
rotkónniens the way he presents (himself) is beautiful, he is elegant,
iakotkwénniens or **iakotkónniens** she
is elegant, **iotkwénniens** or **iotkónniens**
it is elegant, appealing; and NEG:
iah teiotkónniens it is awful, sloppy,
dirty, **iah tehotkónniens** he is sloppy,
not neat.
With CAUS -hst-: **rikonniénhstha'** I
respect him, **wa'khekónnienhste'** I
respected her.
With REFL -atat- and CAUS -hst-:
ratatkonniénhstha' he is proud, stuck-
up, putting on airs, **iontatkonniénhstha'**
she is proud.
With SRF -at-, N -onkwe['t]- person,
human being, and SRF -at-:
rotonkwe'tatkónniens he is an elegant
gentleman, he is distinguished,
iakotonkwe'tatkónniens she is elegant.
With N -rihw- matter, message, and CAUS
-hst-: **kherihwakonniénhstha'** I respect
her, and NMZR -htsher-:
karihwakonnienhstáhtshera' respect.
• Iah tehotkónniens tsi ní:tsi ratia'tahser-
ón:nis. He is sloppy, not neat the way he
dresses.

Cf. Gagonnienston aimer, estimer
(Bruyas: 50); *Gagonnienston* honnorer
(Galissonnière: 49r); *Kekonniēnsta*
respecter (Marcoux: 341); *Iakonnienst*
c'est proper, *kkonienstha* respecter,
honorer, *Katatkonnienstha* se prévaloir,
être arrogant (Cuoq: 151);
a ion tat kon niens te na ko ren esteem

(Diabo: 24, with *akò:ren* somebody else);
rot kwe nions neat (Diabo: 48);
ion tat kon niens tha proud (Diabo: 59);
ka kwe niens tha tse ra respect (Diabo:
64); *Iotenonhwarahtonhtsheratkwéniens*
A respectable drunk (-nonhwar- brain,
-ahton- disappear, NMZR -htsher-)
(Tewaterihwarenia'tha, Summer 1990: 17,
listed under "Fun Words in Kanien'keha")

-kwente- V be an opening, clearing, with DLC
With N -atshat- steam, mist, fog, cloud:
teiotshatakwén:te' there are scattered
clouds (there's space between the clouds).
With N -(h)rh- woods: **teiohrhakwén:te'**
there is a clearing in the woods or in the
bush.

kwéskwes pig

-kwe'niio- V be in charge of
With N -hstien['t]- bone:
kahstien'takwe'ní:io spine.
With N -ia't- body: **raia'takwe'ní:io** he is
in charge, the head, **ieia'takwe'ní:io** she
is in charge, the head.
With N -nat- town, settlement:
ranatakwe'ní:io mayor; and ATTR ='ke,
at: **kanatakwe'niiò:ke** on the main street.
With N -tsinonhiaht- vein:
katsinonhiahtakwe'ní:io the main artery.

-kwe'nonni- fold. *See* -hwe'nonni-/
-kwe'nonni-

-kwe'tar[on]-/-e'tar[on]- V cut, slice off a
piece or chunk: **kkwè:tarons** I slice it, I
cut off a piece (for example, a piece of pie
or fabric), **enkkwè:tare'** I will slice it,
wa'kkwè:tare' I sliced it, **wakkwè:taron**
I have sliced it.
With DISTR -onkw-: **kkwe'tarónkwas** I
am cutting it up, **wa'kkwe'tarón:ko'** I cut
it up.

With N -na'tar[o][k]- bread:
kena'tarakwè:tarons I am slicing bread.
With N -'wahr- meat:
ke'wahrakwè:tarons I am cutting meat into slices, **wa'ke'wahrakwè:tare'** I cut or sliced meat.

-kwir- N tree, sapling: **ó:kwire'**
  With ATTR =shon'a, pluralizer:
  okwire'shòn:'a trees.
  With SRF -at- and V -akenhiat- at the end or peak: **tsi iotkwirakèn:iate'** at the top of the tree.
  With SRF -at-, V -hsa'kt[on]-/-a'kt[on]- bend, and DLC: **teiotkwirà:kton** the tree is bent or crooked.
  With SRF -at- and V -hseronni- dress, prepare: **wahatkwirahserón:ni'** he trimmed the tree.
  With SRF -at- and V -ia'k- cut, sever: **ratkwíria'ks** he is cutting down a tree, **wahatkwíria'ke'** he cut down a tree.
  With V -ot- stand: **iokwí:rote'** there's a tree, standing; and DISTR -on-: **iokwiró:ton** there are trees.

  Cf. oskꝜira branche d'arbre, *kaskꝜiriagon* quitter son pays pour demeurer chez l'ennemi (Bruyas: 98)

kwitó:kwito hairy woodpecker

-kwitsh- N knee: **okwítsha'**
  POSS: **kkwitshà:ke** (on) my knee, **rakwitshà:ke** (on) his knee, **iekwitshà:ke** (on) her knee.
  With V -a- touch, and TRNL, or TRNL and DLC: **iahikwítsha'** or **ia'thikwítsha'** I touched his knee.
  With V -ia'k- hit, bang, and TRNL: **iahonkkwítshia'ke'** I banged my knee.
  With V -ia'[k]- hit, slap: **wahakkwitsháia'ke'** he hit me in the knee.
  With V -nonhwak[t]- be sore, hurt: **wakkwitshanòn:waks** my knee hurts.
  With unclear V, and DLC: **tehakwitsté:ken** he is knock-kneed, **teiekwitsté:ken** she is knock-kneed.
  NOTE: For another (possibly older) root for 'knee', *see* -entshot- kneel.

  Cf. GaꝜitsa le genou (Galissonnière: 23v); *okwītsa* genou (Marcoux: 89); *o kwits ha* knee (Anon: 3); *oh kwihts hah* knee (Jamieson 3: 3)

M

matén:t Aunt! **aktén:t** or **akwatén:t** my aunt
  • Aktent tanon ii watia(tia)terennaienne. My aunt and I are going to church. (Mary Deer's class notes, Nov. 30, 1971)
  Cf. ak tent aunt (Anon: 2); *aktent* my aunt, *satent* your aunt, *onkenitent* our aunt, *matent* aunt (Mary Deer's class notes,

Lesson 5); *Matén:t* or *akwatén:t* My aunt (Horne: 5); *iematénht* aunt (from the French "ma tante") (Gabriel: 10)

menshó: (million) pieces. Probably a borrowing from French *morceaux* 'pieces'.
  • Menshó: tòn:sen'ne'. It fell and broke into a million pieces.

N

náhe' time. For example: **tsi náhe'** since, while, **ken' náhe'** not long after, **wahón:nise' tsi náhe'** a long time ago.

-nahkw- N marriage: **kanáhkwa'**
With V -ati-/-onti- lose, throw: **ronahkóntie's** he walks out on his spouse(s).
With V -hawi-/-enhawi- carry: **ranahkwenhá:wi's** he is living together (with someone) without being married, **ienahkwenhá:wi's** she is living together without being married.
With V -iio be good, nice, and DLC: **teiakeninahkwí:io** we two have a good marriage, **tehninahkwí:io** they have a good marriage.
With V -oreht- judge: **kanahkoréhtha'** matchmaker.

-nahn- V fill: **kanà:non** it is full, **wahá:nahne'** he filled it.

-nahskw- N pet, domestic animal
With V -ien- put down, have: **wakenáhskwaien'** I have a pet.
With V -o'ten- be a kind of, and PART: **Oh na'kanahskò:ten'?** What kind of animal (species) is it?
With V -tshahni[ht]- be industrious, energetic: **ionahskwatshà:ni** (it is) a really frisky, spirited animal.
NOTE: This root is always incorporated; for the unincorporated variant, *see* -tshenen-/-itshenen-.

Cf. Gannask8a esclave, estre esclave (Bruyas: 68); "The third [social class] is (that of) the *Ennaskoua*, that is, of the captives to whom life has been granted, or their children." (Lafitau I: 341); *Gannask8a* Captif (Galissonnière: 16r);

Esclave (Galissonnière: 36r); *enāska* Captif (Marcoux: 55); *Enaska* animal propre au service, animal domestique; captif, esclave, prisonnier (Cuoq: 3); *e-nas-kwa* dom. anim. (Cory: 13); Wendat *Otindasquan* prisonniers (Sagard: Qu1); Wendat *ndask8a* ésclave, prisonnier (Potier: 448); Onondaga *hénachk8a* prisonnier de guerre (Shea: 83); Onondaga *Enàsqua* prisoner (Zeisberger: 149), *Enásqua* slave (Zeisberger: 175)

-nahst- N rafters
With V -her-/-hr- set on top of: **wahanahstà:ren'** he put up the rafters, **kanahstáhere'** (there are) rafters.
With V -takwarihsi-/-kwarihsi- straighten: **kanahstakwaríhsions** something used to shore up or even out the rafters.

-nahstonhkw- N window, windowsill: **onahstónhkwa'**
With V -a'senht-/-enht- drop, and CISL: **tahanahstónhkwenhte'** he lowered the window, he closed the window, **tasenahstónhkwenht** Lower the window!
With V -haratat-/-karatat- lift, raise up: **wahanahstonhkwakará:tate'** he raised the window, he opened the window, **senahstonhkwakará:tat** Raise the window!
With SRF -ate-, V -hna'neta'-/-neta'- line, double, and DLC: **tewatenahstonhkwanéta's** double window, storm window.
With SRF -ate- and V -nohare-/-ohare- wash: **wa'katenahstonhkóhare'** I washed the window sills.

-naie- V be proud, conceited, vain: **kená:ie'** I am proud, conceited, vain, **raná:ie'** he is

proud, conceited, vain, **iená:ie'** she
is proud, conceited, vain.
With ATTR =kowa, great, and REP:
skanaie'kó:wa peacock.
With SRF -ate- and CAUS -hst-:
iontenaiéhstha' she acts proud,
enkatená:iehste' I will show off,
rotenaiéhston he is showing off.
With N -wenn- voice, word:
rawennaná:ie' he boasts, brags,
iewennaná:ie' she boasts, brags.

Cf. Gannaie glorieux, superbe, arrogant
(Bruyas: 66); *Gannáie* Se vanter v.
arrogant (Galissonnière: 82r); *Kenāie*
Vaniteux (Marcoux: 409); *skanaiekōŝa*
Paon (Marcoux: 278); *Kenaie* être fier,
hautain, vain, orgueilleux (Cuoq: 17);
ska na ie ko wa peacock (Anon: 17);
ie na ie conceit (Diabo: 12)

-nak- V scratch, rake, with DLC: **tékenaks**
I am scratching it, raking it, **teká:naks**
rake, **wà:tkenake'** I scratched it, raked
it, **wa'thákenake'** he scratched me,
tewakená:kon I have scratched it,
raked it.
With SRF -ate-: **wa'thátenake'** he got a
scratch, he got scratched.
With REFL -atate-: **wa'tkatátenake'** I
scratched myself.
• kwah aten'enhrakwé:kon wà:tkenake'.
I raked the whole yard. (Letter 1945, Apr)
• Wa'thátenake' rahnho'kwà:ke. He got a
scratch on his cheek.

-nakar- N stick: **kaná:kare'**
With SRF -ate- and V -atiw- be skinny:
iotenakratí:wen blue beech, American
hornbeam.
With V -es- be long: **kanaká:res** (it is)
a long stick.
With V -ia'k- break, cut in two, and DLC:
wa'tkenakária'ke' I broke the stick.

With V -ohar- attach at the end:
kanakaróhare' candy attached to a stick
(hardened maple syrup or a lollipop).
With V -ot- stand; and o'rhótsheri
(-'rhotsher- string bean):
ienakarótha' o'rhótsheri pole bean.

-naker[e]- V reside, be plenty: **kenákere'**
I reside, **kanákere'** there is plenty of it,
kontinákere' there's a lot around.
With CISL: **tkenákere'** I live there.
With CONT -k-: **enkenákereke'** I will
reside.
With PAST -hkwe': **kenákerehkwe'** I
used to reside; and PART: **tsi nón:we
nikenákerehkwe'** where I used to reside.
With INCH -en'-: **wa'kontinákeren'ne'**
there got to be plenty of them.
With CAUS -t-, or SRF -en- and CAUS -t-:
wa'kenákerate' or **wa'kennákerate'**
I was born, **wahanákerate'** or
wahrennákerate' he was born,
ronakerá:ton he was born.
With N -hwist- metal, money:
kahwistanákere' there is plenty of
money; and NEG: **iah tekahwistanákere'**
there isn't a lot of money.
With NMZR -hser-, V -ke- amount to, and
PART: **áhsen nikanakerahserá:ke** three
locations, three places (where people
reside).
With NMZR -hser-, V -o'ten- be a kind of,
and PART: **Oh nisanakerahserò:ten?**
What Nation are you?
With N -rihw- matter, message: **nòn:wa
karihwanákere'** (it's) the latest news.
• Ó:nen ken kontinákere' ne tekonttsirókwas. Are there fireflies around here
now? • Wa'kontinákeren'ne' ne o'nó:wa'.
There got to be a lot of beetles. • Kátke
sanakerá:ton? When were you born?
• Ka' nón:we nisanakerá:ton? Where were
you born?

-nake['t]- N birch bark, canoe: **oná:ke**
canoe; **onakè:ta'** bill (money), dollar.
With V -ke- amount to, and DLC:
tekanakè:take two bills, two dollars.
With SRF -ate-, V -r- put in, and DISTR
-on-: **watenakè:tarons** white birch.
With V -[t]- be one, and REP:
skanakè:ta one bill, one dollar.

nà:kon down, **nà:kon nonkwá:ti** east
With **tiéksaiens** (-ks- dish, plate, -ien-
put down): **nà:kon tiéksaiens** saucer.

-nakt- N bed, place: **kanákta'** bed.
With LOC -kon, inside: **kanáktakon** in
the bed.
With LOC -okon, under: **kanaktó:kon**
under the bed.
With ending -e', and CISL: **tió:nakte'**
that's its place (talking about a dog).
With SRF -ate-, V -ehsak-/-ihsak-/-esak-/
-isak- look for, and PURP -h-:
wahatenaktisákha' he went looking for
a place or spot.
With V -iio- be good, nice: **ronaktí:io** he
has a good spot; and INCH -'-:
wahonaktí:io'ne' he got a nice spot, he
got comfortable.
With V -ot- stand: **ionáktote'** there is
some space or room, **wakenáktote'** I have
time; and NEG: **iah tewakenáktote'** I have
no time; with V -ot- stand, and BEN -ni-/
-hahs-: **wa'khenaktóthahse'** I let her
stay, I gave her a room to stay in,
ionkenaktotá:ni she is letting me stay.
With SRF -ate- and V -tshenri- find:
wahatenaktatshén:ri' he found a place.
• Ohson'karà:ke tió:nakte' ne è:rhar.
The dog's place is on the floor.
• Kanaktí:io wahatshén:ri' ka' nón:we
ahata'tohseró:ten'. He found a nice spot
to put up the tent.

-nat- N town, settlement: **kaná:ta'**

With LOC -kon, inside: **kaná:takon**
right in town.
With SRF -a-, V -ahkwatase-/-tase- go
around, and DLC: **wa'tiakwanatatá:se'**
we went all around town.
With V -akenhiat- at the end or peak:
kanatakèn:iate' on the edge of town.
With V -a'a- be small, **ken'** particle, and
PART: **ken' nikanatà:'a** (it is) a small
town.
With SRF -a-, V -hkw- pick up, and DLC:
wa'tkaná:tahkwe' I moved (from one
place to another), **teiakonatáhkwen** she
has moved; and CAUS -'t-:
teionnatahkwà:tha' she is moving it (to
another place), **wa'thanatáhkwa'te'** he
moved it, **tewakanatahkwà:ton** I have
moved it.
With V -hronhw- go or angle across, and
DLC: **Tekanatà:ronhwe'** Malone, NY.
With V -hseronni- dress, prepare:
wahatinatahserón:ni' they fixed up
(decorated) the town.
With V -ien- put down, have, and CISL:
tkaná:taien' there's a town there; and
PAST -hkwe': **tkanataién:tahkwe'** there
used to be a town there; with V -ien- put
down, have, and ATTR =kowa, great:
Tsi kanataien'kó:wa Philadelphia;
with SRF -ate- and V -ien- put down, have:
wa'katená:taien' I made myself at home,
wahatená:taien' he made himself at
home, **wa'ontená:taien'** she made herself at home.
With V -ihen- be in the middle of, and
COIN and DLC: **sha'tekanatí:hen** centre
of the town, of the village.
With V -kari- bite: **Ranatakárias**
President of the United States (i.e., he
destroys the town); and ATTR =hne, at:
Ranatakariáhsne Washington, D.C.;
with V -kari- bite, and CISL:
takenataká:ri' I made a fuss in town,
I raised Cain.

With V -ke- amount to, and DLC:
tekaná:take two towns or villages.
With V -kha- (variant -okha-) attach, piece
together, DISTR -nion-, and DLC:
tsi tekanatokhánion at the streets.
With V -kwe'niio- be in charge of:
ranatakwe'ní:io mayor; and ATTR ='ke,
at: **kanatakwe'niiò:ke** on the main street.
With SRF -ate- and V -nonhn- mind, guard:
iakwatenatanónhnha' we are minding,
taking care of the town.
With V -oken- merge, fork, and DLC:
tekanató:ken fork (in the road).
With V -r- put in, and INCH -'-:
wa'kená:tara'ne' I came to town.
With V -ti- be on the other side, and REP:
skaná:tati across the road.

Cf. Ganáta village (Bruyas: 68); *Gannáta*
Village (Galissonnière: 83r); *Gannatajen*
góa Philadelphia (Pyrlaeus: 63); *kanāta*
Village, Ville (Marcoux: 416); *Kanata*
ville, village (Cuoq: 10); *Tsi-ka-na-ta-ien-*
ko-wa Philadelphia (Cory: 83);
Tekanatá:ronhwe' Malone (Horne: 62);
Tsi Kanataien'kó:wa Philadelphia, Pa.
(Horne: 61); Laurentian *Canada* town
(Biggar: 245); Wendat *Andata* Ville,
village (Sagard: Vi7); Onondaga
ganatꭍanen ville, *ganataa* vilage (Shea:
102)

-natahr- V visit: **kenatà:re'** I am here to visit,
wa'kenatà:re' I am going to visit,
kenatà:re's I go visiting, **enkenatà:ra'**
I will go and visit, **wa'kenatà:ra'** I went
to visit.
With PAST -hne': **wakenatahrónhne'** I
have gone to visit.
With CISL: **tienatà:re's** she comes to visit.
With an unproductive suffix -n-:
ronatahré:nen he is visiting,
wahanatahré:nawe' he visited; and
akhsótha my grandmother (-hsot- grand-

parent): **akhsótha iakonatahré:nen** it is
(my, her) moon time, monthly (period),
my grandmother (moon) is visiting; with
suffix -n- and BEN -awi-/-hs-:
rinatahrená:wi I am visiting him,
wa'onkenatahré:nahse' she or they
visited me.
With ending (possibly PURP) -en'se'r-:
wa'khenatahren'sè:re' I'm going (on my
way) to visit her or them.

Cf. Gnaθahre je viens visiter (Bruyas: 69);
Gannaθáron Visiter (Galissonnière: 83v);
Kenatares se promener, rôder de maison
en maison, entrer ici et là, simplement
pour passer le temps; faire des visites
(Cuoq: 17); Wendat *Andataret* Ie te vien
visiter (Sagard: Vi9); Onondaga *gnatarre*
Je viens visiter (Shea: 101)

-nato- N black snake: **oná:to**

Cf. Onnãtu oder *onáto* Wasser(?) Schlange
(Pyrlaeus: 202); *ennaton* serpent d'eau
(Cuoq: 3); *onato rasenn* [black snake
resin] (Beauvais: 3); Onondaga *hanadonk*
serpent d'eau (Shea: 93); Cherokee *inata*
snake (Hill: 24)

-nats- N wheat: **onátsa'**
With ATTR =kowa, great: **onatsa'kó:wa**
barley.
With V -ia'k- cut, sever: **wa'kenatsí:ia'ke'**
I cut wheat; and CAUS -st- or -t-:
ienatsiià:kstha' or **ienatsiià:ktha'** sickle.
With V -kenra- be pale: **onatsakén:ra**
rice.

-nats- N slats
With V -ot- stand, and DISTR -on-:
kanatsó:ton sled or truck with boards or
slats on the side that go between upright
posts.
With V -ot- stand, and DISTR -onnion-:
wa'kenatsotónnion' I put the slats up.

With V -ot- stand, and CISL:
entkenatsó:ten' I will resist, brace myself, stand my ground, **takenatsó:ten'**
I resisted, **tahanatsó:ten'** he stood his
ground, **taienatsó:ten'** she stood her
ground.

-naw- N swamp
With LOC -kon, inside: **kaná:wakon** in
the swamp; and DISTR -hshon:
kanawakónhshon all through the swamp.
With V -ien- put down, have, and CISL:
tkaná:waien' there's a swamp there.
With V -ti- be on the other side, and REP:
Skaná:wati Beyond the swamp (Onondaga title name).

-nawa'aht- N post, pole: **kanawa'áhta'**
With V -ot- stand: **wahanawa'ahtó:ten'**
he put up a post, a pole, **kanawa'áhtote'**
there is a post, a pole; and DISTR -onnion-:
wahanawa'ahtotónnion' he put up posts,
poles.
With V -o'ka't- run into, bump against,
and CISL: **tahanawa'ahtò:ka'te'** he hit
the pole, the post.
With V -'rhenien'-/-ienen'- fall down:
wa'kanawa'ahtié:nen'ne' the pole, post
fell down.

-nawa's- N skin on the eyelid up to the eyebrow: **onawà:sa'**

Cf. Onawasa partie de la tête qui porte les
sourcils (Cuoq: 67); *o nah wah sah* eyebrow (Jamieson 3: 3); *ona'wá:sa* eyelids
(Lazore: 58)

-nawa'tst- N mud: **onawà:tsta'**
With V -okw- take out of liquid:
ranawa'tstókwas mud hen.
With V -oskon- be all, pure:
onawa'tstóskon it is mud all over.
With V -otahrhe'- get hooked on some-

thing: **wahanawa'tstotáhrhe'ne'** he got
stuck in the mud.
With V -r- put in: **ronawà:tstare'** he has
got mud on him, **iakonawà:tstare'** she
has got mud on her.
With SRF -ate- and V -ra'nentakt-/-nentakt-
stick something to:
watenawa'tstanentáktha' wasp (it sticks
mud to it [the wall]).

-nawen- be wet. *See* -na'nawen-/-nawen-

-nawir- N tooth: **onawí:ra'**
POSS: **kenawirà:ke** (on) my tooth (still
in my mouth), **akenawí:ra'** my tooth,
raonawí:ra' his tooth, **akonawí:ra'**
her tooth.
With V -(h)nhont- have in one's mouth:
wakenawiráhnhonte' I have dentures.
With V -nonhwak[t]- be sore, hurt:
wakenawiranòn:waks I have a toothache.
With SRF -ate- and V -onni- make:
iontenawirón:ni she is getting teeth,
she is teething.
With V -o'[k]- slap, flutter, flap, DISTR
-hon-, and DLC: **tewakenawiro'ókhons**
my teeth are chattering.

-na'aht- N rib: **ona'áhta'**
POSS: **kena'ahtà:ke** (on) my ribs,
rana'ahtà:ke (on) his ribs, **iena'ahtà:ke**
(on) her ribs.
With SRF -ate-, V -ia'k- break, cut in two,
and DLC: **wa'tkatena'áhtia'ke'** I broke
my rib.
With V -nonhwak[t]- be sore, hurt:
wakena'ahtanòn:waks I have sore ribs.

-na'kar- N horn, antler, dice: **onà:kara'**
With V -ati-/-onti- lose, throw, and TRNL:
iahonkena'karón:ti' I threw the dice.
With V -es- be long, and DLC:
teiotinà:kares oxen.

With V -her-/-hr- set on top of, and DLC:
tenhonwana'karà:ren' they will install
him as chief.

With V -ia'k- break, cut in two, and DLC:
tenhina'kária'ke' I am going to cut off
his horns. *This is an old expression used
by a woman who is fed up with her husband.*

With V -ia'[k]- hit, slap: **iena'karáia'ks**
piano.

With V -ien- put down, have, and DLC:
tekena'kará:iens I am playing dice,
wa'thana'kará:ien' he played dice,
tehona'kará:ien' he has played dice.

With V -ine- lead, and DLC:
Tehana'karí:ne' He is leading it by the
horns, Mohawk title name 7.

With V -ont- attach, DISTR -on-, and DLC:
teiona'karón:ton it has horns; and ATTR
=’a/=ha, diminutive: **teiotina'karontòn:’a**
sheep.

With REFL -atate-, V -ot- stand, DISTR
-onkw-, and DLC:
tetiatatena'karotónkwas the two are
fighting with their horns.

• Rotiianéhshon teiona'karón:ton ne
kahstó:wa'. The chiefs have horns on
their kahstó:wa'.

Cf. Gannagaronni être considérable
(Bruyas: 66); *Hotinnagaronni* Ancestres,
Anciens (Galissonnière: 7v); *deyako-
nakorondon* chiefs she or they have horns
(Hale: 118–9); *Te jotinnagaronton* des
moutons (Bruyas: 66); *Tehotindagaronton*
Mouton (Galissonnière: 7v);
Tiotinagarontoa Schafr (Pyrlaeus: 201);
teiotinakarontōnha Mouton (Marcoux:
255); *Teotinakares* [ox] (Onkweonwe: 3);
Tiotinakarontonah [sheep] (Onkweonwe:
4). Compare Ohswé:ken dialect *sihk sihk*
sheep (Jamieson 1: 6) and Oneida *síksik*
sheep (Michelson and Doxtator: 663)

-na'kerani-/-na'keren- V imitate, copy, with
CISL: **tehshakona'ké:rens** he imitates her,
copies her, **entekhena'ké:ren'** I will
imitate her, **takhena'ké:ren'** I imitated
her, **thona'kerá:ni** he is imitating him.

-na'khw[en]- V get angry: **wakenà:khwens**
I get angry, **enwakenà:khwen'** I will get
angry, **onkenà:khwen'** I got angry,
wahonà:khwen' he got angry,
wakena'khwèn:'en I am angry.
With CISL: **entionà:khwen'** it will get
infected, **taionà:khwen'** it got infected.
With BEN -'s-: **rakena'khwà:se'** he is
mad at me, **wahinà:khwa'se'** I got mad
at him.

-na'kw- N anger
With V -hsnor[e]- be fast:
rana'kwahsnó:re' he gets angry easily,
iena'kwahsnó:re' she gets angry easily.
With V -onni- make: **khena'kón:nis** I
make her angry, **wahakena'kón:ni'** he
angered me; and REFL -atate-:
rotatena'kón:ni he is snarling, growling
(talking about a dog).

-na'kwarohs- N loose, flabby skin
With V -hren't-/-en't- hang down,
iona'kwarohsèn:ton the skin is hanging
loose (like when someone has a turkey
neck, or the turkey's wattle).

-na'nawen-/-nawen- V be wet: **ionà:nawen**
it is wet.
With CAUS -hst-: **wa'onà:nawenhste'**
it got wet.
With N -ahsir- blanket, shawl:
iakohsiraná:wen her shawl is wet; and
CAUS -hst-: **wa'akohsiraná:wenhste'**
her shawl got wet.
With N -atia'tawi- dress, shirt, and NMZR
-'tsher-: **iakotia'tawi'tsheraná:wen** her

dress, shirt is wet; and CAUS -hst-: **onkwatia'tawi'tsheraná:wenhste'** my dress, shirt got wet.

With N -ent- day: **iawentaná:wen** it is a mild day.

With N -haranawen't- sap: **enkaharanawen'taná:wen'** it will start running sap, **ó:nen wa'kaharanawen'taná:wen'** now the sap is melted and running, **ioharanawen'taná:wen** it is running sap.

With N -hiatonhser- book, paper: **iohiatonhseraná:wen** the book or paper is wet.

With N -ia't- body: **watia'taná:wen** I am wet, **iakoia'tá:nawen** she is wet; and CAUS -hst-: **ontia'taná:wenhste'** I got wet, **wa'akoia'taná:wenhste'** she got wet, **wa'kheia'taná:wenhste'** I got her wet.

With N -ient- wood: **ioientaná:wen** (it is) damp or wet wood.

With N -nennio'kw- snowball, and CAUS -ht-: **wa'kenennio'kwaná:wenhte'** I defrosted it.

With N -nia't- throat: **onkenia'taná:wen'** I quenched my thirst.

With N -nonw- bottom water, dregs: **iononwaná:wen** (it is) lukewarm water.

With N -wis- ice, glass: **wa'kawisaná:wen'** the ice melted; and PROG -hatie-: **iowisanawen'enhátie'** the ice is melting.

With N -'nonhkw- bottom of something: **io'nonhkwaná:wen** the bottom is wet or soggy.

See also -wistanawen- melt, thaw.

-na'skw- N body, curled-up
　　With V -her-/-hr- set on top of, and TRNL: **iehana'skwáhere'** he is lying down curled up, **ieiena'skwáhere'** she is lying down; and SRF -ate-: **ia'katena'skwà:ren'** I went to lie down (for a rest),

wà:s ia'satena'skwà:ren Go, lie down! With V -ien- put down, have, INCH -'-, and TRNL: **ia'kena'skwaién:ta'ne'** I fell down, I tumbled down.

-na'tar[o][k]- N bread: **kanà:taro**
　　With **teio'nowákhen** (-'now- hump, padlock, -kha- attach, piece together): **teio'nowákhen kanà:taro** crusty bread.

With ATTR =onwe, genuine: **kana'tarokhón:we** cornbread.

With V -akaion-/-kaion- be old, and INCH -'-: **iona'tarakaiòn:'on** (it is) stale, old bread.

With V -astath[en]-/-ath[en]- dry: **iona'taráthen** (it is) dry bread.

With V -ate'skont- roast, bake: **wa'katena'tarón:ten'** I baked bread; **watenà:taronte'** bread baked in the oven.

With SRF -ate- and V -atonris[t]- be damp, soggy: **iotena'taratón:ris** (it is) damp, soggy bread.

With SRF -ate-, V -atsha'- burn, and CAUS -ht-: **wa'katena'tarátsha'ahte'** I made toast, **rotena'taratsha'áhton** he is making toast, **watena'taratsha'áhton** toast.

With V -ia'ser-/-'ser- stack, and DLC: **tekana'tarà:sere'** sandwich.

With V -kwe'tar[on]-/-e'tar[on]- cut, slice off a piece or chunk: **kena'tarakwè:tarons** I am slicing bread.

With SRF -ate-, V -ohw- put into liquid, and TRNL and DLC: **ia'tekatenà:tarohs** I dunk bread in it, **ia'tkatenà:tarohwe'** I dunked bread.

With V -onni- make : **kena'tarón:nis** I am making bread or cakes.

With V -ot- stand: **kanà:tarote'** offertory (the offering of bread and wine at the Eucharist).

With V -takeri'ta['w]-/-keri'ta['w]- fry, **enkena'tarakerì:ta'we'** I will fry bread, **wa'kena'tarakerì:ta'we'** I made french toast, **kana'tarakerì:ta** fry bread, french toast.

With N -tsikhe't- sweet, V -r- put in, and DLC: **teiona'taratsikhè:tare'** cake.

Cf. Gannátarok pain (Bruyas: 69); *Gannatarok* pain (Galissonnière: 62r); *kanatārŏk* Pain (Marcoux: 277); *Kanatarok* pain (Cuoq: 10); *ka na ta ro* bread (Anon: 7); *kanataro* [bread] (Ledger: 47); *kā-ná-ta-rŏk* Bread (Cory 15); *ga na da ronh* bread (Jamieson 1: 4); Wendat *Andataroni* Pain (Sagard: Vi6); Wendat *ǫndatara* pain (Potier: 449); Susquehannock *Canadra* bread (Holm: 5); Tuscarora *utá'nareh* bread (Rudes: 431)

-na'tkar- N bluff, slope

With V -es- be long, tall, high, and DLC: **tekanà:tkares** (it is) a steep slope, bluff.

See also -atena'tkar- spin (tires).

-na'ton- V call by a name

With TRNL: **iekhenà:tons** I am calling out to her, **ienkhenà:ton'** I will call out to her, **iahinà:ton'** I called out to him, **iehinà:ton** I have called out to him.

With CISL: **tahanà:ton'** he called out (for example, a bingo number), **tahakenà:ton'** he called out to me; and DISTR -nion-: **tahana'tónnion'** he called them out.

With REFL -atate-: **wahatatenà:ton'** he named himself, introduced himself, **wakatatenà:ton** I think highly of myself, **rotatenà:ton** he thinks highly of himself.

With INSTR -hkw-: **khena'tónhkhwa'** I call her by a name (for example, an Indian name, a German name); and DISTR -nion-: **nia'té:kon ronwana'tonhkwánions** they are calling him all kinds of names (like bullies will do).

With PART: **Tó: nihanà:tons?** How much does he charge for it?

With INSTR -hkw- and BEN -en-: **wahakena'tónhkwen' oié:ri nika-**

hwístake he charged me $10; and PART: **Tó: nahiana'tónhkwen'?** How much did he charge you for it?

With BEN -ni-/-hahs-: **khena'tón:ni** I show it to her, **enkonna'tón:hahse'** I will show it to you, **wahonwana'tón:hahse'** she showed it to him.

• Wahatatenà:ton' nahò:ten' roió'te'. He names himself or introduces himself and says what he does, what his work is.

-na'ts- N pail: **kanà:tson'**

With LOC -kon, inside: **kanà:tsakon** inside the pail.

With V -aweron- spill out of: **rana'tsáwerons** he keeps spilling it out of the pail, **wahana'tsáweron'** he spilled the pail.

With V -her-/-hr- set on top of: **kana'tsáhere'** the pot, dinner is on (the stove), it's cooking; and INSTR -hkw-: **iena'tsahráhkhwa'** frying pan.

With V -kahront- make an opening, a hole: **iona'tsakà:ronte'** there is a hole in the pail.

With V -kehron[t]- put down here and there, and TRNL: **iahana'tsakè:ron'** he put pails all around there.

With V -nohare-/-ohare- wash: **Kana'tsóhare** Canajoharie, NY; and ATTR ='ke, at: **Kana'tsoharè:ke** at Canajoharie.

With V -o- be in water: **Kanà:tso** Ottawa.

With V -okha- leak, drip: **iona'tsókhas** the pail is leaking.

With V -[t]- be one, and REP: **skanà:tsa** one pail.

Cf. Gannatsiarʁton chaudière de guerre ou les guerriers chantent (Bruyas: 70); *Kanatsio* aux Chaudières ... Ottawa (Cuoq: 10); *Tsitkanajoh* Ottawa, floating kettle (money) (Brant-Sero and Hill in Boyle: 172); *Ka na tso* Ottawa (Anon: 17);

Kanajo (Ottawa) (Onkweonwe: 3);
Kanátso Ottawa, *Kanatsóhari* Canajoharie (Cory: 83); *Kanà:tso'* Ottawa,
Kana'tsóhare' Canajoharie (Horne: 60,
61); Iroquois *Tsit-ka-na-joh*, floating kettle
(money), is Ottawa (Beauchamp 1907:
266); Onondaga *kanadzia* chaudierre
(Shea: 32)

-na'tsher- N canal
> With LOC -atatie', along, edge of:
> **kana'tsheratátie'** canal, seaway.
> With LOC -kon, inside: **kana'tsherá:kon**
> in the canal, in the seaway.
> With V -onni- make, and PROG -hatie-:
> **kana'tsheronnihátie'** there's a canal,
> the seaway going along.

-na'watsist- N bark, pie crust, breadcrumbs:
> **ona'watsísta'**
> With V -a'senht-/-enht- drop:
> **wahana'watsístenhte'** he took off the
> bark.
> With V -onni- make:
> **wa'kena'watsistón:ni'** I made a crust.
> With V -r- put in: **iona'watsístare'** there
> is bark (on a tree).
> With V -ronkw- remove, scrape off:
> **rana'watsistarónkwas** he takes the bark
> off, **wahana'watsistarón:ko'** he took the
> bark off, **sena'watsistarón:ko** Take the
> bark off!

ne or **n** the, it, they, them, aforementioned
Often contracts with a following word;
for example: **náhsikwe'** the spear;
nì:'i I, me, we, us.

né: assertion particle: it's (the case) that

-ne- KIN spouse: **né: ró:ne'** that's her
husband, his wife.
> With ATTR =kenha, former, late:
> **rone'kénha** her late husband, his late

wife.
> With REFL -atat-: **iatathróna'** the two are
> husband and wife, **iatiatathróna'** we two
> are husband and wife.

Cf. Ronne le mary ou la femme (Galissonnière: 63r); *rōne* epoux, son; (Marcoux:
156); *Rone* son mari; sa femme, Pl. *rotine*
leur époux ou épouses (Cuoq: 39);
ra on ha ro ne wife, *a ka on ha ro ne*
husband (Anon: 2); *Iatathróna* Husband
and wife (Horne: 91); Onondaga *rhôna*
Dame (Shea: 39)

-nehen't-/-nenhen't- N corn mush:
> **kanehèn:ta'** or **kanenhèn:ta'**

Cf. Gannenhenta petit bled (Galissonnière: 12v); *ga nenh hen dah* Dried
corn (green) (Jamieson 2: 3); Onondaga
uninhọⁿda' Parched corn travelling food
(Waugh: 88)

-nehkw- N little bump, sore, pimple
> With V -ont- attach: **ronéhkonte'** he has a
> little bump, a pimple, **iakonéhkonte'** she
> has a little bump, a pimple, **ionéhkonte'**
> it has got a little bump; and DISTR -on-:
> **iakonehkón:ton** she has little bumps,
> pimples, **ionehkón:ton** there are pimples,
> little bumps.
> • Akwé:kon ionehkón:ton ne iehsá:kon.
> She has sores (for example, canker sores,
> thrush) all inside her mouth.

-nehkwa'ehst- V baptize:
> **wahonwanehkwà:'ehste'** they baptized
> him, **wahakenehkwà:'ehste'** he baptized
> me, **wahshakonehkwà:'ehste'** he bap-
> tized her.

Cf. keneksahēsta Baptizer (Marcoux: 35);
a ion ta te ne kwa es te baptism (Anon:
10); *wahonwanehkwá:este'* they baptized
him (Deering and Delisle: 351); *iakote-
nehkwa'éhston* baptized (Gabriel: 11)

-nehohs- N urine: **onehóhsa'**
With V -akera- stink, smell:
ranehohsákeras he smells pissy; and
INCH -'-: **wahanehohsákera'ne'** he got
to smell pissy.
With V -te[ht]- be strong-tasting, energetic:
ronehóhsate' he has strong (smelling)
urine.
Cf. Onnahost citron (Bruyas: 66);
Onnahósa Boüe (Galissonnière: 13v);
onnehost Citron (Galissonnière: 43v)

-nehrakw- V get amazed, surprised:
wakenehrákwas I am amazed, in
wonder, **onkenehrá:ko'** I became
amazed, surprised, **iakonehrakò:'on**
she was amazed, surprised.
With CAUS -ht-: **ionehrákwa** it is amazing; and PAST -'ne': **ionehrakwahtòn:ne'**
it was amazing.
With FACIL -'tskon, easily:
iakonehrakò:tskon she is easily
surprised.
• Ionehrákwa tsi na'á:wen'. It's amazing
what happened.

-nehsio- N cabbage: **onéhsio**. Probably a bor-
rowing from French *chou*.
With CAUS -'t- and V -akera- stink, smell:
kanehsio'tákeras (it is) a smelly cabbage.
NOTE: Compare Ohswé:ken dialect
o non tsi Cabbage (Jamieson 2: 3) and
Oneida *onú·tsi* head, cabbage (Michelson
and Doxtator: 551).
Cf. nēso ou *nēsio* chou (Marcoux: 67);
o ne shio cabbage (Anon: 8); *onesho*
[cabbage] (Ledger: 60); *o ne sho* cabbage
(D'Ailleboust: 23); *onéshio* cabbage
(Cory: 14, 87); *Onéshio* Cabbage
(Horne: 34)

-nehskwa'rh- hip. *See* -niahskwa'rh-

-nehson- N hell: **onéhson'**
With ATTR =hronon, resident of, NMZR
-'tsher-, and V -kowan[en]-/-owan[en]-
be big: **ranehsonhronon'tsherowá:nen**
(he is) a big devil.
Cf. onēson enfer (Marcoux: 148); *Oneshon*
enfer, dans l'abîme (Cuoq: 33); *o nes hon*
hell (Anon: 10); *o nes hon ni tia we non*
na ho ten fiend [*literally*, what has come
from hell] (Diabo: 28); *oonoosooloohnoo*
[oneshonhró:non] Wicked Spirit (Gallatin:
307); Wendat ... *n'ondechon* ... en enfer
(Potier: 287); Wyandot *degh,shunt* Hell
(Johnston: 25); Onondaga *ônêchon* Enfer
(Shea: 51); Onondaga *onèssoch* Hell (Zeisberger: 92)

-nehw- N animal skin, hide: **kanéhon**
With V -hseronni- dress, prepare:
wa'kenehwahserón:ni' I prepared the
skin or hide.
With V -rohro[k]- gather, collect:
ratinehwarò:roks they collect hides.
With V -'rhoro[k]-/-oro[k]- cover:
kanehó:ron or **onehó:ron** water drum;
also Skin Dance, one of the four sacred
ceremonies of the Haudenosaunee.

nek just, **nek tsi** but

-nekar[on]- burst open. *See* -ra'nekar[on]-/
-nekar[on]-

-neken- be side-by-side, next to. *See*
-ra'neken-/-neken-

-nekenhteron- V handsome man with a good
physique (tall, upright, slim):
ranekénhteron (he is) a hansome man.
With NMZR -'tsher-, V -akaion-/-kaion- be
old, and INCH -'-: **ronekenhteron'tsherakaiòn:'on** bachelor.

With N -hson'kar-/-hswen'kar- board,
V -ket- scrape, NMZR -'sher-, and DLC:
tehnihson'karaketa'sheranekénhteron
two young carpenters (*a playful expression
from Mike Norton*).

Cf. Gannigenteron homme de 35 à 40 ans
(Bruyas: 76); *Rannogéchteront* junger
Mann [young man] (Pyrlaeus: 2v);
ranekentenntserīio un joli garcon (Marcoux: 221); *o ne ken te ron tse ra ka io*
bachelor (Anon: 2); *ra ne ken te ron* boy
(D'Ailleboust: 4)

-neker-/-enneker- N hay: **onékeri** or **ennékeri**
With V -ia'k- cut, sever: **ranekerí:ia'ks** he
is cutting hay, **wahanekerí:ia'ke'** or (with
SRF -ate-) **wahatenekerí:ia'ke'** he cut
hay; and CAUS -st-: **iakennekeriià:kstha'**
scythe.
With V -r- put in, and INSTR -hkw-:
ienekeraráhkhwa' hay wagon.
With SRF -ate- and V -statha't-/-atha't- dry:
ratenekerathà:tha' he dries hay,
enkatenekerátha'te' I will dry hay,
wahatenekerátha'te' he dried hay,
rotenekerathà:ton he is drying hay.

-nekerehetsh- N handle: **onekerehétsha'**
With V -ont- attach: **ionekerehétshonte'**
it has a handle (that sticks out, on a frying
pan or axe).
With V -otahrho[k]- hook, and DISTR
-hon-: **tsikenekerehetshotáhrhon** wolverine.

-nekeren't- N tripe (pig or cow stomach):
onekerèn:ta'
NOTE: The words for 'morel' in the
Ohswé:ken dialect and in Ontario Oneida
look like cognates: *o ne ge ren dah*
(Jamieson 2: 11), *oneklá·ta?* (Michelson
and Doxtator: 640). In Wisconsin Oneida
oneklá·ta? is used for 'tripe'. (A morel

mushroom and tripe do look somewhat
similar in texture.)

-nekheren- V find something strange, unusual:
wakenekhé:rens I find it strange,
onkenekhé:ren' I found it strange.
With N -ia't- body:
wa'kheia'tanekhé:ren' I find her strange,
wahiia'tanekhé:ren' I find him strange.
• Iah tewakaterièn:tare' ka' nitiakawé:non,
wa'kheia'tanekhé:ren'. I don't know
where she has come from, I find her
strange.

-nekhwa'- V bleed: **wa'kanékhwa'** it bled,
ionekhwà:'on it is bleeding.

-nekot- N steps, ladder, stairs: **kanekó:ta'**
With LOC -'ke, on, at: **kanekotà:ke** on
the steps or ladder.
With SRF -ate-, V -hsa'kt[on]-/-a'kt[on]-
bend, and DLC: **teiotenekotà:kton** the
stairs have a bend or curve in them.

-neko'rh- N wampum, wampum string:
onekò:rha'. The form **o'nekò:rha'** has
also been heard.
Cf. onekoera sewan, their money (van
den Bogaert: 52); *Onnegorha* porcelaine
(Bruyas: 70); *Onnegꭤrha* porcelaine
(Galissonnière: 67v); *anogórha* sewand
(Pyrlaeus: 210); *Onekorha* porcelaine
(Cuoq: 68); *o ne gor hah* wampum (beads)
(Jamieson 2: 5); *o'nekó:rha'* Wampum
string (Deering and Delisle: 286); Onon-
daga *otgora* Wampum (Zeisberger: 220);
Susquehannock *Ahghoora* (Holm: 5)

-nekw- N pea, pill: **onékwa'**
POSS: **raonékwa'** his pill.
With SRF -ate- and V -ahnehkwan[on]-
swallow: **wahatenekwahnéhkwane'** or
(with TRNL) **iahatenekwahnéhkwane'**

he took the pill, **satenekwahnéhkwan** or (with TRNL) **ia'satenekwahnéhkwan** Take the pill!
With V -ien- put down, have, and TRNL: **ia'senékwaien** Take a pill! Also a mild saying for 'That's enough!'
With V -ohwiha- split in two, and DLC: **wa'tkenekohwíha'** I split the pill.
With SRF -ate-, V -teni[on]- disperse, flurry, and CAUS -'t-: **wahatenekwaténia'te** he talked gibberish, **rotenekwatenià:ton** he is always blabbing, talking gibberish.

-nekwar- N blood clot: **onekwá:ra'**
With V -r- put in, and DISTR -onnion-: **kanekwarónnion** or **ionekwarónnion** it is polka-dotted.
With SRF -ate-, V -ta'-/-eta'- put inside, and CISL: **entewatenekwaráta'** it will get to be a clot, **tontenekwaráta'** it got to be a clot.

-nekwati- V left side, with REP: **skanekwá:ti** the left hand, **skenekwá:ti** my left hand or side, **sehsenekwá:ti** your left.
• Skenekwá:ti kátstha' akhiá:ton'. I use my left hand to write.

-nekwa't- N dancers in the Dipper constellation
With V -ke- amount to, and PART: **tsá:ta nihatinekwà:take** the seven dancers, Big Dipper.
With V -r- put in: **onekwà:tara'** or (with ATTR =shon'a, pluralizer) **onekwa'tara'shòn:'a** Pleiades, Little Dipper

-nekwenhs- N blood: **onekwénhsa'**
POSS: **raonekwénhsa'** his blood, **akonekwénhsa'** her blood.
With **awenhétsha'** (-enhetsh- sausage):

onekwénhsa' awenhétsha' blood sausage.
With V -ia'k- cut, sever: **kanekwénhsia'ks** it stops the blood, the bleeding.
With SRF -ate-, V -ia'k- break, cut in two, and DLC: **tewatenekwénhsia'ks** a kind of plant.
With SRF -ate-, V -rohro[k]- gather, collect, and BEN -hs-: **onkwatenekwenhsarò:rokhse'** the blood pooled on me, **wesatenekwenhsarò:rokhse'** the blood pooled on you (looking at a bruised thumbnail).
With N -tsikhe't- sweet, V -r- put in, and DLC: **teiakonekwenhsatsikhè:tare'** diabetes.
• Onekwá:ra' ón:ton' sanekwénhsa'. Your blood turned into a clot, you have a blood clot.

-nekwenhtar- N red: **onekwénhtara'**
With **niwatahtsherò:ten'** (-atahtsher- twig, yard, -o'ten- be a kind of): **onekwénhtara' niwatahtsherò:ten'** red willow.
With CAUS -ht- and PURP -'n-: **onekwenhtarahtà:ne'** flushed colour that comes with sickness; scarlet fever.
With V -rakew-/-okew- wipe, and DISTR -nion-: **wa'kwanekwenhtarokewánion'** we wiped the blood off you in several places.
• Onekwenhtarahtà:ne' wa'akoié:na'. She got all flushed (with fever, hives).

-nekwenhtont- V attached as a brim: **ionekwénhtonte' anòn:warore'** ball cap (-nonhwar- brain, -'rhoro[k]-/-oro[k]- cover).

-nekwen't- N belly: **onekwèn:ta'**
POSS: **kenekwen'tà:ke** my belly,

ranekwen'tà:ke his belly,
ienekwen'tà:ke her belly.
With V -ia'[k]- hit, slap:
wahonwanekwen'táia'ke' she hit
him in the belly.

né:ne that's the one, the one who

-nenh- N seed: **ká:nen**
    With V -akaion-/-kaion- be old, and INCH
    -'-: **ionenhakaiòn:'on** heirloom seed(s).
    With SRF -ate-, V -areni- spread around,
    disperse, CAUS -'t-, and DLC:
    tekontenenharenià:tha' they are
    spreading seeds, **wa'tkatenenharénia'te'**
    I spread the seeds.
    With V -ati-/-onti- lose, throw:
    onkenenhón:ti' I dropped seeds (in the
    ground).
    With V -kenra- be pale: **onenhakén:ra**
    Indian white corn.
    • Onkenenhón:ti' onenhakén:ra atiéntho'.
    I dropped seeds to plant the Indian corn.

-nenh- N urine: **onénha'**
    With V -ronhkwani-/-ronhkwen- itch:
    wakenenharónhkwani I have the urge to
    pee, **ronenharónhkwani** he has the urge
    to pee, **iakonenharónhkwani** she has
    the urge to pee.
    Cf. onnhenha urine (Bruyas: 74);
    Onnhenha Urine (Galissonnière: 84r);
    onnhēnha Urine (Marcoux: 405);
    Onondaga *onhenha* pissat (Shea: 80)

-nenhontst- N dates: **onénhontste'**
    Cf. katheton onenontste [pounded
    mandrake] (Beauvais: 10); *uną'hųstε'*
    Mandrake (Waugh 1916: 129)

-nenhr- N crowd: **kanèn:ra'**
    With LOC -kon, inside: **kanèn:rakon** in
    the crowd.

    With V -a'a- be small, **ken'** particle, and
    PART: **ken' nikanenhrà:'a** (it is) a small
    crowd.
    With V -es- be long, and DLC: **tekanèn:res**
    square dance.
    With V -hseronni- dress, prepare:
    rotinenhrahserón:ni they lined up,
    sewanenhrahserón:ni Form a line! (pl)
    With V -ia'[k]- hit, slap, and CISL:
    taienenhráia'ke' she treated everyone,
    she paid for everyone.
    With V -ineken'- emerge, and PROG
    -hatie-: **rotinenhrineken'enhátie'** they
    are in a parade.
    With V -kowan[en]-/-owan[en]- be big:
    kanenhrowá:nen (it is) a big crowd.
    With V -ot- stand, and REV -kw-:
    wa'khenenhrotá:ko' I confronted her,
    wa'onkenenhrotá:ko' she confronted
    me.
    With SRF -ate- and V -rohro[k]- gather,
    collect: **ontenenhrarò:roke'** the crowd
    gathered.
    With V -te- be present, exist, and DLC:
    tehotinenhrá:te' there's a line of them;
    and PROG -tie- and CISL:
    tontahotinenhratátie' they are coming
    close together in a line, they are parading.
    Cf. Gannenᶜra armée, bande, troupe de
    guerriers, compagnie (Bruyas: 71);
    Gannenᶜra Armee (Galissonnière: 9r);
    ganáhra ein Trupp Volk (Pyrlaeus: 239);
    kanēnra Bande, troupe (Marcoux: 34);
    Kanenra bande, troupe, armée, multitude,
    rang, rangée (Cuoq: 10); *ka nen ra* crowd
    (Anon: 30); *ka nen ra* crowd (Diabo: 13);
    Wendat *ɋnnenra* armee, troupe, bande
    (Potier: 450); Onondaga *kanenhra gôna*
    Armée (Shea: 22)

-nenhskw- V steal: **kenénhskwas** I steal it,
    wahanénhsko' he stole it,
    wahakenénhsko' he stole it from me,

ronénhskwen he has stolen it; and PROG -hatie-: **ronenhskwenhátie'** he is stealing it.

With N -hiatonhser- book, paper: **wahakhiatonhseranénhsko'** he stole the book from me.

With N -kahr- eye, and DLC: **tehikahranénhskwas** I am snooping on him, spying on him, **wa'thikahranénhsko'** I spied on him.

With N -rihw- matter, message: **kherihwanénhskwas** I am talking about her, **wahakerihwanénhsko'** he talked about me.

With N -'sereht- vehicle, car: **wahi'serehtanénhsko'** I stole a car from him, I stole his car.

-nenhst- N corn: **ó:nenhste'**

With V -akwenhten- be flat: **tsikenenhstakwénhten** a kind of berry, looks almost like a cranberry, smells foul (like smelly feet) but is delicious when cooked (GM 'moose cherry').

With V -attatakw- explode, pop, and CAUS -ht-: **watenenhstatakwáhton** popcorn.

With V -ek-/-ak- eat: **kenénhstaks** I eat corn, **wakenenhstá:kon** I am eating corn.

With V -iio- be good, nice: **kanenhstí:io** (it is) good corn.

With V -kw- pick: **kenenhstákwas** I harvest corn.

With V -nohare-/-ohare- wash: **wa'kenenhstóhare'** I washed the corn.

With V -o- be in water: **kanénhsto** or **onénhsto** corn soup.

With V -ronkw- remove, scrape off: **kenenhstarónkwas** I am shelling corn, **wa'kenenhstarón:ko'** I shelled corn, **ronenhstarónkwen** he has shelled corn.

With V -statha't-/-atha't- dry: **ranenhstathà:tha'** he dries corn; and SRF -ate-: **wahatenenhstátha'te'** he dried the corn, **rotenenhstathà:ton** he is drying

corn; and INSTR -hkw-: **iontenenhstatha'táhkhwa'** corn crib.

With N -tsikhe't- sweet, V -r- put in, and DLC: **teionenhstatsikhè:tare'** sweet corn.

Cf. Onnenste blé (Bruyas: 72); *Onnenste* Bled (Galissonnière: 12v); *Onensto* potage des Indiens (Cuoq: 133); *onǫ́sdo* Hulled Corn Soup (Waugh: 90); *o nenh stoh gwah* Corn soup (Jamieson 2: 3); *onénhsto* corn soup (Horne: 28); Susquehannock *Onaœsta* Indian corn (Holm: 7)

-nenhstia'k- V mash, with DLC: **teienénhstia'ks** she is mashing it (to soften it up, or so she can spread it), **tenhsenénhstia'ke'** you will mash it, **wa'tkenénhstia'ke'** I mashed it, **teiakonenhstià:kon** she has mashed it.

-neni- N stone, rock: **onén:ia'**

With LOC -okon, under, and ATTR ='a/=ha, diminutive: **oneniokón:ha** rock bass.

With V -ahsihara'- get wedged in, stuck, and DLC: **teioneniahsiharà:'on** there is a rock stuck.

With V -a'sen's-/-en's- drop unintentionally: **onkenén:ien'se'** I dropped the stone.

With V -haratat-/-karatat- lift, raise up: **wa'keneniakará:tate'** I wound it (the clock or watch).

With V -hriht- break into pieces, smash, and DLC: **tekeneniahríhtha'** I break up stones, **tekaneniahríhtha'** stone crusher, **wa'thanenià:rihte'** he smashed, broke up stones, **tekaneniahríhton** crushed stone.

With V -ien- put down, have, INSTR -hkw-, and DLC: **teieneniaientáhkhwa'** marbles.

With SRF -ate-, V -kahrhateni- turn around, empty, DISTR -hon-, and DLC: **tewateneniakahrhateníhon** grindstone.

With V -kareni- take back and forth: **keneniakarénie's** I am carrying stones back and forth.

With V -kowan[en]-/-owan[en]- be big: **onenió:wane'** bullet.

With V -oia'[k]- throw straight at: **Shakotinenióia'ks** Little People (you are lucky if you catch sight of them or they appear to you).

With V -ot- stand, and ATTR =haka/=aka, people of: **Oneniote'á:ka** Oneida; with V -ot- stand, and ATTR =hronon, resident of: **roneniothró:non** he belongs to the Rock clan.

With V -o'kwat- dig, and CAUS -st-: **tsi ienenio'kwátstha'** quarry.

With V -r- put in: **ionén:iare'** calcification from water (for example, in a kettle).

With V -(h)rho- coat: **kaneniáhrhon** enamel; and SRF -ate-: **Ateneniáhrhon** Stone Giant.

With V -ri- cook, ripen, and CAUS -ht-: **kaneniaríhton** brick, cement block.

Cf. Onneyuttehage Sinnekens (van den Bogaert: 14); *Atenenhiarhon* et *Iakonenhioiaks*. "Le premier est une sort de loup-garou que quelques-uns supposent avoir un corps moitié pierre et moitié chair … Le second … est un nain qui lance des pierres, que plusiers prétendent avoir aperçu, mais que jamais personne n'a pu saisir." (Cuoq: 174-5); *sa ko nen io iaks* dwarf (Anon: 35); *ia ko nen io iaks* dwarf (Diabo: 21); *sha go di nen yoh yaks* fairies (Jamieson 2: 10); *tsi ie nen io kwats tha* quarry (Anon: 17); *tsi ienenio'kwátstha* quarry (Old Kahnawake: 24)

-nennawen['t]- N tobacco pipe: **kanén:nawen**
POSS: **akenén:nawen** my pipe.

With -ati-/-onti- lose, throw: **wahonennawen'tón:ti'** he lost his pipe.

With V -es- be long: **kanennawèn:tes** (it is) a long pipe.

With V -ke- amount to, and DLC: **tekanennawèn:take** two pipes.

With V -kowan[en]-/-owan[en]- be big, and REP: **Shotinennawen'tó:wane'** Cayugas, as referred to in council.

With V -[t]- be one, and REP: **skanennawèn:ta** one pipe.

Cf. canonou tobacco pipe (van den Bogaert: 60); *Gannonnaꜱan* calumet (Bruyas: 81); *Gannonnaꜱan* Calumet (Galissonnière: 15v); *Ganunawaenta* Tabacco Pipe (Zeisberger in Wheeler-Voegelin: 58); *Kanōnnăꜱan* Pipe (Marcoux: 291); *Kanonnawen* pipe, calumet (Cuoq: 11); *kanennawen* [pipe] (Ledger: 85); *ka nen na wen* pipe (Anon: 8); *ka nen na wen* pipe (D'Ailleboust: 36); *ka non na wen* pipe (Diabo: 56); Wendat *Anondahoin* calumet (Sagard: Me11); *ꜰnnondaꜱoin* calumet (Potier: 156); Onondaga *kanonahꜱenta* Calumet (Shea: 30); Susquehannock *Chanoona* a tobacco pipe (Holm: 5); Tuscarora *kanꜰtawꜰtyà:nꜰ* Tobacco Pipe (Rudes: 368); Cherokee *ganvnowa* pipe (Mithun 1984b: 276)

-nennio'kw- N snowball: **onenniò:kwa'**

With SRF -ate-: **atenenniò:kwa'** snowman.

With V -ati-/-onti- lose, throw, and TRNL: **iahonennio'kón:ti'** he threw a snowball.

With V -hwatase-/-tase- turn, twist, and DLC: **teionennio'kwatá:se** or **teionien'kwatá:se'** (it is) a snowstorm.

With V -na'nawen-/-nawen- be wet, and CAUS -ht-: **wa'kenennio'kwaná:wenhte'** I defrosted it.

With V -no- be cold: **ionenniò:kwano** ice cream; and CAUS -hst-: **kanennio'kwanóhstha'** freezer, **wa'kenenniò:kwanohste'** I froze it.

With V -onni- make: **wa'kenennio'kón:ni'** I made a snowball.

With SRF -ate-, V -ont- attach, and DLC: **teiotenenniò:konte'** there are snowballs

on it, **tehotenenniò:konte' rahsinà:ke**
he has snowballs on his leg (talking about
a dog).

-nennotsher- N package, parcel:
onennótshera'
With V -awi-/-on- give:
wahakenennótsheron' he gave me a
package.
With V -a'a- be small, **ken'** particle, and
PART: **ken' nikanennotsherà:'a** (it is)
a little package.
With V -hwaneren[k]-/-neren[k]- tie up:
wa'kenennotsheránerenke' I tied the
package; and CAUS -st- and INSTR -hkw-:
ienennotsheranerenkstáhkhwa'
ahserí:ie string or cord used to wrap a
package (-ahseriie['t]- string, rope).
With V -kste- be heavy:
ionennotsherákste' (it is) a heavy
package.
With V -nia[k]- wrap around the neck:
wahanennotsherániake' (ne akohsá:tens)
he put the horse collar on (the horse),
senennotsherániak Put the collar on!
With V -onni- make:
wa'kenennotsherón:ni' I made a package.
With V -ota's- receive:
onkenennotsheró:ta'se' I received a
package.
NOTE: The alternative **onerótshera'**
(-nerotsher-) is also common. Another
word for a measure or container is
ska we no tse ra bushel (D'Ailleboust: 29);
cf. *kawennojera* (Onkweonwe: 4).

-nenskari- V get angry, out of control, throw
a tantrum: **ranenskárias** he gets out of
control angry, **wahanenská:ri'** he got out
of control angry, **wa'enenská:ri'** she got
out of control angry.

-nenskonwarar- V have a dirty face, with DLC:
tehonenskón:warare' he has a dirty face,
teiakonenskón:warare' she has a dirty
face.

-nenskwar- green (unripe) fruit, smallpox.
See -nonskwar-/-nenskwar-

-nentahsi- get unstuck. *See* -ra'nentahsi-/
-nentahsi-

-nentak- stick to. *See* -ra'nentak-/-nentak-

-nentakt- stick something to. *See* -ra'nentakt-/
-nentakt-

-nentsh- N arm: **onéntsha'**
POSS: **kenentshà:ke** (on) my arm,
ranentshà:ke (on) his arm, **ienentshà:ke**
(on) her arm.
With V -a- take hold of someone:
wa'khenéntsha' I held her arm, I took her
hand (to shake it); and CISL: **tahinéntsha'**
I took hold of his arm, **tahakenéntsha'**
he took hold of my arm.
With V -a- touch, and TRNL, or TRNL and
DLC: **iahinéntsha'** or **ia'thinéntsha'** I
touched his arm.
With V -atiront- pull, stretch:
kanentshatiróntha' notched stick, invitation wampum; and INSTR -hkw- and CISL:
tiakonentshatirontáhkhwa' they present
wampum as an invitation.
With V -awe'ehst- pierce, and DLC:
wa'tionkenentsháwe'ehste' they gave
me a needle in the arm.
With SRF -a-, V -enton[hw]- move back
and forth, and DLC:
wa'tionnentshén:tonhwe' she moved her
arm back and forth.
With V -esha- be short, **ken'** particle, and
PART and DLC: **ken' na'tekanentshésha**
atià:tawi short-sleeved shirt (-atia'tawi-
dress, shirt).

With SRF -a- and V -haratat-/-karatat- lift, raise up: **wa'kanentshakará:tate'** I raised my arms.

With SRF -ate-, V -hsa'kt[on]-/-a'kt[on]- bend, and DLC: **wa'tkatenentshà:kete'** I bent my arm.

With SRF -ate- and V -hwahnha[k]-/ -hnha[k]- wrap, tie around: **atenentsháhnha'** bracelet, wristwatch.

With SRF -ate-, V -ia'k- break, cut in two, and DLC: **wa'tkatenéntshia'ke'** I broke my arm.

With V -ia'k- hit, bang, and TRNL: **iahonkenéntshia'ke'** I banged my arm.

With V -ia'ser-/-'ser- stack, and DLC: **tekenentshà:sere'** I have my arms crossed; and SRF -ate-: **wa'tkatenentshà:seren'** I crossed my arms.

With SRF -atate-, V -ienawa'k-/-wa'k- hold, support, and DLC: **teionkwatatenentshawà:kon** we are locking our arms, **tehonatatenentshawà:kon** they are locking their arms, Chain Belt, Covenant Belt.

With V -ine- lead: **shakonentshí:ne'** he is going along holding her arm; and REFL -atate- and DLC: **tetiatatenentshí:ne'** you and I are holding arms as we walk.

With V -kwatho- hem, and DLC: **wa'thanentshakwátho'** he rolled up the sleeves (of his shirt, coat).

With V -ronhkwani-/-ronhkwen- itch: **wakenentsharónhkwani** my arm is itchy.

With SRF -a-, V -tenihon- shake, and DLC: **tekanentshateníhon** I am waving my hand or arm, **wa'tkanentshateníhon'** I waved my arm.

NOTE: Both SRF -a- and -ate- occur with this root. *See also* -nentshawi't- wrist.

-nentshawi't- N wrist: **onentshawì:ta'**
POSS: **kenentshawi'tà:ke** (on) my wrist.
With SRF -ate- and V -hwahnha[k]-/

-hnha[k]- wrap, tie around: **atenentshawi'táhnha'** anything tied around the wrist (beads, leather).

With SRF -ate- and V -tahkw- take out: **wa'katenentshawi'tatáhko'** I sprained my wrist.

NOTE: This stem is composed of -nentsharm, -awi- wrap around, and CAUS -'t-.
• Enhsahsónteren' satià:tawi onentshawì:ta'. You will add (sew on) cuffs to your shirt.

-nentstakwar- N dirty laundry: **onentstá:kwara'**
With V -ka'te- have many: **wakenentstakwarakà:te'** I have lots of dirty laundry.

-nen'- N pit, pellet: **onèn:'a'**
With V -a[t]- be inside, and CISL: **tkanèn:'a** there is a pit in it.
With V -ati-/-onti- lose, throw: **enionen'ón:ti'** it will snow ice pellets, **wa'onen'ón:ti'** it snowed ice pellets, **ionen'óntion** it is snowing ice pellets.
• Tkanèn:'a ne tekakenhwhará:ron. The peach has a pit in it.

-nen'onni- N hominy: **kanen'ón:ni**
• Kanen'ón:ni wa'katkátston'. I made hominy soup.

Cf. Gannohon Bled rafiné (Galissonnière: 12v); *ka non on ni* hominy (Anon: 7) *ka nen on ni* cracked corn (D'Ailleboust: 26);

-nen't- N evergreen: **onèn:ta'**
With ATTR =onwe, genuine: **onen'ta'ón:we** hemlock.
With V -akwenhten- be flat, and NMZR -'tsher-: **onen'takwenhtèn:tshera'** cedar.
With V -a'sen'-/-en'- fall down: **kanèn:ten's** tamarack, jack pine.

With SRF -a- and V -ek-/-ak- eat:
anèn:taks porcupine.

With SRF -ate-, V -ia'k- cut, sever, and
DISTR -hon-: **ontenen'tià:khon'** the evergreen (branches) are broken (maybe after
a heavy snowstorm).

With V -ionni- be lying, be extended:
onen'tión:ni low-growing evergreen,
yew.

With V -keri- broth: **onon'tákeri'** or
onen'tákeri' beer.

Cf. Onnentaɡsenta Cedre (Galissonnière:
8v); *Annentaɡsenᶜten* Cedre (Galissonnière: 16v); *onentākĕri* Biere (Marcoux:
40); *Onenta* sapin du Canada (Cuoq: 33);
onentakwenten [cedar] (Beauvais: 4);
kanentens [tarmarack] (Beauvais: 8);
onentakwententshera [cedar] (Beauvais:
16); *o nen ta* pine, *o nen ta kwen ten tse ra*
cedar (Anon: 18); *wana'djy̨'ni'* Hemlock
(Waugh: 147); *o-nen-tion-ni* Taxus canadensis [Canada yew] (Rousseau: 34);
o-nen-ta-wken-ten-tse-ra Thuja occiden-
talis [cedar] (Rousseau: 35); *o-nen-da-
on-we* Tsuga canadensis [Eastern hemlock]
(Rousseau: 36); *onenta'kwènte* cedar
(Gabriel: 20); Onondaga *onendionni* le
genievre (Juniper) (Shea: 22); *O-ne-te-o-
ne* American Yew (Beauchamp 1893: 118)

-ner- V make pregnant: **iené:ron** she is
pregnant, **kané:ron** it is pregnant (an
animal, derogatory).

With N -ihn- skin, leather, and CAUS -'t-:
ohnanerì:ta' vagina; and POSS:
iehnaneri'tà:ke her vagina.

Cf. onera vagina (van den Bogaert: 56);
Gannéron être enceinte (Bruyas: 73);
Gannéris männl. Schaam (Pyrlaeus: 199);
Keneren être grosse, être enciente (Cuoq:
18); Wendat *annérique* enceinte (Sagard:
Ma11); Onondaga *honera* membre viril
(Shea: 70)

-nerahontsh- N wing, shoulder blade:
onerahóntsha'
POSS: **kenerahontshà:ke** (on) my
shoulder blade, **aonerahóntsha'** its wing.
With **kà:sere** (-'sere[ht]- vehicle, car):
kà:sere onerahóntsha' car fender.
With V -her-/-hr- set on top of, and DLC:
tekanerahontsháhere' it has a fender.
With V -ke- amount to, and DLC:
tekanerahóntshake two wings.
With V -ont- attach, with DLC:
tekanerahóntshonte' it (a bird) has
wings.
With SRF -ate-, V -o'[k]- slap, flutter, flap,
DISTR -hon-, and DLC:
tewatenerahontsho'ókhons it is flapping
its wings (for example, a bird in a bird-
bath).

Cf. Gaꙅiahontsa aisle (Bruyas: 65);
onnerahontsa Aisle (Galissonnière: 5v);
onerahōntsa Aile (Marcoux: 12);
Onerahontsa aîle (Cuoq: 33)

-nerahrh- N shoulder blade: **onerà:rha'**

-nerahs- N cork: **oneráhsa'**
With V -ohro[k]- insert:
wa'kenerahsò:roke' I put the cork in it.

Cf. Onnerasa tondre champignons
(Bruyas: 72); *Onᶜneraᶜsa* Champignon
(Galissonnière: 43v); *Onneraᶜsa* Creste
d'un coq (Galissonnière: 26v); *Onerasa*
amadou; liège; crête de coq (Cuoq: 33);
o ne ra sa cork (Anon: 30)

-neraht- N leaf: **ónerahte'**
With V -ase- be fresh, new, ATTR =kowa,
great, and CISL: **tionerahtase'kó:wa**
white pine.
With V -a'awi-/-en'awi- float, drift:
ionerahten'á:wi the leaves are floating.
With V -hstarathe- be shiny, and DLC:
teionerahtahstaráthe' plantain.

With V -itie-/-tie-/-ontie- fly around, float by: **kanerahtóntie'** there are leaves flying around.

With V -kahte- be raw: **onerahtakáhte'** lettuce.

With V -kehron[t]- put down here and there: **kanerahtakè:ron** here and there there are leaves on the ground.

With V -ohw- put into liquid, and TRNL: **iekanerahtóhon** tea.

With V -oken- merge, fork, and DLC: **teionerahtó:ken** clover.

With V -okha- leak, drip: **Onerahtókha** April; and ATTR =kowa, great: **Onerahtohkó:wa** May.

With SRF -ate-, V -onni- make, and CAUS -'t-: **Tsi iontenerahtonnià:tha'** Corpus Christi; with SRF -ate-, V -onni- make, and PURP -'n-: **Iontenerahtonnià:ne'** Palm Sunday.

With V -ont- attach: **onerahtón:ta'** poplar; and ATTR =kowa, great: **onerahtonta'kó:wa** cottonwood poplar (from Rousseau: 39).

With V -rakarere-/-karere- be noise travelling: **ionerahtakaré:re'** the leaves are making noise.

With SRF -ate- and V -teni[on]- disperse, flurry: **iotenerahtaténion** the leaves are falling.

Cf. Sahonteneratōnnĭăte Fête Dieu (Marcoux: 172); *en ion te nen ra ton nia te* corpus christi (Anon: 6); *iontenenrahtonniá:tha* Corpus Christi (Old Kahnawake: 20); *tioneratastarathe* [plantain] (Beauvais: 26); *tio ne ra to ken* clover (Diabo: 10); *te-io-ne-ra-to-ken* Trifolium [clover] (Rousseau: 50); *o-ne-ra-don-da-kowa* Populus deltoides [cottonwood poplar] (Rousseau: 39); *O ne rah don dah* Poplar (Jamieson 2: 3); *Onerahtón:ta'* Poplar (Horne: 112)

-nera'[k]- V mistake

With DLC: **tekenéra'ks** I mistake it, **wa'tkenéra'ke'** I mistook it, **tewakenéren'** I have mistaken it.

With N -ia't- body, and DLC: **wa'tkonia'tanéra'ke'** I mistook you for someone.

With N -rihw- matter, message: **wa'erihwanéra'ke'** she swore, she sinned; and DISTR -hon-: **rarihwanera'ákhons** he is swearing; with N -rihw- matter, message, and NMZR -hser-: **karihwanera'ákhsera'** sin; and V -akaion-/-kaion- be old: **iorihwanera'akhseraká:ion** original sin; and NMZR -hser- and V -ihei[on]-/-enhei[on]- die: **wa'karihwanera'akhserakaionhserénheie'** the woman of ill repute died (*a playful expression from Mike Norton*).

NOTE: *See also* -atahonhsanera'[k]- mishear. The short accented vowel suggests that this root goes back to an earlier form *-ner'a[k]-.

-nerenh- N tapeworm: **onerénha'** worm; **ronerénha'** he has worms, **iakonerénha'** she has worms.

With V -ta'-/-eta'- put inside: **wahonerénhata'ne'** he got worms.

Cf. Onnerénha vers, *Tagnonkȣatseran-honθo gontiagentakȣa onnerenha* donne moy médecine pour faire sortir les vers (Bruyas: 73); *onneraha* Vers (Galissonnière: 82v); *Onerēnha* Ver du corps (Marcoux: 412); *Onerenha* ver intestinal (Cuoq: 33)

-neren[k] tie up. *See* -hwaneren[k]-/-neren[k]-

-neri'tst- N bellybutton, navel: **onerì:tsta'** POSS: **keneri'tstà:ke** (on) my bellybutton.

With V -ke'tot- protrude, and CISL:

tioneri'tstakè:tote' squash.
With V -kowan[en]-/-owan[en]- be big:
saneri'tstowá:nen you have a big belly-button.

-nerokw- N vest, top: **oneró:kwa'**
With V -ien- put down, have:
kaneró:kwaien' it (an animal) is lying down.
With SRF -ate- and V -onni- make:
wa'katenerokón:ni' I curled up,
iotenerokón:ni it is lying down.

-neront- N deer fly: **onerón:ta'**
NOTE: Also 'wasp' Lazore (42).

-ne[t]- be lined, doubled. *See* -hna'ne[t]-/
-ne[t]-

-netahkw- remove a lining, make a copy. *See* -hna'netahkw-/-netahkw-

-neta'- line, double. *See* -hna'neta'-/-neta'-

nè:'e that one

-ne'konhre[k]- V hit with something:
rane'kòn:reks he hits it, he is hammering it, **wa'kene'kòn:reke'** I hammered it, **rone'kòn:re** he has hammered it.
With DISTR -hon-: **rane'konhrékhons** he is hammering.
With CAUS -st-: **iene'konhrékstha'** hammer.

-ne'wara't- V get nauseous, with BEN -ni-/
-en- and DLC: **tewakene'warà:tani** I am nauseous, **tonkene'warà:ten'** I got nauseous.

-(h)nhahsi- V fire someone, let go:
wahonwahnháhsi' they let him go, he got fired.

NOTE: This stem is composed of a root -(h)nha-, which occurs only with suffixes, and REV -hsi-.

-(h)nhaten- V regret, feel bad about, rue:
kehnhá:tens I regret it, I feel bad about it, **wahahnhá:ten'** he regretted it, **wakehnhatèn:'en** I have regretted it, **iohnhá:ten** it's too bad, it's a shame.
• Kehnhá:tens iah teiotòn:'on tho niaonkwé:non. I regret it that I couldn't go there. • Wa'kehnhá:ten' iah í: tha'tewakatèn:tshon'. I was sorry I didn't win.
Cf. Ionhnhá:ten tsi iáhten tehské:iahre oh kwáh na'kakwiró:ten. But it is a shame that I do not remember the [species of] tree. (Old Kahnawake: 2)

-(h)nha'- V hire, order: **róhnha's** he hires him, **enkhéhnha'ne'** I will hire her, **wahíhnha'ne'** I hired him, **rihnhà:'on** I have hired him.
With PURP -ser-: **konhnhà:sere'** I am here to hire you.
With SRF -aten-: **katénhnha's** I am hiring help, **wa'katénhnha'ne'** I hired, I gave orders; and PURP -ser-: **katenhnhà:sere'** I am going to hire.
With NMZR -tsher-: **kahnhà:tshera'** hired work, help, **rahnhà:tshera'** a male worker, **iehnhà:tshera'** a female worker.
With SRF -aten- and NMZR -ser-:
atenhnhà:sera' chief's installation.
NOTE: This stem is composed of a root -(h)nha-, which occurs only with suffixes, and INCH -'-.
• Wahóhnha'ne' tà:rahkwe' kéntskare'. He told, ordered him to pick up the rug.
• Enkhéhnha'ne' aion'therón:ni'. I will hire her to make baskets. • Nahò:ten' wahsaténhnha'ne' áhsake'? What did you order to eat?

-(h)nhe- V defend, with CISL: **tekhéhnhes** I defend her, **tahíhnhe'** I defended him, **tahakéhnhe'** he defended me.
With NEG: **iah tethakehnhè:'on** he didn't defend me.

-(h)nhoh- N door: **kahnhóha'**
With LOC -'ke-: **kahnhohà:ke** on the door.
With V -ahsihara'- get wedged in, stuck, and DLC: **wa'tkahnhohahsíhara'ne'** the door got stuck, **teiohnhohahsiharà:'on** the door is stuck.
With V -akahron- be wide, and DLC: **tekahnhohakà:ron** (it is) a wide door.
With SRF -ate-, V -hna'neta'-/-neta'- line, double, and DLC: **tewatehnhohanéta's** storm door.
With V -ia'[k]- hit, slap: **wa'kehnhoháia'ke'** I knocked on the door; and DISTR -hon-: **kehnhohaia'ákhons** I am knocking on the door, **wa'kehnhohaia'ákhon'** I knocked (gave several knocks) on the door.
With V -ienht- hit against: **wahahnhóhaienhte'** he slammed the door.
With V -kahront- make an opening, a hole: **kehnhohakahróntha'** I am making a hole in the door, **wa'kehnhohakahrón:ten'** I made a hole in the door.
With V -kareni- take back and forth: **rahnhohakarénie's** he goes in and out, **wahahnhohakaré:ni** he went in and out, **rohnhohakarénion** he is going in and out.
With V -ketskw- raise upright: **wa'kehnhohakétsko'** I lifted up the (trap) door.
With V -niiont- hang, suspend: **wa'kehnhohaniión:ten'** I hung the door, I put in a door; and INSTR -hkw-: **iehnhohaniiontáhkhwa'** hinge.

With SRF -ate- and V -'sere-/-i'sere- drag: **watehnhohì:sere's** the door is scraping (the floor, because the floor is uneven, or the door has shifted).

-(h)nhonhtishon- V knock on a door: **wa'kehnhonhtíshon'** I knocked on the door.
With CISL: **thahnhonhtíshon** he is knocking on the door, **tahahnhonhtíshon'** he knocked on the door.
With TRNL: **ia'kehnhonhtíshon'** I knocked on the door.

-(h)nhont- V have in one's mouth: **wakéhnhonte'** I have something in my mouth, **róhnhonte'** he has something in his mouth, **iakóhnhonte'** she has something in her mouth.
With N -hneht- pine: **wakhnehtáhnhonte'** I have gum in my mouth.
With N -ien'kw- tobacco: **roien'kwáhnhonte'** he has tobacco in his mouth.
With N -nawir- tooth: **wakenawiráhnhonte'** I have dentures.
With N -(h)nhoskw- cheeks (inside of the cheeks), jowl: **wakehnhoskwáhnhonte'** I have a mouthful.
With INCH -'-, *see* -(h)nhonta'- put in one's mouth.
With CAUS -ho-, *see* -(h)nhontho- put in someone's mouth.

-(h)nhonta'- V put in one's mouth
With SRF -ate-: **iontehnhónta's** she or someone puts it in her mouth; harmonica, **wa'katehnhónta'** I put it in my mouth.
With SRF -at- and N -ien'kw- tobacco: **ratien'kwahnhónta's** he puts tobacco in his mouth, **wahatien'kwahnhónta'** he put tobacco in his mouth.
With SRF -ate- and N -(h)nhoskw- cheeks, jowl: **wa'ontehnhoskwahnhónta'** she

took a mouthful, **iontehnhoskwahnhónta** Have her take a mouthful!

With N -rist- iron, steel: **wa'keristahnhónta'** I put the bit in (the horse's) mouth, **seristahnhónta** Put the bit in its mouth! and SRF -ate-: **wateristahnhónta's** bit.

With SRF -at- and N -tsikhe't- sweet: **wa'kattsikhe'tahnhónta'** I put candy in my mouth.

NOTE: This stem is composed of -(h)nhont- have in one's mouth, and INCH -'-.

-(h)nhontho- V put in someone's mouth: **khehnhónthos** I am putting food in her mouth, I am feeding her (for example, an elderly person or a baby), **enkhehnhóntho'** I will feed her, **wahonwahnhóntho'** she fed him, **rihnhónthon** I have fed him.

With TRNL: **iahahnhóntho'** he plugged it in, he put it in a socket.

NOTE: This stem is composed of -(h)nhont- have in one's mouth, and CAUS -ho-.

-(h)nhoskw- N cheeks (inside of the cheeks), jowl: **ohnhóskwa'**

With V -kowan[en]-/-owan[en]- be big, and DLC: **teiehnhoskowá:nen's** she has big cheeks.

With V -(h)nhont- have in one's mouth: **wakehnhoskwáhnhonte'** I have a mouthful.

With SRF -ate- and V -(h)nhonta'- put in one's mouth: **wa'ontehnhoskwahnhónta'** she took a mouthful, **iontehnhoskwahnhónta** Have her take a mouthful!

With SRF -ate- and V -nohare-/-ohare- wash: **wa'katehnhoskóhare'** I rinsed my mouth.

With SRF -ate- and V -sera[hw]-/ -osera[hw]- gush, spew: **wa'kheiatehnhoskóserahwe'** I squirted

liquid (water, juice) at her out of my mouth.

See also **tionhnhónskwaron** cow.

Cf. toka iakonawiranonwaks iontenhoskwanhonta ostona tsi nenkati teiaonriakwa [maybe someone has a toothache, have them take a small mouthful on the side it is throbbing] (Beauvais: 2)

-(h)nhoton- V close: **kehnhó:tons** I close it, **enkehnhó:ton'** I will close it, **wa'kehnhó:ton'** I closed it, **wakehnhó:ton** I have closed it; **kehnhó:ton** I am in jail, **rahnhó:ton** he is in jail, **iehnhó:ton** she is in jail, **eniesahnhó:ton'** they will put you in jail, **wahonwahnhó:ton'** they put him in jail, **ronwahnhó:ton** they locked him up, he is in jail; and INSTR -hkw-: **tsi iontatehnhotónhkhwa'** jail.

With SRF -ate-: **wahatehnhó:ton'** he got put away, locked up.

With REFL -atate-: **wahatatehnhó:ton'** he locked himself up, in, or out.

With REV -kw-: **rahnhotónkwas** he opens it, **wa'kehnhotón:ko'** I opened it, **rohnhotónkwen** he has opened it, **kahnhotónkwen** it is open; **kahnhotónkwa'** key(s); and POSS: **akehnhotónkwa'** my keys; and ATTR =shon'a, pluralizer: **akehnhotonkwa'shòn:'a** my keys.

With N -hah- road: **kahahahnhó:ton** the road is closed.

With N -'nerohkw- box, and REV -kw-: **wa'ke'nerohkwahnhotón:ko'** I opened the box.

-(h)nho'kw- N cheek: **ohnhò:kwa'**

POSS: **kehnho'kwà:ke** (on) my cheek, **rahnho'kwà:ke** (on) his cheek, **iehnho'kwà:ke** (on) her cheek.

With V -kahront- make an opening, a

hole: **iakohnho'kwakà:ronte'** she has a dimple; and DISTR -on-: **iakohnho'kwakahrón:ton** she has dimples (on both sides of her face).

-(h)nhr- N sickness, disease: **káhnhra'**
With V -akaion-/-kaion- be old, and BEN -'s-: **wakehnhrakaiòn:se'** I have tuberculosis, **wahohnhraká:ion'se'** he got tuberculosis.
With V -ine- (with the variant -tarine-) lead: **kahnhratarí:ne's** the disease is going around, an epidemic, **wa'kahnhrá:tarine'** the disease went around.
• Iakó:ra's kí:ken kahnhratarí:ne's. This epidemic is contagious.
Cf. Gannᶜra Contagion (Galissonnière: 22v); *Kānnra* Mal, maladie (Marcoux: 238); *Kannra* maladie (Cuoq: 11); *iakonhrakaions* [tuberculosis] (Beauvais: 14); *kannhrakaiontsera* [tuberculosis] (Granger: 2); *kann-ra-ta-ri-nes* there is much sickness (Cory: 49)

-(h)nhra't- V have grey hair: **wakehnhrà:te'** or **wakehnhrà:then'** I have grey hair, **rohnhrà:te'** or **rohnhrà:then'** he has grey hair, **iakohnhrà:te'** or **iakohnhrà:then'** she has grey hair.

-ni- N snow
With V -'rhoro[k]-/-oro[k]- cover: **onkenió:roke'** I got snowed in, **ionkwanió:ron** we are snowed in.
With V -otka'w- go through, channel: **wahaniótka'we'** he went through, channelled through the (deep) snow; and PROG -hatie-: **wakeniotka'wenhátie'** I am going through the snow.

-niahes- V depend on: **keniahé:sen** I depend on it, I rely on it, **konniahé:sen** I am depending on you, relying on you, I trust you, **enkeniáhese'** I will depend on it, rely on it, **wa'keniáhese'** I depended on it, relied on it, **wahiniáhese'** I depended, relied on him.
• Wa'keniáhese' ne iewennahnotáhkhwa' wa'ón:kon'. I depended, relied on the reading material she gave me.

-niahkar- N nape of the neck, with LOC -okon, under: **keniahkaró:kon** my nape, **raniahkaró:kon** his nape, **ieniahkaró:kon** her nape.

-niahkwe'rh- N mane (of a horse): **oniahkwè:rha'**

-niahskwa'rh- N hip: **oniahskwà:rha'**
POSS: **keniahskwa'rhà:ke** my hip, **raniahskwa'rhà:ke** his hip, **ieniahskwa'rhà:ke** her hip.
With V -nonhwak[t]- be sore, hurt: **wakeniahskwa'rhanòn:waks** my hip hurts.
With V -ta'-/-eta'- put inside: **ó:ia' wa'onkeniahskwa'rháta'** they put a new hip in me.
NOTE: There is a lot of speaker variation of this root: GM reported **ononskwárha'** (-nonskwarh-), but in addition there is **ohnhenskwà:rha** (-nhenskwa'rh-, Horne: 99) and **onehskwà:rha** (-nehskwa'rh-thigh, Lazore: 58).
Cf. ononskwārha hanche (Marcoux: 199); *se nonhs kwar ha keh* hip (Jamieson 3: 3)

-niahton- V belong to the Turtle clan: **wakeniáhton** I am Turtle clan.
Cf. Roniáchta er ist aus dem Geschlecht der Schildkroete (Pyrlaeus: 481); *Ratiniahten* (la bande de) la petite tortue (Marcoux: 377); *ratiniahten* la bande de la tortue (Cuoq: 154); Iroquois "The first

is that of the Tortoise, which calls itself *Atiniathin*." (O'Callaghan I: 3)

-nia[k]- V wrap around the neck
   With N -hstaro'kw- necklace, chain:
   wa'khehstaro'kwániake' I put a necklace on her; and SRF -at-:
   wa'katstaro'kwániake' I put on a necklace, **iakotstaro'kwánien** she has on a necklace.
   With N -nennotsher- package, parcel:
   wahanennotsherániake' he put the horse collar on (the horse), **senennotsherániak** Put the collar on!
   With SRF -ate- and N -nia'tar- fabric, material: **enkatenia'tarániake'** I will put on a tie or scarf, **wahatenia'tarániake'** he put on a tie or scarf, **rotenia'taránien** he has on a tie or scarf.
   With N -tsinaren't- hoof:
   rotsinaren'tánien he is a runner or sub-chief; *literally*, he has a hoof around his neck.
   With SRF -ate-, N -'nhehs- silk, satin, and CAUS -st-: **ionte'nhehsaniákstha'** necktie.

-niak- V get married: **wakéniaks** I get married, **enwakéniake'** I will get married, **wahóniake'** he got married, **wakeniá:kon** I am married, **ionkeniniá:kon** we are married.
   With PURP -h-: **roniákhe'** he is going to get married.
   With CAUS -st-: **iakoniákstha'** anything used at a wedding, **iakoniákstha' atià:tawi't** wedding dress, (-atia'tawi- dress, shirt), **iakoniákstha' teiona'taratsikhè:tare'** wedding cake (-na'tar[o][k]-bread, -tsikhe't- sweet).

-niar- N neck: **oniá:ra'**
   POSS: **keniarà:ke** (on) my neck, **raniarà:ke** (on) his neck, **ieniarà:ke** (on) her neck.
   With V -a'senht-/-enht- drop:
   wahskwaniá:renhte' you finished all our food; and SRF -ate-: **kateniarénhtha'** I am dropping my head or neck (because I am moping or feeling dejected), **enkateniá:renhte'** I will drop my neck, **wakateniarénhton** I have dropped my neck; and CISL: **tkateniarénhtha'** I put down my neck (so my chin is on my chest, maybe while exercising), **entkateniá:renhte'** I will put down my neck, **tahateniá:renhte'** he put down his neck, **tasateniá:renht** Put down your neck!
   With V -her-/-hr- set on top of:
   iehnenhsà:ke ieniaráhere' her head is nodding, she is putting her neck towards her shoulder (-hnenhs- shoulder).
   With V -hnir- be hard, solid:
   wakeniarahní:ron I have a strong neck.
   With -hren't-/-en't- hang down:
   wakeniarèn:ton I have my head or neck hanging (to my chest); and AMB -hne-:
   roniaren'tòn:ne' he has his head down walking, **iakoniaren'tòn:ne'** she has her head down walking.
   With V -hwatase-/-tase- turn, twist:
   Wà:s enkonniaratá:se'! Go on, I will wring your neck! (talking to a dog).
   With SRF -ate- and V -ni'e[k]- sprain, pull a muscle: **wa'kateniaranì:'eke'** I sprained my neck, I pulled something in my neck, **wakateniaranì:'e** I have a sprained neck.
   With SRF -ate- and V -nohare-/-ohare-wash: **wahateniaróhare'** he washed his neck.
   With V -nonhwak[t]- be sore, hurt:
   wakeniaranòn:waks my neck hurts.
   With V -otahrho[k]- hook, and CISL:
   thaniarotáhrhoks ship's pilot, captain of a war canoe, **entehseniarotáhrhoke'** you will take control of the handlebars, sleigh

runners, steering wheel, reins,
takeniarotáhrhoke' I took control of the
handlebars, sleigh runners, wheel, reins,
thoniarotáhrhon he is in charge,
tiakoniarotáhrhon she is in charge.

Cf. Onniara tête coupé, *Ganniarenton*
couper la tête, tuer des ambassadeurs ou
autres venus (Bruyas: 75); *ondiara* col,
hoñandiaren^cton on la decollé (Galissonnière: 21r); *Kateniarēntha* baisser la tête
(Marcoux: 387); *thaniarotārhos* Pilote
(Marcoux: 291); *tha nia ro tar hoks* pilot
(Anon: 11)

niá:re' for now, **wa'ts niá:re'** later

-niatar- N river, lake: **oniá:tara'** or
kaniá:tara'
With LOC -akta', near: **kaniatarákta'**
near the river.
With LOC -atatie', along, edge of:
kaniataratátie' there's a river, lake
going along.
With LOC -'ke, at: **kaniatarà:ke** on or
at the river; and ATTR =kowa, great:
kaniatara'kehkó:wa ocean; and
tetiaon'kwara'éhstha' (unknown
composition): **kaniatara'kehkó:wa
tetiaon'kwara'éhstha'** northern lights.
With V -her-/-hr- set on top of:
kaniataráhere' there is a river, a lake.
With V -hren't-/-en't- hang down:
ioniatarèn:ton loon.
With V -iio- be good, nice: **Kaniatarí:io**
Lake Ontario; and REP: **Skaniatarí:io**
name of the Seneca prophet Handsome
Lake and Seneca title name.
With V -kwaront- bulge, lump:
Ioniatarakwá:ronte' Chambly, Québec.
With V -oken- merge, fork, and DLC:
tekaniataró:ken two waterways merging
or forking.
With V -sera[hw]-/-osera[hw]- gush, spew:

Kaniataróseras Kayaderosseras, NY.
With V -ti- be on the other side, and REP:
Skaniatará:ti Lachine, Québec.
Cf. Skandiatarati d'Europe (Bruyas: 52);
Skanniatarate france, au dela du lac
(Galissonnière: 43r); *Skaniatarati*
[Lachine] (Granger: 2); *Ska nien ta ra ti*
Lachine (Anon: 17); *Ska-nien-ta-ra-ti*
Lachine (Cory: 82); *Skanientará:ti
(Skaniatará:ti)* Lachine (Horne: 60)

-niatsteren[k]- V tie, fasten hair:
wa'kheniátsterenke' I put a ribbon in
her hair.
With SRF -ate-: **wa'kateniátsterenke'**
I fastened my hair with a ribbon,
iakoteniátsteren she has a ribbon
fastened in her hair.
With SRF -ate- and CAUS -st-; and
kà:nhehs (-'nhehs- silk, satin):
kà:nhehs ionteniatsterénkstha' ribbon.
Cf. onniatsara porcelaine que les femmes
attachent aux cheveux que leur pendant
derrière la teste (Bruyas: 75); *Onniatsa* la
queue des femmes (Galissonnière: 20r);
Oniatsa couette, queue de cheveaux; le
ruban qui les attache (Cuoq: 34)

niá:wen thanks. **Niá:wen ki' wáhi.** Thank
you very much.
With ATTR =kowa, great: **niawenhkó:wa**
thank you very much.

-nia'kw- N throat: **onià:kwa'**
POSS: **kenia'kwà:ke** my throat.
With CAUS -ht- and CISL:
thonia'kwáhtha' he burps,
tonkenià:kwahte' I burped (and it
came up on me), **thonia'kwáhton**
he has burped.
With V -her-/-hr- set on top of:
onia'kwáhehr camel.

-nia't- N throat

With V -akahron- be wide, and CAUS -hst-:
iakonia'takahrónhstha' cough drop,
mints.

With V -astath[en]-/-ath[en]- dry:
wakenia'táthens I am thirsty,
onkenia'táthen' I got thirsty.

With V -hwawen'e[k]-/-awen'e[k]- wrap,
and DLC: **teiakonia'tawèn:'eks** chokecherry.

With V -na'nawen-/-nawen- be wet:
onkenia'taná:wen' I quenched my thirst.

With V -o- be in water: **kanià:to** beaver
dam.

With V -oren- split open, and DLC:
wa'tewakenia'tó:ren' I burped.

See also -nia'thara'- have something
go down one's throat, choke.

Cf. deyagonia'dawą́ ıks Chokecherry
(Waugh: 128); *te-ia-go-nia-ta-wen-eks*
Prunus virginiana [chokecherry]
(Rousseau: 47); *Teiakonia'tawèn:'eks*
Chokecherry (Horne: 112)

-nia'tar- N fabric, material

With ATTR ='a/=ha, diminutive:
onia'tarà:'a fabric, material.

With ATTR =shon'a , pluralizer:
onia'tara'shòn:'a fabrics, different kinds
of material.

With LOC -'ke: **onia'tarà:ke** on the material or cloth.

With SRF -ate- and V -nia[k]- wrap around
the neck: **enkatenia'tarániake'** I will put
on a tie or scarf, **wahatenia'tarániake'** he
put on a tie or scarf, **rotenia'taránien** he
has on a tie or scarf.

With V -ohar- attach at the end:
kania'taróhare' there is a cloth attached
to it (a flag on a pole, a rag on a stick); and
SRF -ate- and INSTR -hkw-:
iontenia'taroharáhkhwa' flag.

-nia'thara'- V have something go down one's
throat, choke, with DLC:
tewakenia'thá:ra's I choke,
wa'tiakonia'thá:ra'ne' she choked,
tehonia'tharà:'on he is choking.

-nia'ton- V flood: **ranià:tons** he floods it
(maybe when a beaver is making a dam),
enkenià:ton' I will flood it, **wakenià:ton**
I have flooded it.

-nieht- V send with someone, with TRNL:
ienkhéniehte' I will send it with her,
iahíniehte' I sent it with him,
iekheniéhton I have sent it with her.

With SRF -aten-: **iekatenniéhtha'** I send
it, **ienkaténniehte'** I will send it,
ienkheiaténniehte' I will send her,
iewakatenniéhton I have sent it.

With SRF -aten- and BEN -enni-/-en-:
ia'kheiatenniéhten' I sent it to her,
iekheiatenniehtén:ni I have sent it to her.

-nieht- N snow: **óniehte'**

With V -a'senht-/-enht- drop, and TRNL:
iahaniéhtenhte' he moved, threw the
snow off it.

With V -hkw- pick up, and DLC:
wa'tkaniéhtahkwe' the snow left.

With N -hnot- indicating depth, and V -es-
be long, tall: **ioniehtahnó:tes** it is deep
snow.

With V -ien- put down, have: **kaniéhtaien'**
there's snow (on the ground).

With V -kehron[t]- put down here and
there: **kaniehtakè:ron** there are patches
of snow here and there.

With V -kste- be heavy: **ioniehtákste'**
(it is) heavy snow.

With V -ohtahrho- be tidy, and DLC:
tekeniehtohtáhrhos I am removing the
snow, cleaning off the snow,

tekaniehtohtáhrhos snowplow, **wa'tkeniehtohtáhrho'** I shovelled snow. With V -otahrhe- get hooked on something: **wahaniehtotáhrhe'ne'** he got stuck in the snow.
With V -rohro[k]- gather, collect: **ioniehtarò:ron** the snow has piled up, there's a snowdrift; and DISTR -hon-: **ioniehtarohrókhon** there's snowdrifts.

-nieien- V snow on the ground: **kanié:ien'** there is snow on the ground, **wa'kanié:ien'** it snowed.
• Ahsatkáhtho' tsi ní:kon kanié:ien' ne Kahnawà:ke teiotenonhianíhton. You should see how much snow is on the ground in Kahnawà:ke, it's terrible (drastic). (Letter 1945, Jan)

-nient- N shin: **onién:ta'** shin
POSS: **kenientà:ke** (on) my shin.
With V -ia'k- hit, bang, and TRNL: **iahonkeniéntia'ke'** I banged my shin.
With V -ia'[k]- hit, slap: **wahakenientáia'ke'** he hit me in the shin.
With unclear V, and DLC: **tewakenientawí:sas** I have growing pains, **tehonientawí:sas** he has growing pains, **teiakonientawí:sas** she has growing pains.

-nienthahrho[k]- V lock a door: **kenientháhrhoks** I am locking the door, **wa'kenientháhrhoke'** I locked the door, **iakonientháhrhon** she has locked the door, **senientháhrhok** Lock the door!
NOTE: This stem is composed of a root -nienthar-, which occurs only with suffixes, and CAUS -ho-.

-nientharakw- V unlock a door: **enienienthará:ko'** she will unlock the door, **wa'kenienthará:ko'** I unlocked the

door, **ronientharákwen** he has unlocked the door.
NOTE: This stem is composed of a root -nienthar-, which occurs only with suffixes, and REV -kw-.

-nien'- N flint, with ATTR ='ke, at: **Kanièn:ke** a Kanien'kehá:ka community in NY state; and ATTR =haka/=aka, people of: **Kanien'kehá:ka** People of the Flint. With ATTR =keha, way of: **Kanien'kéha** Kanine'kéha (Mohawk) language.
Cf. "first, the Mahakinbas, or, as they call themselves, *Kajingahaga*," (Megapolensis: 172); "that our Indians in the neighborhood, who are generally called Maquaas, but who call themselves *Kajingehaga*," (Megapolensis: 403); *Agniehronons* [Mohawks] (Jogues in Jameson: 262); *Ganniegehage* raꞟennontagon Il parle la langue d'Agnier (Bruyas: 122); *ganniegeronnon* Les Agniers (Bruyas: 36); *Ganniegeronnon* vel *Ganniegehaga* a *Ganniege* (Bruyas: 18); "he resided several years at Tienonderoga among one of the Iroquois Nations of Indians, who call themselves *Caningehage*, and are by the English called Mohocks." (Barclay in O'Callaghan III: 902); *Canyingoes* Mohocks (Boyd: 4); "which being the symbol of their Nation, This Steel they call *Canniah* — & themselves *Canniungaes*, but from hence, little can be deduced, as they had not the use of any instrument in that form before their Commerce with the Whites," (Sir W. Johnson in O'Callaghan IV: 432); *Kanienke* "On s'accorde généralement à expliquer ce mot par: là où il y a de la pierre à fusil, KANNHIA. Les habitants de KANIENKE s'appellent: *Kanienkehaka* vel *Kanienkeronon*" (Cuoq: 164)

-nien'ser- N trigger: **kanièn:sera'**
With V -a'senht-/-enht- drop, and CISL:
tahanièn:serenhte' he pulled the trigger.
With V -'niaken- escape, and INCH -'-:
wa'kanien'sera'niá:ken'ne' the trigger
went off accidentally.

-nien'te- V come for a purpose, a reason:
kenièn:te' I come for a purpose, I am
here for something, **ranièn:te'** he comes
for something, **ienièn:te'** she comes for
something.
• Nahò:ten' senièn:te'? Why are you here?
• Kenièn:te' (tóka') enwá:ton' ken ahstié:-
nawa'se'. I'm here to see if you can help
me.

-ni[h]- V lend: **keníhas** I lend it to someone,
wa'khé:ni' I lent it to her, **wa'ónkeni'**
she or they lent it to me, I borrowed it,
shakoníhen he has lent it to her.
With REFL -atate-: **wa'katáteni'** I borrowed it, **wa'ontáteni'** she borrowed it.
With N -hwist- metal, money:
wa'onkhwístani' she or they lent me
money.
With N -'sereht- car: **wa'khe'seréhtani'**
I lent her my car.
• enhonwatí:ni ne kaión:ni. they will borrow [someone or they will lend it to them]
this wampum (Old Kahnawake: 4)

-niharaht- V take a shortcut, with DLC:
tekeniharáhtha' I am taking a shortcut,
wa'thanihá:rahte' he took a shortcut,
wa'tienihá:rahte' she took a shortcut,
tewakeniharáhton I have taken a shortcut.

-niiont- V hang, suspend: **keniióntha'** I am
hanging it, I am looping it onto something,
enkeniión:ten' I will hang it,
wa'keniión:ten' I hung it, **roní:ionte'**

he has hung it, **kaní:ionte'** it is hanging
(on a hook), **seniión:ten** Hang it!
With DISTR -onnion-: **kaniiontónnion**
they are hanging.
With SRF -ate-: **ateniión:ta'** apron.
With N -(h)nhoh- door:
wa'kehnhohaniión:ten' I hung the door,
I put in a door; and INSTR -hkw-:
iehnhohaniiontáhkhwa' hinge.
With N -'now- hump, padlock:
wa'ke'nowaniión:ten' I locked it,
se'nowaniión:ten Lock it! *This is an
older expression.*
• Ahsonhtà:ke seniión:ten ieià:tare'! Hang
her picture on the wall!

niió:re' extent. For example:
tsi niió:re' while, during, until.

ní:kon amount. For example:
tsi ní:kon that much,
Tó: ní:kon? How many?
thok ní:kon that's all.
With PART, TRNL, and DLC:
nia'té:kon all kinds of, different ones.
With ATTR ='a/=ha, diminutive:
ken' nikón:ha a little bit.
With PROG -hatie-: **ken' nikonhátie'**
a little bit at a time.

ni' also. Short form of **ò:ni'**

-ni'- V be stingy: **ronì:'on** he is stingy,
cheap, a miser, **iakonì:'on** she is stingy.

-ni'e[k]- V sprain, pull a muscle
With SRF -ate- and N -niar- neck:
wa'kateniaranì:'eke' I sprained my neck,
I pulled something in my neck,
wakateniaranì:'e I have a sprained neck.
With SRF -ate- and N -ronhkwe'n- spine,
back: **wa'kateronhkwe'nanì:'eke'** I
sprained my back.

-ni'keronkw- V twitch: **wa'oni'kerón:ko'** it twitched.

With N -kahr- eye: **wakkahrani'kerónkwas** my eye is twitching, **onkkahrani'kerón:ko'** my eye twitched.

• Wa'oni'kerón:ko' ne khsinà:ke. My leg twitched.

-no- V be cold

With N -ahsont- night: **iohsón:tano** it is a cold night; and CAUS -hst-: **enwahsón:tanohste'** the night will cool off.

With V -a'tarih[en]-/-tarih[en]- be hot, warm, NMZR -hser-, and CAUS -hst-: **wa'ka'tarihenhserá:nohste'** I got a cold, **waka'tarihenhseranóhston** I have a cold.

With N -enhniser- day: **iawenhniserá:no** it is a cold day; and PART: **tsi niiawenhniserá:no** it is a really cold day; with N -enhniser- day, and CAUS -hst-: **enwenhniserá:nohste'** the day will cool off.

With N -hnek- liquid: **ohné:kanos** fresh, cold water, **iohné:kano** it is cold water.

With N -i'tonhkw- flame, fever, omen, CAUS -hst-, INSTR -hkw-, and DLC: **teie'tonhkwanohstáhkhwa'** mint (herb) (from Rousseau: 58, who says an infusion of this herb reduces fever in children).

With N -nennio'kw- snowball: **ionenniò:kwano** ice cream; and CAUS -hst-: **kanennio'kwanóhstha'** freezer, **wa'kenenniò:kwanohste'** I froze it.

With N -nonhs- house: **ionónhsano** (it is) a cold house, **ronónhsano** his house is cold.

With N -onhwents-/-onhonts- earth: **shé:kon iaonhontsá:no** the ground is still cold.

With N -wer- wind, air: **iowerá:no** (it is) a chilly wind; and CAUS -hst-: **eniowerá:nohste'** it (the air) will cool off.

With N -'kats- limb, CAUS -hst-, and DLC: **teke'katsanóhstha'** my legs are cold, **wa'tke'kátsanohste'** my legs got cold.

Cf. Probably: *Cuerano* [February] (Wassenaer: 73); *îe-don-wka-nos-ta-kwa* Menthe Canadensis (Rousseau: 58)

-no- KIN stepfather, stepmother, stepchild, with ATTR ='a/=ha, diminutive: **rakenò:'a** my stepfather, **ionkenò:'a** my stepmother, **rinò:'a** my stepson, **khenò:'a** my stepdaughter.

-noha-/-nonha- KIN uncle, with ATTR ='a/=ha, diminutive: **rakenohà:'a** or **rakenonhà:'a** my uncle, **ronohà:'a** or **rononhà:'a** his uncle, **ronwanohà:'a** or **ronwanonhà:'a** her uncle.

NOTE: Mary Deer's 1971 Mohawk class notes (Lesson 5) give **manok** uncle, a borrowing from French *mon oncle* and unrelated to -noha-/-nonha-.

-nohare-/-ohare- V wash: **kenóhares** I wash it, **enkenóhare'** I will wash it, **wa'kenóhare'** I washed it, **wakenóhare** I have washed it.

With DISTR -nion-: **kanoharénion** laundry.

With N -ahi- fruit, berry: **wa'kahióhare'** I washed fruit.

With SRF -at- and N -ahsir- blanket, shawl: **wa'katahsiróhare'** I washed the blanket.

With N -ahsi't- foot: **wahiiahsi'tóhare'** I washed his feet; and SRF -ar-: **wa'karahsi'tóhare'** I washed my feet.

With N -ahts- hand: **enhahtsóhare'** he will wash his hands, **wa'kahtsóhare'** I washed my hands, **iakohtsóhare** she has washed her hands.

With N -atokw-/-atokwahtsher- spoon: **wa'katokwahtsheróhare'** I washed the spoon.

With SRF -at- and N -a'ar- net, curtain, veil: **wa'kata'aróhare'** I washed the curtains; and DISTR -nion-: **wa'kata'aroharénion'** I washed the curtains.

With SRF -at- and N -hna'tsh- buttocks: **Wà:s sathna'tshóhare** Go, wash your butt!

With SRF -at- and N -hnia's- neck, collar: **rathnia'sóhares** he is gargling, **wa'kathnia'sóhare'** I gargled.

With N -kenh- felt: **kakenhóhare** mop.

With SRF -at- and N -konhs- face: **wa'katkonhsóhare'** I washed my face, **satkonhsóhare** Wash your face!

With N -ks- dish, plate: **keksóhares** I am washing dishes, **wa'keksóhare'** I washed dishes, **wakeksóhare** I have washed dishes; and DISTR -nion-: **wa'keksoharénion'** I washed dishes.

With SRF -ate- and N -nahstonhkw- window, windowsill: **wa'katenahstonhkóhare'** I washed the windowsills.

With N -na'ts- pail: **Kana'tsóhare** Canajoharie, NY; and ATTR ='ke, at: **Kana'tsoharè:ke** at Canajoharie. (See Lounsbury 1960: 28 for the etymology.)

With N -nenhst- corn: **wa'kenenhstóhare'** I washed the corn.

With SRF -ate- and N -(h)nhoskw- cheeks, jowl: **wa'katehnhoskóhare'** I rinsed my mouth.

With SRF -ate- and N -niar- neck: **wahateniaróhare'** he washed his neck.

With V -nonhware- soap, and NMZR -'tsher-: **kenonhware'tsheróhares** I am rinsing the soap off (the dishes, the laundry), **wa'enonhware'tsheróhare'** she rinsed it, **wakenonhware'tsheróhare** I have rinsed it.

With N -ronhkwe'n- spine, back: **wahakeronhkwe'nóhare'** he washed my back; and SRF -ate-: **wahateronhkwe'nóhare'** he washed his (own) back.

With N -tsiser- pane of glass: **wa'ktsiseróhare'** I washed the window panes; and DISTR -nion-: **wa'ktsiseroharénion'** I washed the window panes.

Cf. Gannaktohare laver la natte, dit on quand on jette de la porcelaine sur un corps mort (Bruyas: 67); *toka iakoniasanonwaks onekanos tenieieste iontniasoaret* [Maybe someone has a sore throat, they mix in some fresh water and gargle with it] (Beauvais: 2); Wendat *Andatsouharet* Nettoye, laue le chaudron (Sagard: La2)

-nohkw- N bundle, a smaller bundle: **kanóhkwa'**

With V -hwaneren[k]-/-neren[k]- tie up: **kenohkwánerenks** I am tying up the bundle, **wa'kenohkwánerenke'** I tied up the bundle, **kanohkwáneren** (it is) a bundle, tied up, **senohkwánerenk** Tie up the bundle!

With V -keht[e]- carry on the back: **ronohkwakéhte'** he is carrying a bundle on his back; and SRF -ate- and CAUS -t-: **ratenohkwakéhtats** hobo, peddler.

With V -onni- make: **wa'kenohkón:ni'** I made a bundle, **wa'khenohkón:ni'** I bundled her up, **shenohkón:ni** Bundle her up!

With V -rihsi- take apart, take off: **wa'kenohkwaríhsi'** I took the bundle apart.

With V -[t]- be one, and REP: **skanóhkwa** one bundle.

nok and

-nonha- uncle. *See* -noha-/-nonha-

-nonhiani- V be extreme, menacing, drastic, terrible, with DLC
With SRF -ate- and CAUS -ht-: **tenwatenòn:ianihte'** it will be drastic, **teiotenonhianíhton** it is extreme, drastic, terrible.
With N -enhniser- day: **teiawenhniseranòn:iani** it is really drastic weather (raining, snowing, windy).
With N -onkwe['t]- person, human being: **teionkwe'tanòn:iani** she acts inappropriately.
With N -tsi'nonw- insect, bug: **teiotsi'nonwanòn:iani** (it is) a big beast.
• Teiotenonhianíhton tsi na'á:wen'. It's terrible what happened. • Teiotenonhianíhton tsi ní:tsi io'toniotátie'. It's extreme how it's piled all over (talking about a house full of stuff).

Cf. tenioskwanonianiton (with incorporated -ahskw- bridge, talking about the Quebec bridge) (Onkweonwe: 3)

-nonhkar[on]- V cut hair: **rinónhkarons** I am cutting his hair, **shakonónhkarons** he cuts their hair, (he is) a barber, **wa'onkenónhkare'** she cut my hair, **rinónhkaron** I have cut his hair.
With PURP -h-: **wahonwanonhkarónhe'** he is going to get a haircut.
With SRF -ate-: **wa'katenónhkare'** I cut my hair.

Cf. Gannon^c karon faire les cheveux, *Gannon^c karáton* avec quoy on coupe les cheveux (Bruyas: 81); *Gannon^c karon* tondre cheveux (Galissonnière: 79v); *Kenōnkhărons* Couper les Cheveux (Marcoux: 91)

-nonhkeri- V be curls
With DLC: **teionónhkeri** it is curly, **tewakenónhkeri** I have curls, curly hair, **tehonónhkeri** he has curly hair,

teiakonónhkeri she has curly hair.
With CAUS -st- and DLC: **wa'tekhenónhkeriste'** I curled her hair; and REFL -atate-: **wa'tkatatenónhkeriste'** I curled my hair.
With CAUS -'t-: **ononhkerì:ta'** shavings (for example, from using a drawknife).

-nonhkw- KIN relative, kinsman: **ká:nonhkwe'** kinsmanship, family, **khé:nonhkwe'** she is a relation of mine, **rí:nonhkwe'** he is a relation.
With REFL -atate-: **tiatátenonhkwe'** you (sg) and I are relatives, **iatiatátenonhkwe'** we two are relatives, he or she is my relative, **iatátenonhkwe'** his or her (male) relative, **tiatátenonhkwe'** her (female) relative, **iakwatátenonhkwe'** we are all relatives, my relatives, **rontátenonhkwe'** they are related.

Cf. Gannonkᴤe avoir pour parent (Bruyas: 81); *Gannon^ckᴤe* avoir pour parent (Galissonnière: 62v); *Kānŏnkᴤe* Parent (Marcoux: 279)

-nonhkw-/- nonhkwa'tsher- N medicine: **onónhkwa'**
With ATTR =onwe, genuine: **ononhkwa'ón:we** natural medicine.
With SRF -ate- and V -hninon- buy: **ratenonhkwa'tsherahní:nons** he sells medicine; and CAUS -'t-: **tsi iontenonhkwa'tsherahninòn:tha'** drugstore, pharmacy.
With V -o- be in water, and CISL: **tiononhkwà:tsheros** pepper; and ATTR =kowa, great: **tiononhkwa'tsheroskó:wa** green or red bell pepper.
With SRF -ate- and V -onni- make: **wa'katenonhkwa'tsherón:ni'** I made medicine; and BEN -en-: **wa'onkenonhkwa'tsherónnien'** she made medicine for me.

With V -te[ht]- be strong-tasting, energetic: **iononhkwa'tsherá:te'** it is strong-tasting medicine.

NOTE: The incorporating form has the NMZR -'tsher-.

Cf. onnonᶜksat médecine (Bruyas: 81); *teienonksātsĕros* Poivre (Marcoux: 296); *Teienonkwatseros* médecine qu'on met dans le liquid, c.-à-d. poivre (Cuoq: 134); *tiononkwatsheros* [pepper] (Beauvais: 9); *tiononkwatseros* [pepper] (Ledger: 79); *tiononkwátseros* pepper (Cory: 87); *tio-non-kwa-tse-ros* Polygonum Hydropiper [water pepper] (Rousseau: 40); *tiononhkwà:tserohs* pepper (Horne: 29); Wendat *énonquate* medecine, herbe (Sagard: Gu2); Onondaga *hononksatchera* medecinne (Shea: 69)

-nonhkware't- N hair

With V -kowan[en]-/-owan[en]- be big: **rononhkware'towá:nen** he has big hair, **iakononhkware'towá:nen** she has big hair.

Cf. Gannonksarita cheveux brouillés (Bruyas: 81); *ononksarēta* chevelure, *sakenonksaretosānen* avoir une grosse (Marcoux: 66)

-nonhkwen'- N corn cob, cone: **ononhkwèn:'on**

With V -hwaneren[k]-/-neren[k]- tie up, and DLC: **tekanonhkwen'áneren** corn cob game, in which two corn cobs joined by a string are hurled and caught with a bent stick.

With V -ke- amount to, and DLC: **tekanonhkwèn:'ake** two corn cobs.

With V -ohar- attach at the end: **kanonhkwen'ohárhra'** a cone is hanging or attached (describing, for example, a pine or sumac), **enkanonhkwen'ohá:ren'** it will get cones,

wa'kanonhkwen'ohá:ren' it got cones.

With V -ohro[k]- insert: **senonhkwen'ò:rok** Keep quiet!

Cf. Onnonksȇñonte épi de blé (Bruyas: 81); *onnonᶜksaonᶜte* Espy (Galissonnière: 37r); *ononksēnhon* epi (Marcoux: 155); *Ononkwenhon* épi de blé (Cuoq: 34); *Tekanonhkwen'áneren* Corn cob game (Tewaterihwarenia'tha, Summer 1988: 24); *tekanonhkwen'áneren* corn cob game (Lazore: 74)

-nonhkwis[er]- N head hair: **onónhkwis**

POSS: **akenónhkwis** my hair.

With V -es- be long: **rotinonhkwíseres** "the long-haired ones," a conservative group in Kanehsatà:ke; and SRF -ate- and CAUS -t-: **wa'katenonhkwísereste'** I let my hair grow.

With V -hon'tsi- be black, dark-coloured: **rononhkwiserahòn:tsi** he has black hair.

Cf. "There was formerly, among them, a famous hermit named *Shonnonkouiretsi* or 'the very long-haired one' whose memory is still venerated." (Lafitau I: 247)

-nonhkwishar[on]- V pull hair, with DLC: **tehshakononhkwísharons** he pulls her hair, **wa'tehshakononhkwíshare'** he pulled her hair, **wa'thinonhkwíshare'** I pulled his hair.

-nonhn- V mind, guard: **rinónhnha'** I am minding him, **khenónhnha'** I am minding her, **kanónhnha'** it is guarding it (for example, a chicken sitting on its eggs), **enkhenòn:na'** I will mind her, **wahinòn:na'** I minded him.

With PURP -'nh-: **wa'kanonhna'à:nhe'** I am going to a wake.

With SRF -at-: **katenónhnha'** I am minding, **enkatenòn:na'** I will mind.

With N -ia't- body: **kheia'tanónhnha'**

I guard her, **wahoia'tanòn:na'** he guarded him.

With SRF -ate- and N -nat- town, settlement: **iakwatenatanónhnha'** we are minding, taking care of the town.

-nonhs- N house: **kanónhsa'**

With LOC -kon, inside: **kanónhskon** in the house; and POSS: **raonónhskon** in his house; with LOC -kon inside, and DISTR -hshon: **kanonhskónhshon** through the house.

With unclear ending: **kanonhsoharà:ke** upstairs.

With V -a- be a size, and PART: **tho nikanónhsa'** the house is that size.

With SRF -a-, V -ahkwatase-/-tase- go around, and TRNL: **ia'kanonhsatá:se'** I went around the house.

With V -akaion-/-kaion- be old, and INCH -'-: **wa'kanonhsaká:ion'ne'** the house got old, **iononhsakaiòn:'on** (it is) an old house.

With V -akarenhr[e]- lean to one side, slant: **kanonhsakarèn:re'** the house is leaning.

With **asé'tsi** new: **kanonhsasé'tsi** a new house.

With V -ati-/-onti- lose, throw: **wahotinonhsón:ti'** they just left their houses (abandoning them); and CAUS -ht-: **rotinonhsontiéhtha'** they leave, close up the houses, **wahotinonhsóntiehte'** they abandoned their houses.

With SRF -ate- and V -atonris[t]- be damp, soggy: **iotenonhsatón:ris** (it is) a damp house.

With V -es- be long: **kanónhses** long-house.

With V -haratat-/-karatat- lift, raise up: **wahatinonhsakará:tate'** they raised the house.

With V -hnhonter- attach end-to-end, add on: **wahanonhsahnhónteren'** or (with

SRF -ate-) **wahatenonhsahnhónteren'** he added on a room to the house.

With SRF -ate-, V -ieron- make fun of, play, DISTR -nion-, and DLC: **tekatenonhsaierónnions** I decorate my house, **wa'tkatenonhsaierónnion'** I decorated my house.

With V -iio- be good, nice: **kanonhsí:io** (it is) a nice house, **tsi kanonhsí:io** parlour.

With V -ionni- be lying, be extended: **Rotinonhsión:ni** they of the extended house, the Haudenosaunee.

With V -i'tson-/-'tson- be dirty, and DLC: **tewakenonhsá'tson** I have a dirty house.

With V -ke- amount to, and DLC: **tekanónhsake** two houses.

With V -kowan[en]-/-owan[en]- be big: **kanonhsowá:nen** (it is) a big house; and ATTR ='ke, at: **kanonhsowanèn:ke** at the hospital; with SRF -ate-, V -kowan[en]-/-owan[en]- be big, and CAUS -ht-: **wa'katenonhsó:wanahte'** I made the house bigger.

With V -no- be cold: **ionónhsano** (it is) a cold house, **ronónhsano** his house is cold.

With V -oken- merge, fork, and DLC: **tekanonhsó:ken** between the houses.

With V -onni- make: **kenonhsón:ni** or (with SRF -ate-) **katenonhsón:ni** I am building a house; with V -onni- make, and ATTR =onwe, genuine: **Rotinonhsonni'ón:we** the founders of the Confederacy.

With V -ot- stand: **kanónhsote'** there's a house (standing), **wakenónhsote'** I have a house, my house.

With V -r- put in, and INCH -'-: **wa'kenónhsara'ne'** I entered the house; with V -r- put in, and CAUS -hst-: **kanonhsaráhston** a drawing of a house.

With SRF -a-, V -ra'neken-/-neken- be side-by-side, next to, and DLC: **teiatianonhsa-né:ken** we two are neighbours, my neighbour, **tehonnonhsané:ken** they are neighbours.

With SRF -ate-, and SRF -ate-, V -re- extent, distance, and PART and DLC: **tsi na'tetiatenonhsátere'** it is between the houses.

With V -tokenhti- be holy: **ononhsatokénhti** church; and NMZR -'tsher- and LOC -akta', near: **ononhsatokenhti'tsherákta'** near the church; with V -tokenhti- be holy, ATTR ='ke, at; and **kahnià:sakon** (-hnia's- neck, collar): **ononhsatokenhtì:ke kahnià:sakon** part of a church that goes up to the bell tower.

With V -'rhoro[k]-/-oro[k]- cover: **kanonhsó:ron** there's a cover (roof, shingles) on the house; and REP: **ó:ia' sahanonhsó:roke'** he covered the house, put on a new roof or shingles.

With V -'sere-/-i'sere- drag: **kanonhsì:sere'** cutter, a sleigh with a flatbed; snail.

Cf. Gannonsa cabane (Bruyas: 82); *ka non si se re* cutter (Anon: 13); *ka non si se re* cutter (D'Ailleboust: 6); Laurentian *Quanocha/Canocha* house (Biggar: 245); Wendat *Ganonchia* Cabane (Sagard: Ca1)

-nonhskwa'rh- hip. *See* -niahskwa'rh-

-nonhskwekhs- V invade, break in: **wahshakonónhskwekhse'** he invaded, broke into her house, **wahakenónhskwekhse'** he broke into my house.

NOTE: This stem includes -nonhs- house, and BEN -hs-, but it is unclear what the verb root is.

-nonhst[e]- V treasure, protect, shield: **wakenónhste'** I treasure it, **ronónhste'** he treasures it, **iakonónhste'** she treasures it.

With CAUS -t-: **ranónhstats** he is watching over it, protecting it, **enkenónhstate'** I will watch over it, protect it, **wahanónhstate'** he watched over it, protected it, **iakononhstá:ton** she has watched over it, protected it; **Tsi kanonhstá:ton** Reserve, Reservation.

With N -ia't- body: **riia'tanónhstha'** I protect him; and CAUS -t-: **eniakoia'tanónhstate'** it will protect her, aid her, **wahatia'tanónhstate'** he protected me, came to my aid; and NEG: **iah tehonwaia'tanonhstá:ton** she didn't protect him.

-nonhton'k- V tire of waiting, become impatient: **wakenónhton'ks** I am waiting impatiently, **onkenónhton'ke'** I got tired of waiting.

-nonhwak[t]- V be sore, hurt, ache, pain: **iononhwákte'** it hurts.

With BEN -ni-/-en-: **wakenonhwáktani** I am sick, **enwakenonhwákten'** I will get sick, **wa'akononhwákten'** she got sick.

With N -ahonht- ear: **wakahonhtanòn:waks** I have an earache, **onkwahonhtanòn:wake'** I got an earache.

With N -ahsi't- foot: **wakahsi'tanòn:waks** I have a sore foot.

With N -entskwe'n- chest: **wakentskwe'nanòn:waks** my chest hurts, **iakotskwe'nanòn:waks** or **iakawentskwe'nanòn:waks** her chest hurts.

With N -hnia's- neck, collar: **wakhnia'sanòn:waks** my neck hurts.

With N -hnitsh- thigh: **wakhnitshanòn:waks** my thigh hurts.

With N -hs- lips: **wakhsanòn:waks** my lips are sore.

With N -hsienhont-/-hsiahont- stomach:

wakhsienhontanòn:waks I have a
stomach ache, **onkhsienhontanòn:wake'**
I got a stomach ache.
With N -ia't- body, and DISTR -hon-:
watia'tanonhwákhons my body aches.
With N -ienht- gums: **iakoienhtanòn:waks**
she has sore gums.
With N -kwitsh- knee:
wakkwitshanòn:waks my knee hurts.
With N -nawir- tooth:
wakenawiranòn:waks I have a toothache.
With N -na'aht- rib:
wakena'ahtanòn:waks I have sore ribs.
With N -niahskwa'rh- hip:
wakeniahskwa'rhanòn:waks my hip
hurts.
With N -niar- neck: **wakeniaranòn:waks**
my neck hurts.
With N -nonhwar- brain:
wakenonhwaranòn:waks I have a head-
ache.
With N -senenna't- muscle:
wakesenenna'tanòn:waks my muscles
are sore.

-nonhwar- N brain: **onòn:wara'**
POSS: **akenòn:wara'** my brain,
raonòn:wara' his brain, **akonòn:wara'**
her brain.
With LOC -kon, inside: **kenonhwará:kon**
in my brain.
With V -ahton- disappear:
rononhwarahtòn:'on he is drunk; and
CAUS -'t- and NEG:
iah teiakononhwarahtòn:tha' it doesn't
make one drunk.
With SRF -a-, V -awenrie- stir, and DLC:
tekanonhwarawénrie' I am crazy,
tenkanonhwarawénrie' I will get crazy,
wa'tkanonhwarawénrie' I went crazy;
and CAUS -'t-:
teiakononhwarawenriè:tha' it makes her

or someone crazy (maybe from taking
drugs or drinking too much alcohol),
wa'thononhwarawénrie'te' it made him
crazy.
With V -nonhwak[t]- be sore, hurt:
wakenonhwaranòn:waks I have a head-
ache.
With V -ori- drive: **wakenonhwaró:ri** I
am foolish, silly, **rononhwaró:ri** he is
foolish, silly, **iakononhwaró:ri** she is
foolish, silly, **enwakenonhwaró:ri'** I will
be foolish, **Kanonhwaró:ri** a society for
Midwinter, Midwinter ceremony; and SRF
-ate- and CAUS -st-: **ratenonhwarorístha'**
he acts silly, he fools around,
wahatenonhwaró:riste' he acted silly, he
fooled around, **iakotenonhwaroríston**
she is acting silly, fooling around.
With SRF -a- and V -'rhoro[k]-/-oro[k]-
cover: **wa'kanonhwaró:roke'** I put a hat
on, **wa'kheianonhwaró:roke'** I put a hat
on her, **wakanonhwaró:ron** I have a hat
on; **anòn:warore'** hat; and REV -hsi-:
wa'kanonhwarorókhsi' I took off my
hat.

Cf. cannawarori prostitute (van den
Bogaert: 54); "Our Indians call it
Onnonhouarori, that is 'madness' or
'turning of the head,' because they then
appear to be really crazy or to have their
heads askew." (Lafitau I: 235);
gannonh8arori Chanter chanson de mort
ou autre, pourvu qu'on chante seul sans
qu'aucun réponde (Bruyas: 81);
Gannonh8arorige dans la tabagie où l'on
s'entredemande ses desirs (Bruyas: 81);
Onnon8ara Cervelle (Galissonnière: 23r);
tekennon8arasēnries devenir fou (Marcoux: 387); *Wakenonwarori* être fou
(Cuoq: 135); *a-ri-wa-wa-kon ra-o-non-
wa-ro-re* Sagittaria latifolia [broadleaf
arrowhead, Indian potato; *literally*,
bishop's hat] (Rousseau: 65); Onondaga

"but they also hold a special festival to the Demon of dreams ... They call this celebration *honnonouaroria*," (Dablon in Thwaites 42: 155); Wendat *Ononhouaroia* upsetting of brain (Thwaites 23: 53,103)

-nonhware- V soap
  With CAUS -'t-: **ononhwarè:tha'** soap.
  With NMZR -'tsher- and V -nohare-/
  -ohare- wash: **kenonhware'tsheróhares**
  I am rinsing the soap off (the dishes, the laundry), **wa'enonhware'tsheróhare'**
  she rinsed it, **wakenonhware'tsheróhare**
  I have rinsed it.

-nonhwenhsker- N dust: **ononhwénhskeri**
  With V -hkw- pick up, and DLC:
  wa'tkenonhwénhskerahkwe' I picked up the dust, **teienonhwenhskeráhkhwa'**
  dustpan.
  With V -rohro[k]- gather, collect:
  wa'kenonhwenhskerarò:roke' I gathered the dust.
  NOTE: GM translated this stem as 'junk'.
  Cf. Onnaꞵenskeri balieures (Bruyas: 68);
  onnaꞵenskeri Balieures (Galissonnière: 11v); *onaꞵēnskĕri* Balayures (Marcoux: 34); *ononhwénhsera* garbage (Gabriel: 59)

-nonhweraton- V greet, give thanks, with DLC:
  tekhenonhwerá:tons I greet them, give thanks to them, **wa'tekhenonhwerá:ton'**
  I greeted her, thanked her,
  tehshakeninonhwerá:ton we two greet him, we send him our regards.
  With SRF -ate-: **tekatenonhwerá:tons** I give thanks, **tenkatenonhwerá:ton'** I will give thanks; and NMZR -htsher-:
  Atenonhweratónhtshera' Welcome ceremony, thanksgiving salutation.
  Cf. Kannonhꞵeron saluer quelqu'un,
  Kannonhꞵeronton saluer, remercier par q.c. ou pour (Bruyas: 80); *dewadade-*

nonweronh mutual greeting (Hale: 120–1);
da-e-dewadennonweradonh [we] give thanks (Boyle: 130);
ta ion ta te non we ra ton greet (Anon: 38);
ta ion ta te non we ra ton greet (Diabo: 35)

-nonhweron- V bow (incline the head)
  With SRF -ate- and CISL:
  tahatenòn:weron' he bowed (as a gentlemen would bow towards a lady),
  taiontenòn:weron' she bowed.

-nonhwe'- V like: **kenòn:we's** I like it,
  rakenòn:we's he likes me,
  enkenòn:we'ne' I will like it,
  wa'akeninòn:we'ne' the two of us liked it, **wakenonhwè:'on** I have liked it.
  With N -ia't- body, V -ase- be fresh, new, and NMZR -'tsher-:
  raia'tase'tsheranòn:we's he likes women (he is a playboy).
  With N -rihw- matter, message:
  wa'erihwanòn:we'ne' she agreed with it.

-nonhwe'rh- N body hair (usually animal), fuzz: **ononhwè:rhon**
  With V -a'sen'-/-en'- fall down:
  rononhwè:rhen's his hair is falling out, he is shedding hair,
  wahononhwè:rhen'ne' he shed hair.
  With V -ont- attach: **rononhwè:rhonte'**
  he has body hair (usually talking about an animal).
  With V -r- put in: **wakenonhwè:rhare'**
  I have hair on me (maybe from a dog or cat), **rononhwè:rhare'** he has hair on him, **iononhwè:rhare'** it has hair on it.
  • Iononhwè:rhare' ne raotháhsteren. He has fur or hair on his trousers.
  Cf. Onnonhꞵeri poil qui croist sur le corps (Bruyas: 80); *onnonhꞵerhon* poil (Galissonnière: 67r); *Ononꞵērhon* Poil (Marcoux: 295); *ononwerhon* poil (Cuoq: 35)

-nonkot- N weasel: **onón:kote'**

> Cf. *Anúngoti* Wiesel (Pyrlaeus: 201);
> *oh non goh deh* weasel (Jamieson 1: 5);
> *Onón:kote'* Weasel (Horne: 110)

nonkwá:ti on the side of,
> **othorè:ke nonkwá:ti** north,
> **éntie nonkwá:ti** south,
> **nà:kon nonkwá:ti** east,
> **è:neken nonkwá:ti** west

-nonni- N dance: **kanónnia'**
> With **konnón:kwe** (-onkwe['t]- person,
> human being), and POSS: **konnón:kwe**
> **aotinónnia'** women's dance.
> With V -hkw- pick up, and DLC:
> **tekenonniáhkhwa'** I dance,
> **tenkenónniahkwe'** I will dance,
> **wa'tkenónniahkwe'** I danced,
> **tewakenonniáhkwen** I am dancing.
> With SRF -ate-, V -kenni- compete, and
> DLC: **tekatenonniakénnie's** I jig,
> **wa'thatenonniakén:ni'** he jigged,
> **teiakotenonniakénnion** she is jigging.
> With V -ot- stand: **iakwanónniote'** we
> are moving (to the music, maybe tapping
> our feet).
>
> Cf. "the Iroquois call the constellation of
> the Pleïades *Tejennoniakoua*, meaning the
> dancers, male and female." (Lafitau I:
> 258); "They call the Pleiades, *Te Iennon-*
> *niakoua*, 'the dancers, men and women',"
> (Lafitau II: 135)

-nonniani- V get fed up: **wakenonniá:nis** I
> am fed up, **onkenonniá:ni'** I got fed up.
> • Onkenonniá:ni' tsi niieia'tò:ten, iako-
> ia'tón:ta. I got fed up with the way she is,
> she's annoying, underfoot.

-nons- N crouch, squat
> With V -ien- put down, have, and DLC:
> **tekenón:saien'** I am crouching,

tehanón:saien' he is crouching,
teienón:saien' she is crouching.
> With SRF -a-, V -ot- stand, and DLC:
> **wa'tkanonsó:ten'** I squatted.

-nonskwar-/-nenskwar- N green (unripe) fruit,
> smallpox: **onónskwara'** or **onénskwara'**
> With V -a'ker- float, be in water, and
> possibly BEN -en- and INCH -'-:
> **iakonenskwarà:keren's** smallpox.
> With V -ta'-/-eta'- put inside:
> **wa'onkenenskwaráta'** they gave me a
> vaccination.
>
> Cf. *onōnskꝺara* petite verole, *ꝺakenonskꝺa-*
> *rākĕrens* avoir la picotte (Marcoux: 290);
> *Onoskwara* picote, vaccine, variole,
> petite vérole; bouton, pétit bourgeon des
> arbres et des plantes (Cuoq: 34)

-nont- N mountain, hill
> With LOC -kon, inside: **onón:takon**
> bottom of the hill.
> With LOC -'ke, on, at, and ATTR =haka/
> =aka, people of: **Ononta'kehá:ka** Onon-
> daga.
> With unclear ending: **onontoharà:ke** top
> of the hill.
> With SRF -ate- and V -akenhiat- at the end
> or peak: **tsi iotenontakèn:iate'** at the top
> of the mountain or hill.
> With SRF -ate-, V -ati-/-onti- lose, throw,
> and DLC and CISL: **tetiotenontóntie's** a
> big wave comes back in (for example,
> after a tide has gone out),
> **tentiotenontón:ti'** a big wave will come
> back in, **tontaiotenontón:ti'** a big wave
> came back in.
> With SRF -a-, V -atsnenht- go down,
> descend, and TRNL: **iekanontatsnénhtha'**
> I go downhill, **iahanontátsnenhte'** he
> went downhill, **iewakanontatsnénhton**
> I have gone downhill; and PROG -hatie-:
> **iewakanontatsnenhtonhátie'** I am going

downhill.

With V -es- be long, tall: **ionón:tes**
(it is) a high mountain.

With V -her-/-hr- set on top of:
ionontáhere' there's a hill; and DISTR
-onnion-: **ionontahrónnion** there are
mountains; with V -her-/-hr- set on top of,
and INCH -'-: **kenontà:ra's** I go uphill,
enkenontà:ra'ne' I will go uphill,
wa'enontà:ra'ne' she went uphill,
wakenontahrà:'on I have gone uphill;
and PROG -hatie-: **wakenontahra'onhátie'**
I am going uphill.

With SRF -a-, V -ia'k- break, cut in two,
and DLC: **wa'thonnóntia'ke** they dug or
made a ditch.

With V -iio- be good, nice: **Ionontí:io**
Queen, **Ronontí:io** King, the king in a
deck of cards; **ronontí:io raorístatsi**
large, black metal stove (*literally,* king's
stove; *see* **karístatsi** stove).

With V -kowan[en]-/-owan[en]- be big:
ionontowá:nen's (there are) big mountains (for example, the Rockies or Adirondacks); and ATTR =aka'/=aka, people of,
and REP: **Shotinontowane'á:ka** Seneca.

With V -kwaront- bulge, lump, and PROG
-ontie-: **tsi ionontakwarontóntie's** on the
waves.

With V -ot- stand: **ionón:tote'** there is a
hill.

With V -ti- be on the other side, and REP:
Tsonón:tati' or with ATTR =kowa, great:
Tsonontatihkó:wa Vancouver, BC.

Cf. onnontageronnons Onnnontagués
(Bruyas: 28); *Onontiio koꝶa* la grande
belle-montagne, i.e. l'Empereur des
Francais (Cuoq 1866: 90); *Ro non ti io*
King (Anon: 9); *O-non-ti-io* king (French
governor) (Cory: 51)

nón:ta day. *See* -ent- day

-nontar- N soup: **onón:tara'**
With V -aweron- spill out of:
wa'kenontaráweron' I spilled the soup.
With V -a'tarih[en]-/-tarih[en]- be hot,
warm, and CAUS -'t-:
wa'kenontarataríha'te' I heated up the
soup.
With V -eka'[w]-/-ka'[w]- find tasty:
kanontarákon' it is delicious soup.
With V -otsenht- scoop out of, and
INSTR -hkw-: **ienontarotsenhtáhkhwa'**
soup ladle.
With V -r- put in: **kenontaráhrha'** I am
filling in, serving soup,
wa'kenontará:ren' I served the soup;
and BEN -hahs-: **wa'khenontaráhrhahse'**
I served soup to her.

Cf. onnontara sagamité (Bruyas: 82); "The
sagamité of the Indians is only a sort of
stew made of their Indian corn leached in
ashes, ... which the Iroquois call *onnontara*
in their language." (Lafitau II: 59);
Onnontara Bouillie (Galissonnière: 13v);
Onontara potage des Sauvages, consistant
en blé d'inde bouilli avec du lait et de
l'eau (Cuoq: 34); *onón:tara'* soup (Horne:
28)

-nonte- V be a mountain, hill: **ionón:te'**
there is a mountain, a hill.

-nontek- V cover with a lid: **ranón:teks** he
is putting the lid on, covering it with a lid,
wa'kenón:teke' I put the lid on,
iakononté:kon she has put the lid on,
kanonté:kon it has a lid on it, **senón:tek**
Put the lid on it!
With REV -hsi-: **wa'kenontékhsi'** I took
the lid off, I opened it.

-nont[en]- V feed someone: **khenón:tens** I
feed her or them, I give her or them food,

wahí:nonte' I fed him, **wahonwá:nonte'** she fed him, **ó:nen ronwanón:ten** she has already fed him.

With REFL -atate-: **wahatátenonte'** he fed himself.

With PURP -hr-: **wa'khenontèn:re'** I am on my way to feed her, **enhinontèn:ra'** I will go feed him.

With N -hnek- liquid: **khehnekanón:tens** I give her or them water (to drink), **wa'khehné:kanonte'** I gave her or them water.

• Wa'khé:nonte' kana'tarokhón:we tánon' o'wà:ron' wa'tiakwá:tonte'. I fed them cornbread and steak [and] we ate together.

• Khehnekanón:tens ne kaienthóhsera'. I'm watering the plants.

Cf. Gannonton jetter de la porcelaine pour les morts (Bruyas: 83); Laurentian *Taquenonde* give that to someone (Biggar: 245)

-nontsi[st]- N head: **onón:tsi**

POSS: **kenontsì:ne** (on) my head, **ranontsì:ne** (on) his head, **ienontsì:ne** (on) her head; and **tió:to'kte'** (-o'kt- finish): **tió:to'kte' ne ranontsì:ne** he's not all there.

With V -her-/-hr- set on top of: **kanontsistáhere'** it has an engine.

With V -ienht- hit against, and TRNL: **iahonkenontsístaienhte'** I banged my head.

With V -keront-/-okeront- square, and DLC: **Tehotinontsistokerón:te'** (they are) Germans.

With V -onkw- bump, hit, and TRNL and DLC: **ia'tewakenontsistón:ko'** I bumped my head.

With V -ronhkwani-/-ronhkwen- itch: **wakenontsistarónhkwani** my head is itchy.

Cf. Onnontsi, Onnontsista in comp. tête (Bruyas; 83); *Atenontsi* (mot d'injure) en tête! têtu! o quelle tête! (Cuoq: 135); Laurentian *Aggonosy* the head (Biggar: 241); Wendat *Onontsiq* Teste (Sagard: An5)

-nonw- N bottom water that's stirred up, dregs: **onón:wa'**

With LOC -kon, inside: **kanón:wakon** on the bottom (say, when you're diving in water).

With V -a'tarih[en]-/-tarih[en]- be hot, warm: **iononwataríhen** (it is) warm water.

With V -hkw- pick up, and DLC: **tenkanón:wahkwe'** it will get murky, **wa'tkanón:wahkwe'** it got murky.

With SRF -ate- and V -ien- put down, have: **katenón:waiens** I sink, go underwater; and REP: **sahatenón:waien'** he sank back into the water.

With V -kentst- be leftover scraps, refuse: **kenonwakéntstha'** I am draining it, straining it, **enienón:wakentste'** she will drain it, **wa'kenón:wakentste'** I drained it, **iakononwakéntston** she has drained it; and INSTR -hkw-: **ienonwakentstáhkhwa'** colander.

With V -na'nawen-/-nawen- be wet: **iononwaná:wen** (it is) lukewarm water.

With SRF -ate-, V -o- be in water, and CISL; and **watè:skonte'** (-ate'skont- roast, bake): **watè:skonte' tiotenón:io** (there are) browned bits at the bottom (for example, bottom of the pan when making gravy).

With unclear V, and DLC: **teiononwáhwhen** it is murky; and CAUS -'t-: **tehanonwahwhà:tha'** he makes it murky, **wa'thanonwáhwha'te'** he made it murky.

• Kanón:wakon rothonrohátie'. He is diving underwater.

Cf. Gannoña fonds de l'eau (Bruyas: 80); *Gannoña* fonds (Galissonnière: 42v); *kanōnꙅăkon* fond de l'eau (Marcoux: 177); *Ononwa* lie, fond de l'eau (Cuoq: 35); *iononwataríhen entionweron* [pour warm water in] (Beauvais: 18)

nòn:wa now, today

-nonwak- V crave: **kenón:waks** I have a craving for it, I am hungry for it, **wahanón:wake'** he craved it.

-nonwar- wire, nail, needle, pin. *See* -ronwar-/ -nonwar-

nón:we place, **ka' nón:we** where? **tsik nón:we** or **tiok nón:we** everywhere, all over

-nonwe[ht]- N object for witchcraft, spell: **onón:we**
With V -ien- put down, have: **iononwéhtaien'** she has an object that she uses for witchcraft.

-nonwenhserario- V beat up: **ronwanonwenhseráio's** they beat him up, **wahinonwenhseráio'** I beat him up, **wahonwanonwenhseráio'** they beat him up, he got beat up.
NOTE: The *r* of this stem is usually not pronounced.

nonwén:ton ever. Usually with NEG: **iah nonwén:ton** never.

-nonwireht- V disappear, go out of sight, with TRNL: **iewakenonwiréhtha'** I disappear, go out of sight, **ienwakenonwí:rehte'** I will disappear, go out of sight, **iahonkenonwí:rehte'** I went out of sight, **iewakenonwiréhton** I have disappeared.

Cf. Gannonꙅireᶎton tomber dans un abysme (Bruyas: 11); *wat ne ka no wi re tha* iodine (with incorporated -hnek-liquid) (Anon: 18)

-non'ker- V suck milk, nurse: **ienon'kéhrha'** she is sucking (milk), nursing, **enienon'ké:ra'** she will suck milk, **wahanon'ké:ra'** he sucked milk, **iakonon'ké:ren** she is sucking milk.

-non'kwatek- V house fire: **ionon'kwatékha'** the house is burning, on fire, **wa'onòn:kwateke'** the house burned, **ionon'kwatéken** the house has burned.
With CAUS -t-: **ratenon'kwatéktha'** he burns down houses, **wahatenòn:kwatekte'** he burned down the house.
NOTE: This stem includes -atek- burn, but it is unclear what the incorporated noun is.
Cf. Gannongꙅategen cabane se bruler (Bruyas: 32); *ꙅakenōnkꙅăteks* bruler, une maison brule (Marcoux: 48)

-non'onhr- N sod, turf, hair (scalp): **onon'òn:ra'**
With SRF -ate- and V -'rhoro[k]-/-oro[k]- cover: **rotenon'onhró:ron** he has on a wig, **iakotenon'onhró:ron** she has on a wig; and CAUS -st-: **iontenon'onhrorókstha'** wig.

-non'onser- N squash: **onon'ónsera'**
With ATTR =kowa, great: **onon'onsera'kó:wa** pumpkin.
With ATTR =shon'a, pluralizer: **onon'onsera'shòn:'a** all kinds, varieties of squash.
With V -es- be long: **kanon'ónseres** cucumber, zucchini.
With V -hio'tsis[t]- be salty, sour, and DLC: **teionon'onserahiò:tsis** pickles.

With V -kahte- be raw: **onon'onserakáhte'** watermelon.

-non't- N milk: **onòn:ta'** milk
    With V -atken- rot, spoil: **ionon'tátkens** the milk is rotten, curdled, **enionon'tátken'** the milk will rot, **wa'onon'tátken'** the milk rotted, **ionon'tatkèn:'en** the milk has become rotten.
    With V -aweron- spill out of: **wahanon'táweron'** he spilled the milk; and CISL: **tahanon'táweron'** he poured the milk; with V -aweron- spill out of (variant -aweront-) and INSTR -hkw-: **ienon'tawerontáhkhwa'** milk pitcher.
    With V -okha- leak, drip: **kanon'tókhas** milkweed.
    With V -r- put in, and INSTR -hkw-: **ienon'taráhkhwa'** milk container.
    With V -tahkw- take out: **wa'kenon'tatáhko'** I milked (the cow).
    With unclear V: **kanon'tí:sen** buttermilk.

-nor- N husk, braided corn: **onó:ra'**
    With V -astath[en]-/-ath[en]- dry: **enkanoráthen'** the husks will dry, **wa'kanoráthen'** the husks dried, **ionoráthen** the corn is dry.
    With V -a[t]- be inside, and CISL: **tkanó:ra** corn husk mattress.
    With SRF -ate-, V -hwawen'e[k]-/-awen'e[k]- wrap, and DLC: **teiotenorawèn:'en** ground tomato.
    With V -ke- amount to, and DLC: **tekanó:rake** two husks.
    With V -ohtshi- remove, pull out: **wa'kenoróhtshi'** I took off the husk.
    With V -ri- cook, ripen: **wa'kanorá:ri'** the corn ripened.
    With SRF -ate- and V -statha't-/-atha't- dry: **wa'katenorátha'te'** I dried the husks, **rotenorathà:ton** he is drying husks.

-noron- V be expensive, precious: **kanó:ron** it is expensive.
    With PART: **Tó: nikanó:ron?** How much does it cost?
    With DLC: **tekanó:ron** two lovers, sweethearts.
    With INCH -'-: **enkanó:ron'ne'** it will be expensive, **wa'kanó:ron'ne'** it became expensive.
    With PURP -'ser-: **kanoròn:sere'** it is going to be expensive.
    With INSTR -hkw-: **konnorónhkhwa'** I love you (sg), **wahinó:ronhkwe'** I loved him; and REFL -atate-: **katatenorónhkhwa'** I love myself.
    With INSTR -hkw- and NMZR -htsher-: **kanoronhkwáhtshera'** love, compassion.
    With INSTR -hkw-, DISTR -nion-, and DLC: **tekhenoronhkwánions** I am kissing her, **wa'thinoronhkwánion'** I kissed him; and PART: **Tsi na'teiontatenoronhkwánions** New Year's Day (when people went to all the houses to wish everyone happy new year).
    With N -atenna'tsher- groceries: **watenna'tsheranó:ron** they are expensive groceries.
    With V -atahahsteren- put on pants, trousers, and NMZR -'tsher-: **wathahsteren'tsheranó:ron** they are expensive pants.
    With N -hwist- metal, money: **kahwistanó:ron** money is scarce, hard to come by; **ohwistanó:ron** gold.
    With REFL -atat-, N -ia't- body, and CAUS -hst-: **katatia'tanorónhstha'** I take care of myself, **enkatatia'tanó:ronhste'** I will take care of myself.
    With N -io'tenhser- work: **kaio'tenhseranó:ron** jobs are scarce, hard to find.
    With N -'sereht- vehicle: **ka'serehtanó:ron** it is an expensive car.

Cf. Gannóron être difficile, prétieux (Bruyas: 83); *Garistandóron* or, argent métail prétieux (Bruyas: 93); *Tsi Teionta-tenoronkwanion* [New Year] (Granger: 4); *tsi ten ion ta te no ron kwa nion* new year (Anon: 6); *Teiontatenoronhkwánions* New Years (Horne: 52); Wendat *Andoron* il est de valeur, de grand estime (Sagard: Be2); Onondaga *ganoron* precieux (Shea: 82); Susquehannock *Chanooro hiss* I make much of you (Holm: 5)

-noron's- V be tired out, exhausted: **wakenoròn:se'** I am tired out (I lost all my energy), I am exhausted, I am spent, **ronoròn:se'** he is tired out, **iakonoròn:se'** she is tired out, **onkenó:ron'se'** I got exhausted.

-noskorh- N the inside of the cheeks: **onoskóhrha'**

-not- N bulrush spike, brown part of a bulrush: **onó:ta'**
NOTE: The word **kanó:ta'** may also be the name of a medicine or medicinal plant.
Cf. kanota tsini iotsi ionni [kanota, this is how it is made] (Beauvais: 9)

-nowen- V lie: **wakenó:wen** I lie, I am a liar, **ronó:wen** he is a liar; **onó:wen** lie.
With SRF -a- and CAUS -ht-: **ranowénhtha'** he tells lies, **wa'kanó:wenhte'** I lied, **wakanowénhton** I have lied.
With SRF -a-, CAUS -ht-, and DISTR -nion-: **ranowenhtánions** he tells lies.
With SRF -a-, CAUS -ht-, and BEN -en-: **wahiianowénhten'** I lied to him.
With SRF -ate- and CAUS -ht-: **katenowénhtha'** I doubt it, **wahatenó:wenhte'** he doubted it, **iakotenowénhton** she is doubting it.

-no'karanie- V grind one's teeth, with DLC: **tekeno'karánies** I grind my teeth, **wa'thano'karánie'** he ground his teeth.

-no'kwitsher- N boiled and sweetened corn: **ono'kwítshera'**
NOTE: Mike Norton described this as 'corn flour, cornmeal'.
Cf. Onnꙅksisera farine épaisse (Bruyas: 80); *Onnongꙅitsera* farine espaisse (Galissonnière: 40r); *Okwitsera* blé d'inde brûlé et broyé pour faire des pralines (Cuoq: 67, citing Marcoux); *onohkwítshera'* boiled and sweetened corn (Deering and Delisle: 285); Iroquoian "Some people take the coarsest part of the ground maize ... mixed with fat ... This concentrated food ... is called *Quitzera* by the Iroquois (Kalm 1752, in Larsen and Kalm 1935: 114); Seneca *ɁonóɁkhwishæɁ* a sweetened corn preparation (Chafe: 70, 1209)

-no'ts- N tooth: **onò:tsa'**
With V -ot- stand: **kanò:tsot** muskellunge, **ranò:tsote'** he has a tooth, **ienò:tsote'** she has a tooth; and PART:
Tó: niienò:tsote'? How many teeth does she have?
With V -ot- stand and INCH -'-: **wa'eno'tsó:ta'ne'** she (a baby) got a tooth, her tooth came through.
With V -ot- stand, and REV -kw-: **wahakeno'tsotá:ko'** he took out my tooth.
Cf. Onnotsia dent (Bruyas: 83); *ondꙅtsia* Dent (Galissonnière: 29r); *kanotsiōten* denté, à (Marcoux: 114); *cuhnoojuh* Tooth (Gallatin: 315); *Onotsia* les dents (Cuoq: 35); *ka no tsot* sturgeon (Anon: 17); *kanótsiot /kanó:jot/* muskie (Bonvillain and Francis: 23)

O

-o- V be in water

With N -ahi- fruit, berry: **wà:io** jam.

With N -ahskw- bridge (and possibly CAUS -hw-): **wahskóhon** bridge over water.

With SRF -at-, N -a'kenhr- ashes, dirt, and INSTR -hkw-: **ata'kenhróhkwa'** grey; and V -hon'tsi- be black, dark-coloured: **ata'kenhrohkwahòn:tsi** dark grey.

With N -hahser- light, lamp, and INSTR -hkw-; and **kén:ie'** (-iie-/-ien- oil, grease): **iehahseróhkhwa' kén:ie'** oil for a kerosene lamp, coal oil.

With N -hnek- liquid: **kahné:ko** there's water (in the basement, in the creek).

With N -hnenna't- potato: **wa'khnennà:to'** I boiled potatoes; and INSTR -hkw-: **iehnenna'tóhkhwa'** pot for cooking potatoes.

With N -htehr- root: **enkhtè:ro'** I will put the root in water, I will boil the root.

With N -hwist- metal, money: **tsi kahwísto** a mine.

With N -ien'kwar- smoke, BEN -'s-, and DLC: **wa'tewatièn:kwaro'se'** I got smoke in my eyes, **wa'thoièn:kwaro'se'** he got smoke in his eyes.

With SRF -ate- and N -iie-/-ien- oil, grease: **ioteié:no** there is grease or oil drippings (drippings to make gravy or oily spots floating on water).

With N -na'ts- pail: **Kanà:tso** Ottawa.

With N -nenhst- corn: **kanénhsto** or **onénhsto** corn soup.

With N -nia't- throat: **kanià:to** beaver dam.

With N -nonhkw-/-nonhkwa'tsher- medicine, and CISL: **tiononhkwà:tsheros** pepper; and ATTR =kowa, great: **tiononhkwa'tsheroskó:wa** green or red bell pepper.

With SRF -ate-, N -nonw- bottom water, dregs, and CISL; and **watè:skonte'** (-ate'skont- roast or bake): **watè:skonte' tiotenón:io** (there are) browned bits at the bottom (for example, bottom of the pan when making gravy).

With N -rahkw- sun, BEN -'s-, and DLC: **wa'tewakeráhko'se'** I got blinded from the glare from the sun.

With N -ronhi- sky, heaven, blue, and INSTR -hkw-: **ieronhióhkhwa'** bluing for clothes to whiten them.

With SRF -ate- and N -ront- log, beam: **Aterónto** Toronto.

With SRF -at-, N -tsikhe't- sweet, INSTR -hkw-, and DLC: **teionttsikhe'tóhkhwa'** sugar.

With N -wehn- island, and LOC -'ke, at: **Kawehnò:ke** on the island; Cornwall.

With N -'nhonhs- egg: **wa'ke'nhónhso'** I boiled eggs.

With SRF -at- and CAUS -hw-, *see* -ohw- swell. With CAUS -hw- and TRNL, *see* -ohw- put into liquid. With REV -kw-, *see* -okw- take out of liquid. *See also* -'skoht- drown someone, -'skohw- get into water, dunk oneself, and -'sko'- drown.

Oh nahò:ten'? What? Oh nahò:ten' orì:wase'? What is new? Oh nahò:ten' ionnià:ton? What is it made of?

Cf. Susquehannock *Anhooda?* what? (Holm: 5)

Oh ní:ioht? How? *See* -oht-

Oh nontié:ren? or **Oh niiotié:ren?** Why? *See* -ier-

ohà:kwaront crane, blue heron

-ohar- V attach at the end: **koháhrha'** I attach it at the end of something, **enkohá:ren'** I will attach it, **wa'kohá:ren'** I attached it, **wakóhare'** I have attached it.

With REV -kw-, and CISL: **takohará:ko'** I took or cut a piece off the end; and SRF -at-: **tontohará:ko'** it snapped off, it broke off from the end.

With SRF -at-, N -ahsahtahkar- splinter, and INCH -'-: **onkwatahsahtahkarohá:ra'ne'** I got a splinter.

With N -ahseriie['t]- string, rope, thread: **wa'kahseriie'tohá:ren'** I threaded the needle.

With N -ahsi't- foot, and INCH -'-: **wa'kahsi'tohá:ra'ne'** I got something stuck in my foot.

With N -ahskw- bridge: **iohskóhare'** suspension bridge.

With **atátken** mirror (-ken- see), and NMZR -'tsher-: **watatken'tsheróhare'** dresser.

With N -harennaht- lead, purple: **kaharennahtóhare'** lead, lead pencil. *This is an older word for pencil.*

With N -nakar- stick: **kanakaróhare'** candy attached to a stick (hardened maple syrup or a lollipop).

With SRF -ate-, N -ne'rh- (not attested elsewhere), and DLC: **wa'thakwatene'rhohá:ren'** it stung me, **wa'thotene'rhohá:ren'** it stung him.

With N -nia'tar- fabric, material: **kania'taróhare'** there is a cloth attached to it (a flag on a pole, a rag on a stick); and SRF -ate- and INSTR -hkw-: **iontenia'taroharáhkhwa'** flag.

With N -nonhkwen'- corn cob, cone: **kanonhkwen'oháhrha'** a cone is hanging or attached (describing, for example, a pine or sumac), **enkanonhkwen'ohá:ren'** it will get cones, **wa'kanonhkwen'ohá:ren'** it got cones.

With N -rist- iron, steel: **karistóhare'** pick-axe.

With N -'kats- limb, and DLC: **teka'katsóhare'** sleigh with spindles up the sides.

Cf. Io-hsko-ha-re Schoharie, "a natural bridge" as that formed by timber floating down stream and lodging firmly, so as to form a bridge (F. Marcoux in Hough: 180); Onondaga *Sgocharichróhne* German (Zeisberger: 82)

-ohare- wash. *See* -nohare-/-ohare-

ohén:ton in front, ahead. *See* -hente- go ahead, advance

-ohetst- V pass something: **kohétstha'** I pass it, **enkóhetste'** I will pass it, **wa'kóhetste'** I passed it, **wakohétston** I have passed it.

With CISL: **tasóhetst** Pass it this way!

With TRNL: **iahróhetste'** he passed it that way, **ia'sóhetst** Pass it that way!

With SRF -at-: **katohétstha'** I pass by, **wa'katóhetste'** I passed by, **ontóhetste'** it passed by (a vehicle), **enká:r iotohétston ne kaié:ri** a quarter past four.

With SRF -at- and DLC: **tekatohétstha'** I pass through, I graduate, **wa'tkatóhetste'** I passed through, I graduated.

With SRF -at- and BEN -en-: **wa'kheiatohétsten'** or (with REP) **sakheiatohétsten'** I passed her, **wahakwatohétsten'** or (with REP) **sahakwatohétsten'** he passed me.

With SRF -at- and INSTR -hkw-: **ohén:ton iontohetstáhkhwa'** she cuts in front (of a line), **ohén:ton wahatohétstahkwe'** he cut in front, **ohén:ton iakotohetstáhkwen** she has cut in front.

• Wa'tkatóhetste' tsi ioten'enhrakà:ronte'. I passed through the gate.

Ohkí:we Dance for the dead

Cf. Ohkí:we (Lazore: 50)

ohkwesen'tarì:wase' pheasant
NOTE: Includes -ahkwesen- partridge; remainder is uncertain.

ohkwesen'tóia' quail
NOTE: Composed of -ahkwesen- partridge, and possibly -oia'[k]- throw straight at.

ohnà:ken behind, in the back, at the end
With ATTR =kha, characterized by:
ohna'kénhkha the last time.
• Né:ne ohna'kénhkha tentsitewatátken' ken' nikarihwésha. This will be the last time we will see each other for a little while.

Ohniá:kara' Niagara

Cf. oghnyagara (Little Abraham in Claus C-1478, 472); *Niagara Falls* "It means ... the Neck, the term being first applied to the portage, or neck of land, between lakes Erie and Ontario." (Schoolcraft: 220); "Niagara River, *O-ne-ä-ga'-rä,* At the Neck" (Morgan: 394); "The name *Oh-ny-ga-ra,* 'on or at the neck,' is applied to the whole stream of water between Lakes Erie and Ontario, and is derived from *O-ny-ra, 'neck,'* or contraction between head and trunk." (Oronhyatekha: 12); *Ohnyagara,* Niagara (district), Back of the neck, as if in anger (Brant-Sero and Hill in Boyle: 172); *O-nia-ka-ra* Niagara (Cory: 82); Iroquois *Ongiara* Sault (Sanson map 1656); Iroquois *Oꭓniagara Falls* (Evans map 1755); Iroquois "*Ni-ag-a-ra.* It meant simply *the neck* connecting two great lakes, as the body and the head are united." (Beauchamp 1907: 134); Wendat *ȣndiara/ȣngiara* Niagara (Potier: 154); Neutral (?) "but a

days journey from the last village of the Neutral Nation, on the side of the East, which is named *Onguiaahra,* the same as the River." (Jerome Lalemant in Thwaites 21: 209, 211); Onondaga *Ochjagare* Fort Neagra (McIlwain: 57)

-ohrarak- squeeze, press down. *See* -htohrarak-/-ohrarak-

ohrhió:ken chipmunk

Cf. Oriogen Escurieul suisse (Galissonnière: 7v); *ohriōken* Suisse, espèc d'ecureuil (Marcoux: 373); *Ohrioken* suisse, sorte d'écureuil (Cuoq: 31); *Ohrhió:ken* Chipmunk (Horne: 110); Laurentian *Caiognen* A squirrel (Biggar: 243); Wendat *Ohihoin* Escureux suisses (Sagard: An3)

-ohro[k]- V insert: **kò:roks** I insert it, put it between things, **enkò:roke'** I will insert it, **wa'kò:roke'** I inserted it, **wakò:ron** I have inserted it.
With DISTR -hon-: **wahrohrókhon'** he inserted them.
With TRNL: **ia'kò:roke'** I inserted it, **ia'sò:rok** Insert it! and SRF -at-: **ia'ontò:roke'** she inserted herself.
With SRF -ar- and N -ahsi't- foot: **waharahsi'tò:roke'** he slipped on his shoes or slippers; and CAUS -st-: **ionrahsi'tohrókstha'** slippers, slip-on (backless) shoes.
With N -aten'nits-/-aten'nitsher- cane: **roten'nitsherò:ron** he has crutches (under his arms), **iakoten'nitsherò:ron** she has crutches (under her arms).
With N -a'kenhr- ashes, dirt, and REV -hsi-: **enhon'kenhrohrókhsi'** they will do a reading of the Handsome Lake Code.
With SRF -at- and N -hsin- leg: **katshinò:roks** I am putting on leggings,

wa'katshinò:roke' I put on leggings, **wakatshinò:ron** I have put on leggings; **atshinò:ron** leggings.

With SRF -ani- and N -hsnonhs- finger, hand: **anihsnonhsò:ron** or (with CAUS -st-) **ionnihsnonhsohrókstha'** thimble.

With N -ia't- body: **tia'tò:ron** I am inside it, underneath it.

With N -kahkwen't- wheel, tire, and REP: **sakkahkwen'tò:rok**e' I changed the tire.

With N -koh- blockage, clog: **wahatikohò:roke'** they blocked it, **rotikohò:ron** they have blocked it; and DISTR -hon-: **rotikohohrókhon** they filled them in, they blocked it; with SRF -at- and N -koh- blockage, clog: **iotkohò:ron** it is blocked or clogged.

With N -nerahs- cork: **wa'kenerahsò:roke'** I put the cork in it.

With N -nonhkwen'- corn cob, cone: **senonhkwen'ò:rok** Keep quiet!

With N -rist- iron, steel: **raristò:roks** he is bolting it (a door, a gate), **enkaristò:roke'** I will bolt it, **waharistò:roke'** he bolted it, **karistò:ron** it is bolted.

With N -'wahst- little stick, peg: **wa'ke'wahstò:roke'** I inserted the little stick or peg (maybe to keep the door shut), **se'wahstò:rok** Insert the little stick!

With N -'whahs- skirt: **wa'khe'whahsò:roke'** I put a skirt on her; and SRF -ate-: **wa'kate'whahsò:roke'** I put a skirt on, **wakate'whahsò:ron** I have a skirt on, **sate'whahsò:rok** Put a skirt on!

See also -o'tsohrok- get scrunched.

• Aten'enhró:kon ia'ontò:roke'. She went under the fence. • Tkastò:sera ká:iare' tia'tò:ron. I am inside the down (sleeping) bag.

-ohser- N winter, year: **óhsera'** year.

With LOC -'ke, on, at: **akohserà:ke**

(in the) winter, **akohserà:ke nikahá:wi'** wintertime (-hawi-/-enhawi- carry).

With LOC -'ke, on, at, and ATTR =kha, characterized by: **akohsera'kéhkha** winter kind.

With V -ahset- count: **iohserahsé:tas** the count year, appears (as *ionhserahséta's*) on the front cover of a 1979 calendar; see the citation at the end of the entry.

With V -es- be long, and PART: **tsi niióhseres** during the winter.

With V -hon- mid: **Ohséhrhon** Midwinter; and COIN and DLC: **Sha'tekohséhrhon** January, Midwinter.

With V -iahia'k-/-iia'k- cross over, and PART and DLC: **Tó: na'tesohseriià:kon?** How old are you?

With V -ihen- be in the middle of, and COIN and DLC: **sha'teiohserí:hen** middle of the winter.

With SRF -at- and V -o'kt- finish: **ontohserò:kten'** the year ended, winter ended.

With V -o'ten- be a kind of, and PART: **1924 niiohserò:ten** 1924 it's the year.

With V -te- be present, exist, and COIN shi-: **shiiohserá:te' 1901** in the year 1901.

With SRF -at-, V -tiha- be different, and DLC: **Tó: na'tehiatohseratíhen?** How many years difference between them?

• Akohsera'kéhkha wa'kkahkwen'ta-hninòn:re'. I'm going buy winter tires.

Cf. Osera hyver (Bruyas: 123); *oᶜsera* hyver, *koserhenne* dans l'hyver (Galisson-nière: 49r); *Joserãge* Winter (Pyrlaeus: 183); *koserāke* Hiver (Marcoux: 201); *kosērhon* au milieu de l'hyver (Marcoux: 203); *Koserake* en hiver, *Koserhen* au milieu de l'hiver (Cuoq: 137); *Koserake* [winter] (Granger: 4); *a ko se ra ke* winter (Anon: 6); *A-kó-se-rá(-ke)* winter (Cory: 73); *Oh se rah ge neh* Winter (Jamieson 1: 8); *1979 Tióhton iawén:re tewen'niáwe tánon tsá:ta niwáhsen tióhton ionhser-ahséta's* (Calendar 1979, front cover); *Ohséhrhon* [Midwinter] (Lazore: 50)

-ohseronkw- V caress, pat
With N -ia't- body: **kheia'tohserónkwas** I am caressing her, patting her (maybe to quiet or calm her), **wahiia'tohserón:ko'** I caressed him, patted him, **kheia'tohserónkwen** I have caressed her; and REFL -atat- and DLC: **teniontatia'tohserón:ko'** they will caress (condole) each other.
With N -ronhkwe'n- spine, back: **wa'kheronhkwe'nohserón:ko'** I am patting, rubbing her back.
• Wa'kheié:na' wa'kheia'tohserón:ko' tóhsa taionhséntho'. I held her and patted her so she wouldn't cry.

Cf. denyontatyadoghseronko for the mutual embrace of condolence (Hale: 118–9)

ohserón:ni together
• Ohserón:ni wa'ákene'. We two are going together.

ohskaranawèn:ta' honeycomb

óhskare' kà:nen slippery elm

Ohswé:ken Six Nations of the Grand River, Ontario
With ATTR =haka/=aka, people of: **Ohsweken'á:ka** people from Ohswé:ken.

Cf. De yo swe ken outlet of the river, referring to mythical clan towns (Hale: 121); Iroquois "*O-swe'-go, Osh-wa-kee* and *Swa-geh* are forms of a well known name, meaning *flowing out*, or more exactly *small water flowing into that which is large*." (Beauchamp 1907: 171); Onon-daga "*Oswego*, an Onondaga word

signifying a harbor." (Joseph Brant in Boyce: 291)

-oht- V how it is, the way it is, with PART: **tsi ní:ioht** the way it is. Often shortened to **tsi ní:**.
With PAST -'ne': **tsi niiohtòn:ne'** the way it was, how it used to be.
With PROG -hatie-: **tsi niiohtonhátie'** how it's going.

-ohtahrho- V tidy, with DLC: **tehrohtáhrhos** he is cleaning it, tidying it (a house, a yard), **teiohtáhrhon** it is tidy.
With SRF -at-: **teiontohtáhrhos** she is tidying up (her house), **wa'tkatohtáhrho'** I tidied up, **tewakatohtáhrhon** I have tidied up.
With N -ia't- body: **ronwaia'tohtáhrhos** he gets penalties, **wahonwaia'tohtáhrho'** he got a penalty.
With N -nieht- snow: **tekeniehtohtáhrhos** I am removing the snow, cleaning off the snow, **tekaniehtohtáhrhos** snowplow, **wa'tkeniehtohtáhrho'** I shovelled snow.

Cf. sok entiakwatáhsawen teniakwatoh-táhrho ne atsa'któntie ... we started to clean up a certain area along the river ... (Old Kahnawake: 8)

-ohtshi- V remove, pull out: **kóhtshions** I remove it, **wa'kóhtshi'** I removed it, I pulled it out, **wahróhtshi'** he took it out, **wakóhtshion** I have removed it.
With TRNL: **ia'sóhtshi** Pull it out!
With SRF -at-, CAUS -'t-, and CISL: **enthatóhtshia'te'** he will jump or come out, **tahatóhtshia'te'** he jumped out.
With N -ahkar- wood chips, shavings: **wahahkaróhtshi'** he is shaving it (a board or a branch).
With N -ahseriie['t]- string, rope, thread,

and CISL: **takahseriie'tóhtshi'** I pulled out the thread.

With SRF -ar- and N -ahsi't- foot: **wa'karahsi'tóhtshi'** I took my foot out of it; and BEN -en-: **onkwarahsi'tóhtshien'** my foot came out of it (for example, a shoe).

With N -a'kenhr- ashes, dirt: **sa'kenhróhtshi** Take the ashes out (of the stove)!

With N -kahkwen't- wheel, tire: **rokahkwen'tóhtshion** he has taken off the tire(s).

With N -kahreht- eyelash: **wa'kkahrehtóhtshi' ken' niiohontésha** I took off the top of the strawberry.

With N -koh- blockage, clog: **wa'kkohóhtshi'** I unblocked it, unclogged it.

With N -nor- husk, braided corn: **wa'kenoróhtshi'** I took off the husk.

With N -ra'wist- peel: **kera'wistóhtshions** I am peeling it, **enkera'wistóhtshi'** I will peel it, **wa'kera'wistóhtshi'** I peeled it, **iakora'wistóhtshion** she has peeled it, **sera'wistóhtshi** Peel it!

NOTE: This stem is probably composed of -ot- stand, and REV -hsi-.

-ohw- V swell, with SRF -at-: **wá:tos** it swells, **enwá:to'** or **enwá:tohwe'** it will swell up, **ón:tohwe'** it swelled up.

With N -ahsi't- foot: **rarahsì:tos** his foot swells, **waharahsì:to'** his foot swelled, **wakarahsì:to** my feet are swollen.

With N -hnia's- neck, collar: **wakathnià:so** my neck is swollen.

With N -hsin- leg: **wahatshí:no'** his leg swelled, **rotshí:no** his leg is swollen.

With N -hsnonhs- finger, hand: **kanihsnónhsos** my hand swells, **wa'kanihsnónhso'** my hand swelled, **wakanihsnónhso** my hand is swollen.

With N -ia't- body: **iakotià:to** her stomach is swollen.

With N -ienht- gums: **iakotiénhto** her gums are swollen.

NOTE: This stem is composed of -o- be in water, and CAUS -hw-.

-ohw- V put into liquid, with TRNL: **ié:kohs** I put something in liquid, **iè:rohs** he puts it in, **ién:kohwe'** I will put it in, **iahà:kohwe'** or **iahà:ko'** I put it in, **iahà:rohwe'** or **iahà:ro'** he put it in, **iewakóhon** I have put it in.

With SRF -at-: **ieká:tohs** I go into the water, **ia'ká:tohwe'** I went into the water.

With SRF -at- and N -ahskw- bridge: **iahatáhskohwe'** he put in a dock.

With N -honw[ei]- boat: **iahahón:io'** he put the boat into the water.

With N -honro't- pipe, tube: **ia'akwahonrò:tohwe'** we put the tube, the hose in the water.

With N -hstar- drop: **iekhstá:rohs** I am putting a drop into something that's liquid (maybe a drop of food colouring), **ienkhstá:rohwe'** or **ienkhstá:ro'** I will put in a drop, **ia'khstá:rohwe'** or **ia'khstá:ro'** I put in a drop, **ieiakohstaróhon** she has put in a drop.

With SRF -ate-, N -na'tar[o][k]- bread, and DLC: **ia'tekatenà:tarohs** I dunk bread in it, **ia'tkatenà:tarohwe'** I dunked bread.

With N -neraht- leaf: **iekanerahtóhon** tea.

With N -sahe't- bean: **ia'ksahè:tohwe'** or **ia'ksahè:to'** I added beans.

With N -the'ser- flour: **ia'kethè:serohwe'** or **ia'kethè:sero'** I added flour.

With N -'nhontst- dumpling: **kítkit ieka'nhontstóhon** chicken and dumplings.

NOTE: This stem is composed of -o- be in water, and CAUS -hw-.

-ohwiha- V split in two, with DLC:
tekohwíhas I split it in two,
tenhrohwíha' he will split it,
wa'tkohwíha' I split it, **tewakohwíhen**
I have split it, **tesohwíha** Split it!
With DISTR -nion-: **tekohwihánions** I
split things.
With SRF -at-: **wa'tewatohwíha'** it split,
teiotohwíhen it is split; and DISTR -nion-:
tenwatohwihánion' it will split all over,
wa'tewatohwihánion' it split all over.
With N -ahi- fruit, berry: **wa'tkahiohwíha'**
I split the fruit.
With N -ia't- body: **wa'ttia'tohwíha'** I
split it in two (for example, a rabbit).
With N -ient- wood: **tehaientohwíhas** he
is splitting wood, **wa'ttientohwíha'** I split
wood.
With N -nekw- pea, pill:
wa'tkenekohwíha' I split the pill.
With SRF -ate-, N -wis- ice, glass:
wa'tewatewisohwíha' the glass split or
cracked.

ó:ia' another, **ó:ia' ká:ien'** there is another
one, another thing, **ó:ia' ientsóhrhen'ne'**
the day after tomorrow.
With DISTR -shon: **oià:shon** other things.

ó:ia'k instead, else
• Ó:ia'k nahò:ten' sanonhtónnion! Think
of something else!

-oia'[k]- V throw straight at
With DLC: **teióia'ks** movie, **teiaóien'** it is
throwing on it (for example, projecting or
shining light on).
With TRNL and DLC: **ia'tekóia'ks** I throw
it, **ia'thróia'ke'** he threw it, tossed it
aside, **ia'tewakóien'** I have thrown it,
ia'tesóia'k Throw it!
With N -hson'kar-/-hswen'kar- board,
CAUS -ht-, and DLC:
wa'tekhson'karó:ienhte' I threw it on

the floor, **wa'thihson'karó:ienhte'** I
threw him on the floor (as we were wrestling); and REFL -atat- and DISTR -nion-:
tehontatshon'karoienhtánions they
throw each other on the floor.
With N -neni- stone, rock:
Shakotinenióia'ks Little People (you are
lucky if you catch sight of them or they
appear to you).
With N -rahkw- sun, V -ont- attach, NMZR
-hser-, and DLC: **teiorahkontsheróien'**
the sun is shining on it,
wa'tewakerahkontsheróia'ke' the sun
shone on me, I got sunstroke,
wa'thorahkontsheróia'ke' he got sunstroke.
With N -rist- iron, steel, CAUS -ht-, and
DLC: **tekaristoiénhton** bread or pancake
cooked without a pan directly on a (wood)
stove.
With SRF -at- and N -tsihkw- fist, button:
rattsihkóia'ks boxer.
NOTE: The short accented vowel in the
basic aspect forms suggests that this root
goes back to an earlier form *-oi'ak-.

oié:ri ten, **oieríhaton** tenth,
oié:ri nia'ká:ienhte' ten times,
oié:ri tewen'niáwe one thousand.

ok and, just

-ok- V chafe, get a blister: **ió:kas** it is rubbing,
it chafes, **ón:koke'** it chafed me,
wahá:oke' it chafed him.
With N -ahsi't- foot: **onkwahsì:toke'** I got
a blister on my foot.
With N -hsi- palm of the hand:
wakhsió:kas I have a blister on my hand.
With N -hsin- leg: **onkhsí:noke'** it chafed
my leg.
With N -rat- heel: **wakeratò:kas** I have a
blister on my heel, **onkerá:toke'** I got a
blister on my heel.

Okaristiiáhne Thursday, Eucharist

Cf. okaristiāhne jeudi (Marcoux: 220); *Okaristiane* au jour de l'Eucharistie, le jeudi-saint, le jeudi en général (Cuoq: 28); *Okaristiahne* [Thursday] (Granger: 4); *o ka ris ti a ne* thursday (Anon: 6); *o-ka-ris-ti-a-ne* Thursday (Cory: 71)

-oken- V merge, fork
    With SRF -at- and N -hs- lip: **ratshó:ken** he is a liar, **iontshó:ken** she is a liar.
    With N -nat- town, settlement, and DLC: **tekanató:ken** fork (in the road).
    With N -neraht- leaf, and DLC: **teionerahtó:ken** clover.
    With N -niatar- river, lake, and DLC: **tekaniataró:ken** two waterways merging or forking.
    With N -nonhs- house, and DLC: **tekanonhsó:ken** between the houses.
    With N -ren't- leg from hip to knee, and DLC: **tekaren'tó:ken** ginseng.
    With N -rihw- matter, message, and DLC: **Tekarihó:ken** Mohawk title name 1.
    With N -ronto-/-ronto'tsher- wooden box, and DLC: **tekaronto'tsheró:ken** between the cupboards.
    • Tekaronto'tsheró:ken iahòn:sen'ne'. It fell between the cupboards.
    Cf. Tegannosógen entre 2 cabanes, *Te joθahogen* Où il i a 2 chémins fourchus (Bruyas: 118); "Und weil die Mohaks die ersten gewesen sind, die im Bund getreten, so ist ihr Titul im Rath *Tgarihógu*," (Pyrlaeus: 235); "we, the *Tekarihoken*" [the Mohawk] (Deserontyon: 95); *Teyakwari'hō'kěⁿ*' We Tekarihoken(s) (Deserontyon: 100)

-okeri[k]- gather, shirr. *See* -tokeri[k]-/ -okeri[k]-

-okew- wipe. *See* -rakew-/-okew-

-okha- V leak: **iókhas** it leaks, it drips, **enióka'** it will leak, **wa'ókha'** it leaked, **iaokhà:'on** it is leaking.
    With N -honro't- pipe, tube: **iohonro'tókhas** the pipe is leaking.
    With N -na'ts- pail: **iona'tsókhas** the pail is leaking.
    With N -neraht- leaf: **Onerahtókha** April; and ATTR =kowa, great: **Onerahtohkó:wa** May.
    With N -non't- milk: **kanon'tókhas** milkweed.
    Cf. Oneratacka [May], *Oneratack* [June] (Wassenaer: 73); *Iogas agontak* ma chaudière coule (Bruyas: 45); *Onnrᵃ'toᶜka* Mars, *Onnrᵃ'toᶜko* Avril (Galissonnière: 53v); *oneratokha* avril, *oneratokoȣa* mai (Marcoux: 257); *Iokhas* faire eau, prendre eau (Cuoq: 6); *Oneratokha* petite feuille, Avril, *Oneratakowa* grande feuille, Mai (Cuoq: 157); *Oneratokha* April (Granger: 8); *Oneratokowa* May (Granger: 9); *Onerahtók:ha* [April], *Onerahtohkó:wa* [May] (Calendar 1979)

-okon LOC under. For example:
    ahskwen'nó:kon under the porch; **okwiró:kon** under the tree; **kanaktó:kon** under the bed.

=okon or =okon'a ATTR pluralizer. For example: **kheien'okòn:'a** my children; **otsi'ten'okòn:'a** different birds.
    Followed by ATTR =kenha, former, late: **ionkhihsothokon'kénha** our ancestors.

okón:ra' species of elm tree

óksa Hurry up!

óksa'k quickly, right away
    • Óksa'k ken nontá:se! Come quickly, right away!

-okw- V disperse

With SRF -at-, N -ahsahtahkar- splinter, and DLC: **wa'tewatahsahtahkaró:ko'** it splintered.

With N -atshat- steam, mist, fog, cloud: **iotshatókwen** the fog or mist has lifted; and REP: **sontsható:ko'** the fog or mist lifted, went away again.

With SRF -at-, N -hstar- drop, CAUS -ht-, and DLC: **wa'tekheiatstarókwahte'** I splashed her, **wa'thakwatstarókwahte'** he splashed me.

With SRF -at-, N -ien'kwar- smoke, and DLC: **tewatien'kwarókwas** puffball.

With SRF -at-, N -tsir- spark, fire, embers, and DLC: **tekonttsirókwas** fireflies.

With N -wenn- voice, word, and CISL: **tionkewennókwas** she talks back to me, **tahakewennó:ko'** he talked back to me.

With N -wis- ice, glass: **wa'kawisó:ko'** the ice went away, melted.

-okw- V take out of liquid: **kókwas** I take it out of the water, **wahró:ko'** he took it out of the water, **ontó:ko'** or (with REP) **sontó:ko'** the swelling went down. **iakaókwen** she has taken it out of the water.

With SRF -at-, N -a'kenhr- ashes, dirt, and BEN -hs-: **í:wehre' aonkwata'kenhrókwahse'** I feel faint from hunger (-ehr- think, want), **í:wehre' ahota'kenhrókwahse'** he feels faint from hunger.

With N -its- fish: **kentsókwas** pelican; heron (in GM).

With N -nawa'ts- mud: **ranawa'tstókwas** mud hen.

With N -wir- offspring: **iewirókwas** midwife.

With N -wistohser- butter: **kawistohserókwen** cream.

NOTE: This stem is composed of -o- be in water, and REV -kw-.

-on- give. *See* -awi-/-on-

onekwen'tarí:ha something small, cute

ó:nen now, already, good-bye

onennó:ron or **ononnó:ron** sweet flag

With ATTR =kowa, great: **onennoron'kó:wa** water lily

Cf. anennoron [sweet flag] (Beauvais: 9); *a nen no ro ko wa* ginger (D'Ailleboust: 25); *anon-no-ron* Acorus Calamus [sweet flag] (Rousseau: 70); *onennó:ron* sweet flag (Gabriel: 132); *ononó:ron*, *onennó:ron* sweet flag (Lazore: 56)

ó:nen'k tsi have to, must
• Ó:nen'k tsi enskahtén:ti'. I have to go home.

-onha- emphatic pronoun: **raónha** he, **aónha** she, it (usually an animal), **akaónha** she, someone, **ronónha** they (males, or males and females), **onónha** they (females).

With ATTR ='a/=ha, diminutive: **akonhà:'a** I am alone, **raonhà:'a** he is alone, he alone, and NEG: **iah tewakonhà:'a** I am not alone.

With ending -tsiwa: **raonha'tsíwa** he all alone, only he alone.

NOTE: These pronouns are often pronounced with an *m* for the nasal vowel, e.g., [rámha] for **raónha**.

-onhahr- V be really loud, with DLC: **teiaónhahre'** it is really loud, it is making a racket.
• Iote'serehtakà:te' teiaónhahre'. There's a lot of cars [and] they're making noise.

-onhar- N frozen ground

With V -ien- put down, have: **iaonhará:ien'** the ground is frozen.

With V -tens- be thick: **iaonhará:tens** it is a thick or deep frost.

-onhaw- KIN brother- or sister-in-law, between sexes, with ATTR ='a/=ha, diminutive: **rakonháhwha** my brother-in-law (female speaking), **akonhháwha** my sister-in-law (male speaking).

-onhawinon- V drizzle: **iaonhawí:non** it is drizzling.

-onhew- V sweep, with DLC: **tekonhé:was** I am sweeping, **wa'tiakónhewe'** she swept. With DISTR -nion-: **tekonhewánions** I am sweeping here and there, all over. With SRF -at-: **tekatonhé:was** I am sweeping, **tenkatónhewe'** I will sweep, **wa'tkatónhewe'** I swept, **teiakotonhé:wen** she has swept.

ónhka who, anyone, **ónhka'k** someone

-onhkahr- V snore: **rónhkahre'** he snores, **iakónhkahre'** she snores.

-onhnh- N life
  With V -aksen- be bad: **konhnháksen** I don't feel good, I feel sick, **ronhnháksen** he doesn't feel good, **iakonhnháksen** she doesn't feel good; with V -aksen- be bad, and INCH -'-: **wa'konhnháksen'ne'** I got sick; with V -aksen- be bad, and CAUS -'t-: **onkonhnháksa'te'** it made me feel sick.
  With SRF -at-, V -ehsak-/-ihsak-/-esak-/ -isak- look for, and PURP -h-: **wa'katonhnhisákhe'** I am going looking for work, **wa'katonhnhisákha** I went to look for work; and PAST -hne': **rotonhnhisakhónhne'** he has gone looking for work.
  With SRF -at- and V -her-/-hr- set on top of: **wakatonhnháhere'** I am happy, joyful, **rotonhnháhere'** he is happy,

iakotonhnháhere' she is happy, **wa'katonhnhà:ren'** I became happy; and NMZR -htsher-: **atonhnhahráhtshera'** happiness; with SRF -at-, V -her-/-hr- set on top of, and BEN -hahs-: **wahakwatonhnhahéhrhahse'** he made me happy, **wahiiatonhnhahéhrhahse'** I celebrated him (his birthday).
  With V -hseronni- dress, prepare: **konionhnhahserón:ni** I am making you feel better, healthier, **wa'kheionhnhahserón:ni'** I made her feel better.
  With SRF -at-, V -kari- bite, and DLC: **wa'thatonhnhaká:ri'** he was orphaned, **wa'tiontonhnhaká:ri'** she became an orphan, **teiakotonhnhakarì:'on** she is an orphan.
  With V -kowan[en]-/-owan[en]- be big, and CISL: **tsonhnhó:wane'** whale.
  With SRF -at-, V -teni- change, and DLC: **wa'tiontonhnhaté:ni'** she underwent puberty or menopause, a change of life.

-onhnhe[t]- V be alive: **kónhnhe'** I am alive, **rónhnhe'** he is alive, **iakónhnhe'** she is alive.
  With CONT -k-: **enkónhnheke'** I will be alive, **enhrónhnheke'** he will be alive.
  With INSTR -hkw-: **tionhnhéhkwen** we live by it; corn, beans and squash; The Three Sisters; and DLC: **Teionhnhéhkwen** Mohawk title name 5.
  With SRF -at-, PURP -h-, and REP: **Shatonhnhéthe'** Easter.
  See also **atónhnhets** soul. spirit.

Cf. Naie tionnhe^ckon nongsatonnheston notre ame nous fait vivre (Bruyas: 16); *Onnha* vie (Bruyas: 120); *tsi non sahatōnnhĕte* Pâque (Marcoux: 278); *Gudonnhegwen* From whom one lives (Cooke: 430); *tsi non sa ha tonn he te* easter (Anon: 6); *Shatonhnhéthe* Easter

(Horne: 52); Wendat "In so far as it merely animates the body and gives it life, they call it *Khiondhecwi*;" (Brebeuf in Thwaites 10: 141); Onondaga *gonhekkȣi* la Vie (Shea: 102). See also Laurentian *Cudouagny* God (Biggar: 179).

-onhni- N point of land
With SRF -at- and V -te- be present, exist: **iotòn:niate'** peninsula, point of land.
Cf. *On^{c}nia* pointe du terre, *On^{c}niate* il y a une pointe (Bruyas: 12); *Otonnia* pointe (Galissonnière: 67r); *iotōnniăte* Pointe de terre (Marcoux: 295); *Onnia* pointe du terre, butte (Cuoq: 34); *Tsi ionton:iate* Point (Tewaterihwarenia'tha, Summer 1988: 24); Wendat *etiotondiata* au bout d'une pointe (Potier: 358); Iroquois *Otondiata* (Grenadier Island) (Coyne: 81)

-onhonts- earth, world, nation. *See* -onhwents-/-onhonts-

-onhsen- V sigh, moan: **onkónhsene'** I sighed, I moaned, **wahaónhsene'** he sighed, moaned, **wa'akaónhsene'** she sighed, moaned, **wakonhsé:nen** I am sighing, moaning, **iakaonhsé:nen** she is sighing, moaning.
With AMB -hne-: **wakonhsenà:ne's** I go around sighing, moaning.
Cf. *tsi ni iot ne kwes kwes ia ons he nan es* grunt (Diabo: 35, given as the equivalent for 'grunt', *literally,* 'the way a pig sighs')

ónhte could be, must be

-onhwaten- KIN relation of aunt or uncle and nephew or niece, with ATTR ='a/=ha, diminutive: **ionkonhwatèn:'a** my aunt, **rakonhwatèn:'a** my uncle, **riionhwatèn:'a** my nephew, **kheionhwatèn:'a** my niece, **wáten** Nephew! Niece!
With REFL -atat-: **iatatonhwatèn:'a** uncle and nephew, uncle and niece, aunt and nephew, **tiatatonhwatèn:'a** aunt and niece.
NOTE: At one time this term was used only to talk about a nephew or niece. See Deering and Delisle 31–35, Horne: 4–9.
Cf. *rionȣatēnha* Neveu, mon (Marcoux: 261); Laurentian *Yuadin* my nephew (Biggar: 246)

onhwá'tsi just a little while ago
• Onhwá'tsi tahatewennáta'. Just a little while ago he telephoned.

-onhwents-/-onhonts- N earth, world, nation: **onhóntsa'** or **ohóntsa'** or **onhwéntsa'** or **ohwéntsa'**
With LOC -kon, inside: **onhóntsakon** or **onhwéntsakon** underground; and DISTR -hshon: **onhontsakónhshon** or **onhwentsakónhshon** all under the ground.
With LOC -okon, under: **onhontsó:kon** or **onhwentsó:kon** in the basement or cellar, downstairs.
With LOC -'ke, on, at: **onhontsà:ke** or **onhwentsà:ke** on the earth, ground.
With V -are'sen- get fat, and CAUS -hst-: **wa'konhontsáre'senhste'** I fertilized.
With SRF -at- and V -hkhwa- take away from: **rontonhwentsáhkhwas** they take the land away.
With SRF -at-, V -hriht- break into pieces, smash, and DLC: **tehatonhontsahríhtha'** he is breaking up the earth, **wa'thatonhontsà:rihte'** he broke up the earth.
With SRF -at- and V -ia'k- cut, sever: **watonhóntia'ks** landslide, **ontonhóntia'ke'** a landslide happened, **iotonhontià:kon** there was a landslide.

With SRF -at-, V -kahrhateni- turn around, empty, BEN -en-, and DLC: **wa'tewakatonhontsakahrhaténien'** I got disoriented (cited as a "Tongue Twister" in Tewaterihwarenia'tha, Winter 1990: 14).
With V -ke- amount to, and PART: **Ià:ia'k nihononhwentsá:ke** Six Nations.
With V -kwek- be the whole of: **onhontsakwé:kon** the whole world.
With V -no- be cold: **iaonhontsá:no** the ground is cold.
With V -r- put in: **ionhóntsare'** or **ionhwéntsare'** map.
With V -te- be present, exist: **tsi ionhontsá:te'** the earth, the world.

ò:ni' also, and, **tóka' ò:ni' (tóka' ni')** or

-onko- V penetrate
With CAUS -ht-, TRNL and DLC: **ia'tkón:kohte'** I went through it, I penetrated it (for example, drilling a hole in a board), **ia'tewakonkóhton** I have gone through it.
With V -a'tarih[en]-/-tarih[en]- be hot, warm, NMZR -hser-, CAUS -ht-, and DLC: **teka'tarihenhseronkóhtha'** I am sweating, **wa'tha'tarihenhserón:kohte'** he got sweaty, **teiako'tarihenhseronkóhton** she has sweated.
With SRF -at-, N -ia't- body, CAUS -ht-, and DLC: **tewakatia'tonkóhtha'** I have diarrhea, **wa'tewakatia'tón:kohte'** I got diarrhea.
With SRF -ate- and N -rihw- matter, message: **roterihón:ko** he is annoying, bothersome, **iakoterihón:ko** she is annoying, **ioterihón:ko** it is annoying, disgusting; and CAUS -ht- and BEN -ni-/-en-: **wakaterihonkóhtani** I am annoyed, **onkwaterihonkóhten'** I got fed up.
With N -ronhi- sky, heaven, CAUS -ht-, and DLC: **Teioronhión:koht** Cayuga title name 6.

• **Ia'tkón:kohte' wa'kkahrón:ten' ake'nowáta'.** I went through it, I made a hole to put in a lock. • **Katia'tátsha's roterihón:ko.** I'm so irritated, he's annoying. • **Wakaterihonkóhtani né: sha'orì:wa.** I am annoyed, it's the same thing (over and over).

-onkw- V bump, hit, with TRNL and DLC: **ia'tewakónkwas** I bump into it, I hit it, **ia'tewakón:ko'** I bumped into it, I hit it, **ia'thaón:ko'** he bumped into it, **ia'tewakónkwen** I have bumped into it.
With N -hsnonhs- finger, hand: **ia'tewakehsnonhsón:ko'** I bumped or hit my finger, my hand.
With N -ia't- body: **ia'thatia'tón:ko'** he bumped into me, **ia'thiia'tón:ko'** I bumped into him.
With N -nontsi[st]- head: **ia'tewakenontsistón:ko'** I bumped my head.
• **Wa'katia'tátsha' ia'tewakón:ko' io'taríhen (kanà:tson', iena'tsahráhkhwa').** I burned myself, I bumped something hot (a pot, a frying pan). • **Kahnhohà:ke ia'tewakón:ko' ne akhióhsa'.** I bumped my elbow against the door.

-onkwe'ne- V be crowded: **ionkwè:ne'** it is crowded.
With NEG and REP: **iah tetsonkwè:ne'** there's not a lot of people anymore.
With PAST -hne': **ionkwe'néhne'** it was crowded.
With INCH -'-: **enionkwè:ne'ne'** it will get crowded, **wa'onkwè:ne'ne'** it got crowded.
With SRF -at- and CAUS -hst-: **ionkwatonkwe'néhston** we are crowding, loitering.
• **Iah tetsonkwè:ne' né:ne Kahnawà:ke akwé:kon ki' nà:'a Brooklyn ieiakawé:non**

nonkwá: tóhkara' niiátion iakwatenatanónhnha'. There are not a lot of people
left in Kahnawà:ke, everyone has gone to
Brooklyn, only a couple of us are taking
care of the town. (Letter 1945, Jan)

-onkwe['t]- N person, human being: **ón:kwe**
person, **rón:kwe** male person, **iakón:kwe**
or **ión:kwe** female person, **konnón:kwe**
women, female persons.
POSS: **akonkwè:ta'** my people; and ATTR
=shon'a, pluralizer: **raonkwe'ta'shòn:'a**
his people.
With ATTR =onwe, genuine:
Onkwehón:we Native person; and ATTR
=hneha, way of: **Onkwehonwehnéha** the
Native way, Native language.
With LOC -'ke: on, at: **onkwe'tà:ke** the
public.
With SRF -at-, and SRF -at- and V -hteron-
be scared, afraid: **rotonkwe'táthteron** he
is a frightening person, he makes one feel
uncomfortable.
With V -iio- be good, nice: **ronkwe'tí:io**
he is handsome, a good-looking person,
iakonkwe'tí:io she is pretty, beautiful;
with NMZR -hser- and V -iio- be good,
nice: **ronkwehserí:io** he is a kind fellow.
With SRF -at- and V -kareni- take back and
forth: **watonkwe'takarénie's** bus.
With V -ke- amount to, PROG -hatie-,
and DLC: **teionkwe'takehátie'** two by
two, two at a time.
With SRF -at-, and SRF -at- and V
-kwennien-/-konnien- be very clean, neat:
rotonkwe'tatkónniens he is an elegant
gentleman, he is distinguished,
iakotonkwe'tatkónniens she is elegant.
With V -nonhiani- be extreme, menacing,
and DLC: **teionkwe'tanòn:iani** she acts
inappropriately.
Cf. J agongꙮeta C'est ma créature, mon
sujet (Bruyas: 119); "the second [social

class] is (that of) the *Agongoueha* [the
women kind], or the common people;"
(Lafitau I: 341); Laurentian *Aggouetté* a
woman (Biggar: 242); Wendat *onꙮe* etre
homme (Potier: 417); Wendat *Honhouoy*
Vn homme (Sagard: Pa13); Onondaga
ongꙮe homme (Shea: 62), *agongꙮeda* mon
sujet (Shea: 96); Onondaga *unquehúe*
Heathen (Zeisberger: 92)

onkwe'tá:kon grey squirrel
Cf. *Ogꙮetagon* Escurieux noir (Galissson-
nière: 7v); *onh gweh da gonhs* squirrel
(black, grey) (Jamieson 1: 5)

-onni- V make: **kón:ni** I am making it,
kón:nis I am making more than one of
something, **enkón:ni'** I will make it,
wahrón:ni' he made it, **wakón:ni** I have
made it, **tsón:ni** Make it (pl)!
With CAUS -'t-: **konnià:tha'** I make it
with it, **enkónnia'te'** I will make it with
it, **wahrónnia'te'** he made it with it,
ionnià:ton it is made of it.
With BEN -enni-/-en-: **kheionnién:ni** I
am making her (do something),
wahakónnien' he made me (do it).
With SRF -at-: **wahatón:ni'** he was born,
rotón:ni he is born; and PURP -'n-:
ratonnià:ne' he is going to be born,
Christmas.
With SRF -at-: **watón:nis** it grows,
ontón:ni' it grew; and suffix -s-:
ontonnísa' it finished growing, it ripened,
iotonníson' it has finished growing, it is
ripe or ready.
With REFL -atat-: **ratatón:ni** he is putting
on airs, proud of himself, patting himself
on the back, **iontatón:ni** she is putting on
airs.
With SRF -at- and N -ahi- fruit, berry:
iotahión:ni (there are) a lot of fruit or
berries.

With N -ahkwenni- outfit, clothing: **rahkwennión:ni** tailor, **ionhkwennión:ni** seamstress.

With N -atia'tawi- dress, shirt, and NMZR -'tsher-: **enkatia'tawi'tsherón:ni** I will make a dress, a shirt; and BEN -enni-/-en-: **wahiiatia'tawi'tsherónnien'** I made a shirt for him.

With V -atkahri- play, and NMZR -'tsher-: **wakatkahri'tsherón:ni** I am playing.

With N -a'ker- snowflake: **wa'kerón:ni** it is making snow, changing to snow.

With N -a'ser- blade, axe: **O'serón:ni** French; and ATTR =keha, way of: **O'seroni'kéha** French language.

With N -a'ther- basket: **ion'therón:ni** she is making a basket; and SRF -at- and CAUS -'t-: **enhata'therónnia'te'** he will make a basket with it.

With N -honro't- pipe, tube: **wa'khonro'tón:ni'** I made it into a tube.

With SRF -at- and N -hrie'n- pack, load: **wa'kathrie'nón:ni'** I made a pack.

With N -hronw- crevice, ditch, and DLC: **tekahronión:ni** (there is) a ditch; and PROG -hatie-: **tekahronionnihátie'** (there is) a ditch going along.

With N -hsnonhs- finger, hand: **wa'kehsnonhsón:ni'** I made donuts.

With V -hsonw- be a hole: **wahahsonión:ni'** he made a hole.

With V -hsw- be playful, kid, tease, and CAUS -'t: **wahihswa'tón:ni'** I teased him, joked with him.

With N -hwist- metal, money: **rahwistón:ni** blacksmith.

With N -ian- footprint, track, and DLC: **tehatiianón:ni** they leave their footprints, their tracks, **tekaianón:ni** there is a path.

With N -ia't- body: **kaia'tón:ni** doll.

With SRF -at- and N -ien'kwar- smoke: **iotien'kwarón:ni** it is smoky.

With N -ithohkw- bundle: **wa'ethohkón:ni'** she made a bundle.

With SRF -an-, N -i't- excrement, and DLC: **teioni'tón:ni** it is tangled, complicated, a mess; and CAUS -'t-: **wa'thani'tónnia'te'** he messed it up, he complicated things.

With N -kar- cost, value: **onkkarón:ni'** I suffered for it (I went out to eat and now I'm paying!); with N -kar- cost, and CAUS -'t-: **wahokarónnia'te'** it harmed him; with SRF -at- and N -kar- cost, value: **wahatkarón:ni'** he had an expense.

With V -kenhr[on]- act indifferently towards, shun, and NMZR -'ser-: **wahikenhra'serón:ni'** I criticized, belittled him.

With N -khw- food: **wa'kekhón:ni'** I cooked; and SRF -ate-: **katekhón:nis** I eat.

With SRF -at- and N -ko'ts- crest, comb: **wa'katko'tsón:ni'** I fixed my hair.

With SRF -ate- and N -nawir- tooth: **iontenawirón:ni** she is getting teeth.

With N -na'kw- anger: **wahakena'kón:ni'** he angered me; and REFL -atate-: **rotatena'kón:ni** he is snarling, growling (talking about a dog).

With N -na'tar[o][k]- bread: **kena'tarón:nis** I am making bread, cake.

With N -na'tsher- canal, and PROG -hatie-: **kana'tsheronnihátie'** there's a canal, the seaway going along.

With N -na'watsist- bark, pie crust: **wa'kena'watsistón:ni'** I made a crust.

With N -nennio'kw- snowball: **wa'kenennio'kón:ni'** I made a snowball.

With N -nennotshera- package, parcel: **wa'kenennotsherón:ni'** I made a package.

With SRF -ate-, N -neraht- leaf, and CAUS -'t-: **Tsi iontenerahtonnià:tha'** Corpus Christi; with SRF -ate-, N -neraht- leaf, and PURP -'n-: **Iontenerahtonnià:ne'** Palm Sunday.

With SRF -ate- and N -nerokw- vest, top: **iotenerokón:ni** it is lying down.

With N -nohkw- bundle: **wa'kenohkón:ni'**

I made a bundle.
With SRF -ate- and N -nonhkw-/
-nonhkwa'tsher- medicine:
wa'katenonhkwa'tsherón:ni' I made
medicine.
With N -nonhs- house: **kenonhsón:ni** or
(with SRF -ate-) **katenonhsón:ni** I am
building a house; with N -nonhs- house,
and ATTR =onwe, genuine:
Rotinonhsonni'ón:we the founders of
the Confederacy.
With N -ratsken't- braid:
kheratsken'tón:ni I am braiding her hair;
and SRF -ate-: **wa'kateratsken'tón:ni'** I
braided my hair.
With N -ra'wist- peel, pancake:
wa'kera'wistón:ni' I made pancakes.
With N -rihw- matter, message, and BEN
-enni-/-en-: **shakorihonnién:ni** he teaches
them, **wa'kherihónnien'** I taught them;
and NEG: **iah tekarihonnién:ni** nobody
has taught (them), they have no class.
With N -ris[er]- socks: **wa'keriserón:ni'**
I knitted.
With N -rist- iron, steel: **keristón:ni** I am
a metal-maker.
With N -ronto-/-ronto'tsher- wooden box:
karonto'tsherón:ni cabinet(s).
With N -shes[t]- syrup: **wa'keshestón:ni'**
I made syrup.
With N -she'rh- dough, gravy:
wa'keshe'rhón:ni' I made dough, gravy.
With N -the'ser- flour, and CAUS -'t-:
iethe'seronnià:tha' mill.
With SRF -at- and N -tsenh- fire:
wahattsenhón:ni' he made a fire.
With N -tsihkw- fist, button:
wahatsihkón:ni' he made a fist.
With SRF -at- and N -tsi'nahkw- nest:
konttsi'nahkón:ni they are building
nests.
With SRF -at- and N -tsi'ts- flower:
iottsi'tsón:ni (there are) a lot of flowers
growing.

With N -'nhontst- dumpling:
ke'nhontstón:ni I am making dumplings.
With SRF -a-, N -'nikonhr- mind, and NEG:
iah tewaka'nikonhrón:ni I didn't mean
to, didn't intend to.
With SRF -ate- and N -'now- hump,
padlock: **rote'noión:ni** he is hunched
over.
NOTE: This root occurs with many incorporated nouns, and not all the derived or
inflected forms of some of the N plus V
combinations are given here; for the
additional forms, see the N entry. The
suffix -s- in the forms for 'finish growing,
ripen' is called the "eventuative" in
descriptions of Onondaga and Seneca,
and in those languages it has the form -s'-.
• Aió:ha ionnià:ton akwatià:tawi. My coat
is made of mink, my mink coat.

ononnó:ron or **onennó:ron** sweet flag

-onri- N breath
With V -htohrarak-/-ohrarak- squeeze,
press down, and DLC: **teiakaonriò:raraks**
she is wheezing, gasping for breath,
wa'thaonriò:rarake' he wheezed.
With SRF -at- and V -ien- put down, have:
rotonriá:ien' he is whining, sounding
agitated, **iakotonriá:ien'** she is whining.
With SRF -at- and V -o'kt- finish:
katonriò:ktha' I run out of breath,
enhsatonriò:kten' you will run out of
breath, **wa'katonriò:kten'** I ran out of
breath; and PROG -atie-:
wakatonrio'ktátie' I am out of breath,
rotonrio'ktátie' he is out of breath,
iakotonrio'ktátie' she is out of breath.
NOTE: This stem, and -atonrie- breathe,
-atonriser- breath, and -onriahkw- throb,
are all somehow related.

Cf. Atonriajen faire le hé hé au chant des
guerriers (Bruyas: 40); *Aonria* haleine

(Galissonnière: 48r); *teiakaonrioraraks ononkwa eksaa* [asthma medicine for children] (Beauvais: 20)

-onriahkw- V throb, with DLC:
tewakonriáhkhwa' I am throbbing, I am beating (for example, my heart), **tehaonriáhkhwa'** he is throbbing, **teiakaonriáhkhwa'** she is throbbing, **teiaonriáhkhwa'** it is throbbing. *See* -onri- breath.
• Teiaonriáhkhwa' keweionhkarà:ke. My thumb is throbbing.

ons ounce. **énska ons** one ounce, **tékeni ons** two ounces.

-ont- V attach: **kóntha'** I attach it, **wa'kón:ten'** I attached it, **wahrón:ten'** he attached it.
With NEG: **iah tewá:konte'** I didn't attach it.
With REV -kw-: **kontákwas** I detach it, remove it, take it off, **wa'kontá:ko'** I removed it.
With N -ahseriie['t]- string, rope, thread, and DLC: **teiohseriiè:tonte'** fringe.
With N -ahskwen'n- porch: **iohskwèn:nonte'** there's a porch.
With N -ashar- strap, leash: **wa'kasharón:ten'** I put it on a leash.
With V -ato'tsine- slide, NMZR -htsher-, and DLC: **tekato'tsinehtsheróntha'** I am putting on skates, I am skating.
With N -entskwe'n- chest: **oronhia'kó:wa atháhsteren iawentskwè:nonte'** overalls (-ronhi- sky, -athahsteren- put on pants).
With N -hi'kt- thorn, and DISTR -on-: **iohi'któn:ton** it is thorny.
With N -hna't-/-hna'tahtsher- purse: **iohna'táhtsheronte'** pocket.
With N -hnek- liquid: **wakhné:konte'** I am perspiring; with SRF -at-, N -hnek-

liquid, INSTR -hkw-, and DLC; and **akè:ra'** (-akehr-/-kehr- dish, plate): **teionthnekontáhkhwa' akè:ra'** teacup.
With SRF -at-, N -hnenna't- potato, and DLC: **tesathnennà:tonte'** you are so cakey (a Kahnawà:ke expression), you are not all there.
With V -hnio- grow, and INSTR -hkw-: **wa'kahniohkón:ten'** it sprouted.
With N -hnionwar- thistle, picker, bramble, DISTR -on-, and DLC: **teiohnionwarón:ton** it has pickers; with DISTR -onnion- and DLC: **wa'tewakhnionwarontónnion'** I got a pins-and-needles sensation.
With N -hsnonhs- finger, hand, DISTR -on-, and DLC: **teiohsnonhsón:ton** it has fingers.
With N -hsohkw- spout: **iohsóhkonte'** (there is) a spout.
With N -hstar- drop: **khehstaróntha'** I am nursing her.
With N -hsto'ser- small feathers: **iohstò:seronte'** it has feathers.
With SRF -at-, N -hwen'kar- snowshoe, and DLC: **wa'thathwen'karón:ten'** he put on snowshoes.
With N -iahs- cross, and DLC: **teieiahsóntha'** she makes the sign of the cross, she is a Catholic.
With N -ia't- body, REV -kw-, and CAUS -ht-: **riia'tontakwáhtha'** I am leaving him out, **wa'kheia'tontákwahte'** I excluded her; with SRF -at-, N -ia't- body, and INSTR -hkw-: **wahatia'tón:tahkwe'** he faked it, **wakatia'tontáhkwen** I am pretending to be something I am not, I am faking it.
With SRF -an- and N -ihn- skin, leather: **wakaníhnonte'** I have a skin tag.
With SRF -an- and N -ihnhe't[ar]- wart, quill: **wakanihnhè:taronte'** I have a wart.
With N -ihwhar- fur: **rohwhá:ronte'** he has fur.

With N -itahs- tail: **rentáhsonte'** he has a tail, **otsísto kentáhsonte'** comet (-tsisto[hkw]- star).

With N -i'tar- chimney, clan, clay, PROG -atie-, and DLC: **tsi teken'tarontátie'** along the edge of the roof.

With N -kahkwen't- wheel, tire: **énska iokahkwèn:tonte'** wheelbarrow; and DLC: **tekeni teiokahkwèn:tonte'** bicycle.

With N -kahtso't- dry crusty sleep in the eyes, and DLC: **tehokahtsò:tonte'** his eyes are crusty with sleep.

With N -konhston'rh- beard, whiskers, and DLC: **tehokonhstòn:rhonte'** he has a beard or mustache.

With N -na'kar- horn, antler, DISTR -on-, and DLC: **teiona'karón:ton** it has horns; and ATTR ='a/=ha, diminutive: **teiotina'karontòn:'a** sheep.

With N -nehkw- little bump, sore: **ronéhkonte'** he has a little bump, a pimple.

With N -nekerehetsh- handle: **ionekerehétshonte'** it has a handle.

With SRF -ate-, N -nennio'kw- snowball, and DLC: **teiotenenniò:konte'** there are snowballs on it.

With N -nerahontsh- wing, shoulder blade, with DLC: **tekanerahóntshonte'** it (a bird) has wings.

With N -neraht- leaf: **onerahtón:ta'** poplar.

With N -nonhwe'rh- body hair, fuzz: **rononhwè:rhonte'** he has body hair.

With N -rahkw- sun, NMZR -hser- and LOC -'ke, on, at: **orahkontsherà:ke** in the sunshine; with NMZR -hser-, V -oia['k]- throw straight at, and DLC: **teiorahkontsheróien'** the sun is shining on it, **wa'tewakerahkontsheróia'ke'** the sun shone on me, I got sunstroke.

With N -rihw- matter, message: **wahonwarihón:ten'** they appointed him;

and SRF -ate-: **roteríhonte'** he is an official, a faithkeeper; with N -rihw- matter, message, and REV -kw-: **kerihontákwas** I am useful, I accomplish things, get things done, **wa'kerihontá:ko'** I was useful, I got it done.

With SRF -ate- and N -rist- iron, steel: **ateristón:ta** ice cleats.

With N -tar- brim, eaves, and DLC: **teiotá:ronte'** it has a brim; fedora; and PROG -atie-: **teiotarontátie'** eaves.

With N -tshe['t]- bottle, jar: **iotshè:tonte'** blister.

With N -tsihkw- fist, button, knot (tree): **rotsíhkonte'** he has a bump, a lump.

With N -wei- wing: **oweión:ta'** pick (tool).

With SRF -ate-, N -wenn- voice, word, and INSTR -hkw-: **katewennontáhkhwa'** I speak a language.

With N -'nhaht- branch, and DISTR -on-: **io'nhahtón:ton** it has branches.

With N -'nika[ht]- pillar, DISTR -on-, and DLC: **teka'nikahtón:ton** crocodile.

With SRF -ate-, N -'nikahtse'n- laces, and DLC: **tekate'nikahtse'nóntha'** I am doing up the laces.

With N -'nikonhr- mind, INSTR -hkw-, and CAUS -'t-: **iontate'nikonhrontahkwá'tha'** condolence wampum set of fifteen strings.

With N -'nist- stem: **io'nístonte'** straight pins.

NOTE: This root occurs with many incorporated nouns, and not all the inflected forms of some of the N plus V combinations are given here; for the additional forms, see the N entry.

-onta- N kettle, pail: **ón:ta**

Cf. ondach kettles (van den Bogaert: 52); *Ontak* chaudière (Bruyas: 122); *agontak* ma chaudière (Bruyas: 45); *Ontak* Chaudiere (Galissonnière: 18v); *oondahk*

Kettle (Gallatin: 322); *Ontak* chaudière
(Cuoq: 34); *Aon:ta* Pail (Tewaterihwa-
renia'tha, Autumn 1989: 27); Laurentian
Undaccon the earthen pot (Biggar: 245);
Susquehannock *Oωntack* a pot, a kettle
(Holm: 7)

-ontar- N waterway
With V -oken- merge, fork, and DLC:
teiontaró:ken there is a split or fork in
the waterway.
With SRF -at-, V -rik- put together, and
DLC: **Tetiatontarí:kon** Québec City.

Cf. Te jaontarógen Où il y a deux rivières
qui se croisent, qui se rencontrent (Bruyas:
118); *te giatontarigon* Kebec (Bruyas: 41);
Te giatontarigon Kébec, deux rivières que
se reunissent (Bruyas: 90); "Ticonderoga
is from *Teyonderoga* meaning the separa-
tion of two lakes," (Joseph Brant in Boyce:
291); *Tegiettontarĩhco* Quibeck, Haupt-
stadt in Canada (Pyrlaeus: 63);
Tia-on-taro-ken Ticonderoga, "a fork or
point between 2 lakes" (De Lorimier in
Hough: 181); *Dekayadontarigonh* Quebec
... possibly it refers to "sister mountains"
(Brant-Sero and Hill in Boyle: 172);
Tiaontontarikon (Quebec) (Onkweonwe:
3); *Tekyatoñtarí:koñ* Quebec "two rivers
close together" (Lounsbury 1960: 51–52);
Tekoñtaró:keñ or *Teyoñtaró:keñ* Ticonder-
oga "At the Junction, or Forking, of Two
Waterways" (Lounsbury 1960: 51–52);
Wendat *Atontarégué* Kebec (Sagard: Na1);
Gontara Lac (Sagard: Ri2); Wendat
Ontare there is a lake (Chaumonot in
Potier: 741); Wendat *Te,iatontari,e*
Quebec (Potier: 455); *ontara* lac, mer
(Potier: 154); Wyandot *yònta:re'* lake
(Barbeau 1960: 90); Cherokee *v:tali* lake
or large river (Lounsbury 1961: 13)

-ontawe't- V shake, pump, vibrate:
kontawè:tha' I am pumping, shaking,
vibrating it (for example, the pedal of an
old-fashioned sewing machine),
wa'kón:tawe'te' I pumped it, shook it
back and forth.
With SRF -ar-, N -ahsi't- foot, and INSTR
-hkw-: **ionrahsi'tontawe'táhkhwa'** pedal
(of a sewing machine).
With SRF -at-, N -tsir- spark, fire, embers,
and DLC: **teionttsirontawè:tha'** she is
seesawing, **tenkattsirón:tawe'te'** I will
seesaw.

-ontho- V burn, put in the fire
With SRF -at-: **watónthos** it burns; and
ó:iente' (-ient- wood) and **karístatsi**
stove: **ó:iente' watónthos karístatsi**
wood stove; and **kén:ie'** (-iie-/-ien- oil,
grease): **kén:ie' watónthos** it burns oil,
kén:ie' watónthos karístatsi a gas stove,
an oil heater.
With N -ahswen't-/-a'swen't- coal:
ohswèn:ta' watónthos it burns coal,
kahswen'tónthos I am putting coals in
to burn (into a stove or coal oven),
wahahswen'tóntho' he put coals in to
burn, **sahswen'tóntho** Put the coals in!
With N -ient- wood: **tientónthos** I put
wood in the fire, **entientóntho'** I will put
wood in the fire, **wa'tientóntho'** I put
wood in to burn, **roientónthon** he has put
wood in to burn; and REP: **sahaientóntho'**
he is putting more wood in to burn.
With N -ien'kw- tobacco: **enhsien'kóntho'**
you will put tobacco in the fire,
wa'tien'kóntho' I burned tobacco.
NOTE: This stem is composed of a root
-ont- and CAUS -ho-. The root -ont- occurs
also in -ate'skont- roast, bake.

-onti- lose, throw. *See* -ati-/-onti-

-ontie- fly around, float by. *See* -itie-/-tie-/ -ontie-

òn:wa now

=onwe ATTR genuine, authentic
With N -ahta[hkw]- shoe:
ahtahkwa'ón:we moccasin.
With N -hnawer- well, and V -ot- stand:
iohnawerote'ón:we a (natural) spring.
With N -ien'kw- tobacco: **oien'kwa'ón:we**
Indian tobacco.
With N -na'tar[o][k]- bread:
kana'tarokhón:we cornbread.
With N -nonhkw- medicine:
ononhkwa'ón:we natural medicine.
With N -nonhs- house, and V -onni- make:
Rotinonhsonni'ón:we the founders of the
Confederacy.
With N -onkwe['t]- person: **Onkwehón:we**
Native person.
With N -rihw- matter, message and V -iio-
be good, nice: **orihwiio'ón:we** it really is
true, it is unquestionably true.

-on'eskw-/-on'weskw- V enjoy, with
BEN -ni-/-en-: **wakon'éskwani** or
wakon'wéskwani I enjoy it,
raon'éskwani he enjoys it,
iakaon'éskwani she enjoys it,
ionkenon'éskwani we enjoy it,
ronon'éskwani they enjoy it,
onkon'éskwen' I enjoyed it,
wakon'eskwanì:'on I am enjoying it.
With PAST -hkwe': **wakon'eskwaní-
hahkwe'** I used to enjoy it.
• Wakon'éskwani akatahónhsatate'
ratirén:note'. I like to listen to them
sing. • Wakon'eskwanì:'on akaterò:roke'
tahatinónniahkwe'. I am enjoying
watching them dance.

-on'wesen- V be pleasant, agreeable:
ion'wé:sen it is pleasant, nice.

• Ion'wé:sen ahsaterohrókha' tehattsihkwà:'eks tewa'á:raton. It's nice for you
to go and watch him play lacrosse.

-on'weshen- V party, with SRF -at-:
ronton'wéshens they party (they drink,
etc.), **wahaton'wéshen'** he partied.
Cf. ne Raonwesentsera Glory (Cory: 18)

orá:son small black berries, perhaps elderberries
NOTE: According to Mike Norton, these
are used to make wine against asthma.
Cf. Rasek Holunder (elder) (Pyrlaeus:
208); *Orasek* Sureau blanc (Cuoq: 35);
o ra seh elderberry (Jamieson 1: 6)

-oreht- V judge
With N -ia't- body, and DLC:
tetia'toréhtha' I judge, **tehaia'toréhtha'**
he is a judge, **wa'tehshakoia'tó:rehte'** he
judged her or them; and FACIL -'tskon:
tewatia'torehtà:tskon I judge everything.
With N -nahkw- marriage:
kanahkoréhtha' matchmaker.

-oren- V split open, with DLC: **tekó:rens** I
split it open, **wa'tkó:ren'** I split it open,
tewakó:ren I have split it open.
With N -ahi- fruit, berry: **wa'tkahió:ren'**
I split open the fruit.
With N -hson'kar-/-hswen'kar- board:
Tekahson'karó:rens Hogansburg, NY.
With N -nia't- throat:
wa'tewakenia'tó:ren' I burped (from my
throat).
With SRF -ate- and N -wis- ice, glass:
teiotewisó:ren there's a crack in the ice or
glass.

Orenhre'kó:wa Mohawk title name 6

-ori- V drive, drive away

With SRF -at-: **katórie's** I drive (a vehicle), **ratórie's** he drives; falseface (he chases away sickness, or the wind), **iontórie's** she drives, **enkató:ri'** I will drive it, **waható:ri'** he drove it; and PROG -hatie-: **ratorihátie'** he is driving, **iontorihátie'** she is driving.

With SRF -at- and N -heht- field, meadow: **athehtó:ri** scarecrow.

With N -nonhwar- brain: **wakenonhwaró:ri** I am foolish, silly, **rononhwaró:ri** he is foolish, silly, **iakononhwaró:ri** she is foolish, silly, **enwakenonhwaró:ri'** I will be foolish, **Kanonhwaró:ri** a society for Midwinter, Midwinter ceremony; and SRF -ate- and INSTR -st-: **ratenonhwaroríhstha'** he acts silly, he fools around, **wahatenonhwaró:riste'** he acted silly, he fooled around, **iakotenonhwaroríston** she is acting silly, fooling around.

With N -serenht- sleep: **wakeserenhtórie's** it keeps me awake, I have a rough night, a sleepless night, **onkeserenhtó:ri'** it kept me awake, I had a bad night.

With N -'nikonhr- mind: **wahake'nikonhró:ri'** he entertained me, **ionkhi'nikonhró:ri** she is entertaining us; and SRF -ate-: **wa'kate'nikonhró:ri'** I got entertained, I had fun.

• Iontórie's iakoia'takarénie's. She drives the bus. • Wa'kate'nikonhró:ri' ne tewa'á:raton tehonttsihkwà:'eks wakaterohrokhónhne'. I had fun going to watch the lacrosse game.

-oriahneron- V move, shift: **korià:nerons** I move it, I am shifting it, **wa'korià:neron'** I moved it, **wahrorià:neron'** he moved it. With SRF -at-: **katorià:nerons** I move (shaking my body), I am wiggling (I can't sit still), **wahatorià:neron'** he moved (perhaps in his sleep), he wiggled around;

and DISTR -onkw-: **ratoriahnerónkwas** he moves about, **wahatoriahnerón:ko'** he moved around, **wakatoriahnerónkwen** I am moving about.

Órie' friend. According to GM, in older usage a formal term used instead of a name when talking to a male person of any age or standing and irrespective of one's own sex but usually between males. And from Mary Deer's Mohawk class notes, Nov. 1965: *ó-rie* addressing a friend (masc). Today, it can be used by anyone when talking to a friend, male or female.

Cf. Orien Amy (Galissonnière: 6v); "But *Olia* (Comrade, the Stile we give each other)" (Conrad Weiser in Wallace: 467); *orie* mon ami, mon camarade (Cuoq 1866: 141); *ò:rie* friend (old word) (Gabriel: 58); Iroquois "*Arie*, you are Corlaer's Messenger," (Colden: 61); Onondaga *horien* Ami (Shea: 19); Onondaga *óllie/órrie* Friend (Zeisberger: 80)

-oro[k]- cover. *See* -'rhoro[k]-/-oro[k]-

ó:se willow, pussywillow

-osera[hw]- gush, spew. *See* -sera[hw]-/-osera[hw]-

oserakwaròn:ne' bloodsucker

oserennó:ha' marten
• Wà:s sehnhohakétsko ne onhontsó:kon, tánon' ia'sá:ti ne sanawí:ra', tetsatá:ton ne oserennó:ha'. Go lift up the (trap) door to the basement, and throw your tooth, trade it with the marten (his tooth). *What they used to say when a child lost a tooth.*

Cf. seranda marten (van den Bogaert: 53); *Seranóha* Marder (Pyrlaeus: 201); *Serennoah* [marten] (Onkweonwe: 3);

ah ne se ra no hah marten (Jamieson 1: 5); *Oseranó:ha* Marten (Horne: 110)

-oseren'- V sink into, with TRNL and DLC: **ia'teióseren's** it goes in, it sinks (into something soft, like mud, or in a bog).

Oshahrhè:'on Chateauguay, Québec
NOTE: Frank Natawe translated this as 'river mouth narrowed by bulrushes'.
Cf. "... another Creek abᵗ. 3 1/2 leagues up the River Sᵗ. Lawrence on the South Side, called Chateauguay or *Yoroghsarheough*," (Johnson: 805); *Rosahrhekon* à Chateauguay (Cuoq: 39); *O-sar-he-hon.* "... This probably relates to the narrow gorge in the river near the village." (F. Marcoux in Hough: 179); *sharhé:'on* Chateauguay (Williams: 255); *Shahrè:'on* Chateauguay (Horne: 60); *Rosahrèkon* Chateaugay [sic], Quebec (Gabriel: 22)

-oskon- V be all, pure: **aóskon** it is throughout, it is pure.
With V -hon'tsi- be black, dark-coloured, and ending -st-: **kahon'tsistóskon** it is all black.
With N -nawa'tst- mud: **onawa'tstóskon** it is mud all over.
With V -ra'ken- be white, light-coloured, and NMZR -hser-: **kara'kenhseróskon** it is all white.

ostòn:ha or **ostón:ha** a little
Cf. Wendat *Chyuha* Vn peu (Sagard: Pe9); Susquehannock *Stunga* little (Holm: 8)

-ot- V stand (For examples without an incorporated noun, *see* -hniot-/-ot-.)
With SRF -at-, N -ahonht- ear, and DLC: **tekatahonhtótha'** I am really trying to listen.
With V -ahsen- be tens, and NMZR -hser-:

iohsénhserote' hundreds, thousands.
With N -ahsir- blanket, shawl: **wahsí:rote'** sailboat.
With SRF -ar-, N -ahsi't- foot, and DLC: **wa'tkarahsi'tó:ten'** I put my foot up.
With N -ahsonht- wall, and DLC: **tewahsónhtote'** partition, **wa'thahsonhtó:ten'** he put up a wall.
With N -askawe't- barefoot, and DLC: **tehaskawè:tote'** he is barefoot; and PROG -atie-: **tehaskawe'totátie'** he is going barefoot.
With N -aten'nits-/-aten'nitsher- cane: **wakaten'nítsherote'** I am using a cane.
With N -atshat- steam, mist: **iotshá:tote'** it is steaming, there is a mist.
With N -a'eht- claw, and DLC: **teka'éhtote'** I am on my toes; and PROG -atie-: **teka'ehtotátie'** I am on my tiptoes, going along.
With N -a'shar- knife, and DISTR -onkw-: **wahiia'sharotón:ko'** I stabbed him.
With SRF -at- and N -a'tohser- tent, cage: **wa'kata'tohseró:ten'** I put up a tent.
With N -hahser- light, lamp: **wa'khahseró:ten'** I turned on the light, **kaháhserote'** the light is on.
With N -hiohs- elbow, and DLC: **tekhióhsote'** I have my elbow on something; and SRF -at-: **wa'thiiathiohsó:ten'** I nudged him with my elbow.
With N -hnaw- rapid, strong current: **iohná:ote'** it is pouring out.
With N -hnawer- well: **iohnáwerote'** (there is) a well.
With N -hnek- liquid, and CISL: **tiohné:kote'** fountain.
With SRF -at- and N -hnenhs- shoulder: **wa'kathnenhsó:ten'** I put my shoulder up against it (in order to hold it up).
With N -hnia's- neck, collar, and DLC: **wa'tekhnia'só:ten'** I got all dressed up, all done up; with SRF -at- and N -hnia's-

neck, collar: **kathnia'sótha'** I immerse myself (in water) up to my neck; with SRF -at-, N -hnia's- neck, collar, and INSTR -hkw-: **ionthnia'sotáhkhwa'** velvet.
With N -honr- gun: **iohón:rote'** kettle with a spout.
With N -honro't- pipe, tube, and DISTR -on-: **kahonro'tó:ton** organ; dandelion.
With N -hskaw- bush: **kahská:ote'** (there is) a bunch of trees.
With N -hwa'tst- foam: **iohwà:tstote'** (there is) foam.
With N -ia't- body, V -onni- make, NMZR -hser-, and CISL: **tkaia'tonníhserote'** statue, a doll standing over there.
With N -ient- wood, and DLC: **tetientótha'** I stack wood.
With N -ien'kwar- smoke: **ioièn:kwarote'** the smoke is rising.
With N -ithohkw- bundle: **wa'kithohkó:ten'** I made a bundle.
With N -itskw- haunches: **réntskote'** he is sitting; crusty bread; and SRF -an-: **enkanitskó:ten'** I will sit down.
With N -itstenhr- rock, boulder, and DLC: **tenhentstenhró:ten'** he will stack rocks, make a foundation.
With N -itstohkw- pack, pile: **iotstóhkote'** it is piled.
With N -i'tar- chimney, clan, clay: **ken'tá:rote'** there is a chimney.
With N -i'tonw- pile, heap: **wa'ki'tonió:ten'** I made a pile, **io'tón:iote'** there's a pile of something.
With SRF -at- and N -kar- cost, value: **wakatká:rote'** I have a bill, I owe money; with N -kar- cost, value, and BEN -ni-/-hahs-: **khekarotá:ni** I give her credit; with N -kar- cost, value, and REV -hsi-: **rakarotáhsions** he collects money, conductor, cashier; and BEN -enni-/-en-: **rakkarotahsién:nis** he is asking me for his money, he is collecting from me.
With N -konhs- face, INCH -'-, and CONTR

and TRNL: **thiahakonhsó:ta'ne'** he landed on his face, face first.
With N -kont- bridge of the nose: **rokón:tote'** he has a bump on his nose.
With N -kwir- tree, sapling: **iokwí:rote'** there's a tree, standing.
With N -nakar- stick: **ienakarótha' o'rhótsheri** pole bean (-'rhotsher- string bean).
With N -nakt- bed, place: **ionáktote'** there is some space or room, **wakenáktote'** I have time; and BEN -ni-/-hahs-: **wa'khenaktóthahse'** I let her stay, I gave her a room to stay in.
With N -nats- slats, and DISTR -on-: **kanatsó:ton** sled or truck with boards or slats on the side that go between upright posts; with N -nats- slats, and DISTR -onnion-: **wa'kenatsotónnion'** I put the slats up; with N -nats- slats, and CISL: **tahanatsó:ten'** he stood his ground.
With N -nawa'aht- post, pole: **wahanawa'ahtó:ten'** he put up a post, a pole, **kanawa'áhtote'** there is a post, pole.
With REFL -atate-, N -na'kar- horn, antler, DISTR -onkw, and DLC: **tetiatatena'karotónkwas** the two are fighting with their horns.
With N -na'tar[o][k]- bread: **kanà:tarote'** offertory.
With N -nenhr- crowd, and REV -kw-: **wa'khenenhrotá:ko'** I confronted her.
With N -neni- stone, rock, and ATTR =haka/=aka, people of: **Oneniote'á:ka** Oneida; with N -neni- stone, rock, and ATTR =hronon, resident of: **roneniothró:non** he belongs to the Rock clan.
With N -nonhs- house: **wakenónhsote'** I have a house, my house.
With N -nonni- dance: **iakwanónniote'** we are moving (to the music).
With SRF -a-, N -nons- crouch, squat, and

DLC: **wa'tkanonsó:ten'** I squatted.
With N -nont- mountain, hill: **ionón:tote'** there is a hill.
With N -no'ts- tooth: **kanò:tsot** muskellunge, **ranò:tsote'** he has a tooth; and INCH -'-: **wa'eno'tsó:ta'ne'** she (a baby) got a tooth.
With N -rahkw- sun: **ioráhkote'** the sun is shining.
With SRF -ate- and N -rat- heel: **wahaterató:ten'** he stepped on it with his heel, he turned on his heel.
With SRF -ate- and N -reni- bun (hair): **wakaterén:iote'** I have a bun.
With N -renn- music: **kerén:note'** I am singing, **karén:note'** song, music; andSRF -ate-: **katerennótha'** I sing, **waterennótha'** musical instrument, radio, record player.
With N -ren't- leg from hip to knee: **wa'keren'tó:ten'** I put my legs up in the air.
With N -ront- log, beam: **karón:tote'** standing beam, pole.
With N -ronwar-/-nonwar- wire, nail, needle, pin: **kanón:warote'** there is a nail or pin in it, **wa'keronwaró:ten'** I put a nail or pin in it.
With N -tsihkw- fist, button, knot (of a tree): **iotsíhkote'** (there is) a knot in a tree, **wa'ktsihkó:ten'** I put a button on (for example, my coat), I buttoned it.
With N -tsina'ahr- tree stump, and CISL: **tiotsina'à:rote'** there's a stump there.
With N -tsi'nionhker- snot: **waktsi'niónhkerote'** my nose is running.
With N -tsi'nonw- insect, bug, and REV -hsi-: **wahonwatsi'noniotáhsi'** they found him out.
With N -wehn- island: **kawè:note'** island; and DISTR -on-: **wa'kawehnó:ton'** it flooded, **iowehnó:ton** it is a flood; with N -wehn- island, and INCH -'-: **wa'kewehnó:ta'ne'** I became stranded.

With N -wenn- voice, word: **rawén:note'** he is howling, **kawén:note'** echo, it is howling; and INCH -'-: **khewennó:ta's** I suspect her or someone.
With N -'kats- limb, PROG -atie-, and DLC: **teha'katsotátie'** he is going along bare legs.
With N -'nhi- rainbow: **iò:nhiote'** (there is) a rainbow.
With N -'nika[ht]- pillar: **ka'nikáhtote'** (there is) a pillar, a pier.
With SRF -ate-, N -'nikonhr- mind, and CISL: **takate'nikonhró:ten'** I made up my mind.
With N -'nist- stem, bow, rivet, and DLC: **teka'nístote'** it has a bow, a rivet.
With N -'notst- nakedness: **ke'nótstote'** I am naked; and PROG -atie-: **ke'notstotátie'** I am (going along) naked.
With N -'wahst- little stick, peg, and INSTR -hkw-: **ie'wahstotáhkhwa'** clothes peg.
With N -'whahs- skirt, and TRNL and DLC: **ia'teka'wháhsote'** it goes right to the point.
With N -'whar- tunnel, hollow: **io'whá:rote'** hollow (in a tree).
With BEN -'s-, *see* -ota's- receive.
See also -ohtshi- remove, pull out.
NOTE: This root occurs with many incorporated nouns, and not all the inflected forms of some of the N plus V combinations are given here; for the additional forms, see the N entry.

-otahrhe'- V get hooked on something
With N -ia't- body: **tia'totáhrhe's** I get caught on something, hooked on it, **wa'tia'totáhrhe'ne'** I got hooked, snagged on it, **watia'tohahrhè:'on** I have got hooked, snagged on it.
With N -kahr- eye: **wa'kkahrotáhrhe'ne'** I cast my eye on it, I fixated on it, **wahakahrotáhrhe'ne'** he fixed his eye on it.

With N -nawa'tst- mud:
wahanawa'tstotáhrhe'ne' he got stuck in
the mud.
With N -nieht- snow:
wahaniehtotáhrhe'ne' he got stuck in the
snow.
With N -tsi'er- fingernail:
wa'ktsi'erotáhrhe'ne' I snagged my nail
on something.
NOTE: This stem is composed of -otahrhe-
(related to -otarho[k]- hook) and INCH -'-.

Cf. Akohsá:tens senhs ó:ni kontinawatsto-
táhrhes. Even horses got stuck in the mud.
(Old Kahnawake: 20)

-otahrhe's- V get stuck, falter: **onkotáhrhe'se'**
I got hung up, I got stuck (trying to do
something, maybe filling out forms).
With NEG: **iah káneka tehaotahrhè:se'**
he didn't falter, he didn't get stuck.
With N -wenn- voice, word:
wakewennotáhrhè:se' I am having
trouble with my words (stumbling over
them, remembering them).
NOTE: This stem is composed of -otahrhe-
(related to -otarho[k]- hook) and BEN -'s-.
• Karì:wes se' wí iah teshotá:ti tánon'
kwáh iah káneka tehaotahrhè:se'. It's a
long time he didn't speak (Kanien'kéha)
and he didn't falter at all (Letter 1946,
talking about Father Hauser leading a
service).

-otahrho[k]- V hook: **kotáhrhoks** I hook it,
enkotáhrhoke' I will hook it,
wa'kotáhrhoke' I hooked it,
wakotáhrhon I have hooked it.
With SRF -at-: **Atotáhrho** entangled,
Onondaga title name 1.
With SRF -at- and DLC: **tewatotáhrhoks**
hook, safety pin.
With N -hi'kar- gear:
enkhi'karotáhrhoke' I will put it in gear.

With SRF -at-, N -hnenhs- shoulder, and
DISTR -hon-: **athnenhsotáhrhon**
suspenders.
With SRF -at-, N -hsin- leg, and DLC:
wa'thakwatshinotáhrhoke' he tripped
me.
With N -hwist- metal, money, and DLC:
wa'tionkhwistotáhrhoke' they put handcuffs on me, **wa'thihwistotáhrhoke'** I put
handcuffs on him.
With N -ia'kar-/-ia'kwar- midriff, and DLC:
wa'ttia'karotáhrhoke' I draped it over
something (for example, a towel or a belt
over a chair), **wa'tieia'karotáhrhoke'** she
draped it over.
With N -konwar- falseface, face:
wa'kkonwarotáhrhoke' I put the bridle
on (a horse), **skonwarotáhrhok** Put the
bridle on! and SRF -at- and INSTR -st-:
atkonwarotahrhókstha' bridle.
With N -nekerehetsh- handle, and DISTR
-hon-: **tsikenekerehetshotáhrhon**
wolverine.
With N -niar- neck, and CISL:
thaniarotáhrhoks ship's pilot, captain of
a war canoe, **entehseniarotáhrhoke'** you
will take control of the handlebars, sleigh
runners, steering wheel, reins,
takeniarotáhrhoke' I took control of the
handlebars, sleigh runners, wheel, reins,
thoniarotáhrhon he is in charge,
tiakoniarotáhrhon she is in charge.
With N -rihw- matter, message, and DLC:
tekarihotáhrhon argument; and SRF
-ate-: **wa'titiaterihotáhrhoke'** you and I
disagreed, **wa'thiaterihotáhrhoke'** the
two disagreed.
With V -'khar- have on a slip, and DLC:
wa'tekhe'kharotáhrhoke' I put a diaper
on her; and SRF -ate-:
teiakote'kharotáhrhon she has on a
diaper.
NOTE: This stem is composed of a root

-otar-, which occurs only with suffixes, and CAUS -ho- (and with an unclear ending -k-). *See also* -otahrhe'- get hooked on something, and -otahrhe's- get stuck, falter.

• Wa'kotáhrhoke' takatihéntho'. I hooked it [and] I pulled it.

-otarihsi- V unhook: **kotaríhsions** I unhook it, **wa'kotaríhsi'** I unhooked it.
With N -hsi- palm of the hand, and BEN -en-: **onkhsiotaríhsien'** it came out of my hand, I lost my grip, **wahohsiotaríhsien'** he lost his grip.
NOTE: This stem is composed of a root -otar-, which occurs only with suffixes, and REV -hsi-.

-ota's- V receive: **onkó:ta'se'** I received it, **wakotà:se'** I have received it.
With N -hiatonhser- book, paper: **enhohiatonhseró:ta'se'** he will get mail, **onkhiatonhseró:ta'se'** I received a book, I got mail.
With N -nennotsher- package, parcel: **onkenennotsheró:ta'se'** I received a package.
With N -rihw- matter, message: **onkerihó:ta'se'** I got news, I got informed
With N -'nerohkw- box: **onke'nerohkó:ta'se'** I received a box.
NOTE: This stem is composed of -ot- stand, and BEN -'s-.

othé:nen or **thé:nen** something, **iah thé:nen** nothing

ótia'ke' some. *See* -atia'ke-

-otka'w- V go through, channel
With SRF -at- and DLC: **wa'tiótka'we'** it came through (for example, plants), **teiotkà:wen** they are (poking) through.

With SRF -at- and N -a'kenhr- ashes, dirt, and DLC: **tenkonta'kenhrótka'we'** they (plants) will come, poke through the soil.
With N -ni- snow: **wahaniótka'we'** he went through, channelled through the (deep) snow; and PROG -hatie-: **wakeniotka'wenhátie'** I am going through the snow.
With N -(h)rh- woods: **wa'kehrhótka'we'** I went through the woods.

otkénseri leatherwood
Cf. Otkenseri pourriture (Bruyas: 35); *Otkenseri* pourriture; bois de plomb (Cuoq: 37, 64); *o-tken-se-ri* Dirca palustris [leatherwood] (Rousseau: 50)

otokénha' white oak
Cf. Tokenha chêne blanc (Cuoq: 50); *Otokénha'* White oak (Horne: 112)

-otsenh- V go scoop out of
With N -hnek- water: **wa'khnekotsénhe'** I am going to get water; and PAST -hne': **wakhnekotsenhónhne'** I have gone to get water.
NOTE: This stem is composed of a root -otsen-, which occurs only with suffixes, and PURP -h-.

-otsenht- V scoop out of: **iakotsénhtha'** she is scooping it out (water, sugar, flour, with a scoop or dipper), **wa'kótsenhte'** I scooped it out.
With INSTR -hkw-: **iakotsenhtáhkhwa'** dipper.
With N -hnek- water: **wahahnekótsenhte'** he scooped out water.
With N -nontar- soup, and INSTR -hkw-: **ienontarotsenhtáhkhwa'** soup ladle.
NOTE: This stem is composed of a root -otsen-, which occurs only with suffixes, and CAUS -ht-.

Cf. Gatsien plat (Bruyas: 105); *Gatsiehon*
aller a l'eau (Galissonnière: 33r); *Ketsiēn-has* eau, puiser de l' (Marcoux: 135);
Susquehannock *Kaatzie* a dish (Holm: 6)

-otshi- V burn oneself
With SRF -at- and N -en'nahs- tongue:
wa'katen'nahsótshi' I burned my tongue.
With SRF -at- and N -hnia's- neck, collar:
kathnia'sótshions my throat is burning,
wa'kathnia'sótshi' I burned my throat.
• Kathnia'sótshions sò:tsi iononwatariíhen
ne tí:. My throat is burning, the tea water
is too hot.

otsí: ghost *Used mostly when talking to
children.*
Cf. Otsii interj. de crainte, de frayeur
(Cuoq: 37)

otsí:io seal (animal)

otsina'kontahkwà:ne' or
otsi'nahkontahkwà:ne' bee
With **óshes** (-shes[t]- syrup):
otsina'kontahkwà:ne' óshes honey.

otskèn:rha' beech
Cf. Otskenrha hêtre (Cuoq: 38);
otskèn:rha' Beechnut (Horne: 112);
Onondaga *oskenhra* le hetre (Shea: 21)

otsohkó:ton balsam fir
Cf. otshokoton [balsam] (Beauvais: 8);
o-tso-ko-ton Abies balsamea [balsam fir]
(Rousseau: 37); *ohtsohkó:ton* balsam
(Lazore: 61); *Otsho'kó:ton* Balsam,
Spruce tree (Horne: 112)

-owak- V shake, tremble: **ió:waks** it is
shaking.
• Ió:waks tsi rónhnhe'. It's shaking (talk-

ing about a rabbit traumatized by a dog, or
somebody who has MS or tremors).

-owan[en]- be big. *See* -kowan[en]-/
-owan[en]-

-o'[k]- V slap, flutter, flap
With N -athenno-/-athenno'tsher- ball, and
DLC: **tekathénno'ks** I play ball,
tenhonthénno'ke' they will play ball; and
CAUS -st-: **teionthenno'ókstha'** playing
field.
With SRF -at-, N -hsin- leg, and CAUS -ht-:
katshino'káhtha' I am limping,
wahatshinò:kahte' he limped; and PROG
-hatie-: **rotshino'kahtonhátie'** he is
going along limping.
With N -nawir- tooth, DISTR -hon, and
DLC: **tewakenawiro'ókhons** my teeth are
chattering.
With SRF -ate-, N -nerahontsh- wing,
shoulder blade, DISTR -hon-, and DLC:
tewatenerahontsho'ókhons it is flapping
its wings (for example, a bird in a bird-bath).
With N -tsir- spark, fire, embers, and DLC:
tektsíro'ks I am lighting a fire using a
lighter or flint, **wa'tektsíro'ke'** I made a
spark, I lit a fire, **wa'thatsíro'ke'** he made
a spark, he lit a fire; and SRF -at-:
tewattsíro'ks flint (to start a fire), lighter,
tekonttsíro'ks fireflies.
See also -a'sharo'[k]- clap hands,
-attsikenhro'k- blink.

-o'ka't- V run into, bump against, with CISL:
takò:ka'te' I ran into it, I bumped against
it, **tahrò:ka'te'** he bumped against it,
taiakò:ka'te' she bumped against it.
With N -ahsi't- foot: **tahakwahsi'tò:ka'te'**
he (accidently) hit my foot.
With N -ahsonht- wall:
takahsonhtò:ka'te' I ran into the wall.

With **anitskwà:ra** chair (-itskw- haunches, -her-/-hr- set on top of) and NMZR -'tsher-: **takanitskwahra'tsherò:ka'te'** I banged into the chair.

With N -eri[ahs]- heart: **tonkweriahsò:ka'te'** it touched me, it went right to my heart.

With N -kahr- eye, and TRNL: **iahokahrò:ka'te'** it went into his eye (for example, an insect), **iahikahrò:ka'te'** I (accidentally) hit or touched his eye; and REFL -atat-: **ia'katatkahrò:ka'te'** I poked myself in the eye.

With N -nawa'aht- post, the pole: **tahanawa'ahtò:ka'te'** he hit the pole, post.

With N -ront- log, beam: **taharontò:ka'te'** he ran into the beam or post.

With N -ronto-/-ronto'tsher- wooden box: **takeronto'tsherò:ka'te'** I banged against the cupboard.

With N -wenn- voice, word: **tonkewennò:ka'te'** I said it and then *it happened* (and it is usually not a good thing that happened), **tahowennò:ka'te'** he said something and it came back to him because it did come about, **taiakowennò:ka'te'** she said something and it came back to her, **entisawennò:ka'te'** you have to watch what you say since it could happen.

With N -wer- wind, air, and CISL: **takewerò:ka'te'** I went against the wind, **tewakewero'kà:ton** I am facing the wind.
• Taharontò:ka'te' wahaten'enhraríhsi'. He ran into the post or pole [and] and took apart the fence.

-o'kt- V finish: **kò:ktha'** I finish it all or up, **wa'kò:kten'** I finished it, **wahrò:kten'** he finished it.

With TRNL: **iehrò:ktha'** he goes right to the end (of what he is doing), he finishes it, **ienhrò:kten'** he will go right to end, he will finish it, **ia'kò:kten'** I went right to the end (for example, the end of a row of knitting), I finished it, **iewako'ktà:'on** I have finished it, **iehao'ktà:'on** he has finished it.

With SRF -at-: **enkatò:kten'** I will run out of it, **wa'katò:kten'** I ran out of it, **iakoto'ktà:'on** she has run out of it, **ontò:kten'** it ended, **ió:to'kte** it has finished, it has ended, the end.

With SRF -at- and CISL: **tió:to'kte** less than (telling time, for example: *enká:r tió:to'kte' ne kaié:ri* a quarter to four); and **ranontsì:ne** (-nontsi[st]- head): **tió:to'kte' ne ranontsì:ne** he is not all there.

With SRF -at-, INSTR -hkw- and CISL: **takatò:ktahkwe'** I didn't complete something so it's short (for example, I didn't finish the sentence).

With SRF -at- and BEN -ni-/-hahs-: **onkwatò:kthahse'** I ran out of something; and CISL: **tiakoto'ktá:ni** she is short of something, **tonkwatò:kthahse'** I ran short of something.

With SRF -at-, INSTR -hkw-, BEN -ni-/-en- and CISL: **tahshakoto'ktáhkwen'** he didn't give her enough, he "shorted" her, **taionkwato'ktáhkwen'** she didn't give me enough.

With SRF -at- and N -ahseriie['t]- string, rope, thread (variant -hseriie['t]-): **wa'katsheriie'tò:kten'** I ran out of string or thread.

With SRF -at- and N -ahswen't-/-a'swen't- coal: **wa'katahswen'tò:kten'** I ran out of coal.

With SRF -at- and N -akenhnh- summer (variant -kenhnh-): **ontkenhnhò:kten'** summer ended, summer is over.

With N -atonriser- breath: **wahatonriserò:kten'** he took his last breath (and died).

With SRF -at-, N -enhniser- day, BEN -ni-/

-hahs-, and CISL:

tonkwatenhniserò:kthahse' the day was not long enough for me.

With SRF -at- and N -enhni't- moon, month: **ontenhni'tò:kten'** the month ended, the end of the month.

With SRF -at- and N -iahia'khser- week: **ontiahia'ksherò:kten'** the week ended, the end of the week.

With SRF -ate- and N -iie-/-ien- oil, grease: **wa'kateienò:kten'** I ran out of oil or gas.

With N -kar- cost, value: **wahakarò:kten'** he paid off, ended his debt.

With SRF -at- and N -ohser- year, winter: **ontohserò:kten'** the year ended, winter ended.

With SRF -at- and N -onri- breath: **katonriò:ktha'** I am out of breath, **enhsatonriò:kten'** you will run out of breath, **wa'katonriò:kten'** I ran out of breath; and PROG -atie-: **wakatonrio'ktátie'** I am out of breath, **rotonrio'ktátie'** he is out of breath, **iakotonrio'ktátie'** she is out of breath.

With N -rihw- matter, message: **waharihò:kten'** he finished (reading or talking), **wa'erihò:kten'** she finished, **serihò:kton** Shut up!

With SRF -ate- and N -wenn- voice, word: **iotewén:no'kte'** the end of the word.

With SRF -a- and N -'nikonhr- mind: **ka'nikonhrò:ktha'** I am depressed or discouraged, **wa'ka'nikonhrò:kten'** I became depressed, **waka'nikonhro'ktà:'on** I have lost hope, I feel hopeless, **io'nikonhrò:kta** it is useless, futile.

• Iahrò:kten' waha'taníharon' ne otsi'néhtara'. He finished putting the beads on the string. • Onkwatò:kthahse' tó: nikarì:wes wátien' ákhsa'. I ran out of how long I have to finish (i.e., I ran out of time).

-o'kwat- V dig: **kó'kwats** I am digging, **wahró'kwate'** he dug, **wako'kwá:ton** I have dug.

With N -a'kenhr- ashes, dirt: **ka'kenhró'kwats** I am digging up dirt, **wa'ka'kenhró'kwate'** I dug in the dirt.

With N -neni- stone, rock, and CAUS -st-: **tsi ienenio'kwátstha'** quarry.

With N -rihw- matter, message: **wa'kerihó'kwate'** I dug around for information, I did research.

o'náhsar water hemlock

NOTE: According to Mike Norton, it heals broken bones but shrinks or stiffens the muscles if it is left on too long.

Cf. Wendat *Ondachiera* Racine venimeuse (Sagard: PL 3); Onondaga *honachinra* Cigüe (Shea: 33)

o'nonnóhkara' shagbark hickory

Cf. o-non-na Carya cordiformis [butternut hickory] (Rousseau: 39); *Onennóhkara'* Hickory (Horne: 112)

o'só:ra' or **osó:ra'** spruce

Cf. osōrha epenitte (Marcoux: 155); *oneta osora 6 aonts* [6 oz. spruce pitch] (Beauvais: 10); *o-so-ra* Picea sp [spruce] (Rousseau: 36); *osó:ra ohnéhta* spruce gum (-hneht- pine) (Lazore: 56); *o'sò:ra* spruce (Lazore: 62)

-o'te- V be windy: **iaò:te** it is windy.

Cf. iahōte le vent souffler (Marcoux: 411); *Iahote* venter, le vent souffler (Cuoq: 5); *dayao'dǎ'dyɛ'* wind storm coming (Hewitt, n.d.: 2); *Iaòte* Wind (Zeisberger in Wheeler-Voegelin: 57); *Iahó-te, Iahóte* it is windy (Cory: 11, 73); *ia o te* wind (Diabo: 87); *Ya o deh* it is windy (Jamieson 1: 10); *iaó:te* it is windy (Lazore: 51)

-o'ten- V be a kind of, with PART: **nahò:ten'** what?

With N -ahsohkw- colour:
Oh niwahsohkò:ten? What colour is it?

With N -atahtsher- twig, yard (measure); and **onekwénhtara'** (-nekwenhtar- red): **onekwénhtara' niwatahtsherò:ten** red willow.

With N -hnek- liquid, and DISTR -shon-: **tsi nikahneko'tèn:shon** all kinds of drinks.

With N -htehr- root; and **otsì:nekwar** (-tsi'nekwar- yellow): **otsì:nekwar nikahtehrò:ten** goldthread.

With V -ianer[e]- be good, and NMZR -enhser-: **niionkwaianerahserò:ten** our laws, our traditions.

With N -ia't- body: **tsi nihaia'tò:ten** the way he is, **tsi niieia'tò:ten** the way she is.

With N -ieron['t]- body, shape, and COIN: **né: sha'kaieron'tò:ten'** it is the same shape.

With N -io'tenhser- work: **tsi nikaio'tenhserò:ten** what kind of work it is.

With N -i'tar- chimney, clan: **Oh nisen'tarò:ten?** What clan are you?

With N -ko'ts- crest (bird), comb (rooster): **nikko'tsò:ten** my hair style, **niieko'tsò:ten** her hair style.

With N -nahskw- pet, domestic animal: **Oh na'kanahskò:ten'?** What kind of animal (species) is it?

With V -naker[e]- reside, dwell, and NMZR -hser-: **Oh nisanakerahserò:ten?** What Nation are you?

With N -ohser- winter, year: **1924 niiohserò:ten** it's the year 1924.

With N -sahe't- bean; and **onekwénhtara'** (-nekwenhtar- red): **onekwénhtara' nikasahe'tò:ten** kidney beans.

With N -tsi'nionhker- snot: **nihatsi'nionhkerò:ten** he is thought not to be capable or appropriate (for example, not good enough for the job or office). *This is an older expression.*

With N -weienn- manner: **tsi nikeweiennò:ten** (it is) my way (of doing things), my actions, **tsi nihaweiennò:ten** (it is) his way, **tsi niieweiennò:ten** (it is) her way.

-o'thiie- be sharp, pointy. *See* -hio'thiie-/ -o'thiie-

-o'tsirek- V sip, suck: **wa'ko'tsí:reke'** I sipped it, sucked on it (for example, a lollipop), **wahro'tsí:reke'** he sucked on it, **wako'tsiré:kon** I am sucking on it, **iako'tsiré:kon** she is sucking on it.
With CAUS -st-: **iako'tsirékstha'** straw.

-o'tsiskw- V slip on something, with DLC: **tewako'tsískwas** I slip on something, **wa'tewako'tsísko'** I slipped, **wa'thao'tsísko'** he slipped, **wa'tiakao'tsísko'** she slipped, **teiao'tsískwa** it is slippery.

-o'tsohrok- V get scrunched, with DLC: **wa'tio'tsò:roke'** it got scrunched up (say I jumped and when I landed my legs went right up into my body).
NOTE: This stem probably includes -ohro[k]- insert.

R

-r- V put in: **kéhrha'** I put it in (a container), **énkeren'** I will put it in, **wà:keren'** I put it in, **í:kare'** it is in it, **íseren** Put it in! With NEG: **iah thé:nen tewákere'** I didn't put anything in.
With DISTR -onnion-: **kerónnions** I fill them, distribute it, **enkerónnion'** I will distribute it.
With INSTR -hkw-: **ieráhkhwa'** container.
With REV -kw-: **kerákwas** I choose it, **enkerá:ko'** I will choose it, **wahará:ko'** he chose it, **wakerákwen** I have chosen it; and CISL: **entehserá:ko'** you will remove it, **takerá:ko'** I removed it, **taserá:ko** Remove it!
With CAUS -hst-: **keráhstha'** I sketch it, draw it, **énkerahste'** I will draw it, **wà:kerahste'** I drew it, **wakeráhston** I have drawn it, **karáhston** it is drawn; and DISTR -nion-: **kerahstánions** I am drawing, taking pictures, **enkerahstánion'** I will draw, take pictures, **waharahstánion'** he drew, took pictures, **karahstánion** drawings, pictures, artwork, photographs.
With SRF -ate-, CAUS -ht-, DISTR -nion-, and DLC: **tekaterahtánions** I go back and forth, I am pacing; **wa'thaterahtánion'** he paced.
With BEN -ni-/-hahs-: **kherá:ni** I am serving her or them, **wa'khéhrhahse'** I served her or them; and REFL -atate-: **katatherá:ni** I am serving myself, **wa'katatéhrhahse'** I served myself, **satatéhrhahs** Serve yourself!
With BEN -wi-/-hs-, and CISL: **thakerá:wi** he blames me, **tahí:rahse'** I blamed him.
With INCH -'-: **iakó:ra's** it is contagious; and SRF -ate- and DLC: **wa'tiatiátera'ne'** we two ran into one another, we met, **wa'thóntera'ne'** they ran into one other, they had a (car) accident, **tehoterà:'on**

he got a sexually transmitted disease, **teiakoterà:'on** she got a sexually transmitted disease.
With INCH -'- and CISL: **tká:ra's** television, movie; and DLC: **tentká:ra'ne'** it will get filled, full.
With INCH -'- and REP: **ó:nen saká:ra'ne** it is a new moon.
With COIN and REP: **shískare'** the day of the month, the date.
With **éntie** south, and PART: **éntie ní:kare'** (it is) noon.
With DLC: **tekéhrha'** I compare it, **wa'thá:ren'** he compared it, **wa'tié:ren'** she compared it, **téseren** Compare it!
With SRF -ate-: **wakátere'** it is in my dish, **rótere'** he has it in his dish, **iakótere'** she has it in her dish.
With N -ahiakwir- toe, and DLC: **tewahiakwí:rare'** suit of clubs in cards.
With SRF -at- and N -ahsat- dark, shadow: **iotahsá:tare'** (it is) a shadow, **wakatahsá:tare'** I am casting a shadow.
With N -ahseriie['t]- string, rope, thread, DISTR -on-, and DLC: **tekahseriiè:tarons** I am embroidering it, **tewahseriiè:taron** it is embroidered.
With N -atawe- flea, and NMZR -hser-: **wakatawéhserare'** I have fleas on me.
With N -atshat- steam, mist, fog, cloud, and DISTR -onnion-: **iotshatarónnion** there are fluffy clouds here and there.
With N -erahs- moss: **iaweráhsare'** it has moss on it.
With SRF -at- and N -erien't- disposition: **wakaterièn:tare'** I know; and INCH -'-: **onkwaterièn:tara'ne'** I found out, I discovered.
With N -hah- road, and INCH -'-: **wahaháhara'ne'** he got onto the road.
With N -hakenht- soot: **iohakénhtare'**

it is full of soot.

With SRF -at- and N -harennaht- lead, purple: **wakatharennáhtare'** I have a bruise; and INCH -'-: **onkwatharennáhtara'ne'** I got a bruise.

With N -hent- grass, and CAUS -hst-: **iakohentaráhstha'** poison ivy.

With N -hneht- pine: **iohnéhtare'** it has pitch or gum on it.

With N -hnek- water: **kahné:kare'** there is liquid in it.

With N -hniar- snake, and INCH -'-: **wahohniá:rara'ne'** he hallucinated.

With N -hsa'kenser- frost: **iohsa'kénserare'** there is frost on it; and INCH -'-: **wa'ohsa'kénserara'ne'** it got frost on it.

With REFL -atat- and N -hsenn- name: **wa'katatshén:naren'** I signed it.

With N -hstien['t]- bone, and DLC: **tekahstièn:tare'** crossbones.

With N -hwish- burden, effort, and REV -kw-: **onkhwishará:ko'** the burden or weight got lifted off me.

With N -ia't- body: **kaià:tare'** picture, **tià:tare'** a picture of me, **raià:tare'** a picture of him, he is a member, **ieià:tare'** a picture of her, she is a member, **wa'ontià:taren'** they took a picture of me; with N -ia't- body, and INCH -'-: **enhaià:tara'ne'** he will receive communion, **enieià:tara'ne'** she will receive communion; with SRF -at-, N -ia't- body, and INSTR -hkw-; and **ohnà:ken** behind: **ohnà:ken eniakoià:tarahkwe'** she will be late, **ohnà:ken ontià:tarahkwe'** I was late; and PROG -hatie-: **ohnà:ken roia'tarahkwenhátie'** he is (always) late.

With V -ihei[on]-/-enhei[on]- die, CAUS -'t-, and INSTR -hkw-: **iakenheion'taráhkhwa'** coffin.

With N -ihwhar- fur: **iohwhá:rare'** fungus.

With SRF -an-, N -itsker- spit, saliva, and INSTR -hkw-: **ionnitskeraráhkhwa'** spittoon.

With N -itst- fish scale, scab: **wakítstare'** I have scabs; and INCH -'-: **wahótstara'ne'** he got scabs.

With N -kahkwen't- wheel, tire, and DLC: **tenkkahkwèn:taren'** I will put a circle around it.

With N -ke'rh- unkempt, messy hair, and DLC: **tekkè:rhare'** my hair is messy.

With SRF -ate-, N -nake['t]- birch bark, and DISTR -on-: **watenakè:tarons** white birch.

With N -nat- town, settlement, and INCH -'-: **wa'kená:tara'ne'** I came to town.

With N -nawa'tst- mud: **ronawà:tstare'** he has got mud on him.

With N -na'watsist- bark, pie crust: **iona'watsístare'** there is bark (on a tree).

With N -neker-/-enneker- hay, and INSTR -hkw-: **ienekeraráhkhwa'** hay wagon.

With N -nekwar- blood clot, and DISTR -onnion-: **kanekwarónnion** or **ionekwarónnion** it is polka-dotted.

With N -nekwa't- dancers in the Dipper constellation: **onekwà:tara'** or (with ATTR =shon'a, pluralizer) **onekwa'tara'shòn:'a** Pleiades, Little Dipper.

With N -neni- stone, rock: **ionén:iare'** calcification from water.

With N -nonhs- house, and INCH -'-: **wa'kenónhsara'ne'** I entered the house; with N -nonhs- house, and CAUS -hst-: **kanonhsaráhston** a drawing of a house.

With N -nontar- soup: **wa'kenontará:ren'** I served the soup; and BEN -hahs-: **wa'khenontaráhrhahse'** I served soup to her.

With obscure V -nonhwe-: **rarihwanòn:we** he is tiresome, wants to know everything, he is contrary, **ierihwanòn:we** she is tiresome.

With N -nonwe'rh- body hair, fuzz: **wakenonhwè:rhare'** I have hair on me (from a dog or cat).

With N -non't- milk, and INSTR -hkw-:
ienon'taráhkhwa' milk container.

With N -onhwents-/-onhonts- earth, world:
ionhóntsare' or **ionhwéntsare'** map.

With N -rahkw- sun, and DISTR -onnion-:
iakorahkwarónnion she has spots.

With N -rakwaht- callus:
wakerakwáhtare' I have a callus.

With N -rihw- matter, message, INCH -'-,
and CONTR, TRNL, and DLC:
thia'tehorihwarà:'on he is acting foolish.

With N -senenna't- muscle, and DISTR
-onnion-: **wakesenenna'tarónnion** I
have muscles.

With N -serenht- sleep, and INCH -'-:
onkeserénhtara'ne' I got sleepy, drowsy.

With N -sken'rh- rust: **ioskèn:rhare'** it is
rusty or moldy; and PROG -atie- and CISL:
taiosken'rharátie' it is getting rusty,
moldy.

With N -tshe'[t]- bottle, jar: **katshè:tare'**
Big Dipper.

With N -tsikhe't- sweet, and DLC:
teiotsikhè:tare' it is sweet; and N
-na'tar[o][k]- bread: **teiona'taratsi-
khè:tare'** cake; and N -nekwenhs- blood:
teiakonekwenhsatsikhè:tare' diabetes;
and N -nenhst- corn: **teionenhstatsi-
khè:tare'** sweet corn; and N -shes[t]-
syrup: **teioshestatsikhè:tare'** it is sweet
syrup;.

With N -tsiskerot- slime: **iotsiskeró:tare'**
it is slimy; and INCH -'-:
wa'otsiskeró:tara'ne' it got slimy.

With N -tsisto[hkw]- star:
enietsistóhkwaren' she or someone will
put an apostrophe; and DISTR -onnion-:
iotsistohkwarónnion there are stars.

With -tsi'io- be weak, feeble, CAUS -ht-:
rotsi'ióhtare' he is weak, **iotsi'ióhtare'**
it is defective; and INCH -'-:
wahotsi'ióhtara'ne' he got weak.

With N -tsi'nehtar- small bead(s), DISTR
-on-, and DLC: **wa'tektsi'nehtará:ron'**

I beaded it.

With N -tsi'nekwar- yellow:
rotsi'nekwá:rare' he has yellow
jaundice.

With N -tsi'non[ht]- louse, lice:
waktsi'nónhtare' I have lice.

With N -tsi'ts- flower, and INSTR -hkw-:
ietsi'tsaráhkhwa' vase.

With N -wenn- voice, word, and INSTR
-hkw-: **wahiwén:narahkwe'** I heeded
him.

With N -wer- wind, air: **iówerare'** (it is)
a light breeze.

With SRF -ate- and N -wihr- scar:
wakatewì:rare' I have a scar; and INCH
-'-: **ensatewì:rara'ne'** you will get a scar.

With SRF -ate-, N -wir- offspring, and REV
-kw-: **wa'katewirará:ko'** I adopted a
child.

With N -wis- ice: **iowí:sare'** it is icy.

With N -'nehtar- gravel: **io'néhtarare'**
sandpaper.

With N -'nikonhr- mind: **ke'nikòn:rare'**
I am watching over it, I am careful,
ri'nikòn:rare' I am watching over him;
and SRF -aten-: **wa'katen'nikòn:raren'**
I watched over it, **wahiiaten'nikòn:raren'**
I took care of him, I minded him.

With N -'wahr- meat: **io'wà:rare'** it is
fleshy or meaty.

With N -'watsist- rough, outer bark:
io'watsístare' there is bark.

NOTE: This root occurs with many incorporated nouns, and not all the inflected forms
of some of the N plus V combinations are
given here; for the additional forms, see
the N entry.

• Ne kerákwas tóhsa tho nátiere'. I'd
rather not do that. • Wà:tkeren' ne
karahstánion ka' niká:ien' enkenòn:-
we'ne'. I compared the drawings [to see]
which one I like.

rabahbót catfish

rabarowét wheelbarrow. A borrowing from French *la brouette*. Today **énska iokahkwèn:tonte'** (-kahkwen't- wheel, tire, -ont- attach) is mostly used.

raharén: salt herrings. A borrowing from French *le hareng*.

Cf. rearen [herring] (Ledger: 48); *ra a ren* herring (D'Ailleboust: 24); *Raharén:* Herring (from French herring) (Horne: 113)

-rahkw- N sun: **karáhkwa'**
With **ahsonthénhkha** (-ahsonthen- midnight): **ahsonthénhkha karáhkwa'** moon.
With SRF -ate- and V -ahton- disappear: **onterahkwáhton'** eclipse.
With V -awehrho- cover, close off, and CAUS -hst-: **iorahkwawehrhóhston** it is in the shade; and SRF -ate-: **ionterahkwawehrhóhstha'** umbrella, **enhsaterahkwawéhrhohste'** you will get in the shade, **wa'katerahkwawéhrhohste'** I got in the shade, **wakaterahkwawehrhóhston** I am in the shade.
With V -a'sen'-/-en'- fall down, and TRNL: **ia'karáhkwen'ne'** the sun went down; with V -a'sen'-/-en'- fall down, and PROG -hatie-: **ó:nen wa'orahkwen'enhátie'** the sun is going down.
With SRF -ate-, V -her-/-hr- set on top of, and CISL: **tioterahkwáhere'** it is a full moon.
With SRF -ate-, V -ia'ser-/-'ser- stack, and DLC: **wa'tewaterahkwà:seren'** eclipse.
With V -ieri- be right, and TRNL: **iekarahkwaié:ri** it is a full moon, a moonlit night.
With V -ineken'- emerge, and CISL: **tkarahkwíneken's** the sun is rising, **entkarahkwíneken'ne'** the sun will come up, **takarahkwíneken'ne'** the sun came up, **tiorahkwinekèn:'en** the sun has risen.

With V -ka'enion- look closely, scrutinize, and CAUS -'t-: **karahkwaka'eniòn:tha'** clock, sundial.
With V -o- be in water, BEN -'s-, and DLC: **wa'tewakeráhko'se'** I got blinded from the glare from the sun.
With V -ont- attach, NMZR -hser-, and LOC -'ke, on, at: **orahkontsherà:ke** in the sunshine; with NMZR -hser-, V -oia'[k]- throw straight at, and DLC: **teiorahkontsheróien'** the sun is shining on it, **wa'tewakerahkontsheróia'ke'** the sun shone on me, I got sunstroke, **wa'thorahkontsheróia'ke'** he got sunstroke.
With V -ot- stand: **ioráhkote'** the sun is shining; and REP: **sakarahkó:ten'** the sun came out again.
With V -r- put in, and DISTR -onnion-: **iakorahkwarónnion** she has spots, blotches, freckles.
With V -'shatst[e]- be strong: **karahkwa'shátste'** the sun is strong.

Cf. karackwero the sun (van den Bogaert: 58); *Garaksa* le soleil, *Onne ontraksation* nous avons éclipse, *Garaksaserhon* être, se mettre à l'ombre, *Jagotraksaserhosθa* un parasol (Bruyas: 86); *garaksa asontenka* Lune (Galissonnière: 53r); *Tiorᶜksaseron* Ombre (Galissonnière: 61r); *Ontéca garáchqua* Mond (Pyrlaeus: 2r); *Karaksakahenhionthakōsa* Horloge (Marcoux: 202); *Karakwa* le soleil, la lune (Cuoq: 11); *Iorakwawerhostakwa* ombrelle, parasol, *Karakwakahenhiontha* montre (Cuoq: 106); *ka ra kwa a son then kha* moon (Anon: 6); *ka ra kwa ka ion tha* clock (Anon: 13); *ka ra kwa ke en ion ta* watch, *ion te ra kwa we os ta* umbrella (D'Ailleboust: 5); *Karahkwa'ka'iòn:tha'* Clock (Horne: 108); *karakwahka'enhióntha* clock, it examines the sun (Gabriel: 23);

Wendat *Oracot* le soleil luyt (Sagard: Te1); Onondaga *garakkꝶa* soleil (Shea: 94); *karakkꝶa gahenhionk* Montre (Shea: 71)

rahwhút foundry

-rakahr-/-kahr- V make noise: **iorá:kahre'** it is making noise, it is noisy, **eniorá:kahre'** it will make noise.
With CISL: **átste' tiorá:kahre'** there's a noise outside.
With N -ahonht- ear, and DLC: **tekahonhtá:kahre'** I hear ringing in my ears, **wa'tkahonhtá:kahre'** my ears rang.
With N -ahsonht- wall, and DLC: **tewahsonhtá:kahre'** the walls are making noise.
With N -hstien['t]- bone: **iohstien'tá:kahre'** (my) bones are cracking.
With N -hwist- metal, money: **iohwistá:kahre'** a bell is ringing, money is jangling, **wa'ohwistá:kahre'** it rang (for example, church bells).
Cf. Garagarere v. Garagarhe faire du bruit (Bruyas: 58)

rakamí: clerk

Cf. ra ko mi clerk (D'Ailleboust: 31); *ra ken mi* clerk (Diabo: 10)

-rakarehrahst-/-karehrahst- V make noise
With SRF -ate-: **wakaterakarehráhston** I am making noise, **roterakarehráhston** he is making noise, **iakoterakarehráhston** she is making noise; and INSTR -hkw-: **ionterakarehrahstáhkhwa'** rattle.
With SRF -ate-, and N -hsnonhs- finger, hand: **katehsnonhsakarehráhstha'** I am making noise with my hand (for example, snapping my fingers, tapping on the table).

Cf. Gannakꝶagarereraston jouer du trambour, *Garistagareraston* sonner la cloche (Bruyas: 58); *Garagarerasθon* Bruit, en faire (Galissonnière: 14v); *Kalistagarerasta* Cloche (Galissonnière: 20v)

-rakarere-/-karere- V be noise travelling: **iorakaré:re'** it is making noise.
With N -ahiakwir- toe, and DLC: **tehahiakwirakaré:re'** his toes are making noise (talking about a dog).
With N -ahsi't- foot, and DLC: **tekahsi'takaré:re'** my feet are making noise.
With N -neraht- leaf: **ionerahtakaré:re'** the leaves are making noise.
With N -tsi'er- fingernail, and DLC: **tehatsi'erakaré:re'** his toenails are making noise (for example, a dog walking on the floor).

-rakare'ni-/-kare'ni- V be loud: **iorakarè:ni** it is loud.
With N -ahta[hkw]- shoe, and DLC: **teiakohtahkwakarè:ni** she is running around (with different men). This word has also been attested with a level tone, **teiakohtahkwakaré:ni**, *see* -kareni- take back and forth.
With N -wenn- voice, word, and DLC: **tehawennakarè:ni** he has a loud voice, **teiewennakarè:ni** she has a loud voice.

-rakenrie- V rub: **ierakénrie's** or **ierakénie's** she is rubbing it, **wa'kerakénrie'** or **wa'kerakénie'** I rubbed it, **rorakénrie** or **rorakénie** he has rubbed it.
With SRF -ate-: **wakaterakénrie'** I am squirming or wiggling, I am fidgeting, **roterakénrie'** he is squirming, fidgeting, **iakoterakénrie'** she is squirming, fidgeting.

NOTE: The *r* of the last syllable is not always pronounced.

rakerèn:shne barn. A borrowing from French *la grange*.

-rakew-/-okew- V wipe: **keraké:was** I wipe it, **enkerá:kewe'** I will wipe it, **wa'kerá:kewe'** I wiped it, **wakeraké:wen** I have wiped it.
With SRF -ate-, BEN -en-, and REP: **sonkwateraké:wen'** it went away on me, my sins are forgiven, **sesateraké:wen'** your (sg) sins are forgiven.
With SRF -ar-, N -ahsi't- foot, and CAUS -ht-: **ionrahsi'tokewáhta'** foot mat.
With N -atshat- steam, mist, fog, cloud: **katshatoké:was** I wipe away the steam, **wa'katsható:kewe'** I wiped away the steam, **iotshatoké:wen** it is clear (the sky is clear, the windows are unfoggy).
With N -a'kenhr- ashes, dirt: **ka'kenhroké:was** I am dusting, **waha'kenhró:kewe'** he wiped the dust off.
With SRF -at-, N -hnek- liquid, and REP: **shothnekoké:wen** he is sober.
With SRF -at-, N -ia't- body, and CAUS -ht-: **iontia'tokewáhta'** towel(s).
With N -iie-/-ien- oil, grease: **wa'keienó:kewe'** I wiped off the oil or grease.
With SRF -an- and N -i't- excrement: **wahani'tó:kewe'** he wiped his bum, **wà:s sani'tó:kew** Go wipe yourself!
and CAUS -ht-: **ionni'tokewáhta'** toilet paper.
With N -ks- dish, plate, and DISTR -nion-: **wa'keksokewánion'** I wiped (dried) the dishes.
With N -nekwenhtar- red, and DISTR -nion-: **wa'kwanekwenhtarokewánion'** we wiped the blood off you in several places.

With N -sken'rh- rust: **rasken'rhoké:was** he is wiping off the rust, **wahasken'rhó:kewe'** he wiped off the rust, **rosken'rhoké:wen** he has wiped off the rust.
With SRF -at- and N -tsi'nionhker- snot: **wa'kattsi'nionhkeró:kewe'** I wiped my nose.
Cf. wakwanekwenghdarokewanion we wash off the blood marks (Hale: 122–3)

-rakwaht- N callus: **orakwáhta'**
With V -r- put in: **wakerakwáhtare'** I have a callus, **rorakwáhtare'** he has a callus, **iakorakwáhtare'** she has a callus, **iorakwáhtare'** (there is) a callus; and INCH -'-: **onkerakwáhtara'ne'** I got a callus, **wahorakwáhtara'ne'** he got a callus.

ramerá:s molasses
Cf. Ramerass [molasses] (Granger: back cover); *ra me ras* molasses (Anon: 8); *ra mo ras* molasses (D'Ailleboust: 23)

ramorí: salted cod. A borrowing from French *la morue*.
Cf. ramore (Ledger: 54); *ra mo ri* cod (D'Ailleboust: 24)

-ranie-/-karanie- V rub, scrub: **keránies** I am rubbing it, scrubbing it, **enkeránie'** I will rub it, scrub it, **wa'eránie'** she rubbed it, scrubbed it, **iakoránie** she has rubbed it, scrubbed it.
With N -ahsaht- neck of a violin, guitar, fiddle: **wa'kahsahtakaránie'** I played the fiddle; and SRF -at- and CAUS -'t-: **iontahsahtakaraniè:tha'** fiddle.
With N -rist- iron, steel: **raristakaránies** he is filing it, **waharistakaránie'** he filed it; and CAUS -'t-: **ieristakaraniè:tha'** file.

ráonraon or **rámram** hummingbird

raprí:s snuff

Cf. ra pris snuff (Anon: 8); *ra pris* snuff
(D'Ailleboust: 25); *a ion tso ko raB ris*
sniff [*literally*, smoke raprís] (Diabo: 75)

rásen resin, pitch

rasó:s Kahnawà:ke meal of hash meat in a
white flour-and-water sauce served over
potatoes

Cf. ra sos sauce (Anon: 8)

rasosís sausage

Cf. ra so sis sausage (Anon: 7)

-rat- N heel: **orá:ta'**
POSS: **keratà:ke** (on) my heel, **raratà:ke**
(on) his heel, **ieratà:ke** (on) her heel.
With N -hnot- indicating depth, V -es- be
long, tall, and DLC: **teioratahnó:tes** high-
heeled shoes.
With V -ok- chafe, get a blister:
wakeratồ:kas I have a blister on my heel,
onkerá:toke' I got a blister on my heel.
With SRF -ate- and V -ot- stand:
wahaterató:ten' he stepped on it with his
heel, he turned on his heel (and walked
away).

-rat[e]- V have one's foot on something:
íkerate' I am standing on something,
rá:rate' he is standing on something,
ká:rate' it is standing on something,
kerá:te's I am climbing on something,
rará:te's he is climbing, **ierá:te's** she
is climbing.
With CONT -k- and CISL: **tho taserá:tak**
Stand, stay there!
With INCH -'-: **kerá:ta's** I step on it,
wahará:ta'ne' he stepped on it,
wakeratà:'on I have stepped on it; and

REP: **skerá:ta's** I step on it again; and
CISL: **tahará:ta'ne'** he stepped on it.
• Karistà:ke rá:rate'. He is standing on
the (steel) beam. • Kerá:te's tsi wa'tka'-
aratón:ko'. I'm climbing to take off the
cobwebs. • Kahsi'tà:ke wahará:ta'ne'. He
stepped on my foot. • Tewaksterihèn:'en
kwah kheh skerá:ta's. I'm rushing, just
not getting ahead, dropping things,
bumping into things, being a klutz.

-rathen- V climb: **keráthens** I climb,
enkeráthen' I will climb, **waharáthen'**
he climbed, **roráthen** he has climbed.
With PROG -hatie-: **wahorathenhátie'**
he is climbing up.
With TRNL: **iaharáthen'** he climbed, went
up.
With CISL: **taharáthen'** he climbed, came
up; and PROG -hatie-: **tahorathenhátie'**
he is climbing up, coming up.
With CAUS -hst- and TRNL or CISL:
ia'keráthenhste' I brought it up (there),
taharáthenhste' he took it up (here).
• Wa'keráthen' tsi wa'ktsiseróhare'.
I climbed up to wash the windows.
• Ia'keráthenhste' ne à:there'. I brought
up the basket.

-ratsken't- N braid: **oratskèn:ta'**
POSS: **akoratskèn:ta'** her braid.
With V -es- be long: **roratskèn:tes** he
has a long braid, **iakoratsken'té:son's**
she has long braids.
With V -onni- make: **kheratsken'tón:ni**
I am braiding her hair,
wa'keratsken'tón:ni' I braided it; and
SRF -ate-: **wa'kateratsken'tón:ni'** I
braided my hair.

-ratson- V tear, rip: **kerátsons** I tear it,
enharátson' he will tear it, **wa'erátson'**
she tore it, **iakorátson** she has torn it.
With DISTR -onkw-: **keratsónkwas** I am

tearing it up, **waharatsón:ko'** he tore it up.

With SRF -ate-: **onterátson'** it tore, it ripped, **ioterátson** it is torn, it is ripped; and DISTR -onkw-: **ioteratsónkwen** it is torn, ripped all over.

• Iotkà:te' enharátson' raowenhshòn:'a. He's always tearing his things (for example, his shirts).

-rawa't- N muck, sludge, scum: **orawà:ta'**
   With SRF -ate- and V -her-/-hr- set on top of: **ioterawa'táhere'** there is muck, sludge, scum.

-ra'kar- V be leaning against
   With SRF -ate-: **wakaterà:kare'** I am loafing, not doing anything, **roterà:kare'** he is loafing, **kwah nek enkaterà:karen'** I will loaf, just not do anything.
   With SRF -at-, N -hson-/-hsw- back, and TRNL: **ia'katshwarà:karen'** I leaned my back up against something.
   With N -ia't- body: **tia'tarà:kare'** I am leaning up against it, **raia'tarà:kare'** he is leaning up against it, **ieia'tarà:kare'** she is leaning up against it; and TRNL: **iehaia'tarà:kare'** he is leaning up against it (that way); with SRF -at- and N -ia't- body: **wahatia'tarà:karen'** or (with TRNL) **iahatia'tarà:keren'** he leaned against something, **wa'ontia'tarà:karen'** she leaned against it.
   • Raon'éskwani ahaterà:karen'. He likes to loaf. • Karontà:ke iehaia'tarà:kare'. He is leaning against the pole.

-ra'ken- V be white, light-coloured: **karà:ken** it is white, light-coloured.
   With INCH -'-: **enkarà:ken'ne'** it will become white, **wa'karà:ken'ne'** it became white, **iora'kèn:'en** it has gotten white.
   With **arihwawa'konhnéha** purple (-rihw- matter, message, -ienawa'k-/-wa'k- hold,

support) and NMZR -'tsher-: **arihwawa'konhne'tsherarà:ken** lavender.
   With N -ahkwari['t]- bear: **wahkwari'tarà:ken** polar bear.
   With SRF -at- and N -hehs- decayed, rotted wood: **athehsarà:ken** light brown, beige.
   With N -hwist- metal, money: **kahwistarà:ken** silver.
   With N -ihn- skin, leather: **kihnarà:ken** I am a light-skinned person, a White person, **renhnarà:ken** he is light-skinned, **iehnarà:ken** she is light-skinned.
   With N -i'tonhkw- flame, fever: **ken'tonhkwarà:ken** lantern that has a bag inside with naphtha, and the flame is more white than yellow.
   With NMZR -hser- and V -oskon- be all, pure: **kara'kenhseróskon** it is all white.
   With N -sahe't- bean: **kasahe'tarà:ken** white beans.
   With N -'nhehs- silk, satin: **ka'nhehsarà:ken** white silk or satin.
   • Iakoniákstha' atià:tawi kara'kenhseróskon. A wedding dress is all white.

-ra'nekar[on]-/-nekar[on]- V burst open, with DLC: **tekara'neká:rons** it bursts it, it busts, **wa'tkera'né:kare'** I burst it, **tewakera'neká:ron** I have burst it.
   With SRF -ate-: **tewatera'neká:rons** it bursts (a balloon when pierced, pipes that have frozen), **wa'tewatera'né:kare'** it burst, **teiotera'neká:ron** it has burst.
   With N -hnien'tskwir- shrub, small tree: **wa'tkahnien'tskwirané:kare'** the twigs are bursting (with buds or leaves).
   With SRF -at- and N -honro't- pipe, tube: **wa'tewathonro'tané:kare'** the pipe burst.
   With SRF -at- and N -ia't- body: **wa'thatia'tané:kare'** he got a hernia, **tehotia'taneká:ron** he has a hernia.
   With N -skwe'i- bud:

tenkaskwe'iané:kare' the buds will open up, **wa'tkaskwe'iané:kare'** the buds opened up.

With N -tsi'ts- flower: **tekatsi'tsaneká:rons** the flowers are blooming, **tenkatsi'tsané:kare'** the flower will bloom, **wa'tkatsi'tsané:kare'** the flowers bloomed.

Cf. Kan^{c}negaron se crever, s'entrouvrir, *Karan^{c}negaron*, extra comp. (Bruyas: 70); *T8atrandegaron* crever (Galissonnière: 26v); *tekeranekārons* Crever qlqch. (Marcoux: 95); *Tekeranekarons* crever, percer, ouvrir qq. ch. de gonflé, de creux (Cuoq: 46); Onondaga *degranegaronch* je creve quelque chose (Shea: 38)

-ra'neken-/-neken- V be side-by-side, next to, with DLC

With SRF -ate-: **tehiatera'né:ken** the two are (standing) next to each other, they are living together, they are partners, **wa'thiatera'né:ken'** the two got to be next to each other, **wa'thontera'né:ken'** they got to be next to each other, **tetiatera'né:ken** Come get next to me!

With N -ahonht- ear: **taonhtané:ken** or **tehahonhtané:ken** rabbit.

With SRF -ani- and N -hsnonhs- finger, hand: **tenhsanihsnonhsané:ken'** you will put your fingers together (and make a piercing whistle), **wa'tkanihsnonhsané:ken'** I put my fingers together.

With N -ient- wood: **Thaientané:ken** two pieces of wood side-by-side (tied together); name of Mohawk chief Joseph Brant.

With SRF -an- and N -itskw- haunches: **tetianitskwané:ken** you and I are sitting next to teach other.

With SRF -a- and N -nonhs- house: **teiatianonhsané:ken** we two are neighbours, my neighbour, **tehonnonhsané:ken** they are neighbours.

With N -tsi'ts- flower: **tekatsi'tsané:ken** two flowers (are) together.

-ra'nentahsi-/-nentahsi- V unstick: **wa'kera'nentáhsi'** I unstuck it.

With SRF -ate-: **ontera'nentáhsi'** it came off (for example, siding of the house, the patch on a jacket).

With SRF -an- and V -itskar[on]- shoe sole, cover: **onnitskaranentáhsi'** the sole (of a shoe) came off; and BEN -en-: **onkwanitskaranentáhsien'** the sole of my shoe came off on me.

NOTE: This stem is composed of a truncated form of -ra'nentak-/-nentak- stick to, and REV -hsi-.

-ra'nentak-/-nentak- V stick to: **iora'nén:taks** it is sticky, **eniora'nén:take'** it will stick to it, **wa'ora'nén:take'** it got stuck to it, **iora'nentá:kon** it is stuck to it.

With N -i't- excrement: **ro'tanén:taks** he is constipated, **iako'tanén:taks** she is constipated.

With N -rist- iron, steel: **ioristanentá:kon iontianenhtáhkhwa'** sled or sleigh runners (-ian- footprint, track, -a'senht-/-enht- drop).

With N -ronto-/-ronto'tsher- wooden box: **ioronto'tsheranentá:kon** cabinet or cupboards that are on a wall.

With N -'nonhkw- bottom of something, and CISL: **taio'nonhkwanén:take'** it got stuck to the bottom, **tio'nonhkwanentá:kon** something is stuck or caked on the bottom.

With N -'now- hump, padlock: **io'nowanentá:kon** lock (on a door).

With CAUS -t-, *see* -ra'nentakt-/-nentakt- stick something to.

• Rentahsà:ke óhrhohte' iora'nentá:kon. Pickers (burrs) are stuck on his tail.

-ra'nentakt-/-nentakt- V stick something to: **kera'nentáktha'** I am sticking it on (something), **eniera'nén:takte'** she will stick it on, **wahara'nén:takte'** he stuck it on, **rora'nentákton,** he has stuck it on, **sera'nén:takt** Stick it on!
With N -hiatonhser- book, paper: **wa'ehiatonhseranén:takte'** she put up wallpaper; and INSTR -hkw-: **iehiatonhseranentaktáhkhwa'** wall-paper.
With N -ia't- body, and ATTR =hne, at: **Ronwaia'tanentaktónhne** Friday.
With N -ihn- skin, leather: **wa'kihnanén:takte'** I patched it.
With N -konhs- face: **enkkonhsanén:takte'** I will paste a stamp on it, **wahakonhsanén:takte'** he stuck a stamp on it.
With SRF -ate- and N -nawa'tst- mud: **watenawa'tstanentáktha'** wasp (it sticks mud to it [the wall]).
NOTE: This stem is composed of -ra'nentak-/-nentak- stick to, and CAUS -t-.
Cf. enierho oniataraa ne enieranentakte kanoni iakononwaktani [you will rub it on the material, you will plaster it on where they are sick, hurting] (Beauvais: 27); *ia-ko-ta-nen-tak-ta* Rosa Eglanteria (= la plante qui rend constipé) [sweet briar rose] (Rousseau: 47); *ronᵕaiatanentaktōnne* Vendredi (Marcoux: 410); *ronwaiatanentaktonne* quand on l'attache, le vendredi-saint, et par extension, tous les vendredis de l'année (Cuoq: 28); *Ronwaiatanentaktonne* [Friday] (Granger: 4); *Ronwaiatanentaktonne* [Friday] (Granger: 4); *ron wa ia ta nen tak ton ne* Friday (Anon: 6); *ron-wa-ia-ta-nen-tak-tón-ne* Friday (Cory: 71)

-ra'shentho- V oversleep: **onkera'shéntho'** I slept late, I overslept, **wahora'shéntho'** he slept late, **wa'akora'shéntho'** she slept late.

-ra'wist- N peel, pancake: **ora'wísta'**
With V -kahrhatho- turn over: **wa'kera'wistakahrhátho'** I flipped the pancake, **sera'wistakahrhátho** Flip the pancake!
With V -ketskw- raise upright, and CISL: **thara'wistakétskwas** he is turning the page, **takera'wistakétsko'** I turned the page, **tewakera'wistakétskwen** I have turned the page, **tasera'wistakétsko** Turn the page!
With V -ohtshi- remove, pull out: **kera'wistóhtshions** I am peeling it, **wa'kera'wistóhtshi'** I peeled it, **iakora'wistóhtshion** she has peeled it, **sera'wistóhtshi** Peel it!
With V -onni- make: **kera'wistón:nis** I am making pancakes, **wa'kera'wistón:ni'** I made pancakes.
With V -tens- be thick: **iora'wístatens** it has a thick peel or skin.
See also **tsikera'wístak** bat.

-re- V extent, distance
With PART: **tsi niió:re'** while, during, until.
With SRF -ate-, and PART and DLC: **na'tetiátere'** it is between (two things); and DISTR -on-: **ken' na'tekónteron** a little while between, a bit at a time.
With SRF -ate-, and SRF -ate-, N -nonhs-house, and PART and DLC: **tsi na'tetiatenonhsátere'** it is between the houses.
With SRF -ate-, and SRF -ate-, N -'sere[ht]-vehicle, car, and PART and DLC: **tsi na'tetiate'serehtátere'** it is between the cars.

-rehetskw- N back of the knee, with LOC

-okon, under: **kerehetskó:kon** the back
of my knee, **rarehetskó:kon** the back of
his knee, **ierehetskó:kon** the back of her
knee.

-renh- N vine, (tree) limbs: **karénha'**
With V -kowan[en]-/-owan[en]- be big,
and REP: **Sharenhó:wane'** Mohawk title
name 4.

Cf. Garenha cime d'arbre (Bruyas: 88);
karenhakēnhiăte Sommet, des grands
arbres (Marcoux: 367); *Karenhia* bûche,
morceau de gros bois de chauffage (Cuoq:
11); Wendat *ạrenha* cime d'arbre (Potier:
452); Onondaga *garinhaguenhiata* cime
d'un arbre (Shea: 33)

-renhs- N lower leg.
With SRF -ate-, V -ia'ser-/-'ser- stack, and
DLC: **wa'tkaterenhsà:seren'** I crossed my
legs (maybe doing yoga).

Cf. Garensa corde de rassade, chappelet,
jambe (Bruyas: 89); *Orensa* la jambe
(Galissonnière: 24r); *Orensa* jambe depuis
le genou jusqu'au coude pied (Cuoq: 35)

-renhs- N rosary, prayer beads: **karénhsa'**

Cf. Garensa corde de rassade, chappelet,
jambe (Bruyas: 89); *garensa* Corde
(Galissonnière: 23r); *Karēnsa* chapelet
(Marcoux: 61); *Karensa* chapelet, rosaire
(Cuoq: 11); *ka ren sa* beads (Anon: 10)

-renhsaron- V be generous, praise someone,
with DLC: **teharénhsaron** he is generous,
teierénhsaron she is generous,
tekonrénhsarons I praise you, I am proud
of you, **wa'thonwarénhsaron'** she
praised him, she was proud of him.
With REFL -atate-: **wa'tkataterénhsaron'**
I praised myself, I am proud of myself.
• Wa'tekherénhsaron' tsi wa'tiontóhetste'.
I am proud of her that she graduated.

-reni- N bun (hair): **orén:ia'**
With SRF -ate- and V -ot- stand:
wakaterén:iote' I have a bun,
iakoterén:iote' she has a bun,
wa'katerenió:ten' I put my hair in a bun.

-renn- N song, music: **karén:na'**
With V -ahskats[t]- be beautiful:
iorennáhskats it is a beautiful song,
beautiful music.
With SRF -ate- and V -atahonhsat- listen:
wakaterennatahónhsate' I am listening
to music; and CAUS -t-:
katerennatahónhsatats I listen to music.
With SRF -ate- and V -her-/-hr- set on top
of: **waterennahéhrha'** record player.
With SRF -ate- and V -ien- put down, have:
wahaterén:naien' he prayed,
roterén:naien' he is praying;
aterén:naien' prayer; and BEN -ni-/
-hahs-: **wahonwaterennaién:hahse'** she
prayed for him,
wahshakoterennaién:hahse' he prayed
for them, he married them; with SRF -ate-,
V -ien- put down, have, and INSTR -hkw-:
ionterennaientáhkhwa' church.
With V -ot- stand: **karén:note'** or (with
DISTR -on-) **karennó:ton** music;
kerén:note' I am singing; and SRF -ate-:
katerennótha' I sing, I am a singer, I play
a musical instrument, **wa'katerennó:ten'**
I sang, **waterennótha'** musical instrument, radio, record player.
With V -tokeri[k]-/-okeri[k]- gather, shirr:
karennókeri it is a shorter version of the
song(s) or music.
• O'nó:wa' raterennótha'. He plays the
fiddle, the violin.

Cf. "The *Arendiouannens* or
Agotsinnachens, (who are) the successors
of these diviners," (Lafitau I: 238);
garennajenhaga Hurons (Bruyas: 69);
Atrenonnianni Empoisonner (Galisson-

nière: 34r); Wendat *Arendioꝗane* Sorcerers (Brebeuf in Thwaites 10: 35)

-ren'kenni- V know what someone is up to, with DLC: **wa'tekheren'kén:ni'** I know (can predict) what she is up to, what she is about to do, **wa'thakeren'kén:ni'** he knows what I am up to.

-ren'nha- V get used to, make a habit: **rarèn:nha's** he gets used to it, **enkerèn:nha'** I will make it a habit, **wa'kerèn:nha'** I got used to it, I made a habit of it, **roren'nhà:'on** he is used to it. With PART: **tsi niioren'nhà:'on** as usual.
• Wa'kerèn:nha' ohrhon'késtsi akatkétsko'. I got used to getting up early.

Cf. Garennhaon s'accoutumer, s'habituer (Bruyas: 88); *garennháon* S'accoustumer (Galissonnière: 3v); *kerennhas* S'accoutumer à (Marcoux: 6); *Kerennhas* s'accoutumer à (Cuoq: 20)

-ren't- N leg from hip to knee: **orèn:ta'**
With V -oken- merge, fork, and DLC: **tekaren'tó:ken** ginseng.
With V -ot- stand: **kerèn:tote'** I am standing on my head or upside down, **wa'keren'tó:ten'** I put my legs up in the air.
With SRF -ate-, V -'sere-/-i'sere- drag, and DLC: **tehateren'tì:sere's** he is dragging himself (without using his legs, maybe through the grass), **wa'tionteren'tì:sere'** she dragged herself.

Cf. te-ka-ren-to-ken Panox quinquefolium [American ginseng] (Rousseau: 55); *tekarentoken* [ginseng] (Beauvais: 8); *tekaren'tó:ken* gensing (Lazore: 56)

-(h)rh- N woods
With LOC -kon, inside: **kahrhá:kon** in the woods; and DISTR -hshon:

kahrhakónhshon here and there in the woods.
With LOC -kon, inside, and ATTR =kowa, great: **kahrhakonhkó:wa** forest.
With LOC -kon, inside, and ATTR ='a/=ha, diminutive: **Ratihrhakón:ha** Cree.
With V -atek- burn: **iohrhatékha'** (there is) a forest fire.
With SRF -ate-, V -awe'ehst- pierce, and TRNL and DLC: **ia'tkatehrháwe'ehste'** I went into the woods.
With V -her-/-hr- set on top of: **kahrháhere'** there are woods.
With V -kwente- be an opening, clearing, and DLC: **teiohrhakwén:te'** there is a clearing in the woods or in the bush.
With V -otka'w- go through, channel: **wa'kehrhótka'we'** I went through the woods.
NOTE: This root is often pronounced -rh-, without the first (h).

Cf. Garha forest, *Garhagonha* oiseau de proye, vautour (Bruyas: 89); *Garhagonronnon* [forest people] Têtes de Boule (Lafitau I: 358); Wendat *Harhayon* forest (Sagard: Fo); *Chauhaguéronon* Montagnets (Sagard: Na1)

-(h)rhar[e]- V wait for, expect: **wakehrhá:re'** I am waiting for it, I am expecting it, **rohrhá:re'** he is waiting, **iakohrhá:re'** she is waiting.
With PAST -hkw-: **rohrhá:rehkwe'** he was waiting for it.
With CONT -k-: **enionkwahrhá:reke'** we will be waiting.
With SRF -ate- and CAUS -t-: **katehrhá:rats** I wait, **enkatehrhá:rate'** I will wait, **wa'katehrhá:rate'** I waited, **wa'kheiatehrhá:rate'** I waited for her, **satehrhá:rat** Wait!
With CAUS -tst- and BEN -enni-/-en-: **enkonhrharátsten'** I will promise you,

wahakehrharátsten' he promised me, **wahihrharátsten'** I promised him, **khehrharatstén:ni** I have promised her.
• Wakehrhá:re' aiesakè:tohte'. I am waiting for you to to show up. • Wà:kehre' ki' ostòn:ha enkatehrhá:rate' ne more news. I thought I would wait a bit for more news. (Letter 1945, Jan) • Wa'khehrharátsten' teióia'ks eniatiaterohrókha'. I promised her to take her to go to the movies.

Cf. Garhare attendre, espérer, *Garharaston* attendre pour q. chose, *Garharastanni* faire attendre, promettre à quelqu'un (Bruyas: 89); *Garhare* Attendre (Galissonnière: 10r); *8akerhāre* Attendre, esperer (Marcoux: 25); *Wakerhare* espérer s'attendre à, se promettre, conjecturer (Cuoq: 55); *ror ha re* wait (Anon: 43); *karharatsera* hope (Cory: 18); *ia kor ha re* expect (Diabo: 26); *ia kor ha rats ton* promise (Diabo: 59); *ror ha re* wait (Diabo: 84)

-(h)rhat- N hedge: **ohrhá:ta'**
NOTE: This word is not recognized by the third author, but the root is probably a component in **kahrhata'kéha** blueberry.

-(h)rhenht- V stay awake or up all night, with DLC: **tekehrhénhtha'** I stay up all night, **tenkéhrhenhte'** I will stay up all night, **wa'tkéhrhenhte'** I stayed up all night, **tehohrhénhton** he has stayed up all night. With PURP: -'n-: **tekehrhenhtà:ne'** I am going to stay up all night.
NOTE: This stem is composed of a root -(h)rhen-, which occurs only with suffixes, and CAUS -ht-.
• Wa'tkéhrhenhte' wa'katerò:roke' owisà:ke tehonttsihkwà:'eks. I stayed up all night to watch them play hockey.

-(h)rhen'- V dawn, become day:

enióhrhen'ne' tomorrow.
With ATTR ='a/=ha, diminutive, and CISL: **Tiohrhèn:sha** English language.
With ATTR =haka/=aka, people of, and CISL: **Tiohrhen'shá:ka** English.
With TRNL and REP: **ó:ia' ientsóhrhen'ne'** the day after tomorrow.
NOTE: This stem is composed of a root -(h)rhen-, which occurs only with suffixes, and INCH -'-.

Cf. Gareñon être jour (Bruyas: 89); *Tiorhashága* Engländer (Pyrlaeus: 2v); *tiorhēnsa, tiorhensāka* Anglais (Marcoux: 16); *Tiorhensa* anglais, *Tiorhensaka* un anglais, une anglaise (Cuoq: 49); *Tiorensaka* [English] (Onkweonwe: 4); *Tio rhen sa ka ke* England (Anon: 17); *tio rhen sa ka* english (Anon: 19); *Tior-hens-ha ne-ha* English [language] (Cory: 57); *Tiohrhen'shakà:ke* England (Horne: 62); *tiohrhen'shaká:ke* England (Gabriel: 46); Onondaga *tiourhenska* Anglois (Shea: 20)

-(h)rho- V coat: **kéhrhos** I coat it, **ráhrhos** he coats it, **enkéhrho'** I will coat it, **wa'kéhrho'** I coated it, **wa'éhrho'** she coated it, **wakéhrhon** I have coated it, **káhrhon** it is coated; cradleboard.
With N -ahsohkw- colour: **ionhsohkwáhrhos** she is colouring it; and CAUS -hst- and INSTR -hkw-: **ionhsohkwahrhohstáhkhwa'** crayons.
With SRF -at- and N -a'enn- bow: **shakota'ennáhrhos** he witches her, **wa'kheiata'ennáhrho'** I witched her.
With N -harennaht- lead, purple, and INSTR -hst-: **ieharennahtahrhóhstha'** stove polish.
With V -hio'tsis[t]- be salty, sour, and DLC: **wa'tekhio'tsistáhrho'** I salted it, **tekahio'tsistáhrhon** it is covered in salt.
With N -hneht- pine: **kahnehtáhrhon**

linoleum, tablecloth.

With SRF -at-, N -hnek- liquid, and CAUS -hst-: **ionthnekahrhóhstha'** untranslated (Beauvais: 2), probably rubbing alcohol.

With N -hsa'kenser- frost: **wa'kahsa'kenseráhrho'** it got covered in frost.

With N -iie-/-ien- oil, grease: **keienáhrhos** or (with SRF -ate-) **kateienáhrhos** I coat it with oil or grease; and CAUS -hst- (with variant -enien-): **iakenienahrhóhstha'** shellac.

With N -itst- fish scale, scab, and CAUS -hst-: **ietstahrhóhstha'** shingle.

With N -i'tonhkw- flame, fever: **waki'tonhkwáhrhos** I have a fever, **iako'tonhkwáhrhos** she has a fever, **io'tonhkwáhrhos** it is feverish, inflamed, **waho'tonhkwáhrho'** he got a fever; and ATTR =kowa, great: **iako'tonhkwahrhoskó:wa** typhoid fever.

With NMZR -hser-, V -ke- amount to, and DLC: **tekahrhonhserá:ke** two cradleboards.

With N -kontsher- paint: **kkontsheráhrhos** I am painting it, **wahakontsheráhrho'** he painted it, **rokontsheráhrhon** he has painted it.

With N -neni- stone, rock: **kaneniáhrhon** enamel; and SRF -ate-: **Ateneniáhrhon** Stone Giant.

With N -rihw- matter, message: **rakerihwáhrhos** he is accusing me, blaming me, **wahakerihwáhrho'** he accused me, blamed me, **wahirihwáhrho'** I accused him, I blamed him.

With N -rist- iron, steel: **keristáhrhos** I am ironing, **wa'keristáhrho'** I ironed it, **wakeristáhrhon** I have ironed it; and CAUS -hst-: **ieristahrhóhstha'** iron.

With N -wis- ice, glass: **iowisáhrhon** it is covered in ice, it is icy; and PROG -hatie- and CISL: **taiowisahrhonhátie'** it is getting covered in ice.

With N -wistohser- butter: **kewistohseráhrhos** I coat it with butter, I am buttering it, **wa'kewistohseráhrho'** I buttered it.

• Wà:io wa'kéhrho' watena'taratsha'áhton. I spread jam on the toast.

-(h)rhoht- N burrs, pickers: **óhrhohte'**
With ATTR =kowa, great: **ohrhohte'kó:wa** burdock.
With V -ronkw- remove, scrape off: **wa'kehrhohtarón:ko'** I removed the burrs.
• Wa'kehrhohtarón:ko' è:rhar raóhwhare'. I took the burrs off the dog's fur.

-(h)rhokw- N tobacco pipe: **kahrhókwa'**
Cf. Garoksa une pipe, touche de petun, *Atroksaɣahon* être assis les uns près des autres, comme en conseil, à cause qu'ils y petunent (Bruyas: 93); *Kahrokwa* pipe, c.-à-d., le temps de fumer une pipe, temps de repos donné aux rameurs (Cuoq: 9)

-(h)rhonri- N mucus, phlegm: **ohrhónria'**
• Ohrhón'ke wa'káhsa'ke' akwé:kon ohrhónria' takaráthen'. This morning I coughed [and] all this phlegm came up.

-(h)rhon'ke- N morning: **ohrhón'ke** this morning.
With ATTR =hne, at: **ohrhon'kè:ne (nikahá:wi')** in the morning.
With ATTR =tsi, intensifier: **ohrhon'kéhstsi** early morning.
With LOC -'ke, on, at, NMZR -htsher-, V -ke- amount to, and PART, TRNL and DLC, or CONTR, TRNL, and DLC: **nia'teiohrhon'kehtshurá:ke** or **thia'teiohrhon'kehtshurá:ke** every morning.

Cf. Orhongetsi de très grand matin (Bruyas: 89); *orhongetsi* de grand matin

(Galissonnière: 48v); *o ron ke tsi* early
(D'Ailleboust: 20); *Ohrhon'kéhstsi* Early
in the morning (Horne: 53)

-ri- V cook, ripen: **enká:ri'** it will cook,
wa'ká:ri' it got cooked, **ió:ri** or **iorì:'on**
it is cooked, it is done.
 With CAUS -ht-: **keríhtha'** I cook it,
wà:kerihte' I cooked it, **wakeríhton** I
have cooked it, **íseriht** Cook it!
 With N -ahi- fruit, berry: **wahiá:ris**
cantaloupe, **onhiá:ri'** the fruit ripened,
iohiá:ri the fruit is ripe; with N -ahi- fruit,
berry, and ATTR ='a/=ha, diminutive:
Ohiarí:ha June; with N -ahi- fruit, berry,
and ATTR =kowa, great: **Ohiarihkó:wa**
July.
 With N -hnenna't- potato, and CAUS -ht-:
wa'khnennà:tarihte' I cooked potatoes.
 With N -neni- stone, rock, and CAUS -ht-:
kaneniaríhton brick, cement block.
 With N -nor- husk: **wa'kanorá:ri'** the
corn ripened.
 With N -'nhonhs- egg, and CAUS -ht-:
wa'ke'nhónhsarihte' I cooked eggs.

Cf. Aꝸenhet ꝸahiári Juin, *Ataᶜkꝸagáien
ꝸahiári* Juilliet, *Sahies ꝸahiári* Aoust,
(Galissonnière: 53v); *oiariha* juin,
oiarikoꝸa juillet (Marcoux: 257–8);
Oiariha June (Granger: 10); *Oiarikowa*
July (Granger: 11); *Ohiaríha* [June],
Ohiarihkó:wa [July] (Calendar 1979)

-rihsi- V take apart, take off: **keríhsions** I
am taking it apart, I am taking it off,
wa'keríhsi' I took it apart or off,
roríhsion he has taken it apart or off.
 With DISTR -onkw-: **wa'kerihsión:ko'** I
took it all apart.
 With N -aten'enhr- fence:
wahaten'enhraríhsi' he took apart the
fence.
 With N -hnek- liquid: **rahnekaríhsions**

he dilutes it, **wa'khnekaríhsi'** I diluted it,
wakhnekaríhsion I have diluted it.
 With N -ithohkw- bundle:
kithohkwaríhsions I am taking the
bundle apart, **wahenthohkwaríhsi'**
he took the bundle apart.
 With N -nohkw- bundle:
wa'kenohkwaríhsi' I took the bundle
apart.
 With SRF -ate-, N -rihw- matter, message,
and BEN -en-: **onkwaterihwaríhsien'** I
got fouled up (for example, my class didn't
go right).
 With SRF -ate-, N -wenn- voice, word, and
BEN -en-: **onkwatewennaríhsien'** my
words didn't come together (for example,
when I am repeating something too many
times), **wahotewennaríhsien'** his words
didn't come together.
 • Akwé:kon wa'kerihsión:ko' ó:ia'
wà:katste'. I took everything off (and)
I changed into something else.

-rihton- N black oak: **karíhton** black oak;
police, **raríhton** he is a policeman.
 With NMZR -'tsher- and V -ien- put down,
have: **ionkwarihton'tsherá:ien'** we have
police.

Cf. Gariᶜton gland, chesne (Bruyas: 93);
Gariᶜton Chesne (Galissonnière: 8v); "le
nom de *Karithon* donné aux officiers de la
justice et de la force publique" (Cuoq: 11);
ga-ri-don Quercus (Chêne) (Rousseau: 38)

-rihw- N matter, message: **orì:wa'**
 POSS: **raónha raorì:wa'** (it's) his fault,
akáonha akorì:wa' (it's) her fault.
 With LOC -akon, inside, and CONTR:
thiorì:wakon it is futile, it is no use.
 With LOC -'ke, on, at, and POSS:
aorihwà:ke about, concerning the
matter, **raorihwà:ke** concerning him,
akorihwà:ke concerning her.

With CISL: **né: tiorì:wa'** it's the reason.
With NEG: **iah tekarì:wa'** it's nothing,
it doesn't matter, don't mention it!
With SRF -ate- and V -ahnot- tell about:
raterihwahnótha' he preaches, lectures.
With V -ahronk- hear about:
wa'kerihwà:ronke' I heard the news.
With V -ahstoht- reduce, shrink, take in:
wa'kerihwáhstohte' I consider the matter
unimportant, insignificant.
With V -ahsto'se- think small of:
wa'kherihwáhsto'se' I found her issue,
whatever she brought up, insignificant.
With SRF -ate-, V -ahtenti- go away, leave,
and CAUS -'t-: **wa'katerihwahténtia'te'**
I started, I prepared to do something.
With V -ahton- disappear, and CAUS -'t-:
waharihwáhton'te' he put an end to the
matter.
With V -akaion-/-kaion- be old, and ATTR
=hneha, way of: **orihwakaionhnéha** old-
fashioned.
With V -aksen- be bad: **karihwáksen**
(it is) a bad matter.
With SRF -ate-, V -areni- spread around,
disperse, CAUS -'t-, and DLC:
tewaterihwarenià:tha' newspaper.
With V -ase- be fresh, new: **orì:wase'**
news.
With SRF -ate- and V -ate'kw- run away:
wa'katerihwatè:ko' I avoided the matter.
With SRF -ate- and V -ate'waht- miss a
target, and REP: **sakaterihwáte'wahte'**
I did something wrong.
With SRF -ate- and V -atie'ni- be plenty,
hold a lot: **roterihwatiè:ni** he talks a lot.
With V -atihentho- pull, and CISL:
taharihwatihéntho' he pulled or drew
out the matter.
With SRF -ate- and V -atken'serahkw-
put off: **wa'katerihwatkèn:serahkwe'**
I made an excuse.
With SRF -ate- and V -atsterist- bother
with: **wa'katerihwatsté:riste'** I bothered

with the matter.
With V -awe'ehst- pierce, and DLC:
tenkerihwáwe'ehste' I will put the
subject forth, look into it.
With V -awi-/-on- give: **wa'onkeríhon'**
she or they allowed me.
With V -a'a- be small, ATTR =shon'a
pluralizer, **ken'** particle and PART:
ken' niiorihwasa'shòn:'a miscellaneous
matters.
With V -a'senht-/-enht- drop:
shakorihwénhtha' he sentences them, he
is a judge.
With V -ehsak-/-ihsak-/-esak-/-isak- look
for: **wa'kerihwí:sake'** I searched for
information.
With V -ent- wear out, end, and INCH -'-:
karihwén:ta's it wears out; with V -ent-
wear out, end, and CAUS -ho-:
wa'kerihwéntho' I wore it out.
With V -es- be long, tall: **rorì:wes** he is
taking a long time; and NEG:
iah tekarì:wes not long (after), it won't
be long; and PART: **tsi nikarì:wes** while.
With V -haratat-/-karatat- lift, raise up:
waharihwakará:tate' he started the
proceedings.
With V -her-/-hr- set on top of:
wa'erihwà:ren she brought the matter
forth, **karihwáhere'** issue, agenda.
With V -hkw- pick up, and DLC:
teierihwáhkhwa' she sings (hymns),
tekarihwáhkhwa' organ; and CAUS -'t-:
teierihwahkwà:tha' hymnal, hymn book.
With V -hnir- be hard, solid, and CAUS -t-:
waharihwahní:rate' he confirmed it.
With V -hsa'-/-isa'- finish, complete:
wa'kerihwísa' I made a commitment,
I promised; and SRF -ate- and DLC:
tehiaterihwísa'as the two are going out
together, they are dating, they are engaged.
With SRF -ate- and V -hseronni- dress,
prepare: **wahonterihwahserón:ni'** they
made arrangements.

With V -hst- use: **karihwáhsta** it is a useful matter.

With SRF -ate-, V -iehwa-/-ioha- look for in vain, and CAUS -ht-: **wa'katerihwaiè:wahte'** I pretended to not know, I denied it.

With V -iena- hold, catch, touch: **Ratirihwaié:nas** they receive the message; Oneidas and Cayugas as referred to in council, **wa'erihwaié:na'** she agreed to the issue.

With V -ienawa'k-/-wa'k- hold, support: **arihwawà:kon** Bishop; and ATTR =kowa, great: **arihwawa'konhkó:wa** the Pope; with -ienawa'k-/-wa'k- hold, support, and ATTR =hneha, way of: **arihwawa'konhnéha** purple; with V -ienawa'k-/-wa'k- hold, support, and DLC: **teionkenirihwaienawà:kon** he/she and I are a couple, my spouse.

With V -ienawa's-/-wa's- help someone: **wa'kherì:wawa'se'** I helped her find information; and REFL -atate-: **wa'kataterì:wawa'se'** I found information for myself.

With V -ieri- be right, and CISL: **tewakerihwaié:ri** I have good intentions, good morals, I am kind, **tkarihwaié:ri** the issue is right; and ATTR =kowa, great: **Thorihwaieri'kó:wa** begging song they sing on New Year's Eve.

With V -ierit- complete: **wa'kerihwaié:rite'** I completed the task; and CISL: **tierihwaié:rits** she does good deeds.

With V -ieron- make fun of, play, and DLC: **wa'thirihwaierónnion'** I tricked him.

With V -iio- be good, nice: **orihwí:io** really; and ATTR =onwe, genuine: **orihwiio'ón:we** it is unquestionably true; with V -iio- be good, nice: **Karihwí:io** the Good Message; and CAUS -hst-: **Karihwiióhston** Christian religion.

With V -ka'te- have many: **iakorihwakà:te'** she has a lot to say.

With V -ke- amount to, and DLC: **tekarì:wake** two items; or PART, TRNL, and DLC: **nia'teiorì:wake** all kinds of affairs, matters.

With V -kha- attach, piece together, and DLC: **tekarihwákhen** a word or message that is put together.

With V -kowan[en]-/-owan[en]- be big, and CAUS -ht-: **waharihó:wanahte'** he announced it.

With V -kwennien-/-konnien- be very clean, neat, and CAUS -hst-: **kherihwakonniénhstha'** I respect her.

With V -naker[e]- reside, be plenty: **nòn:wa karihwanákere'** (it's) the latest news.

With V -nenhskw- steal: **kherihwanénhskwas** I am talking about her.

With V -nera'[k]- mistake: **wa'erihwanéra'ke'** she swore, she sinned; and NMZR -hser-: **karihwanera'ákhsera'** sin.

With V -nonhwe'- like: **wa'erihwanòn:we'ne'** she agreed with it.

With V -oken- merge, fork, and DLC: **Tekarihó:ken** Mohawk title name 1.

With SRF -ate- and V -onko- penetrate: **roterihón:ko** he is annoying; and CAUS -ht- and BEN -ni-/-en-: **onkwaterihonkóhten'** I got fed up.

With V -onni- make, and BEN -enni-/-en-: **kherihonnién:ni** I teach them, **shakorihonnién:ni** he teaches them, **enhirihónnien'** I will teach him, **wa'kherihónnien'** I taught them; and NEG: **iah tekarihonnién:ni** nobody has taught (them), they have no class.

With V -ont- attach: **wahonwarihón:ten'** they appointed him; and SRF -ate-: **roteríhonte'** he is an official, a faithkeeper; and **ka'nisténhsera'** (-'nisten- mother): **ka'nisténhsera' ionateríhonte'** clan mothers; with V -ont- attach, and REV -kw-: **kerihontákwas** I am useful, I accomplish things, get things done,

enkerihontá:ko' I will accomplish it,
wa'kerihontá:ko' I got it done.
With V -otahrho[k]- hook, and DLC:
tekarihotáhrhon argument; and SRF
-ate-: **wa'tiatiaterihotáhrhoke'** we two
disagreed.
With V -ota's- receive: **onkerihó:ta'se'**
I got news, I got informed.
With V -o'kt- finish: **waharihò:kten'**
he finished (reading or talking).
With V -o'kwat- dig: **wa'kerihó'kwate'**
I dug around for information, I did
research.
With V -r- put in, INCH -'-, and CONTR,
TRNL, and DLC: **thia'tehorihwarà:'on**
he is acting foolish or funny.
With V -(h)rho- coat: **wahakerihwáhrho'**
he accused me, blamed me.
With SRF -ate-, V -rihsi- take apart, take
off, and BEN -en-: **onkwaterihwaríhsien'**
I got fouled up.
With V -[t]- be one, and COIN:
né: sha'orì:wa it's the same thing.
With SRF -ate- and V -takwarihsi-/
-kwarihsi- straighten:
roterihwakwaríhsion he is straight,
trustworthy.
With V -te- be present, exist, and INSTR
-hkw-; and **ohén:ton** front, in front:
Ohén:ton Karihwatéhkwen Preface,
Thanksgiving Address; with V -te- be
present, exist, and COIN and DLC:
Sha'tekarì:wate' the issues are similar,
Mohawk title name 3.
With V -token- be certain: **rorihwató:ken**
he is a reliable person.
With V -tokenhti- be holy, and DLC:
teiorihwatokénhton parable.
With V -tshahni[ht]- be industrious, ener-
getic: **iorihwatshà:ni** it is a drastic matter.
With V -tshenri- find:
wa'kerihwatshén:ri' I found out about it.
With V -weienhon- be good at, capable at:
kerihwaweiénhon I know how to put

things, how to phrase things.
With SRF -ate-, V -weienst- learn, study,
practice: **katerihwaiénstha'** I study, I
am a student; and INSTR -hkw-:
ionterihwaienstáhkhwa' school.
NOTE: This root occurs incorporated into
many verbs, and not all the inflected forms
of some of the N plus V combinations are
given here; for the additional forms, see
the V entry.
• Thiorì:wakon, iah tho thà:ke'. It's no
use, I'm not going there. • Wahshakeni-
ri'wanón:tonhse' ne okahkwèn:ta'
aorihwà:ke. We asked him about the
tires. (Letter 1945, June)

-rihwaka't[en]- V complain
With INCH -'-: **rorihwaka'tèn:'en** he is
complaining, **iakorihwaka'tèn:'en** she
is complaining.
With CAUS -t-: **rarihwakà:tats** he
complains, **waharihwakà:tate'** he
complained.
With SRF -ate- and CAUS -hst-:
wakaterihwaka'ténhston I am chatty,
I talk a lot about nothing,
ionaterihwaka'ténhston they are chatty.
NOTE: This stem includes -rihw- matter,
message, but it is not clear what the verb
root is.
• Terí:teri roterihwaka'ténhston. The blue
jay is chattering away.

-rihwathe't- V make clear, explain, with DLC:
tekerihwathè:tha' I make the issue
clearer, **wa'tharihwáthe'te'** he made it
clearer, he explained it,
tehotirihwathè:ton they have explained
it.
NOTE: This stem is composed of -rihw-
matter, message, a root -the- (also present
in -hstarathe- be shiny, bright), and CAUS
-'t-.

-rihwa'serakw- V answer, respond, reply, with DLC: **teharihwa'serákwas** he is answering, **wa'tierihwa'será:ko'** she answered, **tehorihwa'serákwen** he has answered.

With BEN -enni-/-hs-: **wa'tekherihwa'serákwahse'** I answered her, **wa'thonwarihwa'serákwahse'** she answered him, **tekherihwa'serakwén:ni** I have answered her.

• Nahò:ten' wahsheri'wanón:tonhse' wa'tierihwa'será:ko'. What you asked her, she answered.

-rik- V put together, with DLC: **tékeriks** I put it together (next to one another), **tehá:riks** he puts it together, **ténkerike'** I will put it together, **wà:tkerike'** I put it together, **tewakerí:kon** I have put it together, **téserik** Put it together!

With N -a'ar- net, curtain: **wa'tka'á:rarike'** I put together the curtains, **tesa'á:rarik** Put the curtains together!

With SRF -an-, N -i'tonhkw- flame, fever, and DISTR -hon-: **tewani'tonhkwaríkhons** the flame is flickering, **wa'tewani'tonhkwaríkhon'** the flame flickered.

With N -ontar- waterway: **Tetiatontarí:kon** Quebec City.

With SRF -at-, N -tsir- spark, fire, embers, and DISTR -hon-: **tewattsiraríkhons** there are lightning sparks.

-rik- V bite, be biting: **kontí:riks** (the fish) are biting.

-rio-/-riio- V beat up, kill: **kerí:ios** I kill, **wahário'** he killed it, **wa'konwário'** she killed it, **wahonwário'** she or they beat him up, **kário** wild animal, **kontírio** wild animals. (The English translation 'kill' suggests the action results in death, but the meaning of the Kanien'kéha root is not as strong.)

With SRF -ate-: **katerí:ios** I fight, **wahonterí:io'** they fought, **ronaterí:io** they are fighting, **waterí:io** war; and PURP -hs- and PAST -hne': **ronateriiohsónhne'** they have gone to fight, they went to war.

With CAUS -ht-: **iakorióhtha'** she is dying from it; poison, **eniakóriohte'** she will die from it, **wa'akóriohte'** she died from it, **iakorióhton** she has died from it.

With SRF -ate-, NMZR -hser-, V -ent- wear out, end, and INCH -'-: **onteriiohserén:ta'ne'** the war ended.

With N -ia't- body: **watia'tários** I feel there's a heaviness on me, I am feeling out of sorts.

With N -'nikonhr- mind: **wahi'nikonhrário'** I changed his mind, I discouraged him, convinced him to not do something, **wahshako'nikonhrário'** he changed her mind (the *r* of the root is usually not pronounced in these words).

NOTE: The variant -riio- occurs after prefixes that end in (epenthetic) *e*, such as the first person *ke-* or the SRF *-ate-*.

• Wahi'nikonhráio' tóhsa ahahní:non' thí:ken kà:sere. I convinced him to not buy that car.

Cf. Gario beste fauve, *Gario* tuer, battre (Bruyas: 92); *Gario* Animaux (Galisson-nière: 7r); *Kario* animal des bois, bête fauve (Cuoq: 11); Laurentian *aggayo* dog (Biggar: 244); Wendat *Ayot* bestes de la forest (Sagard: An4); Onondaga *gariô* beste (Shea: 27); Susquehannock *abgarijω* dog (Holm: 5)

-ris[er]- N socks: **ká:ris**
POSS: **ákeris** my socks, **raó:ris** his socks, **akó:ris** her socks; and **a'nó:wara** turtle (-'now- hump, padlock): **a'nó:wara raó:ris** pitcher plant.

With V -akera- stink, smell, and INCH -'-:
wahariserákera'ne' his socks got smelly.
With SRF -ate- and V -har-/-ihar- hang up:
wa'kateriserihá:ren' I hung up my
socks, I got a present for Christmas; with
V -har-/-ihar- hang up, and BEN -hahs-:
wahiriseriháhrhahse' I gave him a
Christmas present.
With V -onni- make: **ieriserón:ni** she is
knitting, **wa'keriserón:ni'** I knitted.
With V -'nikhon- sew, and INSTR -hkw-:
ierisera'nikhónhkhwa' darning needle.
• Watiè:was ská:ti ákeris. I can't find one
sock (one side of my socks). • Wahawerien'tí:io nahò:ten' wahateriserihá:ren'. He
is satisfied what he got for Christmas.
Cf. Caris stocking (van den Bogaert: 53);
Raorisk ses mitasses, *Kariska8e* aller
déchaussé (Bruyas: 91); *Garis* chausse,
Jakoriska8e les jambes nües (Galissonnière: 19r); *akerīskă8e* etre nus jambes
(Marcoux: 264); *Karis* mitasse, *akeriskawe*
être nu-jambes (Cuoq: 11); *ka ris* stocking
(Anon: 5); Wendat *Ariche* Bas de chausses
(Sagard: Ha3); Onondaga *degaderich* je
mets mes bas (Shea: 26); Susquehannock
Khaalis stockings (Holm: 7)

-rist- N iron, steel
With LOC -atatie', along, edge of:
karistatátie' along the steel; and
thio'kéha train: **karistatátie' thio'kéha**
train tracks.
With LOC -kon, inside: **karístakon** in the
stove.
With LOC -'ke, on, at: **karistà:ke** on the
iron or steel; and **rotiió'tens** (-io'te-/
-io'ten- work): **karistà:ke rotiió'tens**
they work on steel, ironworkers.
With V -a'senht-/-enht- drop:
wa'kerístenhte' I pleated it,
karisténhton it is pleated, it has pleats.
With V -a'tarih[en]-/-tarih[en]- be hot,

warm: **ioristataríhen** the stove or iron is
hot.
With SRF -ate- and V -hninon- buy:
rateristahní:nons he is selling something
made of iron or steel (maybe a stove).
With V -htohrarak-/-ohrarak- squeeze,
press down, and DLC:
tewakeristohrará:kon I have printed,
typed, **tekaristò:raraks** printing machine;
and CAUS -st-: **teieristohrarákstha'** typewriter.
With V -iahia'k-/-iia'k- cross over, and
TRNL and DLC: **ia'teharistí:ia'ks** he
goes across the (U.S.-Can.) border,
ia'tenteniristí:ia'ke' you and I will go
across the border, **ia'tewakeristiià:kon**
I have gone across the border.
With SRF -ate-, V -ien- put down, have,
and INSTR -hkw-: **ionteristaientáhkhwa'**
steel trap.
With V -kenra- be pale: **karistakén:ra** tin.
With V -(h)nhonta'- put in one's mouth:
wa'keristahnhónta' I put the bit in (the
horse's) mouth, **seristahnhónta** Put the
bit in its mouth! and SRF -ate-:
wateristahnhónta's bit.
With V -ohar- attach at the end:
karistóhare' pick-axe.
With V -ohr[ok]- insert: **raristò:roks** he is
bolting it (a door, a gate), **enkaristò:roke'**
I will bolt it, **waharistò:roke'** he bolted it,
karistò:ron it is bolted.
With V -oia'[k]- throw straight at, CAUS
-ht-, and DLC: **tekaristoiénhton** bread or
pancake cooked without a pan directly on
a (wood) stove.
With V -onni- make: **keristón:ni** I am a
metal-maker.
With SRF -ate- and V -ont- attach:
ateristón:ta ice cleats.
With V -ranie-/-karanie- rub, scrub:
raristakaránies he is filing it,
waharistakaránie' he filed it; and CAUS

-'t-: **ieristakaraniè:tha'** file.
With V -ra'nentak-/-nentak- stick to:
ioristanentá:kon iontianenhtáhkhwa'
sled or sleigh runners (-ian- footprint,
track, -a'senht-/-enht- drop).
With V -(h)rho- coat: **keristáhrhos** I am
ironing, **wa'keristáhrho'** I ironed it,
wakeristáhrhon I have ironed it; and
CAUS -hst-: **ieristahrhóhstha'** iron.
With V -sera[hw]-/-osera[hw]- gush, spew:
raristóseras welder.
With V -'sere-/-i'sere- drag: **raristì:sere's**
surveyor.
See also **karístatsi** stove, piece of iron or
steel.
Cf. "They call us [the Dutch] *Assirioni,*
that is, cloth-makers, or *Charistooni,*
that is, iron-workers, because our people
first brought cloth and iron among them."
(Megapolensis: 178); *Christittye* iron,
copper, lead (van den Bogaert: 58);
Garistatsi fer, métail (Bruyas: 93);
Kalistasi fer (Galissonnière: 40v);
ka ris ta tsi ro io tens iron worker (Anon:
11); Wendat *statsi* Caillou (Sagard: Te5)

-ri'te- N pigeon: **orì:te'**
With ATTR =hneha, way of: **ori'tehnéha**
pigeon dance.

-ri'wahseht- V have a secret: **rori'wahséhton**
he has a secret, **iakori'wahséhton** she has
a secret, **rotiri'wahséhton** they have a
secret.
NOTE: This stem is composed of a noun
root -ri'w- (meaning uncertain) and
-ahseht- hide, kill.

-ri'wakehnha- V argue, with DLC:
tehari'wakéhnhas he is a lawyer,
teieri'wakéhnhas she is a lawyer,
tehniri'wakéhnhas the two argue,
wa'tiakeniri'wakéhnha' we two argued,

tehotiri'wakéhnhen they are arguing,
tekari'wakéhnhen argument.

-ri'wanont[on]- V ask a question:
keri'wanóntha' I am asking a question,
wahari'wanón:ton' he asked a question,
iakori'wanón:ton she has asked.
With BEN -ni-/-hs-: **rakeri'wanontón:ni**
he asks me a question,
enkonri'wanón:tonhse' I will ask you a
question, **wahiri'wanón:tonhse'** I asked
him a question, **wahakeri'wanón:tonhse'**
he asked me a question.
• Ionkeri'wanontón:ni kátke ó:nen
tontahón:ne'. She is asking me when are
they coming back. (Letter 1945, Apr)

-ri'wen'awiht- V gossip, and DLC:
tehari'wen'awíhtha' he is a gossip,
wa'tieri'wen'á:wihte' she gossiped.
NOTE: This stem is composed of a noun
root -ri'w- (meaning uncertain) and
-a'awi-/-en'awi- float, drift.

-rohro[k]- V gather, collect: **rarò:roks** he is
gathering, collecting things, **enkerò:roke'**
I will gather, collect them, **wa'kerò:roke'**
I gathered, collected them, **wakerò:ron**
I have gathered, collected them.
With SRF -ate-: **katerò:roks** I watch
something going on, **enkaterò:roke'**
I will watch, **wa'katerò:roke'** I watched,
wakaterò:ren I am watching; and PURP
-h-: **katerohrókhe'** I am going to watch,
wa'katerohrókhe' I am going (I am on
my way) to watch, **eniatiaterohrókha'**
we two will go to watch, **wa'katerohrókha'** I went to watch; and
PAST -hne': **wakaterohrokhónhne'** I
have gone to watch.
With N -hsenn- name: **rahsennarò:roks**
he is collecting names, (he is) a census
taker.

With N -hwist- metal, money:
khwistarò:roks I am collecting money,
kahwistarò:roks collection (at church),
enhatihwistarò:roke' they will collect
money.
With N -ihwhar- fur: **renhwhararò:roks**
he collects furs.
With N -karien't- carcass:
rakarien'tarò:roks he collects carcasses,
wahakarien'tarò:roke' he collected carcasses.
With N -nehw- animal skin, hide:
ratinehwarò:roks they collect hides.
With SRF -ate- and N -nenhr- crowd:
ontenenhrarò:roke' the crowd gathered.
With SRF -ate-, N -nekwenhs- blood, and
BEN -hs-: **wesatenekwenhsarò:rokhse'**
the blood pooled on you (looking at a
bruised thumbnail).
With N -nieht- snow: **ioniehtarò:ron** the
snow has piled up, there's a snowdrift; and
DISTR -hon-: **ioniehtarohrókhon** there's
snowdrifts.
With N -nonhwenhsker- dust:
wa'kenonhwenhskerarò:roke' I
gathered the dust.
With N -'nhonhs- egg: **ke'nhonhsarò:roks**
I am gathering, collecting eggs.
• Ó:nen á:re' tà:re' ne tekení: rarò:roks.
The junk collector is coming again.
• Katerohrókhe' tká:ra's. I'm going to
watch television. • Wa'katerohrókhe'
teióia'ks. I'm going to the movies.

Cf. ra te kets he ra ro roks conductor (with
the incorporated borrowed English word
teket 'ticket' and NMZR -hser-) (Anon: 20)

-ronhi- N sky, heaven, blue: **karòn:ia'** sky,
heaven; **oròn:ia'** blue.
With **nika'nahkò:ten** (-'nahkw- drum,
barrel, -o'ten- be a kind of): **oròn:ia'
nika'nahkò:ten** a blue barrel (sometimes
used for rain barrel).

With ATTR =kowa, great; and **atháhsteren**
(-athahsteren- put on pants, trousers):
oronhia'kó:wa atháhsteren jeans.
With LOC -'ke, on, at: **karonhià:ke**
heaven; and ATTR =hronon, resident of:
ieronhia'kehró:non angels; and ATTR
='ke, at: **Ratironhia'kehronòn:ke**
Tuesday; with LOC -'ke, on, at, ATTR
=hronon, resident of, NMZR -'tsher- and
V -kwek- be the whole of:
karonhia'kehronon'tsherakwé:kon all
the angels, kingdom of angels *(a playful
expression from Mike Norton)*.
With V -ienawa'k-/-wa'k- hold, support,
and CISL: **Tharonhiawà:kon** Holder of
the heavens.
With V -kenra- be pale: **oronhiakén:ra**
light blue.
With V -o- be in water, and INSTR -hkw-:
ieronhióhkhwa' bluing for clothes to
whiten them.
With V -te- be present, exist, and CISL:
tsi tkaronhiá:te' in the sky, the heavens.
With V -'rhoro[k]-/-oro[k]- cover:
wa'karonhió:roke' it got cloudy, overcast, **ioronhió:ron** it is cloudy, overcast.

Cf. "They are entire strangers to all religion, but they have a *Tharonhijouaagon*,
(whom they also otherwise call
Athzoockkuatoriaho,) that is, a Genius,
whom they esteem in the place of God;"
(Megapolensis: 177); "The first of these
names is that of *Tharonhiaouagon*, the
literal interpretation of which is: He holds
the sky on all sides." (Lafitau I: 106); at
Oneida "the great God of the Iroquois,
Teharonhiaouagon," (Bruyas in Thwaites
53: 253); at Cayuga "*Taronhiaouagon*,
whom they acknowledge as a Divinity, and
obey as the great Master of their lives;"
(Carheil in Thwaites 54: 65); at Onondaga
"*Taronhiaouago*n ... they declare, is the
mightiest of all spirits, and the Master of

our lives." (Milet in Thwaites 55: 61);
Garonhiager⁵onnon Ange (Gallissonnière:
7r); *ratironhiakeronōnke* Mardi (Marcoux:
243); *Ratironhiakeronon* Les Anges,
Karonhiatsikowane à Longueuil (Cuoq:
106); *Ratironhiakehrononke* [Tuesday]
(Granger: 4); *ra ti ron ia ke ro non* angels
(Anon: 10); *ra ti ron ia ke ro non ke*
tuesday (Anon: 6); *ra-ti-ron-ia-kero-
non-ke* Tuesday (Cory: 71)

-ronhiaken- V suffer: **wakeronhiá:ken** I am
    suffering, in agony, **roronhiá:ken** he is
    suffering, **iakoronhiá:ken** she is suffer
    ing, **waharonhiá:ken'** he suffered.
    With NMZR -hser-: **karonhiakénhsera'**
    suffering, agony.
    With N -'nikonhr- mind:
    wake'nikonhraronhiá:ken my mind is
    suffering, I am stressed.

-ronhkwani-/-ronhkwen- V itch:
    wakerónhkwani I am itchy,
    onkerónhkwen' I got itchy.
    With N -ahonht- ear:
    wakahonhtarónhkwani my ear is itchy.
    With N -ahsi't- foot:
    wakahsi'tarónhkwani my foot is itchy.
    With N -ahtsa'n- palm of the hand:
    wakahtsa'narónhkwani the palm of my
    hand is itchy.
    With N -hsnonhs- finger, hand:
    wakehsnonhsarónhkwani my hands are
    itchy.
    With N -kahr- eye: **wakkahrarónhkwani**
    I have an itchy eye.
    With N -nenh- urine:
    wakenenharónhkwani I have the urge to
    pee, **ronenharónhkwani** he has the urge
    to pee, **iakonenharónhkwani** she has the
    urge to pee.
    With N -nentsh- arm:
    wakenentsharónhkwani my arm is itchy.
    With N -nontsi[st]- head:

wakenontsistarónhkwani my head is
    itchy.
    With N -ronhkwe'n- spine, back:
    wakeronhkwe'narónhkwani my back is
    itchy.

-ronhkwe'n- N spine, back: **oronhkwè:na'**
    POSS: **keronhkwe'nà:ke** (on) my back,
    raronhkwe'nà:ke (on) his back,
    ieronhkwe'nà:ke (on) her back.
    With V -akarenhr[e]- lean to one side,
    slant: **karonhkwe'nakarèn:re'** the roof
    is slanted.
    With SRF -ate-, V -ia'k- break, cut in two,
    and DLC: **wa'thateronhkwè:nia'ke'** he
    broke his back.
    With V -keront- square:
    ioronhkwe'nakerón:te' the roof is
    slanted, pitched.
    With SRF -ate- and V -ni'e[k]- sprain, pull
    a muscle: **wa'kateronhkwe'nanì:'eke'** I
    sprained my back.
    With V -nohare-/-ohare- wash:
    wahakeronhkwe'nóhare' he washed my
    back; and SRF -ate-:
    wahateronhkwe'nóhare' he washed his
    (own) back.
    With V -nonhwak[t]- be sore, hurt:
    wakeronhkwe'nanòn:waks I have a sore
    back.
    With V -ohseronkw- caress, pat:
    wa'kheronhkwe'nohserón:ko' I am
    patting, rubbing her back.
    With V -ronhkwani-/-ronhkwen- itch:
    wakeronhkwe'narónhkwani my back
    is itchy.

-ronhwent[e]- V opening, a little space, with
    DLC: **teioronhwén:te'** there is a space.
    With CAUS -t-: **tekeronhwén:tats** I open
    it a little bit (for example, a window or
    door), **tenhseronhwén:tate'** you will
    make an opening or space,
    wa'tkeronhwén:tate' I made an opening,

tewakeronhwentá:ton I have made an opening.

-ronkw- V remove, scrape off: **kerónkwas** I am taking it off, removing it, **wa'kerón:ko'** I scraped it off, **wakerónkwen** I have scraped it off.
With REP: **sakerón:ko'** I am removing it again.
With CAUS -ht- and REP: **tseronkwáhtha'** eraser.
With BEN -enni-/-hs- and REP: **enshonwarónkwahse'** they will remove his sins, he will confess, **saionkerónkwahse'** I confessed; and PURP -hr-: **sahonwaronkwennì:re'** he is going to confession.
With N -itst- fish scale, scab: **wa'kitstarón:ko'** I took the scab off, **wahentstarón:ko'** he took the scab off, With N -na'watsist- bark: **rana'watsistarónkwas** he takes the bark off, **wahana'watsistarón:ko'** he took the bark off, **sena'watsistarón:ko** Take the bark off!
With N -nenhst- corn: **kenenhstarónkwas** I am shelling corn, **wa'kenenhstarón:ko'** I shelled corn, **ronenhstarónkwen** he has shelled corn.
With N -(h)rhoht- burrs, pickers: **wa'kehrhohtarón:ko'** I removed the burrs.

-ronkwahs- N chain: **oronkwáhsa'**
With V -hroh[o]- block, put across (as a barrier): **tekaronkwahsahróho** (there is) a chain going across.
With V -ke- amount to, and DLC: **tekaronkwáhsake** two chains; and PART: **tóhka nikaronkwáhsake** a few chains.
Cf. Orongwaghsa a string, or strings, of wampum (Deserontyon: 101); oronksāsa chaine; grains de rassade & enfilés

(Marcoux: 195); *Oronkwasa chaine; grains enfilés* (Cuoq: 35); *o ron kwa sa chain* (Diabo: 8)

-ronrot- V reflect, be a reflection, halo, with DLC: **teiorón:rote'** it is reflecting the light (for example, the surface of water).
With SRF -ate-: **tehoterón:rote'** he has a halo, **teiakoterón:rote'** she has a halo, **teioterón:rote'** halo.
Cf. tekateronrōtha Rayonner (Marcoux: 326); Oronra rayon de lumière; auréole boréale; auréole, couronne des Saintes (Cuoq: 36); de yo ron ro deh There is a ring around the moon (Jamieson 2: 6)

-ront- N log, beam: **karón:ta'**
With LOC -'ke, on, at: **karontà:ke** on the log, on the beam.
With ATTR =kowa, great: **Ratironta'kó:wa** Oneidas, as referred to in council.
With V -ek-/-ak- eat: **Atirón:taks** Ojibwe.
With V -hrarak- bore a hole: **kerontahrá:raks** I am boring into wood, **wa'kerontahrá:rake'** I bored into wood.
With V -hroh[o]- block, put across (as a barrier), and DLC: **tekarontahróho** (there is) a beam extended across (for example, at the end of a road, across an entrance or waterway); and DISTR -nion-: **tekarontahrohánion** there are beams extended across; with SRF -ate-, V -hroh[o]- block, put across, CAUS -hst-, and DLC: **tewaterontahrohóhstha'** axle.
With V -hronhw- go across, angle across, and DLC: **tekarontà:ronhwe'** (there are) beams across.
With V -hseronni- dress, prepare: **kerontahserón:ni** I square a log or beam, **waharontahserón:ni'** he squared the log.
With V -ia'ser-/-'ser- stack, DISTR -onnion- and DLC: **wa'tharonta'serónnion'** he

stacked logs, **tekaronta'serónnion** there are stacked logs or beams.

With V -keri- be broth: **orontákeri'** sap, maple syrup.

With V -ketskw- raise upright: **kerontakétskwas** I raise a log.

With SRF -ate- and V -o- be in water: **Aterónto** Toronto.

With V -ot- stand: **karón:tote'** standing beam, pole; and CISL: **tsi tkarón:tote'** at the pole.

With V -o'ka't- run into, bump against, and CISL: **taharontò:ka'te'** he ran into the beam or post.

With V related to -ro'[k]- chop with an axe: **karontakáro'ks** woodpecker.

With V -'rhenien'-/-ienen'- fall down: **wa'karontié:nen'ne'** he passed, he died. *This is an older expression.*

Cf. aderondackx French or English (van der Bogaert: 62); *Garontagetsk8an gaianderesera* lever l'arbre de paix (Bruyas: 49); "the Iroquois give the Algonquin the name of *Rontaks*, that is to say, Tree Eaters." (Lafitau II: 62); *Niharuntagóa* Oneider (Pyrlaeus: 236); *Tho-ron-to-hen* Toronto, "timber on the water" (De Lorimier in Hough: 181); *Rarontaks,* pl. *ratirontaks* algonquin, litt. mange-bois, les mangeurs de bois (Cuoq: 39); "they [Mohawks] saw ... trees standing in the water, hence they called the place *Ka-ron-to,*" (Oronhyatekha: 12); *Karondoh,* Toronto, Log in water. (Brant-Sero and Hill in Boyle: 172); *Aterónto* Toronto (Cory: 83); *Aterónto* Toronto (Horne: 60); *ga-ron-da-non-ne* Hepatica acutiloba [= qui surveille l'érable] (Rousseau: 42; cf. Oneida *kutilu·tánunhe?* hepatica, Michelson and Doxtator: 494, and possibly *go di ron da non* hepatica, Jamieson 2: 11); *Tsi tkarón:tote ierih-owanahtáhkhwa* Pole by the R.C. Church

where news was given on podium (Lazore: 46); *Ratiróntaks* Algonquin Nation (Gabriel: 5); Laurentian *conda* wood (Biggar: 243); Iroquois *Adirondacks* Algonkins (Colden: XV); Iroquois "The Algonquin are sometimes stiled ... by the Five Nations, *Ratirontaks*," (John Norton in Klinck and Talman: 198)

-ronto-/-ronto'tsher- N wooden box: **karón:to** wooden box, **orón:to** dugout canoe.

POSS: **raonhé:ion raorón:to** his coffin (-ihei[on]-/-enhei[on]- die).

With SRF -ate-, V -hna'ne[t]-/-ne[t]- be lined, doubled, INSTR -hkw-, and DLC: **tewateronto'tsheranetáhkhwa'** cover for a vault that holds a coffin.

With V -iio- be good, nice: **iakoronto'tsherí:io** she has a nice casket or coffin, she has nice cupboards.

With V -oken- merge, fork, and DLC: **tekaronto'tsheró:ken** between the cupboards.

With V -onni- make: **keronto'tsherón:ni** I am making a cabinet, **karonto'tsherón:ni** or (with DISTR -nion-) **karonto'tsheronníanion** cabinets (for example, kitchen cabinets).

With V -o'ka't- run into, bump against, and CISL: **takeronto'tsherò:ka'te'** I banged against the cupboard.

With V -ra'nentak-/-nentak- stick to: **ioronto'tsheranentá:kon** cabinet or cupboards that are on a wall.

NOTE: The incorporating form has the NMZR -'tsher-.

-ronwar-/-nonwar- N wire, nail, needle, pin: **karón:ware'** or **kanón:ware'**

With **ie'nikhónhkhwa'** (-'nikhon- sew): **ie'nikhónhkhwa' karón:ware'** sewing needle.

With LOC -'ke, on, at: **karonwarà:ke** on the wire.

With V -her-/-hr- set on top of:
karonwaráhere' there is a wire; and
DISTR -onnion- **karonwarahrónnion**
there are wires up.

With V -hnhonter- attach end-to-end, add
on, and DLC: **teharonwarahnhontéhrha'**
he attaches wires, (he is) an electrician,
wa'tharonwarahnhónteren' he
connected the wires.

With V -hwatase-/-tase- turn, twist, and
CAUS -'t-: **ieronwaratasè:tha'** screwdriver.

With V -ia'k- break, cut in two, and DLC:
wa'tkeronwária'ke' I cut the wire.

With V -ia'k- hit, slap: **karonwaráia'ks**
piano, telegram; and TRNL:
ia'kenonwaráia'ke' I sent a telegram.

With V -ot- stand: **kanón:warote'** there
is a nail or pin in it, **wa'keronwaró:ten'**
I put a nail or pin in it.

-ron'onhkw- N pompom: **oron'ónhkwa'**
With V -ha[w]-/-enha[w]- V hold, bring,
take: **raron'onhkwénhawe'** he is the
champion.

With V -her-/-hr- set on top of:
karon'onhkwáhere' there is a pompom;
and REV -kw-: **wahatiron'onhkwahrá:ko'**
they won the championship.

• Karon'onhkwáhere' akwanòn:warore'.
There is a pompom on my hat.

-ron'se- V be undecided, with DLC:
tewakeròn:se' I am undecided,
tehoròn:se' he is undecided,
teiakoròn:se' she is undecided.

• Tewakeròn:se' ka' niká:ien' akerá:ko'.
I am undecided which one I should take.

-ron'wek- V close one's eyes, be blind, with
DLC: **teharon'wé:kon** he is blind,
teieron'wé:kon she is blind.

With SRF -ate-: **tekateròn:weks** I close
my eyes, **wa'tkateròn:weke'** I closed my
eyes, **tewakateron'wé:kon** my eyes are
closed; and REV -hsi-:
wa'tkateron'wékhsi' I opened my eyes.

-ro'[k]- V chop with an axe: **kéro'ks** I chop,
séro'ks you (sg) chop, **ráro'ks** he chops,
iéro'ks she chops, **enkéro'ke'** I will
chop, **waháro'ke'** he chopped it, **wakéro'**
I have chopped.

With DISTR -hon-: **waharo'ókhon'** he
chopped it.

NOTE: The short accented vowel suggests
that this root goes back to an earlier form
*-r'ok-. This root, or a variant of it, is
present also in **karontakáro'ks** woodpecker (*see* second-to-last subentry
under -ront- log, beam).

S

-sahe't- N bean: **osahè:ta'**
    With ATTR =shon'a, pluralizer:
    osahe'ta'shòn:'a different kinds of beans.
    With V -ate'skont- roast, bake:
    watshahè:tonte' baked beans.
    With N -hnek- liquid, V -ati-/-onti- lose,
    throw, CAUS -ht-, and DLC:
    wa'teksahe'tahnekóntiehte' I boiled
    beans.
    With V -iest- mix, and TRNL:
    ia'ksahè:taieste' I added, mixed in beans.
    With V -ke- amount to, and CONTR, TRNL,
    and DLC: **thia'tekasahè:take** all different
    kinds of beans.
    With V -ohw- put into liquid, and TRNL:
    ia'ksahè:tohwe' or **ia'ksahè:to'** I added
    beans.
    With V -o'ten- be a kind of, and PART; and
    onekwénhtara' (-nekwenhtar- red):
    onekwénhtara' nikasahe'tò:ten kidney
    beans.
    With V -ra'ken- be white, light-coloured:
    kasahe'tarà:ken white beans.

    Cf. ceheda beans (van den Bogaert: 56);
    Osaheta fezolles (Bruyas: 95); *Osahéta
    feves* (Galissonnière: 41v); *Osaheta* Beans
    (Zeisberger in Wheeler-Voegelin: 60);
    Osaheta fève, haricot (Cuoq: 36); *osaeta*
    [beans] (Ledger: 59); *Osaeta* [beans]
    (Onkweonwe: 4); *o sa e ta* beans
    (D'Ailleboust: 22); *osaheta, ossahéta*
    beans (green) (Cory: 14, 85); *o sa he dah*
    beans (Jamieson 1: 4); Laurentian *Sahé*
    Beans (Biggar: 81, 245); Onondaga
    8sahêta Pois (Shea: 81)

sakwè:tsta' You fatty! You're fat!

sáthi Get away!
    • Sáthi nakhén:ton! Move away from in
    front of me!

-sa'w- KIN in-law, different generations, with
    ATTR ='a/=ha, diminutive: **raksà:wha** my
    father-in-law, **ionksà:wha** my mother-in-
    law, **khesà:wha** my daughter-in-law,
    ontatshà:wha her daughter-in-law.
    NOTE: This term is used only when the
    younger member in the in-law relation is
    female; for example **raksà:wha** my father-
    in-law (woman speaking). See Deering and
    Delisle: 31–35, Horne: 4–9.

-senenna't- N muscle: **osenennà:ta'** muscle
    With V -nonhwak[t]- be sore, hurt:
    wakesenenna'tanòn:waks my muscles
    are sore.
    With V -r- put in, and DISTR -onnion-:
    wakesenenna'tarónnion I have muscles,
    iakosenenna'tarónnion she has muscles.

sénha more
    • Ohkwá:ri sénha rakowá:nen tsi ní:ioht
    ne í:se' satshé:nen. Ohkwá:ri is bigger
    than your dog (*literally*, your pet).

-senna'karask- V get a cramp or charley horse:
    onkesennà:karaske' I got a charley
    horse, **wahosennà:karaske'** he got a
    charley horse, **wa'akosennà:karaske'**
    she got a charley horse.

-senonn- N calf: **osenón:na'**

    Cf. ose^cnonna gras de la jambe (Galisson-
    nière: 24r); *osenōnna* le gras de jambe
    (Marcoux: 219); *Osenonna* mollet, gras
    de la jambe (Cuoq: 36); *o se non na* calf
    (Anon: 3); *osená:ta* muscle (Lazore: 59);
    Osenón:na' Calf, *Osenonnà:ta'* Muscle
    (Horne: 99); *iesenon'nàke* calf, which is
    the fleshy part of the back leg (Gabriel: 19)

-sera[hw]-/-osera[hw]- V gush, spew:
wa'késerahwe' I added liquid (water, broth) to something.

With REP: **sakéserahwe'** I added liquid again (maybe when I am reusing a teabag).

With CISL: **tkáseras** water is gushing, **takáserahwe'** the water gushed in.

With CAUS -ht- (but unclear beginning): **tonseráhtha'** or **thonseráhtha'** or **iethonseráhtha'** or **toseráhtha'** vinegar.

With N -hnek- liquid: **wa'khehnekóserahwe'** I threw water at her, **wahakhnekóserahwe'** he squirted water at me.

With SRF -an- and N -itsker- spit, saliva: **enhianitskeróserahwe'** he will spit at you, **wahakwanitskeróserahwe'** he spit at me.

With SRF -at- and N -kahr- eye: **wa'katkahróserahwe'** I rinsed my eyes with water.

With SRF -ate- and N -(h)nhoskw- cheeks, jowl: **wa'kheiatehnhoskóserahwe'** I squirted liquid (water, juice) at her out of my mouth.

With N -niatar- river, lake: **Kaniataróseras** Kayaderosseras, NY.

With N -rist- iron, steel: **raristóseras** welder.

Cf. Gaserhon arroser, jeter l'eau, Katke eskesera8e Quand me baptiseras-tu? (Bruyas: 96); *Oserah8i Mouiller* (Galissonnière: 57v); *K–oseras jeter à qlq.* (Cuoq: 26); Iroquois "*Kay-ad-ros-se-ra* means in the Indian tongue the lake country." (Alfred B. Street in Sylvester: 14); Iroquois "A. Cusick interpreted the word [Ka-ya-de-ros′-se-ras] as it stands as a *long deep hole*." (Beauchamp 1907: 71); *iehontoserātha* vinaigre (Marcoux: 416); *iehentoserata* [vinegar] (Ledger: 74); Onondaga *deyosseraronh8a Digue* (Shea: 45). Also *Caniadereosseros* (Thomas Pownall map 1756); *Caniaderosseras* (1775 map in Siebert catalogue I: #184); "that large Tract called *Kaniadarusseras*" (Little Abraham in Brodhead VII: 436)

seréka almost

• Seréka aiesaia'tienénhton. She almost knocked you down.

-serenht- N sleep

With V -aksen- be bad, and INCH -'-: **roserenhtáksen's** he gets bad dreams, **onkeserenhtáksen'ne'** I had a bad dream, **wa'akoserenhtáksen'ne'** she had a bad dream.

With V -iio- be good, nice, and INCH -'-: **onkeserenhtí:io'ne'** I had a nice dream.

With V -iionhkw- (meaning uncertain): **onkeserenhtí:ionhkwe'** I had a nightmare, **wahoserenhtí:ionhkwe'** he had a nightmare.

With V -ori- drive, drive away: **wakeserenhtórie's** it keeps me awake, I have a rough night, a sleepless night, **onkeserenhtó:ri'** it kept me awake, I had a bad night.

With V -r- put in, and INCH -'-: **wakeserénhtara's** I am sleepy, drowsy, **onkeserénhtara'ne'** I got sleepy, drowsy.

With V -'rhenien'-/-ienen'- fall down: **keserenhtié:nen's** I am nodding off to sleep, **wahaserenhtié:nen'ne'** he nodded off to sleep.

Seskéha August

With ATTR =kowa, great: **Seskehkó:wa** September.

Cf. seskeha aoust, seskeko8a sept. (Marcoux: 258); *Seskeha* August (Granger: 12); *Seskekowa* September (Granger: 13); *Seskéha* [August], *Seskehkó:wa* [September] (Calendar 1979)

-shaion- V be slow: **roshá:ion** he is slow (at doing something), **iakoshá:ion** she is slow, **iotishá:ion** they are slow.
• Iotishá:ion tsi taiohniótie' ne kaienthóhsera'. The plants are slow to grow.

Shawískera' or **Shawískara'** twin brother of Tharonhiawà:kon, Holder of the heavens

Cf. oꞩisk-ra gresle (Bruyas: 66); *Da-wis-ka-ronh* Flint (Newhouse: 300); Wendat "she [Aataentsic] brought forth two boys, *Tawiscaron* and Iouskeha," (Brebeuf in Thwaites 10: 129); Wyandot *ta wegh ske ra* Flints (Johnston: 24)

-sha'kent- N bulrush: **osha'kén:ta'**
With LOC -okon, under: **osha'kentó:kon** under the bulrshes.
With V -hwahnha[k]-/-hnha[k]- wrap, tie around, and DLC: **teiosha'kentáhnhen** (it is) surrounded by bulrushes.

Cf. Osakenta gros foin, foin de savane. De là le nom donné à la paroisse de l'Acadie: *Osakentake* (Cuoq: 36); *osakenta iotonnis* [it grows around the bulrush] (Beauvais: 20); *o-sa-ken-ta* Sparganium eurycarpum [bur-reed] (Rousseau: 71)

sha'té:kon eight

Cf. Laurentian *Addegué* Eight (Biggar: 241)

sha'thí:ken it is calm, quiet

shé:kon again, still; hello
• Shé:kon ken tesatehontsó:ni o'wà:ron'? Do you want more meat?

-shen- V have as kin
With KIN -atere- grandchild: **wakaterè:shen** I have a grandchild; and DLC: **tékeni tewakaterè:shen** I have two grandchildren; or PART:
áhsen niwakaterè:shen I have three grandchildren.
With KIN -hsot- grandparent: **rohsótshen** he has grandparents, **iakohsótshen** she has grandparents, **rotihsótshen** they have grandparents.
With KIN -'ken- younger sibling: **ro'kèn:shen** he has a younger sibling.

-shes[t]- N syrup: **óshes**
With otsina'kontahkwà:ne' bee: **otsi'nahkontahkwà:ne' óshes** honey.
With **wáhta'** hard or sugar maple: **wáhta' óshes** maple syrup.
With V -eka'[w]-/-ka'[w]- find tasty: **kashestákon'** it is tasty syrup.
With V -onni- make: **rashestón:ni** he is making syrup, **wa'keshestón:ni'** I made syrup.
With N -tsikhe't- sweet, V -r- put in, and DLC: **teioshestatsikhè:tare'** it is sweet syrup.

-she'rh- N dough, gravy: **oshè:rha'**
With V -akwenhten- be flat, CAUS -hst-, and DLC: **wa'tkeshe'rhakwénhtenhste'** I rolled out the dough.
With V -awenrie- stir, and DLC: **wa'thashe'rhawénrie'** he stirred the dough, the gravy.
With V -onni- make: **wa'keshe'rhón:ni'** I made dough, gravy.

Cf. Oserha quelque chose liquid qui s'est épaissi (Bruyas: 96); *Oserha* Caillé (Galissonnière: 15v); *Oserha* matiere molle comme pâte, levain; liquide épaissi (Cuoq: 36); *os her ha* dough (Diabo: 20); Onondaga *ꞩesera* Pâte, de la (Shea: 77)

=shon'a ATTR pluralizer

Síta Judah

With ATTR =hronon, resident of:
Sita'ehró:non Jewish.

-skan- N skeleton: **ráskan**

With **raókhwa'** (-khw- food): **ráskan
raókhwa'** mushroom. Compare
e´skan agohʉda' Common mushroom
"ghost's ears" (Waugh: 121) and
ráhska'n raonà:taro mushroom [skel-
eton's bread] (Lazore: 15).

*Cf. Gaskenn corpus a quo discessit anima,
Ti saskennennont* tu as un visage de mort
(Bruyas: 97); *Eskenn, hatiskenn* Esprit des
mort (Galissonnière: 37r); *eskenn*
Squelette (Marcoux: 371); *Eskann* spectre,
fantôme, squelette animée (Cuoq: 4);
ras kann os tien tos kon skeleton
[*ohstien'tóskon* all bone] (Diabo: 73);
Wendat/Iroquois "and they imagine a
country of souls called by the Iroquois
and Huron *Eskennanne*, or the Country
of Ancestors, which has all the appearance
of the hell of the poets." (Lafitau I: 251);
Wendat *Eskeine* L'ame (Sagard: Me6);
Wendat *Esken* Esprit (Brebeuf in Thwaites
10: 68); Wendat "it shows why they call
the bones of the dead, *Atisken*, 'the souls'."
(Brebeuf in Thwaites 10: 287)

skanekwen'tará:nen raspberry

Cf. skanek8entarānen Framboise
(Marcoux: 179); *Skanekwentaranent*
framboise (*onekwentara*) (Cuoq: 41);
skanekwataranen [raspberry] (Beauvais:
4); *ska ne kwen ta ra non* raspberry (Anon:
7); *skanegwʉdara´nʉ* Red raspberry
(Waugh: 127); *ska ne kwen ta ra ne*
raspberries (D'Ailleboust: 22);
ska ne gwenh da ra yenh raspberry
(Jamieson 1: 6); *skanekwen'tará:nen*
raspberry (Old Kahnawake: 20);
Skanekwen'tará:nen Raspberry (Horne:

33); Wendat *Sanguathanen* framboises
(Sagard Pl5)

skáthne together

skén:nen peace

With ATTR =kowa, great: **Skennen'kó:wa
ken?** How are you? **Skennen'kó:wa**
Fine (great peace). **Skennen'kó:wa órie'!**
Hello! (spoken to anyone one feels
affection for). **Skennen'kó:wa íksa!**
Hello! (said to a child).

skennèn:'a or **skenèn:'a** slowly
Also with ATTR =shon'a, pluralizer:
skenen'shòn:'a slowly.

-skenni- V rush
With SRF -at-, CAUS -'t-, and DLC:
wa'tkatskénnia'te' I rushed and rushed
(so much I didn't get ahead).
With N -ia't- body, and DLC:
tehatia'taskénnie's he beats me to it,
wa'thatia'taskén:ni' he beat me to it,
he got there before I did,
wa'tekheia'taskén:ni' I beat her to it.

-skenonton- N deer: **oskenón:ton**

Cf. senadondo fox (van den Bogaert: 53);
Oskennonton Cerf (Bruyas: 97);
oskennonton Chevreuil (Galissonnière:
7v); *Oscanónto* Hirsch (Pyrlaeus: 201);
oskennōnton Chevreüil (Marcoux: 67);
Oskennonton chevreuil (Cuoq: 36);
os ke non ton deer (Anon: 16); *Oskenonton*
[deer] (Onkweonwe: 3); *Os-ke-non-ton*
deer (Cory: 13); *oh skenh non donh* deer
(Jamieson 1: 5); *Oskenón:ton* Deer
(Horne: 109); Laurentian *Asquenondo* does
(Biggar: 244); Wendat *Sconoton* Vn Cerf
(Sagard: An2); Onondaga *scœnontò* Dèer
(Zeisberger: 53)

skentstèn:ri buffalo fish; carp
NOTE: This word includes -itstenhr- rock, boulder, and the REP, but the verb root is unclear.

-sken'rh- N rust: **oskèn:rha'**
With V -r- put in: **ioskèn:rhare'** it is rusty, there's rust or mold on it; and INCH -'-: **wa'oskèn:rhara'ne'** it got rusty, moldy; with V -r- put in, PROG -atie- and CISL: **taiosken'rharátie'** it is getting rusty, moldy.
With V -rakew-/-okew- wipe: **rasken'rhoké:was** he is wiping off the rust, **wahasken'rhó:kewe'** he wiped off the rust, **rosken'rhoké:wen** he has wiped off the rust.
NOTE: *Otskenrah* (with SRF -at-) is given for 'buckwheat' in Onkweonwe (4).

-skohar- N dead wood, dead tree, skeleton: **oskóhara'**
With V -kowan[en]-/-owan[en]- be big: **Shoskoharó:wane'** or **Shoskohrhó:wane'** Mohawk title name 9.
Cf. Oskóhara skeleton (The Eastern Door 2007, Vol. 16, No. 40)

-skwe'i- N bud of a tree: **oskwè:ia'**
With V -ra'nekar[on]-/-nekar[on]- burst open, and DLC: **tenkaskwe'iané:kare'** the buds will open up, **wa'tkaskwe'iané:kare'** the buds opened up.

sok then, **sok nà:'a** already
• Sok nà:'a sà:rawe'. He is already home.

sónhatsi wild duck

só:ra' duck

Só:se Joseph

With ATTR =hne, at: **Soséhne** Wednesday.
Cf. sosēhne Mercredi (Marcoux: 246); *Sosehne* [Wednesday] (Granger: 4); *so she ne* wednesday (Anon); *so-sé-ne* Wednesday (Cory: 71)

sotá:r soldier, **rahsotá:r** he is a soldier. A borrowing from English *soldier*.
Cf. Queen aosodar [Queen's soldiers] (Onkweonwe: 4)

sò:tsi too much
• Sò:tsi kanó:ron. It is too expensive.

-statha't-/-atha't- V dry: **kstathà:tha'** I dry it, **enkstátha'te'** I will dry it, **wahastátha'te'** he dried it, **rostathà:ton** he is drying it, **kastathà:ton** it is dried.
With DISTR -nion-: **wa'kstatha'tánion'** I dried them, **iakostatha'tánion** she has dried them.
With INSTR -hkw-: **iestatha'táhkhwa' ahserí:ie** clothesline (-ahseriie['t]- string, rope).
With SRF -at- and N -ient- wood: **wa'katientátha'te'** I dried wood.
With SRF -ate- and N -neker-/-enneker-hay: **ratenekerathà:tha'** he dries hay, **enkatenekerátha'te'** I will dry hay, **wahatenekerátha'te'** he dried hay, **rotenekerathà:ton** he is drying hay.
With N -nenhst- corn: **ranenhstathà:tha'** he dries corn; and SRF -ate-: **wahatenenhstátha'te'** he dried the corn, **rotenenhstathà:ton** he is drying corn; and INSTR -hkw-: **iontenenhstatha'táhkhwa'** corn crib.
With SRF -ate- and N -nor- husk, braided corn: **wa'katenorátha'te'** I dried the husks, **rotenorathà:ton** he is drying husks.
NOTE: This stem is composed of -astath[en]-/-ath[en]- dry, and CAUS -'t-.

• Karonwarà:ke wa'khá:ren' wakstathà:-ton. I hung it on the clothesline and I'm drying it.

-stawin- N stalk, celery: **ostawí:na'** celery, **teiaontahiò:tsis ostawí:na'** or **tiohontahiò:tsis ostawí:na'** rhubarb (-hont- green, -hio'tsis[t]- be salty, sour).

-steri- V be funny, jolly: **iosté:ris** it is funny, amusing.
With CAUS -st-: **rasterístha'** he is making fun, **raksterístha'** he is making fun of me, he is laughing at me, **wahasté:riste'** he made fun, **wahaksté:riste'** he made fun of me, he laughed at me, **wahshakosté:riste'** he made fun of her, he laughed at her, **shakosteríston** he has made fun of her, he has laughed at her.
With N -ia't- body: **roia'tasté:ris** he is funny, jolly, **iakoia'tasté:ris** she is funny, jolly.
• Tehontierónnions rotiia'tasté:ris. They are in a play and they are funny.

-sterih[en]- V hurry, with DLC:
tewaksteríhens I am in a hurry,
tenwaksteríhen' I will hurry,
wa'tewaksteríhen' I hurried,
tewaksterihèn:'en I am hurrying,
tekasterihèn:'en it is rushed,
tesasteríhen Hurry up!
With DISTR -hser-: **tewaksterihénhsere'** I am all in a hurry.
With CAUS -'t-: **tekhesterihà:tha'** I am rushing her, telling her to hurry, **wa'thisteríha'te'** I told him to hurry.
• Wa'thosteríhen' aonsahahtén:ti'. He's in a hurry to go home.

-sto'kw- N beak: **ostò:kwa'**
POSS: **raostò:kwa'** his beak.
With V -es- be long: **rastò:kwes** his beak is long, **kastò:kwes** stork.

-sto'okhon- V peck: **kasto'ókhons** it is pecking, **wahaksto'ókhon'** he pecked me, **iosto'ókhon** it has pecked.

T

-[t]- V be one, with REP

(In contemporary Kanien'kéha spoken at Kahnawà:ke, *t* is not pronounced when it is at the end of a word; this means that the root -t- is pronounced only when there is something following, like the distributive.) With DISTR -hshon-: **skátshon** one at a time, one by one.

With COIN: **né: shà:ka** it is the same; and NEG: **iah né: shà:ka té:** or **iah né: shà:ka té:ken** it is not the same. With N -ahsi't- foot: **sewahsì:ta** one foot (measure).

With N -ahsohkw- colour, and COIN: **né: shonhsóhkwa** it's the same colour. With N -ahsont- night: **sewahsón:ta** one night.

With N -ahtsa'n- palm of the hand, handful: **sewahtsà:na** one handful. With N -atahtsher- twig, yard (measure): **sewatáhtshera** one yard, one metre. With N -akehr-/-kehr- dish, plate, and NMZR -'tsher-: **skakehrà:tshera** one dish. With N -a'ther- basket: **sewa'thé:ra** one basket.

With N -enhni't- moon, month, and DISTR -hshon-: **sewenhni'tátshon** each month. With N -hrie'n- pack, load: **skahriè:na** one pack, one load.

With N -hstar- drop: **skahstá:ra** one drop. With N -hwist- metal, money: **skahwísta** one dollar.

With N -iahia'khser- week: **tsiahià:khsera** one week.

With N -ian- footprint, track: **tsoiá:na** one pair; and DISTR -hshon-: **tsoianátshon** one step at a time.

With N -iar- bag: **skaiá:ra** one bag. With N -ia't- body: **shaià:ta** one male, **tseià:ta** one female, **skaià:ta** one female or animal.

With N -ithohkw- bundle: **skenthóhkwa** one bundle, one bunch.

With N -kon'tsher- pound: **skakòn:tshera** one pound.

With N -ks- dish, plate: **skáksa** one dish, one measure.

With N -nake['t]- birch bark: **skanakè:ta** one dollar.

With N -nennawen['t]- tobacco pipe: **skanennawèn:ta** one pipe.

With N -na'ts- pail: **skanà:tsa** one pail. With N -nohkw- bundle: **skanóhkwa** one bundle.

With N -rihw- matter, message, and COIN: **né: sha'orì:wa** it's the same thing. With N -tshe['t]- bottle, jar: **skatshè:ta** one jar; and DISTR -hshon-: **skatshe'tátshon** one jar each.

With N -tsi'nonhkwara- bulb (plant): **skatsi'niónhkwara'** one bulb. With N -wei- wing: **skáweia** a measure spanning the arms spread out, one fathom. With N -weionhkar- thumb: **skaweiónhkara** one inch.

With N -wero'kw- jug, bulb, gallon: **skawerò:kwa** one gallon. With N -'khah- step: **tso'kháha** one step; and DISTR -hshon-: **tso'khahátshon** step-by-step.

With N -'nenhar- grape, raisin: **ska'nénhara** one grape.

Cf. Gat in fine vocabuli cui praeponitur par la redup. signat unitatem, *Sajatat* un seul (Bruyas: 102); Wendat ... *at* Signat unitatem unius rei, *Skat* une seule chose (Potier: 357)

-t-/-et- V stand: **í:kete'** I am standing, **ì:rate'** he is standing, **í:iete'** or **í:iente'** she is standing, **í:kate'** it is standing, **ítenete'** you and I are standing, **iákenete'** we two

are standing, **íkenete'** the two (females) are standing, **rón:nete'** they are standing, **kón:nete'** they (females) are standing.
With **ohén:ton** in front, ahead: **ohén:ton ì:rate'** he is the head of it, in charge, **ohén:ton í:iete'** or **í:iente'** she is the head, in charge.
With CISL: **ísi' íthrate'** he is standing over there.
With TRNL: **iékenete'** the two (females) are standing over there.
With INCH -'- and DLC: **tékta's** I stand up, I stop, **ténkta'ne'** I will stand up, **wa'tié:ta'ne'** she stood up, **tewaktà:'on** I have stood up, **tésta'n** Stop!
With CAUS -hst- and DLC: **tsi tekatáhstha'** station; and **ó:tsire'** (-tsir- spark, fire): **ó:tsire' tekatáhstha'** wharf, dock.

tà: ne thóh the end, that's it!

-tahkw-/-etahkw- V take out: **ktáhkwas** I am taking it out, **iakenetáhkwas** we two are taking it out, **iakwatáhkwas** we are taking it out, **enktáhko'** I will take it out, **wa'ktáhko'** I took it out, **wahnetáhko'** the two took it out, **wahonnetáhko'** they took it out, **waktáhkwen** I have taken it out.
With N -ahkar- wood chips, shavings: **ionhkaratáhkwas** she is carving, **wahahkaratáhko'** he carved, **rohkaratáhkwen** he has carved, **sahkaratáhko** Carve! and CAUS -ht-: **ionhkaratahkwáhtha'** chisel.
With N -hiatonhser- book, paper, and CAUS -ht-: **tsi iehiatonhseratahkwáhtha'** post office.
With N -hnek- liquid, and CAUS -ht-: **iehnekatahkwáhtha'** pump.
With SRF -at- and N -hsineko't- ankle: **wa'katshineko'tatáhko'** I sprained my ankle.
With N -hwist- metal, money:

wa'khwistatáhko' I got paid (for doing my job), **wa'ts enhshwistatáhko'** later you will get paid for it, get punished; and TRNL: **ia'khwistatáhko'** I took money out (from) there.
With N -kahrohst- intestine: **wa'kkahrohstatáhko'** I took out the intestines.
With SRF -ate- and N -nentshawi't- wrist: **wa'katenentshawi'tatáhko'** I sprained my wrist.
With N -non't- milk: **wa'kenon'tatáhko'** I milked (the cow).
With SRF -ate- and N -weionhkar- thumb: **wa'kateweionhkaratáhko'** I sprained my thumb.
With N -wenn- voice, word, CAUS -ht-, and CISL: **thowennatahkwáhtha'** he just blurts out with it, **tonkewennatáhkwahte'** I blurted out with it.
With N -wer- wind, air: **wahakeweratáhko'** he took the air out of me (from punching me); and SRF -ate-: **onteweratáhko'** the air went out of it.
With SRF -ate- and N -'nehtar- gravel: **onte'nehtaratáhko'** it got chipped, **iote'nehtaratáhkwen** it is chipped.
NOTE: This stem is composed of a root related to -a[t]- be inside, and REV -hkw-.

táhnon and. *See* **tánon'**

-takeri'ta['w]-/-keri'ta['w]- V fry: **enktakerì:ta'we'** I will fry it, **wahatakerì:ta'we'** he fried it.
With N -hnenna't- potato: **khnenna'takerì:tas** I fry potatoes, **wa'ehnenna'takerì:ta'we'** she fried potatoes, **iakohnenna'takerì:ta** she is frying potatoes.
With N -its- fish: **wa'kitsakerì:ta'we'** I fried fish.
With N -i'tar- chimney, clan, clay: **ken'tarakerì:ta** lime.

With N -na'tar[o][k]- bread:
enkena'tarakerì:ta'we' I will fry bread,
wa'kena'tarakerì:ta'we' I made french
toast, **kana'tarakerì:ta** fry bread, french
toast.
With N -'nhonhs- egg:
wa'ke'nhonhsakerì:ta'we' I fried eggs.
With N -'nionkser- onion:
wa'ke'nionkserakerì:ta'we' I fried
onions.
With N -'wahr- meat:
enke'wahrakerì:ta'we' I will fry meat,
wa'ke'wahrakerì:ta'we' I fried meat,
wake'wahrakerì:ta I am frying meat,
ka'wahrakerì:ta fried meat.
NOTE: Some speakers instead have
-takeri'ta[w]-/-keri'ta[w]-, and still
others have -takeri'ta[hw]-/-keri'ta[hw]-.

-takhe- V be running: **ktákhe'** I am running,
ratákhe' he is running, **ietákhe'** she is
running, **katákhe'** it is running,
enhatákhe' he will run, **a'é:ren
wahatákhe'** he is running over there,
ratákhe's he is running around.
With CISL: **tahatákhe'** he is running this
way.
With TRNL: **tho niewaktakhé:non** I ran
over there, that way.
With DISTR -hshon-: **enhatakhéhshon'** he
will run here and there, **wahatakhéhshon'**
he is running here and there.

Cf. Ktakhes aller plus vite que le pas,
trotter, courir (Cuoq: 26); Laurentian
Quedaqué Walk along (Biggar: 245);
Wendat *onsahataχe* il retourne courant
(Potier: 359); Onondaga *ktakhé* je cours
(Shea: 37)

takò:s cat
With ATTR =kowa, great: **tako'skó:wa**
wildcat, tiger.

-takw- explode, pop. *See* -attatakw-

-takwaras-/-kwaras- V bruise, dent
With SRF -at-: **enwattá:kwarase'** it will
get bruised, dented, **onttá:kwarase'** it
got bruised, it got a dent, **iottakwará:son**
it is bruised, dented.
With SRF -ate- and N -'nehtar- gravel:
iote'nehtarakwará:son it is chipped
(a dish, jar, or glass).
• Onttá:kwarase' ne kenentshawi'tà:ke.
I bruised my wrist.

takwaré:re oyster, clam
Cf. atakꞔarēre coquillage, coquille (Marcoux: 86); *takwarere skati watshaaton*
[clam, one side is burnt] (Beauvais: 6);
ta kwa re re oysters (Anon: 17);
ta kwa re re oyster (D'Ailleboust: 23)

-takwarihsi-/-kwarihsi- V straighten:
ktakwaríhsions I straighten it,
enietakwaríhsi' she will straighten it,
wa'ktakwaríhsi' I straightened it,
waktakwaríhsion I have straightened it,
stakwaríhsi Straighten it!
With SRF -at-: **kattakwaríhsions** I
straighten (myself) up, **enhsattakwaríhsi'**
you will straighten up, **wahattakwaríhsi'**
he straightened up, **rottakwaríhsion** he
is straightening up, **iottakwaríhsion** it is
straight.
With SRF -at-, CAUS -'t-, and TRNL or CISL:
ienkattakwaríhsia'te' I will go straight
there (without stopping),
ia'kattakwaríhsia'te' I went straight
there, **ia'sattakwaríhsia't** Go straight
there! **takattakwaríhsia'te'** I came
straight here, **taiatiattakwaríhsia'te'**
we two came straight here.
With N -nahst- rafters:
kanahstakwaríhsions something used
to shore up or even out the rafters.

With SRF -ate- and N -rihw- matter, message: **wakaterihwakwaríhsion** I am straight in my ways, I am trustworthy, honest, **roterihwakwaríhsion** he is straight, trustworthy, **iakoterihwakwaríhsion** she is straight, trustworthy. NOTE: This stem is composed of a root -takwari-/-kwari-, which occurs only with suffixes, and REV -hsi-.

-takwariht-/-kwariht- V open out, with DLC: **wa'tektá:kwarihte'** I am opening it out. NOTE: This stem is composed of a root -takwari-/-kwari-, which occurs only with suffixes, and CAUS -ht-.
• Wa'tektá:kwarihte' ne áhsire'. I opened out the blanket.

takwa'áhson spider
With **teiota'á:raton** (-a'ar- net, curtain): **takwa'áhson teiota'á:raton** spider web. With **í:waks** (-ek-/-ak- eat): **takwa'áhson í:waks** cancer.
Cf. Takwahasont araignée, chancre, cancer (Cuoq: 42)

takwa'ahtsherón:ni witch hazel

tamétos tomatoes
Cf. tametos [tomatoes] (Ledger: 47); *ta me tos* tomatoes (D'Ailleboust: 22)

tánon' and
NOTE: A few speakers say **táhnon**.

-tar- N brim of a hat, eaves of a house
With V -ont- attach, and DLC: **teiotá:ronte'** it has a brim; fedora. With -ont- attach, PROG -atie- and DLC: **teiotarontátie'** eaves.
Cf. Tiotaronte Chappeau (Galissonnière: 17v); *tiotārŏnte* chapeau (Marcoux: 61); *a non wa ro re te io ta ron te* hat (Anon: 5)

taráktarak cricket

tará:kwi sumac
Cf. Taragsi Sumac (Galissonnière: 8v); *tarakwi otera* [sumac roots] (Beauvais: 4); *ta-ra-kwi* Rhus typhina [staghorn sumac] (Rousseau: 51); *Tará:kwi* Sumac (Horne: 112); *tará:kwi* sumac (Gabriel: 130)

-tarih[en]- be hot, warm. *See* -a'tarih[en]-/-tarih[en]-

tarò:taro mourning dove; lazy person
Cf. ta ro ta ro idle (Diabo: 40); *taró:taro* lazy (Gabriel: 43)

-tase- go around. *See* -ahkwatase-/-tase-

-tase- turn, twist. *See* -hwatase-/-tase-

-tat- V offer, demonstrate
With TRNL: **iéktats** I am showing it (for example, a ticket at the window when I go to a movie, or I'm at the toll booth), **iahà:ktate'** I showed it, I held it out, **è:neken iahá:tate'** he held it up, **iewaktá:ton** I have shown it.
With SRF -at- and TRNL or CISL: **ia'kheiáttate'** I went up to her, **tahakwáttate'** he came up to me.

tawà:son flying squirrel

tawí:ne otter
Cf. tawyne otter (van den Bogaert: 53); *θasine* loutre (Galissonnière: 7r); *tasīnet* Loutre (Marcoux: 233); *Tawine* loutre (Cuoq: 42); *Tawine* [otter] (Onkweonwe: 3); *dah wi nah* otter (Jamieson 1: 5); *Tawí:ne* Otter (Horne: 109); Wendat *Tsabouinecq* Loutre (Sagard: An3); Susquehannock *Saddahvvijnhae* otter (Holm: 8)

tawístawis snipe

-ta'-/-eta'- V put inside: **kéta's** I put it inside, **ráta's** he puts it inside, **iakéta's** she puts it inside, **tenéta's** you and I put it inside, **iakenéta's** we two put it inside, **iakwáta's** we (all) put it inside, **ronnéta's** they put it inside, **konnéta's** they (females) put it inside, **enkéta'** I will put it inside, **wa'kéta'** I put it inside, (with variant -ata'-) **ón:ta'ne'** it got to be inside, **wakéten'** I have put it inside. With **kaià:takon** (-ia't- body, -kon inside): **kaià:takon tiakéta's** dressing (chicken, turkey). With TRNL: **iaháta'** he put it in, **ia'séta** Put it in! With N -ahswahser- fine wood shavings, sawdust: **taionhswahseráta'** or (with a variant -ahsewahser-) **taionhsewahseráta'** she put sawdust inside it (for example, when doing beadwork). With SRF -at- and N -a'ar- net, curtain: **wata'aráta's** screen, **wahata'aráta'** he put in a screen. With N -hnek- liquid: **khnekáta's** I put water in it, **wa'khnekáta'** I put water in it; and SRF -at-: **wathnekáta's** anything you put water in (a trough, pail, barrel), fountain pen. With N -ia't- body: **wahiia'táta'** I buried him, **wahonwaia'táta'** they buried him, **wa'ontatia'táta'** they buried her; and CISL: **tho thaià:ta** he is buried there, **tho tieià:ta** she is buried there; with N -ia't- body, and PURP -'nh-: **ronwaia'tata'à:nhe'** they are going to bury him; with N -ia't- body, and CAUS -hst- and INSTR -hkw-: **iontatia'tata'ahstáhkhwa'** grave, cemetery. With N -iie-/-ien- oil, grease: **enkeienáta'** I will put oil or gas in it, **wa'keienáta'** I put oil or gas in it. With SRF -at- and N -kahr- eye:

wa'katkahráta' I looked at it through a telescope, binoculars; and CAUS -hst- and INSTR -hkw-: **iontkahrata'ahstáhkhwa'** telescope, binoculars. With SRF -ate-, N -nekwar- blood clot, and CISL: **entewatenekwaráta'** it will get to be a clot, **tontenekwaráta'** it got to be a clot. With N -nerenh- tapeworm: **wahonerénhata'ne'** he got worms. With N -niahskwa'rh- hip: **ó:ia' wa'onkeniahskwa'rháta'** they put a new hip in me. With N -nonskwar-/-nenskwar- green fruit, smallpox: **wa'onkenenskwaráta'** they gave me a vaccination. With N -tsiser- pane of glass: **ó:ia' wa'ktsiseráta'** I put in another (new) pane of glass. With SRF -ate-, N -wenn- voice, word, and CISL or TRNL: **tahatewennáta'** or **iahatewennáta'** he telephoned; and BEN -enni-/-'s-: **tahakwatewennáta'se'** or **tahakwatewennátahse'** he telephoned me, **iekheiatewennata'én:ni** I telephone her; with SRF -ate-, N -wenn- voice, word, and CAUS -hst- and INSTR -hkw-: **iontewennata'ahstáhkhwa'** telephone. With N -wer- wind, air: **wa'keweráta'** I put air in it; and SRF -ate-: **wateweráta's** balloon. With N -'now- hump, padlock: **wa'ke'nowáta'** I put in (installed) a lock, **ro'nowáten'** he has put in a lock. NOTE: This stem is composed of a root related to -a[t]- be inside, and INCH -'-. • Kaié:ri nikáksake ia'séta iekanerahtóhon! Put in four cups of tea! • Né: ón:ta'ne' ne kenontsì:ne. I got it, I understood (*literally*, it got put inside my head).

-te- V be present, exist With CONTR: **thiká:te'** it is different, **thihá:te'** he is different, **thiié:te'** she is

different, **thihatí:te'** they are different.
With CONTR and DLC: **iah tha'teká:te'**
there is no difference.
With SRF -at-: **tsi iótte'** at the end, at the
edge.
With SRF -at- and CISL: **è:neken tiótte'**
it is high; and ATTR ='a/=ha, diminutive,
ken' particle, and PART: **ken' nitiottè:'a**
it is low.
With SRF -at-, and COIN, DLC, and CISL:
sha'tetiótte' it is even, the same level.
With N -aten'enhr- fence:
tsi ioten'èn:rate' at the end of the yard.
With N -enhniser- day:
òn:wa wenhniserá:te' today; and DISTR
-nion-: **wenhniseraténion** daily.
With N -hah- road, and CISL:
ísi' nonkwá: tiohá:te' there's a road over
there (this and the following words have
the variant -ha- of -hah-); with N -hah-
road, and PROG -tie-: **iohatátie'** there is a
road; with N -hah- road, and DLC: **tékeni
teiohá:te'** Two Row wampum belt; with
N -hah- road, and DISTR -nion-:
iotihaténion it has stripes, straight lines
or rows, **kahòn:tsi tánon' karà:ken
iotihaténion** black and white stripes.
With SRF -at- and N -hiohs- elbow:
tsi iothióhsate' (at) the corner; and DISTR
-onnion-: **tsi iothiohsatónnion** (at) the
corners.
With N -hnaw- rapid, strong current:
iohná:wate' (it is) swift water, a rapid.
With N -nenhr- crowd, and DLC:
tehotinenhrá:te' there's a line of them;
and PROG -tie- and CISL:
tontahotinenhratátie' they are coming
close together in a line, they are parading.
With N -ohser- winter, year, and COIN shi-:
shiiohserá:te' 1901 in the year 1901.
With SRF -at- and N -onhni- point of land:
iotòn:niate' peninsula, point of land.
With N -onhwents-/-onhonts- earth, world:
tsi ionhontsá:te' the earth, the world.

With N -rihw- matter, message, and INSTR
-hkw-; and **ohén:ton** front, in front:
Ohén:ton Karihwatéhkwen Preface,
Thanksgiving Address; with N -rihw-
matter, message, and COIN and DLC:
Sha'tekarì:wate' the issues are similar,
Mohawk title name 3.
With N -ronhi- sky, heaven, blue, and CISL:
tsi tkaronhiá:te' in the sky, in the
heavens.
• Teskwátho tsi iótte' onia'tarà:'a. Put a
hem at the end of the material.

Tehatiskaró:ras Tuscarora

tehkáhon bittern

-te[ht]- V be strong-tasting, energetic: **ió:te'**
it is strong-tasting, spicy.
With DISTR -nion-: **iotehténion** they are
strong-tasting, spicy.
With N -ian- footprint, track: **roiá:nate'**
he has a heavy step or tred, **iakoiá:nate'**
she has a heavy step or tred.
With N -ia't- body: **roià:tate'** he is hyperactive, always moving, never sits still,
iakoià:tate' she is hyperactive.
With N -nehohs- urine: **ronehóhsate'** he
has strong (smelling) urine.
With N -nonhkw-/-nonhkwa'tsher-
medicine: **iononhkwa'tshherá:te'** it is
strong-tasting medicine.
With N -weienn- manner: **roweién:nate'**
he is rough with things, he has a rough
manner, **iakoweién:nate'** she is rough.

teienekera'wistáhkhwa' pitchfork

teiotenenharà:kton blackcap
Cf. te-io-te-ren-hak-ton Rubus sp.
[brambles] (Rousseau: 48)

teiotién:taron sturgeon

Cf. Teiotientaron éturgeon maillé
(Cuoq: 43)

tekáhstia'ks parrot

tekakenhwhará:ron peach

teka'nón:ton alligator
Cf. Ja'ganõntont Crocodil (Pyrlaeus: 201)

tékeni two, **tékeni iawén:re** twelve, **tékeni
iawenréhaton** twelfth, **tewáhsen tékeni**
twenty-two, **tékeni ia'tká:ienhte'** twice.
Cf. Laurentian *Tigneny* Two (Biggar:
241); Wendat *Téni* 2 (Sagard: No1);
Susquehannock *Tiggene* 2 (Holm: 8)

tekení: rags, scrap
NOTE: Long ago there was a ragman who
would call out *tekení:* and people would
bring out their scrap or junk.
• Ó:nen á:re' tà:re' ne tekení: rarò:roks.
The junk collector is coming again.

Teken'tarèn:re' Cornwall, Ontario
NOTE: According to Louis Curotte,
the meaning is 'clans assembled'. The
third author's uncle Melvin was from
Cornwall, and he referred to Cornwall
as **Kahwenò:ke** (-wehn- island, -o- be
in water).

tekonní'tia'ks little black insects on top
of water in a rain barrel
NOTE: *See* -ani'tia'khon- be wrinkled.

-ten- V fly, with DLC: **téktens** I fly, I am
flying, **teká:tens** it flies, airplane,
tenká:ten' it will fly, **tenkontí:ten'** they
will fly, **wa'tká:ten'** it flew, **teió:ten** it
has flown.
With ATTR =hne, at: **tekaténhsne** airport.

-teni- V change, with DLC: **tekténie's** I
change it, **tenkté:ni'** I will change it,
wa'tekté:ni' I changed it, **tewakténion**
I have changed it.
With SRF -at-: **tekatténie's** I am changing,
wa'thatté:ni' he changed.
With BEN -enni-/-en-: **tehaktenién:nis** he
changes it for me or on me (for example,
the radio station), **wa'thakténien'** he
changed it for me.
With N -hnek- liquid: **wa'tekhnekaté:ni'**
I changed the water; and **tóhka** a few, and
PART: **tóhka na'tekhnekaté:ni'** I changed
the water (rinsed, drained it) a few times.
With SRF -at- and N -onhnh- life:
wa'tiontonhnhaté:ni' she underwent
puberty or menopause, a change of life.
With N -wenn- voice, word:
tekewennaténie's I translate it,
wa'thawennaté:ni' he translated it,
tehowennaténion he has translated it.
• Wa'thakténien' akohsera'kéhkha
okahkwèn:ta' sahrohrókhon'. He changed
it for me, he put on the winter tires.

-tenihon- V wave, with DLC: **tekteníhon** I
am waving it, **wa'tekteníhon'** I waved
it, **tekateníhon** it is waving, flapping.
With SRF -ar- and N -ahsi't- foot:
wa'tkarahsi'tateníhon' I shook my foot
(back and forth, in a circle).
With SRF -ani- and N -hsnonhs- finger,
hand: **tekanihsnonhsateníhon** I am
waving my hand.
With SRF -an- and N -itahs- tail:
tehanitahsateníhon he is wagging his
tail, **wa'thanitahsateníhon'** he wagged
his tail.
With SRF -a- and N -nentsh- arm:
tekanentshateníhon I am waving my
hand or arm, **wa'tkanentshateníhon'**
I waved my arm.

-teni[on]- V disperse, flurry

With SRF -at- and N -a'ker- snowflake: **iota'keraténion** it is starting to snow, there's a flake here and a flake there.

With SRF -at- and N -hstar- drop: **ontstaraté:ni'** it started to rain lightly, drizzle, **iotstaraténion** it is raining lightly.

With SRF -ate-, N -nekw- pea, pill, and CAUS -'t-: **wahatenekwaténia'te'** he talked gibberish, **rotenekwatenià:ton** he is always blabbing, talking gibberish.

With SRF -ate- and N -neraht- leaf: **iotenerahtaténion** the leaves are falling.

With N -tsinonhiaht- vein: **waktsinonhiahtaténion** I have veins all over.

-tens- V be thick: **ká:tens** it is thick.

With INCH -ha'-: **enkaténsha'ne'** it will get thick, **wa'katénsha'ne'** it got thick.

With N -hiatonhser- book, paper: **kahiatonhserá:tens** it is thick paper, cardboard.

With V -itskar- shoe sole, cover: **kentská:ratens** it is a thick sole or rug.

With N -onhar- frozen ground: **iaonhará:tens** it is a thick or deep frost.

With N -ra'wist- peel: **iora'wístatens** it has a thick peel or skin.

• Onttèn:ko' wa'katénsha'ne' oshè:rha'. The dough rose [and] got thick.

teréntsho sén:ts twenty-five cents

NOTE: In French a 25-cent piece is called a *caribou* or *trente sous* 'thirty sous', and the Kanien'kéha term is borrowed from this French term.

Cf. Teréntsho senhs twenty-five cents (Old Kahnawake: 20)

terí:teri blue jay

teró: bull

tetsá:ron both

• Tetsá:ron kátstha' akeshónhsa'. I use both my hands.

Tewa'káhnha' Ojibwe, Chippewa

Cf. Atꙅagannen parler une langue étrangère (Bruyas: 40); *tewakénnha* Delawares (Deering and Delisle: 285); Iroquois " ... a Nation whose only offense consists in its not being Iroquois. It is called *Ontôagannha,* signifying 'the place where people cannot speak' – because of the corrupt Algonquin in use there." (Lalemant in Thwaites 47: 145); Iroquois *Dewagunhas* Outawas (Colden: xvi); Iroquois "the Nippissins [were stiled] by the Five Nations, Ratirontaks, *Dewakanha.*" (John Norton in Klinck and Talman: 198); Wendat *akwaꙧnnen, ꙧnnha* parler une langue mal, avoir l'accent etrange, ꙅtaꙅois (Potier: 168); Seneca ... the *Touguenha,* living on the river Ohio (Galinée in Coyne: 27)

thé:nen or **othé:nen** something, **iah thé:nen** nothing

thetén:re yesterday, **ó:ia' tsthetén:re** the day before yesterday

-the'ser- N flour: **othè:sera'**

With **arawén** oats: **arawén othè:sera'** porridge.

With V -awak- shake: **kethe'será:waks** I am sifting flour, **wa'kethe'será:wake'** I sifted the flour, **wakethe'serawá:kon** I have sifted the flour.

With V -iest- mix, and TRNL: **ia'ethe'será:ieste'** she added, mixed in flour.

With V -ohw- put into liquid, and TRNL: **ia'kethè:serohwe'** or **ia'kethè:sero'** I added flour.

With V -onni- make, and CAUS -'t-: **iethe'seronnià:tha'** mill.

Cf. athesera flour (van den Bogaert: 56); *Oθesera* farine (Bruyas: 103); *ꞷtesera* farine (Galissonnière: 40r); *Otezera* Meal (Zeisberger in Wheeler-Voegelin: 60); *otēsĕra* Farine (Marcoux: 170); *Otesera* farinne (Cuoq: 37); *otheseraionni* [it is made into a powder] (Beauvais: 6); *o the se ra* flour (Anon: 8); *otesera* [flour] (Ledger: 53); *otésera* flour, meal (Cory: 15, 87); Wendat *Ottècha* Bled pilé (Sagard: Vi6); Onondaga *ꞷtetchera* Farinne (Shea: 55)

-the't- V pound: **kethè:tha'** I am pounding, **enkéthe'te'** I will pound, **waháthe'te'** he pounded, **wakethè:ton** I have pounded.

thiákeret chocolate

thiekanakarià:kon any old way, haphazard, whatever!
NOTE: Possibly includes -nakar- stick and -ia'k- cut, sever.

thí:ken or **thí:** that, those
• Ónhka ne thí:ken? Who is that?
Cf. Laurentian *Yca* that one (Biggar: 80)

thio'kéha or **thiio'kéha** or **ohthiio'kéha** train

tho there, thus, then. Short for **eh thó**

thó:ha almost

-thohkw- bundle. *See* -ithohkw-

thontaiawénhstsi (it happened) all of a sudden. *See* -en- happen

-thwenhs- N liver: **othwénhsa'**

POSS: **akwathwénhsa'** my liver, **raothwénhsa'** his liver, **akothwénhsa'** her liver.

tí: tea
Cf. ti thé (Marcoux: 388); *ti* tea (Anon: 7); *ti* tea (Cory: 14); *on whe on we a ko ti* Spiraea latifolia (= thé de l'Indian) (Rousseau: 47)

-ti- V be on the other side, with REP: **ská:ti** one side.
With N -hionh- creek, and PART (instead of REP): **ísi' na'kahiónhati** the other side of the creek.
With N -hneht- pine: **Skahnéhtati** Albany, NY.
With N -nat- town, settlement: **skaná:tati** across the road.
With N -naw- swamp: **Skaná:wati** Beyond the swamp (Onondaga title name).
With N -niatar- river, lake: **Skaniatará:ti** Lachine, Québec.
With N -nont- mountain, hill: **Tsonón:tati** Vancouver, BC.

tiawerón:ko eel
Cf. Tiaweroro͂nco Ale (Pyrlaeus: 201); *Tiaweronko* anguille (Cuoq: 48); *tiaweronkon kaneon* [eel skin] (Beauvais: 17); *tia we ron ko* eel (Anon: 17); *tia-we-ron-ko* eel (Cory: 88); *Tiawerón:ko* Eel (Tewaterihwarenia'tha, Autumn 1989: 28); *Tiawerón:ko* Eel (Horne: 110); Wendat *Tyauoirongo* Anguile (Sagard: Po1)

-tie- fly around, float by. *See* -itie-/-tie-/-ontie-

tien' endearing term used for children or younger relatives

-tiha- V be different, with SRF -at- and DLC: **tetiattíhen** the two are different (for

example, a pen and a pencil, or a bottle and a cup); **tetsattíhen** the two of you are different, **teiatiattíhen** we two are different, **tehonttíhen** they are different, **tekonttíhen** they (females) are different. With CONTR: **iah tha'tetiattíhen** it is not different, **iah tha'tehonttíhen** they are not different.
With DISTR -nion-: **tekonttihánion** they are all different.
With N -ahsohkw- colour: **tetiatahsohkwatíhen** they are different colours.
With N -kahr- eye: **tetiatkahratíhas** you and I see things differently (for example, a colour as red versus yellow), **wa'titiatkahratíha'** we saw it differently, **wa'thiatkahratíha'** the two saw it differently.
With N -ohser- winter, year: **Tó: na'tehiatohseratíhen?** How many years difference between them?
With N -wenn- voice, word: **tehontewennatíhen** their language is different.
• Tehonttíhen tsi ní:tsi rontá:tis. They are different in the way they talk.

tikwaté: pie. A borrowing from French *pâté*.
NOTE: The Kanien'kéha word for 'pie' is **tekahswá:ne** (-hson-/-hsw- back, -hna'ne[t]-/-ne[t]- be lined, doubled).
Cf. ti kwa te pie (Anon: 7)

tiohkarà:nes resin
Cf. tiokaranes watshaaton [burnt resin] (Beauvais: 14); *te io ka ra nes* resin (Anon: 14)

tiohnhónskwaron or **tionhnhónskwaron**
cow
NOTE: Possibly from *tionhónskwaronte' (-(h)nhoskw- cheeks, jowl, -ont- attach).

Cf. *Tionnhonsksaronte* Vache domestique (Galissonnière: 7v); *Tionhosgarónti* Kuh (Pyrlaeus: 12); *teionnhōnsksăron* Vache (Marcoux: 408); *Teionnhonskwaron* bœuf, vache. De là le nom de l'Ile Perrot: *Teionnhonskwaronte* (Cuoq: 43); *tionhonskwaron kaontsi ota* [from the cow, black excrement] (Beauvais: 5); *tionn hons kwa ron* cow (Anon: 16); *Tiononskwaron* [cow] (Onkweonwe: 3); *tio nhon skwa ron* cow (D'Ailleboust: 6, 21); *dyonh honhs gwah ronh* cow (Jamieson 1: 6); *tionn hons' kwa ron* cow (Horne, ca. 1970: 45); *tionhnhónhskwaron* cow, *tionhónhskwaron* cow (Old Kahnawake: 12, 31); *tiohnhónskwaron* cow (Lazore: 35); Lounsbury *tsyonhŭskwarŭt* (undated notes archived at the American Philosophical Society)

Tiohsahróntion Detroit
Cf. Tiochsaróntie a mouth of river (Pyrlaeus: 63); *Deyoghsaghrontyon* [Detroit] (Deserontyon in Claus C-1478, 877); *Tyohsahróñtye'* or *Tyohshróñtyoñ*, Bays, or Mouths of Streams, along it (Lounsbury 1960: 26); *Tiohshahróntion* Detroit, Michigan (Horne: 61); Wendat *taochiarontion/ taochiaronkion* la coté de Detroit (Potier: 154); Iroquois *Teuchsagrondie* Detroit (Colden: xvi); Iroquois "Lake Erie, called by the Indians *Techaronkion*," (Courcelles in Brodhead 9: 76); Iroquois *Tiughsaghrondy* Detroit, place of turning or turned channel (Beauchamp 1907: 267);

Tiohtià:ke Montréal
Cf. te hotiagi Montréal (Bruyas: 50); *Tiochtiáne* Canada oder Neufrankreich, *tiochtiágech/róhna* Canada People, Franzosen (Pyrlaeus: 63); *tyoghtyaki* [Montreal] (Brant in Claus C-1478, 629);

Chocktyhargo (Long: 213); *Teiotiagi* [Montreal] (J. Marcoux in Pilling: 90, 113); *Tiohtiaki* [Montreal] (J. Marcoux in Pilling: 114); *Tiohtiake* [Montreal] (J. Marcoux in Pilling: 115); *Ti-o-ti-a-ke* Montreal, "Deep Water by the Side of Shallow" (F. Marcoux in Hough: 181); *teiontiakon* canal. C'est l'ancien nom de Montreal. Par abréviation on dit maintenant: *Tiotiake* (Cuoq: 43); *Tyohtyakih* Montreal (Brant-Sero and Hill in Boyle: 172); "This word [Tutonaguy], with French pronunciation, appears to be the same as that still given by Mohawks to the Island,—*Tiotiakí*, meaning 'deep water beside shallow,' that is to say, 'below the Rapid'." (Lighthall: 202); *Tiohtiake* Montreal (Granger: 2); *Tio tia ke* Montreal (Anon: 17); *Tiotiáke* Montreal (Cory: 83); *Tiohtià:ke* Montreal (Horne: 60); Wendat *Kyokiayé* Le Saguenay, Prouince du Saguenay (Sagard: No1); *Te ôkia,i* Montreal (Potier: 154); Onondaga *tiotiaguiga* Francois (Shea: 57); Onondaga *tiochtiáge hotinágeri* Inhabitants in Canada (Zeisberger: 103); Seneca *Do-te-a'- ga* Montreal, Almost Broken (Morgan: 474)

tióhton nine, **tióhton iawén:re** nineteen, **tióhton niwáhsen** ninety, **tiohtónhaton** ninth, **tióhton nia'ká:ienhte'** nine times.

tió:konte' always, all the time. *See* -kon[t]- persist, persevere

tiona'tsíia' trillium
Cf. tionatsíha [trillium] (Beauvais: 8); *tso-na-ti-a* Trillium (Rousseau: 66)

tiora'wistáhkhwa' or **tiera'wistáhkhwa'** fork

tiotià:kton trout

tiótkon always. *See* -kon[t]- persist, persevere

Tioweró:ton Ste. Lucie, Doncaster Reserve

tkahnhónhserote' jack-in-the-pulpit

tó: how much? how many? For example: **Tó: ní:kon?** How many? **Tó: nihá:ti?** How many (persons)? **Tó: ní:wa'?** How big? **Tó: nikanó:ron?** How much does it cost? **Tó: niahà:tkene'?** How much did it go for? How much did it come to? **Tó: na'tesohseriià:kon?** How old are you?
Also an exclamative expression, as in (taking to oneself) "let me see!"

tóhka several, a few. Often in combination with **ní:kon** so many: **tóhka ní:kon** several, a few.

tohkára' a few (less than the amount of **tóhka**). Often in combination with **ní:kon** so many: **tohkára' ní:kon** several, a few.

tóhsa do not
• Tóhsa taketshà:ni'k! Don't be afraid of me!

tohtó:wi wooden doll

tó:ka I don't know

tóka' if

tóka' nòn:wa maybe

tóka' ò:ni' (tóka' ni') or

-token- V be certain: **kató:ken** it is certain, definite, it is so.
With CAUS -ht- and DLC:

wa'tektó:kenhte' I aligned them, I lined them up, I made it even.
With N -rihw- matter, message: **rorihwató:ken** he is a reliable person, **iakorihwató:ken** she is a reliable person.

-tokenhti- V be holy
With N -ent- day, and ATTR ='ke, at: **Awentatokenhtì:ke** Sunday.
With N -hahser- light, lamp, and CAUS -ht-: **ohahseratokénhti** (church) candle.
With N -hiatonhser- book, paper: **kahiatonhseratokénhti** gospel, Bible.
With N -ia't- body: **iakoia'tatokénhti** nun.
With N -nonhs- house: **ononhsatokénhti** church; and ATTR ='ke, at; and **kahnià:sakon** (-hnia's- neck, collar): **ononhsatokenhtì:ke kahnià:sakon** part of a church that goes up to the bell tower; with N -nonhs- house, NMZR -'tsher-, and LOC -akta', near: **ononhsatokenhti'tsher-ákta'** near the church.
With N -rihw- matter, message, and DLC: **teiorihwatokénhton** parable.
Cf. ia wen ta to ken ton Sunday (Anon: 6); *a-on-ia-ta-to-ken-ti-ke* Sunday (Cory: 71)

tó:kenske' or **tó:ske'** it is true, certainly

-tokeri[k]-/-okeri[k]- V gather, shirr:
ietókeriks she is gathering it, putting in gathers (in sewing), **wa'któkerike'** I gathered it, **katókeri** it is gathered, shirred.
With DISTR -hon-: **wa'ktokeríkhon'** I put in many gathers.
With SRF -at- and DISTR -hon-: **iottokeríkhon** it is gathered, shirred.
With SRF -an-, N -ihn- skin, leather, and DISTR -hon-: **wakanihnokeríkhon** I am wrinkled, **iakonihnokeríkhon** she is wrinkled.

With REFL -atate- and N -khw- food: **wa'katatekhókerike'** I cut down on eating.
With N -renn- song, music: **karennókeri** it is a shorter version of the song(s) or music.
With N -wenn- voice, word: **kawennókeri** it is a shortened version of a word.

toks a snap (on clothing)

tó:kwahre' cranberry
Cf. Tag8are fruit rouges qui croissent dans leau (Galissonnière: 44r); *Tokware* vel *Aiok* canneberge (Cuoq: 50); *dogwa'herı'* a cranberry (Waugh: 110); *Tó:kwahre'* Cranberry (Horne: 33)

tostostseríneken' song sparrow, nightingale
Cf. Totstotstserineken rossignol (Cuoq: 50); *tsistotserīnĕken* Rossignol (Marcoux: 348)

tóta grandmother, grandfather
Cf. Tóta grandma (or grandpa) (Horne n.d.: 1)

tó:tis salamander
With ATTR =kowa, great: **totiskó:wa** lizard, iguana.
NOTE: Some use **tó:tis** for 'lizard'. In Oneida, **to·tís** is the word for 'spring frog' (Michelson and Doxtator: 714); cf. Ohswé:ken dialect *do dihs* frog (young) (Jamieson 1: 5)

-tsahon- V whisper, with DLC: **tewaktsáhon** I am whispering, **teiakotsáhon** she is whispering, **tehotitsáhon** they are whispering, **wa'tektsáhon'** I whispered.
With BEN -ni-/-hahs-: **tehshakotsahón:ni** he is whispering to her, **wa'thitsahón:hahse'** I whispered to him.

tsanì:to beaver

Cf. sinite beaver (van den Bogaert: 53); *Tsinnitsk* Castor (Galissonnière: 16v); *tsiennīto* Castor (Marcoux: 57); *tsiennito* Castor (Cuoq: 51); *tsa ni to* beaver (Anon: 16); *jenh ni doh* beaver (Jamieson 1: 5); *Tsanì:to* Beaver (Horne: 110)

tsá:ta seven, **tsá:ta iawén:re** seventeen, **tsá:ta niwáhsen** seventy, **tsatáhkhaton** seventh.

Cf. Satach [seven] (Wassenaer: 73); *tsadack* seven (van der Bogaert: 62); *tsiatak* 7 (Galissonnière: 59r); *Joathdack* 7 (Weiser: 386); *tshoátak* 7 (Pyrlaeus: 11r); Laurentian *Judaié/Judayé* Six (Biggar: 241); Wendat *Sotaret* 7 (Sagard: No2); Susquehannock *Tzadack* 7 (Holm: 8)

-tsawenhs- N long leaves (for example, of the bulrush): **otsawénhsa'**

-tsenh- N fire: **otsénha'**
With V -a'tarih[en]-/-tarih[en]- be hot, warm: **iotsenhataríhen** it is a hot fire.
With V -ent- wear out, end, and INCH -'-: **wa'katsenhén:ta'ne'** the fire is out, the meeting is over.
With V -hre[k]- push, and DISTR -hseron-: **ktsenhahréhserons** I poke around in the fire, **wahatsenhahréhseron'** he poked the fire.
With V -iahia'k-/-iia'k- cross over, and DLC: **tenhatitsenhí:ia'ke'** they will cross the fire, they will debate.
With V -ien- put down, have: **ratitsénhaiens** they council; and INSTR -hkw-: **ietsenhaientáhkhwa'** town or council hall; with V -ien- put down, have, and DLC: **teionkenitsénhaien'** we debate across the fire.
With V -kowan[en]-/-owan[en]- be big: **Katsenhowá:nen** Grand Council.

With SRF -at- and V -onni- make: **wahattsenhón:ni'** he made a fire.
Cf. Gatsienha foyer, *Gatsihajen* tenir conseil (Bruyas: 105-6); *Gatsienha* foyer, *Gatsiaien* Conseil, tenir (Galissonnière: 22r); *rotsiēnhăien* Conseil, le tenir (Marcoux: 80); *Atsienha* feu pour se chauffer, feu pour la tenue du conseil (Cuoq: 3)

tsèn:nio Leave it alone!
• Tsèn:nio tóhsa ken' nà:tser! Leave it alone, don't touch it!
Cf. Tsién:nio! Don't touch that! (Tewaterihwarenia'tha, Summer 1988: 24, listed under "Old Words")

-tsen't- V doctor, treat: **enkhétsen'te'** I will doctor her, treat her, **wahakétsen'te'** he treated me.
With DLC: **tehshakotitsèn:tha'** health centre, clinic, hospital.
With SRF -ate-: **katétsen'ts** I am a doctor, or (with a different habitual ending) **katetsèn:tha'** I provide care or aid, **ratétsen'ts** he is a doctor, **enkatétsen'te'** I will doctor.

-tshahni[ht]- V be industrious, energetic, active: **waketshà:ni** I am industrious, I apply myself, **rotshà:ni** he is industrious, **iakotshà:ni** she is industrious.
With PAST -'ne': **waketshahnihtòn:ne'** I used to be energetic.
With INCH -'-: **enwaketshahníhta'ne'** I will get industrious, active, do things, **wahotshahníhta'ne'** he got industrious.
With N -ia't- body: **roia'tatshà:ni** he is energetic, active, **iakoia'tatshà:ni** she is energetic, active.
With N -nahskw- pet, domestic animal: **ionahskwatshà:ni** (it is) a really frisky, spirited animal.
With N -rihw- matter, message:

iorihwatshà:ni it is a drastic matter (my car broke, my glasses broke).
With N -wenn- voice, word: **rowennatshà:ni** his voice is strong.
With N -'nikonhr- mind: **wake'nikonhratshà:ni** I am strong-minded, brave, **ro'nikonhratshà:ni** he is strong-minded, brave.

-tshahni['k]- V fear, be afraid of: **ketshà:nis** I fear it, **ietshà:nis** she is afraid of it, **ronwatshà:nis** she is afraid of him, **enketshà:ni'ke'** I will get afraid, **wa'ketshà:ni'ke** I got afraid, **waketshahnì:kon** I have become afraid, **tóhsa setshà:ni'k** Don't be afraid!
• Nahò:ten' wa'katkáhtho' wa'ketshà:ni'ke'. What I saw scared me.

-tshaht- N bile: **ótshahte'**

-tshenen-/-itshenen- N pet, domestic animal: **katshé:nen**
POSS: **akitshé:nen** my pet, **satshé:nen** your animal, **raotshé:nen** his animal, **akotshé:nen** her animal.
With NEG: **iah í: tewakitshé:nen (thí: takò:s)** it is not my animal (not my cat).
Cf. Gatsennen animal domestique, serviteur, esclave (Bruyas: 105); *gastennen* Animal domes (Galissonnière: 7v); *katsēnen* Animal domestique, mon *aketsēnen* (Marcoux: 16); *Katsenen* animal domestique, esclave (Cuoq: 15); Onondaga *haguetchênen* mon esclave (Shea: 53); Onondaga *agozène* a tame animal, slave (Zeisberger: 11,175)

-tshenri- V find: **ketshénrie's** I find it, **enketshén:ri'** I will find it, **wa'ketshén:ri'** I found it, **rotshénrion** he has found it.
With SRF -at- and N -erien't- disposition:

wa'katerien'tatshén:ri' I got an idea; and FACIL -'tskon, easily: **wakaterien'tatshenriè:tskon** I am creative.
With N -hah- road: **wa'khahatshén:ri'** I found the road.
With N -karien't- carcass: **wa'kkarien'tatshén:ri'** I found a carcass.
With SRF -ate- and N -nakt- bed, place: **wahatenaktatshén:ri'** he found a place.
With N -rihw- matter, message: **wa'kerihwatshén:ri'** I found out about it.

-tshe['t]- N bottle, jar: **kátshe'**
With **káhi** (-ahi- fruit, berry): **kátshe' káhi** pear.
With LOC -kon: **katshè:takon** in the jar; and DISTR -hshon: **katshe'takónhshon** in all the jars.
With SRF -ate-, V -aweron- spill out of, and TRNL and DLC: **ia'tkatetshe'táweron'** I gulped or chugged it down.
With V -her-/-hr- set on top of: **wa'ketshe'tà:ren'** I set down a bottle.
With V -ihen- be in the middle of, and COIN and DLC: **sha'tekatshe'tí:hen** half a bottle or jar.
With V -ke- amount to, and DLC: **tekatshè:take** two jars.
With V -ont- attach: **iotshè:tonte'** blister, **wa'katshe'tón:ten'** it got, bubbled up a blister.
With V -r- put in: **katshè:tare'** Big Dipper.
With V -[t]- be one, REP: **skatshè:ta** one jar; and DISTR -hshon-: **skatshe'tátshon** one jar each.
Cf. Gatsheta v. Katse Courge (Galissonnière: 25v); *kātse* Bouteille (Marcoux: 46); *Katse* bouteille, etc. (Cuoq: 15); *ka tshe ka hi* pear (Anon: 7); Wendat *Asséta* Bouteille (Sagard: Me11)

tsi complementizer. For example:
tsi náhe' since, **tsi nén:we'** everlasting,
forever, **tsi ní:ioht** like, than,
tsi nió:re' while, during, after, until,
tsi nikarì:wes while, **tsi ní:kon** that
much, **tsi ní:wa'** the extent or size,
tsi nón:we the place where
• Wisk niiohserá:ke ó:nen tsi náhe'. It is
five years since then.

=tsi ATTR intensifier. For example: **asé'tsi** it
is new, **thontaiawénhstsi** all of a sudden,
ohrhon'kéhstsi early morning.

-tsihenhst- N crispiness, char: **otsihénhsta'**
With ATTR =tsi, intensifier:
ratsihénhstatsi priest, **ratitsihénhstatsi**
priests.
With V -a'senht-/-enht- drop:
wa'ktsihénhstenhte' I singed the hair
off it, **wahatsihénhstenhte'** he singed
the hair off.
With V -ienta'- get, obtain, and REP:
ó:ia' enshotitsihenhstaién:ta'ne' they
will get another priest [Father Granger
would be replaced] (Old Kahnawake: 4)
Cf. Jesʁs hoñaʁennenhaʁis *hatitsihenstatsi*
Les robes noirs apportent la voix de Jésus
(Bruyas: 52); *hatitsihenst* robes noires
(Bruyas: 83); *Otsihensta* noir,
Gatsihenstatsi être noir, vétu de noir
(Bruyas: 106); *ktsihēnstătsi* Prêtre (Marcoux: 305); *Ktsihenstatsi* être robe-noire,
être prêtre (Cuoq: 66, who says this word
includes an old word *otsihen* related to
kahontsi [black], but this is unlikely);
ra tsi hens ta tsi priest (Anon: 10);
Ra-tsi-ens-tat-tsi minister, priest (Cory:
51); *ratsihénhstatsi* priest (Old Kahnawake: 20); *Ra tsi henhs da jih* Minister
(Jamieson 3: 10); Wendat *Etsihenstatsi*
Jesuit (Fraser: 736)

-tsihkw- N fist, button, knot (of a tree), puck:
otsíhkwa'
With ATTR =kowa, great: **otsihkwa'kó:wa**
turnip (rutabaga).
With SRF -at-, V -hwa'e[k]-/-a'e[k]- hit,
strike, and DLC: **tehattsihkwà:'eks** he
plays hockey or lacrosse, **tewa'á:raton**
tehattsihkwà:'eks he plays lacrosse
(-a'ar- net, curtain), **wa'thattsihkwà:'eke'**
ohahà:ke he played road hockey (-hah-
road), **tehottsihkwà:e'** he has played
hockey, lacrosse; and PURP -h-:
wa'thonttsihkwa'ékhe' owisà:ke they
are going to play hockey (-wis- ice, glass).
With V -ien- put down, have, and DLC:
tektsíhkwaiens I am playing billiards,
checkers (a game with pieces); and PURP
-h-: **tentenitsihkwaiénha'** you and I are
going to go play billiards, pool.
With V -kahte- be raw: **otsihkwakáhte'**
radish.
With SRF -at- and V -oia'[k]- throw
straight at: **rattsihkóia'ks** boxer.
With V -onni- make: **enktsihkón:ni'** I will
make a fist, **wa'ktsihkón:ni'** I made a
fist, **rotsihkón:ni** he is making a fist,
stsihkón:ni Make a fist!
With V -ont- attach: **iakotsíhkonte'** she
has a bump, a lump, **rotsíhkonte'** he has
a bump, a lump.
With V -ot- stand: **iotsíhkote'** (there is)
a knot in a tree, **wa'ktsihkó:ten'** I put a
button on (for example, my coat), I buttoned it, **stsihkó:ten** Do up the buttons!
and REV -kw-: **wa'ktsihkotá:ko'** I unbut-
toned it.

-tsihkwaront- V tie a knot, with DLC:
tektsihkwaróntha' I am tying a knot,
wa'tektsihkwarón:ten' I tied a knot,
teiakotsíhkwaronte' she has tied a knot,
tekatsíhkwaronte' knot,
testsihkwarón:ten Tie a knot!

tsiio'skohió:wane' aspen

tsikeninonhrawísta' or **tsikeninon'rawísta'**
dragonfly

tsikenithè:sera' moth

tsikenitshehwèn:ta' pollywog, tadpole
NOTE: Possibly related to -anitshehwen't-
milkweed.

-tsiker- N cloud: **otsíkeri**
NOTE: This word is not used much any-
more; *see* -atshat- steam, mist, fog, cloud.
Cf. Otsigre nuée (Bruyas: 43); *Iotsigere*
Nuages (Galissonnière: 60r); *Tiochzikere*
Clouds (Zeisberger in Wheeler-Voegelin:
57)

tsikera'wístak bat
NOTE: Probably includes -ra'wist- peel,
pancake.

-tsikhe't- N sweet: **otsikhè:ta'** candy, a
sweet.
With SRF -at- and V -(h)nhonta'- put in
one's mouth: **wa'kattsikhe'tahnhónta'**
I put candy in my mouth.
With SRF -at-, V -ia'k- cut, sever, and
BEN -hs-: **ó:nen wesattsikhè:tia'khse'**
A saying, something like 'Enough already!
That's it! You're done!'
With SRF -at-, V -o- be in water, INSTR
-hkw-, and DLC: **teionttsikhe'tóhkhwa'**
sugar.
With V -r- put in, and DLC:
teiotsikhè:tare' it is sweet; and N -hnek-
liquid: **teiohnekatsikhè:tare'** soda; and
N -na'tar[o][k]- bread: **teiona'taratsi-
khè:tare'** cake; and N -nekwenhs- blood
teiakonekwenhsatsikhè:tare' diabetes;
and N -nenhst- corn: **teionenhstatsi-
khè:tare'** sweet corn; and N -shes[t]-

syrup: **teioshestatsikhè:tare'** it is sweet
syrup.
Cf. Otsikehta sucre; miel (Cuoq: 37);
katsikhetaraken [white sugar] (Beauvais:
5); *otsiketa* [sugar] (Ledger: 47); *o tsi keta*
sugar, *ka tsi ke ta ra ken* granulated sugar
(D'Ailleboust: 23); *o tsik he ta* sugar
(Anon: 7); *tia wen ie na tsi khe ta re*
vaseline [sweet oil] (Anon: 18); *otsikéta,
o-tsi-ké-ta* sugar (Cory: 14, 85); Wendat
otsiketa Sucre ... Sel (Potier: 454);
Onondaga *hotchiketa* sel (Shea: 93)

tsikhnennà:tak toad

tsiki'nhontstókhi ant

tsiktsinén:nawen butterfly
Cf. Tsigennonnaẟen Papillon (Galissonnière: 62r); *tsi ke non na wenh* butterfly
(Jamieson 3: 8); *Tsiktsinén:nawen* Butterfly (Horne: 113)

tsiktsiré:re chickadee
NOTE: Cuoq (47) has an entry *Tektsirere*
which he believes to be a cedar waxing,
and which he says is a label given to
gossips. Cf. *dek tsi re reh* chickadee
(Jamieson 1: 7), Oneida *tsiktsile·lé·*
chickadee (Michelson and Doxtator: 655)

-tsin- V be a male animal: **rá:tsin** male;
kítkit rá:tsin rooster.
With DLC: **tehní:tsin** two male animals.
With REFL -atat- and CAUS -hst-:
ratattsináhstha' he is daring, fearless,
willing to take anybody on,
iontattsináhstha' she is fearless.
Cf. etsi a man (van den Bogaert: 54);
Gatsinn masle, tam de hominibus quam
belluis (Bruyas: 106); *Etshinak* a Man
(Zeisberger in Wheeler-Voegelin: 58);
Etsinn mâle, du sexe masculin, garcón

(Cuoq: 4); Susquehannock *Itæætsin* A man (Holm: 6); Onondaga *hatgina* mâle (Shea: 68)

-tsinahken- V practitioner of medicine: **ratsináhken** he is a practitioner of medicine, an exorcist, **ietsináhken** she is a practitioner of medicine.
NOTE: This must be a very old word since Frank Natawe reported that he knew this word from his father Louis T. Curotte. The third author does not recognize it.
Cf. "*Kitzinacka* which, I suppose, is Priest," (Wassenaer: 68) "*Koutsinacka*, or devil-hunter" (Wassenaer: 87); *sinachkoo* (to) exorcise the devil (van den Bogaert: 61); *Atsinnaχen* jongleur (Bruyas: 43); *rotsinna͡ꭓen* sorcier (Galissonnière: 76v); "and the Iroquois [call them] *Agotsinnachen*, that is to say 'Seers'," (Lafitau I: 237)

-tsinahken't- N charm: **otsinahkèn:ta'**
NOTE: According to Mike Norton, this "charm" looks like a liver, reddish-brown and about one foot long. It has an eye in the centre and thick veins and sinews. It has no legs but it can move. It is found in cellars. It causes illness and wherever it lives, people will wither away. It is an independent entity but it is not an animal. It is assumed to have originated as a caterpillar on a dissipated island at Niagara Falls. The caterpillar was sought by warriors as a hunting charm because it was said to be bloodthirsty.

-tsinaren't-/-tsiniaren't- N hoof: **otsinarèn:ta'** or **otsiniarèn:ta'**
With V -hseronni- dress, prepare: **wa'ktsiniaren'tahserón:ni'** (ne akohsá:tens) I worked on the hoofs (of the horse).

With V -nia[k]- wrap around the neck: **rotsinaren'tánien** he is a runner or sub-chief; *literally,* he has a hoof around his neck.
Cf. otsinarēnta pied fourchu des animaux (Marcoux: 290); *Otsinarenta* sabot, core ou pied du cheval; médaille des petits-chefs (Cuoq: 38)

-tsina'ahr- N tree stump: **otsina'à:ra'**
With LOC -'ke, on at: **otsina'ahrà:ke** on the stump.
With V -ot- stand, and CISL: **tiotsina'à:rote'** there's a stump there.

-tsina'kw- N lung(s): **otsinà:kwa'**
POSS: **aktsinà:kwa'** my lungs, **raotsinà:kwa'** his lungs, **akotsinà:kwa'** her lungs.
With V -tsi'io- be weak, feeble: **rotsina'kwatsi'ió:ha** his lungs are weak.

-tsinonhiaht- N vein: **otsinonhíahton**
POSS: **aktsinonhiáhton** my veins, **raotsinonhiáhton** his veins, **akotsinonhiáhton** her veins.
With LOC -atatie', along: **tsi katsinonhiahtatátie'** veins going along.
With V -kwe'niio- be in charge of: **katsinonhiahtakwe'ní:io** the main artery.
With V -teni[on]- disperse: **waktsinonhiahtaténion** I have veins all over.
Cf. Otsinnonhia͡ꞓta Nerf, Veine (Galissonnière: 59r, 82r); *otsinonhiāhton* Veine (Marcoux: 410); *Otsinonhiaton* veine, artère; nerf muscle (Cuoq: 30); *tsi ia ko tsi non ia ron nion* nerves (Anon: 3); *o tsi non ia ton* vein (Anon: 4); *otsinonhiáhton* veins (Horne: 99); *otsinon'iá:ton* tendons or sinews (Gabriel: 64)

-tsinonhwaratase- V wring out:
    ietsinonhwaratá:ses she is wringing it
out, **wa'ktsinonhwaratá:se'** I wrung it
out.
    With NEG: **iah teiakotsinonhwaratá:se**
she didn't wring it out.

-tsinonhwateni- V get dizzy:
    iakotsinonhwaténie's she gets dizzy,
onktsinonhwaté:ni' I got dizzy
    With CAUS -'t-: **wahaktsinonhwaténia'te'**
he swings me around; and DISTR -nion-:
wahaktsinonhwatenia'tánion' he swung
me around, **wahitsinonhwatenia'tánion'**
I swung him around.
    With SRF -at- and CAUS -'t-:
rattsinonhwatenià:tha' he spins around,
enkattsinonhwaténia'te' I will spin
around, **wa'kattsinonhwaténia'te'** I
spun around, **rottsinonhwatenià:ton**
he is spinning around.

-tsinowen- N mouse: **otsinó:wen**
    With ATTR =kowa, great:
otsinowenhkó:wa rat.

-tsir- N spark, fire, embers: **ó:tsire'**
    With **tekatáhstha'** (-t-/-et- stand):
ó:tsire' tekatáhstha' wharf, dock.
    With ATTR =kowa, great: **otsire'kó:wa**
ferry.
    With V -a[t]- be inside: **rotsí:ra** he is
quick-tempered, ready to get into it,
iakotsí:ra she is quick-tempered.
    With V -awenrie- stir, and DLC:
wa'tektsirawénrie' I stirred the embers,
testsirawénrie Stir the embers!
    With SRF -at- , V -okw- disperse, and DLC:
tekonttsirókwas fireflies.
    With SRF -at-, V -ontawe't- shake, pump,
vibrate, and DLC: **teionttsirontawè:tha'**
she is seesawing, **tenkattsirón:tawe'te'**
I will seesaw.

With V -o'[k]- slap, flutter, flap, and DLC:
tektsíro'ks I am lighting a fire using a
lighter or flint, **wa'tektsíro'ke'** I made a
spark, I lit a fire, **wa'thatsíro'ke'** he made
a spark, he lit a fire; and SRF -at-:
tewattsíro'ks flint (to start a fire), lighter,
tekonttsíro'ks fireflies.
    With SRF -at- , V -rik- put together, DISTR
-hon-, and DLC: **tewattsiraríkhons** there
are lightning sparks.
    NOTE: Both words for 'fireflies' are used.

Cf. o tsi re te ka tas tha wharf (Anon: 17);
o tsi re te ka tas ta dock (Diabo: 19);
o tsi re te ka ia iaks ferry (-iahia'k-/-iia'k-
cross over) (D'Ailleboust: 21)

tsí:s cheese

-tsiser- N pane of glass: **otsísera'**
    With ATTR =shon'a, pluralizer:
otsisera'shòn:'a glass panes.
    With V -nohare-/-ohare- wash:
wa'ktsiseróhare' I washed the window
panes; and DISTR -nion-:
wa'ktsiseroharénion' I washed the window panes.
    With V -ta'-/-eta'- put inside:
ó:ia' wa'ktsiseráta' I put in another
(new) pane of glass.
    With SRF -at- and V -'rhoro[k]-/-oro[k]-
cover: **iottsiseró:ron** there is a film on it,
iottsiseró:ron rakahrà:ke there is a film
on his eye (-kahr- eye), he has cataracts.
    With unclear V, and DLC: **tekatsiserá:ton**
window; and SRF -at- and DISTR -nion-:
tekonttsiseratónnion plaid.

*Cf. Létourneux nok hiatatienha & Co rate-
ristahninons Akera sonha, Otsisera sonha,
Okhontsera sonha, etc.* [L and Sons, he
sells metal, dishes, panes of glass, paints,
etc.] (Granger: inside front cover);
wathtsiseró:roks ne iekahrá:ke she has
cataracts (Old Kahnawake: 2)

-tsiskaionni- V have a cowlick (a section or swirl of hair growing against the direction of the rest of the hair): **rotsiskaión:ni** he has a cowlick, **iakotsiskaión:ni** she has a cowlick.
With CAUS -'t-: **katsiskaionnì:tha'** tornado; **otsiskaionnì:ta'** shell; snail.

tsiské:kek praying mantis

-tsiskerot- N slime: **otsiskeró:ta'**
With V -r- put in: **iotsiskeró:tare'** it is slimy; and INCH -'-: **wa'otsiskeró:tara'ne'** it got slimy.
Cf. otsiskeró:ta slime (Gabriel: 122)

tsiskó:ko robin
Cf. tsiskōko grive [thrush] (Marcoux: 194); *Tsiskoko* grive (Cuoq: 51); *tsis ko ko* robin (Anon: 16); *jihs go goh* robin (Jamieson 1: 7); *Tsiskò:ko* Robin (Horne: 113)

tsiskwaró:kwaro top (toy)

-tsist- N fire: **katsísta'** council fire, bunch of wampum strings.
With SRF -at- and V -ien- put down, have: **Ronattsístaien'** Firekeepers, Onondagas as referred to in council.
Cf. Gatsistaien tenir conseil, allumer le feu du Conseil (Bruyas: 106); *otsista* a fire (Lafitau II: 135); *Kenhenyondatsjistayenhaghse* here they are to kindle a fire (Hale: 118–9); Laurentian *Asista* Fire (Biggar: 245); Wendat *tsista* feu (Potier: 454); Wendat *assista/attista* feu (Sagard: Fe4); Onondaga *ontchichta* Fire (Shea: 56); Susquehannock *Uthsijsta* Fire (Holm: 9)

tsistá:rare' grasshopper

tsistékeri great horned owl

Cf. Tsistekeri chat huant, hibou (Cuoq: 51); *tsis te ke ri* owl (Anon: 17); *jihs deh geh rih* owl (horned) (Jamieson 1: 7); *Tsistékeri* Owl (Horne: 113)

tsistekeriià:kon buffalo
Cf. Tsitekeriakon buffle (Cuoq: 52); *jo de ga ri ya gonh* buffalo (Jamieson 2: 10); *Tsitekerià:kon/Tsistekerià:kon* Buffalo/Bison (Horne: 109); Onondaga *tegueriagui* Boeuf Illinois (Shea: 27)

-tsisto[hkw]- N star: **otsísto**
With **kentáhsonte'** (-itahs- tail, -ont- attach): **otsísto kentáhsonte'** comet.
With ATTR =shon'a, pluralizer: **otsistohkwa'shòn:'a** a lot of stars.
With SRF -at- and V -ahseht- hide, kill: **rottsistohkwahséhton** he is a detective.
With V -itie-/-tie-/-ontie- fly around, float by: **katsistohkóntie'** meteor.
With SRF -at-, V -kahrhateni- turn around, empty, CAUS -'t-, PROG -hatie-, and CISL: **taiottsistohkwakahrhatenia'tonhátie'** stars come rolling out.
With V -r- put in: **enietsistóhkwaren'** she or someone will put (add) an apostrophe; and DISTR -onnion-: **iotsistohkwarónnion** there are stars, it has spots or dots.
NOTE: The playful expression for 'stars come rolling out' is from Mike Norton; it is also given as a "Tongue Twister" in Tewaterihwarenia'tha, Winter 1989: 21, and it appears in Mary Deer's class notes, Feb. 1966.

tsítha bird
Cf. tsit ha bird (Anon: 16); *tsi ta* bird (D'Ailleboust: 6); *Tsĩ-tā* bird (Cory: 13); *Tsítha (Otsi'tèn:'a)* Bird (Horne: 113)

tsítsho fox

Cf. Tsitso Renard (Galissonnière: 7); *Tsĩtso* Renard (Marcoux: 336); *Tsitso* renard (Cuoq: 52); *tsi tsho* fox (Anon: 16); *Jijho* [fox] (Onkweonwe: 3); *tsítso* fox (Cory: 89); *jihts hoh* fox (Jamieson 1: 5); *Tsítsho* Fox (Horne: 109); Susquehannock *Sissω* fox (Holm: 8)

-tsi'er- N fingernail: **otsi'é:ra'**
POSS: **aktsi'é:ra'** my nails, **aotsi'é:ra'** its nails (an animal's).
With V -es- be long, and DLC: **tektsi'eré:son's** I have long nails; and ATTR =kowa, great: **tekatsi'ereskó:wa** eagle.
With V -hio'thiie-/-o'thiie- be sharp, pointy: **rotsi'ero'thí:ie'** he has sharp claws, sharp nails, **iotsi'ero'thí:ie'** it has sharp claws, nails.
With V -ia'k- cut, sever: **wa'khetsi'éria'ke'** I cut her nails; and SRF -at-: **wa'kattsi'éria'ke'** I cut my nails.
With SRF -at-, V -ion't-/-inion't- bring in, and BEN -en-: **onkwattsi'erinión:ten'** I got an ingrown nail, **wahottsi'erinión:ten'** he got an ingrown nail.
With V -otahrhe'- get hooked on something: **wa'ktsi'erotáhrhe'ne'** I snagged my nail on something.
With V -rakarere-/-karere- be noise travelling, and DLC: **tehatsi'erakaré:re'** his toenails are making noise (for example, a dog walking on the floor).

-tsi'eroht- N lobster: **otsi'eróhta'**

-tsi'io- V be weak, feeble: **waktsi'ió:ha** I am weak, feeble, **rotsi'ió:ha** he is weak, feeble, **iotsi'ió:ha** it is weak.
With CAUS -ht- and V -r- put in: **rotsi'ióhtare'** he is weak, there's something wrong with him (usually talking about an animal), **iotsi'ióhtare'** it is

defective; and INCH -'-: **eniakotsi'ióhtara'ne'** she will get weak, **onktsi'ióhtara'ne'** I got weak.
With N -tsina'kw- lung: **rotsina'kwatsi'ió:ha** his lungs are weak.
With N -'nikonhr- mind: **wake'nikonhratsi'ió:ha** I have a weak mind, I am cowardly.
• Onktsi'ióhtara'ne' katonriò:ktha'. I got weak, I am out of breath.

tsí'ks fly

-tsi'nahkw- N nest: **otsi'náhkwa'**
With SRF -at- and V -onni- make: **konttsi'nahkón:ni** they are building nests.

-tsi'nehtar- N small bead(s): **otsi'néhtara'**
With ATTR =shon'a, pluralizer: **otsi'nehtara'shòn:'a** beads.
With V -hwatase-/-tase- turn, twist, and DLC: **teietsi'nehtaratá:ses** she does beadwork, **wa'tektsi'nehtaratá:se'** I did beadwork.
With V -r- put in, DISTR -on-, and DLC: **tektsi'nehtará:rons** I put beads on it, I am doing beadwork, **tenktsi'nehtará:ron'** I will put beads on it, **wa'tektsi'nehtará:ron'** I beaded it, **tekatsi'nehtará:ron** it has all beads on it.

-tsi'nekwar- N yellow: **otsì:nekwar**
With **nikahtehrò:ten'** (-htehr- root, -o'ten- be a kind of): **otsì:nekwar nikahtehrò:ten** goldthread.
With V -r- put in: **rotsi'nekwá:rare'** he has yellow jaundice, **iakotsi'nekwá:rare'** she has yellow jaundice.

Cf. Otsinnigꞗar couleur verte, bile (Bruyas: 106); *Oziniquar* gelb oder grün (Pyrlaeus: 209); *ozit quarocu* yellow (Zeisberger in Wheeler-Voegelin: 61); *Otsinekwar* jaune;

bile (Cuoq: 38); *otsinekwar nikateroten*
[yellow root] (Beauvais: 14); *o tsi ne kwar*
yellow (D'Ailleboust: 17); *o-tsí-na-kwar*
yellow (Cory: 63); *o tsi ne kwar ho non sa*
yolk [yellow egg] (Diabo: 89);
oh tsi neh gwahr yellow (Jamieson 1: 8);
oti-ne-whar-ni-ka-te-ro-ten [goldthread]
(Rousseau: 43); Wendat *Odsinquaraé*
vert (Sagard: Co3); Wendat *otsing8ara*
bile ... verdure (Potier: 454); Onondaga
hotgikk8arogon jaune (Shea: 63); Onondaga *ozitwarócu* yellow (Zeisberger: 236)

-tsi'niokar- N mole: **otsi'nió:kare'**
NOTE: This word has the additional vari-
ants **otsi'nión:karon** and **otsi'nió:karon**
(Horne: 110).

-tsi'nionhker- N snot: **otsi'niónhkeri**
With SRF -at-: **rattsi'niónhkerons** he is
blowing his nose, **wa'kattsi'niónhkere'**
I blew my nose.
With V -ot- stand: **waktsi'niónhkerote'**
my nose is running, **rotsi'niónhkerote'**
his nose is running.
With V -o'ten- be a kind of, and PART:
nihatsi'nionhkerò:ten he is thought not
to be capable or appropriate (for example,
not good enough for the job or office).
This is an older expression.
With SRF -at- and V -rakew-/-okew- wipe:
wa'kattsi'nionhkeró:kewe' I wiped my
nose.

-tsi'nionhkwar- N bulb (plant), wick (bag or
mantle) inside of a coleman lamp:
otsi'niónhkwara' or **otsi'nónhkwara'**
With V -ke- amount to, and DLC:
tekatsi'nionhkwará:ke two (plant) bulbs.
With V -[t]- be one, and REP:
skatsi'niónhkwara' one bulb.
Cf. otsinonkwara [wicks] (Ledger: 74);
o tsin hon kwa ra wicks (D'Ailleboust: 24)

-tsi'non[ht]- N louse, lice: **otsì:non**
With V -ek-/-ak- eat: **katsi'nónhtaks**
monkey; and ATTR =kowa, great:
katsi'nonhtakskó:wa gorilla.
With V -r- fill or be in: **waktsi'nónhtare'**
I have lice, **rotsi'nónhtare'** he has lice,
iakotsi'nónhtare' she has lice.

-tsi'nonw- N insect, bug: **otsi'nón:wa'**
With ATTR =shon'a, pluralizer:
otsi'nonwa'shòn:'a all different kinds
of bugs.
With V -akera- stink, smell:
katsi'nonwákeras bedbug.
With V -nonhiani- be extreme, menacing,
and DLC: **teiotsi'nonwanòn:iani** (it is) a
big beast.
With V -ot- stand, and REV -hsi-:
wahitsi'noniotáhsi' I found him out,
wahonwatsi'noniotáhsi' they found
him out.

-tsi'nonwahnhe't- N earthworm:
otsi'nonwahnhè:ta'

-tsi'tahren- V cry a lot: **rotsi'tà:ren** he cries
a lot, he is a crybaby, **iakotsi'tà:ren** she
is a crybaby.

-tsi'takahre- V squeak: **iotsì:takahre'** it is
squeaking.

-tsi'tawi- V be a crybaby: **ratsì:tawis** he is
a crybaby, **ietsì:tawis** she is a crybaby;
atsì:tawis crybaby.

-tsi'tenht- V be a crybaby, with SRF -at-:
rattsi'ténhtha' he is a crybaby,
ionttsi'ténhtha' she is a crybaby.

-tsi'ten'a N bird: **otsi'tèn:'a**
With ATTR =okon'a, pluralizer:
otsi'ten'okòn:'a different birds.

-tsi'tia'k- V stop crying: **wahatsì:tia'ke'** he stopped crying.

-tsi'tokhenhst- V sob: **waktsi'tokhénhstha'** I am sobbing, **rotsi'tokhénhstha'** he is sobbing, **iakotsi'tokhénhstha'** she is sobbing.

-tsi'tonni- V make cry: **raktsi'tón:nis** he makes me cry, **enhshakotsi'tón:ni'** he will make her cry, **wahaktsi'tón:ni'** he made me cry.

-tsi'ts- N flower, outside of the lips: **otsì:tsa'** POSS: **raotsì:tsa'** his flower; and **bararón:** bullfrog: **bararón: raotsì:tsa'** pond lily.
With V -akera- stink, smell: **katsi'tsákeras** (it is) a smelly plant.
With V -awi-/-on- give: **wahaktsì:tson'** he gave me flowers.
With V -ia'k- cut, sever: **wahatsì:tsia'ke'** he cut the flowers.
With V -ia'[k]- hit, slap, and DLC: **wa'thaktsi'tsáia'ke'** he smacked me in the mouth.
With V -ien- put down, have, and PURP -hn-: **wa'etsi'tsaiénhne'** bridesmaid.
With V -kenra- be pale: **iotsi'tsakén:ra** (it is) a light-coloured flower.
With V -kw- pick: **ktsi'tsákwas** I am picking flowers, **wahatsì:tsako'** he picked flowers.
With SRF -at- and V -onni- make: **iottsi'tsón:ni** (there are) a lot of flowers growing.
With V -r- fill or be in, and INSTR -hkw-:

ietsi'tsaráhkhwa' vase.
With V -ra'nekar[on]-/-nekar[on]- burst open, and DLC: **tekatsi'tsaneká:rons** the flowers are blooming, **tenkatsi'tsané:kare'** the flower will bloom, **wa'tkatsi'tsané:kare'** the flowers bloomed.
With V -ra'neken-/-neken- be side-by-side, next to, and DLC: **tekatsi'tsané:ken** two flowers (are) together.
Cf. Otsitia Bierre (Galissonnière: 12v); *wa-wa-ron ra-o-ti-tsa* Nuphar variegatum (= la flueur du ouaouaron) [pond lily] (Rousseau: 43); *o-tsi-tsia* wine (Cory: 15)

tsohtsó:ron yellow birch

tsó:ka'we' crow
With ATTR =kowa, great: **tsoka'we'kó:wa** raven

tsó:kwaris red-winged blackbird
Cf. jo gwa rihs purple grackle (Jamieson 1: 7)

tsonenskwénrie snakeroot
NOTE: According to Frank Natawe, this can be put it in the mouth and tastes like aniseed; also used as a tea to aid digestion.
Cf. tsonenskwenrie [snakeroot] (Beauvais: 20); *te-io-nien-skwen-re* Asarum canadense [Canadian wild ginger] (Rousseau: 41); *tsohnohskwén:rie* snake root (Lazore: 56)

tso'nawénhes mermaid

W

-w- V arrive: **èn:rawe'** he will arrive, **wà:kewe'** I arrived, **wà:rawe'** he is arriving, he arrived, **wahón:newe'** they are arriving, they arrived, **ì:ro** he has arrived, he is here.

With TRNL: **ién:kewe'** I will get over there, **ièn:rawe'** he will get over there, **iahà:kewe'** I got over there, **iahà:rawe'** he got over there, **ó:nen iewá:ko** I have arrived there.

With TRNL and REP: **iesewá:ko** it's my birthday, **ietsá:ko** it's her birthday.

Cf. Iesewako tsinatewakoseriiakon. It's my birthday. (Mary Deer's 1971 class notes, Lesson 5)

wáhi indeed, of course, isn't it, y'know; **ó:nen ki' wáhi** good-bye

wahón:nise' a long time, **wahón:nise' tsi náhe'** a long time ago
• Wahón:nise' tetiontiatatkénhne'. It's a long time (since) we've seen each other.

wáhta' sugar maple, hard maple

Cf. Oáta Erable (Galissonnière: 8v); *Wáchta* Ahornbaum (Pyrlaeus: 207); *Wahta* érable (Cuoq: 52); *wa-ta* Acer saccharophorum (Rousseau: 52); Wendat *ouhatte* Herable (Sagard: Pl1); Onondaga *óhsatta* erablé (Shea: 21)

wastè:ton maple candy, fudge

Wastonhró:non American(s). A borrowing from English *Boston*, with the ATTR =hronon, resident of.
With ATTR ='ke, at: **Wastonhronòn:ke** United States.

watshirótha' sailboat
NOTE: Other words for sailboat are **wahsí:rote'** (-ahsir- blanket, -ot- stand), and **wattsirótha'** (Lazore: 65).
Cf. *ionts hi ro ta kwa* sail (Diabo: 67).

-wa'k- hold, support. *See* -ienawa'k-/-wa'k-

-wa'se- help someone. *See* -ienawa'se-/-wa'se-

wa'ts or **wa'ts niá:re'** later

Wá'tsok! or **Wá'tsik!** Wait!
• Wá'tsok teniokennhón:ti' ken' na'tekanentshésha atià:tawi enwá:ton' énhsatste'. Just wait it will be summer, you can wear short sleeves.

-wehn- N island
With V -o- be in water, and LOC -'ke, at: **Kawehnò:ke** on the island; Cornwall.
With V -ot- stand: **kawè:note'** island; with V -ot- stand, and DISTR -on-: **enkawehnó:ton'** it will flood, **wa'kawehnó:ton'** it flooded, **iowehnó:ton** it is a flood; with V -ot- stand, and INCH -'-: **wa'kewehnó:ta'ne'** I became stranded, **wahawehnó:ta'ne'** he became stranded.

Cf. Cayanoghe islands (van den Bogaert: 60); *Hatisendogerha* Les Hurons (quia in insula habitabant) (Bruyas: 22, 55); *Gasendo* Isle (Galissonnière: 51r); *Gahsendo* isle, *Kawenote* il y a une île (Cuoq: 16); *Ka-we-no-ke* Cornwall (Cory: 82); *Kawehno:ke* Island (Tewaterihw-arenia'tha, Summer 1988: 24); *kahwehnó:ke* Cornwall Island, on the island (Gabriel: 30); Laurentian *Cohena* island[?] (Biggar: 244); Wendat *Ahoindo* isles (Sagard: Te5); Onondaga *Kaꙩenno* Ilé (Shea: 63)

-wehr- V thunder: **Rawè:ras** mythical Thunderer, **wa'ká:wehre'** it thundered, **iowè:ren** it thunders.
  With PROG -hatie-: **iowehrenhátie'** it is thundering; and CISL: **taiowehrenhátie'** thunder is coming.
  Cf. kaꙩēras Tonner. *Les sauv croyent que ca sont leurs ancêtres qui tonnent, il les appellet Ratiꙩēras.* (Marcoux: 390); *Kaweras* tonner, la foudre gronder (Cuoq: 16); *Ratiweras* les tonneurs (Cuoq: 177, citing Tharonhiakanere J. Marcoux); *ra-we-ras* it thunders (Cory: 75)

-wei- N wing: **óweia'**
  With V -awak- shake: **wa'kheweiá:wake'** I fanned her; and SRF -ate-: **kateweiá:waks** I am fanning myself, **wa'kateweiá:wake'** I fanned myself, **wakateweiawá:kon** I have fanned myself; with V -awak- shake, and CAUS -st-: **ionteweiawákstha'** fan.
  With SRF -ate- and V -her-/-hr- set on top of: **ateweià:ra'** cape, shawl; and DLC: **wa'tkateweià:ren'** I put on a cape, **tewakateweiáhere'** I have a cape on, I am wearing a shawl.
  With V -ke- amount to, and DLC: **tekaweiá:ke** two measures spanning the arms spread out.
  With V -ont- attach: **oweión:ta'** pick (tool).
  With V -[t]- be one, and REP: **skáweia** a measure spanning the arms spread out (cf. English 'fathom').
  Cf. Gaꙩie éventail, *Gaꙩiahontsa* aisle (Bruyas: 65); *ꙩꙩateꙩiat* une brasse (Galissonnière: 14r); *Oweia* bras, aîle

(Cuoq: 38, 142); *Atewia* Brasse (Cuoq: 3); *seꙩateꙩēiat* Brasse (Marcoux: 47)

-weiahthentak- V get the wind or air knocked out of one: **onkeweiahthén:take'** I got the wind or air kocked out of me, **wahoweiahthén:take'** he got the wind or air kocked out of him, **wa'akoweiahthén:take'** she got winded.

-weien- oil, grease. *See* -iie-/-ien-

-weienhara'- V get busy, with DLC: **teieweienhá:ra's** she gets busy, **tenkeweienhá:ra'ne'** I will get busy, **wa'tkeweienhá:ra'ne'** I got busy, **tewakeweienharà:'on** I am busy
  NOTE: In these words, the *en* is pronounced like the *en* in the English word *when*.

-weienhon- V be good at, capable at
  With N -ahkwenni- outfit, clothing: **rahkwenniaweiénhon** he is a good tailor, he knows how to make clothes.
  With N -khw- food: **kekhwaweiénhon** I know how to cook.
  With N -rihw- matter, message: **kerihwaweiénhon** I know how to put things, how to phrase things.

-weienn- N manner
  With V -ent- wear out, end, and INCH -'-: **wa'keweiennén:ta'ne'** I got it ready, I finished doing it, **wa'eweiennén:ta'ne'** she got it ready, **roweiennentà:'on** he is getting it ready, **kaweiennentà:'on** it is ready, it is done; and SRF -ate-: **enwateweiennén:ta'ne'** it will get finished, it will be over, **onteweiennén:ta'ne'** it got finished; with REFL -atate-: **ratateweiennén:ta's** he gets ready, **wa'katateweiennén:ta'ne'** I got ready.
  With V -o'ten- be a kind of, and PART:

tsi nikeweiennò:ten (it is) my way
(of doing things), my actions,
tsi nihaweiennò:ten (it is) his way,
tsi niieweiennò:ten (it is) her way.
With V -te[ht]- be strong-tasting, energetic:
roweién:nate' he is rough with things, he
has a rough manner, **iakoweién:nate'** she
is rough.
• Onteweiennén:ta'ne' akwé:kon wà:khsa'
nahò:ten' wa'tió'te'. It's all done, I
finished all my work. • Tsi nihaweienn-
ò:ten tsi ní:tsi ratoriahnerónkwas. It's his
way of moving (fast, slow).

-weienst- V learn, study, practice
With SRF -ate-: **kateweiénstha'** I am
learning, studying, practicing,
wa'katéweienste' I learned,
roteweiénston he has learned.
With N -ia't- body: **roia'taweiénston**
it looks good on him (what he is wearing),
iakoia'taweiénston it looks good on her.
With SRF -ate-, N -rihw- matter, message,
and variant -ienst-: **katerihwaiénstha'** I
study, I am a student; and INSTR -hkw-:
ionterihwaienstáhkhwa' school.

-weiente- V know how: **keweién:te'** I know
how, **raweién:te'** he knows
how, **ieweién:te'** she knows how.
With CAUS -ht- and INCH -'-:
keweientéhta's I learn,
enkeweientéhta'ne' I will learn,
wa'keweientéhta'ne' I learned,
wakeweientehtà:'on I have learned.
With CAUS -ht-, INSTR -hkw-, and REP:
skeweientehtáhkwen my right hand or
side, **shaweientehtáhkwen** his right hand,
tseweientehtáhkwen her right hand.
• Keweién:te' akaterennó:ten'. I know
how to sing.

-weionhkar- N thumb: **oweiónhkara'**
POSS: **keweionhkarà:ke** (on) my thumb,

raweionhkarà:ke (on) his thumb,
ieweionhkarà:ke (on) her thumb.
With V -ke- amount to, and DLC:
tekaweionhkará:ke two inches.
With V -t- be one, and REP:
skaweiónhkara one inch.
With SRF -ate- and V -tahkw- take out:
wa'kateweionhkaratáhko' I sprained
my thumb.

wè:ne' it seems. *See* -e'ne-

wenhaká:ras sassafras

-wenhnis- V stutter: **rowèn:nis** he stutters,
iakowèn:nis she stutters.

-wenn- N voice, word: **owén:na'** word.
POSS: **akewén:na'** my voice.
With V -ahnot- tell about:
kewennahnótha' I read,
enkewennahnó:ton' or **enkewenna-
hnó:ten'** I will read, **wa'kewenna-
hnó:ton'** or **wa'kewennahnó:ten'** I read,
wakewennà:note' I am reading; and BEN
-ni-/-hahs-: **rakewennahnotá:ni** he is
reading to me, **enkhewennahnóthahse'**
I will read to her; with V -ahnot- tell about,
and INSTR -hkw-: **iewennahnotáhkhwa'**
kahiatónhsera' books, stuff to read
(-hiatonhsera- book, paper).
With V -ahronk- hear about:
khewennahrónkha' I hear her, her voice
(for example, if she is lecturing, or on the
radio), **wahiwennà:ronke'** I heard him,
his voice, **riwennahrón:ken** I have heard
him.
With V -ahsonter- join, connect, DISTR
-onnion-, and DLC: **tekawennahsonterónnion** morphology (*Martin 2016 title)*.
With SRF -ate- and V -ahton- disappear:
wahatewennáhton' he lost his voice.
With V -akaion-/-kaion- be old:
owennaká:ion or (with INCH -'-)

iowennakaiòn:'on (it is) an old word.
With V -ati-/-onti- lose, throw:
shakowennóntie's he disobeys her,
wahiwennón:ti' I disobeyed him,
wahakewennón:ti' he disobeyed me.
With V -es- be long: **kawén:nes** (it is)
a long word.
With V -hkw- pick up, and DLC:
tehakewennáhkhwa' he talks for me, he
speaks on my behalf, **wa'thiwén:nahkwe'**
I spoke for him.
With V -hna'netahkw-/-netahkw- remove
a lining, make a copy, and DLC:
tehawennanetáhkwas he is translating.
With SRF -ate- and V -ia'k- cut, sever:
atewénnia'ke' goose (domesticated).
With V -iio- be good, nice: **Rawenní:io**
God; with REFL -atate- and V -iio- be good,
nice: **katatewenní:io** I am free,
iontatewenní:io she is free; and INCH
-'-: **enkatatewenní:io'ne'** I will become
free; with V -iio- be good, nice, and CAUS
-hst-: **konwenniióhstha'** I give you a free
hand, I allow you, **enkonwenní:iohste'** I
will allow you; and REFL -atate-:
iontatewenniióhstha' she takes something freely (without asking), she helps
herself to it, she takes advantage,
wahatatewenní:iohste' he helped himself to it; with V -iio- be good, nice, and
CONTR: **thikawenní:io** it's alright,
thikawenní:io kátke anytime,
thikawenní:io ka' nón: anywhere, anyplace.
With V -ineken'- emerge, and CISL:
thawenníneken's he speaks up,
takewenníneken'ne' I spoke up.
With V -i'tson-/-'tson- be dirty, and DLC:
teiakowenná'tson she has a dirty mouth
(uses foul language).
With V -naie- be proud, vain:
rawennaná:ie' he boasts, brags,
iewennaná:ie' she boasts, brags.
With V -okw- disperse, and CISL:

tionkewennókwas she talks back to me,
tahakewennó:ko' he talked back to me.
With SRF -ate-, V -ont- attach, and INSTR
-hkw-: **katewennontáhkhwa'** I speak a
language, **wahatewennón:tahkwe'** he
spoke, used the language,
rotewennontáhkwen he is speaking in a
language.
With V -ot- stand: **rawén:note'** he is
howling, **kawén:note'** echo, it is howling
(the wind or a siren); and PROG -atie-:
kawennotátie' it is howling going by;
with SRF -ate- and V -ot- stand:
enhatewennó:ten' he will howl,
wahatewennó:ten' he howled,
ontewennó:ten' it howled, it screamed;
with V -ot- stand, and INCH -'-:
khewennó:ta's I suspect her or someone
(I don't trust their word),
wahiwennó:ta'ne' I suspected him; with
SRF -ate-, V -ot-, stand, and FACIL -'tskon-:
rotewennotà:tskon he is forever doubting.
With V -otahrhe's- get stuck, falter:
wakewennotahrhè:se' I am having
trouble with my words (stumbling over
them, remembering them).
With V -o'ka't- run into, bump against,
and CISL: **tonkewennò:ka'te'** I said it and
then *it happened* (and it is usually not a
good thing that happened),
tahowennò:ka'te' he said something and
it came back to him because it did come
about, **taiakowennò:ka'te'** she said
something and it came back to her,
entisawennò:ka'te' you have to watch
what you say since it could happen.
With SRF -ate- and V -o'kt- finish:
iotewén:no'kte' the end of the word.
With V -r- put in, and INSTR -hkw-:
khewennaráhkhwa' I listen to her, heed
her, **enkhewén:narahkwe'** I will heed
her, **wahiwén:narahkwe'** I heeded him,
ionkewennaráhkwen she has heeded me;

and NEG: **iah tehiwennaráhkwen** I didn't heed him, I didn't listen to him; and SRF -ate-: **wahatewén:narahkwe'** he heeded, listened (to what he was told); with V -r- put in, and FACIL -'tskon, easily: **rotewennarà:tskon** he is obedient. With V -rakare'ni-/-kare'ni- be loud, and DLC: **tehawennakarè:ni** he has a loud voice, **teiewennakarè:ni** she has a loud voice. With SRF -ate-, V -rihsi- take apart, take off, and BEN -en-: **onkwatewennaríhsien'** my words didn't come together (for example, when I am repeating something too many times), **wahotewennaríhsien'** his words didn't come together. With V -tahkw- take out, CAUS -ht-, and CISL: **thowennatahkwáhtha'** he just blurts out with it, **tonkewenna-táhkwahte'** I blurted out with it. With SRF -ate-, V -ta'-/-eta'- put inside, and CISL or TRNL: **tahatewennáta'** or **iahatewennáta'** he telephoned; and BEN -enni-/-'s-: **iekheiatewennata''én:ni** I telephone her, **tahakwatewennáta'se'** or **tahakwatewennátahse'** he telephoned me; with SRF -ate-, V -ta'-/-eta'- put inside, CAUS -hst-, and INSTR -hkw-: **iontewennata'ahstáhkhwa'** telephone. With V -teni- change, and DLC: **tekewennaténie's** I translate, **wa'thawennaté:ni'** he translated it, **tehowennaténion** he has translated it. With SRF -ate-, V -tiha- be different, and DLC: **tehontewennatíhen** their language is different. With V -tokeri[k]-/-okeri[k]- gather, shirr: **kawennókeri** it is a shortened version of a word. With V -tshahni[ht]- be industrious, energetic: **rowennatshà:ni** his voice is strong. With V -'shatst[e]- be strong: **kewenna'shátste'** I mean what I say,

rawenna'shátste' he means what he says, **iewenna'shátste'** she means what she says.
See also -atewennaientonhw- scold.
• Sathón:te' ken kawén:note' átste'? Do you hear the sound outside? • Wahi-wennó:ta'ne' iah tethorihwaié:ri. I am suspicious of him [because] he is not a nice person.
Cf. Gaꞷendio estre le maistre (Bruyas: 65); *Raꞷendio* Dominus est, vox ejus est pulchra seu vim magnam habet (Bruyas: 116); *desawennawenrate* your voice coming through (Hale: 116–7)

wén:so franc, occurs in **áhsen wén:so** fifty cents
Cf. asenꞷēnso ecu, 1/2 piastre i.e. trois vingt sous (Marcoux: 139); *asenꞷenso* 1 écu, *seꞷensotserat* 1 franc (Marcoux 1828: 99), *Wenso* vingt sous, un franc (Cuoq: 58)

Wén:tat Wendat
Cf. Wendat *Hoüandate* Les Wendats (Sagard: Na2); "The general name, and that which is common to these four Nations, in the language of the country is *Wendat;*" (Le Jeune in Thwaites 16: 227); *ꞷendat* Wendat (Potier: 154); Wendat (possibly) "the *Owendaets* (otherwise called the Ionontady-Haga Indians) in conjunction with the other Indians settled on Ohio," (Brodhead 6: 596); Wyandot *wą́ndat* Wyandots (Barbeau 1960: 303)

-wer- N wind, air: **ówera'**
With SRF -ate-, V -atsnenht- go down, descend, and TRNL: **ia'katewerátsnenhte'** I went downwind.
With V -a'senht-/-enht- drop: **wa'káwerenhte'** the air pressure dropped, **iowerénhton** the air is heavy.

With V -a'tarih[en]-/-tarih[en]- be hot, warm: **iowerataríhen** it is a warm wind.
With V -hkw- pick up, and DLC: **tekaweráhkhwa'** the wind comes up, it gets windy, **wa'tkáwerahkwe'** it got windy.
With V -hre[k]- push, and TRNL: **iekewerà:reks** I am blowing out air, **iahawerà:reke'** he blew out air.
With V -hroh[o]- block, put across (as a barrier), and CAUS -hst-: **iowerahrohóhston** it is sheltered from the wind; and SRF -ate-: **wakatewerahrohóhston** I am shielding or sheltering myself from the wind; and PROG -hatie-: **wakatewerahrohohston-hátie'** I am going along sheltering from the wind.
With V -hwatase-/-tase- turn, twist, and DLC: **teioweratá:se** it is very windy, **wa'tkaweratá:se'** it got very windy.
With V -ia'k- break, and DLC: **wa'tkawerí:ia'ke'** the wind died down, it got calm, **teioweriià:kon** the wind has died down, it is calm.
With V -kowan[en]-/-owan[en]- be big, and REP: **skawiró:wane'** or **skaweró:wane'** turkey.
With V -kste- be heavy: **iowerákste'** the air is heavy.
With V -no- be cold: **iowerá:no** (it is) a chilly wind; and CAUS -hst-: **eniowerá:nohste'** it (the air) will cool off.
With V -o'ka't- run into, bump against, and CISL: **takewerò:ka'te'** I went against the wind, **tewakewero'kà:ton** I am facing the wind.
With V -r- put in: **iówerare'** (it is) a light breeze.
With V -tahkw- take out: **wahakeweratáhko'** he took the air out of me (from punching me); and SRF -ate-: **onteweratáhko'** the air went out of it.
With V -ta'-/-eta'- put inside:

wa'keweráta' I put air in it; and SRF -ate-: **wateweráta's** balloon.
With V -'niaken- escape, and BEN -'s-: **wahowera'niá:ken'se'** he farted.
Cf. schawariwane turkey (van den Bogaert: 54); *skaꞩirōꞩăne* dinde (Marcoux: 125); *ska-wi-ró-wa-ne* turkey (Cory: 88); *ska we ro wa neh* turkey (Jamieson 1: 8); *Skawiró:wane'* Turkey (Horne: 111)

-wero'kw- N jug, bulb, lamp chimney, carcass, gallon: **owerò:kwa'**
With V -akera- stink, smell: **kawero'kwákeras** (it is) a smelly carcass.
With V -atken- rot, spoil: **iowero'kwátkens** it is bloating (ready to burst), decaying (for example, an animal in the bush or a drowned person), **wa'owero'kwátken'** it rotted, **iowero'kwatkèn:'en** it has rotted; and PROG -hatie-: **iowero'kwatken'enhátie'** it is rotting.
With V -[t]- be one, and REP: **skawerò:kwa** one gallon.
• Ó:ia' shní:non owerò:kwa'! Buy more light bulbs!
Cf. skaweró:kwa large jug holds one gallon (Gabriel: 59)

Wesá:se' Warrior dance, Thunder ceremony
Cf. Wahsase [Thunder ceremony] (Lazore: 50)

-wihr- N scar, sand bar willow: **owì:ra'**
With SRF -ate- and V -r- put in: **wakatewì:rare'** I have a scar; and DISTR -onnion-: **rotewihrarónnion** he has scars; with SRF -ate-, V -r- put in, and INCH -'-: **ensatewì:rara'ne'** you will get a scar, **onkwatewì:rara'ne'** I got a scar.
Cf. o-wi-ra Alnus incana [alder] (Rousseau: 38)

wíhson plum

> *Cf. o8ison* prunier (Galissonnière: 8v, 43v); *8īson* Prune (Marcoux: 311); *Wison prune, prunier, wisonke* Le village de St. Philippe (Cuoq: 59); *wi son io iat hen* prunes [plum, dried fruit] (Anon: 7); *wi son* plum (D'Ailleboust: 22); *wison, wí-son* plum (Cory: 14, 87); *wi senh ga hihk* plum (Jamieson 1: 6); *wíhson* plum (Lazore: 17)

-wir- N offspring: **owí:ra'** (animal) baby.
> With ATTR ='a/=ha, diminutive: **owirà:'a** baby.
> With V -ase- be fresh, new: **owí:rase'** a new baby.
> With V -hkhwa- take away from: **wahshakowiráhkhwa'** he took her child away from her.
> With V -hninon- buy: **wa'ewirahní:non'** she had a baby; and PURP -hr-: **iewirahninòn:re'** she is going to have a baby.
> With V -ien- put down, have: **wakewí:raien'** I have a child; and SRF -ate-: **watewí:raiens** it gives birth, the interest (from the bank) keeps increasing, keeps giving birth. *This is an old expression.*
> With V -ka'te- have many: **iakowirakà:te'** she has a lot of children.
> With V -okw- take out of liquid: **iewirókwas** midwife.
> With SRF -ate-, V -r- put in, and REV -kw-: **wa'katewirará:ko'** I adopted a child.

-wis- N ice, glass: **ó:wise'**
> With LOC -kon, inside: **owí:sakon** in the glass.
> With LOC -'ke, on, at: **owisà:ke** on the ice.
> With V -ati-/-onti- lose, throw: **eniowisón:ti'** it will hail, **iowisóntion** it is hailing.
> With V -a'awi-/-en'awi- float, drift: **iowisen'á:wi** the ice is floating, (it is) an ice flow.
> With V -a'sen'-/-en'- fall down, and CISL: **takawí:sen'ne'** the glass fell.
> With V -a'sen's-/-en's- drop unintentionally: **onkewí:sen'se'** I dropped the glass.
> With V -her-/-hr- set on top of: **enkewisà:ren'** I will set down the glass, **wa'ewisà:ren'** she set down the glass.
> With V -hren't-/-en't- hang down, and DISTR -onnion-: **iowisen'tónnion** icicles.
> With V -hriht- break into pieces, smash, and DLC: **tehawisahríhtha'** he is breaking up ice, **wa'thawisà:rihte'** he broke the glass.
> With V -hri'- get broken into pieces, shatter, and DLC: **wa'tkawisà:ri'ne'** the glass broke.
> With V -na'nawen-/-nawen- be wet: **wa'kawisaná:wen'** the ice melted; and PROG -hatie-: **iowisanawen'enhátie'** the ice is melting.
> With SRF -ate-, V -ohwiha- split in two, and DLC: **wa'tewatewisohwíha'** the glass split or cracked.
> With V -okw- disperse: **wa'kawisó:ko'** the ice went away, melted.
> With SRF -ate-, V -oren- split open, and DLC: **teiotewisó:ren** there's a crack in the ice or glass.
> With V -r- put in: **iowí:sare'** it is icy.
> With V -(h)rho- coat: **iowisáhrhon** it is covered in ice, it is icy; and PROG -hatie- and CISL: **taiowisahrhonhátie'** it is getting covered in ice.

-wiser- V be ice: **iowísere'** there is ice (a layer of ice on top of it).
> With DISTR -nion-: **iowiserénion** there is ice here and there.
> With CAUS -t-: **enkawíserate'** it will

freeze over, **wa'kawíserate'** it formed ice, it froze over.

wísk five, **wísk iawén:re** fifteen, **wísk niwáhsen** fifty, **wískhaton** fifth, **wísk nia'ká:ienhte'** five times.

> *Cf.* Laurentian *Ouyscon* Five (Biggar: 241); Wendat *Ouyche* 5 (Sagard: No2); Susquehannock *Wisck* 5 (Holm: 9)

-wiskera- V be (smell) musty: **kawískeras** it smells musty.
With INCH -'-: **enkawískera'ne'** it will get musty, **wa'kawískera'ne'** it got musty.

-wiskwenhtare'ehst- V slip on ice: **rowiskwenhtare'éhstha'** he slips on the ice, **onkewiskwenhtáre'ehste'** I slipped on the ice, **seréka aonkewiskwenhtare'éhston** I almost slipped on the ice.

-wistanawen- V melt, thaw: **wa'kawistaná:wen'** it melted, thawed, **iowistaná:wen** it is melted, thawed.
With PROG -hatie-: **iowistanawenhátie'** it is melting, thawing.
With CAUS -ht-: **wa'kewistaná:wenhte'** I melted it.
NOTE: This stem includes a noun root related to -wisto- be cold, and -na'nawen-/ -nawen- be wet.

-wisto- V be cold (not referring to weather): **kewístos** I am cold, **enkewístoske'** I will get cold, **wa'kewístoske'** I got cold, **wakewistóskon** I have gotten cold, **iowísto** it is cold.
With INCH -'- and PROG -hatie-: **iowisto'onhátie'** it is cooling off.
With CAUS -ht-: **kewistóhtha'** I cool it, **kawistóhtha'** refrigerator, **enkawístohte'** it will get cold, **wa'kawístohte'** it got cold, it cooled, **wa'kewístohte'** I cooled it.
With NMZR -hser-, *see* -wistohser- butter.
• Wa'kawístohte' ne káhwhe. The coffee got cold.

-wistohser- N butter: **owistóhsera'**
With V -okw- take out of liquid: **kawistohserókwen** cream.
With V -(h)rho- coat: **kewistohseráhrhos** I coat it with butter, I am buttering it, **wa'kewistohseráhrho'** I buttered it.
NOTE: This stem is composed of -wisto- be cold, and NMZR -hser-.

> *Cf. wistotcera* grease (van den Bogaert: 59); *Oh8istonsera* graisse figée quasi refroidie (Bruyas: 56); *Oh8istonsera* graisse fondüe en pain (Galissonnière: 46v); *o8istōsĕra* beurre (Marcoux: 39); *Owistosera* beurre, suif, crème (Cuoq: 39); *o wis to se ra* butter (Anon: 7); *owistosera* [butter] (Ledger: 47); *Owistosera* [butter] Onkweonwe: 4); *owist^hohsera, owistósera* butter (Cory: 14, 85); *o wihs doh seh rah* butter (Jamieson 1: 4)

,

='a/=ha ATTR diminutive

-'aweien- V be dew: **io'áweien** (there is) dew.

-'ka[ht]- V be fast-moving, with DLC: **teiò:ka**
it is fast, **tewakè:ka** I am fast, **tehò:ka** he
is fast, **teiakò:ka** she is fast.
With PAST -'ne': **tewake'kahtòn:ne'**
I was fast.
With N -'sere[ht]- vehicle, car:
teio'serehtà:ka passenger train.

-'kats- N limb: **o'kátsa'**
With V -no- be cold, CAUS -hst-, and DLC:
teke'katsanóhstha' my legs are cold,
wa'tke'kátsanohste' my legs got cold.
With V -ohar- attach at the end, and DLC:
teka'katsóhare' sleigh with spindles up
the sides.
With V -ot- stand, PROG -atie-, and DLC:
teha'katsotátie' he has bare legs,
teie'katsotátie' she has bare legs.

-'ke LOC on, at

='ke ATTR at

-'ken- KIN younger sibling
With ATTR ='a/=ha, diminutive: **ri'kèn:'a**
my younger brother, **khe'kèn:'a** my
younger sister.
With ATTR ='ke, at, and ATTR ='a/=ha,
diminutive: **ri'ken'kéha** at my younger
brother's place.
With REFL -atate- and ATTR ='a/=ha,
diminutive: **tiatate'kèn:'a** you (sg) and
I are brother and sister, **tewatate'kèn:'a**
you and I are brothers and sisters,
iakwatate'kèn:'a we are brothers and
sisters, **iatate'kèn:'a** the two (are)
brothers, or brother and sister,

tiatate'kèn:'a the two (are) sisters,
rontate'kèn:'a they all (are) brothers
or siblings, **tewatatè:ken** Brothers!
With ATTR =okon'a, pluralizer:
iakwatate'ken'okòn:'a we are brothers
and sisters, my siblings.
With V -shen- have as kin: **ro'kèn:shen**
he has a younger sibling.

-'khah- N step: **o'kháha'**
With V -akahron- be wide, and DLC:
teha'khahakà:ron he has a wide stride
(with legs apart).
With V -aksen- be bad: **ke'khaháksen**
my walk or gait is wrong (I'm limping
or off-balance).
With V -ati-/-onti- lose, throw, and TRNL:
iewake'khahóntie's I am taking steps,
iahonke'khahón:ti' I took a step.
With V -es- be long, tall, and DLC:
teha'khahé:son's he has long strides.
With SRF -ate-, V -hkw- pick up, and DLC:
tenkate'kháhahkwe' I will take a step,
wa'thate'kháhahkwe' he took a step.
With V -ke- amount to, and DLC:
teka'kháhake two steps.
With V -[t]- be one, and REP: **tso'kháha**
one step; and DISTR -hshon-:
tso'khahátshon step-by-step.

-'khar- V have on a slip: **wakè:khare'** I
have on a slip, **kà:khare'** slip; POSS:
akè:khare' my slip.
With SRF -ate-: **wa'kate'khá:ren** I put
on a slip, **sate'khá:ren** Put a slip on!
With V -akera- stink, smell, and DLC:
teie'kharákeras her slip or skirt smells
(talking about someone who doesn't
wash).
With V -otahrho[k]- hook, and DLC:
wa'tekhe'kharotáhrhoke' I put a diaper

on her; and SRF -ate-: **teiakote'khar-
otáhrhon** she has on a diaper.
• Ó:ia' she'kharotáhrhok ne owirà:'a.
Change the baby's diaper.

Cf. "This breech clout which the Iroquois
call *gaccaré* is, for the men, a skin one
foot wide and three or four feet long."
(Lafitau II: 28); *Gaχare* brayer, *Raoχare*
son brayer (Bruyas: 107); *Gaχare, Ageχare*
brayet (Galissonnière- 14r); *Kākăre* Brayer
- Brayet, *akēkăre* mon (Marcoux: 47);
Kakare brayer; jupe (Cuoq: 9); *ka kha re*
slip (Anon: 5)

-'khohkw- N lower part of the body, from the
waist down: **o'khóhkwa'**
POSS: **ke'khohkwà:ke** my lower part,
ra'khohkwà:ke his lower part,
ie'khohkwà:ke her lower part.
• O'khóhkwa' wa'katkáhtho' tsi ioten'èn:-
rate'. I saw a ghost (lower part of a being,
neither male nor female) at the end of the
yard.

-'khoken- V crotch, with DLC: **teha'khó:ken**
his crotch, **teie'khó:ken** her crotch.

-'kohs- N tail of a bird: **o'kóhsa'**
POSS: **ao'kóhsa'** its tail.
With V -es- be long, tall: **ro'kóhses** he is
wearing a long coat, a trench coat (some
use this for a peeping tom, a flasher);
iako'kóhses she is wearing a long coat.

-'nahkw- N drum, barrel: **ka'náhkon**
With V -konhre[k]- hit, punch, and CAUS
-st-: **ie'nahkwakonhrékstha'** drumstick.
With V -o'ten- be a kind of, and PART; and
oròn:ia' (-ronhi- sky, heaven, blue):
oròn:ia' nika'nahkò:ten a blue barrel
(sometimes used for rain barrel).

Cf. o ron ia ni ka na ko ten bucket (Anon:
12)

-'nahs- N feather, plume: **ò:nahs**
With V -kenra- be pale: **o'nahsakén:ra**
swan.

-'nehar[on]- V beat someone at, defeat:
rake'néharons he beats me at it (cards,
a game), **wahshako'néhare'** he beat her
at it.

-'nehkwat- V stand very straight, upright:
ra'néhkwate' he is standing very straight,
really upright, **ie'néhkwate'** she is standing very straight.
With SRF -ate- and CAUS -ho-:
kate'nehkwáthos I arch my back, I lean
back, **wa'onte'nehkwátho'** she arched
her back, **rote'nehkwáthon** he has arched
his back.

-'nehsaronhkw- N sand: **o'nehsarónhkwa'**
With SRF -ate-, V -areni- spread around,
disperse, CAUS -'t-, and DLC:
wa'thonte'nehsaronhkwarénia'te' they
spread sand.
With V -ati-/-onti- lose, throw:
wahoti'nehsaronhkón:ti' they threw
sand on it.

-'nehtar- N gravel: **o'néhtara'**
With SRF -ate-, V -areni- spread around,
disperse, CAUS -'t-, and DLC:
tekate'nehtararenià:tha' I spread gravel.
With V -ati-/-onti- lose, throw:
wahoti'nehtarón:ti' they threw gravel
on it, **ka'nehtaróntion** it is gravelled.
With V -kareni- take back and forth:
ra'nehtarakarénie's he is carrying gravel
back and forth.
With V -r- put in: **io'néhtarare'** sandpaper.
With V -a[t]- be inside: **iako'néhtara** she
has kidney stones, gall stones.
With SRF -ate- and V -tahkw- take out:

onte'nehtaratáhko' it got chipped,
iote'nehtaratáhkwen it is chipped.
With SRF -ate- and V -takwaras-/-kwaras-
bruise: **iote'nehtarakwará:son** it is
chipped (a dish, jar, or glass).

-'nek- V plead, beg: **ke'nékha'** I am pleading
or begging for something, **ra'nékha'** he is
pleading, **ie'nékha'** she is pleading.
With BEN -enni-/-en-: **rake'nekén:ni** he
pleads with me, **wahi'né:ken'** I pleaded
with him, I begged him, **wahake'né:ken'**
he pleaded with me, he begged me.
• Rake'nekén:ni ahaterohrókha'. He keeps
begging me to go to the movies. • Wahake'né:ken' ahiia'takéhnha'. He pleaded
with me that I help him.

-'nekentsi- N rattlesnake: **o'nekén:tsi**

    Cf. Laurentian *Undeguezy* a snake (Biggar:
243)

-'neko'rh- wampum, wampum string. *See*
-neko'rh-

-'nenhar- N grape, raisin: **o'nénhare'**
    With unclear V: **io'nenháhrhare'** grape-
vine.
    With SRF -ate-, V -hwatase-/-tase- turn,
twist, CAUS -'t-, and DISTR -on-:
iote'nenharatasè:ton sprouts from vines
are curling around something (a wall or
fence); with V -hwatase-/-tase- turn, twist,
NMZR -'tsher-, and V -kehron[t]- put down
here and there: **o'nenharatase'tshera-
kè:ron** shoots or vines that are lying on
the ground.
    With V -[t]- be one, and REP: **ska'nénhara**
one grape.
    With SRF -ate- and V -'sere-/-i'sere- drag:
wate'nenharì:sere' vines are travelling
or going along on the ground.

Cf. Oneahharadasehhouhtserakeri
wine (Primer: 62; with NMZR -'tsher-
and incorporated into -keri- be broth);
Onéahháradáschhoúhtserákeri Wine, or
blood red soup (Long: 214); *o nen ha re*
grape (Anon: 7); *onenhare* [raisins]
(Ledger: 47); *wa-te-nen-ha-ri-se-res* Rhus
radicans [poison ivy] (Rousseau: 52)

-'nenhr- N cluster of branches: **o'nèn:ra'**
    With V -a'senht-/-enht- drop, and DLC:
wa'tke'nèn:renhte' I pruned the
branches.

-'nerohkw- N box: **o'neróhkwa'**
    With LOC -kon, inside: **o'neróhkwakon**
inside the box.
    With LOC -'ke, on, at: **o'nerohkwà:ke**
on the box.
    With V -atiront- pull, stretch, and DLC:
teie'nerohkwatiróntha' accordion.
    With V -her-/-hr- set on top of:
ka'nerohkwáhere' there is a box set on
it.
    With V -ia'ser-/-'ser- stack, and DLC:
wa'tha'nerohkwà:seren' he stacked the
box on top of the other,
teka'nerohkwà:sere' the boxes are
stacked on top of one another; and DISTR
-onnion-: **teka'nerohkwa'serónnion** the
boxes are all on top of one another.
    With V -ientot- stack in a pile, and DLC:
wa'tha'nerohkwaientó:ten' he stacked
boxes.
    With SRF -ate- and V -i[k]- fill up:
wahate'neróhkwike' he filled the box.
    With V -ke- amount to, and DLC:
teka'neróhkwake two boxes.
    With SRF -ate-, V -ketskw- raise upright,
and DLC: **tewate'nerohkwakétskwas** cart
(with two wheels, pulled by a horse).
    With V -kste- be heavy: **io'nerohkwákste'**
(it is) a heavy box, and BEN -'s-:

wake'nerohkwakstè:se' I find the box heavy.

With V -(h)nhoton- close, and REV -kw-: **wa'ke'nerohkwahnhotón:ko'** I opened the box.

With V -ota's- receive: **onke'nerohkó:ta'se'** I received a box.

• Wa'ke'nerohkwahnhotón:ko' wa'któhko' nahò:ten' í:wa. I opened the box [and] I took out whatever was inside.

-'nhaht- N branch: **ò:nhahte'**

With V -ia'k- cut, sever: **enke'nháhtia'ke'** I will cut the branch, **waha'nháhtia'ke'** he cut the branch, **wake'nhahtià:kon** I have cut the branch, **se'nháhtia'k** Cut the branch! and DISTR -hon-: **waha'nhahtià:khon'** he cut the branches. With SRF -ate-, V -kwat- curve, and DLC: **teiote'nhahtakwá:ton** it is a crooked branch, there is a curve in the branch. With V -ont- attach, and DISTR -on-: **io'nhahtón:ton** it has branches.

-'nhehs- N silk, satin: **kà:nhehs** or **kà:nheks** With **ionteniatsterénkstha'** (-niatsteren[k]- tie, fasten hair): **kà:nhehs ionteniatsterénkstha'** ribbon. With V -hren't-/-en't- hang down, and DISTR -onnion-: **io'nhehsen'tónnion atià:tawi** ribbon shirt (-atia'tawi- dress, shirt). With SRF -ate-, V -nia[k]- wrap around the neck, and CAUS -st-: **ionte'nhehsaniáкstha'** necktie. With V -ra'ken- be white: **ka'nhehsarà:ken** white silk or satin. • Ka'nhehsarà:ken wa'khninòn:re' iakoniákstha' enkatia'tawi'tsherón:ni'. I am going to buy white silk to make a wedding dress.

-'nhehs-/-'nehs- N snow crust

With V -her-/-hr- set on top of: **io'nhehsáhere'** there is an icy crust on the snow, **wa'ka'nhehsà:ren'** it formed an icy crust.

NOTE: Some pronounce this root -'nehs-.

Cf. Gannesahre la neige porte (Bruyas: 73); *Gan^cnesáren, Ion^cnesahre* la neige porte (Bruyas: 73); *ionesāhěre* Croute sur la neige (Marcoux: 97)

-'nhehsiio V belong to the Snipe clan: **wake'nhehsí:io** I am Snipe clan.

Cf. rotinesiio la bande de l'allouette (Cuoq: 154); Onondaga *ônêchiô* Alouette (Shea: 19)

-'nhehtien- female: **o'nhéhtien** female animal, **io'nhéhtien** she is a female animal.

Cf. coenheckti a woman (van den Bogaert: 54); *Gannhetien* femme (Bruyas: 74); *Onnhetien* femme (Galissonnière: 40r); *onnhētien* Femelle, *otinnhētien* les; *akonnhētien* Femme (Marcoux: 171); Wendat *onnhetien* femme, femelle (Potier: 450); Wendat *Ondequien* Filles (Sagard: Pa14); Onondaga *onhèchti* Female (Zeisberger: 73); Susquehannock *Achonhœffti* a woman (Holm: 5)

-'nhetska- V be soft: **io'nhétska** it is soft. With INCH -'-: **enio'nhétska'ne'** it will get soft, **wa'o'nhétska'ne'** it got soft. With CAUS -ht-: **enke'nhétskahte'** I will soften it, **waha'nhétskahte'** he softened it.

• Enio'nhétska'ne' ne sewahió:wane'. The apples will get soft.

-'nhi- N rainbow

With V -ot- stand: **iò:nhiote'** (there is) a rainbow.

-'nhien- N stick (used for playing, like a hockey stick): **kà:nhien**
With **tewa'á:raton** (-a'ar- net, curtain, veil): **tewa'á:raton ne kà:nhien** lacrosse stick.

Cf. Kannhi grand baston dont on abbat les nids des tourtes [large stick to knock down the nests of doves] (Bruyas: 74); *Gannien* batte feu (Bruyas: 76); *Kannhia* pointe de flesche (Galissonnière: 42r); *Kānnhiĕn* Baton (Marcoux: 36)

-'nhii- V bark: **ra'nhí:ias** he barks, **wahà:nhiie'** he barked, **ro'nhí:ien** he is barking.
With FACIL -'tskon, easily: **ro'nhiià:tskon** he barks a lot, **io'nhiià:tskon** she or it barks a lot.
NOTE: There are two different, though similar, pronunciations of this root; for the alternative forms, *see* -hnih-/-hnii-.

Cf. Gannien japper (Bruyas: 76); *gan^cnien* Aboyer (Galissonnière: 3); *knīha, waknīien, ēnknĭie* Aboyer (Marcoux: 3); *Kniha, waknīhen, enkīha* aboyer, japper (Cuoq: 24); *a kann hi ie* bark (noise) (Anon: 25)

-'nhonhs- N egg: **o'nhónhsa'**
With V -atken- rot, spoil: **io'nhonhsátkens** the eggs are rotten.
With SRF -ate- and V -hninon- buy: **kate'nhonhsahní:nons** I sell eggs.
With V -ia'k- break, cut in two, and DLC: **teka'nhónhsia'ks** it hatches, incubator, **wa'tka'nhónhsia'ke'** it hatched.
With V -iest- put together, mix, and TRNL: **ia'ke'nhónhsaieste'** I added, mixed in eggs.
With V -o- be in water: **wa'ke'nhónhso'** I boiled eggs.
With V -ri- cook, ripen, and CAUS -ht-: **wa'ke'nhónhsarihte'** I cooked eggs.

With V -rohro[k]- gather, collect: **ke'nhonhsarò:roks** I am gathering, collecting eggs.
With V -takeri'ta['w]-/-keri'ta['w]- fry: **wa'ke'nhonhsakerì:ta'we'** I fried eggs.
With SRF -ani- and unclear V: **wani'nhónhsos** it lays eggs, **onni'nhónhso'** it laid an egg, **ioni'nhónhso** it has laid an egg.

-'nhontst- N dumpling: **o'nhóntsta'**
With V -ohw- put into liquid, and TRNL: **kítkit ieka'nhontstóhon** chicken and dumplings.
With V -onni- make: **ke'nhontstón:ni** I am making dumplings, **wa'ke'nhontstón:ni'** I made dumplings.

-'ni- KIN father, with ATTR ='a/=ha, diminutive: **rake'níha** my father, **ia'níha** your (sg) father, **ro'níha** his or her father, **ronwa'níha** her father, **rákeni** Father!

-'niahrha'te- V snoop, with DLC: **tewake'niahrhà:te'** I am snooping, nosing around, into everything, **teho'niahrhà:te'** he is snooping.
With PART: **Ó: na'teiako'niahrhà:te'** Oh, someone is really snooping!

-'niakatste- V be strict: **ra'niakátste'** he is strict, **ie'niakátste'** she is strict.

-'niaken- V escape
With INCH -'-: **ra'niá:ken's** he runs away, **waha'niá:ken'ne'** he ran away, he took off, escaped, **wa'ka'niá:ken'ne'** it took off (*akitshé:nen* my pet), **ro'niakèn:'en** he has run away.
With BEN -'s-: **wahake'niá:ken'se'** he got away from me, he took off on me.
With CAUS -ht-: **khe'niakénhtha'** I rescue her, I save her,

wahake'niá:kenhte' he rescued me, **khe'niakénhton** I have rescued her. With N -nien'ser- trigger, and INCH -'-: **wa'kanien'sera'niá:ken'ne'** the trigger went off accidentally. With N -wer- wind, air, and BEN -'s-: **wahowera'niá:ken'se'** he farted.

-'nika[ht]- N pillar: **ka'ní:ka** With V -ot- stand: **ka'nikáhtote'** (there is) a pillar, a pier. With V -ont- attach, DISTR -on-, and DLC: **teka'nikahtón:ton** crocodile.

-'nikahtse'n- N laces: **a'nikahtsè:na'** With SRF -ate-, V -ont- attach, and DLC: **tekate'nikahtse'nóntha'** I am putting laces on, I am doing up the laces, **wa'tkate'nikahtse'nón:ten'** I did up the laces. Cf. *hennikatsena* or *nekatsena* [laces] (Ledger: 59, 89); *a ni ka tse na* shoe laces (Anon: 5); *enh nih gah je nah* shoe-lace (Jamieson 2: 10)

-'nikhon- V sew: **ke'níkhons** I am sewing, **enke'níkhon'** I will sew it, **wa'e'níkhon'** she sewed it, **wake'níkhon** I have sewn it. With INSTR -hkw-; and **karón:ware'** (-ronwar-/-nonwar- wire, nail, needle, pin): **ie'nikhónhkhwa' karón:ware'** sewing needle; and **ahserí:ie** (-ahseriie['t]- string, rope, thread): **ie'nikhónhkhwa' ahserí:ie** sewing thread. With REV -kw- and REP: **ske'nikhónkwas** I am taking or picking out the stitches, **enhse'nikhón:ko'** you will pick out the stitches, **sewake'nikhónkwen** I have picked out the stitches. With N -ahsir- blanket, shawl: **ionhsira'níkhons** she is sewing a blanket. With N -ris[er]- socks, and INSTR -hkw-: **ierisera'nikhónhkhwa'** darning needle.

-'nikonhkatste- V have a strong will: **ro'nikonhkátste'** he has a strong will, **iako'nikonhkátste'** she has a strong will.

-'nikonhr- N mind: **o'nikòn:ra'** With V -ahton- disappear: **onke'nikonhráhton'** I fainted. With V -aksen- be bad: **ra'nikonhráksen** he is negative, a negative person; with V -aksen- be bad, and INCH -'-: **wake'nikonhráksen's** I feel bad, I am sad, **onke'nikonhráksen'** or **onke'nikonhráksen'ne'** I got sad; with V -aksen- be bad, and CAUS -'t-: **wahi'nikonhráksa'te'** I hurt his feelings. With SRF -ate-, V -ati-/-onti- lose, throw, and TRNL: **ia'kate'nikonhrón:ti'** I expressed myself. With V -atiront- pull, stretch, and CISL: **tho'nikonhratí:ronte'** he is attracted to it, drawn to it. With SRF -ate- and V -attokha- be smart, knowledgeable: **rate'nikonhrattókha'** he has a bright, a wise mind. With SRF -ate-, and SRF -at- and V -ehiahron- raise a child: **wahate'nikonhratehià:ron'** his mind expanded, he matured. With V -ha[w]-/-enha[w]- hold, bring, take, and TRNL: **iahi'nikonhrénhawe'** I swayed, persuaded him. With V -her-/-hr- set on top of, INCH -'-, and DLC: **wa'thi'nikonhrà:ra'ne'** I got suspicious of him. With V -hnir- be hard, solid: **wake'nikonhrahní:ron** I am strong-willed; and CAUS -t-: **wa'khe'nikonhrahní:rate'** I comforted her. With V -hren't-/-en't- hang down: **wake'nikonhrèn:ton** I am depressed. With SRF -ate- and V -hsa'-/-isa'- finish: **wa'kate'nikonhrísa'** I made up my mind, **wakate'nikonhríson'** I have matured;

with V -hsa'-/-isa'- finish, CAUS -ht-, and CISL: **tonke'nikonhráhsa'ahte'** I am focusing on it.

With N -hwish- burden, effort, V -ihei[on]-/-enhei[on]- die, and DLC: **wa'tke'nikonhrahwishénheie'** my mind got tired.

With SRF -a- and V -ia'k- cut, sever: **wa'on'nikòn:ria'ke'** she gave up.

With V -ienta'- get, obtain: **onke'nikonhraién:ta'ne'** I understood it.

With SRF -ate-, V -iio- be good, nice, and CAUS -hst-: **wakate'nikonhriióhston** I am patient.

With V -kenni- compete, with DLC: **wa'thi'nikonhrakén:ni** I convinced him, I won him over.

With V -ketskw- raise upright: **Ka'nikonhrakétskwen** Condolence; and REP: **saionke'nikonhrakétsko'** she lifted my spirits.

With V -kon[t]- persist, and CISL: **tewake'nikòn:rakonte'** I keep at it, **tio'nikòn:rakonte'** it is continuous; and INSTR -hkw-: **tewake'nikonhrakontáhkwen** I have my mind set on it, I am focused on it.

With V -ksten- be old: **ro'nikonhrakstén:ha** he has an old soul or spirit (can be said of younger persons who are ahead of their years).

With SRF -a-, V -onni- make, and NEG: **iah tewaka'nikonhrón:ni** I didn't mean to, didn't intend to.

With V -ont- attach, INSTR -hkw-, and CAUS -'t-: **iontate'nikonhrontahkwá'tha'** condolence wampum set of fifteen strings.

With V -ori- drive, drive away: **wahake'nikonhró:ri'** he entertained me; and SRF -ate-: **wa'kate'nikonhró:ri'** I got entertained, I had fun.

With SRF -ate-, V -ot- stand, and CISL: **takate'nikonhró:ten'** I made up my mind, I know (what I think, what I'll do).

With SRF -a- and V -o'kt- finish: **ka'nikonhrò:ktha'** I am depressed or discouraged, **io'nikonhrò:kta** it is useless, futile.

With V -r- put in: **ke'nikòn:rare'** I am watching over it, I am careful, **ri'nikòn:rare'** I am watching over him; with CONT -k-: **se'nikòn:rarak** Be careful! with PAST -hkwe: **ke'nikòn:rarahkwe'** I was careful, **khe'nikòn:rarahkwe'** I was watching over her; with SRF -aten- and V -r- put in: **enhiiaten'nikòn:raren'** I will look after him, mind him, **wa'katen'nikòn:raren'** I watched over it, **wahiiaten'nikòn:raren'** I took care of him, minded him, **saten'nikòn:raren** Be careful, take care!

With V -rio-/-riio- beat up, kill: **wahi'nikonhrário'** I changed his mind, I discouraged him, convinced him to not do something.

With V -ronhiaken- suffer: **wake'nikonhraronhiá:ken** my mind is suffering, I am stressed.

With V -tshahni[ht]- be industrious, energetic: **ro'nikonhratshà:ni** he is strong-minded, brave.

With V -tsi'io- be weak, feeble: **wake'nikonhratsi'ió:ha** I have a weak mind, I am cowardly.

NOTE: This root occurs incorporated into many verbs, and not all the inflected forms of some of the N plus V combinations are given here; for the additional forms, see the V entry.

• Ke'nikòn:rare' tóhsa akatáthre'ne'. I am careful not to cut myself. • Wa'kate'nikonhró:ri' wakaten'niota'nónhne'. I had a nice time, I went to a wedding.

-'nikonhrhar- V bother, worry, with DLC: **tekhe'nikonhrháhrha'** or (with SRF -a-) **tekheia'nikonhrháhrha'** I am bothering her, being a pest,

wa'thake'nikonhrhá:ren' or (with SRF -a-) **wa'thakwa'nikonhrhá:ren'** he bothered me.
With SRF -a-: **tewaka'nikónhrhare'** I am worried about it, **teho'nikónhrhare'** he worries, he is troubled, **tóhsa tesa'nikonhrhá:ren** Don't worry!
• Wa'tekhe'nikonhrhá:ren' tsi iontewe-iénstha' ó:ia'k wákhthare'. I'm bothering her while she's studying [and] I'm just talking. • Tewaka'nikónhrhare' raorihwà:ke. I'm worried about him.

-'nikonhrha't- V cheat: **ra'nikonhrhà:tha'** he cheats, he is cheating, **wa'e'nikónhrha'te'** she cheated, **ro'nikonhrhà:ton** he has cheated.
With BEN -enni-/-en-: **rake'nikonhrha'tén:nis** he cheats me, **wahia'nikonhrhà:ten'** he cheated you.

-'nikonhrhen- V forget, with REP: **sewake'nikónhrhens** I forget, **sonke'nikónhrhen'** I forgot, **saho'nikónhrhen'** he forgot, **sewake'nikonhrhèn:'en** I have forgotten.
With FACIL -'tskon, easily: **sewake'nikonhrhèn:tskon** I am forgetful.
With NEG: **iah tesho'nikónhrhens** he doesn't forget.
With N -ia't- body: **sahiia'ta'nikónhrhen'** I forgot him.

-'nikonhroht- V become aware, grow to know, mature: **waho'nikòn:rohte'** he became aware, conscious, got to know as he was growing, matured, **wa'ako'nikòn:rohte'** she became aware.

-'nionhr- N inside of a chimney: **o'niòn:ra'**
With V -atek- burn: **io'nionhratékha'** the inside of the chimney is in flames, **wa'o'niòn:rateke'** the inside of the chimney burned, **onke'niòn:rateke'** I had a fire in my chimney.
With V -awehrho- cover, close off: **wa'ke'nionhrawéhrhon'** I closed the damper to the chimney, **waha'nionhrawéhrhon'** he closed the chimney damper.
With V -kahront- make an opening, a hole: **io'nionhrakà:ronte'** there is a hole in the chimney.

-'nionhs- N nose: **o'niónhsa'**
POSS: **ke'nionhsà:ke** (on) my nose, **ra'nionhsà:ke** (on) his nose, **ie'nionhsà:ke** (on) her nose.
With REP: **ska'niónhsa'** moose.

-'nionkha- V get a nosebleed, with DLC: **wa'tke'niónkha'** I got a nosebleed, **wa'tha'niónkha'** he got a nosebleed, **wa'tie'niónkha'** her nose bled, **teho'nionkhà:'on** his nose is bleeding, **teiako'nionkhà:'on** she has a nosebleed.

-'nionkot- V turned-up nose: **ra'nión:kote'** he has a turned-up nose, **ie'nión:kote'** she has a turned-up nose.

-'nionkser- N onion: **o'niónkseri**
With V -hriht- break into pieces, smash, and DLC: **wa'tha'nionkserà:rihte'** he cut up onions.
With V -ke- amount to, and DLC: **teka'nionkserá:ke** two onions.
With V -kenser[on]- plane, slice, and DLC: **wa'tha'nionkserakén:sere'** he sliced onions.
With V -takeri'ta['w]-/-keri'ta['w]- fry: **wa'ke'nionkserakerì:ta'we'** I fried onions.
NOTE: The form **o'nónkseri** has also been reported, which looks like it may include **à:nonk** (from **a'nonk**), a word not used much in Kahnawà:ke nowadays, but it

does occur in some of the sources cited below.

Cf. ānonk, dans la compos. anōnksĕra oignon (Marcoux: 269); *anonk* oignon, ciboule, ciboulette (Cuoq: 2); *Ononkseri* [onions] (Onkweonwe: 4); *o nonk se ri* onions (D'Ailleboust); *ononkseri* onions (Cory: 14); *a nonhk* Onions (Jamieson 2: 3); *o'niónkseri/à:non* onion (Mithun 1977: 56); *o'niónkseri* onion (Lazore: 13); *O'niónkseri* Onions (Horne: 34); Oneida *á:nuk* (Michelson and Doxtator: 319)

-'nionkwarist- N snout: **o'nionkwarísta'**
POSS: **ra'nionkwaristà:ke** (on) his snout.
With V -es- be long: **ra'nionkwarístes** he has a long snout.

-'nionkwek- V blocked nose, with DLC: **tewake'nión:kweks** my nose is blocked, stuffed up, **wa'tho'nión:kweke'** he got a blocked, stuffy nose.
NOTE: This stem includes -kwek- shut, close off.

-'niosken'- V err, make a mistake, with DLC: **teke'niósken's** I make mistakes, **wa'tha'niósken'ne'** he erred, he made a mistake, **tewake'nioskèn:'en** I am making a mistake.

-'niskw- V be late: **enwake'nísko'** I will be late, **onke'nísko'** I was late, **waho'nísko'** he was late.
With PROG -hatie-: **wake'nisko'onhátie'** I am late, **ro'nisko'onhátie'** he is late, **iako'nisko'onhátie'** she is late.
With SRF -aten- and CAUS -ht-: **katen'niskwáhtha'** I am taking my time, **wa'katen'nískwahte'** I took my time.
• Enwake'nísko' iá:kewe' tsi sanónhsote'. I will be late arriving at your house.

-'nisohkw- N youngest member of a family, baby of a family: **o'nisóhkwa'**
POSS: **ake'nisóhkwa'** my youngest child.

Cf. Onisokwa le dernier enfant d'une famille (Cuoq: 34)

-'nist- N stem (of a plant, an apple), bow, rivet: **o'nísta'**
With V -ia'k- cut, sever: **wa'ke'nístia'ke'** I cut the stem.
With V -kwatho- hem, and DLC: **tehati'nistakwáthos** they are riveting, putting in rivets, **tenhati'nistakwátho'** they will put in rivets, **wa'tha'nistakwátho'** he put in rivets.
With V -ont- attach: **io'nístonte'** straight pins.
With V -ot- stand, and DLC: **teka'nístote'** it has a bow on it, a rivet in it (for example, a jeans' pocket), and SRF -ate-: **wa'tkate'nistó:ten'** I made a bow.

Cf. *Gannistigarʒt* faire un boucle (Bruyas: 79)

-'nistaka't- V tickle, with DLC: **tewake'nistakà:tha'** I am ticklish, **tehi'nistakà:tha'** I am tickling him, **wa'thake'nístaka'te'** he tickled me.

-'nisten- KIN mother, with ATTR ='a/=ha, diminutive: **ake'nisténha** my mother, **sa'nisténha** your (sg) mother, **ro'nisténha** his mother, **o'nisténha** her mother, **roti'nisténha** their mother, **istèn:'a** my mother, my auntie, **istá:** Mother!
With NMZR -hser- and **iotiianéhshon** (-iane[r]- be titled) or **ionateríhonte'** (-rihw- matter, message, -ont- attach): **iotiianéhshon ka'nisténhsera'** or **ka'nisténhsera' ionateríhonte'** clan mothers.

-'nonhkw- N bottom of something, bread end: **o'nónhkwa'**

With LOC -'ke, on, at: **ka'nonhkwà:ke** at the bottom of it.

With SRF -ate-, V -atsha'- burn, and CAUS -ht-: **wa'kate'nonhkwátsha'ahte'** I burned the bottom of it.

With V -a'sen's-/-en's- drop unintentionally, and DLC: **wa'tewake'nónhkwen'se'** my pants fell down.

With V -hnir- be hard, solid; and **anòn:warore'** (-nonhwar- brain, -'rhoro[k]-/-oro[k]- cover): **io'nonhkwahní:ron anòn:warore'** top hat.

With V -ien- put down, have, and CISL: **tka'nónhkwaien'** it has a bottom (for example, a basket or a pie).

With V -na'nawen-/-nawen- be wet: **io'nonhkwaná:wen** the bottom is wet or soggy.

With V -ra'nentak-/-nentak- stick to, and CISL: **taio'nonhkwanén:take'** it got stuck to the bottom, **tio'nonhkwanentá:kon** something is stuck or caked on the bottom.
• Taio'nonhkwanén:take' iah tha'tewakawénrie'. It's stuck on the bottom (of the pot), I didn't stir it.

Cf. onōnkwa le fond d'une chaudière (Marcoux: 177); *Ononkwa* fond d'une chaudière (Cuoq: 34)

-'nonhr-/-'nionhr-/-'nhonhr-/-non'onhr- N armpit, with LOC -okon, under: **ke'nonhró:kon** or **ke'nionhró:kon** or **ke'nhonhró:kon** or **kenon'onhró:kon** my armpit, **ra'nionhró:kon** his armpit, **ie'nionhró:kon** her armpit.
NOTE: There is a lot of speaker variation in the pronunciation of this root.

-'nonn- N white ash splints for making baskets: **o'nón:na'**

With SRF -ate-, and CISL: **tiakote'nón:na'** she has a hoop on (under her dress).

Cf. Onnonna bois dont on fait les mannes (Bruyas: 34)

-'nosera- V be scabby: **wake'nóseras** I am scabby.

Cf. Onnꞷsera Galle (Galissonnière: 49r); *onōsĕra* gale (Marcoux: 187); *Onosera* Gale (Cuoq: 35)

-'nosha- V become envious: **ra'nóshas** he is (always) envious, **ri'nóshas** I envy him, **enke'nósha'** I will become envious, **enkhe'nósha'** I will become envious of her, **wa'ke'nósha'** I became envious, **wahi'nósha'** I became envious of him, **wake'nóshen** I am envious, an envious or jealous type of person, **ro'nóshen** he is envious, **iako'nóshen** she is envious.
With NMZR -htsher-: **ka'nosháhtshera'** envy.

-'notst- N nakedness: **o'nótsta'** (used, for example, for a chicken or pig after it has been cleaned and all the hair removed, or a newborn kitten or rabbit that has no fur)
With ATTR =kowa, great: **o'notsta'kó:wa** elephant.

With V -her-/-hr- set on top of: **ra'notstáhere'** he is sitting there naked, **ie'notstáhere'** she is sitting there naked.
With V -ot- stand: **ke'nótstote'** I am naked, **ra'nótstote'** he is naked, **ie'nótstote'** she is naked; and PROG -atie-: **ke'notstotátie'** I am (going along) naked, **ra'notstotátie'** he is (going along) naked, **ie'notstotátie'** she is (going along) naked; with SRF -ate- and V -ot- stand: **wa'kate'notstó:ten'** I got naked.

-'now- N hump, padlock, beetle, ladybug, fiddle, guitar, violin: **o'nó:wa'**

With V -hren't-/-en't- hang down:
io'nowèn:ton there is a lock hanging.
With V -hriht- break into pieces, smash,
and DLC: **wa'tke'nowà:rihte'** I broke,
smashed the padlock.
With V -iahia'k-/-iia'k- cross over, and
DLC: **tewake'nowiià:kon** I am a hunchback, **teho'nowiià:kon** he is a hunchback,
teiako'nowiià:kon she is a hunchback.
With V -ien- put down, have:
ke'nó:waien' I am crouched down; and
SRF -ate-: **wahate'nó:waien'** he crouched
down.
With V -kha- attach, piece together, and
DLC; and **kanà:taro** (-na'tar[o][k]- bread):
teio'nowákhen kanà:taro crusty bread.
With V -kwaront- bulge, lump:
io'nowakwá:ronte' camel.
With V -niiont- hang, suspend:
wa'ke'nowaniión:ten' I locked it,
se'nowaniión:ten Lock it! *This is an
older expression.*
With SRF -ate- and V -onni- make:
rote'noión:ni he is hunched over,
iakote'noión:ni she is hunched over.
With (possibly) V -r- put in: **a'nó:wara**
turtle; the suit of spades in cards; and
raó:ris (-ris[er]- socks):
a'nó:wara raó:ris pitcher plant.
With V -ra'nentak-/-nentak- stick to:
io'nowanentá:kon lock (on a door).
With V -ta'-/-eta'- put inside:
wa'ke'nowáta' I put in (installed) a lock,
ro'nowáten' he has put in a lock.

Cf. "The Mohawk Indians are divided
into three tribes, which are called *Ochkari,
Anaware, Oknaho*, that is the Bear, the
Turtle and the Wolf." (Megapolensis:
178); *Tioton niasendage ennosarane* la
famille de la tortue a 9 voix (Bruyas: 64);
"*Hannoouara*, that is ... the [Great] Turtle"
(Lafitau I: 291); Stamm der Schildkrote
Anowaragóa (Pyrlaeus: 238); "The Tribe

Anowara, the great Tortoise, the most
noble." (Ettwein in Wheeler-Voegelin:
49); *Onowa* poulie, cadenas, écaille de
tortue, courbure du dos, et en général tout
ce qui s'arrondit en bosse (Cuoq: 35);
a-no-wa-ra ra-o-ris Sarracenia purpurea
[purple pitcher plant, turtle socks] (Rousseau: 43); *a'nó:wara raotí:ris* turtle socks,
pitcher plant (Lazore: 80)

-'onwar- N seedling: **o'ón:wara'**
With V -ien- put down, have:
wa'ke'onwará:ien' I started the seedling.

-'rhenienht-/-ienenht- V knock over, knock
down: **ke'rheniénhtha'** I am knocking
them over (for example, the fence poles),
waha'rhé:nienhte' he knocked them
over, **ro'rheniénhton** he has knocked
them over.
With N -ia't- body: **wahatia'tié:nenhte'**
he knocked me down,
wa'kheia'tié:nenhte' I knocked her
down.
NOTE: This stem is composed of a root
-'rhenien-/-ienen-, which occurs only with
suffixes, and CAUS -ht-.

-'rhenien'-/-ienen'- V fall down:
ka'rhé:nien's it falls down,
wa'ka'rhé:nien'ne' it fell down,
io'rhenièn:'en it has fallen down.
With N -hiohs- elbow, and DLC:
wa'tekhiohsié:nen'ne' I am so tired,
just worn out, worn down,
wa'thahiohsié:nen'ne' he is worn out,
wa'tiehiohsié:nen'ne' she is worn out.
With N -ia't- body: **tia'tié:nen's** I fall
down, **raia'tié:nen's** he falls down,
kaia'tié:nen's she or it falls down,
wa'tia'tié:nen'ne' I fell down or over,
watia'tienèn:'en I have fallen down.
With N -nawa'aht- post, pole:

wa'kanawa'ahtié:nen'ne' the pole, post fell down.
With N -ront- log, beam:
wa'karontié:nen'ne' he passed, he died.
This is an older expression.
With N -serenht- sleep: **keserenhtié:nen's** I am nodding off to sleep,
wahaserenhtié:nen'ne' he nodded off to sleep.
NOTE: This stem is composed of a root -'rhenien-/-ienen-, which occurs only with suffixes, and INCH -'-.

-'rheniohkot- V be a shrub: **io'rhenióhkote'** (it is) a shrub.

-'rhiotsh- N chin: **o'rhiótsha'**
POSS: **ke'rhiotshà:ke** (on) my chin,
ra'rhiotshà:ke (on) his chin,
ie'rhiotshà:ke (on) her chin.
With V -ia'[k]- hit, slap:
wahake'rhiotsháia'ke' he hit me in the chin.
With V -ienht- hit against, and TRNL:
iahonke'rhiótshaienhte' I banged my chin.
With V -kahront- make an opening, a hole:
ro'rhiotshakà:ronte' he has a dimple in his chin.

-'rhoro[k]-/-oro[k]- V cover: **ke'rhó:roks** I cover it, **enke'rhó:roke'** I will cover it,
wa'ke'rhó:roke' I covered it,
wahi'rhó:roke' I covered him,
wahshako'rhó:roke' he covered her,
ro'rhó:ron he has covered it, **ka'rhó:ron** it is covered.
With SRF -ate-: **wa'kate'rhó:roke'** I covered myself.
With REV -hsi-: **wahshako'rhorókhsi'** he uncovered her; and SRF -ate-:
wa'kate'rhorókhsi' I uncovered myself.
With N -atekhwahra- table, NMZR -'tsher-,

and CAUS -st-:
iontekhwahra'tsherorókstha' tablecloth.
With V -atkon'ser- use as a pillow or cushion, NMZR -htsher-, and CAUS -st-:
iontkon'serahtsherorókstha' pillow case.
With SRF -at-, N -ia't- body, and CAUS -st-:
watia'torókstha' envelope.
With N -ihn- skin, leather: **ohnó:ron** penis.
With SRF -at- and N -konwar- falseface, face: **iakotkonwaró:ron** she has on a mask; and CAUS -st-:
iontkonwarorókstha' Hallowe'en mask.
With N -nehw- animal skin, hide:
kanehó:ron or **onehó:ron** water drum; also Skin Dance, one of the four sacred ceremonies of the Haudenosaunee.
With N -ni- snow: **onkenió:roke'** I got snowed in, **ionkwanió:ron** we are snowed in.
With N -nonhs- house: **kanonhsó:ron** there's a cover (roof, shingles) on the house; and REP: **ó:ia' sahanonhsó:roke'** he covered the house, put on a new roof or shingles.
With SRF -a- and N -nonhwar- brain:
wa'kanonhwaró:roke' I put a hat on,
wa'kheianonhwaró:roke' I put a hat on her, **wakanonhwaró:ron** I have a hat on; **anòn:warore'** hat; and REV -hsi-:
wa'kanonhwarorókhsi' I took off my hat.
With SRF -ate- and N -non'onhr- sod, turf, hair (scalp): **rotenon'onhró:ron** he has on a wig, **iakotenon'onhró:ron** she has on a wig; and CAUS -st-:
iontenon'onhrorókstha' wig.
With N -ronhi- sky, heaven:
wa'karonhió:roke' it got cloudy, overcast, **ioronhió:ron** it is cloudy, overcast.
With SRF -at- and N -tsiser- pane of glass:

iottsiseró:ron there is a film on it; and
rakahrà:ke (-kahr- eye): **iottsiseró:ron**
rakahrà:ke he has cataracts.

-'rhotsher- N string bean: **o'rhótsheri**
With **ienakarótha'** (-nakar- stick):
ienakarótha' o'rhótsheri pole bean.
With V -kw- pick: **ke'rhotsherákwas**
I am picking beans, **wa'ke'rhotsherá:ko'**
I picked beans.

Cf. Orhotsera la gousse des fezoles
(Bruyas: 90); *orhotsera* Gousse (Galissonnière: 46r); *orhōsĕra* cosse, gousse
de feves (Marcoux: 191); *Orhotsera*
cosse, gousse de pois, de fèves (Cuoq:
35); *o'rhótsheri* green beans/wax beans
(Horne: 34)

-'ser- stack. *See* -ia'ser-/-'ser-

-'sere-/-i'sere- V drag: **kè:sere'** I am
dragging it, **enkè:sere'** I will drag it,
wahà:sere' he dragged it, **rà:sere's** he is
dragging it around.
With SRF -ate-: **ratè:sere'** he is crawling,
wa'ontè:sere' she crawled, **ratè:sere's**
he is crawling around.
With N -ahsir- blanket, shawl:
ionhsirì:sere' she is dragging the blanket.
With SRF -ar-, N -ahsi't- foot, and DLC:
teionrahsi'tì:sere's she is dragging her
feet, **wa'tkarahsi'tì:sere'** I dragged my
feet.
With N -honw[ei]- boat, and DISTR
-hshon-: **onkhonwi'seréhshon'** I am
riding around (in a car); with SRF -at-,
N -honw[ei]- boat, CAUS -ht-, and PURP
-'n-: **wa'kathonwi'serehtà:ne'** I am
going for a car ride.
With SRF -ate- and N -(h)nhoh- door:
watehnhohì:sere's the door is scraping
(the floor, because the floor is uneven, or
the door has shifted).

With N -nonhs- house: **kanonhsì:sere'**
cutter, a sleigh with a flatbed; snail.
With SRF -ate-, N -ren't- leg from hip to
knee, and DLC: **tehateren'tì:sere's** he is
dragging himself (without using his legs,
maybe through the grass),
wa'tionteren'tì:sere' she dragged herself.
With N -rist- iron, steel: **raristì:sere's**
surveyor.
With SRF -ate- and N -'nenhar- grape:
wate'nenharì:sere' vines are travelling
or going along on the ground.
With CAUS -ht-, *see* -'sere[ht]- vehicle, car.

-'sere[ht]- N vehicle, car: **kà:sere**
POSS: **akè:sere** my car, **raò:sere** his car,
akò:sere her car.
With **onerahóntsha'** (-nerahontsh- wing,
shoulder blade): **kà:sere onerahóntsha'**
car fender.
With SRF -ate-, V -ahkwatase-/-tase- go
around, and TRNL: **ia'kate'serehtatá:se'**
I went around the car.
With V -akaion-/-kaion- be old, and INCH
-'-: **wa'ka'serehtaká:ion'ne'** the car got
old, **io'serehtakaiòn:'on** (it is) an old car.
With SRF -ate- and V (otherwise unknown)
-akatenien-: **onkwate'serehtakaténien'** I
got carsick.
With V -atek- burn: **io'serehtatékha'** the
car is burning; and SRF -ate- and CAUS -'t-:
ronte'serehtatekà:tha' they set fire to the
cars.
With V -haratat-/-karatat- lift, raise up:
ro'serehtakaratá:ton he has raised up the
car.
With V -hninon- buy, and PURP -hr-:
ke'serehtahninòn:re' I am going to buy
a car.
With V -hnhonter- attach end-to-end, add
on, and DLC: **teka'serehtahnhón:tere'**
the cars are hooked together; and SRF -ate-:
tewate'serehtahnhontéhrha' double-

runner sleigh with front and back hooked together, a trailer.

With V -hseronni- dress, prepare: **ra'serehtahserón:ni** mechanic; and CAUS -'t-: **ie'serehtahseronnià:tha'** garage (for repairing cars).

With SRF -ate- and V -ien- put down, have: **wa'kate'seréhtaien'** I parked the car; with V -ien- put down, have, and INSTR -hkw-: **ie'serehtaientáhkhwa'** parking garage.

With V -ienta'- get, obtain, and REP: **ó:ia' sonke'serehtaién:ta'ne'** I got a car again, I got another car.

With SRF -ate- and V -kahrhatho- turn over: **onkwate'serehtakahrhátho'** I flipped over in or on my vehicle (in my car, on my bike).

With V -ka'te- have many: **ro'serehtakà:te'** he has a lot of cars; and SRF -ate- **iote'serehtakà:te'** there are a lot of cars.

With V -kste- be heavy: **io'serehtákste'** freight train.

With V -nenhskw- steal: **wahi'serehtanénhsko'** I stole a car from him, I stole his car.

With V -ni[h]- lend: **wa'khe'seréhtani'** I lent her my car.

With V -noron- be expensive, precious: **ka'serehtanó:ron** it is an expensive car.

With SRF -ate-, and SRF -ate-, V -re- extent, distance, and PART and DLC: **tsi na'tetiate'serehtátere'** it is between the cars.

With V -'ka[ht]- be fast-moving, and DLC: **teio'serehtà:ka** passenger train.

-'shatst[e]- V be strong: **ke'shátste'** I am strong, **ra'shátste'** he is strong, **ie'shátste'** she is strong, **ka'shátste'** it is strong; **ro'shátste'** he charges a lot for it. With NEG: **iah sò:tsi teho'shátste'** he doesn't charge a lot.

With NEG and REP: **iah teske'shátste'** I am not strong anymore.

With CONT -k-: **enke'shátsteke'** I will be strong.

With INCH -en'-: **waha'shátsten'ne'** he got strong.

With NMZR -enhser-: **ka'shatsténhsera'** strength.

With NMZR -enhser-, V -a- be a size, and PART: **tsi nike'shatsténhsera'** all my might, **tsi niha'shatsténhsera'** all his might.

With NMZR -enhser- and V -ien- put down, have: **wake'shatstenhserá:ien'** I have strength or energy; and NEG: **iah tewake'shatstenhserá:ien'** I have no strength or energy.

With N -rahkw- sun: **karahkwa'shátste'** the sun is strong.

With N -wenn- voice, word: **kewenna'shátste'** I mean what I say, **rawenna'shátste'** he means what he says, **iewenna'shátste'** she means what she says.

-'shenn- N aim

With V -aksen- be bad: **ra'shennáksen** he has a bad aim.

With V -iio- be good, nice: **ra'shenní:io** he has a good aim.

With SRF -ate-, V -kenni- compete, and TRNL and DLC: **ia'thate'shennakén:ni'** he aimed for it.

-'shenni- V defeat, triumph over: **khe'shénnie's** I defeat her, **wahi'shén:ni'** I defeated him, **wahshako'shén:ni'** he defeated her.

-'shennia't- V throw

With SRF -ate-, TRNL and DLC: **ia'tekate'shennià:tha'** I throw it, **ia'tkate'shénnia'te'** I threw it, **ia'tehote'shennià:ton** he has thrown it.

-'skoht- V put someone in water, drown someone: **wahshakò:skohte'** he drowned her or them.

NOTE: This stem is composed of an empty noun -'sk-, -o- be in water, and CAUS -ht-.

-'skohw- V get into water, dunk oneself With SRF -ate- and TRNL: **iekatè:skohs** I get into water, **ienkatè:skohwe'** I will go into the water, **ia'katè:skohwe'** I went into the water, **iewakate'skóhon** I have gotten into the water.

NOTE: This stem is composed of an empty noun -'sk-, -o- be in water, and CAUS -hw-.

-'skonw- N roasted meat: **o'skón:wa'**

NOTE: A variant of this root probably occurs in -ate'skont- roast bake. Otherwise the root is attested only in Seneca *ga'sgö:wö'* roast meat (Chafe, English-Seneca Dictionary: 139)

-'sko'- V drown: **wahà:sko'ne'** he drowned, **roskò:'on** he has drowned.

NOTE: This stem is composed of an empty noun -'sk-, -o- be in water, and INCH -'-.

-'tehkar- N skin and bones: **o'téhkara'**
• Nek o'téhkara' tsi niiotí:wen. She is so skinny she is just skin and bones.

-'tenn- N bottom part of a tree, butt: **o'tén:na'**
Cf. o ten na trunk (Anon: 18)

-'tsha'- V beat at, defeat, with DLC: **teionkè:tsha's** she beats me at something, **wa'tewakè:tsha'** it beat me, it defeated me, **wa'thakè:tsha'** he beat me, **teionkè:tshon'** she has beaten me.
With CONTR: **iah tha'tehakè:tshon'** he didn't beat me.
With SRF -aten-: **tehatèn:tsha's** he is earning, **wa'tkatèn:tsha'** I earned, I won, I profited, **tewakatèn:tshon'** I have earned, I have won; and PROG -hatie-: **tehoten'tshon'onhátie'** he is making money, he is earning.

-'tskon FACIL, easily. For example: **wakatshennonnià:tskon** I become happy easily.

-'tson- be dirty. *See* -i'tson-/-'tson-

-'wahr- N meat: **o'wà:ron'**
With V -a[t]- be inside, and CISL: **tka'wà:ra** meat pie(s).
With V -awe'ehst- pierce, INSTR -hkw-, and DLC: **teie'wahrawe'ehstáhkhwa'** meat fork.
With V -hio'tsis[t]- be salty, sour, and DLC: **teio'wahrahiò:tsis** salt pork.
With V -hriht- break into pieces, smash, and DLC: **teka'wahrahríhton** hash meat.
With V -kenser[on]- plane, slice, and DLC: **wa'tha'wahrakén:sere'** he sliced meat.
With V -kwe'tar[on]-/-e'tar[on]- cut, slice off a piece or chunk: **ke'wahrakwè:tarons** I am cutting meat into slices, **wa'ke'wahrakwè:tare'** I cut or sliced meat.
With V -r- put in: **io'wà:rare'** it is fleshy or meaty, **é:so io'wà:rare'** there is a lot of meat on it.
With V -takeri'ta['w]-/-keri'ta['w]- fry: **enke'wahrakerì:ta'we'** I will fry meat, **wa'ke'wahrakerì:ta'we'** I fried meat, **wake'wahrakerì:ta** I am frying meat, **ka'wahrakerì:ta** fried meat.

-'wahst- N little stick, peg: **ò:wahste'**
With **ionteka'táhkhwa'** (-atek- burn): **ionteka'táhkhwa' ò:wahste'** match-sticks.
With V -ohro[k]- insert: **wa'ke'wahstò:roke'** I inserted the little

stick or peg (maybe to keep the door shut), **se'wahstò:rok** Insert the little stick!
With V -ot- stand, and DISTR -onnion-: **wa'ke'wahstotónnion'** I fastened the pegs (clothes pegs); with V -ot- stand, and INSTR -hkw-: **ie'wahstotáhkhwa'** clothes peg.

-'watsist- N rough, outer bark: **o'wá:tsiste'**
With V -a'senht-/-enht- drop: **wa'ke'watsístenhte'** I took the bark off, **se'watsístenht** Take the bark off!
With V -r- put in: **io'watsístare'** there is bark.

-'whahs- N skirt: **o'wháhsa'**
POSS: **ake'wháhsa'** my skirt, **ako'wháhsa'** her skirt.
With V -awenren- outgrow, and DLC: **wa'tewake'whahsawén:ren'** I outgrew the skirt.
With V -ohro[k]- insert: **wa'khe'whahsò:roke'** I put a skirt on her; and SRF -ate-: **wa'kate'whahsò:roke'** I put a skirt on, **wakate'whahsò:ron** I have a skirt on, **sate'whahsò:rok** Put a skirt on!

With V -ot- stand, and TRNL and DLC: **ia'teka'wháhsote'** it goes right to the point (*more literally,* the bed skirt goes right to the floor).
• Ia'teka'wháhsote' nahò:ten' rotihtharáhkwen. They get right to the point of what they are saying.

-'whar- N tunnel, hollow: **o'whá:ra'**
With LOC -atatie' along, edge of: **ka'wharatátie'** hallway.
With LOC -kon, inside: **o'whá:rakon** in the tunnel.
With LOC -okon, under: **o'wharó:kon** under, through the tunnel.
With V -es- be long, tall: **ka'whá:res** (it is) a long hall.
With V -kahront- make an opening, a hole: **tsi io'wharakà:ronte'** at the tunnel (in Kahnawà:ke).
With V -ot- stand: **io'whá:rote'** hollow (in a tree); and PROG -atie-: **io'wharotátie'** it is hollow all along.
• O'wharó:kon wa'tkatóhetste'. I passed through the tunnel.

ENGLISH-KANIEN'KÉHA DICTIONARY

The entries in this English-Kanien'kéha dictionary consist of a compilation of the English words used to translate the Kanien'kéha roots, stems, and words in the Kanien'kéha-English side. When an English word is expressed in Kanien'kéha by a root or stem, the entry includes a few inflected forms of the root or stem and, in some cases, examples of productive derivations. These are just representative forms that show which paradigms the Kanien'kéha noun or verb belongs to—primarily the stem class and aspect conjugation. Thus this English-Kanien'kéha side is not the "reverse" of the Kanien'kéha-English dictionary since it does not include all the Kanien'kéha words that are given there, such as additional pro-nominal inflections, forms with one or more prepronominal prefixes, and more forms with derivational endings and incorporated nouns.

Each entry in the English-Kanien'kéha dictionary has an English word at the head, followed by one or more Kanien'kéha words and the Kanien'kéha root in parentheses. If an English meaning is conveyed in Kanien'kéha by a verb with an incorporated noun, both the component verb and noun roots are given at the end of the entry. If no root is given, that means that the word has no structure, or the structure is unknown or uncertain.

When the English entry is a noun in Kanien'kéha, the basic noun form is listed after the English word. For body parts, a possessed form is also given since body parts infrequently occur in isolation. For example, the entry for 'ankle' lists the basic form **ohsinekò:ta'** and the possessed form **khsineko'tà:ke** '(on) my ankle'. (The Kanien'kéha side also gives the possessed forms **rahsineko'tà:ke** '(on) his ankle', **iehsineko'tà:ke** '(on) her ankle', and the incorporation **wa'katshineko'tatáhko'** 'I sprained my ankle'.)

Terms for natural or growing things as well as geological formations more often than not are incorporated into positional or locative verbs such as -ot- 'stand' or -ien- 'put down', and these incorporated forms are included with the stand-alone noun form. For example, the entry for 'snow' gives **óniehte'** 'snow' and **kaniéhtaien'** 'there is snow (on the ground)', and the entry for 'sun' gives **karáhkwa'** 'sun' and **ioráhkote'** 'the sun is shining'. Descriptions concerning the body are often expressed with positional or locative verbs too, for example, **ra'nótstote'** 'he is naked' from **o'nótsta'** 'nakedness'.

English entries that correspond to verbs in Kanien'kéha are a bit more complicated. Which Kanien'kéha forms are given depends on the meaning—whether the meaning has to do with a condition or quality, or rather describes an event or something that happens. Roughly speaking, the distinction is between Kanien'kéha verbs that occur only in the stative aspect (state verbs) and verbs that occur in the habitual and punctual aspects as well as the stative.

If the meaning of the verb has to do with a condition or quality of humans or animals and the verb is a state verb, the first person ('I'), third person masculine ('he'), and feminine ('she') forms are usually given. If the condition applies to an inanimate object, just the 'it' form is given. In addition, sometimes a form that expresses inchoative meaning (that the state came about) or causative meaning (that the state is brought about by an agent) is given as well. For example, the entry for 'shiny' gives the stative form **teiohstaráthe'** 'it is shiny' and also an inchoative example, **wa'tiohstaráthe'ne'** 'it got shiny', and a causative, **wa'tekhstaráthe'te'** 'I shined it'.

Typically, if the meaning of the verb describes an event (an activity or action), at least one form in each of the three basic aspects (habitual, punctual, stative) is given *if the verb root regularly occurs in each of the aspects*. Language learners who are used to seeing verbs inflected in each of the three aspect categories will find many entries lack one of the expected forms. As it turns out, it seems the meaning of some verbs is not compatible or natural with all the aspects. Derived stems—verb roots with an incorporated noun or with a derivational suffix—are typically given with just one or two aspect inflections since additional ones can be regularly created by learning the aspect inflections of the component roots or derivational endings.

When an English verb has both intransitive and transitive uses and equivalent forms exist in Kanien'kéha, an example of each use (intransitive and transitive) is given. For example, the entry for 'ask' includes both **wa'keri'wanón:ton'** 'I asked a question' and **wahiri'wanón:tonhse'** 'I asked him a question' (in this case the form that corresponds to a transitive verb in English has the benefactive suffix but that is not always the case). Nominalized forms of verbs are also included; an example is **karonhiakénhsera'** 'suffering, agony', derived from the verb meaning 'suffer', as in **wakeronhiá:ken** 'I am suffering, in agony'.

As a final note, we ask that readers think about the challenges of translating Kanien'-kéha words into English and likewise English words into Kanien'kéha. Context matters—depending on the context (or the speaker) different Kanien'kéha words may be used. "Translation" suggests an exact one-to-one match between languages, but so often a translation is approximate rather than exact. Finding the most apt translation(s) was one of the biggest challenges for us.

Abbreviations:
s.o. = someone; s.t. = something

abandon: **wahiiatewén:tehte'** I left him (my spouse), **shakotewentéhton** he has abandoned them (-atewenteht-)

Abenakis; Eastern Seaboard Indians: **ronatshá:kanen** (-atshakan-)

able: **kkwénie's** I am able to do, **enkkwé:ni'** I will be able to, I can do it, **wa'kkwé:ni'** I was able, **wakkwénion** I am able, I can (-kweni-)

above: **è:neken**

accomplish: *See* useful; get things done

accordion: **teie'nerohkwatiróntha'** (-'nerohkw-, -atiront-)

accuse; blame: **rakerihwáhrhos** he is accusing me, blaming me, **wahakerihwáhrho'** he accused me, blamed me (-rihw-, -(h)rho-)

ache: *See* hurt; ache

Achilles tendon: **o'kó:tara'** Achilles tendon, **ka'kotarà:ke** my Achilles tendon (-a'kotar-)

acquainted: **wa'konientéhrha'ne'** I made your acquaintance, I got to know you (-ientehrha'-)

acquire: **watién:ta's** I obtain it, **ontién:ta'ne'** I got it, **watientà:'on** I have gotten it (-ienta'-)

across: **tekà:ronhwe'** it is put, angled across (-hronhw-); **wa'tekhróho'** I put something across, I put up a barrier, **tekahróho** it is put across, it is in the way (-hroh[o]-)

act; perform: **tekatierónnions** I am playing a part (in a play), I am performing, **wa'thatierónnion'** he acted, he performed (-ieron-)

active: **roià:tate'** he is hyperactive, always moving, never sits still, **iakoià:tate'** she is hyperactive (-ia't-, -te[ht]-)

active; energetic: **roia'tatshà:ni** he is active, energetic, **iakoia'tatshà:ni** she is active, energetic (-ia't-, -tshahni[ht]-)

Adam's apple; core: **ohà:ta'** (-ha't-)

add extra: **kawénhtats** I add the difference, **wa'kawénhtate'** I added more to it, **wakawenhtá:ton** I have added more to it (-awenht[e]-)

add liquid: **wa'késerahwe'** I added liquid, water, broth to it (-sera[hw]-/-osera[hw]-)

adept; useful; helpful: **ratón:ron** he is useful, helpful, **iontón:ron** she is useful, helpful (-atonron-)

adopt: **wa'katewirará:ko'** I adopted a child (-wir-, -r-)

affection, show affection: **tehakwahrhò:tons** he shows me affection, **wa'thiiahrhò:ton'** I showed him affection, **tehakwahrho'tón:ni** he is showing me affection (-ahrho'ton-)

afraid: *See* scared

after, not long after: **ken' náhe'**

again: **á:re'**

age: **Tó: na'tesohseriià:kon?** How old are you? (-ohser-, -iahia'k-/-iia'k-)

agenda; issue: **karihwáhere'** (-rihw-, -her-/-hr-)

agony: *See* suffer

agree to: *See* consent

agree to: **wa'erihwaié:na'** she agreed to it (-rihw-, -iena-)

agree with: **wa'erihwanòn:we'ne'** she agreed with it (-rihw-, -nonhwe'-)

agree with (food): **iah tha'teiontiatenrò:'on** it didn't agree with me (-atenro-)

ahead; in front: **ohén:ton** (-henton-)

ahead, go ahead: **khén:te'** I am ahead, **waháhente'** he went ahead, **wakhén:ton** I have gone ahead, **rahentéhtha'** he puts it in front, ahead, **wa'khén:tehte'** I put it ahead, I advanced it (-hente-)

Ahkwesáhsne Kanien'kehá:ka (Mohawk) Nation at Ahkwesáhsne (-ahkwesen-)

aim: **ia'thate'shennakén:ni'** he aimed for it (-'shenn-, -kenni-)

air; wind: **ówera'** (-wer-)

air, get knocked out: **onkeweiahthén:take'** I got the wind, the air knocked out of me (-weiahthentak-)

airplane: **teká:tens** (-ten-)

Albany, NY: **Skahnéhtati** (-hneht-, -ti-)

alcohol, rubbing alcohol: **ionthnekahrhóhstha'** (-hnek-, -(h)rho-)

align: **wa'tektó:kenhte'** I aligned them (-token-)

alive: **kónhnhe'** I am alive, **rónhnhe'** he is alive, **iakónhnhe'** she is alive (-onhnhe[t]-)

all: **akwé:kon**

alligator: **teka'nón:ton**

allow: **rakerihwá:wis** he allows me, he gives me permission, **wahiríhon'** I let him (-rihw-, -awi-/-on-); **konwenniióhstha'** I give you a free hand, I allow you, **enkonwenní:iohste'** I will allow you (-wenn-, -iio-)

allow: *See* consent

almanac: **iakentahsetà:tha'** (-ent-, -ahset-)

almost: **seréka; thó:ha**

alone: **akonhà:'a** I am alone, I alone (-onha-)

alone, left alone: **ia'tewatià:tiste'** I was left all alone, **ia'tewatia'tíston** I am all alone (-ia't-, -i-)

already: **sok nà:'a**

also: **ò:ni'**

altar: **tsi iehahsentáhkhwa'** (-hahsen[t]-)

altar boy: **rohahserawà:se'** (-hahser-, -ienawa's-/-wa's-)

always: **tió:konte'; tiótkon** (-kon[t]-)

amazed; surprised: **wakenehrákwas** I am amazed, in wonder, **onkenehrá:ko'** I became amazed, surprised, **iakonehrakò:'on** she was amazed, **ionehrákwa** it is amazing (-nehrakw-)

Amen: **e'thó: naiá:wen'** or **eh tho naiá:wen'** (-en-)

American: **Wastonhró:non**

amount: **ní:kon** so many, so much, **nihá:ti** (there are) so many, that many, **nikón:ti** (there are) so many (females, animals) (-i-)

amulet: **oiá:ron** (-iaron-)

ancestors: **ionkhihsothokon'kénha**, **onkwahsotshera'kénha** our ancestors (-hsot-); **rotikaiónhshon** ancestors (-akaion-/-kaion-)

and: **ok**; **ò:ni'**; **tánon'**

angels: **ieronhia'kehró:non** (-ronhi-)

angry, get angry: **wakenà:khwens** I get angry, **onkenà:khwen'** I got angry, **wakena'khwèn:'en** I am angry, **wahinà:khwa'se'** I got mad at him (-na'khw[en]-)

angry, get angry at one another: **teionkeni'táksen's** we two get mad at each other, **wa'tionkeni'táksen'ne'** we two got mad at each other, **teioti'taksèn:'en** they (females) have gotten mad at each other (-i't-, -aksen-)

angry, get angry easily: **rana'kwahsnó:re'** he gets angry easily, **iena'kwahsnó:re'** she gets angry easily (-na'kw-, -hsnor[e]-)

angry, make s.o. angry: **rakena'kón:nis** he makes me angry, **wahakena'kón:ni'** he made me angry (-na'kw-, -onni-)

angry, out of control angry: **ranenskárias** he gets out of control angry, **wahanenská:ri'** he got out of control angry (-nenskari-)

animal, domestic: **katshé:nen** animal, pet, **akitshé:nen** my pet (-tshenen-)

animal, wild: **kário** wild animal, **kontírio** wild animals (-rio-/-riio-)

ankle: **ohsinekò:ta'** ankle, **khsineko'tà:ke** (on) my ankle (-hsineko't-)

announce: **waharihó:wanahte'** he announced it (-rihw-, -kowan[en]-/-owan[en]-)

annoyed: **onkwatahkónthahse'** I got annoyed, fed up, **rotahkontén:ni** he gets annoyed (-atahkont-)

annoyed: **onkhswà:ten'** I got annoyed, it got to me, **wakhswà:tani** I get annoyed, it gets to me (-hsw[en]-)

annoyed: **tekaterien'takárias** I get irritated, annoyed, it gets on my nerves, **wa'tkaterien'taká:ri'** I got irritated (-erien't-, -kari-)

annoyed: **onkwaterihonkóhten'** I got fed up, **wakaterihonkóhtani** I am annoyed (-rihw-, -onko-)

annoyed: **onkwatia'tónthahse'** s.t. or s.o. got underfoot, in the way, annoying me (-ia'tont[a]-)

another: **ó:ia'** another, **oià:shon** other things

another one; somebody else: **akò:ren** somebody else, another one, **akohren'shòn:'a** other people, the others

answer: **teharihwa'serákwas** he is answering, **wa'tierihwa'será:ko'** she answered, **tehorihwa'serákwen** he has answered, **wa'tekherihwa'serákwahse'** I answered her (-rihwa'serakw-)

ant: **tsiki'nhontstókhi**

antler; horn; dice: **onà:kara'** (-na'kar-)

anxious: **tewakatón'ne** I am anxious, **thotón'ne** he is anxious, **tiakotón'ne** she is anxious (-aton'ne[k]-)

anytime: **thikawenní:io kátke** (-wenn-, -iio-)

anywhere: **thikawenní:io ka' nón:** (-wenn-, -iio-); **ka' nón:we**

anywhere; nowhere: **káneka**

appear: **roke'tóhtha'** he emerges, he appears, **wahokè:tohte'** he appeared, **wakke'tóhton** I have appeared (-ke'toht-)

apple: **sewahió:wane'** (-ahi-, -kowan[en]-/-owan[en]-)

appoint: **wahonwarihón:ten'** they appointed him, **roteríhonte'** he is an official, a faith-keeper (-rihw-, -ont-)

April: **Onerahtókha** (-neraht-, -okha-)

apron: **ateniión:ta'** (-niiont-)

arch of the foot: **tekaia'kwatáhkwen** (-ia'kwatahkw-)

argue: **tehari'wakéhnhas** he argues, he is a lawyer, **wa'tiakeniri'wakéhnha'** we two argued, **tehotiri'wakéhnhen** they are arguing, **tekari'wakéhnhen** argument (-ri'wakehnha-)

argue; disagree: **wa'thiaterihotáhrhoke'** the two disagreed, **tekarihotáhrhon** argument (-rihw-, -otahrho[k]-)

arm: **onéntsha'** arm, **kenentshà:ke** (on) my arm (-nentsh-)

armpit: **ke'nonhró:kon** or **ke'nionhró:kon** or **ke'nhonhró:kon** or **kenon'onhró:kon** my armpit (-'nonhr-/-'nionhr-/-'nhonhr-/-non'onhr-)

arrange: **wa'atiaterihwahserón:ni'** we two arranged it, made arrangements (-rihw-, -hseronni-)

arrive: **èn:rawe'** he will arrive, **wà:kewe'** I arrived, **ì:ro** he has arrived (-w-); **wa'katatià:thewe'** I arrived (I brought my body here), **wahatatià:thewe'** he arrived, **wa'ontatià:thewe'** she arrived (-ia't-, -he[w]-)

arrow: **kaién:kwire'** (-ienkwir-)

arthritis; rheumatism: **athoráhsera'** (-athor[e]-)

as if; instead: **iá:we**

ash, black: **éhsa'**

ash, white: **káneron**

ashamed: *See* embarrassed; ashamed

ashes; dirt: **o'kèn:ra'** (-a'kenhr-)

ask: **keri'wanóntha'** I am asking a question, **wahari'wanón:ton'** he asked a question, **iakori'wanón:ton** she has asked a question, **wahiri'wanón:tonhse'** I asked him a question (-ri'wanont[on]-)

asleep, body part; numb: **wakahsíthens** I get numb, **onkwahsíthen'** it fell asleep on me, I got numb, I got an (electric) shock, **wakahsithèn:'en** it has fallen asleep on me (-ahsithen-)

aspen: **tsiio'skohió:wane'**

attach: **kóntha'** I attach it, **wahrón:ten'** he attached it (-ont-)

attach; attach at the end: **koháhrha'** I attach it at the end of something, **wa'kohá:ren'** I attached it, **wakóhare'** I have attached it (-ohar-)

attach; attach end-to-end; join; connect: **tekahsontéhrha'** I am joining, connecting them, **wa'thahsónteren'** he connected it, **tewakahsón:tere'** I have connected it, **tewahsón:tere'** it is connected (-ahsonter-)

attach; piece together: **tekékhas** I attach things, piece them together, **wa'tiékha'** she pieced it together, **teiakókhen** she has pieced it together, **tekákhen** it is pieced, put together (-kha-)

attach; stick on: **kera'nentáktha'** I am sticking it on (something), **wahara'nén:takte'** he stuck it on, **rora'nentákton**, he has stuck it on (-ra'nentakt-/-nentakt-)

attack, get attacked: **wa'tewákhkwa'te'** something hit me, it attacked me, **teiakohkwà:ton** it has attacked her (-hkw-)

attack; jump s.o.: **tionkwatia'tóntie's** she keeps jumping me, attacking me, **iahiiatia'tón:ti'** I jumped him (-ia't-, -ati-/-onti-)

attractive: **roia'tarà:se'** he is attractive, **iakoia'tarà:se'** she is attractive, **iorà:se'** it is appealing (-ia't-, -ara'se-)

August: **Seskéha**

aunt: **ionkonhwatèn:'a** my aunt (-onhwaten-); **istèn:'a** my mother, my auntie (-'nisten-); **matén:t** Aunt!

autumn; fall: **kanenna'kè:ne**

avoid: **wa'katerihwaté:ko'** I avoided the matter (-rihw-, -ate'kw-)

awake, keep awake: **wakeserenhtórie's** I have a rough night, a sleepless night, **onkeserenhtó:ri'** it kept me awake, I had a bad night (-serenht-, -ori-)

awake, stay awake; stay up: **tekehrhénhtha'** I stay up all night, **wa'tkéhrhenhte'** I stayed up all night, **tehohrhénhton** he has stayed up all night (-(h)rhenht-)

awake, stay awake; stay up: **wa'katiehwá:ton'** I stayed up all night, I woke myself up early, **wahatiehwá:ton'** he stayed up all night, **wa'ontiehwá:ton'** she stayed up all night (-iehwat[on]-)

aware: **waho'nikòn:rohte'** he became aware, conscious, got to know as he was growing, matured (-'nikonhroht-)

axe: **ató:ken'**

axle: **tewaterontahrohóhstha'**
(-ront-, -hroh[o]-)

baby: **owirà:'a** (-wir-)

baby, have a baby: **iewirahninòn:re'** she is
going to have a baby **wa'ewirahní:non'** she
had a baby (-wir-, -hninon-)

bachelor: **ronekenhteron'tsherakaiòn:'on**
(-nekenhteron-, -akaion-/-kaion-)

back: **khsòn:ne** my back, behind me
(-hson-/-hsw-)

back; spine: **oronhkwè:na'** back, spine,
keronhkwe'nà:ke (on) my back
(-ronhkwe'n-)

back, arch the back: **kate'nehkwáthos**
I arch my back, I lean back,
wa'onte'nehkwátho' she arched her back,
rote'nehkwáthon he has arched his back
(-'nehkwat-)

back, in the back: **ohnà:ken**

back s.o. up: **entkonhswanéta'** I will
back you up, take your part,
tahakhswanéta' he backed me up
(-hson-/-hsw-, -hna'neta'-/-neta'-)

bacon; ham: **kahakenhtaríkhton** (-hakenht-)

bad: **io'táksen** it is spoiled, it is bad,
io'táksen's it is going bad,
wa'o'táksen'ne' it went bad,
io'taksèn:'en it has gone bad (-aksen-)

bad: **wahétken** it is bad,
wahétken's it is going bad,
onhétken'ne' it went bad,
iohetkèn:'en it has gone bad (-ahetken-)

bad, feel bad; regret: **kehnhá:tens** I
regret it, I feel bad about it,
wahahnhá:ten' he regretted it,
wakehnhatèn:'en I have regretted it,
iohnhá:ten it's too bad (-(h)nhaten-)

bag: **ká:iare'** (-iar-)

bake: *See* roast; bake

baking powder: **iontten'kwáhtha'** or
iethen'kwáhtha' (-atten'kw-)

ball: **athén:no** (-athenno-/-athenno'tsher-)

ball cap: **ionekwénhtonte' anòn:warore'**
(-nekwenhtont-)

balloon: **wateweráta's** (-wer-, -ta'-/-eta'-)

balsam fir: **otsohkó:ton**

banana: **teiotahià:kton**
(-ahi-, -hsa'kt[on]-/-a'kt[on]-)

bandage: **ratken'tó:rens** he is putting on a
bandage, **wahatken'tó:ren'** he put a bandage
on, **iakotkèn:tore'** she has a bandage on,
iontken'toráhkhwa' bandage (-ken'tor[en]-)

bank: **tsi iehwistaientáhkhwa'**
(-hwist-, -ien-)

baptize: **wahonwanehkwà:'ehste'**
they baptized him (-nehkwa'ehst-)

bar; tavern; boarding house:
iohson'karèn:ton
(-hson'kar-/-hswen'kar-, -hren't-/-en't-)

barber: *See* cut hair

bare: *See* naked

bare legs: **teha'katsotátie'** he has bare legs, **teie'katsotátie'** she has bare legs (-'kats-, -ot-)

barefoot: **tehaskawè:tote'** he is barefoot, **teionskawè:tote'** she is barefoot (-askawe't-, -ot-)

bark; pie crust; breadcrumbs: **ona'watsísta'** (-na'watsist-)

bark, inner: **ó:kare'** (-kar-)

bark, outer: **o'wá:tsiste'** bark, **io'watsístare'** there is bark (-'watsist-, -r-)

bark, peel off: **raká:rons** he is peeling off bark, **énkkare'** I will peel off the bark, **wakká:ron** I have peeled off the bark (-kar[on]-)

bark, remove: **khwáserons** I take the bark off, **wahahwáseron'** he took the bark off, **wakhwáseron** I have removed the bark (-hwaseron-)

bark (dog): **rahní:has** he barks, **wahà:niie'** he barked, **rohní:hen** he is barking (-hnih-/-hnii-, -'nhii-)

barley: **teiotikonhstòn:rhes** (-konhston'rh-, -es-); **onatsa'kó:wa** (-nats-)

barn: **akohsaténhsne** (-hsaten-); **rakerèn:shne**

barrel; drum: **ka'náhkon** (-'nahkw-)

basement; downstairs: **onhontsó:kon** or **onhwentsó:kon** (-onhwents-/-onhonts-)

basket: **à:there'** (-a'ther-)

bass, rock bass: **oneniokón:ha** (-neni-)

basswood: **ohósera'** (-hoser-)

bat: **athén:no iehwa'ékstha'** (-athenno-/ -athenno'tsher- and -hwa'e[k]-/-a'e[k]-)

bat (animal): **tsikera'wístak**

bath, take a bath: *See* swim; bathe

bathroom; outhouse: **átste' ieienhtáhkhwa'** (-eht-); **ionni'tenhtáhkhwa'** (-i't-, -a'senht-/-enht-)

bathtub: **iontawenhstáhkhwa'** (-awen-)

bead: **otsi'néhtara'** bead (-tsi'nehtar-); **tektsi'nehtará:rons** I am doing beadwork, **wa'tektsi'nehtará:ron'** I beaded it, **tekatsi'nehtará:ron** it has all beads on it (-tsi'nehtar-, -r-); **teietsi'nehtaratá:ses** she does beadwork, **wa'tektsi'nehtaratá:se'** I did beadwork (-tsi'nehtar-, -hwatase-/-tase-)

beak: **ostò:kwa'** (-sto'kw-)

beam; log: **karón:ta'** (-ront-)

bean: **osahè:ta'** (-sahe't-)

bean, pole bean: **ienakarótha' o'rhótsheri** (-nakar-, -ot-, and -'rhotsher-)

bean, string bean: **o'rhótsheri** (-'rhotsher-)

beans, baked beans: **watshahè:tonte'** (-sahe't-, -ate'skont-)

bear: **ohkwá:ri** (-ahkwari['t]-)

bear, polar bear: **wahkwari'tarà:ken** (-ahkwari['t]-, -ra'ken-)

Bear clan: **wakhskeré:wake'** I am Bear clan (-hskerewak-)

beard: **okonhstòn:rha'** beard, **tehokonhstòn:rhonte'** he has a beard, a mustache (-konhston'rh-, -ont-)

beast: **teiotsi'nonwanòn:iani** (it is) a big beast (-tsi'nonw-, -nonhiani-)

beat at: **teionkè:tsha's** she beats me at s.t., **wa'thakè:tsha'** he beat me, **teionkè:tshon'** she has beaten me (-'tsha'-); **rake'néharons** he beats me at it, **wahshako'néhare'** he beat her at it (-'nehar[on]-)

beat at: *See* defeat

beat to: **wa'thatia'taskén:ni'** he beat me to it, he got there before I did (-ia't-, -skenni-)

beat up: **ronwanonwenhseráio's** they beat him up, **wahinonwenhseráio'** I beat him up (-nonwenhserario-)

beat up; kill: **kerí:ios** I kill, **wahário'** he killed it, **wahonwário'** they beat him up (-rio-/-riio-)

beautiful; handsome: **ióhskats** it is beautiful, **iakoia'táhskats** she is beautiful, **roia'táhskats** he is handsome (-ahskats[t]-)

beaver: **tsanì:to**

beaver dam: **kanià:to** (-nia't-, -o-)

because: **ase'kén**

bed; place: **kanákta'** (-nakt-)

bedbug: **katsi'nonwákeras** (-tsi'nonw-, -akera-)

bedroom: **tsi ionnonhwétstha'** (-anonhwet-)

bee: **otsina'kontahkwà:ne'** or **otsi'nahkontahkwà:ne'**

beech: **otskèn:rha'**

beech, blue: **iotenakratí:wen** (-nakar-, -atiw-)

beer: **onon'tákeri'** or **onen'tákeri'** (-nen't-, -keri-)

beetle; ladybug; padlock; hump; fiddle: **o'nó:wa'** (-'now-)

beg; plead: **ke'nékha'** I am pleading, begging, **rake'nekén:ni** he pleads with me, **wahi'né:ken'** I pleaded with him, I begged him (-'nek-)

beg: *See* solicit

begin: *See* start

behind: **ohnà:ken**

behind; back: **khsòn:ne** my back, behind me (-hson-/-hsw-)

beige: **athehsarà:ken** (-hehs-, -ra'ken-)

believe: **tkehtáhkhwa'** I believe it, **tahréhtahkwe'** he believed it, **thawehtáhkwen** he has believed it, **tkoniehtáhkhwa'** I believe you (-ehtahkw-)

belittle: *See* insult

bell: **iehwista'ékstha'** (-hwist-, -hwa'e[k]-/-a'e[k]-)

belly: **onekwèn:ta'** belly, **kenekwen'tà:ke** my belly (-nekwen't-)

bellyband: **wa'ttia'kwaráhnhake'** I put the bellyband on (a horse), **tekonwaia'kwarahnhákstha'** bellyband (-ia'kar-/-ia'kwar-, -hwahnha[k]-/-hnha[k]-)

bellybutton: **onerì:tsta'** bellybutton, **keneri'tstà:ke** (on) my bellybutton (-neri'tst-)

belonging: **ì:'i akwá:wen** it is mine, **raónha raó:wen** it is his, **akaónha akó:wen** it is hers (-awen-)

belt: **atia'táhnha'** belt, **wahatia'táhnhake'** he put on a belt (-ia't-, -hwahnha[k]-/-hnha[k]-)

bend; fold: **tekhsà:ktons** I bend it, I fold it, **wa'tekhsà:kete'** I bent it, **tehohsà:kton** he has bent it, **tewakatshà:kton** I am bent over, **teiotshà:kton** it is bent, crooked (-hsa'kt[on]-/-a'kt[on]-)

berry; fruit: **káhi** (-ahi-)

berry, foul-smelling: **tsikenenhstakwénhten** berry that looks almost like a cranberry and smells foul (-nenhst-, -akwenhten-)

best man: **waho'terónhne'** (-i'teron-)

better, get better: **sahatkwatá:ko'** he got better, **iah tetsakotkwatákwen** she didn't get better (-kwatakw-)

better, get better; recover: **satie'wén:ta'ne'** I got better, I recovered, **tsakoie'wentà:on** she has recovered (-ie'wenta'-)

better, make feel better: **wa'kheionhnhahserón:ni'** I made her feel better (-onhnh-, -hseronni-)

between: **na'tetiátere'** it is between, **ken' na'tekónteron** a little while between, a bit at a time (-re-)

Bible: **kahiatonhseratokénhti** (-hiatonhser-, -tokenhti-)

bicycle: **tékeni teiokahkwèn:tonte'** (-kahkwen't-, -ont-)

big: **kkowá:nen** I am big, **rakowá:nen** he is big, **iekowá:nen** she is big, **kkowanáhtha'** I am making it bigger, enlarging it, **wa'ekó:wanahte'** she made it bigger (-kowan[en]-/-owan[en]-)

bile: **ótshahte'** (-tshaht-)

billiards; checkers: **tektsíhkwaiens** I am playing billiards, checkers (a game with pieces) (-tsihkw-, ien-)

binoculars; telescope: **wa'katkahráta'** I looked at it through a telescope, binoculars, **iontkahrata'ahstáhkhwa'** telescope, binoculars (-kahr-, -ta'-/-eta'-)

birch, white: **watenakè:tarons** (-nake['t]-, -r-)

birch, yellow: **tsohtsó:ron**

bird: **otsi'tèn:'a** (-tsi'ten'a); **tsítha**

birth, give birth: **ontéwe'ton'** it gave birth (-atewe't-)

birthday: **wa'tié:rite'** I celebrated my birthday, **tsakoierí:ton** it is her birthday (-ierit-); **ietsá:ko** it is her birthday (-w-)

Bishop: **arihwawà:kon** (-rihw-, -ienawa'k-/-wa'k-)

bit: **wa'keristahnhónta'** I put the bit in (the horse's) mouth, **wateristahnhónta's** bit (-rist-, -(h)nhonta'-)

bite: **katekhwákwas** I take a bite of food, I bite into it, **wa'katekhwá:ko'** I took a bite, **wakatekhwákwen** I have taken a bite (-khw-, -kw-)

bite, be biting: **kontí:riks** (the fish) are biting (-rik-)

bite s.o.: **khekárias** I bite her, **wa'onkká:ri'** she bit me, **ionkkárien** she has bitten me (-kari-)

bitter: **iotská:ra** it is bitter tasting (-atskara-)

bittern: **tehkáhon**

blab: *See* talk; blab

black: **kahòn:tsi** it is black (-hon'tsi-)

blackberry: **wahiahòn:tsi** (-ahi-, -hon'tsi-)

blackcap: **teiotenenharà:kton**

blacksmith: **rahwistón:ni** (-hwist-, -onni-)

blame: **thakerá:wi** he blames me, **tahí:rahse'** I blamed him (-r-)

blame: *See* accuse; blame

blanket; shawl: **áhsire'** (-ahsir-)

bleed: **wa'kanékhwa'** it bled, **ionekhwà:'on** it is bleeding (-nekhwa'-)

bleed, nosebleed: **wa'tha'niónkha'** he got a nosebleed, **teiako'nionkhà:'on** she has a nosebleed (-'nionkha-)

bless: **wahshakoia'taté:riste'** he blessed them, **sheia'taté:rist** Bless them! (-ia'taterist-)

blind: **teharon'wé:kon** he is blind, **teieron'wé:kon** she is blind (-ron'wek-); **iah tehá:ken** he is blind, he doesn't see, **iah teié:ken** she is blind (-ken-)

blink: **tehattsikèn:ro'ks** he is blinking, **wa'tionttsikèn:ro'ke'** she blinked (-attsikenhro'k-)

blister: **wakhsió:kas** I have a blister on my hand, **wake006tó:kas** I have a blister on my heel (-ok-)

blister, bubble up: **wa'katshe'tón:ten'** it bubbled up a blister, **iotshè:tonte'** blister (-tshe['t]-, -ont-)

block: *See* across, put across

block; clog: **wahatikohò:roke'** they blocked it, **iotkohò:ron** it is blocked, clogged (-koh-, -ohro[k]-)

blood: **onekwénhsa'** (-nekwenhs-)

blood clot: **onekwá:ra'** (-nekwar-)

bloodsucker: **oserakwaròn:ne'**

bloom: **tekatsi'tsaneká:rons** the flowers are blooming, **wa'tkatsi'tsané:kare'** the flowers bloomed (-tsi'ts-, -ra'nekar[on]-/-nekar[on]-)

blouse; vest: **oià:kara'** (-ia'kar-/-ia'kwar-)

blue: **oròn:ia'** (-ronhi-)

blue jay: **terí:teri**

blueberry: **kahrhata'kéha**

bluing (for clothes to whiten them): **ieronhióhkhwa'** (-ronhi-, -o-)

blurt out: **thowennatahkwáhtha'** he just blurts out with it, **tonkewennatáhkwahte'** I blurted out with it (-wenn-, -tahkw-)

board: **ohsòn:kare'** or **ohswèn:kare'** (-hson'kar-/-hswen'kar-)

boarding house; tavern; bar: **iohson'karèn:ton** (-hson'kar-/-hswen'kar-, -hren't-/-en't-)

boast; brag: **rawennaná:ie'** he boasts, brags, **iewennaná:ie'** she boasts, brags (-wenn-, -naie-)

boat: **kahonwé:ia'** (-honw[ei]-)

boat, sailboat: **wahsí:rote'** or **watshirótha'** or **wattsirótha'** (-ahsir-, -ot-)

body: **oià:ta'** body, **tia'tà:ke** (on) my body (-ia't-)

body: **oieròn:ta'** body, **tieron'tà:ke** or **tieròn:ke** (on) my body (-ieron['t]-)

body, waist down: **o'khóhkwa'** body, from the waist down, **ke'khohkwà:ke** my body from the waist down (-'khohkw-)

boil (on the body): **okwahrò:ta'** boil, **wakatkwahro'takwá:ronte'** I have a boil, **onkwatkwahro'takwarón:ten'** I got a boil (-kwahro't-, -kwaront-)

boil: **tekhnekontiéhtha'** I am boiling it, **wa'tekhnekóntiehte'** I boiled it, **tekahnekontiéhton** it is boiled (-hnek-, -ati-/-onti-)

boil: **wa'khnennà:to'** I boiled potatoes, **wa'ke'nhónhso'** I boiled eggs (-o-)

bolt: **raristò:roks** he is bolting it, **waharistò:roke'** he bolted it, **karistò:ron** it is bolted (-rist-, -ohro[k]-)

bone: **óhstien** (-hstien['t]-)

bone, gnaw a bone: **rahstio'ká:nonts** he is gnawing at a bone, **wahahstiò:kane'** he gnawed the bone (-hstio'kanont-/-hstio'kan-)

bone marrow: **ohstien'takón:ha** (-hstien['t]-)

book; paper: **kahiatónhsera'** book, paper (-hiatonhser-)

boot lining: **ateráhki** or **ateráhkwi**

boots: **wa'tkarahtahkwanéta'** I put on galoshes, boots, **teionrahtahkwaneta'ahstáhkhwa'** boots, overshoes, galoshes (-ahta[hkw]-, -hna'neta'-/-neta'-)

boots, rubber boots: **teiohnatiróntha' áhta** (-ihn-, -atiront-, and -ahta[hkw]-)

bore: **rahrá:raks** he bores a hole, **wahahrá:rake'** he bored a hole, **wakhrará:kon** I have bored a hole (-hrarak-)

borer: **anihsonwatá:se** (-hsonw-, -hwatase-/-tase-)

born: **wahanákerate'** or **wahrennákerate'** he was born, **ronakerá:ton** he was born (-naker[e]-); **wahatón:ni'** he was born, **rotón:ni** he is born (-onni-)

borrow: *See* lend

both: **tetsá:ron**

bother; fuss with: **katsterístha'** I bother, fuss with it, **wa'katsté:riste'** I bothered with it, **iakotsteríston** she has bothered with it, **wahshakotsté:riste'** he bothered her, he bugged her (-atsterist-)

bother; worry: **tekhe'nikonhrháhrha'** I am bothering her, being a pest, **wa'thake'nikonhrhá:ren'** he bothered me, he worried me, **tewaka'nikónhrhare'** I am worried about it (-'nikonhrhar-)

bottle; jar: **kátshe'** (-tshe['t]-)

bottom: **o'nónhkwa'** bottom, **tka'nónhkwaien'** it has a bottom (-'nonhkw-, -ien-)

boulder; rock: **otstèn:ra'** (-itstenhr-)

bow (and arrow): **a'én:na'** (-a'enn-)

bow: **wa'tke'nistó:ten'** I made a bow, **teka'nístote'** it has a bow on it, **o'nísta'** bow (-'nist-, -ot-)

bow (incline the head): **tahatenòn:weron'** he bowed (-nonhweron-)

bow-legged: **tehahá:kwaien'** he is bow-legged, **teiehá:kwaien'** she is bow-legged (-hakwaien-)

bowl; dish; plate: **akè:ra'** (-akehr-/-kehr-)

box: **o'neróhkwa'** (-'nerohkw-)

box, wooden: **karón:to** (-ronto-/-ronto'tsher-)

boxer: **rattsihkóia'ks** (-tsihkw-, -oia'[k]-)

boy: **raksà:'a** (-ksa['t]-)

brace oneself; resist: **entkenatsó:ten'** I will resist, brace myself, stand my ground, **tahanatsó:ten'** he stood his ground (-nats-, -ot-)

brace with the foot: **tekaráhsarons** I brace it with my foot, **wa'tharáhsaren'** he braced it (-arahsar[on]-)

bracelet; wristwatch: **atenentsháhnha'** (-nentsh-, -hwahnha[k]-/-hnha[k]-)

brag: *See* boast; brag

braid: **oratskèn:ta'** braid, **wa'keratsken'tón:ni'** I braided it, **wa'kateratsken'tón:ni'** I braided my hair (-ratsken't-, -onni-)

brain: **onòn:wara'** (-nonhwar-)

branch: **ò:nhahte'** branch, **io'nhahtón:ton** it has branches (-'nhaht-, -ont-)

branches, cluster of branches: **o'nèn:ra'** (-'nenhr-)

brass instrument: **iehonrawátstha'** (-honrawatst-)

brave: **wake'nikonhratshà:ni** I am brave (-'nikonhr-, -tshahni[ht]-)

bread: **kanà:taro** (-na'tar[o][k]-)

bread, bread or pancake cooked on a wood stove: **tekaristoiénhton** (-rist-, -oia'[k]-)

bread, crusty: **teio'nowákhen kanà:taro** (-'now-, -kha-); **réntskote'** (-itskw-, -ot-)

break: **tétia'ks** I break it, **wà:ttia'ke'** I broke it,

teiakoià:kon she has broken it,
wa'tewátia'ke' it broke,
teiotià:kon it is broken (-ia'k-)

break; smash: **tekhríhtha'** I break it,
smash it, crush it,
wa'tékhrihte' I broke it,
tewakhríhton I have broken it (-hriht-);
wa'tkà:ri'ne' it broke,
teiohrì:'on it is broken (-hri'-)

break in; invade: **wahshakonónhskwekhse'**
he invaded, broke into her house
(-nonhskwekhs-)

breath, run out of: **wa'katonriò:kten'**
I ran out of breath (-onri-, -o'kt-)

breath, take one's last: **wahatonriserò:kten'**
he took his last breath (and he died)
(-atonriser-, -o'kt-)

breathe: **katón:rie'** I am breathing,
wahatón:rie' he breathed,
iakotón:rie' she is breathing, taking
a breath (-atonrie-)

breeze: **iówerare'** (it is) a light breeze
(-wer-, -r-)

brick; cement block: **kaneniaríhton**
(-neni-, -ri-)

bridesmaid: **wa'etsi'tsaiénhne'** bridesmaid
(-tsi'ts-, -ien-)

bridge: **áhskwa'** (-ahskw-)

bridle: **wa'kkonwarotáhrhoke'** I put the
bridle on, **atkonwarotahrhókstha'** bridle
(-konwar-, -otahrho[k]-)

bright: **teiohswáthe'** it is bright,
wa'tiohswáthe'ne' it got bright (-hswathe-)

brightly-coloured: **iotá:kon** it is brightly-
coloured, vivid (-atak-)

brim, of a hat: **teiotá:ronte'** it has a brim,
a fedora hat (-tar-, -ont-)

bring: **tékhas** I bring it, **tákhawe'** I brought
it, **thóha** he has brought it,
entekheia'ténhawe' I will bring her
(-ha[w]-/-enha[w]-);
takhá:wi' I am bringing it (-hawi-)

bring in: **tátion'te'** I brought it in,
tewatiòn:ton I have brought it in,
iahà:tion'te' I brought it in (that way)
(-ion't-/-inion't-)

bring up: **ia'keráthenhste'** I brought it up
(there), **taharáthenhste'** he took it up (here)
(-rathen-)

brooch; badge: **athnió:ta'** brooch, badge,
iakóthniote' she has on a brooch (-hniot-)

broom: **akonhonwà:tha'**

broth: **ohnekákeri'** (-hnek-, -keri-)

brother, older: **rakhtsì:'a** my older brother
(-htsi-)

brother, younger: **ri'kèn:'a** my younger
brother (-'ken-)

brother-in-law: **ontiatióha** my brother-in-law
(man speaking) (-atioha);
rakonháhwha my brother-in-law (woman
speaking) (-onhaw-)

brown: **athéhsa'** (-hehs-)

bruise: **wakatharennáhtare'** I have a bruise,
onkwatharennáhtara'ne' I got a bruise
(-harennaht-, -r-)

bruise; dent: **onttá:kwarase'** it got bruised, it got a dent, **iottakwará:son** it is bruised, dented (-takwaras-/-kwaras-)

buck: **tewanihna'tshakétskwas** it is bucking (an animal) (-hna'tsh-, -ketskw-)

buckle: **ohniáhskari** buckle, **wa'tekhniáhskarike'** I buckled it up (-hniahskari[k]-)

buckwheat: **énnekoks** or **ánekoks**

bud; chaff: **oshé:wa'** (-ashew-)

bud, on a tree: **oskwè:ia'** (-skwe'i-)

buffalo: **tsistekeriià:kon**

buffalo fish; carp: **skentstèn:ri**

bug; insect: **otsi'nón:wa'** (-tsi'nonw-)

bug, a kind of black bug: **atenénha'**

bulb; lamp chimney; carcass; jug; gallon: **owerò:kwa'** (-wero'kw-)

bulb (of a plant): **otsi'niónhkwara'** or **otsi'nónhkwara'** (-tsi'nionhkwara-)

bulge; lump: **iokwá:ronte'** it has a bulge, a lump, **wa'okwarón:ta'ne** a bulge, a lump came up (-kwaront-)

bull: **teró:**

bullet: **onenió:wane'** (-neni-, -kowan[en]-/-owan[en]-)

bullfrog: **bararón:**

bully: **ronwatkóntha'** they bully him, pick on him, **wahiiatkón:ten'** I got after him, **shakótkonte'** he is bullying her (-kon[t]-)

bulrush: **osha'kén:ta'** (-sha'kent-)

bulrush spike: **onó:ta'** (-not-)

bump; lump: **rotsíhkonte'** he has a bump, a lump, **iakotsíhkonte'** she has a bump, a lump (-tsihkw-, -ont-)

bump, little bump: **ronéhkonte'** he has a little bump, a pimple, **iakonehkón:ton** she has little bumps (-nehkw-, -ont-)

bump against; run into: **takò:ka'te'** I ran into it, I bumped against it, **tahrò:ka'te'** he bumped against it, **taiakò:ka'te'** she bumped against it (-o'ka't-)

bump into: **ia'tewakónkwas** I bump into it, **ia'thaón:ko'** he bumped into it, **ia'tewakónkwen** I have bumped into it, **ia'thatia'tón:ko'** he bumped into me (-onkw-)

bump into s.o.: **wahakwatià:taienhte'** he bumped into me (-ia't-, -ienht-)

bump s.o.: **wahákkwahte'** he bumped me (accidentally) (-kwaht-)

bun (hair): **orén:ia'** bun, **wakaterén:iote'** I have a bun (-reni-, -ot-)

bundle: **kenthóhkwa'** (-ithohkw-)

bundle: **kanóhkwa'** bundle, **skanóhkwa** one bundle (-nohkw-)

burden: **onkhwíshen'** it got burdensome or heavy for me, a struggle, **wahohwíshen'** it got burdensome for him (-hwish-)

burdock: **ohrhohte'kó:wa** (-(h)rhoht-)

burn: **wátsha's** it burns, **óntsha'** it burned, **katsha'áhtha'** I burn it, **wa'kátsha'ahte'** I burned it, **wakatsha'áhton** I have burned it, **watsha'áhton** it is burnt, **wa'katia'tátsha'** I got burned (-atsha'-)

burn (a product): **watónthos** it burns (wood, oil) (-ontho-)

burn; be in flames, on fire: **iotékha'** it is burning, **wa'ó:teke'** it burned, **iotéken** it has burned, it is burnt (-atek-)

burn, house fire: **ionon'kwatékha'** the house is burning, on fire, **wa'onòn:kwateke'** the house burned, **ionon'kwatéken** the house has burned (-non'kwatek-)

burn oneself: **wa'katen'nahsótshi'** I burned my tongue, **wa'kathnia'sótshi'** I burned my throat (-otshi-)

burp: **thonia'kwáhtha'** he burps, **tonkenià:kwahte'** I burped, **thonia'kwáhton** he has burped (-nia'kw-); **wa'tewakenia'tó:ren'** I burped (-nia't-, -oren-)

burrs; pickers: **óhrhohte'** (-(h)rhoht-)

burst: **tewatera'neká:rons** it bursts, **wa'tewatera'né:kare'** it burst, it busted, **teiotera'neká:ron** it has burst (-ra'nekar[on]-/-nekar[on]-)

bury: **wahonwaia'táta'** they buried him, **wa'ontatia'táta'** they buried her (-ia't-, -ta'-/-eta'-)

bus: **iakoia'takarénie's** (-ia't-, -kareni-); **watonkwe'takarénie's** (-onkwe['t]-, -kareni-)

bush: **ohská:wakon** in the bush, **kahská:ote'** (there is) a bunch of trees (-hskaw-, -ot-)

busy, get: **teieweienhá:ra's** she gets busy, **wa'tkeweienhá:ra'ne'** I got busy, **tewakeweienharà:'on** I am busy (-weienhara'-)

busybody: **ratáthare'** he is a busybody, **iontáthare'** she is a busybody (-atathar-)

but: **nek tsi**

butter: **owistóhsera'** butter, **wa'kewistohseráhrho'** I buttered it (-wistohser-, -(h)rho-)

butterfly: **tsiktsinén:nawen**

buttermilk: **kanon'tí:sen** (-non't-)

butternut: **atiehwà:ta'**

buttocks: **ohnà:tsha'** buttocks, **khna'tshà:ke** (on) my buttocks (-hna'tsh-); **ohò:kwa'** buttocks, **kho'kwà:ke** (on) my buttocks (-ho'kw-)

button; knot (tree); puck; fist: **otsíhkwa'** button, etc., **wa'ktsihkó:ten'** I put a button on, I buttoned it (-tsihkw-, -ot-)

buy: **khní:nons** I buy, **wahahní:non'** he bought it, **wakhní:non** I have bought it,

wahihní:non' I bought it from him
(-hninon-)

cabbage: **onéhsio** (-nehsio-)

cabinet; cupboard: **ioronto'tsheranentá:kon**
(-ronto-/-ronto'tsher-, -ra'nentak-/-nentak-)

cadaver: **awenheiòn:ta'**
(-ihei[on]-/-enhei[on]-)

cage; tent: **a'tóhsera'** (-a'tohser-)

cake: **teiona'taratsikhè:tare'** (-na'tar[o][k]-,
-tsikhe't-, -r-); **akarè:t**

calcification: **ionén:iare'** (-neni-, -r-)

calendar: **iakenhni'tahsetà:tha'**
(-enhni't-, -ahset-)

calf (leg): **osenón:na'** (-senonn-)

call out to: **iekhenà:tons** I am calling out
to her, **iahinà:ton'** I called out to him,
iehinà:ton I have called out to him (-na'ton-)

call s.o.: **thakì:nonks** he is calling me,
tahakì:nonke' he called me,
iekhè:nonks I am calling her,
iahì:nonke' I called him (-ihnonk-)

callus: **orakwáhta'** callus,
wakerakwáhtare' I have a callus,
onkerakwáhtara'ne' I got a callus
(-rakwaht-, -r-)

calm; quiet: **sha'thí:ken**

camel: **io'nowakwá:ronte'**
(-'now-, -kwaront-);
onia'kwáhehr (-nia'kw-, -her-/-hr-)

Canada: **Koráhne**

Canajoharie, NY: **Kana'tsóhare**
(-na'ts-, -nohare-/-ohare-)

canal; seaway: **kana'tsheratátie'**
(-na'tsher-, -onni-)

canary: **atiaren'tà:'a** (-atiaren't-)

cancer: **takwa'áhson í:waks** (-ek-/-ak-)

candle, church candle: **ohahseratokénhti**
(-hahser-, -tokenhti-)

candy: **otsikhè:ta'** (-tsikhe't-)

candy, attached to a stick; lollipop:
kanakaróhare' (-nakar-, -ohar-)

candy, maple candy: **wastè:ton**

cane: **atèn:nits** cane,
wakaten'nítsherote' I am using a cane
(-aten'nits-/-aten'nitsher-, -ot-)

canoe: **oná:ke** (-nake['t]-)

canoe, dugout canoe: **orón:to** (-ronto-)

cantaloupe: **wahiá:ris** (-ahi-, -ri-)

cap, ball cap: **ionekwénhtonte'**
anòn:warore' (-nekwenhtont-)

cape; shawl: **ateweià:ra'** cape, shawl,
tewakateweiáhere' I have a cape on,
wa'tkateweià:ren' I put on a cape
(-wei-, -her-/-hr-)

captain, war canoe; ship's pilot:
thaniarotáhrhoks (-niar-, -otahrho[k]-)

car: **kà:sere** (-'sere[ht]-)

carcass: **okarièn:ta'** (-karien't-)

carcass; bulb; lamp chimney; jug; gallon: **owerò:kwa'** (-wero'kw-)

cardboard: **kahiatonhserá:tens** (-hiatonhser-, -tens-)

cards, play: **tehatihiatonhserá:iens** they are playing cards, **teiehiatonhseraientáhkhwa'** cards (-hiatonhser-, -ien-)

care, take care of oneself: **katatia'tanorónhstha'** I take care of myself (-ia't-, -noron-)

care, take care of s.o.: **tekhéhsnie'** I take care of her, **wa'tekhéhsnie'ne'** I took care of her, **tehshakohsniè:'on** he has taken care of her (-hsnie-)

careful; watch over: **ke'nikòn:rare'** I am careful, I am watching over it (-'nikonhr-, -r-)

caress; pat: **kheia'tohserónkwas** I am caressing her, patting her, **wahiia'tohserón:ko'** I patted him, **kheia'tohserónkwen** I have caressed her (-ia't-, -ohseronkw-)

caribou; elk: **atená:ti**

carpenter: **rahson'karaké:tas** (he is) a carpenter (-hson'kar-/-hswen'kar-, -ket-)

carpet; rug: **kéntskare'**; **ietskarónhkhwa'** (-itskar[on]-)

carry: **khá:wi'** I am carrying it, **kheia'tenhá:wi'** I am carrying her (-hawi-/-enhawi-)

carry on the back: **wakkéhte'** I am carrying it, I have it on my back, **ratkéhtats** he puts it on his back, **wahatkéhtate'** he carried it on his back (-keht[e]-)

carry s.o. on the back: **khehsá:tens** I carry someone on my back, I am giving someone a ride on my back, **wa'khehsá:ten'** I gave her a ride (-hsaten-)

cart: **tewate'nerohkwakétskwas** (-'nerohkw-, -ketskw-)

carve: **rahkaratáhkwas** he is carving, **wahahkaratáhko'** he carved, **rohkaratáhkwen** he has carved (-ahkar-, -tahkw-)

cashier; conductor: **rakarotáhsions** cashier, conductor (male), **iekarotáhsions** (female) (-kar-, -ot-)

cat: **takò:s**

cataracts: **iottsiseró:ron rakahrà:ke** he has cataracts (-tsiser-, -'rhoro[k]-/-oro[k]-)

catch; hold: **tié:nas** I grab hold of it, **wahaié:na'** he caught it, **watienà:'on** I have gotten hold of it, **wahoié:na'** he caught him (-iena-)

catch up to: **wa'khehnhóntera'ne'** I caught up to her, **rihnhonterà:'on** I have caught up to him (-hnhonter-)

caterpillar: **ohwharà:ne'** (-ihwhar-)

catfish: **rabahbót**

Catholic: **tehaiahsóntha'** he is a Catholic, **teieiahsóntha'** she is a Catholic (-iahs-, -ont-)

cave: **iotstenhrakà:ronte'** (-itstenhr-, -kahront-)

Cayuga: **Kaiokonhá:ka** Cayuga; **Shotinennawen'tó:wane'** Cayugas, as referred to in council (-nennawen['t]-, -kowan[en]-/-owan[en]-); **Ratirihwaié:nas** Oneidas and Cayugas, as referred to in council (-rihw-, -iena-)

cedar: **onen'takwenhtèn:tshera'** (-nen't-, -akwenhten-)

celebrate: **wahiiatonhnhahéhrhahse'** I celebrated him (his birthday) (-onhnh-, -her-/-hr-)

celery; stalk: **ostawí:na'** (-stawin-)

cement block; brick: **kaneniaríhton** (-neni-, -ri-)

cemetery; grave: **iontatia'tata'ahstáhkhwa'** (-ia't-, -ta'-/-eta'-)

census taker: **rahsennarò:roks** (-hsenn-, -rohro[k]-)

certainly; no wonder: **kanekhé:re**

certainly; true: **tó:kenske'; tó:ske'**

chafe: **ió:kas** it is rubbing, it chafes, **ón:koke'** it chafed me (-ok-)

chaff: **okehwhèn:ta'** (-kehwhen't-)

chaff; winnow: **rashé:was** he is separating the chaff, **wa'káshewe'** I separated the chaff, **roshé:wen** he has separated the chaff (-ashew-)

chain: **oronkwáhsa'** (-ronkwahs-)

chair: **anitskwà:ra** (-itskw-, -her-/-hr-)

Chambly, Québec: **Ioniatarakwá:ronte'** (-niatar-, -kwaront-)

champion: **raron'onhkwénhawe'** he is the champion (-ron'onhkw-, -ha[w]-/-enha[w]-); **wahatiron'onhkwahrá:ko'** they won the championship (-ron'onhkw-, -her-/-hr-)

change: **tekténie's** I change it, **wa'tekté:ni'** I changed it, **tewakténion** I have changed it (-teni-)

change (coins): **teiohwistahrì:'on** (-hwist-, -hri'-)

change s.o.'s mind: *See* discourage

charge a lot: **ro'shátste'** he charges a lot for it (-'shatst[e]-)

charge an amount: **Tó: nihanà:tons?** How much does he charge for it? (-na'ton-)

charge, in charge: **raia'takwe'ní:io** he is in charge, **ieia'takwe'ní:io** she is in charge (-ia't-, -kwe'niio-); **thoniarotáhrhon** he is in charge, **tiakoniarotáhrhon** she is in charge (-niar-, -otahrho[k]-)

charge, in charge; head: **ohén:ton ì:rate'** he is the head of it, in charge, **ohén:ton í:iete'** she is the head of it, in charge (-t-/-et-)

charley horse; cramp: **onkesennà:karaske'** I got a charley horse (-senna'karask-)

charm: **otsinahkèn:ta'** (-tsinahken't-)

chase: *See* follow

Chateauguay, Québec: **Oshahrhè:'on**

cheap: *See* stingy

cheat: **ra'nikonhrhà:tha'** he cheats, he is cheating, **wa'e'nikónhrha'te'** she cheated, **ro'nikonhrhà:ton** he has cheated, **wahia'nikonhrhà:ten'** he cheated you (-'nikonhrha't-)

cheek: **ohnhò:kwa'** cheek, **kehnho'kwà:ke** (on) my cheek (-(h)nho'kw-)

cheek; jowl; mouthful: **ohnhóskwa'** (-(h)nhoskw-)

cheek, inside of the cheeks: **onoskóhrha'** (-noskorh-)

cheekbones; temple: **kahranonhsà:ke** or **kehranonhsà:ke** (on) my temples (-ahranonhs-)

cheese: **tsí:s**

cherish: *See* affection, show affection

cherry: **é:ri**

chest: **otskwè:na'** chest, **kentskwe'nà:ke** (on) my chest (-entskwe'n-)

chew: **rohnehtá:kon** he is chewing, **iakohnehtá:kon** she is chewing (-hneht-, -ek-/-ak-)

chickadee: **tsiktsiré:re**

chicken: **kítkit**

chicken and dumplings: **kítkit ieka'nhontstóhon** (-'nhontst-, -ohw-)

chicken pox: *See* measles

chief: **roiá:ner** he is a chief, **rotiianéhshon** they have titles, chiefs (-iane[r]-)

chief, install: **tenhonwana'karà:ren'** they will install him as chief (-na'kar-, -her-/-hr-)

child: **raksà:'a** boy, **eksà:'a** girl, **ratiksa'okòn:'a** children, **kontiksa'okòn:'a** girls, **íkhsa!** Child! (-ksa['t]-)

child, have a child: **wakewí:raien'** I have a child (-wir-, -ien-); **iewirahninòn:re'** she is going to have a baby, **wa'ewirahní:non'** she had a baby (-wir-, -hninon-)

chimney; clan; clay: **o'tá:ra'** chimney, clan, clay, **ken'tá:rote'** there is a chimney (-i'tar-, -ot-)

chimney, inside of a chimney: **o'niòn:ra'** (-'nionhr-)

chimney sweep: **rahakenhtá:waks** (-hakenht-, -awak-)

chin: **o'rhiótsha'** chin, **ke'rhiotshà:ke** (on) my chin (-'rhiotsh-)

chipmunk: **ohrhió:ken**

chipped: **onte'nehtaratáhko'** it got chipped, **iote'nehtaratáhkwen** it is chipped (-'nehtar-, -tahkw-); **iote'nehtarakwará:son** it is chipped (-'nehtar-, -takwaras-/-kwaras-)

Chippewa: **Tewa'káhnha'**

chisel: **ionhkaratahkwáhtha'** (-ahkar-, -tahkw-)

chocolate: **thiákeret**

choke: **tewakenia'thá:ra's** I choke, **wa'tiakonia'thá:ra'ne'** she choked, **tehonia'tharà:'on** he is choking

(-nia'thara'-); **wa'tewakhónria'ke'**
I choked, **wa'tehshakohónria'ke'**
he choked her, strangled her (-honria'k-)

chokecherry: **teiakonia'tawèn:'eks**
(-nia't-, -hwawen'e[k]-/-awen'e[k]-)

choose: **kerákwas** I choose it,
wahará:ko' he chose it,
wakerákwen I have chosen it (-r-)

chop: **kéro'ks** I chop (wood),
waháro'ke' he chopped it,
wakéro' I have chopped (-ro'[k]-)

chop into pieces: *See* break into pieces

Christianity: **Karihwiióhston**
(-rihw-, -iio-)

Christmas: **ratonnià:ne'** (-onni-)

Christmas present: **wa'kateriserihá:ren'**
I got a present for Christmas,
wahiriseriháhrhahse' I gave him a
Christmas present (-ris[er]-, -har-/-ihar-)

church: **ononhsatokénhti** (-nonhs-,
-tokenhti-); **ionterennaientáhkhwa'**
(-renn-, -ien-)

cinnamon: **wahkarákon'**
(-ahkar-, -eka'[w]-/-ka'[w]-)

circle: *See* round

clam; oyster: **takwaré:re**

clan; clay; chimney: **o'tá:ra'** clan, clay,
chimney, **waki'tá:raien'** I have a clan
(-i'tar-, -ien-)

clan, without a clan: **rohsennakéhte'** he
doesn't have a clan, so they give him a

name, **iakohsennakéhte'** she doesn't have a
clan (-hsenn-, -keht[e]-)

clan mothers: **iotiianéhshon ka'nisténhsera'**;
ka'nisténhsera' ionateríhonte' (-'nisten-);
iotiiá:ner (-iane[r]-)

clap hands: **teka'sháro'ks** I clap my hands,
wa'tion'sháro'ke' she clapped,
tewaka'sháro' I am clapping (-a'sharo'[k]-)

claw: **o'éhta'** claw, **rao'éhta'** his claws
(-a'eht-)

clay; clan; chimney: **o'tá:ra'** (-i'tar-)

clear (sky): **iotshatoké:wen** it is clear
(-atshat-, -rakew-/-okew-)

clerk: **rakamí:**

cliff: **ionitstenhrià:kon** (-itstenhr-, -ia'k-)

climb: **keráthens** I climb,
waharáthen' he climbed,
roráthen he has climbed (-rathen-)

climb on s.t.: **kerá:te's** I am climbing on
something (-rat[e]-)

clinic; hospital: **tehshakotitsèn:tha'** (-tsen't-)

clock: **karahkwaka'eniòn:tha'**
(-rahkw-, -ka'enion-)

clog: *See* block; clog

close (a door): **kehnhó:tons** I close it,
wa'kehnhó:ton' I closed it,
wakehnhó:ton I have closed it (-(h)nhoton-)

closet; pantry; cupboard:
iontahkwenniaientáhkhwa'
(-ahkwenni-, -ien-)

clothes peg: **ie'wahstotáhkhwa'**
(-'wahst-, -ot-)

clothing: **atsherónnia'** (-hseronni-)

clothing; outfit: **atahkwénnia'** (-ahkwenni-)

clothing, dressy clothing:
iontia'tahseronnia'táhkhwa'
(-ia't-, -hseronni-)

cloud: **otsíkeri** (-tsiker-)

cloudy: **iotshatarónnion** there are fluffy
clouds here and there (-atshat-, -r-)

cloudy; overcast: **wa'karonhió:roke'**
it got cloudy, overcast,
ioronhió:ron it is cloudy, overcast
(-ronhi-, -'rhoro[k]-/-oro[k]-)

clover: **teionerahtó:ken** (-neraht-, -oken-)

clown: **aié:ron** (-ieron-)

clubs, suit of clubs: **tewahiakwí:rare'**
(-ahiakwir-, -r-)

coal: **ohswèn:ta'** or **o'swèn:ta'**
(-ahswen't-/-a'swen't-)

coal oil: **iehahseróhkhwa' kén:ie'**
(-hahser-, -o-)

coat; dress; shirt; jacket: **atià:tawi**
(-atia'tawi-)

coat; spread: **kéhrhos** I coat it,
wa'kéhrho' I coated it,
wakéhrhon I have coated it (-(h)rho-)

cobweb: **teiota'á:raton** there are cobwebs
(-a'ar-)

cod, salted: **ramorí:**

coffee: **káhwhe**; **ohso'kwákeri'**
(-hso'kw-, -keri-)

coffin: **iakenheion'taráhkhwa'**
(-ihei[on]-/-enhei[on]-, -r-)

coffin cover: **tewateronto'tsheranetáhkhwa'**
cover for a vault that holds a coffin
(-ronto-/-ronto'tsher-, -hna'ne[t]-/-ne[t]-)

colander: **ienonwakentstáhkhwa'**
(-nonw-, -kentst-)

cold: **kewístos** I am cold,
wa'kewístoske' I got cold, **iowísto** it is cold,
wa'kawístohte' it got cold (-wisto-)

cold, get a cold: **wa'ka'tarihenhserá:nohste'**
I got a cold, **waka'tarihenhseranóhston**
I have a cold (-a'tarih[en]-/-tarih[en]-, -no-);
wahothoriáhseron'se' he caught a cold,
wakathoriahseròn:se' I have a cold
(-athoriahseron's-)

cold feet: **tewakahsennì:taks** my feet are
cold, **wa'tewakahsennì:take'** I got cold
feet (-ahsenni'tak-)

cold hands: **tewakahsiò:tanos** I have cold
hands, **wa'tewakahsiò:tanohste'** my hands
got cold (-ahsio'tano-)

cold legs: **teke'katsanóhstha'** my legs are
cold, **wa'tke'kátsanohste'** my legs got cold
(-'kats-, -no-)

cold water: **ohné:kanos** fresh, cold water,
iohné:kano it is cold water (-no-)

cold (weather): **iothó:re'** it is cold,
wathó:rats it gets cold,
onthó:rate' it got cold (-athor[e]-)

collar: **tekahnia'sáhere'** it has a collar
(-hnia's-, -her-/-hr-)

collar (horse): **wahanennotsherániake'**
he put the collar on (the horse)
(-nennotsher-, -nia[k]-)

collect: *See* gather; collect

collect money: **iekarotáhsions** she collects
money, **rakkarotahsién:nis** he is asking me
for his money, he is collecting from me,
wahikarotáhsien' I collected money from
him (-kar-, -ot-)

colour: **ohsóhkwa'** colour (-ahsohkw-);
wa'káhsohwe' I coloured it, dyed it,
wakahsóhon I have coloured it, dyed it,
wahsóhon it is coloured, dyed (-ahso[hw]-)

comb; brush: **atkerothí:ha** comb,
katkerothí:ha I am combing, brushing my
hair, **wa'katkeróthiwe'** I combed, brushed
my hair (-kerothiha-)

comb; crest: **okò:tsa'** crest (of a bird), comb
(of a rooster), **roko'tsáhere'** he (a rooster)
has a comb (-ko'ts-, -her-/-hr-)

come: **éntke'** I will come,
tá:ke' I am coming, I came,
tà:re' he is coming, he came,
ká:ts Come! (-e-)

come back: **sháhkets** he goes back and forth,
tontaháhkete' he came back (-ahket-)

come behind: **ohnà:ken tahoia'ten'tòn:ne'**
he is coming in the back, behind
(-ia't-, -hren't-/-en't-)

come down: *See* descend

come for a purpose: **kenièn:te'** I come
for a purpose, I am here for something,
ranièn:te' he comes for something,
ienièn:te' she comes for something
(-nien'te-)

come for nothing: **ó:kont wa'ká:ton'**
I came for nothing (-aton-)

come forward: **ohén:ton tà:rehte'** he came
forward, **ohén:ton tá:ienhte'** she came forward (-eht-)

come in: *See* enter

Come on! **Hánio!** or **Hánion!**

comet: **otsísto kentáhsonte'**
(-tsisto[hkw]-, and -itahs-, -ont-)

comfort: **wa'khe'nikonhrahní:rate'**
I comforted her (-'nikonhr-, -hnir-)

comfortable: **wahonaktí:io'ne'** he got a
nice spot, he got comfortable (-nakt-, -iio-)

commit: *See* promise; commit

communion: **enhaià:tara'ne'** he will receive
communion (-ia't-, -r-)

compare: **tekéhrha'** I compare,
wà:tkeren' I compared it (-r-)

compete: **tehontkénnie's** they are competing,
wa'thontkén:ni' they competed,
teiakotkénnion she has competed (-kenni-)

complain: **rarihwakà:tats** he complains,
waharihwakà:tate' he complained,
iakorihwaka'tèn:'en she is complaining
(-rihwaka't[en]-)

complete: *See* finish

complete to exhaustion: **wa'kerihwaié:rite'**
I completed the task (to the point of exhaustion), **wakerihwaierí:ton** I am done doing it
(-rihw-, -ierit-)

complicate: **teioni'tón:ni** it is tangled,
complicated, a mess,
tehani'tonnià:tha' he messes it up,
he complicates things,
wa'thani'tónnia'te' he messed it up,
teiakoni'tonnià:ton she has messed it up
(-i't-, -onni-)

compress: **tehrontahní:rats** he is compressing it, packing it down,
wa'throntahní:rate' he compressed it,
tewakontahnirá:ton I have compressed it
(-hnir-)

conceited: *See* proud; conceited

concentrate: *See* focus

conductor: *See* cashier; conductor

conductor; engineer: **rahtentià:tha'**
(-ahtenti-)

cone; corn cob: **ononhkwèn:'on**
(-nonhkwen'-)

confirm: **kerihwahní:rats** I confirm it,
waharihwahní:rate' he confirmed it,
wakerihwahnirá:ton I have confirmed it
(-rihw-, -hnir-)

confirm (into a religion):
wahatken'tsóhkawe' he was confirmed
(-atken'tsohkaw-)

confront: **wa'khenenhrotá:ko'** I confronted
her, **wa'onkenenhrotá:ko'** she confronted
me (-nenhr-, -ot-)

confront; tell off: **sakhehsnó:rahkwe'**
I confronted her, I told her off
(-hsnor[e]-)

connect: *See* attach, end-to-end; join; connect

consent: **kathón:tats** I consent, I agree,
wahathón:tate' he consented,
wakathontá:ton I have consented
(-athont[e]-)

conserve: *See* put away; save

conspicuous: **roià:taken** he stands out,
he is conspicuous, **iakoià:taken** she is
conspicuous (-ia't-, -ken-)

constipated: **ro'tanén:taks** he is constipated,
iako'tanén:taks she is constipated
(-i't-, -ra'nentak-/-nentak-)

contagious: **iakó:ra's** it is contagious (-r-)

container: **ieráhkhwa'** (-r-)

continue: **ienkkón:tahkwe'** I will keep
doing it, **iahakón:tahkwe'** he kept doing it,
he continued (-kon[t]-);
ia'katahsónteren' I am continuing (with
what I am doing) (-ahsonter-)

control: **thanónhtons** he gets his way,
he likes to control things,
tahanónhton' he got his way,
thonónhton he has had his way (-anonhton-)

converse: *See* talk

convince: **wa'thi'nikonhrakén:ni'** I convinced him, I won him over, **wa'thake'nikonhrakén:ni'** he won me over (-'nikonhr-, -kenni-)

cook: **keríhtha'** I cook it, **wà:kerihte'** I cooked it, **wakeríhton** I have cooked it, **wa'ká:ri'** it got cooked, **ió:ri** it is cooked (-ri-)

cook, prepare a meal: **kekhón:nis** I cook, I prepare a meal, **wa'kekhón:ni'** I cooked, **rokhón:ni** he is cooking (-khw-, -onni-)

cool: **kewistóhtha'** I cool it, **wa'kewístohte'** I cooled it, **wa'kawístohte'** it got cold, cooled down, **iowisto'onhátie'** it is cooling off (-wisto-)

copy; imitate: **tehshakona'ké:rens** he imitates her, copies her, **takhena'ké:ren'** I imitated her, **thona'kerá:ni** he is imitating him (-na'kerani-/-na'keren-)

copy; trace: **thate'nienténhstha'** he is tracing it, copying it, **takate'nién:tenhste'** I traced it, copied it, **tiakote'nienténhston** she has traced it, copied it (-ate'nienten-)

copy, make a copy: **tekhna'netáhkwas** I am making a copy, **wa'tekhna'netáhko'** I made a copy, **tehohna'netáhkwen** he has made a copy (-hna'netahkw-/-netahkw-)

corduroy: **barakén:**

core; Adam's apple: **ohà:ta'** (-ha't-)

cork: **oneráhsa'** (-nerahs-)

corn: **ó:nenhste'** (-nenhst-)

corn, boiled and sweetened: **ono'kwítshera'** (-no'kwitsher-)

corn, Green Corn festival: **okahseró:ta'** (-kahserot-)

corn, hominy: **kanen'ón:ni** (-nen'onni-)

corn, Indian white: **onenhakén:ra** (-nenh-, -kenra-)

corn, popcorn: **watenenhstatakwáhton** (-nenhst-, -attatakw-)

corn, sweet: **teionenhstatsikhè:tare'** (-nenhst-, -tsikhe't-, -r-)

corn chaff: **okehwhèn:ta'** (-kehwhen't-)

corn cob; cone: **ononhkwèn:'on** (-nonhkwen'-)

corn cob game: **tekanonhkwen'áneren** (-nonhkwen'-, -hwaneren[k]-/-neren[k]-)

corn crib: **iontenenhstatha'táhkhwa'** (-nenhst-, -statha't-/-atha't-)

corn ear: **ohráhta'** (-hraht-)

corn husk: **onó:ra'** (-nor-)

corn husk face: **katiéhson**

corn mush: **kanehèn:ta'** or **kanenhèn:ta'** (-nehen't-/-nenhen't-)

corn soup: **kanénhsto** or **onénhsto** (-nenhst-, -o-)

corn stalk: **óhere'** (-her-)

corn stalk, cut corn stalks: **wakkéhon** I am harvesting corn, cutting the stalks (-kehon-)

corn tassle: **ókera'** (-ker-)

cornbread: **kana'tarokhón:we** (-na'tar[o][k]-)

cornbread paddle: **a'serawénrie'** (-a'ser-, -awenrie-)

corner: **ohiohsà:ke** corner, **tsi tekahióhsaien'** at the corner, **tsi iothióhsate'** (at) the corner (-hiohs-)

Cornwall, Ontario: **Kawehnò:ke** (-wehn-); **Teken'tarèn:re'**

Corpus Christi: **Tsi iontenerahtonnià:tha'** (-neraht-, -onni-)

cost: **Tó: nikanó:ron?** How much does it cost? (-noron-)

costume, put on: **wa'thatahkwenniaierónnion'** he put on a costume, **tehotahkwenniaierónnion** he has on a costume (-ahkwenni-, -ieron-)

cough: **kahsà:kha'** I cough, **wa'káhsa'ke'** I coughed, **rohsà:ken** he is coughing (-ahsa'k-)

cough drop; mint: **iakonia'takahrónhstha'** (-nia't-, -akahron-)

council: **ratitsénhaiens** they council, **ietsenhaientáhkhwa'** council hall (-tsenh-, -ien-)

count: **tkahsé:tas** I am counting, **takáhsete'** I counted, **tewakahsé:ton** I have counted, **tahshakóhsete'** he counted them (-ahset-)

couple: **tehotirihwaienawà:kon** they are a couple, **teionkenirihwaienawà:kon** he/she and I are a couple, my spouse (-rihw-, -ienawa'k-/-wa'k-)

cousin: **ontiara'sè:'a** my cousin (-ara'se-)

Covenant Belt: **tehonatatenentshawà:kon** (-nentsh-, -ienawa'k-/-wa'k-)

cover: **ke'rhó:roks** I cover it, **wa'ke'rhó:roke'** I covered it, **ro'rhó:ron** he has covered it, **ka'rhó:ron** it is covered, **wahi'rhó:roke'** I covered him, **wa'kate'rhó:roke'** I covered myself (-'rhoro[k]-/-oro[k]-)

cover (a floor): **kítskarons** I put a cover on the floor (a rug, linoleum), **wa'kítskaron'** I put down a cover, **wakítskaron** I have put down a cover, **kéntskare'** cover, linoleum, carpeting (-itskar[on]-)

cover s.o.: **wa'káhkwase'** I covered (myself), **wahakwáhkwase'** he covered me (-ahkwas-)

cover with a lid: **ranón:teks** he is putting the lid on, **wa'kenón:teke'** I put the lid on, **iakononté:kon** she has put the lid on, **kanonté:kon** it has a lid on it (-nontek-)

cow: **tiohnhónskwaron** or **tionhnhónskwaron**

coward: **wake'nikonhratsi'ió:ha** I have a weak mind, I am cowardly (-'nikonhr-, -tsi'io-)

cowlick: **rotsiskaión:ni** he has a cowlick, **iakotsiskaión:ni** she has a cowlick (-tsiskaionni-)

crabapple: **sewahiowane'ón:we** (-ahi-, -kowan[en]-/-owan[en]-)

cradleboard: **káhrhon** (-(h)rho-)

cramp: *See* charley horse; cramp

cranberry: **tó:kwahre'**

crane; blue heron: **ohà:kwaront**

crave: **kenón:waks** I have a craving for it, I am hungry for it, **wahanón:wake'** he craved it (-nonwak-)

crawl: **ratè:sere'** he is crawling, **wa'ontè:sere'** she crawled, **ratè:sere's** he is crawling around (-'sere-)

crayons: **ionhsóhkhwa'** or **ionhsohkwahrhohstáhkhwa'** (-ahsohkw-)

crazy: **tekanonhwarawénrie'** I am crazy, **wa'tkanonhwarawénrie'** I went crazy, **teiakononhwarawenriè:tha'** it makes her or someone crazy (-nonhwar-, -awenrie-)

cream: **kawistohserókwen** (-wistohser-, -okw-)

Creator: **Shonkwaia'tíson'** Our Creator (-hsa'-/-isa'-)

credit, give credit: **khekarotá:ni** I give her credit (towards a bill), **wahikaróthahse'** I gave him credit (-kar-, -ot-)

Cree: **Ratihrhakón:ha** (-(h)rh-)

creek: **kahiónha'** creek, **kahionhatátie'** there's a creek going along (-hionh-)

cricket: **taráktarak**

crispiness: **otsihénhsta'** (-tsihenhst-)

criticize; insult: **wa'khehsénhten'** I criticized her, I insulted her, **rakhsenhtén:ni** he criticizes me (-hs-, -a'senht-/-enht-)

crocodile: **teka'nikahtón:ton** (-'nika[ht]-, -ont-)

crooked: *See* bend; fold

crooked: *See* lean to one side; slant

cross: **kaiáhsa'** (-iahs-)

cross: **tetià:ia'ks** I cross over, **wa'thaià:ia'ke'** he crossed over, **tewatiahià:kon** I have crossed over (-iahia'k-/-iia'k-)

cross the border: **ia'teharistí:ia'ks** he goes across the (U.S.-Can.) border, **ia'tenteniristí:ia'ke'** you and I will go across the border, **ia'tewakeristiià:kon** I have gone across the border (-rist-, -iahia'k-/-iia'k-)

cross-eyed: **rakahkarèn:re'** he is cross-eyed, **iekahkarèn:re'** she is cross-eyed (-kahkarenhre-)

crossbones (indicating poison): **tekahstièn:tare'** (-hstien['t]-, -r-)

crossing guard; traffic cop: **shakohahá:wis** (-hah-, -awi-/-on-)

crotch: **teha'khó:ken** his crotch, **teie'khó:ken** her crotch (-'khoken-)

crouch: **ke'nó:waien'** I am crouched down, **wahate'nó:waien'** he crouched down (-'now-, -ien-)

crouch; squat: **tekenón:saien'** I am crouching, squatting (-nons-, -ien-)

crow: **tsó:ka'we'**

crowbar: **karistatsi'kó:wa**

crowd: **kanèn:ra'** (-nenhr-)

crowded: **ionkwè:ne'** it is crowded, **wa'onkwè:ne'ne'** it got crowded, **ionkwatonkwe'néhston** we are crowding, loitering (-onkwe'ne-)

crutches: **roten'nitsherò:ron** he has crutches (under his arms), **iakoten'nitsherò:ron** she has crutches (-aten'nits-/-aten'nitsher-, -ohro[k]-)

cry: **teionhsénthos** she is crying, **wa'thahséntho'** he cried, **tewakahsénthon** I have cried (-ahsentho-)

cry: *See* sob; cry

cry, make cry: **raktsi'tón:nis** he makes me cry, **wahaktsi'tón:ni'** he made me cry (-tsi'tonni-)

cry, stop crying: **wahatsì:tia'ke'** he stopped crying (-tsi'tia'k-)

crybaby: **rotsi'tà:ren** he is a crybaby, **iakotsi'tà:ren** she is a crybaby (-tsi'tahren-)

crybaby: **ratsì:tawis** he is a crybaby, **ietsì:tawis** she is a crybaby; **atsì:tawis** crybaby (-tsi'tawi-)

crybaby: **rattsi'ténhtha'** he is a crybaby, **ionttsi'ténhtha'** she is a crybaby (-tsi'tenht-)

cucumber; zucchini: **kanon'ónseres** (-non'onser-, -es-)

cuff, of a shoe or moccasin: **ohsaráhkwa'** (-ahsarahkw-)

cupboard; cabinet: **ioronto'tsheranentá:kon** (-ronto'tsher-, -ra'nentak-/-nentak-)

cupboard; pantry; closet: **iontahkwennia-ientáhkhwa'** (-ahkwenni-, -ien-)

curly: **tewakenónhkeri** I have curls, curly hair, **teionónhkeri** it is curly (-nonhkeri-)

current: *See* rapid; current

curtain; net; veil: **à:'are'** (-a'ar-)

curve: **teiotkwá:ton** there is a curve (-kwat-)

cut: **ítia'ks** I am cutting it, **wà:tia'ke'** I cut it, **watià:kon** I have cut it (-ia'k-)

cut; slice: **kkwè:tarons** I slice it, I cut off a piece, **wa'kkwè:tare'** I cut it, **wakkwè:taron** I have sliced it (-kwe'tar[on]-/-e'tar[on]-)

cut hair: **shakonónhkarons** he cuts their hair, (he is) a barber, **wa'onkenónhkare'** she cut my hair, **rinónhkaron** I have cut his hair, **wa'katenónhkare'** I cut my hair (-nonhkar[on]-)

cut into: **khrè:nas** or **khré:nas** I cut into it, I make an incision, **wà:khre'ne'** or **wà:khrene'** I cut it, **wakhrè:nen** or **wakhré:nen** I have made a cut (-hren-/-hre'n-)

cut off: **thá:ia'ks** he is cutting off a piece, **tátia'ke'** I cut some off, **thoià:kon** he has cut it off (-ia'k-)

cute: **onekwen'tarí:ha** expression used to refer to something small, cute, chubby

damp; soggy: **iotón:ris** it is damp, soggy, **wa'otonrísta'ne'** it got damp (-atonris[t]-)

dance: **tekenonniáhkhwa'** I dance, **wa'tkenónniahkwe'** I danced, **tewakenonniáhkwen** I am dancing (-nonni-, -hkw-)

dance, Dance for the Dead: **Ohkí:we**

dance, Great Feather dance: **Ohstowa'kó:wa**

dance, jig: **tekatenonniakénnie's** I jig, **wa'thatenonniakén:ni'** he jigged, **teiakotenonniakénnion** she is jigging (-nonni-, -kenni-)

dance, Skin dance: **kanehó:ron** or **onehó:ron** (-nehw-, -'rhoro[k]-/-oro[k]-)

dance, square dance: **tekanèn:res** (-nenhr-, -es-)

dance, Warrior dance: **Wesá:se'**

dandelion: **kahonro'tó:ton** (-honro't-, -ot-)

dandruff: **rawéharare'** he has dandruff, **iakawéharare'** she has dandruff (-eharar-)

dangerous; scary: **ióthteron** it is dangerous, it is scary (-hteron-)

daring; fearless: **ratattsináhstha'** he is daring, fearless, willing to take anybody on, **iontattsináhstha'** she is fearless (-tsin-)

dark: **tetiò:karas** it is dark, **tontaiò:karahwe'** it got dark, **tetio'karà:'on** it has gotten dark (-a'kara[hw]-)

dark, in the dark: **ahsá:takon** (-ahsat-)

date: **shískare'** the day of the month, the date (-r-)

dates: **onénhontste'** (-nenhontst-)

daughter: **kheièn:'a** my daughter (-ien-)

daughter-in-law: **kheiehnhónsa'** (-ehnhonsa') or **khesà:wha** my daughter-in-law (-sa'w-)

daughter, stepdaughter: **khenò:'a** my stepdaughter (-no-)

dawn: **tontawentahróho'** (it is) early dawn (the sun has not risen) (-ent-, -hroh[o]-)

day: **awenhnísera'** (-enhniser-)

day, all day: **kon'tátie'**

daylight: **wén:te'** it is daylight, **taiawente'onhátie'** it is becoming daylight, it is almost daylight (-ent-)

deaf: **tekahonhtakwé:kon** I am hard of hearing, I am deaf, **tehahonhtakwé:kon** he is deaf, **teionhonhtakwé:kon** she is deaf (-ahonht-, -kwek-)

dear: **tien'** endearing term used for children or younger relatives

deceive: *See* trick; deceive

December: **Tsothóhrha** (-athor[e]-)

decide: **wa'kate'nikonhrísa'** I made up my mind, **rote'nikonhríson'** he has made up his mind (-'nikonhr-, -hsa'-/-isa'-); **takate'nikonhró:ten** I made up my mind (-'nikonhr-, -ot-)

deep: **iohnó:tes** it is deep (-es-)

deer: **oskenón:ton** (-skenonton-)

deer fly: **onerón:ta'** (-neront-)

defeat: **khe'shénnie's** I defeat her, **wahshako'shén:ni'** he defeated her (-'shenni-)

defeat: *See* beat at

defecate: **raní'taiens** he is defecating, **wahaní'taien'** he defecated, **iakoní'taien'** she has defecated (-i't-, -ien-)

defective: *See* weak; feeble

defend: **tekhéhnhes** I defend her, **tahíhnhe'** I defended him (-(h)nhe-)

defrost: **wa'kenennio'kwaná:wenhte'** I defrosted it (-nennio'kw-, -na'nawen-/-nawen-)

delicious: *See* tasty

deliver: *See* spread around

dent: *See* bruise; dent

deny: **ratonhnhí:ias** he denies it, **wahatónhnhiie'** he denied it, **rotonhnhí:hen** he is denying it (-atonhnhii-); **katerihwaiehwáhtha'** I deny it, pretend to not know, **wa'katerihwaiè:wahte'** I denied it, **wakaterihwaiehwáhton** I am pretending to not know (-rihw-, -iehwa-/-ioha-)

depend on; rely; trust: **keniahé:sen** I depend on it, I rely on it, **konniahé:sen** I am depending on you, I trust you, **wahiniáhese'** I depended on him, trusted him (-niahes-)

depressed: **wake'nikonhrèn:ton** I am depressed (-'nikonhr-, -hren't-/-en't-)

depressed: *See* hopeless

descend: **tkatsnénhtha'** I come down, **tahátsnenhte'** he came down, **tewakatsnénhton** I have come down, **tonkwatsnenhtonhátie'** I am on my way down, **iekatsnénhtha'** I go down, **iahátsnenhte'** he went down, **iewakatsnénhton** I have gone down (-atsnenht-)

detective: **rottsistohkwahséhton** he is a detective (-tsisto[hkw]-, -ahseht-)

Detroit: **Tiohsahróntion**

devil; demon: **ótkon** (-atkon-)

dew: **io'áweien** (-'aweien-)

diabetes: **teiakonekwenhsatsikhè:tare'** (-nekwenhs-, -tsikhe't-, -r-)

diamonds, suit of diamonds: **teiotekerón:te'** (-keront-/-okeront-)

diaper: **athwawen'éktha'** or **teionthwawen'ekstáhkhwa'** (-hwawen'e[k]-/-awen'e[k]-)

diaper, put or have on: **wa'tekhe'kharotáhrhoke'** I put a diaper on her, **teiakote'kharotáhrhon** she has on a diaper (-'khar-, -otahrho[k]-)

diarrhea: **tewakatia'tonkóhtha'** I have diarrhea, **wa'tewakatia'tón:kohte'** I got diarrhea (-ia't-, -onko-)

dice, play: **tekena'kará:iens** I am playing dice (-na'kar-, -ien-)

die: **renhé:ions** he is dying, **wahrénheie'** he died, **wa'íheie'** she died, **iakawenhé:ion** she is dead (-ihei[on]-/-enhei[on]-)

die: *See* breath, take one's last

die from: **iakorióhtha'** she is dying from it, **wa'akóriohte'** she died from it, **iakorióhton** she has died from it (-rio-/-riio-)

diet: **katatiwáhtha'** I am dieting, **wa'ontatí:wahte'** she put herself on a diet (-atiw-)

different: **thiká:te'** it is different, **iah tha'teká:te'** there is no difference (-te-); **tetiattíhen** the two are different (-tiha-)

difficult: **wentó:re'** it is difficult, it is hard, **enwató:ren'ne'** it will become difficult (-entor[e]-)

dig: **kó'kwats** I am digging, **wahró'kwate'** he dug, **wako'kwá:ton** I have dug (-o'kwat-)

dig around: *See* rummage

diligent: **wakatste'niá:ron'** I keep at it, I put in a good effort, I am diligent, **rotste'niá:ron'** he is diligent, **iakotste'niá:ron'** she is diligent (-atste'niaron-)

dilute: **rahnekaríhsions** he dilutes it, **wa'khnekaríhsi'** I diluted it, **wakhnekaríhsion** I have diluted it (-hnek-, -rihsi-)

dimples: **iakohnho'kwakà:ronte'** she has dimples (-(h)nho'kw-, -kahront-)

dipper: **iakotsenhtáhkhwa'** (-otsenht-)

dipper, Big Dipper; Pleiades: **tsá:ta nihatinekwà:take** (-nekwa't-, -ke-)

dipper, Little Dipper; Pleiades: **onekwa'tara'shòn:'a** (-nekwa't-, -r-)

dirt; ashes: **o'kèn:ra'** (-a'kenhr-)

dirty: **teió'tson** it is dirty, **wa'tió'tson'ne'** it got dirty, **wa'tkí'tsonhste'** I dirtied it (-i'tson-/-'tson-)

dirty face: **tehonenskón:warare'** he has a dirty face, **teiakonenskón:warare'** she has a dirty face (-nenskonwarar-)

dirty laundry: **onentstá:kwara'** (-nentstakwar-)

disagree: *See* argue; disagree

disappear: **wáhtons** it disappears, **ónhton'** it disappeared, **iohtòn:'on** it has disappeared (-ahton-)

disappear; go out of sight: **iewakenonwiréhtha'** I disappear, go out of sight, **iahonkenonwí:rehte'** I went out of sight, **iewakenonwiréhton** I have disappeared (-nonwireht-)

discourage: **wahi'nikonhrário'** I changed his mind, I discouraged him, convinced him to not do it (-'nikonhr-, -rio-/-riio-)

discouraged: *See* hopeless

disease; sickness: **káhnhra'** (-(h)nhr-)

disease, sexual: **tehoterà:'on** he got a sexually transmitted disease, **teiakoterà:'on** she got a sexually transmitted disease (-r-)

dish; plate: **káksa'** (-ks-)

dish; plate; bowl: **akè:ra'** (-akehr-/-kehr-)

dislike: **íkhswens** I dislike things, **wà:khswen'** I disliked it, **ríhswens** I dislike him, **atathswénhsera'** dislike (-hsw[en]-)

dislike s.o.: **kheiatahkwáhswens** I dislike her, hate her, **wahiiatahkwáhswen'** I disliked him, hated him (-atahkwahswen-)

disobey: **shakowennóntie's** he disobeys her, **wahiwennón:ti'** I disobeyed him (-wenn-, -ati-/-onti-); **iah tehiwennaráhkwen** I didn't heed him, I didn't listen to him (-wenn-, -r-)

disoriented: **wa'tewakatonhontsa-kahrhaténien'** I got disoriented (-onhwents-/-onhonts-, -kahrhateni-)

disperse: **tewattókwas** it goes all over, **wa'tewattó:ko'** it dispersed, it went all over, **teiottókwen** it has gone all over (-attokw-); **tewarénie's** it goes all over, **wa'tewaré:ni'** it fell apart, it went all over, **tonsaiakwaré:ni'** we dispersed (-areni-)

ditch: **tekahronión:ni** (there is) a ditch (-hronw-, -onni-)

ditch, dig: **wa'thonnóntia'ke** they dug, made a ditch (-nont-, -ia'k-)

dive: **rathón:ros** he is diving, **wahathón:ro'** he dove (-athonro-)

dizzy: **iakotsinonhwaténie's** she gets dizzy, **onktsinonhwaté:ni'** I got dizzy (-tsinonhwateni-)

do: **tsi nitiéhrha'** how or what I do, **tsi nà:tiere'** how I did it, **tsi niwatié:ren** how I have done it (-ier-)

do, keep doing: *See* continue

do fast: **kathsnó:rats** I am hurrying up, **wa'kathsnó:rate'** I hurried up, I went fast, **rothsnorá:ton** he has hurried up, **raia'tahsnó:re'** he is fast, he does things fast (-ia't-, -hsnor[e]-)

do good deeds: **tierihwaié:rits** she does good deeds, **tahaierihwaié:rite'** he did good deeds, **thorihwaierí:ton** he has done a good deed (-rihw-, -ierit-)

do good job: **thateweièn:tons** he does a good job, **tahateweièn:ton'** he did a good job, **tewakateweièn:ton** I have done a good job (-ateweien'ton-)

do intensely: **kahkwíhsrons** I try hard, I do it intensely, with effort, **wahahkwíhsron'** he tried hard, **rohkwíhsron** he is trying hard (-ahkwihsron-)

do over: **entkáteratste'** I will do it over, **takáteratste'** I did it over (-ateratst-)

do slowly: **watia'takenhé:ion** I do things slowly, I am a slowpoke (-ia't-, -ihei[on]-/-enhei[on]-)

dock (plant): **ítiete'**

dock; wharf: **ó:tsire' tekatáhstha'** (-tsir- and -t-/-et-)

dock, put in a dock: **iahatáhskohwe'** he put in a dock (-ahskw-, -ohw-)

doctor: **katétsen'ts** I am a doctor, **enkhétsen'te'** I will doctor her, treat her, **wahakétsen'te'** he treated me (-tsen't-)

dodge: **iontahratè:kwas** she is turning her head away, **wa'katahratè:ko'** I turned my head away, I dodged it, **rotahratè:kwen** he has turned his head away (-atahrate'kw-)

dog: **è:rhar**

doll: **kaia'tón:ni** (-ia't-, -onni-)

doll, wooden: **tohtó:wi**

dollar; bill: **onakè:ta'** bill, dollar, **skanakè:ta** one bill, one dollar (-nake['t]-, -[t]-)

dollar; money; metal: **ohwísta'** money, metal, **skahwísta** one dollar (-hwist-, -[t]-)

donkey: **tewahónhtes** (-ahonht-, -es-)

don't: **tóhsa**

donuts, make donuts: **wa'kehsnonhsón:ni'** I made donuts (-hsnonhs-, -onni-)

door: **kahnhóha'** (-(h)nhoh-)

door, close: *See* close (a door)

door, lock: **kenientháhrhoks** I am locking the door, **wa'kenientháhrhoke'** I locked the door, **iakonientháhrhon** she has locked the door (-nienthahrhok-)

door, storm door: **tewatehnhohanéta's** (-(h)nhoh-, -hna'neta'-/-neta'-)

door, unlock: **wa'kenienthará:ko'** I unlocked the door, **ronientharákwen** he has unlocked the door (-nientharakw-)

dot: *See* star; dot

dot, polka-dotted: **kanekwarónnion** or **ionekwarónnion** it is polka-dotted (-nekwar-, -r-)

double; line: **tekahnà:ne** or **teiohnà:ne** it is lined, doubled (-hna'ne[t]-/-ne[t]-); **tenkhna'néta'** I will line it, double it, **wa'tekhna'néta'** I lined it, I doubled it (-hna'neta'-/-neta'-)

doubt: **katenowénhtha'** I doubt it, **wa'hatenó:wenhte'** he doubted it, **iakotenowénhton** she is doubting it (-nowen-)

dough; gravy: **oshè:rha'** (-she'rh-)

down: **nà:kon**

downstairs; basement: **onhontsó:kon** or **onhwentsó:kon** (-onhwents-/-onhonts-)

dozen: **sewatesèn:tshera** one dozen (-atesen-/-atosen-)

drag: **kè:sere'** I am dragging it, **wahà:sere'** he dragged it, **rà:sere's** he is dragging it around (-'sere-)

dragonfly: **tsikeninonhrawísta'** or **tsikeninon'rawísta'**

drain: **kenonwakéntstha'** I am draining it, **wa'kenón:wakentste'** I drained it, **iakononwakéntston** she has drained it (-nonw-, -kentst-); **wa'khné:kentste'** I drained it, **iakohnekéntston** she has drained it (-hnek-, -kentst-)

drape: **wa'ttia'karotáhrhoke'** I draped it over s.t. (-ia'kar-/-ia'kwar-, -otahrho[k]-)

drastic: *See* extreme; drastic; terrible

draw: **keráhstha'** I sketch it, I draw it, **wà:kerahste'** I drew it, **wakeráhston** I have drawn it (-r-)

drawknife: **ionton'wesà:tha'**

dream: **wakatétshens** I dream, **onkwatétshen'** I dreamed, **iakotetshèn:'en** she is dreaming, **wahakwatetshà:ten'** I dreamed of him (-atetsh[en]-)

dream, bad, good: **onkeserenhtáksen'ne'** I had a bad dream (-serenht-, -aksen-); **onkeserenhtí:io'ne'** I had a nice dream (-serenht-, -iio-)

dregs; bottom water: **onón:wa'** (-nonw-)

dress; shirt; jacket; coat: **atià:tawi** (-atia'tawi-)

dress, get dressed: **katsherón:nis** I get dressed, **wa'ontsherón:ni'** she got dressed (-hseronni-)

dress, get dressed: *See* ready, get ready

dress up: **wa'tekhnia'só:ten'** I got all dressed up, all done up, **wa'thahnia'só:ten'** he got all dressed up, **wa'tiehnia'só:ten'** she got all dressed up (-hnia's-, -ot-)

dress warmly: **wakahtà:nawen** I am dressed warmly, **ratahta'nawénhstha'** he dresses warmly, **wa'katahtà:nawenhste'** I got dressed warmly, **rotahta'nawénhston** he has dressed warmly (-ahta'nawen-)

dress well, elegantly: **rawénhsion** he is well-dressed, elegant, **iakawénhsion** she is well-dressed, elegant (-enhsion-)

dresser: **watatken'tsheróhare'** (-ken-, -ohar-)

dressing (chicken, turkey): **kaià:takon tiakéta's** (-ia't-, -ta'-/-eta'-)

drift: *See* float; drift

drill: **iehsonwatase'táhkhwa'** (-hsonw-, -hwatase-/-tase-)

drink: **khnekíhrha'** I drink, **wahahnekì:ra'** he drank, **wakhnekì:ren** I am drinking, I have drunk (-hnekir-/-hnekihra-)

drip: **watshà:rhons** or **watshà:nhons** it is dripping, leaking, **ontshà:rhon'** or **ontshà:nhon'** it dripped (-atsha'rhon-/-atsha'nhon-)

drip: *See* leak; drip

drive: **katórie's** I drive, **waható:ri'** he drove it, **ratorihátie'** he is driving (-ori-)

drizzle: **iaonhawí:non** it is drizzling (-onhawinon-)

drool: **iakótskeren's** she is drooling, **wahótskeren'ne'** he drooled (-itsker-, -a'sen'-/-en'-)

drop: **ieka'sénhtha'** I drop it down or in, **ia'kà:senhte'** I dropped it, **iewaka'sénhton** I have dropped it (-a'senht-/-enht-)

drop uninentionally: **waka'sèn:se'** I drop it, **onkwà:sen'se'** I dropped it (-a'sen's-/-en's-)

drop, a drop: **ohstá:ra'** (-hstar-)

drown: **wahà:sko'ne'** he drowned, **roskò:'on** he has drowned (-'sko'-); **wahshakò:skohte'** he drowned her or them (-'skoht-)

drowsy: *See* sleepy

drugstore: **tsi iontenonhkwa'tshera-hninòn:tha'** (-nonhkw-/-nonhkwa'tsher-, -hninon-)

drum; barrel: **ka'náhkon** (-'nahkw-)

drum, water drum: **kanehó:ron** or **onehó:ron** (-nehw-, -'rhoro[k]-/-oro[k]-); **kana'tsówi**

drumstick: **ie'nahkwakonhrékstha'** (-'nahkw-, -konhre[k]-)

drunk: **rohné:ka** he drank too much, he is drunk (-hnek-, -a[t]-); **rononhwarahtòn:'on** he is drunk (-nonhwar-, -ahton-)

dry: **iostáthen** it is dry, **onstáthen'** it dried, **iostathèn:'en** it has dried (-astath[en]-/-ath[en]-); **kstathà:tha'** I dry it, **wahastátha'te'** he dried it, **rostathà:ton** he is drying it, **kastathà:ton** it is dried (-statha't-/-atha't-)

dry, go dry; evaporate: **ónhsteske'** it evaporated, went dry, **iahónhsteske'** it boiled away, evaporated, **ieiohstéskon** it has evaporated (-ahstesk-)

duck: **só:ra'**

duck, wild: **sónhatsi**

dull: **wa'tekhiò:kete'** I made it dull, **wa'tewathiò:kete'** it got dull, **teiothiò:kton** it is dull (-hio'kt-/-hio'ket-)

dumpling: **o'nhóntsta'** dumpling, **kítkit ieka'nhontstóhon** chicken and dumplings (-'nhontst-)

during; until: **tsi niió:re'** (-re-)

dust: **ononhwénhskeri** (-nonhwenhsker-)

eagle: **à:kweks**; **tekatsi'ereskó:wa** (-tsi'er-, -es-)

ear: **ohónhta'** ear, **kahonhtà:ke** (on) my ear (-ahonht-)

earn; win: **tehatèn:tsha's** he is earning, **wa'tkatèn:tsha'** I earned, I won, I profited, **tewakatèn:tshon** I have earned, I have won (-'tsha'-)

earring: **ate'wáhshare'** earring, **tewakate'wáhshare'** I have on earrings (-ate'wahshar-)

earth; world: **onhóntsa'** or **onhwéntsa'** (-onhwents-/-onhonts-)

east: **nà:kon nonkwá:ti**

Easter: **Shatonhnhéthe'** (-onhnhe[t]-)

easy: **watié:sen** it is easy, **ontié:sen'ne'** it became easy, **iotiesèn:'en** it has become easy (-ies[en]-)

eat: **í:keks** I eat it, **wà:keke'** I ate it, **waké:kon** I have eaten it (-ek-/-ak-)

eat (a meal): **teiontskà:hons** she eats, **wa'thatskà:hon'** he ate, **tewakatskà:hon** I have eaten, I am eating (-atska'hon-)

eat (a prepared meal): **katekhón:nis**
I eat, have a meal, **wa'katekhón:ni'** I ate,
ionkwatekhón:ni we ate, we had a meal
(-khw-, -onni-)

eat, cut down on eating:
wa'katatekhókerike' I cut down on eating
(-khw-, -tokeri[k]-/-okeri[k]-)

eat, finish eating: **kekhwén:ta's** I finish eating, **wa'kekhwén:ta'ne'** I finished eating,
rokhwentà:'on he has finished eating
(-khw-, -ent-)

eat, finish eating; get full: **wakáhta's** I get
full, **onkwáhta'ne'** I finished eating, I got
full, **wakahtà:'on** I have finished eating,
I am done eating (-ahta'-)

eat all the food: **wahskwaniá:renhte'** you
finished all our food (-niar-, -a'senht-/-enht-)

eat gluttonously: **ranítsheho** he likes to eat,
he is a glutton, **wahanitshého'** he ate gluttonously, **anítsheho** glutton (-anitsheho-)

eat together: **wa'tiakwá:tonte'** we ate
together, **teionkwatón:ton** we are eating
together (-atont-)

eat up: **ratekhwísa's** he eats it all,
wa'katekhwísa' I ate it up, I finished it,
rotekhwíson' he has finished eating it
(-khw-, -hsa'-/-isa'-)

eaves: **teiotarontátie'** (-tar-, -ont-)

echo: **kawén:note'** echo, it is howling
(wind, a siren) (-wenn-, -ot-)

eclipse: **wa'tewaterahkwà:seren'**
(-rahkw-, -ia'ser-/-'ser-);
onterahkwáhton' (-rahkw-, -ahton-)

edge; end: **tsi iótte'** at the end, at the edge
(-te-)

eel: **tiawerón:ko**

effort, do with effort: *See* do intensely

egg: **o'nhónhsa'** (-'nhonhs-)

eight: **sha'té:kon**

elastic: **teiohnatiróntha'** it is elastic, an
elastic band (-ihn-, -atiront-)

elbow: **ohióhsa'** elbow, **khiohsà:ke** (on)
my elbow (-hiohs-)

elderberries: **orá:son**

electrician: **teharonwarahnhontéhrha'**
(-ronwar-/-nonwar-, -hnhonter-)

elegant: **iotkwénniens** or **iotkónniens** it
is appealing, elegant,
rotkwénniens or **rotkónniens** he is elegant,
iakotkwénniens or **iakotkónniens** she is
elegant (-kwennien-/-konnien-)

elegant: *See* dress well, elegantly

elephant: **o'notsta'kó:wa** (-'notst-)

elevator: **iakoia'takará:tats**
(-ia't-, -haratat-/-karatat-)

eleven: **énska iawén:re**

elk; caribou: **atená:ti**

elm, American: **aká:ratsi**

elm, slippery: **óhskare' kà:nen**;
ohò:ksera' or **ohò:kseri** (-ho'kser)

elm, species of elm: **okón:ra'**

elsewhere: **ákte'**

elsewhere; over there: **a'é:ren** or **é:ren**

embarrassed; ashamed: **katéhens** I get
embarrassed, ashamed,
wa'katéhen' I got embarrassed, ashamed,
wakatehèn:'en I am embarrassed, ashamed,
wa'kheiatéha'te' I embarrassed her,
iotéha it is shameful (-ateh[en]-)

embers; spark; fire: **ó:tsire'** (-tsir-)

embroider: **tekahseriiè:tarons** I am
embroidering it, **wa'tkahseriiè:taron'**
I embroidered it, **tewahseriiè:taron** it is
embroidered (-ahseriie['t]-, -r-)

empty: **rakahrhaténie's** he is emptying
it, **wahakahrhaté:ni'** he emptied it,
rokahrhaténion he has emptied it
(-kahrhateni-)

enamel: **kaneniáhrhon** (-neni-, -(h)rho-)

encourage: **wa'khehretsá:ron'** I encouraged
her or them, **rihretsá:ron** I am encouraging
him (-hretsaron-)

encourage; urge: **kheiatste'niá:ron** I am
urging, encouraging her to apply herself,
wahiiatste'niá:ron I encouraged him
(-atste'niaron-)

end; edge: **tsi iótte'** at the end, at the edge
(-te-)

end up somewhere: *See* show up

endure: **wakátste'** it lasts long, it endures
(-akatste-)

endure pain: **wakahkátste'** I can endure pain,
rohkátste' he can endure pain,
iakohkátste' she can endure pain (-ahkatste-)

energetic: *See* active; energetic

engine: **kanontsistáhere'** it has an engine
(-nontsi[st]-, -her-/-hr-)

engineer; conductor: **rahtentià:tha'**
(-ahtenti-)

English: **Tiohrhen'shá:ka** (-(h)rhen'-)

enjoy: **wakon'éskwani** or **wakon'wéskwani**
I enjoy it, **onkon'éskwen'** I enjoyed it,
wakon'weskwanì:'on I am enjoying it
(-on'eskw-/-on'weskw-)

enough: **tho ia'tekaié:ri** that's enough,
ia'tewatié:rihse' I had enough,
iah tha'tewatieríhse' I didn't have enough
(-ieri-)

enter: **thataweià:tha'** he comes in,
tahatáweia'te' he came in,
thotaweià:ton he has come in,
iehataweià:tha' he goes in,
iahatáweia'te' he went in,
iehotaweià:ton he has gone in (-ataweia't-)

entertain: **wa'kate'nikonhró:ri'** I got entertained, I had fun, **wahake'nikonhró:ri'** he
entertained me (-'nikonhr-, -ori-)

envelope: **watia'torókstha'**
(-ia't-, -'rhoro[k]-/-oro[k]-)

envy: **ra'nóshas** he is envious,
wa'ke'nósha' I became envious,
wake'nóshen I am envious,
ri'nóshas I envy him,
ka'nosháhtshera' envy (-'nosha-)

epidemic: **kahnhratarí:ne's** epidemic, the disease is going around, **wa'kahnhrá:tarine'** the disease went around (-(h)nhr-, -ine-)

epileptic: **wakhsiá:ra's** I am epileptic, **wahohsiá:ra'ne'** he had a seizure (-hsiara'-)

eraser: **tseronkwáhtha'** (-ronkw-)

escape: **ra'niá:ken's** he runs away, **waha'niá:ken'ne'** he ran away, took off, escaped, **ro'niakèn:'en** he has run away (-'niaken-)

Eucharist; Thursday: **Okaristiiáhne**

evaporate: *See* dry, go dry; evaporate

even; level: **sha'tetiótte'** it is even, the same level (-te-)

evening: **o'karahsnéha** (-a'kara[hw]-)

ever, never: **nonwén:ton** ever, **iah nonwén:ton** never

evergreen: **onèn:ta'** (-nen't-)

everywhere: **tsik nón:we**

examine: **katkèn:se'** I look into it, examine it, **wa'onkwátken'se'** she examined me, **wakatkèn:se'** I have looked into it (-ken-)

excrement: **ó'ta'** (-i't-)

excuse, make excuses: **raterihwatken'seráhkhwa'** he makes excuses, **wa'katerihwatkèn:serahkwe'** I made an excuse, **roterihwatken'seráhkwen** he is making excuses (-rihw-, -atken'serahkw-)

excuse me: **skén:nen sanonhtonniónhak** or **skén:nen sanonhtonniónhek** Have peace as you are thinking (excuse me!) (-anonhton-)

exercise: **katia'tahkariiohstánions** I exercise, **wa'katia'tahkarí:iohste'** I exercised, **iakotia'tahkariióhston** she is exercising (-ia'tahkariio-)

exhale: **ia'katonriserà:reke'** I exhaled (-atonriser, -hre[k]-)

expand: **wattèn:kwas** it expands, it rises (in baking), **onttèn:ko'** it expanded (-atten'kw-)

expect: *See* wait

expensive: **kanó:ron** it is expensive, **wa'kanó:ron'ne'** it became expensive (-noron-)

explain: **tekerihwathè:tha'** I make the issue clearer, **wa'tharihwáthe'te'** he made it clearer, he explained it, **tehotirihwathè:ton** they have explained it (-rihwathe't-)

explode: **onttatá:ko'** it exploded, **wa'kattatákwahte'** I exploded it (-attatakw-)

express oneself: **ia'kate'nikonhrón:ti'** I expressed myself (-'nikonhr-, -ati-/-onti-)

extinguish: **ka'swáhtha'** I extinguish a fire, I turn off the light, **wa'kà:swahte'** I turned off the light, **waka'swáhton** I have turned off the light (-a'swaht-)

extra: **iowénhte'** it is left over, there is an extra amount (-awenht[e]-)

extreme; drastic; terrible: **teiotenonhianíhton** it is extreme, drastic (-nonhiani-)

eye: **okà:ra'** eye, **kkahrà:ke** (on) my eye (-kahr-)

eye, close: **tekateròn:weks** I close my eyes, **wa'tkateròn:weke'** I closed my eyes, **tewakateron'wé:kon** my eyes are closed (-ron'wek-)

eye, get s.t. in: **onkkà:ri'se'** something went into my eye, **wakkahrì:sen** I have something in my eye (-kahri's-)

eye, open: **tekatkahkwaríhsions** I open my eyes, **wa'tiontkahkwaríhsi'** she opened her eyes, **tewakatkahkwaríhsion** I have opened my eyes (-atkahkwarihsi-); **wa'tkateron'wékhsi'** I opened my eyes (-ron'wek-)

eye, open wide: **tekkahríneken's** I open my eyes big or wide, **wa'tiekahríneken'ne'** she opened her eyes wide, **tewakkahrinekèn:'en** my eyes are opened wide (-kahr-, -ineken'-)

eyeball: **okahrò:kwa'** (-kahro'kw-)

eyebrow: **okèn:kera'** eyebrow, **kken'kerà:ke** (on) my eyebrow (-ken'ker-)

eyeglasses: **atkahráhnha'** (-kahr-, -hwahnha[k]-/-hnha[k]-)

eyelash: **okahréhta'** eyelash, **akkahréhta'** my eyelash (-kahreht-)

eyelid skin: **onawà:sa'** skin on the eyelid up to the eyebrow (-nawa's-)

fabric; material: **á:ta'** (-ata-); **onia'tarà:'a** (-nia'tar-)

face: **okónhsa'** face, **kkonhsà:ke** (on) my face (-konhs-)

fail; not go as planned: **onkwatientakahrháthoʼseʼ** it didn't go well for me, not as planned (-ient-, -kahrhatho-)

fail at: **tetewakahtákwas** I try but fail, **tontonkwahtá:ko'** I was unsuccessful and tried again (-ahtakw-)

faint: **onke'nikonhráhton'** I fainted (-'nikonhr-, -ahton-)

faint from hunger: **í:wehre' aonkwata'kenhrókwahse'** I feel faint from hunger (-a'kenhr-, -okw-)

fake: *See* pretend; fake

fall; autumn: **kanenna'kè:ne**

fall apart: *See* disperse

fall backwards: *See* lean back; fall backwards

fall down; fall off: **tewà:sen's** it falls down, **tòn:sen'ne'** it fell down, **tio'sèn:'en** it has fallen down, **ia'tià:ten'ne'** I fell down or off, **iehoia'tèn:'en** he has fallen down (-a'sen'-/-en'-)

fall down; fall over: **ka'rhé:nien's** it falls down or over, **wa'ka'rhé:nien'ne'** it fell down or over, **io'rhenièn:'en** it has fallen down or over, **wa'tia'tié:nen'ne'** I fell down or over (-'rhenienht-/-ienenht-)

fall down; tumble: **ia'kena'skwaién:ta'ne'** I fell down, I tumbled down (-na'skw-, -ien-)

falseface: **ratórie's** (-ori-); **atò:wi** or **hatónwi** (-ato'wi-); **okón:wara'** (-konwar-)

falter; get stuck: **onkotáhrhe'se'** I got hung up, I got stuck (-otahrhe's-)

family: **kahwá:tsire'** (-hwatsir-)

family, be family: **rontenò:sen** they are family (-ateno'sen-)

family, paternal: **akatón:ni** my paternal family, my godfather (-atonni-)

famous: **rahsennowá:nen** he has a big name, he is famous, **wahahsennowáhnha'** he got a big name, a big reputation (-hsenn-, -kowan[en]-/-owan[en]-)

fan: **kateweiá:waks** I am fanning myself, **wa'kateweiá:wake'** I fanned myself, **wakateweiawá:kon** I have fanned myself, **wa'kheweiá:wake'** I fanned her, **ionteweiawákstha'** fan (-wei-, -awak-)

far: **í:non**

farm: **kahehtà:ke** (on) the farm (-heht-)

fart: **wahani'té:ni'** he farted, **roni'ténion** he has farted (-ani'teni-)

fart; pass wind: **wahowera'niá:ken'se'** he farted, he passed wind (-wer-, -'niaken-)

fast: **iohsnó:re'** it is fast, **raia'tahsnó:re'** he is fast, does things fast (-ia't-, -hsnor[e]-)

fast-moving: **teiò:ka** it is fast, **tewakè:ka** I am fast (-'ka[ht]-)

fast; go without: **onkwentóntiehte'** I fasted, I went without, **rawentontiéhton** he has fasted (-ent-, -ati-/-onti-)

fat: **wakáre'sen** I am fat, **wa'ónre'sen'** she got fat, **rore'sèn:'en** he has gotten fat (-are'sen-)

fat: **sakwè:tsta'** you fatty! you're fat!

fat; grease: **o'tónsera'** (-i'tonser-)

father: **rake'níha** my father (-'ni-)

father-in-law: **rakwehnhónsa'** my father-in-law (-ehnhonsa'); **raksà:wha** my father-in-law (-sa'w-)

father, stepfather: **rakenò:'a** my stepfather (-no-)

fathom (measure): **skáweia** a measure spanning the arms spread out (-wei-)

fault: **raónha raorì:wa'** (it's) his fault, **akáonha akorì:wa'** (it's) her fault (-rihw-)

fearless: *See* daring; fearless

feast: *See* wedding; feast

feather: **ò:nahs** (-'nahs-)

feather; down; fluff: **ohstò:seri** small feathers, down, fluff, **iohstò:seronte'** it has feathers (-hsto'ser-, -ont-)

February: **Enníska**

fed up: **wakenonniá:nis** I am fed up, **onkenonniá:ni'** I got fed up (-nonniani-)

fed up: *See* annoyed

feeble: *See* weak; feeble

feed s.o.: **khenón:tens** I feed her or them, **wahí:nonte'** I fed him, **ronwanón:ten** she has fed him (-nont[en]-)

feed s.o.: **khehnhónthos** I am putting food in her mouth, I am feeding her, **wahonwahnhóntho'** she fed him, **rihnhónthon** I have fed him (-(h)nhontho-)

felt (fabric): **okénha'** (-kenh-)

female: **tewakathonwí:sen** I am a female, **tiakothonwí:sen** she is a female (-athonwisen-); **o'nhéhtien** female (animal) (-'nhehtien-)

fence: **aten'èn:ra'** (-aten'enhr-)

fender (car): **tekanerahontsháhere'** it has a fender (-nerahontsh-, -her-/-hr-)

fern: **kahtehrahòn:tsi** (-htehr-, -hon'tsi-); **ietskaronhkhwa'kó:wa** (-itskar[on]-)

ferry: **otsire'kó:wa** (-tsir-)

fever: **waki'tonhkwáhrhos** I have a fever, **io'tonhkwáhrhos** it is feverish, inflamed, **waho'tonhkwáhrho'** he got a fever (-i'tonhkw-, -(h)rho-)

fever, scarlet: **onekwenhtarahtà:ne'** flushed colour that comes with sickness; scarlet fever (-nekwenhtar-)

fever, typhoid: **iako'tonhkwahrhoskó:wa** (-i'tonhkw-, -(h)rho-)

few, a few: **tóhka, tohkára'**

fiddle: **ohsáhta'** neck of a fiddle (guitar, violin), **wa'kahsahtakaránie'** I played the fiddle, **iontahsahtakaraniè:tha'** fiddle (-ahsaht-, -ranie-/-karanie-)

fiddle; beetle; ladybug; padlock; hump: **o'nó:wa'** (-'now-)

fidget: *See* squirm; fidget

field; garden: **kahéhtaien'** there is a field, a garden (-heht-, -ien-)

field; meadow; prairie: **kahén:ta'** field, etc., **kahén:taien'** there is a field (-hent-, -ien-)

fifty cents: **áhsen wén:so**, see **wén:so**

fight: **katerí:ios** I fight, **wahonterí:io'** they fought, **ronaterí:io** they are fighting (-rio-/-riio-)

file: **raristakaránies** he is filing it, **waharistakaránie'** he filed it, **ieristakaraniè:tha'** file (-rist-, -ranie-/-karanie-)

fill: **wahá:nahne'** he filled it, **kanà:non** it is full (-nahn-)

fill; accumulate: **wa'katiè:nihte'** I got plenty of it, I filled it, **rotie'níhton** he has filled it, **iotiè:ni** there's plenty, it holds a lot (-atie'ni-)

fill, be full: **tetkáhere'** it is full (-her-/-hr-)

film: **iottsiseró:ron** there is a film on it (-tsiser-, -'rhoro[k]-/-oro[k]-)

finally: **khá:re' ó:nen**

find: **ketshénrie's** I find it, **wa'ketshén:ri'** I found it, **rotshénrion** he has found it (-tshenri-)

find, can't find s.t.: **watiè:was** I can't find it, **wahoióha'** he couldn't find it, **watiohà:'on** I couldn't find it (-iehwa-/-ioha-)

find out: **wa'kerihwatshén:ri'** I found out about it (-rihw-, -tshenri-)

find out; discover: **onkwaterièn:tara'ne'** I found out, I discovered (-erien't-, -r-)

find s.o. out: **wahonwatsi'noniotáhsi'** they found him out (-tsi'nonw-, -ot-)

finger; hand: **ohsnónhsa'** or **oshónhsa'** finger, hand, **kehsnonhsà:ke** or **keshonhsà:ke** (on) my hand(s) or finger(s) (-hsnonhs-)

finish; complete: **íkhsa's** I finish it, **waháhsa'** he finished it, **róhson'** he has finished it (-hsa'-/-isa'-)

finish; end: **kò:ktha'** I finish it all or up, **wa'kò:kten'** I finished it, **ontò:kten'** it ended (-o'kt-)

finish, go right to the end: **iehrò:ktha'** he goes right to the end, he finishes it, **ia'kò:kten'** I went right to the end, I finished it, **iewako'ktà:'on** I have finished it (-o'kt-)

finish: *See* ready; finish

fire: **otsénha'** (-tsenh-)

fire; spark; embers: **ó:tsire'** (-tsir-)

fire, council fire: **katsísta'** (-tsist-)

fire, extinguish a fire: *See* extinguish

fire, house fire: **wa'onòn:kwateke'** the house burned (-non'kwatek-)
fire, light a fire: **tektsíro'ks** I am lighting a fire using a lighter or flint, **wa'tektsíro'ke'** I lit a fire, **tewattsíro'ks** flint, lighter (-tsir-, -o'[k]-)

fire, start a fire: **katekà:tha'** I start a fire, **wa'katé:ka'te'** I started a fire, **wakatekà:ton** I have started a fire (-atek-)

fire s.o.: **wahonwahnháhsi'** they let him go, he got fired (-(h)nhahsi-)

fireflies: **tekonttsirókwas** (-tsir-, -okw-); **tekonttsíro'ks** (-tsir-, -o'[k]-)

fireplace; stove: **tsi ionteka'táhkhwa'** (-atek-)

first: **tiotierénhton** (-atierenht-)

fish: **kéntson'** (-its-)

fish: **rahriohkawí:ne's** he is fishing, **wahahrióhkawine'** he fished (-ahriohkawine-)

fishhook: **à:ria'** (-ahri-)

fist, make a fist: **wa'ktsihkón:ni'** I made a fist, **rotsihkón:ni** he is making a fist (-tsihkw-, -onni-); **wa'kahtsakwe'nón:ni'** I made a fist, **rohtsakwe'nón:ni** he is making a fist (-ahts-, -hwe'nonni-/-kwe'nonni-)

fit: **ia'tetié:ri** it fits me, **ia'ttié:ri'ne'** it fit me, **iah thia'testié:ris** it doesn't fit me anymore (-ieri-)

five: **wísk**

fix: **rakwatákwas** he is fixing it, **wahakwatá:ko'** he fixed it, **rokwatákwen** he has fixed it (-kwatakw-)

flag: **iontenia'taroharáhkhwa'** (-nia'tar-, -ohar-)

flame; omen: **o'tónhkwa'** (-i'tonhkw-)

flat: **tewatakwénhten** it is flat,
wa'tewatakwénhten'ne' it got flat,
wa'tektakwénhtenhste' I flattened it
(-akwenhten-)

flax: **óhskare'** (-hskar-)

flea: **otá:we** flea, **wakatawéhserare'**
I have fleas on me (-atawe-, -r-)

flexible: **roia'tahkarí:io** he is flexible,
iakoia'tahkarí:io she is flexible
(-ia'tahkariio-)

flick: **wa'tionkkèn:toke'** she flicked her
finger against my forehead,
wa'thikèn:toke' I flicked my finger against
his forehead (-ken'tok-/-ken'to'k-)

flicker: **tewani'tonhkwaríkhons** the flame
is flickering, **wa'tewani'tonhkwaríkhon'**
the flame flickered (-i'tonhkw-, -rik-)

flint: *See* fire, light a fire

flirt: **wahakwara'séhsten'** he flirted with
me, **ronwara'sehstén:ni** she is flirting with
him (-ara'se-)

float: **io'kéhrha'** it is in the water,
io'kerónnion it is in there floating,
wa'katà:kerahkwe' I floated (-a'ker-)

float; drift: **io'á:wi** it is floating, drifting
(-a'awi-)

flood: **wa'kawehnó:ton'** it flooded,
iowehnó:ton it is a flood (-wehn-)

flood s.t.: **ranià:tons** he floods it,
enkenià:ton' I will flood it,
wakenià:ton I have flooded it (-nia'ton-)

floor: **ohson'karà:ke** or **ohswen'karà:ke**
on the floor (-hson'kar-/-hswen'kar-)

flour: **othè:sera'** (-the'ser-)

flower: **otsì:tsa'** (-tsi'ts-); **awénha'**

flute: **teiehonro'tahróhos**
(-honro't-, -hroh[o]-)

fly: **tsí'ks**

fly: **teká:tens** it is flying, airplane,
wa'tká:ten' it flew,
teió:ten it has flown (-ten-)

fly around: **kátie'** it is flying, **ratíties's**
they are flying around (-itie-/-tie-/-ontie-)

foam: **ohwà:tsta'** foam, **iothwa'tstáhere'**
there is foam on top of it (-hwa'tst-, -her-/-hr-)

focus: **tonke'nikonhráhsa'ahte'** I am giving
it my full attention,
tewake'nikonhrahsa'áhton I have given it
my full attention (-'nikonhr-, -hsa'-/-isa'-);
tewake'nikonhrakontáhkwen I have my
mind set on it, **tho'nikonhrakontáhkwen** he
is focused on it, **tiako'nikonhrakontáhkwen**
she is focused on it (-'nikonhr-, -kon[t]-)

fog; steam; mist: **otshá:ta'** steam, etc.,
iotshá:tote' it is steaming,
teiotshá:taien' it is misty, foggy (-atshat-)

fold: **khwe'nón:nis** I fold it,
wahahwe'nón:ni' he folded it,
rohwe'nón:ni he has folded it
(-hwe'nonni-/-kwe'nonni-)

fold: *See* bend; fold

follow: **khéhsere'** I am following her,
wa'khéhsere' I followed her (-hsere-)

food: **kákhwa'** (-khw-)

fool around: *See* play; playful

foolish; silly: **wakenonhwaró:ri** I am
foolish, silly, **ratenonhwarorístha'**
he acts silly, he fools around,
wahatenonhwaró:riste' he fooled around,
iakotenonhwaroríhton she is acting silly,
fooling around (-nonhwar-, -ori-);
thia'tehorihwarà:'on he is acting foolish
(-rihw-, -r-)

foot: **ohsì:ta'** foot, **kahsi'tà:ke** (on) my foot
(-ahsi't-)

foot, arch of the foot: **tekaia'kwatáhkwen**
(-ia'kwatahkw-)

foot, on foot: **ehta'kéhshon**

foot, turned out feet: **tehaianakáhrhate'**
his feet are turned out,
teieianakáhrhate' her feet are turned out,
tekaianakáhrhate' its feet are turned out
(-ian-, -kahrhate-)

footprint; track: **oiá:na'** (-ian-)

forehead: **okèn:kwara'** forehead,
kken'kwarà:ke (on) my forehead
(-ken'kwar-)

forehead, top of the forehead:
okèn:tstara' forehead,
kken'tstarà:ke (on) my forehead
(-ken'star-)

forest: **kahrhakonhkó:wa** (-(h)rh-)

forever; everlasting: **tsi nén:we'**

forge: **ion'tariha'táhkhwa'**
(-a'tarih[en]-/-tarih[en]-)

forget: **sho'nikónhrhens** he forgets,
sonke'nikónhrhen' I forgot,
sewake'nikonhrhèn:'en I have forgotten,
sahiia'ta'nikónhrhen' I forgot him
(-'nikonhrhen-)

fork: **tiora'wistáhkhwa'** or
tiera'wistáhkhwa'

fork, meat fork: **teie'wahrawe'ehstáhkhwa'**
(-'wahr-, -awe'ehst-)

fork, pitchfork: **teienekera'wistáhkhwa'**

Fort Covington, NY: **Kentsa'kowáhne** (-its-)

fouled up: **onkwaterihwaríhsien'** I got
fouled up (-rihw-, -rihsi-)

foundation: **kentskwáhere'**
(-itskw-, -her-/-hr-)

foundry: **rahwhút**

fountain: **tiohné:kote'** (-hnek-, -ot-)

four: **kaié:ri**

fox: **tsítsho**

freckles: **iakorahkwarónnion** she has spots,
freckles (-rahkw-, -r-)

free: **katatewenní:io** I am free,
enkatatewenní:io'ne' I will become
free (-wenn-, -iio-)

freeze: **wa'kenenniò:kwanohste'** I froze it,
kanennio'kwanóhstha' freezer
(-nennio'kw-, -no-)

French: **O'serón:ni** (-a'ser-, -onni-)

French person: **Kanatién**

fresh: **á:se'** it is fresh (-ase-)

Friday: **Ronwaia'tanentaktónhne** (-ia't-, -ra'nentakt-/-nentakt-)

friend: **ontiatén:ro'** we two (are) friends, my friend, **onkwatén:ro'** my friends (-atenro-); **ontiátshi** we two (females) (are) friends, my friend (female speaking) (-atshi-); **ákhskare'** my boyfriend, girlfriend (-hskar-); **Órie!** Friend!

friendship: **aterò:sera'** (-atero'ser-)

frightened: *See* scared

fringe: **teiohseriiè:tonte'** (-ahseriie['t]-, -ont-)

frog: **otskwà:rhe'**

front; ahead: **ohén:ton** in front, ahead, **akhén:ton** in front of me, **raohén:ton** in front of him, **akohén:ton** in front of her (-henton-)

front; downtown: **kanáthen**

frost: **ohsa'kénsera'** frost, **iohsa'kénserare'** there is frost on something (-hsa'kenser-, -r-); **iohsa'kenserá:ien'** there's frost on the ground (-hsa'kenser-, -ien-); **wa'otí:ienhte'** they (plants) got frost (-ienht-)

frostbite: **wa'tewakahsenni'tontá:ko'** I got frostbite, **tehohsenni'tontákwen** he has frostbite (-ahsenni'tontakw-)

frozen ground: **iaonhará:ien'** (-onhar-, -ien-)

fruit; berry: **káhi** (-ahi-)

fruit, green unripe fruit: **onónskwara'** or **onénskwara'** (-nonskwar-/-nenskwar-)

fry: **enktakerì:ta'we'** I will fry it, **wahatakerì:ta'we'** he fried it (-takeri'ta['w]-/-keri'ta['w]-)

frying pan: **iena'tsahráhkhwa'** (-na'ts-, -her-/-hr-)

fun, have fun: *See* entertain

fun, make fun of; laugh at: **rasterístha'** he is making fun, **wahaksté:riste'** he made fun of me, he laughed at me, **shakosteríston** he has made fun of her, laughed at her (-ia't-, -steri-)

fun, make fun of; ridicule: **thiiontié:ron** she or they are making fun of me, **thahatié:ron'** he made fun of me (-ieron-)

funeral parlour: **iontatia'tahráhkhwa'** (-ia't-, -her-/-hr-)

fungus: **iohwhá:rare'** (-ihwhar-, -r-)

funny; jolly: **iosté:ris** it is funny, amusing, **roia'tasté:ris** he is funny, jolly, **iakoia'tasté:ris** she is funny (-ia't-, -steri-)

fur: **óhwhare'** (-ihwhar-)

fuzz; body hair: **ononhwè:rhon** fuzz, **wakenonhwè:rhare'** I have hair on me (from a dog or cat) (-nonhwe'rh-, -r-)

gallon: **skawerò:kwa** one gallon (-wero'kw-)

gallop: **watia'karóntie's** it is galloping, **ontia'karón:ti'** it started galloping (-atia'karonti-)

Gananoque, Ontario: **Kananóhkhwi**

garage: **ie'serehtahseronnià:tha'** garage (for repairing cars) (-'sere[ht]-, -hseronni-);

ie'serehtaientáhkhwa' parking garage
(-'sere[ht]-, -ien-)

garden; field: kahéhtaien' there is a field,
a garden (-heht-, -ien-)

gargle: rathnia'sóhares he is gargling,
wa'kathnia'sóhare' I gargled
(-hnia's-, -nohare-/-ohare-)

garlic: iokháhon

garter: atshíhnha (-hsin-)

gate: ioten'enhrakà:ronte'
(-aten'enhr-, -kahront-)

gather; collect: rarò:roks he is gathering,
collecting things, wa'kerò:roke' I gathered,
collected them, wakerò:ron I have gathered
them (-rohro[k]-)

gather; shirr: ietókeriks she is gathering it,
she is putting in gathers,
wa'któkerike' I gathered it,
katókeri it is gathered, shirred
(-tokeri[k]-/-okeri[k]-)

gear: ohì:kara' (-hi'kar-)

general (military): tekahwistáhere'
(-hwist-, -her-/-hr-)

generous: teharénhsaron he is generous,
teierénhsaron she is generous (-renhsaron-)

German: Tehotinontsistokerón:te'
(-nontsi[st]-, -keront-)

get; obtain: See acquire

get, go get: rakóhe' he is here to get it,
wa'kkóhe' I am going to get it,

kkóhe's I go to get it,
wa'kkóha' I went to get it (-koh-)

get, go get s.o.: rakihnónkhse' he is coming
for me, wa'konhnónkhse' I am going to get
you, wa'khehnónkhsa' I went to get her
(-ihnonk-)

get in: katíta's I get on it, in it,
wahatíta' he got on it, in it,
rotíten' he has gotten on it, in it (-ita'-)

get in the way: See obstruct

get in water: iekatè:skohs I get into water,
ia'katè:skohwe' I went into the water,
iewakate'skóhon I have gotten into the water
(-'skohw-)

get out or off: katitáhkwas I get off it,
out of it, wa'katitáhko' I got off,
rotitáhkwen he has gotten off (-itahkw-)

get up: katkétskwas I get up,
wa'katkétsko' I got up,
wakatkétskwen I have gotten up (-ketskw-)

ghost: See haunted

ghost: otsí:

giant, Stone Giant: Ateneniáhrhon
(-neni-, -(h)rho-)

ginger; snake root: tsonenskwénrie

ginseng: tekaren'tó:ken (-ren't-, -oken-)

giraffe: kahnia'seskó:wa (-hnia's-, -es-)

girl: eksà:'a (-ksa['t]-)

give: koniá:wis I give it to you,

wa'ón:kon' she gave it to me,
rakwá:wi he has given it to me (-awi-/-on-)

give last rites to: **wahoia'tóhka'we'** he gave
him the last rites (-ia'tohka'w-)

give up: **ion'nikòn:ria'ks** she is giving up,
she quits, **wa'on'nikòn:ria'ke'** she gave up,
iako'nikonhrià:kon she has given up
(-'nikonhr-, -ia'k-)

glance: **kkahrahsnó:re'** I am giving it a
quick look, **rakahrahsnó:re'** he gives it a
glance, **iekahrahsnó:re'** she gives it a glance
(-kahr-, -hsnor[e]-)

glare: **wa'tewakeráhko'se'** I got blinded
from the glare from the sun (-rahkw-, -o-)

glass; ice: **ó:wise'** (-wis-)

glass, pane of glass: **otsísera'** (-tsiser-)

gloves: *See* mittens; gloves

glutton: *See* eat gluttonously

go: **í:ke'** I am walking,
tá:ke' I am coming, I came,
tho nonkwá:ti wà:ke' I am going over there
(-e-); **é:ren kéhtha'** I go away from here,
é:ren wà:rehte' he went away (-eht-)

go ahead: *See* ahead, go ahead

go around: **rahkwatá:ses** he keeps going
around, **wa'kahkwatá:se'** I went around,
rohkwatá:se he has gone around
(-ahkwatase-/-tase-)

go away: **kahténtie's** I go away, I walk,
wa'kahtén:ti' I went away, I walked,
wakahténtion I have gone away (-ahtenti-)

go backward: **ohnà:ken sà:rehte'** he went
backward (-eht-)

go down: *See* descend

go in: *See* enter

go in and out: **rahnhohakarénie's** he goes
in and out, **wahahnhohakaré:ni'** he went
in and out, **rohnhohakarénion** he is going
in and out (-(h)nhoh-, -kareni-)

go out: **tiá:ken's** I go out,
wahaiá:ken'ne' he went out,
watiakèn:'en I have gone out (-iaken'-)

go out as one is: **khwaserotátie'** I am
going out just the way I am,
rahwaserotátie' he is going out as is,
iehwaserotátie' she is going out as is
(-hwaserotatie-)

go out of sight: *See* disappear; go out of sight

go over: **ia'thatawèn:rate'** he went over it,
ieiakotawenhrá:ton she has gone over it
(-awenhrat-)

go straight somewhere: **ia'kattakwaríhsia'te'**
I went straight there, **takattakwaríhsia'te'**
I came straight here (-takwarihsi-/-kwarihsi-)

go through: *See* penetrate

go up to s.o.: **ia'kheiáttate'** I went up to her,
tahakwáttate' he came up to me (-tat-)

goat: **kaia'tákeras** (-ia't-, -akera-)

God: **Rawenní:io** (-wenn-, -iio-)

goiter: **iakohnia'sakwá:ronte'**
(-hnia's-, -kwaront-)

gold: **ohwistanó:ron** (-hwist-, -noron-)

goldenrod: **kahontakeraskó:wa** (-hont-, -akera-)

goldthread: **otsì:nekwar nikahtehrò:ten** (-htehr-, -o'ten-)

good: **ioiánere'** it is good (-ianer[e]-)

good-bye: **ó:nen**

goose, domestic: **atewénnia'ke'** (-wenn-, -ia'k-)

goose, wild: **káhonk**

gooseberry: **teiohnionwarontòn:'a** (-hnionwar-, -ont-)

gorilla: **katsi'nonhtakskó:wa** (-tsi'non[ht]-, -ek-/-ak-)

gossip: **tehari'wen'awíhtha'** he is a gossip, **wa'tieri'wen'á:wihte'** she gossiped (-ri'wa'awiht-)

governor: **kó:ra, rakó:ra**

graduate: *See* pass through; graduate

Grand Council: **Katsenhowá:nen** (-tsenh-, -kowan[en]-/-owan[en]-)

grandchild: **riiaterè:'a** my grandson, **kheiaterè:'a** my granddaughter, **aterè:sera'** grandchildren, **teiotere'será:ne** great-grandchild (-atere-)

grandparent: **akhsótha** my grandmother, **rakhsótha** my grandfather, **kahsótshera'** grandparents, grandparents and great-grandparents, **teiohsotshherá:ne** great-grandparent(s) (-hsot-);

tóta grandmother, grandfather

grape; raisin: **o'nénhare'** (-'nenhar-)

grapefruit: **iohiatská:ra** (-ahi-, -atskara-)

grapevine: **io'nenháhrhare'** (-'nenhar-)

grass: **óhente'** (-hent-)

grasshopper: **tsistá:rare'**

grave; cemetery: **iontatia'tata'ahstáhkhwa'** (-ia't-, -ta'-/-eta'-)

gravel: **o'néhtara'** (-'nehtar-)

gravy; dough: **oshè:rha'** dough, gravy (-she'rh-)

grease; fat: **o'tónsera'** (-i'tonser-)

grease; oil: **kén:ie'** (-iie-/-ien-)

Great Law: **Kaianere'kó:wa** or **Kaianerenhsera'kó:wa** (-ianer[e]-)

greedy: **wakatétshen** I am greedy, **rotétshen** he is greedy, **iakotétshen** she is greedy (-atetshen-)

green: **óhonte'** (-hont-)

greet: **tekhenonhwerá:tons** I greet them, give thanks to them, **wa'tekhenonhwerá:ton'** I greeted her, thanked her (-nonhweraton-)

grey: **ata'kenhróhkwa'** (-a'kenhr-, -o-)

grindstone: **tewateneniakahrhateníhon** (-neni-, -kahrhateni-)

groceries: **atennà:tshera'**;
atenna'tshera'shòn:'a
(-atenna'tsher-)

group (of people): **otióhkwa'** (-itiohkw-)

grow: **watón:nis** it grows, **ontón:ni'** it grew,
ontonnísa' it finished growing, it ripened
(-onni-); **wa'kà:nio'** it grew (vegetation),
taiohniótie' it is growing (-hnio-)

grow up: **wahatehià:ron'** he grew up,
rotehià:ron he has grown up (-ehiahron-)

guilty: **wakhníhshen** I am guilty,
rohníhshen he is guilty,
iakohníhshen she is guilty (-hnihshen-)

gulp; chug: **ia'tkatetshe'táweron'**
I gulped, chugged it down
(-tshe['t]-, -aweron-)

gum; pitch; pine: **ohnéhta'** (-hneht-)

gums: **oiénhta'** gums, **atiénhta'** my gums,
tienhtà:ke on my gums (-ienht-)

gun: **káhonre'** (-honr-)

gush: **tkáseras** water is gushing,
takáserahwe' the water gushed in
(-sera[hw]-/-osera[hw]-)

habit: *See* used to, get used to

hail: **iowisóntion** it is hailing
(-wis-, -ati-/-onti-)

hair: **onónhkwis** hair,
akenónhkwis my hair (-nonhkwis[er]-)

hair, big hair: **rononhkware'towá:nen**
he has big hair, **iakononhkware'towá:nen**
she has big hair (-nonhkware't-)

hair, body hair: *See* fuzz; body hair

hair, cowlick: *See* cowlick

hair, curly hair: *See* curly

hair, cut hair: *See* cut hair

hair, fix one's hair: **wa'katko'tsón:ni'**
I fixed my hair, **iakotko'tsón:ni** she
has fixed her hair (-ko'ts-, -onni-)

hair, grey hair: **wakehnhrà:te'** or
wakehnhrà:then' I have grey hair,
rohnhrà:te' or **rohnhrà:then'** he has grey
hair, **iakohnhrà:te'** or **iakohnhrà:then'**
she has grey hair (-(h)nhra't-)

hair, pull s.o.'s hair:
tehshakononhkwísharons he pulls her
hair, **wa'thinonhkwíshare'** I pulled his hair
(-nonhkwishar[on]-)

hair, shed hair: **rononhwè:rhen's** his
hair is falling out, he is shedding hair,
wahononhwè:rhen'ne' he shed hair
(-nonhwe'rh-, -a'sen'-/-en'-)

hair, style: **nikko'tsò:ten** my hair style,
niieko'tsò:ten her hair style
(-ko'ts-, -o'ten-)

hair, tie or fasten hair: **wa'kateniátsterenke'**
I fastened my hair with a ribbon,
iakoteniátsteren she has a ribbon fastened
in her hair (-niatsteren[k]

hair, unkempt hair: **tekkè:rhare'** my hair
is unkempt, every which way,
tehakè:rhare' his hair is messy,
teiekè:rhare' her hair is messy
(-ke'rh-)

half: **ahsén:nen** (-ahsennen-)

hall; hallway: **ka'wharatátie'** (-'whar-)

halo: **tehoterón:rote'** he has a halo, **iakoterón:rote'** she has a halo, **teioterón:rote'** halo (-ronrot-)

hallucinate: **rohniá:rara's** he is having hallucinations, **wahohniá:rara'ne'** he saw things, he hallucinated (-hniar-, -r-)

ham; bacon: **kahakenhtaríkhton** (-hakenht-)

Hamilton, ON: **Ohrón:wakon** (-hronw-)

hammer: **rane'kòn:reks** he is hammering it, **wa'kene'kòn:reke'** I hammered it, **rone'kòn:re** he has hammered it, **iene'konhrékstha'** hammer (-ne'konhre[k]-)

hand; finger: **ohsnónhsa'** or **oshónhsa'** finger, hand, **kehsnonhsà:ke** or **keshonhsà:ke** (on) my hand(s) or finger(s) (-hsnonhs-)

hand, extend: **tontaháhtsatate'** he put out his hand, **ia'tewakáhtsate'** I have put out my hand, my hand is held out (-ahtsat[at]-)

hand, palm: **óhsia'** palm, **khsió:kon** (on) my palm(s) (-hsi-)

handcuff: **wa'thihwistotáhrhoke'** I put handcuffs on him (-hwist-, -otahrho[k]-)

handful; palm: **ohtsà:na'** palm of the hand, handful, **kahtsa'nà:ke** (on) my palm (-ahtsa'n-)

handle: **onekerehétsha'** handle, **ionekerehétshonte'** it has a handle (-nekerehetsh-, -ont-)

handsome: **ranekénhteron** handsome man with a good physique (-nekenhteron-)

handsome; beautiful: **roia'táhskats** he is handsome, **iakoia'táhskats** she is beautiful (-ahskats[t]-)

Handsome Lake: **Skaniatarí:io** (-niatar-, -iio-)

hang: **iohrèn:ton** it is hanging (down) (-hren't-/-en't-)

hang; suspend: **keniióntha'** I am hanging it, **wa'keniión:ten'** I hung it, **roní:ionte'** he has hung it, **kaní:ionte'** it is hanging (-niiont-)

hang up: **kháhrha'** I hang it up, **wa'ehá:ren'** she hung it up (-har-/-ihar-)

happen: **tsi niiá:wens** the way it happens, **tsi na'á:wen'** what happened, **tsi niiawèn:'en** the way it has happened, **tsi niwatià:tawens** what is happening to me, what is wrong with me (-ia't-, -en-)

happy: **katshennón:nis** I become happy, **wahatshennón:ni'** he became happy, **wakatshennón:ni** I am happy (-atshennonni-)

happy; joyful: **wakatonhnháhere'** I am happy, **wa'katonhnhà:ren'** I became happy, **atonhnhahráhtshera'** happiness (-onhnh-, -her-/-hr-)

hard: *See* difficult

hard; solid: **iohní:ron** it is hard, solid, firm, **iohníhrhas** it gets hard, **wa'ohníhrha'** it got hard, **iohnihrhà:'on** it has gotten hard, it is hard (-hnir-)

harm: **wakkaronnià:tha'** it harms me, **wahokarónnia'te'** it harmed him (-kar-, -onni-)

harmonica: **iontehnhónta's** (-(h)nhonta'-)

harness: **akohsá:tens aotahkwénnia'** (-ahkwenni-)

harvest: **tienthókwas** I harvest, **wa'tienthó:ko'** I harvested, **roienthókwen** he has harvested (-ientho-)

hat: **wa'kanonhwaró:roke'** I put a hat on, **wakanonhwaró:ron** I have a hat on, **anòn:warore'** hat (-nonhwar-, -'rhoro[k]-/-oro[k]-)

hat, fedora: **teiotá:ronte'** it has a brim, fedora (-tar-, -ont-)

hat, top hat: **io'nonhkwahní:ron anòn:warore'** top hat (-'nonhkw-, -hnir-)

hatch: **teka'nhónhsia'ks** it hatches, incubator, **wa'tka'nhónhsia'ke'** it hatched (-'nhonhs-, -ia'k-)

hate: *See* dislike

Haudenosaunee: **Rotinonhsión:ni** they of the extended house, the Haudenosaunee (-nonhs-, -ionni-)

haunted: **iakotiáneron's** it is haunted, **iakotianerónhstha'** it is haunted, a ghost (-atianeron-)

have: *See* hold; have

have: *See* put down; have; lie

hawk: **teiakoia'táhkhwa'** (-ia't-, -hkw-)

hay: **onékeri** or **ennékeri** (-neker-/-enneker-)

hazelnut: **ohsóhi'te'** or **ohsóhihte'** (-hsohi't-/-hsohiht-)

head: **onón:tsi** head, **kenontsì:ne** (on) my head (-nontsi[st]-)

head piece: **kahstó:wa'**

healthy: **wakata'karí:te'** I am healthy, **rota'karí:te'** he is well, **iakota'karí:te'** she is well, **saionta'karí:tate'** she got well again (-a'karit[e]-)

heap; pile: **o'tón:wa'** heap, pile, **io'tón:iote'** there's a pile of something (-i'tonw-, -ot-)

hear: **wakathón:te'** I hear it, **onkwathón:te'ne'** I heard it, **rothontè:'on** he has heard it (-athont[e]-)

hear s.o.'s voice: **wahiwennà:ronke'** I heard him, his voice, **riwennahrón:ken** I have heard him (-wenn-, -ahronk-)

hearsay: **iá:ken** it is said

hearse: **wenheion'takarénie's** (-ihei[on]-/-enhei[on]-, -kareni-)

heart: **awé:ri** heart, **akwé:ri** or **akwerià:ne** my heart (-eri[ahs]-)

heaven: **karonhià:ke** (-ronhi-)

heavy: **iókste'** it is heavy, **roia'tákste'** he is heavy, **iakoia'tákste'** she is heavy (-ia't-, -kste-)

heavy feeling: **watia'tários** I feel there's a heaviness on me (-ia't-, -rio-/-riio-)

hedge: **ohrhá:ta'** (-(h)rhat-)

heed: **khewennaráhkhwa'** I listen to her, heed her, **wahiwén:narahkwe'** I heeded him, listened to him, **ionkewennaráhkwen** she has heeded me (-wenn-, -r-)

heel: **orá:ta'** heel, **keratà:ke** (on) my heel (-rat-)

heel, back of the heel: **ohskón:tara'** heel, **kahskontarà:ke** (on) my heel (-ahskontar-)

hell: **onéhson'** (-nehson-)

Hello: **Kwé:** or **Kwé**

Hello; still; more: **Shé:kon**

help: **khehsnié:nens** I help her or someone, **wahshakohsnié:nen'** he helped her, **khehsnié:nen** I am helping her (-hsnienen-)

help; support: **ratia'takéhnhas** he helps me out with it, he supports me, **wahatia'takéhnha** he helped me, **ratia'takéhnhen** he is helping me, **eniontatia'takéhnha'** she will help herself (-ia'takehnha-)

help do s.t.: **ratienawà:se'** he helps me do something, **wa'kheié:nawa'se'** I helped her, **wa'katatié:nawa'se'** I helped myself to it (-ienawa's-/-wa's-)

help oneself to: **iontatewenniióhstha'** she takes without asking, she helps herself to it, **wahatatewenní:iohste'** he helped himself to it (-wenn-, -iio-)

helpful: *See* adept; useful; helpful

hem: **tekkwáthos** I am hemming it, **wa'tiekwátho'** she hemmed it, **teiakokwáthon** she has hemmed it (-kwatho-)

hemlock: **onen'ta'ón:we** (-nen't-)

hemlock, water hemlock: **o'náhsar**

here: **ken** or **kèn:tho**

Here! **Koh!**

hernia: **wa'thatia'tané:kare'** he got a hernia, **tehotia'taneká:ron** he has a hernia (-ia't-, -ra'nekar[on]-/-nekar[on]-)

heron, blue heron; crane: **ohà:kwaront**

herrings, salt herrings: **raharén:**

hiccup: **wakhniò:tskahre'** I have hiccups, **onkhniò:tskahre'** I got the hiccups (-hnio'tskahr-)

hickory: **o'nonnóhkara'**

hide: **ionhséhtha'** she hides it, **wa'káhsehte'** I hid it, **iakohséhton** she has hidden it, **katahséhtha'** I hide, **wa'katáhsehte'** I hid, **wakatahséhton** I have hidden, I am hiding, **wa'kheia'táhsehte'** I hid her, **wa'koniahséhten** I hid it on you, from you (-ahseht-)

hide; skin: **ohnakénhsa'** (-hnakenhs-); **kanéhon** (-nehw-)

high: **è:neken tiótte'** it is high (-te-)

high (sides): **teióhses** it is high (sides) (-es-)

hill: **ionontáhere'** there's a hill
(-nont-, -her-/-hr-); **ionón:te'** there is
a mountain, a hill (-nonte-)

hinder: **tatio'tá:ti** you are wasting my time,
hindering me, **ratio'tá:ti** he is wasting my
time, **iontio'tá:ti** she is wasting my time
(-io'tat-)

hinge: **iehnhohaniiontáhkhwa'**
(-(h)nhoh-, -niiont-)

hip: **oniahskwà:rha'** or **ononhskwà:rha'** or
ohnhenskwà:rha' or **onehskwà:rha'** hip,
keniahskwa'rhà:ke my hip (-niahskwa'rh-);
oháhsa' hip (-hahs-)

hire: **róhnha's** he hires him,
wahíhnha'ne' I hired him,
rihnhà:'on I have hired him,
katénhnha's I am hiring help (-(h)nha'-)

hit; bump: *See* bump

hit; punch: **kkòn:reks** I hit it,
wahakkòn:reke' he hit me, punched me,
wakkonhré:kon or **wakkòn:re** I have hit
it (-konhre[k]-)

hit; strike: *See* strike; hit

hit against: **wà:tienhte'** I hit it with something, **óntienhte'** it hit me,
watiénhton I have hit it (-ienht-)

hobo; peddler: **ratenohkwakéhtats**
(-nohkw-, -keht[e]-)

hockey; lacrosse: **tehattsihkwà:'eks**
he plays hockey, lacrosse,
wa'thattsihkwà:'eke he played hockey,
lacrosse, **tehottsihkwà:e'** he has played
hockey, lacrosse
(-tsihkw-, -hwa'e[k]-/-a'e[k]-)

hoe: **atshò:kten**

Hogansburg, NY: **Tekahson'karó:rens**
(-hson'kar-/-hswen'kar-, -oren-)

hold: **íkhawe'** I am holding it, I have it,
enkhá:wake' I will hold it,
khá:wahkwe' I was holding it
(-ha[w]-/-enha[w]-)

hold: *See* catch; hold

hold; support: **watienawà:kon** I am holding it, **kheienawà:kon** I am holding her
(-ienawa'k-/-wa'k-)

hold, take hold of s.o.: **wahihnià:sa'** I put
my arms around his neck, **tahakenńtsha'**
he took hold of my arm (-a-)

hold down: **wa'ontia'tò:rarake'** she held
me down, **wahoia'tò:rarake'** he held him
down (-ia't-, -htohrarak-/-ohrarak-)

hold out; show: **iéktats** I am showing it,
iahà:ktate' I showed it, I held it out,
iewaktá:ton I have shown it (-tat-)

hole: **iohsón:we'** (there is) a hole (-hsonw-)

hole: *See* opening; hole

hollow: **o'whá:ra'** hollow, tunnel,
io'whá:rote' hollow (in a tree) (-'whar-, -ot-)

home, at home: **tkì:teron** I reside there, I am
home, **entki'terón:take'** I will be home,
tki'terón:tahkwe' I was home (-i'teron[t]-)

home, go home: **sakahtén:ti'** I went home,
shahtentiónhe' he is going to go home,
sahahtentiónhe' he is going home, he is
on his way home,
tontakahtén:ti' I came home (-ahtenti-)

home, make oneself at home: **wa'katená:taien'** I made myself at home (-nat-, -ien-)

hominy: **kanen'ón:ni** (-nen'onni-)

honest: *See* trustworthy; honest

honey: **otsina'kontahkwà:ne' óshes** (-shes[t]-)

honeycomb: **ohskaranawèn:ta'**

honk: **wa'thahenrehtánion'** he honked the horn (-henreht-)

hoof: **otsinarèn:ta'** or **otsiniarèn:ta'** (-tsinaren't-/-tsiniaren't-)

hook: **kotáhrhoks** I hook it, **wa'kotáhrhoke'** I hooked it, **wakotáhrhon** I have hooked it (-otahrho[k]-)

hook: **kahniò:kwa'** (-hnio'kw-)

hook, fishhook: **à:ria'** (-ahri-)

hooked; snagged: **tia'totáhrhe's** I get caught, hooked on it, **wa'tia'totáhrhe'ne'** I got hooked, snagged on it, **watia'tohahrhè:'on** I have got hooked, snagged on it (-otahrhe'-)

hoop: **tiakote'nón:na'** she has a hoop on (under her dress) (-'nonn-)

hope: *See* wish for

hopefully: **aiá:wens**

hopeless: **ka'nikonhrò:ktha'** I am depressed, discouraged, **wa'ka'nikonhrò:kten'** I became depressed, **waka'nikonhro'ktà:'on** I have lost hope,

I feel hopeless, **io'nikonhrò:kta** it is useless, futile (-'nikonhr-, -o'kt-)

horn; antler; dice: **onà:kara'** (-na'kar-)

horn, bullhorn: **teiakohenrehtáhkhwa'** (-henreht-)

hornbeam (tree): **ohtehrò:tsi** (-htehr-)

horse: **akohsá:tens** horse, **wakhsá:tens** I go on horseback (-hsaten-)

hospital: **tehshakotitsèn:tha'** (-tsen't-); **tsi tiakenheion'taientáhkhwa'** (-ihei[on]-/-enhei[on]-, -ien-); **kanonhsowanèn:ke** (-nonhs-, -kowan[en]-/-owan[en]-)

hot; warm: **waka'taríhens** I get hot, **onkwa'taríhen'** I got hot, **waka'tarihèn:'en** I am hot, **io'taríhen** it is hot (-a'tarih[en]-/-tarih[en]-)

hotel; inn: **tsi iontaweia'táhkhwa'** (-ataweia't-)

hour: **enkahwistà:'eke'** one hour, **tékeni tenkahwistà:'eke'** two hours (-hwist-, -hwa'e[k]-/-a'e[k]-)

house: **kanónhsa'** house, **kanónhsote'** there's a house (standing) (-nonhs-, -ot-)

How? **Oh ní:ioht?**

howl: **rawén:note'** he is howling, **wahatewennó:ten'** he howled (-wenn-, -ot-)

hug: **wa'thiia'kwahrhiè:na'** I hugged him, I put my arms around him, **wa'tehshakoia'kwahrhiè:na'** he hugged her (-ia'kwahrhie'n-)

humble: **roniténhton** he is humble, **iakoniténhton** she is humble, **wa'kaní:tenhte'** I humbled myself (-iten[ht]-)

hummingbird: **ráonraon** or **rámram**

hump; padlock; beetle; ladybug; fiddle: **o'nó:wa'** (-'now-)

hunch over: **rote'noión:ni** he is hunched over, **iakote'noión:ni** she is hunched over (-'now-, -onni-)

hunchback: **tewake'nowiià:kon** I am a hunchback, **teho'nowiià:kon** he is a hunch-back, **teiako'nowiià:kon** she is a hunchback (-'now-, -iahia'k-/-iia'k-)

hundred: **tewen'niáwe** hundred (-en'niawe-); **iohsénhserote'** hundreds, thousands (-ahsen-, -ot-)

hungry: **katonhkária'ks** I am hungry, **wahatonhkária'ke'** he got hungry, **wakatonhkarià:kon** I was hungry (-atonhkaria'k-)

hungry for: *See* crave

hunt: **kató:rats** I hunt, **wa'kató:rate'** I hunted, **wakatorá:ton** I have hunted (-atorat-)

hurry: **tewaksteríhens** I am in a hurry, **wa'tewaksteríhen'** I hurried, **tewaksterihèn:'en** I am hurrying, **wa'thisteríha'te'** I'm rushing him (-sterih[en]-)

hurry; rush: **wa'tkatskénnia'te'** I rushed and rushed (-skenni-)

hurry: *See* do fast

Hurry up! **Óksa!**

hurt: **iononhwákte'** it hurts (-nonhwak[t]-)

hurt; ache: **wakahkará:rens** I am aching, I am hurting, **onkwahkará:ren'** I hurt, I ached (-ahkararen-)

hurt; injure: **shakokarewáhtha'** he injures her or them, **wahakkaré:wahte'** he injured me, **wahokaré:wahte'** he got hurt, **shakokarehwáhton** he has hurt her (-karewaht-)

hurt s.o's feelings: **rake'nikonhraksà:tha'** he hurts my feelings, **wahi'nikonhráksa'te'** I hurt his feelings, **rake'nikonhraksà:ton** he has hurt my feelings (-'nikonhr-, -aksen-)

husband: **ró:ne'** her husband, his wife (-ne-); **tiakenì:teron** my husband, my wife (-i'teron-)

husband; spouse: *See* couple

husk, corn husk: **onó:ra'** (-nor-)

husk face: **katiéhson**

hymnal; hymn book: **teierihwahkwà:tha'** (-rihw-, -hkw-)

I; we: **ì:'i; í:, nì:'i**

ice; glass: **ó:wise'** (-wis-)

ice; freeze over: **iowísere'** there is ice (a layer of ice on top of it), **wa'kawíserate'** it formed ice, it froze over (-wiser-)

ice, icy: **iowí:sare'** it is icy (-wis-, -r-)

ice, slip on ice: **rowiskwenhtare'éhstha'** he slips on the ice, **onkewiskwenhtáre'ehste'** I slipped on the ice (-wiskwenhtare'ehst-)

ice cleats: **ateristón:ta** (-rist-, -ont-)

ice cream: **ionennió:kwano** (-nennio'kw-, -no-)

icicles: **iowisen'tónnion** (-wis-, -hren't-/-en't-)

idea, get an idea: **wa'katerien'tatshén:ri'** I got an idea (-erien't-, -tshenri-)

if: **tóka'**

imitate s.o.: *See* copy; imitate s.o.

immerse: **kathnia'sótha'** I immerse myself (in water) up to my neck, **wa'kathnia'só:ten'** I immersed myself (-hnia's-, -ot-)

inch: **skaweiónhkara** one inch (-weionhkar-, -[t]-)

in-law: *See* mother-in-law, father-in-law, etc.

in-laws, stay with: **kehnonhwáhsen** I am living with my in-laws, **rahnonhwáhsen** he is living with his in-laws, **iehnonhwáhsen** she is living with her in-laws (-hnonhwahsen-)

Indian agent: **Étien**

industrious: **waketshà:ni** I am industrious, I apply myself, **rotshà:ni** he is industrious, **iakotshà:ni** she is industrious, **wahotshahníhta'ne'** he got industrious (-tshahni[ht]-)

infected: **taionà:khwen'** it got infected (-na'khw[en]-)

inflamed: *See* fever

inform; warn: **wahiiahronkà:ten'** I informed him, warned him, **shakohronka'tén:ni** he informs them, lets them know (-ahronk-)

inhale: **takatonriseratihéntho'** I inhaled (-atonriser-, -atihentho-)

injure: *See* hurt; injure

insect; bug: **otsi'nón:wa'** (-tsi'nonw-)

insects, little black insects: **tekonní'tia'ks**

insert: **kò:roks** I insert it, put it between things, **wa'kò:roke'** I inserted it, **wakò:ron** I have inserted it (-ohro[k]-)

inside: **í:wa** it is inside it (-a[t]-); **tià:ti** I am in it (-ia't-, -i[t]-)

inside; underneath: **tia'tò:ron** I am inside of it, underneath it (-ia't-, -ohro[k]-)

instead; as if: **iá:we**

insulate: **wa'katahonhtawéhrhon'** I insulated the (outside of) the house (-awehrho-)

insult: **wahikenhra'serón:ni'** I insulted him, belittled him, **wa'khekenhra'serón:ni'** I insulted her, I put her down (-kenhr[on]-)

insult: *See* criticize; insult

intentions, good intentions; good morals; kind: **tewakerihwaié:ri** I have good intentions, I am kind (-rihw-, -ieri-)

intestines: **okahróhsta'** intestines,
akkahróhsta' my intestines (-kahrohst-)

intolerant: **khekenhrón:nis** I am intolerant
of her, **rakkenhrón:nis** he is intolerant of
me (-kenhr[on]-)

introduce: **tenhonwanaterò:seron'** she will
introduce them to each other,
wa'tekheiaterò:seron' I introduced them
to each other (-atero'ser-, -awi-/-on-)

introduce oneself: **wahatatenà:ton'** he
named himself, introduced himself (-na'ton-)

invite: **wakathonkaróntie's** I extend an invitation, **wahothonkarón:ti'** he extended an
invitation, **iakothonkaróntion** she has
extended an invitation (-honkar-, -ati-/-onti-);
kwahonkará:wis I or we are giving you an
invitation, **wa'konhón:karon'** I gave you
an invitation (-honkar-, -awi-/-on)

iron: **keristáhrhos** I am ironing,
wa'keristáhrho' I ironed it,
wakeristáhrhon I have ironed it,
ieristahrhóhstha' iron (-rist-, -(h)rho-)

iron; steel: **karistà:ke** on the iron or steel
(-rist-)

ironworkers: **karístatsi rotiió'te'**
ronhskwahéhrha' (-ahskw-, -her-/-hr-)

irritated: *See* annoyed

island: **kawè:note'** (-wehn-, -ot-)

issue; agenda: **karihwáhere'**
(-rihw-, -her-/-hr-)

itch: **wakerónhkwani** I am itchy,
onkerónhkwen' I got itchy
(-ronhkwani-/-ronhkwen-)

jack pine; tamarack: **kanèn:ten's**
(-nen't-, -a'sen'-/-en'-)

jack-in-the-pulpit: **tkahnhónhserote'**

jacket; dress; shirt; coat: **atià:tawi**
(-atia'tawi-)

jail: **rahnhó:ton** he is in jail,
wahonwahnhó:ton' they put him in jail,
ronwahnhó:ton they locked him up, he is
in jail, **tsi iontatehnhotónhkhwa'** jail
(-(h)nhoton-)

jam: **wà:io** (-ahi-, -o-)

January: **Tsothohrhkó:wa** (-athor[e]-)

January; Midwinter: **Sha'tekohséhrhon**
(-ohser-, -hon-)

jar; bottle: **kátshe'** (-tshe['t]-)

jaundice: **rotsi'nekwá:rare'** he has yellow
jaundice (-tsi'nekwar-, -r-)

jealous: **raten'kéhwhas** he gets jealous,
wahaten'kéhwha' he got jealous,
roten'kéhwhen he is jealous,
wahakwaten'kéhwha' he got jealous of
me (-aten'kehwha-)

jeans: **oronhia'kó:wa atháhsteren**
(-ronhi- and -athahsteren[k]-)

Jewish: **Síta** Judah, **Sita'ehró:non** Jewish

join: *See* attach, end-to-end; join; connect

joint: **ohstónteri** joint, **tewakhstonterónnion**
my joints (-hstonter-)

jolly: *See* funny; jolly

judge: **tehaia'toréhtha'** he is a judge, **wa'tehshakoia'tó:rehte'** he judged her or them (-ia't-, -oreht-)

judge: *See* sentence; judge

jug; bulb; lamp chimney; carcass; gallon: **owerò:kwa'** (-wero'kw-)

juice: **kahnekinekénhton** (-hnek-, -inekenht-)

July: **Ohiarihkó:wa** (-ahi-, -ri-)

jump: **tekani'tsonhkwáhkhwa'** I jump, **wa'tionni'tsónhkwahkwe'** she jumped, **tehoni'tsonhkwáhkwen** he is jumping (-i'tsonhkw-, -hkw-)

jump out: **tahatóhtshia'te'** he jumped out (-ohtshi-)

jump s.o.; attack: *See* attack; jump s.o.

June: **Ohiarí:ha** (-ahi-, -ri-)

Kahnawà:ke (-hnaw-)

Kayaderosseras, NY: **Kaniataróseras** (-niatar-, -sera[hw]-/-osera[hw]-)

kettle: **ón:ta** (-onta-)

kettle, with a spout: **iohón:rote'** (-honr-, -ot-)

key: **kahnhotónkwa'** key(s), **akehnhotónkwa'** my keys (-(h)nhoton-)

kick: **karahsénthos** I kick it, **wa'karahséntho'** I kicked it, **rorahsénthon** he has kicked it or him, **wahiiarahséntho'** I kicked him (-arahsentho-)

kidney: **otstiéhseri** kidney, **akwatstiéhseri** my kidney (-atstiehser-)

kill: **shakohséhtha'** he kills them, **wahshakóhsehte'** he killed her, **shakohséhton** he has killed her (-ahseht-)

kill: *See* beat up

kind: *See* intentions, good intentions; good morals; kind

King: **Ronontí:io** (-nont-, -iio-)

Kingston, Ontario: **Ka'taróhkwen** or **Ken'taróhkwen**

kiss: **tekhenoronhkwánions** I am kissing her, **wa'thinoronhkwánion'** I kissed him (-noron-)

kitchen: **tsi iekhonnià:tha'** (-khw-, -onni-)

kite: **kentahsíhare'** (-itahs-, -har-/-ihar-)

knee: **okwítsha'** knee, **kkwitshà:ke** (on) my knee (-kwitsh-)

knee, back of the knee: **kerehetskó:kon** the back of my knee (-rehetskw-)

knee, knock-kneed: **tehakwitsté:ken** he is knock-kneed, **teiekwitsté:ken** she is knock-kneed (-kwitsh-)

kneel: **tekéntshote'** I am kneeling, **tekatentshótha'** I go on my knees, **wa'tkatentshó:ten'** I got on my knees (-entshot-)

kneeler; prayer bench: **teiontentshotáhkhwa'** (-entshot-)

knife: **à:share'** (-a'shar-)

knit: **ieriserón:ni** she is knitting, **wa'keriserón:ni'** I knitted (-ris[er]-, -onni-)

knock: **thahnhonhtíshon** he is knocking on the door, **tahahnhonhtíshon'** he knocked on the door (-(h)nhonhtishon-); **wa'kehnhoháia'ke'** I knocked on the door (-(h)nhoh-, -ia'k-)

knock down: **tka'sénhtha'** I drop it, pull it down, **takà:senhte'** I brought it down, **tho'sénhton** he has knocked, pulled it down (-a'senht-/-enht-)

knock over, down: **ke'rheniénhtha'** I am knocking them over, **waha'rhé:nienhte'** he knocked them over, **ro'rheniénhton** he has knocked them over, **wahatia'tié:nenhte'** he knocked me down (-'rhenienht-/-ienenht-)

knot: **tektsihkwaróntha'** I am tying a knot, **wa'tektsihkwarón:ten'** I tied a knot, **teiakotsíhkwaronte** she has tied a knot, **tekatsíhkwaronte'** knot (-tsihkwaront-)

knot (tree); fist; button; puck: **otsíhkwa'** knot, etc., **iotsíhkote'** (there is) a knot in a tree (-tsihkw-, -ot-)

know: **wakaterièn:tare'** I know, **roterièn:tare'** he knows, **iakoterièn:tare'** she knows, **onkwaterièn:tara'ne'** I got to know, I found out, **iah tewakaterièn:tare'** I don't know (-erien't-, -r-)

know a language: **kahrónkha'** I speak, understand a language, **wa'kà:ronke'** I learned the language, **wakahronkhà:'on** I have learned, I know the language (-ahronk-)

know how: **keweién:te'** I know how, **raweién:te'** he knows how, **ieweién:te'** she knows how (-weiente-)

know s.o.: **konienté:ri** I know you, **kheienté:ri** I know her (-ienteri-)

know s.o., get to know s.o.: *See* acquainted

know, I don't know: **tó:ka**

knowledgeable; smart: **kattókha'** I am smart, knowledgeable, **rattókha'** he is smart, **ionttókha'** she is smart, **attokháhtshera'** wisdom, knowledge (-attokha-)

laces: **a'nikahtsè:na'** laces, **tekate'nikahtse'nóntha'** I am putting laces on, **wa'tkate'nikahtse'nón:ten'** I did up the laces (-'nikahtse'n-, -ont-)

Lachine, Québec: **Skaniatará:ti** (-niatar-, -ti-)

lacrosse; hockey: **tehattsihkwà:'eks** he plays hockey, lacrosse, **tewa'á:raton tehonttsihkwà:'eks**, lacrosse game (-tsihkw-, -hwa'e[k]-/-a'e[k]-, -a'ar-)

ladder; steps; stairs: **kanekó:ta'** (-nekot-)

ladybug; beetle; padlock; hump; fiddle: **o'nó:wa'** (-'now-)

lake; river: **oniá:tara'** or **kaniá:tara'** (-niatar-)

Lake Ontario: **Kaniatarí:io** (-niatar-, -iio-)

lamp; light: **oháhsera'** (-hahser-)

lamprey: **okontè:na'** (-konte'n-)

land: **ontà:senhte'** it landed (on the ground) (-a'senht-/-enht-)

landslide: **watonhóntia'ks**
(-onhwents-/-onhonts-, -ia'k-)

language, know: *See* know a language

language, speak: **katewennontáhkhwa'**
I speak a language, **wahatewennón:tahkwe'**
he spoke in a language, **rotewennontáhkwen**
he is speaking in a language (-wenn-, -ont-)

lantern: **iehahserénhas** (-hahser-,
-ha[w]-/-enha[w]-); **ken'tonhkwarà:ken**
(-i'tonhkw-, -ra'ken-)

Laprairie, Québec: **Kenhtà:ke** (-iht-)

last: *See* endure

late: **onke'nísko'** I was late,
wake'nisko'onhátie' I am late (-'niskw-);
ohnà:ken ontià:tarahkwe' I was late
(-ia't-, -r-)

later: **wá'ts niá:re. Wá'ts!** Later!

laugh: **ontiéshon'** I laughed,
iakoiéshon she is laughing (-ieshon-)

laugh at: *See* fun, make fun of; laugh at

laugh loudly, uncontrollably:
tekatontaríktha' I laugh loudly,
wa'thatón:tarikte' he laughed loudly,
teiakotontaríkton she is laughing
uncontrollably (-atontarikt-)

lavender (colour):
arihwawa'konhne'tsherarà:ken
(-rihw-, -ienawa'k-/-wa'k-, -ra'ken-)

law: **kaianerénhsera'** (-ianer[e]-)

lawyer: *See* argue

lay s.o. out: **wahonwaia'tà:ren'** they
laid him out, **ieia'táhere'** she is laid out
(-ia't-, -her-/-hr-)

lazy: **kentóhrha'** I am lazy,
wahrentó:ren' he got lazy,
wakentorà:'on I have become lazy (-entor-)

lazy, a lazy person: **tarò:taro**

lead; purple; bruise: **oharennáhta'**
(-harennaht-)

leaf: **ónerahte'** (-neraht-)

leaf, long leaves (bulrush): **otsawénhsa'**
(-tsawenhs-)

leak; drip: **iókhas** it leaks, it drips,
wa'ókha' it leaked,
iaokhà:'on it is leaking (-okha-)

lean against: **tia'tarà:kare'** I am leaning up
against it, **wahatia'tarà:karen'** he leaned
against it (-ra'kar-)

lean back; fall backwards: **iékhsate'** I am
leaning back, **iahahsá:ta'ne'** he fell backwards, **iehohsatà:'on** he has fallen backwards (-hsat-)

lean back: *See* back, arch the back

lean to one side; slant: **wakarèn:re'** it is
leaning, crooked, on a slant,
raia'takarèn:re' he is crooked, lopsided,
ieia'takarèn:re' she is crooked, lopsided
(-ia't-, -akarenhr[e]-)

learn; study; practice: **kateweiénstha'** I am
learning, studying, practicing,
wa'katéweienste' I learned,
roteweiénston he has learned (-weienst-)

learn how: **keweientéhta's** I learn,
wa'keweientéhta'ne' I learned,
wakeweientehtà:'on I have learned
(-weiente-)

leash; strap: **ashá:ra'** (-ashar-)

leather; skin: **óhna'** (-ihn-)

leatherwood: **otkénseri**

leave: *See* go away

leave abruptly: **kateriahtíhtha'** I leave
(abruptly), **wa'kateriáhtihte'** I went
away, removed myself from a situation
(-ateriahtiht-)

leave discreetly: **wahata'á:wihte'** he
removed himself, he (discreetly) made
his way out, **wakata'awíhton** I am on my
way (-a'awi-)

leave for work: **ó:nen ensekhná:wenhte'**
I will leave, go home, go downstream,
look for work (-hnaw-, -a'senht-/-enht-)

Leave it alone! **Tsèn:nio!**

leave s.o. out; exclude s.o.:
riia'tontakwáhtha' I am leaving him out,
wa'kheia'tontákwahte' I excluded her
(-ia't-, -ont-)

leave s.t. with s.o.:
wa'kheiatahkwenniaién:hahse' I left it
in her care, **koniatahkwenniaién:ni** I am
leaving it in your care (-ahkwenni-, -ien-)

lecture: *See* preach

left: **skenekwá:ti** my left hand, left side
(-nekwati-)

left over: **iotatén:ron** it is left,
wa'otá:tenre' it got left over,
onkwatá:tenre' I was left with leftovers,
a surplus, **wakatatén:ron** I have leftovers
(-atatenr-)

left over; extra: **iowénhte'** it is left over,
there is an extra amount (-awenht[e]-)

leftover scraps: **watkéntston** (-kentst-)

leg: **ohsí:na'** leg, **khsinà:ke** (on) my leg
(-hsin-)

leg, hip to knee: **orèn:ta'** (-ren't-)

legend: **iekaratónhkhwa'** (-karaton-)

leggings: **atshinénha'**

leggings, put on: **katshinò:roks** I am putting
on leggings, **wa'katshinò:roke'** I put on
leggings, **wakatshinò:ron** I have put on
leggings, **atshinò:ron** leggings
(-hsin-, -ohro[k]-)

lemon: **teiohiahiò:tsis** (-ahi-, -hio'tsis[t]-)

lend: **kheníhas** I lend it to someone,
wa'ónkeni' she lent it to me,
shakoníhen he has lent it to her,
wa'katáteni' I borrowed it (-ni[h]-)

Lent: **tsi niiakawentontiéhtha'**
(-ent-, -ati-/-onti-)

less than: **kà:ron**

let; allow: *See* allow

let go of: **katkà:was** I let it go,
wa'kátka'we' I did let it go,
riiatkà:wen I have let him go (-atka'w-)

let have: **enkoniatewentéhta'se'** I will let you have some, **wa'onkwatewentéhta'se'** she let me have some (-atewenteht-)

let out: **ietia'tínekenhs** I let it out (an animal), **ia'kheiia'tínekenhwe'** I let her out, **iehiia'tinekénhen** I have let him out (-ia't-, -inekenhw-)

let stay: **wa'khenaktóthahse'** I let her stay, I gave her a room to stay in, **ionkenaktotá:ni** she is letting me stay (-nakt-, -ot-)

letter; number: **ohiatónhkwa'** (-hiaton-)

lettuce: **onerahtakáhte'** (-neraht-, -kahte-)

level; even: **sha'tetiótte'** it is even, the same level (-te-)

level (tool): **kahné:kare'** (-hnek-, -r-)

lick: **rakanónthons** he is licking it, **wahaká:nonte'** he licked it, **rokanónthon** he has licked it (-kanont-)

lie; tell lies: **onó:wen** a lie, **ronó:wen** he lies, he is a liar, **ranowénhtha'** he tells lies, **wa'kanó:wenhte'** I lied, **wakanowénhton** I have lied, **wahiianowénhten'** I lied to him (-nowen-)

lie; tell lies: **ratshó:ken** he is a liar, **iontshó:ken** she is a liar (-hs-, -oken-); **ákte' nihathró:ris** he tells s.t. else, he lies (-hrori-)

lie around: **é:so kakè:ron** lots of things are here and there, all over (-kehron[t]-)

lie down: **ká:rats** I am lying down,

ia'ká:rate' I went to lay down, **ieiakorá:ton** she has gone to lie down (-arat-)

lie down: **tia'tión:ni** I am lying down, **raia'tión:ni** he is lying down, **ieia'tión:ni** she is lying down (-ia't-, -ionni-)

lie down: **iehana'skwáhere'** he is lying down curled up, **ia'ontena'skwà:ren'** she went to lie down (-na'skw-, -her-/-hr-)

lie down: **kaneró:kwaien'** it is lying down (an animal) (-nerokw-, -ien-)

lie on one's side: **tia'tokerón:te'** I am lying on my side, **wa'katia'tokerón:tate'** I got on my side (-ia't-, -keront-/-okeront-)

lie on one's stomach: **tekhra'kwénhtare'** I am on my stomach, **ia'tkathra'kwenhtáhrho'** I lay on my stomach, **ia'thahra'kwénhtara'ne'** he fell down, landing on his belly (-hra'kwenhtar-)

lie on top of: **iahatia'takwenhtáhrho'** he lay down on top of it, **ia'ontia'takwenhtáhrho'** she lay down on top of it (-atia'kwenhtahrho-)

lift: *See* pick up

lift: *See* raise; lift

light, turn off: *See* extinguish

light, turn on: **wa'khahseró:ten'** I turned on the light, **kaháhserote'** the light is on (-hahser-, -ot-)

lighter; flint: *See* fire, light a fire

lighter; matches: **ionteka'táhkhwa'** (-atek-)

lightning: **tewanihne'kara'wánions** it is lightning, **wa'tewanihne'kara'wánion'** it did lightning (-anihne'kara'wanion-)

lightning sparks: **tewattsirarikhons** there are lightning sparks (-tsir-, -rik-)

lightning strike; thunderclap: **wa'ote'serón:ti'** a lightning bolt struck, there was a thunderclap, **iote'seróntie'** lightning is striking (-ate'serontie-)

like: **kenòn:we's** I like it, **wa'akwanòn:we'ne'** we liked it, **wakenonhwè:'on** I have liked it, **rakenòn:we's** he likes me (-nonhwe'-)

lily, pond lily: **bararón: raotsì:tsa'** (-tsi'ts-)

limb: **o'kátsa'** (-'kats-)

lime: **ken'tarakerì:ta** (-i'tar-, -takeri'ta['w]-/-keri'ta['w]-)

limp: **katshino'káhtha'** I am limping, **wahatshinò:kahte'** he limped (-hsin-, -o'[k]-)

lining for a boot, shoe: **ateráhki** or **ateráhkwi**

linoleum; tablecloth: **kahnehtáhrhon** (-hneht-, -(h)rho-)

lion: **kèn:reks**

lip: **óhsa'** (-hs-)

lip: **ohskwèn:ta'** lip, **khskwen'tà:ke** (on) my lip (-hskwen't-)

lip, upper: **ohswèn:kara'** lip, **khswen'karà:ke** (on) my lip (-hswen'kar-)

liquid; water: **ohné:ka'** (-hnek-)

listen: **katahónhsatats** I listen, **wahiiatahónhsatate'** I listened to him, **wakatahónhsate'** I am listening (-atahonhsat-)

listen, try hard: **tekatahonhtótha'** I am trying to listen, **wa'tkatahonhtó:ten'** I tried hard to listen (-ahonht-, -ot-)

listen to: *See* heed

little, a little: **ostòn:ha** or **ostón:ha**

Little People: **Shakotinenióia'ks** (-neni-, -oia'[k]-)

live: *See* alive

live: *See* reside

live together: **ranahkwenhá:wi's** he is living together (with someone) without being married, **ienahkwenhá:wi's** she is living together without being married (-nahkw-, -hawi-/-enhawi-)

live with in-laws: *See* in-laws, live with in-laws

liver: **othwénhsa'** liver, **akwathwénhsa'** my liver (-thwenhs-)

lizard: **totiskó:wa**

load; pack: **skahriè:na** one pack, one load (-hrie'n-)

loaf: **wakaterà:kare'** I am loafing, not doing anything, **roterà:kare'** he is loafing (-ra'kar-)

lobster: **otsi'eróhta'** (-tsi'eroht-)

lock; beetle; ladybub; hump; fiddle: **o'nó:wa'** (-'now-)

lock: **io'nowanentá:kon** (-'now-, -ra'nentak-/-nentak-)

lock: *See* door, lock a door

log; beam: **karón:ta'** log, beam (-ront-)

lollipop; candy attached to a stick: **kanakaróhare'** (-nakar-, -ohar-)

lonesome: **kentón:nis** I am lonesome, **wa'kentón:ni'** I got lonesome (-entonni-)

long: **í:iens** it is long (-es-)

long time: **wahón:nise'**

look: **katkáhthos** I look at it, **wa'katkáhtho'** I looked at it, **rotkáhthon** he has looked at it, **wahiiatkáhtho'** I looked at him (-atkahtho-)

look: **tekkà:nere'** I look at it, **tenkká:nehrake'** I will look at it, **tekkà:nerahkwe'** I was looking at it, **tekhekà:nere'** I am looking at her (-kahner-)

look after oneself: **tekatatahrhò:tons** I look after myself (I don't overdo it) (-ahro'ton-)

look alike: **tetsitiatié:ren** you and I resemble, look like one another (-ieren-)

look away: **katahróntie's** I look the other way, **wa'katahrón:ti'** I looked the other way, **rotahróntion** he is looking the other way, **wa'kheiatahrón:ti'** I looked away from her (-atahronti-)

look closely: **kka'én:ions** I am looking at it closely, carefully, **wahaka'én:ion'** he

looked closely at it, **roka'én:ion** he has looked closely at it (-ka'enion-)

look for: **kéhsaks** or **ké:saks** I am looking for it, **wa'kéhsake'** or **wa'ké:sake'** I looked for it, **wakehsá:kon** or **wakesá:kon** I have looked for it (-ehsak-/-ihsak-/-esak-/-isak-)

look good: **roia'taweiénston** it looks good on him, **iakoia'taweiénston** it looks good on her (-weienst-)

look in or out: **tewatke'tótha'** it keeps looking in, this way (an animal), **tahatke'tó:ten'** he looked in, **thotkè:tote'** he is looking in, **iahatke'tó:ten'** he looked out, that way (-ke'tot-)

look into: *See* examine

look up: **wa'kathon'kwáweron'** I looked up with my head back (-hon'kw-, -aweron-)

loon: **ioniatarèn:ton** (-niatar-, -hren't-/-en't-)

lose: **wakátie's** I lose it, **onkwá:ti'** I lost it, **wakátion** I have lost it (-ati-/-onti-)

lose; misplace: **wahóhton'se'** he lost it, misplaced it, **wakahtón:ni** I have lost it, misplaced it (-ahton-)

lost, get lost: **wahatia'táhton'** he got lost, **iakotia'tahtòn:'on** she is lost (-ia't-, -ahton-)

lots; many: **é:so**

loud; audible: **iohrón:ka** it is audible, loud (-ahronk-)

loud noise: **iorakarè:ni** it is loud (-rakare'ni-/-kare'ni-)

louse, lice: **otsì:non** louse, **waktsi'nónhtare'** I have lice (-tsi'non[ht]-, -r-)

love: **konnorónhkhwa'** I love you, **wahinó:ronhkwe'** I loved him, **kanoronhkwáhtshera'** love, compassion (-noron-)

low: **ken' nitiottè:'a** it is low (-te-)

luck: **aterà:swa'** luck, **rotera'swí:io** he has good luck, he is lucky, **onkwatera'swí:iohste'** I got lucky (-atera'sw-, -iio-)

lump: *See* bulge; lump

lump: *See* bump; lump

lung: **otsinà:kwa'** lung, **aktsinà:kwa'** my lungs (-tsina'kw-)

lye: **o'kenhrákeri'** (-a'kenhr-, -keri-)

mad: *See* angry

maid of honour: **wa'ontati'terónhne'** (-i'teron-)

mailman: **tehathiatonhserarenià:tha'** (-hiatonhser-, -areni-)

make: **kón:ni** I am making it, **kón:nis** I am making more than one, **wahrón:ni'** he made it, **wakón:ni** I have made it (-onni-)

makeup; rouge makeup: **katkonte'ékhons** I am putting rouge on my cheeks, on my cheekbones, **wa'katkonte'ékhon'** I put on rouge, **iakotkonte'ékhon** she has on rouge, **iontkonte'éktha'** rouge (-kontsher-)

male (animal): **rá:tsin** (-tsin-)

male person; warrior: **rohsken'rakéhte'** (-hsken'rakehte-)

Malone, NY: **Tekanatà:ronhwe'** (-nat-, -hronhw-)

mane (horse): **oniahkwè:rha'** (-niahkwe'rh-)

mantel; shelf: **wenniseráhere'** (there is) a shelf, a mantel (-enniser-, -her-/-hr-)

many; lots: **é:so**

many, have many: **wakkà:te'** I have many, **enwakkà:teke'** I will have many, **wakkà:tehkwe'** I used to have many (-ka'te-)

many, How many? **Tó: ní:kon?**

map: **ionhóntsare'** or **ionhwéntsare'** (-onhwents-/-onhonts-, -r-)

maple, soft maple: **ken'takén:ra**

maple, sugar maple: **wáhta**

maple candy: **wastè:ton**

maple sap, syrup: **orontákeri'** (-ront-, -keri-)

marbles: **teieneniaientáhkhwa'** (-neni-, ien-)

March: **Enniskó:wa**

mark: **kaierón:ni** it is marked, **tieronnítstha'** I mark it, **wahaierón:nitste'** he marked it, **roieronnítston** he has marked it (-ieronni-)

marriage: **kanáhkwa'** (-nahkw-)

marry: **wakéniaks** I get married, **wahóniake'** he got married, **wakeniá:kon** I am married (-niak-)

marten: **oserennó:ha'**

mash: **teienénhstia'ks** she is mashing it, **wa'tkenénhstia'ke'** I mashed it, **teiakonenhstià:kon** she has mashed it (-nenhstia'k-)

mask, Hallowe'en: **iontkonwaroróksta'** (-konwar-, -'rhoro[k]-/-oro[k]-)

mask, put on a (Covid) face mask: **teiontkonhsáhnhaks** she is putting on a mask, **tenhsatkonhsáhnhake'** you will put on a mask, **tewakatkonhsáhnhen** I have on a mask (-konhs-, -hwahnha[k]-/-hnha[k]-)

mass, celebrate: **roháhsen** (he says) mass (-hahsen[t]-)

match; go together: **tetiatén:ro'** the two match, they go together, **tetiatén:ro'** the two (females) match (-atenro-)

matches; lighter: **ionteka'táhkhwa'** (-atek-)

matchmaker: **kanahkoréhtha'** (-nahkw-, -oreht-)

matchsticks: **ionteka'táhkhwa' ò:wahste'** (-atek-, -'wahst-)

material; fabric: **á:ta'** (-ata-); **onia'tarà:'a** (-nia'tar-)

matter: **orì:wa'** matter, affair, issue, **iah tekarì:wa'** it's nothing, it doesn't matter, don't mention it! (-rihw-)

mature: **wahate'nikonhratehià:ron'** he matured (-'nikonhr-, -ehiahron-)

May: **Onerahtohkó:wa** (-neraht-, -okha-)

maybe: **tóka' nòn:wa**

mayor: **ranatakwe'ní:io** (-nat-, -kwe'niio-)

meadow; field; prairie: **kahén:ta'** meadow, etc., **kahén:taien'** there is a field (-hent-, -ien-)

mean s.t.: **né: tsí:ton** you mean it (-iton-)

mean what one says: **kewenna'shátste'** I mean what I say, **rawenna'shátste'** he means what he says, **iewenna'shátste'** she means what she says (-wenn-, -'shatst[e]-)

measles: **onkwata'keráhkwen'** I got the measles, chicken pox, **wahota'keráhkwen'** he got the measles, **wa'akota'keráhkwen'** she got the measles (-a'ker-)

measure: **kate'nienténhstha'** I am measuring it, **wa'kate'nién:tenhste'** I measured it, **ionte'nientenhstáhkhwa'** ruler, tape measure (-ate'nienten-)

meat: **o'wà:ron'** (-'wahr-)

meat, roasted: **o'skón:wa'** (-'skonw-)

mechanic: **ra'serehtahserón:ni** (-'sere[ht]-, -hseronni-)

medicine: **onónhkwa'** (-nonhkw-/-nonhkwa'tsher-)

meet: **katkennísa's** I have meetings, **wahontkennísa'** they met, they had a meeting, **ionkwatkenníson'** we are meeting, **watkenníson'** meeting (-atkennis-)

meet; run into: **wa'tiatiátera'ne'** we two ran into one another, we met (-r-)

melt: *See* thaw; melt

melt, ice: **wa'kawisaná:wen'** the ice melted (-wis-, -na'nawen-/-nawen-); **wa'kawisó:ko'** the ice went away, it melted (-wis-, -okw-)

menopause; puberty: **wa'tiontonhnhaté:ni'** she underwent puberty, menopause (-onhnh-, -teni-)

menstruate: **akawenhnì:ta'** her moon time, her monthly (period) (-enhni't-); **akhsótha iakonatahré:nen** it is (my, her) moon time, monthly (period) (-hsot-, -natahr-)

mermaid: **tso'nawénhes**

metal; money: **ohwísta'** (-hwist-)

meteor: **katsistohkóntie'** (-tsisto[hkw]-, -itie-/-tie-/-ontie-)

midnight: **ahsónthen** (-ahsonthen-)

midwife: **iewirókwas** (-wir-, -okw-)

Midwinter; January: **Sha'tekohséhrhon** (-ohser-, -hon-)

Midwinter Society; Midwinter ceremony: **Kanonhwaró:ri** (-nonhwar-, -ori-)

mild: **iawentaná:wen** it is a mild day (-ent-, -na'nawen-/-nawen-)

milk: **onòn:ta'** (-non't-)

milkweed: **anitshehwèn:ta'** (-anitshehwen't-); **kanon'tókhas** (-non't-, -okha-)

mill: **iethe'seronnià:tha'** (-the'ser-, -onni-)

mind; spirit: **o'nikòn:ra'** (-'nikonhr-)

mind s.o.: **khenónhnha'** I am minding her, **wahinòn:na'** I minded him (-nonhn-)

mine: **tsi kahwísto** a mine (-hwist-, -o-)

mink: **aió:ha'**

mint; cough drop: **iakonia'takahrónhstha'** (-nia't-, -akahron-)

mint (herb): **teie'tonhkwanohstáhkhwa'** (-i'tonhkw-, -no-)

minute: **Tó: niwahseriiè:take?** How many minutes? (-ahseriie['t]-, -ke-)

mirror: **atátken** (-ken-)

miser: *See* stingy

miser; wart: **anihnhè:ta'** (-ihnhe't[ar]-)

mishear: **tekatahonhsanéra'ks** I mishear, **wa'tkatahonhsanéra'ke'** I misheard it, **tehotahonhsanéren'** he has misheard it (-atahonhsanera['k]-)

misplace: *See* lose; misplace

miss a target: **skate'wáhtha'** I miss it, **saháte'wahte'** he missed it, **shote'wáhton** he has missed it, **sahiiáte'wahte'** I missed him (-ate'waht-)

miss (a target): *See* sideswipe

miss s.o: **kheia'tíhsaks** or **kheia'tí:saks** I am looking for her, I miss her, **wahiia'tíhsake'** or **wahiia'tí:sake'** I looked for him, missed him, **riia'tihsá:kon** or **riia'tisá:kon** I have looked for him (-ia't-, -ehsak-/-ihsak-/-esak-/-isak-)

miss (bus, train, airplane): **watia'tóntie's**
I miss it, **ontia'tón:ti'** I missed it
(-ia't-, -ati-/-onti-)

mist; steam; fog: **otshá:ta** steam, etc.,
iotshá:tote' it is steaming,
teiotshá:taien' it is misty, foggy
(-atshat-, -ot- or -ien-)

mistake: **tekaterien'tawénrie's** I make mistakes, **wa'tkaterien'tawénrie'** I made a
mistake, **teiakorien'tawenriè:'on** she has
made a mistake (-erien't-, -awenrie-)

mistake; err: **teke'niósken's** I make mistakes,
wa'tha'niósken'ne' he erred, he made a mistake, **tewake'nioskèn:'en** I am making a
mistake (-'niosken'-)

mistake s.t. or s.o.: **tekenéra'ks** I mistake it,
wa'tkenéra'ke' I mistook it,
tewakenéren' I have mistaken it,
wa'tkonia'tanéra'ke' I mistook you for
someone (-nera'[k]-)

mistreat; put down: **shakoiesáhtha'**
he mistreats her, puts her down,
wahonwaié:sahte' she mistreated him
(-ies[en]-)

mistreat; take out on: **tehateriahtíkhons** he
takes it out on something, he slams things
around, **wa'thiiateriahtíkhon'** I mistreated
him, took it out on him (-ateriahtikhon-)

mittens; gloves: **a'niá:nawen** mitten, glove,
tewaka'niá:nawen I have gloves, mitts on,
wa'tka'niá:nawenke' I put gloves, mitts on
(-a'nianawen[k]-)

mix: **tetiéstha'** I am mixing it together,
wà:ttieste' I mixed it,
tewatiéston I have mixed it (-iest-)

mixed parentage: **thiehohonro'takè:tote'**
someone with a Onkwehón:we or Native
father and White mother (-honro't-, -ke'tot-);
wakatientátshon' I have an Onkwehón:we
or Native mother and a White father
(-ient-, -atsha'-)

moan: *See* sigh; moan

moccasin: **ahtahkwa'ón:we** (-ahta[hkw]-)

Mohawk: **Kanien'kehá:ka** People of the
Flint (-nien'-); **Ronathnáwerote'** Mohawks
and Senecas, as referred to in council
(-hnawer-, -ot-)

molasses: **ramerá:s**

mold: *See* rust; mold

mole: **otsi'nió:kare'** or **otsi'nión:karon**
or **otsi'nió:karon** (-tsi'niokar-)

Monday: **Awententa'ón:ke** (-ent-, -ent-)

money; metal: **ohwísta'** (-hwist-)

monkey: **katsi'nónhtaks**
(-tsi'non[ht]-, -ek-/-ak-)

month: **awenhnì:ta'** (-enhni't-)

Montréal: **Tiohtià:ke**

moon: **ahsonthénhkha karáhkwa'**
(-ahsonthen-, -rahkw-);
akhsótha awenhnì:ta'
(-hsot-, -enhni't-)

moon, full: **tioterahkwáhere'** it is a full
moon (-rahkw-, -her-/-hr-);
iekarahkwaié:ri it is a full moon, a moonlit night (-rahkw-, -ieri-)

moon, new: **ó:nen saká:ra'ne** it is a new moon (-r-)

moose: **ska'niónhsa'** (-'nionhs-)

mop: **kakenhóhare** (-kenh-, -nohare-/-ohare-)

morals, good morals: *See* intentions, good intentions; good morals; kind

more (as compared with): **sénha**

more; still: **shé:kon**

morgue: **tsi tiakenheion'taientáhkhwa'** (-ihei[on]-/-enhei[on]-, -ien-)

morning: **ohrhon'kè:ne** in the morning, **ohrhon'kéhstsi** early morning (-(h)rhon'ke-)

morphology: **tekawennahsonterónnion** (-wenn-, -ahsonter-)

morsel; portion: **ken' niwahtsohkwà:'a** (it is) a small morsel, a small portion, **wahtsohkowá:nen** (it is) a big morsel, a large portion (-ahtsohkw-)

mortar: **ka'ní:ka**

mosquito: **okariahtà:ne'** (-kari-)

moss: **aweráhsa'** moss, **iaweráhsare'** it has moss on it (-erahs-, -r-)

most: **aonhà:'a** most

moth: **tsikenithè:sera'**

mother: **ake'nisténha** my mother, **istèn:'a** my mother, my auntie, **Istá:!** Mother! (-'nisten-)

mother-in-law: **ionkwehnhónsa'** my mother-in-law (-ehnhonsa'); **ionksà:wha** my mother-in-law (-sa'w-)

mother, stepmother: **ionkenò:'a** my step-mother (-no-)

mountain; hill: **ionón:te'** there is a mountain, a hill (-nonte-)

mourn: **wakatshon'niónhkwen** I am mourning, **rotshon'niónhkwen** he is mourning, **iakotshon'niónhkwen** she is mourning (-atshon'nionhkw-)

mourning dove: **tarò:taro**

mouse: **otsinó:wen** (-tsinonwen-)

mouth: **tsi khsakà:ronte'** my mouth (-hs-, -kahront-)

mouth, close: **kátskweks** I shut my mouth, **wahátskweke'** he closed his mouth, **iakotskwé:kon** she has closed her mouth (-hs-, -kwek-)

mouth, inside: **khsá:kon** inside my mouth (-hs-)

mouth, open: **wa'tkátskara'we'** I opened my mouth, **teiakotskarà:wen** her mouth is open (-hs-, -kara'w-)

mouth, put in: **róhnhonte'** he has it in his mouth (-(h)nhont-); **iontehnhónta's** she or s.o. puts it in her mouth, **wa'katehnhónta'** I put it in my mouth (-(h)nhonta'-)

mouth, put in s.o.'s mouth: *See* feed s.o.

mouth, rinse: **wa'katehnhoskóhare'** I rinsed my mouth (-(h)nhoskw-, -nohare-/-ohare-)

mouthful: **wakehnhonskwáhnhonte'** I have a mouthful (-(h)nhoskw-, -(h)nhont-); **wa'ontehnhoskwahnhónta'** she took a mouthful (-(h)nhoskw-, -(h)nhonta'-)

move: **korià:nerons** I move it, shift it, **wa'korià:neron'** I moved it, **ratoriahnerónkwas** he moves about, **wahatoriahnerón:ko'** he moved around, **wakatoriahnerónkwen** I am moving about (-oriahneron-)

move: *See* wander

move; relocate: **wa'tkaná:tahkwe'** I moved, **teiakonatáhkwen** she has moved, **teionnatahkwà:tha'** she is moving it, **wa'thanatáhkwa'te'** he moved it, **tewakanatahkwà:ton** I have moved it (-nat-, -hkw-)

move back and forth (a part of the body): **wa'tkarahsi'tén:tonhwe'** I moved my foot back and forth, **tehanitahsén:tons** he is moving his tail back and forth, he is waving, wagging his tail (-enton[hw]-)

move over: **waháthkwi'te'** he moved over (-hkwi't-)

movie: **teióia'ks** (-oia'[k]-)

much, too much: **sò:tsi**

muck; sludge; scum: **orawà:ta'** (-rawa't-)

mucus; phlegm: **ohrhónria'** (-(h)rhonri-)

mud: **onawà:tsta'** (-nawa'tst-)

mud hen: **ranawa'tstókwas** (-nawa'tst-, -okw-)

muscle: **osenennà:ta'** muscle, **wakesenenna'tarónnion** I have muscles (-senenna't-, -r-)

mushroom: **ráskan raókhwa'** (-skan-, -khw-)

music: **karén:note'** music, **waterennótha'** musical instrument, radio, record player (-renn-, -ot-)

muskellunge: **kanò:tsot** (-no'ts-, -ot-)

muskrat: **anò:tien**

must; have to: **ó:nen'k tsi**

musty: **kawískeras** it smells musty, **wa'kawískera'ne'** it got musty (-wiskera-)

nail; wire; needle; pin: **karón:ware'** or **kanón:ware'** (-ronwar-/-nonwar-)

nail: **otsi'é:ra'** nails, **aktsi'é:ra'** my nails (-tsi'er-)

nail, ingrown: **onkwattsi'eriniòn:ten'** I got an ingrown nail (-tsi'er-, -ion't-/-inion't-)

naked: **o'nótsta'** nakedness, **ra'nótstote'** he is naked, **ie'nótstote'** she is naked (-'notst-, -ot-)

name: **kahsén:na'** (-hsenn-); **Oh nahò:ten' ní:se' iesá:iats?** What is your name? (-iat-)

name, call by a name: **khena'tónhkhwa'** I call her by a name (-na'ton-)

nation: **Oh nisanakerahserò:ten?** What Nation are you? (-naker[e]-, -o'ten-)

Native: **Onkwehón:we** Native person,

Onkwehonwehnéha Native way, Native language (-onkwe['t]-)

natural: **sha'oié:ra** it is natural (-ier-)

nauseous: **tewakene'warà:tani** I am nauseous, **tonkene'warà:ten'** I got nauseous (-ne'wara't-)

near: **ákta'**

neck: **oniá:ra'** neck, **keniarà:ke** (on) my neck (-niar-)

neck; collar: **ohnià:sa'** neck, collar, **khnia'sà:ke** (on) my neck, **tekahnia'sáhere'** it has a collar (-hnia's-, -her-/-hr-)

neck, nape of the neck: **keniahkaró:kon** my nape (-niahkar-)

neck, put around the neck: **kaníhtiaks** I put it around my neck, **wa'kaníhtiake'** I put it around my neck, **wakaníhtien** I have it around my neck; **ionnihtiákstha'** necklace, yoke (of a shirt or dress) (-anihtia[k]-)

necklace: **ohstarò:kwa'** necklace, **wa'katstaro'kwániake'** I put on a necklace, **iakotstaro'kwánien** she has on a necklace (-hstaro'kw-, -nia[k]-)

necktie: **wahatenia'tarániake'** he put on a tie, **rotenia'taránien** he has on a tie (-nia'tar-, -nia[k]-); **ionte'nhehsaniákstha'** necktie (-'nhehs-, -nia[k]-)

need; want: **tewakatonhwentsó:ni** or **tewakatehontsó:ni** I want it, need it, **Nahò:ten' tesatehontsó:ni?** What do you want? (-atonhwentsoni-/-atonhontsoni-/-atehontsoni-)

needle; nail; wire; pin: **karón:ware'** or **kanón:ware'** (-ronwar-/-nonwar-)

needle, darning needle: **ierisera'nikhónhkhwa'** (-ris[er]-, -'nikhon-)

negative person: **ra'nikonhráksen** he is a negative person, **ie'nikonhráksen** she is negative (-'nikonhr-, -aksen-)

neighbours: **teiatianonhsané:ken** we two are neighbours, my neighbour (-nonhs-, -ra'neken-/-neken-)

nephew: **riionhwatèn:'a** my nephew (-onhwaten-)

nest: **otsi'náhkwa'** (-tsi'nahkw-)

net; curtain; veil: **à:'are'** (-a'ar-)

never: **iah nonwén:ton**

never mind: **arohátien**

new: **asé'tsi** it is new

New Year's Day: **Tsi na'teiontatenoronhkwánions** (-noron-)

New York City; Manhattan: **Kanón:no**

news: **orì:wase'** news (-rihw-, -ase-)

newspaper: **tewaterihwarenià:tha'** (-rihw-, -areni-)

next to: **tehiatera'né:ken** the two are (standing) next to each other, they are partners (-ra'neken-/-neken-)

Niagara: **Ohniá:kara'**

niece: **kheionhwatèn:'a** my niece (-onhwaten-)

night: **kwa'ahsontè:ke** or **kwa'shontè:ke** nighttime, **tsi niwahsón:tes** during the night (-ahsont-)

night, restless night: *See* awake, keep awake

nightingale: **tostostseríneken'**

nightmare: **onkeserenhtí:ionhkwe'** I had a nightmare (-serenht-)

nine: **tióhton**

nipple: **okónhkwara'** (-konhkwar-)

no; not: **iáhten** or **iah**

nod: **iehnenhsà:ke ieniaráhere'** her head is nodding, she is putting her neck towards her shoulder (-hnenhs-, and -niar-, -her-/-hr-)

noise: **tewakaterien'takária** I am noisy, **wa'thaterien'takáriahte'** he made noise, **tehoterien'takariáhton** he is making noise (-erien't-, -kari-)

noise: **iorá:kahre'** it is making noise, it is noisy (-rakahr-/-kahr-); **wakaterakarehráhston** I am making noise (-rakarehrahst-/-karehrahst-)

noise; racket: **teiaónhahre'** it is making a racket (-onhahr-)

noise, a lot: **iotsharókwen** there's a lot of noise, **katsharokwáhtha'** I make noise, **wahatsharókwahte'** he made a lot of noise, **wakatsharokwáhton** I am making noise (-atsharokw-)

noon: **éntie ní:kare'**

north: **othorè:ke** (-athor[e]-)

northern lights: **kaniatara'kehkó:wa tetiaon'kwara'éhstha'** (-niatar-)

nose: **o'niónhsa'** nose, **ke'nionhsà:ke** (on) my nose (-'nionhs-)

nose, bleed: **wa'tha'niónkha'** he got a nosebleed, **teiako'nionkhà:'on** she has a nosebleed (-'nionkha-)

nose, blocked: **tewake'nión:kweks** my nose is blocked, stuffed up, **wa'tho'nión:kweke'** he got a blocked, stuffy nose (-'nionkwek-)

nose, blow: **wa'kattsi'niónhkere'** I blew my nose, **rottsi'niónhkeren** he is blowing his nose (-tsi'nionhker-)

nose, bridge of the nose: **okón:ta'** (-kont-)

nose, runny: **waktsi'niónhkerote'** my nose is running (-tsi'nionhker-, -ot-)

nose, turned-up: **ra'nión:kote'** he has a turned-up nose, **ie'nión:kote'** she has a turned-up nose (-'nionkot-)

not: **iah, iáhten**

not yet: **áre'kho**

nothing: **iah thé:nen**

notice: **kattó:kas** I notice it, sense it, perceive it, **waháttoke'** he noticed, **wakattó:ken** I have noticed (-attok-)

November: **Kentenhkó:wa** (-iten[ht]-)

now: **nòn:wa**

now; already: **ó:nen**

numb: *See* asleep, body part; numb

nun: **iakoia'tatokénhti** (-ia't-, -tokenhti-)

nurse, suck milk: **ienon'kéhrha'** she
is sucking (milk), nursing,
wahanon'ké:ra' he sucked milk,
iakonon'ké:ren she is sucking milk
(-non'ker-)

nurse s.o.: **khehstaróntha'** I am nursing
her, **wa'khehstarón:ten'** I nursed her
(-hstar-, -ont-)

nut: **ohsò:kwa'** (-hso'kw-)

nutmeg: **iehso'kwaketà:tha'** (-hso'kw-, -ket-)

oak, black: **karíhton** (-rihton-)

oak, white: **otokénha'**

oar; paddle: **aká:we'** (-kawe-)

oats: **arawén**

obey: *See* heed

obstruct: **ieió'tats** she gets in the way of it,
obstructs it, **wahaió'tate'** he got in the way
(-io'tat-)

obtain; get: *See* acquire

ocean: **kaniatara'kehkó:wa** (-niatar-);
teiohnekahio'tsíshne (-hnek-, -hio'tsis[t]-)

October: **Kenténha** (-iten[ht]-)

offend: **thotierà:se'** he gets offended,
tonkwatié:ra'se' I got offended (-ier-)

offertory: **kanà:tarote'** (-na'tar[o][k]-, -ot-)

often: **iotkà:te'** (-ka'te-)

Ohswé:ken Six Nations of the Grand River

oil; grease: **kén:ie'** (-iie-/-ien-)

Ojibwe: **Atirón:taks** (-ront-, -ek-/-ak-);
Tewa'káhnha'

Oka: **Kanehsatà:ke** Kanien'kehá:ka
(Mohawk) territory at Oka, Québec

old: **aká:ion** it is old, **onká:ion'ne'** or
wa'oká:ion'ne' it got old, **iokaiòn:'on**
it has gotten old (-akaion-/-kaion-)

old person: **rokstén:ha** he is old,
iakokstén:ha she is old,
wahokstén:ha'ne' he got old
rokstenha'onhátie' he is getting old
(-ksten-)

older: **ó:nen tewátien'** I am older now,
ó:nen thó:ien' he is older now,
ó:nen tiakó:ien' she is older now (-ien-)

omen: *See* premonition; omen

omen; flame: **o'tónhkwa'** (-i'tonhkw-)

one: **énska**

Oneida: **Oneniote'á:ka** Oneida (-neni-, -ot-);
Ratironta'kó:wa Oneidas, as referred to in
council (-ront-); **Ratirihwaié:nas** Oneidas
and Cayugas as referred to in council
(-rihw-, -iena-)

onion: **o'niónkseri** (-'nionkser-)

Onondaga: **Ononta'kehá:ka** Onondaga
(-nont-); **Ronattsístaien'** Onondagas, as
referred to in council (-tsist-, -ien-)

open (a door): **rahnhotónkwas** he opens it, **wa'kehnhotón:ko'** I opened it, **rohnhotónkwen** he has opened it, **kahnhotónkwen** it is open (-(h)nhoton-)

open (a lid): **wa'kenontékhsi'** I took the lid off, I opened it (-nontek-)

open out: **wa'tektá:kwarihte'** I spread it, I am opening it out (-takwariht-/-kwariht-)

opening; hole: **iokà:ronte'** there is an opening, a hole, **wa'kkahrón:ten'** I made a hole in it (-kahront-)

opening; space: **teioronhwén:te'** there is a space, **wa'tkeronhwén:tate'** I made an opening (-ronhwent[e]-)

opossum: **wenniheià:tha'** (-ihei[on]-/-enhei[on]-)

or: **káton'**; **tóka' ni'**

orange (colour): **atiarèn:ta'** (-atiaren't-)

organ (musical instrument): **tekarihwáhkhwa'** (-rihw-, -hkw-); **kahonro'tó:ton** (-honro't-, -ot-)

oriole: **atiaren'ta'kó:wa** (-atiaren't-)

orphan: **wa'thatonhnhaká:ri'** he was orphaned, **teiakotonhnhakarì:'on** she is an orphan (-onhnh-, -kari-)

other: **akò:ren** somebody else, another one, **akohren'shòn:'a** other people, the others

Ottawa: **Kanà:tso** (-na'ts-, -o-)

otter: **tawí:ne**

ounce: **ons** ounce

outfit; clothing: **atahkwénnia'** (-ahkwenni-)

outgrow: **wa'tewakawén:ren'** I outgrew it, **teiakowenrèn:'en** she has outgrown it, she doesn't fit it (-awenren-)

outhouse; bathroom: **átste' ieienhtáhkhwa'** (-eht-); **ionni'tenhtáhkhwa'** (-i't-, -a'senht-/-enht-);

outside: **átste'**

oval: **í:iens tsi teiothwe'nón:ni** (-es-, -hwe'nonni-/-kwe'nonni-)

over (an amount): **skáhere'** it's over, more than (-her-/-hr-)

overalls: **oronhia'kó:wa atháhsteren iawentskwè:nonte'** (-ronhi- and -athahsteren[k]- and -entskwe'n-, -ont-)

overcast; cloudy: **ioronhió:ron** it is cloudy, overcast (-ronhi-, -'rhoro[k]-/-oro[k]-)

overflow: **tewaréserons** it boils over, flows over, **tonré:sere'** it flowed over, **tioréseron** it has overflowed (-areser[on]-)

overflow s.t.: **kawèn:rats** I overflow it, **wahawèn:rate'** he overflowed it, **wakawenhrá:ton** I have overflowed it (-awenhrat-)

owe: **wakatká:rote'** I have a bill, I owe money, **rotká:rote'** he owes money, **iakotká:rote'** she owes money (-kar-, -ot-)

owl, barn owl: **kwaroró:ha**

owl, great horned owl: **tsistékeri**

oxen: **teiotinà:kares** (-na'kar-, -es-)

oyster; clam: **takwaré:re**

pace: **tekaterahtánions** I go back and forth, I am pacing; **wa'thaterahtánion'** he paced (-r-)

pack: **rathrie'nón:ni** he packs it, **wa'kathrie'nón:ni'** I packed it, (-hrie'n-, -onni-); **skahriè:na** one pack, one load (-hrie'n-, -[t]-)

pack; pile: **otstóhkwa'** pack, pile, **iotstóhkote'** piled (-itstohkw-, -ot-)

pack down: *See* compress

package; parcel: **onennótshera'** or **onerótshera'** (-nennotsher-)

paddle: **raká:wes** he paddles, **wahaká:we'** he paddled, **wakkawehátie'** I am paddling, **aká:we'** paddle, oar (-kawe-)

paddle, for cornbread: **a'serawénrie'** (-a'ser-, -awenrie-)

paddle; flail the arms: **tenhateniá:wake'** he will flail, paddle his arms, **wa'thateniá:wake'** he flailed, paddled his arms (-ateniawak-)

pail: **kanà:tson'** (-na'ts-); **ón:ta** (-onta-)

pain: *See* hurt

pain: *See* hurt; ache

pain, endure pain: *See* endure pain

pain, growing pains: **tewakenientawí:sas** I have growing pains,

tehonientawí:sas he has growing pains, **teiakonientawí:sas** she has growing pains (-nient-)

paint: **okóntshera'** paint, **kkontsheráhrhos** I am painting, **wahakontsheráhrho'** he painted it, **rokontsheráhrhon** he has painted it (-kontsher-, -(h)rho-)

pair: **tsoiá:na** one pair (-ian-)

pale: **wa'thatskennenón:ten'** he got pale, **teiakotskenné:nonte'** she is pale (-atskennenont-)

palm (hand): *See* handful

Palm Sunday: **Iontenerahtonnià:ne'** (-neraht-, -onni-)

pancake; peel: **ora'wísta'** (-ra'wist-)

pantry; cupboard; closet: **iontahkwenniaientáhkhwa'** (-ahkwenni-, -ien-)

pants; trousers: **atháhsteren** pants, trousers, **tehotháhsteren** he has trousers on, **wa'tkatháhsterenke'** I put pants on (-athahsteren[k]-)

paper; book: **kahiatónhsera'** (-hiatonhser-)

parable: **teiorihwatokénhton** (-rihw-, -tokenhti-)

parade: **rotinenhrineken'enhátie'** they are in a parade (-nenhr-, -ineken'-)

paralyzed: **wahaia'takénheie'** he became paralyzed, **wa'eia'takénheie'** she became paralyzed (-ia't-, -ihei[on]-/-enhei[on]-)

parcel; package: **onennótshera'** or **onerótshera'** (-nennotsher-)

parlour: **tsi kanonhsí:io** (-nonhs-, -iio-)

parrot: **tekáhstia'ks**

partition: **tewahsónhtote'** (-ahsonht-, -ot-)

partridge: **ohkwé:sen** (-ahkwesen-)

party: **ronton'wéshens** they party (they drink, etc.), **wahaton'wéshen'** he partied (-on'weshen-)

pass: **kohétstha'** I pass it, **wa'kóhetste'** I passed it, **wakohétston** I have passed it, **wa'kheiatohétsten'** I passed her, **wa'katóhetste'** I passed by, **ontóhetste'** it passed by (a vehicle) (-ohetst-)

pass by; visit: **iehakwáthos** he goes over there, stops by, passes by, visits briefly, **ienkkwátho'** I will visit, pass by, **iahakwátho'** he went by, passed by (-kwatho-)

pass over: **iehawèn:rats** he is putting it over, he is passing it over, **iahawèn:rate'** or **ia'thawèn:rate'** he put it, he passed it over, **ieiakowenhrá:ton** she has passed it over (-awenhrat-)

pass through; graduate: **tekatohétstha'** I pass through, I graduate, **wa'tkatóhetste'** I passed through, I graduated (-ohetst-)

patch: **iokwèn:rare'** a patch, a bunch of things that are together (-kwenhrar-)

patch (sewing): **wa'kihnanén:takte'** I patched it (-ihn-, -ra'nentakt-/-nentakt-)

path: **tekaianón:ni** (-ian-, -onni-)

patient: **wakate'nikonhriióhston** I am patient (-'nikonhr-, -iio-)

paved: **kahnehtóntion** it is paved (-hneht-, -ati-/-onti-)

pay: **rakária'ks** he is paying, **wahakária'ke'** he paid, **rokarià:kon** he has paid, **wahakkária'khse'** he paid me, **khekarià:ki** I have paid her (-kar-, -ia'k-)

pea; pill: **onékwa'** (-nekw-)

peace: **skén:nen**

peach: **tekakenhwhará:ron**

Peach Pit game: **kaientowá:nen** (-ient-, -kowan[en]-/-owan[en]-)

peacock: **skanaie'kó:wa** (-naie-)

pear: **kátshe' káhi** (-tshe['t]- and -ahi-)

peck: **kasto'ókhons** it is pecking, **iosto'ókhon** it has pecked, **wahaksto'ókhon'** he pecked me (-sto'okhon-)

pedal: **iekawe'táhkhwa'** bike pedal (-kawe-); **ionrahsi'tontawe'táhkhwa'** sewing machine pedal (-ahsi't-, -ontawe't-)

peddle; sell: **ratkè:rons** he peddles, sells things, **wahatkè:ron'** he peddled it, sold it, **iakotkè:ron** she is selling (-kehron[t]-)

peddler; hobo: **ratenohkwakéhtats** (-nohkw-, -keht[e]-)

peel: **ora'wísta'** peel,

kera'wistóhtshions I am peeling it,
wa'kera'wistóhtshi' I peeled it,
iakora'wistóhtshion she has peeled it
(-ra'wist-, -ohtshi-)

peg; little stick: **ò:wahste'** (-'wahst-)

pelican: **kentsókwas** (-its-, -okw-)

pellet; pit: **onèn:'a'** (-nen'-)

penalty, get a penalty: **ronwaia'tohtáhrhos**
he gets penalties, **wahonwaia'tohtáhrho'**
he got a penalty (-ia't-, -ohtahrho-)

pencil: **iehiatónhkhwa'** (-hiaton-);
kaharennahtóhare' lead pencil
(-harennaht-, -ohar-)

penetrate; go through: **ia'tkón:kohte'** I went
through it, I penetrated it, **ia'tewakonkóhton**
I have gone through it (-onko-)

penguin: **kwé:nati**

peninsula; point of land: **iotòn:niate'**
(-onhni-, -te-)

penis: **ohnó:ron** (-ihn-, -'rhoro[k]-/-oro[k]-)

pepper: **tiononhkwà:tsheros** pepper;
tiononhkwa'tsheroskó:wa green or red bell
pepper (-nonhkw-/-nonhkwa'tsher-, -o-)

perceive: *See* notice

perch: **oiahè:ta'** (-iahe't-)

perform: *See* act; perform

perfume: **wakatia'takon'ónhston** I have
on perfume, **iontia'takon'onhstáhkhwa'**
perfume (-ia't-, -eka'[w]-/-ka'[w]-)

permit: *See* allow

person: **ón:kwe** person,
rón:kwe male person,
iakón:kwe female person (-onkwe['t]-)

Personal Chant: **Atón:wa**

persuade: **iahi'nikonhrénhawe'** I swayed,
persuaded him (-'nikonhr-, -ha[w]-/-enha[w]-)

pestle: **ahsí:sa'** or **kasí:sa'**

pheasant: **ohkwesen'tarì:wase'**

Philadelphia: **Tsi kanataien'kó:wa**
(-nat-, -ien-)

phlegm; mucus: **ohrhónria'** (-(h)rhonri-)

piano: **iena'karáia'ks** (-na'kar-, -ia'k-);
karonwaráia'ks (-ronwar-/-nonwar-, -ia'k-)

pick: **íkkwas** I am picking it,
wà:kko' I picked it,
wákkwen I have picked it (-kw-)

pick (tool): **oweión:ta'** (-wei-, -ont-)

pick-axe: **karistóhare'** (-rist-, -ohar-)

pick on someone: *See* bully

pick up: **tekéhkhwa'** I pick it up,
wà:tkehkwe' I picked it up,
tewakéhkwen I have picked it up,
wa'tekheià:tahkwe' I picked her up (-hkw-)

pickerel: **skakahráksen** (-kahr-, -aksen-)

pickers: **ohnión:wara'** pickers,
teiohnionwarón:ton it has pickers
(-hnionwar-, -ont-)

pickers; burrs: **óhrhohte'** (-(h)rhoht-)

pickles: **teionon'onserahiò:tsis**
(-non'onser-, -hio'tsis[t]-)

picture: **kaià:tare'** picture, **tià:tare'**
a picture of me, **kerahstánions** I am
drawing, taking pictures (-ia't-, -r-)

pie: **tekahswá:ne** (-hson-/-hsw-,
-hna'ne[t]-/-ne[t]-); **tikwaté:**

pie, fruit pie: **tewà:ia** (-ahi-, -a[t]-)

pie, meat pie: **tka'wà:ra** (-'wahr-, -a[t]-)

pierce: **tekawe'éhstha'** I pierce it,
wa'tháwe'ehste' he pierced it,
tewakawe'éhston I have pierced it
(-awe'ehst-)

pig: **kwéskwes**

pigeon: **orì:te'** (-ri'te-)

pigeon-toed: **tehorahsi'tatá:se** he is pigeon-
toed, **teiakorahsi'tatá:se** she is pigeon-toed
(-ahsi't-, -hwatase-/-tase-)

pike: **tsikónhses** (-konhs-, -es-)

pike, yellow: **skakahráksen** (-kahr-, -aksen-)

pile: *See* heap; pile

pile: *See* pack; pile

pile: *See* stack; pile

pill; pea: **onékwa'** (-nekw-)

pillar: **ka'ní:ka** pillar, **ka'nikáhtote'**
(there is) a pillar, a pier (-'nika[ht]-, -ot-)

pillow; cushion: **atkòn:sera'** (-atkon'ser-)

pilot of a ship; war canoe captain:
thaniarotáhrhoks (-niar-, -otahrho[k]-)

pimple: *See* bump, little bump

pin; nail; wire; needle: **karón:ware'** or
kanón:ware' (-ronwar-/-nonwar-)

pin, safety pin: **tewatotáhrhoks**
(-otahrho[k]-)

pin, straight pin: **io'nístonte'** (-'nist-, -ont-)

pinch: **wa'thihnò:rarake'** I pinched him,
wa'thakihnò:rarake' he pinched me
(-ihn-, -htohrarak-/-ohrarak-);
wahihnatá:se' I twisted his skin, I pinched
him, **wahakihnatá:se'** he pinched me
(-ihn-, -hwatase-/-tase-)

pine; pitch; gum: **ohnéhta'** (-hneht-)

pine, white pine: **tionerahtase'kó:wa**
(-neraht-, -ase-)

pineapple: **ken' niiohontesha'kó:wa**
(-hont-, -esha-)

pink: **weshén:rate'** (it is) pink (-eshenrat-)

pins-and-needles sensation:
tewakhnionwarontónnion I have a pins-
and-needles sensation (-hnionwar-, -ont-)

pipe; tube: **ohonrò:ta'** (-honro't-)

pipe, tobacco pipe: **kanén:nawen**
(-nennawen['t]-); **kahrhókwa'** (-(h)rhokw-)

pistol; handgun: **ken' nikahonrésha**
(-honr-, -esha-)

pit; pellet: **onèn:'a'** (-nen'-)

pitch; pine; gum: **ohnéhta'** pitch, etc., **iohnéhtare'** it has pitch, gum on it (-hneht-, -r-)

pitch: **rásen**

pitcher, milk pitcher: **ienon'tawerontáhkhwa'** (-non't-, -aweron-)

pitcher plant: **a'nó:wara raó:ris** (-'now- and -ris[er]-)

pity: **ritén:ras** I take pity on him, **wa'khé:tenre'** I felt sorry for her, took pity on her, **ritén:ron** I have pitied him, **atatitén:ron** charity, pity (-itenr-)

place; bed: **kanákta'** (-nakt-)

plaid: **tekonttsiseratónnion** (-tsiser-)

plane: **tehakénserons** he is planing it, **wa'tekkén:sere'** I planed it, scraped it, sliced it, **tehokénseron** he has planed it (-kenser[on]-)

plant: **tiénthos** I plant, **wahaiéntho'** he planted, **watiénthon** I have planted (-ientho-)

plant, seedling: **o'ón:wara'** (-'onwar-)

plantain: **teionerahtahstaráthe'** (-neraht-, -hstarathe-)

plate; dish: **káksa'** (-ks-)

plate; dish; bowl: **akè:ra'** (-akehr-/-kehr-)

play: **katkahrì:tha'** I play with it, **wahatkà:ri'te'** he played with it, **wakatkahrì:ton** I am playing with it,

wakatkahri'tsherón:ni I am playing (-atkahri-)

play; gamble: **tehá:iens** he is playing, gambling, **wa'tiakení:ien'** we two played (-ien-)

play; playful: **katswà:tha'** I am playing, I am fooling around, kidding, **wahátswa'te'** he played, fooled around, **ronatswà:ton** they are playing (-hsw-)

plead: *See* beg; plead

pleasant: **ion'wé:sen** it is pleasant, nice (-on'wesen-)

pleat: **wa'kerístenhte'** I pleated it, **karisténhton** it is pleated, it has pleats (-rist-, -a'senht-/-enht-)

Pleiades: *See* dipper

plenty: **kanákere'** there is plenty of it (-naker[e]-)

plenty: *See* fill

plenty, have plenty: *See* many, have many

pliers: **tekahtò:raraks** (-htohrarak-/-ohrarak-)

plough: **ki'tarakahrháthos** I am ploughing, **wahen'tarakahrhátho'** he ploughed, **ken'tarakahráthon** it is ploughed, **ie'tarakahrhathóhstha'** plough (-i'tar-, -kahrhatho-)

plug in: **iahahnhóntho'** he plugged it in, put it in a socket (-(h)nhontho-)

plum: **wíhson**

pneumonia: **amónia**

pocket: **iohna'táhtsheronte'**
(-hna'tahtsher-, -ont-)

point: **iehahtsá:tons** he points to it,
ia'kahtsá:ton' I pointed to it,
iewakahtsá:ton I am pointing to it,
I have pointed to it,
iahiiahtsá:ton' I pointed to him (
-ahtsaton-)

pointy: *See* sharp; pointy

poison: **iakorióhtha'** (-rio-/-riio-)

poison ivy: **iakohentaráhstha'** (-hent-, -r-)

pole; post: **kanawa'áhta'** post, pole,
kanawa'áhtote' there is a pole there
(-nawa'aht-, -ot-)

police; black oak: **karíhton** police, black oak,
raríhton he is a policeman (-rihton-)

polish: *See* shiny

pollywog: **tsikenitshehwèn:ta'**

pompom: **oron'ónhkwa'** pompom,
karon'onhkwáhere' there is a pompom
(-ron'onhkw-, -her-/-hr-)

pond: **iohnhonwá:taien'**

poor: **wakí:ten** I am poor,
ró:ten he is poor, **iakó:ten** she is poor,
wahoténhta'ne' he became poor (-iten[ht]-)

popcorn: **watenenhstatakwáhton**
(-nenhst-, -attatakw-)

Pope: **arihwawa'konhkó:wa**
(-rihw-, -ienawa'k-/-wa'k-)

poplar: **onerahtón:ta'** (-neraht-, -ont-)

porch: **ahskwèn:na'** porch (-ahskwen'n-)

porcupine: **anèn:taks** (-nen't-, -ek-/-ak-)

porridge: **arawén othè:sera'** (-the'ser-)

possible: **wá:tons** it is possible,
ón:ton' it became, it could be,
iotòn:'on it has become possible,
iah thaón:ton' it wasn't possible, it can't be
(-aton-)

post; pole: **kanawa'áhta'** post, pole,
kanawa'áhtote' there is a pole there
(-nawa'aht-, -ot-)

post office: **tsi iehiatonhseratahkwáhtha'**
(-hiatonhser-, -tahkw-)

postpone: **ionsonkwá:ti'** I postponed it,
I put it off (-ati-/-onti-)

potato: **ohnennà:ta'** (-hnenna't-)

pound: **kethè:tha'** I am pounding,
waháthe'te' he pounded,
wakethè:ton I have pounded (-the't-)

pound (weight): **skakòn:tshera** one pound
(-kon'tsher-)

pour: *See* spill

pour out: **iohná:ote'** it is pouring out
(-hnaw-, -ot-)

power, mystical power: **rotia'tátkon** he
is a mystic, he has power (-ia't-, -atkon-)

practice: *See* learn; study; practice

prairie; meadow; field: **kahén:ta'** prairie,
etc., **kahén:taien'** there is a field
(-hent-, -ien-)

praise: **tekonrénhsarons** I praise you, I am proud of you, **wa'thonwarénhsaron'** she praised him (-renhsaron-)

praise; worship: **ronwahsén:naien'** they praise him, worship him (-hsenn-, -ien-)

pray: **roterén:naien'** he is praying, **wahonwaterennaién:hahse'** she prayed for him, **aterén:naien'** prayer (-renn-, -ien-)

praying mantis: **tsiské:kek**

preach; lecture: **raterihwahnótha'** he preaches, lectures, **wahaterihwahnó:ton'** he preached, **wakaterihwà:note'** I have preached (-rihw-, -ahnot-)

pregnant: **iené:ron** she is pregnant (-ner-)

premonition; omen: **kahsòn:nions** it is an omen, **onkhsòn:nion'se'** I got a premonition, **wakhson'niòn:se'** I have a premonition (-hson'nion-)

President of the United States: **Ranatakárias** (-nat-, -kari-)

press down: *See* squeeze

pretend; fake: **rotia'tontáhkwen** he is pretending to be something he is not, **wahatia'tón:tahkwe'** he faked it (-ia't-, -ont-)

pretend to be dead: **wahanihé:ia'te'** he pretended to be dead (-ihei[on]-/-enhei[on]-)

pretend to not know: *See* deny

pretend to sleep: **ranità:stha'** he pretends to be sleeping, **wa'kaní:ta'ste'** I pretended to be sleeping, **wakanità:ston** I am pretending to sleep (-ita'[w]-)

prevent: **enhsheià:riste'** you will urge her, prevent her (from something), **wahiià:riste'** I urged, prevented him (-ahrist-)

priest: **ratsihénhstatsi** (-tsihenhst-)

promise: **wahakehrharátsten'** he promised me, **khehrharatstén:ni** I have promised her (-(h)rhar[e]-)

promise; commit: **kerihwísa's** I make a commitment, I promise, **wa'kerihwísa'** I made a commitment, I promised, **rorihwíson'** he has promised (-rihw-, -hsa'-/-isa'-)

protect: *See* watch over; protect

protrude; stick out: **iokè:tote'** it is protruding, sticking out (-ke'tot-)

proud; conceited: **kená:ie'** I am proud, I am conceited, **raná:ie'** he is proud, conceited, **iená:ie'** she is proud, conceited, **ratenaiéhstha'** he acts proud, **enkatená:iehste'** I will show off, **rotenaiéhston** he is showing off (-naie-)

proud; put on airs: **ratatón:ni** he is putting on airs, proud of himself, patting himself on the back (-onni-)

proud; show off: **rara'séhstha'** he is proud, he admires himself, he is a show-off, **ionra'séhstha'** she is proud, a show-off (-ara'se-)

proud; stuck-up: **ratatkonniénhstha'** he is proud, stuck-up, putting on airs, **iontatkonniénhstha'** she is proud (-kwennien-/-konnien-)

proud of s.o.: *See* praise

puberty; menopause: **wa'tiontonhnhaté:ni'** she underwent puberty, menopause (-onhnh-, -teni-)

puddles: **kahionwa'takè:ron**

puffball: **tewatien'kwarókwas** (-ien'kwar-, -okw-)

pull: **thatiróntha'** he pulls it, **tahatirón:ten'** he pulled it, **thotí:ronte'** he is pulling it (-atiront-)

pull; tug: **tkatihénthos** I pull it, **takatihéntho'** I pulled it, **tewakatihénthon** I have pulled it (-atihentho-)

pull out: *See* remove; pull out

pump: **iehnekatahkwáhtha'** (-hnek-, -tahkw-)

pump: *See* shake back and forth; pump

pumpkin: **onon'onsera'kó:wa** (-non'onser-)

punch: *See* hit; punch

punish: **khehrewáhtha'** I punish her or them, **wa'onkhré:wahte'** she or s.o. punished me, **khehrewáhton** I have punished her (-hrewaht-)

purple: **arihwawa'konhnéha** (-rihw-, -ienawa'k-/-wa'k-)

purple; lead; bruise: **oharennáhta'** (-harennaht-)

purse: **kahnà:ta'** (-hna't-/-hna'tahtsher-)

push: **iékhreks** I push it, **iahà:khreke'** I pushed it, **iewákhre** I have pushed it, **iekhè:reks** I am pushing her (-hre[k]-)

pushy: **rokonhsahní:ron** he is pushy, he has a hard face, **iakokonhsahní:ron** she has a hard face (-konhs-, -hnir-)

put away; save: **kateweièn:tons** I put it away, I save it, **wa'kateweièn:ton'** I put it away, I put it aside, I saved it, **roteweièn:ton** he has saved it (-ateweien'ton-)

put down; have; lie: **ítiens** I put it down, **wà:tien'** I put it down, **wátien'** I have it, **kèn:tho ká:ien'** it is here, **tho tká:ien'** it is there (-ien-)

put down here and there: **kkè:rons** I put it down here and there, I am laying it out, **wahakè:ron'** he put them down, **rokè:ron** he has put them down (-kehron[t]-)

put down one's head: **iontkón:hens** she puts her head down, **wa'katkón:hen'** I put my head down, **iakotkón:hen** she has put her head down (-atkonhen-)

put in: **kéhrha'** I put it in (a container), **wà:keren'** I put it in, **í:kare'** it is in it (-r-)

put inside: **kéta's** I put it inside, **wa'kéta'** I put it inside, **wakéten'** I have put it inside (-ta'-/-eta'-)

put into liquid: **ié:kohs** I put something in liquid, **iahà:kohwe'** or **iahà:ko'** I put it in, **iewakóhon** I have put it in (-ohw-)

put on; set down: **khéhrha'** I put it on the top of it, on the surface of something,

wà:khren' I set it down,
káhere' it is set on top (-her-/-hr-)

put s.o. down: **khé'terons** I put her down,
wahí'teron' I put him down,
khé'teron I have put her down (-i'teron-)

put together, side-by-side: **tékeriks** I put it
together, **wà:tkerike'** I put it together,
tewakerí:kon I have put it together (-rik-)

pyjamas: **iakotà:stha'** (-ita'[w]-)

quail: **ohkwesen'tóia'**

quake; tremble; shiver; shake:
watia'tishónhkhwa' I am quaking, trembling, etc., **ontia'tíshonhkwe'** I shivered
(-ishonhkw-)

quarry: **ienenio'kwátstha'** (-neni-, -o'kwat-)

quarter (measure): **enká:r**

Québec City: **Tetiatontarí:kon** (-ontar-, -rik-)

Queen: **Ionontí:io** (-nont-, -iio-)

Queen (in cards): **kakwín**

question: *See* ask

question, yes-no question marker: **ken**

quick: *See* fast

quick-tempered: **khseró:hen** I am
quick-tempered, **rahseró:hen** he is
quick-tempered, **iehseró:hen** she is
quick-tempered (-hserohen-);
rotsí:ra he is quick-tempered, ready to get
into it, **iakotsí:ra** she is quick-tempered
(-tsir-, -a[t]-)

quickly; right away: **óksa'k**

quiet; calm: **sha'thí:ken**

quiet; still: **teiotó:te'** it is quiet, it is still,
tha'tewakató:te' I am quiet,
tha'tható:tate' he got quiet,
tha'tesató:tat Be quiet!
tó:tek Quiet! (-atot[e]-)

quill: **ohnhè:ta'** (-ihnhe't[ar]-)

quilt: **tekihnakhánions** I am piecing cloth
together, **tekenhnakhánion áhsire'** quilt
(-ihn-, -kha-, and -ahsir-)

rabbit: **taonhtané:ken** or **tehahonhtané:ken**
(-ahonht-, -ra'neken-/-neken-)

raccoon: **atí:ron**

race: **tekaré:rens** I race,
wa'tharé:ren' he raced,
tewakaré:ren I have raced (-areren-)

radish: **otsihkwakáhte'** (-tsihkw-, -kahte-)

radio: *See* music

rafters: **kanahstáhere'** (-nahst-, -her-/-hr-)

rag: **otkaróhkwa'** (-atkarohkw-)

rags; scrap: **tekení:**

raid: **wahonwahsòn:karenhte'** they raided
him, his place, **wa'esahsòn:karenhte'** they
raided you (-hson'kar-/-hswen'kar-,
-a'senht-/-enht-)

rain: **iokennó:re's** it rains,
wa'okén:nore' it rained,
iokennó:ron it is raining,

iokennoronhátie's it is raining off and on (-kennor-)

rain; drizzle: **iaonhawí:non** it is drizzling (-onhawinon-)

rain lightly: **wa'ohstarón:ti'** it started to rain lightly, **iohstaróntion** it is raining lightly (-hstar-, -ati-/-onti-); **ontstaraté:ni'** it started to rain lightly, drizzle, **iotstaraténion** it is raining lightly (-hstar-, -teni-)

rainbow: **iò:nhiote'** (there is) a rainbow (-'nhi-, -ot-)

raincoat: **kahnehtáhrhon atià:tawi** (-hneht-, -(h)rho-)

raise; lift: **khará:tats** I lift it, **wahahará:tate'** he raised it up, **wakharatá:ton** I have raised it up (-haratat-/-karatat-)

raise a child: **enheiehià:ron'** I will raise her, **wahakehià:ron'** he raised me (-ehiahron-)

raise upright: **rakétskwas** he raises it upright, **wahakétsko'** he raised it, **wakkétskwen** I have raised it (-ketskw-)

raisin; grape: **o'nénhare'** (-'nenhar-)

rake: **tékenaks** I am scratching it, raking it, **wà:tkenake'** I scratched it, raked it, **tewakená:kon** I have scratched it, raked it, **wa'thákenake'** he scratched me, **teká:naks** rake (-nak-)

rape: **tahakwanónhton'se'** he forced me to have sex against my will (-anonhton-)

rapid; current: **kahnawáhere'** there is a rapid (-hnaw-, -her-/-hr-);

iohná:wate' (it is) swift water, a strong current (-hnaw-, -te-)

raspberry: **skanekwen'tará:nen**

raspberry, fall raspberry: **ahtahkwaká:ion** (-ahta[hkw]-, -akaion-/-kaion-)

rat: **otsinowenhkó:wa** (-tsinonwen-)

rattle: **ohstá:wen** rattle, **ohstawa'kó:wa** turtle rattle (-hstawen-); **ionterakarehrahstáhkhwa'** rattle (-rakarehrahst-/-karehrahst-)

rattlesnake: **o'nekén:tsi** (-'nekentsi-)

raven: **tsoka'we'kó:wa**

raw: **iokáhte'** it is raw (-kahte-)

razor: **iontkonhston'rhià:kstha'** (-konhston'rh-, -ia'k-)

reach for: **ia'tekatia'karétstha'** I reach over, I stretch over to reach something, **ia'thatià:karetste'** he reached over, **ia'tewakatia'karétston** I am reaching over for it (-atia'karetst-)

read: **kewennahnótha'** I read, **wa'kewennahnó:ton'** I read, **wakewennà:note'** I am reading (-wenn-, -ahnot-)

read Handsome Lake Code: **enhon'kenhrohrókhsi'** they will do a reading of the Handsome Lake Code (-a'kenhr-, -ohro[k]-)

ready; finish: **wa'keweiennén:ta'ne'** I got it ready, I finished doing it, **roweiennentà:'on** he is getting it ready, **kaweiennentà:'on** it is ready, it is done,

ratateweiennén:ta's he gets ready, **wa'katateweiennén:ta'ne'** I got ready (-weienn-, -ent-)

ready, get ready: **ratkwatákwas** he is getting ready, getting dressed, **wahatkwatá:ko'** he got ready, he dressed, **rotkwatákwen** he is ready, dressed (-kwatakw-)

really: **kwah tekèn:'en** or **kwah tokèn:'en**

reason: **né: tiorì:wa'** it's the reason (-rihw-)

rebuke: **riiattehtén:ni** I am rebuking him, warning him not to do it again, **wahakwattéhten'** he rebuked me (-atteht-)

receive: **onkó:ta'se'** I received it, **wakotà:se'** I have received it (-ota's-)

recognize: **tién:tere's** I recognize it, **wahaién:tere'ne'** he recognized it, **kheién:tere's** I recognize her, **kheienterè:'on** I have recognized her (-ientere'-)

recover: *See* better, get better; recover

rectum: **ohétkwa'** (-hetkw-)

red: **onekwénhtara'** (-nekwenhtar-)

red-winged blackbird: **tsó:kwaris**

reduce: *See* shrink

reflect: **teiorón:rote'** it is reflecting the light (-ronrot-)

refrigerator: **kawistóhtha'** (-wisto-)

regret: *See* bad, feel bad; regret

regret: *See* sorry, feel sorry; regret

reins: **iekarenhrakwáhtha'** (-karenhr[on]-)

reject: **onkkenhrà:ten'** I disliked it right away, I rejected it (-kenhr[on]-)

relative: **khé:nonhkwe'** she is a relation of mine, **tiatátenonhkwe'** you and I are relatives (-nonhkw-)

reliable: **rorihwató:ken** he is a reliable person, **iakorihwató:ken** she is a reliable person (-rihw-, -token-)

rely on: *See* depend on; rely; trust

remember: **kè:iahre'** I remember, **rehià:ra's** he remembers, **wa'kehià:ra'ne'** I remembered, **rawehiahrà:'on** he has remembered, **wa'kheiehià:ra'ne'** I remember her (-ehiahr-)

remove; detach: **kontákwas** I detach it, remove it, take it off, **wa'kontá:ko'** I removed it (-ont-)

remove; pull out: **kóhtshions** I remove it, **wa'kóhtshi'** I removed it, I pulled it out, **wakóhtshion** I have removed it (-ohtshi-)

remove; take out: **takerá:ko'** I removed it (-r-)

remove; yank out: **wa'thahsihará:ko'** he yanked it out (-ahsiharakw-)

repent: **sakatathré:wahte'** I repented, **shotathrewáhton** he has repented (-hrewaht-)

reply: *See* answer

rescue: **khe'niakénhtha'** I rescue her, saved her, **wa'khe'niá:kenhte'** I rescued her, saved her, **khe'niakénhton** I have rescued, saved her (-'niaken-)

resemble: *See* look alike

Reserve: **tsi kanonhstá:ton** (-nonhst[e]-)

reside: **kenákere'** I reside, **enkenákereke'** I will reside, **kenákerehkwe'** I used to reside (-naker[e]-)

reside; be home: **kì:teron** I live, reside, **tkì:teron** I reside there, I am home (-i'teron[t]-)

resin; pitch: **tiohkarà:nes**; **rásen**

resist: **rateronhia'táhkhwa'** he resists, he is uncooperative, **wahakwateronhia'táhkwen'** he resisted me (-ateronhia'tahkw-)

resist: *See* brace oneself; resist

respect: **rikonniénhstha'** I respect him, **wa'khekónnienhste'** I respected her, **karihwakonnienhstáhtshera'** respect (-kwennien-/-konnien-)

rest: **katoríshens** I rest, **wahatoríshen'** he rested, he took a break, **wakatoríshen** I am resting (-atorishen-)

restaurant: **teiontska'hónhkhwa'** (-atska'hon-)

rheumatism; arthritis: **athoráhsera'** (-athor[e]-)

rhubarb: **teiaontahiò:tsis ostawí:na'** or **tiohontahiò:tsis ostawí:na'** (-ront-, -hio'tsis[t]-, and -hstawin-)

rib: **ona'áhta'** rib, **kena'ahtà:ke** (on) my ribs (-na'aht-)

ribbon: **kà:nhehs ionteniatsterénkstha'** (-'nhehs-, -niatsteren[k]-)

rice: **onatsakén:ra** (-nats-, -kenra-)

rich: **wakkwátshe'** I am well-off, **rokwátshe'** he is well-off, **iakokwátshe'** she is well-off (-kwatshe-)

ridicule: **thikatiéskwani** I ridicule (someone), **thenkatiéskwani'** I will ridicule, **thiwakatiéskwani** I have ridiculed (-atieskwani-)

ridicule: *See* fun, make fun of; ridicule

right: **tkaié:ri** it is right, **iah tetkaié:ri** it is not right (-ieri-)

right (hand): **skeweientehtáhkwen** my right hand, side (-weiente-)

ring: **kanihsnonhsawì:tha'** I am putting on a ring(s), **wa'kanihsnónhsawi'te'** I put on a ring(s), **wakanihsnonhsawì:ton** I have a ring(s) on, **anihsnónhsawi** ring (-hsnonhs-, -awi-)

rip: *See* tear; rip

ripen: *See* grow

rise (in baking): *See* expand

river; lake: **oniá:tara'** or **kaniá:tara'** (-niatar-)

river, at or by the river: **atsà:kta'**

rivet: **tehati'nistakwáthos** they are putting in rivets, **tenhati'nistakwátho'** they will put in rivets, **o'nísta'** rivet (-'nist-, -kwatho-)

road: **oháha'** road, **iohatátie'** there is a road, **ohahaktóntie'** on the side of the road (-hah-)

roast; bake: **kate'skóntha'** I roast it, **wa'kate'skón:ten'** I roasted it, **wakatè:skonte'** I have roasted it, **watè:skonte'** a roast (-ate'skont-)

robin: **tsiskó:ko**

rock: **wa'tekkarèn:ron'** I rocked it, **wa'tekhekarèn:ron'** I rocked her, **tewatkarèn:ron** it is rocking (-karenhr[on]-)

rock; boulder: **otstèn:ra'** (-itstenhr-)

rock; stone: **onén:ia'** (-neni-)

Rock clan: **roneniothró:non** he belongs to the Rock clan (-neni-, -ot-)

roll: **wahakahrhaténia'te'** he rolled it, **rokahrhatenià:ton** he has rolled it, **wa'katkahrhaténia'te'** I rolled over (-kahrhateni-)

roof: **kanonhsó:ron** (-nonhs-, -'rhoro[k]-/-oro[k]-)

roof edge: **tsi teken'tarontátie'** along the edge of the roof (-i'tar-, -ont-)

rooster: **kítkit rá:tsin**

root: **ohtè:ra'** (-htehr-)

rope; string; thread: **ahserí:ie** (-ahseriie['t]-)

rosary; prayer beads: **karénhsa'** (-renhs-)

rot: **iótkens** it is rotten, **wa'ótken'** it rotted, **iotkèn:'en** it has rotted (-atken-)

rough: **roweién:nate'** he has a rough manner, **iakoweién:nate'** she is rough (-weienn-, -te[ht]-)

round: **teiothwe'nón:ni** it is round, a circle (-hwe'nonni-/-kwe'nonni-)

rows; stripes: **iotihaténion** it has stripes, straight lines or rows (-hah-, -te-)

rub: **ierakénrie's** or **ierakénie's** she is rubbing it, **wa'kerakénrie'** or **wa'kerakénie'** I rubbed it, **rorakénrie** or **rorakénie** he has rubbed it (-rakenrie-)

rub; scrub: **keránies** I am rubbing it, scrubbing, **wa'eránie'** she rubbed it, scrubbed it, **iakoránie** she has rubbed it, scrubbed it (-ranie-/-karanie-)

rug; carpet: **kéntskare'**; **ietskarónhkhwa'** (-itskar[on]-)

ruler; tape measure: **ionte'nientenhstáhkhwa'** (-ate'nient[en]-)

rummage: **tekattokwáhtha'** I go digging around, **wa'tkattókwahte'** I rummaged, I dug around, **tehottokwáhton** he has rummaged (-attokw-)

run: **tekaráhtats** I run, **wa'tharáhtate'** he ran, **tewakarahtá:ton** I have run (-arahtat-)

run: **ktákhe'** I am running, **enhatákhe'** he will run, **wahatákhe'** he is running, **ratákhe's** he is running around (-takhe-)

run: *See* race

run away: **katè:kwas** I run away,
wa'katè:ko' I ran away,
rotè:kwen he has run away (-ate'kw-)

run away: *See* escape

run out of: **wa'katò:kten'** I ran out of it,
onkwatò:kthahse' I ran out of something
(-o'kt-)

rust; mold: **oskèn:rha'** rust, mold,
ioskèn:rhare' there is rust on it, mold on it,
wa'oskèn:rhara'ne' it got rusty, moldy
(-sken'rh-, -r-)

sad: **wake'nikonhráksen's** I feel bad, sad,
onke'nikonhráksen' or
onke'nikonhráksen'ne' I got sad
(-'nikonhr-, -aksen-)

salamander: **tó:tis**

salt: **tiohiò:tsis** salt, **teiohiò:tsis** it is salty,
sour, **wa'tekhio'tsistáhrho'** I salted it
(-hio'tsis[t]-)

same: **né: shà:ka** it is the same,
iah né: shà:ka té: or **iah né: shà:ka té:ken**
it is not the same (-[t]-)

sand: **o'nehsarónhkwa'** (-'nehsaronhkw-)

sandpaper: **io'néhtarare'** (-'nehtar-, -r-)

sandwich: **tekana'tarà:sere'**
(-na'tar[o][k]-, -ia'ser-/-'ser-)

sap: **oharanawèn:ta'** (-haranawen't-)

sap; syrup: **orontákeri'** (-ront-, -keri-)

sarsaparilla: **tsohtè:rese'** (-htehr-, -es-)

Santa Clause: **shakonhstòn:rha**
(-konhston'rh-, -[t]-)

sassafras: **átsta's, wenhaká:ras**

satin; silk: **kà:nhehs** or **kà:nheks** (-'nhehs-)

satisfied: **wakerien'tí:ios** I am satisfied,
onkwerien'tí:io' I became satisfied
(-erien't-, -iio-)

Saturday: **Entákta'** (-ent-)

sauce: **rasó:s**

saucer: **nà:kon tiéksaiens** (-ks-, -ien-)

sausage: **awenhétsha'** (-enhetsh-); **rasosís**

save: **katatién:ni** I am saving it,
ratatién:ni he is saving it,
iontatién:ni she is saving it (-ien-)

save: *See* put away; save

save s.o.: *See* rescue

saw: **teiehson'karià:kstha'**
(-hson'kar-/-hswen'kar-, -ia'k-)

sawdust; fine wood shavings: **ohswáhseri**
(-ahswahser-)

say: **ión:tons** she is saying,
wahèn:ron' he said,
iaká:wen she has said (-aton-/-ihron-/-en-)

scab: **ótsta'** scab, **wakítstare'** I have scabs,
wahótstara'ne' he got scabs (-itst-, -r-)

scabby: **wake'nóseras** I am scabby
(-'nosera-)

scar: **owì:ra'** scar,

wakatewì:rare' I have a scar, **onkwatewì:rara'ne'** I got a scar (-wihr-, -r-)

scarecrow: **athehtó:ri** (-heht-, -ori-)

scared: **ketshà:nis** I fear it, I am afraid of it, **wa'ketshà:ni'ke** I got afraid, **waketshahnì:kon** I have become afraid, **ronwatshà:nis** she is afraid of him (-tshahni['k]-)

scared: **wakhterón:ni** I am scared, **ónkhteron'ne'** I got scared, **wahakhterónhkwen'** he scared me (-hteron-)

scared: **wakateronhienhtén:ni** I am scared, **onkwateronhiénhten'** I got scared (-ateronhienht-)

scared; feel spooky: **wakatiáneron's** I get scared, I feel spooky, **onkwatiáneron'ne'** I got spooked (-atianeron-)

scared; startled: **tkatón'neks** I get startled, **taiontón'neke'** she got a scare (-aton'ne[k]-)

scent; smell: **awénsera'** (-enser-)

school: **ionterihwaienstáhkhwa'** (-rihw-, -weienst-)

scissors: **tewata'sharí:sas** scissors, **teka'sharí:sas** I am using scissors, **wa'tion'shá:rise'** she used scissors (-a'shar-)

scold: **wahshakotewennaién:tonhwe'** he scolded her or them, **wahiiatewennaién:tonhwe'** I scolded him (-atewennaientonhw-)

scoop: **iakotsénhtha'** she is scooping it out, **wa'kótsenhte'** I scooped it out (-otsenht-)

score: **raiòn:tha'** he scores, **wà:tion'te'** I scored, **iah tehoiòn:ton** he didn't score (-ion't-/-inion't-)

Scotland: **Ken'taherè:ke** (-i't-, -her-/-hr-)

scrape; scratch: **raké:tas** he scrapes it, **wahá:kete'** he scraped it, **wakké:ten** I have scraped it, **wahákkete'** he scratched me (-ket-)

scrape; take off: **kerónkwas** I am taking it off, removing it, **wa'kerón:ko'** I scraped it off, **wakerónkwen** I have scraped it off (-ronkw-)

scrape: *See* plane

scratch: *See* rake

scratch: *See* scrape; scratch

screen: **wata'aráta's** screen, **wahata'aráta'** he put in a screen (-a'ar-, -ta'-/-eta'-)

screwdriver: **iehwatasè:tha'** (-hwatase-/-tase-); **ieronwaratasè:tha'** (-ronwar-/-nonwar-, -hwatase-/-tase-)

scrub: *See* rub; scrub

scrunched: **wa'tio'tsò:roke'** it got scrunched up (-o'tsohrok-)

scrutinize: *See* look closely

scum; muck; sludge: **orawà:ta'** (-rawa't-)

scythe: **iakennekeriià:kstha'** (-neker-/-enneker-, -ia'k-)

seagull: **tsohwà:tstaka'we'**
(-hwa'tst-, -eka'[w]-/-ka'[w]-)

seal: **otsí:io**

seamstress: **ionhkwennión:ni**
(-ahkwenni-, -onni-)

search: *See* look for

seaway; canal: **kana'tsheratátie'** (-na'tsher-)

secret: **rori'wahséhton** he has a secret,
iakori'wahséhton she has a secret
(-ri'wahseht-)

see: **íkkens** I see, **wahí:ken'** I saw him,
wahonwatí:ken' she saw them,
ió:ken it is seen, it is visible (-ken-)

seed: **ká:nen** (-nenh-)

seesaw: **teionttsirontawè:tha'** she is seesawing, **tenkattsirón:tawe'te'** I will seesaw
(-tsir-, -ontawe't-)

seizure: *See* epileptic

sell: **katenhní:nons** I am selling s.t.,
wa'katenhní:non' I sold it,
rotenhní:non he has sold it (-hninon-)

sell: *See* peddle; sell

sell, have for sale: **wakatiesénhston** I have it
for sale, **watiesénhston** it is on sale (-iesen-)

sell (go) for an amount: **Tó: niahà:tkene'?**
How much did it go for? (-e-);
Tó: nia'ká:ko'? How much did it go
(sell) for? (-kw-)

send: **iekatenniéhtha'** I send it,

ienkaténniehte' I will send it,
iewakatenniéhton I have sent it,
ienkheiaténniehte' I will send her,
iahíniehte' I sent it with him,
ia'kheiatenniéhten' I sent it to her
(-nieht-)

Seneca: **Shotinontowane'á:ka** Seneca
(-nont-, -kowan[en]-/-owan[en]-);
Ronathnáwerote' Mohawks and Senecas,
as referred to in council (-hnawer-, -ot-)

sense: *See* notice

sentence; judge: **shakorihwénhtha'**
he sentences them, he is a judge,
wahirì:wenhte' I sentenced him
(-rihw-, -a'senht-/-enht-)

separate: **tekekháhsions** I am separating it,
wa'tkekháhsi' I separated it,
tewakekháhsion I have separated it (-kha-)

September: **Seskehkó:wa**

serpent: **ohniare'kó:wa** (-hniar-)

serve food: **kherá:ni** I am serving them,
wa'khéhrhahse' I served them,
kataterá:ni I am serving myself,
wa'katatéhrhahse' I served myself (-r-)

seven: **tsá:ta**

several; a few: **tóhka, tohkára'**

sew: **ke'níkhons** I am sewing,
wa'e'níkhon' she sewed it,
wake'níkhon I have sewn it (-'nikhon-)

shade: **wa'katerahkwawéhrhohste'** I got in
the shade, **wakaterahkwawehrhóhston** I am
in the shade (-rahkw-, -awehrho-)

shadow: **iotahsá:tare'** (it is) a shadow, **wakatahsá:tare'** I have a shadow, I am casting a shadow (-ahsat-, -r-)

shake: **ká:waks** I am shaking it out, **wa'ká:wake'** I shook it, **wakawá:kon** I have shaken it (-awak-)

shake; tremble: **ió:waks** it is shaking (-owak-)

shake: *See* quake; tremble; shiver; shake

shake back and forth; pump: **wa'kón:tawe'te'** I pumped it, shook it back and forth (-ontawe't-)

shake s.o.: **wahiiatihén:tonhwe'** I lightly shook him, (-atihentonhw-)

shallow: **ken' niiohnotésha** it is shallow (-esha-)

share: **tentiátieste'** you and I will share, **wa'tiatiátieste'** we two shared (-iest-)

sharp; pointy: **iohio'thí:ie'** it is sharp, pointy (-hio'thiie-/-o'thiie-); **khio'thí:ions** I am sharpening it, **wa'khio'thí:ion'** I sharpened it, **rohio'thí:ion** he has sharpened it (-hio'thiion-)

shave: **katkonhstòn:rhia'ks** I am shaving, **wahatkonhstòn:rhia'ke'** he shaved, **rotkonhston'rhià:kon** he has shaved (-konhston'rh-, -ia'k-)

shave: **wahahkaróhtshi'** he is shaving it (a board, a branch) (-ahkar-, -ohtshi-)

shawl; blanket: **áhsire'** (-ahsir-)

shed; lean to: **wahskwen'nakarenhrá:ton** (-ahskwen'n-, -akarenhr[e]-)

sheep: **teiotina'karontòn:'a** (-na'kar-, -ont-)

sheets: **ionnitskaráhkhwa'** (-itskar[on]-)

shelf; mantel: **wenniseráhere'** (there is) a shelf, a mantel (-enniser-, -her-/-hr-)

shell; snail: **otsiskaionnì:ta'** (-tsiskaionni-)

shellac: **iakenienahrhóhstha'** (-iie-/-ien-, -(h)rho-)

shelter s.o.: **wahiiatiénawa'ahste'** I took him in, **kheiatienawa'áhston** I am sheltering her (-ienawa'ahst-)

shield: **wahathróhohste'** he shielded himself, **iakothrohóhston** she is turned away, shielding myself, **ionthrohohstáhkhwa'** shield (-hroh[o]-)

shin: **onién:ta'** shin, **kenientà:ke** (on) my shin (-nient-)

shingle: **ietstahrhóhstha'** (-itst-, -(h)rho-)

shiny: **teiohstaráthe'** it is shiny, **teiehstarathè:tha'** she is polishing it, **wa'tekhstaráthe'te'** I shined it, polished it, **tewakhstarathè:ton** I have polished it, **teiehstarathe'táhkhwa'** polish (-hstarathe-)

ship: **kahonweia'kó:wa** (-honw[ei]-)

shirt; dress; jacket; coat: **atià:tawi** (-atia'tawi-)

shiver: *See* quake; tremble; shiver; shake

shock, electric shock: *See* asleep, body part

shoe: **áhta** shoe, **karáhta's** or **tekaráhta's** I am putting on shoes, **wa'karáhta'** or **wa'tkaráhta'** I put on shoes, **roráhten** or **tehoráhten** he has on shoes (-ahta[hkw]-); **tewakahtárion** I have on shoes (-ahtarion-)

shoe lining: **ateráhki** or **ateráhkwi**

shoes, without socks: **tekarahsohá:rens** I am putting on shoes without socks, **wa'tkarahsohá:ren'** I put on shoes without socks (-arahsoharen-)

shoot: **karòn:tats** I shoot, **waharòn:tate'** he shot it, **wakaron'tá:ton** I have shot, **wahakwaròn:tate'** he shot at me (-aron'tat-)

shop: **katkehrontákwas** I am shopping, **wahatkehrontá:ko'** he shopped, **iakotkehrontákwen** she has shopped (-kehron[t]-)

shore, go ashore: **khráhrhos** I go to shore, **wahahráhrho'** he got to shore, **rohráhrhon** he has gotten to shore (-hrahrho-)

short: **ken' niiénsha** it is short (-esha-)

short-changed: **nà:kon taká:ton'** I got short-changed, I overpaid (-aton-)

shortcut: **tekeniharáhtha'** I am taking a shortcut, **wa'thanihá:rahte'** he took a shortcut, **tewakeniharáhton** I have taken a shortcut (-niharaht-)

shorter: **karennókeri** it is a shorter version of the song(s) or music, **kawennókeri** it is a shortened version of a word (-tokeri[k]-/-okeri[k]-)

shoulder: **ohnénhsa'** shoulder, **khnenhsà:ke** (on) my shoulder (-hnenhs-)

shoulder blade; wing: **onerahóntsha'** **kenerahontshà:ke** (on) my shoulder blade, **aonerahóntsha'** its wing (-nerahontsh-)

shoulder blade: **onerà:rha'**

shovel: **iekarenià:tha'** (-kareni-)

show, hold out: *See* hold out, show

show off: *See* proud; show off

show oneself: **ratke'tótha'** he shows himself, he peeks (in), **wahatke'tó:ten'** he showed himself (-ke'tot-)

show s.t. to s.o.: **khena'tón:ni** I show it to her, **wahonwana'tón:hahse'** she showed it to him (-na'ton-)

show up: **tho iahonkhwà:ehste'** I ended up there, I showed up there, **tho iahohwà:'ehste'** he ended up there (-hwa'ehst-)

shrink: **ónhsto'ne'** it shrunk, got small (-ahsto'-); **kahstóhtha'** I reduce it, shrink it, **waháhstohte'** he shrunk it (-ahstoht-)

shrub: **io'rhenióhkote'** (-'rheniohkot-)

shrub; small tree: **ohnièn:tskwire'** shrub, small tree having new buds (-hnien'tskwir-)

shun: **khekèn:rons** I shun her, **wahakkèn:ron'** he shunned me (-kenhr[on]-)

shy: **wakatshé:iaron** I am shy, **rotshé:iaron** he is shy, **iakotshé:iaron** she is shy (-atsheiaron-)

sick: **wakenonhwáktani** I am sick, **wa'akononhwákten'** she got sick (-nonhwak[t]-)

sick; not feel good: **konhnháksen** I don't feel good, I feel sick, **ronhnháksen** he doesn't feel good, **iakonhnháksen** she doesn't feel good (-onhnh-, -aksen-)

sickle: **ienatsiià:kstha'** or **ienatsiià:ktha'** (-nats-, -ia'k-)

sickness; disease: **káhnhra'** (-(h)nhr-)

side, one side: **ská:ti** (-ti-)

sideswipe: **tehawiskwáhtha'** he misses the target, **wa'thawískwahte'** he missed the target, **wa'thakwawískwahte'** he sideswiped me, he brushed by me (-awiskwaht-)

sigh: **tahawenníseren'ne'** he sighed, **taiakawenníseren'ne'** she sighed (-enniseren'-)

sigh; moan: **iakaonhsé:nen** she is sighing, moaning, **onkónhsene'** I sighed, moaned, **wahaónhsene'** he sighed, moaned (-onhsen-)

sign s.t.: **wa'katatshén:naren'** I signed it (-hsenn-, -r-)

silk; satin: **kà:nhehs** or **kà:nheks** (-'nhehs-)

silly: *See* foolish; silly

silver: **kahwistarà:ken** (-hwist-, -ra'ken-)

sin; swear: **wa'erihwanéra'ke'** she swore, she sinned, **rarihwanera'ákhons** he is swearing, **karihwanera'ákhsera'** sin (-rihw-, -nera'[k]-)

sin, confess sins: **enshonwarónkwahse'** they will remove his sins, he will confess, **sahonwaronkwennì:re'** he is going to confession (-ronkw-)

sin, forgive sins: **sonkwateraké:wen'** it went away on me, my sins are forgiven (-rakew-/-okew-)

since: **tsi náhe'**

sing: **katerennótha'** I sing, **wa'katerennó:ten'** I sang, **kerén:note'** I am singing, **karén:na'** song, music (-renn-, -ot-)

sing hymns: **teierihwáhkhwa'** she sings, **wa'tierì:wahkwe'** she sang, **tehorihwáhkwen** he is singing (-rihw-, -hkw-)

singe: **wa'ktsihénhstenhte'** I singed the hair off it (-tsihenhst-, -a'senht-/-enht-)

sink (into s.t. soft): **ia'teióseren's** it goes in, it sinks (into something soft) (-oseren'-)

sink underwater: **katenón:waiens** I sink, go underwater, **sahatenón:waien'** he sank back into the water (-nonw-, -ien-)

sip; suck: **wa'ko'tsí:reke'** I sipped it, sucked on it, **wako'tsiré:kon** I am licking, sucking on it (-o'tsirek-)

sister, older: **akhtsì:'a** my older sister (-htsi-)

sister, younger: **khe'kèn:'a** my younger sister (-'ken-)

sister-in-law: **ontiaríha** my sister-in-law (woman speaking) (-ariha-); **akonháhwha** my sister-in-law (man speaking) (-onhaw-)

sit: **kátiens** I sit down, **wa'kátien'** I sat down, **sátien** Sit! (-ien-)

sit; perch: **kítskote'** I am sitting, **wa'kanitskó:ten'** I sat down (-itskw-, -ot-)

six: **ià:ia'k**

size: **Tó: ní:wa'?** How big is it? **tsi ní:wa'** the size of it, how big it is (-a-)

skate: **ato'tsí:ne** skates, **tekato'tsinehtsheróntha'** I am putting on skates, I am skating, **wa'tkato'tsinehtsherón:ten'** I put on skates (-ato'tsine-, -ont-)

skeleton: **ráskan** (-skan-)

sketch: *See* draw

ski: *See* sled; ski

skin; hide: **kanéhon** (-nehw-); **ohnakénhsa'** (-hnakenhs-)

skin; leather: **óhna'** (-ihn-)

skin, flabby skin: **iona'kwarohsèn:ton** (-na'kwarohs-, -hren't-/-en't-)

skin an animal: **raiénserons** he skins it, **wa'tién:sere'** I skinned it, **roiénseron** he has skinned it (-ienser[on]-)

skin and bones: **o'téhkara'** (-'tehkar-)

skinny; thin: **wakatí:wen** I am skinny, **rotí:wen** he is skinny, **iakotí:wen** she is skinny, **enká:tiwe'** I will be skinny (-atiw-)

skirt: **o'wháhsa'** skirt,

wakate'whahsò:ron I have a skirt on, **wa'kate'whahsò:roke'** I put a skirt on, (-'whahs-, -ohro[k]-)

skunk: **anì:tas** (-i't-)

sky; heaven: **karòn:ia'** (-ronhi-)

slant: *See* lean to one side; slant

sled; ski: **tkatianénhtha'** I am sledding, skiing, **takatiá:nenhte'** I sledded, I skied, **iontianenhtáhkhwa'** sled (-ian-, -a'senht-/-enht-)

sled, with slats: **kanatsó:ton** (-nats-, -ot-)

sleep: **wakí:ta's** I am sleeping, **onkí:ta'we'** I dropped off to sleep, I fell asleep (-ita'[w]-)

sleep, in the eyes: **okahtsò:ta'** dry crusty sleep in the eyes, **tehokahtsò:tonte'** his eyes are crusty with sleep (-kahtso't-, -ont-)

sleep, nod off: **keserenhtié:nien's** I am nodding off to sleep, **wahaserenhtié:nene'ne'** he nodded off (-serenht-, -'rhenien'-/-ienen'-)

sleep late; oversleep: **onkera'shéntho'** I slept late, I overslept (-ra'shentho-)

sleep over: **kanòn:wets** I sleep over, **wahanòn:wete'** he slept over, **wakanonhwé:ton** I have slept over (-anonhwet-)

sleepy; drowzy: **wakeserénhtara's** I am sleepy, drowsy, **onkeserénhtara'ne'** I got sleepy, drowsy (-serenht-, -r-)

sleigh: **kanonhsì:sere'** cutter, a sleigh with a flatbed (-nonhs-, -'sere-/-i'sere-)

sleigh, double-runner; trailer: **tewate'serehtahnhontéhrha'** (-'sere[ht]-, -hnhonter-)

sleigh, with spindles up the sides: **teka'katsóhare'** (-'kats-, -ohar-)

slice: *See* cut; slice

slice: *See* plane

slide: **tekato'tsinéhtha'** I slide, **wa'tkato'tsí:nehte'** I slid, **ia'tewakato'tsinéhton** I have slid that way (-ato'tsine-)

slime: **otsiskeró:ta'** slime, **iotsiskeró:tare'** it is slimy, **wa'otsiskeró:tara'ne'** it got slimy (-tsiskerot-, -r-)

slip: **tewako'tsískwas** I slip, **wa'tewako'tsísko'** I slipped, **teiao'tsískwa** it is slippery (-o'tsiskw-)

slip on ice: *See* ice, slip on ice

slip (clothing): **kà:khare'** slip, **wakè:khare'** I have on a slip, **wa'kate'khá:ren'** I put on my slip (-'khar-)

slippers; slip-on (backless) shoes: **ionrahsi'tohrókstha'** (-ahsi't-, -ohro[k]-)

slow: **roshá:ion** he is slow (at doing s.t.), **iakoshá:ion** she is slow (-shaion-)

slow: *See* do slowly

slowly: **skennèn:'a** or **skenèn:'a**

sludge; muck; scum: **orawà:ta'** (-rawa't-)

small: **ken' niwà:'a** it is small (-a'a-)

smallpox: **iakonenskwarà:keren's** (-nonskwar-/-nenskwar-, -a'ker-)

smart: *See* knowledgeable; smart

smash: *See* break; smash

smell: **wakéhswas** I smell something, **onkésho'** I smelled it (-hsw-)

smell: *See* stink; smell

smell; scent: **awénsera'** (-enser-)

smoke: **oièn:kwara'** (-ien'kwar-)

smoke: **katshókwas** I smoke, **wahatshó:ko'** he smoked, **rotshókwen** he is smoking (-atshokw-)

snail; shell: **otsikaionní:ta'** (-tsiskaionni-)

snake: **ò:niare'** (-hniar-)

snake, black snake: **oná:to** (-nato-)

snakeroot; ginger: **tsonenskwénrie**

snap (on clothing): **toks**

snare: **wahatkahrhá:ren'** he snared it (-atkahrhar-)

snarl; growl: **rotatena'kón:ni** he is snarling, growling (talking about a dog) (-na'kw-)

sneeze: **wa'tewakí'tson'ke'** I sneezed (once), **teiako'tson'kánions** she is sneezing, **wa'tho'tson'kánion'** he sneezed (-i'tson'k-)

snipe: **tawístawis**

Snipe clan: **wake'nhehsí:io** I am Snipe clan
(-'nhehsiio-)

snoop: **tewake'niahrhà:te'** I am snooping, nosing around, into everything,
teho'niahrhà:te' he is snooping,
teiako'niahrhà:te' she is snooping
(-'niahrha'te-)

snoop on s.o.: *See* spy

snore: **rónhkahre'** he snores,
iakónhkahre' she snores (-onhkahr-)

snot: **otsi'niónhkeri** (-tsi'nionhker-)

snout: **o'nionkwarísta'** snout,
ra'nionkwaristà:ke (on) his snout
(-'nionkwarist-)

snow: **óniehte'** snow, **kaniéhtaien'**
there's snow (on the ground)
(-nieht-, -ien-)

snow: **òn:keren'ne'** it snowed,
io'kerèn:'en it is snowing
(-a'ker-, -a'sen'-/-en'-);
iota'keraténion it is starting to snow,
a flake here and there (-a'ker-, -teni-)

snow, icy crust: **io'nhehsáhere'** there is
an icy crust on the snow,
wa'ka'nhehsà:ren' it formed an icy crust
(-'nhehs-/-'nehs-, -her-/-hr-)

snow, on the ground: **wa'kanié:ien'** it
snowed, **kanié:ien'** there's snow on the
ground (-nieien-)

snow ice pellets: **wa'onen'ón:ti'** it snowed
ice pellets, **ionen'óntion** it is snowing ice
pellets (-nen'-, -ati-/-onti-)

snowball: **onenniò:kwa'** (-nennio'kw-)

snowdrift: **ioniehtarohrókhon**
(-nieht-, -rohro[k]-)

snowed in: **onkenió:roke'** I got snowed in,
ionkwanió:ron we are snowed in
(-ni-, -'rhoro[k]-/-oro[k]-)

snowflake: **ò:kera'** (-a'ker-)

snowman: **atenenniò:kwa'** (-nennio'kw-)

snowplow: **tekaniehtohtáhrhos**
(-nieht-, -ohtahrho-)

snowshoe: **kahwèn:kare'** (-hwen'kar-)

snowsnake: **aterawénhta'**

snowstorm: **teionennio'kwatá:se** or
teionien'kwatá:se' (it is) a snowstorm
(-nennio'kw-, -hwatase-/-tase-)

snuff: **raprí:s**

soap: **ononhwarè:tha'** (-nonhware-)

sob: **waktsi'tokhénhstha'** I am sobbing,
rotsi'tokhénhstha' he is sobbing,
iakotsi'tokhénhstha' she is sobbing
(-tsi'tokhenhst-)

sober: **shothnekoké:wen** he is sober
(-hnek-, -rakew-/-okew-)

socks: **ká:ris** (-ris[er]-)

socks, put on: **wa'katsherón:nike'** I put on
stockings, socks, **iakotsherón:ni** she has on
stockings (-hseronni[k]-)

sod; turf: **onon'òn:ra'** (-non'onhr-)

soda; pop: **teiohnekatsikhè:tare'**
(-hnek-, -tsikhe't-);

wathnekatákwas (-hnek-, -attatakw-)

soft: **io'nhétska** it is soft,
wa'o'nhétska'ne' it got soft,
waha'nhétskahte' he softened it
(-'nhetska-)

solicit: **tehontsharí:tes** they are soliciting,
asking, begging for something,
wa'thatshá:rite' he solicited,
tehonatsharí:ton they have solicited
(-atsharit[e]-)

solid: *See* hard; solid

some: **ótia'ke'** (-atia'k-)

someone: **ónhka'k**

someone else: **akò:ren** someone else,
akohren'shòn:'a other people, others

something: **othé:nen** or **thé:nen** something,
iah thé:nen nothing

sometimes: **sewatié:rens** (-ier-)

son: **riièn:'a** my son (-ien-)

son-in-law: **riiehnhónsa'** (-ehnhonsa') or
risà:wha my son-in-law (-sa'w-)

son, stepson: **rinò:'a** my stepson (-no-)

song; music: **karén:na'** (-renn-)

soot: **ohá:kenhte'** soot, **iohakénhtare'**
it is full of soot (-hakenht-, -r-)

sorry, feel sorry; regret: **sakatateri'wáhsten'**
I was sorry, I regretted it (-atateri'wahst-)

sorry, feel sorry for: *See* pity

sort: **tetiestáhsions** I sort it,
wa'thaiestáhsi' he sorted it,
tehoiestáhsion he has sorted it (-iest-)

soul; spirit: **atónhnhets**

soup: **onón:tara'** (-nontar-)

soup, corn soup: **kanénhsto** or **onénhsto**
(-nenhst-, -o-)

soup, eat soup: **katshó:ris** I have soup,
wahatshó:ri' he ate soup,
iakotshó:ri she is having soup (-atshori-)

soup, make soup: **katkátstons** I make soup,
wahatkátston' he made soup,
rotkátston he is making soup (-atkatston-)

sour: *See* salt

south: **éntie nonkwá:ti**

space: **ionáktote'** there is some space,
some room (-nakt-, -ot-)

space: *See* opening; space

spades, suit of spades: **a'nó:wara**
(-'now-)

sparrow, song sparrow: **tostostseríneken'**

speak: **iontá:tis** she speaks,
wa'katá:ti' I spoke (-atati-)

speak: *See* talk

speak a language: *See* know a language

speak for s.o: **tehakewennáhkhwa'**
he talks for me, he speaks on my behalf,
wa'thiwén:nahkwe' I spoke for him
(-wenn-, -hkw-)

speak up: **thawenníneken's** he speaks up, **takewenníneken'ne'** I spoke up (-wenn-, -ineken'-)

spear: **ahsí:kware'** or **áhsikwe'**

spicy: **ió:te'** it is strong-tasting, spicy (-te[ht]-)

spider: **takwa'áhson**

spill: **káwerons** I spill it, **wa'káweron'** I spilled it, **iakóweron** she has spilled it, **tkáwerons** I pour it, **takáweron'** I poured it, **iaháweron'** he spilled it, poured it out (-aweron-)

spin: **rattsinonhwatenià:tha'** he spins, **wa'kattsinonhwaténia'te'** I spun around, **rottsinonhwatenià:ton** he is spinning around (-tsinonhwateni-)

spin wheels, tires: **wa'otenà:tkaren'** it is spinning, **onkwatenà:tkaren'** my wheels, my tires spun, **rotena'tkará:ni** his wheels, his tires are spinning (-atena'tkar-)

spine: **kahstien'takwe'ní:io** (-hstien['t]-, -kwe'niio-)

spine; back: **oronhkwè:na'** spine, back, **keronhkwe'nà:ke** (on) my back (-ronhkwe'n-)

spinster: **iakoia'tase'tsherakaiòn:'on** (-ia't-, -ase-, -akaion-/-kaion-)

spit: **ronitskeróntie's** he is spitting, **onkwanitskerón:ti'** I spit, **ronitskeróntion** he has spit (-itsker-, -ati-/-onti-)

spit; saliva: **ótskeri** (-itsker-)

spit at s.o.: **wahakwanitskeróserahwe'** he spit at me (-itsker-, -sera[hw]-/-osera[hw]-)

splash s.o.: **wa'tekheiatstarókwahte'** I splashed her, **wa'thakwatstarókwahte'** he splashed me (-hstar-, -okw-)

splinter: **wa'tewatahsahtahkaró:ko'** it splintered (-ahsahtahkar-, -okw-)

splinter, get: **wakatahsahtahkariniòn:ton** I have a splinter, **onkwatahsahtahkar-ínion'te'** (-ahsahtahkar-, -ion't-/-inion't-); **onkwatahsahtahkarohá:ra'ne'** I got a splinter (-ahsahtahkar-, -ohar-)

splints, for making baskets: **o'nón:na'** (-'nonn-)

split in two: **tekohwíhas** I split it in two, **wa'tkohwíha'** I split it, **tewakohwíhen** I have split it (-ohwiha-)

split open: **tekó:rens** I split it open, **wa'tkó:ren'** I split it open, **tewakó:ren** I have split it open (-oren-)

spoil: *See* bad

spoon: **atókwa** (-atokw-/-atokwahtsher-)

spouse: **ró:ne'** her husband, his wife (-ne-)

spouse: *See* couple

spout: **iohsóhkonte'** (there is) a spout (-hsohkw-, -ont-)

sprain: **wa'katshineko'tatáhko'** I sprained my ankle, **wa'katenentshawi'tatáhko'** I sprained my wrist (-tahkw-); **wa'kateniaranì:'eke'** I sprained my neck, **wa'kateronhkwe'nanì:'eke'** I sprained my back (-ni'e[k]-)

spread around: **tekarenià:tha'** I spread it around, spread it out, I deliver things, **wa'tkarénia'te'** I spread it around, **tewakarenià:ton** I have spread it around (-areni-)

spread out: *See* open out

spread with: *See* coat; spread

spring: **kenkwitè:ne**

spring: **iohnawerote'ón:we** a (natural) spring (-hnawer-, -ot-)

sprout: **ohnióhkwa'** sprout, **wa'kahniohkón:ten'** it sprouted (-hnio-, -ont-)

spruce: **o'só:ra'** or **osó:ra'**

spy: **tehikahranénhskwas** I am snooping on him, spying on him, **wa'thikahranénhsko'** I spied on him (-kahr-, -nenhskw-)

square: **teiotekerón:te'** it is square (-keront-)

squash: **onon'ónsera'** (-non'onser-); **tio'takè:tote'** (-i't-, -ke'tot-); **tioneri'tstakè:tote'** (-neri'tst-, -ke'tot-)

squat: *See* crouch, squat

squeak: **iotsì:takahre'** it is squeaking (-tsi'takahre-)

squeal on s.o.: *See* tattle

squeal on s.o.: *See* tell about; tell on

squeeze: **tekhtò:raraks** I squeeze it, press down on it, **wa'tekhtò:rarake'** I squeezed it, **tewakhtohrará:kon** I have squeezed it (-htohrarak-/-ohrarak-)

squeeze (juice): **wa'khnekínekenhte'** I squeezed the liquid out of it (-hnek-, -inekenht-)

squirm; fidget: **wakaterakénrie'** I am squirming, wiggling, fidgeting, **roterakénrie'** he is squirming, **iakoterakénrie'** she is squirming (-rakenrie-)

squirrel, flying: **tawà:son**

squirrel, grey: **onkwe'tá:kon**

squirrel, red: **aró:sen**

stab: **kà:'as** I stab it, **wa'kà:'ase'** I stabbed it, **wahshakò:'ase'** he stabbed her (-a'as-); **wahiia'sharotón:ko'** I stabbed him (put the blade in and out several times) (-a'shar-, -ot-)

stack: **tetia'séhrha'** I stack it, **wa'ttià:seren'** I stacked it, **tewatià:sere'** I have stacked it, **tekaià:sere'** it is stacked (-ia'ser-/-'ser-)

stack; pile: **tetientótha'** I stack them, pile them up, **wa'tientó:ten'** I stacked them, **tewatién:tote'** I have stacked (-ientot-)

stairs; steps; ladder: **kanekó:ta'** (-nekot-)

stalk; celery: **ostawí:na'** (-stawin-)

stamp: **wahakonhsanén:takte'** he stuck a stamp on it (-konhs-, -ra'nentakt-/-nentakt-)

stand; stop: **í:kete'** I am standing, **tékta's** I stand up, I stop, **wa'tié:ta'ne'** she stood up, **tewaktà:'on** I have stood up, **tésta'n** Stop! (-t-/-et-)

stand on s.t: **íkerate'** I am standing on it, **rá:rate'** he is standing on it (-rat[e]-)

stand out: *See* conspicuous

stand s.t. up: **khniótha'** I stand it up,
wa'khnió:ten' I stood it up,
kà:niote' it is standing up
(-hniot-)

stand very upright: **ra'néhkwate'** he is
standing very straight, really upright,
ie'néhkwate' she is standing very straight
(-'nehkwat-)

star; dot: **otsísto** star,
otsistohkwa'shòn:'a a lot of stars,
iotsistohkwarónnion there are stars,
it has spots, dots (-tsisto[hkw]-, -r-)

stare: **wa'thatkà:neren'** he stared at it,
wa'thakwatkà:neren' he stared at me
(-kahner-)

start: **tkatahsáhwhas** I start,
tahatáhsawen' he started,
tontáhsawen' it started,
tewakatáhsawe' I have begun,
tiotáhsawe' at the beginning
(-atahsaw-)

start (an engine): **kahtentià:tha'** I start it,
wa'kahténtia'te' I started it, prepared to
do it (-ahtenti-)

startled: *See* scared; startled

station: **tsi tekatáhstha'** (-t-/-et-)

statue: **tkaia'tonníhserote'**
(-ia't-, -onni-, -ot-)

stay with s.o.: **wa'kheiatién:hahse'** I stayed
with them, **wa'onkwatién:hahse'** they
stayed with me (-ien-)

Ste. Lucie, Doncaster Reserve: **Tioweró:ton**

steal: **kenénhskwas** I steal it,
wahanénhsko' he stole it,
ronénhskwen he has stolen it,
wahakenénhsko' he stole it from me
(-nenhskw-)

steam; mist; fog: **otshá:ta'** steam, etc.,
iotshá:tote' it is steaming,
teiotshá:taien' it is misty, foggy
(-atshat-, -ot- or -ien-)

steamroller: **teiontahní:rats** (-hnir-)

steel; iron: **karistà:ke** on the iron or steel
(-rist-)

steep: **tekanà:tkares** (it is) a steep slope,
bluff (-na'tkar-, -es-)

stem (plant); rivet; bow: **o'nísta'** (-'nist-)

step: **o'kháha'** step, **tso'kháha** one step,
tso'khahátshon step by step (-'khah-)

step, take a step: **wa'thate'kháhahkwe'**
he took a step (-'khah-, -hkw-);
iewake'khahóntie's I am taking steps,
iahonke'khahón:ti' I took a step
(-'khah-, -ati-/-onti-)

step on s.t.: **kerá:ta's** I step on it,
wahará:ta'ne' he stepped on it,
wakeratà:'on I have stepped on it (-rat[e]-)

steps; stairs; ladder: **kanekó:ta'** (-nekot-)

stick: **kaná:kare'** (-nakar-)

stick (for playing sports): **kà:nhien** (-'nhien-)

stick; peg: **ò:wahste'** (-'wahst-)

stick; sticky: **iora'nén:taks** it is sticky,
wa'ora'nén:take' it got stuck to it,

iora'nentá:kon it is stuck to it
(-ra'nentak-/-nentak-)

stick on: *See* attach; stick on

stick out: *See* protrude; stick out

stick up, out: **onttá:kara'we'** it stuck up,
stuck out, **iottakarà:wen** it is sticking up,
sticking out (-attakara'w-)

stiff: **iota'tíhon** it is stiff,
wa'kata'tíhonhkwe' I stiffened it
(-ata'tihon-)

still: *See* quiet; still

still; more: **shé:kon**

sting s.o: **wa'thakwatene'rhohá:ren'** it
stung me, **wa'thotene'rhohá:ren'** it stung
him (-atena'rhohar-)

stingy: **ronì:'on** he is stingy,
iakonì:'on she is stingy (-ni'-);
rattókha' he is stingy,
ionttókha' she is stingy (-attokha-)

stink; smell: **wákeras** it stinks, it smells,
ónkera'ne' it started to smell (-akera-)

stir: **tekawénrie's** I stir it,
wa'tkawénrie' I stirred it,
tewakawénrie' I have stirred it, I am
stirring it (-awenrie-)

stomach: **ohsienhón:ta'** or **ohsiahón:ta'**
stomach, **akhsienhón:ta'** my stomach
(-hsienhont-/-hsiahont-)

stone; rock: **onén:ia'** (-neni-)

store: **iontenhninòn:tha'** (-hninon-)

store s.t.: **wa'katahkwenniá:ien'** I stored it,
iontahkwenniaientáhkhwa' storage shed,
cupboard, pantry, closet (-ahkwenni-, -ien-)

stop: *See* stand; stop

stork: **kastò:kwes** (-sto'kw-, -es-)

story: **oká:ra'** (-kar-);
kká:ratons I tell stories,
wahaká:raton' he told a story,
roká:raton he is telling a story, he has told
a story, **wa'onkkaratón:hahse'** she told me
a story (-karaton-)

stove: **karístatsi**

stove; fireplace: **tsi ionteka'táhkhwa'**
(-atek-)

straight: **ktakwaríhsions** I straighten it,
wa'ktakwaríhsi' I straightened it,
waktakwaríhsion I have straightened it,
iottakwaríhsion it is straight
(-takwarihsi-/-kwarihsi-)

stranded: **wa'kewehnó:ta'ne'** I became
stranded (-wehn-, -ot-)

strange, find strange: **wakenekhé:rens** I find
it strange, **onkenekhé:ren'** I found it strange,
wa'kheia'tanekhé:ren' I find her strange
(-nekheren-)

strap; leash: **ashá:ra'** (-ashar-)

straw: **kahwà:'e** (-hwa'e[k]-/-a'e[k]-)

straw, for drinking: **iako'tsirékstha'**
(-o'tsirek-)

strawberry: **ken' niiohontésha**
(-hont-, -esha-)

stream: **kahnawatátie'** (-hnaw-)

stretch: **tekatiróntha'** I stretch it,
tenkatirón:ten' I will stretch it,
tewakatí:ronte' I have stretched it (-atiront-)

strict: **ra'niakátste'** he is strict,
ie'niakátste' she is strict (-'niakatste-)

strike; hit: **khwà:'eks** I hit it, strike it,
wahahwà:'eke' he struck it,
wakhwà:'e I have struck it
(-hwa'e[k]-/-a'e[k]-)

string; rope; thread: **ahserí:ie** (-ahseriie['t]-)

string; twine: **iehwanerénkstha'**
(-hwaneren[k]-/-neren[k]-)

string s.t.: **ra'taníharons** he is stringing
them, **wa'ka'taníharon'** I strung them
(-a'taniharon-)

stripes; rows: **iotihaténion** it has stripes,
straight lines or rows (-hah-, -te-)

stroll: *See* wander

strong: **ke'shátste'** I am strong,
ra'shátste' he is strong,
ie'shátste' she is strong,
ka'shatsténhsera' strength (-'shatst[e]-)

strong-tasting; spicy: **ió:te'** it is strong-
tasting, spicy, **iotehténion** they are
strong-tasting, spicy (-te[ht]-)

strong-willed: **wake'nikonhrahní:ron**
I am strong-willed (-'nikonhr-, -hnir-);
ro'nikonhkátste' he has a strong will,
iako'nikonhkátste' she has a strong will
(-'nikonhkatste-)

struggle: **wa'tiontátienhte'** she struggled,
had a hard time, **tehotatiénhton** he is
struggling, finding it hard to get by (-ienht-)

stuck: *See* wedged

study: **katerihwaiénstha'** I study, I am
a student (-rihw-, -weienst-)

study: *See* learn; study; practice

stump: **otsina'à:ra'** tree stump,
tiotsina'à:rote' there's a stump there
(-tsina'ahr-, -ot-)

sturgeon: **teiotién:taron**

stutter: **rowèn:nis** he stutters,
iakowèn:nis she stutters (-wenhnis-)

suck: *See* sip; suck

sudden, all of a sudden: **thontaiawénhstsi**
(-en-)

suddenly notice: **tha'katié:renk** I was suddenly surprised (-atierenk-)

suffer: **wakeronhiá:ken** I am suffering,
in agony, **waharonhiá:ken'** he suffered,
karonhiakénhsera' suffering, agony
(-ronhiaken-)

suffer; pay for: **onkkarón:ni'** I suffered for
it, I paid for it (-kar-, -onni-)

sugar: **teionttsikhe'tóhkhwa'** (-tsikhe't-, -o-)

suitcase: **ionhtentiéhtha' kahnà:ta'**
(-ahtenti- and -hna't-)

sumac: **tará:kwi**

summer: **akenhnhà:ke** in the summer
(-akenhnh-)

sun: **karáhkwa'** sun, **ioráhkote'** the sun
is shining (-rahkw-, -ot-)

Sunday: **Awentatokenhtì:ke**
(-ent-, -tokenhti-)

sunfish: **atenà:tara'** (-atena'tar-)

sunrise: **tkarahkwíneken's** the sun is coming
up, rising, **takarahkwíneken'ne'** the sun
came up, **tiorahkwinekèn:'en** the sun has
come up (-rahkw-, -ineken'-)

sunrise; daylight: **enwén:te'ne'** it is beginning to be daylight, **iawente'onhátie'** the
sun is rising, the sun is coming up (-ente-)

sunset: **ia'karáhkwen'ne'** the sun went
down (-rahkw-, -a'sen'-/-en'-);
ia'tewatshénthos the sun is going down,
setting, **ia'tewatshéntho'** the sun went down,
the sun set (-atshentho-)

sunstroke: **wa'tewakerahkontsheróia'ke'**
the sun shone on me, I got sunstroke
(-rahkw-, -oia'[k]-)

support: *See* help; support

support: *See* hold; support

surprised: *See* amazed; surprised

surveyor: **raristì:sere's** (-rist-, -'sere-/-i'sere-)

suspect: **khewennó:ta's** I suspect her or s.o.,
wahiwennó:ta'ne' I suspected him
(-wenn-, -ot-)

suspend: *See* hang; suspend

suspenders: **athnenhsotáhrhon**
(-hnenhs-, -otahrho[k]-)

suspicious: **tehi'nikonhrà:ra's** I get suspicious of him, **wa'thi'nikonhrà:ra'ne'**
I got suspicious of him,
tehi'nikonhrahrà:'on I have gotten
suspicious of him, I am suspicious of him
(-'nikonhr-, -her-/-hr-)

swallow: **ken'tarakonhá:ka** (-i'tar-)

swallow: **iehahnehkwá:nons** he is swallowing, **ia'kahnéhkwane'** I swallowed it,
iewakahnehkwá:non I have swallowed it
(-ahnehkwan[on]-)

swamp: **kaná:wakon** in the swamp,
tkaná:waien' there's a swamp there
(-naw-, -ien-)

swan: **o'nahsakén:ra** (-'nahs-, -kenra-)

swear: *See* sin; swear

sweat: **teka'tarihenhseronkóhtha'** I am
sweating, **wa'tha'tarihenhserón:kohte'**
he got sweaty, **teiako'tarihenhseronkóhton**
she has sweated
(-a'tarih[en]-/-tarih[en]-, -onko-)

sweat; perspire: **wakhné:konte'** I am
perspiring, **rohné:konte'** he is perspiring,
iakohné:konte' she is perspiring
(-hnek-, -ont-)

sweep: **tekatonhé:was** I am sweeping,
wa'tkatónhewe' I swept,
teiakotonhé:wen she has swept (-onhew-)

sweet: **otsikhè:ta'** candy, a sweet,
teiotsikhè:tare' it is sweet (-tsikhe't-, -r-)

sweet flag: **onennó:ron** or **ononnó:ron**

sweetgrass: **kahontákon'**
(-hont-, -eka'[w]-/-ka'[w]-)

swell: **wá:tos** it swells,
ón:tohwe' it swelled up (-ohw-);
ontó:ko' the swelling went down (-okw-)

swim; bathe: **katá:wens** I am swimming,
taking a bath, **wahatá:wen'** he swam, took a
bath, **rotá:wen** he has swum, taken a bath
(-awen-)

swing: **kathonwiháhrha'** I swing,
wahathonwihá:ren' he swung,
wakathonwíhare' I am swinging,
ionthonwiharáhkhwa' swing
(-honw[ei]-, -har-/-ihar-)

swing s.o. around: **wahaktsinonhwaténia'te'**
he swings me around,
wahaktsinonhwatenia'tánion' he swung me
around (-tsinonhwateni-)

swipe from s.o.: **tekhehkwén:ni** I swipe it
from her, **wa'thíhkwen'** I took it from him
(-hkw-)

syrup: **óshes** (-shes[t]-)

syrup; sap: **orontákeri'** (-ront-, -keri-)

table: **atekhwà:ra** (-khw-, -her-/-hr-)

tablecloth: **iontekhwahra'tsherorókstha'**
(-atekhwahr-, -'rhoro[k]-/-oro[k]-)

tablecloth; linoleum: **kahnehtáhrhon**
(-hneht-, -(h)rho-)

tadpole: **tsikenitshehwèn:ta'**

tail: **otáhson** (-itahs-)

tail, of a bird: **o'kóhsa'** (-'kohs-)

tailor: **rahkwennión:ni** (-ahkwenni-, -onni-)

take: **iékhas** I take it,
iahà:khawe' I took it,
ia'kheia'ténhawe' I took her there
(-ha[w]-/-enha[w]-)

take apart, take off: **keríhsions** I am
taking it apart, I am taking it off,
wa'keríhsi' I took it apart, off,
roríhsion he has taken it apart, off
(-rihsi-)

take away from: **khéhkhwas** I take it
away from her,
wahíhkhwa' I took it away from him,
rotéhkhwen he has taken things away
(-hkhwa-)

take back and forth: **kkarénie's** I am taking
it back and forth,
wahakaré:ni' he took it back and forth,
iakokarénion she has taken it back and forth
(-kareni-)

take freely: *See* help oneself to

take from s.o.: *See* swipe from s.o.

take off: **rahrákwas** he takes it off of it,
wahahrá:ko' he took it off of it (-her-/-hr-)

take one's time: **katen'niskwáhtha'**
I am taking my time,
wa'katen'nískwahte' I took my time
(-'niskw-)

take outside: **ia'tiá:kenhwe'** I took it outside,
iehoiakénhen he has brought or taken it outside (-iakenhw-)

take s.o. in: *See* shelter s.o.

take s.t. out: **ktáhkwas** I take it out,
wa'ktáhko' I took it out,
waktáhkwen I have taken it out (-tahkw-)

take up: **ia'keráthenhste'** I brought it up
(there), **taharáthenhste'** he took it up (here)
(-rathen-)

talk; converse: **wákhthare'** I am talking,
wa'tiakenihthá:ren' we two talked, con-
versed, **wahakhtháhrhahse'** he talked to me
(-hthar-)

talk; speak: **iontá:tis** she speaks,
wa'katá:ti' I spoke (-atati-)

talk; tell: **kathró:ris** I tell about it,
wa'kathró:ri' I told about it,
rothró:ri he has told, he is telling about it,
kathrorià:tha' I talk about it,
wa'kathrória'te' I talked about it (-hrori-)

talk a lot; blab: **wakaterihwatiè:ni** I talk a
lot, I'm a blabbermouth (-rihw-, -atie'ni-)

talk a lot; chatter: **wakaterihwaka'ténhston**
I am chatty, talk a lot about nothing
(-rihwaka't[en]-)

talk about: **wa'akwahthá:rahkwe'** we talked
about it, **rotihtharáhkwen** they are talking
about it (-hthar-)

talk about s.o.: **kherihwanénhskwas** I am
talking about her, **wahakerihwanénhsko'**
he talked about me (-rihw-, -nenhskw-)

talk back: **rotewennátkon** he talks back,
he has a sassy mouth, **iakotewennátkon**
she talks back, she has a sassy mouth
(-atewennatkon-)

talk back to s.o.: **tionkewennókwas** she talks
back to me, **tahakewennó:ko'** he talked back
to me (-wenn-, -okw-)

talk gibberish; blab: **wahatenekwaténia'te'**
he talked gibberish, **rotenekwatenià:ton**
he is always blabbing, talking gibberish
(-nekw-, -teni-)

tall: **khnén:ies** I am tall,
rahnén:ies he is tall,
iehnén:ies she is tall (-es-)

tamarack; jack pine: **kanèn:ten's**
(-nen't-, -a'sen'-/-en'-)

tangled up: *See* complicate

tar: **kahnehtahòn:tsi** (-hneht-, -hon'tsi-)

taste strong: **ió:te'** it is strong-tasting, spicy
(-te[ht]-)

tasty: **waké:ka's** I find it tasty, I like
the taste of it,
onké:ka'we' I found it tasty,
wakekà:'on I have found it tasty,
iawékon' it is delicious, yummy
(-eka'[w]-/-ka'[w]-)

tattle: **wa'kheiatenhní:non'** I squealed,
tattled on her, **wahakwatenhní:non'** he
squealed on me (-hninon-)

tattle: *See* tell about; tell on

tavern; bar; boarding house:
iohson'karèn:ton
(-hson'kar-/-hswen'kar-, -hren't-/-en't-)

tea: **iekanerahtóhon** (-neraht-, -ohw-); **tí:**

teach: **shakorihonnién:ni** he teaches them,
wa'kherihónnien' I taught them
(-rihw-, -onni-)

teacup: **teionthnekontáhkhwa' akè:ra'**
(-hnek-, -ont-, -akehr-/-kehr-)

tear: **okáhseri** (-kahser-)

tear; rip: **kerátsons** I tear it,
wa'erátson' she tore it,
iakorátson she has torn it,
onterátson' it tore, ripped,
ioterátson it is torn, ripped (-ratson-)

tease: **wákhswa** I like to tease,
wahihswa'tón:ni' I teased him, joked
with him (-hsw-, -onni-)

telegram: **ia'kenonwaráia'ke'** I sent a
telegram (-ronwar-/-nonwar-, -ia'k-)

telephone: **tahatewennáta'** or
iahatewennáta' he telephoned,
tahakwatewennátahse' he telephoned me,
iekheiatewennata'én:ni I telephone her,
iontewennata'ahstáhkhwa' telephone
(-wenn-, -ta'-/-eta'-)

telephone: **teiehtharáhkhwa'** (-hthar-)

telescope: *See* binoculars; telescope

television: **tká:ra's** (-r-)

tell: **khehró:ris** I tell her,
wa'khehró:ri' I told her,
rihró:ri I have told him,
kathró:ris I tell about it,
wa'kathró:ri' I told about it,
rothró:ri he has told, he is telling
about it (-hrori-)

tell about; tell on: **riia'tahnótha'** I tell
about him, I tell on him,
wahatia'tahnó:ton' or
wahatia'tahnó:ten' he squealed on me,
shakoia'tà:note' he is talking about her
(-ia't-, -ahnot-)

tell off: *See* confront; tell off

temple; cheekbones: **kahranonhsà:ke**
or **kehranonhsà:ke** (on) my temples
(-ahranonhs-)

ten: **oié:ri**

tent; cage: **a'tóhsera'** (-a'tohser-)

terrible: *See* extreme; drastic; terrible

thank you: **niá:wen**

thank, give thanks: *See* greet

Thanksgiving Address: **Ohén:ton
Karihwatéhkwen** (-henton-, -rihw-, -hkw-)

that; those: **thí:ken** or **thí:**

thaw; melt: **wa'kawistaná:wen'** it melted,
thawed, **iowistaná:wen** it is melted, thawed,
iowistanawenhátie' it is melting, thawing
(-wistawen-)

then; and then: **e'thó:ne'** or **eh thó:ne'**

then; well; therefore: **káti'**

there: **tho, e'thó:, eh tho**

there; over there: **ísi'**

there; over there; away: **a'é:ren** or **é:ren**

thick: **ká:tens** it is thick,
wa'katénsha'ne' it got thick (-tens-)

thigh: **ohnítsha'** thigh, **khnitshà:ke** (on)
my thigh (-hnitsh-)

thimble: **anihsnonhsò:ron** or
ionnihsnonhsohrókstha'
(-hsnonhs-, -ohro[k]-)

thimbleberry: **shà:iase'** or **shà:iese'**
(-ahi-, -es-)

thin: *See* skinny; thin

think: **kanonhtónnions** I think,
wahanonhtónnion' or
wahanonhtónnionhwe' he thought
(-anonhton-)

think; want: **í:kehre'** I think so, I want to,
wà:kehre' I thought (-ehr-)

thirst, quench: **onkenia'taná:wen'**
I quenched my thirst
(-nia't-, -na'nawen-/-nawen-)

thirsty: **wakenia'táthens** I am thirsty,
onkenia'táthen' I got thirsty
(-nia't-, -astath[en]-/-ath[en]-)

thirteen: **áhsen tewen'niáwe**

thirty: **áhsen niwáhsen** (-ahsen-)

this; these: **kí:ken** or **kí:**

thorn: **ohì:kta'** thorn,
iohi'któn:ton it is thorny (-hi'kt-, -ont-)

thousand: **oié:ri tewen'niáwe** (-en'niawe-)

thread; string; rope: **ahserí:ie** (-ahseriie['t]-)

three: **áhsen**

thrive: **io'karí:te'** it is thriving (-a'karit[e]-)

throat: **onià:kwa'** throat,
kenia'kwà:ke my throat (-nia'kw-)

throat: **ohòn:kwa'** (-hon'kw-)

throat, go around in the throat:
onkwathnekakwe'nónnien' s.t. is going
around and around in my throat (not going
down) (-hnek-, -hwe'nonni-/-kwe'nonni-)

throb: **teiaonriáhkhwa'** it is throbbing,
tewakonriáhkhwa' I am throbbing, I am
beating (-onriahkw-)

throw: **iewakátie's** I throw it away, that way,
iahonkwá:ti' I threw it that way (-ati-/-onti-)

throw: **ia'tekate'shennià:tha'** I throw it,
ia'tkate'shénnia'te' I threw it,
ia'tehote'shennià:ton he has thrown it
(-'shennia't-)

throw straight at: **ia'tekóia'ks** I throw it,
ia'thróia'ke' he threw it, tossed it aside,
ia'tewakóien' I have thrown it (-oia'[k]-)

thumb: **oweiónhkara'** thumb,
keweionhkarà:ke (on) my thumb
(-weionhkar-)

thunder: **iowè:ren** it thunders,
wa'ká:wehre' it thundered,
iowehrenhátie' it is thundering (-wehr-)

thunderclap; lightning strike:
wa'ote'serón:ti' a lightning bolt struck,
there was a thunderclap (-ate'serontie-)

Thunderer: **Rawè:ras** (-wehr-)

Thursday: **Okaristiiáhne**

tickle: **tewake'nistakà:tha'** I am ticklish, **tehi'nistakà:tha'** I am tickling him, **wa'thake'nístaka'te'** he tickled me (-'nistaka't-)

tidy: **teiontohtáhrhos** she is tidying up, **wa'tkatohtáhrho'** I tidied up, **tewakatohtáhrhon** I have tidied up, **teiohtáhrhon** it is tidy (-ohtahrho-)

tie; fasten: **íkhnerenks** I tie it, **wahà:nerenke'** he tied it, **wákhneren** I have tied it (-hneren[k]-)

tie up: **khwánerenks** I tie it up, **wa'khwánerenke'** I tied it up, **wakhwáneren** I have tied it up (-hwaneren[k]-/-neren[k]-)

tiger: **tako'skó:wa**

time: **Tó: niiohwistà:'e?** What time is it? (-a'e[k]-)

time: **nikahá:wi'** it's at this time (-hawi-/ -enhawi-); **ia'káhewe'** it is time (-he[w]-)

time, have time: **wakenáktote'** I have time, **iah tewakenáktote'** I have no time (-nakt-, -ot-)

timid: **wakátshen** I am timid, I shy away from fights, **wahátshenhte'** he backed away, stood down, **rotshénhton** he is backing down (-atshen-)

tin: **karistakén:ra** (-rist-, -kenra-)

tiny: **rotkanón:ni** he is tiny, **iakotkanón:ni** she is tiny (-atkanonni-)

tire; wheel: **okahkwèn:ta'** (-kahkwen't-)

tired: **tekhwishenhé:ions** I get tired, **wa'tekhwishénheie'** I got tired, **tewakhwishenhé:ion** I am tired (-hwish-, -ihei[on]-/-enhei[on]-)

tired; exhausted: **wakenoròn:se'** I am tired out, I am exhausted, **onkenó:ron'se'** I got exhausted (-noron's-)

tired; overtired: **wa'tewakahtahkwitáhkwen'** I got overtired, **wa'thohtahkwitáhkwen'** he got overtired, **wa'tiakohtahkwitáhkwen'** she got overtired (-ahtahkwitahkwen-)

tired; worn out: **wa'tekhiohsié:nen'ne'** I am so tired, just worn out, worn down, **wa'thahiohsié:nen'ne'** he is worn out, **wa'tiehiohsié:nen'ne'** she is worn out (-hiohs-, -'rhenien'-/-ienen'-)

tiresome: **rarihwanòn:we** he is tiresome, wants to know everything, he is contrary, **ierihwanòn:we** she is tiresome (-rihw-)

toad: **tsikhnennà:tak**

toast: **wa'katena'tarátsha'ahte'** I made toast, **watena'taratsha'áhton** toast (-na'tar[o][k]-, -atsha'-)

tobacco: **oièn:kwa'** (-ien'kw-)

toboggan: **teionthonwenhtáhkhwa'** (-honw[ei]-, -a'senht-/-enht-)

today: **òn:wa wenhniserá:te'** (-enhniser-, -te-)

toe: **ohiakwí:ra'** toe, **kahiakwirà:ke** (on) my toe (-ahiakwir-)

toe, on tiptoes: **teka'éhtote'** I am on my toes, **wa'tkata'ehtó:ten'** I stood up on my toes (-a'eht-, -ot-)

together: **skáthne**; **ohserón:ni**

together: **teiakeniiáhse** we two are together, **wa'tiakwatiáhsete'** we all came to be together (-iahse-)

toilet paper: **ionni'tokewáhtha'** (-i't-, -rakew-/-okew-)

tomato: **tamétos**

tomato, ground tomato: **teiotenorawèn:'en** (-nor-, -hwawen'e[k]-/-awen'e[k]-)

tomorrow: **enióhrhen'ne'** tomorrow, **ó:ia' ientsóhrhen'ne'** the day after tomorrow (-(h)rhen'-)

tongue: **awen'náhson** tongue, **akwen'náhson** my tongue (-en'nahs-)

tongue, stick out the tongue: **wa'tkaten'náhkara'we'** I stuck out my tongue, **tehaten'nahkara'wánions** he keeps sticking out his tongue (-aten'nahkara'w-)

too: **ò:ni'**

too much: **sò:tsi**

tooth: **onawí:ra'** tooth, **kenawirà:ke** (on) my tooth (in my mouth), **akenawí:ra'** my tooth (-nawir-)

tooth: **onò:tsa'** tooth, **ranò:tsote'** he has a tooth, **wa'eno'tsó:ta'ne'** she (a baby) got a tooth, her tooth came through (-no'ts-, -ot-)

tooth, chatter: **tewakenawiro'ókhons** my teeth are chattering (-nawir-, -o'[k]-)

tooth, clench: **tekano'seríkhons** I am clenching, gritting my teeth, **wa'tionno'seríkhon'** she clenched her teeth (-ano'serikhon-)

tooth, grind: **tekeno'karánies** I grind my teeth, **wa'thano'karánie'** he ground his teeth (-no'karanie-)

top (clothing); vest: **oneró:kwa'** (-nerokw-)

top (toy): **tsiskwaró:kwaro**

tornado: **katsiskaionnì:tha'** (-tsiskaionni-)

Toronto, Ontario: **Aterónto** (-ront-, -o-)

touch: **ia'tié:na'** I touched it, **iahiié:na'** I touched him, **tóhsa ia'tsé:na** Don't touch it! (-iena-)

touch: **ken' nà:tiere'** I touched it, **tóhsa ken' nà:tser** Don't touch it! (-ier-)

touch s.o. somewhere: **iahihnénhsa'** or **ia'thihénhsa'** I touched his shoulder, **iahikwítsha'** or **ia'thikwítsha'** I touched his knee (-a-)

towel: **iontia'tokewáhtha'** (-ia't-, -rakew-/-okew-)

town: **kaná:ta'** town, settlement, **tkaná:taien'** there's a town there (-nat-, -ien-)

town, downtown; front: **kanáthen**

town hall; council hall: **ietsenhaientáhkhwa'** (-tsenh-, -ien-)

toy: **iontkahri'táhkhwa'** (-atkahri-)

trace: *See* copy; trace

track; footprint: **oiá:na'** (-ian-)

trade: **tentiatá:ton'** I will trade with you, **wa'tiatiatá:ton'** we two traded, **teiontiatatá:wi** we two are trading (-awi-/-on-)

traffic cop; crossing guard: **shakohahá:wis** (-hah-, -awi-/-on-)

trailer; double runner sleigh: **tewate'serehtahnhontéhrha'** (-'sere[ht]-, -hnhonter-)

train: **thio'kéha** or **thiio'kéha** or **ohthiio'kéha**

train, freight: **io'serehtákste'** (-'sere[ht]-, -kste-)

train, passenger: **teio'serehtà:ka** (-'sere[ht]-, -'ka-)

tramp; wanderer: **rathahí:ne's** (-hah-, -ine-)

trample: **wa'thiiaskwa'serónkwahte'** I trampled him, **teioskwa'seronkwáhton** it got trampled, crushed underfoot (-askwa'ser-)

translate: **tekewennaténie's** I translate, **wa'thawennaté:ni'** he translated it, **tehowennaténion** he has translated it (-wenn-, -teni-); **tehawennanetáhkwas** he is translating (-wenn-, -hna'netahkw-/-netahkw-)

trap, steel trap: **ionteristaientáhkhwa'** (-rist-, -ien-)

travel: **teiontstikáhwhas** she is a a traveller, she goes all over, **wa'thatstikáhwha'** he travelled all over, **tewakatstikáhwhen** I have travelled (-atstikahwha-)

treasure: **wakenónhste'** I treasure it, **ronónhste'** he treasures it, **iakonónhste'** she treasures it (-nonhst[e]-)

treasures; riches: **atshohkwáhtshera'**

treat; speak for: **ia'ontá:ti'** she spoke up, she spoke for it (treated somebody) (-atati-)

treat everyone: **taienenhráia'ke'** she treated everyone, paid for everyone (-nenhr-, -ia'k-)

tree: **ó:kwire'** tree, **iokwí:rote'** there's a tree, standing (-kwir-, -ot-); **kéhrhite'** there is a tree (-ehrhit-)

tree, bottom: **o'tén:na'** (-'tenn-)

trees: *See* woods

tremble: *See* quake; tremble; shiver; shake

trick; deceive: **tehakerihwaierónnions** he tricks me, deceives me, **wa'thakerihwaierónnion'** he tricked me (-rihw-, -ieron-)

trigger: **kanièn:sera'** (-nien'ser-)

trillium: **tiona'tsíia'**

trip: **tonkwahsì:tia'ke'** I tripped (-ahsi't-, -ia'k-)

trip s.o.: **wa'thakwatshinotáhrhoke'** he tripped me (-hsin-, -otahrho[k]-)

tripe: **onekerèn:ta'** (-nekeren't-)

trousers: *See* pants; trousers

trout: **tiotià:kton**

true; certainly: **tó:kenske'**; **tó:ske'**

trust: *See* depend on; rely; trust

trustworthy; honest: **wakaterihwakwaríhsion** I am straight in my ways, I am trustworthy, honest (-rihw-, -takwarihsi-/-kwarihsi-)

try, try on: **kate'niéntha'** I am trying, **wa'kate'nién:ten'** I tried it on, **rote'nién:ten** he has tried it on (-ate'nient[en]-)

try again: *See* fail at

try hard: *See* do intensely

tube; pipe: **ohonrò:ta'** (-honro't-)

tuberculosis: **wakehnhrakaiòn:se'** I have tuberculosis, **wahohnhraká:ion'se'** he got tuberculosis (-(h)nhr-, -akaion-/-kaion-)

Tuesday: **Ratironhia'kehronòn:ke** (-ronhi-)

tug-of-war: **tehonahseriie'tatí:ronte'** they are playing tug-of-war (-ahseriie['t]-, -atiront-)

tumble over: **wa'tkanonhwetsháweron'** I tumbled over, I got upside down (-anonhwetshaweron-)

tumpline: **akéhton**

tunnel: **o'whá:ra'** tunnel, hollow, **tsi io'wharakà:ronte'** at the tunnel (in Kahnawà:ke) (-'whar-, -kahront-)

turkey: **skawiró:wane'** or **skaweró:wane'** (-wer-, -kowan[en]-/-owan[en]-)

turn: *See* twist; turn

turn, take turns: **tehontenihà:tha'** they are taking turns, **wa'ttiateníha'te'** you and I took turns, **teiontiatenihà:ton** we two have taken turns (-ateniha't-)

turn a direction: **kkarenhrákwas** I turn, **wa'kkarenhrá:ko'** I turned, **rokarenhrákwen** he has turned (-karenhr[on]-)

turn a page: **thara'wistakétskwas** he is turning the page, **takera'wistakétsko'** I turned the page, **tewakera'wistakétskwen** I have turned the page (-ra'wist-, -ketskw-)

turn around: **tehakahrhaténie's** he is turning it around, **wa'tekkahrhaté:ni'** I turned it around, **tehokahrhaténion** he has turned it around, **wa'tkatkahrhaté:ni'** I turned around, **wa'thikahrhaté:ni'** I turned him around (-kahrhateni-)

turn away: *See* dodge

turn over: **rakahrháthos** he turns it over, **wahakahrhátho'** he turned it over, **wakkahrháthon** I have turned it over, **wa'katkahrhátho'** I turned over (-kahrhatho-)

turnip: **otsihkwa'kó:wa** (-tsihkw-)

turpentine: **kahnehtákeras** (-hneht-, -akera-)

turtle: **a'nó:wara** (-'now-)

Turtle clan: **wakeniáhton** (-niahton-)

Tuscarora: **Tehatiskaró:ras**

twenty: **tewáhsen** (-ahsen-)

twenty-five cents: **teréntsho sén:ts**

twins: **tehníkhen** they are male twins, **tekeníkhen** they are female twins (-kha-)

twist; turn: **khwatá:ses** I am turning, twisting it, **wa'khwatá:se'** I twisted it (-hwatase-/-tase-)

twitch: **wa'oni'kerón:ko'** it twitched (-ni'keronkw-)

two: **tékeni**

two: **tehniiáhse** two males, a male and a female, **tekeniiáhse** two females (-iahse-)

typewriter: **tekaristò:raraks** or **teieristohrarákstha'** (-rist-, -htohrarak-/-ohrarak-)

typhoid fever: **iako'tonhkwahrhoskó:wa** (-i'tonhkw-, -(h)rho-)

ugly: **kahétken** she or it is ugly, **rahétken** he is ugly, **iehétken** she is ugly (-hetken-)

umbrella: **ionterahkwawehrhóhstha'** (-rahkw-, -awehrho-)

uncle: **rakenohà:'a** or **rakenonhà:'a** my uncle (-noha-/-nonha-); **rakonhwatèn:'a** my uncle (-onhwaten-)

undecided: **tewakeròn:se'** I am undecided, **tehoròn:se'** he is undecided, **teiakoròn:se'** she is undecided (-ron'se-)

underground: **onhóntsakon** or **onhwéntsakon** (-onhwents-/-onhonts-)

understand: **wake'nikonhraién:ta's** I understand, **onke'nikonhraién:ta'ne'** I understood it (-'nikonhr-, -ienta'-)

understand; grasp: **iénkhewe'** I will understand, I will get it, **iahà:khewe'** I got it, I remembered, I understood (-he[w]-)

undertaker: **renheion'tahserón:ni** (-ihei[on]-/-enhei[on]-, -hseronni-)

unexpected: **wa'tewakatierónnion'se'** something unexpected happened to me (-rihw-, -ieron-)

United States: **Wastonhronòn:ke**

until; during: **tsi niió:re'** (-re-)

up: **è:neken**

upside down: *See* tumble over

upstairs: **kanonhsoharà:ke** (-nonhs-)

urge not to do: *See* prevent

urinate: **wahanistiá:ke'** he urinated, **wakanistiá:ke** I am urinating (-anistiake-)

urinate, urge for: **wakenenharónhkwani** I have the urge to pee (-nenh-, -ronhkwani-)

urine: **onehóhsa'** (-nehohs-); **onénha'** (-nenh-)

use: **kátstha'** I am using it, **wà:ratste'** he used it, **iakótston** she has used it, she is wearing it (-hst-)

use up: **ieiehsa'áhtha'** she uses it up, **iahà:khsa'ahte'** or **iahà:khsahte'** I used it up, **iewakhsa'áhton** I have used it up (-hsa'-/-isa'-)

used to, get used to: **rarèn:nha's** he gets used to it, he makes a habit of it, **wa'kerèn:nha'** I got used to it, I made a habit of it, **roren'nhà:'on** he has gotten used to it, he is used to it (-ren'nha-)

useful: **íkhsta** I am useful, **ráhsta** he is useful, **káhsta** it is useful (-hst-)

useful: *See* adept; useful; helpful

useful; get things done: **kerihontákwas** I am useful, accomplish things, get things done, **enkerihontá:ko'** I will accomplish it, **wa'kerihontá:ko'** I was useful, I got it done (-rihw-, -ont-)

useless: *See* hopeless

usual: **tsi niioren'nhà:'on** as usual (-ren'nha-)

vaccinate: **wa'onkenenskwaráta'** they gave me a vaccination (-nonskwar-/-nenskwar-, -ta'-/-eta'-)

vagina: **ohnanerì:ta'** vagina, **iehnaneri'tà:ke** her vagina (-ihn-, -ner-)

vain: *See* proud; conceited

Vancouver, BC: **Tsonontatihkó:wa** (-nont-, -ti-)

vase: **ietsi'tsaráhkhwa'** (-tsi'ts-, -r-)

vegetables: **ase'shòn:'a** (-ase-)

veil; net; curtain: **à:'are'** (-a'ar-)

vein: **otsinonhíahton** vein, **aktsinonhiáhton** my veins (-tsinonhiaht-)

velvet: **ionthnia'sotáhkhwa'** (-hnia's-, -ot-)

Venus: **thentenhawíhtha'** (-ent-, -hawi-/-enhawi-)

Vermont: **Tsi iontoratstáhkhwa'** (-atorat-)

vest; blouse: **oià:kara'** (-ia'kar-/-ia'kwar-)

vest; top: **oneró:kwa'** (-nerokw-)

vibrate: *See* shake back and forth

village; town; settlement: **kaná:ta'** (-nat-)

village, in the village: **kanathénhshon**

vinegar: **tonseráhtha'** or **thonseráhtha'** or **iethonseráhtha'** or **toseráhtha'** (-sera[hw]-/-osera[hw]-)

visit: **kenatà:re'** I am here to visit, **kenatà:re's** I go visiting, **wa'kenatà:ra'** I went to visit, **wakenatahrónhne'** I have gone to visit (-natahr-)

visit: *See* pass by; visit

voice: **akewén:na'** my voice (-wenn-)

voice, high-pitched, loud: **wakhsakawén:te'** I have a high-pitched, loud voice, **rohsakawén:te'** he has a high-pitched voice, **iakohsakawén:te'** she has a high-pitched voice (-hsakawente-)

voice, singing: **roha'tí:io** he has a nice voice, **iakoha'tí:io** she has a nice voice (-ha't-, -iio-)

volunteer s.o.: **wa'khehonkária'ke'** I asked her to take on a task, I volunteered her (-honkar-, -ia'k-)

vomit: **thatstí:kons** he is vomiting, **tahátstike'** he vomitted, **thotstí:kon** he has vomited (-atstik[on]-)

vote: **tehonnitiohkwakénnie's** they vote, councilors, **wa'tkanitiohkwakén:ni'** I voted (-itiohkw-, -kenni-)

waist; midriff: **tetià:kares** I am long-waisted, **ken' na'tetia'karésha** I am short-waisted (-ia'kar-/-ia'kwar-)

wait: **wakehrhá:re'** I am waiting for it, expecting it, **katehrhá:rats** I wait, **wa'katehrhá:rate'** I waited, **wa'kheiatehrhá:rate'** I waited for her (-(h)rhar[e]-)

Wait! **Wá'tsok!** or **Wá'tsik!**

wait impatiently: **wakenónhton'ks** I am waiting impatiently, **onkenónhton'ke'** I got tired of waiting (-nonhton'k-)

wake up: **rá:ie's** he wakes up, **wà:tie'** I woke up, **watiè:'on** I am awake, **wahí:iehte'** I woke him up (-ie-)

wake up early: **tiè:wate'** I wake up early, **raiè:wate'** he wakes up early, **ieiè:wate'** she wakes up early (-iehwat[on]-)

wake up suddenly: **ia'tiehwáhtahkwe'** I woke up suddenly (-iehwahtahkw-)

walk: **í:ke'** I am walking, **ì:re'** he is walking, **í:ien'** she is walking, **ì:re's** he is walking around (-e-)

walk: *See* go away

walk fast: **kastó:rons** I walk fast, **wahastó:ron'** he walked fast, **iakostoróntie'** she is walking fast as she is going (-astoron-)

wall: **ahsónhta'** (-ahsonht-)

walleye: **skakahráksen** (-kahr-, -aksen-)

wampum: **onekò:rha'** or **o'nekò:rha'** (-neko'rh-)

wampum belt: **kaión:ni, kahswénhtha'**

wander: **tekatawénrie's** I wander, I stroll, roam, **wa'thatawénrie'** he wandered, he strolled (-awenrie-)

want; need: *See* need; want

want: *See* think; want

warm: *See* hot; warm

warm oneself: **wa'katèn:ion'** or **wa'katèn:rion'** I warmed myself, **wahatèn:ion'** he warmed himself, **wa'ontèn:ion'** she warmed herself (-atenh(r)ion-)

warn: *See* inform; warn

warrior: **rohsken'rakéhte'** (-hsken'rakehte-)

wart: **anihnhè:ta'** wart, **wakanihnhè:taronte'** I have a wart (-ihnhe't[ar]-, -ont-)

wash: **kenóhares** I wash it, **wa'kenóhare'** I washed it, **wakenóhare** I have washed it (-nohare-/-ohare-)

wash, handwash: **teionsharánies** she is washing (something dainty), **wa'tkasharánie'** I washed it (-asharanie-)

Washington, DC: **Ranatakariáhsne** (-nat-, -kari-)

wasp: **watenawa'tstanentáktha'** (-nawa'tst-, -ra'nentakt-/-nentakt-)

waste: **iontiesáhtha'** she wastes things, **wahatié:sahte'** he wasted it, **wakatiesáhton** I am wasting it, I have wasted it (-ies[en]-); **katkaiónhstha'** I waste it (-akaion-/-kaion-)

waste s.o.'s time: *See* hinder

watch: **katerò:roks** I watch something going on, **wa'katerò:roke'** I watched, **wakaterò:ren** I am watching (-rohro[k]-)

watch; have an eye on: **tekkahráhere'** I have my eye on it I am watching it, **tehakahráhere'** he has his eye on it, **teiekahráhere'** she has her eye on it (-kahr-, -her-/-hr-)

watch over; be careful: **ke'nikòn:rare'** I am watching over it, I am careful, **ri'nikòn:rare'** I am watching over him (-'nikonhr-, -r-)

watch over; protect: **ranónhstats** he is watching over it, protecting it, **wahanónhstate'** he watched over it, **iakononhstá:ton** she has watched over it (-nonhst[e]-)

watch s.o.: *See* mind s.o.

watch; bracelet: **atenentsháhnha'** (-nentsh-, -hwahnha[k]-/-hnha[k]-)

water; liquid: **ohné:ka'** liquid, water, **ohné:kanos** fresh, cold water (-hnek-)

water, bottom water; dregs: **onón:wa'** (-nonw-)

water, get into: *See* get into water

water, in the water: **awèn:ke** (-awen-)

water, lukewarm: **iononwaná:wen** it is lukewarm water (-nonw-, -na'nawen-/-nawen-)

water, murky: **wa'tkanón:wahkwe'** it got murky, **teiononwáhwhen** it is murky (-nonw-, -hkw-)

water, warm: **iononwataríhen** it is warm water (-nonw-, -a'tarih[en]-/-tarih[en]-)

water hemlock: **o'náhsar**

water lily: **onennoron'kó:wa**

waterfall: **tewa'sénhtha'** (-a'senht-/-enht-)

watermelon: **onon'onserakáhte'** (-non'onser-, -kahte-)

wave: **tekteníhon** I am waving it, **wa'tekteníhon'** I waved it, **tekateníhon** it is waving, flapping (-tenihon-)

waves, come in: **tontaiotenontón:ti'** a big wave came back in (-nont-, -ati-/-onti-)

waves, go out: **entkahnekatihéntho'** the water will go out (-hnek-, -atihentho-)

we; I: **ì:'i**; **í:**, **nì:'i**

weak; feeble: **waktsi'ió:ha** I am weak,
feeble, **rotsi'ió:ha** he is weak, feeble,
iotsi'ió:ha it is weak,
iotsi'ióhtare' it is defective,
onktsi'ióhtara'ne' I got weak (-tsi'io-, -r-)

wear: *See* use

wear out: **karihwén:ta's** it wears out,
wa'karihwén:ta'ne' it wore out,
iorihwentà:'on it has worn out,
wa'kerihwéntho' I wore it out (-rihw-, -ent-)

weasel: **onón:kote'** (-nonkot-)

web, cobweb: **teiota'á:raton** there are
cobwebs (-a'ar-)

web, spider web: **takwa'áhson teiota'á:raton**
(-a'ar-)

wedding; feast: **wa'katen'nió:ten'** I had a
wedding, **watèn:niote'** there's a wedding,
a feast (-aten'niot-)

wedding cake, dress: **iakoniákstha' atià:tawi**
wedding dress, **iakoniákstha' teiona'tara-**
tsikhè:tare' wedding cake (-niak-)

wedged: **tewahsihá:ra's** it gets wedged in,
stuck, **wa'tewahsíhara'ne'** it got stuck,
teiohsiharà:'on it has gotten stuck
(-ahsihara'-)

Wednesday: **Soséhne**

week: **tsiahià:khsera** one week
(-iahia'khser-)

weigh: **wahakon'tsherihá:ren'** he weighed
it, **wahatatkon'tsherihá:ren'** he weighed
himself (-kon'tsher-, -har-/-ihar-)

welder: **raristóseras**
(-rist-, -sera[hw]-/-osera[hw]-)

well: **ohnáwera'** well, **iohnáwerote'**
(there is) a well (-hnawer-, -ot-)

west: **è:neken nonkwá:ti**

wet: **ionà:nawen** it is wet,
watia'taná:wen I am wet,
wa'onà:nawenhste' it got wet,
ontia'taná:wenhste' I got wet
(-na'nawen-/-nawen-)

wet, s.t. soaking wet: **okoharóhsa'** or
akoharóhsa' (-koharohs-)

whale: **tsonhnhó:wane'**
(-onhnh-, -kowan[en]-/-owan[en]-)

wharf: **tsi iehrahrhóhstha'** (-hrahrho-)

wharf; dock: **ó:tsire' tekatáhstha'**
(-tsir- and -t-/-et-)

What? **Oh nahò:ten'?**

What is the matter? **Oh niiotié:ren?** (-ier-)

wheat: **onátsa'** (-nats-)

wheel; tire: **okahkwèn:ta'** (-kahkwen't-)

wheeze: **teiakaonriò:raraks** she is wheezing, gasping for breath, **wa'thaonriò:rarake'**
he wheezed (-onri-, -htohrarak-/-ohrarak-)

When? **Kátke?**

Where? **Ka' nón:we?**

while: **tsi niió:re'** while, during, until (-re-);
tsi nikarì:wes while, **iah tekarì:wes** not
long (after), it won't be long (-rihw-, -es-)

whine: **rotonriá:ien'** he is whining, sounding agitated, **iakotonriá:ien'** she is whining (-onri-, -ien-)

whippoorwill: **kwa'kóhrien**

whisper: **tewaktsáhon** I am whispering, **wa'tektsáhon'** I whispered, **wa'thitsahón:hahse'** I whispered to him (-tsahon-)

whistle: **renná:kahre'** he is whistling, **iakenná:kahre'** she is whistling, **wahrenná:kahre'** he whistled (-ennakahr-); **atá:tis** a whistle (-atati-)

white; light-coloured: **karà:ken** it is white (-ra'ken-)

white; pale: **iokén:ra** it is pale, light-coloured (-kenra-)

Who? **Ónhka?**

Why? **Oh nontié:ren?** (-ier-)

wide: **tewatakà:ron** it is wide (-akahron-)

widow; widower: **wakatenhrè:'ons** I am a widow(er), **wahotenhrè:'onske'** he became a widower, **wa'akotenhrè:'onske'** she became a widow (-atenhre'ons[k]-); **tehorahsi'takwe'nón:ni** he is a widower (-ahsi't-, -hwe'nonni-/-kwe'nonni-)

wife; husband: **ró:ne'** his wife, her husband (-ne-); **tiakenì:teron** my wife, my husband (-i'teron-)

wife; spouse: *See* couple

wig: **rotenon'onhró:ron** he has on a wig, **iakotenon'onhró:ron** she has on a wig,

iontenon'onhrorókstha' wig (-non'onhr-, -'rhoro[k]-/-oro[k]-)

willow, pussywillow: **ó:se**

willow, red: **onekwénhtara' niwatahtsherò:ten** (-atahtsher-, -o'ten-)

willow, sand bar; scar: **owì:ra'** (-wihr-)

win: **wahatkwé:ni'** he won, **rotkwénion** he has won (-kweni-)

win: *See* beat at; defeat

win: *See* earn; win

wind; air: **ówera'** (-wer-)

wind a clock: **wa'keneniakará:tate'** I wound it (clock, watch) (-neni-, -haratat-/-karatat-)

window, storm window: **tewatenahstonhkwanéta's** (-nahstonhkw-, -hna'neta'-/-neta'-)

window, storm window with vent holes: **watahkarakétskwas** (-ahkar-, -ketskw-)

window, windowsill: **onahstónhkwa'** (-nahstonhkw-)

windy: **iaò:te** it is windy (-o'te-); **tekaweráhkhwa'** the wind comes up, it gets windy, **wa'tkáwerahkwe'** it got windy (-wer-, -hkw-); **teiowerá:se** it is very windy, **wa'tkawerá:se'** it got very windy (-wer-, -hwatase-/-tase-)

wing: **óweia'** (-wei-)

wing: *See* shoulder blade; wing

winnow: *See* chaff, winnow

winter; year: **óhsera'** winter, year, **akohserà:ke** (in the) winter (-ohser-)

wipe: **keraké:was** I wipe it, **wa'kerá:kewe'** I wiped it, **wakeraké:wen** I have wiped it (-rakew-/-okew-)

wire; nail; needle; pin: **karón:ware'** or **kanón:ware'** (-ronwar-/-nonwar-)

wisdom: **attokháhtshera'** (-attok-)

wish for: **kaská:neks** I wish for something, **wa'kaská:neke'** I wished for it, **wakaskanékon** I have wished for it (-askanek-)

witch: **rata'én:naras** he is a witch, **ionta'én:naras** she is a witch, **shakota'ennáhrhos** he witches her, **wa'kheiata'ennáhrho'** I witched her, **ata'ennaráhtshera'** witchcraft (-a'enn-, -(h)rho-)

witch hazel: **takwa'ahtsherón:ni**

witchcraft, practice; make spells: **iontkónhstha'** she dabbles in witchcraft, she makes spells, **enkátkonhste'** I will make a spell, **iakotkónhston** she is dabbling in witchcraft (-atkon-)

witchcraft object: **onón:we** (-nonwe[ht]-)

wolf: **okwáho** (-kwaho-)

Wolf clan: **wakkwáho** I am Wolf clan (-kwaho-); **wakathahión:ni** I am Wolf clan (-athahioni-)

wolverine: **tsikenekerehetshotáhrhon** (-nekerehetsh-, -otahrho[k]-)

wood: **ó:iente'** (-ient-)

wood, block of wood: **okonhrétsha'** (-konhretsh-)

wood, dead wood: **oskóhara'** (-skohar-)

wood, rotted wood: **ohéhsa'** (-hehs-)

wood chips; shaving: **ohká:ra'** (-ahkar-)

wood shavings: **ononhkerì:ta'** (-nonhkeri-); **kahwé:sen** (-hwesen-)

wood shavings; sawdust: **ohswáhseri** (-ahswahser-)

woodchuck: **anonhwaráweron** or **anon'waráweron**

woodpecker: **karontakáro'ks** (-ront-, -ro'[k]-)

woodpecker, hairy: **kwitó:kwito**

woods: **kahrhá:kon** in the woods, **kahrháhere'** there are woods (-(h)rh-, -her-/-hr-)

Wood's Edge: **Teiohnionwarákta'** (-hnionwar-)

wool: **karisé:**

word: **owén:na'** (-wenn-)

work: **watió'te'** I am working, **wahoió'ten'** he worked, **watio'tèn:'en** I have worked,

kaio'ténhsera' work (-io'te-/-io'ten-)

work, leave for work: *See* leave for work

work together: **taiatiatén:rohwe'** we worked together, **tahontén:rohwe'** they worked together (-atenro-); **teiakeniié:nas** we two work together, **wa'tiakeniié:na'** we worked together (-iena-); **teionkeniienawà:kon** we two are working together (-ienawa'k-/-wa'k-)

work, look for work: **wa'katonhnhisákhe'** I am going looking for work, **wa'katonhnhisákha'** I went to look for work (-onhnh-, -ehsak-/-ihsak-/-esak-/-isak-)

world; earth: **tsi ionhontsá:te'** (-onhwents-/-onhonts-, -te-)

worm, earthworm: **otsi'nonwahnhè:ta'** (-tsi'nonwanhe't-)

worm, tapeworm: **onerénha'** worm, **ronerénha'** he has worms, **iakonerénha'** she has worms, (-nerenh-)

worn: **iotká:non** it is worn (it has been used a lot and now it is worn)

worry: **teho'nikónhrhare'** he worries, he is troubled, **tóhsa tesa'nikonhrhá:ren** Don't worry! (-'nikonhrhar-)

worship: *See* praise

wrap: **tekhwawèn:'eks** I wrap it, **wa'tekhwawèn:'eke'** I wrapped it, **tewakhwawèn:'e** I have wrapped it (-hwawen'e[k]-/-awen'e[k]-)

wrap around: **tekhwáhnhaks** I wrap s.t. around s.t., **wa'tekhwáhnhake'** I wrapped it around it, **tewakhwáhnhen** I have wrapped it around it (-hwahnha[k]-/-hnha[k]-)

wrestle: **tehontatié:nas** they are wrestling (-iena-)

wring: **ietsinonhwaratá:ses** she is wringing it out, **wa'ktsinonhwaratá:se'** I wrung it out (-tsinonhwaratase-)

wrinkled: **teioni'tià:khon** it is all wrinkled (-ani'tia'khon-); **wakanihnokeríkhon** I am wrinkled (-ihn-, -tokeri[k]-/-okeri[k]-)

wrist: **onentshawì:ta'** (-nentshawi't-)

write: **khiá:tons** I am writing, **wahahiá:ton'** he wrote, **wakhiá:ton** I have written (-hiaton-)

yard: **aten'èn:rakon** in the yard (-aten'enhr-)

yard; yardstick: **sewatáhtshera** one yard, one metre, **atáhtshera'** yardstick (-atahtsher-)

yawn: **tewakhskara'wahtánions** I am yawning, **wa'tewakhskarà:wahte'** I yawned (-hs-, -kara'w[en]-)

year; winter: **óhsera'** (-ohser-)

yell: **tewakhenréhtha'** I am yelling, **wa'thohén:rehte'** he yelled, **tehohenréhton** he has yelled (-henreht-)

yell; hoop and holler: **rahsakaionhtánions** he yells (a warning), **wahahsakaionhtánion'** he yelled, hollered (-hsakaionhtanion-)

yellow: **otsì:nekwar** (-tsi'nekwar-)

yes: **hén:** or **én:**

yesterday: **thetén:re** yesterday, **ó:ia' tsthetén:re** the day before yesterday yew: **onen'tión:ni** (-nen't-, -ionni-)

yogurt: **okaié:ta'** (-kaiet-)

you (singular, dual, plural): **í:se'**

yoke (of a shirt); necklace: **ionnihtiákstha'**
(-anihtia[k]-)

young: **ken' nithoièn:'a** he is young,
ken' nitiakoièn:'a she is young (-ien-)

young man: **ranekénhteron** (-nekenhteron-)

young woman: **ieià:tase'** (-ia't-, -ase-)

youngest of the family: **o'nisóhkwa'**
(-'nisohkw-)

zucchini; cucumber: **kanon'ónseres**
(-non'onser-, -es-)

References

Abbott, Clifford. 2016. Contact and change in Oneida. In Andrea L. Berez-Kroeker, Diane M. Hintz, and Carmen Jany (eds.), *Language Contact and Change in the Americas: Studies in Honor of Marianne Mithun*, 167–188. Amsterdam: John Benjamins.

Abrams, Percy W. 2006. *Onondaga Pronominal Prefixes*. Buffalo: University at Buffalo dissertation.

Barbeau, Marius. 1949. How the Huron-Wyandot Language Was Saved from Oblivion. *Proceedings of the American Philosophical Society* 93(3): 226–232.

Barbeau, Marius. 1960. *Huron-Wyandot Traditional Narratives in Translations and Native Texts*. National Museum of Canada Bulletin No. 165. Ottawa: Canada Department of Northern Affairs and National Resources.

Barrin de La Galissonnière, Roland-Michel. n.d. *Petit Dictionnaire de la langue des Iroquois de la nation d'Agnié*. Digital copy available from gallica.BnF.fr.

Beauchamp, William M. 1893. *Indian Names in New York, with a Selection from Other States, and some Onondaga Names of Plants, etc.* Fayetteville, N.Y.: H.C. Beauchamp, Recorder Office.

Beauchamp, William M. 1907. *Aboriginal Place Names of New York*. New York State Museum Bulletin 108. Albany: New York State Education Department.

Beauchamp, William M. 1922. *Iroquois Folk Lore, gathered from the Six Nations of New York*. Syracuse, N.Y.: The Dehler Press.

Beauvais, Johnny. 1985. *Kahnawake: A Mohawk Look at Canada and Adventures of Big John Canadian 1840–1919*. Self-published.

Beauvais, Louis Kanonwatase. n.d. (Notebook of recipes for treating ailments and conditions of the body.)

Biggar, H. P. 1924. *The Voyages of Jacques Cartier, Published from the originals with translations, notes and appendices*. Publications of the Public Archives of Canada, No. 11. Ottawa: F. A. Acland.

Bonvillain, Nancy. 1978. Linguistic Change in Akwesasne Mohawk: French and English Influences. *International Journal of American Linguistics* 44: 31–39.

Bonvillain, Nancy, and Beatrice Francis. 1971. *English-Mohawk, Mohawk-English Dictionary*. St. Regis, QC: Mohawk Tribal Council and St. Regis Band Council.

Boyce, Douglas W. 1973. A Glimpse of Iroquois Culture History through the Eyes of Joseph Brant and John Norton. *Proceedings of the American Philosophical Society* 117(4): 286–294.

Boyd, Julian P. (ed). 1938. *Indian Treaties Printed by Benjamin Franklin, 1736–1762*. Philadelphia: Historical Society of Pennsylvania.

Boyle, David. 1898. *The Pagan Iroquois*. Archaeological Report: Being part of Appendix to the Minister of Education, Ontario, 54–205. Toronto.

Brodhead, J. R. 1856–83. *Documents Relative to the Colonial History of New York, procured in Holland, England and France*, edited by E.B. O'Callaghan. Albany: Weed, Parsons & Co.

Bruyas, Jacques. 1862. *Radical Words of the Mohawk Language with their Derivatives*. Shea's Library of American Linguistics X. New York: Cramoisy Press. Republished 1970 by AMS Press, Inc., N.Y.

[Calendar] 1979. Caughnawaga, Québec: Kanien'keha:ka Otiohkwa.

Chafe, Wallace L. 1967. *Seneca Dictionary and Morphology*. Washington, DC: Smithsonian Institution Press.

Chafe, Wallace L. 1980. Consequential verbs in Northern Iroquoian languages and elsewhere. In Kathryn Klar, Margaret Langdon, and Shirley Silver (eds.), *American Indian and Indoeuropean Studies: Papers in Honor of Madison S. Beeler*, 43–49. The Hague: Mouton.

Chafe, Wallace L. n.d. *English–Seneca Dictionary*. Online at senecalanguage.com.

Claus Papers. Ottawa: Public Archives of Canada.

Colden, Cadwallader. 1750. *The History of the Five Indian Nations of Canada*. London: John Whiston, Lockyer Davis, and John Ward.

Cooke, Charles A. 1952. Iroquois Personal Names: Their Classification. *Proceedings of the American Philosophical Society* 96: 427–438.

Cory, Rev. David M. [n.d.] *Mohawk Manual, Dictionary and Phrase-Book, Ka-iatonse-ra On-kwe on-we ne-ha.* American Philosophical Society Floyd Glenn Lounsbury papers, ca. 1935–1998, Mss.Ms.Coll.95.

Coyne, James H. (Translator and Editor). 1903. *Galinee's Narrative and Map.* Ontario Historical Society, Papers and Records Vol. IV, Part 1. Toronto.

Cuoq, J. A. 1866. *Etudes Philologiques sur les quelques Langues Sauvages de L'Amerique.* Montreal: Dawson Brothers.

Cuoq, J. A. 1882. *Lexique de la Langue Iroquoise avec Notes et Appendices.* Montreal: J. Chapleau & Fils.

D'Ailleboust, Annie Katsitsanien Montour. 1921. Noteboook.

Deering, Nora, and Helga Delisle. 1976. *Mohawk: A Teaching Grammar.* Ecowi, QC: Manitou College.

Deserontyon, John. 1928. *A Mohawk Form of Ritual of Condolence, 1782, by John Deserontyon, translated, with an introduction, by J.N.B. Hewitt.* Indian Notes and Monographs, Vol. X, No. 8. New York: Museum of the American Indian Heye Foundation.

Devine, E. J., S. J. 1922. *Historic Caughnawaga.* Montreal: Messenger Press.

Diabo, Louise. 1951. *Mohawk language notebook with alphabetical word list, written by Louise Diabo.* American Philosophical Society Floyd Glenn Lounsbury papers, ca. 1935–1998, Mss.Ms.Coll.95.

Dyck, Carrie, Frances Froman, Alfred Keye, and Lottie Keye. 2023 draft. *A Grammar and Dictionary of Gayogoho:nǫʔ (Cayuga).*

Fenton, William N., and Elizabeth Tooker. 1978. Mohawk. In Bruce T. Trigger (ed.), *Handbook of North American Indians, Vol. 15: Northeast*, 466–480. Washington, DC: Smithsonian Institution.

Forbes, Guillaume. 1906. Etude sur les Noms Iroquois. *Congres International des Americanists*, 301–310. Quebec.

Fraser, Alexander. 1920. *Huron Manuscripts from Rev. Pierre Potier's collection.* Fifteenth Report of the Bureau of Archives for the Province of Ontario, 1918–1919. Toronto: Clarkson W. James.

Gabriel, Harvey Satewas. 2014. *Kanesata'ké:ha Tekawenna'thé:tha/ Kanesatake Mohawk Dictionary.*

Gallatin, Albert. 1836. A Synopsis of the Indian Tribes Within the United States East of the Rocky Mountains, and in the British and Russian Possessions in North America. *American Antiquarian Society's Archaeologia Americana* vol. 2, 1–422.

Granger, S. J. Kenwenteshon, L. S. 1906 *Iakentasethatha Kahnawakeha 1906, Almanach Iroquois 1906.* Tiohtiake

(Montréal), Canada: Teioristorarakon Iesos Raweriasatokenti Teieristoraraksțha Aonosa.

Hale, Horatio. 1883. *The Iroquois Book of Rites*. Brinton's Library of Aboriginal American Literature 2. Philadelphia: D. G. Brinton. Reprinted 1963 by University of Toronto Press.

Hawley, Rev. 1809. Mohawk numbers, by Rev. Mr. Hawley, of Mashpee. From President Stiles' MSS. *Massachusetts Historical Society Collections,* first series, vol. 10, 137.

Hewitt, J. N. B. 1903. *Iroquoian Cosmology.* Twenty-first Annual Report of the Bureau of American Ethnology to the Secretary of the Smithsonian Institution 1899–1900. Washington: Government Printing Office.

Hewitt, J. N. B. n.d. *Vocabulary of "Oneida of Seymoure, Wisconsin"* Ms. 3814, National Anthropological Archives, Smithsonian Institution.

Hill, Sarah H. 1997. *Weaving New Worlds: Southeastern Cherokee Women and their Basketry.* The University of North Carolina Press.

Holm, Thomas Campanius. 1834. *Description of the Province of New Sweden, now called, by the English, Pennsylvania, in America.* Translated from the Swedish, for the Historical Society of Pennsylvania, with notes, by Peter S. Du Ponceau. Philadelphia: M'Carty and Davis. Reprinted 1996 by Evolution Publishing and Manufacturing, Holland, Bucks County, PA.

Horne, Josephine S. n.d. *Questions & Answers in Mohawk and English.* Kahnawake, Canada.

Horne, Josephine S. ca. 1970. *Illustrated Mohawk Vocabulary.* Mimeograph used in language classes in Kahnawà:ke.

Horne, Josephine S. 2003. *Kanien'kéha Iakorihonnién:nis.* Kahnawà:ke, Canada: Kanien'kehaka Onkwawén:na Raotitiohkwa.

Hough, Franklin B. 1853. *A History of St. Lawrence and Franklin Counties, New York, from the Earliest Period to the Present Time.* Albany: Little & Co.

Jameson, J. Franklin (ed). 1909. *Narratives of New Netherland, 1609–1664.* New York: Charles Scribner's Sons. Reprinted by Applewood Books, Bedford, MA.

Jamieson, Julia L. 1958. *The Mohawk Language, Book No. 1.* Jarvis, Ontario: Record Print.

Jamieson, Julia L. 1959. *The Mohawk Language, Book No. 2.* Brantford, Ontario: Convery – Hoover Press.

Jamieson, Julia L. 1960. *The Mohawk Language, Book No. 3.* Hagersville, Ontario: Hagersville Press Print.

Johnson, Sir William. 1951. *The papers of Sir William Johnson.* Prepared for publication by Milton W. Hamilton and Albert B. Corey, Volume X. Albany: The University of the State of New York.

Johnston, John. 1820. Account of the present state of the Indian tribes inhabiting Ohio. *Arcchaeologia Americana: Transactions and Collections of the American Antiquarian Society,* vol. 1, 269–299. Extract reprinted 2003 as *A Vocabulary of Wyandot, American Language Reprints,* vol. 30 by Evolution Publishing.

Ketchum, William. 1864–1865. *An Authentic and Comprehensive History of Buffalo, with some Account of its Early Inhabitants, both Savage and Civilized, comprising historical notices of the Six Nations or Iroquois Indians, including a sketch of the life of Sir William Johnson, and other prominent white men, long resident among the Senecas, arranged in chronological order, in two volumes.* Buffalo: Rockwell, Baker & Hill, Printers.

Klinck, Carl F., and James J. Talman (eds.) 1970. *The Journal of Major John Norton 1816*. Toronto: The Champlain Society.

Lafitau, Father Joseph François. 1974/1977. *Customs of the American Indians Compared with the Customs of Primitive Times*, edited and translated by William N. Fenton and Elizabeth L. Moore, in two volumes. Toronto: The Champlain Society.

Larsen, Esther Louise, and Pehr Kalm. 1935. Pehr Kalm's Description of Maize, How It Is Planted and Cultivated in North America, Together with the Many Uses of This Crop Plant, *Agricultural History* 9: 98–117. Agricultural History Society.

Lazore, Dorothy Karihwénhawe. 1993. *The Mohawk language Standardisation Project, Conference Report*. Ontario: Literacy Ontario.

Lazore, Hazel. 1987 (revised 1991). *Kanien'-kehá:ka Owenna'shón:'a*. Kahnawà:ke, Quebec: Mohawk Language & Curriculum.

Lighthall, W. D. 1899. Hochelagans and Mohawks, A Link in Iroquois History. *The Transactions of the Royal Society of Canada* Vol. V, Section II: 199–211.

Long, John. 1791. *Voyages and Travels of an Indian Interpreter and Trader, Describing The Manners and Customs of the North American Indians; with an Account of the Posts situated on the River Saint Laurence, Lake Ontario, &c. To which is added a Vocabulary of The Chippeway*. Printed for the author.

Lounsbury, Floyd G. 1960. Iroquois place names in the Champlain Valley. *Report of the New York-Vermont Interstate Commission on the Lake Champlain Basin, Legislative Document No. 9*, 23–66. Albany.

Lounsbury, Floyd G. 1961. Iroquois-Cherokee linguistic relations. In W. N. Fenton and J. Gulick (eds.), *Symposium on Cherokee and Iroquois culture*. Bureau of American Ethnology, Bulletin 180, 9–17. Washington: U.S. Govt. Print. Off.

Lukaniec, Megan. 2022. Managing Data from Archival Documentation for Language Reclamation. In Andrea L. Berez-Kroeker, Bradley McDonnell, Eve Koller, and Lauren B. Collister (eds.), *The Open Handbook of Linguistic Data Management*, 315–325. Cambridge, MA: MIT Press.

Maracle, David Kanatawakhon. 2002. *Yonteweyenhstahkwa Kanyen'keha, A Mohawk Language Dictionary: A Root Dictionary to be Used as a Resource and Reference Text for any Mohawk Language Learning Situation*. London, Ontario: Centre for Research and Teaching of Canadian Native Languages, University of Western Ontario.

Marcoux, Joseph. 1826. *Dictionnaire Francais–Iroquois Pour L'Usage des Missionnaires Sauvage des Canadas Par un Missionnaire Canadien. Ouvrage Nouveau*. Sault Saint Louis.

Marcoux, Joseph. 1828 [as cited in Pilling 1988: 115]. *Grammaire Iroquoise ou la Langue Iroquoise reduite en Principes Fixes Par Moi*. Sault Saint Louis [undated online copy available from Bibliothéque Assemblée Nationale du Québec].

Martin, Akwiratékha'. 2016 (2nd edition 2023). *Tekawennahsonterónnion, Kanien'kéha Morphology*. Kahnawà:ke, Québec: Kanien'kehá:ka Onkwawén:na Raotitióhkwa.

McIlwain. See Wraxall.

Megapolensis, Reverend Johannes. 1644. A Short Account of the Mohawk Indians. In Jameson.

Michelson, Gunther. 1973. *A Thousand Words of Mohawk*, Mercury Series,

Ethnology Division, paper no. 5. Ottawa, Canada: National Museum of Man, National Museums of Canada.

Michelson, Gunther. 1988. Wordlist and Linguistic Notes. *A Journey into Mohawk and Oneida Country, 1634–1635*, translated and edited by Charles T. Gehring and William A. Starna, 51–65. Syracuse: Syracuse University Press.

Michelson, Gunther. 2002. Search into the Origin of an Early Mohawk Dictionary. *Algonquian and Iroquoian Linguistics* 27(4): 50–62.

Michelson, Karin. 1981. A philological investigation into seventeenth-century Mohawk. *International Journal of American Linguistics* 47: 91–102.

Michelson, Karin, and Mercy Doxtator. 2002. *Oneida-English, English-Oneida Dictionary*. Toronto: University of Toronto Press.

Mithun, Marianne (ed.). 1977. *Iontenwenna-weienstáhkhwa': Mohawk Spelling Dictionary*. New York State Museum Bulletin 429, Albany: The University of the State of New York, The State Education Department.

Mithun, Marianne. 1979. The consciousness of levels of phonological structure. *International Journal of American Linguistics* 45: 343–348.

Mithun, Marianne. 1981. Stalking the Susquehannocks. *International Journal of American Linguistics* 47: 1–26.

Mithun, Marianne. 1984a. The Mystery of the Vanished Laurentians. In Anders Ahlqvist (ed.), *Papers from the 5th International Conference on Historical Linguistics*, 230–242. Amsterdam: John Benjamins.

Mithun, Marianne. 1984b. The Proto-Iroquoians: Cultural Reconstruction from Lexical Materials. In Michael K. Foster, Jack Campisi, and Marianne Mithun (eds.), *Extending the Rafters: Interdisciplinary Approaches to Iroquoian Studies*, 259–282. Albany: State University of New York Press.

Morgan, Lewis H. 1851. *League of the Ho-De-No-Sau-Nee or Iroquois*. Rochester: Sage and Brother.

Newhouse, Seth (Da-yo-de-ka-ne). 1885. *Cosmogony of the Iroquois Confederacy*. Oshweken. Available from the Public Archives of Canada. [Described in Fenton, William N. 1949. Seth Newhouse's Traditional History and Constitution of the Iroquois Confederacy. *Proceedings of the American Philosophical Society* 93: 141–158]

O'Callaghan, E.B. 1849–1851. *The Documentary History of the State of New York*. Albany: Weed, Parsons & Co. [Includes O'Callaghan, E.B. Papers Relating to the Iroquois and Other Indian Tribes, 1666–1763]

Old Kahnawake: An Oral History of Kahnawake. 1991. Kahnawake: Kanien'kehaka Raotitiohkwa Press.

Onkweonwe Vol. 1, No. 1. October 25, 1900. Ottawa. (Mohawk newspaper developed and written by Charles A. Cooke of Wahta, Ontario.)

Orchard, William C. 1929. Mohawk Burden-Straps. *Indian Notes,* Vol. VI, No. 4: 351–359. Museum of the American Indian, Heye Foundation.

Oronhyatekha, of the Mohawk Nation [Peter Martin]. 1876. The Mohawk Language. *The Canadian Journal. New Series*. No. XC.–April.

Penrose, Maryly B. 1981. Indian Affairs Papers, American Revolution. Franklin Park, N.J.: Liberty Bell Associates.

Pilling, James Constantine. 1888. *Bibliography of the Iroquoian Languages*. Bureau of American Ethnology Bulletin 6. Washington: Government Printing Office.

Potier, Pierre. See Fraser, Alexander.

A Primer for the Use of the Mohawk Children, To acquire the Spelling and Reading of their own: as well as to get acquainted with the English Tongue, which for that purpose is put on the opposite Page. 1781. Montreal: Printed at Fleury Mesplets.

Pyrlaeus, Christopher. 1966. *Lexicon der Macquaischen Sprachen [1742].* See A Guide to Manuscripts Relating to the American Indian in the Library of the American Philosophical Society, compiled by John F. Freeman and Murphy D. Smith, # 2276. Philadelphia: The American Philosophical Society.

Rousseau, Jacques. 1945. Le Folklore Botanique de Caughnawaga. *Études Ethnobotaniques Québécoise*, par Jacques Rousseau et Marcel Raymond, 7–74. Montréal: Université de Montréal, Institut Botanique.

Rudes, Blair A. 1999. *Tuscarora-English, English-Tuscarora Dictionary.* Toronto: University of Toronto Press.

Sagard, Fr. Gabriel. 1866. *Dictionaire de la Langve Hvronne.* Paris: La Librairie Tross.

Schoolcraft, Henry R. 1846. *Notes on the Iroquois or, Contributions to American History, Antiquities, and General Ethnology of Western New York.* New York: Bartlett & Welford.

Shea, John Gilmary. 1860. *A French-Onondaga Dictionary.* New York: Cramoisy Press. Republished 1970 by AMS Press, Inc., N.Y.

Sylvester, N. B. 1876. *Saratoga and Kay-ad-ros-se-ra: An Historical Address.* Troy, N.Y.: William N. Young.

Tewaterihwarenia'tha – the journal of Kaien'kehaka Raotitiohkwa cultural center.

Thomas, Jacob & Yvonne. 1978. *The Friendship Treaty Belt. The Two Row Wampum Treaty Belt.* Library of Jacob & Yvonne Thomas, For educational purposes only.

Thwaites, Reuben Gold (ed.). 1959. *The Jesuit Relations and Allied Documents.* New York: Pageant Book Company.

Torok, C. H. 1965. The Tyendinaga Mohawks. *Ontario History*, LVII, 2: 69–77.

van Wassenaer, Nicolaes. From the "historisch Verhael" 1624–1630. In Jameson.

Wallace, Paul A. W. 1945. *Conrad Weiser, 1696–1760, Friend of Colonist and Mohawk.* Philadelphia: University of Pennsylvania Press.

Waugh, F. W. 1916. *Iroquois Foods and Food Preparation.* Canada Department of Mines, Geological Survey Memoir 86. Ottawa: Government Printing Bureau.

Weiser, Conrad. 1756. Table of the names of numbers of several Indian nations. *Gentleman's magazine,* vol. 26: 386.

Wheeler-Voegelin, Erminie (ed.). 1959. Some Remarks and Annotations concerning the Traditions, Customs, Languages etc. of the Indians in North America, from the Memoirs of the Reverend David Zeisberger, and other Missionaries of the United Brethren. *Ethnohistory* 6(1): 42–69.

Williams, Marianne (ed.). 1976. *Kanien'keha' Okara'shòn:'a. Mohawk Stories.* Albany: New York State Museum Bulletin 427.

Wraxall, Peter. 1915. *An Abridgement of the Indian Affairs Contained in Four Folio Volumes, Transacted in the Colony of New York, from the Year 1678 to the Year 1751,* edited with an introduction by Charles Edward McIlwain. Cambridge, MA: Harvard University Press.

Zeisberger, David. 1982. *Zeisberger's Indian Dictionary.* Ed. E. N. Horsford. Cambridge, MA: John Wilson & Son. Republished 1987 by AMS Press, Inc., N.Y.

About Gunther Michelson

February 16, 1920–February 7, 2005

Gunther Michelson was born in Hamburg, Germany, to Charles and Annie Michelson. He attended the Wilhelm Gymnasium, where reportedly his favourite subjects were Latin and Greek. Like many young boys in Germany, he read the adventure novels by Karl May set in North America. With these began an interest in "America," encompassing eventually its history, traditions, language, and art. In 1939, he was drafted into the German army and spent three years in Russian territory. At the end of the war, he was located in the American "zone" and for about 10 months was held by the Americans; he spoke English well, so he was assigned translation work. He married (Ilse) Eva Jeske (1924–2013), the only child of Anne and Emil Jeske, in 1948. The couple lived in Düsseldorf, with Gunther spending some time in London, England, training with Reuters News Agency. In 1952, Gunther and Eva immigrated to Montréal, Canada, not long after Gunther's older brother, Edgar, had moved to Canada. In Montréal Gunther joined Radio-Canada's (CBC) International Service, which broadcast news about Canada to German-speaking audiences in Europe.

In 1953, I was born and shortly thereafter the family moved to Chateauguay, then a small town south of Montréal and bordering on the Caughnawaga Mohawk reserve, today's territory of Kahnawà:ke. My younger sister, Iris, was born in 1955, and around that time Eva's mother, the only grandparent Iris and I got to know, also relocated to Canada. When Iris and I were young girls, Gunther joined the Society of Friends, or Quakers, a decision likely due to his belief in the futilities of war. He retired from the CBC in the mid

1980s, and several years after retiring, Gunther and Eva moved to Ottawa.

Gunther spent most of his time outside of his professional life at the CBC studying (absorbing, really) anything related to the Haudenosaunee. He began studying the Kanien'kéha language in the early 1960s with Mae Montour and with Mae's father, Louis Curotte, and then her brother, Frank Natawe. He attended Caughnawaga Historical Society meetings, where he met Mike Norton, who also became a consultant in his linguistic studies. Mae and her husband, Mac, and Mike and his wife, Catherine, became good friends of the Michelsons'. Gunther also became friends with Ray Fadden of Onchiota, NY, whom the Michelson family visited often (we even spent a week in a cabin in the woods behind Fadden's Six Nations Indian Museum).

Gunther attended the annual Conference on Iroquois Research starting in the 1960s, where he met archeologists, anthropologists, historians, and linguists, many of whom became lifelong friends. His correspondence includes exchanges with Bill Pendergast, Mike Foster, Bill Fenton, Floyd Lounsbury, Barbara Graymont, and Bill Starna, to mention just a few. These letters demonstrate the extent to which his expertise was consulted and acknowledged. He also forged connections with several Haudenosaunee leaders and artists, whom he greatly admired, such as Alex General, Joseph Logan, Clinton Rickard, and especially Jake Thomas, who visited us in Chateauguay when I was a young girl (and who always remembered me whenever we met later on). Gunther's correspondence includes letters from Chief Deskaheh, Joseph

Logan, Roy Buck, and Jake Thomas. Another good friend, also not an academic by profession, was Pete Hest of Nedrow, NY, who was formally adopted by the Onondaga as a boy.

Gunther's approach to his published—and unpublished—work was focused, exacting, and supremely organized. And because he was not associated with an academic institution, he was independent in his thinking and modest to a fault about his wide-ranging first-hand knowledge and accomplishments. He began his extensive library of Iroquoian works in Chateauguay and added to it until his death. He got to know the bookstore owners who specialized in second-hand and early edition rare books in Montréal, Ottawa, and later in Buffalo. He kept detailed records about when and where each edition was obtained and relevant references to any literature about the item. He read everything he owned (and more of course) including, for example, the entire set of Jesuit Relations, the entire set of Sir William Johnson papers, contemporary academic publications, works by obscure or small presses, and little-known booklets and pamphlets. As he read, he recorded details on index cards for current and what would become future projects. Bill Fenton once said of Gunther that he had a special knack for identifying a good project.

In addition to work and research, Gunther developed an interest in the art of all First Nations in Canada and the U.S. Although throughout his life he acquired and appreciated the works by artisans long gone, he also believed that the work of contemporary artists was as much deserving of attention as the mostly unattributed works of former times.

Gunther and Eva had many friends and entertained often at their bungalow in Chateauguay Heights, at their large apartment on Côte-des-Neiges in Montréal close to Mont Royal, and at their sixteenth floor apartment in Ottawa not far from the Ottawa River.

Gunther's father's side of the family was very musical (an aunt was a professional opera singer, and his brother Edgar a talented pianist), and he played piano by ear. He loved vacationing in the northeast, especially by mountain lakes, and in later years in the American southwest.

If asked about his legacy, Gunther's answer might be that he discovered, assembled, and interpreted facts and observations about the Haudenosaunee and Iroquois-speaking people, obtained from every discipline and from diverse sources. Exchanging knowledge was an ingrained part of who he was. A complete list of his publications is appended below.

1973   *A Thousand Words of Mohawk*, Mercury Series, Ethnology Division, paper no. 5. Ottawa, Canada: National Museum of Man, National Museums of Canada.

1974   Up-streaming Bruyas. *Papers in Linguistics from the 1972 Conference on Iroquoian Research*, Mercury Series, Ethnology Division, paper no. 10, 36–46. Ottawa, Canada: National Museum of Man, National Museums of Canada.

1976   The Legend of Teharahsahkwa. *Man in the Northeast* 12: 3–13.

1977   Iroquois Population Statistics. *Man in the Northeast* 14: 3–17.

1981   The Covenant Chain in Colonial History. *Man in the Northeast* 21: 115–126.

1988   An Account of an Iroquois Condolence Council. *Man in the Northeast* 36: 61–75.

1988   *A Journey into Mohawk and Oneida Country, 1634–1635*, translated and edited by Charles T. Gehring and William A. Starna. Wordlist and Linguistic Notes by Gunther

Michelson. Syracuse: Syracuse University Press.

1989   Two Early Iroquoian Place Names: References and Interpretation. *Algonquian and Iroquoian Linguistics* 14(1): 9–11.

1991   Iroquoian Terms for Wampum. *International Journal of American Linguistics* 57: 108–116.

2000   A Note on *Ehonkeronon*. *Algonquian and Iroquoian Linguistics* 25(1): 6.

2002   Search into the Origin of an Early Mohawk Dictionary. *Algonquian and Iroquoian Linguistics* 27(4): 50–62.

2003   Midwinter at two Onondaga Longhouses. *Northeast Anthropology* 64: 17–29.

2008   *"To Do Justice to Him & Myself," Evert Wendell's Account Book of the Fur Trade with Indians in Albany, New York 1695–1726*, edited and translated by Kees-Jan Waterman with linguistic information by Gunther Michelson. Philadelphia: American Philosophical Society. (This volume received the Hendrick's Manuscript Award of the New Netherland Institute.)

www.ingramcontent.com/pod-product-compliance
Ingram Content Group UK Ltd.
Pitfield, Milton Keynes, MK11 3LW, UK
UKHW052053130825
461675UK00008B/59